Landmarks in Philosophy

LANDMARKS FOR BEGINNERS IN PHILOSOPHY

EDITED BY IRWIN EDMAN
AND HERBERT W. SCHNEIDER

WITH THE ASSISTANCE OF
EDWIN N. GARLAN, GEORGE
C. SEWARD, HENRY M. MAGID

ALL OF COLUMBIA UNIVERSITY

REYNAL & HITCHCOCK · NEW YORK

PRINTED IN THE UNITED STATES OF AMERICA
BY THE CORNWALL PRESS, CORNWALL, N. Y.

13213

Acknowledgments

THE editors are indebted first of all to their associates in this enterprise, Drs. E. N. Garlan, Henry M. Magid, and George C. Seward of the Department of Philosophy of Columbia University. In addition to making selections from the literature of philosophy on the basis of their current experience in teaching an introductory course in philosophy, Drs. Garlan and Seward have prepared an analytical index for cross-reference, which is likewise based on their experience in the classroom and which is intended to be a practical device to help students in tracing the basic themes of philosophy as they arise in the texts selected. Dr. Magid has contributed a new translation of the difficult pages selected from Aristotle's *Physics*. In numerous other ways these three associates have contributed to the editing of the texts and the preparation of the introductions; without their collaboration this work would not have been attempted and could not have been completed.

It may be appropriate here to remark that we have profited by years of experience on the part of a large group of instructors at Columbia in trying to initiate students into philosophical reading and thinking. The works here included have proved to be of particular value and have convinced us that the best way to cultivate systematic and critical thinking is to begin with a variety of the most critical systems instead of with a single academic digest, though it be the quintessence of truth, which the student may "learn" without learning much.

To the following publishers we wish to acknowledge our indebtedness for their generous permission to make use of their publications:

The Clarendon Press, Oxford, and the Jowett trustees for Ben-

v

jamin Jowett's translation of the *Symposium* and the *Protagoras* from *The Dialogues of Plato;* the Macmillan Company, London for J. E. C. Welldon's translation of the *Nichomachean Ethics* of Aristotle; the Clarendon Press, Oxford for Selby-Bigge's edition of the works of Hume, and A. C. Frazer's edition of the works of Berkeley.

J. M. Dent and Company for the use of John Healey's translation of St. Augustine's *City of God.*

Charles Scribner's Sons for J. F. Shaw's translation of St. Augustine's *Enchiridion.*

Burns and Oates for Joseph Rickaby's translation of St. Thomas' *Summa contra Gentiles.*

The Open Court Publishing Company for John Veitch's translation of Nietzsche's *Genealogy of Morals.*

Longmans Green Company for T. K. Abbott's translation of Kant's *Fundamental Principles of the Metaphysics of Morals* and for William James' *Pragmatism* and *The Will to Believe.*

The Macmillan Company for the use of H. B. Samuel's translation of Nietzsche's *Genealogy of Morals.*

Henry Holt and Company for R. A. Audra's and C. Brereton's translation of Henri Bergson's *Two Sources of Religion and Morality.*

Table of Contents

General Introduction

T HE title of this book suggests its double intention. The writings chosen are, in the judgment of the editors, landmarks in the history of philosophy; they are drawn from works clearly in the classical canon of thinkers from the Greeks to the present time. But the selections, in every case extensive and, where possible, complete in themselves, are landmarks in a second and no less important sense. They are statements, eminent for clarity and cogency, of perennial issues and recurrent problems in western philosophy. For the history of philosophy is not simply a study of successive intellectual episodes, of ideas once suggested and then passed by, of problems raised and then forever neglected, or answers given once and thereafter ignored. New problems are raised, and new ways are found for dealing with new issues. But one striking fact about the history of philosophical ideas is their recurrent character. However much the language and the emphasis of philosophical interests differ at different times and among different philosophers of the same time, whenever and wherever men reflect upon first and last things they are contemporaries.

The historic landmarks are not simply high points in a story; they are landmarks also in a permanent landscape, the terrain of thoroughgoing reflection on persistent traits of being. What Plato said is arresting not only as Greek thought but as "the love of wisdom." Plato and Aristotle at the beginning, James and Bergson at the end of this volume, will be addressing the readers on the same or essentially comparable themes—ways of thinking and of knowing, ways of being, and ways of life. And the more recent thinkers are, as Francis Bacon said, the more "ancient," in the sense that they are aware of the fact that in their minds the minds of many generations of readers of Plato, Aristotle, and the rest are still living and that there is a continuous and cumulative life of ideas.

The editors do not claim, indeed they disclaim, any attempt to present an inclusive sampling of the whole history of philosophy.

ix

We have, for example, omitted Spinoza because it seems impossible to present in brief compass in his own words the whole character of his central themes, problems, and solutions. Many philosophers have been omitted because, while high points in a story, they seem to retraverse at second hand what has been said at first hand and in more first-rate intellectual form by others who are included. Thus there is no contemporary metaphysical idealist, but there is Hegel.

Wherever feasible we have tried to include complete works or at least continuous portions of the text. Cutting is always arbitrary, and abuse of this practice produces an aphoristic type of selection which is often obscure and confusing. We have retained passages of minor importance in many cases, therefore, in order to preserve the sequence. In several instances this was not possible. With Schopenhauer, notably, it was necessary, because of the style, to take greater liberties with the text. What we have included of his work represents therefore a compilation of extracts rather than a continuous passage.

The editors have a firm conviction that the great philosophers speak for themselves and to all men in any age. But this book is called and is intended to be landmarks for beginners. The brief essay introductory to each landmark is meant to be simply an introduction, a brief analytical and historical statement that will serve at once to give some inkling of the writer's historical place and some sense of his perennial intellectual significance. We have been guided by the interests, as we conceived them, of minds wakening to philosophical reflection both within and outside the academies.

There have been innumerable "introductions to philosophy." These, however responsible and clear, are inevitably provincial; speak a language of but one school of philosophy, and probably lack the accent of classic and original minds. There is no substitute for contact with the seminal minds of philosophy, those to whom all teachers must turn, and by whom they would wish their students, too, to be instructed. And there is no hope at present that any one philosophy will be a good introduction to all the others.

H. W. S.

I. E.

April, 1941

Plato

Plato

PLATO is, it goes almost without saying, a landmark in philosophy for beginners or for veterans. The very use of the word philosophy and Plato's emphasis on its exact meaning, the love of wisdom, have their source in Plato's writings. Nearly all the issues that have pre-occupied philosophers down to the present have their first seeds planted and their first principles broached in Plato's dialogues: the relation of time and eternity, the meaning of good, the knowledge of the real, the awareness of the beautiful, and the recognition of the truth, on which, however variously these be defined, the good life depends.

It generally surprises the beginner that a thinker properly regarded as the Father of European philosophy should have written not treatises but dialogues. The Plato actually found in the pages of the dialogues rather than in the doctrines of Platonists almost inevitably astonishes and impresses the first reader as a man of letters rather than as a philosopher. The careful student will discover soon enough that the patent literary art is the vehicle for the most searching analysis of the profoundest of questions concerning man's nature and its possible good. Consider the two dialogues selected for this volume. The Protagoras begins in a comic scene and retains elements of comedy throughout, but before the end one has participated in the most subtle and serious discussion of the identity of all the virtues and the identity, also, of virtue and knowledge. In the Symposium, the scene is a gay party, and there is gaiety and wit throughout, but the theme is love and the love of beauty, and before one has finished reading Socrates' famous speech, one finds that the true lover is necessarily wise and virtuous, and that the true object of his love is hardly distinguishable from the good.

Plato is, in the first place and in the last analysis, a dramatic poet of ideas. His career as a writer is said indeed to have begun as a very young man with the writing of verses, which he soon destroyed. Plato, born 427, died 347 B.C., came of one of the most distinguished families of the Periclean Age. His uncle, Charmides (who appears as a beautiful embodiment of youthful temperance in the dialogue of that name) was a powerful figure in the brief anarchic regime that followed on the collapse of Athens at the close of the Peloponnesian War. From about eighteen to about twenty-one Plato was one of the companion-pupils of Socrates, whose trial and execution on the charge of corrupting youth and denying the gods profoundly shocked Plato and disillusioned him with political life. Socrates' life and death may be said to have converted Plato to philosophy from both politics and poetry, though his dialogues and his life show that he was not weaned completely from either. The dialogues may be in fact properly considered, as they were undoubtedly first begun, as a memento to the personality and spirit of that philosophical conversationalist who had first awakened Plato intellectually and seemed to him to exhibit in doctrine and in person the philosophical or the examined life.

After the execution of Socrates, Plato withdrew from Athens to the city of Megara. He soon began to travel for a number of years in Italy, Sicily, Cyrene and Egypt. On his return he founded the Academy, in effect the first European university. Here he lectured and discussed philosophical and mathematical questions with members of the school. At the age of sixty Plato took advantage of an extraordinary opportunity to test on an actual reigning statesman, Dionysius II of Syracuse, some of his ideas concerning the education of a philosopher-king. Plato tried to educate his prince by the mathematical science of the Academy, but the prince because of personal jealousies and weariness of the exacting discipline of his studies abandoned Plato's scheme. Plato returned to the Academy at Athens where he spent the remaining twenty years of his life and there he died at the age of eighty-one. These are the bare known facts, and not all of these certain, about Plato. There are certain legends, that he was called Plato because of his broad brow, that he was born on Apollo's birthday, that he died at a marriage feast, that he was very handsome. His life in its details is as much a secret as Shakespeare's, and since he was a dramatist, we can tell as little about him personally from his dialogues as we can tell about Shakespeare from his plays.

We know more about the age in which Plato lived, an age of discussion, during which political debate was yielding to irresponsible casuistry. The young freemen were being trained in the art of rhetoric by foreign, footloose teachers known as Sophists. Philosophy had been largely physical speculations brought to bear on traditional mythologies. In morals the scepticism and relativism of such thinkers as Protagoras had broken down traditional moral standards.

The dialogues are in large part a picture of the examined life and the method of its examination which Socrates exemplified in his discourses with younger men. The philosophy practised by Socrates is contrasted with the rhetoric taught by the paid teachers. The dialogues are wonderfully charming genre pictures of the life of the Athenian cultivated classes, with their allusions to banquets and the palaestra, their scenes in the homes of the wealthy, their spirited young men, handsome or gifted, or both. But they are, especially the earlier so-called Socratic ones, studies in the philosophical habit, a critique of accepted standards and an attempt to find standards of conduct to which reason can assent. Hence Socrates' rejection, after raising crucial questions, of merely conventional definitions; hence his attempts to find a definition that will adequately cover all instances. Hence the search for the "idea." The definition or standard of conduct sought for by Socrates appears in some of the dialogues, notably in the Symposium, to be an eternal form having its being in eternity and exempt from all the multiplicity of things in space and all the variability of things in time. These "ideas" changeless and single are or appear in Plato to be at once the objects of genuine knowledge and of rational love. They are suggested by beautiful objects, they are broached in memory or learning and in a virtuous life or a just commonwealth. Themselves variations of the idea of the Good, they are patterns or ideals in the light of which an ordered soul or an ordered commonwealth may have its goal defined and its character suggested.

The dialogues may be read at once as drama, as morals and as discussions of knowledge, being and truth. The two dialogues selected present two different aspects of Platonic analysis. One is an instance of Socrates' dialectic method: his exhibition of the method of defining an idea, its consequences and its relations. The other presents the Platonist whom poets have possessed. It is a comedy but in the midst of it shines through the "light that never was on sea or land, the consecration and the poet's dream." The whole gamut of Plato's temper and interests is to be found in these two masterpieces. Here may be found the hints and suggestions which are the seeds of the Platonic and Platonizing traditions in the history of philosophy, and the themes that have ever since engaged philosophical reflection.

Protagoras

PERSONS OF THE DIALOGUE

Socrates, *who is the narrator
of the Dialogue to his
Companion.*
Hippocrates.
Alcibiades.

Critias.
Protagoras,
Hippias, } *Sophists.*
Prodicus,
Callias, *a wealthy Athenian.*

Scene: *The House of Callias.*

COMPANION. Where do you come from, Socrates? And yet I need
hardly ask the question, for I know that you have been in chase of
the fair Alcibiades. I saw him the day before yesterday; and he had
got a beard like a man,—and he is a man, as I may tell you in your
ear. But I thought that he was still very charming.

SOCRATES. What of his beard? Are you not of Homer's opinion,
who says,

"Youth is most charming when the beard appears"?

And that is now the charm of Alcibiades.

COMPANION. Well, and how do matters proceed? Have you
been visiting him, and was he gracious to you?

SOCRATES. Yes, I thought that he was very gracious; and especially
to-day, for I have just come from him, and he has been helping me
in an argument. But shall I tell you a strange thing? I paid no attention to him, and several times I quite forgot that he was present.

COMPANION. What is the meaning of this? Has anything happened between you and him? For surely you cannot have discovered a fairer love than he is; certainly not in this city of Athens.

SOCRATES. Yes, much fairer.

COMPANION. What do you mean—a citizen or a foreigner?

SOCRATES. A foreigner.

COMPANION. Of what country?

SOCRATES. Of Abdera.

COMPANION. And is this stranger really in your opinion a fairer
love than the son of Cleinias?

6

SOCRATES. And is not the wiser always the fairer, sweet friend?

COMPANION. But have you really met, Socrates, with some wise one?

SOCRATES. Say rather, with the wisest of all living men, if you are willing to accord that title to Protagoras.

COMPANION. What! Is Protagoras in Athens?

SOCRATES. Yes; he has been here two days.

COMPANION. And do you just come from an interview with him?

SOCRATES. Yes; and I have heard and said many things.

COMPANION. Then, if you have no engagement, suppose that you sit down and tell me what passed, and my attendant here shall give up his place to you.

SOCRATES. To be sure; and I shall be grateful to you for listening.

COMPANION. Thank you, too, for telling us.

SOCRATES. That is thank you twice over. Listen then:—

Last night, or rather very early this morning, Hippocrates, the son of Apollodorus and the brother of Phason, gave a tremendous thump with his staff at my door; some one opened to him, and he came rushing in and bawled out: Socrates, are you awake or asleep?

I knew his voice, and said: Hippocrates, is that you? and do you bring any news?

Good news, he said; nothing but good.

Delightful, I said; but what is the news? and why have you come hither at this unearthly hour?

He drew nearer to me and said: Protagoras is come.

Yes, I replied; he came two days ago: have you only just heard of his arrival?

Yes, by the gods, he said; but not until yesterday evening.

At the same time he felt for the truckle-bed, and sat down at my feet, and then he said: Yesterday, quite late in the evening, on my return from Oenoe, whither I had gone in pursuit of my runaway slave Satyrus, as I meant to have told you, if some other matter had not come in the way;—on my return, when we had done supper and were about to retire to rest, my brother said to me: Protagoras is come. I was going to you at once, and then I thought that the night was far spent. But the moment sleep left me after my fatigue, I got up and came hither direct.

I, who knew the very courageous madness of the man, said: What is the matter? Has Protagoras robbed you of anything?

He replied, laughing: Yes, indeed he has, Socrates, of the wisdom which he keeps from me.

But, surely, I said, if you give him money, and make friends with him, he will make you as wise as he is himself.

Would to heaven, he replied, that this were the case! He might take all that I have, and all that my friends have, if he pleased. But that is why I have come to you now, in order that you may speak to him on my behalf; for I am young and also I have never seen nor heard him (when he visited Athens before I was but a child); and all men praise him, Socrates; he is reputed to be the most accomplished of speakers. There is no reason why we should not go to him at once, and then we shall find him at home. He lodges, as I hear, with Callias the son of Hipponicus: let us start.

I replied: Not yet, my good friend; the hour is too early. But let us rise and take a turn in the court and wait about there until daybreak; when the day breaks, then we will go. For Protagoras is generally at home, and we shall be sure to find him; never fear.

Upon this we got up and walked about in the court, and I thought that I would make trial of the strength of his resolution. So I examined him and put questions to him. Tell me, Hippocrates, I said, as you are going to Protagoras, and will be paying your money to him, what is he to whom you are going? and what will he make of you? If, for example, you had thought of going to Hippocrates of Cos, the Asclepiad, and were about to give him your money, and some one had said to you: You are paying money to your namesake Hippocrates, O Hippocrates; tell me, what is he that you give him money? how would you have answered?

I should say, he replied, that I gave money to him as a physician.

And what will he make of you?

A physician, he said.

And if you were resolved to go to Polycleitus the Argive, or Pheidias the Athenian, and were intending to give them money, and some one had asked you: What are Polycleitus and Pheidias? and why do you give them this money?—how would you have answered?

I should have answered, that they were statuaries.

And what will they make of you?

A statuary, of course.

Well, now, I said, you and I are going to Protagoras, and we are ready to pay him money on your behalf. If our own means are sufficient, and we can gain him with these, we shall be only too glad; but if not, then we are to spend the money of your friends as well. Now suppose that while we are thus enthusiastically pursuing our object some one were to say to us: Tell me, Socrates, and you Hippocrates, what is Protagoras, and why are you going to pay him money?—how should we answer? I know that Pheidias is a sculptor, and that Homer is a poet; but what appellation is given to Protagoras? how is he designated?

They call him a Sophist, Socrates, he replied.

Then we are going to pay our money to him in the character of a Sophist?

Certainly.

But suppose a person were to ask this further question: And how about yourself? What will Protagoras make of you, if you go to see him?

He answered, with a blush upon his face (for the day was just beginning to dawn, so that I could see him): Unless this differs in some way from the former instances, I suppose that he will make a Sophist of me.

By the gods, I said, and are you not ashamed at having to appear before the Hellenes in the character of a Sophist?

Indeed, Socrates, to confess the truth, I am.

But you should not assume, Hippocrates, that the instruction of Protagoras is of this nature: may you not learn of him in the same way that you learned the arts of the grammarian, or musician, or trainer, not with the view of making any of them a profession, but only as a part of education, and because a private gentleman and freeman ought to know them?

Just so, he said; and that, in my opinion, is a far truer account of the teaching of Protagoras.

I said: I wonder whether you know what you are doing?

And what am I doing?

You are going to commit your soul to the care of a man whom you call a Sophist. And yet I hardly think that you know what a Sophist is; and if not, then you do not even know to whom you are committing your soul and whether the thing to which you commit yourself be good or evil.

I certainly think that I do know, he replied.

Then tell me, what do you imagine that he is?

I take him to be one who knows wise things, he replied, as his name implies.

And might you not, I said, affirm this of the painter and of the carpenter also: Do not they, too, know wise things? But suppose a person were to ask us: In what are the painters wise? We should answer: In what relates to the making of likenesses, and similarly of other things. And if he were further to ask: What is the wisdom of the Sophist, and what is the manufacture over which he presides?—how should we answer him?

How should we answer him, Socrates? What other answer could there be but that he presides over the art which makes men eloquent.

Yes, I replied, that is very likely true, but not enough; for in the answer a further question is involved: Of what does the Sophist make a man talk eloquently? The player on the lyre may be supposed to make a man talk eloquently about that which he makes him understand, that is about playing the lyre. Is not that true?

Yes.

Then about what does the Sophist make him eloquent? Must not he make him eloquent in that which he understands?

Yes, that may be assumed.

And what is that which the Sophist knows and makes his disciples know?

Indeed, he said, I cannot tell.

Then I proceeded to say: Well, but are you aware of the danger which you are incurring? If you were going to commit your body to some one, who might do good or harm to it, would you not carefully consider and ask the opinion of your friends and kindred, and deliberate many days as to whether you should give him the care of your body? But when the soul is in question, which you hold to be of far more value than the body, and upon the good or evil of which depends the well-being of your all,—about this you never consulted either with your father or with your brother or with any one of us who are your companions. But no sooner does this foreigner appear, than you instantly commit your soul to his keeping. In the evening, as you say, you hear of him, and in the morning you go to him, never deliberating or taking the opinion of any one as to whether you ought to entrust yourself to him or not;—you have quite made up your mind that you will at all hazards be a pupil of Protagoras, and are prepared to expend all the property of yourself and of your friends in carrying out at any price this determination, although, as you admit, you do not know him, and have never spoken with him: and you call him a Sophist, but are manifestly ignorant of what a Sophist is; and yet you are going to commit yourself to his keeping.

When he heard me say this, he replied: No other inference, Socrates, can be drawn from your words.

I proceeded: Is not a Sophist, Hippocrates, one who deals wholesale or retail in the food of the soul? To me that appears to be his nature.

And what, Socrates, is the food of the soul?

Surely, I said, knowledge is the food of the soul; and we must take care, my friend, that the Sophist does not deceive us when he praises what he sells, like the dealers wholesale or retail who sell the food of the body; for they praise indiscriminately all their goods, without knowing what are really beneficial or hurtful: neither do their customers knew, with the exception of any trainer or physician who may happen to buy of them. In like manner those who carry about the wares of knowledge, and make the round of the cities, and sell or retail them to any customer who is in want of them, praise them all alike; though I should not wonder, O my friend, if many of them were really ignorant of their effect upon the soul; and their customers equally ignorant, unless he who buys of them happens to be a physician of the soul. If, therefore, you have understanding of what is good and evil, you may safely buy knowledge of Protagoras or of any one; but if not, then, O my friend, pause, and do not hazard your dearest interests at a game of chance. For there is far greater peril in buying knowledge than in buying meat and drink: the one you purchase of the wholesale or retail dealer, and carry them away in other vessels, and before you receive them into the body as food, you may deposit them at home and call in any experienced friend who knows what is good to be eaten or drunken, and what not, and how much, and when; and then the danger of purchasing them is not so great. But you cannot buy the wares of knowledge and carry them away in another vessel; when you have paid for them you must receive them into the soul and go your way, either greatly harmed or greatly benefited; and therefore we should deliberate and take counsel with our elders; for we are still young—too young to determine such a matter. And now let us go, as we were intending, and hear Protagoras; and when we have heard what he has to say, we may take counsel of others; for not only is Protagoras at the house of Callias, but there is Hippias of Elis, and, if I am not mistaken, Prodicus of Ceos, and several other wise men.

To this we agreed, and proceeded on our way until we reached the vestibule of the house; and there we stopped in order to conclude a discussion which had arisen between us as we were going along; and we stood talking in the vestibule until we had finished and come to an understanding. And I think that the doorkeeper, who was a eunuch, and who was probably annoyed at the great inroad of the Sophists, must have heard us talking. At any rate, when we knocked at the door, and he opened and saw us, he grumbled: They are Sophists—he is not at home; and instantly gave the door a hearty bang with both his hands. Again we knocked, and he answered without opening: Did you not hear me say that he is not at home, fellows? But, my friend, I said, you need not be alarmed; for we are not Sophists, and we are not come to see Callias, but we want to see Protagoras; and I must request you to announce us. At last, after a good deal of difficulty, the man was persuaded to open the door.

When we entered, we found Protagoras taking a walk in the cloister; and next to him, on one side, were walking Callias, the son of Hipponicus, and Paralus, the son of Pericles, who, by the mother's side, is his half-brother, and Charmides, the son of Glaucon. On the other side of him were Xanthippus, the other son of Pericles, Philippides, the son of Philomeus; also Antimoerus of Mende, who of all the disciples of Protagoras is the most famous, and intends to make sophistry his profession. A train of listeners followed him; the greater part of them appeared to be foreigners, whom Protagoras had brought with him out of the various cities visited by him in his journeys, he, like Orpheus, attracting them by his voice, and they following. I should mention also that there were some Athenians in the company. Nothing delighted

me more than the precision of their movements: they never got
into his way at all; but when he and those who were with him
turned back, then the band of listeners parted regularly on either
side; he was always in front, and they wheeled round and took
their places behind him in perfect order.

After him, as Homer says, "I lifted my eyes and saw" Hippias
the Elean sitting in the opposite cloister on a chair of state, and
around him were seated on benches Eryximachus, the son of
Acumenus, and Phaedrus the Myrrhinusian, and Andron the son
of Androtion, and there were strangers whom he had brought with
him from his native city of Elis, and some others: they were putting to Hippias certain physical and astronomical questions, and
he, *ex cathedra,* was determining their several questions to them,
and discoursing of them.

Also, "my eyes beheld Tantulus"; for Prodicus the Cean was at
Athens: he had been lodged in a room which, in the days of Hipponicus, was a storehouse; but, as the house was full, Callias had
cleared this out and made the room into a guest chamber. Now
Prodicus was still in bed, wrapped up in sheepskins and bed-
clothes, of which there seemed to be a great heap; and there was
sitting by him on the couches near, Pausanias of the deme of Cera-
meis, and with Pausanias was a youth quite young, who is certainly
remarkable for his good looks, and, if I am not mistaken, is also of
a fair and gentle nature. I thought that I heard him called
Agathon, and my suspicion is that he is the beloved of Pausanias.
There was this youth, and also there were the two Adeimantuses,
one the son of Cepis, and the other of Leucolophides, and some
others. I was very anxious to hear what Prodicus was saying, for
he seems to me to be an all-wise and inspired man; but I was not
able to get into the inner circle, and his fine deep voice made an
echo in the room which rendered his words inaudible.

No sooner had we entered than there followed us Alcibiades
the beautiful, as you say, and I believe you; and also Critias the
son of Callaeschrus.

On entering we stopped a little, in order to look about us, and
then walked up to Protagoras, and I said: Protagoras, my friend
Hippocrates and I have come to see you.

Do you wish, he said, to speak with me alone, or in the presence
of the company?

Whichever you please, I said; you shall determine when you have heard the purpose of our visit.

And what is your purpose? he said.

I must explain, I said, that my friend Hippocrates is a native Athenian; he is the son of Apollodorus, and of a great and prosperous house, and he is himself in natural ability quite a match for anybody of his own age. I believe that he aspires to political eminence; and this he thinks that conversation with you is most likely to procure for him. And now you can determine whether you would wish to speak to him of your teaching alone or in the presence of the company.

Thank you, Socrates, for your consideration of me. For certainly a stranger finding his way into great cities, and persuading the flower of the youth in them to leave the company of their kinsmen or any other acquaintances, old or young, and live with him, under the idea that they will be improved by his conversation, ought to be very cautious; great jealousies are aroused by his proceedings, and he is the subject of many enmities and conspiracies. Now the art of the Sophist is, as I believe, of great antiquity; but in ancient times those who practised it, fearing this odium, veiled and disguised themselves under various names, some under that of poets, as Homer, Hesiod, and Simonides, some, of hierophants and prophets, as Orpheus and Musaeus, and some, as I observe, even under the name of gymnastic masters, like Iccus of Tarentum, or the more recently celebrated Herodicus, now of Selymbria and formerly of Megara, who is a first-rate Sophist. Your own Agathocles pretended to be a musician, but was really an eminent Sophist; also Pythocleides the Cean; and there were many others; and all of them, as I was saying, adopted these arts as veils or disguises because they were afraid of the odium which they would incur. But that is not my way, for I do not believe that they effected their purpose, which was to deceive the government, who were not blinded by them; and as to the people, they have no understanding, and only repeat what their rulers are pleased to tell them. Now to run away, and to be caught in running away, is the very height of folly, and also greatly increases the exasperation of mankind; for they regard him who runs away as a rogue, in addition to any other objections which they have to him; and therefore I take an entirely opposite course, and acknowledge myself to be a

Sophist and instructor of mankind; such an open acknowledgment appears to me to be a better sort of caution than concealment. Nor do I neglect other precautions, and therefore I hope, as I may say, but the favour of heaven that no harm will come of the acknowledgment that I am a Sophist. And I have been now many years in the profession—for all my years when added up are many: there is no one here present of whom I might not be the father. Wherefore I should much prefer conversing with you, if you want to speak with me, in the presence of the company.

As I suspected that he would like to have a little display and glorification in the presence of Prodicus and Hippias, and would gladly show us to them in the light of his admirers, I said: But why should we not summon Prodicus and Hippias and their friends to hear us?

Very good, he said.

Suppose, said Callias, that we hold a council in which you may sit and discuss.—This was agreed upon, and great delight was felt at the prospect of hearing wise men talk; we ourselves took the chairs and benches, and arranged them by Hippias, where the other benches had been already placed. Meanwhile Callias and Alcibiades got Prodicus out of bed and brought in him and his companions.

When we were all seated, Protagoras said: Now that the company are assembled, Socrates, tell me about the young man of whom you were just now speaking.

I replied: I will begin again at the same point, Protagoras, and tell you once more the purport of my visit: this is my friend Hippocrates, who is desirous of making your acquaintance; he would like to know what will happen to him if he associates with you. I have no more to say.

Protagoras answered: Young man, if you associate with me, on the very first day you will return home a better man than you came, and better on the second day than on the first, and better every day than you were on the day before.

When I heard this, I said: Protagoras, I do not at all wonder at hearing you say this; even at your age, and with all your wisdom, if any one were to teach you what you did not know before, you would become better no doubt: but please to answer in a different way—I will explain how by an example. Let me suppose that Hip-

pocrates, instead of desiring your acquaintance, wished to become
acquainted with the young man Zeuxippus of Heraclea, who has
lately been in Athens, and he had come to him as he has come to
you, and had heard him say, as he has heard you say, that every day
he would grow and become better if he associated with him: and
then suppose that he were to ask him, "In what shall I become
better, and in what shall I grow?" Zeuxippus would answer,
"In painting." And suppose that he went to Orthagoras the The-
ban, and heard him say the same thing, and asked him, "In what
shall I become better day by day?" He would reply, "In flute-
playing." Now I want you to make the same sort of answer to this
young man and to me, who am asking questions on his account.
When you say that on the first day on which he associates with you
he will return home a better man, and on every day will grow in
like manner,—in what, Protagoras, will he be better? and about
what?

When Protagoras heard me say this, he replied: You ask questions fairly, and I like to answer a question which is fairly put. If
Hippocrates comes to me he will not experience the sort of
drudgery with which other Sophists are in the habit of insulting
their pupils; who, when they have just escaped from the arts, are
taken and driven back into them by these teachers, and made to
learn calculation, and astronomy, and geometry, and music (he
gave a look at Hippias as he said this); but if he comes to me, he
will learn that which he comes to learn. And this is prudence in
affairs private as well as public; he will learn to order his own
house in the best manner, and he will be able to speak and act for
the best in the affairs of the State.

Do I understand you, I said; and is your meaning that you teach
the art of politics, and that you promise to make men good
citizens?

That, Socrates, is exactly the profession which I make.

Then, I said, you do indeed possess a noble art, if there is no
mistake about this; for I will freely confess to you, Protagoras, that
I have a doubt whether this art is capable of being taught, and yet
I know not how to disbelieve your assertion. And I ought to tell
you why I am of opinion that this art cannot be taught or communicated by man to man. I say that the Athenians are an understanding people, and indeed they are esteemed to be such by the

other Hellenes. Now I observe that when we are met together in the assembly, and the matter in hand relates to building, the builders are summoned as advisers; when the question is one of shipbuilding, then the shipwrights, and the like of other arts which they think capable of being taught and learned. And if some person offers to give them advice who is not supposed by them to have any more skill in the art than they, but to be good-looking, and rich, and noble, they don't listen to him, but laugh at him, and hoot him, until either he is clamoured down and re-tires of himself; or he persists, but is dragged away or put out by the constables at the command of the prytanes. This is their way of behaving about professors of the arts. But when the question is an affair of state, then everybody is free to have a say—carpenter, tinker, cobbler, sailor, passenger; rich and poor, high and low—any one who likes gets up, and no one reproaches him, as in the former case, with not having learned, and having no teacher, and yet giving advice; evidently because they are under the impression that this sort of knowledge cannot be taught. And not only is this true of the State, but of individuals; the best and wisest of our citizens are unable to impart their political wisdom to others: as for example, Pericles, the father of these young men, who gave them excellent instruction in all that could be learned from mas-ters, in his own department of politics neither taught them, nor gave them teachers; but they were allowed to wander at their own free will in a sort of hope that they would light upon virtue of their own accord. Or take another example: there was Cleinias the younger brother of our friend Alcibiades, of whom this very same Pericles was the guardian; and he being in fact under the appre-hension that Cleinias would be corrupted by Alcibiades, took him away, and placed him in the house of Ariphron to be educated; but before six months had elapsed, Ariphron sent him back, not knowing what to do with him. And I could mention numberless other instances of persons who were good themselves, and never yet made any one else good, whether friend or stranger. Now I, Pro-tagoras, having these examples before me, am inclined to think that virtue cannot be taught. But then again, when I listen to your words, I waver; and am disposed to think that there must be some-thing in what you say, because I know that you have great ex-perience, and learning, and invention. And I wish that you would, if possible, show me a little more clearly that virtue can be taught. Will you be so good?

That I will, Socrates, and gladly. But what would you like? Shall I, as an elder, speak to you as younger men in an apologue or myth, or shall I argue out the question?

To this several of the company answered that he should choose for himself.

Well, then, he said, I think that the myth will be more interesting.

Once upon a time there were gods only, and no mortal creatures. But when the time came that these also should be created, the gods fashioned them out of earth and fire and various mixtures of both elements in the interior of the earth; and when they were about to bring them into the light of day, they ordered Prometheus and Epimetheus to equip them, and to distribute to them severally their proper qualities. Epimetheus said to Prometheus: "Let me distribute, and do you inspect." This was agreed, and Epimetheus made the distribution. There were some to whom he gave strength without swiftness, while he equipped the weaker with swiftness; some he armed, and others he left unarmed; and devised for the latter some other means of preservation, making some large, and having their size as a protection, and others small, whose nature was to fly in the air or burrow in the ground; this was to be their way of escape. Thus did he compensate them with the view of preventing any race from becoming extinct. And when he had provided against their destruction by one another, he contrived also a means of protecting them against the seasons of heaven; clothing them with close hair and thick skins sufficient to defend them against the winter cold and able to resist the summer heat, so that they might have a natural bed of their own when they wanted to rest; also he furnished them with hoofs and hair and hard and callous skins under their feet. Then he gave them varieties of food,—herb of the soil to some, to others fruits of trees, and to others roots, and to some again he gave other animals as food. And some he made to have few young ones, while those who were their prey were very prolific; and in this manner the race was preserved. Thus did Epimetheus, who, not being very wise, forgot that he had distributed among the brute animals all the qualities which he had to give,—and when he came to man, who

was still unprovided, he was terribly perplexed. Now, while he was
in this perplexity, Prometheus came to inspect the distribution,
and he found that the other animals were suitably furnished, but
that man alone was naked and shoeless, and had neither bed nor
arms of defence. The appointed hour was approaching when man
in his turn was to go forth into the light of day; and Prometheus,
not knowing how he could devise his salvation, stole the mechanical arts of Hephaestus and Athene, and fire with them (they could
neither have been acquired nor used without fire), and gave them
to man. Thus man had the wisdom necessary to the support of life,
but political wisdom he had not; for that was in the keeping of
Zeus, and the power of Prometheus did not extend to entering into
the citadel of heaven, where Zeus dwelt, who moreover had terrible sentinels; but he did enter by stealth into the common work-
ship of Athene and Hephaestus, in which they used to practise
their favourite arts, and carried off Hephaestus' art of working by
fire, and also the art of Athene, and gave them to man. And in this
way man was supplied with the means of life. But Prometheus is
said to have been afterwards prosecuted for theft, owing to the
blunder of Epimetheus.

Now, man, having a share of the divine attributes, was at first
the only one of the animals who had any gods, because he alone
was of their kindred; and he would raise altars and images of them.
He was not long in inventing articulate speech and names; and he
also constructed houses and clothes and shoes and beds, and drew
sustenance from the earth. Thus provided, mankind at first lived
dispersed, and there were no cities. But the consequence was that
they were destroyed by the wild beasts, for they were utterly weak
in comparison of them, and their art was only sufficient to provide
them with the means of life, and did not enable them to carry on
war against the animals: food they had, but not as yet the art of
government, of which the art of war is a part. After a while the
desire of self-preservation gathered them into cities; but when
they were gathered together, having no art of government, they
evil entreated one another, and were again in process of dispersion
and destruction. Zeus feared that the entire race would be exter-
minated, and so he sent Hermes to them, bearing reverence and
justice to be the ordering principles of cities and the bonds of
friendship and conciliation. Hermes asked Zeus how he should im-

part justice and reverence among men:—Should he distribute them
as the arts are distributed; that is to say, to a favoured few only,
one skilled individual having enough of medicine or of any other
art for many unskilled ones? "Shall this be the manner in which
I am to distribute justice and reverence among men, or shall I give
them to all?" "To all," said Zeus; "I should like them all to have a
share; for cities cannot exist, if a few only share in the virtues, as
in the arts. And further, make a law by my order, that he who
has no part in reverence and justice shall be put to death, for he is
a plague of the State."

And this is the reason, Socrates, why the Athenians and mankind
in general, when the question relates to carpentering or any other
mechanical art, allow but a few to share in their deliberations; and
when any one else interferes, then, as you say, they object, if he be
not of the favoured few; which, as I reply, is very natural. But
when they meet to deliberate about political virtue, which proceeds only by way of justice and wisdom, they are patient enough
of any man who speaks of them, as is also natural, because they
think that every man ought to share in this sort of virtue, and that
States could not exist if this were otherwise. I have explained to
you, Socrates, the reason of this phenomenon.

And that you may not suppose yourself to be deceived in thinking that all men regard every man as having a share of justice or
honesty and of every other political virtue, let me give you a further proof, which is this. In other cases, as you are aware, if a man
says that he is a good flute-player, or skilful in any other art in
which he has no skill, people either laugh at him or are angry with
him, and his relations think that he is mad and go and admonish
him; but when honesty is in question, or some other political virtue, even if they know that he is dishonest, yet, if the man comes
publicly forward and tells the truth about his dishonesty, then,
what in the other case was held by them to be good sense, they
now deem to be madness. They say that all men ought to profess
honesty whether they are honest or not, and that a man is out of
his mind who says anything else. Their notion is, that a man must
have some degree of honesty; and that if he has none at all he
ought not to be in the world.

I have been showing that they are right in admitting every man
as a counsellor about this sort of virtue, as they are of opinion that

every man is a partaker of it. And I will now endeavour to show
further that they do not conceive this virtue to be given by nature,
or to grow spontaneously, but to be a thing which may be taught;
and which comes to a man by taking pains. No one would instruct,
no one would rebuke, or be angry with those whose calamities they
suppose to be due to nature or chance; they do not try to punish or
to prevent them from being what they are; they do but pity them.
Who is so foolish as to chastise or instruct the ugly, or the diminu-
tive, or the feeble? And for this reason. Because he knows that good
and evil of this kind is the work of nature and of chance; whereas
if a man is wanting in those good qualities which are attained by
study and exercise and teaching, and has only the contrary evil
qualities, other men are angry with him, and punish and reprove
him—of these evil qualities one is impiety, another injustice, and
they may be described generally as the very opposite of political
virtue. In such cases any man will be angry with another, and
reprimand him,—clearly because he thinks that by study and learning, the virtue in which the other is deficient may be acquired. If
you will think, Socrates, of the nature of punishment, you will see
at once that in the opinion of mankind virtue may be acquired; no
one punishes the evil-doer under the notion, or for the reason, that
he has done wrong,—only the unreasonable fury of a beast acts in
that manner. But he who desires to inflict rational punishment
does not retaliate for a past wrong which cannot be undone; he has
regard to the future, and is desirous that the man who is punished,
and he who sees him punished, may be deterred from doing wrong
again. He punishes for the sake of prevention, thereby clearly implying that virtue is capable of being taught. This is the notion of
all who retaliate upon others either privately or publicly. And the
Athenians, too, your own citizens, like other men, punish and take
vengeance on all whom they regard as evil-doers; and hence, we
may infer them to be of the number of those who think that virtue
may be acquired and taught. Thus far, Socrates, I have shown you
clearly enough, if I am not mistaken, that your countrymen are
right in admitting the tinker and the cobbler to advise about politics, and also that they deem virtue to be capable of being taught
and acquired.

There yet remains one difficulty which has been raised by you
about the sons of good men. What is the reason why good men

teach their sons the knowledge which is gained from teachers, and make them wise in that, but do nothing towards improving them in virtues which distinguish themselves? And here, Socrates, I will leave the apologue and resume the argument. Please to consider: Is there or is there not some one quality of which all the citizens must be partakers, if there is to be a city at all? In the answer to this question is contained the only solution of your difficulty; there is no other. For if there be any such quality, and this quality or unity is not the art of the carpenter, or the smith, or the potter, but justice and temperance and holiness and, in a word, manly virtue—if this is the quality of which all men must be partakers, and which is the very condition of their learning or doing anything else, and if he who is wanting in this, whether he be a child only or a grown-up man or woman, must be taught and punished, until by punishment he becomes better, and he who rebels against instruction and punishment is either exiled or condemned to death under the idea that he is incurable—if what I am saying be true, good men have their sons taught other things and not this, do consider how extraordinary their conduct would appear to be. For we have shown that they think virtue capable of being taught and cultivated both in private and public; and, notwithstanding, they have their sons taught lesser matters, ignorance of which does not involve the punishment of death: but greater things, of which the ignorance may cause death and exile to those who have no training or knowledge of them—aye, and confiscation as well as death, and, in a word, may be the ruin of families—those things, I say, they are supposed not to teach them,—not to take the utmost care that they should learn. How improbable is this, Socrates!

Education and admonition commence in the first years of childhood, and last to the very end of life. Mother and nurse and father and tutor are vying with one another about the improvement of the child as soon as ever he is able to understand what is being said to him: he cannot say or do anything without their setting forth to him that this is just and that is unjust; this is honourable, that is dishonourable; this is holy, that is unholy; do this and abstain from that. And if he obeys, well and good; if not, he is straightened by threats and blows, like a piece of bent or warped wood. At a later stage they send him to teachers, and enjoin them to see to his manners even more than to his reading and music; and the teachers do as they are desired. And when the boy has learned his letters and is beginning to understand what is written, as before he understood only what was spoken, they put into his hands the works of great poets, which he reads sitting on a bench at school; in these are contained many admonitions, and many tales, and praises, and encomia of ancient famous men, which he is required to learn by heart, in order that he may imitate or emulate them and desire to become like them. Then, again, the teachers of the lyre take similar care that their young disciple is temperate and gets into no mischief; and when they have taught him the use of the lyre, they introduce him to the poems of other excellent poets, who are the lyric poets; and these they set to music, and make their harmonies and rhythms quite familiar to the children's souls, in order that they may learn to be more gentle, and harmonious, and rhythmical, and so fitted for speech and action; for the life of man in every part has need of harmony and rhythm. Then they send them to the master of gymnastic, in order that their bodies may better minister to the virtuous mind, and that they may not be compelled through bodily weakness to play the coward in war or on any other occasion. This is what is done by those who have the means, and those who have the means are the rich; their children begin to go to school soonest and leave off latest. When they have done with masters, the State again compels them to learn the laws, and live after the pattern which they furnish, and not after their own fancies; and just as in learning to write, the writing master first draws lines with a style for the use of the young beginner, and gives him the tablet and makes him follow the lines, so the city draws the laws, which were the invention of good lawgivers living in the olden time; these are given to the young man, in order to guide him in his conduct whether he is commanding or obeying; and he who transgresses them is to be corrected, or, in other words, called to account, which is a term used not only in your country, but also in many others, seeing that justice calls men to account. Now, when there is all this care about virtue private and public, why, Socrates, do you still wonder and doubt whether virtue can be taught? Cease to wonder, for the opposite would be far more surprising.

But why then do the sons of good fathers often turn out ill? There is nothing very wonderful in this; for, as I have been saying, the existence of a State implies that virtue is not any man's private possession. If so—and nothing can be truer—then I will further ask you to imagine, as an illustration, some other pursuit or branch of knowledge which may be assumed equally to be the condition of the existence of a State. Suppose that there could be no state unless we were all flute-players, as far as each had the capacity, and everybody was freely teaching everybody the art, both in private and public, and reproving the bad player as freely and openly as every man now teaches justice and the laws, not concealing them as he would conceal the other arts, but imparting them—for all of us have a mutual interest in the justice and virtue of one another, and this is the reason why every one is so ready to teach justice and the laws;—suppose, I say, that there were the same readiness and liberality among us in teaching one another flute-playing, do you imagine, Socrates, that the sons of good flute-players would be more likely to be good than the sons of bad ones? I think not. Would not their sons grow up to be distinguished or undistinguished according to their own natural capacities as flute-players, and the son of a good player would often turn out to be a bad one, and the son of a bad player to be a good one, and all flute-players would be good enough in comparison of those who were ignorant and unacquainted with the art of flute-playing? In like manner I would have you consider that he who appears to you to be the worst of those who have been brought up in laws and humanities, would appear to be a just man and a master of justice if he were to be compared with men who had no education, or courts of justice, or laws, or any restraints upon them which compelled them to practise virtue—with the savages, for example, whom the poet Pherecrates exhibited on the stage at the last year's Lenaean festival. If you were living among men such as the man-haters in his chorus, you would be only too glad to meet with Eurybates and Phrynondas, and you would sorrowfully long to revisit the rascality of this part of the world. And you, Socrates, are discontented, and why? Because all men are teachers of virtue, each one according to his ability; and you say, Where are the teachers? You might as well ask, Who teaches Greek? For of that too there will not be any teachers found. Or you might ask, Who is to teach the sons of our artisans this same art which they have learned of their fathers? He and his fellow-workmen have taught them to the best of their ability,—but who will carry them further in their arts? And you would certainly have a difficulty, Socrates, in finding a teacher of them; but there would be no difficulty in finding a teacher of those who are wholly ignorant. And this is true of virtue or of anything else; if a man is better able than we are to promote virtue ever so little, we must be content with the result. A teacher of this sort I believe myself to be, and above all other men to have the knowledge which makes a man noble and good; and I give my pupils their money's worth, and even more, as they themselves confess. And therefore I have introduced the following mode of payment: —When a man has been my pupil, if he likes he pays my price, but there is no compulsion; and if he does not like, he has only to go into a temple and take an oath of the value of the instructions, and he pays no more than he declares to be their value.

Such is my apologue, Socrates, and such is the argument by which I endeavour to show that virtue may be taught, and that this is the opinion of the Athenians. And I have also attempted to show that you are not to wonder at good fathers having bad sons, or at good sons having bad fathers, of which the sons of Polycleitus afford an example, who are the companions of our friends here, Paralus and Xanthippus, but are nothing in comparison with their father; and this is true of the sons of many other artists. As yet I ought not to say the same of Paralus and Xanthippus themselves, for they are young and there is still hope of them.

Protagoras ended, and in my ear

"So charming left his voice, that I the while
Thought him still speaking; still stood fixed to hear." [1]

At length, when the truth dawned upon me, that he had really finished, not without difficulty I began to collect myself, and looking at Hippocrates, I said to him: O son of Apollodorus, how deeply grateful I am to you for having brought me hither; I would not have missed the speech of Protagoras for a great deal. For I used to imagine that no human care could make men good; but I know better now. Yet I have still one very small difficulty which I am sure that Protagoras will easily explain, as he has already explained so much. If a man were to go and consult Pericles or any of our great speakers about these matters, he might perhaps hear as fine a discourse; but then when one has a question to ask of any

[1] Borrowed by Milton, Paradise Lost, viii, 2, 3.

of them, like books, they can neither answer nor ask; and if any
one challenges the least particular of their speech, they go ringing
on in a long harangue, like brazen pots, which when they are
struck continue to sound unless some one puts his hand upon
them: whereas our friend Protagoras cannot only make a good
speech, as he has already shown, but when he is asked a question he
can answer briefly; and when he asks he will wait and hear the
answer; and this is a very rare gift. Now I, Protagoras, want to ask
you a little question, which if you will only answer, I shall be quite
satisfied. You were saying that virtue can be taught;—that I will
take upon your authority, and there is no one to whom I am more
ready to trust. But I marvel at one thing about which I should like
to have my mind set at rest. You were speaking of Zeus sending
justice and reverence to men; and several times while you were
speaking, justice, and temperance, and holiness, and all these qualities, were described by you as if together they made up virtue.
Now I want you to tell me truly whether virtue is one whole, of
which justice and temperance and holiness are parts; or whether
all these are only the names of one and the same thing: that is the
doubt which still lingers in my mind.

There is no difficulty, Socrates, in answering that the qualities
of which you are speaking are the parts of virtue which is one.

And are they parts, I said, in the same sense in which mouth,
nose, and eyes, and ears, are the parts of a face; or are they like
parts of gold, which differ from the whole and from one another
only in being larger or smaller?

I should say that they differed, Socrates, in the first way; they
are related to one another as the parts of a face are related to the
whole face.

And do men have some one part and some another part of virtue? Or if a man has one part, must he also have all the others?

By no means, he said; for many a man is brave and not just, or
just and not wise.

You would not deny, then, that courage and wisdom are also
parts of virtue?

Most undoubtedly they are, he answered; and wisdom is the
noblest of the parts.

And they are all different from one another? I said.

Yes.

And has each of them a distinct function like the parts of the face;—the eye, for example, is not like the ear, and has not the same functions; and the other parts are none of them like one another, either in their functions, or in any other way? I want to know whether the comparison holds concerning the parts of virtue. Do they also differ from one another in themselves and in their functions? For that is clearly what the simile would imply.

Yes, Socrates, you are right in supposing that they differ.

Then, I said, no other part of virtue is like knowledge, or like justice, or like courage, or like temperance, or like holiness?

No, he answered.

Well, then, I said, suppose that you and I enquire into their natures. And first, you would agree with me that justice is of the nature of a thing, would you not? That is my opinion: would it not be yours also?

Mine also, he said.

And suppose that some one were to ask us, saying, "O Protagoras, and you, Socrates, what about this thing which you were calling justice, is it just or unjust?"—and I were to answer, just: would you vote with me or against me?

With you, he said.

Thereupon I should answer to him who asked me, that justice is of the nature of the just: would not you?

Yes, he said.

And suppose that he went on to say: "Well, now, is there also such a thing as holiness?"—we should answer, "Yes," if I am not mistaken?

Yes, he said.

Which you would also acknowledge to be a thing—should we not say so?

He assented.

"And is this sort of thing which is of the nature of the holy, or of the nature of the unholy?" I should be angry at his putting such a question, and should say, "Peace, man; nothing can be holy if holiness is not holy." What would you say? Would you not answer in the same way?

Certainly, he said.

And then after this suppose that he came and asked us, "What were you saying just now? Perhaps I may not have heard you rightly, but you seemed to me to be saying that the parts of virtue were not the same as one another." I should reply, "You certainly heard that said, but not, as you imagine, by me; for I only asked the question; Protagoras gave the answer." And suppose that he turned to you and said, "Is this true, Protagoras? and do you maintain that one part of virtue is unlike another, and is this your position?"—how would you answer him?

I could not help acknowledging the truth of what he said, Socrates.

Well, then, Protagoras, we will assume this; and now supposing that he proceeded to say further, "Then holiness is not of the nature of justice, nor justice of the nature of holiness, but of the nature of unholiness; and holiness is of the nature of the not just, and therefore of the unjust, and the unjust is the unholy"; how shall we answer him? I should certainly answer him on my own behalf that justice is holy, and that holiness is just; and I would say in like manner on your behalf also, if you would allow me, that justice is either the same with holiness, or very nearly the same; and above all I would assert that justice is like holiness and holiness is like justice; and I wish that you would tell me whether I may be permitted to give this answer on your behalf, and whether you would agree with me.

He replied, I cannot simply agree, Socrates, to the proposition that justice is holy and that holiness is just, for there appears to me to be a difference between them. But what matter? if you please I please; and let us assume, if you will, that justice is holy, and that holiness is just.

Pardon me, I replied; I do not want this "if you wish" or "if you will" sort of conclusion to be proven, but I want you and me to be proven: I mean to say that the conclusion will be best proven if there be no "if."

Well, he said, I admit that justice bears a resemblance to holiness, for there is always some point of view in which everything is like every other thing; white is in a certain way like black, and hard is like soft, and the most extreme opposites have some qualities in common; even the parts of the face which, as we were saying before, are distinct and have different functions, are still in a certain point of view similar, and one of them is like another of them. And you may prove that they are like one another on the same principle that all things are like one another; and yet things which are alike in some particular ought not to be called alike, nor things which are unlike in some particular, however slight, unlike.

And do you think, I said in a tone of surprise, that justice and holiness have but a small degree of likeness?

Certainly not; any more than I agree with what I understand to be your view.

Well, I said, as you appear to have a difficulty about this, let us take another of the examples which you mentioned instead. Do you admit the existence of folly?

I do.

And is not wisdom the very opposite of folly?

That is true, he said.

And when men act rightly and advantageously they seem to you to be temperate?

Yes, he said.

And temperance makes them temperate?

Certainly.

And they who do not act rightly act foolishly, and in acting thus are not temperate?

I agree, he said.

Then to act foolishly is the opposite of acting temperately?

He assented.

And foolish actions are done by folly, and temperate actions by temperance?

He agreed.

And that is done strongly which is done by strength, and that which is weakly done, by weakness?

He assented.

And that which is done with swiftness is done swiftly, and that which is done with slowness, slowly?

He assented again.

And that which is done in the same manner, is done by the same; and that which is done in an opposite manner by the opposite?

He agreed.

Once more, I said, is there anything beautiful?

Yes.

To which the only opposite is the ugly?

There is no other.

And is there anything good?

There is.

To which the only opposite is the evil?

There is no other.

And there is the acute in sound?

True.

To which the only opposite is the grave?

There is no other, he said, but that.

Then every opposite has one opposite only and no more?

He assented.

Then now, I said, let us recapitulate our admissions. First of all we admitted that everything has one opposite and not more than one?

We did so.

And we admitted also that what was done in opposite ways was done by opposites?

Yes.

And that which was done foolishly, as we further admitted, was done in the opposite way to that which was done temperately?

Yes.

And that which was done temperately was done by temperance, and that which was done foolishly by folly?

He agreed.

And that which is done in opposite ways is done by opposites?

Yes.

And one thing is done by temperance, and quite another thing by folly?

Yes.

And in opposite ways?

Certainly.

And therefore by opposites:—then folly is the opposite of temperance?

Clearly.

And do you remember that folly has already been acknowledged by us to be the opposite of wisdom?

He assented.

And we said that everything has only one opposite?

Yes.

Then, Protagoras, which of the two assertions shall we renounce? One says that everything has but one opposite; the other
that wisdom is distinct from temperance, and that both of them
are parts of virtue; and that they are not only distinct, but dissimilar, both in themselves and in their functions, like the parts of
a face. Which of these two assertions shall we renounce? For both
of them together are certainly not in harmony; they do not accord
or agree: for how can they be said to agree if everything is assumed
to have only one opposite and not more than one, and yet folly,
which is one, has clearly the two opposites—wisdom and temperance? Is not that true, Protagoras? What else would you say?

He assented, but with great reluctance.

Then temperance and wisdom are the same, as before justice and
holiness appeared to us to be nearly the same. And now, Protagoras, I said, we must finish the enquiry, and not faint. Do you
think than an unjust man can be temperate in his unjustice?

I should be ashamed, Socrates, he said, to acknowledge this,
which nevertheless many may be found to assert.

And shall I argue with them or with you? I replied.

I would rather, he said, that you should argue with the many
first, if you will.

Whichever you please, if you will only answer me and say
whether you are of their opinion or not. My object is to test the
validity of the argument; and yet the result may be that I who ask
and you who answer may both be put on our trial.

Protagoras at first made a show of refusing, as he said that the
argument was not encouraging; at length, he consented to answer.

Now then, I said, begin at the beginning and answer me. You
think that some men are temperate, and yet unjust?

Yes, he said; let that be admitted.

And temperance is good sense?

Yes.

And good sense is good counsel in doing injustice?

Granted.

If they succeed, I said, or if they do not succeed?

If they succeed.

And you would admit the existence of good?

Yes.

And is the good that which is expedient for man?

Yes, indeed, he said: and there are some things which may be inexpedient, and yet I call them good.

I thought that Protagoras was getting ruffled and excited; he seemed to be setting himself in an attitude of war. Seeing this, I minded my business, and gently said:—

When you say, Protagoras, that things inexpedient are good, do you mean inexpedient for man only, or inexpedient altogether? and do you call the latter good?

Certainly not the last, he replied; for I know of many things,— meats, drinks, medicines, and ten thousand other things, which are inexpedient for man, and some which are expedient; and some which are neither expedient nor inexpedient for man, but only for horses; and some for oxen only, and some for dogs; and some for no animals, but only for trees; and some for the roots of trees and not for their branches, as for example, manure, which is a good thing when laid about the roots of a tree, but utterly destructive if thrown upon the shoots and young branches; or I may instance olive oil, which is mischievous to all plants, and generally most injurious to the hair of every animal with the exception of man, but beneficial to human hair and to the human body generally; and even in this application (so various and changeable is the nature of the benefit), that which is the greatest good to the outward parts of a man, is a very great evil to his inward parts: and for this reason physicians always forbid their patients the use of oil in their food, except in very small quantities, just enough to extinguish the disagreeable sensation of smell in meats and sauces.

When he had given this answer, the company cheered him. And I said: Protagoras, I have a wretched memory, and when any one makes a long speech to me I never remember what he is talking about. As then, if I had been deaf, and you were going to converse with me, you would have to raise your voice; so now, having such a bad memory, I will ask you to cut your answers shorter, if you would take me with you.

What do you mean? he said: how am I to shorten my answers? shall I make them too short?

Certainly not, I said.

But short enough?

Yes, I said.

Shall I answer what appears to me to be short enough, or what appears to you to be short enough?

I have heard, I said, that you can speak and teach others to speak about the same things at such length that words never seemed to fail, or with such brevity that no one could use fewer of them. Please therefore, if you talk with me, to adopt the latter or more compendious method.

Socrates, he replied, many a battle of words have I fought, and if I had followed the method of disputation which my adversaries desired, as you want me to do, I should have been no better than another, and the name of Protagoras would have been nowhere.

I saw that he was not satisfied with his previous answers, and that he would not play the part of answerer any more if he could help; and I considered that there was no call upon me to continue the conversation; so I said: Protagoras, I do not wish to force the conversation upon you if you had rather not, but when you are willing to argue with me in such a way that I can follow you, then I will argue with you. Now you, as is said of you by others and as you say yourself, are able to have discussions in shorter forms of speech as well as in longer, for you are a master of wisdom; but I cannot manage these long speeches: I only wish that I could. You, on the other hand, who are capable of either, ought to speak shorter as I beg you, and then we might converse. But I see that you are disinclined, and as I have an engagement which will prevent my staying to hear you at greater length (for I have to be in another place), I will depart; although I should have liked to have heard you.

Thus I spoke, and was rising from my seat, when Callias seized me by the right hand, and in his left hand caught hold of this old cloak of mine. He said: We cannot let you go, Socrates, for if you leave us there will be an end of our discussions: I must therefore beg you to remain, as there is nothing in the world that I should like better than to hear you and Protagoras discourse. Do not deny the company this pleasure.

Now, I had got up, and was in the act of departure. Son of Hipponicus, I replied, I have always admired, and do now heartily applaud and love your philosophical spirit, and I would gladly comply with your request, if I could. But the truth is that I cannot. And what you ask is as great an impossibility to me, as if you bade me run a race with Crison of Himera, when in his prime, or with some one of the long or day course runners. To such a request I should reply that I would fain ask the same of my own legs; but they refuse to comply. And therefore if you want to see Crison and me in the same stadium, you must bid him slacken his speed to mine, for I cannot run quickly, and he can run slowly. And in like manner if you want to hear me and Protagoras discoursing, you must ask him to shorten his answers, and to keep to the point, as he did at first; if not, how can there be any discussion? For discussion is one thing, and making an oration is quite another, in my humble opinion.

But you see, Socrates, said Callias, that Protagoras may fairly claim to speak in his own way, just as you claim to speak in yours.

Here Alcibiades interposed, and said: That, Callias, is not a true statement of the case. For our friend Socrates admits that he cannot make a speech—in this he yields the palm to Protagoras: but I should be greatly surprised if he yielded to any living man in the power of holding and apprehending an argument. Now, if Protagoras will make a similar admission, and confess that he is inferior to Socrates in argumentative skill, that is enough for Socrates; but if he claims superiority in argument as well, let him ask and answer—not, when a question is asked, slipping away from the point, and instead of answering, making a speech at such length that most of his hearers forget the question at issue (not that Socrates is likely to forget—I will be bound for that, although he may pretend in fun that he has a bad memory). And Socrates appears to me to be more in the right than Protagoras; that is my view, and every man ought to say what he thinks.

When Alcibiades had done speaking, some one—Critias, I believe—went on to say: O Prodicus and Hippias, Callias appears to me to be a partisan of Protagoras: and this led Alcibiades, who loves opposition, to take the other side. But we should not be partisans either of Socrates or of Protagoras; let us rather unite in entreating both of them not to break up the discussion.

Prodicus added: That, Critias, seems to me to be well said, for those who are present at such discussions ought to be impartial hearers of both the speakers; remembering, however, that impartiality is not the same as equality, for both sides should be impartially heard, and yet an equal meed should not be assigned to both

of them; but to the wiser a higher meed should be given, and a
lower to the less wise. And I as well as Critias would beg you, Protagoras and Socrates, to grant our request, which is, that you will
argue with one another and not wrangle; for friends argue with
friends out of good-will, but only adversaries and enemies wrangle.
And then our meeting will be delightful; for in this way you, who
are the speakers, will be most likely to win esteem, and not praise
only, among us who are your audience; for esteem is a sincere conviction of the hearers' souls, but praise is often an insincere expression of men uttering falsehoods contrary to their conviction. And
thus we who are the hearers will be gratified and not pleased; for
gratification is of the mind when receiving wisdom and knowledge,
but pleasure is of the body when eating or experiencing some other
bodily delight. Thus spoke Prodicus, and many of the company
applauded his words.

Hippias the sage spoke next. He said: All of you who are here
present I reckon to be kinsmen and friends and fellow-citizens, by
nature and not by law; for by nature like is akin to like, whereas
law is the tyrant of mankind, and often compels us to do many
things which are against nature. How great would be the disgrace
then, if we, who know the nature of things, and are the wisest of
the Hellenes, and such are met together in this city, which is the
metropolis of wisdom, and in the greatest and most glorious house
of this city, should have nothing to show worthy of this height of
dignity, but should only quarrel with one another like the meanest
of mankind! I do pray and advise you, Protagoras, and you, Socrates, to agree upon a compromise. Let us be your peacemakers.
And do not you, Socrates, aim at this precise and extreme brevity
in discourse, if Protagoras objects, but loosen and let go the reins
of speech, that your words may be grander and more becoming to
you. Neither do you, Protagoras, go forth on the gale with every
sail set out of sight of land into an ocean of words, but let there be
a mean observed by both of you. Do as I say. And let me also persuade you to choose an arbiter or overseer or president; he will
keep watch over your words and will prescribe their proper length.

This proposal was received by the company with universal approval; Callias said that he would not let me off, and they begged
me to choose an arbiter. But I said that to choose an umpire of discourse would be unseemly; for if the person chosen was inferior,

then the inferior or worse ought not to preside over the better; or if he was equal, neither would that be well; for he who is our equal will do as we do, and what will be the use of choosing him? And if you say, "Let us have a better then,"—to that I answer that you cannot have any one who is wiser than Protagoras. And if you choose another who is not really better, and whom you only say is better, to put another over him as though he were an inferior person would be an unworthy reflection on him; not that, as far as I am concerned, any reflection is of much consequence to me. Let me tell you then what I will do in order that the conversation and discussion may go as you desire. If Protagoras is not disposed to answer let him ask and I will answer; and I will endeavour to show at the same time how, as I maintain, he ought to answer: and when I have answered as many questions as he likes to ask, let him in like manner answer me; and if he seems to be not very ready at answering the precise question asked of him, you and I will unite in entreating him, as you entreated me, not to spoil the discission. And this will require no special arbiter—all of you shall be arbiters.

This was generally approved, and Protagoras, though very much against his will, was obliged to agree that he would ask questions; and when he had put a sufficient number of them, that he would answer in his turn those which he was asked in short replies. He began to put his questions as follows:—

I am of opinion, Socrates, he said, that skill in poetry is the principal part of education; and this I conceive to be the power of knowing what compositions of the poets are correct, and what are not, and how they are to be distinguished, and of explaining when asked the reason of the difference. And I propose to transfer the question which you and I have been discussing to the domain of poetry; we will speak as before of virtue, but in reference to a passage of a poet. Now Simonides says to Scopas the son of Creon the Thessalian:—

"Hardly on the one hand can a man become truly good, built four-square in hands and feet and mind, a work without a flaw."

Do you know the poem? or shall I repeat the whole?

There is no need, I said; for I am perfectly well acquainted with the ode,—I have made a careful study of it.

Very well, he said. And do you think that the ode is a good composition, and true?

Yes, I said, both good and true.

But if there is a contradiction, can the composition be good or true?

No, not in that case, I replied.

And is there not a contradiction? he asked. Reflect.

Well, my friend, I have reflected.

And does not the poet proceed to say, "I do not agree with the word of Pittacus, albeit the utterance of a wise man: Hardly can a man be good"? Now you will observe that this is said by the same poet.

I know it.

And do you think, he said, that the two sayings are consistent?

Yes, I said, I think so (at the same time I could not help fearing that there might be something in what he said). And you think otherwise?

Why, he said, how can he be consistent in both? First of all, premising as his own thought, "Hardly can a man become truly good"; and then a little further on in the poem, forgetting, and blaming Pittacus and refusing to agree with him, when he says, "Hardly can a man be good," which is the very same thing. And yet when he blames him who says the same with himself, he blames himself; so that he must be wrong either in his first or his second assertion.

Many of the audience cheered and applauded this. And I felt at first giddy and faint, as if I had received a blow from the hand of an expert boxer, when I heard his words and the sounds of cheering; and to confess the truth, I wanted to get time to think what the meaning of the poet really was. So I turned to Prodicus and called him. Prodicus, I said, Simonides is a countryman of yours, and you ought to come to his aid. I must appeal to you, like the river Scamander in Homer, who, when beleaguered by Achilles, summons the Simoïs to aid him, saying:

"Brother dear, let us both together stay the force of the hero."

And I summon you, for I am afraid that Protagoras will make an end of Simonides. Now is the time to rehabilitate Simonides, by the application of your philosophy of synonyms, which enables you

to distinguish "will" and "wish," and make other charming distinctions like those which you drew just now. And I should like to
know whether you would agree with me; for I am of opinion that
there is no contradiction in the words of Simonides. And first of
all I wish that you would say whether, in your opinion, Prodicus,
"being" is the same as "becoming."

Not the same, certainly, replied Prodicus.

Did not Simonides first set forth, as his own view, that "Hardly
can a man become truly good"?

Quite right, said Prodicus.

And then he blames Pittacus, not, as Protagoras imagines, for
repeating that which he says himself, but for saying something different from himself. Pittacus does not say as Simonides says, that
hardly can a man become good, but hardly can a man be good: and
our friend Prodicus would maintain that being, Protagoras, is not
the same as becoming; and if they are not the same, then Simonides
is not inconsistent with himself. I dare say that Prodicus and many
others would say, as Hesiod says,

"On the one hand, hardly can a man become good,
  For the gods have made virtue the reward of toil;
  But on the other hand, when you have climbed the height,
  Then, to retain virtue, however difficult the acquisition, is easy."

Prodicus heard and approved; but Protagoras said: Your correction, Socrates, involves a greater error than is contained in the
sentence which you are correcting.

Alas! I said, Protagoras; then I am a sorry physician, and do but
aggravate a disorder which I am seeking to cure.

Such is the fact, he said.

How so? I asked.

The poet, he replied, could never have made such a mistake as
to say that virtue, which in the opinion of all men is the hardest of
all things, can be easily retained.

Well, I said, and how fortunate are we in having Prodicus
among us, at the right moment; for he has a wisdom, Protagoras,
which, as I imagine, is more than human and of very ancient date,
and may be as old as Simonides or even older. Learned as you are
in many things, you appear to know nothing of this; but I know,
for I am a disciple of his. And now, if I am not mistaken, you do

not understand the word "hard" in the sense which Simonides intended; and I must correct you, as Prodicus corrects me when I use the word "awful" as a term of praise. If I say that Protagoras or any one else is an "awfully" wise man, he asks me if I am not ashamed of calling that which is good "awful"; and then he explains to me that the term "awful" is always taken in a bad sense, and that no one speaks of being "awfully" healthy or wealthy, or of "awful" peace, but of "awful" disease, "awful" war, "awful" poverty, meaning by the term "awful," evil. And I think that Simonides and his countrymen the Ceans, when they spoke of "hard" meant "evil," or something which you do not understand. Let us ask Prodicus, for he ought to be able to answer questions about the dialect of Simonides. What did he mean, Prodicus, by the term "hard"?

Evil, said Prodicus.

And therefore, I said, Prodicus, he blames Pittacus for saying, "Hard is the good" just as if that were equivalent to saying, Evil is the good.

Yes, he said, that was certainly his meaning; and he is twitting Pittacus with ignorance of the use of terms, which in a Lesbian, who has been accustomed to speak a barbarous language, is natural.

Do you hear, Protagoras, I asked, what our friend Prodicus is saying? And have you an answer for him?

You are entirely mistaken, Prodicus, said Protagoras; and I know very well that Simonides in using the word "hard" meant what all of us mean, not evil, but that which is not easy—that which takes a great deal of trouble: of this I am positive.

I said: I also incline to believe, Protagoras, that this was the meaning of Simonides, of which our friend Prodicus was very well aware, but he thought that he would make fun, and try if you could maintain your thesis; for that Simonides could never have meant the other is clearly proved by the context, in which he says that God only has this gift. Now, he cannot surely mean to say that to be good is evil, when he afterwards proceeds to say that God only has this gift, and that this is the attribute of him and of no other. For if this be his meaning, Prodicus would impute to Simonides a character of recklessness which is very unlike his countrymen. And I should like to tell you, I said, what I imagine to be the real meaning of Simonides in this poem, if you will test what, in your way of speaking, would be called my skill in poetry; or, if you would rather, I will be the listener.

To this proposal Protagoras replied: As you please;—and Hippias, Prodicus, and the others told me by all means to do as I proposed.

Then now, I said, I will endeavour to explain to you my opinion about this poem of Simonides. There is a very ancient philosophy which is more cultivated in Crete and Lacedaemon than in any other part of Hellas, and there are more philosophers in those countries than anywhere else in the world. This, however, is a secret which the Lacedaemonians deny; and they pretend to be ignorant, just because they do not wish to have it thought that they rule the world by wisdom, like the Sophists of whom Protagoras was speaking, and not by valour of arms; considering that if the reason of their superiority were disclosed, all men would be practising their wisdom. And this secret of theirs has never been discovered by the imitators of Lacedaemonian fashions in other cities, who go about with their ears bruised in imitation of them, and have the caestus bound on their arms and are always in training, and wear short cloaks; for they imagine that these are the practices which have enabled the Lacedaemonians to conquer the other Hellenes. Now, when the Lacedaemonians want to unbend and hold free conversation with their wise men, and are no longer satisfied with mere secret intercourse, they drive out all these laconizers, and any other foreigners who may happen to be in their country, and they hold a philosophical *séance* unknown to strangers; and they themselves forbid their young men to go out into other cities—in this they are like the Cretans—in order that they might not unlearn the lessons which they have taught them. And in Lacedaemon and Crete not only men but also women have a pride in their high cultivation. And hereby you may know that I am right in attributing to the Lacedaemonians this excellence in philosophy and speculation: If a man converses with the most ordinary Lacedaemonian, he will find him seldom good for much in general conversation, but at any point in the discourse he will be darting out some notable saying, terse and full of meaning, with unerring aim; and the person with whom he is talking seems to be like a child in his hands. And many of our own age and of former ages have noted that the true Lacedaemonian type of character has the love of philosophy even stronger than the love of gymnastics; they are conscious that only a perfectly educated man is capable of uttering such expressions. Such were Thales of Miletus, and Pittacus of Mitylene, and Bias of Priene, and our own Solon, and Cleobulus the Lindian, and Myson the Chenian; and seventh in the catalogue of wise men was the Lacedaemonian Chilo. All these were lovers and emulators and disciples of the culture of the Lacedaemonians, and any one may perceive that their wisdom was of this character; consisting of short memorable sentences, which they severally uttered. And they met together and dedicated in the temple of Apollo at Delphi, as the first fruits of their wisdom, the far-famed inscriptions, which are in all men's mouths,—"Know thyself," and "Nothing too much."

Why do I say all this? I am explaining that this Lacedaemonian brevity was the style of primitive philosophy. Now there was a saying of Pittacus which was privately circulated and received the approbation of the wise, "Hard is it to be good." And Simonides, who was ambitious of the fame of wisdom, was aware that if he could overthrow this saying, then, as if he had won a victory over some famous athlete, he would carry off the palm among his contemporaries. And if I am not mistaken, he composed the entire poem with the secret intention of damaging Pittacus and his saying.

Let us all unite in examining his words, and see whether I am speaking the truth. Simonides must have been a lunatic, if, in the very first words of the poem, wanting to say only that to become good is hard, he inserted, "on the one hand" ["on the one hand to become good is hard"] ; there would be no reason for the introduction of "on the one hand," unless you suppose him to speak with a hostile reference to the words of Pittacus. Pittacus is saying "Hard is it to be good," and he, in refutation of this thesis, rejoins that the truly hard thing, Pittacus, is to become good, not joining "truly" with "good," but with "hard." Not, that the hard thing is to be truly good, as though there were some truly good men, and there were others who were good but not truly good (this would be a very simple observation, and quite unworthy of Simonides); but you must suppose him to make a trajection of the word "truly," construing the saying of Pittacus thus (and let us imagine Pittacus to be speaking and Simonides answering him): "O my friends," says Pittacus, "hard is it to be good," and Simonides answers, "In that, Pittacus, you are mistaken; the difficulty is not to be good, but on the one hand, to become good, four-square in hands and feet and mind, without a flaw—that is hard truly." This way of reading the passage accounts for the insertion of, "on the one hand," and for the position at the end of the clause of the word "truly," and all that follows shows this to be the meaning. A great deal might be said in praise of the details of the poem, which is a charming piece of workmanship, and very finished, but such minutiae would be tedious. I should like, however, to point out the general intention of the poem, which is certainly designed in every part to be a refutation of the saying of Pittacus. For he speaks in what follows a little further on as if he meant to argue that although there is a difficulty in becoming good, yet this is possible for a time, and only for a time. But having become good, to remain in a good state and be good, as you, Pittacus, affirm, is not possible, and is not granted to man; God only has this blessing; "but man cannot help being bad when the force of circumstances overpowers him." Now, whom does the force of circumstances overpower in the command of a vessel? Not the private individual, for he is always overpowered; and as one who is already prostrate cannot be overthrown, and only he who is standing upright but not he who is prostrate can be laid prostrate, so the force of circumstances can only overpower him who, at some time or other, has resources, and not him who is at all times helpless. The descent of a great storm may make the pilot helpless, or the severity of the season the husbandman or the physician; for the good may become bad, as another poet witnesses:—

"The good are sometimes good and sometimes bad."

But the bad does not become bad; he is always bad. So that when the force of circumstances overpowers the man of resources and skill and virtue, then he cannot help being bad. And you, Pittacus, are saying, "Hard is it to be good." Now there is a difficulty in becoming good; and yet this is possible: but to be good is an impossibility—

"For he who does well is the good man, and he who does ill is the bad."

But what sort of doing is good in letters? and what sort of doing makes a man good in letters? Clearly the knowing of them. And what sort of well-doing makes a man a good physician? Clearly the knowledge of the art of healing the sick. "But he who does ill is the bad." Now, who becomes a bad physician? Clearly he who is in the first place a physician, and in the second place a good physician; for he may become a bad one also: but none of us unskilled individuals can by any amount of doing ill become physicians, any more than we can become carpenters or anything of that sort; and he who by doing ill cannot become a physician at all, clearly cannot become a bad physician. In like manner the good may become deteriorated by time, or toil, or disease, or other accident (the only real doing ill is to be deprived of knowledge), but the bad man will never become bad, for he is always bad; and if he were to become bad, he must previously have been good. Thus the words of the poem tend to show that on the one hand a man cannot be continuously good, but that he may become good and may also become bad; and again that

"They are the best for the longest time whom the gods love."

All this relates to Pittacus, as is further proved by the sequel. For he adds:—

"Therefore I will not throw away my span of life to no purpose in searching after the impossible, hoping in vain to find a perfectly faultless man among those who partake of the fruit of the broad-bosomed earth: if I find him, I will send you word."

(this is the vehement way in which he pursues his attack upon Pittacus throughout the whole poem):

"But him who does no evil, voluntarily I praise and love;—not even the gods war against necessity."

All this has a similar drift, for Simonides was not so ignorant as to say that he praised those who did no evil voluntarily, as though there were some who did evil voluntarily. For no wise man, as I believe, will allow that any human being errs voluntarily, or voluntarily does evil and dishonourable actions; but they are very well aware that all who do evil and dishonourable things do them against their will. And Simonides never says that he praises him who does no evil voluntarily; the word "voluntarily" applies to himself. For he was under the impression that a good man might often compel himself to love and praise another, and to be the friend and approver of another; and that there might be an involuntary love, such as a man might feel to an unnatural father or mother, or country, or the like. Now, bad men, when their parents or country have any defects, look on them with malignant joy, and find fault with them and expose and denounce them to others, under the idea that the rest of mankind will be less likely to take themselves to task and accuse them of neglect; and they blame their defects far more than they deserve, in order that the odium which is necessarily incurred by them may be increased: but the good man dissembles his feelings, and constrains himself to praise them; and if they have wronged him and he is angry, he pacifies his anger and is reconciled, and compels himself to love and praise his own flesh and blood. And Simonides, as is probable, considered that he himself had often had to praise and magnify a tyrant or the like, much against his will, and he also wishes to imply to Pittacus that he does not censure him because he is censorious.

"For I am satisfied," he says, "when a man is neither bad nor very stupid; and when he knows justice (which is the health of states), and is of sound mind, I will find no fault with him, for I am not given to finding fault, and there are innumerable fools"

(implying that if he delighted in censure he might have abundant opportunity of finding fault).

"All things are good with which evil is unmingled."

In these latter words he does not mean to say that all things are good which have no evil in them, as you might say "All things are white which have no black in them," for that would be ridiculous; but he means to say that he accepts and finds no fault with the moderate or intermediate state.

["I do not hope," he says, "to find a perfectly blameless man among those who partake of the fruits of the broad-bosomed earth (if I find him, I will send you word); in this sense I praise no man. But he who is moderately good, and does no evil, is good enough for me, who love and approve every one"] (and here observe that he uses a Lesbian word meaning "approve," because he is addressing Pittacus,—

"Who love and *approve* every one *voluntarily*, who does no evil":

and that the stop should be put after "voluntarily"); "but there are some whom I involuntarily praise and love. And you, Pittacus, I would never have blamed, if you had spoken what was moderately good and true; but I do blame you because, putting on the appearance of truth, you are speaking falsely about the highest matters."—And this, I said, Prodicus and Protagoras, I take to be the meaning of Simonides in this poem.

Hippias said: I think, Socrates, that you have given a very good explanation of the poem; but I have also an excellent interpretation of my own which I will propound to you, if you will allow me.

Nay, Hippias, said Alcibiades; not now, but at some other time. At present we must abide by the compact which was made between Socrates and Protagoras, to the effect that as long as Protagoras is willing to ask, Socrates should answer; or that if he would rather answer, then that Socrates should ask.

I said: I wish Protagoras either to ask or answer as he is inclined; but I would rather have done with poems and odes, if he does not object, and come back to the question about which I was asking you at first, Protagoras, and by your help make an end of that. The talk about the poets seems to me like a commonplace entertainment to which a vulgar company have recourse; who, because they are not able to converse or amuse one another, while they are drinking, with the sound of their own voices and conversation, by reason of their stupidity, raise the price of flute-girls in the market, hiring for a great sum the voice of a flute instead of their own breath, to be the medium of intercourse among them: but where the company are real gentlemen and men of education, you will see no flute-girls, nor dancing-girls, nor harp-girls; and they have no nonsense or games, but are contented with one another's conversation, of which their own voices are the medium, and which they carry on by turns and in an orderly manner, even though they are very liberal in their potations. And a company like this of ours, and men such as we profess to be do not require the help of another's voice, or of the poets whom you cannot interrogate about the meaning of what they are saying; people who cite them declaring, some that the poet has one meaning, and others that he has another, and the point which is in dispute can never be decided. This sort of entertainment they decline, and prefer to talk with one another, and put one another to the proof in conversation. And these are the models which I desire that you and I should imitate. Leaving the poets, and keeping to ourselves, let us try the mettle of one another and make proof of the truth in conversation. If you have a mind to ask, I am ready to answer; or if you would rather, do you answer, and give me the opportunity of resuming and completing our unfinished argument.

I made these and some similar observations; but Protagoras would not distinctly say which he would do. Thereupon Alcibiades turned to Callias, and said:—Do you think, Callias, that Protagoras is fair in refusing to say whether he will or will not answer? for I certainly think that he is unfair; he ought either to proceed with the argument, or distinctly to refuse to proceed, that we may know his intention; and then Socrates will be able to discourse with some one else, and the rest of the company will be free to talk with one another.

I think that Protagoras was really made ashamed by these words of Alcibiades, and when the prayers of Callias and the company were superadded, he was at last induced to argue, and said that I might ask and he would answer.

So I said: Do not imagine, Protagoras, that I have any other interest in asking questions of you but that of clearing up my own difficulties. For I think that Homer was very right in saying that

"When two go together, one sees before the other,"

for all men who have a companion are readier in deed, word, or thought; but if a man

"Sees a thing when he is alone,"

he goes about straightway seeking until he finds some one to whom he may show his discoveries, and who may confirm him in them. And I would rather hold discourse with you than with any one, because I think that no man has a better understanding of most things which a good man may be expected to understand, and in particular of virtue. For who is there, but you?—who not only claim to be a good man and a gentleman, for many are this, and yet have not the power of making others good—whereas you are not only good yourself, but also the cause of goodness in others. Moreover, such confidence have you in yourself, that although other Sophists conceal their profession, you proclaim in the face of Hellas that you are a Sophist or teacher of virtue and education, and are the first who demanded pay in return. How then can I do otherwise than invite you to the examination of these subjects, and ask questions and consult with you? I must, indeed. And I should like once more to have my memory refreshed by you about the questions which I was asking you at first, and also to have your help in considering them. If I am not mistaken the question was this: Are wisdom and temperance and courage and justice and holiness five names of the same thing? or has each of the names a separate underlying essence and corresponding thing having a peculiar function, no one of them being like any other of them? And you replied that the five names were not the names of the same thing, but that each of them had a separate object, and that all these objects were parts of virtue, not in the same way that the parts of gold are like each other and the whole of which they are parts, but as the parts of the face are unlike the whole of which they are parts and one another, and have each of them a distinct function. I should like to know whether this is still your opinion; or if not, I will ask you to define your meaning, and I shall not take you to task if you now make a different statement. For I dare say that you may have said what you did only in order to make trial of me.

I answer, Socrates, he said, that all these qualities are parts of virtue, and that four out of the five are to some extent similar, and that the fifth of them, which is courage, is very different from the other four, as I prove in this way: You may observe that many men are utterly unrighteous, unholy, intemperate, ignorant, who are nevertheless remarkable for their courage.

Stop, I said; I should like to think about that. When you speak of brave men, do you mean the confident, or another sort of nature?

Yes, he said; I mean the impetuous, ready to go at that which others are afraid to approach.

In the next place, you would affirm virtue to be a good thing, of which good thing you assert yourself to be a teacher.

Yes, he said; I should say the best of all things, if I am in my right mind.

And is it partly good and partly bad, I said, or wholly good?

Wholly good, and in the highest degree.

Tell me, then, who are they who have confidence when diving into a well?

I should say, the divers.

And the reason of this is that they have knowledge?

Yes, that is the reason.

And who have confidence when fighting on horseback—the skilled horsemen or the unskilled?

The skilled.

And who when fighting with light shields—the peltasts or the nonpeltasts?

The peltasts. And that is true of all other things, he said, if that is your point: those who have knowledge are more confident than those who have no knowledge, and they are more confident after they have learned than before.

And have you not seen persons utterly ignorant, I said, of these things, and yet confident about them?

Yes, he said, I have seen such persons far too confident.

And are not these confident persons also courageous?

In that case, he replied, courage would be a base thing, for the men of whom we are speaking are surely madmen.

Then who are the courageous? Are they not the confident?

Yes, he said; to that statement I adhere.

And those, I said, who are thus confident without knowledge are really not courageous, but mad; and in that case the wisest are also the most confident, and being the most confident are also the bravest, and upon that view again wisdom will be courage.

Nay, Socrates, he replied, you are mistaken in your remembrance of what was said by me. When you asked me, I certainly did say that the courageous are the confident; but I was never asked whether the confident are the courageous; if you had asked me, I should have answered "Not all of them": and what I did answer you have not proved to be false, although you proceeded to show that those who have knowledge are more courageous than they were before they had knowledge, and more courageous than others who have no knowledge, and were then led on to think that courage is the same as wisdom. But in this way of arguing you might come to imagine that strength is wisdom. You might begin by asking whether the strong are able, and I should say "Yes"; and then whether those who know how to wrestle are not more able to wrestle than those who do not know how to wrestle, and more able after than before they had learned, and I should assent. And when I had admitted this you might use my admissions in such a way as to prove that upon my view wisdom is strength; whereas in that case I should not have admitted, any more than in the other, that the able are strong, although I have admitted that the strong are able. For there is a difference between ability and strength; the former is given by knowledge as well as by madness or rage, but strength comes from nature and a healthy state of the body. And in like manner I say of confidence and courage, that they are not the same; and I argue that the courageous are confident, but not all the confident courageous. For confidence may be given to men by art, and also, like ability, by madness and rage; but courage comes to them from nature and the healthy state of the soul.

I said: You would admit, Protagoras, that some men live well and other ill?

He assented.

And do you think that a man lives well who lives in pain and grief?

He does not.

But if he lives pleasantly to the end of his life, will he not in that case have lived well?

He will.

Then to live pleasantly is a good, and to live unpleasantly an evil?

Yes, he said, if the pleasure be good and honourable.

And do you, Protagoras, like the rest of the world, call some pleasant things evil and some painful things good?—for I am rather disposed to say that things are good in as far as they are pleasant, if they have no consequences of another sort, and in as far as they are painful they are bad.

I do not know, Socrates, he said, whether I can venture to assert in that unqualified manner that the pleasant is the good and the painful the evil. Having regard not only to my present answer, but also the whole of my life, I shall be safer, if I am not mistaken, in saying that there are some pleasant things which are not good, and that there are some painful things which are good, and some which are not good, and that there are some which are neither good nor evil.

And you would call pleasant, I said, the things which participate in pleasure or create pleasure?

Certainly, he said.

Then my meaning is, that in as far as they are pleasant they are good; and my question would imply that pleasure is a good in itself.

According to your favourite mode of speech, Socrates, "let us reflect about this," he said; and if the reflection is to the point, and the result proves that pleasure and good are really the same, then we will agree; but, if not, then we will argue.

And would you wish to begin the enquiry? I said; or shall I begin?

You ought to take the lead, he said; for you are the author of the discussion.

May I employ an illustration? I said. Suppose some one who is enquiring into the health or some other bodily quality of another: —he looks at his face and at the tips of his fingers, and then he says, Uncover your chest and back to me that I may have a better view: —that is the sort of thing which I desire in this speculation. Having seen what your opinion is about good and pleasure, I am minded to say to you: Uncover your mind to me, Protagoras, and reveal your opinion about knowledge, that I may know whether you agree with the rest of the world. Now, the rest of the world are of opinion that knowledge is a principle not of strength, or of rule, or of command: their notion is that a man may have knowledge, and yet that the knowledge which is in him may be over-mastered by anger, or pleasure, or pain, or love, or perhaps by fear,—just as if knowledge were a slave, and might be dragged about anyhow. Now, is that your view? or do you think that knowledge is a noble and commanding thing, which cannot be overcome, and will not allow a man, if he only knows the difference of good and evil, to do anything which is contrary to knowledge, but that wisdom will have strength to help him?

I agree with you, Socrates, said Protagoras; and not only so, but

I, above all other men, am bound to say that wisdom and knowledge are the highest of human things.

Good, I said, and true. But are you aware that the majority of the world are of another mind; and that men are commonly supposed to know the things which are best, and not to do them when they might? And most persons whom I have asked the reason of this have said that when men act contrary to knowledge they are overcome by pain, or pleasure, or some of those affections which I was just now mentioning.

Yes, Socrates, he replied; and that is not the only point about which mankind are in error.

Suppose, then, that you and I endeavour to instruct and inform them what is the nature of this affection which they call "being overcome by pleasure," and which they affirm to be the reason why they do not always do what is best. When we say to them: Friends, you are mistaken, and are saying what is not true, they would probably reply: Socrates and Protagoras, if this affection of the soul is not to be called "being overcome by pleasure," pray, what is it, and by what name would you describe it?

But why, Socrates, should we trouble ourselves about the opinion of the many, who just say anything that happens to occur to them?

I believe, I said, that they may be of use in helping us to discover how courage is related to the other parts of virtue. If you are disposed to abide by our agreement, that I should show the way in which, as I think, our recent difficulty is most likely to be cleared up, do you follow; but if not, never mind.

You are quite right, he said; and I would have you proceed as you have begun.

Well, then, I said, let me suppose that they repeat their question, What account do you give of that which, in our way of speaking, is termed being overcome by pleasure? I should answer thus: Listen, and Protagoras and I will endeavour to show you. When men are overcome by eating and drinking and other sensual desires which are pleasant, and they, knowing them to be evil, nevertheless indulge in them, would you not say that they were overcome by pleasure? They will not deny this. And suppose that you and I were to go on and ask them again: "In what way do you say that they are evil,—in that they are pleasant and give pleasure at the moment, or because they cause disease and poverty and other like evils in the future? Would they still be evil, if they had no attendant evil consequences, simply because they give the consciousness of pleasure of whatever nature?"—Would they not answer that they are not evil on account of the pleasure which is immediately given by them, but on account of the after consequences —diseases and the like?

I believe, said Protagoras, that the world in general would answer as you do.

And in causing diseases do they not cause pain? and in causing poverty do they not cause pain;—they would agree to that also, if I am not mistaken?

Protagoras assented.

Then I should say to them, in my name and yours: Do you think them evil for any other reason, except because they end in pain and rob us of other pleasures:—there again they would agree?

We both of us thought that they would.

And then I should take the question from the opposite point of view, and say: "Friends, when you speak of goods being painful, do you not mean remedial goods, such as gymnastic exercises, and military service, and the physician's use of burning, cutting, drugging and starving? Are these the things which are good but painful?" They would assent to me?

He agreed.

"And do you call them good because they occasion the greatest immediate suffering and pain; or because, afterwards, they bring health and improvement of the bodily condition and the salvation of States and power over others and wealth?"—they would agree to the latter alternative, if I am not mistaken?

He assented.

"Are these things good for any other reason except that they end in pleasure, and get rid of and avert pain? Are you looking to any other standard but pleasure and pain when you call them good?" They would acknowledge that they were not?

I think so, said Protagoras.

"And do you not pursue after pleasure as a good, and avoid pain as an evil?"

He assented.

"Then you think that pain is an evil and pleasure is a good:

and even pleasure you deem an evil, when it robs you of greater pleasures than it gives, or causes pains greater than the pleasure. If, however, you call pleasure an evil in relation to some other end or standard, you will be able to show us that standard. But you have none to show."

I do not think that they have, said Protagoras.

"And have you not a similar way of speaking about pain? You call pain a good when it takes away greater pains than those which it has, or gives pleasures greater than the pains: then if you have some standard other than pleasure and pain to which you refer when you call actual pain a good, you can show what that is. But you cannot."

True, said Protagoras.

Suppose again, I said, that the world says to me: "Why do you spend many words and speak in many ways on this subject?" Excuse me, friends, I should reply; but in the first place there is a difficulty in explaining the meaning of the expression "overcome by pleasure"; and the whole argument turns upon this. And even now, if you see any possible way in which evil can be explained as other than pain, or good as other than pleasure, you may still retract. Are you satisfied, then, at having a life of pleasure which is without pain? If you are, and if you are unable to show any good or evil which does not end in pleasure and pain, hear the consequences:—If what you say is true, then the argument is absurd which affirms that a man often does evil knowingly, when he might abstain, because he is seduced and overpowered by pleasure; or again, when you say that a man knowingly refuses to do what is good because he is overcome at the moment by pleasure. And that this is ridiculous will be evident if only we give up the use of various names, such as pleasant and painful, and good and evil. As there are two things, let us call them by two names—first, good and evil, and then pleasant and painful. Assuming this, let us go on to say that a man does evil knowing that he does evil. But some one will ask, Why? Because he is overcome, is the first answer. And by what is he overcome? the enquirer will proceed to ask. And we shall not be able to reply "By pleasure," for the name of pleasure has been exchanged for that of good. In our answer, then, we shall only say that he is overcome. "By what?" he will reiterate. By the good, we shall have to reply; indeed we shall.

Nay, but our questioner will rejoin with a laugh, if he be one of the swaggering sort, "This is too ridiculous, that a man should do what he knows to be evil when he ought not, because he is overcome by good. Is that," he will ask, "because the good was worthy or not worthy of conquering the evil?" And in answer to that we shall clearly reply, Because it was not worthy; for if it had been worthy, then he who, as we say, was overcome by pleasure, would not have been wrong. "But how," he will reply, "can the good be unworthy of the evil, or the evil of the good?" Is not the real explanation that they are out of proportion to one another, either as greater and smaller, or more and fewer? This we cannot deny. And when you speak of being overcome—"what do you mean," he will say, "but that you choose the greater evil in exchange for the lesser good?" Admitted. And now substitute the names of pleasure and pain for good and evil, and say, not as before, that a man does what is evil knowingly, but that he does what is painful knowingly, and because he is overcome by pleasure, which is unworthy to overcome. What measure is there of the relations of pleasure to pain other than excess and defect, which means that they become greater and smaller, and more and fewer, and differ in degree? For if any one says: "Yes, Socrates, but immediate pleasure differs widely from future pleasure and pain"— to that I should reply: And do they differ in anything but in pleasure and pain? There can be no other measure of them. And do you, like a skilful weigher, put into the balance the pleasures and the pains, and their nearness and distance, and weigh them, and then say which outweighs the other. If you weigh pleasures against pleasures, you of course take the more and greater; or if you weigh pains against pains, you take the fewer and the less; or if pleasures against pains, then you choose that course of action in which the painful is exceeded by the pleasant, whether the distant by the near or the near by the distant; and you avoid that course of action in which the pleasant is exceeded by the painful. Would you not admit, my friends, that this is true? I am confident that they cannot deny this.

He agreed with me.

Well, then, I shall say, if you agree so far, be so good as to answer me a question: Do not the same magnitudes appear larger to your sight when near, and smaller when at a distance? They will acknowledge that. And the same holds of thickness and number; also sounds, which are in themselves equal, are greater when near, and lesser when at a distance. They will grant that also. Now suppose happiness to consist in doing or choosing the greater, and in not doing or in avoiding the less, what would be the saving principle of human life? Would not the art of measuring be the saving principle; or would the power of appearance? Is not the latter that deceiving art which makes us wander up and down and take the things at one time of which we repent at another, both in our actions and in our choice of things great and small? But the art of measurement would do away with the effect of appearances, and, showing the truth, would fain teach the soul at last to find rest in the truth, and would thus save our life. Would not mankind generally acknowledge that the art which accomplishes this result is the art of measurement?

Yes, he said, the art of measurement.

Suppose, again, the salvation of human life to depend on the choice of odd and even, and on the knowledge of when a man ought to choose the greater or less, either in reference to themselves or to each other, and whether near or at a distance; what would be the saving principle of our lives? Would not knowledge? —a knowledge of measuring, when the question is one of excess and defect, and a knowledge of number, when the question is of odd and even? The world will assent, will they not?

Protagoras himself thought that they would.

Well, then, my friends, I say to them; seeing that the salvation of human life has been bound to consist in the right choice of pleasures and pains,—in the choice of the more and the fewer, and the greater and the less, and the nearer and remoter, must not this measuring be a consideration of their excess and defect and equality in relation to each other?

This is undeniably true.

And this, as possessing measure, must undeniably also be an art and science?

They will agree, he said.

The nature of that art or science will be a matter of future consideration; but the existence of such a science furnishes a demonstrative answer to the question which you asked of me and Protagoras. At the time when you asked the question, if you remember,

both of us were agreeing that there was nothing mightier than
knowledge, and that knowledge, in whatever existing, must have
the advantage over pleasure and all other things; and then you
said that pleasure often got the advantage even over a man who
has knowledge; and we refused to allow this, and you rejoined:
O Protagoras and Socrates, what is the meaning of being overcome
by pleasure if not this?—tell us what you call such a state:—if we
had immediately and at the time answered "Ignorance," you
would have laughed at us. But now, in laughing at us, you will
be laughing at yourselves: for you also admitted that men err in
their choice of pleasures and pains; that is, in their choice of good
and evil, from defect of knowledge; and you admitted further,
that they err, not only from defect of knowledge in general, but
of that particular knowledge which is called measuring. And you
are also aware that the erring act which is done without knowledge
is done in ignorance. This, therefore, is the meaning of being
overcome by pleasure;—ignorance, and that the greatest. And our
friends Protagoras and Prodicus and Hippias declare that they
are the physicians of ignorance; but you, who are under the mistaken impression that ignorance is not the cause, and that the art
of which I am speaking cannot be taught, neither go yourselves,
nor send your children, to the Sophists, who are the teachers of
these things—you take care of your money and give them none;
and the result is, that you are the worse off both in public and
private life:—Let us suppose this to be our answer to the world
in general: And now I should like to ask you, Hippias, and you,
Prodicus, as well as Protagoras (for the argument is to be yours
as well as ours), whether you think that I am speaking the truth
or not?

They all thought that what I said was entirely true.

Then you agree, I said, that the pleasant is the good, and the
painful evil. And here I would beg my friend Prodicus not to
introduce his distinction of names, whether he is disposed to say
pleasurable, delightful, joyful. However, by whatever name he
prefers to call them, I will ask you, most excellent Prodicus, to
answer in my sense of the words.

Prodicus laughed and assented, as did the others.

Then, my friends, what do you say to this? Are not all actions
honourable and useful, of which the tendency is to make life pain-

less and pleasant? The honourable work is also useful and good? This was admitted.

Then I said, if the pleasant is the good, nobody does anything under the idea or conviction that some other thing would be better and is also attainable, when he might do the better. And this inferiority of a man to himself is merely ignorance, as the superiority of a man to himself is wisdom.

They all assented.

And is not ignorance the having a false opinion and being deceived about important matters?

To this also they unanimously assented.

Then, I said, no man voluntarily pursues evil, or that which he thinks to be evil. To prefer evil to good is not in human nature; and when a man is compelled to choose one of two evils, no one will choose the greater when he may have the less.

All of us agreed to every word of this.

Well, I said, there is a certain thing called fear or terror; and here, Prodicus, I should particularly like to know whether you would agree with me in defining this fear or terror as expectation of evil.

Protagoras and Hippias agreed, but Prodicus said that this was fear and not terror.

Never mind, Prodicus, I said; but let me ask whether, if our former assertions are true, a man will pursue that which he fears when he is not compelled? Would not this be in flat contradiction to the admission which has been already made, that he thinks the things which he fears to be evil; and no one will pursue or voluntarily accept that which he thinks to be evil?

That also was universally admitted.

Then, I said, these, Hippias and Prodicus, are our premises; and I would beg Protagoras to explain to us how he can be right in what he said at first. I do not mean in what he said quite at first, for his first statement, as you may remember, was that whereas there were five parts of virtue none of them was like any other of them; each of them had a separate function. To this, however, I am not referring, but to the assertion which he afterwards made that of the five virtues four were nearly akin to each other, but that the fifth, which was courage, differed greatly from the others. And of this he gave me the following proof. He said: You will find, Socrates, that some of the most impious, and unrighteous, and intemperate, and ignorant of men are among the most courageous; which proves that courage is very different from the other parts of virtue. I was surprised at his saying this at the time, and I am still more surprised now that I have discussed the matter with you. So I asked him whether by the brave he meant the confident. Yes, he replied, and the impetuous or goers. (You may remember, Protagoras, that this was your answer.)

He assented.

Well, then, I said, tell us against what are the courageous ready to go—against the same dangers as the cowards?

No, he answered.

Then against something different?

Yes, he said.

Then do cowards go where there is safety, and the courageous where there is danger?

Yes, Socrates, so men say.

Very true, I said. But I want to know against what do you say that the courageous are ready to go—against dangers, believing them to be dangers, or not against dangers?

No, said he; the former case has been proved by you in the previous argument to be impossible.

That, again, I replied, is quite true. And if this has been rightly proven, then no one goes to meet what he thinks to be dangers, since the want of self-control, which makes men rush into dangers, has been shown to be ignorance.

He assented.

And yet the courageous man and the coward alike go to meet that about which they are confident; so that, in this point of view, the cowardly and the courageous go to meet the same things.

And yet, Socrates, said Protagoras, that to which the coward goes is the opposite of that to which the courageous goes; the one, for example, is ready to go to battle, and the other is not ready.

And is going to battle honourable or disgraceful? I said.

Honourable, he replied.

And if honourable, then already admitted by us to be good; for all honourable actions we have admitted to be good.

That is true; and to that opinion I shall always adhere.

True, I said. But which of the two are they who, as you say, are unwilling to go to war, which is a good and honourable thing?

The cowards, he replied.

And what is good and honourable, I said, is also pleasant?

It has certainly been acknowledged to be so, he replied.

And do the cowards knowingly refuse to go to the nobler, and pleasanter, and better?

The admission of that, he replied, would belie our former admissions.

But does not the courageous man also go to meet the better, and pleasanter, and nobler?

That must be admitted.

And the courageous man has no base fear or base confidence?

True, he replied.

And if not base, then honourable?

He admitted this.

And if honourable, then good?

Yes.

But the fear and confidence of the coward or foolhardy or madman, on the contrary, are base?

He assented.

And these base fears and confidences originate in ignorance and uninstructedness?

True, he said.

Then, as to the motive from which the cowards act, do you call it cowardice or courage?

I should say cowardice, he replied.

And have they not been shown to be cowards through their ignorance of dangers?

Assuredly, he said.

And because of that ignorance they are cowards?

He assented.

And the reason why they are cowards is admitted by you to be cowardice?

He again assented.

Then the ignorance of what is and is not dangerous is cowardice?

He nodded assent.

But surely courage, I said, is opposed to cowardice?

Yes.

Then the wisdom which knows what are and are not dangers is opposed to the ignorance of them?

To that again he nodded assent.

And the ignorance of them is cowardice?

To that he very reluctantly nodded assent.

And the knowledge of that which is and is not dangerous is courage, and is opposed to the ignorance of these things?

At this point he would no longer nod assent, but was silent.

And why, I said, do you neither assent nor dissent, Protagoras?

Finish the argument by yourself, he said.

I only want to ask one more question, I said. I want to know whether you still think that there are men who are most ignorant and yet most courageous?

You seem to have a great ambition to make me answer, Socrates, and therefore I will gratify you, and say, that this appears to me to be impossible consistently with the argument.

My only object, I said, in continuing the discussion, has been the desire to ascertain the nature and relations of virtue; for if this were clear, I am very sure that the other controversy which has been carried on at great length by both of us—you affirming and I denying that virtue can be taught—would also become clear. The result of our discussion appears to me as to be singular. For if the argument had a human voice, that voice would be heard laughing at us and saying: "Protagoras and Socrates, you are strange beings; there are you, Socrates, who were saying that virtue cannot be taught, contradicting yourself now by your attempt to prove that all things are knowledge, including justice, and temperance, and courage,—which tends to show that virtue can certainly be taught; for if virtue were other than knowledge, as Protagoras attempted to prove, then clearly virtue cannot be taught; but if virtue is entirely knowledge, as you are seeking to show, then I cannot but suppose that virtue is capable of being taught. Protagoras, on the other hand, who started by saying that it might be taught, is now eager to prove it to be anything rather than knowledge; and if this is true, it must be quite incapable of being taught." Now I, Protagoras, perceiving this terrible confusion of our ideas, have a great desire that they should be cleared up. And I should like to carry on the discussion until we ascertain what virtue is, and whether capable of being taught or not, lest haply

Epimetheus should trip us up and deceive us in the argument, as he forgot us in the story; I prefer your Prometheus to your Epimetheus, for of him I make use, whenever I am busy about these questions, in Promethean care of my own life. And if you have no objection, as I said at first, I should like to have your help in the enquiry.

Protagoras replied: Socrates, I am not of a base nature, and I am the last man in the world to be envious. I cannot but applaud your energy and your conduct of an argument. As I have often said, I admire you above all men whom I know, and far above all men of your age; and I believe that you will become very eminent in philosophy. Let us come back to the subject at some future time; at present we had better turn to something else.

By all means, I said, if that is your wish; for I too ought long since to have kept the engagement of which I spoke before, and only tarried because I could not refuse the request of the noble Callias. So the conversation ended, and we went our way.

Symposium

PERSONS OF THE DIALOGUE

Apollodorus, *who repeats to his companion the Dialogue which he had heard from Aristodemus, and had already once narrated to Glaucon.*

Phaedrus.
Pausanias.
Eryximachus.
Aristophanes.
Agathon.
Socrates.
Alcibiades.
A troop of Revellers.

Scene: *The House of Agathon.*

CONCERNING the things about which you ask to be informed I believe that I am not ill-prepared with an answer. For the day before yesterday I was coming from my own home at Phalerum to the city, and one of my acquaintance, who had caught sight of me from behind, calling out playfully in the distance, said: Apollodorus, O thou Phalerian [1] man, halt! So I did as I was bid; and then he said, I was looking for you, Apollodorus, only just now, that I might ask you about the speeches in praise of love, which were delivered by Socrates, Alcibiades, and others, at Agathon's supper. Phoenix, the son of Philip, told another person who told me of them; his narrative was very indistinct, but he said that you knew, and I wish that you would give me an account of them. Who, if not you, should be the reporter of the words of your friend? And first tell me, he said, were you present at this meeting?

Your informant, Glaucon, I said, must have been very indistinct indeed, if you imagine that the occasion was recent; or that I could have been of the party.

Why, yes, he replied, I thought so.

Impossible: I said. Are you ignorant that for many years Agathon has not resided at Athens; and not three have elapsed since I became acquainted with Socrates, and have made it my daily business to know all that he says and does? There was a time when I was

[1] Probably a play of words on *phalaròs*, "bald-headed."

62

running about the world, fancying myself to be well employed, but I was really a most wretched being, no better than you are now. I thought that I ought to do anything rather than be a philosopher.

Well, he said, jesting apart, tell me when the meeting occurred.

In our boyhood, I replied, when Agathon won the prize with his first tragedy, on the day after that on which he and his chorus offered the sacrifice of victory.

Then it must have been a long while ago, he said; and who told you—did Socrates?

No, indeed, I replied, but the same person who told Phoenix;—he was a little fellow, who never wore any shoes, Aristodemus, of the deme of Cydathenaeum. He had been at Agathon's feast; and I think that in those days there was no one who was a more devoted admirer of Socrates. Moreover, I have asked Socrates about the truth of some parts of his narrative, and he confirmed them. Then, said Glaucon, let us have the tale over again; is not the road to Athens just made for conversation? And so we walked, and talked of the discourses on love; and therefore, as I said at first, I am not ill-prepared to comply with your request, and will have another rehearsal of them if you like. For to speak or to hear others speak of philosophy always gives me the greatest pleasure, to say nothing of the profit. But when I hear another strain, especially that of you rich men and traders, such conversation displeases me; and I pity you who are my companions, because you think that you are doing something when in reality you are doing nothing. And I dare say that you pity me in return, whom you regard as an unhappy creature, and very probably you are right. But I certainly know of you what you only think of me—there is the difference.

COMPANION. I see, Apollodorus, that you are just the same—always speaking evil of yourself, and of others; and I do believe that you pity all mankind, with the exception of Socrates, yourself first of all, true in this to your old name, which, however deserved, I know not how you acquired, of Apollodorus the madman; for you are always raging against yourself and everybody but Socrates.

APOLLODORUS. Yes, friend, and the reason why I am said to be mad, and out of my wits, is just because I have these notions of myself and you; no other evidence is required.

COMPANION. No more of that, Apollodorus; but let me renew my request that you would repeat the conversation.

APOLLODORUS. Well, the tale of love was on this wise:—But perhaps I had better begin at the beginning, and endeavour to give you the exact words of Aristodemus:

He said that he met Socrates fresh from the bath and sandalled; and as the sight of the sandals was unusual, he asked him whither he was going that he had been converted into such a beau:—

To a banquet at Agathon's he replied, whose invitation to his sacrifice of victory I refused yesterday, fearing a crowd, but promising that I would come to-day instead; and so I have put on my finery, because he is such a fine man. What say you to going with me unasked?

I will do as you bid me, I replied.

Follow then, he said, and let us demolish the proverb:—

"To the feasts of inferior men the good unbidden go";

instead of which our proverb will run:—

"To the feasts of the good the good unbidden go";

and this alteration may be supported by the authority of Homer himself, who not only demolishes but literally outrages the proverb. For, after picturing Agamemnon as the most valiant of men, he makes Menelaus, who is but a faint-hearted warrior, come unbidden to the banquet of Agamemnon, who is feasting and offering sacrifices, not the better to the worse, but the worse to the better.

I rather fear, Socrates, said Aristodemus, lest this may still be my case; and that, like Menelaus in Homer, I shall be the inferior person, who

"To the feasts of the wise unbidden goes."

But I shall say that I was bidden of you, and then you will have to make an excuse.

"Two going together,"

he replied, in Homeric fashion, one or other of them may invent an excuse by the way.

This was the style of their conversation as they went along.

Socrates dropped behind in a fit of abstraction, and desired Aristodemus, who was waiting, to go on before him. When he reached the house of Agathon he found the doors wide open, and a comical thing happened. A servant coming out met him, and led him at once into the banqueting-hall in which the guests were reclining, for the banquet was about to begin. Welcome, Aristodemus, said Agathon, as soon as he appeared—you are just in time to sup with us; if you come on any other matter put it off, and make one of us, as I was looking for you yesterday and meant to have asked you, if I could have found you. But what have you done with Socrates?

I turned round, but Socrates was nowhere to be seen; and I had to explain that he had been with me a moment before, and that I came by his invitation to the supper.

You were quite right in coming, said Agathon; but where is he himself?

He was behind me just now, as I entered, he said, and I cannot think what has become of him.

Go and look for him, boy, said Agathon, and bring him in; and do you, Aristodemus, meanwhile take the place by Eryximachus.

The servant then assisted him to wash, and he lay down, and presently another servant came in and reported that our friend Socrates had retired into the portico of the neighbouring house. "There he is fixed," said he, "and when I call to him he will not stir."

How strange, said Agathon; then you must call him again, and keep calling him.

Let him alone, said my informant; he has a way of stopping anywhere and losing himself without any reason. I believe that he will soon appear; do not therefore disturb him.

Well, if you think so, I will leave him, said Agathon. And then, turning to the servants, he added, "Let us have supper without waiting for him. Serve up whatever you please, for there is no one to give you orders; hitherto I have never left you to yourselves. But on this occasion imagine that you are our hosts, and that I and the company are your guests; treat us well, and then we shall commend you." After this, supper was served, but still no Socrates; and during the meal Agathon several times expressed a wish to send for him, but Aristodemus objected; and at last when the feast was about half over—for the fit, as usual, was not of long duration

—Socrates entered. Agathon who was reclining alone at the end of
the table, begged that he would take the place next to him; that "I
may touch you," he said, "and have the benefit of that wise
thought which came into your mind in the portico, and is now in
your possession; for I am certain that you would not have come
away until you had found what you sought."

How I wish, said Socrates, taking his place as he was desired,
that wisdom could be infused by touch, out of the fuller into the
emptier man, as water runs through wool out of a fuller cup into
an emptier one; if that were so, how greatly should I value the
privilege of reclining at your side! For you would have filled me
full with a stream of wisdom plenteous and fair; whereas my own
is of a very mean and questionable sort, no better than a dream.
But yours is bright and full of promise, and was manifested forth
in all the splendour of youth the day before yesterday, in the presence of more than thirty thousand Hellenes.

You are mocking, Socrates, said Agathon, and ere long you and
I will have to determine who bears off the palm of wisdom—of this
Dionysus shall be the judge; but at present you are better occupied
with supper.

Socrates took his place on the couch, and supped with the rest;
and then libations were offered, and after a hymn had been sung
to the god, and there had been the usual ceremonies, they were
about to commence drinking, when Pausanias said, And now, my
friends, how can we drink with least injury to ourselves? I can
assure you that I feel severely the effect of yesterday's potations,
and must have time to recover; and I suspect that most of you are
in the same predicament, for you were of the party yesterday. Consider then: How can the drinking be made easiest?

I entirely agree, said Aristophanes, that we should, by all means,
avoid hard drinking, for I was myself one of those who were yesterday drowned in drink.

I think that you are right, said Eryximachus, the son of Acumenus; but I should still like to hear one other person speak: Is
Agathon able to drink hard?

I am not equal to it, said Agathon.

Then, said Eryximachus, the weak heads like myself, Aristodemus, Phaedrus, and others who never can drink, are fortunate
in finding that the stronger ones are not in a drinking mood. (I do

not include Socrates, who is able either to drink or to abstain, and will not mind, whichever we do.) Well, as none of the company seem disposed to drink much, I may be forgiven for saying, as a physician, that drinking deep is a bad practice, which I never follow, if I can help, and certainly do not recommend to another, least of all to any one who still feels the effects of yesterday's carouse.

I always do what you advise, and especially what you prescribe as a physician, rejoined Phaedrus the Myrrhinusian, and the rest of the company, if they are wise, will do the same.

It was agreed that drinking was not to be the order of the day, but that they were all to drink only so much as they pleased.

Then, said Eryximachus, as you are all agreed that drinking is to be voluntary, and that there is to be no compulsion, I move, in the next place, that the flute-girl, who has just made her appearance, be told to go away and play to herself, or, if she likes, to the women who are within. To-day let us have conversation instead; and, if you will allow me, I will tell you what sort of conversation. This proposal having been accepted, Eryximachus proceeded as follows:—

I will begin, he said, after the manner of Melanippe in Euripides,

"Not mine the word"

which I am about to speak, but that of Phaedrus. For often he says to me in an indignant tone:—"What a strange thing it is, Eryximachus, that, whereas other gods have poems and hymns made in their honour, the great and glorious god, Love, has no encomiast among all the poets who are so many. There are the worthy Sophists too—the excellent Prodicus, for example—who have descanted in prose on the virtues of Heracles and other heroes; and, what is still more extraordinary, I have met with a philosophical work in which the utility of salt has been made the theme of an eloquent discourse; and many other like things have had a like honour bestowed upon them. And only to think that there should have been an eager interest created about them, and yet that to this day no one has ever dared worthily to hymn Love's praises! So entirely has this great deity been neglected." Now in this Phaedrus seems to me to be quite right, and therefore I want to offer him a contribution;

also I think that at the present moment we who are here assembled cannot do better than honour the god Love. If you agree with me, there will be no lack of conversation; for I mean to propose that each of us in turn, going from left to right, shall make a speech in honour of Love. Let him give us the best which he can; and Phaedrus, because he is sitting first on the left hand, and because he is the father of the thought, shall begin.

No one will vote against you Eryximachus, said Socrates. How can I oppose your motion, who profess to understand nothing but matters of love? Nor, I presume, will Agathon and Pausanias; and there can be no doubt of Aristophanes, whose whole concern is with Dionysus and Aphrodite; nor will any one disagree of those whom I see around me. The proposal, as I am aware, may seem rather hard upon us whose place is last; but we shall be contented if we hear some good speeches first. Let Phaedrus begin the praise of Love, and good luck to him. All the company expressed their assent, and desired him to do as Socrates bade him.

Aristodemus did not recollect all that was said, nor do I recollect all that he related to me; but I will tell you what I thought most worthy of remembrance, and what the chief speakers said.

Phaedrus began by affirming that Love is a mighty god, and wonderful among gods and men, but especially wonderful in his birth. For he is the eldest of the gods, which is an honour to him; and a proof of his claim to this honour is, that of his parents there is no memorial; neither poet nor prose-writer has ever affirmed that he had any. As Hesiod says:—

> "First Chaos came, and then broad-bosomed Earth,
> The everlasting seat of all that is,
> And Love."

In other words, after Chaos, the Earth and Love, these two, came into being. Also Parmenides sings of Generation:

> "First in the train of gods, he fashioned Love."

And Acusilaus agrees with Hesiod. Thus numerous are the witnesses who acknowledge Love to be the eldest of the gods. And not only is he the eldest, he is also the source of the greatest benefits to us. For I know not any greater blessing to a young man who is beginning life than a virtuous lover, or to the lover than a beloved youth. For the principle which ought to be the guide of men who would nobly live—that principle, I say, neither kindred, nor honour, nor wealth, nor any other motive is able to implant so well as love. Of what am I speaking? Of the sense of honour and dishonour, without which neither States nor individuals ever do any good or great work. And I say that a lover who is detected in doing any dishonourable act, or submitting through cowardice when any dishonour is done to him by another, will be more pained at being detected by his beloved than at being seen by his father, or by his companions, or by any one else. The beloved too, when he is found in any disgraceful situation, has the same feeling about his lover. And if there were only some way of contriving that a State or an army should be made up of lovers and their loves, they would be the very best governors of their own city, abstaining from all dishonour, and emulating one another in honour; and when fighting at each other's side, although a mere handful, they would overcome the world. For what lover would not choose rather to be seen by all mankind than by his beloved, either when abandoning his post or throwing away his arms? He would be ready to die a thousand deaths rather than endure this. Or who would desert his beloved or fail him in the hour of danger? The veriest coward would become an inspired hero, equal to the bravest, at such a time; Love would inspire him. That courage which, as Homer says, the god breathes into the souls of some heroes, Love of his own nature infuses into the lover.

Love will make men dare to die for their beloved—love alone; and women as well as men. Of this, Alcestis, the daughter of Pelias, is a monument to all Hellas; for she was willing to lay down her life on behalf of her husband, when no one else would, although he had a father and mother; but the tenderness of her love so far exceeded theirs, that she made them seem to be strangers in blood to their own son, and in name only related to him; and so noble did this action of hers appear to the gods, as well as to men, that among the many who have done virtuously she is one of the very few to whom, in admiration of her noble action, they have granted the privilege of returning alive to earth; such exceeding honour is paid by the gods to the devotion and virtue of love. But Orpheus, the son of Oeagrus, the harper, they sent empty away, and presented to him an apparition only of her whom he sought, but her-

self they would not give up, because he showed no spirit; he was
only a harp-player, and did not dare like Alcestis to die for love,
but was contriving how he might enter Hades alive; moreover,
they afterwards caused him to suffer death at the hands of women,
as the punishment of his cowardliness. Very different was the reward of the true love of Achilles towards his lover Patroclus—his
lover and not his love (the notion that Patroclus was the beloved
one is a foolish error into which Aeschylus has fallen, for Achilles
was surely the fairer of the two, fairer also than all the other
heroes; and, as Homer informs us, he was still beardless, and
younger far). And greatly as the gods honour the virtue of love,
still the return of love on the part of the beloved to the lover is
more admired and valued and rewarded by them, for the lover is
more divine; because he is inspired by God. Now Achilles was
quite aware, for he had been told by his mother, that he might
avoid death and return home, and live to a good old age, if he
abstained from slaying Hector. Nevertheless he gave his life to revenge his friend, and dared to die, not only in his defence, but
after he was dead. Wherefore the gods honoured him even above
Alcestis, and sent him to the Islands of the Blest. These are my
reasons for affirming that Love is the eldest and noblest and
mightiest of the gods, and the chiefest author and giver of virtue
in life, and of happiness after death.

This, or something like this, was the speech of Phaedrus; and
some other speeches followed which Aristodemus did not remember; the next which he repeated was that of Pausanias. Phaedrus,
he said, the argument has not been set before us, I think, quite in
the right form;—we should not be called upon to praise Love in
such an indiscriminate manner. If there were only one Love, then
what you said would be well enough; but since there are more
Loves than one, you should have begun by determining which of
them was to be the theme of our praises. I will amend this defect;
and first of all I will tell you which Love is deserving of praise, and
then try to hymn the praiseworthy one in a manner worthy of him.
For we all know that Love is inseparable from Aphrodite, and if
there were only one Aphrodite there would be only one Love; but
as there are two goddesses there must be two Loves. And am I not
right in asserting that there are two goddesses? The elder one, having no mother, who is called the heavenly Aphrodite—she is the

daughter of Uranus; the younger, who is the daughter of Zeus and Dione—her we call common; and the Love who is her fellow-worker is rightly named common, as the other love is called heavenly. All the gods ought to have praise given to them, but not without distinction of their natures; and therefore I must try to distinguish the characters of the two Loves. Now actions vary according to the manner of their performance. Take, for example, that which we are now doing, drinking, singing and talking—these actions are not in themselves either good or evil, but they turn out in this or that way according to the mode of performing them; and when well done they are good, and when wrongly done they are evil; and in like manner not every love, but only that which has a noble purpose, is noble and worthy of praise. The Love who is the offspring of the common Aphrodite is essentially common, and has no discrimination, being such as the meaner sort of men feel, and is apt to be of women as well as of youths, and is of the body rather than of the soul—the most foolish beings are the objects of this love which desires only to gain an end, but never thinks of accomplishing the end nobly, and therefore does good and evil quite indiscriminately. The goddess who is his mother is far younger than the other, and she was born of the union of the male and female, and partakes of both. But the offspring of the heavenly Aphrodite is derived from a mother in whose birth the female has no part,—she is from the male only; this is that love which is of youths, and the goddess being older, there is nothing of wantonness in her. Those who are inspired by this love turn to the male, and delight in him who is the more valiant and intelligent nature; any one may recognize the pure enthusiasts in the very character of their attachments. For they love not boys, but intelligent beings whose reason is beginning to be developed, much about the time at which their beards begin to grow. And in choosing young men to be their companions, they mean to be faithful to them, and pass their whole life in company with them, not to take them in their inexperience, and deceive them, and play the fool with them, or run away from one to another of them. But the love of young boys should be forbidden by law, because their future is uncertain; they may turn out good or bad, either in body or soul, and much noble enthusiasm may be thrown away upon them; in this matter the good are a law to themselves, and the coarser sort

of lovers ought to be restrained by force, as we restrain or attempt
to restrain them from fixing their affections on women of free
birth. These are the persons who bring a reproach on love; and
some have been led to deny the lawfulness of such attachments
because they see the impropriety and evil of them; for surely nothing that is decorously and lawfully done can justly be censured.
Now here and in Lacedaemon the rules about love are perplexing,
but in most cities they are simple and easily intelligible; in Elis
and Boeotia, and in countries having no gifts of eloquence, they
are very straightforward; the law is simply in favour of these connexions, and no one, whether young or old, has anything to say to
their discredit; the reason being, as I suppose, that they are men of
few words in those parts, and therefore the lovers do not like the
trouble of pleading their suit. In Ionia and other places, and generally in countries which are subject to the barbarians, the custom
is held to be dishonourable; loves of youths share the evil repute
in which philosophy and gymnastics are held, because they are in-
imical to tyranny; for the interests of rulers require that their subjects should be poor in spirit; and that there should be no strong
bond of friendship or society among them, which love, above all
other motives, is likely to inspire, as our Athenian tyrants learned
by experience; for the love of Aristogeiton and the constancy of
Harmodius had a strength which undid their power. And, therefore, the ill-repute into which these attachments have fallen is to
be ascribed to the evil condition of those who make them to be
ill-reputed; that is to say, to the self-seeking of the governors and
the cowardice of the governed; on the other hand, the indiscriminate honour which is given to them in some countries is attributable to the laziness of those who hold this opinion of them.
In our own country a far better principle prevails, but, as I was
saying, the explanation of it is rather perplexing. For, observe that
open loves are held to be more honourable than secret ones, and
that the love of the noblest and highest, even if their persons are
less beautiful than others, is especially honourable. Consider, too,
how great is the encouragement which all the world gives to the
lover; neither is he supposed to be doing anything dishonourable;
but if he succeeds he is praised, and if he fail he is blamed. And in
the pursuit of his love the custom of mankind allows him to do
many strange things, which philosophy would bitterly censure if

they were done from any motive of interest, or wish for office or power. He may pray, and entreat, and supplicate, and swear, and lie on a mat at the door, and endure a slavery worse than that of any slave—in any other case friends and enemies would be equally ready to prevent him, but now there is no friend who will be ashamed of him and admonish him, and no enemy will charge him with meanness or flattery; the actions of a lover have a grace which ennobles them; and custom has decided that they are highly commendable and that there is no loss of character in them; and, what is strangest of all, he only may swear and forswear himself (so men say), and the gods will forgive his transgression, for there is no such thing as a lover's oath. Such is the entire liberty which gods and men have allowed the lover, according to the custom which prevails in our part of the world. From this point of view a man fairly argues that in Athens to love and to be loved is held to be a very honourable thing. But when parents forbid their sons to talk with their lovers, and place them under a tutor's care, who is appointed to see to these things, and their companions and equals cast in their teeth anything of the sort which they may observe, and their elders refuse to silence the reprovers and do not rebuke them—any one who reflects on all this will, on the contrary, think that we hold these practices to be most disgraceful. But, as I was saying at first, the truth as I imagine is, that whether such practices are honourable or whether they are dishonourable is not a simple question; they are honourable to him who follows them honourably, dishonourable to him who follows them dishonourably. There is dishonour in yielding to the evil, or in an evil manner; but there is honour in yielding to the good, or in an honourable manner. Evil is the vulgar lover who loves the body rather than the soul, inasmuch as he is not even stable, because he loves a thing which is in itself unstable, and therefore when the bloom of youth which he was desiring is over, he takes wing and flies away, in spite of all his words and promises; whereas the love of the noble disposition is lifelong, for it becomes one with the everlasting. The custom of our country would have both of them proven well and truly, and would have us yield to the one sort of lover and avoid the other, and therefore encourages some to pursue, and others to fly; testing both the lover and beloved in contests and trials, until they show to which of the two classes they respectively belong. And this is the why, in the first place, a hasty attachment is held to be dishonourable, because time is the true test of this as of most other things; and secondly there is a dishonour in being overcome by the love of money, or of wealth, or of political power, whether a man is frightened into surrender by the loss of them, or, having experienced the benefits of money and political corruption, is unable to rise above the seductions of them. For none of these things are of a permanent or lasting nature; not to mention that no generous friendship ever sprang from them. There remains, then, only one way of honourable attachment which custom allows in the beloved, and this is the way of virtue; for as we admitted that any service which the lover does to him is not to be accounted flattery or a dishonour to himself, so the beloved has one way only of voluntary service which is not dishonourable, and this is virtuous service.

For we have a custom, and according to our custom any one who does service to another under the idea that he will be improved by him either in wisdom, or in some other particular of virtue—such a voluntary service, I say, is not to be regarded as a dishonour, and is not open to the charge of flattery. And these two customs, one the love of youth, and the other the practice of philosophy and virtue in general, ought to meet in one, and then the beloved may honourably indulge the lover. For when the lover and beloved come together, having each of them a law, and the lover thinks that he is right in doing any service which he can to his gracious loving one; and the other that he is right in showing any kindness which he can to him who is making him wise and good; the one capable of communicating wisdom and virtue, the other seeking to acquire them with a view to education and wisdom; when the two laws of love are fulfilled and meet in one—then, and then only, may the beloved yield with honour to the lover. Nor when love is of this disinterested sort is there any disgrace in being deceived, but in every other case there is equal disgrace in being or not being deceived. For he who is gracious to his lover under the impression that he is rich, and is disappointed of his gains because he turns out to be poor, is disgraced all the same: for he has done his best to show that he would give himself up to any one's "uses base" for the sake of money; but this is not honourable. And on the same principle, he who gives himself to a lover because he is a good man, and in the hope that he will be improved by his company, shows himself to be virtuous, even though the object of his affection turn out to be a villain, and to have no virtue; and if he is deceived he has committed a noble error. For he has proved that for his part he will do anything for anybody with a view to virtue and improvement, than which there can be nothing nobler. Thus noble in every case is the acceptance of another for the sake of virtue. This is that love which is the the love of the heavenly goddess, and is heavenly, and of great price to individuals and cities, making the lover and the beloved alike eager in the work of their own improvement. But all other loves are the offspring of the other, who is the common goddess. To you, Phaedrus, I offer this my contribution in praise of love, which is as good as I could make extempore.

Pausanias came to a pause—this is the balanced way in which I have been taught by the wise to speak; and Aristodemus said that the turn of Aristophanes was next, but either he had eaten too much, or from some other cause he had the hiccough, and was obliged to change turns with Eryximachus the physician, who was reclining on the couch below him. Eryximachus, he said, you ought either to stop my hiccough, or to speak in my turn until I have left off.

I will do both, said Eryximachus: I will speak in your turn, and do you speak in mine; and while I am speaking let me recommend you to hold your breath, and if after you have done so for some time the hiccough is no better, then gargle with a little water; and if it still continues, tickle your nose with something and sneeze; and if you sneeze once or twice, even the most violent hiccough is sure to go. I will do as you prescribe, said Aristophanes, and now get on.

Eryximachus spoke as follows: Seeing that Pausanias made a fair beginning, and but a lame ending, I must endeavour to supply his deficiency. I think that he has rightly distinguished two kinds of love. But my art further informs me that the double love is not merely an affection of the soul of man towards the fair, or towards anything, but is to be found in the bodies of all animals and in productions of the earth, and I may say in all that is; such is the conclusion which I seem to have gathered from my own art of medicine, whence I learn how great and wonderful and universal is the deity of love, whose empire extends over all things, divine as well as human. And from medicine I will begin that I may do honour to my art. There are in the human body these two kinds of love, which are confessedly different and unlike, and being unlike, they have loves and desires which are unlike; and the desire of the healthy is one, and the desire of the diseased is another; and as Pausanias was just now saying that to indulge good men is honourable, and bad men dishonourable:—so too in the body the good and healthy elements are to be indulged, and the bad elements and the elements of disease are not to be indulged, but discouraged. And this is what the physician has to do, and in this the art of medicine consists: for medicine may be regarded generally as the knowledge of the loves and desires of the body, and how to satisfy them or not; and the best physician is he who is able to separate fair love from foul, or to convert one into the other; and he who knows how to eradicate and how to implant love, whichever is required, and can reconcile the most hostile elements in the constitution and make them loving friends, is a skillful practitioner. Now the most hostile are the most opposite, such as hot and cold, bitter and sweet, moist and dry, and the like. And my ancestor, Asclepius, knowing how to implant friendship and accord in these elements, was the creator of our art, as our friends the poets here tell us, and I believe them; and not only medicine in every branch, but the arts of gymnastic and husbandry are under his dominion. Any one who pays the least attention to the subject will also perceive that in music there is the same reconciliation of opposites; and I suppose that this must have been the meaning of Heracleitus, although his words are not accurate; for he says that The One is united by disunion, like the harmony of the bow and the lyre. Now there is an absurdity in saying that harmony is discord or is composed of elements which are still in a state of discord. But what he probably meant was, that harmony is composed of differing notes of higher or lower pitch which disagreed once, but are now reconciled by the art of music; for if the higher and lower notes still disagreed, there could be no harmony,—clearly not. For harmony is a symphony, and symphony is an agreement; but an agreement of disagreements while they disagree there cannot be; you cannot harmonize that which disagrees. In like manner rhythm is compounded of elements short and long, once differing and now in accord; which accordance, as in the former instance, medicine, so in all these other cases, music implants, making love and unison to grow up among them; and thus music, too, is concerned with the principles of love in their application to harmony and rhythm. Again, in the essential nature of harmony and rhythm there is no difficulty in discerning love which has not yet become double. But when you want to use them in actual life, either in the composition of songs or in the correct performance of airs or metres composed already, which latter is called education, then the difficulty begins, and the good artist is needed. Then the old tale has to be repeated of fair and heavenly love—the love of Urania the fair and heavenly muse, and of the duty of accepting the temperate, and those who are as yet intemperate only that they may become temperate, and of preserving their love; and again, of the vulgar Polyhymnia, who must be used with circumspection that the pleasure be enjoyed, but may not generate licentiousness; just as in my own art it is a great matter so to regulate the desires of the epicure that he may gratify his tastes without the attendant evil of disease. Whence I infer that in music, in medicine, in all other things human as well as divine, both loves ought to be noted as far as may be, for they are both present.

The course of the seasons is also full of both these principles; and when, as I was saying, the elements of hot and cold, moist and dry, attain the harmonious love of one another and blend in temperance and harmony, they bring to men, animals, and plants health and plenty, and do them no harm; whereas the wanton love, getting the upper hand and affecting the seasons of the year, is very destructive and injurious, being the source of pestilence, and bringing many other kinds of diseases on animals and plants; for hoarfrost and hail and blight spring from the excesses and disorders of these elements of love, which to know in relation to the revolutions of the heavenly bodies and the seasons of the year is termed astronomy. Furthermore, all sacrifices and the whole province of divination, which is the art of communion between gods and men—these, I say, are concerned only with the preservation of the good and the cure of the evil love. For all manner of impiety is likely to ensue if, instead of accepting and honouring and reverencing the harmonious love in all his actions, a man honours the other love, whether in his feelings towards gods or parents, towards

the living or the dead. Wherefore the business of divination is to
see to these loves and to heal them, and divination is the peace-
maker of gods and men, working by a knowledge of the religious
or irreligious tendencies which exist in human loves. Such is the
great and mighty, or rather omnipotent force of love in general.
And the love, more especially, which is concerned with the good,
and which is perfected in company with temperance and justice,
whether among gods or men, has the greatest power, and is the
source of all our happiness and harmony, and makes us friends
with the gods who are above us, and with one another. I dare say
that I too have omitted several things which might be said in praise
of Love, but this was not intentional, and you, Aristophanes, may
now supply the omission or take some other line of commendation;
for I perceive that you are rid of the hiccough.

Yes, said Aristophanes, who followed, the hiccough is gone; not,
however, until I applied the sneezing; and I wonder whether the
harmony of the body has a love of such noises and ticklings, for I
no sooner applied the sneezing than I was cured.

Eryximachus said: Beware, friend Aristophanes, although you
are going to speak, you are making fun of me; and I shall have to
watch and see whether I cannot have a laugh at your expense,
when you might speak in peace.

You are quite right, said Aristophanes, laughing. I will unsay my
words; but do you please not to watch me, as I fear that in the
speech which I am about to make, instead of others laughing with
me, which is to the manner born of our muse and would be all the
better, I shall only be laughed at by them.

Do you expect to shoot your bolt and escape, Aristophanes?
Well, perhaps if you are very careful and bear in mind that you
will be called to account, I may be induced to let you off.

Aristophanes professed to open another vein of discourse; he had
a mind to praise Love in another way, unlike that either of Pausanias or Eryximachus. Mankind, he said, judging by their neglect
of him, have never, as I think, at all understood the power of Love.
For if they had understood him they would surely have built noble
temples and altars, and offered solemn sacrifices in his honour; but
this is not done, and most certainly ought to be done: since of all
the gods he is the best friend of men, the helper and the healer of
the ills which are the great impediment to the happiness of the

race. I will try to describe his power to you, and you shall teach the rest of the world what I am teaching you. In the first place, let me treat of the nature of man and what has happened to it; for the original human nature was not like the present, but different. The sexes were not two as they are now, but originally three in number; there was man, woman, and the union of the two, having a name corresponding to this double nature, which had once a real existence, but is now lost, and the word "Androgynous" is only preserved as a term of reproach. In the second place, the primeval man was round, his back and sides forming a circle; and he had four hands and four feet, one head with two faces, looking opposite ways, set on a round neck and precisely alike; also four ears, two privy members, and the remainder to correspond. He could walk upright as men now do, backwards or forwards as he pleased, and he could also roll over and over at a great pace, turning on his four hands and four feet, eight in all, like tumblers going over and over with their legs in the air; this was when he wanted to run fast. Now, the sexes were three, and such as I have described them; because the sun, moon, and earth are three; and the man was originally the child of the sun, the woman of the earth, and the man-woman of the moon, which is made up of sun and earth, and they were all round and moved round and round like their parents. Terrible was their might and strength, and the thoughts of their hearts were great, and they made an attack upon the gods; of them is told the tale of Otys and Ephialtes who, as Homer says, dared to scale heaven, and would have laid hands upon the gods. Doubt reigned in the celestial councils. Should they kill them and annihilate the race with thunderbolts, as they had done the giants, then there would be an end of the sacrifices and worship which men offered to them; but, on the other hand, the gods could not suffer their insolence to be unrestrained. At last, after a good deal of reflection, Zeus discovered a way. He said: "Methinks I have a plan which will humble their pride and improve their manners; men shall continue to exist, but I will cut them in two and then they will be diminished in strength and increased in numbers; this will have the advantage of making them more profitable to us. They shall walk upright on two legs, and if they continue insolent and will not be quiet, I will split them again and they shall hop about on a single leg." He spoke and cut men in two, like a sorb-

apple which is halved for pickling, or as you might divide an egg
with a hair; and as he cut them one after another, he bade Apollo
give the face and the half of the neck a turn in order that the man
might contemplate the section of himself: he would thus learn a
lesson of humility. Apollo was also bidden to heal their wounds
and compose their forms. So he gave a turn to the face and pulled
the skin from the sides all over that which in our language is called
the belly, like the purses which draw in, and he made one mouth
at the centre, which he fastened in a knot (the same which is called
the navel); he also moulded the breast and took out most of the
wrinkles, much as a shoemaker might smooth leather upon a last;
he left a few, however, in the region of the belly and navel, as a
memorial of the primeval state. After the division the two parts of
man, each desiring his other half, came together, and throwing
their arms about one another, entwined in mutual embraces, longing to grow into one; they were on the point of dying from hunger
and self-neglect, because they did not like to do anything apart;
and when one of the halves died and the other survived, the sur-
vivor sought another mate, man or woman, as we call them,—being
the sections of entire men or women,—and clung to that. They
were being destroyed, when Zeus in pity of them invented a new
plan: he turned the parts of generation round to the front, for this
had not been always their position, and they sowed the seed no
longer as hitherto like grasshoppers in the ground, but in one
another; and after the transposition the male generated in the
female in order that by mutual embraces of man and woman they
might breed, and the race might continue; or if man came to man
they might be satisfied, and rest, and go their ways to the business
of life: so ancient is the desire of one another which is implanted
in us, reuniting our original nature, making one of two, and healing the state of man. Each of us when separated, having one side
only, like a flat fish, is but the indenture of a man, and he is always
looking for his other half. Men who are a section of that double
nature which was once called Androgynous are lovers of women;
adulterers are generally of this breed, and also adulterous women
who lust after men: the women who are a section of the woman do
not care for men, but have female attachments; the female companions are of this sort. But they who are a section of the male,
follow the male, and while they are young, being slices of the

original man, they hang about men and embrace them, and they
are themselves the best of boys and youths, because they have the
most manly nature. Some indeed assert that they are shameless, but
this is not true; for they do not act thus from any want of shame,
but because they are valiant and manly, and have a manly countenance, and they embrace that which is like them. And these
when they grow up become our statesmen, and these only, which
is a great proof of the truth of what I am saying. When they reach
manhood they are lovers of youth, and are not naturally inclined
to marry or beget children,—if at all, they do so only in obedience
to the law; but they are satisfied if they may be allowed to live with
one another unwedded; and such a nature is prone to love and
ready to return love, always embracing that which is akin to him.
And when one of them meets with his other half, the actual half of
himself, whether he be a lover of youth or a lover of another sort,
the pair are lost in an amazement of love and friendship and inti-
macy, and one will not be out of the other's sight, as I may say,
even for a moment: these are the people who pass their whole lives
together; yet they could not explain what they desire of one another. For the intense yearning which each of them has towards
the other does not appear to be the desire of lover's intercourse,
but of something else which the soul of either evidently desires and
cannot tell, and of which she has only a dark and doubtful pre-
sentiment. Suppose Hephaestus, with his instruments, to come to
the pair who are lying side by side and to say to them, "What do
you people want of one another?" they would be unable to explain.
And suppose further, that when he saw their perplexity he said:
"Do you desire to be wholly one; always day and night to be in one
another's company? for if this is what you desire, I am ready to melt
you into one and let you grow together, so that being two you shall
become one, and while you live live a common life as if you were a
single man, and after your death in the world below still be one
departed soul instead of two—I ask whether this is what you lov-
ingly desire, and whether you are satisfied to attain this?"—there is
not a man of them who when he heard the proposal would deny or
would not acknowledge that this meeting and melting into one
another, this becoming one instead of two, was the very expression
of his ancient need. And the reason is that human nature was
originally one and we were a whole, and the desire and pursuit of

the whole is called love. There was a time, I say, when we were one, but now because of the wickedness of mankind God has dispersed us, as the Arcadians were dispersed into villages by the Lacedaemonians. And if we are not obedient to the gods, there is a danger that we shall be split up again and go about in *basso-rilievo*, like the profile figures having only half a nose which are sculptured on monuments, and that we shall be like tallies. Wherefore let us exhort all men to piety, that we may avoid evil, and obtain the good, of which Love is to us the lord and minister; and let no one oppose him—he is the enemy of the gods who opposes him. For if we are friends of the god and at peace with him we shall find our own true loves, which rarely happens in this world at present. I am serious, and therefore I must beg Eryximachus not to make fun or to find any allusion in what I am saying to Pausanias and Agathon, who, as I suspect, are both of the manly nature, and belong to the class which I have been describing. But my words have a wider application—they include men and women everywhere; and I believe that if our loves were perfectly accomplished, and each one returning to his primeval nature had his original true love, then our race would be happy. And if this would be best of all, the best in the next degree and under present circumstances must be the nearest approach to such an union; and that will be the attainment of a congenial love. Wherefore, if we would praise him who has given to us the benefit, we must praise the god Love, who is our greatest benefactor, both leading us in this life back to our own nature, and giving us high hopes for the future, for he promises that if we are pious, he will restore us to our original state, and heal us and make us happy and blessed. This, Eryximachus, is my discourse of love, which, although different to yours, I must beg you to leave unassailed by the shafts of your ridicule, in order that each may have his turn; each, or rather either, for Agathon and Socrates are the only ones left.

Indeed, I am not going to attack you, said Eryximachus, for I thought your speech charming, and did I not know that Agathon and Socrates are masters in the art of love, I should be really afraid that they would have nothing to say, after the world of things which have been said already. But, for all that, I am not without hopes.

Socrates said: You played your part well, Eryximachus; but if you were as I am now, or rather as I shall be when Agathon has spoken, you would, indeed, be in a great strait.

You want to cast a spell over me, Socrates, said Agathon, in the hope that I may be disconcerted at the expectation raised among the audience that I shall speak well.

I should be strangely forgetful, Agathon, replied Socrates, of the courage and magnanimity which you showed when your own compositions were about to be exhibited, and you came upon the stage with the actors and faced the vast theatre altogether undismayed, if I thought that your nerves could be fluttered at a small party of friends.

Do you think, Socrates, said Agathon, that my head is so full of the theatre as not to know how much more formidable to a man of sense a few good judges are than many fools?

Nay, replied Socrates, I should be very wrong in attributing to you, Agathon, that or any other want of refinement. And I am quite aware that if you happened to meet with any whom you thought wise, you would care for their opinion much more than for that of the many. But then we, having been a part of the foolish many in the theatre, cannot be regarded as the select wise; though I know that if you chanced to be in the presence, not of one of ourselves, but of some really wise man, you would be ashamed of disgracing yourself before him—would you not?

Yes, said Agathon.

But before the many you would not be ashamed, if you thought that you were doing something disgraceful in their presence?

Here Phaedrus interrupted them, saying: Do not answer him, my dear Agathon; for if he can only get a partner with whom he can talk, especially a good-looking one, he will no longer care about the completion of our plan. Now, I love to hear him talk; but just at present I must not forget the encomium on Love which I ought to receive from him and from every one. When you and he have paid your tribute to the god, then you may talk.

Very good, Phaedrus, said Agathon; I see no reason why I should not proceed with my speech, as I shall have many other opportunities of conversing with Socrates. Let me say first how I ought to speak, and then speak:—

The previous speakers, instead of praising the god Love, or unfolding his nature, appear to have congratulated mankind on the

benefits which he confers upon them. But I would rather praise
the god first, and then speak of his gifts; this is always the right
way of praising everything. May I say without impiety or offence,
that of all the blessed gods he is the most blessed because he is the
fairest and best? And he is the fairest: for, in the first place, he is
the youngest, and of his youth he is himself the witness, fleeing out
of the way of age, who is swift enough, swifter truly than most of
us like:—Love hates him and will not come near him; but youth
and love live and move together—like to like, as the proverb says.
Many things were said by Phaedrus about Love in which I agree
with him; but I cannot agree that he is older than Iapetus and
Cronos:—not so; I maintain him to be the youngest of the gods,
and youthful ever. The ancient doings among the gods of which
Hesiod and Parmenides spoke, if the tradition of them be true,
were done of Necessity and not of Love; had Love been in those
days, there would have been no chaining or mutilation of the gods,
or other violence, but peace and sweetness, as there is now in
heaven, since the rule of Love began. Love is young and also tender; he ought to have a poet like Homer to describe his tenderness, as Homer says of Ate, that she is a goddess and tender:—

>   "Her feet are tender, for she sets her steps,
>   Not on the ground but on the heads of men":

herein is an excellent proof of her tenderness,—that she walks not
upon the hard but upon the soft. Let us adduce a similar proof of
the tenderness of Love; for he walks not upon the earth, nor yet
upon the skulls of men, which are not so very soft, but in the hearts
and souls of both gods and men, which are of all things the softest:
in them he walks and dwells and makes his home. Not in every soul
without exception, for where there is hardness he departs, where
there is softness there he dwells; and nestling always with his feet
and in all manner of ways in the softest of soft places, how can he
be other than the softest of all things? Of a truth he is the tenderest
as well as the youngest, and also he is of flexile form; for if he were
hard and without flexure he could not enfold all things, or wind
his way into and out of every soul of man undiscovered. And a
proof of his flexibility and symmetry of form is his grace, which is
universally admitted to be in an especial manner the attribute of
Love; ungrace and love are always at war with one another. The

fairness of his complexion is revealed by his habitation among the
flowers; for he dwells not amid bloomless or fading beauties,
whether of body or soul or aught else, but in the place of flowers
and scents, there he sits and abides. Concerning the beauty of the
god I have said enough; and yet there remains much more which I
might say. Of his virtue I have now to speak: his greatest glory is
that he can neither do nor suffer wrong to or from any god or any
man; for he suffers not by force if he suffers; force comes not near
him, neither when he acts does he act by force. For all men in all
things serve him of their own free will, and where there is voluntary agreement, there, as the laws which are the lords of the city say,
is justice. And not only is he just but exceedingly temperate, for
Temperance is the acknowledged ruler of the pleasures and desires,
and no pleasure ever masters Love; he is their master and they are
his servants; and if he conquers them he must be temperate indeed.
As to courage, even the God of War is no match for him; he is the
captive and Love is the lord, for love, the love of Aphrodite, masters him, as the tale runs; and the master is stronger than the
servant. And if he conquers the bravest of all others, he must be
himself the bravest. Of his courage and justice and temperance I
have spoken, but I have yet to speak of his wisdom; and according
to the measure of my ability I must try to do my best. In the first
place, he is a poet (and here, like Eryximachus, I magnify my art),
and he is also the source of poesy in others, which he could not be
if he were not himself a poet. And at the touch of him every one
becomes a poet, even though he had no music in him before; this
also is a proof that Love is a good poet and accomplished in all the
fine arts; for no one can give to another that which he has not himself, or teach that of which he has no knowledge. Who will deny
that the creation of the animals is his doing? Are they not all the
works of his wisdom, born and begotten of him? And as to the
artists, do we not know that he only of them whom love inspires
has the light of flame?—he whom Love touches not walks in darkness. The arts of medicine and archery and divination were discovered by Apollo, under the guidance of love and desire; so that
he too is a disciple of Love. Also the melody of the Muses, the
metallurgy of Hephaestus, the weaving of Athene, the empire of
Zeus over gods and men, are all due to Love, who was the inventor
of them. And so Love set in order the empire of the gods—the love

of beauty, as is evident, for with deformity Love has no concern. In the days of old, as I began by saying, dreadful deeds were done among the gods, for they were ruled by Necessity; but now since the birth of Love, and from the love of the beautiful, has sprung every good in heaven and earth. Therefore, Phaedrus, I say of Love that he is the fairest and best in himself, and the cause of what is fairest and best in all other things. And there comes into my mind a line of poetry in which he is said to be the god who

"Gives peace on earth and calms the stormy deep,
Who stills the winds and bids the sufferer sleep."

This is he who empties men of disaffection and fills them with affection, who makes them to meet together at banquets such as these: in sacrifices, feasts, dances, he is our lord—who sends courtesy and sends away discourtesy, who gives kindness ever and never gives unkindness; the friend of the good, the wonder of the wise, the amazement of the gods; desired by those who have no part in him, and precious to those who have the better part in him; parent of delicacy, luxury, desire, fondness, softness, grace; regardful of the good, regardless of the evil: in every word, work, wish, fear—saviour, pilot, comrade, helper; glory of gods and men, leader best and brightest: in whose footsteps let every man follow, sweetly singing in his honour and joining in that sweet strain with which love charms the souls of gods and men. Such is the speech, Phaedrus, half-playful, yet having a certain measure of seriousness, which, according to my ability, I dedicate to the god.

When Agathon had done speaking, Aristodemus said that there was a general cheer; the young man was thought to have spoken in a manner worthy of himself, and of the god. And Socrates, looking at Eryximachus, said: Tell me, son of Acumenus, was there not reason in my fears? and was I not a true prophet when I said that Agathon would make a wonderful oration, and that I should be in a strait?

The part of the prophecy which concerns Agathon, replied Eryximachus, appears to me to be true; but not the other part—that you will be in a strait.

Why, my dear friend, said Socrates, must not I or any one be in a strait who has to speak after he has heard such a rich and varied discourse? I am especially struck with the beauty of the concluding words—who could listen to them without amazement? When I reflected on the immeasurable inferiority of my own powers, I was ready to run away for shame, if there had been a possibility of escape. For I was reminded of Gorgias, and at the end of his speech I fancied that Agathon was shaking at me the Gorginian or Gorgonian head of the great master of rhetoric, which was simply to turn me and my speech into stone, as Homer says, and strike me dumb. And then I perceived how foolish I had been in consenting to take my turn with you in praising love, and saying that I too was a master of the art, when I really had no conception how anything ought to be praised. For in my simplicity I imagined that the topics of praise should be true, and that this being presupposed, out of the true the speaker was to choose the best and set them forth in the best manner. And I felt quite proud, thinking that I knew the nature of true praise, and should speak well. Whereas I now see that the intention was to attribute to Love every species of greatness and glory, whether really belonging to him or not, without regard to truth or falsehood—that was no matter; for the original proposal seems to have been not that each of you should really praise Love, but only that you should appear to praise him. And so you attribute to Love every imaginable form of praise which can be gathered anywhere; and you say that "he is all this," and "the cause of all that," making him appear the fairest and best of all to those who know him not, for you cannot impose upon those who know him. And a noble and solemn hymn of praise have you rehearsed. But as I misunderstood the nature of the praise when I said that I would take my turn, I must beg to be absolved from the promise which I made in ignorance, and which (as Euripides would say) was a promise of the lips and not of the mind. Farewell then to such a strain: for I do not praise in that way; no, indeed, I cannot. But if you like to hear the truth about love, I am ready to speak in my own manner, though I will not make myself ridiculous by entering into any rivalry with you. Say then, Phaedrus, whether you would like to have the truth about love, spoken in any words and in any order which may happen to come into my mind at the time. Will that be agreeable to you?

Aristodemus said that Phaedrus and the company bid him speak in any manner which he thought best. Then, he added, let me have

your permission first to ask Agathon a few more questions, in order
that I may take his admissions as the premises of my discourse.

I grant the permission, said Phaedrus: put your questions. Socrates then proceeded as follows:—

In the magnificent oration which you have just uttered, I think
that you were right, my dear Agathon, in proposing to speak of the
nature of Love first and afterwards of his works—that is a way of
beginning which I very much approve. And as you have spoken so
eloquently of his nature, may I ask you further, Whether love is
the love of something or of nothing? And here I must explain myself: I do not want you to say that love is the love of a father or the
love of a mother—that would be ridiculous; but to answer as you
would, if I asked is a father a father of something? to which you
would find no difficulty in replying, of a son or daughter: and the
answer would be right.

Very true, said Agathon.

And you would say the same of a mother?

He assented.

Yet let me ask you one more question in order to illustrate my
meaning: Is not a brother to be regarded essentially as a brother of
something?

Certainly, he replied.

That is, of a brother or sister?

Yes, he said.

And now said Socrates, I will ask about Love:—Is Love of something or of nothing?

Of something, surely, he replied.

Keep in mind what this is, and tell me what I want to know—
whether Love desires that of which love is.

Yes, surely.

And does he possess, or does he not possess, that which he loves
and desires?

Probably not, I should say.

Nay, replied Socrates, I would have you consider whether "necessarily" is not rather the word. The inference that he who desires
something is in want of something, and that he who desires nothing is in want of nothing, is in my judgment, Agathon, absolutely
and necessarily true. What do you think?

I agree with you, said Agathon.

Very good. Would he who is great, desire to be great, or he who is strong, desire to be strong?

That would be inconsistent with our previous admissions.

True. For he who is anything cannot want to be that which he is?

Very true.

And yet, added Socrates, if a man being strong desired to be strong, or being swift desired to be swift, or being healthy desired to be healthy, in that case he might be thought to desire something which he already has or is. I give the example in order that we may avoid misconception. For the possessors of these qualities, Agathon, must be supposed to have their respective advantages at the time, whether they choose or not; and who can desire that which he has? Therefore, when a person says, I am well and wish to be well, or I am rich and wish to be rich, and I desire simply to have what I have—to him we shall reply: "You, my friend, having wealth and health and strength, want to have the continuance of them; for at this moment, whether you choose or no, you have them. And when you say, I desire that which I have and nothing else, is not your meaning that you want to have what you now have in the future?" He must agree with us—must he not?

He must, replied Agathon.

Then, said Socrates, he desires that what he has at present may be preserved to him in the future, which is equivalent to saying that he desires something which is non-existent to him, and which as yet he has not got?

Very true, he said.

Then he and every one who desires, desires that which he has not already, and which is future and not present, and which he has not, and is not, and of which he is in want;—these are the sort of things which love and desire seek?

Very true, he said.

Then now, said Socrates, let us recapitulate the argument. First, is not love of something, and of something too which is wanting to a man?

Yes, he replied.

Remember further what you said in your speech, or if you do not remember I will remind you: you said that the love of the beautiful set in order the empire of the gods, for that of deformed things there is no love—did you not say something of that kind?

Yes, said Agathon.

Yes, my friend, and the remark was a just one. And if this is true, Love is the love of beauty and not of deformity?

He assented.

And the admission has been already made that Love is of something which a man wants and has not?

True, he said.

Then Love wants and has not beauty?

Certainly, he replied.

And would you call that beautiful which wants and does not possess beauty?

Certainly not.

Then would you still say that love is beautiful?

Agathon replied: I fear that I did not understand what I was saying.

You made a very good speech, Agathon, replied Socrates; but there is yet one small question which I would fain ask:—Is not the good also the beautiful?

Yes.

Then in wanting the beautiful, love wants also the good?

I cannot refute you, Socrates, said Agathon:—Let us assume that what you say is true.

Say rather, beloved Agathon, that you cannot refute the truth; for Socrates is easily refuted.

And now, taking my leave of you, I will rehearse a tale of love which I heard from Diotima of Mantineia, a woman wise in this and in many other kinds of knowledge, who in the days of old, when the Athenians offered sacrifice before the coming of the plague, delayed the disease ten years. She was my instructress in the art of love, and I shall repeat to you what she said to me, beginning with the admissions made by Agathon, which are nearly if not quite the same which I made to the wise woman when she questioned me: I think that this will be the easiest way, and I shall take both parts myself as well as I can. As you, Agathon, suggested, I must speak first of the being and nature of Love, and then of his works. First I said to her in nearly the same words which he used to me, that Love was a mighty god, and likewise fair; and she proved to me as I proved to him that, by my own showing, Love was neither fair nor good. "What do you mean, Diotima," I said, "is Love then evil and foul?" "Hush," she cried; "must that be foul which is not fair?" "Certainly," I said. "And is that which is not wise, ignorant? Do you not see that there is a mean between wisdom and ignorance?" "And what may that be?" I said. "Right opinion," she replied; "which, as you know, being incapable of giving a reason, is not knowledge (for how can knowledge be devoid of reason? nor again, ignorance, for neither can ignorance attain the truth), but is clearly something which is a mean between ignorance and wisdom." "Quite true," I replied. "Do not then insist," she said, "that what is not fair is of necessity foul, or what is not good evil; or infer that because Love is not fair and good he is therefore foul and evil; for he is in a mean between them." "Well," I said, "Love is surely admitted by all to be a great god." "By those who know or by those who do not know?" "By all." "And now, Socrates," she said with a smile, "can Love be acknowledged to be a great god by those who say that he is not a god at all?" "And who are they?" I said. "You and I are two of them," she replied. "How can that be?" I said. "It is quite intelligible," she replied; "for you yourself would acknowledge that the gods are happy and fair—of course you would—would you dare to say that any god was not?" "Certainly not," I replied. "And you mean by the happy, those who are the possessors of things good or fair?" "Yes." "And you admitted that Love, because he was in want, desires those good and fair things of which he is in want?" "Yes, I did." "But how can he be a god who has no portion in what is either good or fair?" "Impossible." "Then you see that you also deny the divinity of Love."

"What then is Love?" I asked. "Is he mortal?" "No." "What then?" "As in the former instance, he is neither mortal nor immortal, but in a mean between the two." "What is he, Diotima?" "He is a great spirit *(daimon)*, and like all spirits he is intermediate between the divine and the mortal." "And what," I said, "is his power?" "He interprets," she replied, "between gods and men, conveying and taking across to the gods the prayers and sacrifices of men, and to men the commands and replies of the gods; he is the mediator who spans the chasm which divides them, and therefore in him all is bound together, and through him the arts of the prophet and the priest, their sacrifices and mysteries and charms,

and all prophecy and incantation, find their way. For God mingles
not with man; but through Love all the intercourse and converse
of God with man, whether awake or asleep, is carried on. The wisdom which understands this is spiritual; all other wisdom, such as
that of arts and handicrafts, is mean and vulgar. Now these spirits
or intermediate powers are many and diverse, and one of them is
Love." "And who," I said, "was his father, and who his mother?"
"The tale," she said, "will take time; nevertheless I will tell you.
On the birthday of Aphrodite there was a feast of the gods, at which
the god Poros, or Plenty, who is the son of Metis, or Discretion, was
one of the guests. When the feast was over, Penia or Poverty, as
the manner is on such occasions, came about the doors to beg. Now
Plenty, who was the worse for nectar (there was no wine in those
days), went into the garden of Zeus and fell into a heavy sleep; and
Poverty considering her own straitened circumstances, plotted to
have a child by him, and accordingly she lay down at his side and
conceived Love, who partly because he is naturally a lover of the
beautiful, and because Aphrodite is herself beautiful, and also because he was born on her birthday, is her follower and attendant.
And as his parentage is, so also are his fortunes. In the first place
he is always poor, and anything but tender and fair, as the many
imagine him; and he is rough and squalid, and has no shoes, nor a
house to dwell in; on the bare earth exposed he lies under the
open heaven, in the streets, or at the doors of houses, taking his
rest; and like his mother he is always in distress. Like his father
too, whom he also partly resembles, he is always plotting against
the fair and good; he is bold, enterprising, strong, a mighty hunter,
always weaving some intrigue or other, keen in the pursuit of wisdom, fertile in resources; a philosopher at all times, terrible as an
enchanter, sorcerer, sophist. He is by nature neither mortal nor
immortal, but alive and flourishing at one moment when he is in
plenty, and dead at another moment, and again alive by reason of
his father's nature. But that which is always flowing in is always
flowing out, and so he is never in want and never in wealth; and,
further, he is in a mean between ignorance and knowledge: The
truth of the matter is this: No god is a philosopher or seeker after
wisdom, for he is wise already; nor does any man who is wise seek
after wisdom. Neither do the ignorant seek after wisdom. For
herein is the evil of ignorance, that he who is neither good nor

wise is nevertheless satisfied with himself: he has no desire for that of which he feels no want." "But who, then, Diotima," I said, "are the lovers of wisdom, if they are neither the wise nor the foolish?" "A child may answer that question," she replied; "they are those who are in a mean between the two; Love is one of them. For wisdom is a most beautiful thing, and Love is of the beautiful; and therefore Love is also a philosopher, or lover of wisdom, and being a lover of wisdom is in a mean between the wise and the ignorant. And of this too his birth is the cause; for his father is wealthy and wise, and his mother poor and foolish. Such, my dear Socrates, is the nature of the spirit Love. The error in your conception of him was very natural, and as I imagine from what you say, has arisen out of a confusion of love and the beloved, which made you think that love was all beautiful. For the beloved is the truly beautiful, and delicate, and perfect, and blessed; but the principle of love is of another nature, and is such as I have described."

I said: "O thou stranger woman, thou sayest well; but, assuming Love to be such as you say, what is the use of him to men?" "That, Socrates," she replied, "I will attempt to unfold: of his nature and birth I have already spoken; and you acknowledge that love is of the beautiful. But some one will say: Of the beautiful in what, Socrates and Diotima?—or rather let me put the question more clearly, and ask: When a man loves the beautiful, what does he desire?" I answered her, "That the beautiful may be his." "Still," she said, "the answer suggests a further question: What is given by the possession of beauty?" "To what you have asked," I replied, "I have no answer ready." "Then," she said, "let me put the word 'good' in the place of the beautiful, and repeat the question once more: If he who loves the good, what is it then that he loves?" "The possession of the good," I said. "And what does he gain who possesses the good?" "Happiness," I replied; "there is less difficulty in answering that question." "Yes," she said, "the happy are made happy by the acquisition of good things. Nor is there any need to ask why a man desires happiness; the answer is already final." "You are right," I said. "And is this wish and this desire common to all? and do all men always desire their own good, or only some men?— what say you?" "All men," I replied; "the desire is common to all." "Why, then," she rejoined, "are not all men, Socrates, said to love, but only some of them? whereas you say that all men are always

loving the same things." "I myself wonder," I said, "why this is."
"There is nothing to wonder at," she replied; "the reason is that
one part of love is separated off and receives the name of the whole,
but the other parts have other names." "Give an illustration," I
said. She answered me as follows: "There is poetry, which, as you
know, is complex and manifold. All creation or passage of non-
being into being is poetry or making, and the processes of all art
are creative; and the masters of arts are all poets or makers." "Very
true." "Still," she said, "you know that they are not called poets,
but have other names; only that portion of the art which is separated off from the rest, and is concerned with music and metre, is
termed poetry, and they who possess poetry in this sense of the
word are called poets." "Very true," I said. "And the same holds of
love. For you may say generally that all desire of good and happiness is only the great and subtle power of love; but they who are
drawn towards him by any other path, whether the path of money-
making or gymnastics or philosophy, are not called lovers—the
name of the whole is appropriated to those whose affection takes
one form only—they alone are said to love, or to be lovers." "I dare
say," I replied, "that you are right." "Yes," she added, "and you
hear people say that lovers are seeking for their other half; but
I say that they are seeking neither for the half of themselves,
nor for the whole, unless the half or the whole be also a good.
And they will cut off their own hands and feet and cast them
away, if they are evil; for they love not what is their own, unless
perchance there be some one who calls what belongs to him the
good, and what belongs to another the evil. For there is nothing
which men love but the good. Is there anything?" "Certainly, I
should say, that there is nothing." "Then," she said, "the simple
truth is, that men love the good." "Yes," I said. "To which must
be added that they love the possession of the good?" "Yes, that
must be added." "And not only the possession, but the everlasting
possession of the good?" "That must be added too." "Then love,"
she said, "may be described generally as the love of the everlasting
possession of the good?" "That is most true."

   "Then if this be the nature of love, can you tell me further,"
she said, "what is the manner of the pursuit? what are they doing
who show all this eagerness and heat which is called love? and what
is the object which they have in view? Answer me." "Nay, Dio-

tima," I replied, "if I had known, I should not have wondered at your wisdom, neither should I have come to learn from you about this very matter." "Well," she said, "I will teach you:—The object which they have in view is birth in beauty, whether of body or soul." "I do not understand you," I said; "the oracle requires an explanation." "I will make my meaning clearer," she replied. "I mean to say, that all men are bringing to the birth in their bodies and in their souls. There is a certain age at which human nature is desirous of procreation—procreation which must be in beauty and not in deformity; and this procreation is the union of man and woman, and is a divine thing; for conception and generation are an immortal principle in the mortal creature, and in the inharmonious they can never be. But the deformed is always inharmonious with the divine, and the beautiful harmonious. Beauty, then, is the destiny or goddess of parturition who presides at birth, and therefore, when approaching beauty, the conceiving power is propitious, and diffusive, and benign, and begets and bears fruit: at the sight of ugliness she frowns and contracts and has a sense of pain, and turns away, and shrivels up, and not without a pang refrains from conception. And this is the reason why, when the hour of conception arrives, and the teeming nature is full, there is such a flutter and ecstasy about beauty whose approach is the alleviation of the pain of travail. For love, Socrates, is not, as you imagine, the love of the beautiful only." "What then?" "The love of generation and of birth in beauty." "Yes," I said. "Yes, indeed," she replied. "But why of generation?" "Because to the mortal creature, generation is a sort of eternity and immortality," she replied; "and if, as has been already admitted, love is of the everlasting possession of the good, all men will necessarily desire immortality together with good: Wherefore love is of immortality."

All this she taught me at various times when she spoke of love. And I remember her once saying to me, "What is the cause, Socrates, of love, and the attendant desire? See you not how all animals, birds, as well as beasts, in their desire of procreation, are in agony when they take the infection of love, which begins with the desire of union; whereto is added the care of offspring, on whose behalf the weakest are ready to battle against the strongest even to the uttermost, and to die for them, and will let themselves be tormented with hunger or suffer anything in order to maintain their young? Man may be supposed to act thus from reason; but why should animals have these passionate feelings? Can you tell me why?" Again I replied that I did not know. She said to me: "And do you expect ever to become a master in the art of love, if you do not know this?" "But I have told you already, Diotima, that my ignorance is the reason why I come to you; for I am conscious that I want a teacher; tell me then the cause of this and of the other mysteries of love." "Marvel not," she said, "if you believe that love is of the immortal, as we have several times acknowledged; for here again, and on the same principle too, the mortal nature is seeking as far as is possible to be everlasting and immortal: and this is only to be attained by generation, because generation always leaves behind a new existence in the place of the old. Nay, even in the life of the same individual there is succession and not absolute unity: a man is called the same, and yet in the short interval which elapses between youth and age, and in which every animal is said to have life and identity, he is undergoing a perpetual process of loss and reparation—hair, flesh, bones, blood, and the whole body are always changing. Which is true not only of the body, but also of the soul, whose habits, tempers, opinions, desires, pleasures, pains, fears, never remain the same in any one of us, but are always coming and going; and equally true of knowledge, and what is still more surprising to us mortals, not only do the sciences in general spring up and decay, so that in respect of them we are never the same; but each of them individually experiences a like change. For what is implied in the word 'recollection,' but the departure of knowledge, which is ever being forgotten, and is renewed and preserved by recollection, and appears to be the same although in reality new, according to that law of succession by which all mortal things are preserved, not absolutely the same, but by substitution, the old worn-out mortality leaving another new and similar existence behind—unlike the divine, which is always the same and not another? And in this way, Socrates, the mortal body, or mortal anything, partakes of immortality; but the immortal in another way. Marvel not then at the love which all men have of their offspring; for that universal love and interest is for the sake of immortality."

I was astonished at her words, and said: "Is this really true, O thou wise Diotima?" And she answered with all the authority of an accomplished Sophist: "Of that, Socrates, you may be assured;—

think only of the ambition of men, and you will wonder at the senselessness of their ways, unless you consider how they are stirred by the love of an immortality of fame. They are ready to run all risks greater far than they would have run for their children, and to spend money and undergo any sort of toil, and even to die, for the sake of leaving behind them a name which shall be eternal. Do you imagine that Alcestis would have died to save Admetus, or Achilles to avenge Patroclus, or your own Codrus in order to preserve the kingdom for his sons, if they had not imagined that the memory of their virtues, which still survives among us, would be immortal? Nay," she said, "I am persuaded that all men do all things, and the better they are the more they do them, in hope of the glorious fame of immortal virtue; for they desire the immortal.

"Those who are pregnant in the body only, betake themselves to women and beget children—this is the character of their love; their offspring, as they hope, will preserve their memory and give them the blessedness and immortality which they desire in the future. But souls which are pregnant—for there certainly are men who are more creative in their souls than in their bodies—conceive that which is proper for the soul to conceive or contain. And what are these conceptions?—wisdom and virtue in general. And such creators are poets and all artists who are deserving of the name inventor. But the greatest and fairest sort of wisdom by far is that which is concerned with the ordering of states and families, and which is called temperance and justice. And he who in youth has the seed of these implanted in him and is himself inspired, when he comes to maturity desires to beget and generate. He wanders about seeking beauty that he may beget offspring—for in deformity he will beget nothing—and naturally embraces the beautiful rather than the deformed body; above all, when he finds a fair and noble and well-nurtured soul, he embraces the two in one person, and to such an one he is full of speech about virtue and the nature and pursuits of a good man; and he tries to educate him; and at the touch of the beautiful which is ever present to his memory, even when absent, he brings forth that which he had conceived long before, and in company with him tends that which he brings forth; and they are married by a far nearer tie and have a closer friendship than those who beget mortal children, for the children who are their common offspring are fairer and more immortal. Who,

when he thinks of Homer and Hesiod and other great poets, would
not rather have their children than ordinary human ones? Who
would not emulate them in the creation of children such as theirs,
which have preserved their memory and given them everlasting
glory? Or who would not have such children as Lycurgus left behind him to be the saviours, not only of Lacedaemon, but of
Hellas, as one may say? There is Solon, too, who is the revered
father of Athenian laws; and many others there are in many other
places, both among Hellenes and barbarians, who have given to
the world many noble works, and have been the parents of virtue
of every kind; and many temples have been raised in their honour
for the sake of children such as theirs; which were never raised in
honour of any one, for the sake of his mortal children.

"These are the lesser mysteries of love, into which even you,
Socrates, may enter; to the greater and more hidden ones which
are the crown of these, and to which, if you pursue them in a right
spirit, they will lead, I know not whether you will be able to attain.
But I will do my utmost to inform you, and do you follow if you
can. For he who would proceed aright in this matter should begin
in youth to visit beautiful forms; and first, if he be guided by his
instructor aright, to love one such form only—out of that he should
create fair thoughts; and soon he will of himself perceive that the
beauty of one form is akin to the beauty of another; and then if
beauty of form in general is his pursuit, how foolish would he be
not to recognize that the beauty in every form is one and the same!
And when he perceives this he will abate his violent love of the
one, which he will despise and deem a small thing, and will become a lover of all beautiful forms; in the next stage he will consider that the beauty of the mind is more honourable than the
beauty of the outward form. So that if a virtuous soul have but a
little comeliness, he will be content to love and tend him, and will
search out and bring to the birth thoughts which may improve the
young, until he is compelled to contemplate and see the beauty of
institutions and laws, and to understand that the beauty of them
all is of one family, and that personal beauty is a trifle; and after
laws and institutions he will go on to the sciences, that he may see
their beauty, being not like a servant in love with the beauty of
one youth or man or institution, himself a slave mean and narrow-
minded, but drawing towards and contemplating the vast sea of

beauty, he will create many fair and noble thoughts and notions
in boundless love of wisdom; until on that shore he grows and
waxes strong, and at last the vision is revealed to him of a single
science, which is the science of beauty everywhere. To this I will
proceed; please to give me your very best attention:

"He who has been instructed thus far in the things of love, and
who has learned to see the beautiful in due order and succession,
when he comes towards the end will suddenly perceive a nature of
wondrous beauty (and this, Socrates, is the final cause of all our
former toils)—a nature which in the first place is everlasting, not
growing and decaying, or waxing and waning; secondly, not fair
in one point of view and foul in another, or at one time or in one
relation or at one place fair, at another time or in another relation or at another place foul, as if fair to some and foul to others,
or in the likeness of a face or hands or any other part of the bodily
frame, or in any form of speech or knowledge, or existing in any
other being, as, for example, in an animal, or in heaven, or in
earth, or in any other place but beauty absolute, separate, simple,
and everlasting, which without diminution and without increase,
or any change, is imparted to the ever-growing and perishing beauties of all other things. He who from these ascending under the
influence of true love, begins to perceive that beauty, is not far
from the end. And the true order of going, or being led by another,
to the things of love, is to begin from the beauties of earth and
mount upwards for the sake of that other beauty, using these as
steps only, and from one going on to two, and from two to all
fair forms, and from fair forms to fair practices, and from fair
practices to fair notions, until from fair notions he arrives at the
notion of absolute beauty, and at last knows what the essence of
beauty is. This, my dear Socrates," said the stranger of Mantineia,
"is that life above all others which man should live, in the contemplation of beauty absolute; a beauty which if you once beheld,
you would see not to be after the measure of gold, and garments,
and fair boys and youths, whose presence now entrances you; and
you and many an one would be content to live seeing them only
and conversing with them without meat or drink, if that were
possible—you only want to look at them and to be with them. But
what if the man had eyes to see the true beauty—the divine beauty,
I mean, pure and clear and unalloyed, not clogged with the pollu-

tions of mortality and all the colours and vanities of human life—
thither looking, and holding converse with the true beauty simple
and divine? Remember how in that communion only, beholding
beauty with the eye of the mind, he will be enabled to bring forth,
not images of beauty, but realities (for he has hold not of an image
but of a reality), and bringing forth and nourishing true virtue
to become the friend of God and be immortal, if mortal man may.
Would that be an ignoble life?"

Such, Phaedrus—and I speak not only to you, but to all of you—
were the words of Diotima; and I am persuaded of their truth.
And being persuaded of them, I try to persuade others, that in
the attainment of this end human nature will not easily find a
helper better than love. And therefore, also, I say that every man
ought to honour him as I myself honour him, and walk in his
ways, and exhort others to do the same, and praise the power and
spirit of love according to the measure of my ability now and ever.

The words which I have spoken, you, Phaedrus, may call an
encomium of love, or anything else which you please.

When Socrates had done speaking, the company applauded, and
Aristophanes was beginning to say something in answer to the
allusion which Socrates had made to his own speech, when suddenly there was a great knocking at the door of the house, as of
revellers, and the sound of a flute-girl was heard. Agathon told the
attendants to go and see who were the intruders. "If they are
friends of ours," he said, "invite them in, but if not, say that the
drinking is over." A little while afterwards they heard the voice of
Alcibiades resounding in the court; he was in a great state of intoxication, and kept roaring and shouting "Where is Agathon?
Lead me to Agathon," and at length, supported by the flute-girl
and some of his attendants, he found his way to them. "Hail,
friends," he said, appearing at the door crowned with a massive
garland of ivy and violets, his head flowing with ribands. "Will you
have a very drunken man as a companion of your revels? Or shall
I crown Agathon, which was my intention in coming, and go away?
For I was unable to come yesterday, and therefore I am here to-
day, carrying on my head these ribands, that taking them from
my own head, I may crown the head of this fairest and wisest of
men, as I may be allowed to call him. Will you laugh at me because I am drunk? Yet I know very well that I am speaking the

truth, although you may laugh. But first tell me; if I come in shall we have the understanding of which I spoke? Will you drink with me or not?"

The company were vociferous in begging that he would take his place among them, and Agathon specially invited him. Thereupon he was led in by the people who were with him; and as he was being led, intending to crown Agathon, he took the ribands from his own head and held them in front of his eyes; he was thus prevented from seeing Socrates, who made way for him, and Alcibiades took the vacant place between Agathon and Socrates, and in taking the place he embraced Agathon and crowned him. Take off his sandals, said Agathon and let him make a third on the same couch.

By all means; but who makes the third partner in our revels? said Alcibiades, turning round and starting up as he caught sight of Socrates. By Heracles, he said, what is this? here is Socrates always lying in wait for me, and always, as his way is, coming out at all sorts of unsuspected places: and now, what have you to say for yourself, and why are you lying here, where I perceive that you have contrived to find a place, not by a joker or lover of jokes, like Aristophanes, but by the fairest of the company.

Socrates turned to Agathon and said: I must ask you to protect me, Agathon; for the passion of this man has grown quite a serious matter to me. Since I became his admirer I have never been allowed to speak to any other fair one, or so much as to look at them. If I do, he goes wild with envy and jealousy, and not only abuses me but can hardly keep his hands off me, and at this moment he may do me some harm. Please to see to this, and either reconcile me to him, or, if he attempts violence, protect me, as I am in bodily fear of his mad and passionate attempts.

There can never be reconciliation between you and me, said Alcibiades; but for the present I will defer your chastisement. And I must beg you, Agathon, to give me back some of the ribands that I may crown the marvellous head of this universal despot—I would not have him complain of me for crowning you, and neglecting him, who in conversation is the conqueror of all mankind; and this not only once, as you were the day before yesterday, but always. Whereupon, taking some of the ribands, he crowned Socrates, and again reclined.

Then he said: You seem, my friends, to be sober, which is a thing not to be endured; you must drink—for that was the agreement under which I was admitted—and I elect myself master of the feast until you are well drunk. Let us have a large goblet, Agathon, or rather, he said, addressing the attendant, bring me that wine-cooler. The wine-cooler which had caught his eye was a vessel holding more than two quarts—this he filled and emptied, and bade the attendant fill it again for Socrates. Observe, my friends, said Alcibiades, that this ingenious trick of mine will have no effect on Socrates, for he can drink any quantity of wine and not be at all nearer being drunk. Socrates drank the cup which the attendant filled for him.

Eryximachus said: What is this, Alcibiades? Are we to have neither conversation nor singing over our cups; but simply to drink as if we were thirsty?

Alcibiades replied: Hail, worthy son of a most wise and worthy sire!

The same to you, said Eryximachus; but what shall we do?

That I leave to you, said Alcibiades.

"The wise physician skilled our wounds to heal"

shall prescribe and we will obey. What do you want?

Well, said Eryximachus, before you appeared we had passed a resolution that each one of us in turn should make a speech in praise of love, and as good a one as he could: the turn was passed round from left to right; and as all of us have spoken, and you have not spoken but have well drunken, you ought to speak, and then impose upon Socrates any task which you please, and he on his right-hand neighbour, and so on.

That is good, Eryximachus, said Alcibiades; and yet the comparison of a drunken man's speech with those of sober men is hardly fair; and I should like to know, sweet friend, whether you really believe what Socrates was just now saying; for I can assure you that the very reverse is the fact, and that if I praise any one but himself in his presence, whether God or man, he will hardly keep his hands off me.

For shame, said Socrates.

Hold your tongue, said Alcibiades, for by Poseidon, there is no one else whom I will praise when you are of the company.

Well, then, said Eryximachus, if you like, praise Socrates.

What do you think, Eryximachus? said Alcibiades: shall I attack him and inflict the punishment before you all?

What are you about? said Socrates; are you going to raise a laugh at my expense? Is that the meaning of your praise?

I am going to speak the truth, if you will permit me.

I not only permit, but exhort you to speak the truth.

Then I will begin at once, said Alcibiades, and if I say anything which is not true, you may interrupt me if you will, and say "That is a lie," though my intention is to speak the truth. But you must not wonder if I speak anyhow as things come into my mind; for the fluent and orderly enumeration of all your singularities is not a task which is easy to a man in my condition.

And now, my boys, I shall praise Socrates in a figure which will appear to him to be a caricature, and yet I speak, not to make fun of him, but only for the truth's sake. I say, that he is exactly like the busts of Silenus, which are set up in the statuaries' shops, holding pipes and flutes in their mouths; and they are made to open in the middle, and have images of gods inside them. I say also that he is like Marsyas the satyr. You yourself will not deny, Socrates, that your face is like that of a satyr. Aye, and there is a resemblance in other points too. For example, you are a bully, as I can prove by witnesses, if you will not confess. And are you not a flute-player? That you are, and a performer far more wonderful than Marsyas. He indeed with instruments used to charm the souls of men by the power of his breath, and the players of his music do so still: for the melodies of Olympus are derived from Marsyas who taught them, and these, whether they are played by a great master or by a miserable flute-girl, have a power which no others have; they alone possess the soul and reveal the wants of those who have need of gods and mysteries, because they are divine. But you produce the same effect with your words only, and do not require the flute: that is the difference between you and him. When we hear any other speaker, even a very good one, he produces absolutely no effect upon us, or not much, whereas the mere fragments of you and your words, even at second-hand, and however imperfectly repeated, amaze and possess the souls of every man, woman, and child who comes within hearing of them. And if I were not afraid that you would think me hopelessly drunk, I would have sworn as well as spoken to the influence which they have always had and still have over me. For my heart leaps within me more than that of any Corybantian reveller, and my eyes rain tears when I hear them. And I observe that many others are affected in the same manner. I have heard Pericles and other great orators, and I thought that they spoke well, but I never had any similar feeling; my soul was not stirred by them, nor was I angry at the thought of my own slavish state. But this Marsyas has often brought me to such a pass, that I have felt as if I could hardly endure the life which I am leading (this, Socrates, you will admit); and I am conscious that if I did not shut my ears against him, and fly as from the voice of the siren, my fate would be like that of others,—he would transfix me, and I should grow old sitting at his feet. For he makes me confess that I ought not to live as I do, neglecting the wants of my own soul, and busying myself with the concerns of the Athenians; therefore I hold my ears and tear myself away from him. And he is the only person who ever made me ashamed, which you might think not to be in my nature, and there is no one else who does the same. For I know that I cannot answer him or say that I ought not to do as he bids, but when I leave his presence the love of popularity gets the better of me. And therefore I run away and fly from him, and when I see him I am ashamed of what I have confessed to him. Many a time have I wished that he were dead, and yet I know that I should be much more sorry than glad, if he were to die: so that I am at my wit's end.

And this is what I and many others have suffered from the flute-playing of this satyr. Yet hear me once more while I show you how exact the image is, and how marvellous his power. For let me tell you; none of you know him; but I will reveal him to you; having begun, I must go on. See you how fond he is of the fair? He is always with them and is always being smitten by them, and then again he knows nothing and is ignorant of all things—such is the appearance which he puts on. Is he not like a Silenus in this? To be sure he is: his outer mask is the carved head of the Silenus; but, O my companions in drink, when he is opened, what temperance there is residing within! Know you that beauty and wealth and honour, at which the many wonder, are of no account with him, and are utterly despised by him: he regards not at all the

persons who are gifted with them; mankind are nothing to him;
all his life is spent in mocking and flouting at them. But when
I opened him, and looked within at his serious purpose, I saw in
him divine and golden images of such fascinating beauty that
I was ready to do in a moment whatever Socrates commanded:
they may have escaped the observation of others, but I saw them.
Now I fancied that he was seriously enamoured of my beauty,
and I thought that I should therefore have a grand opportunity
of hearing him tell what he knew, for I had a wonderful opinion
of the attractions of my youth. In the prosecution of this design,
when I next went to him, I sent away the attendant who usually
accompanied me (I will confess the whole truth, and beg you
to listen; and if I speak falsely, do you, Socrates, expose the falsehood). Well, he and I were alone together, and I thought that
when there was nobody with us, I should hear him speak the
language which lovers use to their loves when they are by themselves, and I was delighted. Nothing of the sort; he conversed
as usual, and spent the day with me and then went away. Afterwards I challenged him to the palaestra; and he wrestled and
closed with me several times when there was no one present; I
fancied that I might succeed in this manner. Not a bit; I made
no way with him. Lastly, as I had failed hitherto, I thought that
I must take stronger measures and attack him boldly, and, as
I had begun, not give him up, but see how matters stood between him and me. So I invited him to sup with me, just as if
he were a fair youth, and I a designing lover. He was not easily
persuaded to come; he did, however, after a while accept the
invitation, and when he came the first time, he wanted to go
away at once as soon as supper was over, and I had not the face
to detain him. The second time, still in pursuance of my design,
after we had supped, I went on conversing far into the night,
and when he wanted to go away, I pretended that the hour was
late and that he had much better remain. So he lay down on
the couch next to me, the same on which he had supped, and
there was no one but ourselves sleeping in the apartment. All
this may be told without shame to any one. But what follows I
could hardly tell you if I were sober. Yet as the proverb says,
"In vino veritas," whether with boys, or without them, and
therefore I must speak. Nor, again, should I be justified in con-

cealing the lofty actions of Socrates when I come to praise him.
Moreover, I have felt the serpent's sting; and he who has suffered, as they say, is willing to tell his fellow-sufferers only, as
they alone will be likely to understand him, and will not be
extreme in judging of the sayings or doings which have been
wrung from his agony. For I have been bitten by a more than
viper's tooth; I have known in my soul, or in my heart, or in
some other part, that worst of pangs, more violent in ingenuous
youth than any serpent's tooth, the pang of philosophy, which
will make a man say or do anything. And you whom I see around
me, Phaedrus and Agathon and Eryximachus and Pausanias and
Aristodemus and Aristophanes, all of you, and I need not say
Socrates himself, have had experience of the same madness and
passion in your longing after wisdom. Therefore listen and excuse my doings then and my sayings now. But let the attendants
and other profane and unmannered persons close up the doors
of their ears.

When the lamp was put out and the servants had gone away,
I thought that I must be plain with him and have no more ambiguity. So I gave him a shake, and I said: "Socrates, are you
asleep?" "No," he said. "Do you know what I am meditating?"
"What are you meditating?" he said. "I think," I replied, "that
of all the lovers whom I have ever had you are the only one who
is worthy of me, and you appear to be too modest to speak. Now
I feel that I should be a fool to refuse you this or any other
favour, and therefore I come to lay at your feet all that I have
and all that my friends have, in the hope that you will assist me
in the way of virtue, which I desire above all things, and in
which I believe that you can help me better than any one else.
And I should certainly have more reason to be ashamed of what
wise men would say if I were to refuse a favour to such as you,
than of what the world, who are mostly fools, would say of me
if I granted it." To these words he replied in the ironical manner which is so characteristic of him:—"O Alcibiades, my friend,
you have indeed an elevated aim if what you say is true, and
if there really is in me any power by which you may become
better; truly you must see in me some rare beauty of a kind
infinitely higher than any which I see in you. And therefore,
if you mean to share with me and to exchange beauty for beauty,

you will have greatly the advantage of me; you will gain true
beauty in return for appearance—like Diomede, gold in exchange for brass. But look again, sweet friend, and see whether
you are not deceived in me. The mind begins to grow critical
when the bodily eye fails, and it will be a long time before you
get old." Hearing this, I said: "I have told you my purpose,
which is quite serious, and do you consider what you think best
for you and me." "That is good," he said; "at some other time
then we will consider and act as seems best about this and about
other matters." Whereupon, I fancied that he was smitten, and
that the words which I had uttered like arrows had wounded
him, and so without waiting to hear more I got up, and throwing my coat about him crept under his threadbare cloak, as the
time of year was winter, and there I lay during the whole night
having this wonderful monster in my arms. This again, Socrates,
will not be denied by you. And yet, notwithstanding all, he was
so superior to my solicitations, so contemptuous and derisive
and disdainful of my beauty—which really, as I fancied, had
some attractions—hear, O judges; for judges you shall be of the
haughty virtue of Socrates—nothing more happened, but in the
morning when I awoke (let all the gods and goddesses be my
witnesses) I arose as from the couch of a father or an elder
brother.

What do you suppose must have been my feelings, after this
rejection, at the thought of my own dishonour? And yet I could
not help wondering at his natural temperance and self-restraint
and manliness. I never imagined that I could have met with a
man such as he is in wisdom and endurance. And therefore I
could not be angry with him or renounce his company, any
more than I could hope to win him. For I well knew that if
Ajax could not be wounded by steel, much less he by money;
and my only chance of captivating him by my personal attractions had failed. So I was at my wit's end: no one was ever more
hopelessly enslaved by another. All this happened before he
and I went on the expedition to Potidaea; there we messed together, and I had the opportunity of observing his extraordinary
power of sustaining fatigue. His endurance was simply marvellous when, being cut off from our supplies, we were compelled
to go without food—on such occasions, which often happen in

time of war, he was superior not only to me but to everybody;
there was no one to be compared to him. Yet at a festival he
was the only person who had any real powers of enjoyment;
though not willing to drink, he could if compelled beat us all
at that,—wonderful to relate! no human being had ever seen
Socrates drunk; and his powers, if I am not mistaken, will be
tested before long. His fortitude in enduring cold was also surprising. There was a severe frost, for the winter in that region
is really tremendous, and everybody else either remained in-
doors, or if they went out had on an amazing quantity of clothes,
and were well shod, and had their feet swathed in felt and
fleeces: in the midst of this, Socrates with his bare feet on the
ice and in his ordinary dress marched better than the other
soldiers who had shoes, and they looked daggers at him because
he seemed to despise them.

I have told you one tale, and now I must tell you another,
which is worth hearing,

"Of the doings and sufferings of the enduring man"

while he was on the expedition. One morning he was thinking
about something which he could not resolve; he would not give
it up, but continued thinking from early dawn until noon—
there he stood fixed in thought; and at noon attention was
drawn to him, and the rumour ran through the wondering
crowd that Socrates had been standing and thinking about something ever since the break of day. At last, in the evening after
supper, some Ionians out of curiosity (I should explain that
this was not in winter but in summer), brought out their mats
and slept in the open air that they might watch him and see
whether he would stand all night. There he stood until the following morning; and with the return of light he offered up a
prayer to the sun, and went his way. I will also tell, if you please
—and indeed I am bound to tell—of his courage in battle; for
who but he saved my life? Now this was the engagement in
which I received the prize of valour: for I was wounded and he
would not leave me, but he rescued me and my arms; and he
ought to have received the prize of valour which the generals
wanted to confer on me partly on account of my rank, and I
told them so (this, again, Socrates will not impeach or deny),

but he was more eager than the generals that I and not he should have the prize. There was another occasion on which his behaviour was very remarkable—in the flight of the army after the battle of Delium, where he served among the heavy-armed,— I had a better opportunity of seeing him than at Potidaea, for I was myself on horseback, and therefore comparatively out of danger. He and Laches were retreating, for the troops were in flight, and I met them and told them not to be discouraged, and promised to remain with them; and there you might see him, Aristophanes, as you describe, just as he is in the streets of Athens, stalking like a pelican, and rolling his eyes, calmly contemplating enemies as well as friends, and making very intelligible to anybody, even from a distance, that whoever attacked him would be likely to meet with a stout resistance; and in this way he and his companion escaped—for this is the sort of man who is never touched in war; those only are pursued who are running away headlong. I particularly observed how superior he was to Laches in presence of mind. Many are the marvels which I might narrate in praise of Socrates; most of his ways might perhaps be paralleled in another man, but his absolute unlikeness to any human being that is or ever has been is perfectly astonishing. You may imagine Brasidas and others to have been like Achilles; or you may imagine Nestor and Antenor to have been like Pericles; and the same may be said of other famous men, but of this strange being you will never be able to find any likeness, however remote, either among men who now are or who ever have been—other than that which I have already suggested of Silenus and the satyrs; and they represent in a figure not only himself, but his words. For, although I forgot to mention this to you before, his words are like the images of Silenus which open; they are ridiculous when you first hear them; he clothes himself in language that is like the skin of the wanton satyr—for his talk is of pack-asses and smiths and cobblers and curriers, and he is always repeating the same things in the same words, so that any ignorant or inexperienced person might feel disposed to laugh at him; but he who opens the bust and sees what is within will find that they are the only words which have a meaning in them, and also of the most divine, abounding in fair images of virtue, and of the widest comprehension, or rather extending to the whole duty of a good and honourable man.

This, friends, is my praise of Socrates. I have added my blame of him for his ill-treatment of me; and he has ill-treated not only me, but Charmides the son of Glaucon, and Euthydemus the son of Diocles, and many others in the same way—beginning as their lover he has ended by making them pay their addresses to him. Wherefore I say to you, Agathon, "Be not deceived by him; learn from me and take warning, and do not be a fool and learn by experience, as the proverb says."

When Alcibiades had finished, there was a laugh at his outspokenness; for he seemed to be still in love with Socrates. You are sober, Alcibiades, said Socrates, or you would never have gone so far about to hide the purpose of your satyr's praises, for all this long story is only an ingenious circumlocution, of which the point comes in by the way at the end; you want to get up a quarrel between me and Agathon, and your notion is that I ought to love you and nobody else, and that you and you only ought to love Agathon. But the plot of this Satyric or Silenic drama has been detected, and you must not allow him, Agathon, to set us at variance.

I believe you are right, said Agathon, and I am disposed to think that his intention in placing himself between you and me was only to divide us; but he shall gain nothing by that move; for I will go and lie on the couch next to you.

Yes, yes, replied Socrates, by all means come here and lie on the couch below me.

Alas, said Alcibiades, how I am fooled by this man; he is determined to get the better of me at every turn. I do beseech you, allow Agathon to lie between us.

Certainly not, said Socrates; as you praised me, and I in turn ought to praise my neighbour on the right, he will be out of order in praising me again when he ought rather to be praised by me, and I must entreat you to consent to this, and not be jealous, for I have a great desire to praise the youth.

Hurrah! cried Agathon, I will rise instantly, that I may be praised by Socrates.

The usual way, said Alcibiades; where Socrates is, no one else has any chance with the fair; and now how readily has he invented a specious reason for attracting Agathon to himself.

Agathon arose in order that he might take his place on the couch by Socrates, when suddenly a band of revellers entered, and spoiled

the order of the banquet. Some one who was going out having left
the door open, they had found their way in, and made themselves
at home; great confusion ensued, and every one was compelled to
drink large quantities of wine. Aristodemus said that Eryximachus,
Phaedrus, and others went away—he himself fell asleep, and as the
nights were long took a good rest: he was awakened towards daybreak by a crowing of cocks, and when he awoke, the others were
either asleep, or had gone away; there remained only Socrates,
Aristophanes, and Agathon, who were drinking out of a large
goblet which they passed round, and Socrates was discoursing to
them. Aristodemus was only half awake, and he did not hear the
beginning of the discourse; the chief thing which he remembered
was Socrates compelling the other two to acknowledge that the
genius of comedy was the same with that of tragedy, and that the
true artist in tragedy was an artist in comedy also. To this they
were constrained to assent, being drowsy, and not quite following
the argument. And first of all Aristophanes dropped off, then,
when the day was already dawning, Agathon. Socrates, having laid
them to sleep, rose to depart; Aristodemus, as his manner was, following him. At the Lyceum he took a bath, and passed the day as
usual. In the evening he retired to rest at his own home.

Aristotle

Aristotle

ARISTOTLE'S treatises are our first encyclopaedia. They present in as systematic a form as was possible in the time of Alexander the Great the various branches of knowledge. But they are a more philosophic enterprise than any subsequent encyclopaedia, with the exception of the great *Encyclopaedia* of the French Enlightenment. They are not merely bodies of information, but expositions and applications of a general method of analysis and of a generalized conception of Being. Some of these books have been lost.

Those that have come down to us present a striking contrast to the dialogues of Plato. They are not finished literary pieces, but discursive and frequently disjointed note-books, the product of academic lectures, probably not all written in their present form by Aristotle himself, and all of them arranged and systematized by his disciples, chiefly Theophrastus and Andronicus of Rhodes. They deal with the widest range of subject: rhetoric, poetics, ethics, politics, analytics, biology, the motion of the heavens, the processes of nature (physics), and certain general considerations, following the works on physics, which, ever since Andronicus invented the label, have been called metaphysics. In fact these various "-ics" are Aristotelian distinctions that have ever since been academic labels for the arts and sciences.

The "meta-physical" treatises, however, are peculiarly philosophical in the sense that they serve as an introduction to any and all branches of knowledge. For here Aristotle attempts to formulate the most general principles and properties of any subject matter of inquiry. Here we have a "primary science," in the sense of having a science of subject matter in general. Here we have the theory of the relation between art and nature, being and becoming, form and material, possibility and actuality, and those other basic distinctions according to which all things are and are conceived. A summary of these basic distinctions in Aristotelian philosophy is given in the brief selection from the books on natural processes (physics).

The *Ethics,* which we have selected as the best introduction to Aristotelian philosophy, illustrates Aristotle's characteristic habits and terms of analysis as these were applied to the inquiry into "the good life." This treatise not only carries on the discussion of the problems raised in Plato's dialogues, but lays the foundation for many of the basic themes of subsequent philosophic thought. Aristotle here first gave to these themes a technical and relatively precise formulation. The relation of ethics to the other philosophic inquiries is suggested in the book itself. The final chapter describes the passage from practical to speculative good, from virtue to contemplation; but its closing paragraphs also indicate the transition in Aristotle's mind from ethics to politics, where the theory of the good life receives its most practical application.

Aristotle (384-322 B.C.) was the son of a Thracian physician, a tutor of Alexander the Great, and a student in Plato's Academy. He shared his father's preoccupation with medicine and biology. He founded the school of the Lyceum at Athens, where his teaching was perpetuated for generations. He is usually regarded as the culmination of ancient Greek philosophy, but his work might equally be regarded as a beginning of systematic, but relatively independent, sciences. For Alexandrian science and medieval scholasticism his treatises became authoritative and they are still one of the most influential formulations of philosophic doctrine.

Physics

Book II

11 Some things can be understood as existing by nature, others in other ways. Thus it is nature that produces animals and the parts of their bodies, plants, earth, air, fire, and water; for we say of these things and all things like them, that they exist by nature. All natural things have in themselves the source of their movement or rest—whether this movement be motion in space, growth and decline, or mere change in quality. A bed, on the other hand, or a cloak, and whatever other things belong to this class, in so far as they are considered for what they are, as products of art, have no inherent tendency to change their state. They have this tendency only accidentally since they are composed of rock, earth, or a mixture of such things. For nature is the source and explanation of the movement and rest of those things in which these exist primarily and not by accident. What "by accident" means can be seen from this example: If an ill man, being a physician, cures himself, I say that it is indirectly and by accident that the physician is cured, for it is not as a physician but as an ill man; the physician is cured only because the physician and the patient happened to be the same person, whereas these two qualities are usually found in different persons. One can say the same for all things which are the products of art. None of them has the source of its production in itself. This source is outside them, in other things, as for example in the case of a house, or any other product of human labor; although sometimes, accidentally, they do have a source of movement within them.

This is what is meant by nature. One says of things that they are natural and that they are by nature when they have in themselves the sources of which I have just spoken. They are properly called entities (*ousia*)[1]; for an entity is a subject, for subjects have char-

---

[1] This term is usually translated "substance."

116

acteristic natures. All things exist in accordance with the laws of
nature, with all their essential properties, in the same way as the
inherent property of fire always to rise exists. For this property is
not nature, nor does it possess a nature; but fire rises by nature and
according to nature. This is what is meant by the nature of a
thing, and what is signified by "by nature" and "according to
nature."

We will not try to prove the existence of nature; this is ridiculous; it is clear to everyone that there are many things of the kind
that we have just indicated; and he who would try to demonstrate
the more apparent by the less apparent shows that he cannot distinguish what is and what is not evident in itself. This inability
is not unknown. We can compare it with the case of a man, blind
from birth, arguing about colors. He could pronounce the words,
but necessarily he would not have the least idea what the words
represent.

There are some who imagine that the natures and entities of
natural things consist in their original constituents which are in
each one of them, without having there any precise form—that is
to say, the material of the thing. Thus for these people, the nature
of a bed, is the wood of which it is made; the nature of a statue is
the bronze of which it is made. Antiphon gives proof of this: he
says, if we plant a bed in the earth, and if, on decaying, it has
sufficient force to sprout, it is not a bed that will be produced,
but wood. Thus there are two distinct aspects of a bed: The first,
which is purely accidental, is the arrangement given to the material by the craftsman and the rules of the craft; the other, which is
the substance of the bed, is that which remains constant in spite
of the modifications which the bed undergoes. These materials
have the same relation with respect to other things, gold and
bronze, for example, with respect to water, or bone and wood to
earth, etc. His general conclusion is that whatever is the material
of a thing is both its nature and its substance.

Along similar lines, some thinkers believe that the nature of
things is the earth, air, fire, water, or combinations of some or all
of these elements. The single element or the several elements of
which these thinkers admit the reality, become for them the single
or multiple substances of things, and all the rest are nothing but
affections, qualities, dispositions of this substance. And further,

they say this substance is eternal, considering that it has not in itself the power of change, while everything else is born and perishes without end.

Thus, in one sense, one can call nature the original material which underlies each thing which has in itself the source of movement and change. But from another point of view, one can hold also that the nature of things is the form which determines their kinds by definition; because, in the same way that one calls art that which conforms to the rules of art, and is a product of art, so one ought to call natural that which accords with the laws and is a product of nature. But just as one does not say of a thing that it conforms to the rules of art, nor that there is art in it, if it is only so potentially, for example, a bed which has not yet received the shape which makes it a bed; so one cannot speak of things as natural which have their nature only potentially. For that which is potentially flesh and bone has not its own nature until it receives the form proper to its definition, which makes explicit what it is to be flesh and bone; nor does it exist by nature.

According to another view the nature of things that have the source of their movement in themselves is their shape and form, which is inseparable from the matter, save in discourse. The compound of these (form and material), for example in the case of a man, is not nature, but is by nature. For it is better to regard this compound as a nature rather than the material. For everyone admits that that which is complete has its nature, rather than that which is only potential. Besides a man comes from a man, while a bed does not come from a bed; and that is how they came to hold, as we have seen, that the nature of the bed is not the shape that art gives it, but the wood of which it is formed, since the wood of the bed, placed in the earth, if it took root again, would produce wood and not a bed. But, if the configuration of the bed is produced by art, we can conclude, since man produces man, that the form of natural things constitutes their nature.

Sometimes the nature and the generation of things are confused; healing, for example, is so called because it is the means, not to the art of healing, but to health; for necessarily the process of healing goes *from* the art of healing and not *to it*. But this is not the relation of nature to nature. The thing which nature produces goes from something to some other thing. To what end does this nat-

ural movement tend? Not to what it started as, but to what it is
going toward. This form then is its nature. Nature and form can
be spoken of in two ways, for an unfulfilment is, in a certain sense,
a form. It remains to know whether unfulfilment is or is not a
contrary form involved in the simpler generation of things, but
this is the object of another study which will come later.

21 . . . If one recognizes two aspects of nature, one can ask with
which of these is the physicist concerned; or is he concerned with
their combination? Then, in order to understand this combination, is it not necessary that he understand the two elements of
which it is composed? And furthermore, can one not inquire
whether the knowledge of these two natures is the task of a single
science, or of distinct sciences? If we look at the ancient philosophers, it would seem that physics is limited to the study of the
material; for Democritus, Empedocles and the others hardly touch
on the question of the form and essential character. But if art imitates nature and studies both the form and to a certain extent the
material (for example, the physician studies health and, in addition, phlegm and bile, the state of which determines health;
and likewise the architect occupies himself at the same time with
both the structure of the house and the material, and similarly
with the other arts), it follows that it is the task of physics to study
both of these in natural processes. Furthermore a single science
studies both the end and the means. And nature is the end and that
for the sake of which things exist, because where the movement is
continuous, there is some end to this movement, it has a final stage
and goal. Hence the exclamation of the poet concerning the death
of one of his characters is ridiculous: "He has achieved the end
for which he was born." The goal does not mean every outcome,
but only the best.

For the arts make their materials—some simply making them,
and the others employing them so that they are fit for use—and we
make use of things as if they existed only for us, for we are also,
in a sense, an end. For, that for the sake of which a thing exists
can be understood in two ways, as I have explained in my books
entitled *Concerning Philosophy*.[1] There are two kinds of arts

---

[1] This is a lost dialogue. The two senses are "good for someone" and "good for
some product." (*Metaphysics*, 1072b2.)

which order their material and know it: the one uses the things, and the other directs the work that makes them. The art of the one who uses things may, in a sense, be called architectonic, but there is this difference between the two arts, that the one, that which determines the usage is only concerned with the form, while the other, that which fashions the things, is only occupied with the material. For example, the pilot who uses the rudder on the ship, knows what must be the form of it and he orders it so; but the builder knows of what wood the rudder must be made, and what are the techniques that have to be applied. In art, we fashion the material with a view to the use to which we will put it; but in natural things, the material is already there.

Furthermore, material is relative, since the material varies with the form, and since a different form corresponds also to a different material. But up to what point ought the physicist study the form and essential character of things? As the physician studies the nerves, and the smith the bronze, so the physicist studies nature up to a certain point. He studies the things which are only separable in thought from the material. As they say, it is man and the sun which produce man. But this investigation concerning what is separable and what is the essential character of a thing belongs to First Philosophy.

3 Having settled these things, we must take up next the causes; [1]

[1] Traditionally *aitia* has been translated into English as "cause." This follows the fashion instituted by Cicero who translated the term into Latin as *causa*. Unless properly understood, however, such a translation is misleading for the reason that while in English a cause signifies usually a force, conditioning circumstance, or agent, for Aristotle this is only one meaning of the equivalent Greek term. In Greek popular usage the term referred to a law suit or a cause of action in a suit at law. Most simply, however, it meant satisfaction of a demand. For example, if one asks, "What kind of a thing is this?", the satisfactory or explanatory answer to this question would give the thing's *aitia*. Aristotle takes this term over and gives it precise and technical meaning.

For Aristotle, knowledge in its truest sense is not merely information or knowledge of the fact; rather it is a knowledge of the "reasoned fact," an understanding of the reasons, explanations, or whys and wherefores of the fact. As the text reveals, for the complete understanding of a natural process it is necessary to investigate four factors or aspects of explanation, to ask and answer four basic types of question concerning it. Aristotle's four causes are thus not four agents or powers which are involved in a process; they are four guides to inquiry.

It would be preferable to translate the word *aitia* as the whys and wherefores of a natural process were it not for the fact that the phrase "four causes" has conventional use and historical significance.

and we must determine their number and kinds. The end of this treatise is to know nature; and as one only knows a thing when one knows why it is, its reason (*prote aitia*), we must do this in studying the generation and destruction of things, and all natural changes. Once we know the principles of these things, we can use them in dealing with the problems that concern us.

In the first place, one calls cause that which composes a thing, and that from which it arises. Thus one can say in this sense that bronze is the cause of the statue, and silver is the cause of the phial; and one applies this way of speaking to all things of the same kind. (Material cause.) In a second sense, the cause is the form and the model of things; it is the essential character of the thing and its kind. Thus in music, the cause of the octave is the ratio 2:1, and, in a more general way, it is number; and with number; it is the part which enters into its definition. (Formal cause.) In a third sense, the cause is the source from which movement or rest comes. Thus he who, in a certain case, has given advice to act is the cause of the acts which are accomplished; the father is the cause of the child; and generally speaking that which acts is the cause of that which is done; that which produces a change is the cause of the change produced. (Efficient cause.) Fourthly, cause signifies the end and the goal of a thing. Thus health is the cause of walking. If we ask, "Why is he walking?" the answer is, "In order to be well," and when we say this, we believe that we have the cause of the walking. This meaning applies to all the intermediaries who contribute to the attainment of the final end, after the first mover has started the movement. For example, dieting and purgation, or drugs and the instruments of the surgeon can be regarded as means to health; and the only difference is that some are acts and others are instruments. (Final cause.)

These are briefly the meanings of the word cause. In accordance with this diversity of senses, a single thing can have several causes at the same time, and not simply. Thus, for the statue, one can assign to it as causes both the art of the sculptor who has made it and the bronze of which it is made and not in any other sense than as a statue. The two causes are not to be understood in the same sense; they differ in that one is the material and the other is the source of the movement. It is also because of this that there can be said to be things that are reciprocally the causes of each other.

Thus exercise is the cause of health, and health is the cause of exercise; but not in the same sense, for, in the first case, health is the end, while in the second health is the source of the movement. Moreover, a single thing is at times the cause of opposite results; for, the same thing which is the cause of a given effect when it is present, can be the cause of an opposite effect when it is absent. For example, the absence of the pilot can be considered the cause of the loss of the ship, because the presence of the same pilot could have guaranteed its safety.

All the causes mentioned can be reduced to these four very obvious kinds. The letters of the alphabet are the cause of the syllables; the material is the cause of the things which art produces; fire and the other elements are the causes of the bodies which they compose; the parts are the cause of the whole, and the propositions are the causes of the conclusions which are drawn from them. Each of these is a cause since it is that out of which the other thing comes. Of these, the causes are either the subject of the thing, as parts relative to the whole; or the essential character of the thing, as the whole and the synthesis and the form; or the source of change or rest, as the germ, the physician, the giver of advice, and in general that which has effects; and finally, in the fourth place, the end and the good of other things; the attainment of the best is that for the sake of which the thing exists, and it would make no difference whether one said the real or the apparent good.

These are the various causes, and such is the number of their kinds. To these four causes it is necessary to add many distinctions which can be made, but not so many that they cannot be grouped under a few headings. (1) Besides the various meanings which we have noted, it is possible that even between causes of the same kind there can be differences of rank, and that one may be prior or posterior to the other. Thus the physician and the technician can both cause health (for the physician is a technician). In the same way, in harmony, it is the ratio 2:1 and more generally number which are the causes of the octave. Thus for the specific may be substituted the more general. (2) There is another distinction referring to the accidental nature of the cause and its kind. Polycleitus and the sculptor are the causes of the statue in different ways. Polycleitus is the name of the sculptor who could have had another name, and Polycleitus is only an accidental cause, since the sculptor is the direct cause. Furthermore, one can generalize and say that man or a living being is the cause of the statue, since Polycleitus and the sculptor are both. Among the accidental causes there are differences of remoteness, as one can say that the white man or the artist is the cause of the statue.

(3) Besides the distinction between causes properly so called and those which are accidental, it is necessary to make a new distinction between the causes which are potential and those which actually are effective. If it is a question, for example, of a house, the cause of the construction is either the builder who can construct it, or the builder who actually does construct it.

These distinctions which we have just enumerated can be extended from causes to their effects; for example, they can apply directly to that statue, more generally to statue, and more generally still to image; or to this particular bronze, to bronze in general, and in a still more general way, to matter. The same holds for the accidental attributes of these effects. Finally one can join several of these causes and distinctions and say, for example, the sculptor Polycleitus, instead of saying separately Polycleitus or the sculptor.

These distinctions then number six and they can each have two senses: The individual and its kind, the accidental and its kind, and these can be taken separately or together. A general distinction for all causes is that between the actual and the potential, for each of the four causes can be either actually effective, or merely potentially active. The only difference is that the actual and particular causes go with the effects they produce, existing or ceasing to exist at the same time as the effects; for example, if the physician cures, it is necessary that the physician in the process of curing exists as long as the sick man who is being cured; or, the builder actually building must exist during the same period that the house is being built. But the case of potential causes is different; here the house and its builder do not perish at the same time.

We must, in the investigation of causes, be as precise as is possible. Thus a man builds a house as an architect, and the architect builds it according to the rules of his art. This last cause then is prior to the others, and so it is in all cases. Kinds, moreover, are the causes of kinds, just as individuals are the causes of individuals. Thus, generically, it is the sculptor that is the cause of the statue;

but a given sculptor is the cause of a particular statue, and in the same way potential causes produce only potential effects, and actual causes actual effects.

We finish here what we have to say on the number of the causes and their distinctions.

The Nicomachean Ethics

Book I

EVERY art and every scientific inquiry, and similarly every action and purpose, may be said to aim at some good. Hence the good has been well defined as that at which all things aim. But it is clear that there is a difference in the ends; for the ends are sometimes activities, and sometimes results beyond the mere activities. Also, where there are certain ends beyond the actions, the results are naturally superior to the activities.

As there are various actions, arts, and sciences, it follows that the ends are also various. Thus health is the end of medicine, a vessel of shipbuilding, victory of strategy, and wealth of domestic economy. It often happens that there are a number of such arts or sciences which fall under a single faculty, as the art of making bridles, and all such other arts as make the instruments of horsemanship, under horsemanship, and this again as well as every military action under strategy, and in the same way other arts or sciences under other faculties. But in all these cases the ends of the architectonic arts or sciences, whatever they may be, are more desirable than those of the subordinate arts or sciences, as it is for the sake of the former that the latter are themselves sought after. It makes no difference to the argument whether the activities themselves are the ends of the actions, or something else beyond the activities as in the above mentioned sciences.

If it is true that in the sphere of action there is an end which we wish for its own sake, and for the sake of which we wish everything else, and that we do not desire all things for the sake of something else (for, if that is so, the process will go on *ad infinitum,* and our desire will be idle and futile) it is clear that this will be the good or the supreme good. Does it not follow then that the knowledge of this supreme good is of great importance for the conduct of life, and that, *if we know it,* we shall be like archers who have a mark

at which to aim, we shall have a better chance of attaining what
we want? But, if this is the case, we must endeavour to comprehend, at least in outline, its nature, and the science or faculty to
which it belongs.

It would seem that this is the most authoritative or architectonic
science or faculty, and such is evidently the political; for it is the
political science or faculty which determines what sciences are
necessary in states, and what kind of sciences should be learnt, and
how far they should be learnt by particular people. We perceive
too that the faculties which are held in the highest esteem, e.g.
strategy, domestic economy, and rhetoric, are subordinate to it.
But as it makes use of the other practical sciences, and also legis-
lates upon the things to be done and the things to be left undone,
it follows that its end will comprehend the ends of all the other
sciences, and will therefore be the true good of mankind. For although the good of an individual is identical with the good of a
state, yet the good of the state, whether in attainment or in preservation, is evidently greater and more perfect. For while in an
individual by himself it is something to be thankful for, it is
nobler and more divine in a nation or state.

These then are the objects at which the present inquiry aims,
and it is in a sense a political inquiry. But our statement of the
case will be adequate, if it be made with all such clearness as the
subject-matter admits; for it would be as wrong to expect the same
degree of accuracy in all reasonings as in all manufactures. Things
noble and just, which are the subjects of investigation in political
science, exhibit so great a diversity and uncertainty that they are
sometimes thought to have only a conventional, and not a natural,
existence. There is the same sort of uncertainty in regard to good
things, as it often happens that injuries result from them; thus
there have been cases in which people were ruined by wealth, or
again by courage. As our subjects then and our premises are of
this nature, we must be content to indicate the truth roughly and
in outline; and as our subjects and premises are true generally
but not universally, we must be content to arrive at conclusions
which are only generally true. It is right to receive the particular
statements which are made in the same spirit; for an educated
person will expect accuracy in each subject only so far as the nature of the subject allows; he might as well accept probable reason-

ing from a mathematician as require demonstrative proofs from a rhetorician. But everybody is competent to judge the subjects which he understands, and is a good judge of them. It follows that in particular subjects it is a person of *special* education, and in general a person of universal education, who is a good judge. Hence the young are not proper students of political science, as they have no experience of the actions of life which form the premisses and subjects of the reasonings. Also it may be added that from their tendency to follow their emotions they will not study the subject to any purpose or profit, as its end is not knowledge but action. It makes no difference whether a person is young in years or youthful in character; for the defect *of which I speak* is not one of time but is due to the emotional character of his life and pursuits. Knowledge is as useless to such a person as it is to an intemperate person. But where the desires and actions of people are regulated by reason the knowledge of these subjects will be extremely valuable.

But having said so much by way of preface as to the students of political science, the spirit in which it should be studied, and the object which we set before ourselves, let us resume our argument as follows:

As every knowledge and moral purpose aspires to some good, what is in our view the good at which the political science aims, and what is the highest of all practical goods? As to its name there is, I may say, a general agreement. The masses and the cultured classes agree in calling it happiness, and conceive that "to live well" or "to do well" is the same thing as "to be happy." But as to the nature of happiness they do not agree, nor do the masses give the same account of it as the philosophers. The former define it as something visible and palpable, e.g. pleasure, wealth, or honour; different people give different definitions of it, and often the same person gives different definitions at different times; for when a person has been ill, it is health, when he is poor, it is wealth, and, if he is conscious of his own ignorance, he envies people who use grand language above his own comprehension. Some philosophers on the other hand have held that, besides these various goods, there is an absolute good which is the cause of goodness in them all. It would perhaps be a waste of time to examine all these opinions, it will be enough to examine such as are most popular or as seem to be more or less reasonable.

But we must not fail to observe the distinction between the reasonings which proceed from first principles and the reasonings which lead up to first principles. For Plato was right in raising the difficult question whether the *true* way was from first principles or to first principles, as in the race-course from the judges to the goal, or *vice versa*. We must begin then with such facts as are known. But facts may be known in two ways, i.e. either relatively to ourselves or absolutely. It is probable then that *we* must begin with such facts as are known to us, *i.e. relatively*. It is necessary therefore, if a person is to be a competent student of what is noble and just and of politics in general, that he should have received a good moral training. For the fact that a thing is so is a first principle or starting-point,[1] and, if the fact is sufficiently clear, it will not be necessary to go on to ask the reason of it. But a person who has received a good moral training either possesses first principles, or will have no difficulty in acquiring them. But if he does not possess them, and cannot acquire them, he had better lay to heart Hesiod's lines:

> "Far best is he who is himself all-wise,
>   And he, too, good who listens to wise words;
>   But whoso is not wise nor lays to heart
>   Another's wisdom is a useless man."

But to return from our digression: It seems not unreasonable that people should derive their conception of the good or of happiness from men's lives. Thus ordinary or vulgar people conceive it to be pleasure, and accordingly approve a life of enjoyment. For there are practically three prominent lives, the sensual, the political, and, thirdly, the speculative. Now the mass of men present an absolutely slavish appearance, as choosing the life of brute beasts, but they meet with consideration because so many persons in authority share the tastes of Sardanapalus. Cultivated and practical people, on the other hand, identify happiness with honour, as honour is the general end of political life. But this appears too superficial for our present purpose; for honour seems to depend more upon the people who pay it than upon the person to whom it

---

[1] Aristotle's reasoning depends in part on the double meaning of *arché* viz. (1) starting-point or beginning, (2) first principle or axiomatic truth.

is paid, and we have an intuitive feeling that the good is something which is proper to a man himself and cannot easily be taken away from him. It seems too that the reason why men seek honour is that they may be confident of their own goodness. Accordingly they seek it at the hands of the wise and of those who know them well, and they seek it on the ground of virtue; hence it is clear that in their judgment at any rate virtue is superior to honour. It would perhaps be right then to look upon virtue rather than honour as being the end of the political life. Yet virtue again, it appears, lacks completeness; for it seems that a man may possess virtue and yet be asleep or inactive throughout life, and, not only so but he may experience the greatest calamities and misfortunes. But nobody would call such a life a life of happiness, unless he were maintaining a paradox. It is not necessary to dwell further on this subject, as it is sufficiently discussed in the popular philosophical treatises. The third life is the speculative which we will investigate hereafter.

The life of money-making is in a sense a life of constraint, and it is clear that wealth is not the good of which we are in quest; for it is useful in part as a means to something else. It would be a more reasonable view therefore that the things mentioned before, viz. *sensual pleasure, honour and virtue,* are ends than that wealth is, as they are things which are desired on their own account. Yet these too are apparently not ends, although much argument has been employed to show that they are.

We may now dismiss this subject; but it will perhaps be best to consider the universal *good,* and to discuss the meaning in which the phrase is used, although there is this difficulty in such an enquiry, that the *doctrine of* ideas has been introduced by our friends. Yet it will perhaps seem the best, and indeed the right course, at least when the truth is at stake, to go so far as to sacrifice what is near and dear to us, especially as we are philosophers. For friends and truth are both dear to us, but it is a sacred duty to prefer the truth.

Now the authors of this theory did not make ideas of things in which they predicated priority and posteriority. Hence they did not constitute an idea of numbers. But good is predicated equally of substance, quality and relation, and the absolute or essential, *i.e. substance,* is in its nature prior to the relative, as relativity is like an offshoot or accident of existence; hence there cannot be an idea which is common to them both. Again, there are as many ways of predicating good as of predicating existence; for it is predicated of substance as e.g. of God or the mind, or of quality as of the virtues, or of quantity as of the mean, or of relativity as of the useful, or of time as of opportunity, or of place as of a habitation, and so on. It is clear then that it cannot be a common universal idea or a unity; otherwise it would not be predicated in all the categories but only in one. Thirdly, as there is a single science of all such things as fall under a single idea, there would have been a single science of all good things, *if the idea of "good" were single;* but in fact there are many sciences even of such good things as fall under a single category, strategy, e.g. being the science of opportunity in war, and medicine the science of opportunity in disease, medicine again being the science of the mean in respect of food, and gymnastic the science of the mean in respect of exercise. It would be difficult, too, to say what is meant by the "absolute" in anything, if in "absolute man" and in "man" there is one and the same conception of man. For there will be no difference between them in respect of manhood, and, if so, neither will there be any difference between "absolute good" and "good" in respect of goodness. Nor again will good be more good if it is eternal, since a white thing which lasts for a long time is not whiter than that which lasts for a single day. There seems to be more plausibility in the doctrine of the Pythagoreans[1] who place unity in the catalogue of goods, and Speusippus apparently agrees with them. However these are questions which may be deferred to another occasion; but there is an objection to my arguments which suggests itself, viz. that the *Platonic* theory does not apply to every good, that the things which in themselves are sought after and welcomed are reckoned as one species and the things which tend to produce or in any sense preserve these or to prevent their opposites are reckoned as goods in a secondary sense as being means to these. It is clear then that there will be two kinds of goods, some being absolute goods, and others secondary. Let us then separate goods which are merely serviceable from absolute goods and consider if they are conceived as falling under a single idea. But what kind of things is it that may be de-

[1] The point is that it is apparently more reasonable to describe unity as a good than to describe good as a unity.

fined as absolute goods? Will it be all such as are sought after independently of their consequences, e.g. wisdom, sight, and certain pleasures and honours? For granting that we seek after these sometimes as means to something else, still we may define them as absolute goods. Or is none of these things an absolute good, nor anything else except the idea? But then the type *or idea* will be purposeless, *i.e. it will not comprise any particulars.* If, on the other hand, these things too are absolute goods, the conception of the good will necessarily appear the same in them all, as the conception of whiteness appears the same in snow and in white lead. But the conception of honour, wisdom and pleasure, are distinct and different in respect of goodness. "Good" then is not a common term falling under one idea. But in what sense is the term used? For it does not seem to be an accidental homonymy.[1] Is it because all goods issue from one source or all tend to one end; or is it rather a case of analogy? for as the sight is to the body, so is the mind to the soul, *i.e. the mind may be called the eye of the soul, and so on.* But it will perhaps be well to leave this subject for the present, as an exact discussion of it would belong rather to a different branch of philosophy. But the same is true of the idea; for even if there is some one good which is predicated of all these things, or some abstract and absolute good, it will plainly not be such as a man finds practicable and attainable, and therefore will not be such a good as we are in search of. It will possibly be held, however, that it is worth while to apprehend this *universal good,* as having a relation to the goods which are attainable and practicable; for if we have this as a model, we shall be better able to know the things which are good relatively to ourselves, and, knowing them, to acquire them. Now although there is a certain plausibility in this theory, it seems not to harmonize with scientific experience; for while all sciences aim at a certain good and seek to supply a deficiency, they omit the knowledge of the universal good. Yet it is not reasonable to suppose that what would be so extremely helpful is ignored, and not sought at all by artists generally. But it is difficult to see what benefit a cobbler or carpenter will get in reference to his art by knowing the absolute good, or how the contemplation of the absolute idea will make a person a better physi-

---

[1] What is meant by an "accidental homonymy" or equivocation is easily seen in the various senses of a single English word such as *bull.*

cian or general. For it appears that a physician does not regard health abstractedly, but regards the health of man or rather perhaps of a particular man, as he gives his medicine to individuals.

But leaving this subject for the present let us revert to the good of which we are in quest and consider what its nature may be. For it is clearly different in different actions or arts; it is one thing in medicine, another in strategy, and so on. What then is the good in each of these instances? It is presumably that for the sake of which all else is done. This in medicine is health, in strategy, victory, in domestic architecture, a house, and so on. But in every action and purpose it is the end, as it is for the sake of the end that people all do everything else. If then there is a certain end of all action, it will be this which is the practicable good, and if there are several such ends it will be these.

Our argument has arrived by a different path at the same conclusion as before; but we must endeavour to elucidate it still further. As it appears that there are more ends than one and some of these, e.g. wealth, flutes, and instruments generally we desire as means to something else, it is evident that they are not all final ends. But the highest good is clearly something final. Hence if there is only one final end, this will be the object of which we are in search, and if there are more than one, it will be the most final of them. We speak of that which is sought after for its own sake as more final than that which is sought after as a means to something else; we speak of that which is never desired as a means to something else as more final than the things which are desired both in themselves and as means to something else; and we speak of a thing as absolutely final, if it is always desired in itself and never as a means to something else.

It seems that happiness preeminently answers to this description, as we always desire happiness for its own sake and never as a means to something else, whereas we desire honour, pleasure, intellect, and every virtue, partly for their own sakes (for we should desire them independently of what might result from them) but partly also as being means to happiness, because we suppose they will prove the instruments of happiness. Happiness, on the other hand, nobody desires for the sake of these things, nor indeed as a means to anything else at all.

We come to the same conclusion if we start from the consideration of self-sufficiency, if it may be assumed that the final good is self-sufficient. But when we speak of self-sufficiency, we do not mean that a person leads a solitary life all by himself, but that he has parents, children, wife, and friends, and fellow-citizens in general, as man is naturally a social being. But here it is necessary to prescribe some limit; for if the circle be extended so as to include parents, descendants, and friends' friends, it will go on indefinitely. Leaving this point, however, for future investigation, we define the self-sufficient as that which, taken by itself, makes life desirable, and wholly free from want, and this is our conception of happiness.

Again, we conceive happiness to be the most desirable of all things, and that not merely as one among other good things. If it were one among other good things, the addition of the smallest good would increase its desirableness; for the accession makes a superiority of goods, and the greater of two goods is always the more desirable. It appears then that happiness is something final and self-sufficient, being the end of all action.

Perhaps, however, it seems a truth which is generally admitted, that happiness is the supreme good; what is wanted is to define its nature a little more clearly. The best way of arriving at such a definition will probably be to ascertain the function of Man. For, as with a flute-player, a statuary, or any artisan, or in fact anybody who has a definite function and action, his goodness, or excellence seems to lie in his function, so it would seem to be with Man, if indeed he has a definite function. Can it be said then that, while a carpenter and a cobbler have definite functions and actions, Man, unlike them, is naturally functionless? The reasonable view is that, as the eye, the hand, the foot, and similarly each several part of the body has a definite function, so Man may be regarded as having a definite function apart from all these. What then, can this function be? It is not life; for life is apparently something which man shares with the plants; and it is something peculiar to him that we are looking for. We must exclude therefore the life of nutrition and increase. There is next what may be called the life of sensation. But this too, is apparently shared by Man with horses, cattle, and all other animals. There remains what I may call the practical life of the rational part *of Man's being*. But the rational part is twofold; it is rational partly in the sense of being obedient to reason, and partly in the sense of possessing reason and intelligence. The practical life too may be conceived of in two ways, *viz.*, *either as a moral state, or as a moral activity:* but we must understand by it the life of activity, as this seems to be the truer form of the conception.

The function of Man then is an activity of soul in accordance with reason, or not independently of reason. Again the functions of a person of a certain kind, and of such a person who is good of his kind e.g. of a harpist and a good harpist, are in our view generically the same, and this view is true of people of all kinds without exception, the superior excellence being only an addition to the function; for it is the function of a harpist to play the harp, and of a good harpist to play the harp well. This being so, if we define the function of Man as a kind of life, and this life as an activity of soul, or a course of action in conformity with reason, if the function of a good man is such activity or action of a good and noble kind, and if everything is successfully performed when it is performed in accordance with its proper excellence, it follows that the good of Man is an activity of soul in accordance with virtue or, if there are more virtues than one, in accordance with the best and most complete virtue. But it is necessary to add the words "in a complete life." For as one swallow or one day does not make a spring, so one day or a short time does not make a fortunate or happy man.

This may be taken as a sufficiently accurate sketch of the good; for it is right, I think, to draw the outlines first and afterwards to fill in the details. It would seem that anybody can carry on and complete what has been satisfactorily sketched in outline, and that time is a good inventor or cooperator in so doing. This is the way in which the arts have made their advances, as anybody can supply a deficiency.

But bearing in mind what has been already said, we must not look for the same degree of accuracy in all subjects; we must be content in each class of subjects with accuracy of such a kind as the subject-matter allows, and to such an extent as is proper to the inquiry. For while a carpenter and a geometrician both want to find a right angle, they do not want to find it in the same sense; the one wants only such an approximation to it as will serve his practical purpose, the other, as being concerned with truth, wants to know its nature or character. We must follow the same course in other subjects, or we shall sacrifice the main points to such as are subordinate. Again, we must not insist with equal emphasis in all subjects upon ascertaining the reason of things. We must sometimes e.g. in dealing with first principles be content with the proper evidence of a fact; the fact itself is a first point or principle. But there are various ways of discovering first principles; some are discovered by induction, others by perception, others by what may be called habituation, and so on. We must try to apprehend them all in the natural *or appropriate* way, and must take pains to define them satisfactorily, as they have a vital influence upon all that follows from them. For it seems that the first principle or beginning is more than half the whole, and is the means of arriving at a clear conception of many points which are under investigation.

In considering the first principle we must pay regard not only to the conclusion and the premisses of our argument, but also to such views as are popularly held about it. For while all experience harmonizes with the truth, it is never long before truth clashes with falsehood.

Goods have been divided into three classes, viz. external goods as they are called, goods of the soul and goods of the body. Of these three classes we consider the goods of the soul to be goods in the strictest or most literal sense. But it is to the soul that we ascribe psychical actions and activities. Thus our definition is a good one, at least according to this theory, which is not only ancient but is accepted by students of philosophy at the present time. It is right too, inasmuch as certain actions and activities are said to be the end; for thus it appears that the end is some good of the soul and not an external good. It is in harmony with this definition that the happy man should live well and do well, as happiness, it has been said, is in fact a kind of living and doing well.

It appears too that the requisite characteristics of happiness are all contained in the definition; for some people hold that happiness is virtue, others that it is prudence, others that it is wisdom of some kind, others that it is these things or one of them conjoined with pleasure or not dissociated from pleasure, others again include external prosperity. Some of these views are held by many ancient thinkers, others by a few thinkers of high repute. It is probable that neither side is altogether wrong, but that in some one point, if not in most points, they are both right.

Now the definition is in harmony with the view of those who hold that happiness is virtue or excellence of some sort; for activity in accordance with virtue implies virtue. But it would seem that there is a considerable difference between taking the supreme good to consist in acquisition or in use, in a moral state or in an activity. For a moral state, although it exists, may produce nothing good, e.g. if a person is asleep, or has in any other way become inactive. But this cannot be the case with an activity, as activity implies action and good action. As in the Olympian games it is not the most beautiful and strongest persons who receive the crown but they who actually enter the lists as combatants—for it is some of these who become victors—so it is they who act rightly that attain to what is noble and good in life. Again, their life is pleasant in itself. For pleasure is a psychical fact, and whatever a man is said to be fond of is pleasant to him, e.g. a horse to one who is fond of horses, a spectacle to one who is fond of spectacles, and similarly just actions to a lover of justice, and virtuous actions in general to a lover of virtue. Now most men find a sense of discord in their pleasures, because their pleasures are not such as are naturally pleasant. But to the lovers of nobleness natural pleasures are pleasant. It is actions in accordance with virtue that are naturally pleasant. Such actions then are pleasant both relatively to these persons and in themselves. Nor does their life need that pleasure should be attached to it as a sort of amulet; it possesses pleasure in itself. For it may be added that a person is not good, if he does not take delight in noble actions, as nobody would call a person just if he did not take delight in just actions, or liberal if he did not take delight in liberal actions, and so on. But if this is so, it follows that actions in accordance with virtue are pleasant in themselves. But they are also good and noble, and good and noble in the highest degree, if the judgment of the virtuous man upon them is right, his judgment being such as we have described. Happiness then is the best and noblest and pleasantest thing in the world, nor is there any such distinction between goodness, nobleness, and pleasure as the epigram at Delos suggests:

"Justice is noblest, Health is best,
To gain one's end is pleasantest."

For these are all essential characteristics of the best activities, and we hold that happiness consists in these or in one and the noblest of these. Still it is clear that happiness requires the addition of external goods, as we said; for it is impossible, or at least difficult for a person to do what is noble unless he is furnished with external means. For there are many things which can only be done through the instrumentality of friends or wealth or political power, and there are some things the lack of which must mar felicity, e.g. noble birth, a prosperous family, and personal beauty. For a person is incapable of happiness if he is absolutely ugly in appearance, or low born, or solitary and childless, and perhaps still more so, if he has exceedingly bad children or friends, or has had good children or friends and has lost them by death. As we said, then, it seems that prosperity of this kind is an indispensable addition to virtue. It is for this reason that some persons identify good fortune, and others virtue, with happiness.

The question is consequently raised whether happiness is something that can be learnt or acquired by habit or discipline of any other kind, or whether it comes by some divine dispensation or even by chance.

Now if there is anything in the world that is a gift of the Gods to men, it is reasonable to suppose that happiness is a divine gift, especially as it is the best of human things. This however is perhaps a point which is more appropriate to another investigation than the present. But even if happiness is not sent by the Gods but is the result of virtue and of learning or discipline of some kind, it is apparently one of the most divine things in the world; for it would appear that that which is the prize and end of virtue is the supreme good and is in its nature divine and blessed. It will also be widely extended; for it will be capable of being produced in all persons, except such as are morally deformed, by a process of study or care. And if it is better that happiness should be produced in this way than by chance, it may reasonably be supposed that it is so produced, as the order of things is the best possible in Nature and so too in art, and in causation generally, and most of all in the highest kind of causation. But it would be altogether inconsistent to leave what is greatest and noblest to chance. But the definition *of happiness* itself helps to clear up the question; for happiness has been defined as a certain kind of activity of the soul in accordance with virtue. Of the other goods, *i.e. of goods besides those of the soul,* some are necessary as antecedent conditions of happiness, others are in their nature co-operative and serviceable as instruments of happiness.

The conclusion at which we have arrived agrees with our original position. For we laid it down that the end of political science is the supreme good; and political science is concerned with nothing so much as with producing a certain character in the citizens, or in other words with making them good, and capable of performing noble actions. It is reasonable then not to speak of an ox, or a horse, or any other animal as happy; for none of them is capable of participating in activity as so defined. For the same reason no child can be happy, as the age of a child makes it impossible for him to display this activity at present, and if a child is ever said to be happy, the ground of the felicitation is his promise, *rather than his actual performance.* For happiness demands, as we said, a complete virtue and a complete life. For there are all sorts of changes and chances in life, and it is possible that the most prosperous of men will, in his old age, fall into extreme calamities as is told of Priam in the heroic legends. But if a person has experienced such chances, and has died a miserable death, nobody calls him happy.

Is it the case then that nobody in the world may be called happy so long as he is alive? Must we adopt Solon's rule of looking to the end? and, if we follow Solon, can it be said that a man is really happy after his death? Surely such a view is wholly absurd, especially for us who define happiness as a species of activity. But if we do not speak of one who is dead as happy, and if Solon's meaning is not this but rather that it is only when a man is dead that it is safe to call him fortunate as being exempt at last from evils and calamities, this again is a view which is open to some objection. For it seems that one who is dead is capable of being affected both by good and by evil in the same way as one who is living but unconscious, e.g. by honours and dishonours and by the successes or reverses of his children and his descendants generally. But here again a difficulty occurs. For if a person has lived a fortunate life up to old age, and has died a fortunate death, it is possible that he may experience many vicissitudes of fortune in the persons of his descendants. Some of them may be good and may enjoy such a life as they deserve; others may be bad and may have a bad life. It is clear, too, that descendants may stand in all sorts of different degrees of relationship to their ancestor. It would be an extraordinary result, if the dead man were to share the vicissitudes of their fortune and to become happy at one time and miserable at another, *as they became either happy or miserable*. But it would be equally extraordinary, if the future of descendants should not affect their parents at all or for a certain time. It will be best, however, to revert to the difficulty which was raised before, as it will perhaps afford an answer to the present question. If it is right to look to the end, and when the end comes to felicitate a person not as being fortunate but as having been so before, surely it is an extraordinary thing that at the time when he is happy we should not speak the truth about him, because we do not wish to call the living happy in view of the vicissitudes to which they are liable and because we have formed a conception of happiness as something that is permanent and exempt from the possibility of change and because the same persons are liable to many revolutions of fortune. For it is clear that, if we follow the changes of fortune, we shall often call the same person happy at one time, and miserable at another, representing the happy man as "a sort of chameleon without any stability of position." It cannot be right to follow the changes of fortune. It is not upon these that good or evil depends; they are necessary accessories of human life, as we said; but it is a man's activities in accordance with virtue that constitute his happiness and the opposite activities that constitute his misery. The difficulty which has now been discussed is itself a witness that this is the true view. For there is no human function so constant as the activities in accordance with virtue; they seem to be more permanent than the sciences themselves. Among these activities, too, it is the most honourable which are the most permanent, as it is in them that the life of the fortunate chiefly and most continuously consists. For this is apparently the reason why such activities are not liable to be forgotten.

The element of permanency which is required will be found in the happy man, and he will preserve his character throughout life; for he will constantly or in a preeminent degree pursue such actions and speculations as accord with virtue; nor is there anybody who will bear the chances of life so nobly, with such a perfect and complete harmony, as he who is truly good and "foursquare with-out a flaw." Now the events of chance are numerous and of differ-ent magnitudes. It is clear then that small incidents of good fortune, or the reverse, do not turn the scale of life, but that such incidents as are great and numerous augment the felicity of life, if they are fortunate, as they tend naturally to embellish it and the use of them is noble and virtuous, and on the other hand, if they are of a contrary character, mar and mutilate its felicity by causing pains and hindrances to various activities. Still even in these cir-cumstances nobility shines out, when a person bears the weight of accumulated misfortunes with calmness, not from insensibility but from innate dignity and magnanimity.

But if it is the activities which determine the life, as we said, nobody who is fortunate can become miserable; for he will never do what is hateful and mean. For our conception of the truly good and sensible man is that he bears all the chances of life with deco-rum and always does what is noblest in the circumstances, as a good general uses the forces at his command to the best advantage in war, a good cobbler makes the best shoe with the leather that is given him, and so on through the whole series of the arts. If this is so, it follows that the happy man can never become miserable; I do not say that he will be fortunate, if he meets such chances of life as Priam. Yet he will not be variable or liable to frequent change, as he will not be moved from his happiness easily or by ordinary misfortunes but only by such misfortunes as are great and numerous; and after them it will not be soon that he will regain his happiness, but, if he regains it at all, it will be only in a long and complete period of time and after attaining in it to great and noble results.

We may safely then define a happy man as one whose activity accords with perfect virtue and who is adequately furnished with external goods, not for a casual period of time but for a complete or perfect lifetime. But perhaps we ought to add, that he will always live so, and will die as he lives; for it is not given us to fore-see the future, but we take happiness to be an end, and to be alto-gether perfect and complete, and, this being so, we shall call people fortunate during their lifetime, if they possess and will possess these characteristics, but fortunate only so far as men may be for-tunate.

But to leave the discussion of this subject: The idea that the fortunes of one's descendants and of one's friends generally have no influence at all upon oneself seems exceedingly harsh, and contrary to received opinions. But as the events of life are numerous and present all sorts of differences, and some are of more concern to us than others, it would be clearly a long, if not an infinite task, to define them individually; we must, I think, be content to describe them generally and in outline. Now, as in personal misfortunes some have a certain weight and influence upon our life, and others, it seems, are comparatively light, so it is with such misfortunes as affect our friends generally. But as the difference between the experiences of the living or the dead is far greater than the difference between terrible crimes when enacted upon the stage in tragedies and the same crimes when merely assumed to have already occurred, it is necessary to take account of this difference also, and still more perhaps of the serious doubt which has been raised as to the participation of the dead in any good or evil. For it is probable in this view that if anything, whether good or evil, reaches the dead at all, it is feeble and insignificant, either absolutely, or in relation to them, or if not, is of such a magnitude and character as to be incapable of making people happy if they are not happy or of depriving them of their felicity, if they are.

It would seem then that the dead are affected or influenced in some way by the prosperity and the adversity of their friends, but that the influence is of such a kind and degree as not to make people happy, if they are not happy, nor to have any similar effect.

Having determined these points, let us consider whether happiness belongs rather to such things as are objects of praise or to such things as are objects of honour. For it is clearly not a mere potential good.

It appears that whatever is an object of praise is praised as possessing a certain character, and standing in a certain relation to something. For we praise one who is just and manly and good in any way, or we praise virtue, because of their actions and productions. We praise one who is strong and swift and so on, as naturally possessing a certain character and standing in a certain relation to something that is itself good and estimable. The truth of this statement becomes clear, if we take the case of praises bestowed upon the Gods. Such praise appears ridiculous as implying a reference

to ourselves, and there must be such a reference, because, as we
said, praise invariably implies a reference *to a higher standard.*
But if this is the nature of praise, it is clear that it is not praise but
something greater and better which is appropriate to all that is
best, as indeed is evident; for we speak of the Gods as "blessed"
and "happy" *rather than as "praiseworthy"* and we speak of the
most godlike men as "blessed." It is the same with goods; for nobody praises happiness as he praises justice, but he calls it blessed,
as being in its nature better and more divine. It is sometimes held
on these grounds that Eudoxus was right in advocating the supremacy of pleasure; for the fact that pleasure is a good and yet is
not praised, indicates, as he thought, that it is higher than the objects of praise, as God and the good are higher, these being the
standards to which everything else is referred. For praises are appropriate to virtue, as it is virtue which makes us capable of noble
deeds; but panegyrics to accomplished results, whether they be
results of the body or of the soul. But it may be said that an exact
discussion of these points belongs more properly to the special
study of panegyrics. We see clearly, however, from what has been
said, that happiness is something honourable and final. And that
it is so seems to follow also from the fact that it is a first principle;
for it is for the sake of happiness that we all do everything else,
and the first principle or the cause of all that is good we regard as
something honourable and divine.

Inasmuch as happiness is an activity of soul in accordance with
complete or perfect virtue, it is necessary to consider virtue, as this
will perhaps be the best way of studying happiness.

It appears that virtue is the object upon which the true statesman has expended the largest amount of trouble, as it is his wish
to make the citizens virtuous and obedient to the laws. We have
instances of such statesmen in the legislators of Crete and Lacedaemon and such other legislators as have resembled them. But if this
inquiry is proper to political science, it will clearly accord with
our original purpose to pursue it. But it is clear that it is human
virtue which we have to consider; for the good of which we are in
search is, as we said, human good, and the happiness, human happiness. By human virtue or excellence we mean not that of the
body, but that of the soul, and by happiness we mean an activity
of the soul.

If this is so, it is clearly necessary for statesmen to have some knowledge of the nature of the soul in the same way as it is necessary for one who is to treat the eye or any part of the body, to have some knowledge of it, and all the more as political science is better and more honourable than medical science. Clever doctors take a great deal of trouble to understand the body, and similarly the statesman must make a study of the soul. But he must study it with a view to his particular object and so far only as his object requires; for to elaborate the study of it further would, I think, be to aggravate unduly the labour of our present undertaking.

There are some facts concerning the soul which are adequately stated in the popular or exoterical discourses, and these we may rightly adopt. It is stated e.g. that the soul has two parts, one irrational and the other possessing reason. But whether these parts are distinguished like the parts of the body and like everything that is itself divisible, or whether they are theoretically distinct, but in fact inseparable, as convex and concave in the circumference of a circle, is of no importance to the present inquiry.

Again, it seems that of the irrational part of the soul one part is common, *i.e. shared by man with all living things,* and vegetative; I mean the part which is the cause of nutrition and increase. For we may assume such a faculty of the soul to exist in all things that receive nutrition, even in embryos, and the same faculty to exist in things that are full grown, as it is more reasonable to suppose that it is the same faculty than that it is different. It is clear then that the virtue or excellence of this faculty is not distinctively human but is shared by man with all living things; for it seems that this part and this faculty are especially active in sleep, whereas good and bad people are never so little distinguishable as in sleep— whence the saying that there is no difference between the happy and the miserable during half their lifetime. And this is only natural; for sleep is an inactivity of the soul in respect of its virtue or vice, except in so far as certain impulses affect it to a slight extent, and make the visions of the virtuous better than those of ordinary people. But enough has been said on this point, and we must now leave the principle of nutrition, as it possesses no natural share in human virtue.

It seems that there is another natural principle of the soul which

is irrational and yet in a sense partakes of reason. For in a continent or incontinent person we praise the reason, and that part of
the soul which possesses reason, as it exhorts men rightly and exhorts them to the best conduct. But it is clear that there is in them
another principle which is naturally different from reason and
fights and contends against reason. For just as the paralysed parts
of the body, when we intend to move them to the right, are drawn
away in a contrary direction to the left, so it is with the soul; the
impulses of incontinent people run counter to reason. But there is
this difference, however, that while in the body we see the part
which is drawn astray, in the soul we do not see it. But it is probably right to suppose with equal certainty that there is in the soul
too something different from reason, which opposes and thwarts it,
although the sense in which it is distinct from reason is immaterial.
But it appears that this part too partakes of reason, as we said; at
all events in a continent person it obeys reason, while in a temperate or courageous person it is probably still more obedient, as
being absolutely harmonious with reason.

It appears then that the irrational part of the soul is itself two-
fold; for the vegetative faculty does not participate at all in reason,
but the faculty of desire or general concupiscence participates in it
more or less, in so far as it is submissive and obedient to reason.
But *it is obedient* in the sense in which we speak of "paying attention to a father" or "to friends," but not in the sense in which we
speak of "paying attention to mathematics." All correction, rebuke
and exhortation is a witness that the irrational part of the soul is
in a sense subject to the influence of reason. But if we are to say
that this part too possesses reason, then the part which possesses
reason will have two divisions, one possessing reason absolutely
and in itself, the other listening to it as a child listens to its father.

Virtue or excellence again, admits of a distinction which depends on this difference. For we speak of some virtues as intellectual and of others as moral, wisdom, intelligence and prudence,
being intellectual, liberality and temperance being moral, virtues.
For when we describe a person's character, we do not say that he is
wise or intelligent but that he is gentle or temperate. Yet we praise
a wise man too in respect of his mental state, and such mental
states as deserve to be praised we call virtuous.

Book II

. . . . The nature of virtue has been now generically described. But it is not enough to state merely that virtue is a moral state, we must also describe the character of that moral state.

It must be laid down then that every virtue or excellence has the effect of producing a good condition of that of which it is a virtue or excellence, and of enabling it to perform its function well. Thus the excellence of the eye makes the eye good and its function good, as it is by the excellence of the eye that we see well. Similarly, the excellence of the horse makes a horse excellent and good at racing, at carrying its rider and at facing the enemy.

If then this is universally true, the virtue or excellence of man will be such a moral state as makes a man good and able to perform his proper function well. We have already explained how this will be the case, but another way of making it clear will be to study the nature or character of this virtue.

Now in everything, whether it be continuous or discrete, it is possible to take a greater, a smaller, or an equal amount, and this either absolutely or in relation to ourselves, the equal being a mean between excess and deficiency. By the mean in respect of the thing itself, or the absolute mean, I understand that which is equally distinct from both extremes; and this is one and the same thing for everybody. By the mean considered relatively to ourselves I understand that which is neither too much nor too little; but this is not one thing, nor is it the same for everybody. Thus if 10 be too much and 2 too little we take 6 as a mean in respect of the thing itself; for 6 is as much greater than 2 as it is less than 10, and this is a mean in arithmetical proportion. But the mean considered relatively to ourselves must not be ascertained in this way. It does not follow that if 10 pounds *of meat* be too much and 2 be too little for a man to eat, a trainer will order him 6 pounds, as this may itself be too much or too little for the person who is to take it; it will be too little e.g. for Milo, but too much for a beginner in gymnastics. It will be the same with running and wrestling; *the right amount will vary with the individual*. This being so, everybody who understands his business avoids alike excess and deficiency; he seeks and chooses the mean, not the absolute mean, but the mean considered relatively to ourselves.

Every science then performs its function well, if it regards the mean and refers the works which it produces to the mean. This is the reason why it is usually said of successful works that it is impossible to take anything from them or to add anything to them, which implies that excess or deficiency is fatal to excellence but that the mean state ensures it. Good artists too, as we say, have an eye to the mean in their works. But virtue, like Nature herself, is more accurate and better than any art; virtue therefore will aim at the mean;—I speak of moral virtue, as it is moral virtue which is concerned with emotions and actions, and it is these which admit of excess and deficiency and the mean. Thus it is possible to go too far, or not to go far enough, in respect of fear, courage, desire, anger, pity, and pleasure and pain generally, and the excess and the deficiency are alike wrong; but to experience these emotions at the right times and on the right occasions and towards the right persons and for the right causes and in the right manner is the mean or the supreme good, which is characteristic of virtue. Similarly there may be excess, deficiency, or the mean, in regard to actions. But virtue is concerned with emotions and actions, and here excess is an error and deficiency a fault, whereas the mean is successful and laudable, and success and merit are both characteristics of virtue.

It appears then that virtue is a mean state, so far at least as it aims at the mean.

Again, there are many different ways of going wrong; for evil is in its nature infinite, to use the Pythagorean [1] figure, but good is finite. But there is only one possible way of going right. Accordingly the former is easy and the latter difficult; it is easy to miss the mark but difficult to hit it. This again is a reason why excess and deficiency are characteristics of vice and the mean state a characteristic of virtue.

> "For good is simple, evil manifold."

Virtue then is a state of deliberate moral purpose consisting in a

---

[1] The Pythagoreans, starting from the mystical significance of number, took the opposite principles of "the finite" (tò péras or tò peperasménon) and "the infinite" (tò ápeiron) to represent good and evil.

mean that is relative to ourselves, the mean being determined by reason, or as a prudent man would determine it.

It is a mean state *firstly as lying* between two vices, the vice of excess on the one hand, and the vice of deficiency on the other, and secondly because, whereas the vices either fall short of or go beyond what is proper in the emotions and actions, virtue not only discovers but embraces the mean.

Accordingly, virtue, if regarded in its essence or theoretical conception, is a mean state, but, if regarded from the point of view of the highest good, or of excellence, it is an extreme.

But it is not every action or every emotion that admits of a mean state. There are some whose very name implies wickedness, as e.g. malice, shamelessness, and envy, among emotions, or adultery, theft, and murder, among actions. All these, and others like them, are censured as being intrinsically wicked, not merely the excesses or deficiencies of them. It is never possible then to be right in respect of them; they are always sinful. Right or wrong in such actions as adultery does not depend on our committing them with the right person, at the right time or in the right manner; on the contrary it is sinful to do anything of the kind at all. It would be equally wrong then to suppose that there can be a mean state or an excess or deficiency in unjust, cowardly or licentious conduct; for, if it were so, there would be a mean state of an excess or of a deficiency, an excess of an excess and a deficiency of a deficiency. But as in temperance and courage there can be no excess or deficiency because the mean is, in a sense, an extreme, so too in these cases there cannot be a mean or an excess or deficiency, but, however the acts may be done, they are wrong. For it is a general rule that an excess or deficiency does not admit of a mean state, nor a mean state of an excess or deficiency.

But it is not enough to lay down this as a general rule; it is necessary to apply it to particular cases, as in reasonings upon actions general statements, although they are broader, are less exact than particular statements. For all action refers to particulars, and it is essential that our theories should harmonize with the particular cases to which they apply.

We must take particular virtues then from the catalogue *of virtues.*

In regard to feelings of fear and confidence, courage is a mean state. On the side of excess, he whose fearlessness is excessive has no name, as often happens, but he whose confidence is excessive is foolhardy, while he whose timidity is excessive and whose confidence is deficient is a coward.

In respect of pleasures and pains, although not indeed of all pleasures and pains, and to a less extent in respect of pains than of pleasures, the mean state is temperance, the excess is licentiousness. We never find people who are deficient in regard to pleasures; accordingly such people again have not received a name, but we may call them insensible.

As regards the giving and taking of money, the mean state is liberality, the excess and deficiency are prodigality and illiberality. Here the excess and deficiency take opposite forms; for while the prodigal man is excessive in spending and deficient in taking, the illiberal man is excessive in taking and deficient in spending.

(For the present we are giving only a rough and summary account *of the virtues,* and that is sufficient for our purpose; we will hereafter determine their character more exactly.)

In respect of money there are other dispositions as well. There is the mean state which is magnificence; for the magnificent man, as having to do with large sums of money, differs from the liberal man who has to do only with small sums; and the excess *corresponding to it* is bad taste or vulgarity, the deficiency is meanness. These are different from the excess and deficiency of liberality; what the difference is will be explained hereafter.

In respect of honour and dishonour the mean state is highmindedness, the excess is what is called vanity, the deficiency littlemindedness. Corresponding to liberality, which, as we said, differs from magnificence as having to do *not with great but* with small sums of money, there is a moral state which has to do with petty honour and is related to highmindedness which has to do with great honour; for it is possible to aspire to honour in the right way, or in a way which is excessive or insufficient, and if a person's aspirations are excessive, he is called ambitious, if they are deficient, he is called unambitious, while if they are between the two, he has no name. The dispositions too are nameless, except that the disposition of the ambitious person is called ambition. The consequence is that the extremes lay claim to the mean or intermediate place. We ourselves speak of one who observes the mean sometimes as ambitious, and at other times as unambitious; we sometimes praise an ambitious, and at other times an unambitious person. The reason for our doing so will be stated in due course, but let us now discuss the other virtues in accordance with the method which we have followed hitherto.

Anger, like other emotions, has its excess, its deficiency, and its mean state. It may be said that they have no names, but as we call one who observes the mean gentle, we will call the mean state gentleness. Among the extremes, if a person errs on the side of excess, he may be called passionate and his vice passionateness, if on that of deficiency, he may be called impassive and his deficiency impassivity.

There are also three other mean states with a certain resemblance to each other, and yet with a difference. For while they are all concerned with intercourse in speech and action, they are different in that one of them is concerned with truth in such intercourse, and the others with pleasantness, one with pleasantness in amusement and the other with pleasantness in the various circumstances of life. We must therefore discuss these states in order to make it clear that in all cases it is the mean state which is an object of praise, and the extremes are neither right nor laudable but censurable. It is true that these mean and extreme states are generally nameless, but we must do our best here as elsewhere to give them a name, so that our argument may be clear and easy to follow.

In the matter of truth then, he who observes the mean may be called truthful, and the mean state truthfulness. Pretence, if it takes the form of exaggeration, is boastfulness, and one who is guilty of pretence is a boaster; but if it takes the form of depreciation it is irony, and he who is guilty of it is ironical.

As regards pleasantness in amusement, he who observes the mean is witty, and his disposition wittiness; the excess is buffoonery, and he who is guilty of it a buffoon, whereas he who is deficient in wit may be called a boor and his moral state boorishness.

As to the other kind of pleasantness, viz. pleasantness in life, he who is pleasant in a proper way is friendly, and his mean state friendliness; but he who goes too far, if he has no ulterior object in view, is obsequious, while if his object is self interest, he is a flatterer, and he who does not go far enough and always makes himself unpleasant is a quarrelsome and morose sort of person.

There are also mean states in the emotions and in the expression of the emotions. For although modesty is not a virtue, yet a modest person is praised as if he were virtuous; for here too one person is said to observe the mean and another to exceed it, as e.g. the bashful man who is never anything but modest, whereas a person who has insufficient modesty or no modesty at all is called shameless, and one who observes the mean modest.

Righteous indignation, again, is a mean state between envy and malice. They are all concerned with the pain and pleasure which we feel at the fortunes of our neighbors. A person who is righteously indignant is pained at the prosperity of the undeserving; but the envious person goes further and is pained at anybody's prosperity, and the malicious person is so far from being pained that he actually rejoices *at misfortunes.*

We shall have another opportunity however of discussing these matters. But in regard to justice, as the word is used in various senses, we will afterwards define those senses and explain how each of them is a mean state. And we will follow the same course with the intellectual virtues.

There are then three dispositions, two being vices, viz. one the vice of excess and the other that of deficiency, and one virtue, which is the mean state between them; and they are all in a sense mutually opposed. For the extremes are opposed both to the mean and to each other, and the mean is opposed to the extremes. For as the equal if compared with the less is greater but if compared with the greater is less, so the mean states, whether in the emotions or in actions, if compared with the deficiencies, are excessive, but if compared with the excesses are deficient. Thus the courageous man appears foolhardy as compared with the coward, but cowardly as compared with the foolhardy. Similarly, the temperate man appears licentious as compared with the insensible but insensible as compared with the licentious, and the liberal man appears prodigal as compared with the illiberal, but illiberal as compared with the prodigal. The result is that the extremes mutually repel and reject the mean; the coward calls the courageous man foolhardy, but the foolhardy man calls him cowardly, and so on in the other cases.

But while there is this mutual opposition between the extremes and the mean, there is greater opposition between the two extremes than between either extreme and the mean; for they are further removed from each other than from the mean, as the great from the small and the small from the great than both from the equal. Again, while some extremes exhibit more or less similarity to the mean, as foolhardiness to courage and prodigality to liberality, there is the greatest possible dissimilarity between the extremes. But things which are furthest removed from each other are defined to be opposites; hence the further things are removed, the greater is the opposition between them.

It is in some cases the deficiency and in others the excess which is the more opposed to the mean. Thus it is not foolhardiness the excess, but cowardice the deficiency which is the more opposed to courage, nor is it insensibility the deficiency, but licentiousness the excess which is the more opposed to temperance. There are two reasons why this should be so. One lies in the nature of the thing itself; for as one of the two extremes is the nearer and more similar to the mean, it is not this extreme, but its opposite, that we chiefly set against the mean. For instance, as it appears that foolhardiness is more similar and nearer to courage than cowardice, it is cowardice that we chiefly set against courage; for things which are further removed from the mean seemed to be more opposite to it. This being one reason which lies in the nature of the thing itself, there is a second which lies in our own nature. It is the things to which we ourselves are naturally more inclined that appear more opposed to the mean. Thus we are ourselves naturally more inclined to pleasures *than to their opposites,* and are more prone therefore to licentiousness than to decorum. Accordingly we speak of those things, in which we are more likely to run to great lengths, as being more opposed to the mean. Hence it follows that licentiousness which is an excess is more opposed to temperance than insensibility.

It has now been sufficiently shown that moral virtue is a mean state, and in what sense it is a mean state; it is a mean state as lying between two vices, a vice of excess on the one side and a vice of deficiency on the other, and as aiming at the mean in the emotions and actions.

That is the reason why it is so hard to be virtuous; for it is always hard work to find the mean in anything, e.g. it is not everybody, but only a man of science, who can find the mean or centre of a circle. So too anybody can get angry—that is an easy matter—and anybody can give or spend money, but to give it to the right persons, to give the right amount of it and to give it at the right time and for the right cause and in the right way, this is not what anybody can do, nor is it easy. That is the reason why it is rare and laudable and noble to do well. Accordingly one who aims at the mean must begin by departing from that extreme which is the more contrary to the mean; he must act in the spirit of Calypso's advice,

> "Far from this smoke and swell keep thou thy bark,"

for of the two extremes one is more sinful than the other. As it is difficult then to hit the mean exactly, we must take the second best course, as the saying is, and choose the lesser of two evils, and this we shall best do in the way that we have described, *i.e. by steering clear of the evil which is further from the mean*. We must also observe the things to which we are ourselves particularly prone, as different natures have different inclinations, and we may ascertain what these are by a consideration of our feelings of pleasure and pain. And then we must drag ourselves in the direction opposite to them; for it is by removing ourselves as far as possible from what is wrong that we shall arrive at the mean, as we do when we pull a crooked stick straight.

But in all cases we must especially be on our guard against what is pleasant and against pleasure, as we are not impartial judges of pleasure. Hence our attitude towards pleasure must be like that of the elders of the people in the *Iliad* towards Helen, and we must never be afraid of applying the words they use; for if we dismiss pleasure as they dismissed Helen, we shall be less likely to go wrong. It is by action of this kind, to put it summarily, that we shall best succeed in hitting the mean.

It may be admitted that this is a difficult task, especially in particular cases. It is not easy to determine e.g. the right manner, objects, occasions, and duration of anger. There are times when we ourselves praise people who are deficient in anger, and call them gentle, and there are other times when we speak of people who exhibit a savage temper as spirited. It is not however one who deviates a little from what is right, but one who deviates a great deal, whether on the side of excess or of deficiency, that is censured; for he is sure to be found out. Again, it is not easy to decide theoretically how far and to what extent a man may go before he becomes censurable, but neither is it easy to define theoretically anything else within the region of perception; such things fall under the head of particulars, and our judgment of them depends upon our perception.

So much then is plain, that the mean state is everywhere laudable, but that we ought to incline at one time towards the excess and at another towards the deficiency; for this will be our easiest manner of hitting the mean, or in other words of attaining excellence.

Book III

As virtue is concerned with emotions and actions, and such emotions and actions as are voluntary are the subjects of praise and blame, while such as are involuntary are the subjects of pardon and sometimes even of pity, it is necessary, I think, in an investigation of virtue to distinguish what is voluntary from what is involuntary. It will also be useful in legislation as bearing upon the honours and punishments which the legislator assigns.

It is generally admitted that acts done under compulsion, or from ignorance, are involuntary. But an act is compulsory, if its origin is external *to the agent or patient,* i.e. if it is one in which the agent or the patient contributes nothing, as e.g. if the wind, or people who have us in their power, were to carry us in a certain direction. But if an action is done from fear of greater evils or for some noble end, e.g. if a tyrant, who had our parents and children in his power, were to order us to do some shameful act, on condition that, if we did it, their lives should be spared, and, if not, they should be put to death, it is a question whether such action is voluntary or involuntary. The case of throwing goods overboard during a storm at sea is similar; for although nobody would voluntarily make such a sacrifice in the abstract, yet every sensible person will make it for his own safety and the safety of his fellow passengers. Actions like this, although they are of a mixed character, are more like voluntary than involuntary actions, as they are chosen at the time of performing them, and the end *or character* of an action depends upon *the choice made at* the moment of performing it. When we speak then of an action as voluntary or involuntary, we must have regard to the time at which a person performs it. The person *whose actions we are considering* acts voluntarily; for in actions like his the original power which sets the instrumentality of his limbs in motion lies in himself, and when the origin of a thing lies in a person himself, it is in his power either to do it or not to do it. Such actions then are *practically* voluntary, although in the abstract they may be said perhaps to be involuntary, as nobody would choose any such action in itself.

Such actions are at times subjects of praise, when people submit to something that is shameful or painful for the sake of gaining what is great and noble; or in the contrary case they are the subjects of censure, as it is only a bad man who would submit to what is utterly shameful, if his object were not noble at all, or were indifferent. There are also some actions which are pardonable, although not laudable, as when a person is induced to do what is wrong by such causes as are too strong for human nature and do not admit of resistance. Yet it is probable that there are some actions where compulsion is an impossibility; a person would rather suffer the most dreadful form of death than do them. Thus the reasons which constrained Alcmæon in Euripides to murder his mother are clearly ridiculous.

It is sometimes difficult to determine what ought to be chosen or endured for the sake of obtaining or avoiding a certain result. But it is still more difficult to abide by our decisions; for it generally happens that, while the consequence which we expect is painful, the act which we are constrained to do is shameful, and therefore we receive censure or praise according as we yield or do not yield to the constraint.

What class of actions then is it that may be rightly called compulsory? Actions it may be said are compulsory in the abstract, whenever the cause is external to the agent and he contributes nothing to it. But if an action, although involuntary in itself, is chosen at a particular time and for a particular end, and if its original cause lies in the agent himself, then, although such an action is involuntary in itself, it is voluntary at that time and for that end. Such an action however is more like a voluntary than an involuntary action; for actions fall under the category of particulars, and *in the supposed case* the particular action is voluntary.

It is not easy to state what kind of actions are to be chosen for certain ends, as particular cases admit of many differences. It might be argued that whatever is pleasant or noble is compulsory, as pleasure and nobleness are external to ourselves and exercise a constraint upon us; but if that were so, every action would be compulsory, as these are the motives of all actions in us all. Again, if a person acts under compulsion and involuntarily, his action is painful to him; but if the motives of his action are pleasure and nobleness, it is pleasant. It is ridiculous to lay the blame of our wrong actions upon external causes, rather than upon the facility with which we ourselves are caught by such causes, and, while we take the credit of our noble actions to ourselves, to lay the blame of our shameful actions upon pleasure. It seems then that an action is compulsory if its origin is external to the agent, i.e. if the person who is the subject of compulsion is in no sense contributory to the action.

An action which is due to ignorance is always non-voluntary; but it is not involuntary, unless it is followed by pain and excites a feeling of regret. For if a person has performed an action, whatever it may be, from ignorance, and yet feels no distress at his action, it is true that he has not acted voluntarily, as he was not aware of what he was doing, but on the other hand, he has not acted involuntarily, so long as he feels no pain.

If a person who has acted from ignorance regrets what he has done, it may be said that he is an involuntary agent; but, if he does not regret it, his case is different, and he may be called a non-voluntary agent, for, as there is this difference, it is better that he should have a special name.

It would seem, too, that there is a difference between acting from ignorance and doing a thing in ignorance. Thus, if a person is intoxicated or infuriated, he is not regarded as acting from ignorance, but as acting from intoxication or fury; yet he does not act consciously but in ignorance.

It must be admitted then that every vicious person is ignorant of what he ought to do, and what he ought to abstain from doing, and that ignorance is the error which makes people unjust and generally wicked. But when we speak of an action as involuntary, we do not mean merely that a person is ignorant of his true interest. The ignorance which is the cause of involuntary action, as distinguished from that which is the cause of vice, is not such ignorance as affects the moral purpose, nor again is it ignorance of the universal; for this is censurable. It is rather ignorance of particulars, i.e. ignorance of the particular circumstances and occasion of the action. Where this ignorance exists, there is room for pity and forgiveness, as one who is ignorant of any such particular is an involuntary agent.

It will perhaps be as well then to define the nature and number of these particulars. They are

    1. the agent,
    2. the act,
    3. the occasion or circumstances of the act.

Sometimes also

    4. the instrument, e.g. a tool,
    5. the object, e.g. safety,

and   6. the manner of doing an act, e.g. gently or violently.

Nobody but a madman can be ignorant of all these particulars. It is clear that nobody can be ignorant of the agent; for how can a person be ignorant of himself? But a person may be ignorant of what he is doing, as when people say that a word escaped them unawares or that they did not know a subject was forbidden, like Æschylus *when he revealed* the mysteries, or that he only meant to show the working of a weapon when he discharged it, like the man who discharged the catapult. Again, a person may take his son for an enemy like Merope, or a pointed foil for a foil that has its button on, or a solid stone for a pumice stone, or he may kill somebody by a blow that was meant to save him, or he may deal a fatal blow while only intending, as in a sparring match, to give a lesson in the art of dealing a blow. As there may be ignorance in regard to all these particular circumstances of an action, it may be said that a person has acted involuntarily, if he was ignorant of any one of them, and especially of such particulars as seem to be most important, i.e. of the circumstances of the action, and of its natural result. But if an action is to be called involuntary in respect of such ignorance, it is necessary that it should be painful to the agent and should excite in him a feeling of regret.

As an action is involuntary if done under compulsion or from ignorance, it would seem to follow that it is voluntary if the agent originates it with a knowledge of the particular circumstances of the action. For it is perhaps wrong to say that actions which are due to passion or desire are involuntary. For in the first place upon that hypothesis none of the lower animals can any more be said to act voluntarily, nor can children; and secondly is it to be argued that nothing which we do from desire or passion is voluntary? or are our noble actions done voluntarily, and our shameful actions involuntarily? Surely the latter view is ridiculous, if one and the same person is the author of both kinds of action. But it would seem irrational to assert that such things as ought to be the objects of desire are desired involuntarily; and there are certain things which ought to be the occasions of anger, and certain things such as health and learning, which ought to be the objects of desire. Again, it seems that what is involuntary is painful, but what is done from desire is pleasant. Again, what difference is there, in respect of involuntariness, between errors of reason and errors of passion? It is our duty to avoid both; but the irrational emotions seem to be as truly human *as the reason itself and therefore we are as truly responsible for our emotions as for our reasoning*. Such actions then as proceed from passion and desire are not less the actions of the man than rational actions; it is absurd therefore to regard these as involuntary.

Having thus distinguished voluntary from involuntary action, we naturally proceed to discuss moral purpose. For it would seem that the moral purpose is most closely related to virtue, and is a better criterion of character than actions themselves are.

It is clear that moral purpose is something voluntary. Still moral purpose and volition are not identical; volition is a term of wider range. For while children and the lower animals participate in volition, they do not participate in moral purpose. Also we speak of actions done on the spur of the moment as being voluntary, but not as being done with moral purpose.

It would appear then that the definition of moral purpose as desire, or passion, or wish, or opinion of some sort is a mistake. For moral purpose is not like desire and passion common to irrational creatures as well as to Man. Again, an incontinent person acts from desire but not from moral purpose. On the other hand a continent person acts from moral purpose but not from desire. Again, desire is contrary to moral purpose, but one desire is not contrary to another. Desire, too, is, but moral purpose is not, directed to pleasures and pains. Still less can moral purpose be the same thing as passion; for there are no actions which seem to be so little directed by moral purpose as those which are due to angry passion. Nor again is moral purpose the same thing as wish, although it is clear that it is nearly allied to it. For moral purpose does not apply to impossibilities, and anybody who should say that he had a purpose of achieving what is impossible would be thought a fool. But there is such a thing as wishing for the impossible, as e.g. for immortality. Again, while we may wish for things which could not possibly be affected by our own action, as e.g. for the victory of a certain actor or athlete, it can never be said that we purpose such things; we only purpose what may, as we think, be possibly effected by our own action. Again, the wish is directed rather to the end, but the moral purpose to the means. Thus we wish to be good in health, but we purpose or choose the means of being in good health. Or again we wish to be happy and admit the wish; but we cannot appropriately say that we purpose or choose to be happy. For it seems to be a general law that our moral purpose is confined to such things as lie within our own power. Nor again can moral purpose be opinion, for it seems that the sphere of opinion is universal; it embraces things which are eternal or impossible as much as things which lie within our own power. Opinion too, unlike moral purpose, is distinguished by being true or false, not by being good or evil. Perhaps there is nobody who maintains that moral purpose is identical with opinion generally; but neither is it identical with opinion of a particular kind. For it is according as we purpose or choose what is good or evil, and not according as we hold particular opinions, that we possess a certain character. Again, we choose to accept or avoid a thing and so on, but we opine what a thing is, or for whom or in what way it is beneficial. We do not opine at all to accept or avoid a thing. Again, whereas moral purpose is praised rather as being directed to a proper end than as being correct, opinion is praised as being true. Again, we purpose or choose such things as we best know to be good; but we form an opinion of things of which we have no knowledge. Again, it is apparently not the same people who make the best choice and who form the best opinions. There are some people who form a better opinion than others, but are prevented by vice from making the right choice. It is possible that opinion may precede moral purpose or follow it, but that is not the point; for the question which we are considering is simply this, whether moral purpose is identical with opinion of a particular kind.

What then is the nature and character of moral purpose, since it is none of the things which have been mentioned? It is clearly voluntary, but there are things which are voluntary and yet are not chosen or purposed. It may be said, I think, that a thing is voluntary, if it is the result of previous deliberation, for moral purpose implies reason and thought. The very name *(proairesis)* seems to indicate previous deliberation, as it denotes something chosen in preference to other things.

The question is, Do we deliberate upon everything? Is everything a matter for deliberation, or are there some things which are not subjects of deliberation?

We must presumably understand by "a matter of deliberation" not that about which a fool or a madman, but that about which a sensible person, would deliberate.

Nobody deliberates about things which are eternal, *i.e. immutable,* as e.g. the universe or the incommensurability of the diagonal and the side of a square; or about things which are in motion but always follow the same course, whether of necessity or by nature or for some other cause, as e.g. the solstices and sunrisings; or about things which are wholly irregular like droughts and showers; or about mere matters of chance such as the finding of a treasure. Nor again are all human affairs matters of deliberation; thus no Lacedaemonian will deliberate upon the best constitution for the Scythians. The reason why we do not deliberate about these things is that none of them can be effected by our action. The matters about which we deliberate are practical matters lying within our power. There is in fact no other class of matters left; for it would seem that the causes of things are nature, necessity, chance, and besides these only intelligence, and human agency in its various forms. But different classes of people deliberate about such practical matters as depend upon their several actions. Further, those sciences, which are exact and complete in themselves, do not admit of deliberation, as e.g. writing; for we are in no doubt as to the proper way of writing. But if a thing depends upon our own action and is not invariable, it is a matter of deliberation, as e.g. questions of medicine, of finance, or of navigation rather than of gymnastic, as being less exactly systematized, and similarly all other arts, and again, the arts more than the sciences, as we are more in doubt about them.

Deliberation occurs in cases which fall under a general rule, if it is uncertain what the issue will be, and in cases which do not admit of an absolute decision. We invite the help of other people in our deliberations upon matters of importance, when we distrust our own ability to decide them.

Again, we deliberate not about ends but about the means to ends. Thus a doctor does not deliberate whether he shall cure his patients, nor an orator whether he shall persuade his audience, nor a statesman whether he shall produce law and order, nor does any one else deliberate about his end. They all propose to themselves a certain end and then consider how and by what means it can be attained, and if it appears capable of attainment by several means, they consider what will be the easiest and best means of attaining it, and if there is only one means of attaining it, how it may be attained by this means, and by what means this means itself can be attained, until they come to the first cause, which in the order of discovery is last. For it seems that deliberation is a process of investigation and analysis such as this: it is like the analysis of a geometrical figure. It appears however that, while investigation is not always deliberation, mathematical investigations, e.g. not being so, deliberation is always investigation, and that that which is last in the order of analysis is first in the order of production.

If *in a deliberation* we come upon an impossibility, we abandon our task, as e.g. if money is required and it is impossible to provide the money; but if it appears to be possible, we set about doing it. By possibilities I mean such things as may be effected by our own actions; for what is done by our friends may be said to be done by ourselves, as the origin of it lies in ourselves. The question is sometimes what instruments are necessary, and at other times how they are to be used. Similarly in all other cases it is sometimes the means of doing a certain thing and at other times the manner or the agency that is in question.

It seems, as has been said, that a man originates his own actions. Deliberation touches such things as may be done by a man himself, and actions are done for the sake of something which lies beyond themselves. Accordingly it is not the end, but the means to the end, that will be matter of deliberation. Nor again will particular questions be matters of deliberation, as e.g. the question whether a particular thing is a loaf or has been properly baked; that is rather a matter of perception, and, if we go on deliberating for ever, we shall never come to an end.

The objects of deliberation and of moral purpose are the same, except that the object of moral purpose is already determined; for it is that which is preferred after deliberation. For everybody gives up inquiring how he shall act when he has traced back the origin of his action to himself and to the dominant part of himself, i.e. to the part which exercises moral choice or purpose. There is an illustration of this principle in the ancient polities which Homer represented, for in them the kings promulgated their purpose, whatever it might be, to the people.

But if the object of our moral purpose is that which, being in our power, is after deliberation the object of our desire, it follows that the moral purpose is a deliberative desire of something which is in our power; for we first deliberate upon a thing and, after passing judgment upon it, we desire it in accordance with our deliberation.

Let us now leave this rough sketch of the moral purpose. We have shown what are the matters with which it deals, and that it is directed to the means *rather than to the ends*.

We have said that the wish is directed to the end; but there are some people who hold that the end is the good, and others that it is what appears to be good. If it is said that the object of wish is the good, it follows that where a person's moral purpose or choice is wrong that which he wishes is not *in the proper sense* an object of wish; for if it is an object of wish it will also be a good, but it was perhaps an evil. If on the other hand, it is said that it is what appears to be good which is the object of wish, it follows that there is no such thing as a natural object of wish, but that it is in every man's case that which seems good to him. But different, and it may be even opposite things, seem good to different people.

If these conclusions are not satisfactory, it will perhaps be best to say that in an absolute or true sense it is the good which is the object of wish, but that in reference to the individual it is that which appears to be good. Hence it is the true good which is good relatively to the virtuous man, and something that need not be defined which is good relatively to the vicious man. The case is much the same as in the body; when people are in a good state of health it is things which are truly wholesome that are wholesome to them, but when they are in a bad state of health it is other things, and so with things that are bitter, sweet, hot, heavy, and the rest. For the virtuous man forms a right judgment of particular cases, and in every case that which is true appears true to him. For every moral state has its own honours and pleasures, nor is there any point perhaps so distinctive of the virtuous man as his power of seeing the truth in all cases, because he is, as it were, the standard and measure of things. It seems to be pleasure which most frequently deceives people, for pleasure appears to be good, although it is not, and the result is that they choose what is pleasant as if it were good, and avoid pain as if it were evil. . . .

Book VIII

. . . . It is the friendship of the good which is friendship in the truest sense, as has been said several times. For it seems that, while that which is good or pleasant in an absolute sense is an object of love and desire, that which is good or pleasant to each individual is an object of love or desire to him; but the love or desire of one good man for another depends upon such goodness and pleasantness as are at once absolute and relative to the good.

Affection resembles an emotion but friendship resembles a moral state. For while affection may be felt for inanimate as much as for animate things, the love of friends for one another implies moral purpose, and such purpose is the outcome of a moral state.

Again, we wish the good of those whom we love for their own sake, and the wish is governed not by emotion but by the moral state. In loving our friend too, we love what is good for ourselves; as when a good man becomes a friend, he becomes a blessing to his friend. Accordingly each of two friends loves what is good for himself, and returns as much as he receives in good wishes and in pleasure; for, as the proverb says, equality is friendship.

These conditions then are best realized in the friendship or love of the good. Among austere and elderly people friendship arises less easily, as they are more peevish and less fond of society; for it is social intercourse which seems to be the principal element and cause of friendship. Thus it is that the young form friendships quickly, but old people do not, as they do not make friends with any body who is not delightful to them, nor do austere people. Such people, it is true, wish each other well; they desire each other's good, and render each other services; but they are not really friends, as they do not satisfy the principal condition of friendship by living together and delighting in each other's society.

It is as impossible to be friends with a number of people in the perfect sense of friendship, as it is to be in love with a number of people at the same time; for perfect friendship is in some sense an excess, and such excess of feeling is natural towards an individual, but it is not easy for a number of people to give intense pleasure to the same person at the same time, or, I may say, to be good at all. Friendship too implies experience and familiarity, which are very difficult. But it is possible to find a number of people who are pleasant, as affording profit or pleasure; for people of this kind are numerous and their services do not occupy much time.

Among such people the friendship which is based upon pleasure more nearly resembles true friendship, when each party renders the same services to the other, and they are delighted with each other or with the same things, as e.g. in the friendships of the young; for a liberal spirit is especially characteristic of these friendships.

The friendship which rests upon utility is commercial in its character. Fortunate people do not want what is useful but what is pleasant. They want people to live with; and although for a short time they may bear pain, nobody would endure it continuously; nobody would endure the good itself continuously, if it were painful to him. Hence it is that they require their friends to be pleasant. They ought perhaps to require them also to be good, and not only so, but good in relation to themselves; for then they will have all the qualities which friends ought to have.

It appears that people in positions of authority make a distinction between their friends. Some are useful to them, and others are pleasant, but the same people are not in general both useful and pleasant. For they do not look for friends who are virtuous as well as pleasant, or who will help them to attain noble ends; they look partly for amusing people when they want to be pleased, and partly for people who are clever at executing their commands, and these qualities are hardly ever united in the same person.

It has been stated that a virtuous man is at once pleasant and useful; but such a man does not become the friend of one who is superior to him, unless he is himself superior to that person in virtue. Otherwise there is no such equality as occurs when his superiority in virtue is proportionate to his inferiority in some other respect. Friendships of this kind however are exceedingly rare.

The friendships which have been described are based upon equality; for the services and sentiments of the two friends to one another are the same, or they exchange one thing for another, e.g. pleasure for profit. It has been already stated that friendships depending on exchange are less true and less permanent than others. As being at once similar and dissimilar to the same thing, such friendships may be said both to be and not to be friendships. They look like friendships in respect of similarity to the friendship which depends upon virtue; for the one possesses pleasure, the other utility, and these are characteristics of virtuous friendships as well. But as virtuous friendship is undisturbed by calumnies, and is permanent, while these are quickly changed, and as there are many other differences between them, it seems that their dissimilarity to virtuous friendship makes them look as if they were not friendships at all.

There is another kind of friendship or love depending upon superiority, e.g. the friendship or love of a father for a son, or of any elder person for a younger, or of a husband for a wife, or of a ruler for a subject. These friendships are of different sorts; for the friendship or love of parents for children is not the same as that of rulers for subjects, nor indeed is the friendship or love of a father for a son the same as that of a son for a father, nor that of a husband for his wife the same as that of a wife for her husband. For in each of these there is a different virtue and a different function, and there are different motives; hence the affections and friendships are also different. It follows that the services rendered by each party to the other in these friendships are not the same, nor is it right to expect that they should be the same; but when children render to parents what is due to the authors of their being, and parents to children what is due to them, then such friendships are permanent and virtuous.

In all such friendships as depend upon the principle of superiority, the affection should be proportionate to the superiority; i.e. the better or the more useful party, or whoever may be the superior, should receive more affection than he gives; for it is when the affection is proportionate to the merit that a sort of equality is established, and this equality seems to be a condition of friendship.

But it is apparently not the same with equality in justice as with equality in friendship. In justice it is proportionate equality which is the first consideration, and quantitative equality which is the second, but in friendship quantitative equality is first and proportionate second. This is clearly seen to be the case, if there be a wide distinction between two persons in respect of virtue, vice, affluence, or anything else. For persons so widely different cease to be friends; they do not even affect to be friends. But it is nowhere so conspicuous as in the case of the Gods; for the Gods enjoy the greatest superiority in all good things. It is clear too in the case of kings; for people who are greatly inferior to them do not expect to be their friends. Nor again do worthless people expect to be the friends of the best or wisest of mankind. No doubt in such cases it is impossible to define exactly the point up to which friendship may be carried; it may suffer many deductions and yet continue, but where there is a great distinction, as between God and man, it ceases to be.

This is a fact which has given rise to the question whether it is true that friends do really wish the greatest good of their friends, e.g. whether they wish them to be Gods; for then they will lose them as friends, and will therefore lose what are goods, as friends are goods.

That being so, if it has been rightly said that a friend wishes his friend's good for the friend's sake, it will be necessary that the friend should remain such as he is. He will wish his friend the greatest good as a man. And yet perhaps he will not wish him every good, as every one wishes good in the highest sense to himself.

It seems that ambition makes most people wish to be loved rather than to love others. That is the reason why most people are fond of flatterers; for a flatterer is an inferior friend, or pretends to be so, and to give more love than he receives. But to be loved seems to approximate to being honoured, and honour is a general object of desire. Not that people, as it appears, desire honour for its own sake, they desire it only accidentally; for it is hope which causes most people to delight in the honours paid them by persons of high position, as they think they will obtain from them whatever they may want, and therefore delight in honour as a symbol of prosperity *in the future*. But they who aspire to gain honour from persons of high character and wide information are eager to confirm their own opinion of themselves; they delight therefore in a sense of their own goodness, having confidence in the judgment so expressed upon it. But people delight in being loved for their own sake. Hence it would seem to follow that it is better to be loved than to be honoured, and that friendship or love is desirable in itself.

But friendship seems to consist rather in loving than in being loved. It may be seen to be so by the delight which mothers have in loving; for mothers sometimes give their own children to be brought up by others, and although they know them and love them, do not look for love in return, if it be impossible both to love and to be loved, but are content, as it seems, to see their children doing well, and to give them their love, even if the children in their ignorance do not render them any such service as is a mother's due.

As friendship consists in loving rather than in being loved, and people who are fond of their friends receive praise, it is in some sense a virtue of friends to love; hence where love is found in due proportion, people are permanent friends, and their friendship is permanent.

It is in this way that, even where people are unequal, they may be friends, as they will be equalized. But equality and similarity constitute friendship, especially the similarity of the virtuous; for the virtuous, being exempt from change in themselves, remain unchanged also in relation to one another, and neither ask others to do wrong nor do wrong themselves to please others. It may even be said that they prevent it; for good people neither do wrong themselves nor allow their friends to do it.

But there is no stability in vicious friends; for they do not remain like themselves, and if they become friends it is only for a short time, and from the gratification which they feel in each other's vice.

But if people are useful and pleasant to each other, they remain friends for a longer time, i.e. they remain friends so long as they afford each other pleasure or assistance.

The friendship which is based upon utility seems more than any other to be an union of opposites. It is e.g. such friendship as arises between a poor man and a rich man, or between an ignorant man and a well informed man; for if a man happens to be in want of something, his desire to get it makes him give something else in exchange. We may perhaps include a lover and his beloved, or a beautiful man and an ugly man, in this class of friends. It is thus that lovers sometimes make themselves look ridiculous by expecting to be loved as much as they love others. Such an expectation would perhaps be reasonable if they were equally lovable; but if there is nothing lovable about them, it is ridiculous. It is true, I think, that one opposite does not desire another in itself, but desires it only accidentally. What it really longs for is the mean, as the mean is a good. Thus it is good for what is dry not to become wet, but to arrive at the mean state, and similarly for what is hot, and so on.

But we may dismiss these questions as being more or less foreign to our present purpose.

It appears, as has been said at the outset, that friendship and justice have the same occasions and the same sphere; for every association seems to involve justice of some kind, and friendship as well. At all events we address our fellow-sailors and fellow-soldiers, and similarly the members of any other association to which we belong, as friends. The friendship too is coextensive with the association, for so also is the justice. The proverbial saying, "Friends' goods are common goods" is right, as friendship depends upon association.

Brothers and comrades have all things in common. Other people have certain definite things in common, some more, some fewer; for some friendships go further than others. Justice too is of different kinds; it is not the same in the relation of parents to children as in that of brothers to each other, or in that of comrades and fellow citizens to each other, and similarly in other friendships. Injustice too assumes various forms in relation to these several classes. It is aggravating, if the friends whom it affects are nearer to each other. Thus it is a more dreadful thing to defraud a comrade of money than to defraud a fellow citizen, or to refuse help to a brother than to a stranger, or to assault a father than any body else.

Justice itself too naturally grows as friendship grows; for they have the same sphere and are equally extensive.

All associations are, as it were, parts of the political association; for when people take a journey together, it is from motives of interest and for the sake of gaining something that their life requires. It seems too that interest was the motive with which the political association was originally formed, and with which it is continued; for this is the goal which legislators have in view, and they describe the interest of the community as just.

Now all other associations aim at some particular interest or success. Thus sailors aim at a successful voyage in the hope of making money or something of the kind, fellow-soldiers in an army at a successful campaign, whether it be spoil or victory or the capture of a city that is their aim, and it is much the same with members of a tribe or township. It seems too that some associations are formed on a basis of pleasure, as when people associate for a fête or a picnic; for there the object is sacrifice and good fellowship. But these are all, as it were, subordinate to the political association; for the aim of the political association is the interest not of the moment but of all a life-time, in the sacrifices which people make and the meetings which they hold in connexion with the sacrifices, in the honours which they pay to the gods, and the pleasure and relaxation which they provide for themselves. For it appears that the ancient sacrifices and meetings take place after the ingathering of the fruits of the earth, e.g. the festival of the first-fruits, these having been the seasons of the greatest leisure.

It appears then that all these associations are parts of the political association, and the proper friendships will correspond to the associations.

There are three kinds of polity and an equal number of perversions, or in other words corruptions, of these three kinds. The polities are kingship, aristocracy, and a third depending upon a property qualification, which it seems proper to describe as timocratic, but it is usually designated as a polity *in the limited sense.* Of these, kingship is the best and timocracy the worst.

The perversion of kingship is tyranny, both being monarchies although they are widely different, as the tyrant considers his own interest, and the king the interest of his subjects; for a king is not a king unless he is self-sufficient and superior to his subjects in all that is good; but if he is such, there is nothing more that he needs. Hence he will consider not his own interest but the interest of his subjects; for if he were not a king after this fashion, he would be a sort of king of the ballot.

Tyranny is the opposite of kingship, as it pursues the good of the tyrant himself. *It is clear that kingship is the best form of polity; but* it is still clearer that tyranny is the worst. The opposite of the best is always worst.

A polity changes from kingship to tyranny; for tyranny is a vicious form of monarchy. Accordingly the vicious king becomes a tyrant.

An aristocracy is converted into an oligarchy through the fault of the ruling class who make an unfair distribution of political honours, who reserve all or nearly all the good things for themselves, and who keep the offices of state continually in the same hands, from the inordinate value that they set upon wealth. The result is that it is only a few people who hold office, and they are not the most virtuous, but wicked people.

A timocracy is converted into a democracy; for they border closely upon each other, as timocracy professes to have a democratic character, and all who possess the requisite property qualification are equals in a timocracy.

Of the perversions democracy is the least vicious, as it departs but slightly from the character of the polity.

These are the ways in which polities are most easily transferred; for these are the least violent transformations.

It is possible to discover models, and so to say patterns, of these constitutions in households. For the association of a father with his sons takes the form of a kingship, as a father cares for his children. It is this care which makes Homer speak of Zeus as "father"; for kingship purports to be a parental rule. But in Persia the rule of the father is tyrannical; for there parents treat their sons as slaves. The association of master and slave is also tyrannical, as it is the master's interest which is realized in it. Now the rule of a slave-master seems to be a right [1] form of tyranny, but the rule of a father in Persia seems to be a perverted form, as different people require to be ruled in different ways.

The association of husband and wife seems to be aristocratical; for the husband's rule depends upon merit, and is confined to its proper sphere. He assigns to the wife all that suitably belongs to her. If the husband is lord of everything, he changes the association to an oligarchy; for then he acts unfairly, and not in virtue of his superior merit.

Sometimes again the wife rules, as being an heiress. Such rule is not based upon merit, but depends upon wealth or power as in oligarchies.

The association of brothers resembles a timocracy; for they are equals except so for as they differ in years; hence if the difference of years is very great, the friendship ceases to be fraternal.

A democracy is chiefly found in such households as have no master, where everybody is equal to everybody else, or where the head of the house is weak, and everybody can do as he chooses.

Now it appears that there is a friendship or love which is proper to each of these several polities in the same degree as there is a justice proper to each.

The friendship or love of a king to his subjects takes the form of superiority in benefaction. He treats his subjects well, as being good, and as caring for their welfare, like a shepherd for the welfare of his flock, whence Homer called Agamemnon "'shepherd of the folk.''

The love of a father for his child is similar in character, although it differs in the magnitude of the benefactions; for a father is the author of the child's existence, which seems to be the greatest of all benefactions, as well as of his nurture and education. These benefactions are ascribed also to ancestors, and it is Nature's law that a father should rule his sons, and ancestors their descendants, and a king his subjects.

These friendships imply superiority; hence parents are not

---

[1] Aristotle believes in a natural class of slaves. Cp. *Politics* i. ch. 5.

only loved but honoured, as being superiors. Justice therefore in these cases implies not identical but proportionate treatment; for so too does friendship.

The friendship or love of husband and wife is the same as exists in an aristocracy; for it depends upon virtue. The better party gets the greater good, and each gets what befits him or her, but this is equally the rule of justice.

The friendship of brothers is like the friendship of comrades; for they are equals and are persons of the same age, and when this is the case, people are generally alike in their feelings and characters. We may compare with this the friendship or love which is characteristic of a timocracy; for in a timocracy the citizens profess to be equal and virtuous; hence they hold office in turn and upon a principle of equality, and accordingly their friendship follows the same law.

But in the perverted forms of polity justice does not go far, neither does friendship, and nowhere is its range so limited as in the worst of them. Friendship does not exist, or hardly exists, in a tyranny; for where there is nothing in common between ruler and subject, there cannot be friendship between them, as there cannot be justice either. The relation is like that of an artisan to a tool, or of soul to body, or of master to servant; for although all these are benefited by the people who use them, there is no possibility of friendship or justice in the relation in which we stand to inanimate things nor indeed in our relation to a horse or an ox or to a slave *qua* slave. For there is nothing in common between a master and his slave; the slave is an animate instrument, and the instrument an inanimate slave. It is impossible therefore to be friends with a slave *qua* slave, but not with a slave *qua* man, for there would seem to be a possibility of justice between every man and any one who is capable of participation in law and covenant, and therefore in friendship, in so far as he is man.

Friendships therefore and justice exist only to a slight extent in tyrannies and have only a narrow range. Their range is widest in democracies, as it is when people are equals that they have most in common. . . .

Book X

It is natural, I think, to discuss pleasure next; for it seems that there is, in a preeminent degree, an affinity between pleasure and our human nature, and that is the reason why, in the education of the young, we steer their course by the rudders of pleasure and pain. It seems too that there is no more important element in the formation of a virtuous character than a rightly directed sense of pleasure and dislike; for pleasure and pain are coextensive with life, and they exercise a powerful influence in promoting virtue and happiness of life, as we choose what is pleasant and avoid what is painful.

Considering, then, the importance of these questions, it would seem to be clearly a duty not to pass them over, especially as they admit of much dispute. For some people say that the good is pleasure; others, on the contrary, that pleasure is something utterly bad, whether, as is possible, they are convinced that it really is so, or they think it better in the interest of human life to represent pleasure as an evil, even if it is not so, feeling that men are generally inclined to pleasure, and are the slaves of their pleasures, and that it is a duty therefore to lead them in the contrary direction, as they will so arrive at the mean *or proper* state.

But I venture to think that this is not a right statement of the case. For in matters of the emotions and actions theories are not so trustworthy as facts; and thus, when theories disagree with the facts of perception, they fall into contempt, and involve the truth itself in their destruction. For if a person censures pleasure and yet is seen at times to make pleasure his aim, he is thought to incline to pleasure as being entirely desirable; for it is beyond the power of ordinary people to make distinctions. It seems then the true theories are exceedingly useful, not only as the means of knowledge but as guides of life; for as being in harmony with facts, they are believed, and being believed they encourage people who understand them to regulate their lives in accordance with them.

Enough then of such considerations; let us review the various doctrines of pleasure.

Eudoxus held that pleasure was the good, because he saw that all things, whether rational or irrational, make pleasure their aim.

He argued that in all cases that which is desirable is good, and that which is most desirable is most good; and hence the fact of all things being drawn to the same object is an indication that that object is the best for all, as everything discovers what is good for itself in the same way as it discovers food; but that that which is good for all, and is the aim of all, is the good.

His theories were accepted, not so much for their intrinsic value as for the excellence of his moral character; for he was regarded as a person of exemplary temperance. It seemed then that he did not put forward these views as being a votary of pleasure, but that the truth was really as he said. He held that this truth resulted with equal clearness from a consideration of the opposite *of pleasure;* for as pain is something which everybody should avoid, so too its opposite is something which everybody should desire. He argued that a thing is in the highest degree desirable, if we do not desire it for any ulterior reason, or with any ulterior motive, and this is admittedly the case with pleasure; for if a person is pleased, nobody asks the further question, What is his motive in being pleased? a fact which proves that pleasure is desirable in itself. And further that the addition of pleasure to any good, e.g. to just or temperate conduct, renders that good more desirable, and it follows that if the good is augmented by a thing, that thing must itself be a good.

It seems then that this argument proves pleasure to be a good, but not to be a good in a higher sense than anything else; for any good whatever is more desirable with the addition of another good than when it stands alone. It is by a precisely similar argument that Plato tries to prove that pleasure is not the good. Pleasure (he says) is not the chief good, for the pleasant life is more desirable with the addition of prudence than without it; but if the combination is better, pleasure is not the good, as the good itself cannot be made more desirable by any addition.

But it is clear that, *if pleasure is not the good,* neither can anything else be which is made more desirable by the addition of any absolute good. What is it then which is incapable of such addition, but at the same time admits of our participating in it? For it is a good of this kind which is the object of our research.

People who argue on the other hand that that which all things aim at is not a good may be said to talk nonsense; for we accept the universal opinion as true, and one who upsets our trust in the universal opinion will find it hard to put forward any opinion that is more trustworthy. If it were only unintelligent beings that longed for pleasure, there would be something in what he says; but if intelligent beings also long for it, how can it be so? It is probable that even in the lower creatures there is some natural principle which is superior to the creatures themselves, and aims at their proper good.

Nor does it seem that these people fairly meet the argument drawn from the opposite of pleasure. They say it does not follow that, if pain is an evil, pleasure is a good, as not only is one evil opposed to another, but both are opposed to that which is neither one nor the other, *but a neutral state.* This is true enough, but it does not apply to pleasure and pain. For if both pleasure and pain were evil, it would have been a duty to avoid both, and if neither were evil, it would have been a duty not to avoid either, or not to avoid one more than the other; whereas in fact it is clear that people avoid one as an evil, and desire the other as a good. It follows then that pleasure and pain are opposed to each other as good and evil.

Nor again does it follow that, if pleasure is not a quality, neither is it a good, for the activities of virtue are not qualities, nor is happiness.

It is argued too that good is definite, but pleasure is indefinite, as it admits of degrees.

Now if the ground of this opinion is that it is possible to be pleased *in a greater or a less degree,* the same thing is true of justice and the other virtues. For here it is evident that we speak of persons as possessing the several virtues in a greater or less degree; some people are just and courageous in a greater *or less* degree than others, and it is possible to act with a greater or less degree of justice and temperance.

If however the meaning is that the indefiniteness resides in the pleasures, this is, I think, not the true explanation, supposing that some pleasures are mixed and others unmixed.

Again, health is definite, yet it admits of degrees; and why should it not be so with pleasure? For health is not the same symmetry or proportion of elements in all people, nor is it always uniform in the same person; it admits of relaxation up to a certain point, and of different degrees, without ceasing to be health. Something of the same kind then may be also true of pleasure.

Again, *the opponents of pleasure,* looking upon the good as perfect or complete, and the processes of movement and production as imperfect or incomplete, try to prove that pleasure is motion or production. But they are wrong, I think, nor is pleasure a motion at all. For quickness and slowness are characteristic, it seems, of every motion, either absolutely, as of the motion of the universe, or else relatively, but neither of them is a condition inherent in pleasure. It is possible to *become* pleased, as it is to *become* angry, quickly, but not to *be* pleased quickly or relatively, *i.e. in comparison with somebody else,* as it is to walk or to grow quickly and so on. The transition then, to a state of pleasure may be quick or slow, but the active experience of pleasure, i.e. the state of being pleased, cannot be quick.

In what sense, too, can pleasure be a process of production? It is apparently not the case that anything can be produced out of anything; it is the case that a thing is resolved into that out of which it is produced. Also, pain is the destruction of that of which pleasure is the production. It is said too that pain is a deficiency of the natural state, and pleasure its satisfaction. But this deficiency and this satisfaction are emotions of the body. If, then, pleasure is a satisfaction of the natural state, it follows that the part which is the seat of the satisfaction will feel pleasure i.e. the body. But this seems not to be the case. We conclude therefore that pleasure is not a satisfaction of the natural state, although one may feel pleasure while the process of satisfaction is going on, as he may feel pain while undergoing an operation.

This view of pleasure, *viz. that it is a process of satisfaction,* seems to have originated in the pleasures and pains of eating and drinking, as in them we first feel a deficiency and an antecedent pain, and then feel pleasure at the satisfaction. But this is not true of all pleasures; the pleasures of mathematics e.g. have no such antecedent pain, nor among the pleasures of the senses have those of the smell, nor again many sound and sights, memories and hopes. What is there then of which these will be processes of production? For in them there has been no deficiency to be satisfied.

But if the instance of immoral pleasures be adduced *to prove that pleasure is a bad thing,* we may answer that these are not really pleasant. They may be pleasant to people who are in a bad condition, but it must not be inferred that they are pleasant except to such people, any more than that things are healthful or sweet or bitter in themselves, because they are so to invalids, or that things are white, because they appear so to people who are suffering from ophthalmia.

Perhaps the truth may be stated thus: Pleasures are desirable, but not if they are immoral in their origin, just as wealth is pleasant, but not if it be obtained at the cost of turning traitor to one's country, or health, but not at the cost of eating any food, however disagreeable. Or it may be said that pleasures are of different kinds, those which are noble in their origin are different from those which are dishonourable, and it is impossible to enjoy the pleasure of the just man without being just, or that of the musician without being musical, and so on. The distinction drawn between a friend and a flatterer seems to bring out clearly the truth that pleasure is not a good, or that there are pleasures of different kinds; for it seems that while the object of the friend in social intercourse is good, that of the flatterer is pleasure, and while the flatterer is censured, the friend for his disinterestedness is praised.

Again, nobody would choose to live all his life with the mind of a child, although he should enjoy the pleasures of childhood to the utmost, or to delight in doing what is utterly shameful, although he were never to suffer pain for doing it. There are many things too upon which we should set our hearts, even if they brought no pleasure with them, e.g. sight, memory, knowledge, and the possession of the virtues; and if it be true that these are necessarily attended by pleasures, it is immaterial, as we should desire them even if no pleasure resulted from them. It seems to be clear then that pleasure is not the good, nor is every pleasure desirable, and that there are some pleasures which are desirable in themselves, and they differ in kind or in origin from the others.

We may regard this as a sufficient account of such views as are held in regard to pleasure and pain.

But the nature or character of pleasure will be more clearly seen, if we resume our argument from the beginning.

It seems that the act of sight is perfect or complete at any time; it does not lack anything which will afterwards be produced, and will make it perfect of its kind. Pleasure appears to resemble sight in this respect; it is a whole, nor is it possible at any time to find a pleasure which will be made perfect of its kind by increased duration.

It follows that pleasure is not a motion; for every motion takes a certain time, and aims at a certain end. Thus the builder's art is perfect or complete when it has accomplished its object. It is complete, either in respect of the whole time which the building took, or in respect of the moment *when it was completed*. But in the various parts of the time the various processes or motions are imperfect and different in kind from the whole and from one another; for the setting of the stones is different from the fluting of the pillar, and both from the building of the temple *as a whole,* and whereas the building of the temple is complete, nothing being wanting to the object proposed, that of the basement and the triglyph is incomplete, as each is only the building of a part of the temple. These processes or motions are therefore different in kind, and it is impossible at any time *when the building is going on* to find a motion which is complete or perfect of its kind. Such a motion, if found at all, will be found only in the whole time.

It is much the same with walking or any other process. For here again, although all locomotion is a motion from one place to another, there are different kinds of locomotion, such as flying, walking, jumping, and the like. And not only so, but walking itself is of different kinds; for the starting-point and the goal are not the same in the whole course, and in a part of it, or in one part of the course and in another; nor is it the same thing to cross one line as to cross another; for it is not only that a person crosses a line, but the line which he crosses is in a certain place, and one line is in a different place from another.

The subject of motion has been accurately discussed in another treatise. Motion is apparently not complete in any and every period of time; on the contrary, most motions are incomplete and different in kind, inasmuch as the starting-point and the goal constitute a difference of kind. Pleasure on the other hand seems to be complete or perfect of its kind in any and every period of time.

It is clear then that motion and pleasure must be distinct from one another, and that pleasure is something which is whole and perfect.

Another reason for holding this view is that motion is impossible except in a period of time, but pleasure is not; for the pleasure of a moment is a whole.

It is clear from these considerations that pleasure is not rightly described as a motion or process of production, for such a description is not appropriate to all things but only to such as are divisible into parts and are not wholes. For there is no process of production in an act of sight or in a mathematical point or in a unit, nor is any one of these things a motion or a process of production. It follows that there is no such process in pleasure, as it is a whole.

Again, every sense exercises its activity upon its own object, and the activity is perfect only when the sense itself is in a sound condition, and the object is the noblest that falls within the domain of that sense; for this seems to be preeminently the character of the perfect activity. We may say that it makes no difference whether we speak of the sense itself or of the organ in which it resides as exercising the activity; in every instance the activity is highest when the part which acts is in the best condition, and the object upon which it acts is the highest of the objects which fall within its domain. Such an activity will not only be the most perfect, but the most pleasant; for there is pleasure in all sensation, and similarly in all thought and speculation, and the activity will be pleasantest when it is most perfect, and it will be most perfect when it is the activity of the part being in a sound condition and acting upon the most excellent of the objects that fall within its domain.

Pleasure perfects the activity, but not in the same way in which the excellence of the sense or of the object of sense perfects it, just as health is the cause of our being in a healthy state in one sense and the doctor is the cause of it in another.

It is clear that every sense has its proper pleasure; for we speak of pleasant sights, pleasant sounds and so on. It is clear too that the pleasure is greatest when the sense is best, and its object is best; but if the sentient subject and the sensible object are at their best, there will always be pleasure so long as there is a subject to act and an object to be acted upon.

When it is said that pleasure perfects the activity, it is not as a state *or quality* inherent in the subject but as a perfection superadded to it, like the bloom of youth to people in the prime of life.

So long then as the object of thought or sensation and the critical or contemplative subject are such as they ought to be, there will be pleasure in the exercise of the activity; for this is the natural result if the agent and the patient remain in the same relation to each other.

It may be asked then, How is it that nobody feels pleasure continuously? It is probably because we grow weary. Human beings are incapable of continuous activity, and as the activity comes to an end, so does the pleasure; for it is a concomitant of the activity. It is for the same reason that some things give pleasure when they are new, but give less pleasure afterwards; for the intelligence is called into play at first, and applies itself to its object with intense activity, as when we look a person full in the face *in order to recognize him,* but afterwards the activity ceases to be so intense and becomes remiss, and consequently the pleasure also fades away.

It may be supposed that everybody desires pleasure, for everybody clings to life. But life is a species of activity and a person's activity displays itself in the sphere and with the means which are after his own heart. Thus a musician exercises his ears in listening to music, a student his intellect in speculation, and so on.

But pleasure perfects the activities; it therefore perfects life, which is the aim of human desire. It is reasonable then to aim at pleasure, as it perfects life in each of us, and life is an object of desire.

Whether we desire life for the sake of pleasure or pleasure for the sake of life, is a question which may be dismissed for the moment. For it appears that pleasure and life are yoked together and do not admit of separation, as pleasure is impossible without activity and every activity is perfected by pleasure.

If this be so, it seems to follow that pleasures are of different kinds, as we hold that things which are different in kind are perfected by things which are themselves different in kind. For this is apparently the rule in the works of nature or of art, e.g. animals, trees, pictures, statues, a house, or a piece of furniture. Similarly we hold that energies which are different in kind are perfected by things which are also different in kind.

Now the pleasures of the intellect are different from the pleasures of the senses, and these again are different in kind from one another. It follows that the pleasures which perfect them will also be different.

This conclusion would appear also to result from the intimate connexion of each pleasure with the activity which it perfects. For the activity is increased by its proper pleasure, as if the activity is pleasant, we are more likely to arrive at a true judgment or an accurate result in any matter. It is so e.g. with people who are fond of geometry; they make better geometricians and understand the various problems of geometry better than other people. It is so too with people who are fond of music or architecture or any other subject; their progress in their particular subject is due to the pleasure which they take in it. Pleasure helps to increase activity, and that which helps to increase a thing must be closely connected with it. Where things then are different in kind, the things which are closely connected with them will also be different in kind.

This becomes still clearer when we observe that the pleasures which spring from one activity are impediments to the exercise of another. Thus people who are fond of the flute are incapable of attending to an argument, if they hear somebody playing the flute, as they take a greater pleasure in flute-playing than in the activity which they are called to exercise at the moment; hence the pleasure of the flute-playing destroys their argumentative activity. Much the same result occurs in other cases, when a person exercises his activity on two subjects simultaneously; the pleasanter of the two drives out the other, especially if it be much the pleasanter, until the activity of the other disappears. Accordingly, if we take intense delight in anything, we cannot do anything else at all. It is only when we do not care much for a thing that we do something else as well, just as people who eat sweetmeats in the theatres do so most when the actors are bad.

As the pleasure then which is proper to an activity refines it and gives it greater permanence and excellence, while alien pleasures impair it, it is clear that there is a wide difference between these pleasures. It may almost be said that the pleasures which are alien to it have the same effect as the pains which are proper to it; for the pains which are proper to an activity destroy it, as, when a person finds writing or thinking unpleasant and painful, he does not write or does not think, as the case may be.

The pleasures and pains then which are proper to an activity have opposite effects upon it. I mean by "proper" such as are the consequences of the activity *per se*. But it has been already stated that alien pleasures have much the same effect as pain; they are destructive of the activity, although not destructive of it in the same way.

Again, as the activities differ in goodness and badness, some being desirable, some undesirable, and some neither the one nor the other, so it is with pleasures, as every activity has its proper pleasure. Thus the pleasure which is proper to a virtuous activity is good, and that which is proper to a low activity is vicious. For the desires of what is noble are themselves laudable, the desires of what is disgraceful are censurable; but the pleasures which reside in the activities are more strictly proper to them than the desires, as the latter are distinct from the activities in time and nature, but the former are closely related in time to the activities, and are so difficult to distinguish from them that it is a question whether the activity is identical with the pleasure.

It seems however that pleasure is not the same thing as thought or sensation; it would be strange if it were so; but the impossibility of separating them makes some people regard them as the same.

As the activities then are different, so are the pleasures. Sight is different from or superior to touch in purity, hearing and smell are superior to taste; there is a corresponding difference therefore in their pleasures. The pleasures of the intellect too are different from or superior to these, and there are different kinds of pleasures of the senses or of the intellect. It seems that there is a pleasure, as there is a function, which is proper to every living thing, *viz.* the pleasure inherent in its activity. If we consider individual living things, we see this is so; for the pleasures of a horse, a dog, and a man are different, and as Heraclitus says, "a donkey would choose a bundle of hay in preference to gold; for fodder is pleasanter to donkeys than gold."

As the pleasures then of beings who are different in kind are themselves different in kind, it would be reasonable to suppose that there is no difference between the pleasures of the same beings. But there is a wide difference, at least in the case of men; the same things give pleasure to some people and pain to others, to some they are painful and hateful, to others pleasant and lovable. This is true of sweet things; the same things do not seem sweet to a person in a fever and to a person in good health, nor does the same thing seem hot to an invalid and to a person in a good physical condition. It is much the same with other things as well.

But in all these cases it seems that the thing really is what it appears to the virtuous man to be. But if this is a true statement of the case, as it seems to be, if virtue or the good man *qua* good is the measure of everything, it follows that it is such pleasures as appear pleasures to the good man that are really pleasures, and the things which afford him delight that are really pleasant. It is no wonder if what he finds disagreeable seems pleasant to somebody else, as men are liable to many corruptions and defilements; but such things are not pleasant except to these people, and to them only when they are in this condition.

It is clear then that we must not speak of pleasures which are admitted to be disgraceful as pleasures, except in relation to people who are thoroughly corrupt. But the question remains, Among such pleasures as are seen to be good, what is the character or nature of the pleasures that deserve to be called the *proper* pleasures of Man? It is plain, I think, from a consideration of the activities; for the activities bring pleasures in their train. Whether then there is one activity or there are several belonging to the perfect and fortunate man, it is the pleasures which perfect these activities that would be strictly described as the *proper* pleasures of Man. All other pleasures are only in a secondary or fractional sense the pleasures of Man, as are all other activities.

After this discussion of the kinds of virtue and friendship and pleasures it remains to give a sketch of happiness, since we defined happiness as the end of human things. We shall shorten our account of it if we begin by recapitulating our previous remarks.

We said that happiness is not a moral state; for, if it were, it would be predicable of one who spends his whole life in sleep, living the life of a vegetable, or of one who is utterly miserable. If then we cannot accept this view if we must rather define happiness as an activity of some kind, as has been said before, and if activities are either necessary and desirable as a means to something else or desirable in themselves, it is clear that we must define happiness as belonging to the class of activities which are desirable in themselves, and not desirable as means to something else; for happiness has no want, it is self-sufficient.

Again, activities are desirable in themselves, if nothing is expected from them beyond the activity. This seems to be the case with virtuous actions, as the practice of what is noble and virtuous is a thing desirable in itself. It seems to be the case also with such amusements as are pleasant, we do not desire them as means to other things; for they often do us harm rather than good by making us careless about our person and our property. Such pastimes are generally the resources of those whom the world calls happy. Accordingly people who are clever at such pastimes are generally popular in the courts of despots, as they make themselves pleasant to the despot in the matters which are the objects of his desire, and what he wants is to pass the time pleasantly.

The reason why these things are regarded as elements of happiness is that people who occupy high positions devote their leisure to them. But such people are not, I think, a criterion. For a high position is no guarantee of virtue or intellect, which are the sources on which virtuous activities depend. And if these people, who have never tasted a pure and liberal pleasure, have recourse to the pleasures of the body, it must not be inferred that these pleasures are preferable; for even children suppose that such things as are valued or honoured among them are best. It is only reasonable then that, as men and children differ in their estimate of what is honourable, so should good and bad people.

As has been frequently said, therefore, it is the things which are honourable and pleasant to the virtuous man that are really honourable and pleasant. But everybody feels the activity which accords with his own moral state to be most desirable, and accordingly the virtuous man regards the activity in accordance with virtue as most desirable.

Happiness then does not consist in amusement. It would be paradoxical to hold that the end of human life is amusement, and that we should toil and suffer all our life for the sake of amusing ourselves. For we may be said to desire all things as means to something else except indeed happiness, as happiness is the end *or perfect state.*

It appears to be foolish and utterly childish to take serious trouble and pains for the sake of amusement. But to amuse oneself with a view to being serious seems to be right, as Anacharsis says; for amusement is a kind of relaxation, and it is because we cannot work for ever that we need relaxation.

Relaxation then is not an end. We enjoy it as a means to activity; but it seems that the happy life is a life of virtue, and such a
life is serious, it is not one of mere amusement. We speak of
serious things too *(for serious things are virtuous)* as better than
things which are ridiculous and amusing, and of the activity of the
better part of man's being or of the better man as always the more
virtuous. But the activity of that which is better is necessarily
higher and happier. Anybody can enjoy bodily pleasures, a slave
can enjoy them as much as the best of men; but nobody would
allow that a slave is capable of happiness unless he is capable of
life; for happiness consists not in such pastimes as I have been
speaking of, but in virtuous activities, as has been already said.

If happiness consists in virtuous activity, it is only reasonable to
suppose that it is the activity of the highest virtue, or in other
words, of the best part of our nature. Whether it is the reason or
something else which seems to exercise rule and authority by a
natural right, and to have a conception of things noble and divine,
either as being itself divine or as relatively the most divine part of
our being, it is the activity of this part in accordance with its
proper virtue which will be the perfect happiness.

It has been already stated that it is a speculative activity, *i.e. an
activity which takes the form of contemplation.* This is a conclusion which would seem to agree with our previous arguments and
with the truth itself; for the speculative is the highest activity,
as the intuitive reason is the highest of our faculties, and the
objects with which the intuitive reason is concerned are the highest of things that can be known. It is also the most continuous;
for our speculation can more easily be continuous than any
kind of action. We consider too that pleasure is an essential element of happiness, and it is admitted that there is no virtuous
activity so pleasant as the activity of wisdom or philosophic reflexion; at all events it appears that philosophy possesses pleasures
of wonderful purity and certainty, and it is reasonable to suppose
that people who possess knowledge pass their time more pleasantly
than people who are seekers after truth.

Self-sufficiency too, as it is called, is preeminently a characteristic
of the speculative activity; for the wise man, the just man, and all
others, need the necessaries of life; but when they are adequately
provided with these things, the just man needs people to whom

and with whom he may do justice, so do the temperate man, the courageous man and everyone else; but the wise man is capable of speculation by himself, and the wiser he is, the more capable he is of such speculation. It is perhaps better for him in his speculation to have fellow-workers; but nevertheless he is in the highest degree self-sufficient.

It would seem too that the speculative is the only activity which is loved for its own sake as it has no result except speculation, whereas from all moral actions we gain something more or less besides the action itself.

Again, happiness, it seems, requires leisure; for the object of our business is leisure, as the object of war is the enjoyment of peace. Now the activity of the practical virtues is displayed in politics or war, and actions of this sort seem incompatible with leisure. This is absolutely true of military actions, as nobody desires war, or prepares to go to war, for its own sake. A person would be regarded as absolutely bloodthirsty if he were to make enemies of his friends for the mere sake of fighting and bloodshed. But the activity of the statesman too is incompatible with leisure. It aims at securing something beyond and apart from politics, *viz.* the power and honour or at least the happiness of the statesman himself and his fellow citizens, which is different from the political activity and is proved to be different by our search for it *as something distinct*.

If then political and military actions are preeminent among virtuous actions in beauty and grandeur, if they are incompatible with leisure and aim at some end, and are not desired for their own sakes, if the activity of the intuitive reason seems to be superior in seriousness as being speculative, and not to aim at any end beyond itself, and to have its proper pleasure, and if this pleasure enhances the activity, it follows that such self-sufficiency and power of leisure and absence of fatigue as are possible to a man and all the other attributes of felicity are found to be realized in this activity. This then will be the perfect happiness of Man, if a perfect length of life is given it, for there is no imperfection in happiness. But such a life will be too good for Man. He will enjoy such a life not in virtue of his humanity but in virtue of some divine element within him, and the superiority of this activity to the activity of any other virtue will be proportionate to the superiority of this divine element in man to his composite *or material* nature.

If then the reason is divine in comparison with *the rest of* Man's nature, the life which accords with reason will be divine in comparison with human life in general. Nor is it right to follow the advice of people who say that the thoughts of men should not be too high for humanity or the thoughts of mortals too high for mortality; for a man, as far as in him lies, should seek immortality and do all that is in his power to live in accordance with the highest part of his nature, as, although that part is insignificant in size, yet in power and honour it is far superior to all the rest.

It would seem too that this is the true self of everyone, if a man's true self is his supreme or better part. It would be absurd then that a man should desire not the life which is properly his own but the life which properly belongs to some other being. The remark already made will be appropriate here. It is what is proper to everyone that is in its nature best and pleasantest for him. It is the life which accords with reason then that will be best and pleasantest for Man, as a man's reason is in the highest sense himself. This will therefore be also the happiest life.

It is only in a secondary sense that the life which accords with other, *i.e. non-speculative,* virtue can be said to be happy; for the activities of such virtue are human, *they have no divine element.* Our just or courageous actions or our virtuous actions of any kind we perform in relation to one another, when we observe the law of propriety in contracts and mutual services and the various moral actions and in our emotions. But all these actions appear to be human affairs. It seems too that moral virtue is in some respects actually the result of physical organization and is in many respects closely associated with the emotions. Again, prudence is indissolubly linked to moral virtue, and moral virtue to prudence, since the principles of prudence are determined by the moral virtues, and moral rectitude is determined by prudence. But the moral virtues, as being inseparably united with the emotions, must have to do with the composite *or material* part *of our nature,* and the virtues of the composite part *of our nature* are human, *and not divine,* virtues. So too therefore is the life which accords with these virtues; so too is the happiness *which accords with them.*

But the happiness *which consists in the exercise* of the reason is separated *from these emotions.* It must be enough to say so much about it; for to discuss it in detail would take us beyond our present purpose. It would seem too to require external resources only to a small extent or to a less extent than moral virtue. It may be granted that both will require the necessaries of life and will require them equally, even if the politician devotes more trouble to his body and his bodily welfare than the philosopher; for the difference will not be important. But there will be a great difference in respect of their activities. The liberal man will want money for the practice of liberality, and the just man for the requital of services which have been done him; for our wishes, *unless they are manifested in actions,* must always be obscure, and even people who are not just pretend that it is their wish to act justly. The courageous man too will want physical strength if he is to perform any virtuous action, and the temperate man liberty, as otherwise it will be impossible for him or for anybody else to show his character.

But if the question be asked whether it is the purpose or the performance that is the surer determinant of virtue, as virtue implies both, it is clear that both are necessary to perfection. But action requires various conditions, and the greater and nobler the action, the more numerous will the conditions be.

In speculation on the other hand there is no need of such conditions, at least for its activity; it may rather be said that they are actual impediments to speculation. It is as a human being and as living in society that a person chooses to perform virtuous actions. Such conditions then will be requisite if he is to live as a man.

That perfect happiness is a species of speculative activity will appear from the following consideration among others. Our conception of the Gods is that they are preeminently happy and fortunate. But what kind of actions do we properly attribute to them? Are they just actions? But it would make the Gods ridiculous to suppose that they form contracts, restore deposits, and so on. Are they then courageous actions? Do the Gods endure dangers and alarms for the sake of honour? Or liberal actions? But to whom should they give money? It would be absurd to suppose that they have a currency or anything of the kind. Again, what will be the nature of their temperate actions? Surely to praise the gods for temperance is to degrade them; they are exempt from low desires.

We may go through the whole category of virtues, and it will appear that whatever relates to moral action is petty and unworthy of the Gods.

Yet the Gods are universally conceived as living and therefore as displaying activity; they are certainly not conceived as sleeping like Endymion. If then action and still more production is denied to one who is alive, what is left but speculation? It follows that the activity of God being preeminently blissful will be speculative, and if so then the human activity which is most nearly related to it will be most capable of happiness.

It is an evidence of this truth that the other animals, as being perfectly destitute of such activity, do not participate in happiness; for while the whole life of the Gods is fortunate or blessed, the life of men is blessed in so far as it possesses a certain resemblance to their speculative activity. But no other animal is happy, as no other animal participates at all in speculation.

We conclude then that happiness is coextensive with speculation, and that the greater a person's power of speculation, the greater will be his happiness, not as an accidental fact but in virtue of the speculation, as speculation is honourable in itself. Hence happiness must be a kind of speculation.

Man, as being human, will require external prosperity. His nature is not of itself sufficient for speculation, it needs bodily health, food, and care of every kind. It must not however be supposed that, because it is impossible to be fortunate without external goods, a great variety of such goods will be necessary to happiness. For neither self-sufficiency nor moral action consists in excess; it is possible to do noble deeds without being lord of land and sea, as moderate means will enable a person to act in accordance with virtue. We may clearly see that it is so; for it seems that private persons practise virtue not less but actually more than persons in high place. It is enough that such a person should possess as much as is requisite for virtue; his life will be happy if he lives in the active exercise of virtue. Solon was right perhaps in his description of the happy man as one "who is moderately supplied with external goods, and yet has performed the noblest actions,"—such was his opinion—"and had lived a temperate life," for it is possible to do one's duty with only moderate means. It seems too that Anaxagoras did not conceive of the happy man as possessing wealth or power when he said that he should not be surprised if the happy man proved a puzzle in the eyes of the world; for the world judges by externals alone, it has no perception of anything that is not external.

The opinions of philosophers then seem to agree with our theories. Such opinions, it is true, possess a sort of authority; but it is the facts of life that are the tests of truth in practical matters, as they possess a supreme authority. It is right then to consider the doctrines which have been already advanced in reference to the facts of life, to accept them if they harmonize with those facts, and to regard them as mere theories if they disagree with them.

Again, he whose activity is directed by reason and who cultivates reason, and is in the best, *i.e. the most rational,* state of mind is also, as it seems, the most beloved of the Gods. For if the Gods care at all for human things, as is believed, it will be only reasonable to hold that they delight in what is best and most related to themselves, i.e. in reason, and that they requite with kindness those who love and honour it above all else, as caring for what is dear to themselves and performing right and noble actions.

It is easy to see that these conditions are found preeminently in the wise man. He will therefore be most beloved of the Gods. We may fairly suppose to that he is most happy; and if so, this is another reason for thinking that the wise man is preeminently happy.

Supposing then that our sketch of these subjects and of the virtues, and of friendship too, and pleasure, has been adequate, are we to regard our object as achieved? Or are we to say in the old phrase that in practical matters the end is not speculation and knowledge but action? It is not enough to know the nature of virtue; we must endeavour to possess it, and to exercise it, and to use whatever other means are necessary for becoming good.

Now, if theories were sufficient of themselves to make men good, they would deserve to receive any number of handsome rewards, as Theognis said, and it would have been our duty to provide them. But it appears in fact that, although they are strong enough to encourage and stimulate youths who are already liberally minded, although they are capable of bringing a soul which is generous and enamoured of nobleness under the spell of virtue, they are impotent to inspire the mass of men to chivalrous action; for it is not the nature of such men to obey honour but terror, nor to abstain from evil for fear of disgrace but for fear of punishment. For, as their life is one of emotion, they pursue their proper pleasures and the means of gaining these pleasures, and eschew the pains which are opposite to them. But of what is noble and truly pleasant they have not so much as a conception, because they have never tasted it. Where is the theory or argument which can reform such people as these? It is difficult to change by argument the settled features of character. We must be content perhaps if, when we possess all the means by which we are thought to become virtuous, we gain some share of virtue.

Some people think that men are made good by nature, others by habit, others again by teaching.

Now it is clear that the gift of Nature is not in our own power, but is bestowed through some divine providence upon those who are truly fortunate. It is probably true also that reason and teaching are not universally efficacious; the soul of the pupil must first have been cultivated by habit to a right spirit of pleasure and aversion, like the earth that is to nourish the seed. For he whose life is governed by emotion would not listen to the dissuasive voice of reason, or even comprehend it, and if this is his state, how is it possible to convert him? Emotion, it seems, never submits to reason but only to force. It is necessary then to presuppose a character which is in a sense akin to virtue, which loves what is noble and dislikes what is dishonourable. But it is difficult for one to receive from his early days a right inclination to virtue, unless he is brought up under virtuous laws; for a life of temperance and steadfastness is not pleasant to most people, least of all to the young. It follows that the nurture and pursuits *of the young* should be regulated by law, as they will not be painful, if he becomes used to them.

But it is not enough, I think, that we should receive a right nurture and control in youth; we must practise what is right and get the habit of doing it when we have come to man's estate. We shall need laws then to teach us what is right, and so to teach us all the duty of life; for most people are moved by necessity rather than by reason, and by the fear of punishment rather than by the love of nobleness.

Accordingly it is sometimes held that legislators should on the one hand invite and exhort men to pursue virtue because it is so noble, as they who have been already trained in virtue will pay heed to them, and on the other hand, if they are disobedient and degenerate, should inflict punishments and chastisements on them and utterly expel them, if they are incurable; for so the good man who lives by the rule of honour will obey reason, and the bad man whose aim is pleasure must be chastened by pain like a beast of burden. Hence too it is said that the pains ought to be such as are most opposed to a person's favourite pleasures.

If then, as has been said, he who is to be a good man should receive a noble nurture and training and then should live accordingly in virtuous pursuits and never voluntarily or involuntarily do evil, this result will only be attained if we live, so to say, in accordance with reason and right order resting upon force.

Now the authority of a father does not possess such force or compulsion, nor indeed does that of any individual, unless he is a king or some such person. But the law has a compulsory power, as being itself in a sense the outcome of prudence and reason; and whereas we hate people who oppose our inclinations, even if they are right in so doing, we do not feel the law to be grievous in its insistence upon virtue.

It is only in the state of Lacedaemon and a few other states that the legislator seems to have undertaken to control the nurture and pursuits of the citizens. In the great majority of states there is an absolute neglect of such matters, and everybody lives as he chooses, "being lawgiver of wife and children" like the Cyclops.

It is best then that the state should undertake the control of these matters and should exercise it rightly and should have the power of giving effect to its control. But if the state altogether neglects it, it would seem to be the duty of every citizen to further the cause of virtue in his own children and friends, or at least to set before himself the purpose of furthering it. It would seem too from what has been said that he will be best able to do this, if he has learnt the principles of legislation; for the control of the state is clearly exercised through the form of laws, and is good if the laws are virtuous. Whether they are written or unwritten laws, and whether they are suited to the education of an individual or of a number of people is apparently a matter of indifference, as it is in music or gymnastic or other studies. For as in a state it is law and custom which are supreme, so in a household it is the paternal

precepts and customs, and all the more because of the father's relationship to the members of his family, and of the benefits which
he has conferred upon them; for the members of a family are naturally affectionate and obedient to the father from the first.

Again, there is a superiority in the individual as against the general methods of education; it is much the same as in medicine
where, although it is the general rule that a feverish patient needs
to be kept quiet and to take no food, there may perhaps be some
exceptions. Nor does a teacher of boxing teach all his pupils to
box in the same style.

It would seem then that a study of individual character is the
best way of perfecting the education of the individual, as then
everyone has a better chance of receiving such treatment as is suitable. Still the individual case may best be treated, whether in
medicine or in gymnastic or in any other subject, by one who
knows the general rule applicable to all people or to people of a
particular kind; for the sciences are said to deal, and do deal, with
general laws. At the same time there is no reason why even without
scientific knowledge a person should not be successful in treating
a particular case if he has made an accurate, although empirical,
observation of the results which follow from a particular course of
treatment, as there are some doctors who seem to be excellent doctors in their own cases, although they would be unable to relieve
anybody else.

Nevertheless if a person wishes to succeed in art or speculation,
it is, I think, his duty to proceed to a universal principle and to
make himself acquainted with it as far as possible; for sciences, as
has been said, deal with universals. Also it is the duty of any one
who wishes to elevate people, whether they be few or many, by his
treatment, to try to learn the principles of legislation, if it is laws
that are the natural means of making us good. So in education it
is not everybody—it is at the most only the man of science—who
can create a noble disposition in all who come to him as patients,
as it is in medicine or in any other art which demands care and
prudence.

Is it not then our next step to consider the sources and means of
learning the principles of legislation? It may be thought that here
as elsewhere we must look *to the persons who practise the principles, i.e.* to statesmen; for legislation, as we saw, is apparently a

branch of politics. But there is this difference between politics and all other sciences and faculties. In these it is the same people who are found to teach the faculties and to make practical use of them, e.g. doctors and painters; whereas in politics it is the sophists who profess to teach, but it is never they who practise. The practical people are the active statesmen who would seem to be guided in practical life by a kind of faculty or experience rather than by intelligence; for we see that they never write or speak on these subjects, although it is perhaps a nobler task than the composition of forensic or parliamentary speeches, nor have they ever made their own sons or any other people whom they care for into statesmen. Yet it might be expected that they should do so, if it were in their power, for they could not have bequeathed any better legacy to their state, nor is there anything which they would have preferred for themselves or their dearest friends to such a faculty. Still it must be admitted that experience does much good; otherwise people could not be made statesmen by familiarity with politics. It follows that, if people desire to understand politics, they need experience as well as theory.

These sophists however who are lavish in their professions appear to be far from teaching *statesmanship;* in fact they are absolutely ignorant of the sphere or nature of statesmanship. If it were not so they would not have made statesmanship identical with, or inferior to, rhetoric; they would not have thought it easy work to form a legislative code by merely collecting such laws as are held in high repute; they would not have supposed that all they have to do is to make a selection of the best laws, as if the selection itself did not demand intelligence, and as if a right judgment were not a thing of the greatest difficulty in legislation no less than in music. For it is only such persons as possess experience of particular arts who can form a correct judgment of artistic works, and understand the means and manner of executing them, and the harmony of particular combinations. Inexperienced persons on the other hand are only too glad if they are alive to the fact that a work has been well or badly executed, as in painting. But laws are like the artistic works of political science. How then should *a mere collection of* laws make a person capable of legislating, or of deciding upon the best laws? It does not appear that *the study* of medical books makes people good doctors; yet medical books affect not only to state methods of treatment, but to state the way of curing people, and the proper method of treating particular cases by classifying the various states of health. But all this, although it seems useful to the experienced, is useless to those who are ignorant of medical science. It may be supposed then that collections of laws and polities would be useful to those who are capable of considering and deciding what is right or wrong, and what is suitable to particular cases; but if people who examine such questions have not *the proper* frame of mind, they will find it impossible to form a right judgment unless indeed by accident, although they may gain a more intelligent appreciation of them.

As previous writers have failed to investigate the subject of legislation, it will perhaps be better to examine it ourselves, and indeed to examine the whole subject of politics, in order that the philosophy of human life may be made as complete as possible.

Let us try then, first of all, to recount such particular opinions as have been rightly expressed by our predecessors, then, in view of the polities which we have collected, to consider the preservatives and destructives of states and of particular polities, and the reasons why some polities are good and others bad. For when we have considered these, it will perhaps be easier to see what kind of polity is best, and what is the best way of ordering it and what are its laws and customs.

Augustine

Augustine

AUGUSTINE is at once one of the first great Christian philosophers and one of the first great philosophers of Christianity. Himself a convert to Christianity, after his conversion he used his pagan learning and particularly his knowledge of the *Enneads* of the Neo-Platonist, Plotinus, as an intellectual instrument and structure to amplify and certify faith, codify doctrine and consolidate the institution of the Church. The terms in which Augustine defined his own faith and by intention that of all Christians, served also to define the chief issues in philosophy for hundreds of years and some of them up to the present day. In formulating the grounds and implications of his belief in God, Augustine found it necessary to treat the relations of time and eternity, of will and intellect, of mind and its objects, of nature and history, of creation and destiny.

Augustine was primarily interested in formulating the Christian faith, its grounds and its consequences, and the way in which that faith was itself the ground of all consequences. But in so doing he found himself involved in the analysis of those principles of knowledge and being which faith itself implied. These principles, subtly and extensively expounded, constitute a philosophy no less philosophical than Christian, an ultimate theory of being, of morals, of knowledge, and of history. In teaching, as he attempts to do in the *Enchiridion* and in the *De Trinitate,* the elements of Christian piety, Augustine broaches the fundamental questions of metaphysics, moral theory and the theory of knowledge. He thus becomes as important in the history of the European mind as in the history of Christian piety.

It is not without importance to an understanding of the intellectual conclusions to which he arrived, to examine Augustine's intellectual origins. He was born in 354 at Carthage, son of a pagan father and a Christian mother. He had the education of a Roman intellectual, not least in the philosophy of the Stoics and the Neo-Platonists. It is furthermore of significance that for many years Augustine was a teacher of rhetoric and that before the end of his life he was a Bishop. His philosophy, as it appears especially in his *Confessions* and in the *City of God,* is stated as a man of letters would state it, and his interest is always partly that of an administrator and "doctor" of the Church. It must also always be remembered that Augustine was a mystical convert to the faith he taught, and the whole moral and intellectual apparatus of his analysis is aimed to provide an instrument for arriving at a serene but intense union with God, a consummation transcending the very intellectual activity which was the necessary way to it.

Augustine tells us with rather proud humility of the profligacies and ambitions which marked his life prior to his conversion. Revulsion from carnality, worldliness and intellectual arrogance he pictures as having led him to Christianity, a revulsion abetted by the prayers of his mother, hastened by the touching death of a Christian friend and the exemplary saintliness of the Christian Bishop Ambrose. But it was his training in, as well as his reaction against, pagan doctrines that determined the philosophical character of his faith after his conversion. For one thing, Augustine's Christianity was a *doctrine,* something to be taught and something, he thought, that might be learned. It was knowledge and the object of that knowledge was God.

Augustine's primary and ultimate concern was salvation. But the problem of salvation in a profound, and not merely a technical, sense was a problem of knowledge. For the soul's felicity lay in knowing God. How was God to be known? God gave the light by which he was known, but to know God one must first believe in him. Adequate knowledge is belief fulfilled.

God as an object of knowledge is Truth revealed and Being known. One must believe in order to know God. But to know, as Augustine had learned from Plotinus, was an intellectual activity. It was the activity of mind beholding authentic being, not the deceptive images revealed through the senses. Knowledge consisted in the beholding of Intelligibles by Intelligence. The Source of Intelligibility was the Perfect Being of God, who was also the source of that light (vouchsafed to man by grace) by virtue of which Perfect Being could come to be known in its transcendent glory. God himself transcends rational distinctions, but has his rational character revealed in the person of His Son in whom is conceived the realm of Platonic ideas. This realm serves as the exemplar and pattern of the universe. The sensible world is an image of this Divine Logos, and it is through this Logos that the sensible world is created. Augustine gives a Neo-Platonic interpretation to the Trinity. God the Father is the One, the Logos is the Son, and the Spirit is the World Soul, or Intelligibility become incarnate, Intelligibility revealed in the image that is the world.

All knowledge is ultimately knowledge of God, which God makes possible as an inner illumination of the soul. The soul, in knowing, implicitly knows God. By gradual steps it is led to know fully its own source, God, in immediate, direct and full vision. It is set on this path by faith. The stages are stages in fullness of Being. Perfect knowledge is a mystical plenitude of vision. It is salvation—perfect knowing and perfect peace.

Such felicity is not only the goal of the intellect but of the will. "Increase of wisdom and virtue go hand in hand." Insofar as man lives in the pursuit of the knowledge of God and in the pursuit of union of his will with that of God, he is already in spirit in the City of God, the mystical and unanimous society of saints in Heaven and members of the believing Church on earth. Those who by faith and knowledge, by will and intellect, by sacramental identification, are one with God are members of that earthly manifestation of the City of God, the Church of God.

No small part of Augustine's writings are concerned with an examination of the soul's gradual path to God. Beginning with the soul's certainty of itself (here he anticipated Descartes), its own thinking reveals the certainty of God's existence and the character of God's being. But the individual path of the soul to God is one instance of what occurs in all believers and one instance of what occurs universally in history. For if knowledge culminates in salvation, divine history culminates in it, too, and accounts for it. There are two cities, one temporal, the other eternal. The City of God is eternal. It is in essence the union of those who timelessly behold God's Being and are one with it. The temporal city is the City of Man, the heritage of Adam's original sin. All earthly nature and civilization is the fruit of original sin and its consequences in generation after generation of sin and death. There was a historical moment when God's Son, Himself eternal, took temporal and human form and died to the flesh, that man might be saved, that his will might be redirected, his intellect turned to God. The Church is the society of those living by faith and eventually to live in fullness as members of God; they are those who are saved to eternal life, risen with the risen Christ.

Augustine died as Bishop of Hippo. The good Bishop had determined the direction, not only of Christian faith, but of Western thought. Every philosopher, including those without Augustine's concern for salvation through Christ, had thenceforward to reckon with his analysis of time and eternity, nature and history, existence and destiny, knowl-

edge and faith, intellect and will. Augustine naturalized
Plotinus in Christian thought, and in thus Platonizing Christianity, made the terms of Neo-Platonism the intellectual
instruments, and its issues part of the intellectual problems,
of all future European philosophy. And whenever thinking
lights upon the relation of time to eternity, of things to ideas,
Augustine's analysis will seem perennially relevant.

Enchiridion[1]

W HAT ought to be man's chief end in life; what he ought, in view of the various heresies, chiefly to avoid; to what extent religion is supported by reason; what there is in reason that lends no support to faith, when faith stands alone; what is the starting-point, what the goal, of religion; what is the sum of the whole body of doctrine; what is the sure and proper foundation of the catholic faith. Now, undoubtedly, you will know the answers to all these questions, if you know thoroughly the proper objects of faith, hope, and love. For these must be the chief, nay, the exclusive objects of pursuit in religion. He who speaks against these is either a total stranger to the name of Christ, or is a heretic. These are to be defended by reason, which must have its starting-point either in the bodily senses or in the intuitions of the mind. And what we have neither had experience of through our bodily senses, nor have been able to reach through the intellect, must undoubtedly be believed on the testimony of those witnesses by whom the Scriptures, justly called divine, were written; and who by divine assistance were enabled, either through bodily sense or intellectual perception, to see or to foresee the things in question.

Moreover, when the mind has been imbued with the first elements of that faith which worketh by love, it endeavors by purity of life to attain unto sight, where the pure and perfect in heart know that unspeakable beauty, the full vision of which is supreme happiness. Here surely is an answer to your question as to what is the starting-point, and what the goal: we begin in faith, and are made perfect by sight. This also is the sum of the whole body of doctrine. But the sure and proper foundation of the catholic faith is Christ. "For other foundation," says the apostle, "can no man lay than that is laid, which is Jesus Christ." (I Cor. iii, 11.) . . .

. . . Faith believes, hope and love pray. But without faith the

[1] Selections from Chapters 4-12.

two last cannot exist, and wherefore we may say that faith also prays. Whence it is written: "How shall they call on Him in whom they have not believed?"

Again, can anything be hoped for which is not an object of faith? It is true that a thing which is not an object of hope may be believed. What true Christian, for example, does not believe in the punishment of the wicked? And yet such an one does not hope for it. And the man who believes that punishment to be hanging over himself, and who shrinks in horror from the prospect, is more properly said to fear than to hope. And these two states of mind the poet carefully distinguishes, when he says: "Permit the fearful to have hope." (Lucan, *Phars*. ii, 15.) Another poet, who is usually much superior to this one, makes a wrong use of the word, when he says: "If I have been able to hope for so great a grief as this." (Virgil, *Aeneid*, iv, 419.) And some grammarians take this case as an example of impropriety of speech, saying, "He said *sperare* (to hope) instead of *timere* (to fear)." Accordingly, faith may have for its object evil as well as good; for both good and evil are believed, and the faith that believes them is not evil, but good. Faith, moreover, is concerned with the past, the present, and the future, all three. We believe, for example, that Christ died,—an event in the past; we believe that He is sitting at the right hand of God,—a state of things which is present; we believe that He will come to judge the quick and the dead,—an event of the future. Again, faith applies both to one's own circumstances and those of others. Every one, for example, believes that his own existence had a beginning, and was not eternal, and he believes the same both of other men and other things. Many of our beliefs in regard to religious matters, again, have reference not merely to other men, but to angels also. But hope has for its object only what is good, only what is future, and only what affects the man who entertains the hope. For these reasons, then faith must be distinguished from hope, not merely as a matter of verbal propriety, but because they are essentially different. The fact that we do not see either what we believe or what we hope for, is all that is common to faith and hope. In the Epistle to the Hebrews, for example, faith is defined (and eminent defenders of the catholic faith have used the definition as a standard) "the evidence of things not seen." (Heb. xi, 1.) Although, should any one say that he believes, that is, has grounded his faith, not on words, nor on witnesses, nor on any reasoning whatever, but on the direct evidence of his own senses, he would not be guilty of such an impropriety of speech as to be justly liable to the criticism, "You saw, therefore you did not believe." And hence it does not follow that an object of faith is not an object of sight. But it is better that we should use the word "faith" as the Scriptures have taught us, applying it to those things which are not seen. Concerning hope, again, the apostle says: "Hope that is seen is not hope; for what a man seeth, why does he yet hope for? But if we hope for that we see not, then do we with patience wait for it." (Rom. viii, 24, 25.) When, then, we believe that good is about to come, this is nothing else but to hope for it. Now what shall I say of love? Without it faith profits nothing; and in its absence, hope cannot exist. The Apostle James says: "The devils also believe, and tremble." (Jas. ii, 19)—that is, they, having neither hope nor love, but believing that what we love and hope for is about to come, are in terror. And so the Apostle Paul approves and commends the "faith that worketh by love"; (Gal. v, 6.) and this certainly cannot exist without hope. Wherefore there is no love without hope, no hope without love, and neither love nor hope without faith.

When, then, the question is asked what we are to believe in regard to religion, it is not necessary to probe into the nature of things, as was done by those whom the Greeks call *physici;* nor need we be in alarm lest the Christian should be ignorant of the force and number of the elements,—the motion, and order, and eclipses of the heavenly bodies; the form of the heavens; the species and the natures of animals, plants, stones, fountains, rivers, mountains; about chronology and distances; the signs of coming storms; and a thousand other things which those philosophers either have found out, or think they have found out. For even these men themselves, endowed though they are with so much genius, burning with zeal, abounding in leisure, tracking some things by the aid of human conjecture, searching into others with the aids of history and experience, have not found out all things; and even their boasted discoveries are oftener mere guesses than certain knowledge. It is enough for the Christian to believe that the only cause of all created things, whether heavenly or earthly, whether visible or invisible, is the goodness of the creator, the one true God; and

that nothing exists but Himself that does not derive its existence
from Him; and that He is the Trinity—to wit, the Father, and the
Son begotten of the Father, and the Holy Spirit proceeding from
the same Father, but one and the same Spirit of Father and Son.

By the Trinity, thus supremely and equally and unchangeably
good, all things were created; and these are not supremely and
equally and unchangeably good, but yet they are good, even taken
separately. Taken as a whole, however, they are very good, because
their *ensemble* constitutes the universe in all its wonderful order
and beauty.

And in the universe, even that which is called evil, when it is
regulated and put in its own place, only enhances our admiration
of the good; for we enjoy and value the good more when we compare it with the evil. For the Almighty God, who, as even the
heathen acknowledge, has supreme power over all things, being
Himself supremely good, would never permit the existence of
anything evil among His works, if He were not so omnipotent and
good that he can bring good even out of evil. For what is that
which we call evil but the absence of good? In the bodies of animals, disease and wounds mean nothing but the absence of health;
for when a cure is effected, that does not mean that the evils which
were present—namely, the diseases and wounds—go away from the
body and dwell elsewhere: they altogether cease to exist; for the
wound or disease is not a substance, but a defect in the fleshly substance,—the flesh itself being a substance, and therefore something
good, of which those evils—that is, privations of the good which
we call health—are accidents. Just in the same way, what are called
vices in the soul are nothing but privations of natural good. And
when they are cured, they are not transferred elsewhere; when
they cease to exist in the healthy soul, they cannot exist anywhere
else.

All things that exist, therefore, seeing that the Creator of them
all is supremely good, are themselves good. But because they are
not, like their Creator, supremely and unchangeably good, their
good may be diminished and increased. But for good to be diminished is an evil, although, however much it may be diminished, it
is necessary, if the being is to continue, that some good should
remain to constitute the being. For however small or of whatever
kind the being may be, the good which makes it a being cannot be

destroyed without destroying the being itself. An uncorrupted nature is justly held in esteem. But if, still further, it be incorruptible, it is undoubtedly considered of still higher value. When it is corrupted, however, its corruption is an evil, because it is deprived of some sort of good. For if it be deprived of no good, it receives no injury; but it does receive injury, therefore it is deprived of good. Therefore, so long as a being is in process of corruption, there is in it some good of which it is being deprived; and if a part of the being should remain which cannot be corrupted, this will certainly be an incorruptible being, and accordingly the process of corruption will result in the manifestation of this great good. But if it do not cease to be corrupted, neither can it cease to possess good of which corruption may deprive it. But if it should be thoroughly and completely consumed by corruption, there will then be no good left, because there will be no being. Wherefore corruption can consume the good only by consuming the being. Every being, therefore, is a good; a great good, if it can not be corrupted; a little good, if it can: but in any case, only the foolish or ignorant will deny that it is a good. And if it be wholly consumed by corruption, then the corruption itself must cease to exist, as there is no being left in which it can dwell.

The City of God

X:1] IT IS the decided opinion of all who use their brains, that all men desire to be happy. But who are happy, or how they become so, these are question about which the weakness of human understanding stirs endless and angry controversies, in which philosophers have wasted their strength and expended their leisure. To adduce and discuss their various opinion would be tedious, and is unnecessary. . . . For we made selection of the Platonists, justly esteemed the noblest of the philosophers, because they had the wit to perceive that the human soul, immortal and rational, or intellectual, as it is, cannot be happy except by partaking of the light of that God by whom both itself and the world were made; and also that the happy life which all men desire cannot be reached by any who does not cleave with a pure and holy love to that one supreme god, the unchangeable God. . . .

2] But with these more estimable philosophers we have no dispute in this matter. For, they perceived, and in various forms abundantly expressed in their writings, that these spirits have the same source of happiness as ourselves,—a certain intelligible light, which is their God, and is different from themselves, and illumines them that they may be penetrated with light, and enjoy perfect happiness in the participation of God. Plotinus, commenting on Plato, repeatedly and strongly asserts that not even the soul which they believe to be the soul of the world, derives its blessedness from any other source than we do, viz., from that light which is distinct from it and created it, and by whose intelligible illumination it enjoys light in things intelligible. He also compares those spiritual things to the vast and conspicuous heavenly bodies, as if God were the sun, and the soul the moon; for they suppose that the moon derives its light from the sun. That great Platonist, therefore, says that the rational soul, or rather the intellectual soul,—in which class he comprehends the souls of the blessed immortals who inhabit heaven,—has no nature superior to it save God, the Creator of the world and the soul itself, and that these heavenly spirits derive their blessed life, and the light of truth, from the same source as ourselves. . . .

12] . . . For we cannot listen to those who maintain that the invisible God works no visible miracles; for even they believe that he made the world, which surely they will not deny to be visible. Whatever marvel happens in this world, it is certainly less marvelous than this whole world itself,—I mean the sky and earth, and all that is in them,—and these God certainly made. But, as the Creator Himself is hidden and incomprehensible to man, so also is the manner of creation. Although, therefore, the standing miracle of this visible world is little thought of, because always before us, yet, when we arouse ourselves to contemplate it, it is a greater miracle than the rarest and most unheard-of marvels. For man himself is a greater miracle than any miracle done through his instrumentality. Therefore God, who made the visible heaven and earth, does not disdain to work visible miracles in heaven or earth, that He may thereby awaken the soul which is immersed in things visible to worship Himself, the Invisible. But the pace and time of these miracles are dependent on his unchangeable will, in which things future are ordered as if already they were accomplished. For he moves things temporal without Himself moving in time. He does not in one way know things that are to be, and, in another, things that have been; neither does He listen to those who pray otherwise than as He sees those that will pray. For, even when His angels hear us, it is He Himself who hears us in them, as in His true temple not made with hands, as in those men who are His saints; and His answers, though accomplished in time, have been arranged by His eternal appointment.

32] This is the religion which possesses the universal way for delivering the soul; for, except by this way, none can be delivered. This is a kind of royal way, which alone leads to a kingdom which does not totter like all temporal dignities, but stands firm on eternal foundations. And when Porphyry says, towards the end of the first book *De Regressu Animae,* that no system of doctrine which furnishes the universal way for delivering the soul has as yet been received, either from the truest philosophy, or from the ideas and practices of the Indians, or from the reasoning of the Chaldaeans, or from any source whatever, and that no historical reading had made him acquainted with that way, he manifestly acknowledges that there is such a way, but that as yet he was not acquainted with it. Nothing of all that he had so laboriously learned concerning the deliverance of the soul, nothing of all that he seemed to others, if not to himself, to know and believe, satisfied him. For he perceived that there was still wanting a commanding authority which it might be right to follow in a matter of such importance. And when he says that he had not learned from any truest philosophy a system which possessed the universal way of the soul's deliverance, he shows plainly enough, as it seems to me, either that the philosophy of which he was a disciple was not the truest, or that it did not comprehend such a way. And how can that be the truest philosophy which does not possess this way? For what else is the universal way of the soul's deliverance than that by which all souls universally are delivered, and without which, therefore, no soul is delivered? . . .

XI:1] The city of God we speak of is the same to which testimony is borne by that Scripture, which excels all the writing of all nations by its divine authority, and has brought under its influence all kinds of minds, and this not by a casual intellectual movement, but obviously by an express providential arrangement. . . .

2] It is a great and very rare thing for a man, after he has contemplated the whole creation, corporeal and incorporeal, and has discerned its mutability, to pass beyond it, and, by the continuing soaring of his mind, to attain to the unchangeable substance of God, and, in that height of contemplation, to learn from God Himself that none but He has made all that is not of the divine essence. For God speaks with a man not by means of some audible creature dinning in his ears, so that atmospheric vibrations connect Him that makes with him that hears the sound, nor even by means of a spiritual being, with the semblance of a body, such as we see in dreams or similar states; for even in this case He speaks as if to the ears of the body, because it is by means of the semblance of a body He speaks, and with the appearance of a real interval of space,—for visions are exact representations of bodily objects. Not by these, then, does God speak, but by the truth itself, if any one is prepared to hear with the mind rather than with the body. For He speaks to that part of man which is better than all else that is in him, and than which God Himself alone is better. For since man is most properly understood (or, if that cannot be, then, at least, *believed*) to be made in God's image, no doubt it is that part of him by which he rises above those lower parts he has in common with the beasts, which brings him nearer to the Supreme. But since the mind itself, though naturally capable of reason and intelligence, is disabled by besotting and inveterate vices not merely from delighting and abiding in, but even from tolerating His unchangeable light, until it has been gradually healed, and renewed, and made capable of such felicity, it had, in the first place, to be impregnated with faith, and so purified. And that in this faith it might advance the more confidently towards the truth, the truth itself, God, God's Son, assuming humanity without destroying His divinity, established and founded this faith, that there might be a way for man to man's God through a God-man. For this is the Mediator between God and men, the man Christ Jesus. For it is as man that He is the Mediator and the Way. Since, if the way lieth between him who goes, and the place whither he goes, there is hope of his reaching it; but if there be no way, or if he know not where it is, what boots it to know whither he should go. Now the only way that is infallibly secured against all mistakes, is when the very same person is at once God and man, God our end, and man our way.

41 Of all visible things, the world is the greatest; of all invisible, the greatest is God. But, that the world is, we see; that God is, we believe. That God made the world, we can believe from no one more safely than from God Himself. But where have we heard Him? Nowhere more distinctly than in the Holy Scriptures, where His prophet said, "In the beginning God created the heavens and the earth." (Gen. i, 1.) Was the prophet present when God made the heavens and the earth? No; but the wisdom of God, by whom all things were made, was there, and wisdom insinuates itself into holy souls, and makes them the friends of God and His prophets, and noiselessly informs them of His works. They are taught also by the angels of God, who always behold the face of the Father, and announce His will to whom it befits. Of these prophets was he who said and wrote, "In the beginning God created the heavens and the earth." And so fit a witness was he of God, that the same Spirit of God, who revealed these things to him, enabled him also so long before to predict that our faith also would be forthcoming.

But why did God choose then to create the heavens and earth which up to that time He had not made? If they who put this question wish to make out that the world is eternal and without beginning, and that consequently it has not been made by God, they are strangely deceived, and rave in the incurable madness of impiety. For, though the voices of the prophets were silent, the world itself, by its well-ordered changes and movement, and by the fair appearance of all visible things, bears testimony of its own, both that it has been created, and also that it could not have been created save by God, whose greatness and beauty are unutterable and invisible. As for those who own, indeed, that it was made by God, and yet ascribe to it not a temporal but only a creational beginning, so that in some scarcely intelligible way the world should always have existed a created world they make an assertion which seems to them to defend God from the charge of arbitrary hastiness, or of suddenly conceiving the idea of creating the world as a quite new idea, or of casually changing His will, though He be unchangeable. But I do not see how this supposition of theirs can stand in other respects, and chiefly in respect of the soul; for if they contend that it is co-eternal with God, they will be quite at a loss to explain when there has accrued to it a new misery, which through a previous eternity had not existed. For if they said that its happiness and misery ceaselessly alternate, they must say, further, that this alternation will continue for ever; whence will result this absurdity, that, though the soul is called blessed, it is not so in this, that it foresees its own misery and disgrace. And yet, if it does not foresee it, and supposes that it will be neither disgraced nor wretched, but always blessed, then it is blessed because it is deceived; and a more foolish statement one cannot make. But if their idea is that the soul's misery has alternated with its bliss during the ages of the past eternity, but that now, when once the soul has been set free, it will return henceforth no more to misery, they are nevertheless of the opinion that it has never been truly blessed before, but begins at last to enjoy a new and uncertain happiness; that is to say, they must acknowledge that some new thing, and that an important and signal thing, happens to the soul which never in a whole past eternity happened it before. And if they deny that God's eternal purpose included this new experience of the soul, they deny that He is the Author of its blessedness, which is unspeakable impiety. If, on the other hand, they say that the future blessedness of the soul is the result of a new decree of God, how will they show that God is not chargeable with that mutability which displeases them? Further, if they acknowledge that it was created in time, but will never perish in time,—that it has, like number, a beginning but no end, —and that, therefore, having once made trial of misery, and been delivered from it, it will never again return thereto, they will certainly admit that this takes place without any violation of the immutable counsel of God. Let them, then, in like manner believe regarding the world that it too could be made in time, and yet that God, in making it, did not alter His eternal design.

51 Next, we must see what reply can be made to those who agree that God is the Creator of the world, but have difficulties about the time of its creation, and what reply, also they can make to difficulties we might raise about the place of its creation. For, as they demand why the world was created then and no sooner, we may ask why it was created just here where it is, and not elsewhere. For if they imagine infinite spaces of time before the world, during which God could not have been idle, in like manner they may conceive outside the world infinite realms of space, in which if any one says that the Omnipotent cannot hold His hand from working, will it now follow that they must adopt Epicurus' dream of innumerable worlds? with this difference only, that he asserts that they are formed and destroyed by the fortuitous movements of atoms, while they will hold that they are made by God's hand, if they maintain that, through the boundless immensity of space, stretching interminably in every direction round the world, God cannot rest, and that the worlds which they suppose Him to make cannot be destroyed. For here the question is with those who, with ourselves, believe that God is spiritual, and the Creator of all existences but Himself. As for others, it is a condescension to dis-

pute with them on a religious question, for they have acquired a reputation only among men who pay divine honors to a number of gods, and have become conspicuous among the other philosophers for no other reason than that, though they are still far from the truth, they are near it in comparison with the rest. While these, then, neither confine in any place, nor limit, nor distribute the divine substance, but, as is worthy of God, own it to be wholly though spiritually present everywhere, will they perchance say that this substance is absent from such immense spaces outside the world, and is occupied in one only, (and that a very little one compared with the infinity beyond), the one, namely, in which is the world? I think they will not proceed to this absurdity. Since they maintain that there is but one world, of vast material bulk, indeed, yet finite, and in its own determinate position, and that this was made by the working of God, let them give the same account of God's resting in the infinite times before the world as they give of His resting in the infinite spaces outside of it. And as it does not follow that God set the world in the very spot it occupies and no other by accident rather than by divine reason, although no human reason can comprehend why it was so set, and though there was not merit in the spot chosen to give it the precedence of infinite others, so neither does it follow that we should suppose that God was guided by chance when He created the world in that and no earlier time, although previous times had been running by during an infinite past, and though there was no difference by which one time could be chosen in preference to another. But if they say that the thoughts of men are idle when they conceive infinite places, since there is no place beside the world, we reply that, by the same showing, it is vain to conceive of the past times of God's rest, since there is no time before the world.

6] For if eternity and time are rightly distinguished by this, that time does not exist without some movement and transition, while in eternity there is no change, who does not see that there could have been no time had not some creature been made, which by some motion could give birth to change,—the various parts of which motion and change, as they cannot be simultaneous, succeed one another,—and thus, in these shorter or longer intervals of duration, time would begin? Since then, God, in whose eternity is no change at all, is the Creator and Ordainer of time, I do not see how He can be said to have created the world after spaces of time had elapsed, unless it be said that prior to the world there was some creature by whose movement time could pass. And if the sacred and infallible Scriptures say that in the beginning God created the heavens and the earth, in order that it may be understood that He had made nothing previously,—for if He had made anything before the rest, this thing would rather be said to have been made "in the beginning,"—then assuredly the world was made, not in time, but simultaneously with time. For that which is made in time is made both after and before some time,—after that which is past, before that which is future. But none could then be past, for there was no creature by whose movements its duration could be measured. But simultaneously with time the world was made, if in the world's creation change and motion were created, as seems evident from the order of the first six or seven days. For in these days the morning and the evening are counted, until, on the sixth day, all things which God then made were finished, and on the seventh the rest of God was mysteriously and sublimely signalized. What kind of days these were it is extremely difficult, or perhaps impossible for us to conceive, and how much more to say!

21] For what else is to be understood by that invariable refrain, "And God saw that it was good," than the approval of the work in its design, which is the wisdom of God? For certainly God did not in the actual achievement of the work first learn that it was good, but, on the contrary, nothing would have been made had it not been first known by Him. While, therefore, He sees that that is good which, had He not seen it before it was made, would never have been made, it is plain that He is not discovering, but teaching that it is good. Plato, indeed, was bold enough to say that, when the universe was completed, God was, as it were, elated with joy. And Plato was not so foolish as to mean by this that God was rendered more blessed by the novelty of His creation; but he wished thus to indicate that the work now completed met with its Maker's approval, as it had while yet in design. It is not as if the knowledge of God were of various kinds, knowing in different ways things which as yet are not, things which are, and things which have been. For not in our fashion does He look forward to what is future, nor at what is present, nor back upon what is past; but in a manner quite different and far and profoundly remote from our way of thinking. For He does not pass from this to that by transition of thought, but beholds all things with absolute unchangeableness; so that of those things which emerge in time, the future, indeed, are not yet, and the present are now, and the past no longer are; but all of these are by Him comprehended in His stable and eternal presence. Neither does He see in one fashion by the eye, in another by the mind, for He is not composed of mind and body; nor does His present knowledge differ from that which it ever was or shall be, for those variations of time, past, present, and future, though they alter our knowledge, do not affect His, "with whom is no variableness, neither shadow of turning." (Jas. i, 17.) Neither is there any growth from thought to thought in the conceptions of Him in whose spiritual vision all things which He knows are at once embraced. For as without any movement that time can measure, He Himself moves all temporal things, so He knows all times and a knowledge that time cannot measure. And therefore He saw that what He had made was good, when He saw that it was good to make it. And when He saw it made, He had not on that account a twofold nor any way increased knowledge of it; as if He had less knowledge before He made what He saw. For certainly He would not be the perfect worker He is, unless His knowledge were so perfect as to receive no addition from His finished works. Wherefore, if the only object had been to inform us who made the light, it had been enough to say, "God made the light"; and if further information regarding the means by which it was made had been intended, it would have sufficed to say, "And God said, Let there be light, and there was light," that we might know not only that God had made the world, but also that He had made it by the word. But because it was right that three leading truths regarding the creature be intimated to us, viz., who made it, by what means, and why, it is written, "God said, Let there be light, and there was light. And God saw the light that it was good." If, then, we ask who made it, it was "God." If, by what means, He said "Let it be," and it was. If we ask, why He made it, "it was good." Neither is there any author more

excellent than God, nor any skill more efficacious than the word
of God, nor any cause better than that good might be created by
the good God. This also Plato has assigned as the most sufficient
reason for the creation of the world, that good works might be
made by a good God; whether he read this passage, or, perhaps,
was informed of these things by those who had read them, or, by
his quick-sighted genius, penetrated to things spiritual and invisible through the things that are created, or was instructed regarding them by those who had discerned them.

221 This cause, however, of a good creation, namely, the goodness
of God,—this cause, I say, so just and fit, which when piously and
carefully weighed, terminates all the controversies of those who
inquire into the origin of the world, has not been recognized by
some heretics, because there are, forsooth, many things, such as
fire, frost, wild beast, and so forth, which do not suit but injure
this thin-blooded and frail mortality of our flesh, which is at
present under just punishment. They do not consider how admirable these things are in their own places, how excellent in their
own natures, how beautifully adjusted to the rest of creation, and
how much grace they contribute to the universe by their own
contributions as to a commonwealth; and how serviceable they
are even to ourselves, if we use them with a knowledge of their fit
adaptations,—so that even poisons, which are destructive when
used injudiciously, become wholesome and medicinal when used
in conformity with their qualities and design; just as, on the other
hand, those things which give us pleasure, such as food, drink, and
the light of the sun, are found to be hurtful when immoderately
or unseasonably used. And thus divine providence admonishes us
not foolishly to vituperate things, but to investigate their utility
with care; and, when our mental capacity or infirmity is at fault,
to believe that there is a utility, though hidden, as we have experienced that there were other things which we all but failed to discover. For this concealment of the use of things is itself either an
exercise of our humility or a levelling of our pride; for no nature
at all is evil, and this is a name for nothing but the want of good.
But from things earthly to things heavenly, from the visible to
the invisible, there are some things better than others; and for
this purpose are they unequal, in order that they might all exist.

Now God is in such sort a greater worker in great things, that He is not less in little things,—for these little things are to be measured not by their own greatness (which does not exist), but by the wisdom of their Designer; as, in the visible appearance of a man, if one eyebrow be shaved off, how nearly nothing is taken from the body, but how much from the beauty!—for that is not constituted by bulk, but by the proportion and arrangement of the members. But we do not greatly wonder that persons, who suppose that some evil nature has been generated and propagated by a kind of opposing principle proper to it, refuse to admit that the cause of the creation was this, that the good God produced a good creation. For they believe that He was driven to this enterprise of creation by the urgent necessity of repulsing the evil that warred against Him, and that He mixed His good nature with the evil for the sake of restraining and conquering it; and that this nature of His, being thus shamefully polluted, and most cruelly oppressed and held captive, He labors to cleanse and deliver it, and with all His pains does not wholly succeed; but such part of it as could not be cleansed from that defilement is to serve as a prison and chain of the conquered and incarcerated enemy. The Manichaeans would not drivel, or rather, rave in such a style as this, if they believed the nature of God to be, as it is, unchangeable and absolutely incorruptible, and subject to no injury; and if, moreover, they held in Christian sobriety, that the soul which has shown itself capable of being altered for the worse by its own will, and of being corrupted by sin, and so of being deprived of the light of eternal truth,—that this soul, I say, is not a part of God, nor of the same nature as God, but is created by Him and is far different from its Creator.

241 We believe, we maintain, we faithfully preach, that the Father begat the Word, that is, Wisdom, by which all things were made, the only-begotten Son, one as the Father is one, eternal as the Father is eternal, and, equally with the Father, supremely good; and that the Holy Spirit is the Spirit alike of Father and of Son, and is Himself consubstantial and co-eternal with both; and that this whole is a Trinity by reason of the individuality of the persons, and one God by reason of the indivisible divine substance, as also one Almighty by reason of the indivisible omnipotence;

yet so that, when we inquire regarding each singly, it is said that there are not three gods, nor three almighties, but one God Almighty; so great is the indivisible unity of these Three, which requires that it be so stated. But, whether the Holy Spirit of the Father, and of the Son, who are both good, can be with propriety called the goodness of both, because He is common to both, I do not presume to determine hastily. Nevertheless, I would have less hesitation in saying that He is the holiness of both, not as if He were a divine attribute merely, but Himself also the divine substance, and the third person in the Trinity. I am the rather emboldened to make this statement, because, though the Father is a spirit, and the Son a spirit, and the Father holy, and the Son holy, yet the third person is distinctively called the Holy Spirit, as if He were the substantial holiness consubstantial with the other two. But if the divine goodness is nothing else than the divine holiness, then certainly it is a reasonable studiousness, and not presumptuous intrusion, to inquire whether the same Trinity be not hinted at in an enigmatical mode of speech, by which our inquiry is stimulated, when it is written who made each creature, and by what means, and why. For it is the Father of the Word who said, Let there be. And that which was made when He spoke was certainly made by means of the Word. And by the words, "God saw that it was good," it is sufficiently intimated that God made what was made not from any necessity, nor for the sake of supplying any want, but solely from His own goodness, i.e., because it was good. And this is stated after the creation had taken place, that there might be no doubt that the thing made satisfied the goodness on account of which it was made. And if we are right in understanding that this goodness is the Holy Spirit, then the whole Trinity is revealed to us in the creation. In this, too, is the origin, the enlightenment, the blessedness of the holy city which is above among the holy angels. For if we inquire whence it is, God created it; or whence its wisdom, God illumined it; or whence its blessedness, God is its bliss. It has its form by subsisting in Him; its enlightenment by contemplating Him; its joy by abiding in Him. It is; it sees; it loves. In God's eternity is its life; in God's truth its light; in God's goodness its joy.

25] As far as one can judge, it is for the same reason that philosophers have aimed at a three-fold division of science, or rather, were enabled to see that there was a threefold division (for they did not invent, but only discovered it), of which one part is called physical, another logical, the third ethical. The Latin equivalents of these names are now naturalized in the writings of many authors, so that these divisions are called natural, rational, and moral. Not that I would conclude that these philosophers, in this threefold division, had any thought of a trinity in God, although Plato is said to have been the first to discover and promulgate this distribution, and he saw that God alone could be the author of nature, the bestower of intelligence, and the kindler of love by which life becomes good and blessed. But certain it is that, though philosophers disagree both regarding the nature of things, and the mode of investigating truth, and of the good to which all our actions ought to tend, yet in these three great general questions all their intellectual energy is spent. And though there be a confusing diversity of opinion, every man striving to establish his own opinion in regard to each of these questions, yet no one of them all doubts that nature has some cause, science some method, life some end and aim. Then, again, there are three things which every artificer must possess if he is to effect anything,—nature, education, practice. Nature is to be judged by capacity, education by knowledge, practice by its fruit. I am aware that, properly speaking, fruit is what one enjoys, use (practice) what one uses. And this seems to be the difference between them, that we are said to *enjoy* that which in itself, and irrespective of other ends, delights us; to *use* that which we seek for the sake of some end beyond. For which reason the things of time are to be used rather than enjoyed, that we may deserve to enjoy things eternal; and not as those perverse creatures who would fain enjoy money and use God,—not spending money for God's sake, but worshipping God for money's sake. However, in common parlance, we both use fruits and enjoy uses. For we correctly speak of the "fruits of the field," which certainly we all use in the present life. And it was in accordance with this usage that I said that there were three things to be observed in a man, nature, education, practice. For these the philosophers have elaborated, as I said, the threefold division of that science by which a blessed life is attained; the natural having respect to nature, the rational to education, the moral to practice. If, then, we were ourselves the authors of our nature, we should have generated knowledge in ourselves, and should not require to reach it by education, i.e., by learning it from others. Our love, too, proceeding from ourselves and returning to us, would suffice to make our life blessed, and would stand in need of no extraneous enjoyment. But now, since our nature has God as its requisite author, it is certain that we must have Him for our teacher that we may be wise; Him, too, to dispense to us spiritual sweetness that we may be blessed.

26] And we indeed recognize in ourselves the image of God, that is, of the supreme Trinity, an image which though it be not equal to God, or rather, though it be very far removed from Him,— being neither co-eternal, nor, to say all in a word, consubstantial with Him,—is yet nearer to Him in nature than any other of His works, and is destined to be yet restored, that it may bear a still closer resemblance. For we both are, and know that we are, and delight in our being, and our knowledge of it. Moreover, in these three things no true-seeming illusion disturbs us; for we do not come into contact with these by some bodily sense, as we perceive the things outside of us,—colors, e.g., by seeing, sounds by hearing, smells by smelling, tastes by tasting, hard and soft objects by touching,—of all which sensible objects it is the images resembling them, but not themselves which we perceive in the mind and hold in the memory, and which excite us to desire the objects. But, without any delusive representation of images or phantasms, I am most certain that I am, and that I know and delight in this. In respect of these truths, I am not at all afraid of the arguments of the Academicians, who say, What if you are deceived? For if I am deceived, I am. For he who is not, cannot be deceived; and if I am deceived, by this same token I am. And since I am if I am deceived, How am I deceived in believing that I am? for it is certain that I am if I am deceived. Since, therefore, I, the person deceived, should be, even if I were deceived, certainly I am not deceived in this knowledge that I am. And, consequently, neither am I deceived in knowing that I know. And when I love these two things, I add to them a certain third thing, namely, my love, which is of equal moment. For neither am I deceived in this, that I love, since

in those things which I love I am not deceived; though even if
these were false, it would still be true that I *loved* false things.
For how could I justly be blamed and prohibited from loving
false things, if it were false that I loved them? But, since they are
true and real, who doubts that when they are loved, the love of
them is itself true and real? Further, as there is no one who does
not wish to be happy, so there is no one who does not wish to be.
For how can he be happy, if he is nothing?

27] And truly the very fact of existing is by some natural spell so
pleasant, that even the wretched are, for no other reason, unwilling
to perish; and, when they feel that they are wretched, wish not
that they themselves be annihilated, but that their misery be so.
Take even those who, both in their own esteem, and in point of
fact, are utterly wretched, and who are reckoned so, not only by
wise men on account of their folly, but by those who count themselves blessed, and who think them wretched because they are poor
and destitute,—if any one should give these men an immortality,
in which their misery should be deathless, and should offer the
alternative, that if they shrank from existing eternally in the
same misery they might be annihilated, and exist nowhere at all,
nor in any condition, on the instant they would joyfully, nay
exultantly, make election to exist always, even in such a condition,
rather than not exist at all. The well-known feeling of such men
witnesses to this. For when we see that they fear to die, and will
rather live in such misfortune than end it by death, is it now obvious enough how nature shrinks from annihilation? And, accordingly, when they know that they must die, they seek, as a great
boon, that this mercy be shown them, that they may a little longer
live in the same misery, and delay to end it by death. And so they
indubitably prove with what glad alacrity they would accept immortality, even though it secured to them endless destruction.
What! do not even all irrational animals, to whom such calcula-
tions are unknown, from the huge dragons down to the least
worms, all testify that they wish to exist, and therefore shun death
by every movement in their power? Nay, the very plants and
shrubs, which have no such life as enables them to shun destruction by movements we can see, do not they all seek in their own
fashion to conserve their own existence, by rooting themselves

more and more deeply in the earth, that so they may draw nourishment, and throw out healthy branches towards the sky? In fine, even the lifeless bodies, which want not only sensation but seminal life, yet either seek the upper air or sink deep, or are balanced in an intermediate position, so that they may protect their existence in that situation where they can exist in most accordance with their nature.

And how much human nature loves the knowledge of its existence, and how it shrinks from being deceived, will be sufficiently understood from this fact, that every man prefers to grieve in a sane mind, rather than to be glad in madness. And this grand and wonderful instinct belongs to men alone of all animals; for, though some of them have keener eyesight than ourselves for this world's light, they cannot attain to that spiritual light with which our mind is somehow irradiated, so that we can form right judgments of all things. For our power to judge is proportioned to our acceptance of this light. Nevertheless, the irrational animals, though they have not knowledge, have certainly something resembling knowledge; whereas the other material things are said to be sensible, not because they have senses, but because they are the objects of our senses. Yet among plants, their nourishment and generation have some resemblance to sensible life. However, both these and all material things have their causes hidden in their nature; but their outward forms, which lend beauty to this visible structure of the world, are perceived by our senses, so that they too wish to compensate for their own want of knowledge by providing us with knowledge. But we perceive them by our bodily senses in such a way that we do not judge of them by these senses. For we have another and far superior sense, belonging to the inner man, by which we perceive what things are just, and what unjust,—just by means of an intelligible idea, unjust by the want of it. This sense is aided in its functions neither by the eyesight, nor by the orifice of the ear, nor by the air-holes of the nostrils, nor by the palate's taste, nor by any bodily touch. By it I am assured both that I am, and that I know this; and these two I love, and in the same manner I am assured that I love them.

28] We have said as much as the scope of this work demands regarding these two things, to wit, our existence, and our knowledge

of it, and how much they are loved by us, and how there is found
even in the lower creatures a kind of likeness of these things, and
yet with a difference. We have yet to speak of the love wherewith
they are loved, to determine whether this love is itself loved. And
doubtless it is; and this is the proof. Because in men who are justly
loved, it is rather love itself that is loved; for he is not justly called
a good man who knows what is good, but who loves it. Is it not
then obvious that we love in ourselves the very love wherewith we
love whatever good we love? For there is also a love wherewith we
love that which we ought not to love; and this love is hated by him
who loves that wherewith he loves what ought to be loved. For it
is quite possible for both to exist in one man. And this co-existence
is good for a man, to the end that this love which conduces to our
living well may grow, and the other, which leads us to evil may
decrease, until our whole life be perfectly healed and transmuted
into good. For if we were beasts, we should love the fleshly and
sensual life, and this would be our sufficient good; and when it
was well with us in respect of it, we should seek nothing beyond.
In like manner, if we were trees, we could not, indeed, in the
strict sense of the word, love anything; nevertheless we should
seem, as it were, to long for that by which we might become more
abundantly and luxuriantly fruitful. If we were stones, or waves,
or wind, or flame, or anything of that kind, we should want, indeed, both sensation and life, yet should possess a kind of attraction towards our own proper position and natural order. For the
specific gravity of bodies is, as it were, their love, whether they are
carried downwards by their weight, or upwards by their levity.
For the body is borne by its gravity, as the spirit by love, whither-
soever it is borne. But we are men, created in the image of our
Creator, whose eternity is true, and whose truth is eternal, whose
love is eternal and true, and who Himself is the eternal, true, and
adorable Trinity, without confusion, without separation; and,
therefore, while, as we run over all the works which He has established, we may detect, as it were, His footprints, now more and
now less distinct even in those things that are beneath us, since
they could not so much as exist, or be bodied forth in any shape,
or follow and observe any law, had they not been made by Him
who supremely is, and is supremely good and supremely wise; yet
in ourselves beholding His image, let us, like that younger son of

the gospel, come to ourselves, and arise and return to Him from whom by our sin we had departed. There our being will have no death, our knowledge no error, our love no mishap. . . .

XII:1] . . . Accordingly we say that there is no unchangeable good but the one, true, blessed God; that the things which He made are indeed good because from Him, yet mutable because not made out of Him, but out of nothing. Although, therefore, they are not the supreme good, for God is a greater good, yet those mutable things which can adhere to the immutable good, and so be blessed, are very good; for so completely is He their good, that without Him they cannot but be wretched. And the other created things in the universe are not better on this account, that they cannot be miserable. For no one would say that the other members of the body are superior to the eyes, because they cannot be blind. But as the sentient nature, even when it feels pain, is superior to the stony, which can feel none, so the rational nature, even when wretched, is more excellent than that which lacks reason or feeling, and can therefore experience no misery. And since this is so, then in this nature which has been created so excellent, that though it be mutable itself, it can yet secure its blessedness by adhering to the immutable good, the supreme God; and since it is not satisfied unless it be perfectly blessed, and cannot be thus blessed save in God,—in this nature, I say, not to adhere to God, is manifestly a fault. Now every fault injures the nature, and is consequently contrary to the nature. The creature, therefore, which cleaves to God, differs from those who do not, not by nature, but by fault; and yet by this very fault the nature itself is proved to be very noble and admirable. For that nature is certainly praised, the fault of which is justly blamed. For we justly blame the fault because it mars the praiseworthy nature. As, then, when we say that blindness is a defect of the eyes, we prove that sight belongs to the nature of the eyes; and when we say that deafness is a defect of the ears, hearing is thereby proved to belong to their nature;—so, when we say that it is a fault of the angelic creature that it does not cleave to God, we hereby most plainly declare that it pertained to its nature to cleave to God. And who can worthily conceive or express how great a glory that is, to cleave to God, so as to live to Him, to draw wisdom from Him, to delight in Him, and to enjoy this so great good, without death, error, or grief? And thus, since every vice is an injury of the nature, that very vice of the wicked angels, their departure from God, is sufficient proof that God created their nature so good, that it is an injury to it not to be with God.

2] This may be enough to prevent any one from supposing, when we speak of the apostate angels, that they could have another nature, derived, as it were, from some different origin, and not from God. From the great impiety of this error we shall disentangle ourselves the more readily and easily, the more distinctly we understand that which God spoke by the angel when He sent Moses to the children of Israel: "I am that I am." (Ex. iii, 14.) For since God is the supreme existence, that is to say, supremely is, and is therefore unchangeable, the things that He made He empowered to be, but not to be supremely like Himself. To some He communicated a more ample, to others a more limited existence, and thus arranged the natures of beings in ranks. For as from *sapere* comes *sapientia,* so from *esse* comes *essentia,*—a new word indeed, which the old Latin writers did not use, but which is naturalized in our day, that our language may not want an equivalent for the Greek *ousia.* For this is expressed word for word by *essentia.* Consequently, to that nature which supremely is, and which created all else that exists, no nature is contrary save that which does not exist. For nonentity is the contrary of that which is. And thus there is no being contrary to God, the Supreme Being, and Author of all beings whatsoever.

4] But it is ridiculous to condemn the faults of beasts and trees, and other such mortal and mutable things as are void of intelligence, sensation, or life, even though these faults should destroy their corruptible nature; for these creatures received, at their Creator's will, an existence fitting them, by passing away and giving place to others, to secure that lowest form of beauty, the beauty of seasons, which in its own place is a requisite part of this world. For things earthly were neither to be made equal to things heavenly, nor were they, though inferior, to be quite omitted from the universe. Since, then, in those situations where such things are appropriate, some perish to make way for others that are born in

their room, and the less succumb to the greater, and the things
that are overcome are transformed into the quality of those that
have the mastery, this is the appointed order of things transitory.
Of this order the beauty does not strike us, because by our mortal
frailty we are so involved in a part of it, that we cannot perceive
the whole, in which these fragments that offend us are harmonized
with the most accurate fitness and beauty. And therefore, where
we are not so well able to perceive the wisdom of the creator, we
are very properly enjoined to believe it, lest in the vanity of human
rashness we presume to find any fault with the work of so great an
Artificer. At the same time, if we attentively consider even these
faults of earthly things, which are neither voluntary nor penal,
they seem to illustrate the excellence of the nature themselves,
which are all originated and created by God; for it is that which
pleases us in this nature which we are displeased to see removed
by the fault,—unless even the natures themselves displease men, as
often happens when they become hurtful to them, and then men
estimate them not by their nature, but by their utility; as in the
case of those animals whose swarms scourged the pride of the
Egyptians. But in this way of estimating, they may find fault with
the sun itself; for certain criminals or debtors are sentenced by the
judges to be set in the sun. Therefore it is not with respect to our
convenience or discomfort, but with respect to their own nature,
that the creatures are glorifying their Artificer. Thus even the
nature of the eternal fire, penal though it be to the condemned
sinners, is most assuredly worthy of praise. For what is more beautiful than fire flaming, blazing, and shining? What more useful
than fire for warming, restoring, cooking, though nothing is more
destructive than fire burning and consuming? The same thing,
then, when applied in one way, is destructive, but when applied
suitably, is most beneficial. For who can find words to tell its uses
throughout the whole world? We must not listen, then, to those
who praise the light of fire but find fault with its heat, judging it
not by its nature, but by their convenience or discomfort. For they
wish to see, but not to be burnt. But they forget that this very
light which is so pleasant to them disagrees with and hurts weak
eyes; and in that heat which is disagreeable to them, some animals
find the most suitable conditions of a healthy life.

5] All natures, then, inasmuch as they are, and have therefore a rank and species of their own, and a kind of internal harmony, are certainly good. And when they are in the places assigned to them by the order of their nature, they preserve such beings as they have received. And those things which have not received everlasting being, are altered for better or for worse, so as to suit the wants and motions of those things to which the Creator's law has made them subservient; and thus they tend in the divine providence to that end which is embraced in the general scheme of the government of the universe. So that, though the corruption of transitory and perishable things brings them to utter destruction, it does not prevent their producing that which was designed to be their result. And this being so, God who supremely is, and who therefore created every being which has not supreme existence (for that which was made of nothing could not be the equal to Him, and indeed could not be at all had He not made it), is not to be found fault with on account of the creatures faults, but is to be praised in view of the natures He has made.

6] Thus the true cause of the blessedness of the good angels is found to be this, that they cleave to Him who supremely is. And if we ask the cause of the misery of the bad, it occurs to us, and not unreasonably, that they are miserable because they have forsaken Him who supremely is, and have turned to themselves who have no such essence. And this vice, what else is it called than pride? For "pride is the beginning of sin." (Eccles. x, 13.) They were unwilling, then, to preserve their strength for God; and as adherence to God was the condition of their enjoying an ampler being, they diminished it by preferring themselves to Him. This was the first defect, and the first impoverishment, and the first flaw of their nature, which was created, not indeed supremely existent, but finding its blessedness in the enjoyment of the Supreme Being; whilst by abandoning Him it should become, not indeed no nature at all, but a nature with a less ample existence, and therefore wretched.

If the further question be asked, What was the efficient cause of their evil will? there is none. For what is it which makes the will bad, when it is the will itself which makes the action bad? And consequently the bad will is the cause of the bad action, but nothing is the efficient cause of the bad will. For if anything is the cause, this thing either has or has not a will. If it has, the will is either good or bad. If good, who is so left to himself as to say that a good will makes a will bad? For in this case a good will would be the cause of sin; a most absurd supposition. On the other hand, if this hypothetical thing has a bad will, I wish to know what made it so; and that we may not go on forever, I ask at once, what made the *first* evil will bad? For that is not the first which was itself corrupted by an evil will, but is the first which was made evil by no other will. For if it were preceded by that which made it evil, that will was first which made the other evil. But if it is replied, "Nothing made it evil; it always was evil," I ask if it has been existing in some nature. For if not, then it did not exist at all; and if it did exist in some nature, then it vitiated and corrupted it, and injured it, and consequently deprived it of good. And therefore the evil will could not exist in an evil nature, but in a nature at once good and mutable, which this vice could injure. For if it did no injury, it was no vice; and consequently the will in which it was, could not be called evil. But if it did injury, it did it by taking away or diminishing good. And therefore there could not be from eternity, as was suggested, an evil will in that thing in which there had been previously a natural good, which the evil will was able to diminish by corrupting it. If, then, it was not from eternity, who, I ask, made it? The only thing that can be suggested in reply is, that something which itself had no will made the will evil. I ask, then, whether this thing was superior, inferior, or equal to it? If superior, then it is better. How, then, has it no will, and not rather a good will? The same reasoning applies if it was equal; for so long as two things have equally a good will, the one cannot produce in the other an evil will. Then remains the supposition that that which corrupted the will of the angelic nature which first sinned, was itself an inferior thing without a will. But that thing, be it of the lowest and most earthly kind is certainly itself good, since it is a nature and being, with a form and rank of its own in its own kind and order. How, then, can a good thing be the efficient cause of an evil will? How, I say, can good be the cause of evil? For when the will abandons what is above itself, and turns to what is lower, it becomes evil—not because that is evil to which it turns, but because the turning itself is wicked. There-

fore it is not an inferior thing which has made the will evil, but it
is itself which has become so by wickedly and inordinately desiring
an inferior thing. For if two men, alike in physical and moral constitution, see the same corporeal beauty, and one of them is excited
by the sight to desire an illicit enjoyment while the other steadfastly maintains a modest restraint of his will, what do we suppose
brings it about, that there is an evil will in the one and not in the
other? What produces it in the man in whom it exists? Not the
bodily beauty, for that was presented equally to the gaze of both,
and yet did not produce in both an evil will. Did the flesh of the
one cause the desire as he looked? But why did not the flesh of the
other? Or was it the disposition? But why not the disposition of
both? For we are supposing that both were of a like temperament
of body and soul. Must we, then, say that the one was tempted by
a secret suggestion of the evil spirit? As if it was not by his own
will that he consented to this suggestion and to any inducement
whatever! This consent, then, this evil will which he presented to
the evil suasive influence,—what was the cause of it, we ask? For,
not to delay on such a difficulty as this, if both are tempted equally
and one yields and consents to the temptation while the other remains unmoved by it, what other account can we give of the matter than this, that the one is willing, the other unwilling, to fall
away from chastity? And what causes this but their own wills, in
cases at least such as we are supposing, where the temperament is
identical? The same beauty was equally obvious to the eyes of
both; the same secret temptation pressed on both with equal violence. However minutely we examine the case, therefore, we can
discern nothing which caused the will of the one to be evil. For if
we say that the man himself made his will evil, what was the man
himself before his will was evil but a good nature created by God,
the unchangeable good? Here are two men who, before the temptation, were alike in body and soul, and of whom one yielded to the
tempter who persuaded him, while the other could not be persuaded to desire that lovely body which was equally before the
eyes of both. Shall we say of the successfully tempted man that he
corrupted his own will, since he was certainly good before his will
became bad? Then, why did he do so? Was it because his will was
a nature, or because it was made of nothing? We shall find that the
latter is the case. For if a nature is the cause of an evil will, what

else can we say than that evil arises from good or that good is the cause of evil? And how can it come to pass that a nature, good though mutable, should produce any evil—that is to say, should make the will itself wicked?

71 Let no one, therefore, look for an efficient cause of the vile will; for it is not efficient, but deficient, as the will itself is not an effecting of something else, but a defect. For defection from that which supremely is, to that which has less of being—this is to begin to have an evil will. Now, to seek to discover the causes of these defections,—causes, as I have said, not efficient, but deficient,—is as if some one sought to see darkness, or hear silence. Yet both of these are known by us, and the former by means only of the eye, the latter only by the ear; but not by their positive actuality, but by their want of it. Let no one, then seek to know from me what I know that I do not know; unless he perhaps wishes to learn to be ignorant of that which all we know is, that it cannot be known. For those things which are known not by their actuality, but by their want of it, are known, if our expression may be allowed and understood, by not knowing them, that by knowing them they may be not known. For when the eyesight surveys objects that strike the sense, it nowhere sees darkness but where it begins not to see. And so no other sense but the ear can perceive silence, and yet it is only perceived by not hearing. Thus, too, our mind perceives intelligible forms by understanding them; but when they are deficient, it knows them by not knowing them; for "who can understand defects?" (Ps. xix, 12.)

81 This I do know, that the nature of God can never, nowhere, nowise be defective, and that natures made of nothing can. These latter, however, the more being they have, and the more good they do (for then they do have something positive), the more they have efficient causes; but in so far as they are defective in being, and consequently do evil (for then what is their work but vanity?), they have deficient causes. . . .

221 And God was not ignorant that man would sin, and that, being himself made subject now to death, he would propagate men doomed to die, and that these mortals would run to such enormities in sin, that even the beasts devoid of rational will, and who

were created in numbers from the waters and the earth, would live more securely and peaceable with their own kind than men, who had been propagated from one individual for the very purpose of commending concord. For not even lions or dragons have ever waged with their kind such wars as men have waged with one another. But God foresaw also that by His grace a people would be called to adoption, and that they, being justified by the remission of their sins, would be united by the Holy Ghost to the holy angels in eternal peace, the last enemy, death, being destroyed; and He knew that this people would derive profit from the consideration that God had caused all men to be derived from one, for the sake of showing how highly He prizes unity in a multitude.

27] . . . In this first man, who was created in the beginning there was laid the foundation, not indeed evidently, but in God's fore-knowledge, of these two cities or societies, so far as regards the human race. For from that man all men were to be derived—some of them to be associated with the good angels in their reward, others with the wicked in their punishment; all being ordered by the secret yet just judgment of God. For since it is written, "All the paths of the Lord are mercy and truth," neither can His grace be unjust, nor His justice cruel.

XIV:28] Accordingly, two cities have been formed by two loves: the earthly by the love of self, even to the contempt of God; the heavenly by the love of God, even to the contempt of self. The former, in a word, glories in itself, the latter in the Lord. For the one seeks glory from men; but the greatest glory of the other is God, the witness of conscience. The one lifts up its head in its own glory; the other says to its God, "Thou art my glory, and the lifter up of mine head." (Ps. iii, 3.) In the one, the princes and the nations it subdues are ruled by the love of ruling; in the other, the princes and the subjects serve one another in love, the latter obeying, while the former take thought for all. The one delights in its own strength, represented in the persons of its rulers; the other says to its God, "I will love Thee, O Lord, my strength." (Ps. xviii, 1.) And therefore the wise men of the one city, living according to man, have sought for profit to their own bodies or souls, or both, and those who have known God "glorified Him not as God, neither were thankful, but became vain in their imaginations, and their foolish heart was darkened; professing themselves to be wise,"—that is, glorying in their own wisdom, and being possessed by pride,—"they became fools, and changed the glory of the incorruptible God into an image made like to corruptible man, and to birds, and four-footed beasts, and creeping things." For they were either leaders or followers of the people in adoring images, "and worshipped and served the creature more than the Creator, who is blessed forever." (Rom. i, 21-25.) But in the other city there is no human wisdom, but only godliness, which offers due worship to the true God, and looks for its reward in the society of the saints, of holy angels as well as holy men, "that God may be all in all." (I Cor. xv, 28.)

XIX:5] We give a much more unlimited approval to their idea that the life of the wise man must be social. For how could a city of God (concerning which we are already no less that the nineteenth book of this work) either take a beginning or be developed, or attain its proper destiny, if the life of the saints were not a social life? But who can enumerate all the great grievances with which human society abounds in the misery of this mortal state? Who can weigh them? Hear how one of their comic writers makes one of his characters express the common feelings of all men in this matter: "I am married; this is one misery. Children are born to me; they are additional cares." (Terent. *Adelph.* v, 4.) What shall I say of the miseries of love which Terence also recounts—"slights, suspicions, quarrels, war to-day, peace to-morrow?" *(Eunuch,* i, 1.) Is not human life full of such things? Do they not often occur even in honorable friendships? On all hands we experience these slights, suspicions, quarrels, war, all of which are undoubted evils; while, on the other hand, peace is a doubtful good, because we do not know the heart of our friend, and though we did know it to-day, we should be as ignorant of what it might be to-morrow. Who ought to be, or who are more friendly than those who live in the same family? And yet who can rely even upon this friendship, seeing that secret treachery has often broken it up, and produced enmity as bitter as the amity was sweet, or seemed sweet by the most perfect dissimulation? It is on this account that the words of Cicero so move the heart of every one, and provoke a sigh: "There are no snares more dangerous than those which lurk under the guise

of duty or the name of relationship. For the man who is your declared foe you can easily baffle by precaution; but this hidden,
intestine, and domestic danger not merely exists, but overwhelms
you before you can foresee and examine it." (*In Verrem,* ii, 1. 15.)
It is also to this that allusion is made by the divine saying, "A
man's foes are those of his own household," (Matt. x, 36)—words
which one cannot hear without pain; for though a man have sufficient fortitude to endure it with equanimity, and sufficient sagacity
to baffle the malice of a pretended friend, yet if he himself is a
good man, he cannot but be greatly pained at the discovery of the
perfidy of wicked men, whether they have always been wicked and
merely feigned goodness, or have fallen from a better to a malicious disposition. If, then, home, the natural refuge from the ills
of life, is itself not safe, what shall we say of the city, which, as it
is larger, is so much the more filled with lawsuits civil and criminal, and is never free from the fear, if sometimes from the actual
outbreak, of disturbing and bloody insurrections and civil wars?

6] What shall I say of these judgments which men pronounce on
men, and which are necessary in communities, whatever outward
peace they enjoy? Melancholy and lamentable judgments they are,
since the judges are men who cannot discern the consciences of
those at their bar, and are therefore frequently compelled to put
innocent witnesses to the torture to ascertain the truth regarding
the crimes of other men. What shall I say of the torture applied
to the accused himself? He is tortured to discover whether he is
guilty, so that, though innocent, he suffers most undoubted punishment for crime that is still doubtful, not because it is proved
that he committed it, but because it is not ascertained that he did
not commit it. Thus the ignorance of the judge frequently involves an innocent person in suffering. And what is still more
unendurable—a thing, indeed, to be bewailed, and, if that were
possible, watered with fountains of tears—is this, that when the
judge puts the accused to the question, that he may not unwittingly put an innocent man to death, the result of this lamentable
ignorance is that this very person, whom he tortured that he might
not condemn him if innocent, is condemned to death both tortured and innocent. For if he has chosen, in obedience to the philosophical instructions to the wise man, to quit this life rather than

endure any longer such tortures, he declares that he has committed the crime which in fact he has not committed. And when he has been condemned and put to death, the judge is still in ignorance whether he has put to death an innocent or a guilty person, though he put the accused to the torture for the very purpose of saving himself from condemning the innocent; and consequently he has both tortured an innocent man to discover his innocence, and has put him to death without discovering it. If such darkness shrouds social life, will a wise judge take his seat on the bench or no? Beyond question he will. For human society, which he thinks it a wickedness to abandon, constrains him and compels him to this duty. And he thinks it no wickedness that innocent witnesses are tortured regarding the crimes of which other men are accused; or that the accused are put to the torture, so that they are often overcome with anguish, and, though innocent, make false confessions regarding themselves, and are punished; or that, though they be not condemned to die, they often die during, or in consequence of, the torture; or that sometimes the accusers, who perhaps have been prompted by a desire to benefit society by bringing criminals to justice, are themselves condemned through the ignorance of the judge, because they are unable to prove the truth of their accusations though they are true, and because the witnesses lie, and the accused endures the torture without being moved to confession. These numerous and important evils he does not consider sins; for the wise judge does these things, not with any intention of doing harm, but because human society claims him as a judge. But though we must therefore acquit the judge of malice, we must none the less condemn human life as miserable. And if he is compelled to torture and punish the innocent because his office and his ignorance constrain him, is he a happy as well as guiltless man? Surely it were proof of more profound considerateness and finer feeling were he to recognize the misery of these necessities, and shrink from his own implication in that misery; and had he any piety about him, he would cry to God "From my necessities deliver Thou me." (Ps. xxv, 17.)

71 After the state or city comes the world, the third circle of human society,—the first being the house, and the second the city. And the world, as it is larger, so it is fuller of dangers, as the

greater sea is the more dangerous. And here, in the first place, man is separated from man by the difference of languages. For if two men, each ignorant of the other's language, meet, and are not compelled to pass, but, on the contrary, to remain in company, dumb animals, though of different species, would more easily hold intercourse than they, human being though they be. For their common nature is no help to friendliness when they are prevented by diversity of language from conveying their sentiments to one another; so that a man would more readily hold intercourse with his dog than with a foreigner. But the imperial city has endeavored to impose on subject nations not only her yoke, but her language, as a bond of peace, so that interpreters, far from being scarce, are numberless. This is true; but how many great wars, how much slaughter and bloodshed, have provided this unity! And though these are past, the end of these miseries has not yet come. For though there have never been wanting, nor are yet wanting, hostile nations beyond the empire, against whom wars have been and are waged, yet, supposing there were no such nations, the very extent of the empire itself has produced wars of a more obnoxious description—social and civil wars—and with these the whole race has been agitated, either by the actual conflict or the fear of a renewed outbreak. If I attempted to give an adequate description of these threefold disasters, these stern and lasting necessities, though I am quite unequal to the task, what limit could I set? But, say they, the wise man will wage just wars. As if he would not all the rather lament the necessity of just wars, if he remembers that he is a man; for if they were not just he would not wage them, and would therefore be delivered from all wars. For it is the wrong-doing of the opposing party which compels the wise man to wage just wars; and this wrong-doing, even though it gave rise to no war, would still be matter of grief to man because it is man's wrong-doing. Let every one, then, who thinks with pain on all these great evils, so horrible, so ruthless, acknowledge that this is misery. And if any one either endures or thinks of them without mental pain, this is a more miserable plight still, for he thinks himself happy because he has lost human feeling.

81 In òur present wretched condition we frequently mistake a friend for an enemy, and an enemy for a friend. And if we escape

this pitiable blindness, is not the unfeigned confidence and mutual
love of true and good friends our one solace in human society,
filled as it is with misunderstandings and calamities? And yet the
more friends we have, and the more widely they are scattered, the
more numerous are our fears that some portion of the vast masses
of the disasters of life may light upon them. For we are not only
anxious lest they suffer from famine, war, disease, captivity, or the
inconceivable horrors of slavery, but we are also affected with the
much more painful dread that their friendship may be changed
to perfidy, malice, and injustice. And when these contingencies actually occur,—as they do the more frequently the more friends we
have, and the more widely they are scattered,—and when they
come to our knowledge, who but the man who has experienced it
can tell with what pangs the heart is torn? We would, in fact, prefer to hear that they were dead, although we could not without
anguish hear of even this. For if their life has solaced us with the
charms of friendship, can it be that their death should affect us
with no sadness? He who will have none of this sadness must, if
possible, have no friendly intercourse. Let him interdict or extinguish friendly affection; let him burst with ruthless insensibility
the bonds of every human relationship; or let him contrive so to
use them that no sweetness shall distil into his spirit. But if this is
utterly impossible, how shall we contrive to feel no bitterness
in the death of those whose life has been so sweet to us? Hence
arises that grief which affects the tender heart like a wound or a
bruise, and which is healed by the application of kindly consolation. For though the cure is affected all the more easily and rapidly
the better condition the soul is in, we must not on this account
suppose that there is nothing at all to heal. Although, then, our
present life is afflicted, sometimes in a milder, sometimes in a more
painful degree, by the death of those very dear to us, and especially of useful public men, yet we would prefer to hear that
such men were dead rather than to hear or perceive that they had
fallen from the faith, or from virtue,—in other words, that they
were spiritually dead. Of this vast material for misery the earth is
full, and therefore it is written, "Is not human life upon earth a
trial?" (Job vii, 1.) . . .

11] And thus we may say of peace, as we have said of eternal life, that it is the end of our good; and the rather because the Psalmist says of the city of God, the subject of this laborious work, "Praise the Lord, O Jerusalem; praise thy God, O Zion; for He hath strengthened the bars of thy gates; He hath blessed thy children within thee; who hath made thy borders peace." (Ps. cxlvii, 12-14.) For when the bars of her gates shall be strengthened, none shall go in or come out from her; consequently we ought to understand the peace of her borders as that final peace we are wishing to declare. For even the mystical name of the city itself, that is, *Jerusalem,* means, as I have already said, "Vision of Peace." But as the word peace is employed in connection with things in this world in which certainly life eternal has no place, we have preferred to call the end or supreme good of this city life eternal rather than peace. Of this end the apostle says, "But now, being freed from sin, and become servants to God, ye have your fruit unto holiness, and the end life eternal." (Rom. vi, 22.) But, on the other hand, as those who are not familiar with Scripture may suppose that the life of the wicked is eternal life, either because of the immortality of the soul, which some of the philosophers even have recognized, or because of the endless punishment of the wicked, which forms a part of our faith, and which seems impossible unless the wicked live for ever, it may therefore be advisable, in order that every one may readily understand what we mean, to say that the end or supreme good of this city is either peace in eternal life, or eternal life in peace. For peace is a good so great, that even in this earthly and mortal life, there is no word we hear with such pleasure, nothing we desire with such great zest, or find to be more thoroughly gratifying. So that if we dwell for a little longer on this subject, we shall not, in my opinion, be wearisome to our readers, who will attend both for the sake of understanding what is the end of this city of which we speak, and for the sake of the sweetness of peace which is dear to all.

20] Since, then, the supreme good of the city of God is perfect and eternal peace, not such as mortals pass into and out of by birth and death, but the peace of freedom from all evil, in which the immortals ever abide, who can deny that that future life is most blessed, or that, in comparison with it, this life which now we live is most wretched, be it filled with all blessings of body and soul and external things? And yet, if any man uses this life with a reference to that other which he ardently loves and confidently hopes for, he may well be called even now blessed, though not in reality so much as in hope. But the actual possession of the happiness of this life, without the hope of what is beyond, is but a false happiness and profound misery. For the true blessings of the soul are not now enjoyed; for that is no true wisdom which does not direct all its prudent observations, manly actions, virtuous self-restraint, and just arrangements, to that end in which God shall be all and all in a secure eternity and perfect peace.

Thomas Aquinas

Thomas Aquinas

IN ST. THOMAS'S philosophy the Christian faith is given an Aristotelian expression. But this philosophy is more than an exposition of the Christian faith. It reflects the work of generations and centuries of meticulous commentators on the Aristotelian writings, in the course of which these writings had become a language of scholastic exposition rather than a system of scientific enquiry. The very idea of science had become identified with the idea of certainty. To know, for scholasticism, is to be able to prove; to prove requires first principles and accurate reasoning. The search for principles of proof and modes of syllogistic argument became the primary concern of scholastic philosophy. Thomas's system represents the culmination of this search, for in it are to be found the most careful definition of terms, the most elaborate demonstrations, and the most conscientious consideration of difficulties.

At the starting-point of both philosophy and theology is the idea of God. Since, according to Aristotle, human nature culminates in reason, the culmination of reason, according to Thomas, is to know God. But God's essence can not be known. It can be defined formally: "God's essence is his existence." God necessarily (or by definition) exists. To prove that there must be a being that necessarily exists was one of the favorite tasks of medieval schoolmen, and has worried most philosophers ever since their proofs became logically tantalizing. Thomas Aquinas is relatively cautious. He approaches the knowledge of God by negatives and comes to the negative conclusion that God is best known through his

power, acts or will. This is a negative conclusion in the sense
that philosophers and theologians usually wish to know not
merely *that* God does all things but *why* and *how*. Thomas
had more confidence than Augustine had in human reason's
ability to understand God's acts and he even tried to prove
that God by his nature must be reasonable, and that hence
faith and reason, both God-given, could never conflict,
though they have independent functions and subject-matters.
Some things can be known by faith only, others by reason
only, and still others by both revelation and proof.

There is a second major theme in the philosophy of St.
Thomas, namely, that ultimately being and value are one
(ens et bonum convertuntur) and that consequently the mind
of man in seeking truth is also seeking the final good in which
human nature finds perfect happiness. As St. Augustine gave
this Christian doctrine a Platonic form, so St. Thomas made
it Aristotelian. Whereas St. Augustine found it useful to his
version of the Faith to emphasize the Platonic separation of
soul and body, St. Thomas follows as far as he can the Aristotelian conception of the soul as the "principle" of the
body's life. Though he regards the soul as an incorporeal and
immortal substance, he insists that body and soul must be in
"substantial union" and it is this union that constitutes the
real being of the individual agent. The perfection of the rational soul, therefore, is presented in his philosophy as the
natural goal of human life.

Thomas was born in 1225 of the noble family of Aquino.
His early education he received in the famous Benedictine
monastery of Monte Cassino and at the University of Naples.
In 1243 he entered the Dominican Order of Preachers and
soon thereafter went to Cologne to study under Albertus
Magnus, the first of a distinguished line of Dominican
teachers. At Paris Albert and Thomas continued their teaching and writing, Thomas soon becoming the most famous
expositor and defender of Christian philosophy. He died in
1274. His most systematic work is the *Summa Theologica*.

His *Summa contra Gentiles,* from which the following selection is taken, was composed about ten years earlier (c. 1260) and was directed primarily against those Arabian Aristotelians (notably Averroës) and heretical scholastics who could not reconcile Aristotle with the doctrine of creation *ex nihilo* and other basic tenets of Christian faith.

St. Thomas is now the official philosopher of the Roman Catholic Church and the Jesuits are especially active in using Thomistic philosophy as a basis for their teaching of a *"philosophia perennis,"* much as Thomas Aquinas used Aristotle for the same purpose.

Summa Contra Gentiles

1:8] O*F THE Relation of Human Reason to the first Truth of Faith.* The things of sense, from whence human reason takes its beginning of knowledge, retain in themselves some trace of imitation of God, inasmuch as they *are*, and are *good;* yet so imperfect is this trace that it proves wholly insufficient to declare the substance of God Himself. Since every agent acts to the producing of its own likeness, effects in their several ways bear some likeness to their causes: nevertheless the effect does not always attain to the perfect likeness of the agent that produces it. In regard then to knowledge of the truth of faith, which can only be thoroughly known to those who behold the substance of God, human reason stands so conditioned as to be able to argue some true likenesses to it: which like nesses however are not sufficient for any sort of demonstrative or intuitive comprehension of the aforesaid truth. Still it is useful for the human mind to exercise itself in such reasonings, however feeble, provided there be no presumptuous hope of perfect comprehension or demonstration. . . .

9] *The Order and Mode of Procedure in this Work.* There is then a twofold sort of truth in things divine for the wise man to study: one that can be attained by rational enquiry, another than transcends all the industry of reason. This truth of things divine I do not call twofold on the part of God, who is one simple Truth, but on the part of our knowledge, as our cognitive faculty has different aptitudes for the knowledge of divine things. To the declaration therefore of the first sort of truth we must proceed by demonstrative reasons that may serve to convince the adversary. But because such reasons are not forthcoming for truth of the second sort, our aim ought not to be to convince the adversary by reasons, but to refute his reasonings against the truth, which we may hope to do, since natural reason cannot be contrary to the truth of faith. The special mode of refutation to be employed against an opponent of this second sort of truth is by alleging the authority of Scripture confirmed from heaven by miracles. There are however some probable reasons available for the declaration of this truth, to the exercise and consolation of the faithful, but not to the convincing of opponents, because the mere insufficiency of such reasoning would rather confirm them in their error, they thinking that we assented to the truth of faith for reasons so weak.

According then to the manner indicated we will bend our endeavour, first, to the manifestation of that truth which faith professes and reason searches out, alleging reasons demonstrative and probable, some of which we have gathered from the books of philosophers and saints, for the establishment of the truth and the confutation of the opponent. Then, to proceed from what is more to what is less manifest in our regard, we will pass to the manifestation of that truth which transcends reason, solving the arguments of opponents, and by probable reasons and authorities, so far as God shall enable us, declaring the truth of faith.

Taking therefore the way of reason to the pursuit of truths that human reason can search out regarding God, the first consideration that meets us is of the attributes of God in Himself; secondly of the coming forth of creatures from God; thirdly of the order of creatures to God as their last end.

10] Of the Opinion of those who say that the Existence of God cannot be proved, being a Self-evident Truth. This opinion rests on the following grounds:

1] Those truths are self-evident which are recognized at once, as soon as the terms in which they are expressed are known. Such a truth is the assertion that God exists: for by the name "God" we understand something greater than which nothing can be thought. This notion is formed in the understanding by whoever hears and understands the name "God," so that God must already exist at least in the mind. Now He cannot exist in the mind only: for what is in the mind and in reality is greater than that which is in the mind only; but nothing is greater than God, as the very meaning of the name shows: it follows that the existence of God is a self-evident truth, being evidenced by the mere meaning of the name.

2] The existence of a being is conceivable, that could not be conceived not to exist; such a being is evidently greater than another that could be conceived not to exist. Thus then something greater than God is conceivable if He could be conceived not to exist; but anything "greater than God" is against the meaning of the name "God." It remains then that the existence of God is a self-evident truth.

3] Those propositions are most self-evident which are either identities, as "Man is man," or in which the predicates are included in the definitions of the subjects, as "Man is an animal." But in God of all beings this is found true, but His existence is His essence, as will be shown later (Chap. 22); and thus there is one and the same answer to the question "What is He?" and "Whether He is." Thus then, when it is said "God is," the predicate is either the same with the subject or at least is included in the definition of the subject; and thus the existence of God will be a self-evident truth.

4] Things naturally known are self-evident: for the knowledge of them is not attained by enquiry and study. But the existence of God is naturally known, since the desire of man tends naturally to God as his last end, as will be shown further on (B. III, Chap. 25).

5] That must be self-evident whereby all other things are known; but such is God; for as the light of the sun is the principle of all visual perception, so the divine light is the principle of all intellectual cognition.

11] *Rejection of the aforesaid Opinion, and Solution of the aforesaid Reasons.* The above opinion arises partly from custom, men being accustomed from the beginning to hear and invoke the name of God. Custom, especially that which is from the beginning, takes the place of nature; hence the notions wherewith the mind is imbued from childhood are held as firmly as if they were naturally known and self-evident. Partly also it owes its origin to the neglect of a distinction between what is self-evident *of itself absolutely* and what is self-evident *relatively to us.* Absolutely indeed the existence of God is self-evident, since God's essence is His existence. But since we cannot mentally conceive God's essence, his existence is not self-evident relatively to us.

1] Nor is the existence of God necessarily self-evident as soon as the meaning of the name "God" is known. First, because it is not evident, even to all who admit the existence of God, that God is something greater than which nothing can be conceived, since many of the ancients said that this world was God. Then granting that universal usage understands by the name "God" something greater than which nothing can be conceived, it will not follow that there exists *in rerum natura* something greater than which nothing can be conceived. For "thing" and "notion implied in the name of the thing" must answer to one another. From the conception in the mind of what is declared by this name "God" it does not follow that God exists otherwise than in the mind. Hence there will be no necessity either of that something, greater than which nothing can be conceived, existing otherwise than in the mind; and from this it does not follow that there is anything *in rerum natura* greater than which nothing can be conceived. And so the supposition of the non-existence of God goes untouched. For the possibility of our thought outrunning the greatness of any given object, whether of the actual or of the ideal order, has nothing in it to vex the soul of any one except of him alone who already grants the existence *in rerum natura* of something than which nothing can be conceived greater.

2] Nor is it necessary for something greater than God to be conceivable, if His non-existence is conceivable. For the possibility of conceiving Him not to exist does not arise from the imperfection or uncertainty of His Being, since His Being is of itself most manifest, but from the infirmity of our understanding, which cannot discern Him as He is of Himself, but only by the effects which He produces; and so it is brought by reasoning to the knowledge of Him.

3] As it is self-evident to us that the whole is greater than its part, so the existence of God is most self-evident to them that see the divine essence, inasmuch as His essence is His existence. But because we cannot see His essence, we are brought to the knowledge of His existence, not by what He is in Himself but by the effects which He works.

4] Man knows God naturally as he desires him naturally. Now man desires Him naturally inasmuch as he naturally desires happiness, which is a certain likeness to the divine goodness. Thus it is not necessary that God, considered in Himself, should be naturally known to man, but a certain likeness of God. Hence man must be led to a knowledge of God through the likenesses of Him that are found in the effects which He works.

5] God is that wherein all things are known, not as though other things could not be known without His being known first, as happens in the case of self-evident principles, but because through His influence all knowledge is caused in us.

12] *Of the Opinion of those who say that the Existence of God is a Tenet of Faith alone and cannot be demonstrated.* The falseness of this opinion is shown to us as well by the art of demonstration, which teaches us to argue causes from effects, as also by the order of the sciences,—for if there be no knowable substances above the sensible substances, there will be no science above physical science; as also by the efforts of philosophers, directed to the proof of the existence of God; as also by apostolic truth asserting: "The invisible things of God are clearly seen, being understood by the things that are made." (Rom. i, 20.)

The axiom that in God essence and existence are the same is to be understood of the existence whereby God subsists in Himself, the manner of which is unknown to us, as also is His essence; not of the existence which signifies an affirmative judgment of the understanding. For in the form of such affirmative judgment the fact that *there is a God* falls under demonstration; as our mind is led by demonstrative reasons to form such a proposition declaratory of the existence of God. In the reasonings whereby the existence of God is demonstrated it is not necessary to assume for a premise the essence or *quiddity* of God: but instead of the quiddity the effect is taken for a premise, as is done in demonstration *a posteriori* from effect to cause. All the names of God are imposed either on the principle of denying of God Himself certain effects of His power, or from some habitude of God towards those effects. Althought God transcends sense and the objects of sense, nevertheless sensible effects are the basis of our demonstration of the existence of God. Thus the origin of our own knowledge is in sense, even of things that transcend sense.

131 Reasons in Proof of the Existence of God. We will put first the reasons by which Aristotle proceeds to prove the existence of God from the consideration of motion as follows. Everything that is in motion is put and kept in motion by some other thing. It is evident to sense that there are beings in motion. A thing is in motion because something else puts and keeps it in motion. That mover therefore is either itself in motion or not. If it is not in motion, our point is gained which we proposed to prove, namely, that we must posit something which moves other things without being itself in motion, and this we call God. But if the mover is itself in motion, then it is moved by some other mover. Either then we have to go on to infinity, or we must come to some mover which is motionless; but it is impossible to go on to infinity, therefore we must posit some motionless prime mover. In this argument there are two propositions to be proved: that everything which is in motion is put and kept in motion by something else; and that in the series of movers and things moved it is impossible to go on to infinity.

The Philosopher also goes about in another way to show that it is impossible to proceed to infinity in the series of efficient causes, but we must come to one first cause, and this we call God. The way is more or less as follows. In every series of efficient causes, the first term is cause of the intermediate, and the intermediate is cause of the last. But if in efficient causes there is a process to infinity, none of the causes will be the first: therefore all the others will be taken away which are intermediate. But this is manifestly not the case; therefore we must posit the existence of some first efficient cause, which is God.

Another argument is brought by St. John Damascene (*De Fid. Orthod.* I, 3), thus: It is impossible for things contrary and discordant to fall into one harmonious order always or for the most part, except under some one guidance, assigning to each and all a tendency to a fixed end. But in the world we see things of different natures falling into harmonious order, not rarely and fortuitously, but always or for the most part. Therefore there must be some Power by whose providence the world is governed; and that we call God.

14] *That in order to a Knowledge of God we must use the Method of Negative Differentiation.* After showing that there is a First Being, whom we call God, we must enquire into the conditions of His existence. We must use the method of negative differentiation, particularly in the consideration of the divine substance. For the divine substance, by its immensity, transcends every form that our intellect can realize; and thus we cannot apprehend it by knowing what it is, but we have some sort of knowledge of it by knowing what it is not. The more we can negatively differentiate it, or the more attributes we can strike off from it in our mind, the more we approach to a knowledge of it: for we know each thing more perfectly, the fuller view we have of its differences as compared with other things; for each thing has in itself a proper being, distinct from all others. Hence in dealing with things that we can define, we first place them in some genus, by which we know in general what the thing is; and afterwards we add the differentias whereby the thing is distinguished from other things; and thus is achieved a complete knowledge of the substance of the thing. But because in the study of the divine substance we cannot fix upon anything for a genus, nor can we mark that substance off from other things by affirmative differentias, we must determine it by negative differentias. In affirmative differentias one limits the extension of another, and brings us nearer to a complete designation of the thing under enquiry, inasmuch as it makes that thing differ from more and more things. And the same holds good also of negative differentias. For example, we may say that God is not an *accident,* in that He is distinguished from all accidents; then if we add that He is not a *body,* we shall further distinguish Him from some substances; and so in order by such negations He will be further distinguished from everything besides Himself; and then there will be a proper notion of His substance, when He shall be known as distinct from all. Still it will not be a perfect knowledge, because He will not be known for what He is in Himself.

To proceed therefore in the knowledge of God by way of negative differentiation, let us take as a principle what has been shown in a previous chapter, that God is altogether immovable. . . .

21] That God is His own Essence. In everything that is not its own essence, quiddity, or nature, there must be some composition. For since in everything its own essence is contained,—if in anything there were contained nothing but its essence, the whole of that thing would be its essence, and so itself would be its own essence. If then anything is not its own essence, there must be something in that thing besides its essence, and so there must be in it composition. Hence also the essence in compound things is spoken of as a part, as humanity in man. But it has been shown that in God there is no composition. God therefore is His own essence.

2] That alone is reckoned to be beyond the essence of a thing, which does not enter into its definition: for the definition declares what the thing essentially is. But the accidents of a thing are the only points about it which fall not within the definition: therefore the accidents are the only points about a thing besides its essence. But in God there are no accidents: therefore there is nothing in Him besides His essence.

3] The forms that are not predicable of subsistent things, whether in the universal or in the singular, are forms that do not of themselves subsist singly individualised in themselves. It is not said that Socrates or man or animal is whiteness; because whiteness is not anything subsisting singly in itself, but is individualised by the substance in which it exists. Also the essences or quiddities of genera or species are individualised according to the definite matter of this or that individual, although the generic or specific quiddity includes form and matter in general: hence it is not said that Socrates or man is humanity. But the Divine Essence is something existing singly by itself, and individualised in itself. The Divine Essence therefore is predicated of God in such a way that it can be said: "God is His own essence."

22] That in God Existence and Essence is the same. It has been shown that there is an Existence which of itself necessarily is; and that is God. If this existence, which necessarily is, is contained in some essence not identical with it, then either it is dissonant and at variance with that essence, as subsistent existence is at variance with the essence of whiteness; or it is consonant with and akin to that essence, as existence in something other than itself is consonant with whiteness. In the former case, the existence which of itself necessarily is will not attach to that essence, any more than subsistent existence will attach to whiteness. In the latter case, either such existence must depend on the essence, or both existence and essence depend on another cause, or the essence must depend on the existence. The former two suppositions are against the idea of a being which of itself necessarily is; because, if it depends on another thing, it no longer is necessarily. From the third supposition it follows that that essence is accidental and adventitious to the thing which of itself necessarily is; because all that follows upon the being of a thing is accidental to it; and thus the supposed essence will not be the essence at all. God therefore has no essence that is not His existence.

2] Everything is by its own existence. Whatever then is not its own existence does not of itself necessarily exist. But God does of Himself necessarily exist: therefore God is His own existence.

4] "Existence" denotes a certain actuality: for a thing is not said to "be" for what it is potentially, but for what it is actually. But everything to which there attaches an actuality, existing as something different from it, stands to the same as potentiality to actuality. If then the divine essence is something else than its own existence, it follows that essence and existence in God stand to one another as potentiality and actuality. But it has been shown that in God there is nothing of potentiality, but that He is pure actuality. Therefore God's essence is not anything else but His existence.

5] Everything that cannot be except by the concurrence of several things is compound. But nothing in which essence is one thing, and existence another, can be except by the concurrence of several things, to wit, essence and existence. Therefore everything in which essence is one thing, and existence another, is compound. But God is not compound. Therefore the very existence of God is His essence. . . .

28] *That God is Universal Perfection.* As all perfection and nobility is in a thing inasmuch as the thing is, so every defect is in a thing inasmuch as the thing in some manner is not. As then God has being in its totality, so not-being is totally removed from Him, because the measure in which a thing has being is the measure of its removal from not-being. Therefore all defect is absent from God: He is therefore universal perfection.

2] Everything imperfect must proceed from something perfect: therefore the First Being must be most perfect.

3] Everything is perfect inasmuch as it is in actuality; imperfect, inasmuch as it is in potentiality, with privation of actuality. That then which is nowise in potentiality, but is pure actuality, must be most perfect; and such is God.

4] Nothing acts except inasmuch as it is in actuality: action therefore follows the measure of actuality in the agent. It is impossible therefore for any effect that is brought into being by action to be of a nobler actuality than is the actuality of the agent. It is possible though for the actuality of the effect to be less perfect than the actuality of the acting cause, inasmuch as action may be weakened on the part of the object to which it is terminated, or upon which it is spent. Now in the category of efficient causation everything is reducible ultimately to one cause which is God, of whom are all things. Everything therefore that actually is in any other thing must be found in God much more eminently than in the thing itself; God then is the most perfect.

II:8] That God's Power is His Substance. Active power belongs to the perfection of a thing. But every divine perfection is contained in God's own being (I:28). God's power therefore is not different from His being. But God is His own being (I:22); He is therefore His own power.

4] In things the powers of which are not their substance, the said powers are accidents. But there can be no accident in God, who is therefore His own power.

9] That God's Power is His Action. God's power is His substance, as has been shown in the previous chapter: also His action is His substance, as has been shown of His intellectual activity, and the same argument holds for His other activities. Therefore in God power and action are not two different things.

2] The action of any being is a complement of its power; for it stands to power as the second actuality to the first. But the divine power, being God's very essence, has no other complement than itself. And therefore in God action and power are not distinct.

4] Any action that is not the agent's very substance is in the agent as an accident in its subject. But in God there can be nothing accidental. Therefore in God His action is none other than His substance and His power.

34] *Reasons alleged for the Eternity of the World on the part of the Creative Process itself, with Answers to the same. Arg. 1.* It is the common opinion of all philosophers, and therefore it must be true, that nothing is made of nothing (Aristotle, *Physics,* I: 7, 8). Whatever is made, then, must be made of something; and that again, if it is made at all, must be made of something else. But this process cannot go on to infinity; and therefore we must come to something that was not made. But every being that has not always been must have been made. Therefore that out of which all things are first made must be something everlasting. That cannot be God, because He cannot be the material of anything. Therefore there must be something eternal outside God, namely, primordial matter. . . .

37] *Reply.* The common position of philosophers, that nothing is made of nothing, is true of the sort of making that they considered. For all our knowledge begins in sense, which is of singular objects; and human investigation has advanced from particular to general considerations. Hence, in studying the beginning of things, men gave their attention to the making of particular things in detail. The making of one sort of being out of another sort is the making of some particular being, inasmuch as it is "this being," not as it is "being" generally: for some prior being there was that now is changed into "this being." But entering more deeply into the origin of things, philosophers came finally to consider the issuing of all created being from one first cause. In this origin of all created being from God, it is impossible to all any making out of pre-existent material: for such making out of pre-existent material would not be a making of the whole being of the creature. This first making of the universe was not attained to in the thought of the early physicists, whose common opinion it was that nothing was made of nothing: or if any did attain to it, they considered that such a term as "making" did not properly apply to it, since the name "making" implies movement or change, whereas in this origin of all being from one first being there can be no question of the transmutation of one being into another. Therefore it is not the concern of physical science to study this first origin of all things: that study belongs to the metaphysician, who deals with being in general and realities apart from motion. We may however by a figure of speech apply the name of "making" to creation, and speak of things as "made," whatsoever they are, the essence or nature whereof has its origin from other being.

Arg. 2. Everything that takes a new being is now otherwise than as it was before: that must come about by some movement or change: but all movement or change is in some subject: therefore before anything is made there must be some subject of motion.

Reply. The notion of motion or change is foisted in here to no purpose: for what nowise is, is not anywise, and affords no hold for the conclusion that, when it begins to be, it is otherwise than as it was before.

These then are the reasons which some hold to as demonstrative, and necessarily evincing that creatures have always existed, wherein they contradict the Catholic faith, which teaches that nothing but God has always existed, and that all else has had a beginning of being except the one eternal God. Thus then it evidently appears that there is nothing to traverse our assertion, that the world has not always existed. . . .

38] *Arguments wherewith some try to show that the World is not Eternal, and Solutions of the same. Arg. 1.* God is the cause of all things. But a cause must be prior in duration to the effects of its action.

Reply. That is true of things that act by motion, for the effect is not till the termination of the motion: but with causes that act instantaneously there is no such necessity.

Arg. 2. Since the whole of being is created by God, it cannot be said to be made out of any being: whence the conclusion follows that it is made out of nothing, and consequently that it has existence after not existing.

Reply. To the notion of *being made out of something,* if that is not admitted, one must supply the contradictory notion: which contradictory notion is *not being made out of nothing,* except in the former sense of *not being made out of anything.*

Arg. 3. It is not possible to pass through infinity. But if the world always had been, infinity would have been passed through by this time, there being infinite days, or daily rounds of the sun, if the world always has been.

Reply. An infinite quantity, though not existing in simultaneous actual realisation, may nevertheless be in succession, because every infinite, so taken, is really finite. Any given round of the sun could be passed, because so far the number of them was finite: but when they are all viewed together, on the supposition that the world had always existed, it would be impossible to fix upon any first day, and so to make any transition from that to the present day, since transition always requires two extreme points.

Arg. 4. It would follow that addition is made to the infinite, because to past days, or sun-rounds, a new round is daily added.

Reply. There is nothing to hinder addition to the infinite on that side on which it is finite. Supposing time eternal, it must be infinite as preceding, but finite as succeeding, for the present is the limit of the past.

Arg. 5. It would follow in a world always existing that we should have an infinite series of efficient causes, father being cause of child, and grandfather to father, and so to infinity.

Reply. The impossibility of an infinite series of efficient causes, according to philosophers (Aristotle, *Metaph.* ii, 2), holds for causes acting together: because then the effect has to depend on an infinity of co-existent actions; and the infinity of causes there is essential, the whole infinite multitude of them being requisite for the production of the effect. But in the case of causes not acting together no such impossibility holds, in the opinion of those who suppose an endless series of generations. The infinity in this case is accidental to the causes: for to Socrates' father, as such, it is quite an accident whether he be the son of another man or no: whereas to a stick, inasmuch as it moves a stone, it is not an accident whether it be moved by an hand: for it only moves inasmuch as it is moved.

Arg. 6. It would follow that an infinite multitude exists, to wit, the immortal souls of infinite men who have been in the past.

Reply. This objection is more difficult: nevertheless the argument is not of much use, because it supposes many things.

Since these reasons, alleged by some to prove that the world has not always existed, are not necessarily conclusive, though they have a certain probability, it is sufficient to touch on them slightly, without insisting too much, that the Catholic faith may not seem to rest on empty reasonings, and not rather on the solid basis of the teaching of God.

41] *That the Variety of Creatures does not arise from any Contrariety of Prime Agents.* If the diversity of things proceeds from diversity or contrariety of diverse agents, this would seem to hold especially of the contrariety of good and evil, so that all good things should proceed from a good principle, and evils from an evil principle. Now there is good and evil in all genera. But there cannot be one first principle of all evils: for the very essence of such a principle would be evil, and that is impossible. Everything that is, inasmuch as it is a being, must necessarily be good: for it loves and strives to preserve its own being, a sign whereof is this fact, that everything fights against its own destruction: now what all things seek is good. It is impossible therefore for the diversity of things to arise from two principles, one good and one evil.

9] What in no manner of way is, is neither good nor evil: while everything that is, in so far as it is, is good. A thing can be evil therefore only inasmuch as it is not-being, that is, *privative* being; and the evil is precisely the privation. Now privation never comes of the ordinary action of any cause: because every cause acts inasmuch as it is endowed with "form"; and thus the ordinary effect of its action must also be endowed with "form," since every agent acts to the production of its own likeness, unless it be accidentally hindered. It follows that evil does not come of the ordinary action of any cause, but is accidentally incident among the effects of ordinary causation. There is therefore no one primary and essential principle of all evil: but the first principle of all is one primary good, among the effects of which there ensues evil incidentally. . . .

Hereby is excluded the error of those who suppose two primitive contrary principles, good and evil. This error of the early philosophers some evil-minded men have presumed to introduce into Christian teaching, the first of whom was Marcion, and afterwards the Manicheans, who have done most to spread this error.

44] *That the Variety of Creatures has not arisen from Variety of Merits and Demerits.* Origen in his book *Perì Archōn* says that God out of mere bounty in His first production of creatures made them all equal, all spiritual and rational, and they by free will behaved in various ways, some adhering to God more or less, and others receding from Him more or less; and thus by order of divine justice various grades ensued among spiritual substances, some appearing as angels of various orders, some as human could also of various states and conditions, some again as demons in various states. He also said that it was through this variety of rational creatures that God instituted a variety also of material creatures, so that the nobler spiritual substances should be united to the nobler bodies, and that in divers other ways the material creation might serve to express the variety of spiritual substances. According to Origen, man, sun, and stars are composed of rational substances united with corresponding bodies. Now all this opinion can be shown to be manifestly false.

1] The better a thing is, the higher place does it hold in the intention of the agent who produces it. But the best thing in creation is the perfection of the universe, which consists in the orderly variety of things: for in all things the perfection of the whole is preferable to the perfection of parts and details. Therefore the diversity of creatures does not arise from diversity of merits, but was primarily intended by the prime agent.

2] If all rational creatures were created equal from the beginning, we should have allowed that they do not depend for their activity one on another. What arises by the concurrence of divers causes working independently of one another is matter of chance; and thus the diversity and order of creation comes by chance, which is impossible.

12] Since a spiritual creature, or angel, does not deserve to be degraded except for sin,—and it is degraded from its high, invisible estate, by being united with a visible body,—it seems that visible bodies have been added to these spiritual creatures because of sin; which comes near to the error of the Manicheans, who laid it down that the visible creation proceeded from an evil principle.

Origen seems to have given sufficient weight to the consideration that, when we give, not in discharge of any debt, but out of liberality, it is not contrary to justice if we give in unequal measure: but God brought things into being under no debt, but of sheer liberality: therefore the variety of creatures does not presuppose variety of merits.

45] *The Real Prime Cause of the Variety of Creatures.* Since every agent intends to induce its own likeness in the effect, so far as the effect can receive it, an agent will do this more perfectly the more perfectly itself is. But God is the most perfect of agents: therefore it will belong to Him to induce His likeness in creation most perfectly, so far as befits created nature. But creatures cannot attain to any perfect likeness of God so long as they are confined to one species of creature; because, since the cause exceeds the effect, what is in the cause simply as one thing is found in the effect in a composite and manifest way, unless the effect be of the same species as the cause; which is impossible in the case before us, for no creature can be equal to God. Multiplicity therefore and variety was needful in creation, to the end that the perfect likeness of God might be found in creatures according to their measure.

2] As the things that are made of any material are contained in the potentiality of the material, so the things done by any agent must be in the active power of the agent. But the potentiality of the material would not be perfectly reduced to actuality, if out of the material were made only one of those things to which the material is in potentiality. Therefore if any agent whose power extends to various effects were to produce only one of those effects, his power would not be so completely reduced to actuality as by making many. But by the reduction of active power to actuality the effect attains to the likeness of the agent. Therefore the likeness of God would not be perfect in the universe, if there was only one grade of all beings.

3] A creature approaches more perfectly to the likeness of God by being not only good itself, but able to act for the good of others. But no creature could do anything for the good of another creature, unless there were plurality and inequality

among creatures, because the agent must be other than the patient and in a position of advantage *(honorabilius)* over it.

5] The goodness of the species transcends the goodness of the
individual. Therefore the multiplication of species is a greater
addition to the good of the universe than the multiplication of
individuals of one species.

7] To a work contrived by sovereign goodness there ought
not to lacking the height of perfection proper to it. But the good
of order in variety is better than the isolated good of any one
of the things that enter into the order: therefore the good of
order ought not to be wanting to the work of God; which good
could not be, if there were no diversity and inequality between
creatures, not by chance, not from diversity of elements, not by
the intervention of any (inferior) cause, or consideration of
merit, but by the special intention of God, wishing to give the
creature such perfection as it was capable of having. . . .

III:2] *That every Agent acts to some End.* In the case of agents that
manifestly act to some end, we call that the end to which the effort
of the agent tends. Gaining that, he is said to gain his end; and
missing that, he is said to miss his intended end. Nor on this point
does it make any difference whether the end be tended to with
knowledge or not: for as the target is the end of the archer, so is it
also the path of the arrow. The effort of every agent tends to some
certain end. Not any and every action can proceed from any and
every power. Action is sometimes terminated to some product,
sometimes not. When action is terminated to some product, the
effort of the agent tends to the same. When action is not terminated to any product, the effort of the agent tends to the action
itself. Every agent therefore must intend some end in his action,
sometimes the action itself, sometimes something produced by the
action.

3] It is impossible for the chain of action to extend to infinity: there must then be something, in the getting of which the
effort of the agent comes to rest. Therefore every agent acts to
some end.

6] Actions are open to criticism only so far as they are taken
to be done as means to some end. It is not imputed as a fault to
any one, if he fails in effecting that for which his work is not

intended. A physician is found fault with if he fails in healing,
but not a builder or a grammarian. We find fault in points of
art, as when a grammarian does not speak correctly; and also in
points of nature, as in monstrous births. Therefore both the
natural agent, and the agent who acts according to art and with
a conscious purpose, acts for an end.

7] To an agent that did not tend to any definite effect, all
effects would be indifferent. But what is indifferent to many
things, does not do one of them rather than another: Hence
from an agent open to both sides of an alternative (a contin-
gente ad utrumque) there does not follow any effect, unless by
some means it comes to be determined to one above the rest:
otherwise it could not act at all. Every agent therefore tends to
some definite effect, and that is called its end.

Still there are action that do not seem to be for any end, as
things done for sport, and acts of contemplation, and things
done without advertence, as the stroking of the beard and the
like: from which instances one may suppose that there is such
a thing as an agent acting not for any end. But we must observe
that though acts of contemplation are not for any other end,
they are an end in themselves: as for things done in sport, sometimes they are their own end, as when one plays solely for the
amusement that he finds in play; sometimes they are for an end,
as when we play that afterwards we may resume work more
vigorously: while things done without advertence proceed not
from the understanding, but from some phantasy or physical
principle; yet even these acts tend to certain ends, though beyond the scope of the intellect of the agent.

Hereby is banished the error of certain natural philosophers
(Empedocles and Democritus, mentioned by Aristotle, *Physics,*
II, ii, 6) who supposed all things to happen by necessity of mat-
ter, and eliminated final causes from the universe.

)] *That every Agent acts to some Good.* That to which an agent
definitely tends must be suited to it: for it would not tend to a
thing except for some suitability to itself. But what is suitable to
a thing is good for it. Therefore every agent acts to some good.

6] An intellectual agent acts for an end by determining its
own end. A physical agent, though acting for an end, does not

determine its own end, having no idea of an end, but moves in the direction of an end determined for it by another. Now an intellectual agent does not fix for itself an end except under some aspect of good, which is the object of will. Therefore a physical agent also does not move or act to any end except inasmuch as it is good. Such an agent has its end determined by some natural appetite or tendency.

7] It is part of the same plan of action to shun evil and to seek good. But all things are found to shun evil. Intellectual agents shun a thing for this reason, that they apprehend it as evil: while all physical agents, to the full extent of the power that is in them, resist destruction, because that is the evil of everything. All things therefore act to some good.

4] *That Evil in things is beside the Intention of the Agent.* What follows from an action different from what was intended by the agent, manifestly happens beside his intention. But evil is different from good, which every agent intends. Therefore evil happens beside the intention.

2] Failure in effect and action follows upon some defect in the principle of action, as a halting gait follows upon crookedness of legs. Now an agent acts by whatever of active power he has, not by what defect of active power he suffers; and according as he acts, so does he intend his end. He intends therefore an end answering to his power. Anything therefore that ensues answering to defect of power will be beside the intention of the agent. But such is evil.

4] In agents that act by intellect, or by any sort of judgment, intention follows apprehension: for intention tends to that which is apprehended as an end. If then experience lights upon something not of the species apprehended, the event will be beside the intention: thus if one intends to eat honey, and eats gall, taking it for honey, that will be beside the intention. But every intellectual agent intends a thing according as he takes it for something good: if then it turns out not to be good but evil, that will be beside the intention.

7] *That Evil is not a Nature or Essence.* Evil is nothing else than a privation of that which a thing is naturally apt to have and ought to have. But a privation is not an essence, but a negation in a substance.

5] Every essence is natural to some thing. If the essence ranks as a substance, it is the very nature of the thing. If it ranks as an accident, it must be caused by the principle of some substance, and thus will be natural to that substance, though perhaps not natural to some other substance. But what is in itself evil cannot be natural to anything: for the essence of evil is privation of that which is naturally apt to be in a thing and is due to it. Evil then, being a privation of what is natural, cannot be natural to anything. Hence whatever is naturally in a thing is good, and the want of it an evil. No essence then is in itself evil.

6] Whatever has any essence is either itself a form or has a form, for by form everything is assorted in some genus, or species. But form, as such, has a character of goodness, being the principle of action and the end which every maker intends, and the actuality whereby every subject of form is perfected. Whatever therefore has any essence, as such, is good.

7] Being is divided into actuality and potentiality. Actuality, as such, is good, because everything is perfected by that whereby it actually is. Potentiality too is something good: for potentiality tends to actuality, and is proportionate to actuality, not contrary to it; and is of the same genus with actuality; and privation does not attach to it except accidentally. Everything therefore that is, in whatsoever way it is, in so far as it is a being, is good.

8] All being, howsoever it be, is from God. But God is perfect goodness. Since then evil cannot be the effect of goodness, it is impossible for any being, as being, to be evil.

10] *That the Cause of Evil is good.* What is not, is cause of nothing: every cause must be some being. But evil is not any being (Chap. 7): therefore evil cannot be the cause of anything. If then evil is caused by anything, what causes it must be good.

4] Every cause is either material, formal, efficient, or final. But evil can be neither matter nor form: for it has been shown (Chap. 7) that both actual being and potential being is good. In like manner evil cannot be an efficient cause, since everything acts according as it is actually and has a form. Nor can it be a final cause, since it is beside the intention (Chap. 4). Evil therefore cannot be the cause of anything; and therefore, if there be any cause of evil, it must be caused by good.

But since good and evil are opposites, and one opposite cannot be cause of another except accidentally, it follows that good cannot be the active cause of evil except accidentally. In physics, this accident may happen either on the part of the agent or on the party of the effect. On the part of the agent, when the agent suffers from a lack of power, whence it follows that the action is defective and the effect deficient. But to an agent, as such, it is quite an accident to suffer from a lack of power: for an agent does not act inasmuch as power is lacking to him, but according as he has anything of power. Thus then evil is caused accidentally on the part of the agent, inasmuch as the agent runs short of power: therefore it is said that evil has not got an efficient cause, but a deficient cause, because evil does not follow from an efficient cause except in so far as it is deficient in power, and in this respect it is not efficient. It comes to the same thing if the defect of the action and effect arises from some defect of the instrument, or of any other thing requisite for the agent's action, as when motive power produces halting through crookedness of the shin-bone: for the agent acts by both the power and the instrument. On the part of the effect evil is caused accidentally as well in respect of the matter of the effect as also in respect of its form. For if the matter is indisposed to receive the impression of the agent, some defect must follow in the effect. Nor is it imputable to any defect of the agent, that it does not transmute an indisposed matter to a perfect act: for the power of every natural agent is determined according to the limit of its nature; and its failure to transcend that cannot be brought in against it as a defect in power: such defect can then only be argued when it falls short of the measure of power due to it by nature. On the part of the form of the effect evil is accidentally incident, inasmuch as one form necessarily involves the privation of another form, and with the production of one thing there must needs ensue the destruction of another. But this evil does not belong to the effect intended by the agent, but attaches to something else. In the processes of nature therefore evil is caused

by good only accidentally. The same is the case also in the
processes of art: for art in its operation imitates nature, and
is at fault in the same way as nature.

But in moral matters the case seems to be different. For a flaw
in morals does not follow from any lack of power, seeing that
weakness either entirely removes, or at least diminishes, more
reprehensibleness: for weakness does not deserve the punishment which is due to fault, but rather compassion and indulgence: to be blameworthy, a point of conduct must be a
voluntary act, not an inevitable necessity. On careful consideration we find that the case of morals is in some respects like, in
some respects unlike the case of physics. The unlikeness consists in this, that a moral fault is viewed as consisting in the
action alone, not in any effect produced: for moral virtues are
not effective, but active, while arts are effective; and therefore
it has been said that art is at fault in the same way as nature.
Moral evil therefore is not estimated according to the matter
and form of the effect, but follows simply from the agent. Now
in moral actions there are found in orderly enumeration four
active principles. One principle is the executive power, namely,
the motor power which moves the limbs to execute the command of the will. This power is moved by the judgment of the
apprehensive faculty, which judges the particular thing proposed to be good or bad—*good* and *bad* being the (formal) objects of the will, the one object of seeking, the other of avoidance.
Lastly, the apprehensive faculty is moved by the thing apprehended. The first active principle then in moral actions is the
thing apprehended; the second is the apprehensive faculty; the
third is the will; the fourth is motor power which executes the
command of reason. But the act of the executive power already
presupposes moral good or evil: for these exterior acts bear a
moral character only in so far as they are voluntary. Hence if
the act of the will is good, the exterior act will also be called
good; and evil, if the volition is evil. It would be no point of
moral badness for the exterior act to fail by some defect un-
connected with the will: thus lameness is not a moral but a
natural blemish. Such a lack of executive power diminishes, if
it does not totally excuse from, moral blemish. Again, the act
whereby the object moves the apprehensive faculty is exempt

from moral blemish: for it is according to the order of nature that what is visible effects the sight, and every object affects the corresponding passive potentiality. Even the act of the apprehensive faculty, considered in itself, is nowise morally blameworthy, as we see that any defect in it excuses from or diminishes moral blame, like the lack of executive power: for infirmity and ignorance alike excuse from sin, or diminish it. It remains then that moral blameworthiness is found first and foremost in the act of the will alone; and reasonably so, since an act is called "moral" from being voluntary. In the act of the will then is to be sought the root and origin of what in the moral order is sin.

But this investigation leads us into an apparent difficulty. On the understanding that defect in an act arises from some defect in the principle of action, some defect in the will must be presupposed before there can be any moral fault. If this defect is natural, it is ever inherent in the will; and the consequence is that the will must always do wrong in action, a consequence proved false by the fact of there being such things as acts of virtue. On the other hand, if the defect is voluntary, that is already a moral fault, the cause of which must stand over for further enquiry; and so we shall have a running account to infinity. We must therefore say that the defect pre-existing in the will is no natural necessity, otherwise it would follow that the will sinned in every act: nor again is a thing of chance and ill luck, for at that rate there could be in us no moral fault, since events of chance are unpremeditated and beyond the control of reason. The defect therefore is voluntary, but not a moral fault: so we must suppose to save the account running to infinity.

Now we must consider how that can be. In every active principle the perfection of its power depends on some superior active principle: for a secondary agent acts by virtue of the power of the prime agent. So long then as the secondary agent remains under the power of the prime agent, it will act unfailingly: but it will fail in its action whenever it happens to swerve from the order of the prime agent, as appears in an instrument when it ceases to respond to the movement of the agent who uses it. Now it has been said above that in order of moral action two principles go before volition, the apprehensive faculty and the object apprehended, which is the end in view. But since to everything movable there corresponds a proper motive power, not any and every apprehensive faculty is the due motive power of any and every appetite, but one apprehension is the proper motive of one appetite, another of another. As then the sensible apprehensive faculty is the proper motive power of the sensible appetite, so the proper motive power of the will is reason itself. Further, as reason can apprehend many sorts of good things and many ends of action; as moreover every power has its own proper end; the will also must have some object and end of action and prime motive, and that must be not any and every sort of good, but some definite good. Whenever then the will tends to act under the motive of apprehension of reason representing to it its own proper good, a due action ensues. But when the will bursts out into action upon the apprehension of the sensible apprehensive faculty, or even upon the apprehension of reason itself, representing some other good than the proper good of the will, there ensues in the action of the will a moral fault. Therefore any faulty action in the will is preceded by a lack of due regard to reason and to the proper end of willing. I say "a lack of due regard to reason," in such cases as when, upon some sudden apprehension of sense, the will tends to some good that is pleasant according to sense. I say "a lack of due regard to the proper end of willing," in cases when the reason arrives by reasoning at some good, which is not either *now* or *in this way* good, and still the will tends to it as though it were its proper good. Now this lack of due regard is voluntary: for it is in the power of the will to will and not to will: it is likewise in its power to direct reason actually to consider or to cease from considering, or to consider this or that. Still this failure of due consideration is not a moral evil: for, consideration or no consideration, or whatever the consideration be on reason's part, there is no sin until the will comes to tend to some undue end, which then is an act of will.—Thus it remains true that in moral as well as in physical actions, evil is not caused by good except accidentally.

161 *That the End in View of everything is some Good.* That to which a thing tends when in absence from it, and in which it rests when in possession of it, is the scope and aim and end in view.

But everything, so long as it lacks the perfection proper to it, moves towards gaining that perfection, so far as it depends upon itself so to do; and when it has gained that perfection, therein it rests. The end then of everything is its perfection. But the perfection of everything is its own good. Everything therefore is ordained to good as to its end.

4] Things that are aware of an end and things that are unaware of an end are alike ordained to an end, with this difference, that things that are aware of an end tend to an end of themselves, while things that are unaware of an end tend to an end under the direction of an another, as appears in the case of archer and arrow. But things that are aware of an end are always ordained to good for their end: for the will, which is the appetite of a fore-known end, never tends to anything except under the aspect of good, which is its object. Therefore things also which are unaware of an end are ordained to good for their end; and so good is the end of all things.

17] *That all Things are ordained to one End, which is God.* The sovereign good, which is God, is the cause of goodness in all good things. He is therefore also the cause of every end being an end, since whatever is an end is such inasmuch as it is good. But that whereby another thing has an attribute, has more of that attribute itself. Therefore God above all things is the end of all.

4] In every series of end the last end must be the end of all the ends preceding. But we find all things arranged in various grades of goodness under one sovereign good, which is the cause of all goodness; and thereby, since good bears the character of an end, all things are ordered under God as ends preceding under the last end.

5] Private good is subordinated to the end of the common good: for the being of a part is for the sake of the being of the whole: hence the good of the race is more godlike than the good of the individual man. But the sovereign good, which is God, is the common good, since the good of the whole community depends on Him: while the goodness which marks any given thing is its own private good, and also the good of other things which depend upon it. All things therefore are subordinate to the end of one good, which is God.

7] The last end of every producer, in so far as he is a producer, is himself: for the things produced by us we use for ourselves; and if ever a man makes anything for another man, that is referred to his own good,—his utility, his pleasure, or his honour. But God is the productive cause of all things, either immediately or mediately. And therefore His is the end of all.

18] *How God is the End of all Things.* God is at once the last end of all things, and is nevertheless before all things in being. There is an end which, while holding the first place in causation according as it is in intention, is nevertheless posterior in being; and this is the case with every end that an agent establishes by his action, as the physician establishes health by his action in the sick man, which health nevertheless is his end. There is again an end which is prior in causation, and also is prior in being: such an end one aims at winning by one's action or movement, as a king hopes to win a city by fighting. God then is the end of things, as being something which everything has to gain in its own way.

2] God is the last end of things and the prime agent of all (Chap. 17). But an end established by the action of an agent cannot be the prime agent: rather it is the effect produced by the agent. God therefore cannot be the end of things as though He were anything established in being thereby, but only as some pre-existent objects for them to attain.

4] An effect tends to an end in the same way that the producer of the effect acts for that end. But God, the first producer of all things, does not act in view of acquiring anything by His action, but in view of bestowing something by His action: for He is not in potentiality to acquire anything, but only in perfect actuality, whereby He can give and bestow. Things then are not directed to God as though God were an end unto which any accretion or acquisition were to be made: they are directed to Him so that in their own way they may gain From God Himself, since He Himself is their end.

25] *That the End of every Subsistent Intelligence is to understand God.* The proper act of everything is its end, as being its second perfection: hence what is well disposed to its own proper act is said to be virtuous and good. But to understand is the proper act of a subsistent intelligence: that then is its end. And the most perfect instance of this act is its final end and perfection: this is particularly true of acts which are not directed to production, acts such as understanding and feeling. But since such acts take their species from their objects, and are known through their objects, any given one of these acts will be the more perfect, the more perfect its object is. Consequently, to understand the most perfect intelligible object, which is God, will be the most perfect instance of the activity of understanding. To know God then by understanding is the final end of every subsistent intelligence.

But one may say: "It is true that the last end of a subsistent intelligence consists in understanding the best intelligible object, still the best intelligible object, absolutely speaking, is not the best object for *this* or *that* subsistent intelligence; but the higher any subsistent intelligence is, the higher is its best intelligible object; and therefore the highest subsistent intelligence created has for its best intelligible object that which is best absolutely; hence its happiness will be in understanding God; but the happiness of a lower subsistent intelligence will be to understand some lower intelligible object, which is at the same time the highest of the object that can be understood by it. And particularly it seems to be the lot of the human understanding, on account of its weakness, not to understand the absolutely best intelligible object: for in respect of the knowledge of that truth of which there is most to be known the human intellect is as the bat's eye to the sun."

Nevertheless it may be manifestly shown that the end of every subsistent intelligence, even the lowest, is to understand God. For (a) the final end of all being, to which they tend, is God (Ch. 18). But the human understanding, however it be lowest in the order of subsistent intelligences, is nevertheless superior to all beings devoid of understanding. Since then the nobler substance has not the ignobler end, God Himself will be the end elso of the human understanding. But every intelligent being gains its last end by understanding it. Therefore it is by understanding that the human intellect attains God as its end.

(c). Everything most of all desires its own last end. But the human mind is moved to more desire and love and delight over the knowledge of divine things, little as it can discern about them, than over the perfect knowledge that it has of the lowest things.

(e). All sciences and arts and practical faculties are attractive only for the sake of something else: for in them the end is not knowledge but production of a work. But speculative sciences are attractive for their own sake. for their end is sheer knowledge. Nor is there found any action in human life, with the exception of speculative study, which is not directed to some other and further end. Even actions done is sport, which seem to be done in view of no end, have a due end, which is refreshment of mind, to enable us thereby to return stronger to serious occupations: otherwise we should play always, if play was sought for its own sake, which would be unbefitting. Therefore the practical arts are ordained to the speculative, and all human activity has intellectual speculation for its end. In all due ordination of sciences and arts, the character of final end attaches to that science or art which issues precepts as master-builder to the rest: thus the art of navigation, to which belongs the management of a ship, lays down precepts for ship-building. In this relation Metaphysics (philosophia prima) stand to all speculative sciences. On metaphysics they all depend, and from that science they receive their principles and directions how to proceed against deniers of principles. This first philosophy is wholly directed to the final end of the knowledge of God: hence it is called a divine science. The knowledge of God therefore is the final end of all human study and activity.

(f). In all series of agents and causes of change the end of the prime agent and mover must be the ultimate end of all, as the end of a general is the end of all the soldiers who serve under him. But among all the component parts of man we find the intellect to be the superior moving power: for the intellect moves the appetite, putting its object before it; and the intellectual appetite, or will, moves the sensible appetites, the irascible and concupiscible: hence we do not obey concupiscence except under the command of the will. The sensitive appetite, crowned by the consent of the will, proceeds to move the body. The end therefore of the intellect is the end of all human actions. But the end and good of the intellect is truth; and consequently its last end is the first truth. The last end then of the whole man and of all his activities and desires is to know the first truth, which is God.

(g). There is a natural desire in all men of knowing the causes of the things that they see. It was through wonder at seeing things,

the causes of which were unseen, that men first began to philoso-
phise. Nor does enquiry cease until we arrive at the first cause:
then we consider our knowledge perfect, when we know the first
cause. Man then naturally desires so to know the first cause as his
last end. But the first cause is God; and the last end of man, and of
every subsistent intelligence, is called blessedness or happiness. To
know God then is the blessedness and happiness of every subsistent
intelligence. . . .

40] *That Happiness does not consist in the Knowledge of God by
Faith.* Happiness is the perfect activity of the human intellect. But
in the knowledge that is of faith, though there is high perfection
on the part of the object so apprehended, there is great imperfection on the side of intellect, for intellect does not understand that
to which it assents in believing.

2] Final happiness does not consist principally in any act of
will. But in the knowledge of faith the will has a leading part:
for the understanding assents by faith to the things proposed to
it, because it wills to do so, without being necessarily drawn by
the direct evidence of truth.

3] He who believes, yields assent to things proposed to him by
another, which himself he does not see: hence the knowledge of
faith is more like hearing than seeing. Since then happiness consists in the highest knowledge of God, it cannot consist in the
knowledge of faith.

4] Happiness being the last end, all natural desire is thereby
appeased. But the knowledge of faith, far from appeasing desire,
rather excites it, since every one desires to see that which he
believes.

48] *That the Final Happiness of Man is not in this Life.* If then
human happiness does not consist in the knowledge of God,
whereby He is commonly known by all or most men according to
some vague estimate, nor again in the knowledge of God whereby
He is known demonstratively in speculative science, nor in the
knowledge of God whereby He is known by faith, as has been
shown above; if again it is impossible in this life to arrive at a
higher knowledge of God so as to know Him in His essence, or to
understand other pure spirits, and thereby attain to a nearer

knowledge of God; and still final happiness must be placed in some knowledge of God; it follows that it is impossible for the final happiness of man to be in this life.

2] The last end of man bounds his natural desire, so that, when that is reached, nothing further is sought: for if there is still a tendency to something else, the end of rest is not yet gained. But that cannot be in this life: for the more one understands, the more is the desire of understanding, natural to all men, increased.

3] When one gains happiness, he gains also stability and rest. All have this idea of happiness, that it involves stability as a necessary condition: hence the philosopher says that we do not take man for a chameleon. But in this life there is no stability: for however happy a man be called, sicknesses and misfortunes may always happen to debar him from that activity, whatever it is, wherein happiness consists.

4] It seems unfitting and irrational that the period of development should be great and the period of duration small: for it would follow that nature for the greater part of its time went without its final perfection. Hence we see that animals that live for a short time take a short time in arriving at maturity. But if human happiness consists in perfect activity according to perfect virtue, whether intellectual or moral, such happiness cannot accrue to man till after a long lapse of time; and this is especially apparent in speculative activity, in which the happiness of man is ultimately placed. For scarcely in extreme age can a man arrive a perfect view of scientific truth; and then for the most part there is little of human life left.

5] That is the perfect good of happiness, which is absolutely free from admixture of evil, as that is perfect whiteness, which is absolutely unmingled with black. But it is impossible for man in the state of this life to be altogether free from evils,—not to say bodily evils, as hunger, thirst, cold and heat, but even from evils of the soul. There is no man living who is not at times disturbed by inordinate passions, who does not at times overstep the mean in which virtue consists, or fall short of it, who is not in some things deceived, or ignorant of what he wishes to know, or driven to weak surmises on points where he would like absolute certainty.

6] Man naturally shrinks from death, and is sad at the thought of it. Yet man must die, and therefore cannot be perfectly happy while here he lives.

7] Happiness consists, not in habit, but activity: for habits are for the sake of acts. But it is impossible in this life to do any act continually.

8] The more a thing is desired and loved, the greater grief and sadness does its loss bring. But if final happiness be in this world, it will certainly be lost, at least by death; and it is uncertain whether it will last till death, since to any man there may possibly happen in this life diseases totally debarring him from any virtuous activity, such as insanity. Such happiness therefore must always have a natural pendent of sadness.

But it may be replied that whereas happiness is the good of an intelligent nature, true and perfect happiness belongs to those in whom intelligent nature is found in its perfection, that is in pure spirits; but in man it is found imperfectly by way of a limited participation. And this seems to have been the mind of Aristotle: hence, enquiring whether misfortunes take away happiness, after showing that happiness lies in virtuous activities, which are the most permanent things in this life, he concludes that they who enjoy such perfection in this life are "happy for men," meaning that they do not absolutely attain happiness, but only in a human way.

Now it is demonstrable that the aforesaid answer is not to the undoing of the arguments above alleged. For (a) though man is inferior in the order of nature to pure spirits, yet he is superior to irrational creatures; and therefore he must gain his final end in a more perfect way than they. But they gain their final end so perfectly as to seek nothing further. Thus the natural desire of dumb animals is at rest in the enjoyment of sensual delights. Much more must the natural desire of man be put at rest by his arrival at his last end. But that is impossible in this life: therefore it must be attained after this life.

(b) It is impossible for a natural desire to be empty and vain: for nature does nothing in vain. But the desire of nature (for happiness) would be empty and vain, if it never possibly could be fulfilled. Therefore this natural desire of man is fulfillable. But not in this life. Therefore it must be fulfilled after this life.

Alexander and Averroes laid it down that the final happiness of man is not in such knowledge as is possible to man through the speculative sciences, but in a knowledge gained by conjunction with a separately subsistent intelligence, which conjunction they conceived to be possible to man in this life. But because Aristotle saw that there was no other knowledge for man in this life than that which is through the speculative sciences, he supposed man not to gain perfect happiness, but a limited measure of happiness suited to his state. In all which investigation it sufficiently appears how hard pressed on this side and on that these fine geniuses *(praeclara ingenia)* were. From this stress of difficulty we shall find escape in positing, according to the proofs already given, that man can arrive at true happiness after this life, the soul of man being immortal. In this disembodied state the soul will understand in the way in which pure spirits understand. The final happiness of man then will be in the knowledge of God, which the human soul has after this life according to the manner in which pure spirits know Him. . . .

52] *That no Created Substance can of its natural power arrive to see God as He essentially is.* The property of a higher nature cannot be attained by a lower nature except by the action of that higher nature to which it properly belongs. But to see God by the divine essence is the property of the divine nature: for it is proper to every agent to act by its own proper form. Therefore no subsistent intelligence can see God by the divine essence except through the action of God bringing it about.

5] To see the substance of God transcends the limits of every created nature: for it is proper to every intelligent created nature to understand according to the mode of its substance: but the divine substance is not intelligible according to the mode of any created substance.

64] *That God governs things by His Providence.* The foregoing conclusions sufficiently show that God is the end of all things. Hence it may be further gathered that by His providence He governs and rules all things. For whatever things are referred to an end, are all subject to His management to whom principally that end belongs, as appears in any army: for all the components of the army and all their works are referred to one last end, the good of the general, which is victory, and therefore it belongs to the general to govern the whole army. In like manner the art which is concerned with the end gives commands and laws to the art which is concerned with the means, as politics to the art of war, the art of war to the management of cavalry, navigation to shipbuilding. Since therefore all things are referred to an end, which is the divine goodness, God, to whom that goodness principally belongs,— as being His own substance, possessed, understood, and loved,— must have the chief control of all things.

5] Things that are distinct in their natures do not combine into one system, unless they be bound up in one by one directing control *(ab uno ordinante)*. But in the universe there are things, having distinct and contrary natures, which nevertheless all combine in one system, some things taking up the activities of other things, some things being aided or even wrought by others. There must then be one ordainer and governor of the universe.

8] Every agent that intends an end cares more for that which is nearer to the last end. But the last end of the divine will is the divine goodness, and the nearest thing to that in creation is the goodness of the order of the entire universe, that being the end to which every particular good of this or that thing is referred, as the less perfect is referred to the more perfect, and every part is for its whole. What therefore God most cares for in creation is the order of the universe. He is therefore its controller. . . .

71] *That the Divine Providence is not wholly inconsistent with the Presence of Evil in Creation.* Perfect goodness could not be in creation if there were not found an order of goodness among creatures, some being better than others: or else all possible grades of goodness would not be filled up; nor would any creature be like God in having pre-eminence over another. Thus a great beauty would be lost to creation in the removal of the order of distinct and dissimilar beings, one better than the other. A dead level of goodness would be a manifest derogation to the perfection of creation. A higher grade of goodness consists in there being something which cannot fall away from goodness; a lower grade, in there being that which can fall away. The perfection of the universe requires both grades of goodness. But it is the care of the ruler to uphold perfection in the subjects of his government, not to make it less. Therefore it is no part of divine providence wholly to exclude from creation the capability of falling away from good. But upon this capability evil ensues: for what is capable of falling away, sometimes does fall away; and the mere lack of good is evil.

3] The best rule in any government is to provide for everything under government according to the mode of its nature: just administration consists in this. As then it would be contrary to any rational plan of human administration for the civil government to debar its subjects from acting according to their offices and conditions of life, except perhaps in an occasional hour of emergency, so it would be contrary to the plan of divine government not to allow creatures to act according to the mode of their several natures. But by the very fact of creatures so acting there follows destruction and evil in the world, since by reason of mutual contrariety and inconsistency one thing is destructive of another.

5] There are many good things in creation which would find no place there, unless evils were there also. Thus there would be no patience of the just, if there were not the malice of persecutors: no room for vindictive justice, if there were no offences: and in the physical order one thing cannot come to be unless something else is destroyed. If then evil were wholly excluded from the universe by divine providence, the number of good things would be proportionally diminished: which ought not to be, because good is more vigorous in goodness than evil in badness (*virtuosius est bonum in bonitate quam in malitia malum*).

6] The good of the whole takes precedence of the good of the part. It belongs then to a prudent ruler to neglect some defect of goodness in the part for the increase of goodness in the whole, as an architect buries the foundation under the earth for the strengthening of the whole house. But if evil were removed from certain portions of the universe, much perfection would be lost to the universe, the beauty of which consists in the orderly blending of things good and evil (*pulcritudo ex ordinata bonorum et malorum adunatione consurgit*), while evil things have their origin in the breaking down of good things, and still from them good things again take their rise by the providence of the ruler, as an interval of silence makes music sweet.

71 Other things, and particularly inferior things, are ordained to the end of the good of man. But if there were no evils in the world, much good would be lost to man, as well in respect of knowledge, as also in respect of desire and love of good: for good is better known in contrast with evil; and while evil results come about, we more ardently desire good results: as sick men best know what a blessing health is. . . .

Boethius (*De consolatione,* Lib. I, prosa 4) introduces a philosopher asking the question: "If there is a God, how comes evil?" The argument should be turned the other way: "If there is evil, there is a God." For there would be no evil, if the order of goodness were taken away, the privation of which is evil; and this order would not be, if God were not.

Hereby is taken away the occasion of the error of the Manicheans, who supposed two primary agents, good and evil, as though evil could not have place under the providence of a good God.

We have also the solution of a doubt raised by some, whether evil actions are of God. Since it has been shown that every agent produces its action inasmuch as it acts by divine power, and that thereby God is the cause of all effects and of all actions; and it has been further shown that in things subject to divine providence evil and deficiency happens from some condition of secondary causes, in which there may be defect; it is clear that evil actions, inasmuch as they are defective, are not of God, but of defective proximate causes; but so far as the action and entity contained in them goes, they must be of God,—as lameness is of motive power, so far as it has anything of motion, but so far as it has anything of defect, it comes of curvature of the leg.

72] *That Divine Providence is not inconsistent with an element of Contingency in Creation.* As divine providence does not exclude all evil from creation, neither does it exclude contingency, or impose necessity upon all things. The operation of providence does not exclude secondary causes, but is fulfilled by them, inasmuch as they act in the power of God. Now effects are called "necessary" or "contingent" according to their proximate causes, not according to their remote causes. Since then among proximate causes there are many that may fail, not all effects subject to providence will be necessary, but many will be contingent.

6] On the part of divine providence no hindrance will be put to the failure of the power of created things, or to an obstacle arising through the resistance of something coming in the way. But from such failure and such resistance the contingency occurs of a natural cause not always acting in the same way, but sometimes failing to do what it is naturally competent to do; and so natural effects do not come about of necessity.

73] *That Divine Providence is not Inconsistent with Freedom of the Will.* The government of every prudent governor is ordained to the perfection of the things governed, to the gaining, or increasing, or maintenance of that perfection. An element of perfection then is more worthy of being preserved by providence than an element of imperfection and defect. But in inanimate things the contingency of causes comes of imperfection and defect: for by their nature they are determined to one effect, which they always gain, unless there be some let or hindrance arising either from limitation of power, or the interference of some external agent, or indisposition of subject matter; and on this account natural causes in their action are not indifferent to either side of an alternative, but for the most part produce their effects uniformly, while they fail in a minority of instances. But that the will is a contingent cause comes of its very perfection, because its power is not tied to one effect, but it rests with it to produce this effect or that, wherefore it is contingent either way. Therefore providence is more concerned to preserve the liberty of the will than to preserve contingency in natural causes.

2] It belongs to divine providence to use things according to their several modes. But a thing's mode of action depends upon its form, which is the principle of action. But the form whereby a voluntary agent acts is not determinate: for the will acts through a form apprehended by the intellect; and the intellect has not one determined form of effect under its consideration, but essentially embraces a multitude of forms; and therefore the will can produce multiform effects.

3] The last end of every creature is to attain to a likeness of God: therefore it would be contrary to providence to withdraw from a creature that whereby it attains the divine likeness. But a voluntary agent attains the divine likeness by acting freely, as it has been shown that there is free will in God.

4] Providence tends to multiply good things in the subjects of its government. But if free will were taken away, many good things would be withdrawn. The praise of human virtue would be taken away, which is nullified where good is not done freely: the justice of rewards and punishments would be taken away, if man did not do good and evil freely: wariness and circumspection in counsel would be taken away, as there would be no need of taking counsel about things done under necessity. It would be therefore contrary to the plan of providence to withdraw the liberty of the will.

Hereby is excluded the error of the Stoics, who said that all things arose of necessity, according to an indefeasible order, which the Greeks called *eimarmene*.

Rene Descartes

Descartes

DESCARTES' little *Discourse on Method* is at once a declaration of independence and a confession of faith in mathematical analysis. It reflects the search for certainty by means of clear deductions from self-evident propositions, a search which not only dominated the physical science and mechanistic philosophies of the seventeenth and eighteenth centuries, but in general lies close to the heart of all disciples of Socrates in all ages. The faith in an infallible method as a substitute for an infallible authority has sustained all attempts at systematic, demonstrative knowledge.

The starting-point of such a system must be a methodological scepticism, a doubting of everything that can be doubted in order to arrive at the indubitable. Having discovered the indubitable, the expert in rational proof can then build up a system of necessary consequences which will constitute a body of certain truth. Descartes made the boldest and most cavalier attempt to carry out this enterprise and out of his attempt grew some of the most persistent problems and basic distinctions of modern philosophy.

As the *Discourse* relates the discovery, Descartes arrived at his first principles by getting "clear and distinct ideas." He found that the simple mathematical formulae expressing the laws of masses in motion could be extended to all things existing in space and that hence the universe is mechanical. Algebra can express geometric forms (analytic geometry), hence becomes the basic method of analysis and proof in optics, mechanics and all forms of motion. There is theoretically a single science of bodies in motion *(res extensa)* based

282

on the self-evident principle that effects must have adequate causes. Such a science is not derived from the senses, for the testimony of the senses is not indubitable.

But thought itself cannot be explained in mechanical terms. The mere fact of doubting is sufficient to establish the existence of thinking *(res cogitans)* independent of the search for causal explanations. The mind contains its own principles of certainty. The order of "extended substance" and the order of "thinking substance" are each an independent order of being and a system of certain truth. But both depend on God, the absolute substance, who unites the order of nature (mechanics) with the order of thought (logic) in the universal reign of reason.

In the end Descartes gave new proofs for old convictions, but in pretending to discover certainty for himself by rigorous precision of method, by self-examination, and by observation of the "book of the world," instead of by appeal to tests, faith and schools, he formulated the principles of a secular philosophy of nature and for an unrestrained confidence in human reason.

René Descartes (1596-1650) ran away from his French Jesuit school of La Flèche at the age of 16, joined the armies operating in the German states, and after nine years of campaigning and travel settled down in Paris and Holland to devote himself to his favorite mathematical studies. His *Discourse on Method* appeared in 1637 together with his *Dioptrics, Meteors,* and *Geometry.* A few years later he published his *Meditationes de prima philosophia* and his *Principia Philosophia.* An early work entitled *Le monde ou traité de la lumière* was not published until after his death, the author fearing the Inquisition which condemned Galileo's doctrines in 1632. Similar reasons of prudence induced Descartes to postpone writing on ethics, but he had reasons of principle as well. Though he regarded ethics as the highest branch of the tree of philosophy, it presupposed for that very reason the "trunk of physics" and the "roots of metaphysics";

hence moral certainty would be obliged to wait until certainty in these basic sciences had been achieved.

The Cartesian school of philosophy became rapidly the most influential system of thought for those who wished to be free from scholasticism. Though its physics was soon eclipsed by the Newtonian, its metaphysics dominated modern philosophy until Hume and Kant. Spinoza, Leibniz and Pierre Bayle were directly inspired by Cartesian ideas and made them serve the cause of the Enlightenment. Even among Catholic Platonists Descartes' influence was felt and gained a foothold among the French Oratorians (Malebranche) and the Jansenists and Port Royal School (Pascal).

Discourse on Method

GOOD sense is, of all things among men, the most equally distributed; for every one thinks of himself so abundantly provided with it, that those even who are the most difficult to satisfy in everything else, do not usually desire a larger measure of this quality than they already possess. And in this it is not likely that all are mistaken: the conviction is rather to be held as testifying that the power of judging aright and of distinguishing Truth from Error, which is properly what is called Good Sense or Reason, is by nature equal in all men; and that the diversity of our opinions, consequently, does not arise from some being endowed with a larger share of Reason than others, but solely from this, that we conduct our thoughts along different ways, and do not fix our attention on the same objects. For to be possessed of a vigorous mind is not enough; the prime requisite is rightly to apply it. The greatest minds, as they are capable of the highest excellencies, are open likewise to the greatest aberrations; and those who travel very slowly may yet make far greater progress, provided they keep always to the straight road, than those who, while they run, forsake it.

For myself, I have never fancied my mind to be in any respect more perfect than those of the generality; on the contrary, I have often wished that I were equal to some others in promptitude of thought, or in clearness and distinctness of imagination, or in fulness and readiness of memory. And besides these, I know of no other qualities that contribute to the perfection of the mind; for as to the Reason or Sense, inasmuch as it is that alone which constitutes us men, and distinguishes us from the brutes, I am disposed to believe that it is to be found complete in each individual; and on this point to adopt the common opinion of philosophers, who say that the difference of greater and less holds only among the *accidents,* and not among the *forms* or *natures* of *individuals* of the same *species.*

I will not hesitate, however, to avow my belief that it has been my singular good fortune to have very early in life fallen in with certain tracks which have conducted me to considerations and maxims, of which I have formed a Method that gives me the means, as I think, of gradually augmenting my knowledge, and of raising it by little and little to the highest point which the mediocrity of my talents and the brief duration of my life will permit me to reach. For I have already reaped from it such fruits that, although I have been accustomed to think lowly enough of myself, and although when I look with the eye of a philosopher at the varied courses and pursuits of mankind at large, I find scarcely one which does not appear vain and useless, I nevertheless derive the highest satisfaction from the progress I conceive myself to have already made in the search after truth, and cannot help entertaining such expectations of the future as to believe that if, among the occupations of men as men, there is any one really excellent and important, it is that which I have chosen.

After all, it is possible I may be mistaken; and it is but a little copper and glass, perhaps, that I take for gold and diamonds. I know how very liable we are to delusion in what relates to ourselves, and also how much the judgments of our friends are to be suspected when given in our favour. But I shall endeavour in this Discourse to describe the paths I have followed, and to delineate my life as in a picture, in order that each one may be able to judge of them for himself, and that in the general opinion entertained of them, as gathered from current report, I myself may have a new help towards instruction to be added to those I have been in the habit of employing.

My present design, then, is not to teach the Method which each ought to follow for the right conduct of his reason, but solely to describe the way in which I have endeavoured to conduct my own. They who set themselves to give precepts must of course regard themselves as possessed of greater skill than those to whom they prescribe; and if they err in the slightest particular, they subject themselves to censure. But as this Tract is put forth merely as a history, or, if you will, as a tale, in which, amid some examples worthy of imitation, there will be found, perhaps, as many more which it were advisable not to follow, I hope it will prove useful to some without being hurtful to any, and that my openness will find some favour with all.

From my childhood, I have been familiar with letters; and as I was given to believe that by their help a clear and certain knowledge of all that is useful in life might be acquired, I was ardently desirous of instruction. But as soon as I had finished the entire course of study, at the close of which it is customary to be admitted into the order of the learned, I completely changed my opinion. For I found myself involved in so many doubts and errors, that I was convinced I had advanced no farther in all my attempts at learning, than the discovery at every turn of my own ignorance. And yet I was studying in one of the most celebrated Schools in Europe, in which I thought there must be learned men, if such were anywhere to be found. I had been taught all that others learned there; and not contented with the sciences actually taught us, I had, in addition, read all the books that had fallen into my hands, treating of such branches as are esteemed the most curious and rare. I knew the judgment which others had formed of me; and I did not find that I was considered inferior to my fellows, although there were among them some who were already marked out to fill the places of our instructors. And, in fine, our age appeared to me as flourishing, and as fertile in powerful minds as any preceding one. I was thus led to take the liberty of judging of all other men by myself, and of concluding that there was no science in existence that was of such a nature as I had previously been given to believe.

I still continued, however, to hold in esteem the studies of the Schools. I was aware that the Languages taught in them are necessary to the understanding of the writings of the ancients; that the grace of Fable stirs the mind; that the memorable deeds of History elevate it; and, if read with discretion, aid in forming the judgment; that the perusal of all excellent books is, as it were, to interview with the noblest men of past ages, who have written them, and even a studied interview, in which are discovered to us only their choicest thoughts; that Eloquence has incomparable force and beauty; that Poesy has its ravishing graces and delights; that in the Mathematics there are many refined discoveries eminently suited to gratify the inquisitive, as well as further all the arts and lessen the labour of man; that numerous highly useful precepts and exhortations to virtue are contained in treatises on Morals; that Theology points out the path to heaven; that Philosophy affords the means of discoursing with an appearance of truth on all matters, and commands the admiration of the more simple; that Jurisprudence, Medicine, and the other Sciences, secure for their cultivators honours and riches; and, in fine, that it is useful to bestow some attention upon all, even upon those abounding the most in superstition and error, that we may be in a position to determine their real value, and guard against being deceived.

But I believed that I had already given sufficient time to Languages, and likewise to the reading of the writings of the ancients, to their Histories and Fables. For to hold converse with those of other ages and to travel, are almost the same thing. It is useful to know something of the manners of different nations, that we may be able to form a more correct judgment regarding our own, and be prevented from thinking that everything contrary to our customs is ridiculous and irrational,—a conclusion usually come to by those whose experience has been limited to their own country. On the other hand, when too much time is occupied in travelling, we become strangers to our native country; and the over curious in the customs of the past are generally ignorant of those of the present. Besides, fictitious narratives lead us to imagine the possibility of many events that are impossible; and even the most faithful histories, if they do not wholly misrepresent matters, or exaggerate their importance to render the account of them more worthy of perusal, omit, at least, almost always the meanest and least striking of the attendant circumstances; hence it happens that the remainder does not represent the truth, and that such as regulate their conduct by examples drawn from this source, are apt to fall into the extravagances of the knight-errants of Romance, and to entertain projects that exceed their powers.

I esteemed Eloquence highly, and was in raptures with Poesy; but I thought that both were gifts of nature rather than fruits of study. Those in whom the faculty of Reason is predominant, and who most skilfully dispose their thoughts with a view to render them clear and intelligible, are always the best able to persuade others of the truth of what they lay down, though they should speak only in the language of Lower Brittany, and be wholly ignorant of the rules of Rhetoric; and those whose minds are stored with the most agreeable fancies, and who can give expression to them with the greatest embellishment and harmony, are still the best poets, though unacquainted with the Art of Poetry.

I was especially delighted with the Mathematics, on account of the certitude and evidence of their reasonings: but I had not as yet a precise knowledge of their true use; and thinking that they but contributed to the advancement of the mechanical arts, I was astonished that foundations, so strong and solid, should have had no loftier superstructure reared on them. On the other hand, I compared the disquisitions of the ancient Moralists to very towering and magnificent palaces with no better foundation than sand and mud: they laud the virtues very highly, and exhibit them as estimable far above anything on earth; but they give us no adequate criterion of virtue, and frequently that which they designate with so fine a name is but apathy, or pride, or despair, or parricide.

I revered our Theology, and aspired as much as any one to reach heaven: but being given assuredly to understand that the way is not less open to the most ignorant than to the most learned, and that the revealed truths which lead to heaven are above our comprehension, I did not presume to subject them to the impotency of my Reason; and I thought that in order competently to undertake their examination, there was need of some special help from heaven, and of being more than man.

Of Philosophy I will say nothing, except that when I saw that it had been cultivated for many ages by the most distinguished men, and that yet there is not a single matter within its sphere which is not still in dispute, and nothing, therefore, which is above doubt, I did not presume to anticipate that my success would be greater in it than that of others; and further, when I considered the number of conflicting opinions touching a single matter that may be upheld by learned men, while there can be but one true, I reckoned as well-nigh false all that was only probable.

As to the other Sciences, inasmuch as these borrow their principles from Philosophy, I judged that no solid superstructures could be reared on foundations so infirm; and neither the honour nor the gain held out by them was sufficient to determine me to their cultivation: for I was not, thank heaven, in a condition which compelled me to make merchandise of Science for the bettering of my fortune; and though I might not profess to scorn glory as a

Cynic, I yet made very slight account of that honour which I hoped to acquire only through fictitious titles. And, in fine, of false Sciences I thought I knew the worth sufficiently to escape being deceived by the professions of an alchemist, the predictions of an astrologer, the impostures of a magician, or by the artifices and boasting of any of those who profess to know things of which they are ignorant.

For these reasons, as soon as my age permitted me to pass from under the control of my instructors, I entirely abandoned the study of letters, and resolved no longer to seek any other science than the knowledge of myself, or of the great book of the world. I spent the remainder of my youth in travelling, in visiting courts and armies, in holding intercourse with men of different dispositions and ranks, in collecting varied experience, in proving myself in the different situations into which fortune threw me, and, above all, in making such reflection on the matter of my experience as to secure my improvement. For it occurred to me that I should find much more truth in the reasonings of each individual with reference to the affairs in which he is personally interested, and the issue of which must presently punish him if he has judged amiss, than in those conducted by a man of letters in his study, regarding speculative matters that are of no practical moment, and followed by no consequences to himself, farther, perhaps, than that they foster his vanity the better the more remote they are from common sense; requiring, as they must in this case, the exercise of greater ingenuity and art to render them probable. In addition, I had always a most earnest desire to know how to distinguish the true from the false, in order that I might be able clearly to discriminate the right path in life, and proceed in it with confidence.

It is true that, while busied only in considering the manners of other men, I found here, too, scarce any ground for settled conviction, and remarked hardly less contradiction among them than in the opinions of the philosophers. So that the greatest advantage I derived from the study consisted in this, that, observing many things which, however extravagant and ridiculous to our apprehension, are yet by common consent received and approved by other great nations, I learned to entertain too decided a belief in regard to nothing of the truth of which I had been persuaded merely by example and custom: and thus I gradually extricated myself from many errors powerful enough to darken our Natural Intelligence, and incapacitate us in great measure from listening to Reason. But after I had been occupied several years in thus studying the book of the world, and in essaying to gather some experience, I at length resolved to make myself an object of study, and to employ all the powers of my mind in choosing the paths I ought to follow; an undertaking which was accompanied with greater success than it would have been had I never quitted my country or my books.

Part II

I was then in Germany, attracted thither by the wars in that country, which have not yet been brought to a termination; and as I was returning to the army from the coronation of the Emperor, the setting in of winter arrested me in a locality where, as I found no society to interest me, and was besides fortunately undisturbed by any cares or passions, I remained the whole day in seclusion, with full opportunity to occupy my attention with my own thoughts. Of these one of the very first that occurred to me was, that there is seldom so much perfection in works composed of many separate parts, upon which different hands have been employed, as in those completed by a single master. Thus it is observable that the buildings which a single architect has planned and executed, are generally more elegant and commodious than those which several have attempted to improve, by making old walls serve for purposes for which they were not originally built. Thus also, those ancient cities which, from being at first only villages, have become, in course of time, large towns, are usually but ill laid out compared with the regularly constructed towns which a professional architect has freely planned on an open plain; so that although the several buildings of the former may often equal or surpass in beauty those of the latter, yet when one observes their indiscriminate juxtaposition, there a large one and here a small, and the consequent crookedness and irregularity of the streets, one is disposed to allege that chance rather than any human will guided by reason, must have led to such an arrangement. And if we consider that nevertheless there have been at all times certain officers whose duty it was to see that private buildings contributed to public ornament, the difficulty of reaching high perfection with but the materials of others to operate on, will be readily acknowledged. In the same way I fancied that those nations which, starting from a semi-barbarous state and advancing to civilisation by slow degrees, have had their laws successively determined, and, as it were, forced upon them simply by experience of the hurtfulness of particular crimes and disputes, would by this process come to be possessed of less perfect institutions than those which, from the commencement of their association as communities, have followed the appointments of some wise legislator. It is thus quite certain that the constitution of the true religion, the ordinances of which are derived from God, must be incomparably superior to that of every other. And, to speak of human affairs, I believe that the past pre-eminence of Sparta was due not to the goodness of each of its laws in particular, for many of these were very strange, and even opposed to good morals, but to the circumstance that, originated by a single individual, they all tended to a single end. In the same way I thought that the sciences contained in books, (such of them at least as are made up of probable reasonings, without demonstrations,) composed as they are of the opinions of many different individuals massed together, are farther removed from truth than the simple inferences which a man of good sense using his natural and unprejudiced judgment draws respecting the matters of his experience. And because we have all to pass through a state of infancy to manhood, and have been of necessity, for a length of time, governed by our desires and preceptors, (whose dictates were frequently conflicting, while neither perhaps always counselled us for the best,) I further concluded that it is almost impossible that our judgments can be so correct or solid as they would have been, had our Reason been mature from the moment of our birth, and had we always been guided by it alone.

It is true, however, that it is not customary to pull down all the houses of a town with the single design of rebuilding them differently, and thereby rendering the streets more handsome; but it often happens that a private individual takes down his own with the view of erecting it anew, and that people are even sometimes constrained to this when their houses are in danger of falling from age, or when the foundations are insecure. With this before me by way of example, I was persuaded that it would indeed he preposterous for a private individual to think of reforming a state by fundamentally changing it throughout, and overturning it in order to set it up amended; and the same I thought was true of any similar project for reforming the body of the Sciences, or the order of teaching them established in the Schools: but as for the opinions which up to that time I had embraced, I thought that I could not do better than resolve at once to sweep them wholly away, that I might afterwards be in a position to admit either others more correct, or even perhaps the same when they had undergone the scrutiny of Reason. I firmly believed that in this way I should much better succeed in the conduct of my life, than if I built only upon old foundations, and leant upon principles which, in my youth, I had taken upon trust. For although I recognised various difficulties in this undertaking, these were not, however, without remedy, nor once to be compared with such as attend the slightest reformation in public affairs. Large bodies, if once overthrown, are with great difficulty set up again, or even kept erect when once seriously shaken, and the fall of such is always disastrous. Then if there are any imperfections in the constitutions of states, (and that many such exist the diversity of constitutions is alone sufficient to assure us,) custom has without doubt materially smoothed their inconveniences, and has even managed to steer altogether clear of, or insensibly corrected a number which sagacity could not have provided against with equal effect; and, in fine, the defects are almost always more tolerable than the change necessary for their removal; in the same manner that highways which wind among mountains, by being much frequented, become gradually so smooth and commodious, that it is much better to follow them than to seek a straighter path by climbing over the tops of rocks and descending to the bottom of precipices.

Hence it is that I cannot in any degree approve of those restless and busy meddlers who, called neither by birth nor fortune to take part in the management of public affairs, are yet always projecting reforms; and if I thought that this Tract contained aught which might justify the suspicion that I was a victim of such folly, I would by no means permit its publication. I have never contemplated anything higher than the reformation of my own opinions, and basing them on a foundation wholly my own. And although my own satisfaction with my work has led me to present here a

draft of it, I do not by any means therefore recommend to every
one else to make a similar attempt. Those whom God has endowed
with a larger measure of genius will entertain, perhaps, designs
still more exalted; but for the many I am much afraid lest even the
present undertaking be more than they can safely venture to imitate. The single design to strip one's self of all past beliefs is one
that ought not to be taken by every one. The majority of men is
composed of two classes, for neither of which would this be at all
a befitting resolution: in the *first* place, of those who with more
than a due confidence in their own powers, are precipitate in their
judgments and want the patience requisite for orderly and circum-
spect thinking; whence it happens, that if men of this class once
take the liberty to doubt of their accustomed opinions, and quit
the beaten highway, they will never be able to thread the byeway
that would lead them by a shorter course, and will lose themselves
and continue to wander for life; in the *second* place, of those who,
possessed of sufficient sense or modesty to determine that there are
others who excel them in the power of discriminating between
truth and error, and by whom they may be instructed, ought
rather to content themselves with the opinions of such than trust
for more correct to their own Reason.

For my own part, I should doubtless have belonged to the latter
class, had I received instruction from but one master, or had I
never known the diversities of opinion that from time immemorial
have prevailed among men of the greatest learning. But I had become aware, even so early as during my college life, that no opinion, however absurd and incredible, can be imagined, which has
not been maintained by some one of the philosophers; and afterwards in the course of my travels I remarked that all those whose
opinions are decidedly repugnant to ours are not on that account
barbarians and savages, but on the contrary that many of these
nations make an equally good, if not a better, use of their Reason
than we do. I took into account also the very different character
which a person brought up from infancy in France or Germany
exhibits, from that which, with the same mind originally, this individual would have possessed had he lived always among the Chinese or with savages, and the circumstance that in dress itself the
fashion which pleased us ten years ago, and which may again, perhaps, be received into favour before ten years have gone, appears

to us at this moment extravagant and ridiculous. I was thus led to infer that the ground of our opinions is far more custom and example than any certain knowledge. And, finally, although such be the ground of our opinions, I remarked that a plurality of suffrages is no guarantee of truth where it is at all of difficult discovery, as in such cases it is much more likely that it will be found by one than by many. I could, however, select from the crowd no one whose opinions seemed worthy of preference, and thus I found myself constrained, as it were, to use my own Reason in the conduct of my life.

But like one walking alone and in the dark, I resolved to proceed so slowly and with such circumspection, that if I did not advance far, I would at least guard against falling. I did not even choose to dismiss summarily any of the opinions that had crept into my belief without having been introduced by Reason, but first of all took sufficient time carefully to satisfy myself of the general nature of the task I was setting myself, and ascertain the true Method by which to arrive at the knowledge of whatever lay within the compass of my powers.

Among the branches of Philosophy, I had, at an earlier period, given some attention to Logic, and among those of the Mathematics to Geometrical Analysis and Algebra,—three arts or Sciences which ought, as I conceived, to contribute something to my design. But, on examination, I found that, as for Logic, its syllogisms and the majority of its other precepts are of avail rather in the communication of what we already know, or even as the Art of Lully, in speaking without judgment of things of which we are ignorant, than in the investigation of the unknown; and although this Science contains indeed a number of correct and very excellent precepts, there are, nevertheless, so many others, and these either injurious or superfluous, mingled with the former, that it is almost quite as difficult to effect a severance of the true from the false as it is to extract a Diana or a Minerva from a rough block of marble. Then as to the Analysis of the ancients and the Algebra of the moderns, besides that they embrace only matters highly abstract, and, to appearance, of no use, the former is so exclusively restricted to the consideration of figures, that it can exercise the Understanding only on condition of greatly fatiguing the Imagination; and, in the latter, there is so complete a subjection to certain rules and formulas, that there results an art full of confusion and obscurity calculated to embarrass, instead of a science fitted to cultivate the mind. By these considerations I was induced to seek some other Method which would comprise the advantages of the three and be exempt from their defects. And as a multitude of laws often only hampers justice, so that a state is best governed when, with few laws, these are rigidly administered; in like manner, instead of the great number of precepts of which Logic is composed, I believed that the four following would prove perfectly sufficient for me, provided I took the firm and unwavering resolution never in a single instance to fail in observing them.

The *first* was never to accept anything for true which I did not clearly know to be such; that is to say, carefully to avoid precipitancy and prejudice, and to comprise nothing more in my judgment than what was presented to my mind so clearly and distinctly as to exclude all ground of doubt.

The *second,* to divide each of the difficulties under examination into as many parts as possible, and as might be necessary for its adequate solution.

The *third,* to conduct my thoughts in such order that, by commencing with objects the simplest and easiest to know, I might ascend by little and little, and, as it were, step by step, to the knowledge of the more complex; assigning in thought a certain order even to those objects which in their own nature do not stand in a relation of antecedence and sequence.

And the *last,* in every case to make enumerations so complete, and reviews so general, that I might be assured that nothing was omitted.

The long chains of simple and easy reasonings by means of which geometers are accustomed to reach the conclusions of their most difficult demonstrations, had led me to imagine that all things, to the knowledge of which man is competent, are mutually connected in the same way, and that there is nothing so far removed from us as to be beyond our reach, or so hidden that we cannot discover it, provided only we abstain from accepting the false for the true, and always preserve in our thoughts the order necessary for the deduction of one truth from another. And I had little difficulty in determining the objects with which it was necessary to commence, for I was already persuaded that it must be with the simplest and easiest to know, and, considering that of all those who have hitherto sought truth in the Sciences, the mathematicians alone have been able to find any demonstrations, that is, any certain and evident reasons, I did not doubt but that such must have been the rule of their investigations. I resolved to commence, therefore, with the examination of the simplest objects, not anticipating, however, from this any other advantage than that to be found in accustoming my mind to the love and nourishment of truth, and to a distaste for all such reasonings as were unsound. But I had no intention on that account of attempting to master all the particular Sciences commonly denominated Mathematics: but observing that, however difference their objects, they all agree in considering only the various relations or proportions subsisting among those objects, I thought it best for my purpose to consider these proportions in the most general form possible, without referring them to any objects in particular, except such as would most facilitate the knowledge of them, and without by any means restricting them to these, that afterwards I might thus be the better able to apply them to every other class of objects to which they are legitimately applicable. Perceiving further, that in order to understand these relations I should sometimes have to consider them one by one, and sometimes only to bear them in mind, or embrace them in the aggregate, I thought that, in order the better to consider them individually, I should view them as subsisting between straight lines, than which I could find no objects more simple, or capable of being more distinctly represented to my imagination and senses; and on the other hand, that in order to retain them in the memory, or embrace an aggregate of many, I should express them by certain characters the briefest possible. In this way I believed that I could borrow all that was best both in Geometrical Analysis and in Algebra, and correct all the defects of the one by help of the other.

And, in point of fact, the accurate observance of these few precepts gave me, I take the liberty of saying, such ease in unravelling all the questions embraced in these two sciences, that in the two or three months I devoted to their examination, not only did I reach solutions of questions I had formerly deemed exceedingly difficult, but even as regards questions of the solution of which I continued ignorant, I was enabled, as it appeared to me, to determine the means whereby, and the extent to which, a solution was possible; results attributable to the circumstance that I commenced with the simplest and most general truths, and that thus each truth discovered was a rule available in the discovery of subsequent ones. Nor in this perhaps shall I appear too vain, if it be considered that, as the truth on any particular point is one, whoever apprehends the truth, knows all that on that point can be known. The child, for example, who has been instructed in the elements of Arithmetic, and has made a particular addition, according to rule, may be assured that he has found, with respect to the sum of the numbers before him, all that in this instance is within the reach of human genius. Now, in conclusion, the Method which teaches adherence to the true order, and an exact enumeration of all the conditions of the thing sought, includes all that gives certitude to the rules of Arithmetic.

But the chief ground of my satisfaction with this Method, was the assurance I had of thereby exercising my reason in all matters, if not with absolute perfection, at least with the greatest attainable by me: besides, I was conscious that by its use my mind was becoming gradually habituated to clearer and more distinct conceptions of its objects; and I hoped, also, from not having restricted this Method to any particular matter, to apply it to the difficulties of the other Sciences, with not less success than to those of Algebra. I should not, however, on this account have ventured at once on the examination of all the difficulties of the Sciences which presented themselves to me, for this would have been contrary to the order prescribed in the Method, but observing that the knowledge of such is dependent on principles borrowed from Philosophy, in which I found nothing certain, I thought it necessary first of all to endeavour to establish its principles. And because I observed, besides, that an inquiry of this kind was of all others of the greatest moment, and one in which precipitancy and anticipation in judgment were most to be dreaded, I thought that I ought not to approach it till I had reached a more mature age, (being at that time but twenty-three,) and had first of all employed much of my time in preparation for the work, as well by eradicating from my mind all the erroneous opinions I had up to that moment accepted, as by amassing variety of experience to afford materials for my reasonings, and by continually exercising myself in my chosen Method with a view to increased skill in its application.

Part III

And, finally, as it is not enough, before commencing to rebuild the house in which we live, that it be pulled down, and materials and builders provided, or that we engage in the work ourselves, according to a plan which we have beforehand carefully drawn out, but as it is likewise necessary that we be furnished with some other house in which we may live commodiously during the operations, so that I might not remain irresolute in my actions, while my Reason compelled me to suspend my judgment, and that I might not be prevented from living thenceforward in the greatest possible felicity, I formed a provisory code of Morals, composed of three or four maxims, with which I am desirous to make you acquainted.

The *first* was to obey the laws and customs of my country, adhering firmly to the Faith in which, by the grace of God, I had been educated from my childhood, and regulating my conduct in every other matter according to the most moderate opinions, and the farthest removed from extremes, which should happen to be adopted in practice with general consent of the most judicious of those among whom I might be living. For, as I had from that time begun to hold my own opinions for nought because I wished to subject them all to examination, I was convinced that I could not do better than follow in the meantime the opinions of the most judicious; and although there are some perhaps among the Persians and Chinese as judicious as among ourselves, expediency seemed to dictate that I should regulate my practice conformably to the opinions of those with whom I should have to live; and it appeared to me that, in order to ascertain the real opinions of such, I ought rather to take cognizance of what they practised than of what they said, not only because, in the corruption of our manners, there are few disposed to speak exactly as they believe, but also because very many are not aware of what it is that they really believe; for, as the act of mind by which a thing is believed is different from that by which we know that we believe it, the one act is often found without the other. Also, amid many opinions held in equal repute, I chose always the most moderate, as much for the reason that these are always the most convenient for practice, and probably the best, (for all excess is generally vicious,) as that, in the event of my falling into error, I might be at less distance from the truth than if, having chosen one of the extremes, it should turn out to be the other which I ought to have adopted. And I placed in the class of extremes especially all promises by which somewhat of our freedom is abridged; not that I disapproved of the laws which, to provide against the instability of men of feeble resolution, when what is sought to be accomplished is some good, permit engagements by vows and contracts binding the parties to persevere in it, or even, for the security of commerce, sanction similar engagements where the purpose sought to be realized is indifferent: but because I did not find anything on earth which was wholly superior to change, and because, for myself in particular, I hoped gradually to perfect my judgments, and not to suffer them to deteriorate, I would have deemed it a grave sin against good sense, if, for the reason that I approved of something at a particular time, I therefore bound myself to hold it for good at a subsequent time, when perhaps it had ceased to be so, or I had ceased to esteem it such.

My *second* maxim was to be as firm and resolute in my actions as I was able, and not to adhere less steadfastly to the most doubtful opinions, when once adopted, than if they had been highly certain; imitating in this the example of travellers who, when they have lost their way in a forest, ought not to wander from side to side, far less remain in one place, but proceed constantly towards the same side in as straight a line as possible, without changing their direction for slight reasons, although perhaps it might be chance alone which at first determined the selection; for in this way, if they do not exactly reach the point they desire, they will come at least in the end to some place that will probably be preferable to the middle of a forest. In the same way, since in action it frequently happens that no delay is permissible, it is very certain that, when it is not in our power to determine what is true, we ought to act according to what is most probable; and even although we should not remark a greater probability in one opinion than in another, we ought notwithstanding to choose one or the other, and afterwards consider it, in so far as it relates to practice, as no longer dubious, but manifestly true and certain, since the reason by which our choice has been determined is itself possessed of these qualities. This principle was sufficient thenceforward to rid me of all those repentings and pangs of remorse that usually disturb the consciences of such feeble and uncertain minds as, destitute of any clear and determinate principle of choice, allow themselves one day to adopt a course of action as the best, which they abandon the next, as the opposite.

My *third* maxim was to endeavour always to conquer myself rather than fortune, and change my desires rather than the order of the world, and in general, accustom myself to the persuasion that, except our own thoughts, there is nothing absolutely in our power; so that when we have done our best in respect of things external to us, all wherein we fail of success is to be held, as regards us, absolutely impossible: and this single principle seemed to me sufficient to prevent me from desiring for the future anything which I could not obtain, and thus render me contented; for since our will naturally seeks those objects alone which the understanding represents as in some way possible of attainment, it is plain, that if we consider all external goods as equally beyond our power, we shall no more regret the absence of such goods as seem due to our birth, when deprived of them without any fault of ours, than our not possessing the kingdoms of China or Mexico; and thus making, so to speak, a virtue of necessity, we shall no more desire health in disease, or freedom in imprisonment, than we now do bodies incorruptible as diamonds, or the wings of birds to fly with. But I confess there is need of prolonged discipline and frequently repeated meditation to accustom the mind to view all objects in this light; and I believe that in this chiefly consisted the secret of the power of such philosophers as in former times were enabled to rise superior to the influence of fortune, and, amid suffering and poverty, enjoy a happiness which their gods might have envied. For, occupied incessantly with the consideration of the limits prescribed to their power by nature, they became so entirely convinced that nothing was at their disposal except their own thoughts, that this conviction was of itself sufficient to prevent their entertaining any desire of other objects; and over their thoughts they acquired a sway so absolute, that they had some ground on this account for esteeming themselves more rich and more powerful, more free and more happy, than other men who, whatever be the favours heaped on them by nature and fortune, if destitute of this philosophy, can never command the realization of all their desires.

In fine, to conclude this code of Morals, I thought of reviewing the different occupations of men in this life, with the view of making choice of the best. And, without wishing to offer any remarks on the employments of others, I may state that it was my conviction that I could not do better than continue in that in which I was engaged, viz., in devoting my whole life to the culture of my Reason, and in making the greatest progress I was able in the knowledge of truth, on the principles of the Method which I had prescribed to myself. This Method, from the time I had begun to apply it, had been to me the source of satisfaction so intense as to lead me to believe that more perfect or more innocent could not be enjoyed in this life; and as by its means I daily discovered truths that appeared to me of some importance, and of which other men were generally ignorant, the gratification thence arising so occupied my mind that I was wholly indifferent to every other object. Besides, the three preceding maxims were founded singly on the design of continuing the work of self-instruction. For since God has endowed each of us with some Light of Reason by which to distinguish truth from error, I could not have believed that I ought for a single moment to rest satisfied with the opinions of another, unless I had resolved to exercise my own judgment in examining these whenever I should be duly qualified for the task. Nor could I have proceeded on such opinions without scruple, had I supposed that I should thereby forfeit any advantage for attaining still more accurate, should such exist. And, in fine, I could not have restrained my desires, nor remained satisfied, had I not followed a path in which I thought myself certain of attaining all the knowledge to the acquisition of which I was competent, as well as the largest amount of what is truly good which I could ever hope to secure. Inasmuch as we neither seek nor shun any object except in so far as our understanding represents it as good or bad, all that is necessary to right action is right judgment, and to the best action the most correct judgment,—that is, to the acquisition of all the virtues with all else that is truly valuable and within our reach;

and the assurance of such an acquisition cannot fail to render us contented.

Having thus provided myself with these maxims, and having placed them in reserve along with the truths of Faith, which have ever occupied the first place in my belief, I came to the conclusion that I might with freedom set about ridding myself of what remained of my opinions. And, inasmuch as I hoped to be better able successfully to accomplish this work by holding intercourse with mankind, than by remaining longer shut up in the retirement where these thoughts had occurred to me, I betook me again to travelling before the winter was well ended. And, during the nine subsequent years, I did nothing but roam from one place to another, desirous of being a spectator rather than an actor in the plays exhibited on the theatre of the world; and, as I made it my business in each matter to reflect particularly upon what might fairly be doubted and prove a source of error, I gradually rooted out from my mind all the errors which had hitherto crept into it. Not that in this I imitated the Sceptics who doubt only that they may doubt, and seek nothing beyond uncertainty itself; for, on the contrary, my design was singly to find ground of assurance, and cast aside the loose earth and sand, that I might reach the rock or the clay. In this, as appears to me, I was successful enough; for, since I endeavoured to discover the falsehood or incertitude of the propositions I examined, not by feeble conjectures, but by clear and certain reasonings, I met with nothing so doubtful as not to yield some conclusion of adequate certainty, although this were merely the inference, that the matter in question contained nothing certain. And, just as in pulling down an old house, we usually reserve the ruins to contribute towards the erection, so, in destroying such of my opinions as I judged to be ill-founded, I made a variety of observations and acquired an amount of experience of which I availed myself in the establishment of more certain. And further, I continued to exercise myself in the Method I have prescribed; for, besides taking care in general to conduct all my thoughts according to its rules, I reserved some hours from time to time which I expressly devoted to the employment of the Method in the solution of Mathematical difficulties, or even in the solution likewise of some questions belonging to other Sciences, but which, by my having detached them from such principles of these

Sciences as were of inadequate certainty, were rendered almost Mathematical: the truth of this will be manifest from the numerous examples contained in this volume.[1] And thus, without in appearance living otherwise than those who, with no other occupation than that of spending their lives agreeably and innocently, study to sever pleasure from vice, and who, that they may enjoy their leisure without ennui, have recourse to such pursuits as are honourable, I was nevertheless prosecuting my design, and making greater progress in the knowledge of truth, than I might, perhaps, have made had I been engaged in the perusal of books merely, or in holding converse with men of letters.

These nine years passed away, however, before I had come to any determinate judgment respecting the difficulties which form matter of dispute among the learned, or had commenced to seek the principles of any Philosophy more certain than the vulgar. And the examples of many men of the highest genius, who had, in former times, engaged in this inquiry, but, as appeared to me, without success, led me to imagine it to be a work of so much difficulty, that I would not perhaps have ventured on it so soon had I not heard it currently rumoured that I had already completed the inquiry. I know not what were the grounds of this opinion; and, if my conversation contributed in any measure to its rise, this must have happened rather from my having confessed my ignorance with greater freedom than those are accustomed to do who have studied a little, and expounded, perhaps, the reasons that led me to doubt of many of those things that by others are esteemed certain, than from my having boasted of any system of Philosophy. But, as I am of a disposition that makes me unwilling to be esteemed different from what I really am, I thought it necessary to endeavour by all means to render myself worthy of the reputation accorded to me; and it is now exactly eight years since this desire constrained me to remove from all those places where interruption from any of my acquaintances was possible, and betake myself to this country,[2] in which the long duration of the war has led to the establishment of such discipline, that the armies maintained seem to be of use only in enabling the inhabitants to enjoy more securely the

[1] The Discourse on Method was originally published along with Descartes' Dioptrics, Meteorics, and Geometry.

[2] Holland; to which country he withdrew in 1629.

blessings of peace; and where, in the midst of a great crowd actively engaged in business, and more careful of their own affairs than curious about those of others, I have been enabled to live without being deprived of any of the conveniences to be had in the most populous cities, and yet as solitary and as retired as in the midst of the most remote deserts.

Part IV

I am in doubt as to the propriety of making my first meditations in the place above mentioned matter of discourse; for these are so metaphysical, and so uncommon, as not, perhaps, to be acceptable to every one. And yet, that it may be determined whether the foundations that I have laid are sufficiently secure, I find myself in a measure constrained to advert to them. I had long before remarked that, in relation to practice, it is sometimes necessary to adopt, as if above doubt, opinions which we discern to be highly uncertain, as has been already said; but as I then desired to give my attention solely to the search after truth, I thought that a procedure exactly the opposite was called for, and that I ought to reject as absolutely false all opinions in regard to which I could suppose the least ground for doubt, in order to ascertain whether after that there remained aught in my belief that was wholly indubitable. Accordingly, seeing that our senses sometimes deceive us, I was willing to suppose that there existed nothing really such as they presented to us; and because some men err in reasoning, and fall into paralogisms, even on the simplest matters of Geometry, I, convinced that I was as open to error as any other, rejected as false all the reasonings I had hitherto taken for demonstrations; and finally, when I considered that the very same thoughts (presentations) which we experience when awake may also be experienced when we are asleep, while there is at that time not one of them true, I supposed that all the objects (presentations) that had ever entered into my mind when awake, had in them no more truth than the illusions of my dreams. But immediately upon this I observed that, whilst I thus wished to think that all was false, it was absolutely necessary that I, who thus thought, should be somewhat; and as I observed that this truth, *I think, hence I am,* was so certain and of such evidence, that no ground of doubt, however extravagant, could be alleged by the Sceptics capable of shaking it, I concluded that I might, without scruple, accept it as the first principle of the Philosophy of which I was in search.

In the next place, I attentively examined what I was, and as I observed that I could suppose that I had no body, and that there was no world nor any place in which I might be; but that I could not therefore suppose that I was not; and that, on the contrary, from the very circumstance that I thought to doubt of the truth of other things, it most clearly and certainly followed that I was; while, on the other hand, if I had only ceased to think, although all the other objects which I had ever imagined had been in reality existent, I would have had no reason to believe that I existed; I thence concluded that I was a substance whose whole essence or nature consists only in thinking, and which, that it may exist, has need of no place, nor is dependent on any material thing; so that "I," that is to say, the mind by which I am what I am, is wholly distinct from the body, and is even more easily known than the latter, and is such, that although the latter were not, it would still continue to be all that it is.

After this I inquired in general into what is essential to the truth and certainty of a proposition; for since I had discovered one which I knew to be true, I thought that I must likewise be able to discover the ground of this certitude. And as I observed that in the words *I think, hence I am,* there is nothing at all which gives me assurance of their truth beyond this, that I see very clearly that in order to think it is necessary to exist, I concluded that I might take, as a general rule, the principle, that all the things which we very clearly and distinctly conceive are true, only observing, however, that there is some difficulty in rightly determining the objects which we distinctly conceive.

In the next place, from reflecting on the circumstance that I doubted, and that consequently my being was not wholly perfect, (for I clearly saw that it was a greater perfection to know than to doubt,) I was led to inquire whence I had learned to think of something more perfect than myself; and I clearly recognised that I must hold this notion from some Nature which in reality was more perfect. As for the thoughts of many other objects external to me, as of the sky, the earth, light, heat, and a thousand more, I was less at a loss to know whence these came; for since I remarked in them nothing which seemed to render them superior to myself, I could believe that, if these were true, they were dependencies on my own nature, in so far as it possessed a certain perfection, and, if they were false, that I held them from nothing, that is to say, that they were in me because of a certain imperfection of my nature. But this could not be the case with the idea of a Nature more perfect than myself; for to receive it from nothing was a thing manifestly impossible; and, because it is not less repugnant that the more perfect should be an effect of, and dependence on the less perfect, than that something should proceed from nothing, it was equally impossible that I could hold it from myself: accordingly, it but remained that it had been placed in me by a Nature which was in reality more perfect than mine, and which even possessed within itself all the perfections of which I could from any idea; that is to say, in a single word, which was God. And to this I added that, since I knew some perfections which I did not possess, I was not the only being in existence, (I will here, with your permission, freely use the terms of the schools); but, on the contrary, that there was of necessity some other more perfect Being upon whom I was dependent, and from whom I had received all that I possessed; for if I had existed alone, and independently of every other being, so as to have had from myself all the perfection, however little, which I actually possessed, I should have been able, for the same reason, to have had from myself the whole remainder of perfection, of the want of which I was conscious, and thus could of myself have become infinite, eternal, immutable, omniscient, all-powerful, and, in fine, have possessed all the perfections which I could recognise in God. For in order to know the nature of God, (whose existence has been established by the preceding reasonings,) as far as my own nature permitted, I had only to consider in reference to all the properties of which I found in my mind some idea, whether their possession was a mark of perfection; and I was assured that no one which indicated any imperfection was in him, and that none of the rest was wanting. Thus I perceived that doubt, inconstancy, sadness, and such like, could not be found in God, since I myself would have been happy to be free from them. Besides, I had ideas of many sensible and corporeal things; for although I might suppose that I was dreaming, and that all which I saw or imagined was false, I could not, nevertheless, deny that the ideas were in reality in my thoughts. But, because I had already very clearly recognised in myself that the intelligent nature is distinct from the corporeal, and as I observed that all composition is an evidence of dependency, and that a state of dependency is manifestly a state of imperfection, I therefore determined that it could not be a perfection in God to be compounded of these two natures, and that consequently he was not so compounded; but that if there were any bodies in the world, or even any intelligences, or other natures that were not wholly perfect, their existence depended on his power in such a way that they could not subsist without him for a single moment.

I was disposed straightway to search for other truths; and when I had represented to myself the object of the geometers, which I conceived to be a continuous body, or a space indefinitely extended in length, breadth, and height or depth, divisible into divers parts which admit of different figures and sizes, and of being moved or transposed in all manner of ways, (for all this the geometers suppose to be in the object they contemplate,) I went over some of their simplest demonstrations. And, in the first place, I observed, that the great certitude which by common consent is accorded to these demonstrations, is founded solely upon this, that they are clearly conceived in accordance with the rules I have already laid down. In the next place, I perceived that there was nothing at all in these demonstrations which could assure me of the existence of their object: thus, for example, supposing a triangle to be given, I distinctly perceived that its three angles were necessarily equal to two right angles, but I did not on that account perceive anything which could assure me that any triangle existed: while, on the contrary, recurring to the examination of the idea of a Perfect Being, I found that the existence of the Being was comprised in the idea in the same way that the equality of its three angles to two right angles is comprised in the idea of a triangle, or as in the idea of a sphere, the equidistance of all points on its surface from the centre, or even still more clearly; and that consequently it is at least as certain that God, who is this Perfect Being, is, or exists, as any demonstration of Geometry can be.

But the reason which leads many to persuade themselves that

there is a difficulty in knowing this truth, and even also in knowing what their mind really is, is that they never raise their thoughts above sensible objects, and are so accustomed to consider nothing except by way of imagination, which is a mode of thinking limited to material objects, that all that is not imaginable seems to them not intelligible. The truth of this is sufficiently manifest from the single circumstance, that the philosophers of the Schools accept as a maxim that there is nothing in the Understanding which was not previously in the Senses, in which however it is certain that the ideas of God and of the soul have never been; and it appears to me that they who make use of their imagination to comprehend these ideas do exactly the same thing as if, in order to hear sounds or smell odours, they strove to avail themselves of their eyes; unless indeed that there is this difference, that the sense of sight does not afford us an inferior assurance to those of smell or hearing; in place of which, neither our imagination nor our senses can give us assurance of anything unless our Understanding intervene.

Finally, if there be still persons who are not sufficiently persuaded of the existence of God and of the soul, by the reasons I have adduced, I am desirous that they should know that all the other propositions, of the truth of which they deem themselves perhaps more assured, as that we have a body, and that there exist stars and an earth, and such like, are less certain; for, although we have a moral assurance of these things, which is so strong that there is an appearance of extravagance in doubting of their existence, yet at the same time no one, unless his intellect is impaired, can deny, when the question relates to a metaphysical certitude, that there is sufficient reason to exclude entire assurance, in the observation that when asleep we can in the same way imagine ourselves possessed of another body and that we see other stars and another earth, when there is nothing of the kind. For how do we know that the thoughts which occur in dreaming are false rather than those other which we experience when awake, since the former are often not less vivid and distinct than the latter? And though men of the highest genius study this question as long as they please, I do not believe that they will be able to give any reason which can be sufficient to remove this doubt, unless they presuppose the existence of God. For, in the first place, even the principle which I have already taken as a rule, viz., that all the things which we

clearly and distinctly conceive are true, is certain only because
God is or exists, and because he is a Perfect Being, and because all
that we possess is derived from him: whence it follows that our
ideas or notions, which to the extent of their clearness and distinctness are real, and proceed from God, must to that extent be true.
Accordingly, whereas we not unfrequently have ideas or notions
in which some falsity is contained, this can only be the case with
such as are to some extent confused and obscure, and in this proceed from nothing, (participate of negation,) that is, exist in us
thus confused because we are not wholly perfect. And it is evident
that it is not less repugnant that falsity or imperfection, in so far
as it is imperfection, should proceed from God, than that truth or
perfection should proceed from nothing. But if we did not know
that all which we possess of real and true proceeds from a Perfect
and Infinite Being, however clear and distinct our ideas might be,
we should have no ground on that account for the assurance that
they possessed the perfection of being true.

But after the knowledge of God and of the soul has rendered us
certain of this rule, we can easily understand that the truth of the
thoughts we experience when awake, ought not in the slightest
degree to be called in question on account of the illusions of our
dreams. For if it happened that an individual, even when asleep,
had some very distinct idea, as, for example, if a geometer should
discover some new demonstration, the circumstance of his being
asleep would not militate against its truth; and as for the most
ordinary error of our dreams, which consists in their representing
various objects in the same way as our external senses, this is not
prejudicial, since it leads us very properly to suspect the truth of
the ideas of sense, for we are not unfrequently deceived in the
same manner when awake; as when persons in the jaundice see all
objects yellow, or when the stars or bodies at a great distance appear to us much smaller than they are. For, in fine, whether awake
or asleep, we ought never to allow ourselves to be persuaded of the
truth of anything unless on the evidence of our Reason. And it
must be noted that I say of our *Reason,* and not of our imagination
or of our senses: thus, for example, although we very clearly see the
sun, we ought not therefore to determine that it is only of the size
which our sense of sight presents; and we may very distinctly imagine the head of a lion joined to the body of a goat, without being

therefore shut up to the conclusion that a chimæra exists; for it is not a dictate of Reason that what we thus see or imagine is in reality existent; but it plainly tells us that all our ideas or notions contain in them some truth; for otherwise it could not be that God, who is wholly perfect and veracious, should have placed them in us. And because our reasonings are never so clear or so complete during sleep as when we are awake, although sometimes the acts of our imagination are then as lively and distinct, if not more so than in our waking moments, Reason further dictates that, since all our thoughts cannot be true because of our partial imperfection, those possessing truth must infallibly be found in the experience of our waking moments rather than in that of our dreams.

Thomas Hobbes

Thomas Hobbes

LIKE Descartes, Hobbes (1588-1679) was inspired by the achievements of mechanical science and like his contemporaries wrote enthusiastically *de corpore* and *de homine,* explaining human nature in terms of its forces, passions, and motives. His distinctive contribution, however, was to carry this method into the theory of law and morals. He had studied Aristotle at Oxford, and the new mechanists at Paris, but he was a lawyer by profession and carried his philosophic studies into the field of jurisprudence and politics. Hobbes transformed the nominalism of the Oxford Occamites into an argument for the sacredness of the civil state.

Hobbes conceived of the commonwealth as an "artificial animal" created by an act of compact or contract for the enforcement of the law of nature. And the law of nature he expounded as dictates of prudence or utility. Thus Hobbes arrived at a radically secular theory of moral and political obligation, to take the place of divine right theories. To the sovereign or government, created by voluntary contract of subjection and authorization on the part of the subjects, belongs, according to Hobbes, unlimited right to command in all matters temporal and spiritual. To divide authority between church and state was, he thought, to create a "Kingdom of darkness" and was the chief cause of the civil wars which were disrupting England and the Continent.

As a contrast to civil order and peace by contract or law, he portrayed man in a "state of nature," governed merely by his natural powers and passions, each individual inevitably clashing with others, as would any other kind of natural body in "free motion." By bitter experience a rational man learns to surrender his "natural liberty" as a natural body in return for whatever "liberties" the government of his body politic may see fit to allow him. Thus the political order is represented as the embodiment of reason, a "mortal god."

Hobbes went further than his contemporaries in regarding the realm of natural law as a reign of universal necessity. "God's kingdom by nature," as he expressed it, contains no special providences or miracles and has neither beginning in time nor intelligible end. God is simply the Almighty. Man, too, is completely in God's power or rather he exhibits God's power.

The classic exposition of Hobbes philosophy is his *Leviathan,* published in 1651 at a time when he was suspected of monarchism by the Puritans, of independency by the Royalists, and of atheism by both. The first part of the selections that follow is taken from an earlier work on the *Elements of Philosophy.*

Elements of Philosophy

Chapter I

Of Philosophy

91 THE principal parts of philosophy are two. For two chief kinds of bodies, and very different from one another, offer themselves to such as search after their generation and properties; one whereof being the work of nature, is called a *natural body,* the other is called a *commonwealth,* and is made by the wills and agreement of men. And from these spring the two parts of philosophy, called *natural* and *civil.* But seeing that, for the knowledge of the porperties of a commonwealth, it is necessary first to know the dispositions, affections, and manners of men, civil philosophy is again commonly divided into two parts, whereof one, which treats of men's dispositions and manners, is called *ethics;* and the other, which takes cognizance of their civil duties, is called *politics,* or simply *civil philosophy.* In the first place, therefore (after I have set down such premises as appertain to the nature of philosophy in general), I will discourse of *bodies natural;* in the second, of the *dispositions and manners of men;* and in the third, of the *civil duties of subjects. . . .*

Chapter VII

Of Place and Time

11 In the teaching of natural philosophy, I cannot begin better (as I have already shewn) than from *privation;* that is, from feigning the world to be annihilated. But, if such annihilation of all things be supposed, it may perhaps be asked, what would remain for any man (whom only I except from this universal annihilation of things) to consider as the subject of philosophy, or at all to reason upon; or what to give names unto for ratiocination's sake.

I say, therefore, there would remain to that man ideas of the world, and of all such bodies as he had, before their annihilation, seen with his eyes, or perceived by any other sense; that is to say, the memory and imagination of magnitudes, motions, sounds, colours, &c. as also of their order and parts. All which things, though they be nothing but ideas and phantasms, happening internally to him that imagineth; yet they will appear as if they were external, and not at all depending upon any power of the mind. And these are the things to which he would give names, and subtract them from, and compound them with one another. For seeing, that after the destruction of all other things, I suppose man still remaining, and namely that he thinks, imagines, and remembers, there can be nothing for him to think of but what is past; nay, if we do but observe diligently what it is we do when we consider and reason, we shall find, that though all things be still remaining in the world, yet we compute nothing but our own phantasms. For when we calculate the magnitude and motions of heaven or earth, we do not ascend into heaven that we may divide it into parts, or measure the motions thereof, but we do it sitting still in our closets or in the dark. Now things may be considered, that is, be brought into account, either as internal accidents of our mind, in which manner we consider them when the question is about some faculty of the mind; or as species of external things, not as really existing, but appearing only to exist, or to have a being without us. And in this manner we are now to consider them.

2] If therefore we remember, or have a phantasm of any thing that was in the world before the supposed annihilation of the same; and consider, not that the thing was such or such, but only that it had a being without the mind, we have presently a conception of that we call *space:* an imaginary space indeed, because a mere phantasm, yet that very thing which all men call so. For no man calls it space for being already filled, but because it may be filled; nor does any man think bodies carry their places away with them, but that the same space contains sometimes one, sometimes another body; which could not be of space should always accompany the body which is once in it. And this is of itself so manifest, that I should not think it needed any explaining at all, but that I find space to be falsely defined by certain philosophers who infer from thence, one, that the world is infinite (for taking *space* to be the extension of bodies and thinking extension may encrease continually, he infers that bodies may be infinitely extended); and, another, from the same definition, concludes rashly, that it is impossible even to God himself to create more worlds than one; for, if another world were to be created, he says, that seeing there is nothing without this world, and therefore (according to his definition) no space, that new world must be placed in nothing; but in nothing nothing can be placed; which he affirms only, without showing any reason for the same; whereas the contrary is the truth: for more cannot be put into a space already filled, so much is empty space fitter than that, which is full, for the receiving of new bodies. Having therefore spoken thus much for these men's sakes, and for theirs that assent to them, I return to my purpose, and define *space* thus: SPACE *is the phantasm of a thing existing without the mind simply;* that is to say, that phantasm, in which we consider no other accident, but only that it appears without us.

³¹ As a body leaves a phantasm of its magnitude in the mind, so also a moved body leaves a phantasm of its motion, namely, an idea of that body passing out of one space into another by continual succession. And this idea, or phantasm, is that, which (without receding much from the common opinion, or from *Aristotle's* definition) I call *Time.* For seeing all men confess a year to be time, and yet do not think a year to be the accident or affection of any body, they must needs confess it to be, not in the things without us, but only in the thought of the mind. So when they speak of the times of their predecessors, they do not think after their predecessors are gone, that their times can be any where else than in the memory of those that remember them. And as for those that say, days, years, and months are the motions of the sun and moon, seeing it is all one to say, motion *past* and motion *destroyed,* and that *future* motion is the same with motion which *is not yet begun,* they say that, which they do not mean, that there neither is, nor has been, nor shall be any time: for of whatsoever it may be said, *it has been* or *it shall* be, of the same also it might have been said heretofore, or may be said hereafter *it is.* What then can days, months, and years, be, but the names of such computations made in our mind? *Time* therefore is a phantasm, but a phantasm of

motion, for if we would know by what moments time passes away, we make use of some motion or other, as of the sun, of a clock, of the sand in an hourglass, or we mark some line upon which we imagine something to be moved, there being no other means by which we can take notice of any time at all. And yet, when I say *time* is a phantasm of motion, I do not say this is sufficient to define it by; for this word *time* comprehends the motion of *former* and *latter,* or of succession in the motion of a body, in as much as it is first *here* then *there.* Wherefore a complete definition of *time* is such as this, TIME *is the phantasm of before and after in motion;* which agrees with this definition of *Aristotle, time is the number of motion according to former and latter;* for that numbering is an act of the mind; and therefore it is all one to say, *time is the number of motion according to former and latter;* and *time is a phantasm of motion numbered.* But that other definition, *time is the measure of motion,* is not so exact, for we measure time by motion and not motion by time.

4] One space is called *part* of another space, and one time *part* of another time, when this contains that and something besides. From whence it may be collected, that nothing can rightly be called a PART, but that which is compared with something that contains it.

5] And therefore to *make parts,* or to *part* or DIVIDE space or *time,* is nothing else but to consider one and another within the same; so that if any man *divide* space or time, the diverse conceptions he has are more, by one, than the parts he makes; for his first conception is of that which is to be divided, then of some part of it, and again of some other part of it, and so forwards as long as he goes on in dividing.

But it is to be noted, that here, by *division,* I do not mean the severing or pulling asunder of one space or time from another (for does any man think that one hemisphere may be separated from the other hemisphere, or the first hour from the second?) but diversity of consideration; so that division is not made by the operation of the hands but of the mind.

6] When space or time is considered among other spaces or times, it is said to be ONE, namely *one of them;* for except one space might be added to another, and subtracted from another space, and so of time, it would be sufficient to say space or time simply, and superfluous to say one space or one time, if it could not be conceived that there were another. The common definition of *one*, namely, that *one is that which is undivided,* is obnoxious to an absurd consequence; for it may thence be inferred, that whatsoever is divided is many things, that is, that every divided thing, is divided things, which is insignificant.

7] NUMBER is *one* and *one,* or *one one* and *one,* and so forwards; namely, *one* and *one* make the number *two,* and *one one* and *one* the number *three;* so are all other numbers made; which is all one as if we should say, *number is unities.*

8] To COMPOUND space of spaces, or time of times, is first to consider them one after another, and then altogether as one; as if one should reckon first the head, the feet, the arms, and the body, severally, and then for the account of them all together put *man.* And that which is so put for all the severals of which it consists, is called the WHOLE; and those severals, when by the division of the whole they come again to be considered singly, are parts thereof; and therefore the *whole* and *all the parts taken together* are the same thing. And as I noted above, that in *division* it is not necessary to pull the parts asunder; so in *composition,* it is to be understood, that for the making up of a whole there is no need of putting the parts together, so as to make them touch one another, but only of collecting them into one sum in the mind. For thus all men, being considered together, make up the whole of mankind, though never so much dispersed by time and place; and twelve hours, though the hours of several days, may be compounded into one number of twelve.

9] This being well understood, it is manifest, that nothing can rightly be called a whole, that is not conceived to be compounded of parts, and that it may be divided into parts; so that if we deny that a thing has parts, we deny the same to be a whole. For example, if we say the soul can have no parts, we affirm that no soul can be a whole soul. Also it is manifest, that nothing has parts till it be divided; and when a thing is divided, the parts are only so many as the division makes them. Again, that a part of a part is a part of the whole; and thus any part of the number *four,* as *two,* is a part of the number *eight;* for *four* is made of *two* and *two;* but eight is compounded of *two, two,* and *four,* and therefore *two,* which is a part of the part *four,* is also a part of the whole *eight.* . . .

12] . . . Of infinite space or time, it cannot be said that it is a *whole* or *one:* not a *whole,* because not compounded of parts: for seeing parts, how many soever they be, are severally finite, they will also, when they are all put together, make a whole finite: nor *one,* because nothing can be said to be one, except there be another to compare it with; but it cannot be conceived that there are two spaces, or two times, infinite. Lastly, when we make question whether the world be finite or infinite, we have nothing in our mind answering to the name *world;* for whatsoever we imagine, is therefore finite, though our computation reach the fixed stars, or the ninth or tenth, nay, the thousandth sphere. The meaning of the question is this only, whether God has actually made so great an addition of body to body, as we are able to make of space to space.

13] And, therefore, that which is commonly said, that space and time may be divided infinitely, is not to be so understood, as if there might be any infinite or external division; but rather to be taken in this sense, *whatsoever is divided, is divided into such parts as may again be divided;* or thus, *the least divisible thing is not to be given;* or, as geometricians have it, *no quantity is so small, but a less may be taken;* which may easily be demonstrated in this manner. Let any space or time, that which was thought to be the least divisible, be divided into two equal parts, A and B. I say either of them, as A, may be divided again. For suppose the part A to be contiguous to the part B of one side, and of the other side to some other space equal to B. This whole space, therefore, being greater than the space given, is divisible. Wherefore, if it be divided into two equal parts, the part in the middle, which is A, will be also divided into two equal parts; and therefore A was divisible.

Chapter VIII
Of Body and Accident

1] Having understood what imaginary space is, in which we supposed nothing remaining without us, but all those things to be
destroyed, that, by existing heretofore, left images of themselves in
our minds; let us now suppose some one of those things to be
placed again in the world, or created anew. It is necessary, therefore, that this new-created or replaced thing do not only fill some
part of the space above mentioned, or be coincident and coextended with it, but also that it have no dependence upon our
thought. And this is that which, for the extension of it, we commonly call *body;* and because it depends not upon our thought,
we say is *a thing subsisting of itself;* as also *existing,* because without us; and, lastly, it is called the *subject,* because it is so placed in
and *subjected* to imaginary space, that it may be understood by
reason, as well as perceived by sense. The definition, therefore of
body may be this, *a body is that, which having no dependence
upon our thought, is coincident or coextended with some part of
space. . . .*

4] The *extension* of a body, is the same thing with the *magnitude*
of it, or that which some call *real space.* But this *magnitude* does
not depend upon our cogitation, as imaginary space doth; for this
is an effect of our imagination, but *magnitude* is the cause of it;
this is an accident of the mind, that of a body existing out of the
mind.

5] That space, by which word I here understand imaginary space,
which is coincident with the magnitude of any body, is called the
place of that body; and the body itself is that which we call the
thing placed. Now *place,* and the *magnitude* of the *thing placed,*
differ. First in this, that a body keeps always the same *magnitude,*
both when it is at rest, and when it is moved; but when it is
moved, it does not keep the same *place.* Secondly in this, that
place is a phantasm of any body of such and such quantity and
figure; but *magnitude* is the peculiar accident of every body; for
one body may at several times have several places, but has always

one and the same magnitude. Thirdly in this, that *place* is nothing out of the mind, nor magnitude any thing within it. And lastly, *place* is feigned extension, but *magnitude* true extension; and a placed body is not extension, but a thing extended. Besides, *place is immovable;* for, seeing that which is moved, is understood to be carried from place to place, if place were moved, it would also be carried from place to place, so that one place must have another place, and that place another place, and so on infinitely, which is ridiculous. And as for those, that, by making *place* to be of the same nature with *real space,* would from thence maintain it to be immovable, they also make place, though they do not perceive they make it so, to be a mere phantasm. For whilst one affirms that place is therefore said to be immovable, because space in general is considered there; if he had remembered that nothing is general or universal besides names or signs, he would easily have seen that that space, which he says is considered in general, is nothing but a phantasm, in the mind or the memory, of a body of such magnitude and such figure. And whilst another says: real space is made immovable by the understanding; as when, under the superficies of running water, we imagine other and other water to come by continual succession, that superficies fixed there by the understanding, is the *immovable place* of the river: what else does he make it to be but a phantasm, though he do it obscurely and in perplexed words? Lastly, the nature of place does not consist in the *superficies of the ambient,* but in *solid space;* for the whole placed body is coextended with its whole place, and every part of it with every answering part of the same place; but seeing every placed body is a solid thing, it cannot be understood to be coextended with superficies. Besides, how can any whole body be moved, unless all its parts be moved together with it? Or how can the internal parts of it be moved, but by leaving their place? But the internal parts of a body cannot leave the superficies of an external part contiguous to it; and, therefore, it follows, that if place be the superficies of the ambient, then the parts of a body moved, that is, bodies moved, are not moved.

6] Space, or place, that is possessed by a body, is called *full,* and that which is not so possessed, is called *empty.*

Chapter IX
Of Cause and Effect

1] A body is said to work upon or *act,* that is to say, *do* something
to another body, when it either generates or destroys some accident
in it: and the body in which an accident is generated or destroyed
is said to *suffer,* that is, to have something *done* to it by another
body; as when one body by putting forwards another body generates motion in it, it is called the AGENT; and the body in which
motion is so generated, is called the PATIENT; so fire that warms the
hand is the *agent,* and the hand, which is warmed, is the *patient.*
That accident, which is generated in the patient, is called the
EFFECT.

2] When an agent and patient are contiguous to one another, their
action and passion are then said to be *immediate,* otherwise, medi-
ate; and when another body, lying betwixt the agent and patient,
is contiguous to them both, it is then itself both an agent and a
patient; an agent in respect of the body next after it, upon which
it works, and a patient in respect of the body next before it, from
which it suffers. Also, if many bodies be so ordered that every two
which are next to one another be contiguous, then all those that
are betwixt the first and the last are both agents and patients, and
the first is an agent only, and the last a patient only.

3] An agent is understood to *produce* its determined or certain
effect in the patient, according to some certain accident or accidents, with which both it and the patient are affected; that is to
say, the agent hath its effect precisely such, not because it is a body,
but because such a body, or so moved. For otherwise all agents,
seeing they are all bodies alike, would produce like effects in all
patients. And therefore the fire, for example, does not warm, because it is a body, but because it is hot; nor does one body put
forward another body because it is a body, but because it is moved
into the place of that other body. The cause, therefore, of all effects
consists in certain accidents both in the agents and in the patients;
which when they are all present, the effect is produced; but if any
one of them be wanting, it is not produced; and that accident

either of the agent or patient, without which the effect cannot be produced, is called *causa sine qua non,* or *cause necessary by supposition,* as also the *cause requisite for the production of the effect.* But a CAUSE simply, or *an entire cause, is the aggregate of all the accidents both of the agents how many soever they be, and of the patient, put together; which when they are all supposed to be present, it cannot be understood but that the effect is produced at the same instant; and if any one of them be wanting, it cannot be understood but that the effect is not produced.*

4] The aggregate of accidents in the agent or agents, requisite for the production of the effect, the effect being produced, is called the *efficient cause* thereof; and the aggregate of accidents in the patient, the effect being produced, is usually called the *material cause;* I say the effect being produced; for where there is no effect, there can be no cause; for nothing can be called a cause, where there is nothing that can be called an effect. But the efficient and material causes are both but partial causes, or parts of that cause, which in the next precedent article I called an entire cause. And from hence it is manifest, that the effect we expect, though the agents be not defective on their part, may nevertheless be frustrated by a defect in the patient; and when the patient is sufficient, by a defect in the agents.

5] An entire cause is always sufficient for the production of its effect, if the effect be at all possible. For let any effect whatsoever be propounded to be produced; if the same be produced, it is manifest that the cause which produced it was a sufficient cause; but if it be not produced, and yet be possible, it is evident that something was wanting either in some agent, or in the patient, without which it could not be produced; that is, that some accident was wanting which was requisite for its production; and therefore, that cause was not *entire,* which is contrary to what was supposed.

It follows also from hence, that in whatsoever instant the cause is entire, in the same instant the effect is produced. For if it be not produced, something is still wanting, which is requisite for the production of it; and therefore the cause was not entire, as was supposed.

And seeing a necessary cause is defined to be that, which being supposed, the effect cannot but follow; this also may be collected, that whatsoever effect is produced at any time, the same is produced by a necessary cause. For whatsoever is produced, in as much as it is produced, had an entire cause, that is, had all those things, which being supposed, it cannot be understood but that the effect follows; that is, it had a necessary cause. And in the same manner it may be shown, that whatsoever effects are hereafter to be produced, shall have a necessary cause; so that all the effects that have been, or shall be produced, have their necessity in things antecedent.

6] And from this, that whensoever the cause is entire, the effect is produced in the same instant, it is manifest that causation and the production of effects consist in a certain continual progress; so that as there is a continual mutation in the agent or agents, by the working of other agents upon them, so also the patient, upon which they work, is continually altered and changed. For example: as the heat of the fire increases more and more, so also the effects thereof, namely, the heat of such bodies as are next to it, and again, of such other bodies as are next to them, increase more and more accordingly; which is already no little argument that all mutation consists in motion only; the truth whereof shall be further demonstrated in the ninth article. But in this progress of causation, that is of action and passion, if any man comprehend in his imagination a part thereof, and divide the same into parts, the first part or beginning of it cannot be considered otherwise than as action or cause; for, if it should be considered as effect or passion, then it would be necessary to consider something before it, for its cause or action; which cannot be, for nothing can be before the beginning. And in like manner, the last part is considered only as effect; for it cannot be called cause, if nothing follow it; but after the last, nothing follows. And from hence it is, that in all action the beginning and cause are taken for the same thing. But every one of the intermediate parts are both action and passion, and cause and effect, according as they are compared with the antecedent or subsequent part.

7] There can be no cause of motion, except in a body contiguous and moved. For let there be any two bodies which are not contiguous, and betwixt which the intermediate space is empty, or, if filled, filled with another body which is at rest; and let one of the propounded bodies be supposed to be at rest; I say it shall always be at rest. For if it shall be moved, and the cause of that motion, by the 8th chapter, article 19, will be some external body; and, therefore, if between it and that external body there be nothing but empty space, then whatsoever the disposition be of that external body or the patient itself, yet if it be supposed to be now at rest, we may conceive it will continue so till it be touched by some other body. But seeing cause, by the definition, is the aggregate of all such accidents, which being supposed to be present, it cannot be conceived but that the effect will follow, those accidents, which are either in external bodies, or in the patient itself, cannot be the cause of future motion. And in like manner, seeing we may conceive that whatsoever is at rest will still be at rest, though it be touched by some other body, except that other body is moved; therefore in a contiguous body, which is at rest, there can be no cause of motion. Wherefore there is no cause of motion in any body, except it be contiguous and moved.

The same reason may serve to prove that whatsoever is moved, will always be moved on in the same way and with the same velocity, except it be hindered by some other contiguous and moved body; and consequently that no bodies, either when they are at rest, or when there is an interposition of vacuum, can generate or extinguish or lessen motion in other bodies. There is one that has written that things moved are more resisted by things at rest, than by things contrarily moved; for this reason, that he conceived motion not to be so contrary to motion as rest. That which deceived him was, that the words *rest* and *motion* are but contradictory names; whereas motion, indeed, is not resisted by rest, but by contrary motion.

8] But if a body work upon another body at one time, and afterwards the same body work upon the same body at another time, so that both the agent and patient, and all their parts, be in all things as they were; and there be no difference, except only in time, that is, that one action be former, the other later in time; it is manifest itself, that the effects will be equal and like, as not differing in anything besides time. And as effects themselves proceed from their causes, so the diversity of them depends upon the diversity of their causes also.

9] This being true, it is necessary that mutation can be nothing else but motion of the parts of that body which is changed. For first, we do not say anything is changed, but that which appears to our senses otherwise than it appeared formerly. Secondly, both those appearances are effects produced in the sentient; and, therefore, if they be different, it is necessary, by the preceding article, that either some part of the agent, which was formerly at rest, is now moved, and so the mutation consists in this motion; or some part, which was formerly moved, is now otherwise moved, and so also the mutation consists in this new motion; or which, being formerly moved, is now at rest, which, as I have shewn above, cannot come to pass without motion; and so again, mutation is motion; or lastly, it happens in some of these manners to the patient, or some of its parts; so the mutation, howsoever it be made, will consist in the motion of the parts, either of the body which is perceived, or of the sentient body, or of both. Mutation therefore is motion, namely, of the parts either of the agent or of the patient; which was to be demonstrated. And to this it is consequent, that rest cannot be the cause of anything, nor can any action proceed from it; seeing neither motion nor mutation can be caused by it. . . .

Chapter X

Of Power and Act

1] Correspondent to *cause* and *effect,* are POWER and ACT; nay, those and these are the same things; though, for divers considerations, they have divers names. For whensoever any agent has all those accidents which are necessarily requisite for the production of some effect in the patient, then we say that agent has *power* to produce that effect, if it be applied to a patient. But, as I have shewn in the precedent chapter, those accidents constitute the efficient cause; and therefore the same accidents, which constitute the efficient cause, constitute also the *power* of the agent. Wherefore the *power of the agent* and the *efficient cause* are the same thing. But they are considered with this difference, that *cause* is so called in respect of the effect already produced, and power in respect of the same effect to be produced hereafter; so that *cause* respects the past, *power* the future time. Also, the *power of the agent* is that which is commonly called *active power*.

In like manner, whensoever any patient has all those accidents which it is requisite it should have, for the production of some effect in it, we say it is in the *power* of that patient to produce that effect, if it be applied to a fitting agent. But those accidents, as is defined in the precedent chapter, constitute the material cause; and therefore the *power of the patient,* commonly called *passive power,* and *material cause,* are the same thing; but with this different consideration, that in cause the past time, and in power the future, is respected. Wherefore the power of the agent and patient together, which may be called entire or *plenary power,* is the same thing with *entire cause;* for they both consist in the sum or aggregate of all the accidents, as well in the agent as in the patient, which are requisite for the production of the effect. Lastly, as the accident produced is, in respect of the cause, called an effect, so in respect of the power, it is called an *act.* . . .

6] . . . All active power consists in motion also; and that power is not a certain accident, which differs from all acts, but is, indeed, an act, namely, motion, which is therefore called power, because another act shall be produced by it afterwards. For example, if of three bodies the first put forward the second, and this the third, the motion of the second, in respect of the first which produceth it, is the act of the second body; but, in respect of the third, it is the active power of the same second body.

7] The writers of metaphysics reckon up two other causes besides the *efficient* and *material,* namely, the ESSENCE, which some call the *formal cause,* and the END, or *final cause;* both which are nevertheless efficient causes. For when it is said the essence of a thing is the cause thereof, *as to be rational is the cause of man,* it is not intelligible; for it is all one, as if it were said, *to be a man is the cause of man;* which is not well said. And yet the knowledge of the *essence* of anything, is the cause of the knowledge of the thing itself; for, if I first know that a thing is *rational,* I know from thence, that the same is *man;* but this is no other than an efficient cause. A *final cause* has no place but in such things as have sense and will; and this also I shall prove hereafter to be an efficient cause. . . .

Chapter XXV

Of Sense and Animal Motion

11 I have, in the first chapter, defined philosophy to be *knowledge of effects acquired by true ratiocination, from knowledge first had of their causes and generation; and of such causes or generations as may be, from former knowledge of their effects or appearances.* There are, therefore, two methods of philosophy; one, from the generation of things to their possible effects; and the other, from their effects or appearances to some possible generation of the same. In the former of these the truth of the first principles of our ratiocination, namely definitions, is made and constituted by ourselves, whilst we consent and agree about the appellations of things. And this part I have finished in the foregoing chapters; in which, if I am not deceived, I have affirmed nothing, saving the definitions themselves, which hath not good coherence with the definitions I have given; that is to say, which is not sufficiently demonstrated to all those, that agree with me in the use of words and appellations; for whose sake only I have written the same. I now enter upon the other part; which is the finding out by the appearances or effects of nature, which we know by sense, some ways and means by which they may be, I do not say they are, generated. The principles, therefore, upon which the following discourse depends, are not such as we ourselves make and pronounce in general terms, as definitions; but such, as being placed in the things themselves by the Author of Nature, are by us observed in them; and we make use of them in single and particular, not universal propositions. Nor do they impose upon us any necessity of constituting theorems; their use being only, though not without such general propositions as have been already demonstrated, to show us the possibility of some production or generation. Seeing therefore, the science, which is here taught, hath its principles in the appearances of nature, and endeth in the attaining of some knowledge of natural causes, I have given to this part the title of PHYSICS, or the *Phenomena of Nature.* Now such things as appear, or are shown to us by nature, we call phenomena or appearances.

Of all the phenomena or appearances which are near us, the

most admirable is apparition itself, *tò phainesthai;* namely, that some natural bodies have in themselves the patterns almost of all things, and others of none at all. So that if the appearances be the principles by which we know all other things, we must needs acknowledge sense to be the principle by which we know those principles, and that all the knowledge we have is derived from it. And as for the causes of sense, we cannot begin our search of them from any other phenomenon than that of sense it-self. But you will say, by what sense shall we take notice of sense? I answer, by sense itself, namely, by the memory which for some time remains in us of things sensible, though they themselves pass away. For he that perceives that he hath perceived, remembers.

In the first place, therefore, the causes of our perception, that is, the causes of those ideas and phantasms which are perpetually gen-erated within us whilst we make use of our senses, are to be en-quired into; and in what manner their generation proceeds. To help which inquisition, we may observe first of all, that our phan-tasms or ideas are not always the same; but that new ones appear to us, and old ones vanish, according as we apply our organs of sense, now to one object, now to another. Wherefore they are gen-erated, and perish. And from hence it is manifest, that they are some change or mutation in the sentient.

2] Now that all mutation or alteration is motion or endeavour (and endeavour also is motion) in the internal parts of the thing that is altered, hath been proved from this, that whilst even the least parts of any body remain in the same situation in respect of one another, it cannot be said that any alteration, unless perhaps that the whole body together hath been moved, hath happened to it; but that it both appeareth and is the same it appeared and was before. Sense, therefore, in the sentient, can be nothing else but motion in some of the internal parts of the sentient; and the parts so moved are parts of the organs of sense. For the parts of our body, by which we perceive any thing, are those we commonly call the organs of sense. And so we find what is the subject of our sense, namely, that in which are the phantasms; and partly also we have discovered the nature of sense, namely, that it is some internal mo-tion in the sentient.

I have shown besides (in chap. IX, art. 7) that no motion is generated but by a body contiguous and moved: from whence it is manifest, that the immediate cause of sense or perception consists in this, that the first organ of sense is touched and pressed. For when the uttermost part of the organ is pressed, it no sooner yields, but the part next within it is pressed also; and, in this manner, the pressure or motion is propagated through all the parts of the organ to the innermost. And thus also the pressure of the uttermost part proceeds from the pressure of some more remote body, and so continually, till we come to that from which, as from its fountain, we derive the phantasm or idea that is made in us by our sense. And this, whatsoever it be, is that we commonly call *the object*. Sense, therefore, is some internal motion in the sentient, generated by some internal motion of the parts of the object, and propagated through all the media to the innermost part of the organ. By which words I have almost defined what sense is.

Moreover, all resistance is endeavour opposite to another endeavour, that is to say, reaction. Seeing, therefore, there is in the whole organ, by reason of its own internal natural motion, some resistance or reaction against the motion which is propagated from the object to the innermost part of the organ, there is also in the same organ an endeavour opposite to the endeavour which proceeds from the object; so that when that endeavour inwards is the last action in the act of sense, then from the reaction, how little soever the duration of it be, a phantasm or idea hath its being; which, by reason that the endeavour is now outwards, doth always appear as something situate without the organ. So that now I shall give you the whole definition of sense, as it is drawn from the explication of the causes thereof and the order of its generation, thus: SENSE *is a phantasm, made by the reaction and endeavour outwards in the organ of sense, caused by an endeavour inwards from the object, remaining for some time more or less.*

31 The *subject* of sense is the *sentient* itself, namely, some living creature; and we speak more correctly, when we say a living creature seeth, than when we say the eye seeth. The object is the thing received; and it is more accurately said, that we see the sun, than that we see the light. For light and colour, and heat and sound, and other qualities which are commonly called sensible, are not objects, but phantasms in the sentients. For a phantasm is the act

of sense, and differs no otherwise from sense than *fieri,* that is, being a doing, differs from *factum esse,* that is, being done; which difference, in things that are done in an instant, is none at all; and a phantasm is made in an instant. For in all motion which proceeds by perpetual propagation, the first part being moved moves the second, the second the third, and so on to the last, and that to any distance, how great soever. And in what point of time the first or foremost part proceeded to the place of the second, which is thrust on, in the same point of time the last save one proceeded into the place of the last yielding part; which by reaction, in the same instant, if the reaction be strong enough, makes a phantasm; and a phantasm being made, perception is made together with it.

4] The *organs* of sense, which are in the sentient, are such parts thereof, that if they be hurt, the very generation of phantasms is thereby destroyed, though all the rest of the parts remain entire. Now these parts in the most of living creatures are found to be certain spirits and membranes, which, proceeding from the *pia mater,* involve the brain and all the nerves; also the brain itself, and the arteries which are in the brain; and such other parts, as being stirred, the heart also, which is the fountain of all sense, is stirred together with them. For whensoever the action of the object reacheth the body of the sentient, that action is by some nerve propagated to the brain; and if the nerve leading thither be so hurt or obstructed, that the motion can be propagated no further, no sense follows. Also if the motion be intercepted between the brain and the heart by the defect of the organ by which the action is propagated, there will be no perception of the object.

5] But though all sense, as I have said, be made by reaction, nevertheless it is not necessary that every thing that reacteth should have sense. I know there have been philosophers, and those learned men, who have maintained that all bodies are endued with sense. Nor do I see how they can be refuted, if the nature of sense be placed in reaction only. And, though by the reaction of bodies inanimate a phantasm might be made, it would nevertheless cease, as soon as ever the object were removed. For unless those bodies had organs, as living creatures have, fit for the retaining of such motion as is made in them, their sense would be such, as that they should never remember the same. And therefore this hath nothing to do with that sense which is the subject of my discourse. For by sense, we commonly understand the judgment we make of objects by their phantasms; namely, by comparing and distinguishing those phantasms; which we could never do, if that motion in the organ, by which the phantasm is made, did not remain there for some time, and make the same phantasm return. Wherefore sense, as I here understand it, and which is commonly so called, hath necessarily some memory adhering to it, by which former and later phantasms may be compared together, and distinguished from one another.

Sense, therefore, properly so called, must necessarily have in it a perpetual variety of phantasms, that they may be discerned one from another. For if we should suppose a man to be made with clear eyes, and all the rest of his organs of sight well disposed, but endued with no other sense; and that he should look only upon one thing, which is always of the same colour and figure, without the least appearance of variety, he would seem to me, whatsoever others may say, to see, no more than I seem to myself to feel the bones of my own limbs by my organs of feeling; and yet those bones are always and on all sides touched by a most sensible membrane. I might perhaps say he were astonished, and looked upon it; but I should not say he saw it; it being almost all one for a man to be always sensible of one and the same thing, and not to be sensible at all of any thing.

61 And yet such is the nature of sense, that it does not permit a man to discern many things at once. For seeing the nature of sense consists in motion; as long as the organs are employed about one object, they cannot be so moved by another at the same time, as to make by both their motions one sincere phantasm of each of them at once. And therefore two several phantasms will not be made by two objects working together, but only one phantasm compounded from the action of both.

Besides, as when we divide a body, we divide its place; and when we reckon many bodies, we must necessarily reckon as many places; and contrarily, as I have shown in the seventh chapter; so what number soever we say there be of times, we must understand the same number of motions also; and as oft as we count many motions, so oft we reckon many times. For though the object we look upon be of divers colours, yet with those divers colours it is but one varied object, and not variety of objects.

Moreover, whilst those organs which are common to all the senses, such as are those parts of every organ which proceed in men from the root of the nerves to the heart, are vehemently stirred by a strong action from some one object, they are, by reason of the contumacy which the motion, they have already, gives them against the reception of all other motion, made the less fit to receive any other impression from whatsoever other objects, to what sense so-ever those objects belong. And hence it is, that an earnest studying of one object, takes away the sense of all other objects for the present. For *study* is nothing else but a possession of the mind, that is to say, a vehement motion made by some one object in the organs of sense, which are stupid to all other motions as long as this last-eth; according to what was said by Terence, *"Populus studio stupidus in funambulo animum occuparat."* For what is *stupor* but that which the Greeks call *ánaisthesía,* that is, a cessation from the sense of other things? Wherefore at one and the same time, we cannot by sense perceive more than one single object; as in reading, we see the letters successively one by one, and not all together, though the whole page be presented to our eye; and though every several letter be distinctly written there, yet when we look upon the whole page at once, we read nothing.

From hence it is manifest, that every endeavour of the organ outwards, is not to be called sense, but that only, which at several times is by vehemence made stronger and more predominant than the rest; which deprives us of the sense of other phantasms, no otherwise than the sun deprives the rest of the stars of light, not by hindering their action, but by obscuring and hiding them with his excess of brightness.

7] But the motion of the organ, by which a phantasm is made, is not commonly called sense, except the object be present. And the phantasm remaining after the object is removed or past by, is called *fancy,* and in Latin *imaginatio;* which word, because all phantasms are not images, doth not fully answer the signification of the word *fancy* in its general acceptation. Nevertheless I may use it safely enough, by understanding it for the Greek *phantasía.*

IMAGINATION therefore is nothing else but *sense decaying,* or *weakened,* by the absence of the object. But what may be the cause of this decay or weakening? Is the motion the weaker, because the object is taken away? If it were, then phantasms would always and necessarily be less clear in the imagination, than they are in sense; which is not true. For in dreams, which are the imaginations of those that sleep, they are no less clear than in sense itself. But the reason why in men waking the phantasms of things past are more obscure than those of things present, is this, that their organs being at the same time moved by other present objects, those phantasms are the less predominant. Whereas in sleep, the passages being shut up, external action doth not at all disturb or hinder internal motion.

If this be true, the next thing to be considered, will be, whether any cause may be found out, from the supposition whereof it will follow, that the passage is shut up from the external objects of sense to the internal organ. I suppose, therefore, that by the continual action of objects, to which a reaction of the organ, and more especially of the spirits, is necessarily consequent, the organ is wearied, that is, its parts are no longer moved by the spirits without some pain; and consequently the nerves being abandoned and grown slack, they retire to their fountain, which is the cavity either of the brain or of the heart; by which means the action which proceeded by the nerves is necessarily intercepted. For action upon a patient, that retires from it, makes but little impression at the first; and at last, when the nerves are by little and little slackened, none at all. And therefore there is no more reaction, that is, no more sense, till the organ being refreshed by rest, and by a supply of new spirits recovering strength and motion, the sentient awaketh. And thus it seems to be always, unless some other preternatural cause intervene; as heat in the internal parts from lassitude, or from some disease stirring the spirits and other parts or the organ in some extraordinary manner.

8] Now it is not without cause, nor so casual a thing as many perhaps think it, that phantasms in this their great variety proceed from one another; and that the same phantasms sometimes bring into the mind other phantasms like themselves, and at other times extremely unlike. For in the motion of any continued body, one part follows another by cohesion; and therefore, whilst we turn our eyes and other organs successively to many objects, the motion which was made by every one of them remaining, the phantasms are renewed as often as any one of those motions cames to be predominant above the rest; and they become predominant in the same order in which at any time formerly they were generated by sense. So that when by length of time very many phantasms have been generated within us by sense, then almost any thought may arise from any other thought; insomuch that it may seem to be a thing indifferent and casual, which thought shall follow which. But for the most part this is not so uncertain a thing to waking as to sleeping men. For the thought or phantasm of the desired end brings in all the phantasms, that are means conducing to that end, and that in order backwards from the last to the first, and again forwards from the beginning to the end. But this supposes both appetite, and judgment to discern what means conduce to the end, which is gotten by experience; and experience is store of phantasms, arising from the sense of very many things. For *phantá-zesthai* and *meminisse, fancy* and *memory,* differ only in this, that memory supposeth the time past, which fancy doth not. In memory, the phantasms we consider are as if they were worn out with time; but in our fancy we consider them as they are; which distinction is not of the things themselves, but of the considerations of the sentient. For there is in memory something like that which happens in looking upon things at a great distance; in which as the small parts of the object are not discerned, by reason of their remoteness; so in memory, many accidents and places and parts of things, which were formerly perceived by sense, are by length of time decayed and lost.

The perpetual arising of phantasms, both in sense and imagination, is that which we commonly call discourse of the mind, and is common to men with other living creatures. For he that thinketh, compareth the phantasms that pass, that is, taketh notice of their likeness or unlikeness to one another. And as he that observes readily the likenesses of things of different natures, or that are very remote from one another, is said to have a good fancy; so he is said to have a good judgment, that finds out the unlikenesses or differences of things that are like one another. Now this observation of differences is not perception made by a common organ of sense, distinct from sense or perception properly so called, but is memory of the differences of particular phantasms remaining for some time; as the distinction between hot and lucid, is nothing else but the memory both of a heating, and of an enlightening object. . . .

12] But there is another kind of sense, of which I will say something in this place, namely, the sense of pleasure and pain, proceeding not from the reaction of the heart outwards, but from continual action from the outermost part of the organ towards the heart. For the original of life being in the heart, that motion in the sentient, which is propagated to the heart, must necessarily make some alteration or diversion of vital motion, namely, by quickening or slackening, helping or hindering the same. Now when it helpeth, it is pleasure; and when it hindereth, it is pain, trouble, grief, &c. And as phantasms seem to be without, by reason of the endeavour outwards, so pleasure and pain, by reason of the endeavour of the organ inwards, seem to be within; namely, there where the first cause of the pleasure or pain is; as when the pain proceeds from a wound, we think the pain and the wound are both in the same place.

Now vital motion is the motion of the blood, perpetually circulating (as hath been shown from many infallible signs and marks by Doctor Harvey, the first observer of it) in the veins and arteries. Which motion, when it is hindered by some other motion made by the action of sensible objects, may be restored again either by bending or setting strait the parts of the body; which is done when the spirits are carried now into these, now into other nerves, till the pain, as far as is possible, be quite taken away. But if vital motion be helped by motion made by sense, then the parts of the organ will be disposed to guide the spirits in such manner as conduceth most to the preservation and augmentation of that motion, by the help of the nerves. And in animal motion this is the very first endeavour, and found even in the embryo; which while it is in the womb, moveth its limbs with voluntary motion, for the avoiding of whatsoever troubleth it, or for the pursuing of what pleaseth it. And this first endeavour, when it tends towards such things as are known by experience to be pleasant, is called *appetite,* that is, an approaching; and when it shuns what is troublesome, *aversion,* or flying from it. And little infants, at the beginning and as soon as they are born, have appetite to very few things, as also they avoid very few, by reason of their want of experience and memory; and therefore they have not so great a variety of animal motion as we see in those that are more grown. For it is not possible, without such knowledge as is derived from sense, that is, without experience and memory, to know what will prove pleasant or hurtful; only there is some place for conjecture from the looks or aspects of things. And hence it is, that though they do not know what may do them good or harm, yet sometimes they approach and sometimes retire from the same thing, as their doubt prompts them. But afterwards, by accustoming themselves by little and little, they come to know readily what is to be pursued and what to be avoided; and also to have a ready use of their nerves and other organs, in the pursuing and avoiding of good and bad. Wherefore appetite and aversion are the first endeavours of animal motion.

Consequent to this first endeavour, is the impulsion into the nerves and retraction again of animal spirits, of which it is necessary there be some receptacle or place near the original of the nerves; and this motion or endeavour is followed by a swelling and relaxation of the muscles; and lastly, these are followed by contraction and extension of the limbs, which is animal motion.

13] The considerations of appetites and aversions are divers. For seeing living creatures have sometimes appetite and sometimes aversion to the same thing, as they think it will either be for their good or their hurt; while that vicissitude of appetites and aversions remains in them, they have that series of thoughts which is called *deliberation;* which lasteth as long as they have it in their power to obtain that which pleaseth, or to avoid that which displeaseth them. Appetite, therefore, and aversion are simply so called as long as they follow not deliberation. But if deliberation have gone before, then the last act of it, if it be appetite, is called *will;* if aversion, *unwillingness.* So that the same thing is called both will and appetite; but the consideration of them, namely, before and after deliberation, is divers. Nor is that which is done within a man whilst he willeth any thing, different from that which is done in other living creature, whilst, deliberation having preceded, they have appetite.

Neither is the freedom of willing or not willing, greater in man,

than in other living creatures. For where there is appetite, the entire cause of appetite hath preceded; and, consequently, the act of
appetite could not choose but follow, that is, hath of necessity followed (as is shown in chap. IX, art. 5). And therefore such a liberty
as is free from necessity, is not to be found in the will either of
men or beasts. But if by liberty we understand 'the faculty or
power, not of willing, but of doing what they will, then certainly
that liberty is to be allowed to both, and both may equally have it,
whensoever it is to be had.

Again, when appetite and aversion do with celerity succeed one
another, the whole series made by them hath its name sometimes
from one, sometimes from the other. For the same deliberation,
whilst it inclines sometimes to one, sometimes to the other, is from
appetite called *hope,* and from aversion, *fear.* For where there is
no hope, it is not to be called fear, but *hate;* and where no fear,
not hope, but *desire.* To conclude, all the passions, called passions
of the mind, consist of appetite and aversion, except pure pleasure
and pain, which are a certain fruition of good or evil; as anger is
aversion from some imminent evil, but such as is joined with appetite of avoiding that evil by force. . . .

Leviathan

Chapter IV

Of Speech

THE invention of *printing*, though ingenious, compared with
the invention of *letters,* is no great matter. But who was the first
that found the use of letters, is not known. He that first brought
them into Greece, men say was Cadmus, the son of Agenor, king of
Phœnicia. A profitable invention for continuing the memory of
time passed, and the conjunction of mankind, dispersed into so
many, and distant regions of the earth; and withal difficult, as proceeding from a watchful observation of the divers motions of the
tongue, palate, lips, and other organs of speech; whereby to make
as many differences of characters, to remember them. But the most
noble and profitable invention of all other, was that of SPEECH,
consisting of *names* or *appellations,* and their connexion; whereby
men register their thoughts; recall them when they are past; and
also declare them one to another for mutual utility and conversation; without which, there had been amongst men, neither commonwealth, nor society, nor contract, nor peace, no more than
amongst lions, bears, and wolves. The first author of *speech* was
God himself, that instructed Adam how to name such creatures
as he presented to his sight; for the Scripture goeth no further in
this matter. But this was sufficient to direct him to add more
names, as the experience and use of the creatures should give him
occasion; and to join them in such manner by degrees, as to make
himself understood; and so by succession of time, so much language might be gotten, as he had found use for; though not so
copious, as an orator or philosopher has need of: for I do not find
anything in the Scripture, out of which, directly or by consequence, can be gathered, that Adam was taught the names of all
figures, numbers, measures, colours, sounds, fancies, relations;

much less the names of words and speech, as *general, special, affirmative, negative, interrogative, optative, infinitive,* all which are useful; and least of all, of *entity, intentionality, quiddity,* and other insignificant words of the school.

But all this language gotten, and augmented by Adam and his posterity, was again lost at the Tower of Babel, when, by the hand of God, every man was stricken, for his rebellion, with an oblivion of his former language. And being hereby forced to disperse themselves into several parts of the world, it must needs be, that the diversity of tongues that now is proceeded by degrees from them, in such manner, as need, the mother of all inventions, taught them; and in tract of time grew everywhere more copious.

The general use of speech, is to transfer our mental discourse, into verbal; or the train of our thoughts, into a train of words; and that for two commodities, whereof one is the registering of the consequences of our thoughts; which being apt to slip out of our memory, and put us to a new labour, may again be recalled, by such words as they were marked by. So that the first use of names is to serve for *marks,* or *notes* of remembrance. Another is, when many use the same words, to signify, by their connexion and order, one to another, what they conceive, or think of each matter; and also what they desire, fear, or have any other passion for. And for this use they are called *signs.* Special uses of speech are these: first, to register, what by cogitation, we find to be the cause of anything, present or past; and what we find things present or past may produce, or effect; which in sum, is acquiring of arts. Secondly, to show to others that knowledge which we have attained, which is, to counsel and teach one another. Thirdly, to make known to others our wills and purposes, that we may have the mutual help of one another. Fourthly, to please and delight ourselves and others, by playing with our words, for pleasure or ornament, innocently.

To these uses, there are also four correspondent abuses. First, when men register their thoughts wrong, by the inconstancy of the signification of their words; by which they register for their conception, that which they never conceived, and so deceive themselves. Secondly, when they use words metaphorically; that is, in other sense than that they are ordained for; and thereby deceive others. Thirdly, by words, when they declare that to be their will, which is not. Fourthly, when they use them to grieve one another; for seeing nature hath armed living creatures, some with teeth, some with horns, and some with hands, to grieve an enemy, it is but an abuse of speech, to grieve him with the tongue, unless it be one whom we are obliged to govern; and then it is not to grieve, but to correct and amend.

The manner how speech serveth to the remembrance of the consequence of causes and effects, consisteth in the imposing of *names,* and the *connexion* of them.

Of names, some are *proper,* and singular to one only thing, as *Peter, John, this man, this tree;* and some are *common* to many things, *man, horse, tree;* every of which, though but one name, is nevertheless the name of divers particular things; in respect of all which together, it is called an *universal;* there being nothing in the world universal but names; for the things named are every one of them individual and singular.

One universal name is imposed on many things, for their similitude in some quality, or other accident; and whereas a proper name bringeth to mind one thing only, universals recall any one of those many.

And of names universal, some are of more, and some of less extent; the larger comprehending the less large; and some again of equal extent, comprehending each other reciprocally. As for example: the name *body* is of larger signification than the word *man,* and comprehendeth it; and the names *man* and *rational,* are of equal extent, comprehending mutually one another. But here we must take notice, that by a name is not always understood, as in grammar, one only word; but sometimes, by circumlocution, many words together. For all these words, *he that in his actions observeth the laws of his country,* make but one name, equivalent to this one word, *just.*

By this imposition of names, some of larger, some of stricter signification, we turn the reckoning of the consequences of things imagined in the mind, into a reckoning of the consequences of appellations. For example: a man that hath no use of speech at all, such as is born and remains perfectly deaf and dumb, if he set before his eyes a triangle, and by it two right angles, such as are the corners of a square figure, he may, by mediation, compare and find, that the three angles of that triangle, are equal to those two right angles that stand by it. But if another triangle be shown him, different in shape from the former, he cannot know, without a new labour, whether the three angles of that also be equal to the same. But he that hath the use of words, when he observes, that such quality was consequent, not to the length of the sides, nor to any other particular thing in his triangle; but only to this, that the sides were straight, and the angles three; and that that was all, for which he named it a triangle; will boldly conclude universally, that such equality of angles is in all triangles whatsoever; and register his invention in these general terms, *every triangle hath its three angles equal to two right angles.* And thus the consequence found in one particular, comes to be registered and remembered, as a universal rule, and discharges our mental reckoning, of time and place, and delivers us from all labour of the mind, saving the first, and makes that which was found true *here,* and *now,* to be true in *all times* and *places.*

But the use of words in registering our thoughts is in nothing so evident as in numbering. A natural fool that could never learn by heart the order of numeral words, as *one, two,* and *three,* may observe every stroke of the clock, and nod to it, or say *one, one, one,* but can never know what hour it strikes. And it seems, there was a time when those names of number were not in use; and men were fain to apply their fingers of one or both hands, to those things they desired to keep account of; and that thence it proceeded, that now our numeral words are but ten, in any nation, and in some but five; and then they begin again. And he that can tell ten, if he recite them out of order, will lose himself, and not know when he has done. Much less will he be able to add, and subtract, and perform all other operations of arithmetic. So that without words there is no possibility of reckoning of numbers; much less of magnitudes, of swiftness, of force, and other things, the reckonings whereof are necessary to the being, or well-being of mankind.

When two names are joined together into a consequence, or affirmation, as thus, *a man is a living creature;* or thus, *if he be a man, he is a living creature;* if the latter name, *living creature,* signify all that the former name *man* signifieth, then the affirmation, or consequence, is *true;* otherwise *false.* For *true* and *false* are attributes of speech, not of things. And where speech is not, there is neither *truth* nor *falsehood; error* there may be, as when we expect that which shall not be, or suspect what has not been; but in neither case can a man be charged with untruth.

Seeing then that truth consisteth in the right ordering of names in our affirmations, a man that seeketh precise truth had need to remember what every name he uses stands for, and to place it accordingly, or else he will find himself entangled in words, as a bird in lime twigs, the more he struggles the more belimed. And therefore in geometry, which is the only science that it hath pleased God hitherto to bestow on mankind, men begin at settling the significations of their words; which settling of significations they call *definitions,* and place them in the beginning of their reckoning.

By this it appears how necessary it is for any man that aspires to true knowledge, to examine the definitions of former authors; and either to correct them, where they are negligently set down, or to make them himself. For the errors of definitions multiply themselves according as the reckoning proceeds, and lead men into absurdities, which at last they see, but cannot avoid, without reckoning anew from the beginning, in which lies the foundation of their errors. From whence it happens, that they which trust to books do as they that cast up many little sums into a greater, without considering whether those little sums were rightly cast up or not; and at last finding the error visible, and not mistrusting their first grounds, know not which way to clear themselves, but spend time in fluttering over their books; as birds that entering by the chimney, and finding themselves enclosed in a chamber, flutter at the false light of a glass window, for want of wit to consider which way they came in. So that in the right definition of names lies the first use of speech; which is the acquisition of science: and in wrong, or no definitions, lies the first abuse; from which proceed all false and senseless tenets; which make those men that take their instruction from the authority of books, and not from their own meditation, to be as much below the condition of ignorant men, as men endued with true science are above it. For between true science and erroneous doctrines, ignorance is in the middle. Natural sense and imagination are not subject to absurdity. Nature itself cannot err; and as men abound in copiousness of language, so they become more wise, or more mad than ordinary. Nor is it possible without letters for any man to become either excellently wise, or, unless his memory be hurt by disease or ill constitution of organs, excellently foolish. For words are wise men's counters, they do but reckon by them; but they are the money of fools, that value them by the authority of an Aristotle, a Cicero, or a Thomas, or any other doctor whatsoever, if but a man.

Subject to names, is whatsoever can enter in to or be considered in an account, and be added one to another to make a sum, or subtracted one from another and leave a remainder. The Latins called accounts of money *rationes,* and accounting *ratiocinatio;* and that which we in bills or books of account call *items,* they call *nomina,* that is *names;* and thence it seems to proceed, that they extended the word *ratio* to the faculty of reckoning in all other things. The Greeks have but one word, *lógos* for both *speech* and *reason;* not that they thought there was no speech without reason, but no reasoning without speech: and the act of reasoning they called *syllogism,* which signifieth summing up of the consequences of one saying to another. And because the same thing may enter into account for divers accidents, their names are, to show that diversity, diversely wrested and diversified. This diversity of names may be reduced to four general heads.

First, a thing may enter into account for *matter* or *body;* as *living, sensible, rational, hot, cold, moved, quiet;* with all which names the word *matter,* or *body,* is understood; all such being names of matter.

Secondly, it may enter into account, or be considered, for some accident or quality which we conceive to be in it; as for *being moved,* for *being so long,* for *being hot,* &c.; and then, of the name of the thing itself, by a little change or wresting, we make a name for that accident, which we consider; and for *living* put into the account *life;* for *moved, motion;* for *hot, heat;* for *long, length;* and the like: and all such names are the names of the accidents and properties by which one matter and body is distinguished from another. These are called *names abstract,* because severed, not from matter, but from the account of matter.

Thirdly, we bring into account the properties of our own bodies, whereby we make such distinction; as when anything is seen by us, we reckon not the thing itself, but the sight, the colour, the idea of it in the fancy: and when anything is heard, we reckon it not, but the hearing or sound only, which is our fancy or conception of it by the ear; and such are names of fancies.

Fourthly, we bring into account, consider, and give names, to *names* themselves, and to *speech:* for *general, universal, special, equivocal,* are names of names. And *affirmation, interrogation, commandment, narration, syllogism, sermon, oration,* and many other such, are names of speeches. And this is all the variety of names *positive;* which are put to mark somewhat which is in nature, or may be feigned by the mind of man, as bodies that are, or may be conceived to be; or of bodies, the properties that are, or may be feigned to be; or words and speech.

There be also other names, called *negative,* which are notes to signify that a word is not the name of the thing in question; as these words, *nothing, no man, infinite, indocible, three want four,* and the like; which are nevertheless of use in reckoning, or in correcting of reckoning, and call to mind our past cogitations, though they be not names of anything, because they make us refuse to admit of names not rightly used.

All other names are but insignificant sounds; and those of two sorts. One when they are new, and yet their meaning not explained by definition; whereof there have been abundance coined by schoolmen, and puzzled philosophers.

Another, when men make a name of two names, whose significations are contradictory and inconsistent; as this name, an *incorporeal body,* or, which is all one, an *inoorporeal substance,* and a great number more. For whensoever any affirmation is false, the two names of which it is composed, put together and made one, signify nothing at all. For example, if it be a false affirmation to say *a quadrangle is round,* the word *round quadrangle* signifies nothing, but is a mere sound. So likewise, if it be false to say that virtue can be poured, or blown up and down, the words *inpoured virtue, inblown virtue,* are as absurd and insignificant as a *round quadrangle.* And therefore you shall hardly meet with a senseless and insignificant word, that is not made up of some Latin or Greek names. A Frenchman seldom hears our Saviour called by the name of *parole,* but by the name of *verbe* often; yet *verbe* and *parole* differ no more, but that one is Latin and the other French.

When a man, upon the hearing of any speech, hath those thoughts which the words of that speech and their connexion were ordained and constituted to signify, then he is said to understand it; *understanding* being nothing else but conception caused by speech. And therefore if speech be peculiar to man, as for ought I know it is, then is understanding peculiar to him also. And therefore of absurd and false affirmations, in case they be universal, there can be no understanding; though many think they understand then, when they do but repeat the words softly, or con them in their mind.

What kinds of speeches signify the appetites, aversions, and passions of man's mind; and of their use and abuse, I shall speak when I have spoken of the passions.

The names of such things as affect us, that is, which please and displease us, because all men be not alike affected with the same thing, nor the same man at all times, are in the common discourses of men of *inconstant* signification. For seeing all names are imposed to signify our conceptions, and all our affections are but conceptions, when we conceive the same things differently, we can hardly avoid different naming of them. For though the nature of that we conceive, be the same; yet the diversity of our reception of it, in respect of different constitutions of body, and prejudices of opinion, gives every thing a tincture of our different passions. And therefore in reasoning a man must take heed of words; which besides the signification of what we imagine of their nature, have a signification also of the nature, disposition, and interest of the speaker; such as are the names of virtues and vices; for one man calleth *wisdom,* what another calleth *fear;* and one *cruelty,* what another *justice;* one *prodigality,* what another *magnanimity;* and one *gravity,* what another *stupidity,* &c. And therefore such names can never be true grounds of any ratiocination. No more can metaphors, and tropes of speech; but these are less dangerous, because they profess their inconstancy; which the other do not.

Chapter V

Of Reason and Science

When a man *reasoneth,* he does nothing else but conceive a sum total, from *addition* of parcels; or conceive a remainder, from *subtraction* of one sum from another; which, if it be done by words, is conceiving of the consequence of the names of all the parts, to the name of the whole; or from the names of the whole and one part, to the name of the other part. And though in some things, as in numbers, besides adding and subtracting, men name other operations, as *multiplying* and *dividing,* yet they are the same; for multiplication, is but adding together of things equal; and division, but subtracting of one thing, as often as we can. These operations are not incident to numbers only, but to all manner of things that can be added together, and taken one out of another. For as arithmeticians teach to add and subtract in *numbers;* so the geometricians teach the same in *lines, figures,* solid and superficial, *angles, proportions, times,* degrees of *swiftness, force, power,* and the like; the logicians teach the same in *consequences of words;* adding together two *names* to make an *affirmation,* and two *affirmations* to make a *syllogism;* and many *syllogisms* to make a *demonstration;* and from the *sum,* or *conclusion* of a *syllogism,* they subtract one *proposition* to find the other. Writers of politics add together *pactions* to find men's *duties;* and lawyers, *laws* and *facts,* to find what is *right* and *wrong* in the actions of private men. In sum, in what matter soever there is place for *addition* and *subtraction,* there also is place for *reason;* and where these have no place, there *reason* has nothing at all to do.

Out of all which we may define, that is to say determine, what that is, which is meant by this word *reason,* when we reckon it amongst the faculties of the mind. For REASON, in this sense, is nothing but *reckoning,* that is adding and subtracting, of the consequences of general names agreed upon for the *marking* and *signifying* of our thoughts; I say *marking* them when we reckon by ourselves, and *signifying,* when we demonstrate or approve our reckonings to other men.

And, as in arithmetic, unpractised men must, and professors themselves may often, err, and cast up false; so also in any other subject of reasoning, the ablest, most attentive, and most practised men may deceive themselves, and infer false conclusions; not but that reason itself is always right reason, as well as arithmetic is a certain and infallible art: but no one man's reason, nor the reason of any one number of men, makes the certainty; no more than an account is therefore well cast up, because a great many men have unanimously approved it. And therefore, as when there is a controversy in an account, the parties must by their own accord, set up, for right reason, the reason of some arbitrator, or judge, to whose sentence they will both stand, or their controversy must either come to blows, or be undecided, for want of a right reason constituted by nature; so it is also in all debates of what kind soever. And when men that think themselves wiser than all others, clamour and demand right reason for judge, yet seek no more, but that things should be determined, by no other men's reason but their own, it is as intolerable in the society of men, as it is in play after trump is turned, to use for trump on every occasion, that suite whereof they have most in their hand. For they do nothing else, that will have every of their passions, as it comes to bear sway in them, to be taken for right reason, and that in their own controversies: bewraying their want of right reason, by the claim they lay to it.

The use and end of reason, is not the finding of the sum and truth of one, or a few consequences, remote from the first definitions, and settled significations of names, but to begin at these, and proceed from one consequence to another. For there can be no certainty of the last conclusion, without a certainty of all those affirmations and negations, on which it was grounded and inferred. As when a master of a family, in taking an account, casteth up the sums of all the bills of expense into one sum, and not regarding how each bill is summed up, by those that give them in account; nor what it is he pays for; he advantages himself no more, than if he allowed the account in gross, trusting to every of the accountants' skill and honesty: so also in reasoning of all other things, he that takes up conclusions on the trust of authors, and doth not fetch them from the first items in every reckoning, which are the significations of names settled by definitions, loses his labour; and does not know anything, but only believeth.

When a man reckons without the use of words, which may be done in particular things, as when upon the sight of any one thing, we conjecture what was likely to have preceded, or is likely to follow upon it; if that which he thought likely to follow, follows not, or that which he thought likely to have preceded it, hath not preceded it, this is called *error;* to which even the most prudent men are subject. But when we reason in words of general signification, and fall upon a general inference which is false, though it be commonly called *error,* it is indeed an *absurdity,* or senseless speech.

For error is but a deception, in presuming that somewhat is passed, or to come; of which, though it were not past, or not to come, yet there was no impossibility discoverable. But when we make a general assertion, unless it be a true one, the possibility of it is inconceivable. And words whereby we conceive nothing but the sound, are those we call *absurd, insignificant,* and *nonsense.* And therefore if a man should talk to me of a *round quadrangle;* or, *accidents of bread in cheese;* or *immaterial substances;* or of *a free subject*; *a free will*; or any *free,* but free from being hindered by opposition, I should not say he were in an error, but that his words were without meaning, that is to say, absurd.

I have said before, in the second chapter, that a man did excel all other animals in this faculty, that when he conceived any thing whatsoever, he was apt to enquire the consequences of it, and what effects he could do with it. And now I add this other degree of the same excellence, that he can by words reduce the consequences he finds to general rules, called *theorems,* or *aphorisms*; that is, he can reason, or reckon, not only in number, but in all other things, whereof one may be added unto, or subtracted from another.

But this privilege is allayed by another; and that is, by the privilege of absurdity; to which no living creature is subject, but man only. And of men, those are of all most subject to it, that profess philosophy. For it is most true that Cicero saith of them somewhere; that there can be nothing so absurd, but may be found in the books of philosophers. And the reason is manifest. For there is not one of them that begins his ratiocination from the definitions, or explications of the names they are to use; which is a method that hath been used only in geometry; whose conclusions have thereby been made indisputable.

1. The first cause of absurd conclusions I ascribe to the want of method; in that they begin not their ratiocination from definitions; that is, from settled significations of their words: as if they could cast account, without knowing the value of the numeral words, *one, two,* and *three.*

And whereas all bodies enter into account upon divers considerations, which I have mentioned in the precedent chapter; these considerations being diversely named, divers absurdities proceed from the confusion, and unfit connexion of their names into assertions. And therefore,

II. The second cause of absurd assertions, I ascribe to the giving of names of *bodies* to *accidents;* or of *accidents* to *bodies;* as they do, that say, *faith is infused,* or *inspired;* when nothing can be *poured,* or *breathed* into anything, but body; and that, *extension is body;* that *phantasms* are *spirits,* &c.

III. The third I ascribe to the giving of the names of the *accidents* of *bodies without us,* to the *accidents* of our *own bodies;* as they do that say, the *colour is in the body; the sound is in the air,* &c.

IV. The fourth, to the giving of the names of *bodies* to *names,* or *speeches;* as they do that say, that *there be things universal;* that *a living creature is genus,* or *a general thing,* &c.

V. The fifth, to the giving of the names of *accidents* to *names* and *speeches;* as they do that say, *the nature of a thing is its definition; a man's command is his will;* and the like.

VI. The sixth, to the use of metaphors, tropes, and other rhetorical figures, instead of words proper. For though it be lawful to say, for example, in common speech, *the way goeth, or leadeth hither, or thither; the proverb says this or that,* whereas ways cannot go, nor proverbs speak; yet in reckoning, and seeking of truth, such speeches are not to be admitted.

VII. The seventh, to names that signify nothing; but are taken up, and learned by rote from the schools, as *hypostatical, transubstantiate, consubstantiate, eternal-now,* and the like canting of schoolmen.

To him that can avoid these things it is not easy to fall into any absurdity, unless it be by the length of an account; wherein he may perhaps forget what went before. For all men by nature reason alike, and well, when they have good principles. For who is so stupid, as both to mistake in geometry, and also to persist in it, when another detects his error to him?

By this it appears that reason is not, as sense and memory, born with us; nor gotten by experience only, as prudence is; but attained by industry; first in apt imposing of names; and secondly by getting a good and orderly method in proceeding from the elements, which are names, to assertions make by connexion of one of them to another; and so to syllogisms, which are the connexions of one assertion to another, till we come to a knowledge of all the consequences of names appertaining to the subject in hand; and that is it, men call SCIENCE. And whereas sense and memory are but knowledge of fact, which is a thing past and irrevocable. *Science* is the knowledge of consequences, and dependence of one fact upon another: by which, out of that we can presently do, we know how to do something else when we will, or the like another time; because when we see how anything comes about, upon what causes, and by what manner; when the like causes come into our power, we see how to make it produce the like effects.

Children therefore are not endued with reason at all, till they have attained the use of speech; but are called reasonable creatures, for the possibility apparent of having the use of reason in time to come. And the most part of men, though they have the use of reasoning a little way, as in numbering to some degree; yet it serves them to little use in common life; in which they govern themselves, some better, some worse, according to their differences of experience, quickness of memory, and inclinations to several ends; but specially according to good or evil fortune, and the errors of one another. For as for *science*, or certain rules of their actions, they are so far from it, they know not what it is. Geometry they have thought conjuring; but for other sciences, they who have not been taught the beginnings and some progress in them, that they may see how they be acquired and generated, are in this point like children, that having no thought of generation, are made believe by the women that their brothers and sisters are not born, but found in the garden.

But yet they that have no *science,* are in better, and nobler condition, with their natural prudence; than men, that by mis-reasoning, or by trusting them that reason wrong, fall upon false and absurd general rules. For ignorance of causes, and of rules, does not set men so far out of their way, as relying on false rules, and taking for causes of what they aspire to, those that are not so, but rather causes of the contrary.

To conclude, the light of human minds is perspicuous words, but by exact definitions first snuffed, and purged from ambiguity; *reason* is the *pace;* increase of *science,* the *way;* and the benefit of mankind, the *end.* And, on the contrary, metaphors, and senseless and ambiguous words, are like *ignes fatui;* and reasoning upon them is wandering amongst innumerable absurdities; and their end, contention and sedition, or contempt.

As much experience is *prudence;* so, is much science *sapience.* For though we usually have one name of wisdom for them both, yet the Latins did always distinguish between *prudentia* and *sapientia;* ascribing the former to experience, the latter to science. But to make their difference appear more clearly, let us suppose one man endued with an excellent natural use and dexterity in handling his arms; and another to have added to that dexterity, and acquired science, of where he can offend, or be offended by his adversary, in every possible posture or guard: the ability of the former, would be to the ability of the latter, as prudence to sapience; both useful; but the latter infallible. But they that trusting only to the authority of books, follow the blind blindly, are like him that, trusting to the false rules of a master of fence, ventures presumptuously upon an adversary, that either kills or disgraces him.

The signs of science are some, certain and infallible; some, uncertain. Certain, when he that pretendeth the science of anything, can teach the same: that is to say, demonstrate the truth thereof perspicuously to another; uncertain, when only some particular events answer to his pretence, and upon many occasions prove so as he says they must. Signs of prudence are all uncertain; because to observe by experience, and remember all circumstances that may alter the success, is impossible. But in any business, whereof a man has not infallible science to proceed by; to forsake his own natural judgment, and be guided by general sentences read in authors, and subject to many exceptions, is a sign of folly, and generally scorned by the name of pedantry. And even of those men themselves, that in councils of the commonwealth love to show their reading of politics and history, very few do it in their domestic affairs, where their particular interest is concerned; having prudence enough for their private affairs: but in public they study more the reputation of their own wit, than the success of another's business.

Chapter X

Of Power, Worth, Dignity, Honour, and Worthiness

The power *of a man,* (to take it universally,) is his present means, to obtain some future apparent good. And is either *original,* or *instrumental.*

Natural power, is the eminence of the faculties of body, or mind: as extraordinary strength, form, prudence, arts, eloquence, liberality, nobility. *Instrumental* are those powers, which acquired by these, or by fortune, are means and instruments to acquire more: as riches, reputation, friends, and the secret working of God, which men call good luck. For the nature of power, is in this point, like to fame, increasing as it proceeds; or like the motion of heavy bodies, which the further they go, make still the more haste.

The greatest of human powers, is that which is compounded of the powers of most men, united by consent, in one person, natural, or civil, that has the use of all their powers depending on his will; such as is the power of a common-wealth: Or depending on the wills of each particular; such as is the power of a faction, or of divers factions leagued. Therefore to have servants, is power; to have friends, is power: for they are strengths united.

Also riches joined with liberality, is power; because it procureth friends, and servants: without liberality, not so; because in this case they defend not; but expose men to envy, as a prey.

Reputation of power, is power; because it draweth with it the adherence of those that need protection.

So is reputation of love of a man's country, (called popularity,) for the same reason.

Also, what quality soever maketh a man beloved, or feared of many; or the reputation of such quality, is power; because it is a means to have the assistance, and service of many.

Good success is power; because it maketh reputation of wisdom, or good fortune; which makes men either fear him, or rely on him.

Affability of men already in power, is increase of power; because it gaineth love.

Reputation of prudence in the conduct of peace or war, is

power; because to prudent men, we commit the government of ourselves, more willingly than to others.

Nobility is power, not in all places, but only in those commonwealths, where it has privileges: for in such privileges consisteth their power.

Eloquence is power; because it is seeming prudence.

Form is power; because being a promise of good, it recommendeth men to the favour of women and strangers.

The sciences, are small power; because not eminent; and therefore, not acknowledged in any man; nor are at all, but in a few; and in them, but of a few things. For science is of that nature, as none can understand it to be, but such as in a good measure have attained it.

Arts of public use, as fortification, making of engines, and other instruments of war; because they confer to defence, and victory, are power: and though the true mother of them, be science, namely the mathematics; yet, because they are brought into the light, by the hand of the artificer, they be esteemed (the midwife passing with the vulgar for the mother,) as his issue.

The *value,* or WORTH of a man, is as of all other things, his price; that is to say, so much as would be given for the use of his power: and therefore is not absolute; but a thing dependent on the need and judgment of another. An able conductor of soldiers, is of great price in time of war present, or imminent; but in peace not so. A learned and uncorrupt judge, is much worth in time of peace; but not so much in war. And as in other things, so in men, not the seller, but the buyer determines the price. For let a man (as most men do,) rate themselves at the highest value they can; yet their true value is no more than it is esteemed by others.

The manifestation of the value we set on one another, is that which is commonly called honouring, and dishonouring. To value a man at a high rate, is to *honour* him; at a low rate, is to *dishonour* him. But high, and low, in this case, is to be understood by comparison to the rate that each man setteth on himself.

The public worth of a man, which is the value set on him by the common-wealth, is that which men commonly call DIGNITY. And this value of him by the common-wealth, is understood, by offices of command, judicature, public employment; or by names and titles, introduced for distinction of such value.

To pray to another, for aid of any kind, is *to* HONOUR; because a sign we have an opinion he has power to help; and the more difficult the aid is, the more is the honour.

To obey, is to honour; because no man obeys them, whom they think have no power to help, or hurt them. And consequently to disobey, is to *dishonour*.

To give great gifts to a man, is to honour him; because 'tis buying of protection, and acknowledging of power. To give little gifts, is to dishonour; because it is but alms, and signifies an opinion of the need of small helps.

To be sedulous in promoting another's good; also to flatter, is to honour; as a sign we seek his protection or aid. To neglect, is to dishonour.

To give way, or place to another, in any commodity, is to honour; being a confession of greater power. To arrogate, is to dishonour.

To show any sign of love, or fear of another, is to honour; for both to love, and to fear, is to value. To contemn, or less to love or fear, than he expects, is to dishonour; for 'tis undervaluing.

To praise, magnify, or call happy, is to honour; because nothing but goodness, power, and felicity is valued. To revile, mock, or pity, is to dishonour.

To speak to another with consideration, to appear before him with decency, and humility, is to honour him; as signs of fear to offend. To speak to him rashly, to do any thing before him obscenely, slovenly, impudently, is to dishonour.

To believe, to trust, to rely on another, is to honour him; sign of opinion of his virtue and power. To distrust, or not believe, is to dishonour.

To hearken to a man's counsel, or discourse of what kind soever, is to honour; as a sign we think him wise, or eloquent, or witty. To sleep, or go forth, or talk the while, is to dishonour.

To do those things to another, which he takes for signs of honour, or which the law or custom makes so, is to honour; because in approving the honour done by others, he acknowledgeth the power which others acknowledge. To refuse to do them, is to dishonour.

To agree with in opinion, is to honour; as being a sign of approving his judgment, and wisdom. To dissent, is dishonour; and an upbraiding of error; and (if the dissent be in many things) of folly.

To imitate, is to honour; for it is vehemently to approve. To imitate one's enemy, is to dishonour.

To honour those another honours, is to honour him; as a sign of approbation of his judgment. To honour his enemies, is to dishonour him.

To employ in counsel, or in actions of difficulty, is to honour; as a sign of opinion of his wisdom, or other power. To deny employment in the same cases, to those that seek it, is to dishonour.

All these ways of honouring, are natural; and as well within, as without common-wealths. . . .

Chapter XI

Of the difference of Manners

By manners, I mean not here, decency of behaviour; as how one man should salute another, or how a man should wash his mouth, or pick his teeth before company, and such other points of the *small morals;* but those qualities of man-kind, that concern their living together in peace, and unity. To which end we are to consider, that the felicity of this life, consisteth not in the repose of a mind satisfied. For there is no such *finis ultimus,* (utmost aim,) nor *summum bonum,* (greatest good,) as is spoken of in the books of the old moral philosophers. Nor can a man any more live, whose desires are at an end, than he, whose senses and imaginations are at a stand. Felicity is a continual progress of the desire, from one object to another; the attaining of the former, being still but the way to the latter. The cause whereof is, that the object of man's desire, is not to enjoy once only, and for one instant of time; but to assure forever, the way of his future desire. And therefore the voluntary actions, and inclinations of all men, tend, not only to the procuring, but also to the assuring of a contented life; and differ only in the way; which ariseth partly from the diversity of passions, in divers men; and partly from the difference of the knowledge, or opinion each one has of the causes, which produce the effect desired.

So that in the first place, I put for a general inclination of all mankind, a perpetual and restless desire of power after power, that ceaseth only in death. And the cause of this, is not always that a man hopes for a more intensive delight, than he has already attained to; or that he cannot be content with a moderate power: but because he cannot assure the power and means to live well, which he hath present, without the acquisition of more. And from hence it is, that kings, whose power is greatest, turn their endeavours to the assuring it at home by laws, or abroad by wars: and when that is done, there succeedeth a new desire; in some, of fame from new conquest; in others, of ease and sensual pleasure; in others, of admiration, or being flattered for excellence in some art, or other ability of the mind.

Competition of riches, honour, command, or other power, inclineth to contention, enmity, and war: because the way of one competitor, to the attaining of his desire, is to kill, subdue, supplant, or repell the other. Particularly, competition of praise, inclineth to a reverence of antiquity. For men contend with the living, not with the dead; to these ascribing more than due, that they may obscure the glory of the other.

Desire of ease, and sensual delight, disposeth men to obey a common power: because by such desires, a man doth abandon the protection might be hoped for from his own industry, and labour. Fear of death, and wounds, disposeth to the same; and for the same reason. On the contrary, needy men, and hardy, not contented with their present condition: as also, all men that are ambitious of military command, are inclined to continue the causes of war; and to stir up trouble and sedition: for there is no honour military but by war; nor any such hope to mend an ill game, as by causing a new shuffle.

Desire of knowledge, and arts of peace, inclineth men to obey a common power: for such desire, containeth a desire of leisure; and consequently protection from some other power than their own.

Desire of praise, disposeth to laudable actions, such as please them whose judgment they value; for of those men whom we contemn, we contemn also the praises. Desire of fame after death does the same. And though after death, there be no sense of the praise given us on earth, as being joys, that are either swallowed up in the unspeakable joys of heaven, or extinguished in the extreme torments of hell: yet is not such fame vain; because men have a present delight therein, from the foresight of it, and of the benefit that may redound thereby to their posterity: which though they now see not, yet they imagine; and any thing that is pleasure in the sense, the same also is pleasure in the imagination.

To have received from one, to whom we think ourselves equal, greater benefits than there is hope to requite, disposeth to counterfeit love; but really secret hatred; and puts a man into the estate of a desperate debtor, than in declining the sight of his creditor, tacitly wishes him there, where he might never see him more. For benefits oblige; and obligation is thraldom; and unrequitable obligation, perpetual thraldom; which is to one's equal, hateful. But to have received benefits from one, whom we acknowledge for superiour, inclines to love; because the obligation is no new depression: and cheerful acceptation, (which men call *gratitude,*) is such an honour done to the obliger, as is taken generally for retribution. Also to receive benefits, though from an equal, or inferiour, as long as there is hope of requital, disposeth to love: for in the intention of the receiver, the obligation is of aid, and service mutual; from whence proceedeth an emulation of who shall exceed in benefiting; the most noble and profitable contention possible; wherein the victor is pleased with his victory, and the other revenged by confessing it.

To have done more hurt to a man, than he can, or is willing to expiate, inclineth the doer to hate the sufferer. For he must expect revenge, or forgiveness; both which are hateful.

Fear of oppression, disposeth a man to anticipate, or to seek aid by society; for there is no other way by which a man can secure his life and liberty.

Men that distrust their own subtlety, are in tumult, and sedition, better disposed for victory, than they that suppose themselves wise, or crafty. For these love to consult, the other (fearing to be circumvented,) to strike first. And in sedition, men being always in the precincts of battle, to hold together, and use all advantages of force, is a better strategem, than any that can proceed from subtlety of wit.

Vain-glorious men, such as without being conscious to themselves of great sufficiency, delight in supposing themselves gallant men, are inclined only to ostentation; but not to attempt: Because when danger or difficulty appears, they look for nothing but to have their insufficiency discovered.

Vain-glorious men, such as estimate their sufficiency by the flattery of other men, or the fortune of some precedent action, without assured ground of hope from the true knowledge of themselves, are inclined to rash engaging; and in the approach of danger, or difficulty, to retire if they can: because not seeing the way of safety, they will rather hazard their honour, which may be salved with an excuse; than their lives, for which no salve is sufficient.

Men that have a strong opinion of their own wisdom in matter of government, are disposed to ambition. Because without public employment in counsel or magistracy, the honour of their wisdom is lost. And therefore eloquent speakers are inclined to ambition; for eloquence seemeth wisdom, both to themselves and others.

Pusillanimity disposeth men to irresolution, and consequently to lose the occasions, and fittest opportunities of action. For after men have been in deliberation till the time of action approach, if it be not then manifest what is best to be done, 'tis a sign, the difference of motives, the one way and the other, are not great: Therefore not to resolve then, is to lose the occasion by weighing of trifles; which is pusillanimity.

Frugality, (though in poor men a virtue,) maketh a man unapt to achieve such actions, as require the strength of many men at once: for it weakeneth their endeavour, which is to be nourished and kept in vigor by reward.

Eloquence, with flattery, disposeth men to confide in them that have it; because the former is seeming wisdom, the latter seeming kindness. Add to them military reputation, and it disposeth men to adhere, and subject themselves to those men that have them. The two former, having given them caution against danger from him; the latter given them caution against danger from others.

Want of science, that is, ignorance of causes, disposeth, or rather constraineth a man to rely on the advise, and authority of others. For all men whom the truth concerns, if they rely not on their own, must rely on the opinion of some other, whom they think wiser than themselves, and see not why he should deceive them.

Ignorance of the signification of words; which is, want of understanding, disposeth men to take on trust, not only the truth they know not; but also the errors; and which is more, the nonsense of them they trust: for neither error, nor nonsense, can without a perfect understanding of words, be detected.

From the same it proceedeth, that men give different names, to one and the same thing, from the difference of their own passions: as they that approve a private opinion, call it opinion; but they that mislike it, heresy: and yet heresy signifies no more than private opinion; but has only a greater tincture of choler.

From the same also it proceedeth, that men cannot distinguish, without study and great understanding, between one action of many men, and many actions of one multitude; as for example, between the one action of all the Senators of *Rome* in killing *Catiline,* and the many actions of a number of Senators in killing *Cæsar;* and therefore are disposed to take for the action of the people, that which is a multitude of actions done by a multitude of men, led perhaps by the persuasion of one.

Ignorance of the causes, and original constitution of right, equity, law, and justice, disposeth a man to make custom and example the rule of his actions; in such manner, as to think that unjust which it hath been the custom to punish; and that just, of the impunity and approbation whereof they can produce an example, or (as the lawyers which only use this false measure of justice barbarously call it) a precedent; like little children, that have no other rule of good and evil manners, but the correction they receive from their parents, and masters; save that children are constant to their rule, whereas men are not so; because grown strong, and stubborn, they appeal from custom to reason, and from reason to custom, as it serves their turn; receding from custom when their interest requires it, and setting themselves against reason, as oft as reason is against them: Which is the cause, that the doctrine of right and wrong, is perpetually disputed, both by the pen and the sword: Whereas the doctrine of lines, and figures, is not so; because men care not, in that subject what be truth, as a thing that crosses no man's ambition, profit, or lust. For I doubt not, but if it had been a thing contrary to any man's right of dominion, or to the interest of men that have dominion, *That the three angles of a triangle, should be equal to two angles of a square;* that doctrine should have been, if not disputed, yet by the burning of all books of geometry, suppressed, as far as he whom it concerned was able.

Ignorance of remote causes, disposeth men to attribute all events, to the causes immediate, and instrumental; for these are all the causes they perceive. And hence it comes to pass, that in all places, men that are grieved with payments to the public, discharge their anger upon the publicans, that is to say, farmers, collectors, and other officers of the public revenue; and adhere to such as find fault with the public government; and thereby, when they have engaged themselves beyond hope of justification, fall also upon the supreme authority, for fear of punishment, or shame of receiving pardon.

Ignorance of natural causes disposeth a man to credulity, so as to believe many times impossibilities: For such know nothing to the contrary, but that they may be true; being unable to detect the impossibility. And credulity, because men love to be hearkened unto in company, disposeth them to lying: so that ignorance itself without malice, is able to make a man both to believe lies, and tell them; and sometimes also to invent them.

Anxiety for the future time, disposeth men to inquire into the causes of things: because the knowledge of them, maketh men the better able to order the present to their best advantage.

Curiosity, or love of the knowledge of causes, draws a man from consideration of the effect, to seek the cause; and again, the cause of that cause; till of necessity he must come to this thought at last, that there is some cause, whereof there is no former cause, but is eternal; which is it men call God. So that it is impossible to make any profound inquiry into natural causes, without being inclined thereby to believe there is one God Eternal; though they cannot have any idea of him in their mind, answerable to his nature. For as a man that is born blind, hearing men talk of warming themselves by the fire, and being brought to warm himself by the same, may easily conceive, and assure himself, there is somewhat there, which men call *fire,* and is the cause of the heat he feels; but cannot imagine what it is like; nor have an idea of it in his mind, such as they have that see it: so also, by the visible things of this world, and their admirable order, a man may conceive there is a cause of them, which men call God; and yet not have an idea, or image of him in his mind.

And they that make little, or no inquiry into the natural causes of things, yet from the fear that proceeds from the ignorance itself, of what it is that hath the power to do them much good or harm, are inclined to suppose, and feign unto themselves, several kinds of Powers Invisible; and to stand in awe of their own imaginations; and in time of distress to invoke them; as also in the time of an expected good success, to give them thanks; making the creatures of their own fancy, their gods. By which means it hath come to pass, that from the innumerable variety of fancy, men have created in the world innumerable sorts of gods. And this fear of things invisible, is the natural seed of that, which every one in himself calleth religion; and in them that worship, or fear that power otherwise than they do, superstition.

And this seed of religion, having been observed by many; some of those that have observed it, have been inclined thereby to nourish, dress, and form it into laws; and to add to it of their own invention, any opinion of the causes of future events, by which they thought they should best be able to govern others, and make unto themselves the greatest use of their powers.

Chapter XII

Of Religion

Seeing there are no signs, nor fruit of *religion,* but in man only; there is no cause to doubt, but that the seed of *religion,* is also only in man; and consisteth in some peculiar quality, or at least in some eminent degree thereof, not to be found in any other living creatures.

And first, it is peculiar to the nature of man, to be inquisitive into the causes of the events they see, some more, some less; but all men so much, as to be curious in the search of the causes of their own good and evil fortune.

Secondly, upon the sight of anything that hath a beginning, to think also it had a cause, which determined the same to begin, then when it did, rather than sooner or later.

Thirdly, whereas there is no other felicity of beasts, but the enjoying of their quotidian food, ease, and lusts; as having little or no foresight of the time to come, for want of observation, and memory of the order, consequence, and dependence of the things they see; man observeth how one event hath been produced by another; and remembereth in them antecedence and consequence; and when he cannot assure himself of the true causes of things, (for the causes of good and evil fortune for the most part are invisible,) he supposes causes of them, either such as his own fancy suggesteth; or trusteth the authority of other men, such as he thinks to be his friends, and wiser than himself.

The two first, make anxiety. For being assured that there be causes of all things that have arrived hitherto, or shall arrive hereafter; it is impossible for a man, who continually endeavoureth to secure himself against the evil he fears, and procure the good he desireth, not to be in a perpetual solicitude of the time to come; so that every man, especially those that are over provident, are in a state like to that of Prometheus. For as Prometheus, which interpreted, is, *the prudent man,* was bound to the hill Caucasus, a place of large prospect, where, an eagle feeding on his liver, devoured in the day, as much as was repaired in the night: so that man, which looks too far before him, in the care of future time, hath his heart all the day long, gnawed on by fear of death, poverty, or other calamity; and has no repose, nor pause of his anxiety, but in sleep.

This perpetual fear, always accompanying mankind in the ignorance of causes, as it were in the dark, must needs have for subject something. And therefore when there is nothing to be seen, there is nothing to accuse, either of their good, or evil fortune, but some *power,* or agent *invisible:* in which sense perhaps it was, that some of the old poets said, that the gods were at first created by human fear: which spoken of the gods, that is to say, of the many gods of the Gentiles, is very true. But the acknowledging of one God, eternal, infinite, and omnipotent, may more easily be derived, from the desire men have to know the causes of natural bodies, and their several virtues, and operations; than from the fear of what was to befall them in time to come. For he that from any effect he seeth come to pass, should reason to the next and immediate cause thereof, and from thence to the cause of that cause, and plunge himself profoundly in the pursuit of causes; shall at last come to this, that there must be, as even the heathen philosophers confessed, one first mover; that is, a first, and an eternal cause of all things; which is that which men mean by the name of God: and all this without thought of their fortune; the solicitude whereof, both inclines to fear, and hinders them from the search of the causes of other things; and thereby gives occasion of feigning of as many gods, as there be men that feign them.

And for the matter, or substance of the invisible agents, so fancied; they could not by natural cogitation, fall upon any other conceit, but that it was the same with that of the soul of man; and that the soul of man, was of the same substance, with that which appeareth in a dream, to one that sleepeth; or in a looking-glass, to one that is awake; which, men not knowing that such apparitions are nothing else but creatures of the fancy, think to be real, and external substances; and therefore call them ghosts; as the Latins called them *imagines,* and *umbrae;* and thought them spirits, that is, thin aerial bodies; and those invisible agents, which they feared, to be like them; save that they appear, and vanish when they please. But the opinion that such spirits were incorporeal, or immaterial, could never enter into the mind of any man by nature; because, though men may put together words of contradictory signification, as *spirit,* and *incorporeal;* yet they can never have the imagination of any thing answering to them: and therefore, men that by their own meditation, arrive to the acknowledgment of one infinite, omnipotent, and eternal God, chose rather to confess he is incomprehensible, and above their understanding, than to define his nature by *spirit incorporeal,* and then confess their definition to be unintelligible: or if they give him such a title, it is not *dogmatically,* with intention to make the divine nature understood; but *piously,* to honour him with attributes, of significations, as remote as they can from the grossness of bodies visible.

Then, for the way by which they think these invisible agents wrought their effects; that is to say, what immediate causes they used, in bringing things to pass, men that know not what it is that we call *causing,* that is, almost all men, have no other rule to guess by, but by observing, and remembering what they have seen to precede the like effect at some other time, or times before, without seeing between the antecedent and subsequent event, any dependence or connexion at all: and therefore from the like things past, they expect the like things to come; and hope for good or evil luck, superstitiously, from things that have no part at all in the causing of it: as the Athenians did for their war at Lepanto, demand another Phormio; the Pompeian faction for their war in Africa, another Scipio; and others have done in divers other occasions since. In like manner they attribute their fortune to a stander-by, to a lucky or unlucky place, to words spoken, especially if the name of God be amongst them; as charming and conjuring, the liturgy of witches; insomuch as to believe, they have power to turn a stone into bread, bread into a man, or any thing into any thing.

Thirdly, for the worship which naturally men exhibit to powers invisible, it can be no other, but such expressions of their reverence, as they would use towards men; gifts, petitions, thanks, submission of body, considerate addresses, sober behaviour, premeditated words, swearing, that is, assuring one another of their promises, by invoking them. Beyond that reason suggesteth nothing; but leaves then either to rest there; or for further ceremonies, to rely on those they believe to be wiser than themselves.

Lastly, concerning how these invisible powers declare to men the things which shall hereafter come to pass, especially concerning their good or evil fortune in general, or good or ill success in any particular undertaking, men are naturally at a stand; save that using to conjecture of the time to come, by the time past, they are very apt, not only to take casual things, after one or two encounters, for prognostics of the like encounter ever after, but also to believe the like prognostics from other men, of whom they have once conceived a good opinion.

And in these four things, opinion of ghosts, ignorance of second causes, devotion towards what men fear, and taking of things casual for prognostics, consisteth the natural seed of *religion*, which by reason of the different fancies, judgments, and passions of several men, hath grown up into ceremonies so different, that those which are used by one man, are for the most part ridiculous to another.

For these seeds have received culture from two sorts of men.

One sort have been they, that have nourished, and ordered them, according to their own invention. The other have done it, by God's commandment, and direction; but both sorts have done it, with a purpose to make those men that relied on them, the more apt to obedience, laws, peace, charity, and civil society. So that the religion of the former sort, is a part of human politics; and teacheth part of the duty which earthly kings require of their subjects. And the religion of the latter sort is divine politics; and containeth precepts to those that have yielded themselves subjects in the kingdom of God. Of the former sort, were all the founders of commonwealths, and the law-givers of the Gentiles: of the latter sort, were Abraham, Moses, and our blessed Saviour; by whom have been derived unto us the laws of the kingdom of God. . . .

From the propagation of religion, it is not hard to understand the causes of the resolution of the same into its first seeds, or principles; which are only an opinion of a deity, and powers invisible, and supernatural; that can never be so abolished out of human nature, but that new religions may again be made to spring out of them, by the culture of such men, as for such purpose are in reputation.

For seeing all formed religion, is founded at first, upon the faith which a multitude hath in some one person, whom they believe not only to be a wise man, and to labour to procure their happiness, but also to be a holy man, to whom God himself vouchsafeth to declare his will supernaturally; it followeth necessarily, when they that have the government of religion, shall come to have either the wisdom of those men, their sincerity, or their love suspected; or when they shall be unable to show any probable token of divine revelation; that the religion which they desire to uphold, must be suspected likewise; and, without the fear of the civil sword, contradicted and rejected.

That which taketh away the reputation of wisdom, in him that formeth a religion, or addeth to it when it is already formed, is the enjoining of a belief of contradictories: for both parts of a contradiction cannot possibly be true: and therefore to enjoin the belief of them, is an argument of ignorance; which detects the author in that; and discredits him in all things else he shall propound as from revelation supernatural: which revelation a man may indeed have of many things above, but of nothing against natural reason.

That which taketh away the reputation of sincerity, is the doing or saying of such things, as appear to be signs, that what they require other men to believe, is not believed by themselves; all which doings, or sayings are therefore called scandalous, because they be stumbling blocks, that make men to fall in the way of religion; as injustice, cruelty, profaneness, avarice, and luxury. For who can believe, that he that doth ordinarily such actions as proceed from any of these roots, believeth there is any such invisible power to be feared, as he affrighteth other men withal, for lesser faults?

That which taketh away the reputation of love, is the being detected of private ends: as when the belief they require of others, conduceth or seemeth to conduce to the acquiring of dominion, riches, dignity, or secure pleasure, to themselves only, or specially. For that which men reap benefit by to themselves, they are thought to do for their own sakes, and not for love of others.

Lastly, the testimony that men can render of divine calling, can be no other, than the operation of miracles; or true prophecy, which also is a miracle; or extraordinary felicity. And therefore, to those points of religion, which have been received from them that did such miracles; those that are added by such, as approve not their calling by some miracle, obtain no greater belief, than what the custom and laws of the places, in which they be educated, have wrought into them. For as in natural things, men of judgment require natural signs, and arguments; so in supernatural things, they require signs supernatural, which are miracles before they consent inwardly, and from their hearts.

All which causes of the weakening of men's faith, do manifestly appear in the examples following. First, we have the example of the children of Israel: who when Moses, that had approved his calling to them by miracles, and by the happy conduct of them out of Egypt, was absent but forty days, revolted from the worship of the true God, recommended to them by him; and setting up (Exod. xxxiii, 1, 2) a golden calf for their god, relapsed into the idolatry of the Egyptians; from whom they had been so lately delivered. And again, after Moses, Aaron, Joshua, and that generation which had seen the great works of God in Israel, (Judges ii,

11) were dead; another generation arose, and served Baal. So that miracles failing, faith also failed.

Again, when the sons of Samuel, (1 Sam. viii, 3) being constituted by their father judges in Bersabee, received bribes, and judged unjustly, the people of Israel refused any more to have God to be their king, in other manner than he was king of other people; and therefore cried out to Samuel, to choose them a king after the manner of the nations. So that justice failing, faith also failed: insomuch, as they deposed their God, from reigning over them.

And whereas in the planting of Christian religion, the oracles ceased in all parts of the Roman empire, and the number of Christians increased wonderfully every day, and in every place, by the preaching of the Apostles, and Evangelists; a great part of that success, may reasonably be attributed, to the contempt, into which the priests of the Gentiles of that time, had brought themselves by their uncleanness, avarice, and juggling between princes. Also the religion of the church of Rome, was partly, for the same cause abolished in England, and many other parts of Christendom; insomuch, as the failing of virtue in the pastors, maketh faith fail in the people: and partly from bringing of the philosophy, and doctrine of Aristotle into religion, by the Schoolmen; from whence there arose so many contradictions, and absurdities, as brought the clergy into a reputation both of ignorance, and of fraudulent intention; and inclined people to revolt from them, either against the will of their own princes, as in France and Holland; or with their will, as in England.

Lastly, amongst the points by the church of Rome declared necessary for salvation, there be so many, manifestly to the advantage of the Pope, and of his spiritual subjects, residing in the territories of other Christian princes, that were it not for the mutual emulation of those princes, they might without war, or trouble, exclude all foreign authority, as easily as it has been excluded in England. For who is there that does not see, to whose benefit it conduceth, to have it believed, that a king hath not his authority from Christ, unless a bishop crown him? That a king, if he be a priest, cannot marry? That whether a prince be born in lawful marriage, or not, must be judged by authority from Rome? That subjects may be freed from their allegiance, if by the court of

Rome, the king be judged an heretic? That a king, as Chilperic of France, may be deposed by a pope, as Pope Zachary, for no cause; and his kingdom given to one of his subjects? That the clergy and regulars, in what country soever, shall be exempt from the jurisdiction of their king in cases criminal? Or who does not see, to whose profit redound the fees of private masses, and vales of purgatory; with other signs of private interest, enough to mortify the most lively faith, if, as I said, the civil magistrate, and custom did not more sustain it, than any opinion they have of the sanctity, wisdom, or probity of their teachers? So that I may attribute all the changes of religion in the world, to one and the same cause; and that is, unpleasing priests; and those not only amongst Catholics, but even in that church that hath presumed most of reformation.

Chapter XII

Of the Natural Condition of Mankind as Concerning Their Felicity, and Misery

Nature hath made men so equal, in the faculties of the body, and mind; as that though there be found one man sometimes manifestly stronger in body, or of quicker mind than another; yet when all is reckoned together, the difference between man, and man, is not so considerable, as that one man can thereupon claim to himself any benefit, to which another may not pretend, as well as he. For as to the strength of body, the weakest has strength enough to kill the strongest, either by secret machination, or by confederacy with others, that are in the same danger with himself.

And as to the faculties of the mind, setting aside the arts grounded upon words, and especially that skill of proceeding upon general, and infallible rules, called science; which very few have, and but in few things; as being not a native faculty, born with us; nor attained, as prudence, while we look after somewhat else, I find yet a greater equality amongst men, than that of strength. For prudence, is but experience; which equal time, equally bestows on all men, in those things they equally apply themselves unto. That which may perhaps make such equality incredible, is but a vain conceit of one's own wisdom, which almost all men think they have in a greater degree, than the vulgar; that is, than all men but themselves, and a few others, whom by fame, or for concurring with themselves, they approve. For such is the nature of men, that howsoever they may acknowledge many others to be more witty, or more eloquent, or more learned; yet they will hardly believe there be many so wise as themselves; for they see their own wit at hand, and other men's at a distance. But this proveth rather that men are in that point equal, than unequal. For there is not ordinarily a greater sign of the equal distribution of any thing, than that every man is contented with his share.

From this equality of ability, ariseth equality of hope in the attaining of our ends. And therefore if any two men desire the same thing, which nevertheless they cannot both enjoy, they become enemies; and in the way to their end, which is principally their own conservation, and sometimes their delectation only, endeavour to destroy, or subdue one another. And from hence it comes to pass, that where an invader hath no more to fear, than another man's single power; if one plant, sow, build, or possess a convenient seat, others may probably be expected to come prepared with forces united, to dispossess, and deprive him, not only of the fruit of his labour, but also of his life, or liberty. And the invader again is in the like danger of another.

And from this diffidence of one another, there is no way for any man to secure himself, so reasonable, as anticipation; that is, by force, or wiles, to master the persons of all men he can, so long, till he see no other power great enough to endanger him: and this is no more than his own conservation requireth, and is generally allowed. Also because there be some, that taking pleasure in contemplating their own power in the acts of conquest, which they pursue farther than their security requires; if others, that otherwise would be glad to be at ease within modest bounds, should not by invasion increase their power, they would not be able, long time, by standing only on their defence, to subsist. And by consequence, such augmentation of dominion over men being necessary to a man's conservation, it ought to be allowed him.

Again, men have no pleasure, but on the contrary a great deal of grief, in keeping company, where there is no power able to over-awe them all. For every man looketh that his companion should value him, at the same rate he sets upon himself: and upon all signs of contempt, or undervaluing, naturally endeavours, as far as he dares, (which amongst them that have no common power to keep them in quiet, is far enough to make them destroy each other), to extort a greater value from his contemners, by damage; and from others, by the example.

So that in the nature of man, we find three principal causes of quarrel. First, competition; second, diffidence; thirdly, glory.

The first, maketh men invade for gain; the second, for safety; and the third, for reputation. The first use violence, to make themselves masters of other men's persons, wives, children, and cattle; the second, to defend them; the third, for trifles, as a word, a smile, a different opinion, and any other sign of undervalue, either direct in their persons, or by reflection in their kindred, their friends, their nation, their profession, or their name.

Hereby it is manifest, that during the time men live without a common power to keep them all in awe, they are in that condition which is called war; and such a war, as is of every man, against every man. For WAR, consisteth not in battle only, or the act of fighting; but in a tract of time, wherein the will to contend by battle in sufficiently known: and therefore the notion of *time*, is to be considered in the nature of war; as it is in the nature of weather. For as the nature of foul weather, lieth not in a shower or two of rain; but in an inclination thereto of many days together: so the nature of war, consisteth not in actual fighting; but in the known disposition thereto, during all the time there is no assurance to the contrary. All other time is PEACE.

Whatsoever therefore is consequent to a time of war, where every man is enemy to every man; the same is consequent to the time, wherein men live without other security, than what their own strength, and their own invention shall furnish them withal. In such condition, there is no place for industry; because the fruit thereof is uncertain: and consequently no culture of the earth; no navigation, nor use of the commodities that may be imported by sea; no commodious building; no instruments of moving, and removing, such things as require much force; no knowledge of the face of the earth; no account of time; no arts; no letters; no society; and which is worst of all, continual fear, and danger of violent death; and the life of man, solitary, poor, nasty, brutish, and short.

It may seem strange to some man, that has not well weighed

these things; that nature should thus dissociate, and render men apt to invade, and destroy one another: and he may therefore, not trusting to this inference, made from the passions, desire perhaps to have the same confirmed by experience. Let him therefore consider with himself, when taking a journey, he arms himself, and seeks to go well accompanied; when going to sleep, he locks his doors; when even in his house he locks his chests; and this when he knows there be laws, and public officers, armed, to revenge all injuries shall be done him; what opinion he has of his fellow-subjects, when he rides armed; of his fellow citizens, when he locks his doors; and of his children, and servants, when he locks his chests. Does he not there as much accuse mankind by his actions, as I do by my words? But neither of us accuse man's nature in it. The desires, and other passions of man, are in themselves no sin. No more are the actions, that proceed from those passions, till they know a law that forbids them: which till laws be made they cannot know: nor can any law be made, till they have agreed upon the person that shall make it.

It may peradventure be thought, there was never such a time, nor condition of war as this; and I believe it was never generally so, over all the world: but there are many places, where they live so now. But the savage people in many places of America, except the government of small families, the concord whereof dependeth on natural lust, have no government at all; and live at this day in that brutish manner, as I said before. Howsoever, it may be perceived what manner of life there would be, where there were no common power to fear, by the manner of life, which men that have formerly lived under a peaceful government, use to degenerate into, in a civil war.

But though there had never been any time, wherein particular men were in a condition of war one against another; yet in all times, kings, and persons of sovereign authority, because of their independency, are in continual jealousies, and in the state and posture of gladiators; having their weapons pointing, and their eyes fixed on one another; that is, their forts, garrisons, and guns upon the frontiers of their kingdoms; and continual spies upon their neighbours; which is a posture of war. But because they uphold thereby, the industry of their subjects; there does not follow from it, that misery, which accompanies the liberty of particular men.

To this war of every man, against every man, this also is consequent; that nothing can be unjust. The notions of right and wrong, justice and injustice have there no place. Where there is no common power, there is no law: where no law, no injustice. Force, and fraud, are in war the two cardinal virtues. Justice, and injustice are none of the faculties neither of the body, nor mind. If they were, they might be in a man that were alone in the world, as well as his senses, and passions. They are qualities, that relate to men in society, not in solitude. It is consequent also to the same condition, that there be no propriety, no dominion, no *mine* and *thine* distinct; but only that to be every man's, that he can get; and for so long, as he can keep it. And thus much for the ill condition, which man by mere nature is actually placed in; though with a possibility to come out of it, consisting partly in the passions, partly in his reason.

The passions that incline men to peace, are fear of death; desire of such things as are necessary to commodious living; and a hope by their industry to obtain them. And reason suggesteth convenient articles of peace, upon which men may be drawn to agreement. These articles, are they, which otherwise are called the Laws of Nature: whereof I shall speak more particularly, in the two following chapters.

Chapter XIV

Of the First and Second Natural Laws, and of Contracts

The right of nature, which writers commonly call *jus naturale,* is the liberty each man hath, to use his own power, as he will himself, for the preservation of his own nature; that is to say, of his own life; and consequently, of doing anything, which in his own judgment, and reason, he shall conceive to be the aptest means thereunto.

By LIBERTY, is understood, according to the proper signification of the word, the absence of external inpediments: which impediments, may oft take away part of a man's power to do what he would; but cannot hinder him from using the power left him, according as his judgment, and reason shall dictate to him.

A LAW OF NATURE, *lex naturalis,* is a precept or general rule, found out by reason, by which a man is forbidden to do that, which is destructive of his life, or taketh away the means of preserving the same; and to omit that, by which he thinketh it may be best preserved. For though they that speak of this subject, use to confound *jus,* and *lex, right* and *law:* yet they ought to be distinguished; because RIGHT, consisteth in liberty to do, or to forbear; whereas LAW, determineth, and bindeth to one of them: so that law, and right, differ as much, as obligation, and liberty; which in one and the same matter are inconsistent.

And because the condition of man, as hath been declared in the precedent chapter, is a condition of war of every one against every one; in which case every one is governed by his own reason; and there is nothing he can make use of, that may not be a help unto him, in preserving his life against his enemies; it followeth, that in such a condition, every man has a right to every thing; even to one another's body. And therefore, as long as this natural right of every man to every thing endureth, there can be no security to any man, how strong or wise soever he be, of living out the time, which nature ordinarily alloweth men to live. And consequently it is a precept, or general rule of reason, *that every man, ought to endeavour peace, as far as he has hope of obtaining it; and when he cannot obtain it, that he may seek, and use, all helps, and advantages of war.* The first branch of which rule, containeth the first, and fundamental law of nature; which is, *to seek peace, and follow it.* The second, the sum of the right of nature; which is, *by all means we can, to defend ourselves.*

From this fundamental law of nature, by which men are commanded to endeavour peace, is derived this second law; *that a man be willing, when others are so too, as far forth, as for peace, and defence of himself he shall think it necessary, to lay down this right to all things; and be contented with so much liberty against other men, as he would allow other men against himself.* For as long as every man holdeth this right, of doing any thing he liketh; so long are all men in the condition of war. But if other men will not lay down their right, as well as he; then there is no reason for anyone, to divest himself of his: for that were to expose himself to prey, which no man is bound to, rather than to dispose himself to peace. This is that law of the Gospel; *whatso-*

ever you require that others should do to you, that do ye to them. And that law of all men, *quod tibi fieri non vis, alteri ne feceris.*

To *lay down* a man's *right* to any thing, is to *divest* himself of the *liberty*, of hindering another of the benefit of his own right to the same. For he that renounceth, or passeth away his right, giveth not to any other man a right which he had not before; because there is nothing to which every man had not right by nature: but only standeth out of his way, that he may enjoy his own original right, without hindrance from him; not without hindrance from another. So that the effect which redoundeth to one man, by another man's defect of right, is but so much diminution of impediments to the use of his own right original.

Right is laid aside, either by simply renouncing it; or by transferring it to another. By *simply* RENOUNCING; when he cares not to whom the benefit thereof redoundeth. By TRANSFERRING; when he intendeth the benefit thereof to some certain person, or persons. And when a man hath in either manner abandoned, or granted away his right; then is he said to be OBLIGED, or BOUND, not to hinder those, to whom such right is granted, or abandoned, from the benefit of it: and that he *ought*, and it is his DUTY, not to make void that voluntary act of his own: and that such hindrance is INJUSTICE, and INJURY, as being *sine jure;* the right being before renounced, or transferred. So that *injury,* or *injustice,* in the controveries of the world, is somewhat like to that, which in the disputations of scholars is called *absurdity.* For as it is there called an absurdity, to contradict what one maintained in the beginning: so in the world, it is called injustice, and injury, voluntarily to undo that, which from the beginning he had voluntarily done. The way by which a man either simply renounceth, transferreth his right, is a declaration, or signification, by some voluntary and sufficient sign, or signs, that he doth so renounce, or transfer; or hath so renounced, or transferred the same, to him that accepteth it. And these signs are either words only, or actions only; or, as it happeneth most often, both words, and actions. And the same are the BONDS, by which men are bound, and obliged: bonds, that have their strength, not from their own nature, for nothing is more easily broken than a man's word, but from fear of some evil consequence upon the rupture.

Whensoever a man transferreth his right, or renounceth it; it is either in consideration of some right reciprocally transferred to himself; or for some other good he hopeth for thereby. For it is a voluntary act: and of the voluntary acts of every man, the object is some *good to himself*. And therefore there be some rights, which no man can be understood by any words, or other signs, to have abandoned, or transferred. As first a man cannot lay down the right of resisting them, that assault him by force, to take away his life; because he cannot be understood to aim thereby, at any good to himself. The same may be said of wounds, and chains, and imprisonment; both because there is no benefit consequent to such patience; as there is to the patience of suffering another to be wounded, or imprisoned: as also because a man cannot tell, when he seeth men proceed against him by violence, whether they intend his death or not. And lastly the motive, and end for which this renouncing, and transferring of right is introduced, is nothing else but the security of a man's person, in his life, and in the means of so preserving life, as not to be weary of it. And therefore if a man by words, or other signs, seem to despoil himself of the end, for which those signs were intended; he is not to be understood as if he meant it, or that it was his will; but that he was ignorant of how such words and actions were to be interpreted.

The mutual transferring of right, is that which men call CON-TRACT.

Chapter XV

Of Other Laws of Nature

From that law of nature, by which we are obliged to transfer to another, such rights, as being retained, hinder the peace of mankind, there followeth a third; which is this, *that men perform their covenants made:* without which, covenants are in vain, and but empty words; and the right of all men to all things remaining, we are still in the condition of war.

And in this law of nature, consisteth the fountain and original of JUSTICE. For where no covenant hath preceded, there hath no right been transferred, and every man has right to every thing; and consequently, no action can be unjust. But when a covenant is made, then to break it is *unjust:* and the definition of INJUSTICE, is no other than *the not performance of covenant*. And whatsoever is not unjust, is *just*.

But because covenants of mutual trust, where there is a fear of not performance on either part, as hath been said in the former chapter, are invalid; though the original of justice be the making of covenants; yet injustice actually there can be none, till the cause of such fear be taken away; which while men are in the natural condition of war, cannot be done. Therefore before the names of just, and unjust can have place, there must be some coercive power, to compel men equally to the performance of their covenants, by the terror of some punishment, greater than the benefit they expect by the breach of their covenant; and to make good that propriety, which by mutual contract men acquire, in recompense of the universal right they abandon: and such power there is none before the erection of a commonwealth. And this is also to be gathered out of the ordinary definition of justice in the Schools: for they say, that *justice is the constant will of giving to every man his own*. And therefore where there is no *own*, that is no propriety, there is no injustice; and where is no coercive power erected, that is, where there is no commonwealth, there is no propriety; all men having right to all things: therefore where there is no commonwealth, there nothing is unjust. So that the nature of justice, consisteth in keeping of valid covenants: but the validity of covenants begins not but with the constitution of a civil power, sufficient to compel men to keep them: and then it is also that propriety begins.

The fool hath said in his heart, there is no such thing as justice; and sometimes also with his tongue; seriously alleging, that every man's conservation, and contentment, being committed to his own care, there could be no reason, why every man might not do what he thought conduced thereunto: and therefore also to make, or not make; keep, or not keep covenants, was not against reason, when it conduced to one's benefit. He does not therein deny, that there be covenants; and that they are sometimes broken, sometimes kept; and that such breach of them may be called injustice, and the observance of them justice: but he questioneth, whether injustice, taking away the fear of God, (for the same fool hath said in his heart there is no God) may not sometimes stand with that reason, which dictateth to every man his own good;

and particularly then, when it conduceth to such a benefit, as
shall put a man in a condition, to neglect not only the dispraise,
and revilings, but also the power of other men. The kingdom of
God is gotten by violence: but what if it could be gotten by unjust
violence? were it against reason so to get it, when it is impossible
to receive hurt by it? and if it be not against reason, it is not
against justice; or else justice is not to be approved for good. From
such reasoning as this, successful wickedness hath obtained the
name of virtue: and some that in all other things have disallowed
the violation of faith; yet have allowed it, when it is for the getting
of a kingdom. . . .

These are the laws of nature, dictating peace, for a means of
the conservation of men in multitudes; and which only concern
the doctrine of civil society. There be other things tending to the
destruction of particular men; as drunkenness, and all other parts
of intemperance; which may therefore also be reckoned amongst
those things which the law of nature hath forbidden; but are not
necessary to be mentioned, nor are pertinent enough to this place.

And though this may seem too subtle a deduction of the laws
of nature, to be taken notice of by all men; whereof the most part
are too busy in getting food, and the rest too negligent to understand; yet to leave all men inexcusable, they have been contracted
into one easy sum, intelligible even to the meanest capacity; and
that is, *Do not that to another, which thou wouldst not have done
to thyself;* which sheweth him, that he has no more to do in learning the laws of nature, but, when weighing the actions of other
men with his own, they seem too heavy, to put them into the other
part of the balance, and his own into their place, that his own
passions, and self-love, may add nothing to the weight; and then
there is none of these laws of nature that will not appear unto him
very reasonable.

The laws of nature oblige *in foro interno;* that is to say, they
bind to a desire they should take place: but *in foro externo;* that
is, to the putting them in act, not always. For he that should be
modest, and tractable, and perform all he promises, in such time,
and place, where no man else should do so, should but make himself a prey to others, and procure his own certain ruin, contrary
to the ground of all laws of nature, which tend to nature's preservation. And again, he that having sufficient security, that others

shall observe the same laws towards him, observes them not himself, seeketh not peace, but war; and consequently the destruction of his nature by violence.

And whatsoever laws bind *in foro interno,* may be broken, not only by a fact contrary to the law, but also by a fact according to it, in case a man think it contrary. For though his action in this case, be according to the law; yet his purpose was against the law; which, where the obligaton is *in foro interno,* is a breach.

The laws of nature are immutable and eternal; for injustice, ingratitude, arrogance, pride, iniquity, acception of persons, and the rest, can never be made lawful. For it can never be that war shall preserve life, and peace destroy it.

The same laws, because they oblige only to a desire, and endeavour, I mean an unfeigned and constant endeavour, are easy to be observed. For in that they require nothing but endeavour, he that endeavoureth their performance, fulfilleth them, and he that fulfilleth the law, is just.

And the science of them, is the true and only moral philosophy. For moral philosophy is nothing else but the science of what is *good,* and *evil,* in the conversation, and society of mankind. *Good,* and *evil,* are names that signify our appetites, and aversions; which in different tempers, customs, and doctrines of men, are different: and divers men, differ not only in their judgment, on the senses of what is pleasant, and unpleasant to the taste, smell, hearing, touch, and sight; but also of what is conformable, or disagreeable to reason, in the actions of common life. Nay, the same man, in divers times, differs from himself; and one time praiseth, that is, calleth good, what another time he dispraiseth, and calleth evil: from whence arise disputes, controversies, and at last war. And therefore so long as a man is in the condition of mere nature, which is a condition of war, his private appetite is the measure of good, and evil: and consequently all men agree on this, that peace is good, and therefore also the way, or means of peace, which, as I have shewed before, are *justice, gratitude, modesty, equity, mercy,* and the rest of the laws of nature, are good; that is to say; *moral virtues;* and their contrary *vices,* evil. Now the science of virtue and vice, is moral philosophy; and therefore the true doctrine of the laws of nature, is the true moral philosophy. But the writers of moral philosophy, though they acknowledge the same virtues and vices; yet not seeing wherein consisted their goodness; nor that they come to be praised, as the means of peaceable, sociable, and comfortable living, place them in a mediocrity of passions: as if not the cause, but the degree of daring, made fortitude; or not the cause, but the quantity of a gift, made liberality.

These dictates of reason, men used to call by the name of laws, but improperly: for they are but conclusions, or theorems concerning what conduceth to the conservation and defence of themselves; whereas law, properly, is the word of him, that by right hath command over others. But yet if we consider the same theorems, as delivered in the word of God, that by right commandeth all things; then are they properly called laws. . . .

Chapter XVII

Of the Causes, Generation, and Definition of a Commonwealth

The final cause, end, or design of men, who naturally love liberty, and dominion over others, in the introduction of that restraint upon themselves, in which we see them live in commonwealths, is the foresight of their own preservation, and of a more contented life thereby; that is to say, of getting themselves out from that miserable condition of war, which is necessarily consequent, as hath been shown in chapter xiii, to the natural passions of men, when there is no visible power to keep them in awe, and tie them by fear of punishment to the performance of their covenants, and observation of those laws of nature set down. . . .

It is true, that certain living creatures, as bees, and ants, live sociably one with another, which are therefore by Aristotle numbered amongst political creatures; and yet have no other direction, than their particular judgments and appetites; nor speech, whereby one of them can signify to another, what he thinks expedient for the common benefit: and therefore some man may perhaps desire to know, why mankind cannot do the same. To which I answer,

First, that men are continually in competition for honour and dignity, which these creatures are not; and consequently amongst men there ariseth on that ground, envy and hatred, and finally war; but amongst these not so.

Secondly, that amongst these creatures, the common good differeth not from the private; and being by nature inclined to their private, they procure thereby the common benefit. But man, whose joy consisteth in comparing himself with other men, can relish nothing but what is eminent.

Thirdly, that these creatures, having not, as man, the use of reason, do not see, nor think they see any fault, in the administration of their common business; whereas amongst men, there are very many, that think themselves wiser, and able to govern the public, better than the rest; and these strive to reform and innovate, one this way, another that way; and thereby bring it into distraction and civil war.

Fourthly, that these creatures, though they have some use of voice, in making known to one another their desires, and other affections; yet they want that art of words, by which some men can represent to others, that which is good, in the likeness of evil; and evil, in the likeness of good; and augment, or diminish the apparent greatness of good and evil; discontenting men, and troubling their peace at their pleasure.

Fifthly, irrational creatures cannot distinguish between *injury*, and *damage;* and therefore as long as they be at ease, they are not offended with their fellows: whereas man is then most troublesome, when he is most at ease: for then it is that he loves to shew his wisdom, and control the actions of them that govern the commonwealth.

Lastly, the agreement of these creatures is natural; that of men, is by covenant only, which is artificial: and therefore it is no wonder if there be somewhat else required, besides covenant, to make their agreement constant and lasting; which is a common power, to keep them in awe, and to direct their actions to the common benefit.

The only way to erect such a common power, as may be able to defend them from the invasion of foreigners, and the injuries of one another, and thereby to secure them in such sort, as that by their own industry, and by the fruits of the earth, they may nourish themselves and live contentedly; is, to confer all their power and strength upon one man, or upon one assembly of men, that may reduce all their wills, by plurality of voices, unto one will: which is as much as to say, to appoint one man, or assembly of men, to bear their person; and every one to own, and acknowledge himself to be author of whatsoever he that so beareth their person, shall act, or cause to be acted, in those things which concern the common peace and safety; and therein to submit their wills, every one to his will, and their judgments, to his judgment. This is more than consent, or concord; it is a real unity of them all, in one and the same person, made by covenant of every man with every man, in such manner, as if every man should say to every man, *I author-ize and give up my right of governing myself, to this man, or to this assembly of men, on this condition, that thou give up thy right to him, and authorize all his actions in like manner.* This done, the multitude so united in one person, is called a COMMONWEALTH, in Latin CIVITAS. This is the generation of that great LEVIATHAN, or rather, to speak more reverently, of that *mortal god,* to which we owe under the *immortal God,* our peace and defence. For by this authority, given him by every particular man in the common-wealth, he hath the use of so much power and strength conferred on him, that by terror thereof, he is enabled to perform the wills of them all, to peace at home, and mutual aid against their ene-mies abroad. And in him consisteth the essence of the common-wealth; which, to define it, is *one person, of whose acts a great multitude, by mutual covenants one with another, have made themselves every one the author, to the end he may use the strength and means of them all, as he shall think expedient, for their peace and common defence.*

And he that carrieth this person, is called SOVEREIGN, and said to have *sovereign power;* and every one besides, his SUBJECT.

The attaining to this sovereign power, is by two ways. One, by natural force; as when a man maketh his children, to submit them-selves, and their children, to his government, as being able to de-stroy them if they refuse; or by war subdueth his enemies to his will, giving them their lives on that condition. The other, is when men agree amongst themselves, to submit to some man, or assem-bly of men, voluntarily, on confidence to be protected by him against all others. This latter, may be called a political common-wealth, or commonwealth by *institution;* and the former, a commonwealth by *acquisition.* . . .

Chapter XXI

Of the Liberty of Subjects

Liberty, or Freedom, signifieth, properly, the absence of opposition; by opposition, I mean external impediments of motion; and may be applied no less to irrational, and inanimate creatures, than to rational. For whatsoever is so tied, or environed, as it cannot move but within a certain space, which space is determined by the opposition of some external body, we say it hath not liberty to go further. And so of all living creatures, whilst they are imprisoned, or restrained, with walls, or chains; and of the water whilst it is kept in by banks, or vessels, that otherwise would spread itself into a larger space, we use to say, they are not at liberty, to move in such manner, as without those external impediments they would. But when the impediment of motion, is in the constitution of the thing itself, we use not to say; it wants the liberty; but the power to move; as when a stone lieth still, or a man is fastened to his bed by sickness.

And according to this proper, and generally received meaning of the word, a FREEMAN, *is he, that in those things, which by his strength and wit he is able to do, is not hindered to do what he has a will to.* But when the words *free,* and *liberty,* are applied to any thing but bodies, they are abused; for that which is not subject to motion is not subject to impediment: and therefore, when it is said, for example, the way is free, no liberty of the way is signified, but of those that walk in it without stop. And when we say a gift is free, there is not meant any liberty of the gift, but of the giver, that was not bound by any law or covenant to give it. So when we *speak freely,* it is not the liberty of voice, or pronunciation, but of the man, whom no law hath obliged to speak otherwise than he did. Lastly, from the use of the word *free-will,* no liberty can be inferred of the will, desire, or inclination, but the liberty of the man; which consisteth in this, that he finds no stop, in doing what he has the will, desire, or inclination to do.

Fear and liberty are consistent; as when a man throweth his goods into the sea for *fear* the ship should sink, he doth it nevertheless very willingly, and may refuse to do it if he will; it is therefore the action of one that was *free:* so a man sometimes pays his debt, only for *fear* of imprisonment, which because nobody hindered him from detaining, was the action of a man at *liberty.* And generally all actions which men do in commonwealths, for *fear* of the law, are actions, which the doers had *liberty* to omit.

Liberty, and *necessity* are consistent: as in the water, that hath not only *liberty,* but a *necessity* of descending by the channel; so likewise in the actions which men voluntarily do: which, because they proceed from their will, proceed from *liberty;* and yet, because every act of man's will, and every desire, and inclination proceedeth from some cause, and that from another cause, in a continual chain, whose first link is in the hand of God the first of all causes, proceed from *necessity.* So that to him that could see the connexion of those causes, the *necessity* of all men's voluntary actions, would appear manifest. And therefore God, that seeth, and disposeth all things, seeth also that the liberty of man in doing what he will, is accompanied with the *necessity* of doing that which God will, and no more, nor less. For though men may do many things, which God does not command, nor is therefore author of them; yet they can have no passion, nor appetite to anything, of which appetite God's will is not the cause. And did not his will assure the *necessity* of man's will, and consequently of all that on man's will dependeth, the *liberty* of men would be a contradiction, and impediment to the omnipotence and *liberty* of God. And this shall suffice, as to the matter in hand, of that natural *liberty,* which only is properly called *liberty.*

But as men, for the attaining of peace, and conservation of themselves thereby, have made an artificial man, which we call a commonwealth; so also have they made artificial chains, called *civil laws,* which they themselves, by mutual covenants, have fastened at one end, to the lips of that man, or assembly, to whom they have given the sovereign power; and at the other end to their own ears. These bonds, in their own nature but weak, may nevertheless be made to hold, by the danger, though not by the difficulty of breaking them.

In relation to these bonds only it is, that I am to speak now, of the *liberty* of *subjects.* For seeing there is no commonwealth in the world, wherein there be rules enough set down, for the regulating of all the actions, and words of men; as being a thing impossible:

it followeth necessarily, that in all kinds of actions by the laws praetermitted, men have the liberty, of doing what their own reasons shall suggest, for the most profitable to themselves. For if we take liberty in the proper sense, for corporal liberty; that is to say, freedom from chains and prison; it were very absurd for men to clamour as they do, for the liberty they so manifestly enjoy. Again, if we take liberty, for an exemption from laws, it is no less absurd, . for men to demand as they do, that liberty, by which all other men may be masters of their lives. And yet, as absurd as it is, this is it they demand; not knowing that the laws are of no power to protect them, without a sword in the hands of a man, or men, to cause those laws to be put in execution. The liberty of a subject, lieth therefore only in those things, which in regulating their actions, the sovereign hath praetermitted: such as is the liberty to buy, and sell, and otherwise contract with one another; to choose their own abode, their own diet, their own trade of life, and institute their children as they themselves think fit; and the like.

Nevertheless we are not to understand, that by such liberty, the sovereign power of life and death, is either abolished, or limited. For it has been already shown, that nothing the sovereign representative can do to a subject, on what pretence soever, can properly be called injustice, or injury; because every subject is author of every act the sovereign doth; so that he never wanteth right to anything, otherwise, than as he himself is the subject of God, and bound thereby to observe the laws of nature. And therefore it may, and doth often happen in commonwealths, that a subject may be put to death, by the command of the sovereign power; and yet neither do the other wrong; as when Jephtha caused his daughter to be sacrificed: in which, and the like cases, he that so dieth, had liberty to do the action, for which he is nevertheless, without injury put to death. And the same holdeth also in a sovereign prince, that putteth to death an innocent subject. For though the action be against the law of nature, as being contrary to equity, as was the killing of Uriah, by David; yet it was not an injury to Uriah, but to God. Not to Uriah, because the right to do what he pleased was given him by Uriah himself: and yet to God, because David was God's subject, and prohibited all iniquity by the law of nature: which distinction, David himself, when he repented the fact, evidently confirmed, saying, *To thee only have I sinned.* In the same manner, the people of Athens, when they banished the most potent of their commonwealth for ten years, thought they committed no injustice; and yet they never questioned what crime he had done; but what hurt he would do: nay they commanded the banishment of they knew not whom; and every citizen bringing his oystershell into the market place, written with the name of him he desired should be banished, without actually accusing him, sometimes banished an Aristides, for his reputation of justice; and sometimes a scurrilous jester, as Hyperbolus, to make a jest of it. And yet a man cannot say, the sovereign people of Athens wanted right to banish them; or an Athenian the liberty to jest, or to be just.

The liberty, whereof there is so frequent and honourable mention, in the histories, and philosophy of the ancient Greeks, and Romans, and in the writings, and discourse of those that from them have received all their learning in the politics, is not the liberty of particular men; but the liberty of the commonwealth: which is the same with that which every man then should have, if there were no civil laws, nor commonwealth at all. And the effects of it also be the same. For as amongst masterless men, there is perpetual war, of every man against his neighbour; no inheritance, to transmit to the son, nor to expect from the father; no propriety of goods, or lands; no security; but a full and absolute liberty in every particular man: so in states, and commonwealths not dependent on one another, every commonwealth, not every man, has an absolute liberty, to do what it shall judge, that is to say, what that man, or assembly that representeth it, shall judge most conducing to their benefit. But withal, they live in the condition of a perpetual war, and upon the confines of battle, with their frontiers armed, and cannons planted against their neighbours round about. The Athenians, and Romans were free; that is, free commonwealths: not that any particular men had the liberty to resist their own representative; but that their representative had the liberty to resist, or invade other people. There is written on the turrets of the city of Lucca in great characters at this day, the word LIBERTAS; yet no man can thence infer, that a particular man has more liberty, or immunity from the service of the commonwealth there, than in Constantinople. Whether a commonwealth be monarchical, or popular, the freedom is still the same.

But it is an easy thing, for men to be deceived, by the specious name of liberty; and for want of judgment to distinguish, mistake that for their private inheritance, and birth-right, which is the right of the public only. And when the same error is confirmed by the authority of men in reputation for their writings on this subject, it is no wonder if it produce sedition, and change of government. In these western parts of the world, we are made to receive our opinions concerning the institution, and rights of commonwealths, from Aristotle, Cicero, and other men, Greeks and Romans, that living under popular states, derived those rights, not from the principles of nature, but transcribed them into their books, out of the practice of their own commonwealths, which were popular; as the grammarians describe the rules of language, out of the practice of the time; or the rules of poetry, out of the poems of Homer and Virgil. And because the Athenians were taught, to keep them from desire of changing their government, that they were freemen, and all that lived under monarchy were slaves; therefore Aristotle puts it down in his *Politics, (lib. 6. cap. ii.) In democracy,* LIBERTY *is to be supposed: for it is commonly held, that no man is* FREE *in any other government.* And as Aristotle; so Cicero, and other writers have grounded their civil doctrine, on the opinions of the Romans, who were taught to hate monarchy, at first, by them that having deposed their sovereign, shared amongst them the sovereignty of Rome; and afterwards by their successors. And by reading of these Greek, and Latin authors, men from their childhood have gotten a habit, under a false show of liberty, of favouring tumults, and of licentious controlling the actions of their sovereigns, and again of controlling those controllers; with the effusion of so much blood, as I think I may truly say, there was never any thing so dearly bought, as these western parts have bought the learning of the Greek and Latin tongues.

To come now to the particulars of the true liberty of a subject; that is to say, what are the things, which though commanded by the sovereign, he may nevertheless, without injustice, refuse to do; we are to consider, what rights we pass away, when we make a commonwealth; or, which is all one, what liberty we deny ourselves, by owning all the actions, without exception, of the man, or assembly, we make our sovereign. For in the act of our *submission,* consisteth both our *obligation,* and our *liberty;* which must therefore be inferred by arguments taken from thence; there being no obligation on any man, which ariseth not from some act of his own; for all men equally, are by nature free. And because such arguments, must either be drawn from the express words, *I authorize all his actions,* or from the intention of him that submitteth himself to his power, which intention is to be understood by the end for which he so submitteth; the obligation, and liberty of the subject, is to be derived, either from those words, or others equivalent; or else from the end of the institution of sovereignty, namely, the peace of the subjects within themselves, and their defence against a common enemy.

First therefore, seeing sovereignty by institution, is by covenant of every one to every one; and sovereignty by acquisition, by covenants of the vanquished to the victor, or child to the parent; it is manifest, that every subject has liberty in all those things, the right whereof cannot by covenant be transferred. I have shewn before in the 14th chapter, that covenants, not to defend a man's own body, are void. Therefore,

If the sovereign command a man, though justly condemned, to kill, wound, or maim himself; or not to resist those that assault him; or to abstain from the use of food, air, medicine, or any other thing, without which he cannot live; yet hath that man the liberty to disobey.

If a man be interrogated by the sovereign, or his authority, concerning a crime done by himself, he is not bound, without assurance of pardon, to confess it; because no man, as I have shown in the same chapter, can be obliged by covenant to accuse himself.

Again, the consent of a subject to sovereign power, is contained in these words, *I authorize, or take upon me, all his actions;* in which there is no restriction at all, of his own former natural liberty: for by allowing him to *kill me,* I am not bound to kill myself when he commands me. It is one thing to say, *kill me, or my fellow, if you please;* another thing to say, *I will kill myself, or my fellow.* It followeth therefore, that

No man is bound by the words themselves, either to kill himself, or any other man; and consequently, that the obligation a man may sometimes have, upon the command of the sovereign to execute any dangerous, or dishonourable office, dependeth not on the words of our submission; but on the intention, which is to be understood by the end thereof. When therefore our refusal to obey, frustrates the end for which the sovereignty was ordained; then there is no liberty to refuse: otherwise there is.

Upon this ground, a man that is commanded as a soldier to fight against the enemy, though his sovereign have right enough to punish his refusal with death, may nevertheless in many cases refuse, without injustice; as when he substituteth a sufficient soldier in his place: for in this case he deserteth not the service of the commonwealth. And there is allowance to be made for natural timorousness; not only to women, of whom no such dangerous duty is expected, but also to men of feminine courage. When armies fight, there is on one side, or both, a running away; yet when they do it not out of treachery, but fear, they are not esteemed to do it unjustly, but dishonourably. For the same reason, to avoid battle, is not injustice, but cowardice. But he that inrolleth himself a soldier, or taketh imprest money, taketh away the excuse of a timorous nature; and is obliged, not only to go to the battle, but also not to run from it, without his captain's leave. And when the defence of the commonwealth, requireth at once the help of all that are able to bear arms, every one is obliged; because otherwise the institution of the commonwealth, which they have not the purpose, or courage to preserve, was in vain.

To resist the sword of the commonwealth, in defence of another man, guilty, or innocent, no man hath liberty; because such liberty, takes away from the sovereign, the means of protecting us; and is therefore destructive of the very essence of government. But in case a great many men together, have already resisted the sovereign power unjustly, or committed some capital crime, for which every one of them expecteth death, whether have they not the liberty then to join together, and assist, and defend one another? Certainly they have: for they but defend their lives, which the guilty man may as well do, as the innocent. There was indeed injustice in the first breach of their duty; their bearing of arm subsequent to it, though it be to maintain what they have done, is no new unjust act. And if it be only to defend their persons, it is not unjust at all. But the offer of pardon taketh from them, to whom it is offered, the plea of self-defence, and maketh their perseverance in assisting, or defending the rest, unlawful.

As for other liberties, they depend on the silence of the law. In cases where the sovereign has prescribed no rule, there the subject hath the liberty to do, or forbear, according to his own discretion. And therefore such liberty is in some places more, and in some less; and in some times more, in other times less, according as they that have the sovereignty shall think most convenient. As for example, there was a time, when in England a man might enter into his own land, and dispossess such as wrongfully possessed it, by force. But in after times, that liberty of forcible entry, was taken away by a statute made, by the king, in parliament. And in some places of the world, men have the liberty of many wives: in other places, such liberty is not allowed.

If a subject have a controversy with his sovereign of debt, or of right of possession of lands or goods, or concerning any service required at his hands, or concerning any penalty, corporal, or pecuniary, grounded on a precedent law; he hath the same liberty to sue for his right, as if it were against a subject; and before such judges, as are appointed by the sovereign. For seeing the sovereign demandeth by force of a former law, and not by virtue of his power; he declareth thereby, that he requireth no more, than shall appear to be due by that law. The suit therefore is not contrary to the will of the sovereign; and consequently the subject hath the liberty to demand the hearing of his cause; and sentence, according to that law. But if he demand, or take anything by pretence of his power; there lieth, in that case, no action of law; for all that is done by him in virtue of his power, is done by the authority of every subject, and consequently he that brings an action against the sovereign, brings it against himself.

If a monarch, or sovereign assembly, grant a liberty to all, or any of his subjects, which grant standing, he is disabled to provide for their safety, the grant is void; unless he directly renounce, or transfer the sovereignty to another. For in that he might openly, if it had been his will, and in plain terms, have renounced, or transferred it, and did not; it is to be understood it was not his will, but that the grant proceeded from ignorance of the repugnancy between such a liberty and the sovereign power; and therefore the sovereignty is still retained; and consequently all those powers, which are necessary to the exercising thereof; such as are the power of war, and peace, of judicature, of appointing officers, and councillors, of levying money, and the rest named in the 18th chapter.

The obligation of subjects to the sovereign, is understood to last as long, and no longer, than the power lasteth, by which he is able to protect them. For the right men have by nature to protect themselves, when none else can protect them, can by no covenant be relinquished. The sovereignty is the soul of the commonwealth; which once departed from the body, the members do no more receive their motion from it. The end of obedience is protection; which, wheresoever a man seeth it, either in his own, or in another's sword, nature applieth his obedience to it, and his endeavour to maintain it. And though sovereignty, in the intention of them that make it, be immortal; yet it is in its own nature, not only subject to violent death, by foreign war; but also through the ignorance, and passions of men, it hath in it, from the very institution, many seeds of a natural mortality, by intestine discord.

If a subject be taken prisoner in war; or his person or his means of life be within the guards of the enemy, and hath his life and corporal liberty given him, on condition to be subject to the victor, he hath liberty to accept the condition; and having accepted it, is the subject of him that took him; because he had no other way to preserve himself. The case is the same, if he be detained on the same terms, in a foreign country. But if a man be held in prison, or bonds, or is not trusted with the liberty of his body; he cannot be understood to be bound by covenant to subjection; and therefore may, if he can, make his escape by any means whatsoever.

If a monarch shall relinquish the sovereignty, both for himself, and his heirs; his subjects return to the absolute liberty of nature; because, though nature may declare who are his sons, and who are the nearest of his kin; yet it dependeth on his own will, as hath been said in the precedent chapter, who shall be his heir. If therefore he will have no heir, there is no sovereignty, nor subjection. The case is the same, if he die without known kindred, and without declaration of his heir. For then there can no heir be known, and consequently no subjection be due.

If the sovereign banish his subject; during the banishment, he is not subject. But he that is sent on a message, or hath leave to travel, is still subject; but it is, by contract between sovereigns, not by virtue of the covenant of subjection. For whosoever entereth into another's dominion, is subject to all the laws thereof; unless he have a privilege of the amity of the sovereigns, or by special licence.

If a monarch subdued by war, render himself subject to the victor; his subjects are delivered from their former obligation, and become obliged to the victor. If he be held prisoner, or have not the liberty of his own body; he is not understood to have given away the right of sovereignty; and therefore his subjects are obliged to yield obedience to the magistrates formerly placed, governing not in their own name, but in his. For, his right remaining, the question is only of the administration; that is to say, of the magistrates and officers; which, if he have not means to name, he is supposed to approve those, which he himself had formerly appointed. . . .

Chapter XXVI

Of Civil Laws

41 The law of nature, and the civil law, contain each other, and are of equal extent. For the laws of nature, which consist in equity, justice, gratitude, and other moral virtues on these depending, in the condition of mere nature (as I have said before in the end of the 15th chapter,) are not properly laws, but qualities that dispose men to peace, and to obedience. When a commonwealth is once settled, then are they actually laws, and not before; as being then the commands of the common-wealth; and therefore also civil laws: for it is the sovereign power that obliges men to obey them. For in the differences of private men, to declare, what is equity, what is justice, and what is moral virtue, and to make them binding, there is need of the ordinances of sovereign power, and punishments to be ordained for such as shall break them; which ordinances are therefore part of the civil law. The law of nature therefore is a part of the civil law in all common-wealths of the world. Reciprocally also, the civil law is a part of the dictates of nature. For justice, that is to say, performance of covenant, and giving to every man his own, is a dictate of the law of nature. But every subject in a common-wealth, hath covenanted to obey the civil law, (either one with another, as when they assemble to make a common representative, or with the representative itself

one by one, when subdued by the sword they promise obedience, that they may receive life;) And therefore obedience to the civil law is part also of the law of nature. Civil, and natural law are not different kinds, but different parts of law; whereof one part being written, is called civil, the other unwritten, natural. But the right of nature, that is, the natural liberty of man, may by the civil law be abridged, and restrained: nay, the end of making laws, is no other, but such restraint; without the which there cannot possibly be any peace. And law was brought into the world for nothing else, but to limit the natural liberty of particular men, in such manner, as they might not hurt, but assit one another, and join together against a common enemy.

George Berkeley

George Berkeley

THE philosophy of Bishop Berkeley (1685-1753) was born of a desire to refute the scepticism, materialism, and the atheism which he felt to be implicit in the world-view which was expounded early by Descartes, given enormous support by the the success of Newtonian physics, and accepted without serious question by the influential and widely read British philosopher, John Locke. What was this world-view which captured the imaginations of the men of the 18th century and still holds a prominent position in the minds of many today? The Newtonian world-view, for such it has come to be called, conceived the universe to be very different from the world which the individual perceives. The real world as distinguished from the world of sense perception was a world of matter in motion in an absolute space and time governed by a few simple mathematical laws. More technically, as the student saw in Descartes' *Discourse on Method,* the external world consisted in essence of a material substance whose primary quality or attribute was extension. In Locke this is modified to include more specifically size, figure, motion, and impenetrability as the primary qualities of the material substance. This matter, the sole reality or substance besides the human and divine mind, was the support and operated as the cause or the occasion for all sense perception. Sense perception, however, apprehended matter in terms of qualities which were secondary—colors, sounds, tastes being only the effects of the power of matter operating on our sense organs and not literal representations of matter as were the primary qualities. All physical science, and especially Newton's physics, was a study of this ultimate external reality, known only as the inertia of mass, and scientific laws were formulations of its powers and interrelations.

In this conception of the external world, Berkeley saw materialism implied, for in such a world there is little room for man and spiritual values. Already Locke had been led to ask whether it was not possible for matter to think even though he had rejected the notion himself. Atheism, too, was sanctioned by such a view for it relegated God, the Father, to the position of God, the original clockmaker, if it gave even this much place to the Supreme Being. Men would soon perceive that all the basic attributes of God such as eternality, immutability, perfection, infinity, were also attributes of space. Finally, the dualism instituted between mind and matter was bound to lead to an impasse in which the very possibility of knowledge was questioned. Scepticism was inevitable once it was shown that the weak but direct contact man supposedly had with the external world, whose primary qualities were supposed to be apprehended by the senses, is no more direct than the contact gained through such secondary qualities as sounds and colors, since primary and secondary qualities are apprehended in the same way. Both were effects produced on human minds, and there was no satisfactory rational ground for distinguishing between them. Then, with all ideas confined to the mind, knowledge of the external world becomes truly a problem.

The man in whose writings Berkeley saw these tendencies, John Locke (1632-1704), the eminent British empiricist, never thought his position to be either sceptical, materialistic, or atheistical. In Locke's own mind, his *Essay Concerning the Human Understanding* cleared the ground of vain disputes and provided the incentive for a fruitful pursuit of scientific knowledge of the world by stating clearly the nature, powers, and limitations of human knowledge. The conclusion of his book had been that though man cannot know all things (especially about matters of theological speculation), he can learn much concerning the world about him and can direct such knowledge to the improvement of man's conditions. The reason why knowledge of the world should be preeminently the object of man's attention resides in the fact that all knowledge is the result of experience. The mind can have no knowledge of anything but what is first given in experience through sense perception, but since sense perception is the result of the interaction of man and the world, or rather of the impact of bodies upon man, the world of physics is properly man's object of study.

This doctrine that the origin and the test of all knowledge is in experience Berkeley accepted wholeheartedly and without question. He even accepted it in the form Locke had stated it. Experience, Locke had argued, is an affair of receiving ideas; knowledge is solely the perception of the agreement of ideas with one another; and ideas are simply "whatsoever is the object of the understanding when a man thinks." But whereas for Locke the result of such thought was a knowledge of the external world of matter, for Berkeley such knowledge remained a knowledge of ideas. For there was no world of matter; the notion of matter was merely an abstraction derived by progressively stripping the perceived world of its perceived qualities, leaving only the idea of matter as the substance of the world, a substance which was not perceived nor perceivable and therefore a meaningless idea. Similarly Berkeley attacked the doctrine of absolute space. In *Towards a New Theory of Vision,* he formulated a theory of relative space. We learn to recognize distance by experience and do not see it directly. In brief, Berkeley keeps Locke's doctrines of experience, renders them more consistent, and drops the context which Locke had assumed for that experience, namely the world of matter. In place of matter conceived as the support of the perceived world, matter is reinterpreted to mean the sum total of the conjoined qualities of what is presented to sense perception. Science instead of describing a world beyond sense perception, instead of being a science of necessary causes, becomes a generalized description of the course of observed events. God takes the place of matter as the cause of sense perception and as the ultimate explanation of the ordered uniformity of the perceived world which science describes.

Such is the tenor of Berkeley's philosophy, summed up in his famous formula that to be is to be perceived, *esse est percipi*. Three principles are involved in this phrase. These are: 1) that what we perceive is real; 2) that what we perceive are ideas; 3) that the having of ideas necessarily supposes mind as the haver, and mind becomes the sole substance of reality. The first is a statement of realism concerning our contact with the world; it expresses a common sense attitude of the relation of man to nature in the act of perceiving and knowing. The second principle pursued logically leads to a subjective idealism and ultimately to solipsism, for in identifying existence with being perceived, by making the existence of the world dependent upon someone's perception of it, the perceiver becomes as it were the author of all that is, and all that is becomes ultimately the percipient himself—consciousness swallows the world. The third principle, by emphasizing mind or spirit as the sole substance leads to a spiritualism in which God becomes the inclusive category, and all is contained as part of God's essence and being. Philosophers since Berkeley have frequently taken one or the other of these ideas as a partial basis of their thought. Especially in German idealism, in men such as Fichte and Schopenhauer, Berkeley's thought has provided fundamental insight.

Berkeley had conceived the main tenets of his philosophy at the age of 23. He published three works stating his philosophy by 1713 when he was 28. The three volumes which he published between 1709 and 1713 are: the *Essay Toward a New Theory of Vision* (1709); *The Principles of Human Nature* (1710), his most systematic statement of his philosophy; and *Three Dialogues Between Hylas and Philonous* (1713). In 1720 he published *De Motu,* a thoroughgoing criticism of

the concepts of Newtonian physics, which was supplemented
in 1734 by the *Analyst,* a similar criticism of the concepts of
mathematics. In 1732 he published *Alciphron* or the *Minute
Philosopher,* a defense of religion against scepticism. This
was followed by a *Vindication of the Theory of Visual Language* (1733). In his later years, Berkeley altered his philosophical emphasis in the direction of Platonic idealism; a
Platonist account of ideas took the place of his earlier empirical treatment of sense and thought. This change is expressed in his last work, *Siris: A chain of Philosophical Reflections* (1744). His *Commonplace Book* (published in 1871)
contain his notes recording the progress of his thought prior
to his first publications.

Berkeley was Irish born and bred. He spent 13 years as a
student, fellow and tutor at Trinity College, Dublin. In 1713,
he went to England, and for 15 years he spent his time between England and the continent. In 1728, he embarked for
America where he remained for several years waiting in vain
for the English Parliament to provide funds which had been
promised him to establish a College in the Bermudas from
which center culture and religion was to be spread among
the inhabitants of the New World. Upon the failure of this
mission, Berkeley returned to Ireland. Here he remained as
the Bishop of Cloyne during the remaining twenty years of
his life. He retired to Oxford a few months before his death.
His philosophy was introduced into America by his friend
Samuel Johnson, first president of King's College, New York,
who incorporated Berkeley's idealism into his text-book, *Ele-
menta Philosophica* (1752), published by Benjamin Franklin
—the first American text-book of philosophy.

*   *   *

NOTE: Heavy-faced square brackets enclose words or sentences added by
Berkeley in later editions; light-face brackets contain material omitted in
later editions.

Of the
Principles of Human Knowledge

The Preface

WHAT I here make public has, a long and scrupulous inquiry, seemed to me evidently true and not unuseful to be known; particularly to those who are tainted with Scepticism, or want a demonstration of the existence and immateriality of God, or the natural immortality of the Soul. Whether it be so or no I am content the reader should impartially examine; since I do not think myself any farther concerned for the success of what I have written than as it is agreeable to truth. But, to the end this may not suffer, I make it my request that the reader suspend his judgment till he has once at least read the whole through, with that degree of attention and thought which the subject-matter shall seem to deserve. For, as there are some passages that, taken by themselves, are very liable (nor could it be remedied) to gross misinterpretation, and to be charged with most absurd consequences, which, nevertheless, upon an entire perusal will appear not to follow from them; so likewise, though the whole should be read over, yet, if this be done transiently, it is very probable my sense may be mistaken: but to a thinking reader, I flatter myself it will be throughout clear and obvious.

As for the characters of novelty and singularity which some of the following notions may seem to bear, it is, I hope, needless to make any apology on that account. He must surely be either very weak, or very little acquainted with the sciences, who shall reject a truth that is capable of demonstration, for no other reason but because it is newly known, and contrary to the prejudices of mankind.

Thus much I thought fit to premise, in order to prevent, if possible, the hasty censures of a sort of men who are too apt to condemn an opinion before they rightly comprehend it.

Introduction

1] PHILOSOPHY being nothing else but the study of Wisdom and Truth, it may with reason be expected that those who have spent most time and pains in it should enjoy a greater calm and serenity of mind, a greater clearness and evidence of knowledge, and be less disturbed with doubts and difficulties than other men. Yet, so it is, we see the illiterate bulk of mankind, that walk the highroad of plain common sense, and are governed by the dictates of nature, for the most part easy and undisturbed. To them nothing that is familiar appears unaccountable or difficult to comprehend. They complain not of any want of evidence in their senses, and are out of all danger of becoming Sceptics. But no sooner do we depart from sense and instinct to follow the light of a superior principle —to reason, meditate, and reflect on the nature of things, but a thousand scruples spring up in our minds, concerning those things which before we seemed fully to comprehend. Prejudices and errors of sense do from all parts discover themselves to our view; and, endeavouring to correct these by reason, we are insensibly drawn into uncouth paradoxes, difficulties, and inconsistencies, which multiply and grow upon us as we advance in speculation; till at length, having wandered through many intricate mazes, we find ourselves just where we were, or, which is worse, sit down in a forlorn Scepticism.

2] The cause of this is thought to be the obscurity of things, or the natural weakness and imperfection of our understandings. It is said the faculties we have are few, and those designed by nature for the support and pleasure of life, and not to penetrate into the inward essence and constitution of things: besides, the mind of man being finite, when it treats of things which partake of Infinity, it is not to be wondered at if it run into absurdities and contradictions, out of which it is impossible it should ever extricate itself; it being of the nature of Infinite not to be comprehended by that which is finite.

31 But, perhaps, we may be too partial to ourselves in placing the fault originally in our faculties, and not rather in the wrong use we make of them. It is a hard thing to suppose that right deductions from true principles should ever end in consequences which cannot be maintained or made consistent. We should believe that God has dealt more bountifully with the sons of men than to give them a strong desire for that knowledge which he had placed quite out of their reach. This were not agreeable to the wonted indulgent methods of Providence, which, whatever appetites it may have implanted in the creatures, doth usually furnish them with such means as, if rightly made use of, will not fail to satisfy them. Upon the whole, I am inclined to think that the far greater part, if not all, of those difficulties which have hitherto amused philosophers, and blocked up the way to knowledge, are entirely owing to ourselves. We have first raised a dust, and then complain we cannot see.

41 My purpose therefore is, to try if I can discover what those Principles are which have introduced all that doubtfulness and uncertainty, those absurdities and contractions, into the several sects of philosophy; insomuch that the wisest men have thought our ignorance incurable, conceiving it to arise from the natural dulness and limitation of our faculties. And surely it is a work well deserving our pains to make a strict inquiry concerning the First Principles of Human Knowledge; to sift and examine them on all sides: especially since there may be some grounds to suspect that those lets and difficulties, which stay and embarrass the mind in its search after truth, do not spring from any darkness and intricacy in the objects, or natural defect in the understanding, so much as from false Principles which have been insisted on, and might have been avoided.

51 How difficult and discouraging soever this attempt may seem, when I consider what a number of very great and extraordinary men have gone before me in the like designs, yet I am not without some hopes; upon the consideration that the largest views are not always the clearest, and that he who is short-sighted will be obliged to draw the object nearer, and may, perhaps, by a close and narrow survey, discern that which had escaped far better eyes.

6] In order to prepare the mind of the reader for the easier conceiving what follows, it is proper to premise somewhat, by way of Introduction, concerning the nature and abuse of Language. But the unravelling this matter leads me in some measure to anticipate my design, by taking notice of what seems to have had a chief part in rendering speculation intricate and perplexed, and to have occasioned innumerable errors and difficulties in almost all parts of knowledge. And that is the opinion that the mind hath a power of framing *abstract* ideas or notions of things. He who is not a perfect stranger to the writings and disputes of philosophers must needs acknowledge that no small part of them are spent about abstract ideas. These are in a more especial manner thought to be the object of those sciences which go by the name of logic and metaphysics, and of all that which passes under the notion of the most abstracted and sublime learning; in all which one shall scarce find any question handled in such a manner as does not suppose their existence in the mind, and that it is well acquainted with them.

Part First

1] It is evident to any one who takes a survey of the *objects of human knowledge,* that they are either *ideas* actually imprinted on the senses; or else such as are perceived by attending to the passions and operations of the mind; or lastly, *ideas* formed by help of memory and imagination—either compounding, dividing, or barely representing those originally perceived in the aforesaid ways. By sight I have the ideas of light and colours, with their several degrees and variations. By touch I perceive hard and soft, heat and cold, motion and resistance; and of all these more and less either as to quantity or degree. Smelling furnishes me with odours; the palate with tastes; and hearing conveys sounds to the mind in all their variety of tone and composition.

And as several of these are observed to accompany each other, they come to be marked by one name, and so to be reputed as one *thing*. Thus, for example, a certain colour, taste, smell, figure and consistence having been observed to go together, are accounted one distinct thing, signified by the name apple; other collections of ideas constitute a stone, a tree, a book, and the like sensible things;

which as they are pleasing or disagreeable excite the passions of love, hatred, joy, grief, and so forth.

2] But, besides all that endless variety of ideas or objects of knowledge, there is likewise Something which knows or perceives them; and exercises divers operations, as willing, imagining, remembering, about them. This perceiving, active being is what I call *mind, spirit, soul,* or *myself.* By which words I do not denote any one of my ideas, but a thing entirely distinct from them, wherein they exist, or, which is the same thing, whereby they are perceived; for the existence of an idea consists in being perceived.

3] That neither our thoughts, nor passions, nor ideas formed by the imagination, exist without the mind is what everybody will allow. And to me it seems no less evident that the various sensations or ideas imprinted on the Sense, however blended or combined together (that is, whatever objects they compose), cannot exist otherwise than in a mind perceiving them. I think an intuitive knowledge may be obtained of this, by any one that shall attend to what is meant by the term *exist* when applied to sensible things. The table I write on I say exists; that is, I see and feel it: and if I were out of my study I should say it existed; meaning thereby that if I was in my study I might perceive it, or that some other spirit actually does perceive it. There was an odour, that is, it was smelt; there was a sound, that is, it was heard; a colour or figure, and it was perceived by sight or touch. This is all that I can understand by these and the like expressions. For as to what is said of the *absolute* existence of unthinking things, without any relation to their being perceived, that is to me perfectly unintelligible. Their *esse* is *percipi*; nor is it possible they should have any existence out of the minds or thinking things which perceive them.

4] It is indeed an opinion strangely prevailing amongst men, that houses, mountains, rivers, and in a word all sensible objects, have an existence, natural or real, distinct from their being perceived by the understanding. But, with how great an assurance and acquiescence soever this Principle may be entertained in the world, yet whoever shall find in his heart to call it in question may, if I mistake not, perceive it to involve a manifest contradiction. For,

what are the forementioned objects but the things we perceive by
sense? and what do we perceive besides our own ideas or sensations? and is it not plainly repugnant that any one of these, or any
combination of them, should exist unperceived?

5] If we thoroughly examine this tenet it will, perhaps, be found
at bottom to depend on the doctrine of *abstract ideas*. For can
there be a nicer strain of abstraction than to distinguish the existence of sensible objects from their being perceived, so as to
conceive them existing unperceived? Light and colours, heat and
cold, extension and figures—in a word the things we see and feel
—what are they but so many sensations, notions, ideas, or impressions on the sense? and is it possible to separate, even in thought,
any of these from perception? For my part, I might as easily divide
a thing from itself. I may, indeed, divide in my thoughts, or conceive apart from each other, those things which perhaps I never
perceived by sense so divided. Thus, I imagine the trunk of a
human body without the limbs, or conceive the smell of a rose
without thinking on the rose itself. So far, I will not deny, I can
abstract; if that may properly be called *abstraction* which extends
only to the conceiving separately such objects as it is possible may
really exist or be actually perceived asunder. But my conceiving or
imagining power does not extend beyond the possibility of real
existence or perception. Hence, as it is impossible for me to see or
feel anything without an actual sensation of that thing, so is it
impossible for me to conceive in my thoughts any sensible thing or
object distinct from the sensation or perception of it. [In truth,
the object and the sensation are the same thing, and cannot therefore be abstracted from each other.]

6] Some truths there are so near and obvious to the mind that a
man need only open his eyes to see them. Such I take this important one to be, viz. that all the choir of heaven and furniture
of the earth, in a word all those bodies which compose the mighty
frame of the world, have not any subsistence without a mind; that
their *being* is to be perceived or known; that consequently so long
as they are not actually perceived by me, or do not exist in my
mind, or that of any other created spirit, they must either have no
existence at all, or else subsist in the mind of some Eternal Spirit:
it being perfectly unintelligible, and involving all the absurdity of

abstraction, to attribute to any single part of them an existence independent of a spirit. [To be convinced of which, the reader need only reflect, and try to separate in his own thoughts the *being* of a sensible thing from its *being perceived*.]

7] From what has been said it is evident there is not any other Substance than *Spirit,* or that which perceives. But, for the fuller proof of this point, let it be considered the sensible qualities are colour, figure, motion, smell, taste, and such like, that is, the ideas perceived by sense. Now, for an idea to exist in an unperceiving thing is a manifest contradiction; for to have an idea is all one as to perceive: that therefore wherein colour, figure, and the like qualities exist must perceive them. Hence it is clear there can be no unthinking substance or *substratum* of those ideas.

8] But, say you, though the ideas themselves do not exist without the mind, yet there may be things like them, whereof they are copies or resemblances; which things exist without the mind, in an unthinking substance. I answer, an idea can be like nothing but an idea; a colour or figure can be like nothing but another colour or figure. If we look but never so little into our thoughts, we shall find it impossible for us to conceive a likeness except only between our ideas. Again, I ask whether those supposed *originals,* or external things, of which our ideas are the pictures or representations, be themselves perceiveable or no? If they are, then *they* are ideas, and we have gained our point: but if you say they are not, I appeal to any one whether it be sense to assert a colour is like something which is invisible; hard or soft, like something which is intangible; and so of the rest.

9] Some there are who make a distinction betwixt *primary* and *secondary* qualities. By the former they mean extension, figure, motion, rest, solidity or impenetrability, and number; by the latter they denote all other sensible qualities, as colours, sounds, tastes, and so forth. The ideas we have of these last they acknowledge not to be the resemblances of anything existing without the mind, or unperceived; but they will have our ideas of the *primary qualities* to be patterns or images of things which exist without the mind, in an unthinking substance which they call Matter. By Matter, therefore, we are to understand an inert, senseless sub-

stance, in which extension, figure, and motion do actually subsist.
But it is evident, from what we have already shewn, that extension,
figure and motion are only ideas existing in the mind, and that an
idea can be like nothing but another idea; and that consequently
neither they nor their archetypes can exist in an unperceiving substance. Hence, it is plain that the very notion of what is called
Matter or *corporeal substance,* involves a contradiction in it. [In-
somuch that I should not think it necessary to spend more time in
exposing its absurdity. But, because the tenet of the existence of
Matter seems to have taken so deep a root in the minds of philosophers, and draws after it so many ill consequences, I choose
rather to be thought prolix and tedious than omit anything that
might conduce to the full discovery and extirpation of that prejudice.]

10] They who assert that figure, motion, and the rest of the primary or original qualities do exist without the mind, in unthinking
substances, do at the same time acknowledge that colours, sounds,
heat, cold, and such-like secondary qualities, do not; which they
tell us are sensations, existing in the mind alone, that depend on
and are occasioned by the different size, texture, and motion of the
minute particles of matter. This they take for an undoubted truth,
which they can demonstrate beyond all exception. Now, if it be
certain that those *original* qualities are inseparably united with the
other sensible qualities, and not, even in thought, capable of being
abstracted from them, it plainly follows that *they* exist only in the
mind. But I desire any one to reflect, and try whether he can, by
any abstraction of thought, conceive the extension and motion of
a body without all other sensibles qualities. For my own part, I
see evidently that it is not in my power to frame an idea of a body
extended and moving, but I must withal give it some colour or
other sensible quality, which is acknowledged to exist only in the
mind. In short, extension, figure, and motion, abstracted from all
other qualities, are inconceivable. Where therefore the other sensible qualities are, there must these be also, to wit, in the mind and
nowhere else.

11] Again, *great* and *small, swift* and *slow,* are allowed to exist
nowhere without the mind; being entirely relative, and changing
as the frame or position of the organs of sense varies. The exten-

sion therefore which exists without the mind is neither great nor small, the motion neither swift nor slow; that is, they are nothing at all. But, say you, they are extension in general, and motion in general. Thus we see how much the tenet of extended moveable substances existing without the mind depends on that strange doctrine of *abstract ideas*. And here I cannot but remark how nearly the vague and indeterminate description of Matter, or corporeal substance, which the modern philosophers are run into by their own principles, resembles that antiquated and so much ridiculed notion of *materia prima*, to be met with in Aristotle and his followers. Without extension solidity cannot be conceived: since therefore it has been shewn that extension exists not in an unthinking substance, the same must also be true of solidity.

12] That *number* is entirely the creature of the mind, even though the other qualities be allowed to exist without, will be evident to whoever considers that the same thing bears a different denomination of number as the mind views it with different respects. Thus, the same extension is one, or three, or thirty-six, according as the mind considers it with reference to a yard, a foot, or an inch. Number is so visibly relative, and dependent on men's understanding, that it is strange to think how any one should give it an absolute existence without the mind. We say one book, one page, one line, &c.; all these are equally units, though some contain several of the others. And in each instance, it is plain, the unit relates to some particular combination of ideas *arbitrarily* put together by the mind.

13] Unity I know some will have to be a simple or uncompounded idea, accompanying all other ideas into the mind. That I have any such idea answering the word *unity* I do not find; and if I had, methinks I could not miss finding it; on the contrary, it should be the most familiar to my understanding, since it is said to accompany all other ideas, and to be perceived by all the ways of sensation and reflexion. To say no more, it is an *abstract idea*.

14] I shall farther add, that, after the same manner as modern philosophers prove certain sensible qualities to have no existence in Matter, or without the mind, the same thing may be likewise proved of all other sensible qualities whatsoever. Thus, for in-

stance, it is said that heat and cold are affections only of the mind, and not at all patterns of real beings, existing in the corporeal substances which excite them; for that the same body which appears cold to one hand seems warm to another. Now, why may we not as well argue that figure and extension are not patterns or resemblances of qualities existing in Matter; because to the same eye at different stations, or eyes of a different texture at the same station, they appear various, and cannot therefore be the images of anything settled and determinate without the mind? Again, it is proved that sweetness is not really in the sapid thing; because the thing remaining unaltered the sweetness is changed into bitter, as in case of a fever or otherwise vitiated palate. Is it not as reasonable to say that motion is not without the mind; since if the succession of ideas in the mind become swifter, the motion, it is acknowledged, shall appear slower, without any alteration in any external object?

15] In short, let any one consider those arguments which are thought manifestly to prove that colours and tastes exist only in the mind, and he shall find they may with equal force be brought to prove the same thing of extension, figure, and motion. Though it must be confessed this method of arguing does not so much prove that there is no extension or colour in an outward object, as that we do not know by sense which is the true extension or colour of the object. But the arguments foregoing plainly shew it to be impossible that any colour or extension at all, or other sensible quality whatsoever, should exist in an unthinking subject without the mind, or in truth that there should be any such thing as an outward object.

16] But let us examine a little the received opinion. It is said extension is a *mode* or *accident* of Matter, and that Matter is the *substratum* that supports it. Now I desire that you would explain to me what is meant by Matter's *supporting* extension. Say you, I have no idea of Matter; and therefore cannot explain it. I answer, though you have no positive, yet, if you have any meaning at all, you must at least have a relative idea of Matter; though you know not what it is, yet you must be supposed to know what relation it bears to accidents, and what is meant by its supporting them. It is evident *support* cannot here be taken in its usual or literal sense, as when we say that pillars support a building. In what sense therefore must it be taken? [For my part, I am not able to discover any sense at all that can be applicable to it.]

17] If we inquire into what the most accurate philosophers declare themselves to mean by *material substance,* we shall find them acknowledge they have no other meaning annexed to those sounds but the idea of Being in general, together with the relative motion of its supporting accidents. The general idea of Being appeareth to me the most abstract and incomprehensible of all other; and as for its supporting accidents, this, as we have just now observed, cannot be understood in the common sense of those words: it must therefore be taken in some other sense, but what that is they do not explain. So that when I consider the two parts or branches which make the signification of the words *material substance,* I am convinced there is no distinct meaning annexed to them. But why should we trouble ourselves any farther, in discussing this material *substratum* or support of figure and motion and other sensible qualities? Does it not suppose they have an existence without the mind? And is not this a direct repugnancy, and altogether inconceivable?

18] But, though it were possible that solid, figured, moveable substances may exist without the mind, corresponding to the ideas we have of bodies, yet how is it possible for us to know this? Either we must know it by Sense or by Reason. As for our senses, by them we have the knowledge only of our sensations, ideas, or those things that are immediately perceived by sense, call them what you will: but they do not inform us that things exist without the mind, or unperceived, like to those which are perceived. This the materialists themselves acknowledge.—It remains therefore that if we have any knowledge at all of external things, it must be by reason inferring their existence from what is immediately perceived by sense. But [I do not see] what reason can induce us to believe the existence of bodies without the mind, from what we perceive, since the very patrons of Matter themselves do not pretend there is any necessary connexion betwixt them and our ideas? I say it is granted on all hands (and what happens in dreams, frensies, and the like, puts it beyond dispute) that it is possible we might be affected with all the ideas we have now, though no bodies existed

without resembling them. Hence it is evident the supposition of external bodies is not necessary for the producing our ideas; since it is granted they are produced sometimes, and might possibly be produced always, in the same order we see them in at present, without their concurrence.

19] But, though we might possibly have all our sensations without them, yet perhaps it may be thought easier to conceive and explain the manner of their production, by supposing external bodies in their likeness rather than otherwise; and so it might be at least probable there are such things as bodies that excite their ideas in our minds. But neither can this be said. For, though we give the materialists their external bodies, they by their own confession are never the nearer knowing how our ideas are produced; since they own themselves unable to comprehend in what manner body can act upon spirit, or how it is possible it should imprint any idea in the mind. Hence it is evident the production of ideas or sensations in our minds, can be no reason why we should suppose Matter or corporeal substances; since that is acknowledged to remain equally inexplicable with or without this supposition. If therefore it were possible for bodies to exist without the mind, yet to hold they do so must needs be a very precarious opinion; since it is to suppose, without any reason at all, that God has created innumerable beings that are entirely useless, and serve to no manner of purpose.

20] In short, if there were external bodies, it is impossible we should ever come to know it; and if there were not, we might have the very same reasons to think there were that we have now. Suppose—what no one can deny possible—an intelligence, without the help of external bodies, to be affected with the same train of sensations or ideas that you are, imprinted in the same order and with like vividness in his mind. I ask whether that intelligence hath not all the reason to believe the existence of Corporeal Substances, represented by his ideas, and exciting them in his mind, that you can possibly have for believing the same thing? Of this there can be no question. Which one consideration were enough to make any reasonable person suspect the strength of whatever arguments he may think himself to have, for the existence of bodies without the mind.

21] Were it necessary to add any farther proof against the existence of Matter, after what has been said, I could instance several
of those errors and difficulties (not to mention impieties) which
have sprung from that tenet. It has occasioned numberless controversies and disputes in philosophy, and not a few of far greater
moment in religion. But I shall not enter into the detail of them
in this place, as well because I think arguments *a posteriori* are
unnecessary for confirming what has been, if I mistake not, sufficiently demonstrated *a priori,* as because I shall hereafter find
occasion to speak somewhat of them.

22] I am afraid I have given cause to think I am needlessly prolix
in handling this subject. For, to what purpose is it to dilate on that
which may be demonstrated with the utmost evidence in a line or
two, to any one that is capable of the least reflexion? It is but looking into your own thoughts, and so trying whether you can conceive it possible for a sound, or figure, or motion, or colour to
exist without the mind or unperceived. This easy trial may perhaps make you see that what you contend for is a downright contradiction. Insomuch that I am content to put the whole upon this
issue:—If you can but conceive it possible for one extended moveable substance, or in general for any one idea, or anything like an
idea, to exist otherwise than in a mind perceiving it, I shall readily
give up the cause. And, as for all that compages of external bodies
you contend for, I shall grant you its existence, though you cannot either give me any reason why you believe it exists, or assign
any use to it when it is supposed to exist. I say, the bare possibility
of your opinions being true shall pass for an argument that it is so.

23] But, say you, surely there is nothing easier than for me to
imagine trees, for instance, in a park, or books existing in a closet,
and nobody by to perceive them. I answer, you may so, there is no
difficulty in it. But what is all this, I beseech you, more than framing in your mind certain ideas which you call *books* and *trees,* and
at the same time omitting to frame the idea of any one that may
perceive them? But do not you yourself perceive or think of them
all the while? This therefore is nothing to the purpose: it only
shews you have the power of imagining, or forming ideas in your
mind; but it does not shew that you can conceive it possible the
objects of your thought may exist without the mind. To make out

this, it is necessary that you conceive them existing unconceived or unthought of; which is a manifest repugnancy. When we do our utmost to conceive the existence of external bodies, we are all the while only contemplating our own ideas. But the mind, taking no notice of itself, is deluded to think it can and does conceive bodies existing unthought of, or without the mind, though at the same time they are apprehended by, or exist in, itself. A little attention will discover to any one the truth and evidence of what is here said, and make it unnecessary to insist on any other proofs against the existence of *material substance*.

24] [Could men but forbear to amuse themselves with words, we should, I believe, soon come to an agreement in this point.] It is very obvious, upon the least inquiry into our own thoughts, to know whether it be possible for us to understand what is meant by the *absolute existence of sensible objects in themselves*, or *without the mind*. To me it is evident those words mark out either a direct contradiction, or else nothing at all. And to convince others of this, I know no readier or fairer way than to entreat they would calmly attend to their own thoughts; and if by this attention the emptiness or repugnancy of those expressions does appear, surely nothing more is requisite for their conviction. It is on this therefore that I insist, to wit, that the *absolute existence of unthinking things* are words without a meaning, or which include a contradiction. This is what I repeat and inculcate, and earnestly recommend to the attentive thoughts of the reader.

25] All our ideas, sensations, notions, or the things which we perceive, by whatsoever names they may be distinguished, are visibly inactive: there is nothing of power or agency included in them. So that one idea or object of thought cannot produce or make any alteration in another. To be satisfied of the truth of this, there is nothing else requisite but a bare observation of our ideas. For, since they and every part of them exist only in the mind, it follows that there is nothing in them but what is perceived: but whoever shall attend to his ideas, whether of sense or reflexion, will not perceive in them any power or activity; there is, therefore, no such thing contained in them. A little attention will discover to us that the very being of an idea implies passiveness and inertness in it; insomuch that it is impossible for an idea to do anything, or, strictly speaking, to be the cause of anything: neither can it be the resemblance or pattern of any active being, as is evident from sect. 8. Whence it plainly follows that extension, figure, and motion cannot be the cause of our sensations. To say, therefore, that these are the effects of powers resulting from the configuration, number, motion, and size of corpuscles, must certainly be false.

26] We perceive a continual succession of ideas; some are anew excited, others are changed or totally disappear. There is therefore, *some* cause of these ideas, whereon they depend, and which produces and changes them. That this cause cannot be any quality or idea or combination of *ideas,* is clear from the preceding section. It must therefore be a *substance;* but it has been shewn that there is no corporeal or material substance: it remains therefore that the cause of ideas is an incorporeal active substance or Spirit.

27] A Spirit is one simple, undivided, active being—as it perceives ideas it is called the *understanding,* and as it produces or otherwise operates about them it is called the *will.* Hence there can be no *idea* formed of a soul or spirit; for all ideas whatever, being passive and inert (vid. sect. 25), they cannot represent unto us, by way of image or likeness, that which acts. A little attention will make it plain to any one, that to have an idea which shall be *like* that active Principle of motion and change of ideas is absolutely impossible. Such is the nature of Spirit, or that which acts, that it cannot be of itself perceived, but only by the effects which it produceth. If any man shall doubt of the truth of what is here delivered, let him but reflect and try if he can frame the idea of any power or active being; and whether he has ideas of two principal powers, marked by the names *will* and *understanding,* distinct from each other, as well as from a third idea of Substance or Being in general, with a relative notion of its supporting or being the subject of the aforesaid powers—which is signified by the name *soul* or *spirit.* This is what some hold; but, so far as I can see, the words *will,* [*understanding, mind,*] *soul, spirit,* do not stand for different ideas, or, in truth, for any idea at all, but for something which is very different from ideas, and which, being an agent, cannot be like unto, or represented by, any idea whatsoever. [Though it must be owned at the same time that we have some *notion* of soul, spirit, and the operations of the mind, such as willing, loving, hating—inasmuch as we know or understand the meaning of these words.]

28] I find I can excite ideas in my mind at pleasure, and vary and shift the scene as oft as I think fit. It is no more than *willing,* and straightway this or that idea arises in my fancy; and by the same power it is obliterated and makes way for another. This making and unmaking of ideas doth very properly denominate the mind active. Thus much is certain and grounded on experience: but when we talk of unthinking agents, or of exciting ideas exclusive of volition, we only amuse ourselves with words.

29] But, whatever power I may have over my own thoughts, I find the ideas actually perceived by Sense have not a like dependence of *my* will. When in broad daylight I open my eyes, it is not in my power to choose whether I shall see or no, or to determine what particular objects shall present themselves to my view: and so likewise as to the hearing and other senses; the ideas imprinted on them are not creatures of *my* will. There is therefore some other Will or Spirit that produces them.

30] The ideas of Sense are more strong, lively, and distinct than those of the Imagination; they have likewise a steadiness, order, and coherence, and are not excited at random, as those which are the effects of human wills often are, but in a regular train or series —the admirable connexion whereof sufficiently testifies the wisdom and benevolence of its Author. Now the set rules, or established methods, wherein the Mind we depend on excites in us the ideas of Sense, are called *the laws of nature*; and these we learn by experience, which teaches us that such and such ideas are attended with such and such other ideas, in the ordinary course of things.

31] This gives us a sort of foresight, which enables us to regulate our actions for the benefit of life. And without this we should be eternally at a loss: we could not know how to act anything that might procure us the least pleasure, or remove the least pain of sense. That food nourishes, sleep refreshes, and fire warms us; that to sow in the seed-time is the way to reap in the harvest; and in general that to obtain such or such ends, such or such means are conducive—all this we know, not by discovering any *necessary connexion* between our ideas, but only by the observation of the *settled laws* of nature; without which we should be all in uncertainty and confusion, and a grown man no more know how to manage himself in the affairs of life than an infant just born.

32] And yet this consistent uniform working, which so evidently displays the Goodness and Wisdom of that Governing Spirit whose Will constitutes the laws of nature, is so far from leading our thoughts to Him, that it rather sends them wandering after second causes. For, when we perceive certain ideas of Sense constantly followed by other ideas, and we know this is not of our own doing, we forthwith attribute power and agency to the ideas themselves, and make one the cause of another, than which nothing can be more absurd and unintelligible. Thus, for example, having observed that when we perceive by sight a certain round luminous figure, we at the same time perceive by touch the idea or sensation called heat, we do from thence conclude the sun to be the *cause* of heat. And in like manner perceiving the motion and collision of bodies to be attended with sound, we are inclined to think the latter the *effect* of the former.

33] The ideas imprinted on the Senses by the Author of nature are called *real things:* and those excited in the imagination, being less regular, vivid, and constant, are more properly termed *ideas* or *images of* things, which they copy and represent. But then our *sensations,* be they never so vivid and distinct, are nevertheless ideas: that is, they exist in the mind, or are perceived by it, as truly as the ideas of its own framing. The ideas of Sense are allowed to have more reality in them, that is, to be more strong, orderly, and coherent than the creatures of the mind; but this is no argument that they exist without the mind. They are also less dependent on the spirit or thinking substance which perceives them, in that they are excited by the will of another and more powerful Spirit: yet still they are *ideas:* and certainly no idea, whether faint or strong, can exist otherwise than in a mind perceiving it.

34] Before we proceed any farther it is necessary we spend some time in answering Objections which may probably be made against the Principles we have hitherto laid down. In doing of which, if I seem too prolix to those of quick apprehensions, I desire I may be excused, since all men do not equally apprehend things of this nature; and I am willing to be understood by every one.

First, then, it will be objected that by the foregoing principles all that is real and substantial in nature is banished out of the world, and instead thereof a chimerical scheme of *ideas* takes place. All things that exist exist only in the mind; that is, they are purely notional. What therefore becomes of the sun, moon, and stars? What must we think of houses, rivers, mountains, trees, stones; nay, even of our own bodies? Are all these but so many chimeras and illusions on the fancy?—To all which, and whatever else of the same sort may be objected, I answer, that by the Principles premised we are not deprived of any one thing in nature. Whatever we see, feel, hear, or any wise conceive or understand, remains as secure as ever, and is as real as ever. There is a *rerum natura,* and the distinction between realities and chimeras retains its full force. This is evident from sect. 29, 30, and 33, where we have shewn what is meant by *real things,* in opposition to *chimeras* or *ideas of our own framing;* but then they both equally exist in the mind, and in that sense are alike *ideas.*

35] I do not argue against the existence of any one thing that we can apprehend, either by sense or reflection. That the things I see with my eyes and touch with my hands do exist, really exist, I make not the least question. The only thing whose existence we deny is that which *philosophers* call Matter or corporeal substance. And in doing of this there is no damage done to the rest of mankind, who, I dare say, will never miss it. The Atheist indeed will want the colour of an empty name to support his impiety; and the Philosophers may possibly find they have lost a great handle for trifling and disputation. [But that is all the harm that I can see done.]

36] If any man thinks this detracts from the existence or reality of things, he is very far from understanding what hath been premised in the plainest terms I could think of. Take here an abstract of what has been said:—There are spiritual substances, minds, or human souls, which will or excite ideas in themselves at pleasure; but these are faint, weak, and unsteady in respect of others they perceive by sense: which, being impressed upon them according to certain rules or laws of nature, speak themselves the effects of a

Mind more powerful and wise than human spirits. These latter are said to have *more reality* in them than the former;—by which is meant that they are more affecting, orderly, and distinct, and that they are not fictions of the mind perceiving them. And in this sense the sun that I see by day is the real sun, and that which I imagine by night is the idea of the former. In the sense here given of *reality,* it is evident that every vegetable, star, mineral, and in general each part of the mundane system, is as much a *real being* by our principles as by any other. Whether others mean anything by the term *reality* different from what I do, I entreat them to look into their own thoughts and see.

37] It will be urged that thus much at least is true, to wit, that we take away all *corporeal substances.* To this my answer is, that if the word *substance* be taken in the vulgar sense, for a *combination* of sensible qualities, such as extension, solidity, weight, and the like—this we cannot be accused of taking away: but if it be taken in a philosophic sense, for the support of accidents or qualities without the mind—then indeed I acknowledge that we take it away, if one may be said to take away that which never had any existence, not even in the imagination.

38] But after all, say you, it sounds very harsh to say we eat and drink ideas, and are clothed with ideas. I acknowledge it does so— the word *idea* not being used in common discourse to signify the several combinations of sensible qualities which are called *things;* and it is certain that any expression which varies from the familiar use of language will seem harsh and ridiculous. But this doth not concern the truth of the proposition, which in other words is no more than to say, we are fed and clothed with those things which we perceive immediately by our senses. The hardness or softness, the colour, taste, warmth, figure, and suchlike qualities, which combined together constitute the several sorts of victuals and apparel, have been shewn to exist only in the mind that perceives them: and this is all that is meant by calling them *ideas;* which word, if it was as ordinarily used as *thing,* would sound no harsher nor more ridiculous than it. I am not for disputing about the propriety, but the truth of the expression. If therefore you agree with me that we eat and drink and are clad with the immediate objects of sense, which cannot exist unperceived or without the mind, I shall readily grant it is more proper or conformable to custom that they should be called *things* rather than *ideas*.

39] If it be demanded why I make use of the word *idea,* and do not rather in compliance with custom call them *things*; I answer, I do it for two reasons:—First, because the term *thing,* in contradistinction to *idea,* is generally supposed to denote somewhat existing without the mind: Secondly, because *thing* hath a more comprehensive signification than *idea,* including spirits, or thinking things, as well as ideas. Since therefore the objects of sense exist only in the mind, and are withal thoughtless and inactive, I chose to mark them by the word *idea*; which implies those properties.

40] But, say what we can, some one perhaps may be apt to reply, he will still believe his senses, and never suffer any arguments, how plausible soever, to prevail over the certainty of them. Be it so; assert the evidence of sense as high as you please, we are willing to do the same. That what I see, hear, and feel doth exist, that is to say, is perceived by me, I no more doubt than I do of my own being. But I do not see how the testimony of sense can be alleged as a proof for the existence of anything which is *not* perceived by sense. We are not for having any man turn sceptic and disbelieve his senses; on the contrary, we give them all the stress and assurance imaginable; nor are there any principles more opposite to Scepticism than those we have laid down, as shall be hereafter clearly shewn.

41] *Secondly,* it will be objected that there is a great difference betwixt real fire for instance, and the idea of fire, betwixt dreaming or imagining oneself burnt, and actually being so. [If you suspect it to be only the idea of fire which you see, do but put your hand into it and you will be convinced with a witness.] This and the like may be urged in opposition to our tenets.—To all which the answer is evident from what hath been already said; and I shall only add in this place, that if real fire be very different from the idea of fire, so also is the real pain that it occasions very different from the idea of the same pain, and yet nobody will pretend that real pain either is, or can possibly be, in an unperceiving thing, or without the mind, any more than its idea.

42] *Thirdly,* it will be objected that we see things actually without or at a distance from us, and which consequently do not exist in the mind; it being absurd that those things which are seen at the distance of several miles should be as near to us as our own thoughts.—In answer to this, I desire it may be considered that in a dream we do oft perceive things as existing at a great distance off, and yet for all that, those things are acknowledged to have their existence only in the mind.

43] But, for the fuller clearing of this point, it may be worth while to consider how it is that we perceive distance, and things placed at a distance, by sight. For, that we should in truth *see* external space, and bodies actually existing in it, some nearer, others farther off, seems to carry with it some opposition to what hath been said of their existing nowhere without the mind. The consideration of this difficulty it was that gave birth to my *Essay towards a New Theory of Vision,* which was published not long since. Wherein it is shewn that distance or outness is neither immediately of itself perceived by sight, nor yet apprehended or judged of by lines and angles, or anything that hath a necessary connexion with it; but that it is only suggested to our thoughts by certain visible ideas, and sensations attending vision, which in their own nature have no manner of similitude or relation either with distance or things placed at a distance; but, by a connexion taught us by experience, they come to signify and suggest them to us, after the same manner that words of any language suggest the ideas they are made to stand for. Insomuch that a man born blind, and afterwards made to see, would not, at first sight, think the things he saw to be without his mind, or at any distance from him. See sect. 41 of the forementioned treatise.

44] The ideas of sight and touch make two species entirely distinct and heterogeneous. The former are marks and prognostics of the latter. That the proper objects of sight neither exist without the mind, nor are the images of external things, was shewn even in that treatise. Though throughout the same the contrary be supposed true of *tangible objects;*—not that to suppose that vulgar error was necessary for establishing the notion therein laid down, but because it was beside my purpose to examine and refute it, in a discourse concerning *Vision.* So that in strict truth the ideas of sight, when we apprehend by them distance, and things placed at a distance, do not suggest or mark out to us things actually existing at a distance, but only admonish us what ideas of touch will be imprinted in our minds at such and such distances of time, and in consequence of such or such actions. It is, I say, evident, from what has been said in the foregoing parts of this Treatise, and in sect. 147 and elsewhere of the Essay concerning Vision, that visible ideas are the Language whereby the Governing Spirit on whom we depend informs us what tangible ideas he is about to imprint upon us, in case we excite this or that motion in our own bodies. But for a fuller information in this point I refer to the Essay itself.

45] *Fourthly,* it will be objected that from the foregoing principles it follows things are every moment annihilated and created anew. The objects of sense exist only when they are perceived: the trees therefore are in the garden, or the chairs in the parlour, no longer than while there is somebody by to perceive them. Upon shutting my eyes all the furniture in the room is reduced to nothing, and barely upon opening them it is again created.—In answer to all which, I refer the reader to what has been said in sect. 3, 4, &c.; and desire he will consider whether he means anything by the actual existence of an idea distinct from its being perceived. For my part, after the nicest inquiry I could make, I am not able to discover that anything else is meant by those words; and I once more entreat the reader to sound his own thoughts, and not suffer himself to be imposed on by words. If he can conceive it possible either for his ideas or their archetypes to exist without being perceived, then I give up the cause. But if he cannot, he will acknowledge it is unreasonable for him to stand up in defence of he knows not what, and pretend to charge on me as an absurdity, the not assenting to those propositions which at bottom have no meaning in them.

46] It will not be amiss to observe how far the received principles of philosophy are themselves chargeable with those pretended absurdities. It is thought strangely absurd that upon closing my eyelids all the visible objects around me should be reduced to nothing; and yet is not this what philosophers commonly acknowledge, when they agree on all hands that light and colours, which alone are the proper and immediate objects of sight, are mere sen-

sations that exist no longer than they are perceived? Again, it may
to some perhaps seem very incredible that things should be every
moment creating; yet this very notion is commonly taught in the
schools. For the Schoolmen, though they acknowledge the existence of Matter, and that the whole mundane fabric is framed out
of it, are nevertheless of opinion that it cannot subsist without
the divine conservation; which by them is expounded to be a continual creation.

47] Farther, a little thought will discover to us that, though we
allow the existence of Matter or corporeal substance, yet it will
unavoidably follow, from the principles which are now generally
admitted, that the particular bodies, of what kind soever, do none
of them exist whilst they are not perceived. For, it is evident, from
sect. 11 and the following sections, that the Matter philosophers
contend for is an incomprehensible Somewhat, which hath none
of those particular qualities whereby the bodies falling under our
senses are distinguished one from another. But, to make this more
plain, it must be remarked that the infinite divisibility of Matter
is now universally allowed, at least by the most approved and considerable philosophers, who on the received principles demonstrate
it beyond all exception. Hence, it follows there is an infinite
number of parts in each particle of Matter which are not perceived
by sense. The reason therefore that any particular body seems to
be of a finite magnitude, or exhibits only a finite number of parts
to sense, is, not because it contains no more, since in itself it contains an infinite number of parts, but because the sense is not acute
enough to discern them. In proportion therefore as the sense is
rendered more acute, it perceives a greater number of parts in
the object, that is, the object appears greater; and its figure varies,
those parts in its extremities which were before unperceivable appearing now to bound it in very different lines and angles from
those perceived by an obtuser sense. And at length, after various
changes of size and shape, when the sense becomes infinitely acute,
the body shall seem infinite. During all which there is no alteration in the body, but only in the sense. Each body therefore,
considered in itself, is infinitely extended, and consequently void
of all shape and figure. From which it follows that, though we
should grant the existence of Matter to be never so certain, yet it

is withal as certain, the materialists themselves are by their own principles forced to acknowledge, that neither the particular bodies perceived by sense, nor anything like them, exists without the mind. Matter, I say, and each particle thereof, is according to them infinite and shapeless; and it is the mind that frames all that variety of bodies which compose the visible world, any one whereof does not exist longer than it is perceived.

48] But, after all, if we consider it, the objection proposed in sect. 45 will not be found reasonably charged on the Principles we have premised, so as in truth to make any objection at all against our notions. For, though we hold indeed the objects of sense to be nothing else but ideas which cannot exist unperceived, yet we may not hence conclude they have no existence except only while they are perceived by *us;* since there may be some other spirit that perceives them though we do not. Wherever bodies are said to have no existence without the mind, I would not be understood to mean this or that particular mind, but all minds whatsoever. It does not therefore follow from the foregoing Principles that bodies are annihilated and created every moment, or exist not at all during the intervals between *our* perception of them.

49] *Fifthly*, it may perhaps be objected that if extension and figure exist only in the mind, it follows that the mind is extended and figured; since extension is a mode or attribute which (to speak with the Schools) is predicated of the subject in which it exists.— I answer, those qualities are in the mind only as they are perceived by it;—that is, not by way of *mode* or *attribute,* but only by way of *idea*. And it no more follows the soul or mind is extended, because extension exists in it alone, than it does that it is red or blue, because those colours are on all hands acknowledged to exist in it, and nowhere else. As to what philosophers say of subject and mode, that seems very groundless and unintelligible. For instance, in this proposition "a die is hard, extended, and square," they will have it that the word *die* denotes a subject or substance, distinct from the hardness, extension, and figure which are predicated of it, and in which they exist. This I cannot comprehend: to me a die seems to be nothing distinct from those things which are termed its modes or accidents. And, to say a die is hard, extended, and square is not to attribute those qualities to a subject distinct from and supporting them, but only an explication of the meaning of the word *die*.

50] *Sixthly*, you will say there have been a great many things explained by matter and motion; take away these and you destroy the whole corpuscular philosophy, and undermine those mechanical principles which have been applied with so much success to account for the phenomena. In short, whatever advances have been made, either by accident or modern philosophers, in the study of nature do all proceed on the supposition that corporeal substance or Matter doth really exist.—To this I answer that there is not any one phenomenon explained on that supposition which may not as well be explained without it, as might easily be made appear by an induction of particulars. To explain the phenomena, is all one as to shew why, upon such and such occasions, we are affected with such and such ideas. But how Matter should operate on a Spirit, or produce any idea in it, is what no philosopher will pretend to explain; it is therefore evident there can be no use of Matter in natural philosophy. Besides, they who attempt to account for things do it, not by corporeal substance, but by figure, motion, and other qualities; which are in truth no more than mere ideas, and therefore cannot be the cause of anything, as hath been already shewn. See sect. 25.

51] *Seventhly*, it will upon this be demanded whether it does not seem absurd to take away natural causes, and ascribe everything to the immediate operation of spirits? We must no longer say upon these principles that fire heats, or water cools, but that a spirit heats, and so forth. Would not a man be deservedly laughed at, who should talk after this manner?—I answer, he would so: in such things we ought to think with the learned, and speak with the vulgar. They who to demonstration are convinced of the truth of the Copernican system do nevertheless say "the sun rises," "the sun sets," or "comes to the meridian"; and if they affected a contrary style in common talk it would without doubt appear very ridiculous. A little reflection on what is here said will make it manifest that the common use of language would receive no manner of alteration or disturbance from the admission of our tenets. . . .

85] Having done with the Objections, which I endeavoured to propose in the clearest light, and gave them all the force and weight I could, we proceed in the next place to take a view of our tenets in their Consequences. Some of these appear at first sight—as that several difficult and obscure questions, on which abundance of speculation has been thrown away, are entirely banished from philosophy. Whether corporeal substance can think? Whether Matter be infinitely divisible? And how it operates on spirit?—these and the like inquiries have given infinite amusement to philosophers in all ages. But, depending on the existence of Matter, they have no longer any place on our Principles. Many other advantages there are, as well with regard to religion as the sciences, which it is easy for any one to deduce from what has been premised. But this will appear more plainly in the sequel.

86] From the Principles we have laid down it follows human knowledge may naturally be reduced to two heads—that of *ideas* and that of *Spirits*. Of each of these I shall treat in order.

And First as to *ideas,* or *unthinking things.* Our knowledge of these has been very much obscured and confounded, and we have been led into very dangerous errors, by supposing a two-fold existence of sense—the one *intelligible* or in the mind, the other *real* and without the mind. Whereby unthinking things are thought to have a natural subsistence of their own, distinct from being perceived by spirits. This, which, if I mistake not, hath been shewn to be a most groundless and absurd notion, is the very root of Scepticism; for, so long as men thought that real things subsisted without the mind, and that their knowledge was only so far forth *real* as it was *conformable to real things,* it follows they could not be certain that they had any real knowledge at all. For how can it be known that the things which are perceived are conformable to those which are not perceived, or exist without the mind?

87] Colour, figure, motion, extension, and the like, considered only as so many *sensations* in the mind, are perfectly known; there being nothing in them which is not perceived. But, if they are looked on as notes or images, referred to *things* or *archetypes existing without the mind,* then are we involved all in scepticism. We see only the appearances, and not the real qualities of things. What may be the extension, figure, or motion of anything really and absolutely, or in itself, it is impossible for us to know, but only the proportion or relation they bear to our senses. Things remaining the same, our ideas vary; and which of them, or even whether any of them at all, represent the true quality really existing in the thing, it is out of our reach to determine. So that, for aught we know, all we see, hear, and feel, may be only phantom and vain chimera, and not at all agree with the real things existing in *rerum natura*. All this scepticism follows from our supposing a difference between *things* and *ideas,* and that the former have a subsistence without the mind, or unperceived. It were easy to dilate on this subject, and shew how the arguments urged by sceptics in all ages depend on the supposition of external objects. [But this is too obvious to need being insisted on.]

88] So long as we attribute a real existence to unthinking things, distinct from their being perceived, it is not only impossible for us to know with evidence the nature of any real unthinking being, but even that it exists. Hence it is that we see philosophers distrust their senses, and doubt of the existence of heaven and earth, of everything they see or feel, even of their own bodies. And after all their labouring and struggle of thought, they are forced to own we cannot attain to any self-evident or demonstrative knowledge of the existence of sensible things. But, all this doubtfulness, which so bewilders and confounds the mind and makes philosophy ridiculous in the eyes of the world, vanishes if we annex a meaning to our words, and do not amuse ourselves with the terms *absolute, external, exist,* and such like, signifying we know not what. I can as well doubt of my own being as of the being of those things which I actually perceive by sense: it being a manifest contradiction that any sensible object should be immediately perceived by sight or touch, and at the same time have no existence in nature; since the very existence of an *unthinking being* consists in *being perceived.*

89] Nothing seems of more importance towards erecting a firm system of sound and real knowledge, which may be proof against the assaults of Scepticism, than to lay the beginning in a distinct explication of *what is meant* by *thing, reality, existence;* for in vain shall we dispute concerning the real existence of things, or pretend to any knowledge thereof, so long as we have not fixed the meaning of those words. *Thing* or *being* is the most general name of all: it comprehends under it two kinds, entirely distinct and heterogeneous, and which have nothing common but the name, viz. *spirits* and *ideas*. The former are active, indivisible, [incorruptible] substances: the latter are inert, fleeting, [perishable passions,] or dependent beings; which subsist not by themselves, but are supported by, or exist in, minds or spiritual substances.

[We comprehend our own existence by inward feeling or reflection, and that of other spirits by reason. We may be said to have some knowledge or *notion* of our own minds, of spirits and active beings; whereof in a strict sense we have not *ideas*. In like manner, we know and have a *notion* of relations between things or ideas; which relations are distinct from the ideas or things related, inasmuch as the latter may be perceived by us without our perceiving the former. To me it seems that *ideas, spirits,* and *relations* are all in their respective kinds the object of human knowledge and subject of discourse; and that the term *idea* would be improperly extended to signify *everything* we know or have any notion of.]

90] Ideas imprinted on the senses are *real* things, or do really exist: this we do not deny; but we deny they *can* subsist without the minds which perceive them, or that they are resemblances of any archetypes existing without the mind; since the very being of a sensation or idea consists in being perceived, and an idea can be like nothing but an idea. Again, the things perceived by sense may be termed *external,* with regard to their origin; in that they are not generated from within by the mind itself, but imprinted by a Spirit distinct from that which perceives them. Sensible objects may likewise be said to be "without the mind" in another sense, namely when they exist in some other mind. Thus, when I shut my eyes, the things I saw may still exist; but it must be in another mind.

91] It were a mistake to think that what is here said derogates in the least from the reality of things. It is acknowledged, on the received principles, that extension, motion, and in a word all sensible qualities, have need of a support, as not being able to subsist by themselves. But the objects perceived by sense are allowed to be nothing but combinations of those qualities, and consequently cannot subsist by themselves. Thus far it is agreed on all hands. So that in denying the things perceived by sense an existence independent of a substance or support wherein they may exist, we detract nothing from the received opinion of their *reality,* and are guilty of no innovaton in that respect. All the difference is that, according to us, the unthinking beings perceived by sense have no existence distinct from being perceived, and cannot therefore exist in any other substance than those unextended indivisible substances, or *spirits,* which act, and think and perceive them. Whereas philosophers vulgarly hold that the sensible qualities do exist in an inert, extended, unperceiving Substance, which they call *Matter,* to which they attribute a natural subsistence, exterior to all thinking beings, or distinct from being perceived by any mind whatsoever, even the Eternal Mind of the Creator; wherein they suppose only Ideas of the corporeal substances created by Him: if indeed they allow them to be at all *created.*

92] For, as we have shewn the doctrine of Matter or Corporeal Substance to have been the main pillar and support of Scepticism, so likewise upon the same foundation have been raised all the impious schemes of Atheism and Irreligion. Nay, so great a difficulty has it been thought to conceive Matter produced out of nothing, that the most celebrated among the ancient philosophers, even of those who maintained the being of a God, have thought Matter to be uncreated and co-eternal with Him. How great a friend *material substance* has been to Atheists in all ages were needless to relate. All their monstrous systems have so visible and necessary a dependence on it, that when this cornerstone is once removed, the whole fabric cannot choose but fall to the ground; insomuch that it is no longer worth while to bestow a particular consideration on the absurdities of every wretched sect of Atheists.

93] That impious and profane persons should readily fall in with those systems which favour their inclinations, by deriding *immaterial substance,* and supposing the soul to be divisible, and subject to corruption as the body; which exclude all freedom, intelligence, and design from the formation of things, and instead thereof make a self-existent, stupid, unthinking substance the root and origin of all beings; that they should hearken to those who deny a Providence, or inspection of a Superior Mind, over the affairs of the world, attributing the whole series of events either to blind chance or fatal necessity, arising from the impulse of one body on another —all this is very natural. And, on the other hand, when men of better principles observe the enemies of religion lay so great a stress on *unthinking Matter,* and all of them use so much industry and artifice to reduce everything to it; methinks they should rejoice to see them deprived of their grand support, and driven from that only fortress, without which your Epicureans, Hobbists, and the like, have not even the shadow of a pretence, but become the most cheap and easy triumph in the world.

94] The existence of Matter, or bodies unperceived, has not only been the main support of Atheists and Fatalists, but on the same principle doth Idolatry likewise in all its various forms depend. Did men but consider that the sun, moon, and stars, and every other object of the senses, are only so many sensations in their minds, which have no other existence but barely being perceived, doubtless they would never fall down and worship *their own ideas;* but rather address their homage to that Eternal Invisible Mind which produces and sustains all things.

95] The same absurd principle, by mingling itself with the articles of our faith, hath occasioned no small difficulties to Christians. For example, about the Resurrection, how many scruples and objections have been raised by Socinians and others? But do not the most plausible of them depend on the supposition that a body is denominated the *same,* with regard not to the form, or that which is perceived by sense, but the material substance, which remains the same under several forms? Take away this *material substance*— about the identity whereof all the dispute is—and mean by *body* what every plain ordinary person means by that word, to wit, that which is immediately seen and felt, which is only a combination of sensible qualities or ideas: and then their most unanswerable objections come to nothing.

96] Matter being once expelled out of nature drags with it so many sceptical and impious notions, such an incredible number of disputes and puzzling questions, which have been thorns in the sides of divines as well as philosophers, and made so much fruitless work for mankind, that if the arguments we have produced against it are not found equal to demonstration (as to me they evidently seem), yet I am sure all friends to knowledge, peace, and religion have reason to wish they were.

97] Beside the external existence of the objects of perception, another great source of errors and difficulties with regard to ideal knowledge is the doctrine of *abstract ideas,* such as it hath been set forth in the Introduction. The plainest things in the world, those we are most intimately acquainted with and perfectly know, when they are considered in an abstract way, appear strangely difficult and incomprehensible. Time, place, and motion, taken in particular or concrete, are what everybody knows; but, having passed through the hands of a metaphysician, they become too abstract and fine to be apprehended by men of ordinary sense. Bid your servant meet you at such a *time,* in such a *place,* and he shall never stay to deliberate on the meaning of those words. In conceiving that particular time and place, or the motion by which he is to get thither, he finds not the least difficulty. But if *time* be taken exclusive of all those particular actions and ideas that diversify the day, merely for the continuation of existence or duration in abstract, then it will perhaps gravel even a philosopher to comprehend it.

98] For my own part, whenever I attempt to frame a simple idea of *time,* abstracted from the succession of ideas in my mind, which flows uniformly, and is participated by all beings, I am lost and embrangled in inextricable difficulties. I have no notion of it at all: only I hear others say it is infinitely divisible, and speak of it in such a manner as leads me to harbour odd thoughts of my existence: since that doctrine lays one under an absolute necessity of thinking, either that he passes away innumerable ages without a thought, or else that he is annihilated every moment of his life: both which seem equally absurd. Time therefore being nothing, abstracted from the succession of ideas in our minds, it follows that the duration of any finite spirit must be estimated by the number of ideas or actions succeeding each other in that same spirit of mind. Hence, it is a plain consequence that the soul always thinks. And in truth whoever shall go about to divide in his thoughts or abstract the *existence* of a spirit from its *cogitation,* will, I believe, find it no easy task.

99] So likewise when we attempt to abstract *extension* and *motion* from all other qualities, and consider them by themselves, we presently lose sight of them, and run into great extravagances. [Hence spring those odd paradoxes, that the fire is not hot, nor the wall white; or that heat and colour are in the objects nothing but figure and motion.] All which depend on a two-fold abstraction: first, it is supposed that extension, for example, may be abstracted from all other sensible qualities; and, secondly, that the entity of extension may be abstracted from its being perceived. But, whoever shall reflect, and take care to understand what he says, will, if I mistake not, acknowledge that all sensible qualities are alike *sensations,* and alike *real;* that where the extension is, there is the colour too, to wit, in his mind, and that their archetypes can exist only in some other *mind:* and that the objects of sense are nothing but those sensations, combined, blended, or (if one may so speak) concreted together; none of all which can be supposed to exist unperceived. [And that consequently the wall is as truly white as it is extended, and in the same sense.]

100] What it is for a man to be happy, or an object good, every one may think he knows. But to frame an abstract idea of happiness, prescinded from all particular pleasure, or of goodness from everything that is good, this is what few can pretend to. So likewise a man may be just and virtuous without having precise ideas of justice and virtue. The opinion that those and the like words stand for general notions, abstracted from all particular persons and actions, seems to have rendered morality difficult, and the study thereof of less use to mankind. [And in effect one may make a great progress in school-ethics without ever being the wiser or better man for it, or knowing how to behave himself in the affairs of life more to the advantage of himself or his neighbours than he did before.] And in effect the doctrine of *abstraction* has not a little contributed towards spoiling the most useful parts of knowledge.

101] The two great provinces of speculative science conversant about ideas received from sense and their relations, are Natural Philosophy and Mathematics. With regard to each of these I shall make some observations.

And first I shall say somewhat of Natural Philosophy. On this subject it is that the sceptics triumph. All that stock of arguments they produce to depreciate our faculties and make mankind appear ignorant and low, are drawn principally from this head, namely, that we are under an invincible blindness as to the *true* and *real* nature of things. This they exaggerate, and love to enlarge on. We are miserably bantered, say they, by our senses, and amused only with the outside and shew of things. The real essence, the internal qualities and constitution of even the meanest object, is hid from our view: something there is in every drop of water, every grain of sand, which it is beyond the power of human understanding to fathom or comprehend. But, it is evident from what has been shewn that all this complaint is groundless, and that we are influenced by false principles to that degree as to mistrust our senses, and think we know nothing of those things which we perfectly comprehend.

102] One great inducement to our pronouncing ourselves ignorant of the nature of things is, the current opinion that every thing includes *within itself* the cause of its properties: or that there is in each object an inward essence, which is the source whence its discernible qualities flow, and whereon they depend. Some have pretended to account for appearances by occult qualities; but of late they are mostly resolved into mechanical causes, to wit, the figure, motion, weight, and suchlike qualities, of insensible particles: whereas, in truth, there is no other agent or efficient cause than *spirit* it being evident that motion, as well as all other *ideas,* is perfectly inert. See sect. 25. Hence, to endeavour to explain the production of colours or sounds, by figure, motion, magnitude, and the like, must needs be labour in vain. And accordingly we see the attempts of that kind are not at all satisfactory. Which may be said in general of those instances wherein one idea or quality is assigned for the cause of another. I need not say how many hypotheses and speculations are left out, and how much the study of nature is abridged by this doctrine.

103] The great mechanical principle now in vogue is *attraction.* That a stone falls to the earth, or the sea swells towards the moon, may to some appear sufficiently explained thereby. But how are we enlightened by being told this is done by attraction? Is it that that word signifies the manner of the tendency, and that it is by the mutual drawing of bodies instead of their being impelled or protruded towards each other? But nothing is determined of the manner or action, and it may as truly (for aught we know) be

termed *impulse,* or *protrusion,* as *attraction.* Again, the parts of
steel we see cohere firmly together, and this also is accounted for
by attraction; but, in this, as in the other instances, I do not perceive that anything is signified besides the effect itself; for as to
the manner of the action whereby it is produced, or the cause
which produces it, these are not so much as aimed at.

104] Indeed, if we take a view of the several phenomena, and
compare them together, we may observe some likeness and conformity between them. For example, in the falling of a stone to
the ground, in the rising of the sea towards the moon, in cohesion
and crystallization, there is something alike; namely, an union
or mutual approach of bodies. So that any one of these or the like
phenomena may not seem strange or surprising to a man who has
nicely observed and compared the effects of nature. For that only
is thought so which is uncommon, or a thing by itself, and out of
the ordinary course of our observation. That bodies should tend
towards the centre of the earth is not thought strange, because it
is what we perceive every moment of our lives. But that they
should have a like gravitation towards the centre of the moon may
seem odd and unaccountable to most men, because it is discerned
only in the tides. But a philosopher, whose thoughts take in a
larger compass of nature, having observed a certain similitude of
appearances, as well in the heavens as the earth, that argue innumerable bodies to have a mutual tendency towards each other,
which he denotes by the general name *attraction,* whatever can be
reduced to that, he thinks justly accounted for. Thus he explains
the aides by the attraction of the terraqueous globe towards the
moon; which to him doth not appear odd or anomalous, but only
a particular example of a general rule or law of nature.

105] If therefore we consider the difference there is betwixt natural
philosophers and other men, with regard to their knowledge of
the phenomena, we shall find it consists, not in an exacter knowledge of the efficient cause that produces them—for that can be no
other than the *will of a spirit*—but only in a greater largeness of
comprehension, whereby analogies, harmonies, and agreements
are discovered in the works of nature, and the particular effects
explained, that is, reduced to general rules, see sect. 62: which
rules, grounded on the analogy and uniformness observed in the

production of natural effects, are most agreeable and sought after by the mind; for that they extend our prospect beyond what is present and near to us, and enable us to make very probable conjectures touching things that may have happened at very great distances of time and place, as well as to predict things to come: which sort of endeavour towards Omniscience is much affected by the mind.

106] But we should proceed warily in such things: for we are apt to lay too great a stress on analogies, and, to the prejudice of truth, humour that eagerness of the mind, whereby it is carried to extend its knowledge into general theorems. For example, gravitation or mutual attraction, because it appears in many instances, some are straightway for pronouncing *universal;* and that to attract and be attracted by every other body is an essential quality inherent in all bodies whatsoever. Whereas it is evident the fixed stars have no such tendency towards each other; and, so far is that gravitation from being *essential* to bodies that in some instances a quite contrary principle seems to shew itself; as in the perpendicular growth of plants, and the elasticity of the air. There is nothing necessary or essential in the case; but it depends entirely on the will of the Governing Spirit, who causes certain bodies to cleave together or tend towards each other according to various laws, whilst He keeps others at a fixed distance; and to some He gives a quite contrary tendency to fly asunder, just as He sees convenient.

107] After what has been premised, I think we may lay down the following conclusions. First, it is plain philosophers amuse themselves in vain, when they enquire for any natural efficient cause, distinct from a *mind* or *spirit*. Secondly, considering the whole creation is the workmanship of a *wise and good Agent,* it should seem to become philosophers to employ their thoughts (contrary to what some hold) about the final causes of things. [For, besides that this would prove a very pleasing entertainment to the mind, it might be of great advantage, in that it not only discovers to us the attributes of the Creator, but may also direct us in several instances to the proper uses and applications of things.] And I must confess I see no reason why pointing out the various ends to which natural things are adapted, and for which they were originally with unspeakable wisdom contrived, should not be thought one good way of accounting for them, and altogether worthy a philosopher. Thirdly, from what has been premised, no reason can be drawn why the history of nature should not still be studied, and observations and experiments made; which, that they are of use to mankind, and enable us to draw any general conclusions, is not the result of any immutable habitudes or relations between things themselves, but only of God's goodness and kindness to men in the administration of the world. See sects. 30 and 31. Fourthly, by a diligent observation of the phenomena within our view, we may discover the general laws of nature, and from them deduce other phenomena. I do not say *demonstrate;* for all deductions of that kind depend on a supposition that the Author of Nature always operates uniformly, and in a constant observance of those rules *we* take for principles, which we cannot evidently know.

108] [It appears from sect. 66, &c. that the steady consistent methods of nature may not unfitly be styled the Language of its Author, whereby He discovers His attributes to our view and directs us how to act for the convenience and felicity of life.] Those men who frame general rules from the phenomena, and afterwards derive the phenomena from those rules, seem to consider signs rather than causes. A man may well understand natural signs without knowing their analogy, or being able to say by what rule a thing is so or so. And, as it is very possible to write improperly, through too strict an observance of general grammar-rules; so, in arguing from general laws of nature, it is not impossible we may extend the analogy too far, and by that means run into mistakes.

109] [To carry on the resemblance.] As in reading other books a wise man will choose to fix his thoughts on the sense and apply it to use, rather than lay them out in grammatical remarks on the language; so, in perusing the volume of nature, methinks it is beneath the dignity of the mind to affect an exactness in reducing each particular phenomenon to general rules, or shewing how it follows from them. We should propose to ourselves nobler views, such as to recreate and exalt the mind with a prospect of the beauty, order, extent, and variety of natural things: hence, by proper inferences, to enlarge our notions of the grandeur, wisdom, and beneficence of the Creator: and lastly, to make the several parts of the creation, so far as in us lies, subservient to the ends they were designed for—God's glory, and the sustentation and comfort of ourselves and fellow-creatures.

110] [The best key for the aforesaid analogy, or natural Science, will be easily acknowledged to be a certain celebrated Treatise of *Mechanics.*[1]] In the entrance of which justly admired treatise, Time, Space, and Motion are distinguished into *absolute* and *relative, true* and *apparent, mathematical* and *vulgar:* which distinction, as it is at large explained by the author, does suppose those quantities to have an existence without the mind: and that they are ordinarily conceived with relation to sensible things, to which nevertheless in their own nature they bear no relation at all.

111] As for *Time,* as it is there taken in an absolute, or abstracted sense, for the duration or perseverance of the existence of things, I have nothing more to add concerning it after what has been already said on that subject. Sects. 97 and 98. For the rest, this celebrated author holds there is an *absolute Space,* which, being unperceivable to sense, remains in itself similar and immoveable; and relative space to be the measure thereof, which, being moveable and defined by its situation in respect of sensible bodies, is vulgarly taken for immovable space. *Place* he defines to be that part of space which is occupied by any body: and according as the space is absolute or relative so also is the place. *Absolute Motion* is said to be the translation of a body from absolute place to absolute place, as relative motion is from one relative place to another. And because the parts of absolute space do not fall under our senses, instead of them we are obliged to use their sensible measures; and so define both place and motion with respect to bodies which we regard as immoveable. But it is said, in philosophical matters we must abstract from our senses; since it may be that none of those bodies which seem to be quiescent are truly so; and the same thing which is moved relatively may be really at rest. As

[1]In the first edition, the section begins as follows: "The best grammar of the kind we are speaking of will be easily acknowledged to be a treatise of *Mechanics,* demonstrated and applied to Nature, by a philosopher of a neighbouring nation, whom all the world admire. I shall not take upon me to make remarks on the performance of that extraordinary person: only some things he has advanced so directly opposite to the doctrine we have hitherto laid down, that we should be wanting in the regard due to the authority of so great a man did we not take some notice of them." The reference is to Newton whose *Principia* was published in 1787.

likewise one and the same body may be in relative rest and motion, or even moved with contrary relative motions at the same time, according as its place is variously defined. All which ambiguity is to be found in the apparent motions; but not at all in the true or absolute, which should therefore be alone regarded in philosophy. And the true we are told are distinguished from apparent or relative motions by the following properties. First, in true or absolute motion, all parts which preserve the same position with respect of the whole, partake of the motions of the whole. Secondly, the place being moved, that which is placed therein is also moved: so that a body moving in a place which is in motion doth participate the motion of its place. Thirdly, true motion is never generated or changed otherwise than by force impressed on the body itself. Fourthly, true motion is always changed by force impressed on the body moved. Fifthly, in circular motion, barely relative, there is no centrifugal force, which nevertheless, in that which is true or absolute, is proportional to the quantity of motion.

112] But, notwithstanding what hath been said, I must confess it does not appear to me that there can be any motion other than *relative:* so that to conceive motion there must be conceived at least two bodies; whereof the distance or position in regard to each other is varied. Hence, if there was one only body in being it could not possibly be moved. This seems evident, in that the idea I have of motion doth necessarily include relation.—[Whether others can conceive it otherwise, a little attention may satisfy them.]

113] But, though in every motion it be necessary to conceive more bodies than one, yet it may be that one only is moved, namely, that on which the force causing the change in the distance or situation of the bodies is impressed. For, however some may define relative motion, so as to term that body *moved* which changes it distance from some other body whether the force [or action] causing that change were impressed on it or no, yet, as relative motion is that which is perceived by sense, and regarded in the ordinary affairs of life, it follows that every man of common sense knows what it is as well as the best philosopher. Now, I ask any one whether, in his sense of motion as he walks along the streets, the stones he passes over may be said to *move*, because they change distance with his feet? To me it appears that though motion includes a relation of one thing to another, yet it is not necessary that each term of the relation be denominated from it. As a man may think of somewhat which does not think, so a body may be moved to or from another body which is not therefore itself in motion, [I mean relative motion, for other I am not able to conceive.]

114] As the place happens to be variously defined, the motion which is related to it varies. A man in a ship may be said to be quiescent with relation to the sides of the vessel, and yet move with relation to the land. Or he may move eastward in respect of the one, and westward in respect of the other. In the common affairs of life, men never go beyond the Earth to define the place of any body; and what is quiescent in respect of *that* is accounted *absolutely* to be so. But philosophers, who have a greater extent of thought, and juster notions of the system of things, discover even the Earth itself to be moved. In order therefore to fix their notions, they seem to conceive the Corporeal World as finite, and the utmost unmoved walls or shell thereof to be the place whereby they estimate true motions. If we sound our own conceptions, I believe we may find all the absolute motion we can frame an idea of to be at bottom no other than relative motion thus defined. For, as has been already observed, absolute motion, exclusive of *all* external relation, is incomprehensible: and to this kind of relative motion all the above-mentioned properties, causes, and effects ascribed to absolute motion will, if I mistake not, be found to agree. As to what is said of the centrifugal force, that it does not at all belong to circular relative motion, I do not see how this follows from the experiment which is brought to prove it. See Newton's *Philosophiae Naturalis Principia Mathematica, in Schol. Def. VIII.* For the water in the vessel, at that time wherein it is said to have the greatest relative circular motion, hath, I think, no motion at all: as is plain from the foregoing section.

115] For, to denominate a body *moved,* it is requisite, first, that it change its distance or situation with regard to some other body: and secondly, that the force occasioning that change be applied to it. If either of these be wanting, I do not think that, agreeably to the sense of mankind, or the propriety of language, a body can be said to be in motion. I grant indeed that it is possible for us to think a body, which we see change its distance from some other, to be moved, though it have no force applied to it (in which sense there may be apparent motion); but then it is because the force causing the change of distance is imagined by us to be [applied or] impressed on that body thought to move. Which indeed shews we are capable of mistaking a thing to be in motion which is not, and that is all. [But it does not prove that, in the common acceptation of motion, a body is moved merely because it changes distance from another; since as soon as we are undeceived, and find that the moving force was not communicated to it, we no longer hold it to be moved. So, on the other hand, when one only body (the parts whereof preserve a given position between themselves) is imagined to exist, some there are who think that it can be moved all manner of ways, though without any change of distance or situation to any other bodies; which we should not deny, if they meant only that it might have an impressed force, which, upon the bare creation of other bodies, would produce a motion of some certain quantity and determination. But that an actual motion (distinct from the impressed force, or power, productive of change of place in case there were bodies present whereby to define it) can exist in such a single body, I must confess I am not able to comprehend.]

116] From what has been said, it follows that the philosophic consideration of motion doth not imply the being of an *absolute Space,* distinct from that which is perceived by sense, and related to bodies: which that it cannot exist without the mind is clear upon the same principles that demonstrate the like of all other objects of sense. And perhaps, if we inquire narrowly, we shall find we cannot even frame an idea of *pure Space exclusive of all body.* This I must confess seems impossible, as being a most abstract idea. When I excite a motion in some part of my body, if it be free or without resistance, I say there is *Space.* But if I find a resistance, then I say there is *Body:* and in proportion as the resistance to motion is lesser or greater, I say the space is more or less *pure.* So that when I speak of pure or empty space, it is not to be supposed that the word *space* stands for an idea distinct from, or conceivable without, body and motion. Though indeed we are apt to think every noun substantive stands for a distinct idea that may be separated from all others; which hath occasioned infinite mistakes.

When, therefore, supposing all the world to be annihilated besides my own body, I say there still remains *pure Space;* thereby nothing else is meant but only that I conceive it possible for the limbs of my body to be moved on all sides without the least resistance: but if that too were annihilated then there could be no motion, and consequently no Space. Some, perhaps, may think the sense of seeing doth furnish them with the idea of pure space; but it is plain from what we have elsewhere shewn, that the ideas of space and distance are not obtained by that sense. See the *Essay concerning Vision.*

117] What is here laid down seems to put an end to all those disputes and difficulties that have sprung up amongst the learned concerning the nature of *pure Space.* But the chief advantage arising from it is that we are freed from that dangerous dilemma, to which several who have employed their thoughts on that subject imagine themselves reduced, viz. of thinking either that Real Space is God, or else that there is something beside God which is eternal, uncreated, infinite, indivisible, immutable. Both which may justly be thought pernicious and absurd notions. It is certain that not a few divines, as well as philosophers of great note, have, from the difficulty they found in conceiving either limits or annihilation of space, concluded it must be *divine.* And some of late have set themselves particularly to shew that the incommunicable attributes of God agree to it. Which doctrine, how unworthy soever it may seem of the Divine Nature, yet I must confess I do not see how we can get clear of it, so long as we adhere to the received opinions.

118] Hitherto of Natural Philosophy. We come now to make some inquiry concerning that other great branch of speculative knowledge, to wit, Mathematics. These, how celebrated soever they may be for their clearness and certainty of demonstration, which is hardly anywhere else to be found, cannot nevertheless be supposed altogether free from mistakes, if in their principles there lurks some secret error which is common to the professors of those sciences with the rest of mankind. Mathematicians, though they deduce their theorems from a great height of evidence, yet their first principles are limited by the consideration of Quantity. And they do not ascend into any inquiry concerning those transcendental maxims which influence all the particular sciences; each part whereof, Mathematics not excepted, doth consequently participate of the errors involved in them. That the principles laid down by mathematicians are true, and their way of deduction from those principles clear and incontestible, we do not deny. But we hold there may be certain erroneous maxims of greater extent than the object of Mathematics, and for that reason not expressly mentioned, though tacitly supposed, throughout the whole progress of that science; and that the ill effects of those secret unexamined errors are diffused through all the branches thereof. To be plain, we suspect the mathematicians are no less deeply concerned than other men in the errors arising from the doctrine of abstract general ideas, and the existence of objects without the mind.

119] Arithmetic hath been thought to have for its object abstract ideas of *number*. Of which to understand the properties and mutual habitudes, is supposed no mean part of speculative knowledge. The opinion of the pure and intellectual nature of numbers in abstract has made them in esteem with those philosophers who seem to have affected an uncommon fineness and elevation of thought. It hath set a price on the most trifling numerical speculations, which in practice are of no use, but serve only for amusement; and hath heretofore so far infected the minds of some, that they have dreamed of mighty *mysteries* involved in numbers, and attempted the explication of natural things by them. But, if we narrowly inquire into our own thoughts, and consider what has been premised, we may perhaps entertain a low opinion of those high flights and abstractions, and look on all inquiries about numbers only as so many *difficiles nugae*, so far as they are not subservient to practice, and promote the benefit of life.

120] Unity in abstract we have before considered in sect. 13; from which, and what has been said in the Introduction, it plainly follows there is not any such idea. But, number being defined a *collection of units*, we may conclude that, if there be no such thing as unity, or unit in abstract, there are no *ideas* of number in abstract, denoted by the numeral names and figures. The theories therefore in Arithmetic, if they are abstracted from the names and figures, as likewise from all use and practice, as well as from the particular things numbered, can be supposed to have nothing at all for their object. Hence we may see how entirely the science of numbers is subordinate to practice, and how jejune and trifling it becomes when considered as a matter of mere speculation.

121] However, since there may be some who, deluded by the specious show of discovering abstracted verities, waste their time in arithmetical theorems and problems which have not any use, it will not be amiss if we more fully consider and expose the vanity of that pretence. And this will plainly appear by taking a view of Arithmetic in its infancy, and observing what it was that originally put men on the study of that science, and to what scope they directed it. It is natural to think that at first, men, for ease of memory and help of computation, made use of counters, or in writing of single strokes, points, or the like, each whereof was made to signify an unit, *i.e.* some one thing of whatever kind they had occasion to reckon. Afterwards they found out the more compendious ways of making one character stand in place of several strokes or points. And, lastly, the notation of the Arabians or Indians came into use; wherein, by the repetition of a few characters or figures, and varying the signification of each figure according to the place it obtains, all numbers may be most aptly expressed. Which seems to have been done in imitation of language, so that an exact analogy is observed betwixt the notation by figures and names, the nine simple figures answering the nine first numeral names and places in the former, corresponding to denominations in the latter. And agreeably to those conditions of the simple and local value of figures, were contrived methods of finding, from the given figures or marks of the parts, what figures and how placed are proper to denote the whole, or *vice versa*. And having found the sought figures, the same rule or analogy being observed throughout, it is easy to read them into words; and so the number becomes perfectly known. For then the number of any particular things is said to be known, when we know the name or figures (with their due arrangement) that according to the standing analogy belong to them. For, these signs being known, we can by the operations of arithmetic know the signs of any part of the particular sums signified by them; and thus computing in signs, (because of the connexion established betwixt them and the distinct multitudes of things, whereof one is taken for an unit), we may be able rightly to sum up, divide, and proportion the things themselves that we intend to number.

122] In Arithmetic, therefore, we regard not the *things* but the *signs;* which nevertheless are not regarded for their own sake, but because they direct us how to act with relation to things, and dispose rightly of them. Now, agreeably to what we have before observed of Words in general (sect. 19, Introd.), it happens here likewise, that abstract ideas are thought to be signified by numeral names or characters, while they do not suggest ideas of particular things to our minds. I shall not at present enter into a more particular dissertation on this subject; but only observe that it is evident from what has been said, those things which pass for abstract truths and theorems concerning numbers, are in reality conversant about no object distinct from particular numerable things; except only names and characters, which originally came to be considered on no other account but their being *signs,* or capable to represent aptly whatever particular things men had need to compute. Whence it follows that to study them for their own sake would be just as wise, and to as good purpose, as if a man, neglecting the true use or original intention and subserviency of language, should spend his time in impertinent criticisms upon words, or reasonings and controversies purely verbal.

123] From numbers we proceed to speak of *extension,* which, considered as relative, is the object of Geometry. The *infinite* divisibility of *finite* extension, though it is not expressly laid down either as an axiom or theorem in the elements of that science, yet is throughout the same everywhere supposed, and thought to have so inseparable and essential a connexion with the principles and demonstrations in Geometry that mathematicians never admit it into doubt, or make the least question of it. And as this notion is the source from whence do spring all those amusing geometrical paradoxes which have such a direct repugnancy to the plain common sense of mankind, and are admitted with so much reluctance into a mind not yet debauched by learning; so is it the principal occasion of all that nice and extreme subtilty, which renders the study of Mathematics so very difficult and tedious. Hence, if we can make it appear that no *finite* extension contains innumerable parts, or is infinitely divisible, it follows that we shall at once clear the science of Geometry from a great number of difficulties and contradictions which have ever been esteemed a reproach to human reason, and withal make the attainment thereof a business of much less time and pains than it hitherto hath been.

124] Every particular finite extension which may possibly be the object of our thought is an *idea* existing only in the mind; and consequently each part thereof must be perceived. If, therefore, I cannot *perceive* innumerable parts in any finite extension that I consider, it is certain they are not contained in it. But it is evident that I cannot distinguish innumerable parts in any particular line, surface, or solid, which I either perceive by sense, or figure to myself in my mind. Wherefore I conclude they are not contained in it. Nothing can be plainer to me than that the extensions I have in view are no other than my own ideas; and it is no less plain that I cannot resolve any one of my ideas into an infinite number of other ideas; that is, that they are not infinitely divisible. If by *finite extension* be meant something distinct from a finite idea, I declare I do not know what that is, and so cannot affirm or deny anything of it. But if the terms *extension, parts,* and the like, are taken in any sense conceivable—that is, for *ideas,*—then to say a finite quantity or extension consists of parts infinite in number is so manifest and glaring a contradiction, that every one at first sight acknowledges it to be so. And it is impossible it should ever gain the assent of any reasonable creature who is not brought to it by gentle and slow degrees, as a converted Gentile to the belief of transubstantiation. Ancient and rooted prejudices do often pass into principles. And those propositions which once obtain the force and credit of a *principle,* are not only themselves, but likewise whatever is deducible from them, thought privileged from all examination. And there is no absurdity so gross, which, by this means, the mind of man may not be prepared to swallow.

125] He whose understanding is prepossessed with the doctrine of abstract general ideas may be persuaded that (whatever be thought of the ideas of sense) *extension in abstract* is infinitely divisible. And one who thinks the objects of sense exist without the mind will perhaps, in virtue thereof, be brought to admit that a line but an inch long may contain innumerable parts really existing, though too small to be discerned. These errors are grafted as well in the minds of geometricians as of other men, and have a like influence on their reasonings; and it were no difficult thing to shew how the arguments from Geometry made use of to support the infinite divisibility of extension are bottomed on them. [But this, if it be thought necessary, we may hereafter find a proper place to treat of in a particular manner.] At present we shall only observe in general whence it is the mathematicians are all so fond and tenacious of that doctrine.

126] It has been observed in another place that the theorems and demonstrations in Geometry are conversant about universal ideas (sect. 15, Introd.): where it is explained in what sense this ought to be understood, to wit, the particular lines and figures included in the diagram are supposed to stand for innumerable others of different sizes; or, in other words, the geometer considers them abstracting from their magnitude: which doth not imply that he forms an abstract idea, but only that he cares not what the particular magnitude is, whether great or small, but looks on that as a thing indifferent to the demonstration. Hence it follows that a line in the scheme but an inch long must be spoken of as though it contained ten thousand parts, since it is regarded not in itself, but as it is universal; and it is universal only in its signification, whereby it *represents* innumerable lines greater than itself, in which may be distinguished ten thousand parts or more, though there may not be above an inch in *it*. After this manner, the properties of the lines signified are (by a very usual figure) transferred to the sign; and thence, through mistake, thought to appertain to it considered in its own nature.

127] Because there is no number of parts so great but it is possible there may be a line containing more, the inch-line is said to contain parts more than any assignable number; which is true, not of the inch taken absolutely, but only for the things signified by it. But men, not retaining that distinction in their thoughts, slide into a belief that the small particular line described on paper contains in itself parts innumerable. There is no such thing as the ten thousandth part of an inch; but there is of a mile or diameter of the earth, which may be signified by that inch. When therefore I delineate a triangle on paper, and take one side, not above an inch for example in length, to be the radius, this I consider as divided into 10,000 or 100,000 parts, or more. For, though the ten thousandth part of that line considered in itself, is nothing at all, and consequently may be neglected without any error or inconveniency, yet these described lines, being only marks standing for greater quantities, whereof it may be the ten thousandth part is very considerable, it follows that, to prevent notable errors in practice, the radius must be taken of 10,000 parts, or more.

128] From what has been said the reason is plain why, to the end any theorem may become universal in its use, it is necessary we speak of the lines described on paper as though they contained parts which really they do not. In doing of which, if we examine the matter thoroughly, we shall perhaps discover that we cannot conceive an inch itself as consisting of, or being divisible into, a thousand parts, but only some other line which is far greater than an inch, and represented by it; and that when we say a line is *infinitely divisible,* we must mean *a line which is infinitely great.* What we have here observed seems to be the chief cause, why to suppose the *infinite* divisibility of *finite extension* has been thought necessary in geometry.

129] The several absurdities and contradictions which flowed from this false principle might, one would think, have been esteemed so many demonstrations against it. But, by I know not what logic, it is held that proofs *a posteriori* are not to be admitted against propositions relating to Infinity. As though it were not impossible even for an Infinite Mind to reconcile contradictions; or as if anything absurd and repugnant could have a necessary connexion with truth, or flow from it. But whoever considers the weakness of this pretence, will think it was contrived on purpose to humour the laziness of the mind, which had rather acquiesce in an indolent scepticism than be at the pains to go through with a severe examination of those principles it has ever embraced for true.

130] Of late the speculations about Infinites have run so high, and grown to such strange notions, as have occasioned no small scruples and disputes among the geometers of the present age. Some there are of great note who, not content with holding that finite lines may be divided into an infinite number of parts, do yet farther maintain, that each of those Infinitesimals is itself subdivisible into an infinity of other parts, or Infinitesimals of a second order, and so on *ad infinitum*. These, I say, assert there are Infinitesimals of Infinitesimals of Infinitesimals, without ever coming to an end. So that according to them an inch does not barely contain an infinite number of parts, but an infinity of an infinity of an infinity *ad infinitum* of parts. Others there be who hold all orders of Infinitesimals below the first to be nothing at all; thinking it with good reason absurd to imagine there is any positive quantity or part of extension which, though multiplied infinitely, can ever equal the smallest given extension. And yet on the other hand it seems no less absurd to think the square, cube, or other power of a positive real root, should itself be nothing at all; which they who hold Infinitesimals of the first order, denying all of the subsequent orders, are obliged to maintain.

131] Have we not therefore reason to conclude they are *both* in the wrong, and that there is in effect no such thing as parts infinitely small, or an infinite number of parts contained in any finite quantity? But you will say that if this doctrine obtains it will follow the very foundations of Geometry are destroyed, and those great men who have raised that science to so astonishing a height, have been all the while building a castle in the air. To this it may be replied, that whatever is useful in geometry, and promotes the benefit of human life, does still remain firm and unshaken on our Principles; that science considered as practical will rather receive advantage than any prejudice from what has been said. But to set this in a due light, [and shew how lines and figures may be measured, and their properties investigated, without supposing finite extension to be infinitely divisible,] may be the proper business of another place. For the rest, though it should follow that some of the more intricate and subtle parts of Speculative Mathematics may be pared off without any prejudice to truth, yet I do not see what damage will be thence derived to mankind. On the contrary, I think it were highly to be wished that men of great abilities and obstinate application would draw off their thoughts from those amusements, and employ them in the study of such things as lie nearer the concerns of life, or have a more direct influence on the manners.

132] If it be said that several theorems, undoubtedly true, are discovered by methods in which Infinitesimals are made use of, which could never have been if their existence included a contradiction in it:—I answer that upon a thorough examination it will not be found that in any instance it is necessary to make use of or conceive *infinitesimal* parts of *finite* lines, or even quantities less than the *minimum sensible:* nay, it will be evident this is never done, it being impossible. [And whatever mathematicians may think of Fluxions, or the Differential Calculus, and the like, a little reflexion will shew them that, in working by those methods, they do not conceive or imagine lines or surfaces less than what are perceivable to sense. They may indeed call those little and almost insensible quantities Infinitesimals, or Infinitesimals of Infinitesimals, if they please. But at bottom this is all, they being in truth finite; nor does the solution of problems require the supposing any other. But this will be more clearly made out hereafter.]

133] By what we have hitherto said, it is plain that very numerous and important errors have taken their rise from those false Principles which were impugned in the foregoing parts of this Treatise; and the opposites of those erroneous tenets at the same time appear to be most fruitful Principles, from whence do flow innumerable consequences, highly advantageous to true philosophy as well as to religion. Particularly *Matter,* or *the absolute existence of corporeal objects,* hath been shewn to be that wherein the most avowed and pernicious enemies of all knowledge, whether human or divine, have ever placed their chief strength and confidence. And surely if by distinguishing the real existence of unthinking things from their being perceived, and allowing them a subsistence of their own, out of the minds of spirits, no one thing is explained in nature, but on the contrary a great many inexplicable difficulties arise; if the supposition of Matter is barely precarious, as not being grounded on so much as one single reason; if its consequences cannot endure the light of examination and free inquiry, but screen themselves under the dark and general pretence of *infinites being incomprehensible;* if withal the removal of *this* Matter be not attended with the least evil consequence; if it be not even missed in the world, but everything as well, nay much easier conceived without it; if, lastly, both Sceptics and Atheists are for ever silenced upon supposing only spirits and ideas, and this scheme of things is perfectly agreeable both to Reason and Religion: methinks we may expect it should be admitted and firmly embraced, though it were proposed only as an *hypothesis,* and the existence of Matter had been allowed possible: which yet I think we have evidently demonstrated that it is not.

134] True it is that, in consequence of the foregoing Principles, several disputes and speculations which are esteemed no mean parts of learning are rejected as useless [and in effect conversant about nothing at all]. But how great a prejudice soever against our notions this may give to those who have already been deeply engaged, and made large advances in studies of that nature, yet by others we hope it will not be thought any just ground of dislike to the principles and tenets herein laid down, that they abridge the labour of study, and make human sciences more clear, compendious, and attainable than they were before. . . .

145] From what hath been said, it is plain that we cannot know the existence of *other spirits* otherwise than by their operations, or the ideas by them, excited in us. I perceive several motions, changes, and combinations of ideas, that inform me there are certain particular agents, like myself, which accompany them, and concur in their production. Hence, the knowledge I have of other spirits is not immediate, as is the knowledge of my ideas; but depending on the intervention of ideas, by me referred to agents or spirits distinct from myself, as effects or concomitant signs.

146] But, though there be some things which convince us human agents are concerned in producing them, yet it is evident to every one that those things which are called the Works of Nature, that is, the far greater part of the ideas or sensations perceived by us, are *not* produced by, or dependent on, the wills of *men.* There is therefore some other Spirit that causes them; since it is repugnant that they should subsist by themselves. See sect. 29. But, if we attentively consider the constant regularity, order, and concatenation of natural things, the surprising magnificence, beauty and perfection of the larger, and the exquisite contrivance of the smaller parts of the creation, together with the exact harmony and correspondence of the whole, but above all the never-enough-admired laws of pain and pleasure, and the instincts or natural inclinations, appetites, and passions of animals;—I say if we consider all these things, and at the same time attend to the meaning and import of the attributes One, Eternal, Infinitely Wise, Good, and Perfect, we shall clearly perceive that they belong to the aforesaid Spirit, "who works all in all" and "by whom all things consist." . . .

155] We should rather wonder that men can be found so stupid as to neglect, than that neglecting they should be unconvinced of such an evident and momentous truth. And yet it is to be feared that too many of parts and leisure, who live in Christian countries, are, merely through a supine and dreadful negligence, sunk into a sort of Atheism. [They cannot say there is not a God, but neither are convinced that there is. For what else can it be but some lurking infidelity, some secret misgivings of mind with regard to the existence and attributes of God, which permits sinners to grow and harden in impiety?] Since it is downright impossible that a soul pierced and enlightened with a thorough sense of the omnipresence, holiness, and justice of that Almighty Spirit, should persist in a remorseless violation of His laws. We ought, therefore, earnestly to meditate and dwell on those important points; that so we may attain conviction without all scruple "that the eyes of the Lord are in every place, beholding the evil and the good; that He is with us and keepeth us in all places whither we go, and giveth us bread to eat and raiment to put on"; that He is present and conscious to our innermost thoughts; and, that we have a most absolute and immediate dependence on Him. A clear view of which great truths cannot choose but fill our hearts with an awful circumspection and holy fear, which is the strongest incentive to Virtue, and the best guard against Vice.

156] For, after all, what deserves the first place in our studies is, the consideration of GOD and our DUTY; which to promote, as it was the main drift and design of my labours, so shall I esteem them altogether useless and ineffectual if, by what I have said, I cannot inspire my readers with a pious sense of the Presence of God; and, having shewn the falseness or vanity of those barren speculations which make the chief employment of learned men, the better dispose them to reverence and embrace the salutary truths of the Gospel; which to know and to practise is the highest perfection of human nature.

David Hume

David Hume

I F PHILOSOPHY is a criticism of those basic ideas in terms of which the world, our experience, and our knowledge are made intelligible, David Hume (1711-1776) is a preëminent philosopher, one who perhaps more than any other single individual in modern times has awakened others from their "dogmatic slumbers." After Hume men have been forced to re-examine the fundamental assumptions upon which all their other convictions rest, assumptions which are usually taken as almost self-evident, and they have done so primarily in terms of the problems Hume raised. Berkeley had anticipated some of Hume's criticisms, but because Berkeley had done so in the interest of his own religious faith, it remained for Hume, who served no special interest, to express most clearly and without limitation the precarious character of our assumptions in all respects.

Most men do not doubt that there is ample rational justification and empirical evidence for such beliefs as the belief in the existence of the external world, in the uniformity, unity, and order of nature, and the belief that science can attain certain knowledge which is both a representation of this external world and a knowledge of necessary causes and effects. The beliefs in personal identity, in principles of morality, and in a provident God, though perhaps less generally held than in Hume's day, are still widespread fundamental convictions. In an age when faith in reason was supreme, when beliefs about everything from God to the atom were felt to be rationally demonstrable (as illustrated in Descartes), Hume showed that not only is there little rational justification for these beliefs, but, what is more, there is not even adequate empirical evidence for them (as Locke had supposed). Hume showed that nether on an empirical basis nor on a rationalistic basis were the beliefs in spiritual souls, material substances, necessary causes, and God well founded. The result of Hume's criticisms of these ideas was that if our ordinary assumptions about knowledge, man, and the world are to be justified men must reinterpret the meanings of these several beliefs and find other kinds of justification for them than had been provided.

The problem for Hume was not whether men will continue to act upon these beliefs; human beings will certainly do that. The problem was to render these beliefs intelligible. Hume, therefore, undertook to give positive explanations for our beliefs and to put to rest those doubts which had been raised by his own criticisms. When Hume as a young man in his twenties began to write his *Treatise of Human Nature* he was convinced that in the principles of human nature, especially in the psychological laws of association which he compared to the laws of attraction in physics, and in a thoroughgoing empiricism he could find the explanations needed. Yet even before he finished the first volume, he was becoming less sure that he had a complete answer to his doubts. When he rewrote parts of his *Treatise* in more readable and popular form as the *Enquiry Concerning The Human Understanding* (1748) and as *An Enquiry Concerning the Principles of Morals* (1751), selections from both of which follow this introduction, many of the problems and explanations earlier proposed were omitted. His scepticism became firmer as his own suggestions were seen to be at best only partial answers. Even his *Dialogues Concerning Natural Religion* (published posthumously in 1779) are ambiguous concerning his positive position. Though some of his scepticism was intended to shock the reading public much of it remained to trouble him. He could not escape entirely his own doubts. So far as morality is concerned, however, he remained convinced that its roots were to be found in the sentiment of sympathy and in the prudence and beauty of utility, and that the method of moral science is empirical, as the method of any true science must be. Religion for Hume finds its justification, if at all, in faith and its origin in fear. Science has its justification in action but does not give us more than probable knowledge. Mathematics, it is true, is certain, but that is because it is dependent only on definitions. Thus Hume began by seeking justifications for beliefs by tracing those beliefs back to their origin in experience; he ended by suggesting that beliefs had only practical validity. Some see this as scepticism; others see it as opening one of the roads leading to modern experimentalism. To answer Hume is, however, for those who refuse to accept his philosophy, the first and primary task of philosophical thought.

Hume was born and educated in Scotland. After studying at Edinburgh, reading for the bar, and trying business, he determined to win fame for himself as a writer. Though his *Treatise of Human Nature* (1739) was far from being a success, his two *Enquiries* (1748 and 1751) together with his *Essays Political and Moral* (1741-42), *Political Discourses* (1751), and his monumental *History of England* (1754-1761) established a wide reputation for him both in England and on the Continent. In Scotland Hume became the center of the influential Scottish group of thinkers among whom was Hume's close friend, the economist Adam Smith. It is interesting to note that while Hume was a radical in philosophy, his *History of England* was a thoroughgoing defense of the conservative Tory party in English history.

An Enquiry Concerning Human Understanding

As, AFTER all, the abstractedness of these speculations is no recommendation, but rather a disadvantage to them, and as this difficulty may perhaps be surmounted by care and art, and the avoiding of all unnecessary detail, we have, in the following enquiry, attempted to throw some light upon subjects, from which uncertainty has hitherto deterred the wise, and obscurity the ignorant. Happy, if we can unite the boundaries of the different species of philosophy, by reconciling profound enquiry with clearness, and truth with novelty! And still more happy, if, reasoning in this easy manner, we can undermine the foundations of an abstruse philosophy, which seems to have hitherto served only as a shelter to superstition, and a cover to absurdity and error!

Section II

Of the Origin of Ideas

11] Every one will readily allow, that there is a considerable difference between the perceptions of the mind, when a man feels the pain of excessive heat, or the pleasure of moderate warmth, and when he afterwards recalls to his memory this sensation, or anticipates it by his imagination. These faculties may mimic or copy the perceptions of the senses; but they never can entirely reach the force and vivacity of the original sentiment. The utmost we say of them, even when they operate with greatest vigour, is, that they represent their object in so lively a manner, that we could *almost* say we feel or see it: But, except the mind be disordered by disease or madness, they never can arrive at such a pitch of vivacity, as to render these perceptions altogether undistinguishable. All the colours of poetry, however splendid, can never paint natural objects in such a manner as to make the description be taken for a real landskip. The most lively thought is still inferior to the dullest sensation.

We may observe a like distinction to run through all the other perceptions of the mind. A man in a fit of anger, is actuated in a very different manner from one who only thinks of that emotion. If you tell me, that any person is in love, I easily understand your meaning, and form a just conception of his situation; but never can mistake that conception for the real disorders and agitations of the passion. When we reflect on our past sentiments and affections, our thought is a faithful mirror, and copies its objects truly; but the colours which it employs are faint and dull, in comparison of those in which our original perceptions were clothed. It requires no nice discernment or metaphysical head to mark the distinction between them.

12] Here therefore we may divide all the perceptions of the mind into two classes or species, which are distinguished by their different degrees of force and vivacity. The less forcible and lively are commonly denominated *Thoughts* or *Ideas*. The other species want a name in our language, and in most others; I suppose, because it was not requisite for any, but philosophical purposes, to rank them under a general term or appellation. Let us, therefore, use a little freedom, and call them *Impressions;* employing that word in a sense somewhat different from the usual. By the term *impression,* then, I mean all our more lively perceptions, when we hear, or see, or feel, or love, or hate, or desire, or will. And impressions are distinguished from ideas, which are the less lively perceptions, of which we are conscious, when we reflect on any of those sensations or movements above mentioned.

13] Nothing, at first view, may seem more unbounded than the thought of man, which not only escapes all human power and authority, but is not even restrained within the limits of nature and reality. To form monsters, and join incongruous shapes and appearances, costs the imagination no more trouble than to conceive the most natural and familiar objects. And while the body is confined to one planet, along which it creeps with pain and difficulty;

the thought can in an instant transport us into the most distant regions of the universe; or even beyond the universe, into the unbounded chaos, where nature is supposed to lie in total confusion. What never was seen, or heard of, may yet be conceived; nor is anything beyond the power of thought, except what implies an absolute contradiction.

But though our thought seems to possess this unbounded liberty, we shall find, upon a nearer examination, that it is really confined within very narrow limits, and that all this creative power of the mind amounts to no more than the faculty of compounding, transposing, augmenting, or diminishing the materials afforded us by the senses and experience. When we think of a golden mountain, we only join two consistent ideas, *gold,* and *mountain,* with which we were formerly acquainted. A virtuous horse we can conceive; because, from our own feeling, we can conceive virtue; and this we may unite to the figure and shape of a horse, which is an animal familiar to us. In short, all the materials of thinking are derived either from our outward or inward sentiment: the mixture and composition of these belongs alone to the mind and will. Or, to express myself in philosophical language, all our ideas or more feeble perceptions are copies of our impressions or more lively ones. . . .

17] Here, therefore, is a proposition, which not only seems, in itself, simple and intelligible; but, if a proper use were made of it, might render every dispute equally intelligible, and banish all that jargon, which has so long taken possession of metaphysical reasonings, and drawn disgrace upon them. All ideas, especially abstract ones, are naturally faint and obscure: the mind has but a slender hold of them: they are apt to be confounded with other resembling ideas; and when we have often employed any term, though without a distinct meaning, we are apt to imagine it has a determinate idea annexed to it. On the contrary, all impressions, that is, all sensations, either outward or inward, are strong and vivid: the limits between them are more exactly determined: nor is it easy to fall into any error or mistake with regard to them. When we entertain, therefore, any suspicion that a philosophical term is employed without any meaning or idea (as is but too frequent), we need but enquire, *from what impression is that supposed idea derived?* And if it be impossible to assign any, this will serve to confirm our suspicion. By bringing ideas into so clear a light we may reasonably hope to remove all dispute, which may arise, concerning their nature and reality.[1]

Section III

Of the Association of Ideas

18] It is evident that there is a principle of connexion between the different thoughts or ideas of the mind, and that, in their appearance to the memory or imagination, they introduce each other with a certain degree of method and regularity. In our more serious thinking or discourse this is so observable that any particular thought, which breaks in upon the regular tract or chain of ideas, is immediately remarked and rejected. And even in our wildest and most wandering reveries, nay in our very dreams, we shall find, if we reflect, that the imagination ran not altogether at adventures, but that there was still a connexion upheld among the different ideas, which succeeded each other. Were the loosest and

---

[1] It is probable that no more was meant by those, who denied innate ideas, than that all ideas were copies of our impressions; though it must be confessed, that the terms, which they employed, were not chosen with such caution, nor so exactly defined, as to prevent all mistakes about their doctrine. For what is meant by *innate?* If innate be equivalent to natural, then all the perceptions and ideas of the mind must be allowed to be innate or natural, in whatever sense we take the latter word, whether in opposition to what is uncommon, artificial, or miraculous. If by innate, be meant, contemporary to our birth, the dispute seems to be frivolous; nor is it worth while to enquire at what time thinking begins, whether before, at, or after our birth. Again, the word *idea,* seems to be commonly taken in a very loose sense, by LOCKE and others; as standing for any of our perceptions, our sensations and passions, as well as thoughts. Now in this sense, I should desire to know, what can be meant by asserting, that self-love, or resentment of injuries, or the passion between the sexes is not innate?

But admitting these terms, *impressions* and *ideas,* in the sense above explained, and understanding by *innate,* what is original or copied from no precedent perception, then may we assert that all our impressions are innate, and our ideas not innate.

To be ingenuous, I must own it to be my opinion, that LOCKE was betrayed into this question by the schoolmen, who, making use of undefined terms, draw out their disputes to a tedious length, without ever touching the point in question. A like ambiguity and circumlocution seem to run through that philosopher's reasonings on this as well as most other subjects.

freest conversation to be transcribed, there would immediately be observed something which connected it in all its transitions. Or where this is wanting, the person who broke the thread of discourse might still inform you, that there had secretly revolved in his mind a succession of thought, which had gradually led him from the subject of conversation. Among different languages, even where we cannot suspect the least connexion or communication, it is found, that the words, expressive of ideas, the most compounded, do yet nearly correspond to each other: a certain proof that the simple ideas, comprehended in the compound ones, were bound together by some universal principle, which had an equal influence on all mankind.

19] Though it be too obvious to escape observation, that different ideas are connected together; I do not find that any philosopher has attempted to enumerate or class all the principles of association; a subject, however, that seems worthy of curiosity. To me, there appear to be only three principles of connexion among ideas, namely, *Resemblance, Contiguity* in time or place, and *Cause* or *Effect.*

That these principles serve to connect ideas will not, I believe, be much doubted. A picture naturally leads our thoughts to the original: [1] the mention of one apartment in a building naturally introduces an enquiry or discourse concerning the others: [2] and if we think of a wound, we can scarcely forbear reflecting on the pain which follows it.[3] But that this enumeration is complete, and that there are no other principles of association except these, may be difficult to prove to the satisfaction of the reader, or even to a man's own satisfaction. All we can do, in such cases, is to run over several instances, and examine carefully the principle which binds the different thoughts to each other, never stopping till we render the principle as general as possible.[4] The more instances we examine, and the more care we employ, the more assurance shall we ac-

[1] Resemblance.
[2] Contiguity.
[3] Cause and effect.
[4] For instance, Contrast or Contrariety is also a connexion among Ideas: but it may, perhaps, be considered as a mixture of *Causation* and *Resemblance.* Where two objects are contrary, the one destroys the other; that is, the cause of its annihilation, and the idea of the annihilation of an object, implies the idea of its former existence.

quire, that the enumeration, which we form from the whole, is complete and entire.

Section IV

Sceptical Doubts Concerning the Operations of the Understanding

Part I

20] All the objects of human reason or enquiry may naturally be divided into two kinds, to wit, *Relations of Ideas,* and *Matters of Fact.* Of the first kind are the sciences of Geometry, Algebra, and Arithmetic; and in short, every affirmation which is either intuitively or demonstratively certain. *That the square of the hypothenuse is equal to the square of the two sides,* is a proposition which expresses a relation between these figures. *That three times five is equal to the half of thirty,* expresses a relation between these numbers. Propositions of this kind are discoverable by the mere operation of thought, without dependence on what is anywhere existent in the universe. Though there never were a circle or triangle in nature, the truths demonstrated by Euclid would for ever retain their certainty and evidence.

21] Matters of fact, which are the second objects of human reason, are not ascertained in the same manner; nor is our evidence of their truth, however great, of a like nature with the foregoing. The contrary of every matter of fact is still possible; because it can never imply a contradiction, and is conceived by the mind with the same facility and distinctness, as if ever so conformable to reality. *That the sun will not rise to-morrow* is no less intelligible a proposition, and implies no more contradiction than the affirmation, *that it will rise.* We should in vain, therefore, attempt to demonstrate its falsehood. Were it demonstratively false, it would imply a contradiction, and could never be distinctly conceived by the mind.

It may, therefore, be a subject worthy of curiosity, to enquire what is the nature of that evidence which assures us of any real existence and matter of fact, beyond the present testimony of our senses, or the records of our memory. This part of philosophy, it is observable, has been little cultivated, either by the ancients or moderns; and therefore our doubts and errors, in the prosecution of so important an enquiry, may be the more excusable; while we march through such difficult paths without any guide or direction. They may even prove useful, by exciting curiosity, and destroying that implicit faith and security, which is the bane of all reasoning and free enquiry. The discovery of defects in the common philosophy, if any such there be, will not, I presume, be a discouragement, but rather an incitement, as is usual, to attempt something more full and satisfactory than has yet been proposed to the public.

22] All reasonings concerning matter of fact seem to be founded on the relation of *Cause and Effect*. By means of that relation alone we can go beyond the evidence of our memory and senses. If you were to ask a man, why he believes any matter of fact, which is absent; for instance, that his friend is in the country, or in France; he would give you a reason; and this reason would be some other fact; as a letter received from him, or the knowledge of his former resolutions and promises. A man finding a watch or any other machine in a desert island, would conclude that there had once been men in that island. All our reasonings concerning fact are of the same nature. And here it is constantly supposed that there is a connexion between the present fact and that which is inferred from it. Were there nothing to bind them together, the inference would be entirely precarious. The hearing of an articulate voice and rational discourse in the dark assures us of the presence of some person: Why? because these are the effects of the human make and fabric, and closely connected with it. If we anatomize all the other reasonings of this nature, we shall find that they are founded on the relation of cause and effect, and that this relation is either near or remote, direct or collateral. Heat and light are collateral effects of fire, and the one effect may justly be inferred from the other.

23] If we would satisfy ourselves, therefore, concerning the nature of that evidence, which assures us of matters of fact, we must enquire how we arrive at the knowledge of cause and effect.

I shall venture to affirm, as a general proposition, which admits of no exception, that the knowledge of this relation is not, in any instance, attained by reasonings *a priori;* but arises entirely from experience, when we find that any particular objects are constantly conjoined with each other. Let an object be presented to a man of ever so strong natural reason and abilities; if that object be entirely new to him, he will not be able, by the most accurate examination of its sensible qualities, to discover any of its causes or effects. Adam, though his rational faculties be supposed, at the very first, entirely perfect, could not have inferred from the fluidity and transparency of water that it would suffocate him, or from the light and warmth of fire that it would consume him. No object ever discovers, by the qualities which appear to the senses, either the causes which produced it, or the effects which will arise from it; nor can our reason, unassisted by experience, ever draw any inference concerning real existence and matter of fact.

24] This propostiion, *that causes and effects are discoverable, not by reason but by experience,* will readily be admitted with regard to such objects, as we remember to have once been altogether unknown to us; since we must be conscious of the utter inability, which we then lay under, of foretelling what would arise from them. Present two smooth pieces of marble to a man who has no tincture of natural philosophy; he will never discover that they will adhere together in such a manner as to require great force to separate them in a direct line, while they make so small a resistance to a lateral pressure. Such events, as bear little analogy to the common course of nature, are also readily confessed to be known only by experience; nor does any man imagine that the explosion of gunpowder, or the attraction of a loadstone, could ever be discovered by arguments *a priori.* In like manner, when an effect is supposed to depend upon an intricate machinery or secret structure of parts, we make no difficulty in attributing all our knowledge of it to experience. Who will assert that he can give the ultimate reason, why milk or bread is proper nourishment for a man, not for a lion or a tiger? . . .

Part II

28] But we have not yet attained any tolerable satisfaction with regard to the question first proposed. Each solution still gives rise to a new question as difficult as the foregoing, and leads us on to farther enquiries. When it is asked, *What is the nature of all our reasonings concerning matter of fact?* the proper answer seems to be, that they are founded on the relation of cause and effect. When again it is asked, *What is the foundation of all our reasonings and conclusions concerning that relation?* it may be replied in one word, Experience. But if we still carry on our sifting humour, and ask, *What is the foundation of all conclusions from experience?* this implies a new question, which may be of more difficult solution and explication. Philosophers, that give themselves airs of superior wisdom and sufficiency, have a hard task when they encounter persons of inquisitive dispositions, who push them from every corner to which they retreat, and who are sure at last to bring them to some dangerous dilemma. The best expedient to prevent this confusion, is to be modest in our pretensions; and even to discover the difficulty ourselves before it is objected to us. By this means, we may make a kind of merit of our very ignorance.

I shall content myself, in this section, with an easy task, and shall pretend only to give a negative answer to the question here proposed. I say then, that, even after we have experience of the operations of cause and effect, our conclusions from that experience are *not* founded on reasoning, or any process of the understanding. This answer we must endeavour both to explain and to defend.

29] It must certainly be allowed, that nature has kept us at a great distance from all her secrets, and has afforded us only the knowledge of a few superficial qualities of objects; while she conceals from us those powers and principles on which the influence of those objects entirely depends. Our senses inform us of the colour, weight, and consistence of bread; but neither sense nor reason can ever inform us of those qualities which fit it for the nourishment and support of a human body. Sight or feeling conveys an idea of the actual motion of bodies; but as to that wonderful force or power, which would carry on a moving body for ever in a continued change of place, and which bodies never lose but by communicating it to others; of this we cannot form the most distant conception. But notwithstanding this ignorance of natural powers[1]

---

[1] The word, Power, is here used in a loose and popular sense. The more accurate explication of it would give additional evidence to this argument. See Sect. 7.

and principles, we always presume, when we see like sensible qualities, that they have like secret powers, and expect that effects,
similar to those which we have experienced, will follow from
them. If a body of like colour and consistence with that bread,
which we have formerly eat, be presented to us, we make no scruple of repeating the experiment, and foresee, with certainty, like
nourishment and support. Now this is a process of the mind or
thought, of which I would willingly know the foundation. It is
allowed on all hands that there is no known connexion between
the sensible qualities and the secret powers; and consequently, that
the mind is not led to form such a conclusion concerning their
constant and regular conjunction, by anything which it knows of
their nature. As to past *Experience,* it can be allowed to give *direct*
and *certain* information of those precise objects only, and that
precise period of time, which fell under its cognizance: but why
this experience should be extended to future times, and to other
objects, which for aught we know, may be only in appearance
similar; this is the main question on which I would insist. The
bread, which I formerly eat, nourished me; that is, a body of such
sensible qualities was, at that time, endued with such secret
powers: but does it follow, that other bread must also nourish me
at another time, and that like sensible qualities must always be
attended with like secret powers? The consequence seems nowise
necessary. At least, it must be acknowledged that there is here a
consequence drawn by the mind; that there is a certain step taken;
a process of thought, and an inference, which wants to be explained. These two propositions are far from being the same, *I
have found that such an object has always been attended with such
an effect,* and *I foresee, that other objects, which are, in appearance, similar, will be attended with similar effects.* I shall allow,
if you please, that the one proposition may justly be inferred from
the other: I know, in fact, that it always is inferred. But if you insist that the inference is made by a chain of reasoning, I desire you
to produce that reasoning. The connexion between these propositions is not intuitive. There is required a medium, which may
enable the mind to draw such an inference, if indeed it be drawn
by reasoning and argument. What that medium is, I must confess,
passes my comprehension; and it is incumbent on those to pro-

duce it, who assert that it really exists, and is the origin of all our conclusions concerning matter of fact. . . .

When a man says, *I have found, in all past instances, such sensible qualities conjoined with such secret powers:* And when he says, *Similar sensible qualities will always be conjoined with similar secret powers,* he is not guilty of a tautology, nor are these propositions in any respect the same. You say that the one proposition is an inference from the other. But you must confess that the inference is not intuitive; neither is it demonstrative: Of what nature is it, then? To say it is experimental, is begging the question. For all inferences from experience suppose, as their foundation, that the future will resemble the past, and that similar powers will be conjoined with similar sensible qualities. If there be any suspicion that the course of nature may change, and that the past may be no rule for the future, all experience becomes useless, and can give rise to no inference or conclusion. It is impossible, therefore, that any arguments from experience can prove this resemblance of the past to the future; since all these arguments are founded on the supposition of that resemblance. Let the course of things be allowed hitherto ever so regular; that alone, without some new argument or inference, proves not that, for the future, it will continue so. In vain do you pretend to have learned the nature of bodies from your past experience. Their secret nature, and consequently all their effects and influence, may change, without any change in their sensible qualities. This happens sometimes, and with regard to some objects: Why may it not happen always, and with regard to all objects? What logic, what process of argument secures you against this supposition? My practice, you say, refutes my doubts. But you mistake the purport of my question. As an agent, I am quite satisfied in the point; but as a philosopher, who has some share of curiosity, I will not say scepticism, I want to learn the foundation of this inference. No reading, no enquiry has yet been able to remove my difficulty, or give me satisfaction in a matter of such importance. Can I do better than propose the difficulty to the public, even though, perhaps, I have small hopes of obtaining a solution? We shall at least, by this means, be sensible of our ignorance, if we do not augment our knowledge. . . .

Section V

Sceptical Solution of These Doubts

Part I

³⁴¹ The passion for philosophy, like that for religion, seems liable
to this inconvenience, that, though it aims at the correction of our
manners, and extirpation of our vices, it may only serve, by imprudent management, to foster a predominant inclination, and
push the mind, with more determined resolution, towards that
side which already *draws* too much, by the bias and propensity of
the natural temper. It is certain that, while we aspire to the magnanimous firmness of the philosophic sage, and endeavour to confine our pleasures altogether within our own minds, we may, at
last, render our philosophy like that of Epictetus, and other *Stoics*,
only a more refined system of selfishness, and reason ourselves out
of all virtue as well as social enjoyment. While we study with attention the vanity of human life, and turn all our thoughts towards
the empty and transitory nature of riches and honours, we are,
perhaps, all the while flattering our natural indolence, which,
hating the bustle of the world, and drudgery of business, seeks a
pretence of reason to give itself a full and uncontrolled indulgence. There is, however, one species of philosophy which seems
little liable to this inconvenience, and that because it strikes in
with no disorderly passion of the human mind, nor can mingle
itself with any natural affection or propensity; and that is the
Academic or Sceptical philosophy. The academics always talk of
doubt and suspense of judgement, of danger in hasty determinations, of confining to very narrow bounds the enquiries of the
understanding, and of renouncing all speculations which lie not
within the limits of common life and practice. Nothing, therefore,
can be more contrary than such a philosophy to the supine indolence of the mind, its rash arrogance, its lofty pretensions, and
its superstitious credulity. Every passion is mortified by it, except
the love of truth; and that passion never is, nor can be, carried to
too high a degree. It is surprising, therefore, that this philosophy,
which, in almost every instance, must be harmless and innocent,

should be the subject of so much groundless reproach and ob-
loquy. But, perhaps, the very circumstance which renders it so
innocent is what chiefly exposes it to the public hatred and resentment. By flattering no irregular passion, it gains few partizans: By
opposing so many vices and follies, it raises to itself abundance of
enemies, who stigmatize it as libertine, profane, and irreligious.

Nor need we fear that this philosophy, while it endeavours to
limit our enquiries to common life, should ever undermine the
reasonings of common life, and carry its doubts so far as to destroy
all action, as well as speculation. Nature will always maintain her
rights, and prevail in the end over any abstract reasoning whatsoever. Though we should conclude, for instance, as in the foregoing section, that, in all reasonings from experience, there is a
step taken by the mind which is not supported by any argument
or process of the understanding; there is no danger that these
reasonings, on which almost all knowledge depends, will ever be
affected by such a discovery. If the mind be not engaged by argument to make this step, it must be induced by some other principle
of equal weight and authority; and that principle will preserve
its influence as long as human nature remains the same. What that
principle is may well be worth the pains of enquiry.

35] Suppose a person, though endowed with the strongest faculties
of reason and reflection, to be brought on a sudden into this
world; he would, indeed, immediately observe a continual succession of objects, and one event following another; but he would
not be able to discover anything farther. He would not, at first, by
any reasoning, be able to reach the idea of cause and effect; since
the particular powers, by which all natural operations are performed, never appear to the senses; nor is it reasonable to conclude, merely because one event, in one instance, precedes another,
that therefore the one is the cause, the other the effect. Their conjunction may be arbitrary and casual. There may be no reason to
infer the existence of one from the appearance of the other. And
in a word, such a person, without more experience, could never
employ his conjecture or reasoning concerning any matter of fact,
or be assured of anything beyond what was immediately present to
his memory and senses.

Suppose, again, that he has acquired more experience, and has lived so long in the world as to have observed familiar objects or events to be constantly conjoined together; what is the consequence of this experience? He immediately infers the existence of one object from the appearance of the other. Yet he has not, by all his experience, acquired any idea or knowledge of the secret power by which the one object produces the other; nor is it, by any process of reasoning, he is engaged to draw this inference. But still he finds himself determined to draw it: And though he should be convinced that his understanding has no part in the operation, he would nevertheless continue in the same course of thinking. There is some other principle which determines him to form such a conclusion.

36] This principle is Custom or Habit. For wherever the repetition of any particular act or operation produces a propensity to renew the same act or operation, without being impelled by any reasoning or process of the understanding, we always say, that this propensity is the effect of *Custom*. By employing that word, we pretend not to have given the ultimate reason of such a propensity. We only point out a principle of human nature, which is universally acknowledged, and which is well known by its effects. Perhaps we can push our enquiries no farther, or pretend to give the cause of this cause; but must rest contented with it as the ultimate principle, which we can assign, of all our conclusions from experience. It is sufficient satisfaction, that we can go so far, without repining at the narrowness of our faculties because they will carry us no farther. And it is certain we here advance a very intelligible proposition at least, if not a true one, when we assert that, after the constant conjunction of two objects—heat and flame, for instance, weight and solidity—we are determined by custom alone to expect the one from the appearance of the other. This hypothesis seems even the only one which explains the difficulty, why we draw, from a thousand instances, an inference which we are not able to draw from one instance, that is, in no respect, different from them. Reason is incapable of any such variation. The conclusions which it draws from considering one circle are the same which it would form upon surveying all the circles in the universe. But no man, having seen only one body move after being impelled by another, could infer that every other body will move after a like impulse. All inferences from experience, therefore, are effects of custom, not of reasoning.[1]

Custom, then, is the great guide of human life. It is that principle alone which renders our experience useful to us, and makes us expect, for the future, a similar train of events with those which have appeared in the past. Without the influence of custom, we should be entirely ignorant of every matter of fact beyond what is immediately present to the memory and senses. We should never know how to adjust means to ends, or to employ our natural powers in the production of any effect. There would be an end at once of all action, as well as of the chief part of speculation.

[1] Nothing is more useful than for writers, even, on *moral, political,* or *physical* subjects, to distinguish between *reason* and *experience,* and to suppose, that these species of argumentation are entirely different from each other. The former are taken for the mere result of our intellectual faculties, which, by considering *à priori* the nature of things, and examining the effects, that must follow from their operation, establish particular principles of science and philosophy. The latter are supposed to be derived entirely from sense and observation, by which we learn what has actually resulted from the operation of particular objects, and are thence able to infer, what will, for the future, result from them. Thus, for instance, the limitations and restraints of civil government, and a legal constitution, may be defended, either from *reason,* which reflecting on the great frailty and corruption of human nature, teaches, that no man can safely be trusted with unlimited authority; or from *experience* and history, which inform us of the enormous abuses, that ambition, in every age and country, has been found to make of so imprudent a confidence.

The same distinction between reason and experience is maintained in all our deliberations concerning the conduct of life; while the experienced statesman, general, physician, or merchant is trusted and followed; and the unpractised novice, with whatever natural talents endowed, neglected and despised. Though it be allowed, that reason may form very plausible conjectures with regard to the consequences of such a particular conduct in such particular circumstances; it is still supposed imperfect, without the assistance of experience, which is alone able to give stability and certainty to the maxims, derived from study and reflection.

But notwithstanding that this distinction be thus universally received, both in the active speculative scenes of life, I shall not scruple to pronounce, that it is, at bottom, erroneous, at least, superficial.

If we examine those arguments, which, in any of the sciences above mentioned, are supposed to be the mere effects of reasoning and reflection, they will be found to terminate, at last, in some general principle or conclusion, for which we can assign no reason but observation and experience. The only difference between them and those maxims, which are vulgarly esteemed the result of pure experience, is, that the former cannot be established without some process of thought, and some reflection on what we have observed, in order to distinguish its circumstances, and trace its consequences: Whereas in the latter, the experienced event is exactly and fully familiar to that which we infer as the result of any particular situation. The history of a TIBERIUS or a NERO makes us dread a like tyranny, were our monarchs freed from the restraints of laws and senates: But the observation of any fraud or

37] But here it may be proper to remark, that though our conclusions from experience carry us beyond our memory and senses,
and assure us of matters of fact which happened in the most distant places and most remote ages, yet some fact must always be
present to the senses or memory, from which we may first proceed
in drawing these conclusions. A man, who should find in a desert
country the remains of pompous buildings, would conclude that
the country had, in ancient times, been cultivated by civilized inhabitants; but did nothing of this nature occur to him, he could
never form such an inference. We learn the events of former ages
from history; but then we must peruse the volumes in which this
instruction is contained, and thence carry up our inferences from
one testimony to another, till we arrive at the eyewitnesses and
spectators of these distant events. In a word, if we proceed not
upon some fact, present to the memory or senses, our reasonings
would be merely hypothetical; and however the particular links
might be connected with each other, the whole chain of inferences
would have nothing to support it, nor could we ever, by its means,
arrive at the knowledge of any real existence. If I ask why you believe any particular matter of fact, which you relate, you must tell
me some reason; and this reason will be some other fact, connected
with it. But as you cannot proceed after this manner, *in infinitum*,
you must at last terminate in some fact, which is present to your

---

cruelty in private life is sufficient, with the aid of a little thought, to give us the
same apprehension; while it serves as an instance of the general corruption of
human nature, and shows us the danger which we must incur by reposing an entire
confidence in mankind. In both cases, it is experience which is ultimately the foundation of our inference and conclusion.

There is no man so young and unexperienced, as not to have formed, from observation, many general and just maxims concerning human affairs and the conduct
of life; but it must be confessed, that, when a man comes to put these in practice,
he will be extremely liable to error, till time and farther experience both enlarge
these maxims, and teach him their proper use and application. In every situation or
incident, there are many particular and seemingly minute circumstances, which the
man of greatest talent is, at first, apt to overlook, though on them the justness of
his conclusions, and consequently the prudence of his conduct, entirely depend.
Not to mention, that, to a young beginner, the general observations and maxims
occur not always on the proper occasions, nor can be immediately applied with due
calmness and distinction. The truth is, an unexperienced reasoner could be no
reasoner at all, were he absolutely unexperienced; and when we assign that character to any one, we mean it only in a comparative sense, and suppose him possessed
of experience, in a smaller and more imperfect degree.

memory or senses; or must allow that your belief is entirely without foundation.

38] What, then, is the conclusion of the whole matter? A simple one; though, it must be confessed, pretty remote from the common theories of philosophy. All belief of matter of fact or real existence is derived merely from some object, present to the memory or senses, and a customary conjunction between that and some other object. Or in other words; having found, in many instances, that any two kinds of objects—flame and heat, snow and cold—have always been conjoined together; if flame or snow be presented anew to the senses, the mind is carried by custom to expect heat or cold, and to *believe* that such a quality does exist, and will discover itself upon a nearer approach. This belief is the necessary result of placing the mind in such circumstances. It is an operation of the soul, when we are so situated, as unavoidable as to feel the passion of love, when we receive benefits; or hatred, when we meet with injuries. All these operations are a species of natural instincts, which no reasoning or process of the thought and understanding is able either to produce or to prevent.

At this point, it would be very allowable for us to stop our philosophical researches. In most questions we can never make a single step farther; and in all questions we must terminate here at last, after our most restless and curious enquiries. But still our curiosity will be pardonable, perhaps commendable, if it carry us on to still farther researches, and make us examine more accurately the nature of this *belief,* and of the *customary conjunction,* whence it is derived. By this means we may meet with some explications and analogies that will give satisfaction; at least to such as love the abstract sciences, and can be entertained with speculations, which, however accurate, may still retain a degree of doubt and uncertainty. As to readers of a different taste; the remaining part of this section is not calculated for them, and the following enquiries may well be understood, though it be neglected.

Part II

391 Nothing is more free than the imagination of man; and though
it cannot exceed that original stock of ideas furnished by the internal and external senses, it has unlimited power of mixing, compounding, separating, and dividing these ideas, in all the varieties
of fiction and vision. It can feign a train of events, with all the
appearance of reality, ascribe to them a particular time and place,
conceive them as existent, and paint them out to itself with every
circumstance, that belongs to any historical fact, which it believes
with the greatest certainty. Wherein, therefore, consists the difference between such a fiction and belief? It lies not merely in any
peculiar idea, which is annexed to such a conception as commands
our assent, and which is wanting to every known fiction. For as
the mind has authority over all its ideas, it could voluntarily annex
this particular idea to any fiction, and consequently be able to believe whatever it pleases; contrary to what we find by daily experience. We can, in our conception, join the head of a man to
the body of a horse; but it is not in our power to believe that
such an animal has ever really existed.

It follows, therefore, that the difference between *fiction* and
belief lies in some sentiment or feeling, which is annexed to the
latter, not to the former, and which depends not on the will, nor
can be commanded at pleasure. It must be excited by nature, like
all other sentiments; and must arise from the particular situation,
in which the mind is placed at any particular juncture. Whenever
any object is presented to the memory or senses, it immediately,
by the force of custom, carries the imagination to conceive that
object, which is usually conjoined to it; and this conception is
attended with a feeling or sentiment, different from the loose
reveries of the fancy. In this consists the whole nature of belief.
For as there is no matter of fact which we believe so firmly that
we cannot conceive the contrary, there would be no difference between the conception assented to and that which is rejected, were
it not for some sentiment which distinguishes the one from the
other. If I see a billiard-ball moving towards another, on a smooth
table, I can easily conceive it to stop upon contact. This conception implies no contradiction; but still it feels very differently

from that conception by which I represent to myself the impulse and the communication of motion from one ball to another.

40] Were we to attempt a *definition* of this sentiment, we should, perhaps, find it a very difficult, if not an impossible task; in the same manner as if we should endeavour to define the feeling of cold or passion of anger, to a creature who never had any experience of these sentiments. Belief is the true and proper name of this feeling; and no one is ever at a loss to know the meaning of that term; because every man is every moment conscious of the sentiment represented by it. It may not, however, be improper to attempt a *description* of this sentiment; in hopes we may, by that means, arrive at some analogies, which may afford a more perfect explication of it. I say, then, that belief is nothing but a more vivid, lively, forcible, firm, steady conception of an object, than what the imagination alone is ever able to attain. This variety of terms, which may seem so unphilosophical, is intended only to express that act of the mind, which renders realities, or what is taken for such, more present to us than fictions, causes them to weigh more in the thought, and gives them a superior influence on the passions and imagination. Provided we agree about the thing, it is needless to dispute about the terms. The imagination has the command over all its ideas, and can join and mix and vary them, in all the ways possible. It may conceive fictitious objects with all the circumstances of place and time. It may set them, in a manner, before our eyes, in their true colours, just as they might have existed. But as it is impossible that this faculty of imagination can ever, of itself, reach belief, it is evident that belief consists not in the peculiar nature or order of ideas, but in the *manner* of their conception, and in their *feeling* to the mind. I confess, that it is impossible perfectly to explain this feeling or manner of conception. We may make use of words which express something near it. But its true and proper name, as we observed before, is *belief;* which is a term that every one sufficiently understands in common life. And in philosophy, we can go no farther than assert, that *belief* is something felt by the mind, which distinguishes the ideas of the judgment from the fictions of the imagination. It gives them more weight and influence; makes them appear of greater importance; enforces them in the mind; and renders them the governing principle of our actions. I hear at present, for instance, a person's voice, with whom I am acquainted; and the sound comes as from the next room. This impression of my senses immediately conveys my thought to the person, together with all the surrounding objects. I paint them out to myself as existing at present, with the same qualities and relations, of which I formerly knew them possessed. These ideas take faster hold of my mind than ideas of an enchanted castle. They are very different to the feeling, and have a much greater influence of every kind, either to give pleasure or pain, joy or sorrow. . . .

Section VI

Of Probability[1]

461 Though there be no such thing as *Chance* in the world; our ignorance of the real cause of any event has the same influence on the understanding, and begets a like species of belief or opinion.

There is certainly a probability, which arises from a superiority of chances on any side; and according as this superiority encreases, and surpasses the opposite chances, the probability receives a proportionable encrease, and begets still a higher degree of belief or assent to that side, in which we discover the superiority. If a dye were marked with one figure or number of spots on four sides, and with another figure or number of spots on the two remaining sides, it would be more probable, that the former would turn up than the latter; though, if it had a thousand sides marked in the same manner, and only one side different, the probability would be much higher, and our belief or expectation of the event more steady and secure. This process of the thought or reasoning may seem trivial and obvious; but to those who consider it more narrowly, it may, perhaps, afford matter for curious speculation.

It seems evident, that, when the mind looks forward to discover the event, which may result from the throw of such a dye, it con-

---

[1] Mr. Locke divides all arguments into demonstrative and probable. In this view, we must say, that it is only probable all men must die, or that the sun will rise to-morrow. But to conform our language more to common use, we ought to divide arguments into *demonstrations, proofs,* and *probabilities.* By proofs meaning such arguments from experience as leave no room for doubt or opposition.

siders the turning up of each particular side as alike probable; and this is the very nature of chance, to render all the particular events, comprehended in it, entirely equal. But finding a greater number of sides concur in the one event than in the other, the mind is carried more frequently to that event, and meets it oftener, in revolving the various possibilities or chances, on which the ultimate result depends. This concurrence of several views in one particular event begets immediately, by an inexplicable contrivance of nature, the sentiment of belief, and gives that event the advantage over its antagonist, which is supported by a smaller number of views, and recurs less frequently to the mind. If we allow, that belief is nothing but a firmer and stronger conception of an object than what attends the mere fictions of the imagination, this operation may, perhaps, in some measure, be accounted for. The concurrence of these several views or glimpses imprints the idea more strongly on the imagination; gives it superior force and vigour; renders its influence on the passions and affections more sensible; and in a word, begets that reliance or security, which constitutes the nature of belief and opinion.

47] The case is the same with the probability of causes, as with that of chance. There are some causes, which are entirely uniform and constant in producing a particular effect; and no instance has ever yet been found of any failure or irregularity in their operation. Fire has always burned, and water suffocated every human creature: The production of motion by impulse and gravity is an universal law, which has hitherto admitted of no exception. But there are other causes, which have been found more irregular and uncertain; nor has rhubarb always proved a purge, or opium a soporific to every one, who has taken these medicines. It is true, when any cause fails of producing its usual effect, philosophers ascribe not this to any irregularity in nature; but suppose, that some secret causes, in the particular structure of parts, have prevented the operation. Our reasonings, however, and conclusions concerning the event are the same as if this principle had no place. Being determined by custom to transfer the past to the future, in all our inferences; where the past has been entirely regular and uniform, we expect the event with the greatest assurance, and leave no room for any contrary supposition. But where different effects have been found to follow from causes, which are to *appearance* exactly similar, all these various effects must occur to the mind in transferring the past to the future, and enter into our consideration, when we determine the probability of the event. Though we give the preference to that which has been found most usual, and believe that this effect will exist, we must not overlook the other effects, but must assign to each of them a particular weight and authority, in proportion as we have found it to be more or less frequent. It is more probable, in almost every country of Europe, that there will be frost sometime in January, than that the weather will continue open throughout that whole month; though this probability varies according to the different climates, and approaches to a certainty in the more northern kingdoms. Here then it seems evident, that, when we transfer the past to the future, in order to determine the effect, which will result from any cause, we transfer all the different events, in the same proportion as they have appeared in the past, and conceive one to have existed a hundred times, for instance, another ten times, and another once. As a great number of views do here concur in one event, they fortify and confirm it to the imagination, beget that sentiment which we call *belief,* and give its object the preference above the contrary event, which is not supported by an equal number of experiments, and recurs not so frequently to the thought in transferring the past to the future. Let any one try to account for this operation of the mind upon any of the received systems of philosophy, and he will be sensible of the difficulty. For my part, I shall think it sufficient, if the present hints excite the curiosity of philosophers, and make them sensible how defective all common theories are in treating of such curious and such sublime subjects.

Section VII

Of the Idea of Necessary Connexion

Part I

48] The great advantage of the mathematical sciences above the moral consists in this, that the ideas of the former, being sensible, are always clear and determinate, the smallest distinction between them is immediately perceptible, and the same terms are still expressive of the same ideas, without ambiguity or variation. An oval is never mistaken for a circle, nor an hyperbola for an ellipsis. The isosceles and scalenum are distinguished by boundaries more exact than vice and virtue, right and wrong. If any term be defined in geometry, the mind readily, of itself, substitutes, on all occasions, the definition for the term defined: Or even when no definition is employed, the object itself may be presented to the senses, and by that means be steadily and clearly apprehended. But the finer sentiments of the mind, the operations of the understanding, the various agitations of the passions, though really in themselves distinct, easily escape us, when surveyed by reflection; nor is it in our power to recal the original object, as often as we have occasion to contemplate it. Ambiguity, by this means, is gradually introduced into our reasonings: Similar objects are readily taken to be the same: And the conclusion becomes at last very wide of the premises.

One may safely, however, affirm, that, if we consider these sciences in a proper light, their advantages and disadvantages nearly compensate each other, and reduce both of them to a state of equality. If the mind, with greater facility, retains the ideas of geometry clear and determinate, it must carry on a much longer and more intricate chain of reasoning, and compare ideas much wider of each other, in order to reach the abstruser truths of that science. And if moral ideas are apt, without extreme care, to fall into obscurity and confusion, the inferences are always much shorter in these disquisitions, and the intermediate steps, which lead to the conclusion, much fewer than in the sciences which treat of quantity and number. In reality, there is scarcely a proposition in Euclid so simple, as not to consist of more parts, than are to be found in any moral reasoning which runs not into chimera and conceit. Where we trace the principles of the human mind through a few steps, we may be very well satisfied with our progress; considering how soon nature throws a bar to all our enquiries concerning causes, and reduces us to an acknowledgment of our ignorance. The chief obstacle, therefore, to our improvement in the moral or metaphysical sciences is the obscurity of the ideas, and ambiguity of the terms. The principal difficulty in the mathematics is the length of inferences and compass of thought, requisite to the forming of any conclusion. And, perhaps, our progress in natural philosophy is chiefly retarded by the want of proper experiments and phaenomena, which are often discovered by chance, and cannot always be found, when requisite, even by the most diligent and prudent enquiry. As moral philosophy seems hitherto to have received less improvement than either geometry or physics, we may conclude, that, if there be any difference in this respect among these sciences, the difficulties, which obstruct the progress of the former, require superior care and capacity to be surmounted.

49] There are no ideas, which occur in metaphysics, more obscure and uncertain, than those of *power, force, energy* or *necessary connexion,* of which it is every moment necessary for us to treat in all our disquisitions. We shall, therefore, endeavour, in this section, to fix, if possible, the precise meaning of these terms, and thereby remove some part of that obscurity, which is so much complained of in this species of philosophy.

It seems a proposition, which will not admit of much dispute, that all our ideas are nothing but copies of our impressions, or, in other words, that it is impossible for us to *think* of anything, which we have not antecedently *felt,* either by our external or internal senses. I have endeavoured [1] to explain and prove this proposition, and have expressed my hopes, that, by a proper application of it, men may reach a greater clearness and precision in philosophical reasonings, than what they have hitherto been able to attain. Complex ideas may, perhaps, be well known by definition, which is nothing but an enumeration of those parts or simple ideas, that compose them. But when we have pushed up definitions to the most simple ideas, and find still some ambiguity and obscurity; what resource are we then possessed of? By what invention can we throw light upon these ideas, and render them altogether precise and determinate to our intellectual view? Produce the impressions or original sentiments, from which the ideas are copied. These impressions are all strong and sensible. They admit not of ambiguity. They are not only placed in a full light themselves, but may throw light on their correspondent ideas, which lie in obscurity. And by this means, we may, perhaps, attain a new micro-

[1] Section II.

scope or species of optics, by which, in the moral sciences, the most minute, and most simple ideas may be so enlarged as to fall readily under our apprehension, and be equally known with the grossest and most sensible ideas, that can be the object of our enquiry.

50] To be fully acquainted, therefore, with the idea of power or necessary connexion, let us examine its impression; and in order to find the impression with greater certainty, let us search for it in all the sources, from which it may possibly be derived.

When we look about us towards external objects, and consider the operation of causes, we are never able, in a single instance, to discover any power or necessary connexion; any quality, which binds the effect to the cause, and renders the one an infallible consequence of the other. We only find, that the one does actually, in fact, follow the other. The impulse of one billiard-ball is attended with motion in the second. This is the whole that appears to the *outward* senses. The mind feels no sentiment or *inward* impression from this succession of objects: Consequently, there is not, in any single, particular instance of cause and effect, any thing which can suggest the idea of power or necessary connexion.

From the first appearance of an object, we never can conjecture what effect will result from it. But were the power or energy of any cause discoverable by the mind, we could foresee the effect, even without experience; and might, at first, pronounce with certainty concerning it, by mere dint of thought and reasoning.

In reality, there is no part of matter, that does ever, by its sensible qualities, discover any power or energy, or give us ground to imagine, that it could produce any thing, or be followed by any other object, which we could denominate its effect. Solidity, extension, motion; these qualities are all complete in themselves, and never point out any other event which may result from them. The scenes of the universe are continually shifting, and one object follows another in an uninterrupted succession; but the power of force, which actuates the whole machine, is entirely concealed from us, and never discovers itself in any of the sensible qualities of body. We know, that, in fact, heat is a constant attendant of flame; but what is the connexion between them, we have no room so much as to conjecture or imagine. It is impossible, therefore, that the idea of power can be derived from the contemplation of

bodies, in single instances of their operation; because no bodies
ever discover any power, which can be the original of this idea.[1]

51] Since, therefore, external objects as they appear to the senses,
give us no idea of power or necessary connexion, by their operation in particular instances, let us see, whether this idea be derived
from reflection on the operations of our own minds, and be copied
from any internal impression. It may be said, that we are every
moment conscious of internal power; while we feel, that, by the
simple command of our will, we can move the organs of our body,
or direct the faculties of our mind. An act of volition produces
motion in our limbs, or raises a new idea in our imagination. This
influence of the will we know by consciousness. Hence we acquire
the idea of power or energy; and are certain, that we ourselves and
all other intelligent beings are possessed of power. This idea, then,
is an idea of reflection, since it arises from reflecting on the operations of our own mind, and on the command which is exercised
by will, both over the organs of the body and faculties of the soul.

52] We shall proceed to examine this pretension; and first with regard to the influence of volition over the organs of the body. This
influence, we may observe, is a fact, which, like all other natural
events, can be known only by experience, and can never be foreseen from any apparent energy or power in the cause, which
connects it with the effect, and renders the one an infallible consequence of the other. The motion of our body follows upon the
command of our will. Of this we are every moment conscious. But
the means, by which this is effected; the energy, by which the will
performs so extraordinary an operation; of this we are so far from
being immediately conscious, that it must for ever escape our most
diligent enquiry.

For *first;* is there any principle in all nature more mysterious
than the union of soul with body; by which a supposed spiritual
substance acquires such an influence over a material one, that the
most refined thought is able to actuate the grossest matter? Were

[1] Mr. Locke, in his chapter on power, says that, finding from experience, that
there are several new productions in matter, and concluding that there must somewhere be a power capable of producing them, we arrive at last by this reasoning at
the idea of power. But no reasoning can ever give us a new, original, simple idea;
as this philosopher himself confesses. This, therefore, can never be the origin of
that idea.

we empowered, by a secret wish, to remove mountains, or control the planets in their orbit; this extensive authority would not be more extraordinary, nor more beyond our comprehension. But if by consciousness we perceived any power or energy in the will, we must know this power; we must know its connexion with the effect; we must know the secret union of soul and body, and the nature of both these substances; by which the one is able to operate, in so many instances, upon the other.

Secondly, We are not able to move all the organs of the body with a like authority; though we cannot assign any reason besides experience, for so remarkable a difference between one and the other. Why has the will an influence over the tongue and fingers, not over the heart or liver? This question would never embarrass us, were we conscious of a power in the former case, not in the latter. We should then perceive, independent of experience, why the authority of will over the organs of the body is circumscribed within such particular limits. Being in that case fully acquainted with the power or force, by which it operates, we should also know, why its influence reaches precisely to such boundaries, and no farther.

A man, suddenly struck with palsy in the leg or arm, or who had newly lost those members, frequently endeavours, at first to move them, and employ them in their usual offices. Here he is as much conscious of power to command such limbs, as a man in perfect health is conscious of power to actuate any member which remains in its natural state and condition. But consciousness never deceives. Consequently, neither in the one case nor in the other, are we ever conscious of any power. We learn the influence of our will from experience alone. And experience only teaches us, how one event constantly follows another; without instructing us in the secret connexion, which binds them together, and renders them inseparable.

Thirdly, We learn from anatomy, that the immediate object of power in voluntary motion, is not the member itself which is moved, but certain muscles, and nerves, and animal spirits, and, perhaps, something still more minute and more unknown, through which the motion is successively propagated, ere it reach the member itself whose motion is the immediate object of volition. Can there be a more certain proof, that the power, by which this whole operation is performed, so far from being directly and fully known by an inward sentiment or consciousness, is, to the last degree, mysterious and untelligible? Here the mind wills a certain event: Immediately another event, unknown to ourselves, and totally different from the one intended, is produced: This event produces another, equally unknown: Till at last, through a long succession, the desired event is produced. But if the original power were felt, it must be known: Were it known, its effect also must be known; since all power is relative to its effect. And *vice versa,* if the effect be not known, the power cannot be known nor felt. How indeed can we be conscious of a power to move our limbs, when we have no such power; but only that to move certain animal spirits, which, though they produce at last the motion of our limbs, yet operate in such a manner as is wholly beyond our comprehension?

We may, therefore, conclude from the whole, I hope, without any temerity, though with assurance; that our idea of power is not copied from any sentiment or consciousness of power within ourselves, when we give rise to animal motion, or apply our limbs to their proper use and office. That their motion follows the command of the will is a matter of common experience, like other natural events: But the power or energy by which this is effected, like that in other natural events, is unknown and inconceivable.[1]

53 Shall we then assert, that we are conscious of a power or energy in our own minds, when, by an act or command of our will, we raise up a new idea, fix the mind to the contemplation of it, turn it on all sides, and at last dismiss it for some other idea, when we think that we have surveyed it with sufficient accuracy? I believe

---

[1] It may be pretended, that the resistance which we meet with in bodies, obliging us frequently to exert our force, and call up all our power, this gives us the idea of force and power. It is this *nisus,* or strong endeavour, of which we are conscious, that is the original impression from which this idea is copied. But, first, we attribute power to a vast number of objects, where we never can suppose this resistance or exertion of force to take place; to the Supreme Being, who never meets with any resistance; to the mind in its command over its ideas and limbs, in common thinking and motion, where the effect follows immediately upon the will, without any exertion or summoning up of force; to inanimate matter, which is not capable of this sentiment. *Secondly,* This sentiment of an endeavour to overcome resistance has no known connexion with any event: What follows it, we know by experience; but could not know it *à priori.* It must, however, be confessed, that the animal *nisus,* which we experience, though it can afford no accurate precise idea of power, enters very much into that vulgar, inaccurate idea, which is formed of it.

the same arguments will prove, that even this command of the will gives us no real idea of force or energy.

First, it must be allowed, that, when we know a power, we know that very circumstance in the cause, by which it is enabled to produce the effect: For these are supposed to be synonimous. We must, therefore, know both the cause and effect, and the relation between them. But do we pretend to be acquainted with the nature of the human soul and the nature of an idea, or the aptitude of the one to produce the other? This is a real creation; a production of something out of nothing: Which implies a power so great, that it may seem, at first sight, beyond the reach of any being, less than infinite. At least it must be owned, that such a power is not felt, nor known, nor even conceivable by the mind. We only feel the event, namely, the existence of an idea, consequent to a command of the will: But the manner, in which this operation is performed, the power by which it is produced, is entirely beyond our comprehension.

Secondly, The command of the mind over itself is limited, as well as its command over the body; and these limits are not known by reason, or any acquaintance with the nature of cause and effect, but only by experience and observation, as in all other natural events and in the operation of external *objects*. Our authority over our sentiments and passions is much weaker than that over our ideas; and even the latter authority is circumscribed within very narrow boundaries. Will any one pretend to assign the ultimate reason of these boundaries, or show why the power is deficient in one case, not in another.

Thirdly, This self-command is very different at different times. A man in health possesses more of it than one languishing with sickness. We are more master of our thoughts in the morning than in the evening: Fasting, than after a full meal. Can we give any reason for these variations, except experience? Where then is the power, of which we pretend to be conscious? Is there not here, either in a spiritual or material substance, or both, some secret mechanism or structure of parts, upon which the effect depends, and which, being entirely unknown to us, renders the power or energy of the will equally unknown and incomprehensible?

Volition is surely an act of the mind, with which we are sufficiently acquainted. Reflect upon it. Consider it on all sides. Do you find anything in it like this creative power, by which it raises from nothing a new idea, and with a kind of *Fiat,* imitates the omnipotence of its Maker, if I may be allowed so to speak, who called forth into existence all the various scenes of nature? So far from being conscious of this energy in the will, it requires as certain experience as that of which we are possessed, to convince us that such extraordinary effects do ever result from a simple act of volition.

54] The generality of mankind never find any difficulty in accounting for the more common and familiar operations of nature—such as the descent of heavy bodies, the growth of plants, the generation of animals, or the nourishment of bodies by food: But suppose that, in all these cases, they perceive the very force or energy of the cause, by which it is connected with its effect, and is for ever infallible in its operation. They acquire, by long habit, such a turn of mind, that, upon the appearance of the cause, they immediately expect with assurance its usual attendant, and hardly conceive it possible that any other event could result from it. It is only on the discovery of extraordinary phenomena such as earthquakes, pestilence, and prodigies of any kind, that they find themselves at a loss to assign a proper cause, and to explain the manner in which the effect is produced by it. It is usual for men, in such difficulties, to have recourse to some invisible intelligent principle as the immediate cause of that event which surprises them, and which, they think, cannot be accounted for from the common powers of nature. But philosophers, who carry their scrutiny a little farther, immediately perceive that, even in the most familiar events, the energy of the cause is as unintelligible as in the most unusual, and that we only learn by experience the frequent *Conjunction* of objects, without being ever able to comprehend anything like *Connexion* between them.

55] Here, then, many philosophers think themselves obliged by reason to have recourse, on all occasions, to the same principle, which the vulgar never appeal to but in cases that appear miraculous and supernatural. They acknowledge mind and intelligence to be, not only the ultimate and original cause of all things, but the immediate and sole cause of every event which appears in nature. They pretend that those objects which are commonly denominated *causes,* are in reality nothing but *occasions;* and that the true and direct principle of every effect is not any power or force in nature, but a volition of the Supreme Being, who wills that such particular objects should for ever be conjoined with each other. Instead of saying that one billiard-ball moves another by a force which it has derived from the author of nature, it is the Deity himself, they say, who, by a particular volition, moves the second ball, being determined to this operation by the impulse of the first ball, in consequence of those general laws which he has laid down to himself in the government of the universe. But philosophers advancing still in their inquiries, discover that, as we are totally ignorant of the power on which depends the mutual operation of bodies, we are no less ignorant of that power on which depends the operation of mind on body, or of body on mind; nor are we able, either from our senses or consciousness, to assign the ultimate principle in one case more than in the other. The same ignorance, therefore, reduces them to the same conclusion. They assert that the Deity is the immediate cause of the union between soul and body; and that they are not the organs of sense, which, being agitated by external objects, produce sensations in the mind; but that it is a particular volition of our omnipotent Maker, which excites such a sensation, in consequence of such a motion in the organ. In like manner, it is not any energy in the will that produces local motion in our members: It is God himself, who is pleased to second our will, in itself impotent, and to command that motion which we erroneously attribute to our own power and efficacy. Nor do philosophers stop at this conclusion. They sometimes extend the same inference to the mind itself, in its internal operations. Our mental vision or conception of ideas is nothing but a revelation made to us by our Maker. When we voluntarily turn our thoughts to any object, and raise up its image in the fancy, it is not the will which creates that idea: It is the universal Creator, who discovers it to the mind, and renders it present to us.

56] Thus, according to these philosophers, every thing is full of God. Not content with the principle, that nothing exists but by his will, that nothing possesses any power but by his concession: They rob nature, and all created beings, of every power, in order to render their dependence on the Deity still more sensible and immediate. They consider not that, by this theory, they diminish, instead of magnifying, the grandeur of those attributes, which they affect so much to celebrate. It argues surely more power in the Deity to delegate a certain degree of power to inferior creatures than to produce every thing by his own immediate volition. It argues more wisdom to contrive at first the fabric of the world with such perfect foresight that, of itself, and by its proper operation, it may serve all the purposes of providence, than if the great Creator were obliged every moment to adjust its parts, and animate by his breath all the wheels of that stupendous machine.

But if we would have a more philosophical confutation of this theory, perhaps the two following reflections may suffice.

57] *First,* it seems to me that this theory of the universal energy and operation of the Supreme Being is too bold ever to carry conviction with it to a man, sufficiently apprized of the weakness of human reason, and the narrow limits to which it is confined in all its operations. Though the chain of arguments which conduct to it were ever so logical, there must arise a strong suspicion, if not an absolute assurance, that it has carried us quite beyond the reach of our faculties, when it leads to conclusions so extraordinary, and so remote from common life and experience. We are got into fairy land, long ere we have reached the last steps of our theory; and *there* we have no reason to trust our common methods of argument, or to think that our usual analogies and probabilities have any authority. Our line is too short to fathom such immense abysses. And however we may flatter ourselves that we are guided, in every step which we take, by a kind of verisimilitude and experience, we may be assured that this fancied experience has no authority when we thus apply it to subjects that lie entirely out of the sphere of experience. But on this we shall have occasion to touch afterwards.[1]

Secondly, I cannot perceive any force in the arguments on which this theory is founded. We are ignorant, it is true, of the manner in which bodies operate on each other: Their force or energy is entirely incomprehensible: But are we not equally ignorant of the manner or force by which a mind, even the supreme mind, operates either on itself or on body? Whence, I beseech you, do we acquire any idea of it? We have no sentiment or consciousness of

[1] Section XII.

this power in ourselves. We have no idea of the Supreme Being but what we learn from reflection on our own faculties. Were our ignorance, therefore, a good reason for rejecting any thing, we should be led into that principle of denying all energy in the Supreme Being as much as in the grossest matter. We surely comprehend as little the operations of one as of the other. Is it more difficult to conceive that motion may arise from impulse than that it may arise from volition? All we know is our profound ignorance in both cases.[1]

Part II

58] But to hasten to a conclusion of this argument, which is already drawn out to too great a length: We have sought in vain for an idea of power or necessary connexion in all the sources from which we could suppose it to be derived. It appears that, in single instances of the operation of bodies we never can, by our utmost scrutiny, discover any thing but one event following another, without being able to comprehend any force or power by which the cause operates, or any connexion between it and its supposed effect. The same difficulty occurs in contemplating the operations of mind on body—where we observe the motion of the latter to follow upon the volition of the former, but are not able to observe or

---

[1] I need not examine at length the *vis inertiae* which is so much talked of in the new philosophy, and which is ascribed to matter. We find by experience, that a body at rest or in motion continues for ever in its present state, till put from it by some new cause; and that a body impelled takes as much motion from the impelling body as it acquires itself. These are facts. When we call this a *vis inertiae*, we only mark these facts, without pretending to have any idea of the inert power; in the same manner as, when we talk of gravity, we mean certain effects, without comprehending that active power. It was never the meaning of Sir ISAAC NEWTON to rob second causes of all force or energy; though some of his followers have endeavoured to establish that theory upon his authority. On the contrary, that great philosopher had recourse to an etherial active fluid to explain his universal attraction; though he was so cautious and modest as to allow, that it was a mere hypothesis, not to be insisted on, without more experiments. I must confess, that there is something in the fate of opinions a little extraordinary. DES CARTES insinuated that doctrine of the universal and sole efficacy of the Deity, without insisting on it. MALEBRANCHE and other CARTESIANS made it the foundation of all their philosophy. It had, however, no authority in England. LOCKE, CLARKE, and CUDWORTH, never so much as take notice of it, but suppose all along, that matter has a real, though subordinate and derived power. By what means has it become so prevalent among our modern metaphysicians?

conceive the tie which binds together the motion and volition, or the energy by which the mind produces this effect. The authority of the will over its own faculties and ideas is not a whit more comprehensible: So that, upon the whole, there appears not, throughout all nature, any one instance of connexion which is conceivable by us. All events seem entirely loose and separate. One event follows another; but we never can observe any tie between them. They seem *conjoined,* but never *connected.* And as we can have no idea of any thing which never appeared to our outward sense or inward sentiment, the necessary conclusion *seems* to be that we have no idea of connexion or power at all, and that these words are absolutely without any meaning, when employed either in philosophical reasonings or common life.

59] But there still remains one method of avoiding this conclusion, and one source which we have not yet examined. When any natural object or event is presented, it is impossible for us, by any sagacity or penetration, to discover, or even conjecture, without experience, what event will result from it, or to carry our foresight beyond that object which is immediately present to the memory and senses. Even after one instance or experiment where we have observed a particular event to follow upon another, we are not entitled to form a general rule, or foretell what will happen in like cases; it being justly esteemed an unpardonable temerity to judge of the whole course of nature from one single experiment, however accurate or certain. But when one particular species of event has always, in all instances, been conjoined with another, we make no longer any scruple of foretelling one upon the appearance of the other, and of employing that reasoning, which can alone assure us of any matter of fact or existence. We then call the one object, *Cause;* the other, *Effect.* We suppose that there is some connexion between them; some power in the one, by which it infallibly produces the other, and operates with the greatest certainty and strongest necessity.

It appears, then, that this idea of a necessary connexion among events arises from a number of similar instances which occur of the constant conjunction of these events; nor can that idea ever be suggested by any one of these instances, surveyed in all possible lights and positions. But there is nothing in a number of instances, different from every single instance, which is supposed to be exactly similar; except only, that after a repetition of similar instances, the mind is carried by habit, upon the appearance of one event, to expect its usual attendant, and to believe that it will exist. This connexion, therefore, which we *feel* in the mind, this customary transition of the imagination from one object to its usual attendant, is the sentiment or impression from which we form the idea of power or necessary connexion. Nothing farther is in the case. Contemplate the subject on all sides; you will never find any other origin of that idea. This is the sole difference between one instance, from which we can never receive the idea of connexion, and a number of similar instances, by which it is suggested. The first time a man saw the communication of motion by impulse, as by the shock of two billiard balls, he could not pronounce that the one event was *connected:* but only that it was *conjoined* with the other. After he has observed several instances of this nature, he then pronounces them to be *connected.* What alteration has happened to give rise to this new idea of *connexion?* Nothing but that he now *feels* these events to be *connected* in his imagination, and can readily foretell the existence of one from the appearance of the other. When we say, therefore, that one object is connected with another, we mean only that they have acquired a connexion in our thought, and give rise to this inference, by which they become proofs of each other's existence: A conclusion which is somewhat extraordinary, but which seems founded on sufficient evidence. Nor will its evidence be weakened by any general diffidence of the understanding, or sceptical suspicion concerning every conclusion which is new and extraordinary. No conclusions can be more agreeable to scepticism than such as make discoveries concerning the weakness and narrow limits of human reason and capacity.

60] And what stronger instance can be produced of the surprising ignorance and weakness of the understanding than the present? For surely, if there be any relation among objects which it imports to us to know perfectly, it is that of cause and effect. On this are founded all our reasonings concerning matter of fact or existence. By means of it alone we attain any assurance concerning objects which are removed from the present testimony of our memory and

senses. The only immediate utility of all sciences, is to teach us, how to control and regulate future events by their causes. Our thoughts and enquiries are, therefore, every moment, employed about this relation: Yet so imperfect are the ideas which we form concerning it, that it is impossible to give any just definition of cause, except what is drawn from something extraneous and foreign to it. Similar objects are always conjoined with similar. Of this we have experience. Suitably to this experience, therefore, we may define a cause to be *an object, followed by another, and where all the objects similar to the first are followed by objects similar to the second.* Or in other words where, *if the first object had not been, the second never had existed.* The appearance of a cause always conveys the mind, by a customary transition, to the idea of the effect. Of this we have experience. We may, therefore, suitably to this experience, form another definition of cause, and call it, *an object followed by another, and whose appearance always conveys the thought to that other.* But though both these definitions be drawn from circumstances foreign to the cause, we cannot remedy this inconvenience, or attain any more perfect definition, which may point out that circumstance in the cause, which gives it a connexion with its effect. We have no idea of this connexion, nor even any distinct notion what it is we desire to know, when we endeavour at a conception of it. We say, for instance, that the vibration of this string is the cause of this particular sound. But what do we mean by that affirmation? We either mean *that this vibration is followed by this sound, and that all similar vibrations have been followed by similar sounds:* Or, *that this vibration is followed by this sound, and that upon the appearance of one the mind anticipates the senses, and forms immediately an idea of the other.* We may consider the relation of cause and effect in either of these two lights; but beyond these, we have no idea of it.[1]

611 To recapitulate, therefore, the reasonings of this section: Every idea is copied from some preceding impression or sentiment; and where we cannot find any impression, we may be certain that

---

[1] According to these explications and definitions, the idea of *power* is relative as much as that of *cause;* and both have a reference to an effect, or some other event constantly conjoined with the former. When we consider the *unknown* circumstance of an object, by which the degree or quantity of its effect is fixed and determined, we call that its power: And accordingly, it is allowed by all philosophers, that the

there is no idea. In all single instances of the operation of bodies or minds, there is nothing that produces any impression, nor consequently can suggest any idea of power or necessary connexion. But when many uniform instances appear, and the same object is always followed by the same event; we then begin to entertain the notion of cause and connexion. We then *feel* a new sentiment or impression, to wit, a customary connexion in the thought or imagination between one object and its usual attendant; and this sentiment is the original of that idea which we seek for. For as this idea arises from a number of similar instances, and not from any single instance, it must arise from that circumstance, in which the number of instances differ from every individual instance. But this customary connexion or transition of the imagination is the only circumstance in which they differ. In every other particular they are alike. The first instance which we saw of motion communicated by the shock of two billiard balls (to return to this obvious illustration) is exactly similar to any instance that may, at present, occur to us; except only, that we could not, at first, *infer* one event from the other; which we are enabled to do at present, after so long a course of uniform experience. I know not whether the reader will readily apprehend this reasoning. I am afraid that, should I multiply words about it, or throw it into a greater variety

---

effect is the measure of the power. But if they had any idea of power, as it is in itself, why could not they Measure it in itself? The dispute whether the force of a body in motion be as its velocity, or the square of its velocity; this dispute, I say, need not be decided by comparing its effects in equal or unequal times; but by a direct mensuration and comparison.

As to the frequent use of the words, Force, Power, Energy, &c., which every where occur in common conversation, as well as in philosophy; that is no proof, that we are acquainted, in any instance, with the connecting principle between cause and effect, or can account ultimately for the production of one thing to another. These words, as commonly used, have very loose meanings annexed to them; and their ideas are very uncertain and confused. No animal can put external bodies in motion without the sentiment of a *nisus* or endeavour; and every animal has a sentiment or feeling from the stroke or blow of an external object, that is in motion. These sensations, which are merely animal, and from which we can *à priori* draw no inference, we are apt to transfer to inanimate objects, and to suppose, that they have some such feelings, whenever they transfer or receive motion. With regard to energies, which are exerted, without our annexing to them any idea of communicated motion, we consider only the constant experienced conjunction of the events; and as we *feel* a customary connexion between the ideas, we transfer that feeling to the objects; as nothing is more usual than to apply to external bodies every internal sensation, which they occasion.

of lights, it would only become more obscure and intricate. In all abstract reasonings there is one point of view which, if we can happily hit, we shall go farther towards illustrating the subject than by all the eloquence and copious expression in the world. This point of view we should endeavour to reach, and reserve the flowers of rhetoric for subjects which are more adapted to them.

Section VIII

Of Liberty and Necessity

Part I

62] It might reasonably be expected in questions which have been canvassed and disputed with great eagerness, since the first origin of science and philosophy, that the meaning of all the terms, at least, should have been agreed upon among the disputants; and our enquiries, in the course of two thousand years, been able to pass from words to the true and real subject of the controversy. For how easy may it seem to give exact definitions of the terms employed in reasoning, and make these definitions, not the mere sound of words, the object of future scrutiny and examination? But if we consider the matter more narrowly, we shall be apt to draw a quite opposite conclusion. From this circumstance alone, that a controversy has been long kept on foot, and remains still undecided, we may presume that there is some ambiguity in the expression, and that the disputants affix different ideas to the terms employed in the controversy. For as the faculties of the mind are supposed to be naturally alike in every individual; otherwise nothing could be more fruitless than to reason or dispute together; it were impossible, if men affix the same ideas to their terms, that they could so long form different opinions of the same subject; especially when they communicate their views, and each party turn themselves on all sides, in search of arguments which may give them the victory over their antagonists. It is true, if men attempt the discussion of questions which lie entirely beyond the reach of human capacity, such as those concerning the origin of worlds, or the economy of the intellectual system or region of spirits, they may long beat the air in their fruitless contests, and never arrive at any determinate conclusion. But if the question regard any subject of common life and experience, nothing, one would think, could preserve the dispute so long undecided but some ambiguous expressions, which keep the antagonists still at a distance, and hinder them from grappling with each other.

63] This has been the case in the long disputed question concerning liberty and necessity; and to so remarkable a degree that, if I be not much mistaken, we shall find, that all mankind, both learned and ignorant, have always been of the same opinion with regard to this subject, and that a few intelligible definitions would immediately have put an end to the whole controversy. I own that this dispute has been so much canvassed on all hands, and has led philosophers into such a labyrinth of obscure sophistry, that it is no wonder, if a sensible reader indulge his ease so far as to turn a deaf ear to the proposal of such a question, from which he can expect neither instruction or entertainment. But the state of the argument here proposed may, perhaps, serve to renew his attention; as it has more novelty, promises at least some decision of the controversy, and will not much disturb his ease by any intricate or obscure reasoning.

I hope, therefore, to make it appear that all men have ever agreed in the doctrine both of necessity and of liberty, according to any reasonable sense, which can be put on these terms; and that the whole controversy has hitherto turned merely upon words. We shall begin with examining the doctrine of necessity.

64] It is universally allowed that matter, in all its operations, is actuated by a necessary force, and that every natural effect is so precisely determined by the energy of its cause that no other effect, in such particular circumstances, could possibly have resulted from it. The degree and direction of every motion is, by the laws of nature, prescribed with such exactness that a living creature may as soon arise from the shock of two bodies as motion in any other degree or direction than what is actually produced by it. Would we, therefore, form a just and precise idea of *necessity*, we must consider whence that idea arises when we apply it to the operation of bodies.

It seems evident that, if all the scenes of nature were continually shifted in such a manner that no two events bore any resemblance to each other, but every object was entirely new, without any similitude to whatever had been seen before, we should never, in that case, have attained the least idea of necessity, or of a connexion among these objects. We might say, upon such a supposition, that one object or event has followed another; not that one was produced by the other. The relation of cause and effect must be utterly unknown to mankind. Inference and reasoning concerning the operations of nature would, from that moment, be at an end; and the memory and senses remain the only canals, by which the knowledge of any real existence could possibly have access to the mind. Our idea, therefore, of necessity and causation arises entirely from the uniformity observable in the operations of nature, where similar objects are constantly conjoined together, and the mind is determined by custom to infer the one from the appearance of the other. These two circumstances form the whole of that necessity, which we ascribe to matter. Beyond the constant *conjunction* of similar objects, and the consequent *inference* from one to the other, we have no notion of any necessity or connexion.

If is appear, therefore, that all mankind have ever allowed, without any doubt or hesitation, that these two circumstances take place in the voluntary actions of men, and in the operations of mind; it must follow, that all mankind have ever agreed in the doctrine of necessity, and that they have hitherto disputed, merely for not understanding each other.

65] As to the first circumstance, the constant and regular conjunction of similar events, we may possibly satisfy ourselves by the following considerations. It is universally acknowledged that there is a great uniformity among the actions of men, in all nations and ages, and that human nature remains still the same, in its principles and operations. The same motives always produce the same actions: The same events follow from the same causes. Ambition, avarice, self-love, vanity, friendship, generosity, public spirit: these passions, mixed in various degrees, and distributed through society, have been, from the beginning of the world, and still are, the source of all the actions and enterprises, which have ever been observed among mankind. Would you know the sentiments, inclinations, and course of life of the Greeks and Romans? Study well the temper and actions of the French and English: You cannot be much mistaken in transferring to the former *most* of the observations which you have made with regard to the latter. Mankind are so much the same, in all times and places, that history informs us of nothing new or strange in this particular. Its chief use is only to discover the constant and universal principles of human nature, by showing men in all varieties of circumstances and situations, and furnishing us with materials from which we may form our observations and become acquainted with the regular springs of human action and behaviour. These records of wars, intrigues, factions, and revolutions, are so many collections of experiments, by which the politician or moral philosopher fixes the principles of his science, in the same manner as the physician or natural philosopher becomes acquainted with the nature of plants, minerals, and other external objects, by the experiments which he forms concerning them. Nor are the earth, water, and other elements, examined by Aristotle, and Hippocrates, more like to those which at present lie under our observation than the men described by Polybius and Tacitus are to those who now govern the world.

Should a traveller, returning from a far country, bring us an account of men, wholly different from any with whom we were ever acquainted; men, who were entirely divested of avarice, ambition, or revenge; who knew no pleasure but friendship, generosity, and public spirit; we should immediately, from these circumstances, detect the falsehood, and prove him a liar, with the same certainty as if he had stuffed his narration with stories of centaurs and dragons, miracles and prodigies. And if we would explode any forgery in history, we cannot make use of a more convincing argument, than to prove, that the actions ascribed to any person are directly contrary to the course of nature, and that no human motives, in such circumstances, could ever induce him to such a conduct. The veracity of Quintus Curtius is as much to be suspected, when he describes the supernatural courage of Alexander, by which he was hurried on singly to attack multitudes, as when he describes his supernatural force and activity, by which he was able to resist them. So readily and universally do we acknowledge a uniformity in human motives and actions as well as in the operations of body.

Hence likewise the benefit of that experience, acquired by long life and a variety of business and company, in order to instruct us in the principles of human nature, and regulate our future conduct, as well as speculation. By means of this guide, we mount up to the knowledge of men's inclinations and motives, from their actions, expressions, and even gestures; and again descend to the interpretation of their actions from our knowledge of their motives and inclinations. The general observations treasured up by a course of experience, give us the clue of human nature, and teach us to unravel all its intricacies. Pretexts and appearances no longer deceive us. Public declarations pass for the specious colouring of a cause. And though virtue and honour be allowed their proper weight and authority, that perfect disinterestedness, so often pretended to, is never expected in multitudes and parties; seldom in their leaders; and scarcely even in individuals of any rank or station. But were there no uniformity in human actions, and were every experiment which we could form of this kind irregular and anomalous, it were impossible to collect any general observations concerning mankind; and no experience, however accurately digested by reflection, would ever serve to any purpose. Why is the aged husbandman more skilful in his calling than the young beginner but because there is a certain uniformity in the operation of the sun, rain, and earth towards the production of vegetables; and experience teaches the old practitioner the rules by which this operation is governed and directed.

66] We must not, however, expect that this uniformity of human actions should be carried to such a length as that all men, in the same circumstances, will always act precisely in the same manner, without making any allowance for the diversity of characters, prejudices, and opinions. Such a uniformity in every particular, is found in no part of nature. On the contrary, from observing the variety of conduct in different men, we are enabled to form a greater variety of maxims, which still suppose a degree of uniformity and regularity.

Are the manners of men different in different ages and countries? We learn thence the great force of customs and education, which mould the human mind from its infancy and form it into a fixed and established character. Is the behaviour and conduct of the one sex very unlike that of the other? Is it thence we become acquainted with the different characters which nature has impressed upon the sexes, and which she preserves with constancy and regularity? Are the actions of the same person much diversified in the different periods of his life, from infancy to old age? This affords room for many general observations concerning the gradual change of our sentiments and inclinations, and the different maxims which prevail in the different ages of human creatures. Even the characters, which are peculiar to each individual, have a uniformity in their influence; otherwise our acquaintance with the persons and our observation of their conduct could never teach us their dispositions, or serve to direct our behaviour with regard to them.

67] I grant it possible to find some actions, which seem to have no regular connexion with any known motives, and are exceptions to all the measures of conduct which have ever been established for the government of men. But if we would willingly know what judgment should be formed of such irregular and extraordinary actions, we may consider the sentiments commonly entertained with regard to those irregular events which appear in the course of nature, and the operations of external objects. All causes are not conjoined to their usual effects with like uniformity. An artificer, who handles only dead matter, may be disappointed of his aim, as well as the politician, who directs the conduct of sensible and intelligent agents.

The vulgar, who take things according to their first appearance, attribute the uncertainty of events to such an uncertainty in the causes as makes the latter often fail of their usual influence; though they meet with no impediment in their operation. But philosophers, observing that, almost in every part of nature, there is contained a vast variety of springs and principles, which are hid, by reason of their minuteness or remoteness, find, that it is at least possible the contrariety of events may not proceed from any contingency in the cause, but from the secret operation of contrary causes. This possibility is converted into certainty by farther observation, when they remark that, upon an exact scrutiny, a contrariety of effects always betrays an exact contrariety of causes, and proceeds from their mutual opposition. A peasant can give no better reason for the stopping of any clock or watch than to say that it does not commonly go right: But an artist easily perceives that the same force in the spring or pendulum has always the same influence on the wheels; but fails of its usual effect, perhaps by reason of a grain of dust, which puts a stop to the whole movement. From the observation of several parallel instances, philosophers form a maxim that the connexion between all causes and effects is equally necessary, and that its seeming uncertainty in some instances proceeds from the secret opposition of contrary causes.

Thus, for instance, in the human body, when the usual symptoms of health or sickness disappoint our expectation; when medicines operate not with their wonted powers; when irregular events follow from any particular cause; the philosopher and physician are not surprised at the matter, nor are ever tempted to deny, in general, the necessity and uniformity of those principles by which the animal economy is conducted. They know that a human body is a mighty complicated machine: That many secret powers lurk in it, which are altogether beyond our comprehension: That to us it must often appear very uncertain in its operations: And that therefore the irregular events, which outwardly discover themselves, can be no proof that the laws of nature are not observed with the greatest regularity in its internal operations and government.

68] The philosopher, if he be consistent, must apply the same reasoning to the actions and volitions of intelligent agents. The most irregular and unexpected resolutions of men may frequently be accounted for by those who know every particular circumstance of their character and situation. A person of an obliging disposition gives a peevish answer: But he has the toothache, or has not dined. A stupid fellow discovers an uncommon alacrity in his carriage: But he has met with a sudden piece of good fortune. Or even when an action, as sometimes happens, cannot be particularly accounted for, either by the person himself or by the others; we know, in general, that the characters of men are, to a certain degree, inconstant and irregular. This is, in a manner, the constant character of human nature; though it be applicable, in a more particular manner, to some persons who have no fixed rule for their conduct, but proceed in a continued course of caprice and inconstancy. The internal principles and motives may operate in a uniform manner,

notwithstanding these seeming irregularities; in the same manner
as the winds, rain, clouds, and other variations of the weather
are supposed to be governed by steady principles; though not
easily discoverable by human sagacity and enquiry.

69] Thus it appears, not only that the conjunction between motives
and voluntary actions is as regular and uniform as that between
the cause and effect in any part of nature; but also that this regular
conjunction has been universally acknowledged among mankind,
and has never been the subject of dispute, either in philosophy or
common life. Now, as it is from past experience that we draw all
inferences concerning the future, and as we conclude that objects
will always be conjoined together which we find to have always
been conjoined; it may seem superfluous to prove that this experienced uniformity in human actions is a source whence we draw
inferences concerning them. But in order to throw the argument
into greater variety of lights we shall also insist, though briefly,
on this latter topic.

The mutual dependence of men is so great in all societies that
scarce any human action is entirely complete in itself, or is performed without some reference to the actions of others, which are
requisite to make it answer fully the intention of the agent. The
poorest artificer, who labours alone, expects at least the protection
of the magistrate, to ensure him the enjoyment of the fruits of his
labour. He also expects that, when he carries his goods to market,
and offers them at a reasonable price, he shall find purchasers, and
shall be able, by the money he acquires, to engage others to supply
him with those commodities which are requisite for his subsistence.
In proportion as men extend their dealings, and render their intercourse with others more complicated, they always comprehend, in
their schemes of life, a greater variety of voluntary actions, which
they expect, from the proper motives, to co-operate with their
own. In all these conclusions they take their measures from past
experience, in the same manner as in their reasonings concerning
external objects; and firmly believe that men, as well as all the
elements, are to continue, in their operations, the same that they
have ever found them. A manufacturer reckons upon the labour
of his servants for the execution of any work as much as upon the
tools which he employs, and would be equally surprised were his

expectations disappointed. In short, this experimental inference
and reasoning concerning the actions of others enters so much into
human life that no man, while awake, is ever a moment without
employing it. Have we not reason, therefore, to affirm that all
mankind have always agreed in the doctrine of necessity according
to the foregoing definition and explication of it?

70] Nor have philosophers ever entertained a different opinion
from the people in this particular. For, not to mention that almost
every action of their life supposes that opinion, there are even few
of the speculative parts of learning to which it is not essential.
What would become of *history,* had we not a dependence on the
veracity of the historian according to the experience which we
have had of mankind? How could *politics* be a science, if laws
and forms of government had not a uniform influence upon
society? Where would be the foundation of *morals,* if particular
characters had no certain or determinate power to produce particular sentiments, and if these sentiments had no constant operation
on actions? And with what pretence could we employ our *criticism* upon any poet or polite author, if we could not pronounce
the conduct and sentiments of his actors either natural or unnatural to such characters, and in such circumstances? It seems almost
impossible, therefore, to engage either in science or action of any
kind without acknowledging the doctrine of necessity, and this
inference from motive to voluntary actions, from characters to
conduct.

And indeed, when we consider how aptly *natural* and *moral*
evidence link together, and form only one chain of argument, we
shall make no scruple to allow that they are of the same nature,
and derived from the same principles. A prisoner who has neither
money nor interest, discovers the impossibility of his escape, as
well when he considers the obstinacy of the gaoler, as the walls and
bars with which he is surrounded; and, in all attempts for his freedom, chooses rather to work upon the stone and iron of the one,
than upon the inflexible nature of the other. The same prisoner,
when conducted to the scaffold, foresees his death as certainly from
the constancy and fidelity of his guards, as from the operation of
the axe or wheel. His mind runs along a certain train of ideas:
The refusal of the soldiers to consent to his escape; the action of

the executioner; the separation of the head and body; bleeding, convulsive motions, and death. Here is a connected chain of natural causes and voluntary actions; but the mind feels no difference between them in passing from one link to another: Nor is less certain of the future event than if it were connected with the objects present to the memory or senses, by a train of causes, cemented together by what we are pleased to call a *physical* necessity. The same experienced union has the same effect on the mind, whether the united objects be motives, volition, and actions; or figure and motion. We may change the name of things; but their nature and their operation on the understanding never change.

Were a man, whom I know to be honest and opulent, and with whom I live in intimate friendship, to come into my house, where I am surrounded with my servants, I rest assured that he is not to stab me before he leaves it in order to rob me of my silver standish; and I no more suspect this event than the falling of the house itself, which is new, and solidly built and founded.—*But he may have been seized with a sudden and unknown frenzy.*—So may a sudden earthquake arise, and shake and tumble my house about my ears. I shall therefore change the suppositions. I shall say that I know with certainty that he is not to put his hand into the fire and hold it there till it be consumed: And this event, I think I can foretell with the same assurance, as that, if he throw himself out at the window, and meet with no obstruction, he will not remain a moment suspended in the air. No suspicion of an unknown frenzy can give the least possibility to the former event, which is so contrary to all the known principles of human nature. A man who at noon leaves his purse full of gold on the pavement at Charing-Cross, may as well expect that it will fly away like a feather, as that he will find it untouched an hour after. Above one half of human reasonings contain inferences of a similar nature, attended with more or less degrees of certainty proportioned to our experience of the usual conduct of mankind in such particular situations.

71] I have frequently considered, what could possibly be the reason why all mankind, though they have ever, without hesitation, acknowledged the doctrine of necessity in their whole practice and reasoning, have yet discovered such a reluctance to acknowledge it in words, and have rather shown a propensity, in all ages, to profess the contrary opinion. The matter, I think, may be accounted for after the following manner. If we examine the operations of body, and the production of effects from their causes, we shall find that all our faculties can never carry us farther in our knowledge of this relation than barely to observe that particular objects are *constantly conjoined* together, and that the mind is carried, by a *customary transition,* from the appearance of one to the belief of the other. But though this conclusion concerning human ignorance be the result of the strictest scrutiny of this subject, men still entertain a strong propensity to believe that they penetrate farther into the powers of nature, and perceive something like a necessary connexion between the cause and the effect. When again they turn their reflections towards the operations of their own minds, and *feel* no such connexion of the motive and the action; they are thence apt to suppose, that there is a difference between the effects which result from material force, and those which arise from thought and intelligence. But being once convinced that we know nothing farther of causation of any kind than merely the *constant conjunction* of objects, and the consequent *inference* of the mind from one to another, and finding that these two circumstances are universally allowed to have place in voluntary actions; we may be more easily led to own the same necessity common to all causes. And though this reasoning may contradict the systems of many philosophers, in ascribing necessity to the determinations of the will, we shall find, upon reflection, that they dissent from it in words only, not in their real sentiment. Necessity, according to the sense in which it is here taken, has never yet been rejected, nor can ever, I think, be rejected by any philosopher. It may only, perhaps, be pretended that the mind can perceive, in the operations of matter, some farther connexion between the cause and effect; and connexion that has not place in voluntary actions of intelligent beings. Now whether it be so or not, can only appear upon examination; and it is incumbent on these philosophers to make good their assertion, by defining or describing that necessity, and pointing it out to us in the operations of material causes.

72] It would seem, indeed, that men begin at the wrong end of this question concerning liberty and necessity, when they enter upon it by examining the faculties of the soul, the influence of the understanding, and the operations of the will. Let them first discuss a more simple question, namely, the operations of body and of brute unintelligent matter; and try whether they can there form any idea of causation and necessity, except that of a constant conjunction of objects, and subsequent inference of the mind from one to another. If these circumstances form, in reality, the whole of that necessity, which we conceive in matter, and if these circumstances be also universally acknowledged to take place in the operations of the mind, the dispute is at an end; at least, must be owned to be thenceforth merely verbal. But as long as we will rashly suppose, that we have some farther idea of necessity and causation in the operations of external objects; at the same time, that we can find nothing farther in the voluntary actions of the mind; there is no possibility of bringing the question to any determinate issue, while we proceed upon so erroneous a supposition. The only method of undeceiving us is to mount up higher; to examine the narrow extent of science when applied to material causes; and to convince ourselves that all we know of them is the constant conjunction and inference above mentioned. We may, perhaps, find that it is with difficulty we are induced to fix such narrow limits to human understanding: But we can afterwards find no difficulty when we come to apply this doctrine to the actions of the will. For as it is evident that these have a regular conjunction with motives and circumstances and characters, and as we always draw inferences from one to the other, we must be obliged to acknowledge in words that necessity, which we have already avowed, in every deliberation of our lives, and in every step of our conduct and behaviour.[1]

[1] The prevalence of the doctrine of liberty may be accounted for, from another cause, viz. a false sensation or seeming experience which we have, or may have, of liberty or indifference, in many of our actions. The necessity of any action, whether of matter or of mind, is not, properly speaking, a quality in the agent, but in any thinking or intelligent being, who may consider the action; and it consists chiefly in the determination of his thoughts to infer the existence of that action from some preceding objects; as liberty, when opposed to necessity, is nothing but the want of that determination, and a certain looseness or indifference, which we feel, in passing, or not passing, from the idea of one object to that of any succeeding one. Now we may observe, that, though, in *reflecting* on human actions, we seldom feel such a looseness, or indifference, but are commonly able to infer them with considerable certainty from their motives, and from the dispositions of the agent; yet it frequently

73] But to proceed in this reconciling project with regard to the question of liberty and necessity; the most contentious question of metaphysics, the most contentious science; it will not require many words to prove, that all mankind have ever agreed in the doctrine of liberty as well as in that of necessity, and that the whole dispute, in this respect also, has been hitherto merely verbal. For what is meant by liberty, when applied to voluntary actions? We cannot surely mean that actions have so little connexion with motives, inclinations, and circumstances, that one does not follow with a certain degree of uniformity from the other, and that one affords no inference by which we can conclude the existence of the other. For these are plain and acknowledged matters of fact. By liberty, then, we can only mean *a power of acting or not acting, according to the determinations of the will;* that is, if we choose to remain at rest, we may; if we choose to move, we also may. Now this hypothetical liberty is universally allowed to belong to every one who is not a prisoner and in chains. Here, then, is no subject of dispute.

74] Whatever definition we may give of liberty, we should be careful to observe two requisite circumstances; *first,* that it be consistent with plain matter of fact; *secondly,* that it be consistent with itself. If we observe these circumstances, and render our definition intelligible, I am persuaded that all mankind will be found of one opinion with regard to it.

It is universally allowed that nothing exists without a cause of

---

happens, that in *performing* the actions themselves, we are sensible of something like it: And as all resembling objects are readily taken for each other, this has been employed as a demonstrative and even intuitive proof of human liberty. We feel, that our actions are subject to our will, on most occasions; and imagine we feel, that the will itself is subject to nothing, because, when a denial of it we are provoked to try, we feel, that it moves easily every way, and produces an image of itself (or a *Velleïty,* as it is called in the schools) even on that side, on which it did not settle. This image, or faint motion, we persuade ourselves, could, at that time, have been compleated into the thing itself; because, should that be denied, we find, upon a second trial, that, at present, it can. We consider not, that the fantastical desire of shewing liberty, is here the motive of our actions. And it seems certain, that, however we may imagine we feel a liberty within ourselves, a spectator can commonly infer our actions from our motives and character; and even where he cannot, he concludes in general, that he might, were he perfectly acquainted with every circumstance of our situation and temper, and the most secret springs of our complexion and disposition. Now this is the very essence of necessity, according to the foregoing doctrine.

its existence, and that chance, when strictly examined, is a mere negative word, and means not any real power which has anywhere a being in nature. But it is pretended that some causes are necessary, some not necessary. Here then is the advantage of definitions. Let any one *define* a cause, without comprehending, as a part of the definition, a *necessary connexion* with its effect; and let him show distinctly the origin of the idea, expressed by the definition; and I shall readily give up the whole controversy. But if the foregoing explication of the matter be received, this must be absolutely impracticable. Had not objects a regular conjunction with each other, we should never have entertained any notion of cause and effect; and this regular conjunction produces that inference of the understanding, which is the only connexion, that we can have any comprehension of. Whoever attempts a definition of cause, exclusive of these circumstances, will be obliged either to employ unintelligible terms or such as are synonymous to the term which he endeavours to define.[1] And if the definition above mentioned be admitted; liberty, when opposed to necessity, not to constraint, is the same thing with chance; which is universally allowed to have no existence.

Part II

75] There is no method of reasoning more common, and yet none more blameable, than, in philosophical disputes, to endeavour the refutation of any hypothesis, by a pretence of its dangerous consequences to religion and morality. When any opinion leads to absurdities, it is certainly false; but it is not certain that an opinion is false, because it is of dangerous consequence. Such topics, therefore, ought entirely to be forborne; as serving nothing to the discovery of truth, but only to make the person of an antagonist odious. This I observe in general, without pretending to draw any advantage from it. I frankly submit to an examination of this kind,

---

[1] Thus, if a cause be defined, *that which produces any thing;* it is easy to observe, that *producing* is synonomous to *causing.* In like manner, if a cause be defined, *that by which any thing exists;* this is liable to the same objection. For what is meant by these words, *by which?* Had it been said, that a cause is *that* after which *any thing constantly exists;* we should have understood the terms. For this is, indeed, all we know of the matter. And this constancy forms the very essence of necessity, nor have we any other idea of it.

and shall venture to affirm that the doctrines, both of necessity and
of liberty, as above explained, are not only consistent with morality, but are absolutely essential to its support.

Necessity may be defined two ways, conformably to the two definitions of *cause,* of which it makes an essential part. It consists
either in the constant conjunction of like objects or in the inference of the understanding from one object to another. Now necessity, in both these senses, (which, indeed, are at bottom the same)
has universally, though tacitly, in the schools, in the pulpit, and in
common life, been allowed to belong to the will of man; and no
one has ever pretended to deny that we can draw inferences concerning human actions, and that those inferences are founded on
the experienced union of like actions, with like motives, inclinations, and circumstances. The only particular in which any one
can differ, is, that either, perhaps, he will refuse to give the name
of necessity to this property of human actions: But as long as the
meaning is understood, I hope the word can do no harm: Or that
he will maintain it possible to discover something farther in the
operations of matter. But this, it must be acknowledged, can be of
no consequence to morality or religion, whatever it may be to natural philosophy or metaphysics. We may here be mistaken in asserting that there is no idea of any other necessity or connexion in
the actions of body: But surely we ascribe nothing to the actions of
the mind, but what everyone does, and must readily allow of. We
change no circumstance in the received orthodox system with regard to the will, but only in that with regard to material objects
and causes. Nothing, therefore, can be more innocent, at least,
than this doctrine.

761 All laws being founded on rewards and punishments, it is supposed as a fundamental principle, that these motives have a regular
and uniform influence on the mind, and both produce the good
and prevent the evil actions. We may give to this influence what
name we please; but, as it is usually conjoined with the action, it
must be esteemed a *cause,* and be looked upon as an instance of
that necessity, which we would here establish.

The only proper object of hatred or vengeance is a person or
creature, endowed with thought and consciousness; and when any
criminal or injurious actions excite that passion, it is only by their

relation to the person, or connexion with him. Actions are, by their very nature, temporary and perishing; and where they proceed not from some *cause* in the character and disposition of the person who performed them, they can neither redound to his honour, if good; nor infamy, if evil. The actions themselves may be blameable; they may be contrary to all the rules of morality and religion: But the person is not answerable for them; and as they proceeded from nothing in him that is durable and constant, and leave nothing of that nature behind them, it is impossible he can, upon their account, become the object of punishment or vengeance. According to the principle, therefore, which denies necessity, and consequently causes, a man is as pure and untainted, after having committed the most horrid crime, as at the first moment of his birth, nor is his character anywise concerned in his actions, since they are not derived from it, and the wickedness of the one can never be used as a proof of the depravity of the other.

Men are not blamed for such actions as they perform ignorantly and casually, whatever may be the consequences. Why? but because the principles of these actions are only momentary, and terminate in them alone. Men are less blamed for such actions as they perform hastily and unpremeditately than for such as proceed from deliberation. For what reason? but because a hasty temper, though a constant cause or principle in the mind, operates only by intervals, and infects not the whole character. Again, repentance wipes off every crime, if attended with a reformation of life and manners. How is this to be accounted for? but by asserting that actions render a person criminal merely as they are proofs of criminal principles in the mind; and when, by an alteration of these principles, they cease to be just proofs, they likewise cease to be criminal. But, except upon the doctrine of necessity, they never were just proofs, and consequently never were criminal.

77] It will be equally easy to prove, and from the same arguments, that *liberty,* according to that definition above mentioned, in which all men agree, is also essential to morality, and that no human actions, where it is wanting, are susceptible of any moral qualities, or can be the objects either of approbation or dislike. For as actions are objects of our moral sentiment, so far only as they are indications of the internal character, passions, and affections; it is impossible that they can give rise either to praise or blame, where they proceed not from these principles, but are derived altogether from external violence.

781 I pretend not to have obviated or removed all objections to this theory, with regard to necessity and liberty. I can foresee other objections, derived from topics which have not here been treated of. It may be said, for instance, that, if voluntary actions be subjected to the same laws of necessity with the operations of matter, there is a continued chain of necessary causes, pre-ordained and pre-determined, reaching from the original cause of all to every single volition of every human creature. No contingency anywhere in the universe; no indifference; no liberty. While we act, we are, at the same time, acted upon. The ultimate Author of all our volitions is the Creator of the world, who first bestowed motion on this immense machine, and placed all beings in that particular position, whence every subsequent event, by an inevitable necessity, must result. Human actions, therefore, either can have no moral turpitude at all, as proceeding from so good a cause; or if they have any turpitude, they must involve our Creator in the same guilt, while he is acknowledged to be their ultimate cause and author. For as a man, who fired a mine, is answerable for all the consequences whether the train he employed be long or short; so wherever a continued chain of necessary causes is fixed, that Being, either finite or infinite, who produces the first, is likewise the author of all the rest, and must both bear the blame and acquire the praise which belonged to them. Our clear and unalterable ideas of morality establish this rule, upon unquestionable reasons, when we examine the consequences of any human action; and these reasons must still have greater force when applied to the volitions and intentions of a Being infinitely wise and powerful. Ignorance or impotence may be pleaded for so limited a creature as man; but those imperfections have no place in our Creator. He foresaw, he ordained, he intended all those actions of men, which we so rashly pronounce criminal. And we must therefore conclude, either that they are not criminal, or that the Deity, not man, is accountable for them. But as either of these positions is absurd and impious, it follows, that the doctrine from which they are deduced cannot possibly be true, as being liable to all the same objections.

An absurd consequence, if necessary, proves the original doctrine to be absurd; in the same manner as criminal actions render criminal the original cause, if the connexion between them be necessary and evitable.

This objection consists of two parts, which we shall examine separately; *First,* that, if human actions can be traced up, by a necessary chain, to the Deity, they can never be criminal; on account of the infinite perfection of that Being from whom they are derived, and who can intend nothing but what is altogether good and laudable. Or, *Secondly,* if they be criminal, we must retract the attribute of perfection, which we ascribe to the Deity, and must acknowledge him to be the ultimate author of guilt and moral turpitude in all his creatures.

79] The answer to the first objection seems obvious and convincing. There are many philosophers who, after an exact scrutiny of all the phenomena of nature, conclude, that the WHOLE, considered as one system, is, in every period of its existence, ordered with perfect benevolence; and that the utmost possible happiness will, in the end, result to all created beings, without any mixture of positive or absolute ill or misery. Every physical ill, say they, makes an essential part of this benevolent system, and could not possibly be removed, even by the Deity himself, considered as a wise agent, without giving entrance to greater ill, or excluding greater good, which will result from it. From this theory, some philosophers, and the ancient *Stoics* among the rest, derived a topic of consolation under all afflictions, while they taught their pupils that those ills under which they laboured were, in reality, goods to the universe; and that to an enlarged view, which could comprehend the whole system of nature, every event became an object of joy and exultation. But though this topic be specious and sublime, it was soon found in practice weak and ineffectual. You would surely more irritate than appease a man lying under the racking points of the gout by preaching up to him the rectitude of those general laws, which produced the malignant humours in his body, and led them through the proper canals, to the sinews and nerves, where they now excite such acute torments. These enlarged views may, for a moment, please the imagination of a speculative man, who is placed in ease and security; but neither can they dwell with constancy on his mind, even though undisturbed by the emotions of pain or passion; much less can they maintain their ground when attacked by such powerful antagonists. The affections take a narrower and more natural survey of their object; and by an economy, more suitable to the infirmity of human minds, regard alone the beings around us, and are actuated by such events as appear good or ill to the private system.

80] The case is the same with *moral* as with *physical* ill. It cannot reasonably be supposed, that those remote considerations, which are found of so little efficacy with regard to one, will have a more powerful influence with regard to the other. The mind of man is so formed by nature that, upon the appearance of certain characters, dispositions, and actions, it immediately feels the sentiment of approbation or blame; nor are there any emotions more essential to its frame and constitution. The characters which engage our approbation are chiefly such as contribute to the peace and security of human society; as the characters which excite blame are chiefly such as tend to public detriment and disturbance: Whence it may reasonably be presumed, that the moral sentiments arise, either mediately or immediately, from a reflection of these opposite interests. What though philosophical meditations establish a different opinion or conjecture; that everything is right with regard to the WHOLE, and that the qualities, which disturb society, are, in the main, as beneficial, and are as suitable to the primary intention of nature as those which more directly promote its happiness and welfare? Are such remote and uncertain speculations able to counterbalance the sentiments which arise from the natural and immediate view of the objects? A man who is robbed of a considerable sum; does he find his vexation for the loss anywise diminished by these sublime reflections? Why then should his moral resentment against the crime be supposed incompatible with them? Or why should not the acknowledgment of a real distinction between vice and virtue be reconcileable to all speculative systems of philosophy, as well as that of a real distinction between personal beauty and deformity? Both these distinctions are founded in the natural sentiments of the human mind: And these sentiments are not to be controlled or altered by any philosophical theory or speculation whatsoever.

81] The *second* objection admits not of so easy and satisfactory an answer; nor is it possible to explain distinctly, how the Deity can be the mediate cause of all the actions of men, without being the author of sin and moral turpitude. These are mysteries, which mere natural and unassisted reason is very unfit to handle; and whatever system she embraces, she must find herself involved in inextricable difficulties, and even contradictions, at every step which she takes with regard to such subjects. To reconcile the indifference and contingency of human actions with prescience; or to defend absolute decrees, and yet free the Deity from being the author of sin, has been found hitherto to exceed all the power of philosophy. Happy, if she be thence sensible of her temerity, when she pries into these sublime mysteries; and leaving a scene so full of obscurities and perplexities, return, with suitable modesty, to her true and proper province, the examination of common life; where she will find difficulties enough to employ her enquiries, without launching into so boundless an ocean of doubt, uncertainty, and contradiction! . . .

Section XI

Of a Particular Providence and of a Future State

102] I was lately engaged in conversation with a friend who loves sceptical paradoxes; where, though he advanced many principles, of which I can by no means approve, yet as they seem to be curious, and to bear some relation to the chain of reasoning carried on throughout this enquiry, I shall here copy them from my memory as accurately as I can, in order to submit them to the judgement of the reader.

Our conversation began with my admiring the singular good fortune of philosophy, which, as it requires entire liberty above all other privileges, and chiefly flourishes from the free opposition of sentiments and argumentation, received its first birth in an age and country of freedom and toleration, and was never cramped, even in its most extravagant principles, by any creeds, concessions, or penal statutes. For, except the banishment of Protagoras, and the death of Socrates, which last event proceeded partly from other motives, there are scarcely any instances to be met with, in ancient history, of this bigotted jealousy, with which the present age is so much infested. Epicurus lived at Athens to an advanced age, in peace and tranquillity: Epicureans were even admitted to receive the sacerdotal character, and to officiate at the altar, in the most sacred rites of the established religion: And the public encouragement of pensions and salaries was afforded equally, by the wisest of all the Roman emperors, to the professors of every sect of philosophy. How requisite such kind of treatment was to philosophy, in her early youth, will easily be conceived, if we reflect, that, even at present, when she may be supposed more hardy and robust, she bears with much difficulty the inclemency of the seasons, and those harsh winds of calumny and persecution, which blow upon her.

You admire, says my friend, as the singular good fortune of philosophy, what seems to result from the natural course of things, and to be unavoidable in every age and nation. This pertinacious bigotry, of which you complain, as so fatal to philosophy, is really her offspring, who, after allying with superstition, separates himself entirely from the interest of his parent, and becomes her most inveterate enemy and persecutor. Speculative dogmas of religion, the present occasions of such furious dispute, could not possibly be conceived or admitted in the early ages of the world; when mankind, being wholly illiterate, formed an idea of religion more suitable to their weak apprehension, and composed their sacred tenets of such tales chiefly as were the objects of traditional belief, more than of argument or disputation. After the first alarm, therefore, was over, which arose from the new paradoxes and principles of the philosophers; these teachers seem ever after, during the ages of antiquity, to have lived in great harmony with the established superstition, and to have made a fair partition of mankind between them; the former claiming all the learned and wise, the latter possessing all the vulgar and illiterate.

103] It seems then, say I, that you leave politics entirely out of the question, and never suppose, that a wise magistrate can justly be jealous of certain tenets of philosophy, such as those of Epicurus, which, denying a divine existence, and consequently a providence and a future state, seem to loosen, in a great measure, the ties of morality, and may be supposed, for that reason, pernicious to the peace of civil society.

I know, replied he, that in fact these persecutions never, in any age, proceeded from calm reason, or from experience of the pernicious consequences of philosophy; but arose entirely from passion and prejudice. But what if I should advance farther, and assert, that if Epicurus had been accused before the people, by any of the *sycophants* or informers of those days, he could easily have defended his cause, and proved his principles of philosophy to be as salutary as those of his adversaries, who endeavoured, with such zeal, to expose him to the public hatred and jealousy?

I wish, said I, you would try your eloquence upon so extraordinary a topic, and make a speech for Epicurus, which might satisfy, not the mob of Athens, if you will allow that ancient and polite city to have contained any mob, but the more philosophical part of his audience, such as might be supposed capable of comprehending his arguments.

The matter would not be difficult, upon such conditions, replied he: And if you please, I shall suppose myself Epicurus for a moment, and make you stand for the Athenian people, and shall deliver you such an harangue as will fill all the urn with white beans, and leave not a black one to gratify the malice of my adversaries.

Very well: Pray proceed upon these suppositions.

104] I come hither, O ye Athenians, to justify in your assembly what I maintained in my school, and I find myself impeached by furious antagonists, instead of reasoning with calm and dispassionate enquirers. Your deliberations, which of right should be directed to questions of public good, and the interest of the commonwealth, are diverted to the disquisitions of speculative philosophy; and these magnificent, but perhaps fruitless enquiries, take place of your more familiar but more useful occupations. But so far as in me lies, I will prevent this abuse. We shall not here dispute concerning the origin and government of worlds. We shall only enquire how far such questions concern the public interest. And if I can persuade you, that they are entirely indifferent to the peace of society and security of government, I hope that you will presently send us back to our schools, there to examine, at leisure, the question the most sublime, but at the same time, the most speculative of all philosophy.

The religious philosophers, not satisfied with the tradition of your forefathers, and doctrine of your priests (in which I willingly acquiesce), indulge a rash curiosity, in trying how far they can establish religion upon the principles of reason; and they thereby excite, instead of satisfying, the doubts, which naturally arise from a diligent and scrutinous enquiry. They paint, in the most magnificent colours, the order, beauty, and wise arrangement of the universe; and then ask, if such a glorious display of intelligence could proceed from the fortuitous concourse of atoms, or if chance could produce what the greatest genius can never sufficiently admire. I shall not examine the justness of this argument. I shall allow it to be as solid as my antagonists and accusers can desire. It is sufficient, if I can prove, from this very reasoning, that the question is entirely speculative, and that, when, in my philosophical disquisitions, I deny a providence and a future state, I undermine not the foundations of society, but advance principles, which they themselves, upon their own topics, if they argue consistently, must allow to be solid and satisfactory.

105] You then, who are my accusers, have acknowledged, that the chief or sole argument for a divine existence (which I never questioned) is derived from the order of nature; where there appear such marks of intelligence and design, that you think it extravagant to assign for its cause, either chance, or the blind and unguided force of matter. You allow, that this is an argument drawn from effects to causes. From the order of the work, you infer, that there must have been project and forethought in the workman. If you cannot make out this point, you allow, that your conclusion fails; and you pretend not to establish the conclusion in a greater latitude than the phenomena of nature will justify. These are your concessions. I desire you to mark the consequences.

When we infer any particular cause from an effect, we must proportion the one to the other, and can never be allowed to ascribe to the cause any qualities, but what are exactly sufficient to produce the effect. A body of ten ounces raised in any scale may serve as a proof, that the counterbalancing weight exceeds ten ounces; but can never afford a reason that it exceeds a hundred. If the cause, assigned for any effect, be not sufficient to produce it, we must either reject that cause, or add to it such qualities as will give it a just proportion to the effect. But if we ascribe to it farther qualities, or affirm it capable of producing other effects, we can only indulge the licence of conjecture, and arbitrarily suppose the existence of qualities and energies, without reason or authority.

The same rule holds, whether the cause assigned be brute unconscious matter, or a rational intelligent being. If the cause be known only by the effect, we never ought to ascribe to it any qualities, beyond what are precisely requisite to produce the effect: Nor can we, by any rules of just reasoning, return back from the cause, and infer other effects from it, beyond those by which alone it is known to us. No one, merely from the sight of one of Zeuxis's pictures, could know, that he was also a statuary or architect, and was an artist no less skilful in stone and marble than in colours. The talents and taste, displayed in the particular work before us; these we may safely conclude the workman to be possessed of. The cause must be proportioned to the effect; and if we exactly and precisely proportion it, we shall never find in it any qualities, that point farther, or afford an inference concerning any other design or performance. Such qualities must be somewhat beyond what is merely requisite for producing the effect, which we examine.

106] Allowing, therefore, the gods to be the authors of the existence or order of the universe; it follows, that they possess that precise degree of power, intelligence, and benevolence, which appears in their workmanship; but nothing farther can ever be proved, except we call in the assistance of exaggeration and flattery to supply the defects of argument and reasoning. So far as the traces of any attributes, at present, appear, so far may we conclude these attributes to exist. The supposition of farther attributes is more hypothesis; much more the supposition, that, in distant regions of space or periods of time, there has been, or will be, a more magnificent display of these attributes, and a scheme of administration more suitable to such imaginary virtues. We can never be allowed to mount up from the universe, the effect, to Jupiter, the cause; and then descend downwards, to infer any new effect from that cause; as if the present effects alone were not entirely worthy of the glorious attributes, which we ascribe to that deity. The knowledge of the cause being derived solely from the effect, they must be exactly adjusted to each other; and the one can never refer to anything farther, or be the foundation of any new inference and conclusion.

You find certain phenomena in nature. You seek a cause or author. You imagine that you have found him. You afterwards become so enamoured of this offspring of your brain, that you imagine it impossible, but he must produce something greater and more perfect than the present scene of things, which is so full of ill and disorder. You forget, that this superlative intelligence and benevolence are entirely imaginary, or, at least, without any foundation in reason; and that you have no ground to ascribe to him any qualities, but what you see he has actually exerted and displayed in his productions. Let your gods, therefore, O philosophers, be suited to the present appearances of nature: and presume not to alter these appearances of arbitrary suppositions, in order to suit them to the attributes, which you so fondly ascribe to your deities.

107] When priests and poets, supported by your authority, O Athenians, talk of a golden or silver age, which preceded the present reverence. But when philosophers, who pretend to neglect author-state of vice and misery, I hear them with attention and with ity, and to cultivate reason, hold the same discourse, I pay them not, I own, the same obsequious submission and pious deference. I ask; who carried them into the celestial regions, who admitted them into the councils of the gods, who opened to them the book of fate, that they thus rashly affirm, that their deities have executed, or will execute, any purpose beyond what has actually appeared? If they tell me, that they have mounted on the steps or by the gradual ascent of reason, and by drawing inferences from effects to causes, I still insist, that they have aided the ascent of reason by the wings of imagination; otherwise they could not thus change their manner of inference, and argue from causes to effects; presuming, that a more perfect production than the present world would be more suitable to such perfect beings as the gods, and forgetting that they have no reason to ascribe to these celestial beings any perfection or any attribute, but what can be found in the present world.

Hence all the fruitless industry to account for the ill appearances of nature, and save the honour of the gods; while we must acknowledge the reality of that evil and disorder, with which the world so much abounds. The obstinate and intractable qualities of matter, we are told, or the observance of general laws, or some such reason, is the sole cause, which controlled the power and benevolence of Jupiter, and obliged him to create mankind and every sensible creature so imperfect and so unhappy. These attributes then, are, it seems, beforehand, taken for granted, in their greatest latitude. And upon that supposition, I own that such conjectures may, perhaps, be admitted as plausible solutions of the ill phenomena. But still I ask; Why take these attributes for granted, or why ascribe to the cause any qualities but what actually appear in the effect? Why torture your brain to justify the course of nature upon suppositions, which, for aught you know, may be entirely imaginary, and of which there are to be found no traces in the course of nature?

The religious hypothesis, therefore, must be considered only as a particular method of accounting for the visible phenomena of the universe: but no just reasoner will ever presume to infer from it any single fact, and alter or add to the phenomena, in any single particular. If you think, that the appearances of things prove such causes, it is allowable for you to draw an inference concerning the existence of these causes. In such complicated and sublime subjects, every one should be indulged in the liberty of conjecture and argument. But here you ought to rest. If you come backward, and arguing from your inferred causes, conclude, that any other fact has existed, or will exist, in the course of nature, which may serve as a fuller display of particular attributes; I must admonish you, that you have departed from the method of reasoning, attached to the present subject, and have certainly added something to the attributes of the cause, beyond what appears in the effect; otherwise you could never, with tolerable sense or propriety, add anything to the effect, in order to render it more worthy of the cause.

108] Where, then, is the odiousness of that doctrine, which I teach in my school, or rather, which I examine in my gardens? Or what do you find in this whole question, wherein the security of good morals, or the peace and order of society, is in the least concerned?

I deny a providence, you say, and supreme governor of the
world, who guides the course of events, and punishes the vicious
with infamy and disappointment, and rewards the virtuous with
honour and success, in all their undertakings. But surely, I deny
not the course itself of events, which lies open to every one's inquiry and examination. I acknowledge, that, in the present order
of things, virtue is attended with more peace of mind than vice,
and meets with a more favourable reception from the world. I am
sensible, that, according to the past experience of mankind, friendship is the chief joy of human life, and moderation the only source
of tranquillity and happiness. I never balance between the virtuous and the vicious course of life; but am sensible, that, to a
well-disposed mind, every advantage is on the side of the former.
And what can you say more, allowing all your suppositions and
reasonings? You tell me, indeed, that this disposition of things proceeds from intelligence and design. But whatever it proceeds from,
the disposition itself, on which depends our happiness or misery,
and consequently our conduct and deportment in life is still the
same. It is still open for me, as well as you, to regulate my behaviour, by my experience of past events. And if you affirm, that,
while a divine providence is allowed, and a supreme distributive
justice in the universe, I ought to expect some more particular
regard of the good, and punishment of the bad, beyond the ordinary course of events; I here find the same fallacy, which I have
before endeavoured to detect. You persist in imagining, that, if we
grant that divine existence, for which you so earnestly contend,
you may safely infer consequences from it, and add something to
the experienced order of nature, by arguing from the attributes
which you ascribe to your gods. You seem not to remember, that
all your reasonings on this subject can only be drawn from effects
to causes; and that every argument, deducted from causes to effects,
must of necessity be a gross sophism; since it is impossible for you
to know anything of the cause, but what you have antecedently,
not inferred, but discovered to the full, in the effect.

109] But what must a philosopher think of those vain reasoners,
who, instead of regarding the present scene of things as the sole
object of their contemplation, so far reverse the whole course of
nature, as to render this life merely a passage to something farther;

a porch, which leads to a greater, and vastly different building; a prologue, which serves only to introduce the piece, and give it more grace and propriety? Whence, do you think, can such philosophers derive their idea of the gods? From their own conceit and imagination surely. For if they derived it from the present phenomena, it would never point to anything farther, but must be exactly adjusted to them. That the divinity may *possibly* be endowed with attributes, which we have never seen exerted; may be governed by principles of action, which we cannot discover to be satisfied: all this will freely be allowed. But still this is mere *possibility* and hypothesis. We never can have reason to *infer* any attributes, or any principles of action in him, but as far as we know them to have been exerted and satisfied.

Are there any marks of a distributive justice in the world? If you answer in the affirmative, I conclude, that, since justice here exerts itself, it is satisfied. If you reply in the negative, I conclude, that you have then no reason to ascribe justice, in our sense of it, to the gods. If you hold a medium between affirmation and negation, by saying, that the justice of the gods, at present, exerts itself in part, but not in its full extent; I answer, that you have no reason to give it any particular extent, but only so far as you see it, *at present,* exert itself.

110] Thus I bring the dispute, O Athenians, to a short issue with my antagonists. The course of nature lies open to my contemplation as well as to theirs. The experienced train of events is the great standard, by which we all regulate our conduct. Nothing else can be appealed to in the field, or in the senate. Nothing else ought ever to be heard of in the school, or in the closet. In vain would our limited understanding break through those boundaries, which are too narrow for our fond imagination. While we argue from the course of nature, and infer a particular intelligent cause, which first bestowed, and preserves order in the universe, we embrace a principle, which is both uncertain and useless. It is uncertain; because the subject lies entirely beyond the reach of human experience. It is useless; because our knowledge of this cause being derived entirely from the course of nature, we can never, according to the rules of just reasoning, return back from the cause with any new inference, or making additions to the common and experienced course of nature, establish any new principles of conduct and behaviour.

111] I observe (said I, finding he had finished his harangue) that you neglect not the artifice of the demagogues of old; and as you were pleased to make me stand for the people, you insinuate yourself into my favour by embracing those principles, to which, you know, I have always expressed a particular attachment. But allowing you to make experience (as indeed I think you ought) the only standard of our judgement concerning this, and all other questions of fact; I doubt not but, from the very same experience, to which you appeal, it may be possible to refute this reasoning, which you have put into the mouth of Epicurus. If you saw, for instance, a half-finished building, surrounded with heaps of brick and stone and mortar, and all the instruments of masonry; could you not *infer* from the effect, that it was a work of design and contrivance? And could you not return again, from this inferred cause, to infer new additions to the effect, and conclude, that the building would soon be finished, and receive all the further improvements, which art could bestow upon it? If you saw upon the sea-shore the print of one human foot, you would conclude, that a man had passed that way, and that he had also left the traces of the other foot, though effaced by the rolling of the sands or inundation of the waters. Why then do you refuse to admit the same method of reasoning with regard to the order of nature? Consider the world and the present life only as an imperfect building, from which you can infer a superior intelligence; and arguing from that superior intelligence, which can leave nothing imperfect; why may you not infer a more finished scheme or plan, which will receive its completion in some distant point of space or time? Are not these methods of reasoning exactly similar? And under what pretence can you embrace the one, while you reject the other?

112] The infinite difference of the subjects, replied he, is a sufficient foundation for this difference in my conclusions. In works of *human* art and contrivance, it is allowable to advance from the effect to the cause, and returning back from the cause, to form new inferences concerning the effect, and examine the alterations, which it has probably undergone, or may still undergo. But what is the foundation of this method of reasoning? Plainly this; that man is a being, whom we know by experience, whose motives and designs we are acquainted with, and whose projects and inclinations have a certain connexion and coherence, according to the laws which nature has established for the government of such a creature. When, therefore, we find, that any work has proceeded from the skill and industry of man; as we are otherwise acquainted with the nature of the animal, we can draw a hundred inferences concerning what may be expected from him; and these inferences will all be founded in experience and observation. But did we know man only from the single work or production which we examine, it were impossible for us to argue in this manner; because our knowledge of all the qualities, which we ascribe to him, being in that case derived from the production, it is impossible they could point to anything farther, or be the foundation of any new inference. The print of a food in the sand can only prove, when considered alone, that there was some figure adapted to it, by which it was produced: but the print of a human foot proves likewise, from our other experience, that there was probably another foot, which also left its impression, though effaced by time or other accidents. Here we mount from the effect to the cause; and descending again from the cause, infer alterations in the effect; but this is not a continuation of the same simple chain of reasoning. We comprehend in this case a hundred other experiences and observations, concerning the *usual* figure and members of that species of animal, without which this method of argument must be considered as fallacious and sophistical.

113] The case is not the same with our reasonings from the works of nature. The Deity is known to us only by his productions, and is a single being in the universe, not comprehended under any species or genus, from whose experienced attributes or qualities, we can, by analogy, infer any attribute or quality in him. As the universe shews wisdom and goodness, we infer wisdom and goodness. As it shews a particular degree of these perfections, we infer a particular degree of them, precisely adapted to the effect which we examine. But farther attributes or farther degrees of the same attributes, we can never be authorised to infer or suppose, by any rules of just reasoning. Now, without some such licence of supposition, it is impossible for us to argue from the cause, or infer any alteration in the effect, beyond what has immediately fallen under our observation. Greater good produced by this Being must still prove a greater degree of goodness: a more impartial distribution of rewards and punishments must proceed from a greater regard to justice and equity. Every supposed addition to the works of nature makes an addition to the attributes of the Author of nature; and consequently, being entirely unsupported by any reason or argument, can never be admitted but as mere conjecture and hypothesis.[1]

The great source of our mistake in this subject, and of the unbounded licence of conjecture, which we indulge, is, that we tacitly consider ourselves, as in the place of the Supreme Being, and conclude, that he will, on every occasion, observe the same conduct, which we ourselves, in his situation, would have embraced as reasonable and eligible. But, besides that the ordinary course of nature may convince us, that almost everything is regulated by principles and maxims very different from ours; besides this, I say, it must evidently appear contrary to all rules of analogy to reason, from the intentions and projects of men, to those of a Being so different, and so much superior. In human nature, there is a certain experienced coherence of designs and inclinations; so that when, from any fact, we have discovered one intention of any man, it may often be reasonable, from experience, to infer another, and draw a long chain of conclusions concerning his past or future conduct. But this method of reasoning can never have place with regard to a Being, so remote and incomprehensible,

---

[1] In general, it may, I think, be established as a maxim, that where any cause is known only by its particular effects, it must be impossible to infer any new effects from that cause; since the qualities, which are requisite to produce these new effects along with the former, must either be different, or superior, or of more extensive operation, than those which simply produced the effect, whence alone the cause is supposed to be known to us. We can never, therefore, have any reason to suppose the existence of these qualities. To say, that the new effects proceed only from a continuation of the same energy, which is already known from the first effects, will not remove the difficulty. For even granting this to be the case (which can seldom be supposed), the very continuation and exertion of a like energy (for it is impossible it can be absolutely the same), I say, this exertion of a like energy, in a different period of space and time, is a very arbitrary supposition, and what there cannot possibly be any traces of in the effects, from which all our knowledge of the cause is originally derived. Let the *inferred* cause be exactly proportioned (as it should be) to the known effect; and it is impossible that it can possess any qualities, from which new or different effects can be *inferred*.

who bears much less analogy to any other being in the universe than the sun to a waxen taper, and who discovers himself only by some faint traces or outlines, beyond which we have no authority to ascribe to him any attribute or perfection. What we imagine to be a superior perfection, may really be a defect. Or were it ever so much a perfection, the ascribing of it to the Supreme Being, where it appears not to have been really exerted, to the full, in his works, savours more of flattery and panegyric, than of just reasoning and sound philosophy. All the philosophy, therefore, in the world, and all the religion, which is nothing but a species of philosophy, will never be able to carry us beyond the usual course of experience, or give us measures of conduct and behaviour different from those which are furnished by reflections on common life. No new fact can ever be inferred from the religious hypothesis; no event foreseen or foretold; no reward or punishment expected or dreaded, beyond what is already known by practice and observation. So that my apology for Epicurus will still appear solid and satisfactory; nor have the political interests of society any connexion with the philosophical disputes concerning metaphysics and religion.

114] There is still one circumstance, replied I, which you seem to have overlooked. Though I should allow your premises, I must deny your conclusion. You conclude, that religious doctrines and reasonings *can* have no influence on life, because they *ought* to have no influence; never considering, that men reason not in the same manner you do, but draw many consequences from the belief of a divine Existence, and suppose that the Deity will inflict punishments on vice, and bestow rewards on virtue, beyond what appear in the ordinary course of nature. Whether this reasoning of theirs be just or not, is no matter. Its influence on their life and conduct must still be the same. And, those, who attempt to disabuse them of such prejudices, may, for aught I know, be good reasoners, but I cannot allow them to be good citizens and politicians; since they free men from one restraint upon their passions, and make the infringement of the laws of society, in one respect, more easy and secure.

After all, I may, perhaps, agree to your general conclusion in favour of liberty, though upon different premises from those, on which you endeavour to found it. I think, that the state ought to tolerate every principle of philosophy; nor is there an instance, that any government has suffered in its political interests by such indulgence. There is no enthusiasm among philosophers; their doctrines are not very alluring to the people; and no restraint can be put upon their reasonings, but what must be of dangerous consequence to the sciences, and even to the state, by paving the way for persecution and oppression in points, where the generality of mankind are more deeply interested and concerned.

115] But there occurs to me (continued I) with regard to your main topic, a difficulty, which I shall just propose to you without insisting on it; lest it lead into reasonings of too nice and delicate a nature. In a word, I much doubt whether it be possible for a cause to be known only by its effect (as you have all along supposed) or to be of so singular and particular a nature as to have no parallel and no similarity with any other cause or object, that has ever fallen under our observation. It is only when two *species* of objects are found to be constantly conjoined, that we can infer the one from the other; and were an effect presented, which was entirely singular, and could not be comprehended under any known *species*, I do not see, that we could form any conjecture or inference at all concerning its cause. If experience and observation and analogy be, indeed, the only guides which we can reasonably follow in inferences of this nature; both the effect and cause must bear a similarity and resemblance to other effects and causes, which we know, and which we have found, in many instances, to be conjoined with each other. I leave it to your own reflection to pursue the consequences of this principle. I shall just observe, that, as the antagonists of Epicurus always suppose the universe, an effect quite singular and unparelleled, to be the proof of a Deity, a cause no less singular and unparalleled; your reasonings, upon that supposition, seem, at least, to merit our attention. There is, I own, some difficulty, how we can ever return from the cause to the effect, and, reasoning from our ideas of the former, infer any alteration on the latter, or any addition to it.

Section XII
Of the Academical or Sceptical Philosophy
Part I

116] There is not a greater number of philosophical reasonings, displayed upon any subject, than those, which prove the existence of a Deity, and refute the fallacies of *Atheists*; and yet the most religious philosophers still dispute whether any man can be so blinded as to be a speculative atheist. How shall we reconcile these contradictions? The knights-errant, who wandered about to clear the world of dragons and giants, never entertained the least doubt with regard to the existence of these monsters.

The *Sceptic* is another enemy of religion, who naturally provokes the indignation of all divines and graver philosophers; though it is certain, that no man ever met with any such absurd creature, or conversed with a man, who had no opinion or principle concerning any subject, either of action or speculation. This begets a very natural question; What is meant by a sceptic? And how far it is possible to push these philosophical principles of doubt and uncertainty?

There is a species of scepticism, *antecedent* to all study and philosophy, which is much inculcated by Des Cartes and others, as a soverign preservative against error and precipitate judgement. It recommends an universal doubt, not only of all our former opinions and principles, but also of our very faculties; of whose veracity, say they, we must assure ourselves, by a chain of reasoning, deduced from some original principle, which cannot possibly be fallacious or deceitful. But neither is there any such original principle, which has a prerogative above others, that are self-evident and convincing: or if there were, could we advance a step beyond it, but by the use of those very faculties, of which we are supposed to be already diffident. The Cartesian doubt, therefore, were it ever possible to be attained by any human creature (as it plainly is not) would be entirely incurable; and no reasoning could ever bring us to a state of assurance and conviction upon any subject.

It must, however, be confessed, that this species of scepticism, when more moderate, may be understood in a very reasonable sense, and is a necessary preparative to the study of philosophy, by preserving a proper impartiality in our judgements, and weaning our mind from all those prejudices, which we may have imbibed from education or rash opinion. To begin with clear and self-evident principles, to advance by timorous and sure steps, to review frequently our conclusions, and examine accurately all their consequences; though by these means we shall make both a slow and a short progress in our systems; are the only methods, by which we can ever hope to reach truth, and attain a proper stability and certainty in our determinations.

117] There is another species of scepticism, *consequent* to science and enquiry, when men are supposed to have discovered, either the absolute fallaciousness of their mental faculties, or their unfitness to reach any fixed determination in all those curious subjects of speculation, about which they are commonly employed. Even our very senses are brought into dispute, by a certain species of philosophers; and the maxims of common life are subjected to the same doubt as the most profound principles or conclusions of metaphysics and theology. As these paradoxical tenets (if they may be called tenets) are to be met with in some philosophers, and the refutation of them in several, they naturally excite our curiosity, and make us enquire into the arguments, on which they may be founded.

I need not insist upon the more trite topics, employed by the sceptics in all ages, against the evidence of *sense*; such as those which are derived from the imperfection and fallaciousness of our organs, on numberless occasions; the crooked appearance of an oar in water; the various aspects of objects, according to their different distances; the double images which arise from the pressing one eye; with many other appearances of a like nature. These sceptical topics, indeed, are only sufficient to prove, that the senses alone are not implicitly to be depended on; but that we must correct their evidence by reason, and by considerations, derived from the nature of the medium, the distance of the object, and the disposition of the organ, in order to render them, within their sphere, the proper *criteria* of truth and falsehood. There are other more profound arguments against the senses, which admit not of so easy a solution.

118] It seems evident, that men are carried, by a natural instinct or prepossession, to repose faith in their senses; and that, without any reasoning, or even almost before the use of reason, we always suppose an external universe, which depends not on our perception, but would exist, though we and every sensible creature were absent or annihilated. Even the animal creation are governed by a like opinion, and preserve this belief of external objects, in all their thoughts, designs, and actions.

It seems also evident, that, when men follow this blind and powerful instinct of nature, they always suppose the very images, presented by the senses, to be the external objects, and never entertain any suspicion, that the one are nothing but representations of the other. This very table, which we see white, and which we feel hard, is believed to exist, independent of our perception, and to be something external to our mind, which perceives it. Our presence bestows not being on it: our absence does not annihilate it. It preserves its existence uniform and entire, independent of the situation of intelligent beings, who perceive or contemplate it.

But this universal and primary opinion of all men is soon destroyed by the slightest philosophy, which teaches us, that nothing can ever be present to the mind but an image or perception, and that the senses are only the inlets, through which these images are conveyed, without being able to produce any immediate intercourse between the mind and the object. The table, which we see, seems to diminish, as we remove farther from it: but the real table, which exists independent of us, suffers no alteration: it was, therefore, nothing but its image, which was present to the mind. These are the obvious dictates of reason; and no man, who reflects, ever doubted, that the existences, which we consider, when we say, *this house* and *that tree,* are nothing but perceptions in the mind, and fleeting copies or representations of other existences, which remain uniform and independent.

119] So far, then, are we necessitated by reasoning to contradict or depart from the primary instincts of nature, and to embrace a new system with regard to the evidence of our senses. But here philosophy finds herself extremely embarrassed, when she would justify this new system, and obviate the cavils and objections of the sceptics. She can no longer plead the infallible and irresistible instinct of nature: for that led us to a quite different system, which is acknowledged fallible and even erroneous. And to justify this pretended philosophical system, by a chain of clear and convincing argument, or even any appearance of argument, exceeds the power of all human capacity.

By what argument can it be proved, that the perceptions of the mind must be caused by external objects, entirely different from them, though resembling them (if that be possible) and could not arise either from the energy of the mind itself, or from the suggestion of some invisible and unknown spirit, or from some other cause still more unknown to us? It is acknowledged, that, in fact, many of these perceptions arise not from anything external, as in dreams, madness, and other diseases. And nothing can be more inexplicable than the manner, in which body should so operate upon mind as ever to convey an image of itself to a substance, supposed of so different, and even contrary a nature.

It is a question of fact, whether the perceptions of the senses be produced by external objects, resembling them: how shall this question be determined? By experience surely; as all other questions of a like nature. But here experience is, and must be entirely silent. The mind has never anything present to it but the perceptions, and cannot possibly reach any experience of their connexion with objects. The supposition of such a connexion is, therefore, without any foundation in reasoning.

120] To have recourse to the veracity of the supreme Being, in order to prove the veracity of our senses, is surely making a very unexpected circuit. If his veracity were at all concerned in this matter, our senses would be entirely infallible; because it is not possible that he can ever deceive. Not to mention, that, if the external world be once called in question, we shall be at a loss to find arguments, by which we may prove the existence of that Being or any of his attributes.

121] This is a topic, therefore, in which the profounder and more philosophical sceptics will always triumph, when they endeavour to introduce an universal doubt into all subjects of human knowledge and enquiry. Do you follow the instincts and propensities of nature, may they say, in assenting to the veracity of sense? But these lead you to believe that the very perception or sensible image is the external object. Do you disclaim this principle, in order to embrace a more rational opinion, that the perceptions are only representations of something external? You here depart from your natural propensities and more obvious sentiments; and yet are not able to satisfy your reason, which can never find any convincing argument from experience to prove, that the perceptions are connected with any external objects.

122] There is another sceptical topic of a like nature, derived from the most profound philosophy; which might merit our attention, were it requisite to dive so deep, in order to discover arguments and reasonings, which can so little serve to any serious purpose. It is universally allowed by modern enquirers, that all the sensible qualities of objects, such as hard, soft, hot, cold, white, black, &c. are merely secondary, and exist not in the objects themselves, but are perceptions of the mind, without any external archetype or model, which they represent. If this be allowed, with regard to secondary qualities, it must also follow, with regard to the supposed primary qualities of extension and solidity; nor can the latter be any more entitled to that denomination than the former. The idea of extension is entirely acquired from the senses of sight and feeling; and if all the qualities, perceived by the senses, be in the mind, not in the object, the same conclusion must reach the idea of extension, which is wholly dependent on the sensible ideas or the ideas of secondary qualities. Nothing can save us from this conclusion, but the asserting, that the ideas of those primary qualities are attained by *Abstraction,* an opinion, which, if we examine it accurately, we shall find to be unintelligible, and even absurd. An extension, that is neither tangible nor visible, cannot possibly be conceived: and a tangible or visible extension, which is neither hard nor soft, black nor white, is equally beyond the reach of human conception. Let any man try to conceive a triangle in general, which is neither *Isosceles* nor *Scalenum,* nor has any particular length or proportion of sides; and he will soon perceive

the absurdity of all the scholastic notions with regard to abstraction and general ideas.[1]

123] Thus the first philosophical objection to the evidence of sense
or to the opinion of external existence consists in this, that such
an opinion, if rested on natural instinct, is contrary to reason, and
if referred to reason, is contrary to natural instinct, and at the same
time carries no rational evidence with it, to convince an impartial
enquirer. The second objection goes farther, and represents this
opinion as contrary to reason: at least, if it be a principle of reason,
that all sensible qualities are in the mind, not in the object. Be-
reave matter of all its intelligible qualities, both primary and secondary, you in a manner annihilate it, and leave only a certain
unknown, inexplicable *something*, as the cause of our perceptions;
a notion so imperfect, that no sceptic will think it worth while to
contend against it.

Part II

124] It may seem a very extravagant attempt of the sceptics to
destroy *reason* by argument and ratiocination; yet is this the grand
scope of all their enquiries and disputes. They endeavour to find
objections, both to our abstract reasonings, and to those which
regard matter of fact and existence.

The chief objection against all *abstract* reasonings is derived
from the ideas of space and time; ideas, which, in common life and
to a careless view, are very clear and intelligible, but when they
pass through the scrutiny of the profound sciences (and they are
the chief object of these sciences) afford principles, which seem full
of absurdity and contradiction. No priestly *dogmas*, invented on
purpose to tame and subdue the rebellious reason of mankind,
ever shocked common sense more than the doctrine of the infinitive divisibility of extension, with its consequences; as they are

[1] This argument is drawn from Dr. Berkeley; and indeed most of the writings of
that very ingenious author form the best lessons of scepticism, which are to be
found either among the ancient or modern philosophers, Bayle not excepted. He
professes, however, in his title-page (and undoubtedly with great truth) to have
composed his book against the sceptics as well as against the atheists and free-
thinkers. But that all his arguments, though otherwise intended, are, in reality,
merely sceptical, appears from this, *that they admit of no answer and produce no
conviction*. Their only effect is to cause that momentary amazement and irresolution
and confusion, which is the result of sceptism.

pompously displayed by all geometricians and metaphysicians, with a kind of triumph and exultation. A real quantity, infinitely less than any finite quantity, containing qualities infinitely less than itself, and so on *in infinitum;* this is an edifice so bold and prodigious, that it is too weighty for any pretended demonstration to support, because it shocks the clearest and most natural principles of human reason.[1] But what renders the matter more extraordinary, is, that these seemingly absurd opinions are supported by a chain of reasoning, the clearest and most natural; nor is it possible for us to allow the premises without admitting the consequences. Nothing can be more convincing and satisfactory than all the conclusions concerning the properties of circles and triangles; and yet, when these are once received, how can we deny, that the angle of contact between a circle and its tangent is infinitely less than any rectilineal angle, that as you may increase the diameter of the circle *in infinitum,* this angle of contact becomes still less, even *in infinitum,* and that the angle of contact between other curves and their tangents may be infinitely less than those between any circle and its tangent, and so on, *in infinitum?* The demonstration of these principles seems as unexceptionable as that which proves the three angles of a triangle to be equal to two right ones, though the latter opinion be natural and easy, and the former big with contradiction and absurdity. Reason here seems to be thrown into a kind of amazement and suspense, which, without the suggestions of any sceptic, gives her a diffidence of herself, and of the ground on which she treads. She sees a full light, which illuminates certain places; but that light borders upon the most profound darkness. And between these she is so dazzled and confounded, that she scarcely can pronounce with certainty and assurance concerning any one object.

125] The absurdity of these bold determinations of the abstract sciences seems to become, if possible, still more palpable with

[1] Whatever disputes there may be about mathematical points, we must allow that there are physical points; that is, parts of extension, which cannot be divided or lessened, either by the eye or imagination. These images, then, which are present to the fancy or senses, are absolutely indivisible, and consequently must be allowed by mathematicians to be infinitely less than any real part of extension; and yet nothing appears more certain to reason, than that an infinite number of them composes an infinite extension. How much more an infinite number of those infinitely small parts of extension, which are still supposed infinitely divisible.

regard to time than extension. An infinite number of real parts of time, passing in succession, and exhausted one after another, appears so evident a contradiction, that no man, one should think, whose judgement is not corrupted, instead of being improved, by the sciences, would ever be able to admit of it.

Yet still reason must remain restless, and unquiet, even with regard to that scepticism, to which she is driven by these seeming absurdities and contradictions. How any clear, distinct idea can contain circumstances, contradictory to itself, or to any other clear, distinct idea, is absolutely incomprehensible; and is, perhaps, as absurd as any proposition, which can be formed. So that nothing can be more sceptical, or more full of doubt and hesitation, than this scepticism itself, which arises from some of the paradoxical conclusions of geometry or the science of quantity.[1]

126] The sceptical objections to *moral* evidence, or to the reasonings concerning matter of fact, are either *popular* or *philosophical*. The popular objections are derived from the natural weakness of human understanding; the contradictory opinions, which have been entertained in different ages and nations; the variations of our judgement in sickness and health, youth and old age, prosperity and adversity; the perpetual contradiction of each particular man's opinions and sentiments; with many other topics of that kind. It is needless to insist farther on this head. These objections are but weak. For as, in common life, we reason every moment concerning fact and existence, and cannot possibly sub-

---

[1] It seems to me not impossible to avoid these absurdities and contradictions, if it be admitted, that there is no such thing as abstract or general ideas, properly speaking; but that all general ideas are, in reality, particular ones, attached to a general term, which recalls, upon occasion, other particular ones, that resemble, in certain circumstances, the idea, present to the mind. Thus when the term Horse is pronounced, we immediately figure to ourselves the idea of a black or a white animal, of a particular size or figure: But as that term is also usually applied to animals of other colours, figures and sizes, these ideas, though not actually present to the imagination, are easily recalled; and our reasoning and conclusion proceed in the same way, as if they were actually present. If this be admitted (as seems reasonable) it follows that all the ideas of quantity, upon which mathematicians reason, are nothing but particular, and such as are suggested by the senses and imagination, and consequently, cannot be infinitely divisible. It is sufficient to have dropped this hint at present, without prosecuting it any farther. It certainly concerns all lovers of science not to expose themselves to the ridicule and contempt of the ignorant by their conclusions; and this seems the readiest solution of these difficulties.

sist, without continually employing this species of argument, any popular objections, derived from thence, must be insufficient to destroy that evidence. The great subverter of *Pyrrhonism* or the excessive principles of scepticism is action, and employment, and the occupations of common life. These principles may flourish and triumph in the schools; where it is, indeed, difficult, if not impossible, to refute them. But as soon as they leave the shade, and by the presence of the real objects, which actuate our passions and sentiments, are put in opposition to the more powerful principles of our nature, they vanish like smoke, and leave the most determined sceptic in the same condition as other mortals.

127] The sceptic, therefore, had better keep within his proper sphere, and display those *philosophical* objections, which arise from more profound researches. Here he seems to have ample matter of triumph; while he justly insists, that all our evidence for any matter of fact, which lies beyond the testimony of sense or memory, is derived entirely from the relation of cause and effect; that we have no other idea of this relation than that of two objects, which have been frequently *conjoined* together; that we have no argument to convince us, that objects, which have, in our experience, been frequently conjoined, will likewise, in other instances, be conjoined in the same manner; and that nothing leads us to this inference but custom or a certain instinct of our nature; which it is indeed difficult to resist, but which, like other instincts, may be fallacious and deceitful. While the sceptic insists upon these topics, he shows his force, or rather, indeed, his own and our weakness; and seems, for the time at least, to destroy all assurance and conviction. These arguments might be displayed at greater length, if any durable good or benefit to society could ever be expected to result from them.

128] For here is the chief and most confounding objection to *excessive* scepticism, that no durable good can ever result from it; while it remains in its full force and vigour. We need only ask such a sceptic, *What his meaning is? And what he proposes by all these curious researches?* He is immediately at a loss, and knows not what to answer. A Copernican or Ptolemaic, who supports each his different system of astronomy, may hope to produce a conviction, which will remain constant and durable, with his audience. A Stoic or Epicurean displays principles, which may not be durable, but which have an effect on conduct and behaviour. But a Pyrrhonian cannot expect, that his philosophy will have any constant influence on the mind: or if it had, that its influence would be beneficial to society. On the contrary, he must acknowledge, if he will acknowledge anything, that all human life must perish, were his principles universally and steadily to prevail. All discourse, all action would immediately cease; and men remain in a total lethargy, till the necessities of nature, unsatisfied, put an end to their miserable existence. It is true; so fatal an event is very little to be dreaded. Nature is always too strong for principle. And though a Pyrrhonian may throw himself or others into a momentary amazement and confusion by his profound reasonings; the first and most trival event in life will put to flight all his doubts and scruples, and leave him the same, in every point of action and speculation, with the philosophers of every other sect, or with those who never concerned themselves in any philosophical researches. When he awakes from his dream, he will be the first to join in the laugh against himself, and to confess, that all his objections are mere amusement, and can have no other tendency than to show the whimsical condition of mankind, who must act and reason and believe; though they are not able, by their most diligent enquiry, to satisfy themselves concerning the foundation of these operations, or to remove the objections, which may be raised against them.

Part III

129] There is, indeed, a more *mitigated* scepticism or *academical* philosophy, which may be both durable and useful, and which may, in part, be the result of this Pyrrhonism, or *excessive* scepticism, when its undistinguished doubts are, in some measure, corrected by common sense and reflection. The greater part of mankind are naturally apt to be affirmative and dogmatical in their opinions; and while they see objects only on one side, and have no idea of any counterpoising argument, they throw themselves precipitately into the principles, to which they are inclined; nor have they any indulgence for those who entertain opposite sentiments. To hesitate or balance perplexes their understanding, checks their passion, and suspends their action. They are, therefore, impatient till they escape from a state, which to them is so uneasy: and they think, that they could never remove themselves far enough from it, by the violence of their affirmations and obstinacy of their belief. But could such dogmatical reasoners become sensible of the strange infirmities of human understanding, even in its most perfect state, and when most accurate and cautious in its determinations; such a reflection would naturally inspire them with more modesty and reserve, and diminish their fond opinion of themselves, and their prejudice against antagonists. The illiterate may reflect on the disposition of the learned, who, amidst all the advantages of study and reflection, are commonly still diffident in their determinations: and if any of the learned be inclined, from their natural temper, to haughtiness and obstinacy, a small tincture of Pyrrhonism might abate their pride, by showing them, that the few advantages, which they may have attained over their fellows, are but inconsiderable, if compared with the universal perplexity and confusion, which is inherent in human nature. In general, there is a degree of doubt, and caution, and modesty, which, in all kinds of scrutiny and decision, ought for ever to accompany a just reasoner.

130] Another species of *mitigated* scepticism which may be of advantage to mankind, and which may be the natural result of the Pyrrhonian doubts and scruples, is the limitation of our enquiries to such subjects as are best adapted to the narrow capacity of human understanding. The *imagination* of man is naturally sublime, delighted with whatever is remote and extraordinary, and running, without control, into the most distant parts of space and time in order to avoid the objects, which custom has rendered too familiar to it. A correct *Judgement* observes a contrary method, and avoiding all distant and high enquiries, confines itself to common life, and to such subjects as fall under daily practice and experience; leaving the more sublime topics to the embellishment of poets and orators, or to the arts of priests and politicians. To bring us to so salutary a determination, nothing can be more serviceable, than to be once thoroughly convinced of the force of the Pyrrhonian doubt, and of the impossibility, that anything, but the strong power of natural instinct, could free us from it. Those who have a propensity to philosophy, will still continue their researches; because they reflect, that, besides the immediate pleasure, attending such an occupation, philosophical decisions are nothing but the reflections of common life, methodized and corrected. But they will never be tempted to go beyond common life, so long as they consider the imperfection of those faculties which they employ, their narrow reach, and their inaccurate operations. While we cannot give a satisfactory reason, why we believe, after a thousand experiments, that a stone will fall, or fire burn; can we ever satisfy ourselves concerning any determination, which we may form, with regard to the origin of worlds, and the situation of nature, from, and to eternity?

This narrow limitation, indeed, of our enquiries, is, in every respect, so reasonable, that it suffices to make the slightest examination into the natural powers of the human mind and to compare them with their objects, in order to recommend it to us. We shall then find what are the proper subjects of science and enquiry.

131] It seems to me, that the only objects of the abstract science or of demonstration are quantity and number, and that all attempts to extend this more perfect species of knowledge beyond these bounds are mere sophistry and illusion. As the component parts of quantity and number are entirely similar, their relations become intricate and involved; and nothing can be more curious, as well as useful, than to trace, by a variety of mediums, their equality or inequality, through their different appearances. But as all other ideas are clearly distinct and different from each other, we can never advance farther, by our utmost scrutiny, than to observe this diversity, and, by an obvious reflection, pronounce one thing not to be another. Or if there be any difficulty in these decisions, it proceeds entirely from the undeterminate meaning of words, which is corrected by juster definitions. That *the square of the hypothenuse is equal to the squares of the other two sides*, cannot be known, let the terms be ever so exactly defined, without a train of reasoning and enquiry. But to convince us of this proposition, *that where there is no property, there can be no injustice*, it is only necessary to define the terms, and explain injustice, to be a violation of property. This proposition is, indeed, nothing but a more imperfect definition. It is the same case with all those pretended syllogistical reasonings, which may be found in every other branch of learning, except the sciences of quantity and number; and these may safely, I think, be pronounced the only proper objects of knowledge and demonstration.

132] All other enquiries of men regard only matter of fact and existence; and these are evidently incapable of demonstration. Whatever *is* may *not be*. No negation of a fact can involve a contradiction. The non-existence of any being, without exception, is as clear and distinct an idea as its existence. The proposition, which affirms it not to be, however false, is no less conceivable and intelligible, than that which affirms it to be. The case is different with the sciences, properly so called. Every proposition, which is not true, is there confused and unintelligible. That the cube root of 64 is equal to the half of 10, is a false proposition, and can never be distinctly conceived. But that Cæsar, or the angel Gabriel, or any being never existed, may be a false proposition, but still is perfectly conceivable, and implies no contradiction.

The existence, therefore, of any being can only be proved by arguments from its cause or its effect; and these arguments are founded entirely on experience. If we reason *a priori*, anything may appear able to produce anything. The falling of a pebble may, for aught we know, extinguish the sun; or the wish of a man control the planets in their orbits. It is only experience, which teaches us the nature and bounds of cause and effect, and enables us to infer the existence of one object from that of another.[1] Such is the foundation of moral reasoning, which forms the greater part of human knowledge, and is the source of all human action and behaviour.

Moral reasonings are either concerning particular or general facts. All deliberations in life regard the former; as also all disquisitions in history, chronology, geography, and astronomy.

The sciences, which treat of general facts, are politics, natural philosophy, physic, chemistry, &c. where the qualities, causes and effects of a whole species of objects are enquired into.

---

[1] That impious maxim of the ancient philosophy, *Ex nihilo, nihil fit*, by which the creation of matter was excluded, ceases to be a maxim, according to this philosophy. Not only the will of the supreme Being may create matter; but, for aught we know *a priori*, the will of any other being might create it, or any other cause, that the most whimsical imagination can assign.

Divinity or Theology, as it proves the existence of a Deity, and the immortality of souls, is composed partly of reasonings concerning particular, partly concerning general facts. It has a foundation in *reason*, so far as it is supported by experience. But its best and most solid foundation is *faith* and divine revelation.

Morals and criticism are not so properly objects of the understanding as of taste and sentiment. Beauty, whether moral or natural, is felt, more properly than perceived. Or if we reason concerning it, and endeavour to fix its standard, we regard a new fact, to wit, the general tastes of mankind, or some such fact, which may be the object of reasoning and enquiry.

When we run over libraries, persuaded of these principles, what havoc must we make? If we take in our hand any volume; of divinity or school metaphysics, for instance; let us ask, *Does it contain any abstract reasoning concerning quantity or number?* No. *Does it contain any experimental reasoning concerning matter of fact and existence?* No. Commit it then to the flames: for it can contain nothing but sophistry and illusion.

An Enquiry Concerning the Principles of Morals

Section I

Of the General Principles of Morals

133] Dᴉsᴘᴜᴛᴇs with men, pertinaciously obstinate in their principles, are, of all others, the most irksome; except, perhaps, those with persons, entirely disingenuous, who really do not believe the opinions they defend, but engage in the controversy, from affectation, from a spirit of opposition, or from a desire of showing wit and ingenuity, superior to the rest of mankind. The same blind adherence to their own arguments is to be expected in both; the same contempt of their antagonists; and the same passionate vehemence, in inforcing sophistry and falsehood. And as reasoning is not the source, whence either disputant derives his tenets; it is in vain to expect, that any logic, which speaks not to the affections, will ever engage him to embrace sounder principles.

Those who have denied the reality of moral distinctions, may be ranked among the disingenuous disputants; nor is it conceivable, that any human creature could ever seriously believe, that all characters and actions were alike entitled to the affection and regard of everyone. The difference, which nature has placed between one man and another, is so wide, and this difference is still so much farther widened, by education, example, and habit, that, where the opposite extremes come at once under our apprehension, there is no scepticism so scrupulous, and scarce any assurance so determined, as absolutely to deny all distinction between them. Let a man's insensibility be ever so great, he must often be touched with the images of Right and Wrong; and let his prejudices be ever so obstinate, he must observe, that others are susceptible of like impressions. The only way, therefore, of converting an antag-

onist of this kind, is to leave him to himself. For, finding that
nobody keeps up the controversy with him, it is probable he will,
at last, of himself, from mere weariness, come over to the side of
common sense and reason.

134] There has been a controversy started of late, much better
worth examination, concerning the general foundation of Morals;
whether they be derived from Reason, or from Sentiment; whether
we attain the knowledge of them by a chain of argument and induction, or by an immediate feeling and finer internal sense;
whether, like all sound judgement of truth and falsehood, they
should be the same to every rational intelligent being; or whether,
like the perception of beauty and deformity, they be founded
entirely on the particular fabric and constitution of the human
species.

  The ancient philosophers, though they often affirm, that virtue
is nothing but conformity to reason, yet, in general, seem to consider morals as deriving their existence from taste and sentiment.
On the other hand, our modern enquirers, though they also talk
much of the beauty of virtue, and deformity of vice, yet have commonly endeavoured to account for these distinctions by metaphysical reasonings, and by deductions from the most abstract
principles of the understanding. Such confusion reigned in these
subjects, that an opposition of the greatest consequence could prevail between one system and another, and even in the parts of
almost each individual system; and yet nobody, till very lately, was
ever sensible of it. The elegant Lord Shaftesbury, who first gave occasion to remark this distinction, and who, in general, adhered to
the principles of the ancients, is not, himself, entirely free from the
same confusion.

135] It must be acknowledged, that both sides of the question are
susceptible of specious arguments. Moral distinctions, it may be
said, are discernible by pure *reason*: else, whence the many disputes that reign in common life, as well as in philosophy, with
regard to this subject: the long chain of proofs often produced on
both sides; the examples cited, the authorities appealed to, the
analogies employed, the fallacies detected, the inferences drawn,
and the several conclusions adjusted to their proper principles.
Truth is disputable; not taste: what exists in the nature of things

is the standard of our judgement; what each man feels within himself is the standard of sentiment. Propositions in geometry may be proved, systems in physics may be controverted; but the harmony of verse, the tenderness of passion, the brilliancy of wit, must give immediate pleasure. No man reasons concerning another's beauty; but frequently concerning the justice or injustice of his actions. In every criminal trial the first object of the prisoner is to disprove the facts alleged, and deny the actions imputed to him: the second to prove, that, even if these actions were real, they might be justified, as innocent and lawful. It is confessedly by deductions of the understanding, that the first point is ascertained: how can we suppose that a different faculty of the mind is employed in fixing the other?

136] On the other hand, those who would resolve all moral determinations into *sentiment,* may endeavour to show, that it is impossible for reason ever to draw conclusions of this nature. To virtue, say they, it belongs to be *amiable,* and *vice odious.* This forms their very nature or essence. But can reason or argumentation distribute these different epithets to any subjects, and pronounce beforehand, that this must produce love, and that hatred? Or what other reason can we ever assign for these affections, but the original fabric and formation of the human mind, which is naturally adapted to receive them?

The end of all moral speculations is to teach us our duty; and, by proper representations of the deformity of vice and beauty of virtue, beget correspondent habits, and engage us to avoid the one, and embrace the other. But is this ever to be expected from inferences and conclusions of the understanding, which of themselves have no hold of the affections or set in motion the active powers of men? They discover truths: but where the truths which they discover are indifferent, and beget no desire or aversion, they can have no influence on conduct and behaviour. What is honourable, what is fair, what is becoming, what is noble, what is generous, takes possession of the heart, and animates us to embrace and maintain it. What is intelligible, what is evident, what is probable, what is true, procures only the cool assent of the understanding; and gratifying a speculative curiosity, puts an end to our researches.

Extinguish all the warm feelings and prepossessions in favour of virtue, and all disgust or aversion to vice: render men totally indifferent towards these distinctions; and morality is no longer a practical study, nor has any tendency to regulate our lives and actions.

137] These arguments on each side (and many more might be produced) are so plausible, that I am apt to suspect, they may, the one as well as the other, be solid and satisfactory, and that *reason* and *sentiment* concur in almost all moral determinations and conclusions. The final sentence, it is probable, which pronounces characters and actions amiable or odious, praise-worthy or blame-able; that which stamps on them the mark of honour or infamy, approbation or censure; that which renders morality an active principle and constitutes virtue our happiness, and vice our misery: it is probable, I say, that this final sentence depends on some internal sense or feeling, which nature has made universal in the whole species. For what else can have an influence of this nature? But in order to pave the way for such a sentiment, and give a proper discernment of its object, it is often necessary, we find, that much reasoning should precede, that nice distinctions be made, just conclusions drawn, distant comparisons formed, complicated relations examined, and general facts fixed and ascertained. Some species of beauty, especially the natural kinds, on their first appearance, command our affection and approbation; and where they fail of this effect, it is impossible for any reasoning to redress their influence, or adapt them better to our taste and sentiment. But in many orders of beauty, particularly those of the finer arts, it is requisite to employ much reasoning, in order to feel the proper sentiment; and a false relish may frequently be corrected by argument and reflection. There are just grounds to conclude, that moral beauty partakes much of this latter species, and demands the assistance of our intellectual faculties, in order to give it a suitable influence on the human mind.

138] But though this question, concerning the general principles of morals, be curious and important, it is needless for us, at present, to employ farther care in our researches concerning it. For if we can be so happy, in the course of this enquiry, as to discover the true origin of morals, it will then easily appear how far either sentiment or reason enters into all determinations of this nature.[1] In order to attain this purpose, we shall endeavour to follow a very simple method: we shall analyse that complication of mental qualities, which form what, in common life, we call Personal Merit: we shall consider every attribute of the mind, which renders a man an object either of esteem and affection, or of hatred and contempt; every habit or sentiment or faculty, which, if ascribed to any person, implies either praise or blame, and may enter into any panegyric or satire of his character and manners. The quick sensibility, which, on this head, is so universal among mankind, gives a philosopher sufficient assurance, that he can never be considerably mistaken in framing the catalogue, or incur any danger of misplacing the objects of his contemplation: he needs only enter into his own breast for a moment, and consider whether or not he should desire to have this or that quality ascribed to him, and whether such or such an imputation would proceed from a friend or an enemy. The very nature of language guides us almost infallibly in forming a judgement of this nature; and as every tongue possesses one set of words which are taken in a good sense, and another in the opposite, the least acquaintance with the idiom suffices, without any reasoning, to direct us in collecting and arranging the estimable or blameable qualities of men. The only object of reasoning is to discover the circumstances on both sides, which are common to these qualities; to observe that particular in which the estimable qualities agree on the one hand, and the blameable on the other; and thence to reach the foundation of ethics, and find those universal principles, from which all censure or approbation is ultimately derived. As this is a question of fact, not of abstract science, we can only expect success, by following the experimental method, and deducing general maxims from a comparison of particular instances. The other scientific method, where a general abstract principle is first established, and is afterwards branched out into a variety of inferences and conclusions, may be more perfect in itself, but suits less the imperfection of human nature, and is a common source of illusion and mistake in this as well as in other subjects. Men are not cured of their passion for hypotheses and systems in natural philosophy,

[1] See Appendix I, immediately following this selection.

and will hearken to no arguments but those which are derived from experience. It is full time they should attempt a like reformation in all moral disquisitions; and reject every system of ethics, however subtle or ingenious, which is not founded on fact and observation.

We shall begin our enquiry on this head by the consideration of the social virtues, Benevolence and Justice. The explication of them will probably give us an opening by which the others may be accounted for.

Section II

Of Benevolence

Part I

139] It may be esteemed, perhaps, a superfluous task to prove, that the benevolent or softer affections are estimable; and wherever they appear, engage the approbation and good-will of mankind. The epithets *sociable, good-natured, humane, merciful, grateful, friendly, generous, beneficent,* or their equivalents, are known in all languages, and universally express the highest merit, which *human nature* is capable of attaining. Where these amiable qualities are attended with birth and power and eminent abilities, and display themselves in the good government or useful instruction of mankind, they seem even to raise the possessors of them above the rank of *human nature,* and make them approach in some measure to the divine. Exalted capacity, undaunted courage, prosperous success; these may only expose a hero or politician to the envy and ill-will of the public: but as soon as the praises are added of humane and beneficent; when instances are displayed of lenity, tenderness or friendship; envy itself is silent, or joins the general voice of approbation and applause. . . .

140] But I forget, that it is not my present business to recommend generosity and benevolence, or to paint, in their true colours, all the genuine charms of the social virtues. These, indeed, sufficiently engage every heart, on the first apprehension of them; and it is difficult to abstain from some sally of panegyric, as often as they occur in discourse or reasoning. But our object here being more the speculative, than the practical part of morals, it will suffice to remark, (what will readily, I believe, be allowed) that no qualities are more intitled to the general good-will and approbation of mankind than beneficence and humanity, friendship and gratitude, natural affection and public spirit, or whatever proceeds from a tender sympathy with others, and a generous concern for our kind and species. These wherever they appear, seem to transfuse themselves, in a manner, into each beholder, and to call forth, in their own behalf, the same favourable and affectionate sentiments, which they exert on all around.

Part II

141] We may observe that, in displaying the praises of any humane, beneficent man, there is one circumstance which never fails to be amply insisted on, namely, the happiness and satisfaction, derived to society from his intercourse and good offices. To his parents, we are apt to say, he endears himself by his pious attachment and duteous care still more than by the connexions of nature. His children never feel his authority, but when employed for their advantage. With him, the ties of love are consolidated by beneficence and friendship. The ties of friendship approach, in a fond observance of each obliging office, to those of love and inclination. His domestics and dependants have in him a sure resource; and no longer dread the power of fortune, but so far as she exercises it over him. From him the hungry receive food, the naked clothing, the ignorant and slothful skill and industry. Like the sun, an inferior minister of providence he cheers, invigorates, and sustains the surrounding world.

If confined to private life, the sphere of his activity is narrower; but his influence is all benign and gentle. If exalted into a higher station, mankind and posterity reap the fruit of his labours.

As these topics of praise never fail to be employed, and with success, where we would inspire esteem for any one; may it not thence be concluded, that the utility, resulting from the social virtues, forms, at least, a *part* of their merit, and is one source of that approbation and regard so universally paid to them?

142] When we recommend even an animal or a plant as *useful* and *beneficial,* we give it an applause and recommendation suited to its nature. As, on the other hand, reflection on the baneful influence of any of these inferior beings always inspires us with the sentiment of aversion. The eye is pleased with the prospect of corn-fields and loaded vineyards; horses grazing, and flocks pasturing: but flies the view of briars and brambles, affording shelter to wolves and serpents.

A machine, a piece of furniture, a vestment, a house well contrived for use and conveniency, is so far beautiful, and is contemplated with pleasure and approbation. An experienced eye is here sensible to many excellencies, which escape persons ignorant and uninstructed.

Can anything stronger be said in praise of a profession, such as merchandize or manufacture, than to observe the advantages which it procures to society; and is not a monk and inquisitor enraged when we treat his order as useless or pernicious to mankind?

The historian exults in displaying the benefit arising from his labours. The writer of romance alleviates or denies the bad consequences ascribed to his manner of composition.

In general, what praise is implied in the simple epithet *useful!* What reproach in the contrary! . . .

144] Upon the whole, then, it seems undeniable, *that* nothing can bestow more merit on any human creature than the sentiment of benevolence in an eminent degree; and *that* a *part,* at least, of its merit arises from its tendency to promote the interests of our species, and bestow happiness on human society. We carry our view into the salutary consequences of such a character and disposition; and whatever has so benign an influence, and forwards so desirable an end, is beheld with complacency and pleasure. The social virtues are never regarded without their beneficial tendencies, nor viewed as barren and unfruitful. The happiness of mankind, the order of society, the harmony of families, the mutual support of friends, are always considered as the result of their gentle dominion over the breasts of men.

How considerable a *part* of their merit we ought to ascribe to their utility, will better appear from future disquisitions; as well as the reason, why this circumstance has such a command over our esteem and approbation.

Section III
Of Justice
Part I

145] That Justice is useful to society, and consequently that *part* of its merit, at least, must arise from that consideration, it would be a superfluous undertaking to prove. That public utility is the *sole* origin of justice, and that reflections on the beneficial consequences of this virtue are the *sole* foundation of its merit; this proposition, being more curious and important, will better deserve our examination and enquiry.

Let us suppose that nature has bestowed on the human race such profuse *abundance* of all *external* conveniences, that, without any uncertainty in the event, without any care or industry on our part, every individual finds himself fully provided with whatever his most voracious appetites can want, or luxurious imagination wish or desire. His natural beauty, we shall suppose, surpasses all acquired ornaments: the perpetual clemency of the seasons renders useless all clothes or covering: the raw herbage affords him the most delicious fare; the clear fountain, the richest beverage. No laborious occupation required: no tillage: no navigation. Music, poetry, and contemplation form his sole business: conversation, mirth, and friendship his sole amusement.

It seems evident that, in such a happy state, every other social virtue would flourish, and receive tenfold increase; but the cautious, jealous virtue of justice would never once have been dreamed of. For what purpose make a partition of goods, where every one has already more than enough? Why give rise to property, where there cannot possibly be any injury? Why call this object *mine*, when upon the seizing of it by another, I need but stretch out my hand to possess myself to what is equally valuable? Justice, in that case, being totally useless, would be an idle ceremonial, and could never possibly have place in the catalogue of virtues.

We see, even in the present necessitous condition of mankind, that, wherever any benefit is bestowed by nature in an unlimited abundance, we leave it always in common among the whole human race, and make no subdivisions of right and property. Water and air, though the most necessary of all objects, are not challenged as the property of individuals; nor can any man commit injustice by the most lavish use and enjoyment of these blessings. In fertile extensive countries, with few inhabitants, land is regarded on the same footing. And no topic is so much insisted on by those, who defend the liberty of the seas, as the unexhausted use of them in navigation. Were the advantages, procured by navigation, as inexhaustible, these reasoners had never had any adversaries to refute; nor had any claims ever been advanced of a separate, exclusive dominion over the ocean.

It may happen, in some countries, at some periods, that there be established a property in water, none in land;[1] if the latter be in greater abundance than can be used by the inhabitants, and the former be found, with difficulty, and in very small quantities.

146] Again; suppose, that, though the necessities of human race continue the same as at present, yet the mind is so enlarged, and so replete with friendship and generosity, that every man has the utmost tenderness for every man, and feels no more concern for his own interest than for that of his fellows; it seems evident, that the use of justice would, in this case, be suspended by such an extensive benevolence, nor would the divisions and barriers of property and obligation have ever been thought of. Why should I bind another, by a deed or promise, to do me any good office, when I know that he is already prompted, by the strongest inclination, to seek my happiness, and would, of himself, perform the desired service; except the hurt, he thereby receives, be greater the benefit accruing to me? in which case, he knows, that, from my innate humanity and friendship, I should be the first to oppose myself to his imprudent generosity. Why raise land-marks between my neighbour's field and mine, when my heart has made no division between our interests; but shares all his joys and sorrows with the same force and vivacity as if originally my own? Every man, upon this suppositon, being a second self to another, would trust all his interests to the discretion of every man; without jealousy, without partition, without distinction. And the whole human race would form only one family; where all would lie in

[1] Genesis, chaps. xiii and xxi.

common, and be used freely, without regard to property; but cautiously too, with as entire regard to the necessities of each individual, as if our own interests were most intimately concerned.

In the present disposition of the human heart, it would, perhaps, be difficult to find complete instances of such enlarged affections; but still we may observe, that the case of families approaches towards it; and the stronger the mutual benevolence is among the individuals, the nearer it approaches; till all distinction of property be, in a great measure, lost and confounded among them. Between married persons, the cement of friendship is by the laws supposed so strong as to abolish all division of possessions; and has often, in reality, the force ascribed to it. And it is observable, that, during the ardour of new enthusiasms, when every principle is inflamed into extravagance, the commuity of goods has frequently been attempted; and nothing but experience of its inconveniences, from the returning or disguised selfishness of men, could make the imprudent fanatics adopt anew the ideas of justice and of separate property. So true is it, that this virtue derives its existence entirely from its necessary *use* to the intercourse and social state of mankind.

147] To make this truth more evident, let us reverse the foregoing suppositions; and carrying everything to the opposite extreme, consider what would be the effect of these new situations. Suppose a society to fall into such want of all common necessaries, that the utmost frugality and industry cannot preserve the greater number from perishing, and the whole from extreme misery; it will readily, I believe, be admitted, that the strict laws of justice are suspended, in such a pressing emergence, and give place to the stronger motives of necessity and self-preservation. Is it any crime, after a shipwreck, to seize whatever means or instrument of safey one can lay hold of, without regard to former limitations of property? Or if a city besieged were perishing with hunger; can we imagine, that men will see any means of preservation before them, and lose their lives, from a scrupulous regard to what, in other situations, would be the rules of equity and justice? The use and tendency of that virtue is to procure happiness and security, by preserving order in society: but where the society is ready to perish from extreme necessity, no greater evil can be dreaded from violence and injustice; and every man may now provide for himself by all the means, which prudence can dictate, or humanity permit. The public, even in less urgent necessities, opens granaries, without the consent of proprietors; as justly supposing, that the authority of magistracy may, consistent with equity, extend so far: but were any number of men to assemble, without the tie of laws or civil jurisdiction; would an equal partition of bread in a famine, though effected by power and even violence, be regarded as criminal or injurious?

148] Suppose likewise, that it should be a virtuous man's fate to fall into the society of ruffians, remote from the protection of laws and government; what conduct must he embrace in that melancholy situation? He sees such a desperate rapaciousness prevail; such a disregard to equity, such contempt of order, such stupid blindness to future consequences, as must immediately have the most tragical conclusion, and must terminate in destruction to the greater number, and in a total dissolution of society to the rest. He, meanwhile, can have no other expedient than to arm himself, to whomever the sword he seizes, or the buckler, may belong: To make provision of all means of defence and security: And his particular regard to justice being no longer of use to his own safety or that of others, he must consult the dictates of self-preservation alone, without concern for those who no longer merit his care and attention.

When any man, even in political society, renders himself by his crimes, obnoxious to the public, he is punished by the laws in his goods and person; that is, the ordinary rules of justice are, with regard to him, suspended for a moment, and it becomes equitable to inflict on him, for the *benefit* of society, what otherwise he could not suffer without wrong or injury.

The rage and violence of public war; what is it but a suspension of justice among the warring parties, who perceive, that this virtue is now no longer of any *use* or advantage to them? The laws of war, which then succeed to those of equity and justice, are rules calculated for the *advantage* and *utility* of that particular state, in which men are now placed. And were a civilized nation engaged with barbarians, who observed no rules even of war, the former must also suspend their observance of them, where they no longer serve to any purpose; and must render every action or rencounter as bloody and pernicious as possible to the first aggressors.

149] Thus, the rules of equity or justice depend entirely on the particular state and condition in which men are placed, and owe their origin and existence to that utility, which results to the public from their strict and regular observance. Reverse, in any considerable circumstance, the condition of men: Produce extreme abundance or extreme necessity: Implant in the human breast perfect moderation and humanity, or perfect rapaciousness and malice: By rendering justice totally *useless,* you thereby totally destroy its essence, and suspend its obligation upon mankind.

The common situation of society is a medium amidst all these extremes. We are naturally partial to ourselves, and to our friends; but are capable of learning the advantage resulting from a more equitable conduct. Few enjoyments are given us from the open and liberal hand of nature; but by art, labour, and industry, we can extract them in great abundance. Hence the ideas of property become necessary in all civil society: Hence justice derives its usefulness to the public: And hence alone arises its merit and moral obligation.

150] These conclusions are so natural and obvious, that they have not escaped even the poets, in their descriptions of the felicity attending the golden age or the reign of Saturn. The seasons, in that first period of nature, were so temperate, if we credit these agreeable fictions, that there was no necessity for men to provide themselves with clothes and houses, as a security against the violence of heat and cold: The rivers flowed with wine and milk: The oaks yielded honey; and nature spontaneously produced her greatest delicacies. Nor were these the chief advantages of that happy age. Tempests were not alone removed from nature; but those more furious tempests were unknown to human breasts, which now cause such uproar, and engender such confusion. Avarice, ambition, cruelty, selfishness, were never heard of: Cordial affection, compassion, sympathy, were the only movements with which the mind was yet acquainted. Even the punctilious distinction of *mine* and *thine* was banished from among that happy race of mortals, and carried with it the very notion of property and obligation, justice and injustice.

151] This *poetical* fiction of the *golden age* is, in some respects, of a piece with the *philosophical* fiction of the *state of nature;* only that the former is represented as the most charming and most peaceable condition, which can possibly be imagined; whereas the latter is painted out as a state of mutual war and violence, attended with the most extreme necessity. On the first origin of mankind, we are told, their ignorance and savage nature were so prevalent, that they could give no mutual trust, but must each depend upon himself and his own force or cunning for protection and security. No law was heard of: No rule of justice known: No distinction of property regarded: Power was the only measure of right; and a perpetual war of all against all was the result of men's untamed selfishness and barbarity.[1]

Whether such a condition of human nature could ever exist, or if it did, could continue so long as to merit the appelation of a *state,* may justly be doubted. Men are necessarily born in a family-society, at least; and are trained up by their parents to some rule of conduct and behaviour. But this must be admitted, that, if such a state of mutual war and violence was ever real, the suspension of all laws of justice, from their absolute inutility, is a necessary and infallible consequence. . . .

160] The dilemma seems obvious: As justice evidently tends to promote public utility and to support civil society, the sentiment of justice is either derived from our reflecting on that tendency, or like hunger, thirst, and other appetites, resentment, love of life, attachment to offspring, and other passions, arises from a simple original instinct in the human breast, which nature has implanted for like salutary purposes. If the latter be the case, it follows, that property, which is the object of justice, is also distinguished by a simple original instinct, and is not ascertained by any argument or reflection. But who is there that ever heard of such an instinct? Or is this a subject in which new discoveries can be made? We may as well expect to discover, in the body, new senses, which had before escaped the observation of all mankind.

---

[1] This fiction of a state of nature, as a state of war, was not first started by Mr. Hobbes, as is commonly imagined. Plato endeavours to refute an hypothesis very like it in the second, third, and fourth books de republica. Cicero, on the contrary, supposes it certain and universally acknowledged.

161] But farther, though it seems a very simple proposition to say, that nature, by an instinctive sentiment, distinguishes property, yet in reality we shall find, that there are required for that purpose ten thousand different instincts, and these employed about objects of the greatest intricacy and nicest discernment. For when a definition of *property* is required, that relation is found to resolve itself into any possession acquired by occupation, by industry, by prescription, by inheritance, by contract, &c. Can we think that nature, by an original instinct, instructs us in all these methods of acquisition?

These words too, inheritance and contract, stand for ideas infinitely complicated; and to define them exactly, a hundred volumes of laws, and a thousand volumes of commentators, have not been found sufficient. Does nature, whose intincts in men are all simple, embrace such complicated and artificial objects, and create a rational creature, without trusting anything to the operation of his reason?

But even though all this were admitted, it would not be satisfactory. Positive laws can certainly transfer property. It is by another original instinct, that we recognize the authority of kings and senates, and mark all the boundaries of their jurisdiction? Judges too, even though their sentence be erroneous and illegal, must be allowed, for the sake of peace and order, to have decisive authority, and ultimately to determine property. Have we original innate ideas of praetors and chancellors and juries? Who sees not, that all these institutions arise merely from the necessities of human society?

All birds of the same species in every age and country, built their nests alike: In this we see the force of instinct. Men, in different times and places, frame their houses differently: Here we perceive the influence of reason and custom. A like inference may be drawn from comparing the instinct of generation and the institution of property.

How great soever the variety of municipal laws, it must be confessed, that their chief out-lines pretty regularly concur; because the purposes, to which they tend, are everywhere exactly similar. In like manner, all houses have a roof and walls, windows and chimneys; though diversified in their shape, figure, and materials. The purposes of the latter, directed to the conveniences of human life, discover not more plainly their origin from reason and reflection, than do those of the former, which point all to a like end.

I need not mention the variations, which all the rules of property receive from the finer turns and connexions of the imagination, and from the subtilties and abstractions of law-topics and reasonings. There is no possibility of reconciling this observation to the notion of original instincts.

162] What alone will beget a doubt concerning the theory, on which I insist, is the influence of education and acquired habits, by which we are so accustomed to blame injustice, that we are not, in every instance, conscious of any immediate reflection on the pernicious consequences of it. The views the most familiar to us are apt, for that very reason, to escape us; and what we have very frequently performed from certain motives, we are apt likewise to continue mechanically, without recalling, on every occasion, the reflections, which first determined us. The convenience, or rather necessity, which leads to justice is so universal, and everywhere points so much to the same rules, that the habit takes place in all societies; and it is not without some scrutiny, that we are able to ascertain its true origin. The matter, however, is not so obscure, but that even in common life we have every moment recourse to the principle of public utility, and ask, *What must become of the world, if such practices prevail? How could society subsist under such disorders?* Were the distinction or separation of possessions entirely useless, can any one conceive, that it ever should have obtained in society?

163] Thus we seem, upon the whole, to have attained a knowledge of the force of that principle here insisted on, and can determine what degree of esteem or moral approbation may result from reflections on public interest and utility. The necessity of justice to the support of society is the sole foundation of that virtue; and since no moral excellence is more highly esteemed, we may conclude that this circumstance of usefulness has, in general, the strongest energy, and most entire command over our sentiments. It must, therefore, be the source of a considerable part of the merit ascribed to humanity, benevolence, friendship, public spirit, and other social virtues of that stamp; as it is the sole source of the moral approbation paid to fidelity, justice, veracity, integrity, and those other estimable and useful qualities and principles. It is entirely agreeable to the rules of philosophy, and even of common reason; where any principle has been found to have a great force and energy in one instance, to ascribe to it a like energy in all similar instances. This indeed is Newton's chief rule of philosophizing [1]. . . .

[1] Principia, Lib. iii.

Appendix I

Concerning Moral Sentiment

234] If the foregoing hypothesis be received, it will now be easy for us to determine the question first started [1], concerning the general principles of morals; and though we postponed the decision of that question, lest it should then involve us in intricate speculations, which are unfit for moral discourses, we may resume it at present, and examine how far either *reason* or *sentiment* enters into all decisions of praise or censure.

One principal foundation of moral praise being supposed to lie in the usefulness of any quality or action, it is evident that *reason* must enter for a considerable share in all decisions of this kind; since nothing but that faculty can instruct us in the tendency of qualities and actions, and point out their beneficial consequences to society and to their possessor. In many cases this is an affair liable to great controversy: doubts may arise; opposite interests may occur; and a preference must be given to one side, from very nice views, and a small overbalance of utility. This is particularly remarkable in questions with regard to justice; as is, indeed, natural to suppose, from that species of utility which attends this virtue. Were every single instance of justice, like that of benevolence, useful to society; this would be a more simple state of the case, and seldom liable to great controversy. But as single instances of justice are often pernicious in their first and immediate tendency, and as the advantage to society results only from the observance of the general rule, and from the concurrence and combination of several persons in the same equitable conduct; the case here becomes more intricate and involved. The various circumstances of society; the various consequences of any practice; the various interests which may be proposed; these, on many

[1] Sect. I.

occasions, are doubtful, and subject to great discussion and inquiry. The object of municipal laws is to fix all the questions with regard to justice: the debates of civilians; the reflections of politicians; the precedents of history and public records, are all directed to the same purpose. And a very accurate *reason* or *judgement* is often requisite, to give the true determination, amidst such intricate doubts arising from obscure or opposite utilities.

235] But though reason, when fully assisted and improved, be sufficient to instruct us in the pernicious or useful tendency of qualities and actions; it is not alone sufficient to produce any moral blame or approbation. Utility is only a tendency to a certain end; and were the end totally indifferent to us, we should feel the same indifference towards the means. It is requisite *a sentiment* should here display itself, in order to give a preference to the useful above the pernicious tendencies. This sentiment can be no other than a feeling for the happiness of mankind, and a resentment of their misery; since these are the different ends which virtue and vice have a tendency to promote. Here therefore *reason* instructs us in the several tendencies of actions, and *humanity* makes a distinction in favour of those which are useful and beneficial.

236] This partition between the faculties of understanding and sentiment, in all moral decisions, seems clear from the preceding hypothesis. But I shall suppose that hypothesis false: it will then be requisite to look out for some other theory that may be satisfactory; and I dare venture to affirm that none such will ever be found, so long as we suppose reason to be the sole source of morals. To prove this, it will be proper to weigh the five following considerations.

I. It is easy for a false hypothesis to maintain some appearance of truth, while it keeps wholly in generals, makes use of undefined terms, and employs comparisons, instead of instances. This is particularly remarkable in that philosophy, which ascribes the discernment of all moral distinctions to reason alone, without the concurrence of sentiment. It is impossible that, in any particular instance, this hypothesis can so much as be rendered intelligible, whatever specious figure it may make in general declamations and discourses. Examine the crime of *ingratitude,* for instance; which has place, wherever we observe good-will, expressed and known, together with good-offices performed, on the one side, and a return of ill-will or indifference, with ill-offices or neglect on the other: anatomize all these circumstances, and examine, by your reason alone, in what consists the demerit or blame. You never will come to any issue or conclusion.

237] Reason judges either of *matter of fact* or of *relations*. Enquire then, *first,* where is that matter of fact which we here call *crime;* point it out; determine the time of its existence; describe its essence or nature; explain the sense or faculty to which it discovers itself. It resides in the mind of the person who is ungrateful. He must, therefore, feel it, and be conscious of it. But nothing is there, except the passion of ill-will or absolute indifference. You cannot say that these, of themselves, always, and in all circumstances, are crimes. No, they are only crimes when directed towards persons who have before expressed and displayed good-will towards us. Consequently, we may infer, that the crime of ingratitude is not any particular individual *fact;* but arises from a complication of circumstances, which, being presented to the spectator, excites the *sentiment* of blame, by the particular structure and fabric of his mind.

238] This representation, you say, is false. Crime, indeed, consists not in a particular *fact,* of whose reality we are assured by *reason;* but it consists in certain *moral relations,* discovered by reason, in the same manner as we discover by reason the truths of geometry or algebra. But what are the relations, I ask, of which you here talk? In the case stated above, I see first good-will and good-offices in one person; then ill-will and ill-offices in the other. Between these, there is a relation of *contrariety.* Does the crime consist in that relation? But suppose a person bore me ill-will or did me ill-offices; and I, in return, were indifferent towards him, or did him good-offices. Here is the same relation of *contrariety;* and yet my conduct is often highly laudable. Twist and turn this matter as much as you will, you can never rest the morality on relation; but must have recourse to the decisions of sentiment.

When it is affirmed that two and three are equal to the half of ten, this relation of equality I understand perfectly. I conceive, that if ten be divided into two parts, of which one has as many units as the other; and if any of these parts be compared to two added to three, it will contain as many units as that compound number. But when you draw thence a comparison to moral relations, I own that I am altogether at a loss to understand you. A moral action, a crime, such as ingratitude, is a complicated object. Does the morality consist in the relation of its parts to each other? How? After what manner? Specify the relation: be more particular and explicit in your propositions, and you will easily see their falsehood.

239] No, say you, the morality consists in the relation of actions to the rule of right; and they are denominated good or ill, according as they agree or disagree with it. What then is this rule of right? In what does it consist? How is it determined? By reason, you say, which examines the moral relations of actions. So that moral relations are determined by the comparison of action to a rule. And that rule is determined by considering the moral relations of objects. Is not this fine reasoning?

All this is metaphysics, you cry. That is enough; there needs nothing more to give a strong presumption of falsehood. Yes, reply I, here are metaphysics surely; but they are all on your side, who advance an abstruse hypothesis, which can never be made intelligible, nor quadrate with any particular instance or illustration. The hypothesis which we embrace is plain. It maintains that morality is determined by sentiment. It defines virtue to be *whatever mental action or quality gives to a spectator the pleasing sentiment of approbation;* and vice the contrary. We then proceed to examine a plain matter of fact, to wit, what actions have this influence. We consider all the circumstances in which these actions agree, and thence endeavour to extract some general observations with regard to these sentiments. If you call this metaphysics, and find anything abstruse here, you need only conclude that your turn of mind is not suited to the moral sciences.

240] II. When a man, at any time, deliberates concerning his own conduct (as, whether he had better, in a particular emergence, assist a brother or a benefactor), he must consider these separate relations, with all the circumstances and situations of the persons, in order to determine the superior duty and obligation; and in order to determine the proportion of lines in any triangle, it is necessary to examine the nature of that figure, and the relation which its several parts bear to each other. But notwithstanding this appearing similarity in the two cases, there is, at bottom, an extreme difference between them. A speculative reasoner concerning triangles or circles considers the several known and given relations of the parts of these figures, and thence infers some unknown relation, which is dependent on the former. But in moral deliberations we must be acquainted beforehand with all the objects, and all their relations to each other; and from a comparison of the whole, fix our choice or approbation. No new fact to be ascertained; no new relation to be discovered. All the circumstances of the case are supposed to be laid before us, ere we can fix any sentence of blame or approbation. If any material circumstance be yet unknown or doubtful, we must first employ our inquiry or intellectual faculties to assure us of it; and must suspend for a time all moral decision or sentiment. While we are ignorant whether a man were aggressor or not, how can we determine whether the person who killed him be criminal or innocent? But after every circumstance, every relation is known, the understanding has no further room to operate, nor any object on which it could employ itself. The approbation or blame which then ensues, cannot be the work of the judgement, but of the heart; and is not a speculative proposition or affirmation, but an active feeling or sentiment. In the disquisitions of the understanding, from known circumstances and relations, we infer some new and unknown. In moral decisions, all the circumstances and relations must be previously known; and the mind, from the contemplation of the whole, feels some new impression of affection or disgust, esteem or contempt, approbation or blame.

241] Hence the great difference between a mistake of *fact* and one of *right;* and hence the reason why the one is commonly criminal and not the other. When Oedipus killed Laius, he was ignorant of the relation, and from circumstances, innocent and involuntary, formed erroneous opinions concerning the action which he committed. But when Nero killed Agrippina, all the relations between himself and the person, and all the circumstances of the fact, were previously known to him; but the motive of revenge, or fear, or interest, prevailed in his savage heart over the sentiments of duty and humanity. And when we express that detestation against him

to which he himself, in a little time, became insensible, it is not
that we see any relations, of which he was ignorant; but that, for
the rectitude of our disposition, we feel sentiments against which
he was hardened from flattery and a long perseverance in the most
enormous crimes. In these sentiments then, not in a discovery of
relations of any kind, do all moral determinations consist. Before
we can pretend to form any decision of this kind, everything must
be known and ascertained on the side of the object or action.
Nothing remains but to feel, on our part, some sentiment of blame
or approbation; whence we pronounce the action criminal or
virtuous.

242] III. This doctrine will become still more evident, if we compare moral beauty with natural, to which in many particulars it
bears so near a resemblance. It is on the proportion, relation, and
position of parts, that all natural beauty depends; but it would be
absurd thence to infer, that the perception of beauty, like that of
truth in geometrical problems, consists wholly in the perception
of relations, and was performed entirely by the understanding or
intellectual faculties. In all the sciences, our mind from the known
relations investigates the unknown. But in all decisions of taste or
external beauty, all the relations are beforehand obvious to the
eye; and we thence proceed to feel a sentiment of complacency or
disgust, according to the nature of the object, and disposition of
our organs.

Euclid has fully explained all the qualities of the circle; but has
not in any proposition said a word of its beauty. The reason is
evident. The beauty is not a quality of the circle. It lies not in any
part of the line, whose parts are equally distant from a common
centre. It is only the effect which that figure produces upon the
mind, whose peculiar fabric of structure renders it susceptible of
such sentiments. In vain would you look for it in the circle, or
seek it, either by your senses or by mathematical reasoning, in all
the properties of that figure.

Attend to Palladio and Perrault, while they explain all the parts
and proportions of a pillar. They talk of the cornice, and frieze,
and base, and entablature, and shaft and architrave; and give the
description and position of each of these members. But should you
ask the description and position of its beauty, they would readily

reply, that the beauty is not in any of the parts or members of a pillar, but results from the whole, when that complicated figure is presented to an intelligent mind, susceptible to those finer sensations. Till such a spectator appear, there is nothing but a figure of such particular dimensions and proportions: from his sentiments alone arise its elegance and beauty.

Again; attend to Cicero, while he paints the crimes of a Verres or a Catiline. You must acknowledge that the moral turpitude results, in the same manner, from the contemplation of the whole, when presented to a being whose organs have such a particular structure and formation. The orator may paint rage, insolence, barbarity on the one side; meekness, suffering, sorrow, innocence on the other. But if you feel no indignation or compassion arise in you from this complication of circumstances, you would in vain ask him, in what consists the crime or villainy, which he so vehemently exclaims against? At what time, or on what subject it first began to exist? And what has a few months afterwards become of it, when every disposition and thought of all the actors is totally altered or annihilated? No satisfactory answer can be given to any of these questions, upon the abstract hypothesis of morals; and we must at last acknowledge, that the crime or immorality is no particular fact or relation, which can be the object of the understanding, but arises entirely from the sentiment of disapprobation, which, by the structure of human nature, we unavoidably feel on the apprehension of barbarity or treachery.

243] IV. Inanimate objects may bear to each other all the same relations which we observe in moral agents; though the former can never be the object of love or hatred, nor are consequently susceptible of merit or iniquity. A young tree, which over-tops and destroys its parent, stands in all the same relations with Nero, when he murdered Agrippina; and if morality consisted merely in relations, would no doubt be equally criminal.

244] V. It appears evident that the ultimate ends of human actions can never, in any case, be accounted for by *reason,* but recommend themselves entirely to the sentiments and affections of mankind, without any dependence on the intellectual faculties. Ask a man *why he uses exercise;* he will answer, *because he desires to keep his health.* If you then enquire, *why he desires health,* he will

readily reply, *because sickness is painful.* If you push your enquiries farther, and desire a reason *why he hates pain,* it is impossible he can ever give any. This is an ultimate end, and is never
referred to any other object.

Perhaps to your second question, *why he desires health,* he may
also reply, that *it is necessary for the exercise of his calling.* If you
ask, *why he is anxious on that head,* he will answer, *because he
desires to get money.* If you demand *Why? It is the instrument of
pleasure,* says he. And beyond this it is an absurdity to ask for a
reason. It is impossible there can be a progress *in infinitum;* and
that one thing can always be a reason why another is desired.
Something must be desirable on its own account, and because of
its immediate accord or agreement with human sentiment and affection.

245] Now as virtue is an end, and is desirable on its own account,
without fee and reward, merely for the immediate satisfaction
which it conveys; it is requisite that there should be some sentiment which it touches, some internal taste or feeling, or whatever
you may please to call it, which distinguishes moral good and evil,
and which embraces the one and rejects the other.

246] Thus the distinct boundaries and offices of *reason* and of
taste are easily ascertained. The former conveys the knowledge of
truth and falsehood: the latter gives the sentiment of beauty and
deformity, vice and virtue. The one discovers objects as they really
stand in nature, without addition or diminution: the other has a
productive faculty, and gilding or staining all natural objects with
the colours, borrowed from internal sentiment, raises in a manner
a new creation. Reason being cool and disengaged, is no motive to
action, and directs only the impulse received from appetite or inclination, by showing us the means of attaining happiness or avoiding misery: Taste, as it gives pleasure or pain, and thereby constitutes happines or misery, becomes a motive to action, and is the
first spring or impulse to desire and volition. From circumstances
and relations, known or supposed, the former leads us to the discovery of the concealed and unknown: after all circumstances and
relations are laid before us, the latter makes us feel from the whole
a new sentiment of blame or approbation. The standard of the
one, being founded on the nature of things, is eternal and inflex-

ible, even by the will of the Supreme Being: the standard of the other, arising from the eternal frame and constitution of animals, is ultimately derived from that Supreme Will, which bestowed on each being its peculiar nature, and arranged the several classes and orders of existence.

Immanuel Kant

Immanuel Kant

KANT declared that he had effected a Copernican revolution in philosophy. By that he meant that just as Copernicus had indicated the true relations of the movement of the earth around the sun, so he had revealed that knowledge is determined not by the nature of the object known but by the nature of the knowing subject, by the nature of knowledge itself. Kant might equally well have boasted himself a defender of faith, of two faiths, that of the validity of science as over against scepticism, and that of religion and morals as over against the doubts engendered by inquiry. He radically delimited two realms—one, that of "pure reason," the domain of time and space and causality; the other, that of practical reason or faith, the domain in which were to be found (eternally beyond the inquiry or criticism of science) God, freedom and immortality. By validating scientific inquiry in terms of the *a priori* nature of knowing, Kant saved science and the whole Newtonian world of time, space and causation from the destructive scalpel of Hume's scepticism. On the other hand, Kant saved the realm of religion and morals from the disintegrations of empirical discovery and scientific relativism in ethics and belief. If experience is not the source of cause and time and space, God and freedom were certainly not be to be found there either, nor the obligations felt as conscience or duty, nor that immortality which was in Kant's Protestant piety inseparably associated with them. They were not to be found in the world of time and space because that world was of appearances only. The conditions of knowing under which the external world appeared could neither reveal the realities of religion and morals nor be used to disprove their reality. For it was not reason but faith, not inquiry but conscience, which established the realities of God, freedom and immortality. These transcended the "appearances" revealed in knowledge; Kant saved science against Hume and religion against science.

It was David Hume, Kant declared in another famous statement, who had roused him from his dogmatic slumber. The orthodox sleep from which Kant regarded himself as having been wakened was acceptance of the absolute necessity of cause and the iron objectivity of the Newtonian world. Hume had made Kant see how much a matter of assumption was anything beyond the immediate datum, the sensation, the impression given here and now. That it was given was all that could be said. For even the self or the mind to which Locke referred was just as much a matter of going beyond what was actually given as was causality, an assumption engendered by habit, or time and space, objectifications of succession and contiguity. Hume had practically pulverized knowledge. All that of which we could be certain was the momentary impression.

But Kant realized (as for that matter did Hume himself) that if we could only trust the impression, immediate, discrete and without consequence, knowledge would be impossible. There could be no security to any future, no reliance on the necessary consequence of any fact, any action, or any moment. Hume solaced himself with probability. There was no necessity in cause, but we could trust to the habitual and therefore plausibly predictable conjunction of events. To Kant, who had been bred intellectually in the Continental tradition of mathematical certainty, probability was not enough. He sought necessity, and experience could not provide it. He found it in another quarter, in the nature of knowing itself. What Hume had destroyed in the constitution of the external world, Kant restored in the constitution of knowing. Time and space, undiscoverable in experience, were yet indispensable to the possibility of experience at all. The necessities of cause and effect could never be derived from the most scrupulous inspection of sensations. But without causality sensations did not constitute experience. Without time, space, and cause, experience was chaos. Kant re-established time and space as intuitions and cause as a category of understanding. Science was secure because its form was predetermined by the very constitution of knowing. The earth of the external world revolved around the sun of the knowing subject. The Copernican revolution was achieved in philosophy.

At the same time, faith was defended. For the external world, now secure, is secure only as an order of appearances. It is not through knowledge that reality is to be sought or found, nor can the criteria of knowledge be used to discredit the real. The very nature of the forms of knowing preclude and exclude the revelation of realities. The forms of knowing determine the nature of *appearance*, and the objects known are by definition not realities. They are, in Kant's language, phenomena, not noumena. Realities are not known. They are revealed in the inner voice of duty and conscience. The categorical imperative, the moral law within us, testifies to a moral order. The sense of duty points to a world of freedom where duty is not impeded by empirical necessity. The categorical imperative points to God, the source of that divine and immitigable demand. And, finally, conscience points to a realm in which duty may be adequately and endlessly fulfilled, exempt from the limitations of time as well as space. Conscience points thus to Immortality as well as to Freedom and God.

Are physical objects real? Is cause necessary? Are time and space absolute? They are all appearances, determined by the *a priori* structure of the knowing subject. But beyond the forms of knowledge and the structure of appearances are the realities of religion and morality revealed in the demands made by conscience, duty and practical reason or faith. Immanuel Kant from the off-center provincial city of Koenigsberg, where he spent his long untravelled professorial life, legislated for philosophy as he thought knowledge legislated for experience. In his analysis he broached issues that are still alive in philosophy, the relation of the empirically discoverable facts to the assumption by which they are organized and understood, the relation of empirical necessities to moral demands that seem to be absolute, the relation of appearance to reality. Kant asked, "How is experience possible?" On his answer to that question, it turns out, depends the validity of science, and of morals and religion as well in their separate spheres. His answers and his questions may be dealt with or circumvented, but to this day they cannot be ignored.

The Fundamental Principles of the Metaphysics of Morals (1785), printed here in its entirety, is a more popular exposition of the Kantian ethics than that contained in the later *Critique of Practical Reason*. Kant here attempts to approach the problems of ethics from the side of ordinary experience, to advance from common knowledge to critical understanding.

Fundamental Principles of the
Metaphysic of Morals

Preface

ANCIENT GREEK PHILOSOPHY was divided into three sciences: Physics, Ethics, and Logic. This division is perfectly suitable to the nature of the thing, and the only improvement that can be made in it is to add the principle on which it is based, so that we may both satisfy ourselves of its completeness, and also be able to determine correctly the necessary subdivisions.

All rational knowledge is either *material* or *formal:* the former considers some object, the latter is concerned only with the form of the understanding and of the reason itself, and with the universal laws of thought in general without distinction of its objects. Formal philosophy is called Logic. Material philosophy, however, which has to do with determinate objects and the laws to which they are subject, is again two-fold; for these laws are either laws of *nature* or of *freedom*. The science of the former is Physics, that of the latter, Ethics; they are also called *natural philosophy* and *moral philosophy* respectively.

Logic cannot have any empirical part; that is, a part in which the universal and necessary laws of thought should rest on grounds taken from experience: otherwise it would not be logic, *i.e.* a canon for the understanding or the reason, valid for all thought, and capable of demonstration. Natural and moral philosophy, on the contrary, can each have their empirical part, since the former has to determine the laws of nature as an object of experience; the latter the laws of the human will, so far as it is affected by nature: the former, however, being laws according to which everything does happen; the latter, laws according to which everything ought to happen. Ethics, however, must also consider the conditions under which what ought to happen frequently does not.

We may call all philosophy *empirical,* so far as it is based on grounds of experience: on the other hand, that which delivers its doctrines from *à priori* principles alone we may call *pure* philosophy. When the latter is merely formal it is *logic;* if it is restricted to definite objects of the understanding it is *metaphysic.*

In this way there arises the idea of a two-fold metaphysic—a *metaphysic of nature* and a *metaphysic of morals.* Physics will thus have an empirical and also a rational part. It is the same with Ethics; but here the empirical part might have the special name of *practical anthropology,* the name *morality* being appropriated to the rational part.

All trades, arts, and handiworks have gained by division of labour, namely, when, instead of one man doing everything, each confines himself to a certain kind of work distinct from others in the treatment it requires, so as to be able to perform it with greater facility and in the greatest perfection. Where the different kinds of work are not so distinguished and divided, where everyone is a jack-of-all-trades, there manufactures remain still in the greatest barbarism. It might deserve to be considered whether pure philosophy in all its parts does not require a man specially devoted to it, and whether it would not be better for the whole business of science if those who, to please the tastes of the public, are wont to blend the rational and empirical elements together, mixed in all sorts of proportions unknown to themselves, and who call themselves independent thinkers, giving the name of minute philosophers to those who apply themselves to the rational part only—if these, I say, were warned not to carry on two employments together which differ widely in the treatment they demand, for each of which perhaps a special talent is required, and the combination of which in one person only produces bunglers. But I only ask here whether the nature of science does not require that we should always carefully separate the empirical from the rational part, and prefix to Physics proper (or empirical physics) a metaphysic of nature, and to practical anthropology a metaphysic of morals, which must be carefully cleared of everything empirical, so that we may know how much can be accomplished by pure reason in both cases, and from what sources it draws this its *à priori* teaching, and that whether the latter inquiry is conducted by all moralists (whose name is legion), or only by some who feel a calling thereto.

As my concern here is with moral philosophy, I limit the question suggested to this: Whether it is not of the utmost necessity to construct a pure moral philosophy, perfectly cleared of everything which is only empirical, and which belongs to anthropology? for that such a philosophy must be possible is evident from the common idea of duty and of the moral laws. Everyone must admit that if a law is to have moral force, *i.e.* to be the basis of an obligation, it must carry with it absolute necessity; that, for example, the precept, "Thou shalt not lie," is not valid for men alone, as if other rational beings had no need to observe it; and so with all the other moral laws properly so called; that, therefore, the basis of obligation must not be sought in the nature of man, or in the circumstances in the world in which he is placed, but *à priori* simply in the conceptions of pure reason; and although any other precept which is founded on principles of mere experience may be in certain respects universal, yet, in as far as it rests even in the least degree on an empirical basis, perhaps only as to a motive, such a precept, while it may be a practical rule, can never be called a moral law.

Thus not only are moral laws with their principles essentially distinguished from every other kind of practical knowledge in which there is anything empirical, but all moral philosophy rests wholly on its pure part. When applied to man, it does not borrow the least thing from the knowledge of man himself (anthropology), but gives laws *à priori* to him as a rational being. No doubt these laws require a judgment sharpened by experience, in order on the one hand to distinguish in what cases they are applicable, and on the other to procure for them access to the will of the man, and effectual influence on conduct; since man is acted on by so many inclinations that, though capable of the idea of a practical pure reason, he is not so easily able to make it effective *in concreto* in his life.

A metaphysic of morals is therefore indispensably necessary, not merely for speculative reasons, in order to investigate the sources of the practical principles which are to be found *à priori* in our reason, but also because morals themselves are liable to all sorts of corruption, as long as we are without that clue and supreme canon by which to estimate them correctly. For, in order that an action should be morally good, it is not enough that it *conform* to the moral law, but it must also be done *for the sake of the law,* otherwise that conformity is only very contingent and uncertain; since a principle which is not moral, although it may now and then produce actions conformable to the law, will also often produce actions which contradict it. Now it is only in a pure philosophy that we can look for the moral law in its purity and genuineness (and, in a practical matter, this is of the utmost consequence): we must, therefore, begin with pure philosophy (metaphysic), and without it there cannot be any moral philosophy at all. That which mingles these pure principles with the empirical does not deserve the name of philosophy (for what distinguishes philosophy from common rational knowledge is, that it treats in separate sciences what the latter only comprehends confusedly); much less does it deserve that of moral philosophy, since by this confusion it even spoils the purity of morals themselves, and counteracts its own end.

Let it not be thought, however, that what is here demanded is already extant in the propædeutic prefixed by the celebrated Wolf to his moral philosophy, namely, his so-called *general practical philosophy,* and that, therefore, we have not to strike into an entirely new field. Just because it was to be a general practical philosophy, it has not taken into consideration a will of any particular kind —say one which should be determined solely from *à priori* principles without any empirical motives, and which we might call a pure will, but volition in general, with all the actions and conditions which belong to it in this general signification. By this it is distinguished from a metaphysic of morals, just as general logic, which treats of the acts and canons of thought *in general,* is distinguished from transcendental philosophy, which treats of the particular acts and canons of *pure* thought, *i.e.* that whose cognitions are altogether *à priori.* For the metaphysic of morals has to examine the idea and the principles of a possible *pure* will, and not the acts and conditions of human volition generally, which for the most part are drawn from psychology. It is true that moral laws and duty are spoken of in the general practical philosophy (contrary indeed to all fitness). But this is no objection, for in this respect also the authors of that science remain true to their idea of it; they do not distinguish the motives which are prescribed as such by reason alone altogether *à priori,* and which are properly moral, from the empirical motives which the understanding raises to general conceptions merely by comparison of experiences; but without noticing the difference of their sources, and looking on them all as homogeneous, they consider only their greater or less amount. It is in this way they frame their notion of *obligation,* which, though anything but moral, is all that can be asked for in a philosophy which passes no judgment at all on the *origin* of all possible practical concepts, whether they are *à priori,* or only *à posteriori.*

Intending to publish hereafter a metaphysic of morals, I issue in the first instance these fundamental principles. Indeed there is properly no other foundation for it than the *critical examination of a pure practical reason;* just as that of metaphysics is the critical examination of the pure speculative reason, already published. But in the first place the former is not so absolutely necessary as the latter, because in moral concerns human reason can easily be brought to a high degree of correctness and completeness, even in the commonest understanding, while on the contrary in its theoretic but pure use it is wholly dialectical; and in the second place if the critique of a pure practical reason is to be complete, it must be possible at the same time to show its identity with the speculative reason in a common principle, for it can ultimately be only one and the same reason which has to be distinguished merely in its application. I could not, however, bring it to such completeness here, without introducing considerations of a wholly different kind, which would be perplexing to the reader. On this account I have adopted the title of *Fundamental Principles of the Metaphysics of Morals,* instead of that of a *Critical Examination of the pure practical Reason.*

But in the third place, since a metaphysic of morals, in spite of the discouraging title, is yet capable of being presented in a popular form, and one adapted to the common understanding, I find it useful to separate from it this preliminary treatise on its fundamental principles, in order that I may not hereafter have need to introduce these necessarily subtle discussions into a book of a more simple character.

The present treatise is, however, nothing more than the investigation and establishment of *the supreme principle of morality,* and this alone constitutes a study complete in itself, and one which ought to be kept apart from every other moral investigation. No doubt my conclusions on this weighty question, which has hitherto been very unsatisfactorily examined, would receive much light from the application of the same principle to the whole system, and would be greatly confirmed by the adequacy which it exhibits throughout; but I must forego this advantage, which indeed would be after all more gratifying than useful, since the easy applicability of a principle and its apparent adequacy give no very certain proof of its soundness, but rather inspire a certain partiality, which prevents us from examining and estimating it strictly in itself, and without regard to consequences.

I have adopted in this work the method which I think most suitable, proceeding analytically from common knowledge to the determination of its ultimate principle, and again descending synthetically from the examination of this principle and its sources to the common knowledge in which we find it employed. The division will, therefore, be as follows:—

1. *First section.*—Transition from the common rational knowledge of morality to the philosophical.
2. *Second section.*—Transition from popular moral philosophy to the metaphysic of morals.
3. *Third section.*—Final step from the metaphysic of morals to the critique of the pure practical reason.

First Section

Transition From the Common Rational Knowledge of Morality to the Philosophical

Nothing can possibly be conceived in the world, or even out of it, which can be called good without qualification, except a Good Will. Intelligence, wit, judgment, and the other *talents* of the mind, however they may be named, or courage, resolution, perseverance, as qualities of temperament, are undoubtedly good and desirable in many respects; but these gifts of nature may also become extremely bad and mischievous if the will which is to make use of them, and which, therefore, constitutes what is called *character,* is not good. It is the same with the *gifts of fortune.* Power, riches, honour, even health, and the general well-being and contentment with one's condition which is called *happiness,* inspire pride, and often presumption, if there is not a good will to correct the influence of these on the mind, and with this also to rectify the whole principle of acting, and adapt it to its end. The sight of a being who is not adorned with a single feature of a pure and good will, enjoying unbroken prosperity, can never give pleasure to an impartial rational spectator. Thus a good will appears to constitute the indispensable condition even of being worthy of happiness.

There are even some qualities which are of service to this good will itself, and may facilitate its action, yet which have no intrinsic unconditional value, but always presuppose a good will, and this qualifies the esteem that we justly have for them, and does not permit us to regard them as absolutely good. Moderation in the affections and passions, self-control and calm deliberation are not only good in many respects, but even seem to constitute part of the intrinsic worth of the person; but they are far from deserving to be called good without qualification, although they have been so unconditionally praised by the ancients. For without the principles of a good will, they may become extremely bad, and the coolness of a villain not only makes him far more dangerous, but also directly makes him more abominable in our eyes than he would have been without it.

A good will is good not because of what it performs or effects, not by its aptness for the attainment of some proposed end, but simply by virtue of the volition, that is, it is good in itself, and considered by itself is to be esteemed much higher than all that can be brought about by it in favour of any inclination, nay, even of the sum total of all inclinations. Even if it should happen that, owing to special disfavour of fortune, or the niggardly provision of a step-motherly nature, this will should wholly lack power to accomplish its purpose, if with its greatest efforts it should yet achieve nothing, and there should remain only the good will (not, to be sure, a mere wish, but the summoning of all means in our power), then, like a jewel, it would still shine by its own light, as a thing which has its whole value in itself. Its usefulness or fruitlessness can neither add to nor take away anything from this value.

It would be, as it were, only the setting to enable us to handle it the more conveniently in common commerce or to attract to it the attention of those who are not yet connoisseurs, but not to recommend it to true connoisseurs, or to determine its value.

There is, however, something so strange in this idea of the absolute value of the mere will, in which no account is taken of its utility, that notwithstanding the thorough assent of even common reason to the idea, yet a suspicion must arise that it may perhaps really be the product of mere high-flown fancy, and that we may have misunderstood the purpose of nature in assigning reason as the governor of our will. Therefore we will examine this idea from this point of view.

In the physical constitution of an organized being, that is, a being adapted suitably to the purposes of life, we assume it as a fundamental principle that no organ for any purpose will be found but what is also the fittest and best adapted for that purpose. Now in a being which has reason and a will, if the proper object of nature were its *conservation*, its *welfare,* in a word, its *happiness,* then nature would have hit upon a very bad arrangement in selecting the reason of the creature to carry out this purpose. For all the actions which the creature has to perform with a view to this purpose, and the whole rule of its conduct, would be far more surely prescribed to it by instinct, and that end would have been attained thereby much more certainly than it ever can be by reason. Should reason have been communicated to this favoured creature over and above, it must only have served it to contemplate the happy constitution of its nature, to admire it, to congratulate itself thereon, and to feel thankful for it to the beneficient cause, but not that it should subject its desires to that weak and delusive guidance, and meddle bunglingly with the purpose of nature. In a word, nature would have taken care that reason should not break forth into *practical exercise,* nor have the presumption, with its weak insight, to think out for itself the plan of happiness, and of the means of attaining it. Nature would not only have taken on herself the choice of the ends, but also of the means, and with wise foresight would have entrusted both to instinct.

And, in fact, we find that the more a cultivated reason applies itself with deliberate purpose to the enjoyment of life and happiness, so much the more does the man fail of true satisfaction. And from this circumstance there arises in many, if they are candid enough to confess it, a certain degree of *misology,* that is, hatred of reason, especially in the case of those who are most experienced in the use of it, because after calculating all the advantages they derive, I do not say from the invention of all the arts of common luxury, but even from the sciences (which seem to them to be after all only a luxury of the understanding), they find that they have, in fact, only brought more trouble on their shoulders, rather than gained in happiness; and they end by envying, rather than despising, the more common stamp of men who keep closer to the guidance of mere instinct, and do not allow their reason much influence on their conduct. And this we must admit, that the judgment of those who would very much lower the lofty eulogies of the advantages which reason gives us in regard to the happiness and satisfaction of life, or who would even reduce them below zero, is by no means morose or ungrateful to the goodness with which the world is governed, but that there lies at the root of these judgments the idea that our existence has a different and far nobler end, for which, and not for happiness, reason is properly intended, and which must, therefore, be regarded as the supreme condition to which the private ends of man must, for the most part, be postponed.

For as reason is not competent to guide the will with certainty in regard to its objects and the satisfaction of all our wants (which it to some extent even multiplies), this being an end to which an implanted instinct would have led with much greater certainty; and since, nevertheless, reason is imparted to us as a practical faculty, *i.e.* as one which is to have influence on the *will,* therefore, admitting that nature generally in the distribution of her capacities has adapted the means to the end, its true destination must be to produce a *will,* not merely good as a *means* to something else, but *good in itself,* for which reason was absolutely necessary. This will then, though not indeed the sole and complete good, must be the supreme good and the condition of every other, even of the desire of happiness. Under these circumstances, there is nothing inconsistent with the wisdom of nature in the fact that the cultivation of the reason, which is requisite for the first and unconditional purpose, does in many ways interfere, at least in this life, with the attainment of the second, which is always conditional, namely, happiness. Nay, it may even reduce it to nothing, without nature thereby failing of her purpose. For reason recognises the establishment of a good will as its highest practical destination, and in attaining this purpose is capable only of a satisfaction of its own proper kind, namely, that from the attainment of an end, which end again is determined by reason only, notwithstanding that this may involve many a disappointment to the ends of inclination.

We have then to develop the notion of a will which deserves to be highly esteemed for itself, and is good without a view to anything further, an notion which exists already in the sound natural understanding, requiring rather to be cleared up than to be taught, and which in estimating the value of our actions always takes the first place, and constitutes the condition of all the rest. In order to do this we will take the notion of duty, which includes that of a good will, although implying certain subjective restrictions and hindrances. These, however, far from concealing it, or rendering it unrecognisable, rather bring it out by contrast, and make it shine forth so much the brighter.

I omit here all actions which are already recognised as inconsistent with duty, although they may be useful for this or that purpose, for with these the question whether they are done *from duty* cannot arise at all, since they even conflict with it. I also set aside those actions which really conform to duty, but to which men have *no* direct *inclination,* performing them because they are impelled thereto by some other inclination. For in this case we can readily distinguish whether the action which agrees with duty is done *from duty,* or from a selfish view. It is much harder to make this distinction when the action accords with duty, and the subject has besides a *direct* inclination to it. For example, it is always a matter of duty that a dealer should not overcharge an inexperienced purchaser, and wherever there is much commerce the prudent tradesman does not overcharge, but keeps a fixed price for everyone, so that a child buys of him as well as any other. Men are thus *honestly* served; but this is not enough to make us believe that the tradesman has so acted from duty and from principles of honesty: his own advantage required it; it is out of the question in this case to suppose that he might besides have a direct inclination in favour of the buyers, so that, as it were, from love he should give no advantage to one over another. Accordingly the action was done neither from duty nor from direct inclination, but merely with a selfish view.

On the other hand, it is a duty to maintain one's life; and, in addition, every one has also a direct inclination to do so. But on this account the often anxious care which most men take for it has no intrinsic worth, and their maxim has no moral import. They preserve their life *as duty requires,* no doubt, but not *because duty requires.* On the other hand, if adversity and hopeless sorrow have completely taken away the relish for life, if the unfortunate one, strong in mind, indignant at his fate rather than desponding or dejected, wishes for death, and yet preserves his life without loving it—not from inclination or fear, but from duty—then his maxim has a moral worth.

To be beneficent when we can is a duty; and besides this, there are many minds so sympathetically constituted that, without any other motive of vanity or self-interest, they find a pleasure in spreading joy around them, and can take delight in the satisfaction of others so far as it is their own work. But I maintain that in such a case an action of this kind, however proper, however amiable it may be, has nevertheless no true moral worth, but is on a level with other inclinations, *e. g.* the inclination to honour, which, if it is happily directed to that which is in fact of public utility and accordant with duty, and consequently honourable, deserves praise and encouragement, but not esteem. For the maxim lacks the moral import, namely, that such actions be done *from duty,* not from inclination. Put the case that the mind of that philanthropist were clouded by sorrow of his own extinguishing all sympathy with the lot of others, and that while he still has the power to benefit others in distress, he is not touched by their trouble because he is absorbed with his own; and now suppose that he tears himself out of this dead insensibility, and performs the action without any inclination to it, but simply from duty, then first has his action its genuine moral worth. Further still; if nature has put little sympathy in the heart of this or that man; if he, supposed to be an upright man, is by temperament cold and indifferent to the sufferings of others, perhaps because in respect of his own he is provided with the special gift of patience and fortitude, and supposes, or even requires, that others should have the same—and such a man would certainly not be the meanest product of nature—but if nature had not specially framed him for a philanthropist, would he not still find in himself a source from whence to give himself a far higher worth than that of a good-natured temperament could be? Unquestionably. It is just in this that the moral worth of the character is brought out which is incomparably the highest of all, namely, that he is beneficent, not from inclination, but from duty.

To secure one's own happiness is a duty, at least indirectly; for discontent with one's condition, under a pressure of many anxieties and amidst unsatisfied wants, might easily become a great *temptation to transgression of duty*. But here again, without looking to duty, all men have already the strongest and most intimate inclination to happiness, because it is just in this idea that all inclinations are combined in one total. But the precept of happiness is often of such a sort that it greatly interferes with some inclinations, and yet a man cannot form any definite and certain conception of the sum of satisfaction of all of them which is called happiness. It is not then to be wondered at that a single inclination, definite both as to what it promises and as to the time within which it can be gratified, is often able to overcome such a fluctuating idea, and that a gouty patient, for instance, can choose to enjoy what he likes, and to suffer what he may, since, according to his calculation, on this occasion at least, he has [only] not sacrificed the enjoyment of the present moment to a possibly mistaken expectation of a happiness which is supposed to be found in health. But even in this case, if the general desire for happiness did not influence his will, and supposing that in his particular case health was not a necessary element in this calculation, there yet remains in this, as in all other cases, this law, namely, that he should promote his happiness not from inclination but from duty, and by this would his conduct first acquire true moral worth.

It is in this manner, undoubtedly, that we are to understand those passages of Scripture also in which we are commanded to love our neighbour, even our enemy. For love, as an affection, cannot be commanded, but beneficence for duty's sake may; even though we are not impelled to it by any inclination—nay, are even repelled by a natural and unconquerable aversion. This is *practical* love, and not *pathological*—a love which is seated in the will, and

not in the propensions of sense—in principles of action and not
of tender sympathy; and it is this love alone which can be commanded.

The second proposition is: That an action done from duty derives its moral worth, *not from the purpose* which is to be attained
by it, but from the maxim by which it is determined, and therefore
does not depend on the realization of the object of the action, but
merely on the *principle of volition* by which the action has taken
place, without regard to any object of desire. It is clear from what
precedes that the purposes which we may have in view in our
actions, or their effects regarded as ends and springs of the will,
cannot give to actions any unconditional or moral worth. In what,
then, can their worth lie, if it is not to consist in the will and in
reference to its expected effect? It cannot lie anywhere but in the
principle of the will without regard to the ends which can be
attained by the action. For the will stands between its *à priori*
principle, which is formal, and its *à posteriori* spring, which is
material, as between two roads, and as it must be determined by
something, it follows that it must be determined by the formal
principle of volition when an action is done from duty, in which
case every material principle has been withdrawn from it.

The third proposition, which is a consequence of the two preceding, I would express thus: *Duty is the necessity of acting from
respect for the law.* I may have *inclination* for an object as the
effect of my proposed action, but I cannot have *respect* for it, just
for this reason, that it is an effect and not an energy of will. Similarly, I cannot have respect for inclination, whether my own or
another's; I can at most, if my own, approve it; if another's,
sometimes even love it; *i.e.* look on it as favourable to my own
interest. It is only what is connected with my will as a principle,
by no means as an effect—what does not subserve my inclination,
but overpowers it, or at least in case of choice excludes it from
its calculation—in other words, simply the law of itself which
can be an object of respect, and hence a command. Now an
action done from duty must wholly exclude the influence of inclination, and with it every object of the will, so that nothing
remains which can determine the will except objectively the *law,*
and subjectively *pure respect* for this practical law, and conse-

quently the maxim[1] that I should follow this law even to the thwarting of all my inclinations.

Thus the moral worth of an action does not lie in the effect expected from it, nor in any principle of action which requires to borrow its motive from this expected effect. For all these effects—agreeableness of one's condition, and even the promotion of the happiness of others—could have been also brought about by other causes, so that for this there would have been no need of the will of a rational being; whereas it is in this alone that the supreme and unconditional good can be found. The pre-eminent good which we call moral can therefore consist in nothing else than *the conception of law* in itself, *which certainly is only possible in a rational being*, in so far as this conception, and not the expected effect, determines the will. This is a good which is already present in the person who acts accordingly, and we have not to wait for it to appear first in the result.[2]

But what sort of law can that be, the conception of which must determine the will, even without paying any regard to the effect expected from it, in order that this will may be called good ab-

---

[1] A *maxim* is the subjective principle of volition. The objective principle (*i.e.* that which would also serve subjectively as a practical principle to all rational beings if reason had full power over the faculty of desire) is the practical *law*.

[2] It might be here objected to me that I take refuge behind the word *respect* in an obscure feeling, instead of giving a distinct solution of the question by a concept of the reason. But although respect is a feeling, it is not a feeling *received* through influence, but is *self-wrought* by a rational concept, and, therefore, is specifically distinct from all feelings of the former kind, which may be referred either to inclination or fear. What I recognise immediately as a law for me, I recognise with respect. This merely signifies the consciousness that my will is *subordinate* to a law, without the intervention of other influences on my sense. The immediate determination of the will by the law, and the consciousness of this is called *respect*, so that this is regarded as an *effect* of the law on the subject, and not as the *cause* of it. Respect is properly the conception of a worth which thwarts my self-love. Accordingly it is something which is considered neither as an object of inclination nor of fear, although it has something analogous to both. The *object* of respect is the *law* only, and that, the law which we impose on *ourselves*, and yet recognise as necessary in itself. As a law, we are subjected to it without consulting self-love; as imposed by us on ourselves, it is a result of our will. In the former aspect it has an analogy to fear, in the latter to inclination. Respect for a person is properly only respect for the law (of honesty, &c.), of which he gives us an example. Since we also look on the improvement of our talents as a duty, we consider that we see in a person of talents, as it were, the *example of a law* (viz. to become like him in this by exercise), and this constitutes our respect. All so-called moral *interest* consists simply in *respect* for the law.

solutely and without qualification? As I have deprived the will of
every impulse which could arise to it from obedience to any law,
there remains nothing but the universal conformity of its actions
to law in general, which alone is to serve the will as a principle,
i. e. I am never to act otherwise than so *that I could also will that
my maxim should become a universal law*. Here now, it is the
simple conformity to law in general, without assuming any particular law applicable to certain actions, that serves the will as its
principle, and must so serve it, if duty is not to be a vain delusion
and a chimerical notion. The common reason of men in its practical judgments perfectly coincides with this, and always has in
view the principle here suggested. Let the question be, for example: May I when in distress make a promise with the intention
not to keep it? I readily distinguish here between the two significations which the question may have: Whether it is prudent, or
whether it is right, to make a false promise. The former may undoubtedly often be the case. I see clearly indeed that it is not
enough to extricate myself from a present difficulty by means of
this subterfuge, but it must be well considered whether there may
not hereafter spring from this lie much greater inconvenience than
that from which I now free myself, and as, with all my supposed
cunning, the consequences cannot be so easily foreseen but that
credit once lost may be much more injurious to me than any
mischief which I seek to avoid at present, it should be considered
whether it would not be more *prudent* to act herein according to
a universal maxim, and to make it a habit to promise nothing except with the intention of keeping it. But it is soon clear to me
that such a maxim will still only be based on the fear of consequences. Now it is a wholly different thing to be truthful from
duty, and to be so from apprehension of injurious consequences.
In the first case, the very notion of the action already implies a
law for me; in the second case, I must first look about elsewhere to see what results may be combined with it which would
affect myself. For to deviate from the principle of duty is beyond
all doubt wicked; but to be unfaithful to my maxim of prudence may often be very advantageous to me, although to abide
by it is certainly safer. The shortest way, however, and an unerring
one, to discover the answer to this question whether a lying promise is consistent with duty, is to ask myself, Should I be content

that my maxim (to extricate myself from difficulty by a false promise) should hold good as a universal law, for myself as well as for others? and should I be able to say to myself, "Every one may make a deceitful promise when he finds himself in a difficulty from which he cannot otherwise extricate himself"? Then I presently become aware that while I can will the lie, I can by no means will that lying should be a universal law. For with such a law there would be no promises at all, since it would be in vain to allege my intention in regard to my future actions to those who would not believe this allegation, or if they over-hastily did so would pay me back in my own coin. Hence my maxim, as soon as it should be made a universal law, would necessarily destroy itself.

I do not, therefore, need any far-reaching penetration to discern what I have to do in order that my will may be morally good. Inexperienced in the course of the world, incapable of being prepared for all its contingencies, I only ask myself: Canst thou also will that thy maxim should be a universal law? If not, then it must be rejected, and that not because of a disadvantage accruing from it to myself or even to others, but because it cannot enter as a principle into a possible universal legislation, and reason extorts from me immediate respect for such legislation. I do not indeed as yet *discern* on what this respect is based (this the philosopher may inquire), but at least I understand this, that it is an estimation of the worth which far outweighs all worth of what is recommended by inclination, and that the necessity of acting from *pure* respect for the practical law is what constitutes duty, to which every other motive must give place, because it is the condition of a will being good *in itself,* and the worth of such a will is above everything.

Thus, then, without quitting the moral knowledge of common human reason, we have arrived at its principle. And although, no doubt, common men do not conceive it in such an abstract and universal form, yet they always have it really before their eyes, and use it as the standard of their decision. Here it would be easy to show how, with this compass in hand, men are well able to distinguish, in every case that occurs, what is good, what bad, conformably to duty or inconsistent with it, if, without in the least teaching them anything new, we only, like Socrates, direct their attention to the principle they themselves employ; and that therefore we do not need science and philosophy to know what we should do to be honest and good, yea, even wise and virtuous. Indeed we might well have conjectured beforehand that the knowledge of what every man is bound to do, and therefore also to know, would be within the reach of every man, even the commonest. Here we cannot forbear admiration when we see how great an advantage the practical judgment has over the theoretical in the common understanding of men. In the latter, if common reason ventures to depart from the laws of experience and from the perceptions of the senses it falls into mere inconceivabilities and self-contradictions, at least into a chaos of uncertainty, obscurity, and instability. But in the practical sphere it is just when the common understanding excludes all sensible springs from practical laws that its power of judgment begins to show itself to advantage. It then becomes even subtle, whether it be that it chicanes with its own conscience or with other claims respecting what is to be called right, or whether it desires for its own instruction to determine honestly the worth of actions; and, in the lattter case, it may even have as good a hope of hitting the mark as any philosopher whatever can promise himself. Nay, it is almost more sure of doing so, because the philosopher cannot have any other principle, while he may easily perplex his judgment by a multitude of considerations foreign to the matter, and so turn aside from the right way. Would it not therefore be wiser in moral concerns to asquiesce in the judgment of common reason, or at most only to call in philosophy for the purpose of rendering the system of morals more complete and intelligible, and its rules more convenient for use (especially for disputation), but not so as to draw off the common understanding from its happy simplicity, or to bring it by means of philosophy into a new path of inquiry and instruction?

Innocence is indeed a glorious thing, only, on the other hand, it is very sad that it cannot well maintain itself, and is easily seduced. On this account even wisdom—which otherwise consists more in conduct than in knowledge—yet has need of science, not in order to learn from it, but to secure for its precepts admission and permanence. Against all the commands of duty which reason represents to man as so deserving of respect, he feels in himself a powerful counterpoise in his wants and inclinations, the entire satisfaction of which he sums up under the name of happiness. Now reason issues its commands unyieldingly, without promising anything to the inclinations, and, as it were, with disregard and contempt for these claims, which are so impetuous, and at the same time so plausible, and which will not allow themselves to be suppressed by any command. Hence there arises a natural *dialectic,* i.e. a disposition to argue against these strict laws of duty and to question their validity, or at least their purity and strictness; and, if possible, to make them more accordant with our wishes and inclinations, that is to say, to corrupt them at their very source, and entirely to destroy their worth—a thing which even common practical reason cannot ultimately call good.

Thus is the *common reason of man* compelled to go out of its sphere, and to take a step into the field of a *practical philosophy,* not to satisfy any speculative want (which never occurs to it as long as it is content to be mere sound reason), but even on practical grounds, in order to attain in it information and clear instruction respecting the source of its principle, and the correct determination of it in opposition to the maxims which are based on wants and inclinations, so that it may escape from the perplexity of opposite claims, and not run the risk of losing all genuine moral principles through the equivocation into which it easily falls. Thus, when practical reason cultivates itself, there insensibly arises in it a dialectic which forces it to seek aid in philosophy, just as happens to it in its theoretic use; and in this case, therefore, as well as in the other, it will find rest nowhere but in a thorough critical examination of our reason.

Second Section

Transition From Popular Moral Philosophy to the Metaphysic of Morals

If we have hitherto drawn our notion of duty from the common use of our practical reason, it is by no means to be inferred that we have treated it as an empirical notion. On the contrary, if we attend to the experience of men's conduct, we meet frequent and, as we ourselves allow, just complaints that one cannot find a single certain example of the disposition to act from pure duty. Although many things are done in *conformity* with what *duty* prescribes, it is nevertheless always doubtful whether they are done strictly *from duty,* so as to have a moral worth. Hence there have, at all times, been philosophers who have altogether denied that this disposition actually exists at all in human actions, and have ascribed everything to a more or less refined self-love. Not that they have on that account questioned the soundness of the conception of morality; on the contrary, they spoke with sincere regret of the frailty and corruption of human nature, which though noble enough to take as its rule an idea so worthy of respect, is yet too weak to follow it, and employs reason, which ought to give it the law only for the purpose of providing for the interest of the inclinations, whether singly or at the best in the greatest possible harmony with one another.

In fact, it is absolutely impossible to make out by experience with complete certainty a single case in which the maxim of an action, however right in itself, rested simply on moral grounds and on the conception of duty. Sometimes it happens that with the sharpest self-examination we can find nothing beside the moral principle of duty which could have been powerful enough to move us to this or that action and to so great a sacrifice; yet we cannot from this infer with certainty that it was not really some secret impulse of self-love, under the false appearance of duty, that was the actual determining cause of the will. We like then to flatter ourselves by falsely taking credit for a more noble motive; whereas in fact we can never, even by the strictest examination, get completely behind the secret springs of action; since when the question is of moral worth, it is not with the actions which we see that we are concerned, but with those inward principles of them which we do not see.

Moreover, we cannot better serve the wishes of those who ridicule all morality as a mere chimera of human imagination overstepping itself from vanity, than by conceding to them that notions of duty must be drawn only from experience (as, from indolence, people are ready to think is also the case with all other notions); for this is to prepare for them a certain triumph. I am willing to admit out of love of humanity that even most of our actions are correct, but if we look closer at them we everywhere come upon the dear self which is always prominent, and it is this they have in view, and not the strict command of duty which would often require self-denial. Without being an enemy of virtue, a cool observer, one that does not mistake the wish for good, however lively, for its reality, may sometimes doubt whether true virtue is actually found anywhere in the world, and this especially as years increase and the judgment is partly made wiser by experience, and partly also more acute in observation. This being so, nothing can secure us from falling away altogether from our ideas of duty, or maintain in the soul a well-grounded respect for its law, but the clear conviction that although there should never have been actions which really sprang from such pure sources, yet whether this or that takes place is not at all the question; but that reason of itself, independent on all experience, ordains what ought to take place, that accordingly actions of which perhaps the world has hitherto never given an example, the feasibility even of which might be very much doubted by one who founds everything on experience, are nevertheless inflexibly commanded by reason; that, *ex. gr.* even though there might never yet have been a sincere friend, yet not a whit the less is pure sincerity in friendship required of every man, because, prior to all experience, this duty is involved as duty in the idea of a reason determining the will by *à priori* principles.

When we add further that, unless we deny that the notion of morality has any truth or reference to any possible object, we must admit that its law must be valid, not merely for men, but for all *rational creatures generally,* not merely under certain contingent conditions or with exceptions, but *with absolute necessity,* then it is clear that no experience could enable us to infer even the possibility of such apodictic laws. For with what right could we bring into unbounded respect as a universal precept for every rational nature that which perhaps holds only under the contingent conditions of humanity? Or how could laws of the determination of *our* will be regarded as laws of the determination of the will of rational beings generally, and for us only as such, if they were merely empirical, and did not take their origin wholly *à priori* from pure but practical reason?

Nor could anything be more fatal to morality than that we should wish to derive it from examples. For every example of it that is set before me must be first itself tested by principles of morality, whether it is worthy to serve as an original example, *i.e.* as a pattern, but by no means can it authoritatively furnish the conception of morality. Even the Holy One of the Gospels must first be compared with our ideal of moral perfection before we can recognise Him as such; and so He says of Himself, "Why call ye Me (whom you see) good; none is good (the model of good) but God only (whom ye do not see)?" But whence have we the conception of God as the supreme good? Simply from the *idea* of moral perfection, which reason frames *à priori*, and connects inseparably with the notion of a free-will. Imitation finds no place at all in morality, and examples serve only for encouragement, *i.e.* they put beyond doubt the feasibility of what the law commands, they make visible that which the practical rule expresses more generally, but they can never authorize us to set aside the true original which lies in reason, and to guide ourselves by examples.

If then there is no genuine supreme principle of morality but but what must rest simply on pure reason, independent on all experience, I think it is not necessary even to put the question, whether it is good to exhibit these concepts in their generality *(in abstracto)* as they are established *à priori* along with the principles belonging to them, if our knowledge is to be distinguished from the *vulgar,* and to be called philosophical. In our times indeed this might perhaps be necessary; for if we collected votes, whether pure rational knowledge separated from everything empirical, that is to say, metaphysic of morals, or whether popular practical philosophy is to be preferred, it is easy to guess which side would preponderate.

This descending to popular notions is certainly very commendable, if the ascent to the principles of pure reason has first taken place and been satisfactorily accomplished. This implies that we first *found* Ethics on Metaphysics, and then, when it is firmly established, procure a *hearing* for it by giving it a popular character. But it is quite absurd to try to be popular in the first inquiry, on which the soundness of the principles depends. It is not only that this proceeding can never lay claim to the very rare merit of a true *philosophical popularity*, since there is no art in being intelligible if one renounces all thoroughness of insight;

but also it produces a disgusting medley of compiled observations and half-reasoned principles. Shallow pates enjoy this because it can be used for every-day chat, but the sagacious find in it only confusion, and being unsatisfied and unable to help themselves, they turn away their eyes, while philosophers, who see quite well through this delusion, are little listened to when they call men off for a time from this pretended popularity, in order that they might be rightfully popular after they have attained a definite insight.

We need only look at the attempts of moralists in that favourite fashion, and we shall find at one time the special constitution of human nature (including, however, the idea of a rational nature generally), at one time perfection, at another happiness, here moral sense, there fear of God, a little of this, and a little of that, in marvellous mixture without its occurring to them to ask whether the principles of morality are to be sought in the knowledge of human nature at all (which we can have only from experience); and, if this is not so, if these principles are to be found altogether à priori free from everything empirical, in pure rational concepts only, and nowhere else, not even in the smallest degree; then rather to adopt the method of making this a separate inquiry, as pure practical philosophy, or (if one may use a name so decried) as metaphysic of morals,[1] to bring it by itself to completeness, and to require the public, which wishes for popular treatment, to await the issue of this undertaking.

Such a metaphysic of morals, completely isolated, not mixed with any anthropology, theology, physics, or hyperphysics, and still less with occult qualities (which we might call hypophysical), is not only an indispensable substratum of all sound theoretical knowledge of duties, but is at the same time a desideratum of the highest importance to the actual fulfilment of their precepts. For the pure conception of duty, unmixed with any foreign addition of empirical attractions, and, in a word, the conception of

---

[1] Just as pure mathematics are distinguished from applied, pure logic from applied, so if we choose we may also distinguish pure philosophy of morals (metaphysic) from applied (viz. applied to human nature). By this designation we are also at once reminded that moral principles are not based on properties of human nature, but must subsist à priori of themselves, while from such principles practical rules must be capable of being deduced for every rational nature, and accordingly for that of man.

the moral law, exercises on the human heart, by way of reason alone (which first becomes aware with this that it can of itself be practical), an influence so much more powerful than all other springs[1] which may be derived from the field of experience, that in the consciousness of its worth, it despises the latter, and can by degrees become their master; whereas a mixed ethics, compounded partly of motives drawn from feelings and inclinations, and partly also of conceptions of reason, must make the mind waver between motives which cannot be brought under any principle, which lead to good only by mere accident, and very often also to evil.

From what has been said, it is clear that all moral conceptions have their seat and origin completely *à priori* in the reason, and that, moreover, in the commonest reason just as truly as in that which is in the highest degree speculative; that they cannot be obtained by abstraction from any empirical, and therefore merely contingent knowledge; that it is just this purity of their origin that makes them worthy to serve as our supreme practical principle, and that just in proportion as we add anything empirical, we detract from their genuine influence, and from the absolute value of actions; that it is not only of the greatest necessity, in a purely speculative point of view, but is also of the greatest practical importance to derive these notions and laws from pure reason, to present them pure and unmixed, and even to determine the compass of this practical or pure rational knowledge, *i.e.* to determine the whole faculty of pure practical reason; and, in doing so, we must not make its principles dependent on the

---

[1] I have a letter from the late excellent Sulzer, in which he asks me what can be the reason that moral instruction, although containing much that is convincing for the reason, yet accomplishes so little? My answer was postponed in order that I might make it complete. But it is simply this, that the teachers themselves have not got their own notions clear, and when they endeavour to make up for this by raking up motives of moral goodness from every quarter, trying to make their physic right strong, they spoil it. For the commonest understanding shows that if we imagine, on the one hand, an act of honesty done with steadfast mind, apart from every view to advantage of any kind in this world or another, and even under the greatest temptations of necessity or allurement, and, on the other hand, a similar act which was affected, in however low a degree, by a foreign motive, the former leaves far behind and eclipses the second; it elevates the soul, and inspires the wish to be able to act in like manner oneself. Even moderately young children feel this impression, and one should never represent duties to them in any other light.

particular nature of human reason, though in speculative philosophy this may be permitted, or may even at times be necessary; but since moral laws ought to hold good for every rational creature, we must derive them from the general concept of a rational being. In this way, although for its *application* to man morality has need of anthropology, yet, in the first instance, we must treat it independently as pure philosophy, *i.e.* as metaphysic, complete in itself (a thing which in such distinct branches of science is easily done); knowing well that unless we are in possession of this, it would not only be vain to determine the moral element of duty in right actions for purposes of speculative criticism, but it would be impossible to base morals on their genuine principles, even for common practical purposes, especially of moral instruction, so as to produce pure moral dispositions, and to engraft them on men's minds to the promotion of the greatest possible good in the world.

But in order that in this study we may not merely advance by the natural steps from the common moral judgment (in this case very worthy of respect) to the philosophical, as has been already done, but also from a popular philosophy, which goes no further than it can reach by groping with the help of examples, to metaphysic (which does not allow itself to be checked by anything empirical, and as it must measure the whole extent of this kind of rational knowledge, goes as far as ideal conceptions, where even examples fail us), we must follow and clearly describe the practical faculty of reason, from the general rules of its determination to the point where the notion of duty springs from it.

Everything in nature works according to laws. Rational beings alone have the faculty of acting according *to the conception* of laws, that is according to principles, *i.e.* have a *will*. Since the deduction of actions from principles requires *reason,* the will is nothing but practical reason. If reason infallibly determines the will, then the actions of such a being which are recognised as objectively necessary are subjectively necessary also, *i.e.* the will is a faculty to choose *that only* which reason independent on inclination recognises as practically necessary, *i.e.* as good. But if reason of itself does not sufficiently determine the will, if the latter is subject also to subjective conditions (particular impulses) which do not always coincide with the objective conditions; in a word, if the will does not *in itself* completely accord with reason (which is actually the case with men), then the actions which objectively are recognised as necessary are subjectively contingent, and the determination of such a will according to objective laws is *obligation,* that is to say, the relation of the objective laws to a will that is not thoroughly good is conceived as the determination of the will of a rational being by principles of reason, but which the will from its nature does not of necessity follow.

The conception of an objective principle, in so far as it is obligatory for a will, is called a command (of reason), and the formula of the command is called an Imperative.

All imperatives are expressed by the word *ought* [or *shall*], and thereby indicate the relation of an objective law of reason to a will, which from its subjective constitution is not necessarily determined by it (an obligation). They say that something would be good to do or to forbear, but they say it to a will which does not always do a thing because it is conceived to be good to do it. That is practically *good,* however, which determines the will by means of the conceptions of reason, and consequently not from subjective causes, but objectively, that is on principles which are valid for every rational being as such. It is distinguished from the *pleasant,* as that which influences the will only by means of sensation from merely subjective causes, valid only for the sense of this or that one, and not as a principle of reason, which holds for every one.[1]

A perfectly good will would therefore be equally subject to objective laws (viz. laws of good), but could not be conceived as *obliged* thereby to act lawfully, because of itself from its subjective

---

[1] The dependence of the desires on sensations is called inclination, and this accordingly always indicates a *want.* The dependence of a contingently determinable will on principles of reason is called an *interest.* This therefore is found only in the case of a dependent will, which does not always of itself conform to reason; in the Divine will we cannot conceive any interest. But the human will can also *take an interest* in a thing without therefore acting *from interest.* The former signifies the *practical* interest in the action, the latter the *pathological* in the object of the action. The former indicates only dependence of the will on principles of reason in themselves; the second, dependence on principles of reason for the sake of inclination, reason supplying only the practical rules how the requirement of the inclination may be satisfied. In the first case the action interests me; in the second the object of the action (because it is pleasant to me). We have seen in the first section that in an action done from duty we must look not to the interest in the object, but only to that in the action itself, and in its rational principle (viz. the law).

constitution it can only be determined by the conception of good. Therefore no imperatives hold for the Divine will, or in general for a *holy* will; *ought* is here out of place, because the volition is already of itself necessarily in unison with the law. Therefore imperatives are only formulæ to express the relation of objective laws of all volition to the subjective imperfection of the will of this or that rational being, *e.g.* the human will.

Now all *imperatives* command either *hypothetically* or *categorically*. The former represent the practical necessity of a possible action as means to something else that is willed (or at least which one might possibly will). The categorical imperative would be that which represented an action as necessary of itself without reference to another end, *i.e.* as objectively necessary.

Since every practical law represents a possible action as good, and on this account, for a subject who is practically determinable by reason, necessary, all imperatives are formulæ determining an action which is necessary according to the principle of a will good in some respects. If now the action is good only as a means *to something else*, then the imperative is *hypothetical;* if it is conceived as good *in itself* and consequently as being necessarily the principle of a will which of itself conforms to reason, then it is *categorical.*

Thus the imperative declares what action possible by me would be good, and presents the practical rule in relation to a will which does not forthwith perform an action simply because it is good, whether because the subject does not always know that it is good, or because, even if it know this, yet its maxims might be opposed to the objective principles of practical reason.

Accordingly the hypothetical imperative only says that the action is good for some purpose, *possible* or *actual.* In the first case it is a Problematical, in the second an Assertorial practical principle. The categorical imperative which declares an action to be objectively necessary in itself without reference to any purpose, *i.e.* without any other end, is valid as a (practical) Apodictic principle.

Whatever is possible only by the power of some rational being may also be conceived as a possible purpose of some will; and therefore the principles of action as regards the means necessary to attain some possible purpose are in fact infinitely numerous. All sciences have a practical part, consisting of problems expressing that some end is possible for us, and of imperatives directing how it may be attained. These may, therefore, be called in general imperatives of skill. Here there is no question whether the end is rational and good, but only what one must do in order to attain it. The precepts for the physician to make his patient thoroughly healthy, and for a poisoner to ensure certain death, are of equal value in this respect, that each serves to effect its purpose perfectly. Since in early youth it cannot be known what ends are likely to occur to us in the course of life, parents seek to have their children taught a *great many things,* and provide for their *skill* in the use of means for all sorts of arbitrary ends, of none of which can they determine whether it may not perhaps hereafter be an object to their pupil, but which it is at all events *possible* that he might aim at; and this anxiety is so great that they commonly neglect to form and correct their judgment on the value of the things which may be chosen as ends.

There is *one* end, however, which may be assumed to be actually such to all rational beings (so far as imperatives apply to them, viz. as dependent beings), and therefore, one purpose which they not merely *may* have, but which we may with certainty assume that they all actually *have* by a natural necessity, and this is *happiness*. The hypothetical imperative which expresses the practical necessity of an action as means to the advancement of happiness is Assertorial. We are not to present it as necessary for an uncertain and merely possible purpose, but for a purpose which we may presuppose with certainty and *à priori* in every man, because it belongs to his being. Now skill in the choice of means to his own great well-being may be called *prudence,*[1] in the narrowest sense. And thus the imperative which refers to the choice of means to one's own happiness, *i.e.* the precept of prudence, is still always *hypothetical;* the action is not commanded absolutely, but only as means to another purpose.

Finally, there is an imperative which commands a certain con-

[1] The word prudence is taken in two senses: in the one it may bear the name of knowledge of the world, in the other that of private prudence. The former is a man's ability to influence others so as to use them for his own purposes. The latter is the sagacity to combine all these purposes for his own lasting benefit. This latter is properly that to which the value even of the former is reduced, and when a man is prudent in the former sense, but not in the latter, we might better say of him that he is clever and cunning, but, on the whole, imprudent.

duct immediately, without having as its condition any other purpose to be attained by it. This imperative is Categorical. It concerns not the matter of the action, or its intended result, but its form and the principle of which it is itself a result; and what is essentially good in it consists in the mental disposition, let the consequence be what it may. This imperative may be called that of Morality.

There is a marked distinction also between the volitions on these three sorts of principles in the *dissimilarity* of the obligation of the will. In order to mark this difference more clearly, I think they would be most suitably named in their order if we said they are either *rules* of skill, or *counsels* of prudence, or *commands (laws)* of morality. For it is *law* only that involves the conception of an *unconditional* and objective necessity, which is consequently universally valid; and commands are laws which must be obeyed, that is, must be followed, even in opposition to inclination. *Counsels*, indeed, involve necessity, but one which can only hold under a contingent subjective condition, viz. they depend on whether this or that man reckons this or that as part of his happiness; the categorical imperative, on the contrary, is not limited by any condition, and as being absolutely, although practically, necessary, may be quite properly called a command. We might also call the first kind of imperatives *technical* (belonging to art), the second *pragmatic*[1] (to welfare), the third *moral* (belonging to free conduct generally, that is, to morals).

Now arises the question, how are all these imperatives possible? This question does not seek to know how we can conceive the accomplishment of the action which the imperative ordains, but merely how we can conceive the obligation of the will which the imperative expresses. No special explanation is needed to show how an imperative of skill is possible. Whoever wills the end, wills also (so far as reason decides his conduct) the means in his power which are indispensably necessary thereto. This proposition is, as regards the volition, analytical; for, in willing an object as

---

[1] It seems to me that the proper signification of the word *pragmatic* may be most accurately defined in this way. For *sanctions* are called pragmatic which flow properly not from the law of the states as necessary enactments, but from *precaution* for the general welfare. A history is composed pragmatically when it teaches *prudence, i.e.* instructs the world how it can provide for its interests better, or at least as well, as the men of former time.

my effect, there is already thought the causality of myself as an acting cause, that is to say, the use of the means; and the imperative educes from the conception of volition of an end the conception of actions necessary to this end. Synthetical propositions must no doubt be employed in defining the means to a proposed end; but they do not concern the principle, the act of the will, but the object and its realization. *Ex. gr.*, that in order to bisect a line on an unerring principle I must draw from its extremities two intersecting arcs; this no doubt is taught by mathematics only in synthetical propositions; but if I know that it is only by this process that the intended operation can be performed, then to say that if I fully will the operation, I also will the action required for it, is an analytical proposition; for it is one and the same thing to conceive something as an effect which I can produce in a certain way, and to conceive myself as acting in this way.

If it were only equally easy to give a definite conception of happiness, the imperatives of prudence would correspond exactly with those of skill, and would likewise be analytical. For in this case as in that, it could be said, whoever wills the end, wills also (according to the dictate of reason necessarily) the indispensable means thereto which are in his power. But, unfortunately, the notion of happiness is so indefinite that although every man wishes to attain it, yet he never can say definitely and consistently what it is that he really wishes and wills. The reason of this is that all the elements which belong to the notion of happiness are altogether empirical, *i.e.* they must be borrowed from experience, and nevertheless the idea of happiness requires an absolute whole, a maximum of welfare in my present and all future circumstance. Now it is impossible that the most clear-sighted, and at the same time most powerful being (supposed finite) should frame to himself a definite conception of what he really wills in this. Does he will riches, how much anxiety, envy, and snares might he not thereby draw upon his shoulders? Does he will knowledge and discernment, perhaps it might prove to be only an eye so much the sharper to show him so much the more fearfully the evils that are now concealed from him and that cannot be avoided, or to impose more wants on his desires, which already give him concern enough. Would he have long life, who guarantees to him that it would not be a long misery? Would he at least have health? how often has uneasiness of the body restrained from excesses into which perfect health would have allowed one to fall? and so on. In short he is unable, on any principle, to determine with certainty what would make him truly happy; because to do so he would need to be omniscient. We cannot therefore act on any definite principles to secure happiness, but only on empirical counsels, *ex. gr.* of regimen, frugality, courtesy, reserve, &c., which experience teaches do, on the average, most promote well-being. Hence it follows that the imperatives of prudence do not, strictly speaking command at all, that is, they cannot present actions objectively as practically *necessary;* that they are rather to be regarded as counsels *(consilia)* than precepts *(præcepta)* of reason, that the problem to determine certainly and universally what action would promote the happiness of a rational being is completely insoluble, and consequently no imperative respecting it is possible which should, in the strict sense, command to do what makes happy; because happiness is not an ideal of reason but of imagination, resting solely on empirical grounds, and it is vain to expect that these should define an action by which one could attain the totality of a series of consequences which is really endless. This imperative of prudence would however be an analytical proposition if we assume that the means to happiness could be certainly assigned; for it is distinguished from the imperative of skill only by this, that in the latter the end is merely possible, in the former it is given; as however both only ordain the means to that which we suppose to be willed as an end, it follows that the imperative which ordains the willing of the means to him who wills the end is in both cases analytical. Thus there is no difficulty in regard to the possibility of an imperative of this kind either.

On the other hand the question, how the imperative of *morality* is possible, is undoubtedly one, the only one, demanding a solution, as this is not at all hypothetical, and the objective necessity which it presents cannot rest on any hypothesis, as is the case with the hypothetical imperatives. Only here we must never leave out of consideration that we *cannot* make out *by any example,* in other words empirically, whether there is such an imperative at all; but it is rather to be feared that all those which seem to be categorical may yet be at bottom hypothetical. For instance, when the precept is: Thou shalt not promise deceitfully; and it is assumed that the necessity of this is not a mere counsel to avoid some other evil, so that it should mean: thou shalt not make a lying promise, lest if it become known thou shouldst destroy thy credit, but that an action of this kind must be regarded as evil in itself, so that the imperative of the prohibition is categorical; then we cannot show with certainty in any example that the will was determined merely by the law, without any other spring of action, although it may appear to be so. For it is always possible that fear of disgrace, perhaps also obscure dread of other dangers, may have a secret influence on the will. Who can prove by experience the non-existence of a cause when all that experience tells us is that we do not perceive it? But in such a case the so-called moral imperative, which as such appears to be categorical and unconditional, would in reality be only a pragmatic precept, drawing our attention to our own interests, and merely teaching us to take these into consideration.

We shall therefore have to investigate *à priori* the possibility of a categorical imperative, as we have not in this case the advantage of its reality being given in experience, so that [the elucidation of] its possibility should be requisite only for its explanation, not for its establishment. In the meantime it may be discerned beforehand that the categorical imperative alone has the purport of a practical law: all the rest may indeed be called *principles* of the will but not laws, since whatever is only necessary for the attainment of some arbitrary purpose may be considered as in itself contingent, and we can at any time be free from the precept if we give up the purpose: on the contrary, the unconditional command leaves the will no liberty to choose the opposite; consequently it alone carries with it that necessity which we require in a law.

Secondly, in the case of this categorical imperative or law of morality, the difficulty (of discerning its possibility) is a very profound one. It is an *à priori* synthetical practical proposition;[1] and as there is so much difficulty in discerning the possibility of specu-

---

[1] I connect the act with the will without presupposing any condition resulting from any inclination, but *à priori*, and therefore necessarily (though only objectively, *i.e.* assuming the idea of a reason possessing full power over all subjective motives). This is accordingly a practical proposition which does not deduce the willing of an action by mere analysis from another already presupposed (for we have not such a perfect will), but connects it immediately with the conception of the will of a rational being, as something not contained in it.

lative propositions of this kind, it may readily be supposed that the difficulty will be no less with the practical.

In this problem we will first inquire whether the mere conception of a categorical imperative may not perhaps supply us also with the formula of it, containing the proposition which alone can be a categorical imperative; for even if we know the tenor of such an absolute command, yet how it is possible will require further special and laborious study, which we postpone to the last section.

When I conceive a hypothetical imperative in general I do not know beforehand what it will contain until I am given the condition. But when I conceive a categorical imperative I know at once what it contains. For as the imperative contains besides the law only the necessity that the maxims[1] shall conform to this law, while the law contains no conditions restricting it, there remains nothing but the general statement that the maxim of the action should conform to a universal law, and it is this conformity alone that the imperative properly represents as necessary.

There is therefore but one categorical imperative, namely this: *Act only on that maxim whereby thou canst at the same time will that it should become a universal law.*

Now if all imperatives of duty can be deduced from this one imperative as from their principle, then, although it should remain undecided whether what is called duty is not merely a vain notion, yet at least we shall be able to show what we understand by it and what this notion means.

Since the universality of the law according to which effects are produced constitutes what is properly called *nature* in the most general sense (as to form), that is, the existence of things so far as it is determined by general laws, the imperative of duty may be expressed thus: *Act as if the maxim of thy action were to become by thy will a Universal Law of Nature.*

We will now enumerate a few duties, adopting the usual divi-

[1] A MAXIM is a subjective principle of action, and must be distinguished from the *objective principle*, namely, practical law. The former contains the practical rule set by reason according to the conditions of the subject (often its ignorance or its inclinations), so that it is the principle on which the subject *acts;* but the law is the objective principle valid for every rational being, and is the principle on which it *ought to act,* that is, an imperative.

sion of them into duties to ourselves and to others, and into perfect and imperfect duties.[1]

1] A man reduced to despair by a series of misfortunes feels wearied of life, but is still so far in possession of his reason that he can ask himself whether it would not be contrary to his duty to himself to take his own life. Now he inquires whether the maxim of his action could become a universal law of nature. His maxim is: From self-love I adopt it as a principle to shorten my life when its longer duration is likely to bring more evil than satisfaction. It is asked then simply whether this principle founded on self-love can become a universal law of nature. Now we see at once that a system of nature of which it should be a law to destroy life by means of the very feeling whose special nature it is to impel to the improvement of life would contradict itself, and therefore could not exist as a system of nature; hence that maxim cannot possibly exist as a universal law of nature, and consequently would be wholly inconsistent with the supreme principle of all duty.

2] Another finds himself forced by necessity to borrow money. He knows that he will not be able to repay it, but sees also that nothing will be lent to him, unless he promises stoutly to repay it in a definite time. He desires to make this promise, but he has still so much conscience as to ask himself: Is it not unlawful and inconsistent with duty to get out of a difficulty in this way? Suppose however that he resolves to do so, then the maxim of his action would be expressed thus: When I think myself in want of money, I will borrow money and promise to repay it, although I know that I never can do so. Now this principle of self-love or of one's own advantage may perhaps be consistent with my whole future welfare; but the question now is, is it right? I change then the suggestion of self-love into a universal law, and state the question thus:

---

[1] It must be noted here that I reserve the division of duties for a future *metaphysic of morals;* so that I give it here only as an arbitrary one (in order to arrange my examples). For the rest, I understand by a perfect duty one that admits no exception in favour of inclination, and then I have not merely external, but also internal perfect duties. This is contrary to the use of the word adopted in the schools; but I do not intend to justify it here, as it is all one for my purpose whether it is admitted or not. [*Perfect* duties are usually understood to be those which can be enforced by external law; *imperfect,* those which cannot be enforced. They are also called respectively *determinate* and *indeterminate, officia juris* and *officia virtutis.*]

How would it be if my maxim were a universal law? Then I see at once that it could never hold as a universal law of nature but would necessarily contradict itself. For supposing it to be a universal law that everyone when he thinks himself in a difficulty should be able to promise whatever he pleases, with the purpose of not keeping his promise, the promise itself would become impossible, as well as the end that one might have in view in it, since no one would consider that anything was promised to him, but would ridicule all such statements as vain pretences.

3] A third finds in himself a talent which with the help of some culture might make him a useful man in many respects. But he finds himself in comfortable circumstances, and prefers to indulge in pleasure rather than to take pains in enlarging and improving his happy natural capacities. He asks, however, whether his maxim of neglect of his natural gifts, besides agreeing with his inclination to indulgence, agrees also with what is called duty. He sees then that a system of nature could indeed subsist with such a universal law although men (like the South Sea islanders) should let their talents rust, and resolve to devote their lives merely to idleness, amusement, and propagation of their species—in a word, to enjoyment; but he cannot possibly *will* that this should be a universal law of nature, or be implanted in us as such by a natural instinct. For, as a rational being, he necessarily wills that his faculties be developed, since they serve him, and have been given him, for all sorts of possible purposes.

4] A fourth, who is in prosperity, while he sees that others have to contend with great wretchedness and that he could help them, thinks: What concern is it of mine? Let everyone be as happy as heaven pleases, or as he can make himself; I will take nothing from him nor even envy him, only I do not wish to contribute anything to his welfare or to his assistance in distress! Now no doubt if such a mode of thinking were a universal law, the human race might very well subsist, and doubtless even better than in a state in which every one talks of sympathy and good-will, or even takes care occasionally to put it into practice, but on the other side, also cheats when he can, betrays the rights of men, or otherwise violates them. But although it is possible that a universal law of nature might exist in accordance with that maxim, it is impossible to *will* that such a principle should have the universal validity of a law of nature. For a will which resolved this would contradict itself, inasmuch as many cases might occur in which one would have need of the love and sympathy of others, and in which, by such a law of nature, sprung from his own will, he would deprive himself of all hope of the aid he desires.

These are a few of the many actual duties, or at least what we regard as such, which obviously fall into two classes on the one principle that we have laid down. We must be *able to will* that a maxim of our action should be a universal law. This is the canon of the moral appreciation of the action generally. Some actions are of such a character that their maxim cannot without contradiction be even *conceived* as a universal law of nature, far from it being possible that we should *will* that it *should* be so. In others this intrinsic impossibility is not found, but still it is impossible to *will* that their maxim should be raised to the universality of a law of nature, since such a will would contradict itself. It is easily seen that the former violate strict or rigorous (inflexible) duty; the latter only laxer (meritorious) duty. Thus it has been completely shown by these examples how all duties depend as regards the nature of the obligation (not the object of the action) on the same principle.

If now we attend to ourselves on occasion of any transgression of duty, we shall find that we in fact do not will that our maxim should be a universal law, for that is impossible for us; on the contrary we will that the opposite should remain a universal law, only we assume the liberty of making an *exception* in our own favour or (just for this time only) in favour of our inclination. Consequently if we considered all cases from one and the same point of view, namely, that of reason, we should find a contradiction in our own will, namely, that a certain principle should be objectively necessary as a universal law, and yet subjectively should not be universal, but admit of exceptions. As however we at one moment regard our action from the point of view of a will wholly conformed to reason, and then again look at the same action from the point of view of a will affected by inclination, there is not really any contradiction, but an antagonism of inclination to the precept of reason, whereby the universality of the principle is changed into a mere generality, so that the practical principle of reason shall meet the maxim half way. Now, although this cannot be justified in our own impartial judgment, yet it proves that we do really recognise the validity of the categorical imperative and (with all respect for it) only allow ourselves a few exceptions, which we think unimportant and forced from us.

We have thus established at least this much, that if duty is a conception which is to have any import and real legislative authority for our actions, it can only be expressed in categorical, and not at all in hypothetical imperatives. We have also, which is of great importance, exhibited clearly and definitely for every practical application the content of the categorical imperative, which must contain the principle of all duty if there is such a thing at all. We have not yet, however, advanced so far as to a prove *à priori* that there actually is such an imperative, that there is a practical law which commands absolutely of itself, and without any other impulse, and that the following of this law is duty.

With the view of attaining to this it is of extreme importance to remember that we must not allow ourselves to think of deducing the reality of this principle from the *particular attributes of human nature*. For duty is to be a practical, unconditional necessity of action; it must therefore hold for all rational beings (to whom an imperative can apply at all) and *for this reason only* be also a law for all human wills. On the contrary, whatever is deduced from the particular natural characteristics of humanity, from certain feelings and propensities, nay even, if possible, from any particular tendency proper to human reason, and which need not necessarily hold for the will of every rational being; this may indeed supply us with a maxim, but not with a law; with a subjective principle on which we may have a propension and inclination to act, but not with an objective principle on which we should be *enjoined* to act, even though all our propensions, inclinations, and natural dispositions were opposed to it. In fact the sublimity and intrinsic dignity of the command in duty are so much the more evident, the less the subjective impulses favour it and the more they oppose it, without being able in the slightest degree to weaken the obligation of the law or to diminish its validity.

Here then we see philosophy brought to a critical position, since it has to be firmly fixed, notwithstanding that it has nothing to support it either in heaven or earth. Here it must show its purity as absolute dictator of its own laws, not the herald of those which are whispered to it by an implanted sense or who knows what tutelary nature. Although these may be better than nothing, yet they can never afford principles dictated by reason, which must have their source wholly *à priori,* and thence their commanding authority, expecting everything from the supremacy of the law and the due respect for it, nothing from inclination, or else condemning the man to self-contempt and inward abhorrence.

Thus every empirical element is not only quite incapable of being an aid to the principle of morality, but is even highly prejudicial to the purity of morals, for the proper and inestimable worth of an absolutely good will consists just in this, that the principle of action is free from all influence of contingent grounds, which alone experience can furnish. We cannot too much or too often repeat our warning against this lax and even mean habit of thought which seeks for its principle amongst empirical motives and laws; for human reason in its weariness is glad to rest on this pillow, and in a dream of sweet illusions (in which instead of Juno, it embraces a cloud) it substitutes for morality a bastard patched up from limbs of various derivation, which looks like anything one chooses to see in it; only not like virtue to one who has once beheld her in her true form.[1]

The question then is this: Is it a necessary law *for all rational beings* that they should always judge of their actions by maxims of which they can themselves will that they should serve as universal laws? If it is so, then it must be connected (altogether *à priori*) with the very conception of the will of a rational being generally. But in order to discover this connexion we must, however reluctantly, take a step into metaphysic, although into a domain of it which is distinct from speculative philosophy, namely, the metaphysic of morals. In a practical philosophy, where it is not the reasons of what *happens* that we have to ascertain, but the laws of what *ought to happen,* even although it never does, *i.e.* objective practical laws, there it is not necessary to inquire into

---

[1] To behold virtue in her proper form is nothing else but to contemplate morality stripped of all admixture of sensible things and of every spurious ornament of reward or self-love. How much she then eclipses everything else that appears charming to the affections, every one may readily perceive with the least exertion of his reason, if it be not wholly spoiled for abstraction.

the reasons why anything pleases or displeases, how the pleasure of mere sensation differs from taste, and whether the latter is distinct from a general satisfaction of reason; on what the feeling of pleasure or pain rests, and how from it desires and inclinations arise, and from these again maxims by the co-operation of reason: for all this belongs to an empirical psychology, which would constitute the second part of physics, if we regard physics as the *philosophy of nature,* so far as it is based on *empirical laws.* But here we are concerned with objective practical laws, and consequently with the relation of the will to itself so far as it is determined by reason alone, in which case whatever has reference to anything empirical is necessarily excluded; since if *reason of itself alone* determines the conduct (and it is the possibility of this that we are now investigating), it must necessarily do so *à priori.*

The will is conceived as a faculty of determining oneself to action *in accordance with the conception of certain laws.* And such a faculty can be found only in rational beings. Now that which serves the will as the objective ground of its self-determination is the *end,* and if this is assigned by reason alone, it must hold for all rational beings. On the other hand, that which merely contains the ground of possibility of the action of which the effect is the end, this is called the *means.* The subjective ground of the desire is the *spring,* the objective ground of the volition is the motive; hence the distinction between subjective ends which rest on springs, and objective ends which depend on motives valid for every rational being. Practical principles are *formal* when they abstract from all subjective ends, they are *material* when they assume these, and therefore particular springs of action. The ends which a rational being proposes to himself at pleasure as *effects* of his actions (material ends) are all only relative, for it is only their relation to the particular desires of the subject that gives them their worth, which therefore cannot furnish principles universal and necessary for all rational beings and for every volition, that is to say practical laws. Hence all these relative ends can give rise only to hypothetical imperatives.

Supposing, however, that there were something *whose existence* has *in itself* an absolute worth, something which, being *an end in itself,* could be a source of definite laws, then in this and this alone would lie the source of a possible categorical imperative, *i.e.* a practical law.

Now I say: man and generally any rational being *exists* as an end in himself, *not merely as a means* to be arbitrarily used by this or that will, but in all his actions, whether they concern himself or other rational beings, must be always regarded at the same time as an end. All objects of the inclinations have only a conditional worth, for if the inclinations and the wants founded on them did not exist, then their object would be without value. But the inclinations themselves being sources of want, are so far from having an absolute worth for which they should be desired, that on the contrary it must be the universal wish of every rational being to be wholly free from them. Thus the worth of any object which is *to be acquired* by our action is always conditional. Beings whose existence depends not on our will but on nature's, have nevertheless, if they are irrational beings, only a relative value as means, and are therefore called *things;* rational beings, on the contrary, are called *persons,* because their very nature points them out as ends in themselves, that is as something which must not be used merely as means, and so far therefore restricts freedom of action (and is an object of respect). These, therefore, are not merely subjective ends whose existence has a worth *for us* as an effect of our action, but *objective ends,* that is things whose existence is an end in itself: an end moreover for which no other can be substituted, which they should subserve *merely* as means, for otherwise nothing whatever would possess *absolute worth;* but if all worth were conditioned and therefore contingent, then there would be no supreme practical principle of reason whatever.

If then there is a supreme practical principle or, in respect of the human will, a categorical imperative, it must be one which, being drawn from the conception of that which is necessarily an end for every one because it is *an end in itself,* constitutes an *objective* principle of will, and can therefore serve as a universal practical law. The foundation of this principle is: *rational nature exists as an end in itself.* Man necessarily conceives his own existence as being so: so far then this is a *subjective* principle of human actions. But every other rational being regards its existence similarly, just on the same rational principle that holds for me: [1] so that it is at the same time an objective principle, from which as a supreme practical law all laws of the will must be capable of being deduced. Accordingly the practical imperative will be as follows: *So act as to treat humanity, whether in thine own person or in that of any other, in every case as an end withal, never as means only.* We will now inquire whether this can be practically carried out.

To abide by the previous examples:

Firstly, under the head of necessary duty to oneself: He who contemplates suicide should ask himself whether his action can be consistent with the idea of humanity *as an end in itself.* If he destroys himself in order to escape from painful circumstances, he uses a person merely as a *mean* to maintain a tolerable condition up to the end of life. But a man is not a thing, that is to say, something which can be used merely as means, but must in all his actions be always considered as an end in himself. I cannot, therefore, dispose in any way of a man in my own person so as to mutilate him, to damage or kill him. (It belongs to ethics proper to define this principle more precisely so as to avoid all misunderstanding, *e.g.* as to the amputation of the limbs in order to preserve myself; as to exposing my life to danger with a view to preserve it, &c. This question is therefore omitted here.)

Secondly, as regards necessary duties, or those of strict obligation, towards others; he who is thinking of making a lying promise to others will see at once that he would be using another man *merely as a mean,* without the latter containing at the same time the end in himself. For he whom I propose by such a promise to use for my own purposes cannot possibly assent to my mode of acting towards him, and therefore cannot himself contain the end of this action. This violation of the principle of humanity in other men is more obvious if we take in examples of attacks on the freedom and property of others. For then it is clear that he who transgresses the rights of men, intends to use the person of others merely as means, without considering that as rational beings they ought always to be esteemed also as ends, that is, as beings who

---

[1] This proposition is here stated as a postulate. The grounds of it will be found in the concluding section.

must be capable of containing in themselves the end of the very same action.[1]

Thirdly, as regards contingent (meritorious) duties to oneself; is not enough that the action does not violate humanity in our own person as an end in itself, it must also *harmonize with* it. Now there are in humanity capacities of greater perfection, which belong to the end that nature has in view in regard to humanity in ourselves as the subject: to neglect these might perhaps be consistent with the *maintenance* of humanity as an end in itself, but not with the *advancement* of this end.

Fourthly, as regards meritorious duties towards others: the natural end which all men have is their own happiness. Now humanity might indeed subsist, although no one should contribute anything to the happiness of others, provided he did not intentionally withdraw anything from it; but after all this would only harmonise negatively not positively with *humanity as an end in itself,* if every one does not also endeavour, as far as in him lies, to forward the ends of others. For the ends of any subject which is an end in himself, ought as far as possible to be *my* ends also, if that conception is to have its *full* effect with me.

This principle, that humanity and generally every rational nature is *an end in itself* (which is the supreme limiting condition of every man's freedom of action), is not borrowed from experience, *firstly,* because it is universal, applying as it does to all rational beings whatever, and experience is not capable of determining anything about them; *secondly,* because it does not present humanity as an end to men (subjectively), that is as an object which men do of themselves actually adopt as an end; but as an objective end, which must as a law constitute the supreme limiting condition of all our subjective ends, let them be what we will; it must therefore spring from pure reason. In fact the objective principle of all practical legislation lies (according to the first principle) in *the rule* and its form of universality which makes it capable of being a law

---

[1] Let it not be thought that the common: *quod tibi non vis fieri, &c.,* could serve here as the rule or principle. For it is only a deduction from the former, though with several limitations; it cannot be a universal law, for it does not contain the principle of duties to oneself, nor of the duties of benevolence to others (for many a one would gladly consent that others should not benefit him, provided only that he might be excused from showing benevolence to them), nor finally that of duties of strict obligation to one another, for on this principle the criminal might argue against the judge who punishes him, and so on.

(say *e.g.*, a law of nature); but the *subjective* principle is in the *end;* now by the second principle the subject of all ends is each rational being, inasmuch as it is an end in itself. Hence follows the third practical principle of the will, which is the ultimate condition of its harmony with the universal practical reason, viz.: the idea of *the will of every rational being as a universally legislative will.*

On this principle all maxims are rejected which are inconsistent with the will being itself universal legislator. Thus the will is not subject simply to the law, but so subject that it must be regarded *as itself giving the law,* and on this ground only, subject to the law (of which it can regard itself as the author).

In the previous imperatives, namely, that based on the conception of the conformity of actions to general laws, as in a *physical system of nature,* and that based on the universal *prerogative* of rational beings as *ends* in themselves—these imperatives just because they were conceived as categorical, excluded from any share in their authority all admixture of any interest as a spring of action; they were however only *assumed* to be categorical, because such an assumption was necessary to explain the conception of duty. But we could not prove independently that there are practical propositions which command categorically, nor can it be proved in this section; one thing however could be done, namely, to indicate in the imperative itself by some determinate expression, that in the case of volition from duty all interest is renounced, which is the specific criterion of categorical as distinguished from hypothetical imperatives. This is done in the present (third) formula of the principle, namely, in the idea of the will of every rational being as a *universally legislating will.*

For although a will *which is subject to laws* may be attached to this law by means of an interest, yet a will which is itself a supreme lawgiver so far as it is such cannot possibly depend on any interest, since a will so dependent would itself still need another law restricting the interest of its self-love by the condition that it should be valid as universal law.

Thus the *principle* that every human will is *a will which in all its maxims gives universal laws,*[1] provided it be otherwise justified,

[1] I may be excused from adducing examples to elucidate this principle, as those which have already been used to elucidate the categorical imperative and its formula would all serve for the like purpose here.

would be very *well adapted* to be the categorical imperative, in this respect, namely, that just because of the idea of universal legislation it is *not based on any interest,* and therefore it alone among all possible imperatives can be *unconditional.* Or still better, converting the proposition, if there is a categorical imperative *(i.e.,* a law for the will of every rational being), it can only command that everything be done from maxims of one's will regarded as a will which could at the same time will that it should itself give universal laws, for in that case only the practical principle and the imperative which it obeys are unconditional, since they cannot be based on any interest.

Looking back now on all previous attempts to discover the principle of morality, we need not wonder why they all failed. It was seen that man was bound to laws by duty, but it was not observed that the laws to which he is subject are *only those of his own giving,* though at the same time they are *universal,* and that he is only bound to act in conformity with his own will; a will, however, which is designed by nature to give universal laws. For when one has conceived man only as subject to a law (no matter what), then this law required some interest, either by way of attraction or constraint, since it did not originate as a law from *his own* will, but this will was according to a law obliged by *something else* to act in a certain manner. Now by this necessary consequence all the labour spent in finding a supreme principle of *duty* was irrevocably lost. For men never elicited duty, but only a necessity of acting from a certain interest. Whether this interest was private or otherwise, in any case the imperative must be conditional, and could not by any means be capable of being a moral command. I will therefore call this the principle of *Autonomy* of the will, in contrast with every other which I accordingly reckon as *Heteronomy.*

The conception of every rational being as one which must consider itself as giving in all the maxims of its will universal laws, so as to judge itself and its actions from this point of view—this conception leads to another which depends on it and is very fruitful, namely, that of *a kingdom of ends.*

By a *kingdom* I understand the union of different rational beings in a system by common laws. Now since it is by laws that ends are determined as regards their universal validity, hence, if we abstract from the personal differences of rational beings, and likewise from all the content of their private ends, we shall be able to conceive all ends combined in a systematic whole (including both rational beings as ends in themselves, and also the special ends which each may propose to himself), that is to say, we can conceive a kingdom of ends, which on the preceding principles is possible.

For all rational beings come under the *law* that each of them must treat itself and all others *never merely as means,* but in every case *at the same time as ends in themselves.* Hence results a systematic union of rational beings by common objective laws, *i.e.,* a kingdom which may be called a kingdom of ends, since what these laws have in view is just the relation of these beings to one another as ends and means. It is certainly only an ideal.

A rational being belongs as a *member* to the kingdom of ends when, although giving universal laws in it, he is also himself subject to these laws. He belongs to it *as sovereign* when, while giving laws, he is not subject to the will of any other.

A rational being must always regard himself as giving laws either as member or as sovereign in a kingdom of ends which is rendered possible by the freedom of will. He cannot, however, maintain the latter position merely by the maxims of his will, but only in case he is a completely independent being without wants and with unrestricted power adequate to his will.

Morality consists then in the reference of all action to the legislation which alone can render a kingdom of ends possible. This legislation must be capable of existing in every rational being, and of emanating from his will, so that the principle of this will is, never to act on any maxim which could not without contradiction be also a universal law, and accordingly always so to act *that the will could at the same time regard itself as giving in its maxims universal laws.* If now the maxims of rational beings are not by their own nature coincident with this objective principle, then the necessity of acting on it is called practical necessitation, i.e., *duty.* Duty does not apply to the sovereign in the kingdom of ends, but it does to every member of it and to all in the same degree.

The practical necessity of acting on this principle, *i.e.,* duty, does not rest at all on feelings, impulses, or inclinations, but solely on the relation of rational beings to one another, a relation in which the will of a rational being must always be regarded as *legislative,* since otherwise it could not be conceived as *an end in itself.* Reason then refers every maxim of the will, regarding it as legislating universally, to every other will and also to every action towards oneself; and this not on account of any other practical motive, or any future advantage, but from the idea of the *dignity* of a rational being, obeying no law but that which he himself also gives.

In the kingdom of ends everything has either Value or Dignity. Whatever has a value can be replaced by something else which is *equivalent;* whatever, on the other hand, is above all value, and therefore admits of no equivalent, has a dignity.

Whatever has reference to the general inclinations and wants of mankind has a *market value;* whatever, without presupposing a want, corresponds to a certain taste, that is to a satisfaction in the mere purposeless play of our faculties, has a *fancy value;* but that which constitutes the condition under which alone anything can be an end in itself, this has not merely a relative worth, *i.e.,* value, but an intrinsic worth, that is *dignity.*

Now morality is the condition under which alone a rational being can be an end in himself, since by this alone is it possible that he should be a legislating member in the kingdom of ends. Thus morality, and humanity as capable of it, is that which alone has dignity. Skill and diligence in labour have a market value; wit, lively imagination, and humour, have fancy value; on the other hand, fidelity to promises, benevolence from principle (not from instinct), have an intrinsic worth. Neither nature nor art contains anything which in default of these it could put in their place, for their worth consists not in the effects which spring from them, not in the use and advantage which they secure, but in the disposition of mind, that is, the maxims of the will which are ready to manifest themselves in such actions, even though they should not have the desired effect. These actions also need no recommendation from any subjective taste or sentiment, that they may be looked on with immediate favour and satisfaction: they need no immediate propension or feeling for them; they exhibit the will that performs them as an object of an immediate respect, and nothing but reason is required to *impose* them on the will, not to *flatter* it into them, which, in the case of duties, would be a contradiction. This estimation therefore shows that the worth of such a disposition is dignity, and places it infinitely above all value, with which it cannot for a moment be brought into comparison or competition without as it were violating its sanctity.

What then is it which justifies virtue or the morally good disposition, in making such lofty claims? It is nothing less than the privilege it secures to the rational being of participating in the giving of universal laws, by which it qualifies him to be a member of a possible kingdom of ends, a privilege to which he was already destined by his own nature as being an end in himself, and on that account legislating in the kingdom of ends; free as regards all laws of physical nature, and obeying those only which he himself gives, and by which his maxims can belong to a system of universal law, to which at the same time he submits himself. For nothing has any worth except what the law assigns it. Now the legislation itself which assigns the worth of everything, must for that very reason possess dignity, that is an unconditional incomparable worth, and the word *respect* alone supplies a becoming expression for the esteem which a rational being must have for it. *Autonomy* then is the basis of the dignity of human and of every rational nature.

The three modes of presenting the principle of morality that have been adduced are at bottom only so many formulæ of the very same law, and each of itself involves the other two. There is, however, a difference in them, but it is rather subjectively than objectively practical, intended namely to bring an idea of the reason nearer to intuition (by means of a certain analogy), and thereby nearer to feeling. All maxims, in fact, have—

1] A *form*, consisting in universality; and in this view the formula of the moral imperative is expressed thus, that the maxims must be so chosen as if they were to serve as universal laws of nature.

2] A *matter*, namely, an end, and here the formula says that the rational being, as it is an end in itself, must in every maxim serve as the condition limiting all merely relative and arbitrary ends.

3] A *complete characterisation* of all maxims by means of that formula, namely, that all maxims ought by their own legislation to harmonise with a possible kingdom of ends as with a kingdom of nature.[1] There is a progress here in the order of the categories of *unity* of the form of the will (its universality), *plurality* of the matter (the objects, *i.e.,* the ends), and *totality* of the system of these. In forming our moral *judgment* of actions it is better to proceed always on the strict method, and start from the general formula of the categorical imperative: *Act according to a maxim which can at the same time make itself a universal law.* If, however, we wish to gain an *entrance* for the moral law, it is very useful to bring one and the same action under the three specified conceptions, and thereby as far as possible to bring it nearer to intuition.

We can now end where we started at the beginning, namely, with the conception of a will unconditionally good. *That will* is *absolutely good* which cannot be evil, in other words, whose maxim, if made a universal law, could never contradict itself. This principle then is its supreme law: Act always on such a maxim as thou canst at the same time will to be a universal law; this is the sole condition under which a will can never contradict itself; and such an imperative is categorical. Since the validity of the will as a universal law for possible actions is analogous to the universal connexion of the existence of things by general laws, which is the formal notion of nature in general, the categorical imperative can also be expressed thus: *Act on maxims which can at the same time have for their object themselves as universal laws of nature.* Such then is the formula of an absolutely good will.

Rational nature is distinguished from the rest of nature by this, that it sets before itself an end. This end would be the matter of every good will. But since in the idea of a will that is absolutely good without being limited by any condition (of attaining this or that end) we must abstract wholly from every end *to be effected* (since this would make every will only relatively good), it follows that in this case the end must be conceived, not as an end to be effected, but as an *independently* existing end. Consequently it is conceived only negatively, *i.e.,* as that which we must never act

[1] Teleology considers nature as a kingdom of ends; Ethics regards a possible kingdom of ends as a kingdom of nature. In the first case, the kingdom of ends is a theoretical idea, adopted to explain what actually is. In the latter it is a practical idea, adopted to bring about that which is not yet, but which can be realised by our conduct, namely, if it conforms to this idea.

against, and which, therefore, must never be regarded merely as means, but must in every volition be esteemed as an end likewise. Now this end can be nothing but the subject of all possible ends, since this is also the subject of a possible good will; for such a will cannot without contradiction be postponed to any other object. The principle: So act in regard to every rational being (thyself and others), that he may always have place in thy maxim as an end in himself, is accordingly essentially identical with this other: Act upon a maxim which, at the same time, involves its own universal validity for every rational being. For that in using means for every end I should limit my maxim by the condition of its holding good as a law for every subject, this comes to the same thing as that the fundamental principle of all maxims of action must be that the subject of all ends, *i.e.*, the rational being himself, be never employed merely as means, but as the supreme condition restricting the use of all means, that is in every case as an end likewise.

It follows incontestably that, to whatever laws any rational being may be subject, he being an end in himself must be able to regard himself as also legislating universally in respect of these same laws, since it is just this fitness of his maxims for universal legislation that distinguishes him as an end in himself; also it follows that this implies his dignity (prerogative) above all mere physical beings, that he must always take his maxims from the point of view which regards himself, and likewise every other rational being, as lawgivings beings (on which account they are called persons). In this way a world of rational beings (*mundus intelligibilis*) is possible as a kingdom of ends, and this by virtue of the legislation proper to all persons as members. Therefore every rational being must so act as if he were by his maxims in every case a legislating member in the universal kingdom of ends. The formal principle of these maxims is: So act as if thy maxim were to serve likewise as the universal law (of all rational beings). A kingdom of ends is thus only possible on the analogy of a kingdom of nature, the former however only by maxims, that is self-imposed rules, the latter only by the laws of efficient causes acting under necessitation from without. Nevertheless, although the system of nature is looked upon as a machine, yet so far as it has reference to rational beings as its ends, it is given on this account the name of a kingdom of nature. Now such a kingdom of ends would be actually realised by means of maxims conforming to the canon which the categorical imperative prescribes to all rational beings, *if they were universally followed.* But although a rational being, even if he punctually follows this maxim himself, cannot reckon upon all others being therefore true to the same, nor expect that the kingdom of nature and its orderly arrangements shall be in harmony with his as a fitting member, so as to form a kingdom of ends to which he himself contributes, that is to say, that it shall favour his expectation of happiness, still that law: Act according to the maxims of a member of a merely possible kingdom of ends legislating in it universally, remains in its full force, inasmuch as it commands categorically. And it is just in this that the paradox lies; that the mere dignity of man as a rational creature, without any other end or advantage to be attained thereby, in other words, respect for a mere idea, should yet serve as an inflexible precept of the will, and that it is precisely in this independence of the maxim on all such springs of action that its sublimity consists; and it is this that makes every rational subject worthy to be a legislative member in the kingdom of ends: for otherwise he would have to be conceived only as subject to the physical law of his wants. And although we should suppose the kingdom of nature and the kingdom of ends to be united under one sovereign, so that the latter kingdom thereby ceased to be a mere idea and acquired true reality, then it would no doubt gain the accession of a strong spring, but by no means any increase of its intrinsic worth. For this sole absolute lawgiver must, nothwithstanding this, be always conceived as estimating the worth of rational beings only by their disinterested behaviour, as prescribed to themselves from that idea [the dignity of man] alone. The essence of things is not altered by their external relations, and that which abstracting from these, alone constitutes the absolute worth of man, is also that by which he must be judged, whoever the judge may be, and even by the Supreme Being. *Morality* then is the relation of actions to the autonomy of the will, that is, to the potential universal legislation by its maxims. An action that is consistent with the autonomy of the will is *permitted;* one that does not agree therewith is *forbidden.* A will whose maxims necessarily coincide with the laws of autonomy is a *holy* will, good absolutely. The dependence of a will not absolutely good on the principle of autonomy (moral necessitation) is obligation. This then cannot be applied to a holy being. The objective necessity of actions from obligation is called *duty*.

From what has just been said, it is easy to see how it happens that although the conception of duty implies subjection to the law, we yet ascribe a certain *dignity* and sublimity to the person who fulfils all his duties. There is not, indeed, any sublimity in him, so far as he is *subject* to the moral law; but inasmuch as in regard to that very law he is likewise a *legislator*, and on that account alone subject to it, he has sublimity. We have also shown above that neither fear nor inclination, but simply respect for the law, is the spring which can give actions a moral worth. Our own will, so far as we suppose it to act only under the condition that its maxims are potentially universal laws, this ideal will which is possible to us is the proper object of respect, and the dignity of humanity consists just in this capacity of being universally legislative, though with the condition that it is itself subject to this same legislation.

The Autonomy of the Will as the Supreme Principle of Morality

Autonomy of the will is that property of it by which it is a law to itself (independently on any property of the objects of volition). The principle of autonomy then is: Always so to choose that the same volition shall comprehend the maxims of our choice as a universal law. We cannot prove that this practical rule is an imperative, *i.e.*, that the will of every rational being is necessarily bound to it as a condition, by a mere analysis of the conceptions which occur in it, since it is a synthetical proposition; we must advance beyond the cognition of the objects to a critical examination of the subject, that is of the pure practical reason, for this synthetic proposition which commands apodictically must be capable of being cognised wholly *à priori*. This matter, however, does not belong to the present section. But that the principle of autonomy in question is the sole principle of morals can be readily shown by mere analysis of the conceptions of morality. For by this analysis we find that its principle must be a categorical imperative, and that what this commands is neither more nor less than this very autonomy.

Heteronomy of the Will as the Source of all spurious Principles of Morality

If the will seeks the law which is to determine it *anywhere else* than in the fitness of its maxims to be universal laws of its own dictation, consequently if it goes out of itself and seeks this law in the character of any of its objects, there always results *heteronomy*. The will in that case does not give itself the law, but it is given by the object through its relation to the will. This relation whether it rests on inclination or on conceptions of reason only admits of hypothetical imperatives: I ought to do something *because I wish for something else*. On the contrary, the moral, and therefore categorical, imperative says: I ought to do so and so, even though I should not wish for anything else. *Ex. gr.,* the former says: I ought not to lie if I would retain my reputation; the latter says: I ought not to lie although it should not bring me the least discredit. The latter therefore must so far abstract from all objects that they shall have no *influence* on the will, in order that practical reason (will) may not be restricted to administering an interest not belonging to it, but may simply show its own commanding authority as the supreme legislation. Thus, *ex. gr.,* I ought to endeavour to promote the happiness of others, not as if its realization involved any concern of mine (whether by immediate inclination or by any satisfaction indirectly gained through reason), but simply because a maxim which excludes it cannot be comprehended as a universal law in one and the same volition.

CLASSIFICATION

Of all Principles of Morality which can be founded on the Conception of Heteronomy

Here as elsewhere human reason in its pure use, so long as it was not critically examined, has first tried all possible wrong ways before it succeeded in finding the one true way.

All principles which can be taken from this point of view are either *empirical* or *rational*. The *former*, drawn from the principle of *happiness*, are built on physical or moral feelings; the *latter*, drawn from the principle of *perfection*, are built either on the rational conception of perfection as a possible effect, or on that of an independent perfection (the will of God) as the determining cause of our will.

Empirical principles are wholly incapable of serving as a foundation for moral laws. For the universality with which these should hold for all rational beings without distinction, the unconditional practical necessity which is thereby imposed on them is lost when their foundation is taken from the *particular constitution of human nature*, or the accidental circumstances in which it is placed. The principle of *private happiness*, however, is the most objectionable, not merely because it is false, and experience contradicts the supposition that prosperity is always proportioned to good conduct, nor yet merely because it contributes nothing to the establishment of morality—since it is quite a different thing to make a prosperous man and a good man, or to make one prudent and sharp-sighted for his own interests, and to make him virtuous —but because the springs it provides for morality are such as rather undermine it and destroy its sublimity, since they put the motives to virtue and to vice in the same class, and only teach us to make a better calculation, the specific difference between virtue and vice being entirely extinguished. On the other hand, as to moral feeling, this supposed special sense,[1] the appeal to it is indeed superficial when those who cannot *think* believe that *feeling* will help them out, even in what concerns general laws: and besides, feelings which naturally differ infinitely in degree cannot furnish a uniform standard of good and evil, nor has any one a right to form judgments for others by his own feelings: nevertheless this moral feeling is nearer to morality and its dignity in this respect, that it pays virtue the honour of ascribing to her *immediately* the satisfaction and esteem we have for her, and does not, as it were, tell her to her face that we are not attached to her by her beauty but by profit.

[1] I class the principle of moral feeling under that of happiness, because every empirical interest promises to contribute to our well-being by the agreeableness that a thing affords, whether it be immediately and without a view to profit, or whether profit be regarded. We must likewise, with Hutcheson, class the principle of sympathy with the happiness of others under his assumed moral sense.

Amongst the *rational* principles of morality, the ontological conception of *perfection,* notwithstanding its defects, is better than the theological conception which derives morality from a Divine absolutely perfect will. The former is, no doubt, empty and indefinite, and consequently useless for finding in the boundless field of possible reality the greatest amount suitable for us; moreover, in attempting to distinguish specifically the reality of which we are now speaking from every other, it inevitably tends to turn in a circle, and cannot avoid tacitly presupposing the morality which it is to explain; it is nevertheless preferable to the theological view, first, because we have no intuition of the Divine perfection, and can only deduce it from our own conceptions, the most important of which is that of morality, and our explanation would thus be involved in a gross circle; and, in the next place, if we avoid this, the only notion of the Divine will remaining to us is a conception made up of the attributes of desire of glory and dominion, combined with the awful conceptions of might and vengeance, and any system of morals erected on this foundation would be directly opposed to morality.

However, if I had to choose between the notion of the moral sense and that of perfection in general (two systems which at least do not weaken morality, although they are totally incapable of serving as its foundation), then I should decide for the latter, because it at least withdraws the decision of the question from the sensibility and brings it to the court of pure reason; and although even here it decides nothing, it at all events preserves the indefinite idea (of a will good in itself) free from corruption, until it shall be more precisely defined.

For the rest I think I may be excused here from a detailed refutation of all these doctrines; that would only be superfluous labour, since it is so easy, and is probably so well seen even by those whose office requires them to decide for one of these theories (because their hearers would not tolerate suspension of judgment). But what interests us more here is to know that the prime foundation of morality laid down by all these principles is nothing but heteronomy of the will, and for this reason they must necessarily miss their aim.

In every case where an object of the will has to be supposed, in order that the rule may be prescribed which is to determine the will, there the rule is simply heteronomy; the imperative is conditional, namely, *if* or *because* one wishes for this object, one should act so and so: hence it can never command morally, that is categorically. Whether the object determines the will by means of inclination, as in the principle of private happiness, or by means of reason directed to objects of our possible volition generally, as in the principle of perfection, in either case the will never determines itself *immediately* by the conception of the action, but only by the influence which the foreseen effect of the action has on the will; *I ought to do something, on this account, because I wish for something else;* and here there must be yet another law assumed in me as its subject, by which I necessarily will this other thing, and this law again requires an imperative to restrict this maxim. For the influence which the conception of an object within the reach of our faculties can exercise on the will of the subject in consequence of its natural properties, depends on the nature of the subject, either the sensibility (inclination and taste), or the understanding and reason, the employment of which is by the peculiar constitution of their nature attended with satisfaction. It follows that the law would be, properly speaking, given by nature, and as such, it must be known and proved by experience, and would consequently be contigent, and therefore incapable of being an apodictic practical rule, such as the moral rule must be. Not only so, but it is *inevitably only heteronomy;* the will does not give itself the law, but it is given by a foreign impulse by means of a particular natural constitution of the subject adapted to receive it. An absolutely good will then, the principle of which must be a categorical imperative, will be indeterminate as regards all objects, and will contain merely the *form of volition* generally, and that as autonomy, that is to say, the capability of the maxims of every good will to make themselves a universal law, is itself the only law which the will of every rational being imposes on itself, without needing to assume any spring or interest as a foundation.

How such a synthetical practical à priori *proposition is possible* and why it is necessary, is a problem whose solution does not lie within the bounds of the metaphysic of morals; and we have not here affirmed its truth, much less professed to have a proof of it in our power. We simply showed by the development of the universally received notion of morality that an autonomy of the will is inevitably connected with it, or rather is its foundation. Whoever then holds morality to be anything real, and not a chimerical idea without any truth, must likewise admit the principle of it that is here assigned. This section then, like the first, was merely analytical. Now to prove that morality is no creation of the brain, which it cannot be if the categorical imperative and with it the autonomy of the will is true, and as an *à priori* principle absolutely necessary, this supposes the *possibility of a synthetic use of pure practical reason,* which however we cannot venture on without first giving a critical examination of this faculty of reason. In the concluding section we shall give the principal outlines of this critical examination as far as is sufficient for our purpose.

Third Section

Transition From the Metaphysic of Morals to the Critique of Pure Practical Reason

The Concept of Freedom is the Key that explains the Autonomy of the Will

The *will* is a kind of causality belonging to living beings in so far as they are rational, and *freedom* would be this property of such causality that it can be efficient, independently on foreign causes *determining* it; just as *physical necessity* is the property that the causality of all irrational beings has of being determined to activity by the influence of foreign causes.

The preceding definition of freedom is *negative,* and therefore unfruitful for the discovery of its essence; but it leads to a *positive* conception which is so much the more full and fruitful. Since the conception of causality involves that of laws, according to which, by something that we call cause, something else, namely, the effect, must be produced [laid down]; hence, although freedom is not a property of the will depending on physical laws, yet it is not for that reason lawless; on the contrary it must be a causality acting according to immutable laws, but of a peculiar kind; otherwise a free will would be an absurdity. Physical necessity is a heteronomy of the efficient causes, for every effect is possible only according to this law, that something else determines the efficient cause to exert its causality. What else then can freedom of the will be but autonomy, that is the property of the will to be a law to itself? But the proposition: The will is in every action a law to itself, only expresses the principle, to act on no other maxim than that which can also have as an object itself as a universal law. Now this is precisely the formula of the categorical imperative and is the principle of morality, so that a free will and a will subject to moral laws are one and the same.

On the hypothesis then of freedom of the will, morality together with its principle follows from it by mere analysis of the conception. However the latter is still a synthetic proposition; viz., an absolutely good will is that whose maxim can always include itself regarded as a universal law; for this property of its maxim can never be discovered by analysing the conception of an absolutely good will. Now such synthetic propositions are only possible in this way: that the two cognitions are connected together by their union with a third in which they are both to be found. The *positive* concept of freedom furnishes this third cognition, which cannot, as with physical causes, be the nature of the sensible world (in the concept of which we find conjoined the concept of something in relation as cause to *something else* as effect). We cannot now at once show what this third is to which freedom points us, and of which we have an idea *à priori*, nor can we make intelligible how the concept of freedom is shown to be legitimate from principles of pure practical reason. And with it the possibility of a categorical imperative; but some further preparation is required.

FREEDOM

Must be presupposed as a Property of the Will of all Rational Beings

It is not enough to predicate freedom of our own will, from whatever reason, if we have not sufficient grounds for predicating the same of all rational beings. For as morality serves as a law for us only because we are *rational beings,* it must also hold for all rational beings; and as it must be deduced simply from the property of freedom, it must be shown that freedom also is a property of all rational beings. It is not enough then to prove it from certain supposed experiences of human nature (which indeed is quite impossible, and it can only be shown *à priori*), but we must show that it belongs to the activity of all rational beings endowed with a will. Now I say every being that cannot act except *under the idea of freedom* is just for that reason in a practical point of view really free, that is to say, all laws which are inseparably connected with freedom have the same force for him as if his will had been shown to be free in itself by a proof theoretically conclusive.[1] Now I affirm that we must attribute to every rational being which has a will that it has also the idea of freedom and acts entirely under this idea. For in such a being we conceive a reason that is practical, that is, has causality in reference to its objects. Now we cannot possibly conceive a reason consciously receiving a bias from any other quarter with respect to its judgments, for then the subject would ascribe the determination of its judgment not to its own reason, but to an impulse. It must regard itself as the author of its principles independent on foreign influences. Consequently as practical reason or as the will of a rational being it must regard itself as free, that is to say, the will of such a being cannot be a will of its own except under the idea of freedom. This idea must therefore in a practical point of view be ascribed to every rational being.

Of the Interest attaching to the Ideas of Morality

We have finally reduced the definite conception of morality to the idea of freedom. This latter, however, we could not prove to be actually a property of ourselves or of human nature; only we saw that it must be presupposed if we would conceive a being as rational and conscious of its causality in respect of its actions, *i.e.*, as endowed with a will; and so we find that on just the same grounds we must ascribe to every being endowed with reason and will this attribute of determining itself to action under the idea of its freedom.

[1] I adopt this method of assuming freedom merely *as an idea* which rational beings suppose in their actions, in order to avoid the necessity of proving it in its theoretical aspect also. The former is sufficient for my purpose; for even though the speculative proof should not be made out, yet a being that cannot act except with the idea of freedom is bound by the same laws that would oblige a being who was actually free. Thus we can escape here from the onus which presses on the theory.

Now it resulted also from the presupposition of this idea that we became aware of a law that the subjective principles of action, *i.e.,* maxims, must always be so assumed that they can also hold as objective, that is, universal principles, and so serve as universal laws of our own dictation. But why then should I subject myself to this principle and that simply as a rational being, thus also subjecting to it all other beings endowed with reason? I will allow that no interest *urges* me to this, for that would not give a categorical imperative, but I must *take* an interest in it and discern how this comes to pass; for this 'I ought' is properly an 'I would,' valid for every rational being, provided only that reason determined his actions without any hindrance. But for beings that are in addition affected as we are by springs of a different kind, namely, sensibility, and in whose case that is not always done which reason alone would do, for these that necessity is expressed only as an 'ought,' and the subjective necessity is different from the objective.

It seems then as if the moral law, that is, the principle of autonomy of the will, were properly speaking only presupposed in the idea of freedom, and as if we could not prove its reality and objective necessity independently. In that case we should still have gained something considerable by at least determining the true principle more exactly than had previously been done; but as regards its validity and the practical necessity of subjecting oneself to it, we should not have advanced a step. For if we were asked why the universal validity of our maxim as a law must be the condition restricting our actions, and on what we ground the worth which we assign to this manner of acting—a worth so great that there cannot be any higher interest; and if we were asked further how it happens that it is by this alone a man believes he feels his own personal worth, in comparison with which that of an agreeable or disagreeable condition is to be regarding as nothing, to these questions we could give no satisfactory answer.

We find indeed sometimes that we can take an interest in a personal quality which does not involve any interest of external condition, provided this quality makes us capable of participating in the condition in case reason were to effect the allotment; that is to say, the mere being worthy of happiness can interest of itself even without the motive of participating in this happiness. This judgment, however, is in fact only the effect of the importance of the moral law which we before presupposed (when by the idea of freedom we detach ourselves from every empirical interest); but that we ought to detach ourselves from these interests, *i.e.,* to consider ourselves as free in action and yet as subject to certain laws, so as to find a worth simply in our own person which can compensate us for the loss of everything that gives worth to our condition; this we are not yet able to discern in this way, nor do we see how it is possible so to act—in other words, *whence the moral law derives its obligation.*

It must be freely admitted that there is a sort of circle here from which it seems impossible to escape. In the order of efficient causes we assume ourselves free, in order that in the order of ends we may conceive ourselves as subject to moral laws: and we afterwards conceive ourselves as subject to these laws, because we have attributed to ourselves freedom of will: for freedom and self-legislation of will are both autonomy, and therefore are reciprocal conceptions, and for this very reason one must not be used to explain the other or give the reason of it, but at most only for logical purposes to reduce apparently different notions of the same object to one single concept (as we reduce different fractions of the same value to the lowest terms).

One resource remains to us, namely, to inquire whether we do not occupy different points of view when by means of freedom we think ourselves as causes efficient *à priori,* and when we form our conception of ourselves from our actions as effects which we see before our eyes.

It is a remark which needs no subtle reflection to make, but which we may assume that even the commonest understanding can make, although it be after its fashion by an obscure discernment of judgment which it calls feeling, that all the 'ideas' that come to us involuntarily (as those of the senses) do not enable us to know objects otherwise than as they affect us; so that what they may be in themselves remains unknown to us, and consequently that as regards 'ideas' of this kind even with the closest attention and clearness that the understanding can apply to them, we can by them only attain to the knowledge of *appearances*, never to that of *things in themselves*. As soon as this distinction has once been made (perhaps merely in consequence of the difference observed between the ideas given us from without, and in which we are passive, and those that we produce simply from ourselves, and in which we show our own activity), then it follows of itself that we must admit and assume behind the appearance something else that is not an appearance, namely, the things in themselves, although we must admit that as they can never be known to us except as they affect us, we can come no nearer to them, nor can we ever know what they are in themselves. This must furnish a distinction, however crude, between a *world of sense* and the *world of under-standing*, of which the former may be different according to the difference of the sensuous impressions in various observers, while the second which is its basis always remains the same. Even as to himself, a man cannot pretend to know what he is in himself from the knowledge he has by internal sensation. For as he does not as it were create himself, and does not come by the conception of himself *à priori* but empirically, it naturally follows that he can obtain his knowledge even of himself only by the inner sense, and consequently only through the appearances of his nature and the way in which his consciousness is affected. At the same time beyond these characteristics of his own subject, made up of mere appearances, he must necessarily suppose something else as their basis, namely, his *ego,* whatever its characteristics in itself may be. Thus in respect to mere perception and receptivity of sensations he must reckon himself as belonging to the *world of sense,* but in respect of whatever there may be of pure activity in him (that which reaches consciousness immediately and not through affecting the senses) he must reckon himself as belonging to the *intellectual world,* of which however he has no further knowledge. To such a conclusion the reflecting man must come with respect to all the things which can be presented to him: it is probably to be met with even in persons of the commonest understanding, who, as is well known, are very much inclined to suppose behind the objects of the senses something else invisible and acting of itself. They spoil it however by presently sensualizing this invisible again; that is to say, wanting to make it an object of intuition, so that they do not become a whit the wiser.

Now man really finds in himself a faculty by which he distinguishes himself from everything else, even from himself as affected by objects, and that is *Reason.* This being pure spontaneity is even elevated above the *understanding.* For although the latter is a spontaneity and does not, like sense, merely contain intuitions that arise when we are affected by things (and are therefore passive), yet it cannot produce from its activity any other conceptions than those which merely serve *to bring the intuitions of sense under rules,* and thereby to unite them in one consciousness, and without this use of the sensibility it could not think at all, whereas, on the contrary, Reason shows so pure a spontaneity in the case of what I call Ideas [Ideal Conceptions] that it thereby far transcends everything that the sensibility can give it, and exhibits its most important function in distinguishing the world of sense from that of understanding, and thereby prescribing the limits of the understanding itself.

For this reason a rational being must regard himself *qua* intelligence (not from the side of his lower faculties) as belonging not to the world of sense, but to that of understanding; hence he has two points of view from which he can regard himself, and recognise laws of the exercise of his faculties, and consequently of all his actions: *first,* so far as he belongs to the world of sense, he finds himself subject to laws of nature (heteronomy); *secondly,* as belonging to the intelligible world, under laws which being independent on nature have their foundation not in experience but in reason alone.

As a rational being, and consequently belonging to the intelligible world, man can never conceive the causality of his own will otherwise than on condition of the idea of freedom, for independence on the determining causes of the sensible world (an independence which Reason must always ascribe to itself) is freedom. Now the idea of freedom is inseparably connected with the conception of *autonomy,* and this again with the universal principle of morality which is ideally the foundation of all actions of *rational* beings, just as the law of nature is of all phenomena.

Now the suspicion is removed which we raised above, that there was a latent circle involved in our reasoning from freedom to autonomy, and from this to the moral law, viz.: that we lay down the idea of freedom because of the moral law only that we might afterwards in turn infer the latter from freedom, and that consequently we could assign no reason at all for this law, but could only [present] it as a *petitio principii* which well disposed minds would gladly concede to us, but which we could never put forward as a provable proposition. For now we see that when we conceive ourselves as free we transfer ourselves into the world of understanding as members of it, and recognise the autonomy of the will with its consequence, morality; whereas, if we conceive ourselves as under obligation we consider ourselves as belonging to the world of sense, and at the same time to the world of understanding.

How is a Categorical Imperative Possible?

Every rational being reckons himself *qua* intelligence as belonging to the world of understanding, and it is simply as an efficient cause belonging to that world that he calls his causality a *will*. On the other side he is also conscious of himself as a part of the world of sense in which his actions which are mere appearances [phenomena] of that causality are displayed; we cannot however discern how they are possible from this causality which we do not know; but instead of that, these actions as belonging to the sensible world must be viewed as determined by other phenomena, namely, desires and inclinations. If therefore I were only a member of the world of understanding, then all my actions would perfectly conform to the principle of autonomy of the pure will; if I were only a part of the world of sense they would necessarily be assumed to conform wholly to the natural law of desires and inclinations, in other words, to the heteronomy of nature. (The former would rest on morality as the supreme principle, the latter on happiness.) Since however *the world of understanding contains the foundation of the world of sense, and consequently of its laws also,* and accordingly gives the law to my will (which belongs wholly to the world of understanding) directly, and must be conceived as doing so, it follows that, although on the one side I must regard myself as a being belonging to the world of sense, yet on the other side I must recognise myself as subject as an intelligence to the law of the world of understanding, *i.e.,* to reason, which contains this law in the idea of freedom, and therefore as subject to the autonomy of the will: consequently I must regard the laws of the world of understanding as imperatives for me, and the actions which conform to them as duties.

And thus what makes categorical imperatives possible is this, that the idea of freedom makes me a member of an intelligible world, in consequence of which if I were nothing else all my actions *would* always conform to the autonomy of the will; but as I at the same time intuite myself as a member of the world of sense, they *ought* so to conform, and this *categorical* 'ought' implies a synthetic *à priori* proposition, inasmuch as besides my will as affected by sensible desires there is added further the idea of the same will but as belonging to the world of the understanding, pure and practical of itself, which contains the supreme condition according to Reason of the former will; precisely as to the intuitions of sense there are added concepts of the understanding which of themselves signify nothing but regular form in general, and in this way synthetic *à priori* propositions become possible, on which all knowledge of physical nature rests.

The practical use of common human reason confirms this reasoning. There is no one, not even the most consummate villain, provided only that he is otherwise accustomed to the use of reason, who, when we set before him examples of honesty of purpose, of steadfastness in following good maxims, of sympathy and general benevolence (even combined with great sacrifices of advantages and comfort), does not wish that he might also possess these qualities. Only on account of his inclinations and impulses he cannot attain this in himself, but at the same time he wishes to be free from such inclinations which are burdensome to himself. He proves by this that he transfers himself in thought with a will free from the impulses of the sensibility into an order of things wholly different from that of his desires in the field of the sensibility, since he cannot expect to obtain by that wish any gratification of his desires, nor any position which would satisfy any of his actual or supposable inclinations (for this would destroy the pre-eminence of the very idea which wrests that wish from him): he can only expect a greater intrinsic worth of his own person. This better person, however, he imagines himself to be when he transfers himself to the point of view of a member of the world of the understanding, to which he is involuntarily forced by the idea of freedom, *i.e.,* of independence on *determining* causes of the world of sense; and from this point of view he is conscious of a good will, which by his own confession constitutes the law for the bad will that he possesses as a member of the world of sense—a law whose authority he recognises while trangressing it.

What he morally 'ought' is then what he necessarily 'would' as a member of the world of the understanding, and is conceived by him as an 'ought' only inasmuch as he likewise considers himself as a member of the world of sense.

On the Extreme Limits of all Practical Philosophy

All men attribute to themselves freedom of will. Hence come all judgments upon actions as being such as *ought to have been done,* although they *have not been* done. However this freedom is not a conception of experience, nor can it be so, since it still remains, even though experience shows the contrary of what on supposition of freedom are conceived as its necessary consequences. On the other side it is equally necessary that everything that takes place should be fixedly determined according to laws of nature. This necessity of nature is likewise not an empirical conception, just for this reason, that it involves the motion of necessity and consequently of *à priori* cognition. But this conception of a system of nature is confirmed by experience, and it must even be inevitably presupposed if experience itself is to be possible, that is, a connected knowledge of the objects of sense resting on general laws. Therefore freedom is only an Idea [Ideal Conception] of Reason, and its objective reality in itself is doubtful, while nature is a *concept* of the *understanding* which proves, and must necessarily prove, its reality in examples of experience.

There arises from this a dialectic of Reason, since the freedom attributed to the will appears to contradict the necessity of nature, and placed between these two ways Reason for *speculative purposes* finds the road of physical necessity much more beaten and more appropriate than that of freedom; yet for *practical purposes* the narrow footpath of freedom is the only one on which it is possible to make use of reason in our conduct; hence it is just as impossible for the subtlest philosophy as for the commonest reason of men to argue away freedom. Philosophy must then assume that no real contradiction will be found between freedom and physical necessity of the same human actions, for it cannot give up the conception of nature any more than that of freedom.

Nevertheless, even though we should never be able to comprehend how freedom is possible, we must at least remove this ap-

parent contradiction in a convincing manner. For if the thought
of freedom contradicts either itself or nature, which is equally
necessary, it must in competition with physical necessity be entirely given up.

It would, however, be impossible to escape this contradiction
if the thinking subject, which seems to itself free, conceived itself
in the same sense or in *the very same relation* when it calls itself
free as when in respect of the same action it assumes itself to be
subject to the law of nature. Hence it is an indispensable problem
of speculative philosophy to show that its illusion respecting the
contradiction rests on this, that we think of man in a different
sense and relation when we call him free, and when we regard him
as subject to the laws of nature as being part and parcel of nature.
It must therefore show that not only *can* both these very well
co-exist, but that both must be thought *as necessarily united* in
the same subject, since otherwise no reason could be given why we
should burden reason with an idea which, though it may possibly
without contradiction be reconciled with another that is sufficiently established, yet entangles us in a perplexity which sorely
embarrasses Reason in its theoretic employment. This duty, however, belongs only to speculative philosophy, in order that it may
clear the way for practical philosophy. The philosopher then has
no option whether he will remove the apparent contradiction or
leave it untouched; for in the latter case the theory respecting
this would be *bonum vacans* into the possession of which the
fatalist would have a right to enter, and chase all morality out
of its supposed domain as occupying it without title.

We cannot, however, as yet say that we are touching the bounds
of practical philosophy. For the settlement of that controversy
does not belong to it; it only demands from speculative reason
that it should put an end to the discord in which it entangles
itself in theoretical questions, so that practical reason may have
rest and security from external attacks which might make the
ground debatable on which it desires to build.

The claims to freedom of will made even by common reason are
founded on the consciousness and the admitted supposition that
reason is independent on merely subjectively determined causes
which together constitute what belongs to sensation only, and
which consequently come under the general designation of sensi-

bility. Man considering himself in this way as an intelligence, places himself thereby in a different order of things and in a relation to determining grounds of a wholly different kind when on the one hand he thinks of himself as an intelligence endowed with a will, and consequently with causality, and when on the other he perceives himself as a phenomenon in the world of sense (as he really is also), and affirms that his causality is subject to external determination according to laws of nature. Now he soon becomes aware that both can hold good, nay, must hold good at the same time. For there is not the smallest contradiction in saying that a *thing in appearance* (belonging to the world of sense) is subject to certain laws, on which the very same *as a thing* or being *in itself* is independent; and that he must conceive and think of himself in this two-fold way, rests as to the first on the consciousness of himself as an object affected through the senses, and as to the second on the consciousness of himself as an intelligence, *i.e.*, as independent on sensible impressions in the employment of his reason (in other words as belonging to the world of understanding).

Hence it comes to pass that man claims the possession of a will which takes no account of anything that comes under the head of desires and inclinations, and on the contrary conceives actions as possible to him, nay, even as necessary, which can only be done by disregarding all desires and sensible inclinations. The causality of such actions lies in him as an intelligence and in the laws of effects and actions [which depend] on the principles of an intelligible world, of which indeed he knows nothing more than that in it pure reason alone independent on sensibility gives the law; moreover since it is only in that world, as an intelligence, that he is his proper self (being as man only the appearance of himself) those laws apply to him directly and categorically, so that the incitements of inclinations and appetites (in other words the whole nature of the world of sense) cannot impair the laws of his volition as an intelligence. Nay, he does not even hold himself responsible for the former or ascribe them to his proper self, *i.e.*, his will: he only ascribes to his will any indulgence which he might yield them if he allowed them to influence his maxims to the prejudice of the rational laws of the will.

When practical Reason *thinks* itself into a world of understanding it does not thereby transcend its own limits, as it would if it tried to enter it by *intuition* or *sensation*. The former is only a negative thought in respect of the world of sense, which does not give any laws to reason in determining the will, and is positive only in this single point that this freedom as a negative characteristic is at the same time conjoined with a (positive) faculty and even with a causality of reason, which we designate a will, namely, a faculty of so acting that the principle of the actions shall conform to the essential character of a rational motive, *i.e.*, the condition that the maxim have universal validity as a law. But were it to borrow an *object of will*, that is, a motive from the world of understanding, then it would overstep its bounds and pretend to be acquainted with something of which it knows nothing. The conception of a world of the understanding is then only a *point of view* which Reason finds itself compelled to take outside the appearances in order to *conceive itself as practical*, which would not be possible if the influences of the sensibility had a determining power on man, but which is necessary unless he is to be denied the consciousness of himself as an intelligence, and consequently as a rational cause, energizing by reason, that is, operating freely. This thought certainly involves the idea of an order and a system of laws different from that of the mechanism of nature which belongs to the sensible world, and it makes the conception of an intelligible world necessary (that is to say, the whole system of rational beings as things in themselves). But it does not in the least authorise us to think of it further than as to its *formal* condition only, that is, the universality of the maxims of the will as laws and consequently the autonomy of the latter, which alone is consistent with its freedom, whereas, on the contrary, all laws that refer to a definite object give heteronomy which only belongs to laws of nature, and can only apply to the sensible world.

But Reason would overstep all its bounds if it undertook to *explain how* pure reason can be practical, which would be exactly the same problem as to explain *how freedom is possible*.

For we can explain nothing but that which we can reduce to laws, the object of which can be given in some possible experience. But freedom is a mere Idea [Ideal Conception], the objective reality of which can in no wise be shown according to laws of nature, and consequently not in any possible experience; and for this reason it can never be comprehended or understood, because we cannot support it by any sort of example or analogy. It holds good only as a necessary hypothesis of reason in a being that believes itself conscious of a will, that is, of a faculty distinct from mere desire (namely a faculty of determining itself to action as an intelligence, in other words, by laws of reason independently on natural instincts). Now where determination according to laws of nature ceases, there all *explanation* ceases also, and nothing remains but *defence, i.e.,* the removal of the objections of those who pretend to have seen deeper into the nature of things, and thereupon boldly declare freedom impossible. We can only point out to them that the supposed contradiction that they have discovered in it arises only from this, that in order to be able to apply the law of nature to human actions, they must necessarily consider man as an appearance: then when we demand of them that they should also think of him *qua* intelligence as a thing in itself, they still persist in considering him in this respect also as an appearance. In this view it would no doubt be a contradiction to suppose the causality of the same subject (that is, his will) to be withdrawn from all the natural laws of the sensible world. But this contradiction disappears, if they would only bethink themselves and admit, as is reasonable, that behind the appearances there must also lie at their root (although hidden) the things in themselves, and that we cannot expect the laws of these to be the same as those that govern their appearances.

The subjective impossibility of explaining the freedom of the will is identical with the impossibility of discovering and explaining an interest[1] which man can take in the moral law. Nevertheless he does actually take an interest in it, the basis of which in us we call the moral feeling, which some have falsely assigned as the

[1] Interest is that by which reason becomes practical, *i.e.,* a cause determining the will. Hence we say of rational beings only that they take an interest in a thing; irrational beings only feel sensual appetites. Reason takes a direct interest in action then only when the universal validity of its maxims is alone sufficient to determine the will. Such an interest alone is pure. But if it can determine the will only by means of another object of desire or on the suggestion of a particular feeling of the subject, then Reason takes only an indirect interest in the action, and as Reason by itself without experience cannot discover either objects of the will or a special feeling actuating it, this latter interest would only be empirical, and not a pure rational interest. The logical interest of Reason (namely, to extend its insight) is never direct, but presupposes purposes for which reason is employed.

standard of our moral judgment whereas it must rather be viewed as the *subjective* effect that the law exercises on the will, the objective principle of which is furnished by Reason alone.

In order indeed that a rational being who is also affected through the senses should will what Reason alone directs such beings that they ought to will, it is no doubt requisite that reason should have a power *to infuse a feeling of pleasure* or satisfaction in the fulfilment of duty, that is to say, that it should have a causality, by which it determines the sensibility according to its own principles. But it is quite impossible to discern, *i.e.* to make it intelligible *à priori,* how a mere thought, which itself contains nothing sensible, can itself produce a sensation of pleasure or pain; for this is a particular kind of causality of which as of every other causality we can determine nothing whatever *à priori;* we must only consult experience about it. But as this cannot supply us with any relation of cause and effect except between two objects of experience, whereas in this case, although indeed the effect produced lies within experience, yet the cause is supposed to be pure reason acting through mere ideas which offer no object to experience, it follows that for us men it is quite impossible to explain how and why the *universality of the maxim as a law,* that is, morality, interests. This only is certain, that is not *because it interests* us that it has validity for us (for that would be heteronomy and dependence of practical reason on sensibility, namely, on a feeling as its principle, in which case it could never give moral laws), but that it interests us because it is valid for us as men, inasmuch as it had its source in our will as intelligences, in other words in our proper self, *and what belongs to mere appearance is necessarily subordinated by reason the nature of the thing in itself.*

The question then: How a categorical imperative is possible can be answered to this extent that we can assign the only hypothesis on which it is possible, namely, the idea of freedom; and we can also discern the necessity of this hypothesis, and this is sufficient for the *practical exercise* of reason, that is, for the conviction of the *validity of this imperative,* and hence of the moral law; but how this hypothesis itself is possible can never be discerned by any human reason. On the hypothesis, however, that the will of an intelligence is free, its *autonomy,* as the essential formal condition of its determination, is a necessary consequence. Moreover, this freedom of will is not merely quite *possible* as a hypothesis (not involving any contradiction to the principle of physical necessity in the connexion of the phenomena of the sensible world) as speculative philosophy can show: but further, a rational being who is conscious of a causality through reason, that is to say, of a will (distinct from desires), must *of necessity* make it practically, that is, in idea, the condition of all his voluntary actions. But to explain how pure reason can be of itself practical without the aid of any spring of action that could be derived from any other source, *i.e.* how the mere principle of the *universal validity of all its maxims as laws* (which would certainly be the form of a pure practical reason) can of itself supply a spring, without any matter (object) of the will in which one could antecedently take any interest; and how it can produce an interest which would be called purely *moral;* or in other words, *how pure reason can be practical*—to explain this is beyond the power of human reason, and all the labour and pains of seeking an explanation of it are lost.

It is just the same as if I sought to find out how freedom itself is possible as the causality of a will. For then I quit the ground of philosophical explanation, and I have no other to go upon. I might indeed revel in the world of intelligences which still remains to me, but although I have an *idea* of it which is well founded, yet I have not the least *knowledge* of it, nor can I ever attain to such knowledge with all the efforts of my natural faculty of reason. It signifies only a something that remains over when I have eliminated everything belonging to the world of sense from the actuating principles of my will, serving merely to keep in bounds the principles of motives taken from the field of sensibility; fixing its limits and showing that it does not contain all in all within itself, but that there is more beyond it; but his something more I know no further. Of pure reason which frames this ideal, there remains after the abstraction of all matter, *i.e.* knowledge of objects, nothing but the form, namely, the practical law of the universality of the maxims, and in conformity with this the conception of reason in reference to a pure world of understanding as a possible efficient cause, that is a cause determining the will. There must here be a total absence of springs; unless this idea of an intelligible world is itself the spring, or that in which reason primarily takes an interest; but to make this intelligible is precisely the problem that we cannot solve.

Here now is the extreme limit of all moral inquiry, and it is of great importance to determine it even on this account, in order that reason may not on the one hand, to the prejudice of morals, seek about in the world of sense for the supreme motive and an interest comprehensible but empirical; and on the other hand, that it may not impotently flap its wings without being able to move in the (for it) empty space of transcendent concepts which we call the intelligible world, and so lose itself amidst chimeras. For the rest, the idea of a pure world of understanding as a system of all intelligences, and to which we ourselves as rational beings belong (although we are likewise on the other side members of the sensible world), this remains always a useful and legitimate idea for the purposes of rational belief, although all knowledge stops at its threshold, useful, namely, to produce in us a lively interest in the moral law by means of the noble ideal of a universal kingdom of *ends in themselves* (rational beings), to which we can belong as members then only when we carefully conduct ourselves according to the maxims of freedom as if they were laws of nature.

Concluding Remark

The speculative employment of reason *with respect to nature* leads to the absolute necessity of some supreme cause of *the world:* the practical employment of reason *with a view to freedom* leads also to absolute necessity, but only *of the laws of the actions* of a rational being as such. Now it is an essential *principle* of reason, however employed, to push its knowledge to a consciousness of its *necessity* (without which it would not be rational knowledge). It is however an equally essential *restriction* of the same reason that it can neither discern the *necessity* of what is or what happens, nor of what ought to happen, unless a condition is supposed on which it is or happens or ought to happen. In this way, however, by the constant inquiry for the condition, the satisfaction of reason is only further and further postponed. Hence it unceasingly seeks the unconditionally necessary, and finds itself forced to assume it, although without any means of making it comprehensible to itself, happy enough if only it can discover a conception which agrees with this assumption. It is therefore no fault in our deduction of the supreme principle of morality, but an objection that should be made to human reason in general, that it cannot enable us to conceive the absolute necessity of an unconditional practical law (such as the categorical imperative must be). It cannot be blamed for refusing to explain this necessity by a condition, that is to say, by means of some interest assumed as a basis, since the law would then cease to be a moral law, *i.e.* a supreme law of freedom. And thus while we do not comprehend the practical unconditional necessity of the moral imperative, we yet comprehend its *incomprehensibility,* and this is all that can be fairly demanded of a philosophy which strives to carry its principles up to the very limit of human reason.

Georg Wilhelm Friedrich Hegel

Hegel

THE German idealistic tradition of the early nineteenth century, of which Hegel's work was the culmination, inherited from Kant the problem of the systematization of philosophy. In this were involved two questions, one of ultimate reality and one of method; to both of these Hegel gave the fullest expositions.

For Hegel, as for Aristotle, philosophy was an encyclopaedic undertaking. Philosophy, he said, is the science of the Absolute. The Absolute is the whole of reality; Hegel speaks of it variously as absolute Reason, Idea, and Spirit or Mind. In contradistinction to Spinoza's absolute substance Hegel's Absolute may be characterized as absolute Subject. The universe of which absolute mind is the ultimate reality, is a rational system; what is rational is real and what is real is rational. A systematic description of the universe which is rational, which makes sense, is therefore true. Philosophy, therefore, may be defined as knowledge of the universe as a rational system.

True knowledge in its strictest sense could only be knowledge of the whole of reality; adequate, or to use Hegel's term, concrete, knowledge of the relations of the parts to the whole. The method of philosophy should be adapted to its subject; it should be designed to express in itself the articulation of reality. Descartes' mathematical method was adapted to a mechanical universe; Hegel's dialectic method was designed to express the organic quality of reality as he conceived it.

The relation of the parts to the whole is the definition or specification of parts within the whole. Definition is limita-

tion, and a concrete definition is one which expresses not only
the positive but also the negative aspects of this limitation.
In Hegel's terms the thesis implies the antithesis and both
are raised to a unity which at the same times preserves their
distinctions in the synthesis. This synthesis is again a particular, a thesis which implies its antithesis and so on until the
highest unity is reached in Absolute Mind.

Hegel's philosophic system, then, is the interpretation of
reality in terms of this method from the most abstract undifferentiated expression in pure being to the most concrete
and differentiated expression in philosophy. It represents a
description of the stages of reality from the Idea in itself
(Logic), the Idea for itself (Nature), to the Idea in and for
itself (Mind or Spirit); the self-realization of reality, the
coming to self-consciousness of mind.

The selection offered her, part of the Introduction to *The
Philosophy of History,* demonstrates the application of the
dialectical method and suggests the wealth of interesting and
often profound insights quite apart from the value of the
total system. Philosophy of history is an attempt not to gain
morals from history nor to use history to prove the validity
of any preconceived moral system but to interpret the meaning of the historical events themselves. The philosopher of
history regards history as an involved drama and himself as
a critic whose function it is to explain the plot. *The Philosophy of History* represents a compilation by Hegel's students
of lectures delivered at the University of Berlin (1818-1830),
where Hegel gathered about himself a large and influential
group of followers.

Hegel (1770-1831) spent most of his life as professor in the
universities of Jena, Heidelberg, and Berlin. During an in-
terim of eight years after his first professorship he was editor
of a newspaper and principal of a boys' school. He published
only four works during his lifetime: *Phenomenology of Mind*
(1807), *Science of Logic* (1812), *Encyclopaedia of the Philo-*

sophic Sciences (1817,) and *Philosophy of Right* (1821). His lectures on fine arts, religion, and the history of philosophy, as well as those on the interpretation of history, were published after his death during a cholera epidemic in 1831.

Introduction to the Philosophy
of History

THE enquiry into the *essential destiny* of Reason—as far as it is considered in reference to the world—is identical with the question, *what is the ultimate purpose of the world?* And the expression implies that that purpose is to be realised. Two points of consideration suggest themselves: first, the *import* of this desgin —its abstract definition; and secondly, its *realisation*.

It must be observed at the outset, that the object we investigate —universal history—belongs to the realm of *Spirit*. The term "world," includes both physical and psychical nature. Physical nature also plays its part in the world's history, and from the very beginning attention will have to be paid to the fundamental natural relations thus involved. But Spirit, and the course of its development, is our substantial object. Our task does not require us to contemplate nature as a rational system in itself—though in its own proper domain it proves itself such—but simply in its relation to *Spirit*. On the stage on which we are observing it,— universal history—Spirit displays itself in its most concrete actuality. Notwithstanding this (or rather for the very purpose of comprehending the *general* principles which this, its form of *concrete actuality*, embodies) we must premise some abstract characteristics of the *nature of Spirit*. Such an explanation, however, cannot be given here under any other form than that of bare assertion. The present is not the occasion for unfolding the idea of Spirit speculatively; for whatever has a place in an introduction, must, as already observed, be taken as simply historical; something assumed as having been explained and proved elsewhere; or whose demonstration awaits the sequel of the Science of History itself.

We have therefore to mention here:

(1.) The abstract characteristics of the nature of Spirit.

(2.) What means Spirit uses in order to realise its Idea.

(3.) Lastly, we must consider the shape which the perfect embodiment of Spirit assumes—the state.

11 The nature of Spirit may be understood by a glance at its direct opposite—*Matter*. As the essence of matter is gravity, so, on the other hand, we may affirm that the substance, the essence of Spirit is freedom. All will readily assent to the doctrine that Spirit, among other properties, is also endowed with freedom; but philosophy teaches that all the qualities of Spirit exist only through freedom; that all are but means for attaining freedom; that all seek and produce this and this alone. It is a perception of speculative philosophy, that freedom is the sole truth of Spirit. Matter possesses gravity in virtue of its tendency towards a central point. It is essentially composite; consisting of parts that *exclude* each other. It seeks its unity; and therefore exhibits the tendency towards self-destruction, towards its opposite [an indivisible point]. If it could attain this, it would be matter no longer, it would have perished. It strives after the realisation of its Idea; for in unity it exists *ideally*. Spirit, on the contrary, may be defined as that which has its centre in itself. It has not a unity beyond itself, but has already found it; it exists *in* and *with itself*. Matter has its essence out of itself; Spirit is *self-contained existence* (Bei-sich-selbst-seyn). Now this is freedom, exactly. For if I am dependent, my being is referred to something else which I am not; I cannot exist independently of something external. I am free, on the contrary, when my existence depends upon myself. This self-contained existence of Spirit is none other than self-consciousness—consciousness of one's own being. Two things must be distinguished in consciousness; first, the fact *that I know*; secondly, *what I know*. In *self* consciousness these are merged in one; for Spirit *knows itself*. It involves an appreciation of its own nature, as also an energy enabling it to realise itself; to make itself *actually* that which it is *potentially*. According to this abstract definition it may be said of universal history, that it is the exhibition of Spirit in the process of working out the knowledge of that which it is potentially. And as the germ bears in itself the whole nature of the tree, and the taste and form of its fruits, so do the first traces of Spirit virtually contain the whole of that history. The Orientals have not attained the knowledge that Spirit—Man *as such*—is free; and because they do not know this they are not free. They only know that *one is free*. But on this very account, the freedom of that one is only caprice; ferocity—brutal recklessness or passion, or a mildness and tameness of the desires, which is itself only an accident of nature or mere caprice like the former.—That *one* is therefore only a despot; not a *free man*. The consciousness of freedom first arose among the Greeks, and therefore they were free; but they, and the Romans likewise, knew only that *some* are free,—not man as such. Even Plato and Aristotle did not know this. The Greeks, therefore, had slaves; and their whole life and the maintenance of their splendid liberty, was implicated with the institution of slavery: a fact moreover, which made that liberty on the one hand only an accidental, transient and limited growth; on the other hand, constituted it a rigorous thraldom of our common nature—of the human. The German nations, under the influence of Christianity, were the first to attain the consciousness, that man, as man, is free: that it is the *freedom* of Spirit which constitutes its essence. This consciousness arose first in religion, the inmost region of Spirit; but to introduce the principle into the various relations of the actual world, involves a more extensive problem than its simple implantation; a problem whose solution and application require a severe and lengthened process of culture. As an example of this, we may note that slavery did not cease immediately on the reception of Christianity. Still less did liberty predominate in states; or governments and constitutions adopt a rational organization, or recognise freedom as their basis. That application of the principle to political relations; the thorough moulding and interpenetration of the constitution of society by it, is a process identical with history itself. I have already directed attention to the distinction here involved, between a principle as such, and its *application; i.e.* its introduction and carrying out in the actuality of Spirit and life. This is a point of fundamental importance in our science, and one which must be constantly respected as essential. And in the same way as this distinction has attracted attention in view of the *Christian* principle of self-consciousness—freedom; it also shews itself as an essential one, in view of the principle of freedom *generally*. The history of the world is none other than the progress in the consciousness of freedom; a progress whose development according to the necessity of its nature, it is our business to investigate.

The general statement given above, of the various grades in the consciousness of freedom—and which we applied in the first instance to the fact that the Eastern nations knew only that *one* is free; the Greek and Roman world only that *some* are free; whilst *we* know that all men absolutely (man *as man*) are free,—supplies us with the natural division of universal history, and suggests the mode of its discussion. This is remarked, however, only incidentally and anticipatively; some other ideas must be first explained.

The destiny of the spiritual world, and,—since this is the *substantial world,* while the physical remains subordinate to it, or, in the language of speculation, has no truth *as against* the spiritual, —the *final cause of the world at large,* we allege to be the *consciousness* of its own freedom on the part of Spirit, and *ipso facto,* the *reality* of that freedom. But that this term "freedom," without further qualification, is an indefinite, and incalculable ambiguous term; and that while that which it represents is the *ne plus ultra* of attainment, it is liable to an infinity of misunderstandings, confusions and errors, and to become the occasion for all imaginable excesses,—has never been more clearly known and felt than in modern times. Yet, for the present, we must content ourselves with the term itself without farther definition. Attention was also directed to the importance of the infinite difference between a principle in the abstract, and its actualization in the concrete. In the process before us, the essential nature of freedom—which involves in it absolute necessity,—is to be displayed as coming to a consciousness of itself (for it is in its very nature, self-consciousness) and thereby actualizing its existence. Itself is its own object of attainment, and the sole aim of Spirit. This result it is, at which the process of the world's history has been continually aiming; and to which the sacrifices that have ever and anon been laid on the vast altar of the earth, through the long lapse of ages, have been offered. This is the only aim that sees itself realised and fulfilled; the only pole of repose amid the ceaseless change of events and conditions, and the truly efficient principle that pervades them. This final aim is God's purpose with the world; but

God is the absolutely perfect being, and can, therefore, will nothing other than himself—his own will. The nature of His will—that is, His nature itself—is what we here call the idea of freedom; translating the language of religion into that of thought. The question, then, which we may next put, is: What means does this principle of freedom use for its realisation? This is the second point we have to consider.

2] The question of the *means* by which freedom develops itself to a world, conducts us to the phenomenon of history itself. Although freedom is, primarily, an undeveloped idea, the means it uses are external and phenomenal; presenting themselves in history to our sensuous vision. The first glance at history convinces us that the actions of men proceed from their needs, their passions, their interests, their characters and talents; and impresses us with the belief that such needs, passions and interests are the sole springs of action—the efficient agents in this scene of activity. Among these may, perhaps, be found aims of a liberal or universal kind—benevolence it may be, or noble patriotism; but such virtues and general views are but insignificant as compared with the world and its doings. We may perhaps see the ideal of Reason actualized in those who adopt such aims, and within the spheres of their influence; but they bear only a trifling proportion to the mass of the human race; and the extent of that influence is limited accordingly. Passions, private aims, and the satisfaction of selfish desires, are on the other hand, most effective springs of action. Their power lies in the fact that they respect none of the limitations which justice and morality would impose on them; and that these natural impulses have a more direct influence over man than the artificial and tedious discipline that tends to order and self-restraint, law and morality. When we look at this display of passions, and the consequences of their violence; the unreason which is associated not only with them, but even (rather we might say *especially*) with *good* designs and righteous aims; when we see the evil, the vice, the ruin that has befallen the most flourishing kingdoms which the mind of man ever created, we can scarce avoid being filled with sorrow at this universal taint of corruption: and, since this decay is not the work of mere nature, but of the human will—a moral embitterment—a revolt of the good spirit (if it have a place within us) may well be the result of our reflections. Without rhetorical exaggeration, a simply truthful combination of the miseries that have overwhelmed the noblest of nations and polities, and the finest exemplars of private virtue,—forms a picture of most fearful aspect, and excites emotions of the profoundest and most hopeless sadness, counter-balanced by no consolatory result. We endure in beholding it a mental torture, allowing no defence or escape but the consideration that what has happened could not be otherwise; that it is a fatality which no intervention could alter. And at last we draw back from the intolerable disgust with which these sorrowful reflections threaten us, into the more agreeable environment of our individual life—the present formed by our private aims and interests. In short we retreat into the selfishness that stands on the quiet shore, and thence enjoy in safety the distant spectacle of "wrecks confusedly hurled." But even regarding history as the slaughter-bench at which the happiness of peoples, the wisdom of states, and the virtue of individuals have been victimised—the question involuntarily arises—to what principle, to what final aim these enormous sacrifices have been offered. From this point the investigation usually proceeds to that which we have made the general commencement of our enquiry. Starting from this we pointed out those events which made up a picture so suggestive of gloomy emotions and thoughtful reflections—as *the very field* which we, for our part, regard as exhibiting only the means for realising what we assert to be the essential destiny—the absolute aim, or—which comes to the same thing—the true *result* of the world's history. We have all along purposely eschewed "moral reflections" as a method of rising from the scene of particular historical events to the general principles which they embody. Besides, it is not the interest of such sentimentalities, really to rise above those depressing emotions; and to solve the enigmas of providence which the considerations that occasioned them, present. It is essential to their character to find a gloomy satisfaction in the empty and fruitless sublimities of that negative result. We return then to the point of view which we have adopted; observing that the successive steps (Momente) of the analysis to which it will lead us, will also evolve the conditions requisite for answering the enquiries suggested by the panorama of sin and suffering that history unfolds.

The *first* remark we have to make, and which—though already presented more than once—cannot be too often repeated when the occasion seems to call for it,—is that what we call *principle, aim, destiny,* or the nature and idea of Spirit, is something merely general and abstract. Principle—plant of existence—law—is an undeveloped essence, which *as such*—however true in itself—is not completely actual. Aims, principles, &c., have a place in our thoughts, in our subjective design only; but not yet in the sphere of actuality. That which exists for itself only, is a possibility, a potentiality; but has not yet emerged into existence. A *second* element must be introduced in order to produce actuality—viz. actuation, realization; and whose principle is the will—the activity of man in the widest sense. It is only by this activity that that Idea as well as abstract characteristics generally, are realised, actualised; for of themselves they are powerless. The motive power that puts them in operation, and gives them determinate existence, is the need, instinct, inclination, and passion of man. That some conception of mine should be developed into act and existence, is my earnest desire: I wish to assert my personality in connection with it: I wish to be satisfied by its execution. If I am to exert myself for any object, it must in some way or other be *my* object. In the accomplishment of such or such designs I must at the same time find *my* satisfaction; although the purpose for which I exert myself includes a complication of results, many of which have no interest for me. This is the absolute right of personal existence—to find *itself* satisfied in its activity and labour. If men are to interest themselves for anything, they must (so to speak) have part of their existence involved in it; find their individuality gratified by its attainment. Here a mistake must be avoided. We intend blame, and justly impute it as a fault, when we say of an individual, that he is "interested" (in taking part in such or such transactions) that is, seeks only his private advantage. In reprehending this we find fault with him for furthering his personal aims without any regard to a more comprehensive design; of which he takes advantage to promote his own interest, or which he even sacrifices with this view. But he who is active in *promoting an object,* is not simply "interested," but interested in that object itself. Language faithfully expresses this distinction.—Nothing therefore happens, nothing is accomplished, unless the individuals concerned, seek their own satisfaction in the issue. They are particular units of society; *i.e.* they have special needs, instincts, and interests generally, peculiar to themselves. Among these needs are not only such as we usually call necessities—the stimuli of individual desire and volition—but also those connected with individual views and convictions; or—to use a term expressing less decision—leanings of opinion; supposing the impulses of reflection, understanding, and reason, to have been awakened. In these cases people demand, if they are to exert themselves in any direction, that the object should commend itself to them; that in point of opinion,—whether as to its goodness, justice, advantage, profit,—they should be able to "enter into it" (dabei seyn). This is a consideration of especial importance in our age, when people are less than formerly influenced by reliance on others, and by authority; when, on the contrary, they devote their activities to a cause on the ground of their own understanding, their independent conviction and opinion.

We assert then that nothing has been accomplished without interest on the part of the actors; and—if interest be called passion, inasmuch as the whole individuality, to the neglect of all other actual or possible interests and aims, is devoted to an object with every fibre of volition, concentrating all its desires and powers upon it—we may affirm absolutely that *nothing great* in *the world* has been accomplished without *passion*. Two elements, therefore, enter into the object of our investigation; the first the Idea, the second the complex of human passions; the one the warp, the other the woof of the vast tapestry of universal history. The concrete mean and union of the two is liberty, under the conditions of morality in a state. We have spoken of the idea of freedom as the nature of Spirit, and the absolute goal of history. Passion is regarded as a thing of sinister aspect, as more or less immoral. Man is required to have no passions. Passion, it is true, is not quite the suitable word for what I wish to express. I mean here nothing more than human activity as resulting from private interests—special, or if you will, self-seeking designs—with this qualification, that the whole energy of will and character is devoted to their attainment; that other interests (which would in themselves constitute attractive aims), or rather all things else, are sacrificed to them. The object in question is so bound up with the man's will, that it entirely and alone determines the "hue of resolution," and

is inseparable from it. It has become the very essence of his volition. For a person is a specific existence; not man in general (a
term to which no real existence corresponds), but a particular
human being. The term "character" likewise expresses this idiosyncrasy of will and intelligence. But *character* comprehends all
peculiarities whatever; the way in which a person conducts himself
in private relations, &c., and is not limited to his idiosyncrasy in
its practical and active phase. I shall, therefore, use the term "passion"; understanding thereby the particular bent of character, as
far as the peculiarities of volition are not limited to private interest, but supply the impelling and actuating force for accomplishing
deeds shared in by the community at large. Passion is in the first
instance the *subjective,* and therefore the *formal* side of energy,
will, and activity—leaving the object or aim still undetermined.
And there is a similar relation of formality to reality in merely
individual conviction, individual views, individual conscience. It
is always a question, of essential importance, what is the purport
of my conviction, what the object of my passion, in deciding
whether the one or the other is of a true and substantial nature.
Conversely, if it is so, it will inevitably attain actual existence—be
actualized.

From this comment on the second essential element in the historical embodiment of an aim, we infer—glancing at the institution of the state in passing—that a state is then well constituted and
internally powerful, when the private interest of its citizens is one
with the common interest of the state; when the one finds its gratification and realization in the other,—a proposition in itself very
important. But in a state many institutions must be adopted, much
political machinery invented, accompanied by appropriate political arrangements,—necessitating long struggles of the understanding before what is really appropriate can be discovered,—involving,
moreover, contentions with private interest and passions, and a
tedious discipline of these latter, in order to bring about the desired harmony. The epoch when a state attains this harmonious
condition, marks the period of its bloom, its virtue, its vigour, and
its prosperity. But the history of mankind does not begin with a
conscious aim of any kind, as it is the case with the particular
circles into which men form themselves of set purpose. The mere
social instinct implies a conscious purpose of security for life and

property; and when society has been constituted, this purpose becomes more comprehensive. The history of the world begins with its general aim—the realization of the idea of Spirit—only in an *implicit* form *(an sich)* that is, as nature; an inmost, unconscious instinct; and the whole process of history (as already observed), is directed to rendering this unconscious impulse a conscious one. Thus appearing in the form of merely natural existence, natural will—that which has been called the subjective side,—physical craving, instinct, passion, private interest, as also opinion and subjective conception,—spontaneously present themselves at the very commencement. This vast congeries of volitions, interests and activities, constitute the instruments and means of the world-spirit for attaining its object; bringing it to consciousness, and realising it. And this aim is none other than finding itself—coming to itself—and contemplating itself in concrete actuality. But that those manifestations of vitality on the part of individuals and peoples, in which they seek and satisfy their own purposes, are, at the same time, the means and instruments of a higher and broader purpose of which they know nothing,—which they realise unconsciously,—might be made a matter of question; rather has been questioned, and in every variety of form negatived, decried and contemned as mere dreaming and "philosophy." But on this point I announced my view at the very outset, and asserted our hypothesis,—which, however, will appear in the sequel, in the form of a legitimate inference,—and our belief, that Reason governs the world, and has consequently governed its history. In relation to this independently universal and substantial existence—all else is subordinate, subservient to it, and the means for its development. But moreover this Reason is immanent in historical existence and attains to its own perfection in and through that existence. The union of universal abstract existence generally with the individual, —the subjective—that is this alone is truth, belongs to the department of speculation, and is treated in this general form in logic.— But in the process of the world's history itself,—as still incomplete, —the abstract final aim of history is not yet made the distinct object of desire and interest. While these limited sentiments are still unconscious of the purpose they are fulfilling, the universal principle is implicit in them, and is realizing itself through them. The question also assumes the form of the union of *freedom and neces-*

sity; the latent abstract process of Spirit being regarded as *necessity,* while that which exhibits itself in the conscious will of men, as their interest, belongs to the domain of *freedom.* As the metaphysical connection (*i.e.* the connection in the Idea) of these forms of thought, belongs to logic, it would be out of place to analyse it here. The chief and cardinal points only shall be mentioned.

Philosophy shows that the Idea advances to an infinite antithesis; that, viz. between the Idea in its free, universal form—in which it exists for itself—and the contrasted form of abstract reflection on itself, which is formal existence-for-self, ego, formal freedom, such as belongs to Spirit only. The universal Idea exists thus as the substantial totality of things on the one side, and as the abstract essence of free volition on the other side. This reflection of the mind on itself is individual self-consciousness—the polar opposite of the Idea in its general form, and therefore existing in absolute limitation. This polar opposite is consequently limitation, particularization, for the universal absolute being; it is the side of its *definite existence;* the sphere of its formal reality, the sphere of the reverence paid to God.—To comprehend the absolute connection of this antithesis, is the profound task of metaphysics. This limitation originates all forms of particularity of whatever kind. The formal volition [of which we have spoken] wills itself; desires to make its own personality valid in all that it purposes and does: even the pious individual wishes to be saved and happy. This pole of the anthithesis, existing for itself, is—in contrast with the absolute universal being—a special separate existence, taking cognizance of speciality only, and willing that alone. In short it plays its part in the region of mere phenomena. This is the sphere of particular purposes, in effecting which individuals exert themselves on behalf of their individuality—give it full play and objective actualization. This is also the sphere of happiness and its opposite. He is happy who finds his condition suited to his special character, will, and fancy, and so enjoys himself in that condition. The history of the world is not the theatre of happiness. Periods of happiness are blank pages in it, for they are periods of harmony,—periods when the antithesis is in abeyance. Reflection on self,—the freedom above described—is abstractly defined as the formal element of the activity of the absolute Idea. The realizing *activity* of which we have spoken is the middle term of the syllogism, one of whose extremes is the universal essence, the *Idea*, which reposes in the penetralia of Spirit; and the other, the complex of external things, objective matter. That activity is the medium by which the universal latent principle is translated into the domain of objectivity.

I will endeavour to make what has been said more vivid and clear by examples.

The building of a house is, in the first instance, a subjective aim and design. On the other hand we have, as means, the several substances required for the work,—iron, wood, stones. The elements are made use of in working up this material: fire to melt the iron, wind to blow the fire, water to set wheels in motion, in order to cut the wood, &c. The result is, that the wind, which has helped to build the house, is shut out by the house; so also are the violence of rains and floods, and the destructive powers of fire, so far as the house is made fire-proof. The stones and beams obey the law of gravity,—press downwards,—and so high walls are carried up. Thus the elements are made use of in accordance with their nature, and yet co-operate for a product, by which their operation is limited. Thus the passions of men are gratified; they develop themselves and their aims in accordance with their natural tendencies, and build up the edifice of human society; thus fortifying a position for right and order *against themselves*.

The connection of events above indicated, involves also the fact, that in history an additional result is commonly produced by human actions beyond that which they aim at and obtain—that which they immediately recognise and desire. They gratify their own interest; but something farther is thereby accomplished, latent in the actions in question, though not present to their consciousness, and not included in their design. An analogous example is offered in the case of a man who, from a feeling of revenge,—perhaps not an unjust one, but produced by injury on the other's part,—burns that other man's house. A connection is immediately established between the deed itself and a train of circumstances not directly included in it, taken abstractedly. In itself it consisted in merely presenting a small flame to a small portion of a beam. Events not involved in that simple act follow of themselves. The part of the beam which was set fire to is connected with its remote portions; the beam itself is united with the woodwork of the house generally, and this with other houses; so that a wide conflagration ensues, which destroys the goods and chattels of many other persons besides his against whom the act of revenge was first directed; perhaps even costs not a few men their lives. This lay neither in the deed abstractedly, nor in the design of the man who committed it. But the action has a further general bearing. In the design of the doer it was only revenge executed against an individual in the destruction of his property, but it is moreover a crime, and that involves punishment also. This may not have been present to the mind of the perpetrator, still less in his intention; but his deed itself, the general principles it calls into play, its substantial content entails it. By this example I wish only to impress on you the consideration, that in a simple act, something further may be implicated than lies in the intention and consciousness of the agent. The example before us involves, however, this additional consideration, that the substance of the act, consequently we may say the act itself, recoils upon the perpetrator,—reacts upon him with destructive tendency. This union of the two extremes—the embodiment of a general idea in the form of direct actuality, and the elevation of a particularity into connection with universal truth— is brought to pass, at first sight, under the conditions of an utter diversity of nature between the two, and an indifference of the one extreme towards the other. The aims which the agent set before them are limited and special; but it must be remarked that the agents themselves are intelligent thinking beings. The purport of their aims is interwoven with *general, essential* considerations of justice, good, duty, &c.; for mere desire—volition in its rough and savage forms—falls not within the scene and sphere of universal history. Those general considerations, which form at the same time a norm for directing aims and actions, have a determinate purport; for such an abstraction as "good for its own sake," has no place in living actuality. If men are to act, they must not only intend the good, but must have decided for themselves whether this or that particular thing is a good. What special course of action, however, is good or not, is determined, as regards the ordinary contingencies of private life, by the laws and customs of a state; and here no great difficulty is presented. Each individual has his position; he knows on the whole what a just, honourable course of conduct is. As to ordinary, private relations, the assertion that it is difficult to choose the right and good,—the regarding it as the mark of an exalted morality to find difficulties and raise scruples on that score, —may be set down to an evil or perverse will, which seeks to evade duties not in themselves of a perplexing nature; or, at any rate, to an idly reflective habit of mind—where a feeble will affords no sufficient exercise to the faculties,—leaving them therefore to find occupation within themselves, and to expend themselves on moral self-adulation.

It is quite otherwise with the comprehensive relations that history has to do with. In this sphere are presented those momentous collisions between existing, acknowledged duties, laws, and rights, and those contingencies which are adverse to this fixed system; which assail and even destroy its foundations and existence; whose tenor may nevertheless seem good,—on the large scale advantageous,—yes, even indispensable and necessary. These contingencies realise themselves in history: they involve a general principle of a different order from that on which depends the *permanence* of a people or a state. This principle is an essential phase in the development of the *creating* Idea, of truth striving and urging towards [consciousness of] itself. Historical men—*world-historical individuals*—are those in whose aims such a general principle lies.

Caesar, in danger of losing a position, not perhaps at that time of superiority, yet at least of equality with the others who were at the head of the state, and of succumbing to those who were just on the point of becoming his enemies,—belongs essentially to this category. These enemies—who were at the same time pursuing *their* personal aims—had the form of the constitution, and the power conferred by an appearance of justice, on their side. Caesar was contending for the maintenance of his position, honour, and safety; and, since the power of his opponents included the sovereignty over the provinces of the Roman Empire, his victory secured for him the conquest of that entire empire; and he thus became—though leaving the form of the constitution—the autocrat of the state. That which secured for him the execution of a design, which in the first instance was of negative import—the autocracy of Rome,—was, however, at the same time an independently necessary feature in the history of Rome and of the world. It was not, then, his private gain merely, but an unconscious impulse that occasioned the accomplishment of that for which the time was ripe. Such are all great historical men,—whose own particular aims involve those large issues which are the will of the world-spirit. They may be called heroes, inasmuch as they have derived their purposes and their vocation, not from the calm, regular course of things, sanctioned by the existing order; but from a concealed fount—one which has not attained to phenomenal, present existence,—from that inner Spirit, still hidden beneath the surface, which, impinging on the outer world as on a shell, bursts it in pieces, because it is another kernel than that which belonged to the shell in question. They are men, therefore, who appear to draw the impulse of their life from themselves; and whose deeds have produced a condition of things and a complex of historical relations which appear to be only *their* interest, and *their* work.

Such individuals had no consciousness of the general Idea they were unfolding, while prosecuting those aims of theirs; on the contrary, they were practical, political men. But at the same time they were thinking men, who had an insight into the requirements of the time—*what was ripe for development.* This was the very truth for their age, for their world; the species next in order, so to speak, and which was already formed in the womb of time. It was theirs to know this nascent principle; the necessary, directly sequent step in progress, which their world was to take; to make this their aim, and to expend their energy in promoting it. World-historical men—the heroes of an epoch—must, therefore, be recognised as its clear-sighted ones; *their* deeds, *their* words are the best of that time. Great men have formed purposes to satisfy themselves, not others. Whatever prudent designs and counsels they might have learned from others, would be the more limited and inconsistent features in their career; for it was they who best understood affairs; from whom *others* learned, and approved, or at least acquiesced in —their policy. For that Spirit which had taken this fresh step in history is the inmost soul of all individuals; but in a state of unconsciousness which the great men in question aroused. Their fellows, therefore, follow these soul-leaders; for they feel the irresistible power of their own inner spirit thus embodied. If we go on to cast a look at the fate of these world-historical persons, whose vocation it was to be the agents of the world-spirit,—we shall find it to have been no happy one. They attained no calm enjoyment; their whole life was labour and trouble; their whole nature was nought else but their master-passion. When their object is attained they fall off like empty hulls from the kernel. They die early, like Alexander; they are murdered, like Caesar; transported to St. Helena, like Napoleon. This fearful consolation—that historical men have not enjoyed what is called happiness, and of which only private life (and this may be passed under very various external circumstances) is capable,—this consolation those may draw from history, who stand in need of it; and it is craved by envy—vexed at what is great and transcendant,—striving, therefore, to depreciate it, and to find some flaw in it. Thus in modern times it has been demonstrated *ad nauseam* that princes are generally unhappy on their thrones; in consideration of which the possession of a throne is tolerated, and men acquiesce in the fact that not themselves but the personages in question are its occupants. The free man, we may observe, is not envious, but gladly recognises what is great and exalted, and rejoices that it exists.

It is in the light of those common elements which constitute the interest and therefore the passions of individuals, that these historical men are to be regarded. They are *great* men, because they willed and accomplished something great; not a mere fancy, a mere intention, but that which met the case and fell in with the needs of the age. This mode of considering them also excludes the so-called "psychological" view, which—serving the purpose of envy most effectually—contrives so to refer all actions to the heart,—to bring them under such a subjective aspect—as that their authors appear to have done everything under the impulse of some passion, mean or grand,—some *morbid craving*,—and on account of these passions and cravings to have been not moral men. Alexander of Macedon partly subdued Greece, and then Asia; therefore he was possessed by a *morbid craving* for conquest. He is alleged to have acted from a craving for fame, for conquest; and the proof that these were the impelling motives is that he did that which resulted in fame. What pedagogue has not demonstrated of Alexander the Great—of Julius Caesar—that they were instigated by such passions, and were consequently immoral men?—whence the conclusion immediately follows that he, the pedagogue, is a better man than they, because he has not such passions; a proof of which lies in the fact that he does not conquer Asia,—vanquish Darius and Porus,—but while he enjoys life himself lets others enjoy it too.

These psychologists are particularly fond of contemplating those peculiarities of great historical figures which appertain to them as private persons. Man must eat and drink; he sustains relations to friends and acquaintances; he has passing impulses and ebullitions of temper. "No man is a hero to his valet-de-chambre," is a well-known proverb; I have added—and Goethe repeated it ten years later—"but not because the former is no hero, but because the latter is a valet." He takes off the hero's boots, assists him to bed, knows that he prefers champagne, &c. Historical personages waited upon in historical literature by such psychological valets, come poorly off; they are brought down by these their attendants to a level with—or rather a few degrees below the level of—the morality of such exquisite discerners of spirits. The Thersites of Homer who abuses the kings is a standing figure for all times. Blows—that is beating with a solid cudgel—he does not get in every age, as in the Homeric one; but his envy, his egotism, is the thorn which he has to carry in his flesh; and the undying worm that gnaws him is the tormenting consideration that his excellent views and vituperations remain absolutely without result in the world. But our satisfaction at the fate of thersitism also, may have its sinister side.

A world-historical individual is not so unwise as to indulge a variety of wishes to divide his regards. He is devoted to the one aim, regardless of all else. It is even possible that such men may treat other great, even sacred interests, inconsiderately; conduct which is indeed obnoxious to moral reprehension. But so mighty a form must trample down many an innocent flower—crush to pieces many an object in its path.

The special interest of passion is thus inseparable from the active development of a general principle: for it is from the special and determinate and from its negation, that the universal results. Particularity contends with its like, and some loss is involved in the issue. *It* is not the general idea that is implicated in opposition and combat, and that is exposed to danger. It remains in the background, untouched and uninjured. This may be called the *cunning of reason,*—that it sets the passions to work for itself, while that which develops its existence through such impulsion pays the penalty, and suffers loss. For it is *phenomenal* being that is so treated, and of this, part is of no value, part is positive and real. The particular is for the most part of too trifling value as compared with the general: individuals are sacrificed and abandoned. The Idea pays the penalty of determinate existence and of corruptibility, not from itself, but from the passions of individuals.

But though we might tolerate the idea that individuals, their desires and the gratification of them, are thus sacrificed, and their happiness given up to the empire of chance, to which it belongs; and that as a general rule, individuals come under the category of means to an ulterior end,—there is one aspect of human individuality which we should hesitate to regard in that subordinate light, even in relation to the highest; since it is absolutely no subordinate element, but exists in those individuals as inherently eternal and divine. I mean *morality, ethics, religion.* Even when speaking of the realization of the great ideal aim by means of individuals, the *subjective* element in them—their interest and that of their cravings and impulses, their views and judgments, though exihibited as the merely formal side of their existence,—was spoken of as having an infinite right to be consulted. The first idea that presents itself in speaking of *means* is that of something external to the object, and having no share in the object itself. But merely natural things—even the commonest lifeless objects—used as means, must be of such a kind as adapts them to their purpose; they must possess something in common with it. Human beings least of all, sustain the bare external relation of mere means to the great ideal aim. Not only do they in the very act of realising it, make it the occasion of satisfying personal desires, whose purport is diverse from that aim—but they share in that ideal aim itself; and are for that very reason objects of their own existence; not *formally* merely, as the world of living beings generally is—whose individual life is essentially subordinate to that of man, and is properly used *up* as an instrument. Men, on the contrary, are objects of existence to themselves, as regards the intrinsic import of the aim in question. To this order belongs that in them which we would exclude from the category of mere means,—morality, ethics, religion. That is to say, man is an object of existence in himself only in virtue of the divine that is in him,—that which was designated at the outset as *Reason;* which, in view of its activity and power of self-determination, was called *freedom.* And we affirm—without entering at present on the proof of the assertion—that religion, morality, &c. have their foundation and source in that principle, and so are essentially elevated above all alien necessity and chance. And here we must remark that individuals, to the extent of their freedom, are responsible for the depravation and enfeeblement of morals and religion. This is the seal of the absolute and sublime destiny of man—that he knows what is good and what is evil; that his destiny *is* his very ability to will either good or evil,—in one word, that he is the subject of moral imputation, imputation not only of evil, but of good; and not only concerning this or that particular matter, and all that happens *ab extrâ*, but *also* the good and evil attaching to his individual freedom. The brute alone is simply innocent. It would, however, demand an extensive explanation—as extensive as the analysis of moral freedom itself—to preclude or obviate all the misunderstandings which the statement that what is called innocent imports the entire unconsciousness of evil—is wont to occasion.

In contemplating the fate which virtue, morality, even piety experience in history, we must not fall into the litany of lamentations, that the good and pious often—or for the most part—fare ill in the world, while the evil-disposed and wicked prosper. The term *prosperity* is used in a variety of meanings—riches, outward honour, and the like. But in speaking of something which in and for itself constitutes an aim of existence, that so-called well or ill-faring of these or those isolated individuals cannot be regarded as an essential element in the rational order of the universe. With more justice than happiness,—or a fortunate environment for individuals,—it is demanded of the grand aim of the world's existence, that it should foster, nay involve the execution and ratification of good, moral, righteous purposes. What makes men morally discontented (a discontent, by the by, on which they somewhat pride themselves), is that they do not find the present adapted to the realization of aims which they hold to be right and just (more especially in modern times, ideals of political constitutions); they contrast unfavourably things as they *are*, with their idea of things as they *ought* to be. In this case it is not private interest nor passion that desires gratification, but reason, justice, liberty; and equipped with this title, the demand in question assumes a lofty bearing, and readily adopts a position not merely of discontent, but of open revolt against the actual condition of the world. To estimate such a feeling and such views aright, the demands insisted upon, and the very dogmatic opinions asserted, must be examined. At no time so much as in our own, have such general principles and notions been advanced, or with greater assurance. If in days gone by, history seems to present itself as a struggle of passions; in our time—though displays of passion are not wanting —it exhibits partly a predominance of the struggle of notions assuming the authority of principles; partly that of passions and interests essentially subjective, but under the mask of such higher sanctions. The pretensions thus contended for as legitimate in the name of that which has been stated as the ultimate aim of Reason, pass accordingly, for absolute aims,—to the same extent as religion, morals, ethics. Nothing, as before remarked, is now more common than the complaint that the *ideals* which imagination sets up are not realised—that these glorious dreams are destroyed by cold actuality. These ideals—which in the voyage of life founder on the rocks of hard reality—may be in the first instance only subjective, and belong to the idiosyncrasy of the individual, imagining himself the highest and wisest. Such do not properly belong to this category. For the fancies which the individual in his isolation indulges, cannot be the model for universal reality; just as *universal* law is not designed for the units of the mass. These as such may, in fact, find their interests decidedly thrust into the background. But by the term "Ideal," we also understand the ideal of reason, of the good, of the true. Poets, as *e.g.* Schiller, have painted such ideals touchingly and with strong emotion, and with the deeply melancholy conviction that they could not be realised. In affirming, on the contrary that the universal Reason *does* realise itself, we have indeed nothing to do with the individual empirically regarded. That admits of degrees of better and worse, since here chance and particularity have received authority from the Idea to exercise their monstrous power. Much, therefore, in particular aspects of the grand phenomenon might be found fault with. This subjective fault-finding,—which, however, only keeps in view the individual and its deficiency, without taking notice of Reason pervading the whole,—is easy; and inasmuch as it asserts an excellent intention with regard to the good of the whole, and seems to result from a kindly heart, it feels authorized to give itself airs and assume great consequence. It is easier to discover a deficiency in individuals, in states, and in providence, than to see their real import and value.

For in this merely negative fault-finding a proud position is taken,
—one which overlooks the object, without having entered into it,—
without having comprehended its positive aspect. Age generally
makes men more tolerant; youth is always discontented. The toler-
ance of age is the result of the ripeness of a judgment which, not
merely as the result of indifference, is satisfied even with what is
inferior; but, more deeply taught by the grave experience of life,
has been led to perceive the substantial, solid worth of the object
in question. The insight then to which—in contradistinction from
those ideals—philosophy is to lead us, is, that the actual world is
as it ought to be—that the truly good—the universal divine reason
—is not a mere abstraction, but a vital principle capable of realising itself. This *good,* this *Reason,* in its most concrete form, is
God. God governs the world; the actual working of his government—the carrying out of his plan—is the history of the world.
This plan philosophy strives to comprehend; for only that which
has been developed as the result of it, possesses *bonâ fide* reality.
That which does not accord with it, is negative, worthless existence. Before the pure light of this divine Idea—which is no mere
ideal—the phantom of a world whose events are an incoherent
concourse of fortuitous circumstances, utterly vanishes. Philosophy
wishes to discover the substantial purport, the actual side of the
divine idea, and to justify the so much despised actuality of things;
for Reason is the comprehension of the divine work. But as to
what concerns the perversion, corruption, and ruin of religious,
ethical and moral purposes, and states of society generally, it must
be affirmed, that in their *essence* these are infinite and eternal;
but that the forms they assume may be of a limited order, and consequently belong to the domain of mere nature, and be subject
to the sway of chance. They are therefore perishable, and exposed
to decay and corruption. Religion and morality—in the same way
as inherently universal essences—have the peculiarity of being
present in the individual soul, in the full extent of their Idea, and
therefore truly and really; although they may not manifest themselves in it *in extenso,* and are not applied to fully developed relations. The religion, the morality of a limited sphere of life—that
of a shepherd or a peasant, *e.g.*—in its intensive concentration and
limitation to a few perfectly simple relations of life,—has infinite
worth; the same worth as the religion and morality of extensive

knowledge, and of an existence rich in the compass of its relations and actions. This inner focus—this simple region of the claims of subjective freedom,—the home of volition, resolution, and action, —the abstract sphere of conscience,—that which comprises the responsibility and moral value of the individual, remains untouched; and is quite shut out from the noisy din of the world's history— including not merely external and temporal changes, but also those entailed by the absolute necessity inseparable from the realization of the Idea of freedom itself. But as a general truth this must be regarded as settled, that whatever in the world possesses claims as noble and glorious, has nevertheless a higher existence above it. The claim of the world-spirit rises above all special claims.

These observations may suffice in reference to the means which the world-spirit uses for realising its Idea. Stated simply and abstractly, this mediation involves the activity of personal existences in whom Reason is present as their absolute, substantial being; but a basis, in the first instance, still obscure and unknown to them. But the subject becomes more complicated and difficult when we regard individuals not merely in their aspect of activity, but more concretely, in conjunction with a particular manifestation of that activity in their religion and morality,—forms of existence which are intimately connected with Reason, and share in its absolute claims. Here the relation of mere means of an end disappears, and the chief bearings of this seeming difficulty in reference to the absolute aim of Spirit, have been briefly considered.

31 The third point to be analysed is, therefore—what is the object to be realised by these means; *i.e.* what is the form it assumes in the realm of the actual. We have spoken of *means;* but in the carrying out of a subjective, limited aim, we have also to take into consideration the element of a *material,* either already present or which has to be procured. Thus the question would arise: What is the material in which the ideal of Reason is wrought out? The primary answer would be,—personality itself—human desires—subjective generally. In human knowledge and volition, as its material element, Reason attains positive existence. We have considered subjective volition where it has an object which is the truth and essence of a reality, viz. where it constitutes a great world-historical

passion. As a subjective will, occupied with limited passions, it is dependent, and can gratify its desires only within the limits of this dependence. But the subjective will has also a substantial life—a reality,—in which it moves in the region of *essential* being and has the essential itself as the object of its existence. This essential being is the union of the *subjective* with the *rational* will: it is the moral whole, the state, which is that form of actuality in which the individual has and enjoys his freedom; but on the condition of his recognition, believing in and willing that which is common to the whole. And this must not be understood as if the subjective will of the social unit attained its gratification and enjoyment through that common Will; as if this were a means provided for its benefit; as if the individual, in his relations to other individuals, thus limited his freedom, in order that this universal limitation— the mutual constraint of all—might secure a small space of liberty for each. Rather, we affirm, are law, morality, government, and they alone, the positive fact and completion of freedom. Freedom of a low and limited order, is mere caprice; which finds its exercise in the sphere of particular and limited desires.

Subjective volition—passion—is that which sets men in activity, that which effects "practical" actualization. The Idea is the inner spring of action; the state is the actually existing, realised moral life. For it is the unity of the universal, essential will, with that of the individual; and this is "morality." The individual living in this unity has a moral life; possesses a value that consists in this substantiality alone. Sophocles in his Antigone, says, "The divine commands are not of yesterday, nor of today; no, they have an infinite existence, and no one could say whence they came." The laws of morality are not accidental, but are the essentially rational. It is the very object of the state that what is essential in the practical activity of men, and in their dispositions, should be duly recognised; that it should have a manifest existence, and maintain its position. It is the absolute interest of Reason that this moral whole should exist; and herein lies the justification and merit of heroes who have founded states,—however rude these may have been. In the history of the world, only those peoples can come under our notice which form a state. For it must be understood that this latter is the realization of freedom, *i.e.* of the absolute final aim, and that it exists for its own sake. It must further be understood that all the worth which the human being possesses —all spiritual actuality, he possesses only through the state. For his spiritual actuality consists in this, that his own essence—Reason— is objectively present to him, that it possesses objective immediate existence for him. Thus only is he fully conscious; thus only is he a partaker of morality—of a just and moral social and political life. For truth is the unity of the universal and subjective will; and the universal is to be found in the state, in its laws, its universal and rational arrangements. The state is the divine Idea as it exists on earth. We have in it, therefore, the object of history in a more definite shape than before; that in which freedom obtains objectivity, and lives in the enjoyment of this objectivity. For law is the objectivity of spirit; volition in its true form. Only that will which obeys law, is free; for it obeys itself—it is independent and so free. When the state or our country constitutes a community of existence; when the subjective will of man submits to laws,—the contradiction between liberty and necessity vanishes. The rational has necessary existence, as being the reality and substance of things, and we are free in recognising it as law, and following it as the substance of our own being. The objective and the subjective will are then reconciled, and present one identical homogeneous whole. For the morality (Sittlichkeit) of the state is not of that ethical (moralische) reflective kind, in which one's own conviction bears sway; this latter is rather the peculiarity of the modern time, while the true antique morality is based on the principle of abiding by one's duty [to the state at large]. An Athenian citizen did what was required of him, as it were from instinct; but if I reflect on the object of my activity, I must have the consciousness that my will has been called into exercise, But morality is duty—substantial right—a *"second* nature" as it has been justly called; for the *first* nature of man is his primary merely animal existence.

The development *in extenso* of the Idea of the state belongs to the philosophy of jurisprudence; but it must be observed that in the theories of our time various errors are current respecting it, which pass for established truths, and have become fixed prejudices. We will mention only a few of them, giving prominence to such as have a reference to the object of our history.

The error which first meets us is the direct contradictory of our principle that the state presents the realization of freedom; the opinion, viz., that man is free by *nature,* but that in *society,* in the state—to which nevertheless he is irresistibly impelled—he must limit this natural freedom. That man is free by nature is quite correct in one sense; viz., that he is so according to the idea of humanity; but we imply thereby that he is such only in virtue of his destiny—that he has an undeveloped power to become such; for the "nature" of an object is exactly synonymous with its "Idea." But the view in question imports more than this. When man is spoken of as "free by nature," the mode of his existence as well as his destiny is implied. His merely natural and primary condition is intended. In this sense a "state of nature" is assumed in which mankind at large are in the possession of their natural rights with the unconstrained exercise and enjoyment of their freedom. This assumption is not indeed raised to the dignity of the historical fact; it would indeed be difficult, were the attempt seriously made, to point out any such condition as actually existing, or as having ever occurred. Examples of a savage state of life can be pointed out, but they are marked by brutal passions and deeds of violence; while, however rude and simple their conditions, they involve social arrangements which (to use the common phrase) *restrain* freedom. That assumption is one of those nebulous images which theory produces; an idea which it cannot avoid originating, but which it fathers upon real existence, without sufficient historical justification.

What we find such a state of nature to be in actual experience, answers exactly to the idea of a *merely* natural condition. Freedom as the *ideal* of that which is original and natural, does not exist *as original and natural.* Rather must it be first sought out and won; and that by an incalculable medial discipline of the intellectual and moral powers. The state of nature is, therefore, predominantly that of injustice and violence, of untamed natural impulses, of inhuman deeds and feelings. Limitation is certainty produced by society and the state, but it is a limitation of the mere brute emotions and rude instincts; as also, in a more advanced stage of culture, of the premeditated self-will of caprice and passion. This kind of constraint is part of the instrumentality by which only, the consciousness of freedom and the desire for its attainment, in its true—that is rational and ideal form—can be obtained. To the notion of freedom, law and morality are indispensably requisite; and they are in and for themselves, universal existences, objects and aims; which are discovered only by the activity of thought, separating itself from the merely sensuous, and developing itself, in opposition thereto; and which must on the other hand, be introduced into and incorporated with the originally sensuous will, and that contrarily to its natural inclination. The perpetually recurring misapprehension of freedom consists in regarding that term only in its *formal*, subjective sense, abstracted from its essential objects and aims; thus a constraint put upon impulse, desire, passion—pertaining to the particular individual as such—a limitation of caprice and self-will is regarded as a fettering of freedom. We should on the contrary look upon such limitation as the indispensable proviso of emancipation. Society and the state are the very conditions in which freedom is realised.

We must notice a second view, contravening the principle of the development of moral relations into a legal form. The *patriarchal* condition is regarded—either in reference to the entire race of man, or to some branches of it—as exclusively that condition of things, in which the legal element is combined with a due recognition of the moral and emotional parts of our nature; and in which justice as united with these, truly and really influences the intercourse of the social units. The basis of the patriarchal condition is the family relation; which develops the *primary* form of conscious morality, succeeded by that of the state as its *second* phase. The patriarchal condition is one of transition, in which the family has already advanced to the position of a race or people; where the union, therefore, has already ceased to be simply a bond of love and confidence, and has become one of plighted service. We must first examine the ethical principle of the family. The family may be reckoned as virtually a single person; since its members have either mutually surrendered their individual personality, (and consequently their legal position towards each other, with the rest of their particular interests and desires) as in the case of the parents; or have not yet attained such an independent personality,—(the children,—who are primarily in that merely natural condition already mentioned). They live, therefore, in a unity of feeling, love, confidence, and faith in each other. And in a relation of mutual love, the one individual has the consciousness of himself in the consciousness of the other; he lives out of self; and in this mutual self-renunciation each regains the life that had been virtually transferred to the other; gains, in fact, that other's existence and his own, as involved with that other. The further interests connected with the necessities and external concerns of life, as well as the development that has to take place within their circle, *i.e.* of the children, constitute a common object for the members of the family. The spirit of the family—the Penates—form one substantial being, as much as the spirit of a people in the state; and morality in both cases consists in a feeling, a consciousness, and a will, not limited to individual personality and interest, but embracing the common interests of the members generally. But this unity is in the case of the family essentially one of *feeling;* not advancing beyond the limits of the merely *natural.* The piety of the family relation should be respected in the highest degree by the state; by its means the state obtains as its members individuals who are already moral (for as mere *persons* they are not) and who in uniting to form a state bring with them that sound basis of a political edifice—the capacity of feeling one with a whole. But the expansion of the family to a patriarchal unity carries us beyond the ties of blood-relationship—the simply natural elements of that basis; and outside of these limits the members of the community must enter upon the position of independent personality. A review of the patriarchal condition, *in extenso,* would lead us to give special attention to the theocratical constitution. The head of the patriarchal clan is also its priest. If the family in its general relations, is not yet separated from civic society and the state, the separation of religion from it has also not yet taken place; and so much the less since the piety of the hearth is itself a profoundly subjective state of feeling.

We have considered two aspects of freedom,—the objective and the subjective; if, therefore, freedom is asserted to consist in the individuals of a state all agreeing in its arrangements, it is evident that only the subjective aspect is regarded. The natural inference from this principle is, that no law can be valid without the approval of all. This difficulty is attempted to be obviated by the decision that the minority must yield to the majority; the majority therefore bear the sway. But long ago J. J. Rousseau remarked, that in that case there would be no longer freedom, for the will of the *minority* would cease to be respected. At the Polish Diet each single member had to give his consent before any political step could be taken; and this kind of freedom it was that ruined the state. Besides, it is a dangerous and false prejudice, that the people *alone* have reason and insight, and know what justice is; for each popular faction may represent itself as the people, and the questions as to what constitutes the state is one of advanced science, and not of popular decision.

If the principle of regard for the individual will is recognised as the only basis of political liberty, viz., that nothing should be done by or for the state to which all the members of the body politic have not given their sanction, we have, properly speaking, no *constitution*. The only arrangement that would be necessary, would be, first, a centre having no *will* of its own, but which should take into consideration what appeared to be the necessities of the state; and, secondly, a contrivance for calling the members of the state together, for taking the votes, and for performing the arithmetical operations of reckoning and comparing the number of votes for the different propositions, and thereby deciding upon them. The state is an *abstraction,* having its generic existence in its citizens; but it is an actuality, and its simply generic existence must embody itself in individual will and activity. The want of government and political administration in general is felt; this necessitates the selection and separation from the rest of those who have to take the helm in political affairs, to decide concerning them, and to give orders to other citizens, with a view to the execution of their plans. If, *e. g.,* even the people in a democracy resolve on a war, a general must head the army. It is only by a constitution that the *abstraction*—the state—attains life and actuality; but this involves the distinction between those who command and those who obey.—Yet obedience seems inconsistent with liberty, and those who command appear to do the very opposite of that which the fundamental notion of the state, viz., that of freedom, requires. It is, however, urged that,—though the distinction between commanding and obeying is absolutely necessary, because affairs could not go on without it—and indeed this seems only a compulsory limitation, external to and even contravening freedom in the abstract—the constitution should be at least so framed, that the citizens may obey as little as possible, and the smallest modicum of free volition be left to the commands of the superiors;—that the substance of that for which subordination is necessary, even in its most important bearings, should be decided and resolved on by the people—by the will of many or of all the citizens; though it is supposed to be thereby provided that the state should be possessed of vigour and strength as an actuality— an individual unity.—The primary consideration is, then, the distinction between the governing and the governed, and political constitutions in the abstract have been rightly divided into monarchy, aristocracy, and democracy; which gives occasion, however, to the remark that monarchy itself must be further divided into despotism and monarchy proper; that in all the divisions to which the leading notion gives rise, only the generic character is to be made prominent,—it being not intended thereby that the particular category under review should be exhausted as a form, order, or kind in its *concrete* development. But especially it must be observed, that the above-mentioned divisions admit of a multitude of particular modifications,—not only such as lie within the limits of those classes themselves,—but also such as are mixtures of several of these essentially distinct classes, and which are consequently misshapen, unstable, and inconsistent forms. In such a collision, the concerning question is, what is the *best constitution;* that is, by what arrangement, organization, or mechanism of the power of the state its object can be most surely attained. This object may indeed be variously understood; for instance, as the calm enjoyment of life on the part of the citizens, or as universal happiness. Such aims have suggested the so-called ideals of constitution, and,—as a particular branch of the subject,—ideals of the education of princes (Fenelon), or of the governing body—the aristocracy at large (Plato); for the chief point they treat of is the condition of those subjects who stand at the head of affairs; and in these ideals the concrete details of political organization are not at all considered. The inquiry into the best constitution is frequently treated as if not only the theory were an affair of subjective independent conviction, but as if the introduction of a constitution recognised as the best,—or as superior to others,— could be the result of a resolve adopted in this theoretical manner; as if the form of a constitution were a matter of free choice, determined by nothing else but reflection. Of this artless fashion was that deliberation,—not indeed of the Persian *people,* but of the Persian *grandees,* who had conspired to overthrow the pseudo-Smerdis and the Magi, after their undertaking had succeeded, and when there was no scion of the royal family living,—as to what constitution they should introduce into Persia; and Herodotus gives an equally naïve account of this deliberation.

In the present day, the constitution of a country and people is not represented as so entirely dependent on free and deliberate choice. The fundamental but abstractly (and therefore imperfectly) entertained conception of freedom, has resulted in the republic being very generally regarded—in *theory*—as the only just and true political constitution. Many even, who occupy elevated official positions under monarchical constitutions—so far from being opposed to this idea—are actually its supporters; only they see that such a constitution, though the best, cannot be realised under all circumstances; and that—while men are what they are—we must be satisfied with less freedom; the monarchical constitution—under the given circumstances, and the present moral condition of the people—being even regarded as the most advantageous. In this view also, the necessity of a particular constitution is made to depend on the condition of the people in such a way as if the latter were non-essential and accidental. This representation is founded on the distinction which the reflective understanding makes between a notion and the corresponding reality; holding to an abstract and consequently untrue notion; not grasping it in its completeness, or—which is virtually, though not in point of form, the same—not taking a concrete view of a people and a state. We shall have to shew further on, that the constitution adopted by a people makes one substance—one spirit—with its religion, its art and philosophy, or, at least, with its conceptions and thoughts —its culture generally; not to expatiate upon the additional influences, *ab extrâ,* of climate, of neighbours, of its place in the world. A state is an individual totality, of which you cannot select any particular side, although a supremely important one, such as its political constitution; and deliberate and decide respecting it in that isolated form. Not only is that constitution most intimately connected with and dependent on those other spiritual forces; but the form of the entire moral and intellectual individuality—comprising all the forces it embodies—is only a step in the development of the grand whole,—with its place preappointed in the process; a fact which gives the highest sanction to the constitution in question, and establishes its absolute necessity.—The origin of a state involves imperious lordship on the one hand, instinctive submission on the other. But even obedience—lordly power, and the fear inspired by a ruler—in itself implies some degree of voluntary connection. Even in barbarous states this is the case; it is not the isolated will of individuals that prevails; individual pretensions are relinquished, and the general will is the essential bond of political union. This unity of the general and the particular is the Idea itself, manifesting itself as a *state,* and which subsequently undergoes further development within itself. The abstract yet necessitated process in the development of truly independent states is as follows:—They begin with regal power, whether of patriarchal or military origin. In the next phase, particularity and individuality assert themselves in the form of aristocracy and democracy. Lastly, we have the subjection of these separate interests to a single power; but which can be absolutely none other than one outside of which those spheres have an independent position, viz., the monarchical. Two phases of royalty, therefore, must be distinguished,—a primary and a secondary one. This process is necessitated, so that the form of government assigned to a particular stage of development *must* present itself: it is therefore no matter of choice, but is that form which is adapted to the spirit of the people.

In a constitution the main feature of interest is the self-development of the *rational,* that is, the *political* condition of a people; the setting free of the successive elements of the Idea: so that the several powers in the state manifest themselves as separate,—attain their appropriate and special perfection,—and yet in this independent condition, work together for one object, and are held together by it—*i.e.,* form an organic whole. The state is thus the embodiment of rational freedom, realizing and recognizing itself in an objective form. For its objective consists in this,—that its successive stages are not merely ideal, but are present in an appropriate reality; and that in their separate and several working, they are absolutely merged in that agency by which the totality—

the soul—the individual unity—is produced, and of which it is the result.

The state is the idea of Spirit in the external manifestation of human will and its freedom. It is to the state, therefore, that change in the aspect of history indissolubly attaches itself; and the successive phases of the Idea manifest themselves in it as distinct political *principles*. The constitutions under which world-historical peoples have reached their culmination, are peculiar to them; and therefore do not present a generally applicable political basis. Were it otherwise, the differences of similar constitutions would consist only in a peculiar method of expanding and developing that generic basis; whereas they really originate in diversity of principle. From the comparison therefore of the political institutions of the ancient world-historical peoples, it so happens, that for the most recent principle of a constitution—for the principle of our own times—nothing (so to speak) can be learned. In science and art it is quite otherwise; *e. g.*, the ancient philosophy is so decidedly the basis of the modern, that it is inevitably contained in the latter, and constitutes its basis. In this case the relation is that of a continuous development of the same structure, whose foundation-stone, walls, and roof have remained what they were. In art, the Greek itself, in its original form, furnishes us the best models. But in regard to political constitution, it is quite otherwise: here the ancient and the modern have not their essential principle in common. Abstract definitions and dogmas respecting just government,—importing that intelligence and virtue ought to bear sway—are, indeed, common to both. But nothing is so absurd as to look to Greeks, Romans, or Orientals, for models for the political arrangements of our time. From the East may be derived beautiful pictures of a patriarchal condition, of paternal government, and of devotion to it on the part of peoples; from Greeks and Romans, descriptions of popular liberty. Among the latter we find the idea of a free constitution admitting all the citizens to a share in deliberations and resolves respecting the affairs and laws of the commonwealth. In our times, too, this is its general acceptation; only with this modification, that—since our states are so large, and there are so many of "the many," the latter,—direct action being impossible,—should by the indirect method of elective substitution express their concurrence with resolves affecting the common weal; that is, that for legislative purposes generally, the people should be represented by deputies. The so-called representative constitution is that form of government with which we connect the idea of a free constitution, and this notion has become a rooted prejudice. On this theory people and government are separated. But there is a perversity in this antithesis; an ill-intentioned *ruse* designed to insinuate that the people are the totality of the state. Besides, the basis of this view is the principle of isolated individuality—the absolute validity of the subjective will—a dogma which we have already investigated. The great point is, that freedom in its ideal conception has not subjective will and caprice for its principle, but the recognition of the universal will; and that the process by which freedom is realised is the free development of its successive stages. The subjective will is a merely formal determination—*a carte blanche*—not including what it is that is willed. Only the *rational* will is that universal principle which independently determines and unfolds its own being, and develops its successive elemental phases as organic members. Of this Gothic-cathedral architecture the ancients knew nothing.

At an earlier stage of the discussion, we established the two elemental considerations: first, the *idea* of freedom as the absolute and final aim; secondly, the *means* for realising it, *i. e.* the subjective side of knowledge and will, with its life, movement, and activity. We then recognised the state as the moral whole and the reality of freedom, and consequently as the objective unity of these two elements. For although we make this distinction into two aspects for our consideration, it must be remarked that they are intimately connected; and that their connection is involved in the idea of each when examined separately. We have, on the one hand, recognised the Idea in the definite form of freedom conscious of and willing itself,—having itself alone as its object: involving at the same time, the pure and simple idea of Reason, and likewise, that which we have called subject—self-consciousness—Spirit actually existing in the world. If, on the other hand, we consider subjectivity, we find that subjective knowledge and will is thought. But by the very act of thoughtful cognition and volition, I will the universal object—the substance of absolute Reason. We observe, therefore, an essential union between the objective side—the

Idea,—and the subjective side—the personality that conceives and wills it.—The *objective* existence of this union is the state, which is therefore the basis and centre of the other concrete elements of the life of a people,—of art, of law, of morals, of religion, of science. All the activity of Spirit has only this object—the becoming conscious of this union, *i.e.*, of its own freedom. Among the forms of this conscious union *religion* occupies the highest position. In it, Spirit—rising above the limitations of temporal and secular existence—becomes conscious of the Absolute Spirit, and in this consciousness of the self-existent Being, renounces its individual interest; it lays this aside in devotion—a state of mind in which it refuses to occupy itself any longer with the limited and particular. By sacrifice man expresses his renunciation of his property, his will, his individual feelings. The religious concentration of the soul appears in the form of feeling; it nevertheless passes also into reflection; a form of worship (*cultus*) is a result of reflection. The second form of the union of the objective and subjective in the human spirit is art. This advances farther into the realm of the actual and sensuous than religion. In its noblest walk it is occupied with representing, not indeed, the spirit of God, but certainly the form of God; and in its secondary aims, that which is divine and spiritual generally. Its office is to render visible the divine; presenting it to the imaginative and intuitive faculty. But the true is the object not only of conception and feeling, as in religion,—and of intuition, as in art,—but also of the thinking faculty; and this gives us the third form of the union in question—*philosophy*. This is consequently the highest, freest, and wisest phase. Of course we are not intending to investigate these three phases here; they have only suggested themselves in virtue of their occupying the same general ground as the object here considered —the state.

The general principle which manifests itself and becomes an object of consciousness in the state,—the form under which all that the state includes is brought,—is the whole of that cycle of phenomena which constitutes the *culture* of a nation. But the definite *substance* that receives the form of universality, and exists in that concrete actuality which is the state,—is the spirit of the people itself. The actual state is animated by this spirit, in all its particular affairs—its wars, institutions, &c. But man must also attain a conscious realization of this his Spirit and essential nature, and of his original identity with it. For we said that moralty is the identity of the *subjective* or *personal* with the *universal* will. Now the mind must give itself an express consciousness of this; and the focus of this knowledge is *religion*. Art and science are only various aspects and forms of the same substantial being. In considering religion, the chief point of enquiry is, whether it recognises the true—the Idea—only in its separate, abstract form, or in its true unity; in *separation*—God being represented in an abstract form as the highest being, lord of heaven and earth, living in a remote region far from human actualities,—or in its *unity*,—God, as unity of the universal and individual; the individual itself assuming the aspect of positive and real existence in the idea of the incarnation. Religion is the sphere in which a nation gives itself the definition of that which it regards as the true. A definition contains everything that belongs to the essence of an object; reducing its nature to its simple characteristic predicate, as a mirror for every predicate,—the generic soul pervading all its details. The conception of God, therefore, constitutes the general basis of a people's character.

In this aspect, religion stands in the closest connection with the political principle. Freedom can exist only where individuality is recognised as having its positive and real existence in the divine being. The connection may be further explained thus:—secular existence, as merely temporal—occupied with particular interests— is consequently only relative and unauthorized; and receives its validity only in as far as the universal soul that pervades it—its principle—receives absolute validity; which it cannot have unless it is recognised as the definite manifestation, the phenomenal existence of the divine essence. On this account it is that the state rests on religion. We hear this often repeated in our times, though for the most part nothing further is meant than that individual subjects as God-fearing men would be more disposed and ready to perform their duty; since obedience to king and law so naturally follows in the train of reverence for God. This reverence, indeed, since it exalts the general over the special, may even turn upon the latter,—become fanatical,—and work with incendiary and destructive violence against the state, its institutions, and arrangements. Religious feeling, therefore, it is thought, should be sober—kept in a certain degree of coolness,—that it may not storm against and bear down that which should be defended and preserved by it. The possibility of such a catastrophe is at least latent in it.

While, however, the correct sentiment is adopted, that the state is based on religion, the position thus assigned to religion supposes the state already to exist; and that subsequently, in order to maintain it, religion must be brought into it—buckets and bushels as it were—and impressed upon people's hearts. It is quite true that men must be trained to religion, but not as to something whose existence has yet to begin. For in affirming that the state is based on religion—that it has its roots in it—we virtually assert that the former has proceeded from the latter; and that this derivation is going on now and will always continue; i. e., the principles of the state must be regarded as valid in and for themselves, which can only be in so far as they are recognised as determinate manifestations of the divine nature. The form of religion, therefore, decides that of the state and its constitution. The latter acually originated in the partcular religion adopted by the nation; so that, in fact, the Athenian or the Roman state was possible only in connection with the specific form of heathenism existing among the respective peoples; just as a Catholic state has a spirit and constitution different from that of a Protestant one.

If that outcry—that urging and striving for the implantation of religion in the community—were an utterance of anguish and a call for help, as it often seems to be, expressing the danger of religion having vanished, or being about to vanish entirely from the state,—that would be fearful indeed,—worse, in fact, than this outcry supposes; for it implies the belief in a resource against the evil, viz., the implantation and inculcation of religion; whereas religion is by no means a thing to be so produced; its *self-production* (and there can be no other) lies much deeper.

Another and opposite folly which we meet with in our time, is that of pretending to invent and carry out political constitutions independently of religion. The Catholic confession, although sharing the Christian name with the Protestant, does not concede to the state an inherent justice and morality,—a concession which in the Protestant principle is fundamental. This tearing away of the political morality of the constitution from its natural connection, is necessary to the genius of that religion, inasmuch as it does not recognise justice and morality as independent and substantial. But thus excluded from intrinsic worth,—torn away from their last refuge—the sanctuary of conscience—the calm retreat where religion has its abode,—the principles and institutions of political legislation are destitute of a real centre, to the same degree as they are compelled to remain abstract and indefinite.

Summing up what has been said of the state, we find that we have been led to call its vital principle, as actuating the individuals who compose it,—morality. The state, its laws, its arrangements, constitute the rights of its members; its natural features, its mountains, air, and waters, are *their* country, their fatherland, their outward material property; the history of this state, *their* deeds; what their ancestors have produced, belongs to them and lives in their memory. All is their possession, just as they are possessed by it; for it constitutes their existence, their being.

Their imagination is occupied with the ideas thus presented, while the adoption of these laws, and of a fatherland so conditioned is the expression of their will. It is this matured totality which thus constitutes *one* being, the spirit of *one* people. To it the individual members belong; each unit is the son of his nation, and at the same time—in as far as the state to which he belongs is undergoing development—the son of his age. None remains behind it, still less advances beyond it. This spiritual being (the spirit of his time) is his; he is a representative of it; it is that in which he originated, and in which he lives. Among the Athenians the word Athens had a double import; suggesting primarily, a complex of political institutions, but no less, in the second place, that goddess who represented the spirit of the people and its unity.

This spirit of a people is a *determinate* and particular spirit, and is, as just stated, further modified by the degree of its historical development. This spirit, then, constitutes the basis and substance of those other forms of a nation's consciousness, which have been noticed. For Spirit in its self-consciousness must become an object of contemplation to itself, and objectivity involves, in the first instance, the rise of differences which make up a total of distinct spheres of objective spirit; in the same way as the soul exists only as the complex of its faculties, which in their form of concentration in a simple unity produce that soul. It is thus *One In-*

dividuality which, presented in its essence as God, is honoured and enjoyed in *religion;* which is exhibited as an object of sensuous contemplation in *art;* and is apprehended as an intellectual conception, in *philosophy.* In virtue of the original identity of their essence, purport, and object, these various forms are inseparably united with the spirit of the state. Only in connection with this particular religion, can this particular political constitution exist; just as in such or such a state, such or such a philosophy or order of art.

The remark next in order is, that each particular national genius is to be treated as only one individual in the process of universal history. For that history is the exhibition of the divine, absolute development of Spirit in its highest forms,—that gradation by which it attains its truth and consciousness of itself. The forms which these grades of progress assume are the characteristic "national spirits" of history; the peculiar tenor of their moral life, of their government, their art, religion, and science. To realise these grades is the boundless impulse of the World-Spirit—the goal of its irresistible urging; for this division into organic members, and the full development of each, is its Idea.—Universal history is exclusively occupied with shewing how Spirit comes to a recognition and adoption of the truth: the dawn of knowledge appears; it begins to discover salient principles, and at last it arrives at full consciousness.

Having, therefore, learned the abstract characteristics of the nature of Spirit, the means which it uses to realize its Idea, and the shape assumed by it in its complete realisation in phenomenal existence—namely, the state—nothing further remains for this introductory section to contemplate but the course of the world's history.

The mutations which history presents have been long characterised in the general, as an advance to something better, more perfect. The changes that take place in nature—how infinitely manifold soever they may be—exhibit only a perpetually self-repeating cycle; in nature there happens "nothing new under the sun," and the multiform play of its phenomena so far induces a feeling of *ennui;* only in those changes which take place in the region of Spirit does anything new arise. This peculiarity in the world of mind has indicated in the case of man an altogether different destiny from that of merely natural objects—in which we find always one and the same stable character, to which all change reverts;—namely, a *real* capacity for change, and that for the better, —an impulse of *perfectibility*. This principle, which reduces change itself under a law, has met with an unfavorable reception from religions—such as the Catholic—and from states claiming as their just right a stereotyped, or at least a stable position. If the mutability of worldly things in general—political constitutions, for instance—is conceded, either religion (as the religion of *truth*) is absolutely excepted, or the difficulty escaped by ascribing changes, revolutions, and abrogations of immaculate theories and institutions, to accidents or imprudence,—but principally to the levity and evil passions of man. The principle of perfectibility indeed is almost as indefinite a term as mutability in general; it is without scope or goal, and has no standard by which to estimate the changes in question: the improved, more perfect, state of things towards which it professedly tends is altogether undetermined.

The principle of *development* involves also the existence of a latent germ of being—a capacity or potentiality striving to actualize itself. This formal conception finds actual existence in Spirit; which has the history of the world for its theatre, its possession, and the sphere of its actualization. It is not of such a nature as to be tossed to and fro amid the superficial play of accidents, but is rather the absolute arbiter of things; entirely unmoved by contingencies, which, indeed, it applies and manages for its own purposes. Development, however, is also a property of organized natural objects. Their existence presents itself, not as an exclusively dependent one, subjected to external changes, but as one which expands itself in virtue of an external unchangeable principle; a simple essence,—whose existence, *i. e.*, as a germ, is primarily simple,—but which subsequently develops a variety of parts, that become involved with other objects, and consequently live through a continuous process of changes;—a process nevertheless, that results in the very contrary of change, and is even transformed into a *vis conservatrix* of the organic principle, and the form embodying it. Thus the organized *individuum* produces itself; it expands itself *actually* to what it was always *potentially:* So Spirit is only that which it attains by its own efforts; it makes itself *actually* what it always was *potentially*.—That development (of *natural organisms*) takes place in a direct, unopposed, unhindered manner. Between the notion and its actualization—the essential constitution of the original germ and the conformity to it of the existence derived from it—no disturbing influence can intrude. But in relation to Spirit it is quite otherwise. The actualization of *its* idea is mediated by consciousness and will; these very faculties are, in the first instance, sunk in their primary *merely* natural life; the first object and goal of their striving is the realisation of their merely natural destiny,—but which, since it is Spirit that animates it, is possessed of vast attractions and displays great power and [moral] richness. Thus Spirit is at war with itself; it has to overcome itself as its most formidable obstacle. That development which in the sphere of nature is a peaceful growth, is in that of Spirit, a severe, a mighty conflict with itself. What Spirit really strives for is the realisation of its ideal being; but in doing so, it hides that goal from its own vision, and is proud and well satisfied in this alienation from it.

Its expansion, therefore, does not present the harmless tranquillity of mere growth, as does that of organic life, but a stern reluctant working against itself. It exhibits, moreover, not the mere formal conception of development, but the attainment of a definite result. The goal of attainment we determined at the outset: it is Spirit in its *completeness*, in its essential nature, *i. e.*, freedom. This is the fundamental object, and therefore also the leading principle of the development,—that whereby it receives meaning and importance (as in the Roman history, Rome is the object—consequently that which directs our consideration of the facts related); as, conversely, the phenomena of the process have resulted from this principle alone, and only as referred to it, possess a sense and value. There are many considerable periods in history in which this development seems to have been intermitted; in which, we might rather say, the whole enormous gain of previous culture appears to have been entirely lost; after which, unhappily, a new commencement has been necessary, made in the hope of recovering—by the assistance of some remains saved from the wreck of a former civilization, and by dint of a renewed incalculable expenditure of strength and time,—one of the regions which had been an ancient possession of that civilization. We behold also *continued* processes of growth; structures and systems of culture in particular spheres, rich in kind, and well developed in every direction. The merely formal and indeterminate view of development in general can neither assign to one form of expansion superiority over the other, nor render comprehensible the object of that decay of older periods of growth; but must regard such occurrences,—or, to speak more particularly, the retrocessions they exhibit,—as external contingencies; and can only judge of particular modes of development from indeterminate points of view; which—since the development as such, is all in all—are relative and not absolute goals of attainment.

Universal history exhibits the *gradation* in the development of that principle whose substantial *purport* is the consciousness of freedom. The analysis of the successive grades, in their abstract form, belongs to logic; in their concrete aspect to the philosophy of spirit. Here it is sufficient to state that the first step in the process presents that immersion of Spirit in nature which has been already referred to; the second shows it as advancing to the consciousness of its freedom. But this initial separation from nature is imperfect and partial, since it is derived immediately from the merely natural state, is consequently related to it, and is still encumbered with it as an essentially connected element. The third step is the elevation of the soul from this still limited and special form of freedom to its pure universal form; that state in which the spiritual essence attains the consciousness and feeling of itself. These grades are the ground-principles of the general process; but how each of them on the other hand involves within *itself* a process of formation,—constituting the links in a dialectic of transition,—to particularise this may be reserved for the sequel.

Here we have only to indicate that Spirit begins with a germ of infinite possibility, but *only* possibility,—containing its substantial existence in an undeveloped form, as the object and goal which it reaches only in its resultant—full actuality. In actual existence progress appears as an advancing from the imperfect to the more perfect; but the former must not be understood abstractly as *only* the imperfect, but as something which involves the very opposite of itself—the so-called perfect—as a *germ* or impulse. So—reflectively, at least—*possibility* points to something destined to become actual; the Aristotelian *dúnamis* is also *potentia,* power and might. Thus the imperfect, as involving its opposite, is a contradiction, which certainly exists, but which is continually annulled and solved; the instinctive movement—the inherent impulse in the life of the soul—to break through the rind of mere nature, sensuousness, and that which is alien to it, and to attain to the light of consciousness, *i. e.* to itself.

We have already made the remark how the commencement of the history of Spirit must be conceived so as to be in harmony with its idea—in its bearing on the representations that have been made of a primitive *"natural* condition," in which freedom and justice are supposed to exist, or to have existed. This was, however, nothing more than an assumption of historical existence, conceived in the twilight of theorising reflection. A pretension of quite another order,—not a mere inference of reasoning, but making the claim of historical fact, and that supernaturally confirmed, —is put forth in connection with a different view that is now widely promulgated by a certain group. This view takes up the the idea of the primitive paradisaical condition of man, which had been previously expanded by the theologians, after their fashion, —involving, *e.g.,* the supposition that God spoke with Adam in Hebrew,—but re-modelled to suit other requirements. The high authority appealed to in the first instance is the biblical narrative. But this depicts the primitive condition, partly only in the few well-known traits, but partly either as in man generically,—human nature at large,—or, so far as Adam is to be taken as an individual, and consequently one person,—as existing and completed in *this one,* or *only in one* human pair. The biblical account by no means justifies us in imagining a *people,* and an historical condition of such people, existing in that primitive form; still less does it warrant us in attributing to them the possession of a perfectly developed knowledge of God and nature. "Nature," so the fiction runs, "like a clear mirror of God's creation, had originally lain revealed and transparent to the unclouded eye of man."[1] Divine truth is imagined to have been equally manifest. It is even hinted, though left in some degree of obscurity, that in this primary condition men were in possession of an indefinitely extended and already expanded body of religious truths immediately revealed by

[1] Fr. von Schlegel, "Philosophy of History," p. 91, Bohn's Standard Library.

God. This theory affirms that all religions had their historical commencement in this primitive knowledge, and that they polluted and obscured the original truth by the monstrous creations of error and depravity; though in all the mythologies invented by error, traces of that origin and of those primitive true dogmas are supposed to be present and cognizable. An important interest, therefore, accrues to the investigation of the history of ancient peoples, that, viz., of the endeavour to trace their annals up to the point where such fragments of the primary revelation are to be met with in greater purity than lower down.[1]

We owe to the interest which has occasioned these investigations, very much that is valuable; but this investigation bears direct testimony against itself, for it would seem to be awaiting the issue of an historical demonstration of that which is presupposed by it as historically established. That advanced condition of the knowledge of God, and of other scientific, *e.g.*, astronomical knowledge (such as has been falsely attributed to the Hindoos); and the assertion that such a condition occurred at the very be-

[1] We have to thank this interest for many valuable discoveries in Oriental literature, and for a renewed study of treasures previously known, in the department of ancient Asiatic culture, mythology, religions, and history. In Catholic countries, where a refined literary taste prevails, governments have yielded to the requirements of speculative inquiry, and have felt the necessity of allying themselves with learning and philosophy. Eloquently and impressively has the Abbé Lamennais reckoned it among the criteria of the true religion, that it must be the universal—that is, catholic—and the oldest in date; and the congregation has laboured zealously and diligently in France towards rendering such assertions no longer mere pulpit tirades and authoritative dicta, such as were deemed sufficient formerly. The religion of Buddha—a god man—which has prevailed to such an enormous extent, has especially attracted attention. The Indian Timûrtis, as also the Chinese abstraction of the trinity, has furnished clearer evidence in point of subject matter. The savants, M. Abel Remusat and M. Saint Martin, on the one hand, have undertaken the most meritorious investigations in the Chinese literature, with a view to make this also a base of operations for researches in the Mongolian and, if such were possible, in the Thibetian; on the other hand, Baron von Eckstein, in his way (*i.e.*, adopting from Germany superficial physical conceptions and mannerisms, in the style of Fr. v. Schlegel, though with more geniality than the latter) in his periodical, "Le Catholique,"—has furthered the cause of that primitive Catholicism generally, and in particular has gained for the savants of the congregation the support of the government; so that it has even set on foot expeditions to the East, in order to discover there treasures still concealed; (from which further disclosures have been anticipated, respecting profound theological questions, particularly on the higher antiquity and sources of Buddhism), and with a view to promote the interest of Catholicism by this circuitous but scientifically interesting method.

ginning of history,—or that the religions of various nations were traditionally derived from it, and have developed themselves in degeneracy and depravation (as is represented in the rudely-conceived so-called "emanation system,");—all these are suppositions which neither have, nor,—if we may contrast with their arbitrary subjective origin, the true conception of history,—can attain historical confirmation.

The only consistent and worthy method which philosophical investigation can adopt, is to take up history where rationality begins to manifest itself in the actual conduct of the world's affairs (not where it is merely an undeveloped potentiality),—where a condition of things is present in which it realises itself in consciousness, will and action. The inorganic existence of Spirit—that of abstract freedom—unconscious *torpidity* in respect to good and evil (and consequently to laws), or, if we please to term it so, "blessed ignorance,"—is itself not a subject of history. *Natural,* and at the same time *religious* morality, is the piety of the *family.* In this social relation, morality consists in the members behaving towards each other *not as individuals*—possessing an independent will; not as persons. The family therefore, is excluded from that process of development in which history takes its rise. But when this self-involved spiritual unity steps beyond this circle of feeling and natural love, and first attains the consciousness of personality, we have that dark, dull centre of indifference, in which neither nature nor Spirit is open and transparent; and for which nature and Spirit can become open and transparent only by means of a further process,—a very lengthened culture of that will at length become self-conscious. Consciousness alone is clearness; and is that alone for which God (or any other existence) can be revealed. In its true form,—in absolute universality—nothing can be manifested except to consciousness made percipient of it. Freedom is nothing but the recognition and adoption of such universal substantial objects as right and law, and the production of a reality that is accordant with them—the state. Nations may have passed a long life before arriving at this their destination, and during this period, they may have attained considerable culture in some directions. This ante-historical period—consistently with what has been said—lies out of our plan; whether a real history followed it, or the peoples in question never attained a political constitution.—It is a great discovery in history—as of a new world—which has been made within rather more than the last twenty years, respecting the Sanscrit and the connection of the European languages with it. In particular, the connection of the German and Indian peoples has been demonstrated, with as much certainty as such subjects allow of. Even at the present time we know of peoples which scarcely form a society, much less a state, but that have been long known as existing; while with regard to others, which in their advanced condition excite our especial interest, tradition reaches beyond the record of the founding of the state, and they experienced many changes prior to that epoch. In the connection just referred to, between the languages of nations so widely separated, we have a result before us, which proves the diffusion of those nations from Asia as a centre, and the so dissimilar development of what had been originally related, as an incontestable fact; not *as* an inference deduced by that favourite method of combining, and reasoning from, circumstances grave and trivial, which has already enriched and will continue to enrich history with so many fictions given out as facts. But that apparently so extensive range of events lies beyond the pale of history; in fact preceded it.

In our language the term history[1] unites the objective with the subjective side, and denotes quite as much the *historia rerum gestarum,* as the *res gestae* themselves; on the other hand it comprehends not less what has *happened,* than the *narration* of what has happened. This union of the two meanings we must regard as of a higher order than mere outward accident; we must suppose historical narrations to have appeared contemporaneously with historical deeds and events. It is an internal vital principle common to both that produces them synchronously. Family memorials, patriarchal traditions, have an interest confined to the family and the clan. The uniform course of events which such a condition implies, is no subject of serious remembrance; though distinct transactions or turns of fortune, may rouse Mnemosyne to form conceptions of them,—in the same way as love and the religious emotions provoke imagination to give shape to a previously formless impulse. But it is the state which first presents subject-matter

---

[1] German, "Geschichte," from "geschehen," to happen.

that is not only *adapted* to the prose of history, but involves the production of such history in the very progress of its own being. Instead of merely subjective mandates on the part of government, —sufficing for the needs of the moment,—a community that is acquiring a stable existence, and exalting itself into a state, requires formal commands and laws—comprehensive and universally binding prescriptions; and thus produces a record as well as an interest concerned with intelligent, definite—and, in their results—lasting transactions and occurrences; on which Mnemosyne, for the behoof of the perennial object of the formation and constitution of the state, is impelled to confer perpetuity. Profound sentiments generally, such as that of love, as also religious intuition and its conceptions, are in themselves complete—constantly present and satisfying; but that outward existence of a political constitution which is enshrined in its rational laws and customs, is an *imperfect* present; and cannot be thoroughly understood without a knowledge of the past.

The periods—whether we suppose them to be centuries or millennia—that were passed by nations before history was written among them,—and which may have been filled with revolutions, nomadic wanderings, and the strangest mutations,—are on that very account destitute of *objective* history, because they present no *subjective* history, no annals. We need not suppose that the records of such periods have accidentally perished; rather, because they were not possible, do we find them wanting. Only in a state cognizant of laws, can distinct transactions take place, accompanied by such a clear consciousness of them as supplies the ability and suggests the necessity of an enduring record. It strikes every one, in beginning to form an acquaintance with the treasures of Indian literature, that a land so rich in intellectual products, and those of the profoundest order of thought, has no history; and in this respect contrasts most strongly with China—an empire possessing one so remarkable, one going back to the most ancient times. India has not only ancient books relating to religion, and splendid poetical productions, but also ancient codes; the existence of which latter kind of literature has been mentioned as a condition necessary to the origination of history—and yet history itself is not found. But in that country the impulse of organization, in beginning to develop social distinctions, was immediately petrified in the merely natural classfication according to *castes;* so that although the laws concern themselves with civil rights, they make even these dependent on natural distinctions; and are especially occupied with determining the relations (wrongs rather than rights) of those classes towards each other, *i.e.,* the privileges of the higher over the lower. Consequently, the element of morality is banished from the pomp of Indian life and from its political institutions. Where that iron bondage of distinctions derived from nature prevails, the connection of society is nothing but wild arbitrariness,—transient activity,—or rather the play of violent emotion without any goal of advancement or development. Therefore no intelligent reminiscence, no object for Mnemosyne presents itself; and imagination—confused though profound—expatiates in a region, which, to be capable of history, must have had an aim within the domain of actuality, and, at the same time, of substantial freedom.

Since such are the conditions indispensable to a history, it has happened that the growth of families to clans, of clans to peoples, and their local diffusion consequent upon this numerical increase, —a series of facts which itself suggests so many instances of social complication, war, revolution, and ruin,—a process which is so rich in interest, and so comprehensive in extent,—has occurred without giving rise to history: moreover, that the extension and organic growth of the empire of articulate sounds has itself remained voiceless and dumb,—a stealthy, unnoticed advance. It is a fact revealed by philological monuments, that languages, during a rude condition of the nations that have spoken them, have been very highly developed; that the human understanding occupied this theoretical region with great ingenuity and completeness. For grammar, in its extended and consistent form, is the work of thought, which makes its categories distinctly visible therein. It is, moreover, a fact, that with advancing social and political civilization, this systematic completeness of intelligence suffers attrition, and language thereupon becomes poorer and ruder: a singular phenomenon—that the progress towards a more highly intellectual condition, while expanding and cultivating rationality, should disregard that intelligent amplitude and expressiveness—should find it an obstruction and contrive to do without it. Speech is the act of theoretic intelligence in a special sense; it is its *external* manifestation. Exercises of memory and imagination, without language, are direct, [non-speculative] manifestations. But this act of theoretic intelligence itself, as also its subsequent development, and the more concrete class of facts connected with it,—viz. the spreading of peoples over the earth, their separation from each other, their comminglings and wanderings—remain involved in the obscurity of a voiceless past. They are not acts of will becoming self-conscious—of freedom, mirroring itself in a phenomenal form, and creating for itself a proper actuality. Not partaking of this element of substantial, veritable existence, those nations—notwithstanding the develepment of language among them—never advanced to the possession of a *history*. The rapid growth of language, and the progress and dispersion of nations, assume importance and interest for concrete Reason, only when they have come in contact with states, or begin to form political constitutions themselves.

After these remarks, relating to the form of the *commencement* of the world's history, and to that ante-historical period which must be excluded from it, we have to state the direction of its course: though here only formally. The further definition of the subject in the concrete, comes under the head of arrangement.

Universal history—as already demonstrated—shews the development of the consciousness of freedom on the part of Spirit, and of the consequent realization of that freedom. This development implies a gradation—a series of increasingly adequate expressions or manifestations of freedom, which result from its Idea. The logical, and—as still more prominent—the *dialectical* nature of the Idea in general, viz. that it is self-determined—that it assumes successive forms which it successively transcends; and by this very process of transcending its earlier stages, gains an affirmative, and, in fact, a richer and more concrete shape;—this necessity of its nature, and the necessary series of pure abstract forms which the Idea successively assumes—is exhibited in the department of logic. Here we need adopt only one of its results, viz. that every step in the process, as differing from any other, has its determinate peculiar principle. In history this principle is idiosyncrasy of Spirit—peculiar national genius. It is within the limitations of this idiosyncrasy that the spirit of the nation, concretely manifested, expresses every aspect of its consciousness and will—the whole cycle of its realization. Its religion, its polity, its ethics, its legislation, and even its science, art, and mechanical skill, all bear its stamp. These special peculiarities find their key in that common peculiarity,—the particular principle that characterises a people; as, on the other hand, in the facts which history presents in detail, that common characteristic principle may be detected. That such or such a specific quality constitutes the peculiar genius of a people, is the element of our inquiry which must be derived from experience, and historically proved. To accomplish this, pre-supposes not only a disciplined faculty of abstraction, but an intimate acquaintance with the Idea. The investigator must be familiar *à priori* (if we like to call it so), with the whole circle of conceptions to which the principles in question belong—just as Keppler (to name the most illustrious example in this mode of philosophizing) must have been familiar *à priori* with ellipses, with cubes and squares, and with ideas of their relations, before he could discover, from the empirical data, those immortal "laws" of his, which are none other than forms of thought pertaining to those classes of conceptions. He who is unfamiliar with the science that embraces these abstract elementary conceptions, is as little capable —though he may have gazed on the firmament and the motions of the celestial bodies for a life-time—of *understanding* those laws, as of *discovering* them. From this want of acquaintance with the ideas that relate to the development of freedom, proceed a part of those objections which are brought against the philosophical consideration of a science usually regarded as one of mere experience; the so-called *à priori* method, and the attempt to insinuate ideas into the empirical data of history, being the chief points in the indictment. Where this deficiency exists, such conceptions appear alien—not lying within the object of investigation. To minds whose training has been narrow and merely subjective,— which have not an acquaintance and familiarity with ideas,—they are something strange—not embraced in the notion and conception of the subject which their limited intellect forms. Hence the statement that philosophy does not understand such sciences. It must, indeed, allow that it has not that kind of understanding which is the prevailing one in the domain of those sciences that it does not proceed according to the categories of such understanding, but according to the categories of *Reason*—though at the same time recognising that Understanding, and its true value and position. It must be observed that in this very process of scientific *understanding*, it is of importance that the essential should be distinguished and brought into relief in contrast with the so-called non-essential. But in order to render this possible, we must know what *is essential;* and that is—in view of the history of the world in general—the consciousness of freedom, and the phases which this consciousness assumes in developing itself. The bearing of historical facts on this category, is their bearing on the truly essential. Of the difficulties stated, and the opposition exhibited to comprehensive conceptions in science, part must be referred to the inability to grasp and understand ideas. If in natural history some monstrous hybird growth is alleged as an objection to the recognition of clear and indubitable classes or species, a sufficient reply is furnished by a sentiment often vaguely urged,—that "the exception confirms the rule;" *i.e.,* that is the part of a well-defined rule, to shew the conditions in which it applies, or the deficiency or hybridism of cases that are abnormal. Mere nature is too weak to keep its genera and species pure, when conflicting with alien elementary influences. If, *e.g.,* on considering the human organization in its concrete aspect, we assert that brain, heart, and so forth are essential to its organic life, some miserable abortion may be adduced, which has on the whole the human form, or parts of it,—which has been conceived in a human body and has breathed after birth therefrom,—in which nevertheless no brain and no heart is found. If such an instance is quoted against the general conception of a human being—the objector persisting in using the name, coupled with a superficial idea respecting it—it can be proved that a real, concrete human being, is a truly different object; that such a being must have a brain in its head, and a heart in its breast.

A similar process of reasoning is adopted, in reference to the correct assertion that genius, talent, moral virtues, and sentiments, and piety, may be found in every zone, under all political constitutions and conditions; in confirmation of which examples are forthcoming in abundance. If in this assertion, the accompanying distinctions are intended to be repudiated as unimportant or non-essential, reflection evidently limits itself to abstract categories; and ignores the particulars of the object in question, which certainly fall under no principle recognised by such categories. That intellectual position which adopts such merely formal points of view, presents a vast field for ingenious questions, erudite views, and striking comparisons; for profound seeming reflections and declamations, which may be rendered so much the more brilliant in proportion as the subject they refer to is indefinite, and are susceptible of new and varied forms in inverse proportion to the importance of the results that can be gained from them, and the certainty and rationality of their issues. Under such an aspect the well known Indian epopees may be compared with the Homeric; perhaps—since it is the vastness of the imagination by which poetical genius proves itself—preferred to them; as, on account of the similarity of single strokes of imagination in the attributes of the divinities, it has been contended that Greek mythological forms may be recognised in those of India. Similarly the Chinese philosophy, as adopting the One [tōen] as its basis, has been alleged to be the same as at a later period appeared as Eleatic philosophy and as the Spinozistic system; while in virtue of its expressing itself also in abstract numbers and lines, Pythagorean and Christian principles have been supposed to be detected in it. Instances of bravery and indomitable courage,—traits of magnanimity, of self-denial, and self-sacrifice, which are found among the most savage and the most pusillanimous nations,—are regarded as sufficient to support the view that in these nations as much of social virtue and morality may be found as in the most civilized Christian states, or even more. And on this ground a doubt has been suggested whether in the progress of history and of general culture mankind have become better; whether their morality has been increased,—morality being regarded in a subjective aspect and view, as founded on what the agent holds to be right and wrong, good and evil; not on a principle which is considered to be in and for itself right and good, or a crime and evil, or on a particular religion believed to be the true one.

We may fairly decline on this occasion the task of tracing the formalism and error of such a view, and establishing the true principles of morality, or rather of social virtue in opposition to false morality. For the history of the world occupies a higher ground than that on which morality has properly its position, which is personal character,—the conscience of individuals,—their particular will and mode of action; *these* have a value, imputation, reward or punishment proper to themselves. What the absolute aim of Spirit requires and accomplishes,—what providence does,— transcends the obligations, and the liability to imputation and the ascription of good or bad motives, which attach to individuality in virtue of its social relations. They who on moral grounds, and consequently with noble intention, have resisted that which the advance of the spiritual Idea makes necessary, stand higher in moral worth than those whose crimes have been turned into the means—under the direction of a superior principle—of realising the purposes of that principle. But in such revolutions both parties generally stand within the limits of the same circle of transient and corruptible existence. Consequently it is only a formal rectitude—deserted by the living Spirit and by God—which those who stand upon ancient right and order maintain. The deeds of great men, who are the Individuals of the world's history, thus appear not only justified in view of that intrinsic result of which they were not conscious, but also from the point of view occupied by the secular moralist. But looked at from this point, moral claims that are irrelevant, must not be brought into collision with world-historical deeds and their accomplishment. The litany of private virtues—modesty, humility, philanthropy and forbear- ance—must be raised against them. The history of the world might, on principle, entirely ignore the circle within which morality and the so much talked of distinction between the moral and the politic lies—not only in abstaining from judgments, for the principles in- volved, and the necessary reference of the deeds in question to those principles, are a sufficient judgment of them—but in leaving individuals quite out of view and unmentioned. What it has to record is the activity of the spirit of peoples, so that the individual forms which that spirit has assumed in the sphere of outward actuality, might be left to the delineation of special histories.

The same kind of formalism avails itself in its peculiar manner of the indefiniteness attaching to genius, poetry, and even philoso- phy; thinks equally that it finds these everywhere. We have here products of reflective thought; and it is familiarity with those general conceptions which single out and name real distinctions without fathoming the true depth of the matter,—that we call culture. It is something merely formal, inasmuch as it aims at nothing more than the analysis of the subject, whatever it be, into its constituent parts, and the comprehension of these in their logical definitions and forms. It is not the free universality of conception necessary for making an abstract principle the object of consciousness. Such a consciousness of thought itself, and of its forms isolated from a particular object, is philosophy. This has, indeed, the condition of its existence in culture; that condition being the taking up of the object of thought, and at the same time clothing it with the form of universality, in such a way that the material content and the form given by the intellect are held in an inseparable state;—inseparable to such a degree that the object in question—which, by the analysis of one conception into a multitude of conceptions, is enlarged to an incalculable treasure of thought—is regarded as a merely empirical datum in whose formation thought has had no share.

But it is quite as much an act of thought—of the understanding in particular—to embrace in one simple conception object which of itself comprehends a concrete and large significance (as earth, man,—Alexander or Caesar) and to designate it by one word,—as to *resolve* such a conception—duly to isolate in idea the conceptions which it contains, and to give them particular names. And in reference to the view which gave occasion to what has just been said, thus much will be clear,—that as reflection produces what we include under the general terms genius, talent, art, science,— formal culture on every grade of intellectual development, not only can, but must grow, and attain a mature bloom, while the grade in question is developing itself to a state, and on this basis of civilization is advancing to intelligent reflection and to general forms of thought,—as in laws, so in regard to all else. In the very association of men in a state, lies the necessity of formal culture— consequently of the rise of the sciences and of a cultivated poetry and art generally. The arts designated "plastic," require besides, even in their technical aspects, the civilized association of men. The poetic art—which has less need of external requirements and means, and which has the element of immediate existence, the voice, as its material—steps forth with great boldness and with matured expression, even under the conditions presented by a people not yet united in a political combination; since, as re-marked above, language attains on its own particular ground a high intellectual development, prior to the commencement of civilization.

Philosophy also must make its appearance where political life exists; since that in virtue of which any series of phenomena is reduced within the spheres of culture, as above stated, is the form strictly proper to thought; and thus for philosophy, which is nothing other than the consciousness of this form itself—the thinking of thinking,—the material of which its edifice is to be constructed, is already prepared by *general* culture. If in the development of the state itself, periods are necessitated which impel the soul of nobler natures to seek refuge from the present in ideal regions,—in order to find in them that harmony with itself which it can no longer enjoy in the discordant real world, where the reflective intelligence attacks all that is holy and deep, which had been spontaneously inwrought into the religion, laws and manners of nations, and brings them down and attenuates them to abstract godless generalities,—thought will be compelled to become thinking Reason, with the view of effecting in its own element, the restoration of its principles from the ruin to which they had been brought.

We find then, it is true, among all world-historical peoples, poetry, plastic art, science, even philosophy; but not only is there a diversity in style and bearing generally, but still more remarkably in subject-matter; and this is a diversity of the most important kind, affecting the rationality of that subject-matter. It is useless for a pretentious aesthetic criticism to demand that our good pleasure should not be made to rule for the matter—the substantial part of their contents—and to maintain that it is the beautiful form as such, the grandeur of the fancy, and so forth, which fine art aims at, and which must be considered and enjoyed by a liberal taste and cultivated mind. A healthy intellect does not tolerate such abstractions, and cannot assimilate productions of the kind above referred to. Granted that the Indian epopees might be placed on a level with the Homeric, on account of a number of those qualities of form—grandeur of invention and imaginative power, liveliness of images and emotions, and beauty of diction; yet the infinite difference of matter remains; consequently one of substantial importance and involving the interest of Reason, which is immediately concerned with the consciousness of the idea of freedom, and its expression in individuals. There is not only a classical *form,* but a classical order of *subject-matter;* and in a work of art form and subject-matter are so closely united that the former can only be classical to the extent to which the latter is so. With a fantastical, indeterminate material—the *rule* is the essence of *Reason*—the form becomes measureless and formless, or mean and contracted. In the same way, in that comparison of the various systems of philosophy of which we have already spoken, the only point of importance is overlooked, namely, the character of that unity which is found alike in the Chinese, the Eleatic, and the Spinozistic philosophy—the distinction between the recognition of that unity as abstract and as concrete—concrete to the extent of being a unity in and by itself—a unity synonymous with Spirit. But that co-ordination proves that it recognises only such an abstract unity; so that while it gives judgment respecting philosophy, it is ignorant of that very point which constitutes the interest of philosophy.

But there are also spheres which, amid all the variety that is presented in the substantial content of a particular form of culture, remain the same. The difference above mentioned in art, science, philosophy, concerns the thinking Reason and freedom, which is the self-consciousness of the former, and which has the same one root with thought. As it is not the brute, but only the man that thinks, he only—and only because he is a thinking being—has freedom. *His* consciousness imports this, that the individual comprehends itself as a *person,* that is, recognises itself in its single existence as possessing universality,—as capable of abstraction from, and of surrendering all speciality; and, therefore, as inherently infinite. Consequently those spheres of intelligence which lie beyond the limits of this consciousness are a common ground among those substantial distinctions. Even morality, which is so intimately connected with the consciousness of freedom, can be very pure while that consciousness is still wanting; as far, that is to say, as it expresses duties and rights only as *objective* commands; or even as far as it remains satisfied with the merely formal elevation of the soul—the surrender of the sensual, and of all sensual motives—in a purely negative, self-denying fashion. The *Chinese* morality—since Europeans have become acquainted with it and with the writings of Confucius—has obtained the greatest praise and proportionate attention from those who are familiar with the Christian morality. There is a similar acknowledgement of the sublimity with which the *Indian* religion and poetry, (a statement that must, however, be limited to the higher kind), but especially the Indian philosophy, expatiate upon and demand the removal and sacrifice of sensuality. Yet both these nations are, it must be confessed, *entirely* wanting in the essential consciousness of the idea of freedom. To the Chinese their moral laws are just like natural laws,—external, positive commands,—claims established by force,—compulsory duties or rules of courtesy towards each other. Freedom, through which alone the essential determinations of Reason become moral sentiments, is wanting. Morality is a political affair, and its laws are administered by officers of government and legal tribunals. Their treatises upon it (which are not law books, but are certainly addressed to the subjective will and individual disposition) read,—as do the moral writings of the Stoics,— like a string of commands stated as necessary for realising the goal of happiness; so that it seems to be left free to men, on their part, to adopt such commands,—to observe them or not; while the conception of an abstract subject, "a wise man" [sapiens] forms the culminating point among the Chinese, as also among the Stoic moralists. Also in the Indian doctrine of the renunciation of the sensuality of desires and earthly interests, positive moral freedom is not the object and end, but the annihilation of consciousness— spiritual and even physical privation of life.

It is the concrete spirit of a people which we have distinctly to recognise, and since it is Spirit it can only be comprehended spiritually, that is, by thought. It is this alone which takes the lead in all the deeds and tendencies of that people, and which is occupied in realising itself,—in satisfying its ideal and becoming self-conscious,—for its great business is self-production. But for spirit, the highest attianment is self-knowledge; an advance not only to the *intuition*, but to the *thought*—the clear conception of itself. This it must and is also destined to accomplish; but the accomplishment is at the same time its dissolution, and the rise of another spirit, another world-historical people, another epoch of universal history. This transition and connection leads us to the connection of the whole—the idea of the world's history as such—which we have now to consider more closely, and of which we have to give a representation.

History in general is therefore the development of Spirit in *time,* as nature is the development of the Idea in *space.*

If then we cast a glance over the world's history generally, we see a vast picture of changes and transactions; of infinitely manifold forms of peoples, states, individuals, in unresting succession. Everything that can enter into and interest the soul of man—all our sensibility to *goodness, beauty, and greatness*—is called into play. On every hand aims are adopted and pursued, which we recognise, whose accomplishment we desire—we hope and fear for them. In all these occurrences and changes we behold human action and suffering predominant; everywhere something akin to ourselves, and therefore everywhere something that excites our interest for or against. Sometimes it attracts us by beauty, freedom, and rich variety, sometimes by energy such as enables even vice to make itself interesting. Sometimes we see the more comprehensive mass of some general interest advancing with comparative slowness, and subsequently sacrified to an infinite complication of trifling circumstances, and so dissipated into atoms. Then, again, with a vast expenditure of power a trivial result is produced; while from what appears unimportant a tremendous issue proceeds. On every hand there is the motliest throng of events drawing us within the circle of its interest, and when one combination vanishes another immediately appears in its place.

The general thought—the category which first presents itself in this restless mutation of individuals and peoples, existing for a time and then vanishing—is that of *change* at large. The sight of the ruins of some ancient sovereignty directly leads us to contemplate this thought of change in its negative aspect. What traveller among the ruins of Carthage, of Palmyra, Persepolis, or Rome, has not been stimulated by reflections on the transiency of kingdoms and men, and to sadness at the thought of a vigorous and rich life now departed—a sadness which does not expend itself on personal losses and the uncertainty of one's own undertakings, but is a disinterested sorrow at the decay of a splendid and highly cultured national life! But the next consideration which allies itself with that of change, is, that change while it imports dissolution, involves at the same time the rise of a *new life*—that while death is the issue of life, life is also the issue of death. This is a grand conception; one which the Oriental thinkers attained, and which is perhaps the highest in their metaphysics. In the idea of *metempsychosis* we find it evolved in its relation to individual existence; but a myth more generally known, is that of the *Phoenix* as a type of the life of *nature;* eternally preparing for itself its funeral pile, and consuming itself upon it; but so that from its ashes is produced the new, renovated, fresh life. But this image is only Asiatic; oriental not occidental. Spirit—consuming the envelope of its existence—does not merely pass into another envelope, nor rise rejuvenescent from the ashes of its previous form; it comes forth exalted, glorified, a purer spirit. It certainly makes war upon itself—consumes its own existence; but in this very destruction it works up with existence into a new form, and each successive phase becomes in its turn a material, working on which it exalts itself to a new grade.

If we consider Spirit in this aspect—regarding its changes not merely as rejuvenescent transitions, *i.e.,* returns to the same form, but rather as manipulations of itself, by which it multiplies the material for future endeavours—we see it exerting itself in a variety of modes and directions; developing its powers and gratifying its desires in a variety which is inexhaustible; because every one of its creations, in which it has already found gratification, meets it anew as material, and is a new stimulus to plastic activity. The abstract conception of mere change gives place to the thought of Spirit manifesting, developing, and perfecting its powers in every direction which its manifold nature can follow. What powers it inherently possesses we learn from the variety of products and formations which it originates. In this pleasurable activity, it has to do only with itself. As involved with the conditions of mere nature—internal and external—it will indeed meet in these not only opposition and hindrance, but will often see its endeavours thereby fail; often sink under the complications in which it is entangled either by nature or by itself. But in such case it perishes in fulfilling its own destiny and proper function, and even thus exhibits the spectacle of self-demonstration as spiritual activity.

The very essence of Spirit is activity; it actualizes its potentiality —makes itself its own deed, its own work—and thus becomes an object to itself; contemplates itself as an objective existence. Thus is it with the Spirit of a people: it is a Spirit having strictly defined characteristics, which erects itself into an objective world, that exists and persists in a particular religious form of worship, customs, constitution and political laws,—in the whole complex of its institutions,—in the events and transactions that make up its history. That is its work—that is what this particular nation *is*. Nations are what their deeds are. Every Englishman will say: We are the men who navigate the ocean, and have the commerce of the world; to whom the East Indies belong and their riches; who have a parliament, juries, &c.—The relation of the individual to that Spirit is that he appropriates to himself this substantial existence; that it becomes his character and capability, enabling him to have a definite place in the world—to be *something*. For he finds the being of the people to which he belongs an already established, firm world—objectively present to him—with which he has to incorporate himself. In this its work, therefore—its world—the spirit of the people enjoys its existence and finds its satisfaction.—A nation is moral—virtuous—vigorous—while it is engaged in realising its grand objects, and defends its work against external violence during the process of giving to its purposes an objective existence. The contradiction between its potential, subjective being—its inner aim and life—and its *actual* being is removed; it has attained full actuality, has itself objectively present to it. But this having been attained, the activity displayed by the Spirit of the people in question is no longer needed; it has its desire. The nation can still accomplish much in war and peace at home and abroad; but the living substantial soul itself may be said to have ceased its activity. The essential, supreme interest has consequently vanished from its life, for interest is present only where there is opposition. The nation lives the same kind of life as the individual when passing from maturity to old age,—in the enjoyment of itself,—in the satisfaction of being exactly what it desired and was able to attain. Although its imagination might have transcended that limit, it nevertheless abandoned any such aspirations as objects of *actual endeavour*, if the real world was less than favourable to their attainment—and restricted its aim by the conditions thus imposed. This mere *customary life* (the watch wound up and going on of itself) is that which brings on natural death. Custom is activity without opposition, for which there remains only a formal duration; in which the fulness and zest that originally characterised the aim of life is out of the question,—a merely external sensuous existence which has ceased to throw itself enthusiastically into its object. Thus perish individuals, thus perish peoples by a natural death; and though the latter may continue in being, it is an existence without intellect or vitality; having no need of its institutions, because the need for them is satisfied,—a political nullity and tedium. In order that a truly universal interest may arise, the spirit of a people must advance to the adoption of some new purpose: but whence can this new purpose originate? It would be a higher, more comprehensive conception of itself—a transcending of its principle—but this very act would involve a principle of a new order, a new national spirit.

Such a new principle does in fact enter into the spirit of a people that has arrived at full development and self-realization; it dies not a simply natural death,—for it is not a mere single individual, but a spiritual, generic life; in its case natural death appears to imply destruction through its own agency. The reason of this difference from the single natural individual, is that the spirit of a people exists as a *genus,* and consequently carries within it its own negation, in the very generality which characterises it. A people can only die a violent death when it has become naturally dead in itself, as *e.g.,* the German imperial cities, the German imperial constitution.

It is not of the nature of the all-pervading Spirit to die this merely natural death; it does not simply sink into the senile life of mere custom, but—as being a national spirit belonging to universal history—attains to the consciousness of what its work is; it attains to a conception of itself. In fact, it is world-historical only in so far as a *universal principle* has lain in its fundamental element,—in its grand aim: only so far is the work which such a spirit produces, a moral, political organization. If it be mere desires that impel nations to activity, such deeds pass over without leaving a trace; or their traces are only ruin and destruction. Thus, it was first Chronos—Time—that ruled; the Golden Age, without moral products; and what was produced—the offspring of that Chronos—was devoured by it. It was Jupiter—from whose head Minerva sprang, and to whose circle of divinities belong Apollo and the Muses—that first put a constraint upon time, and set a bound to its principle of decadence. He is the political god, who produced a moral work—the state.

In the very element of an achievement the quality of generality, of thought, is contained; without thought it has no objectivity; that is its basis. The highest point in the development of a people is this,—to have gained a conception of its life and condition,—to have reduced its laws, its idea of justice and morality to a science; for in this unity [of the objective and subjective] lies the most intimate unity that Spirit can attain to in and with itself. In its work it is employed in rendering itself an object of its own contemplation; but it cannot develop itself objectively in its essential nature, except in *thinking* itself.

At this point, then, Spirit is acquainted with its principles—the general character of its acts. But at the same time, in virtue of its very generality, this work of thought is different in point of form from the actual achievements of the national genius, and from the vital agency by which those achievements have been performed. We have then before us a *real* and an *ideal* existence of the spirit of the nation. If we wish to gain the general idea and conception of what the Greeks were, we find it in Sophocles and Aristophanes, in Thucydides and Plato. In these individuals the Greek spirit conceived and thought itself. This is the profounder kind of satisfaction which the spirit of a people attains; but it is "ideal," and distinct from its "real" activity.

At such a time, therefore, we are sure to see a people finding satisfaction in the *idea* of virtue; putting *talk* about virtue partly side by side with actual virtue, but partly in the place of it. On the other hand pure, universal thought, since its nature is universality, is apt to bring the special and spontaneous—belief, trust, customary morality—to reflect upon itself, and its primitive simplicity; to shew up the limitation with which it is fettered,—partly suggesting reasons for renouncing duties, partly itself *demanding reasons,* and the connection of such requirements with universal thought; and not finding that connection, seeking to impeach the authority of duty generally, as destitute of a sound foundation.

At the same time the isolation of individuals from each other and from the whole makes its appearance; their aggressive selfishness and vanity; their seeking personal advantage and consulting this at the expense of the state at large. That inward principle in transcending its outward manifestations is subjective also in *form* —viz., selfishness and corruption in the unbound passions and egotistic interests of men.

Zeus, therefore, who is represented as having put a limit to the devouring agency of time, and staid this transiency by having established something inherently and independently durable—Zeus and his race are themselves swallowed up, and that by the very power that produced them—the principle of thought, perception, reasoning, insight derived from rational grounds, and the requirement of such grounds.

Time is the negative element in the sensuous world. Thought is the same negativity, but it is the deepest, the infinite form of it, in which therefore all existence generally is dissolved; first *finite* existence,—*determinate*, limited form: but existence *generally*, in its objective character, is limited; it appears therefore as a mere datum—something immediate—authority;—and is either intrinsically finite and limited, or presents itself as a limit for the thinking subject, and its infinite reflection on itself [unlimited abstraction].

But first we must observe how the life which proceeds from death, is itself, on the other hand, only individual life; so that, regarding the species as the real and substantial in this vicissitude, the perishing of the individual is a regress of the species into individuality. The perpetuation of the race is, therefore, none other than the monotonous repetition of the same kind of existence. Further, we must remark how perception,—the comprehension of being by thought,—is the source and birthplace of a new, and in fact higher form, in a principle which while it preserves, dignifies its material. For thought is that *universal*—that *species* which is immortal, which preserves identity with itself. The particular form of Spirit not merely passes away in the world by natural causes in time, but is annulled in the automatic self-mirroring activity of consciousness. Because this annulling is an activity of thought, it is at the same time conservative and elevating in its operation. While then, on the one side, Spirit annuls the reality, the permanence of that which it *is*, it gains on the other side, the essence, the thought, the universal element of that which *it only was* [its transient conditions]. Its principle is no longer that immediate import and aim which it was previously, but the *essence* of that import and aim.

The result of this process is then that Spirit, in rendering itself objective and making this its being an object of thought, on the one hand destroys the determinate form of its being, on the other hand gains a comprehension of the universal element which it involves, and thereby gives a new form to its inherent principle. In virtue of this, the substantial character of the national spirit has been altered,—that is, its principle has risen into another, and in fact a higher principle.

It is of the highest importance in apprehending and comprehending history to have and to understand the thought involved in this transition. The individual traverses as a unity various grades of development, and remains the same individual; in like manner also does a people, till the Spirit which it embodies reaches the grade of universality. In this point lies the fundamental, the ideal necessity of transition. This is the soul—the essential consideration—of the philosophical comprehension of history.

Spirit is essentially the result of its own activity; its activity is the transcending of immediate, simple, unreflected existence,— the negation of that existence, and the returning into itself. We may compare it with the seed; for with this the plant begins, yet it is also the result of the plant's entire life. But the weak side of life is exhibited in the fact that the commencement and the result are disjoined from each other. Thus also is it in the life of individuals and peoples. The life of a people ripens a certain fruit; its activity aims at the complete manifestation of the principle which it embodies. But this fruit does not fall back into the bosom of the people that produced and matured it; on the contrary, it becomes a poison-draught to it. That poison-draught it cannot let alone, for it has an insatiable thirst for it: the taste of the draught is its annihilation, though at the same time the rise of a new principle.

We have already discussed the final aim of progression. The principles of the successive phases of Spirit that animate the nations in a necessitated gradation, are themselves only steps in the development of the one universal Spirit, which through them elevates and completes itself to a self-comprehending *totality*.

While we are thus concerned exclusively with the idea of Spirit, and in the history of the world regard everything as only its manifestation, we have, in traversing the past,—however extensive its periods,—only to do with what is *present;* for philosophy, as occupying itself with the true, has to do with the *eternally present.* Nothing in the past is lost for it, for the Idea is ever present; Spirit is immortal; with it there is no past, no future, but an essential *now.* This necessarily implies that the present form of Spirit comprehends within it all earlier steps. These have indeed unfolded themselves in succession independently; but what Spirit is it has always been essentially; distinctions are only the development of this essential nature. The life of the ever present Spirit is a circle of progressive embodiments, which looked at in one respect still exist beside each other, and only as looked at from another point of view appear as past. The grades which Spirit seems to have left behind it, it still possesses in the depths of its present.

Arthur Schopenhauer

Schopenhauer

ARTHUR SCHOPENHAUER has the distinction of being one of the philosophers most widely read by men of letters and men of affairs not commonly addicted to philosophy; he is also widely known among many general readers who know and care nothing for any other philosopher. His popularity is not the measure of his importance, which lies rather in the fact that he is a classic statement of romantic pessimism and romantic egoism in philosophy. He is almost alone in Western thought in having come to conclusions almost nihilistic in their despair. He is one of the first modern philosophers to have insisted upon the primacy of will over intellect, and to have combined technical arguments with wisdom of life, to have united the vocabulary of literary picturesqueness with that of theoretical analysis.

Schopenhauer has never been held in unqualified esteem by professional philosophers. Much that to the general reader seems fresh, the trained student sees as borrowed—from Kant, from Plato, from the East Indians, as Schopenhauer himself does not hesitate to point out. But though his technical contributions are secondary and derivative, his borrowings do make a fusion that constitutes unquestionably original insights, insights which such diverse spirits as Wagner and Nietzsche were quick to recognize. His emphasis on the primacy of assertive life and irrational will had their influence, too, on philosophers as various as Bergson in France and William James and John Dewey in America. And his theory of the momentary escape in the absorption in objects of timeless art has had innumerable repercussions in aesthetics and criticism.

Schopenhauer remained all his life an outsider among the professionals. Schopenhauer, born in 1788 at Danzig, was the son of a German merchant and a mother who was a popular novelist and a tempestuous lady with whom her son eventually broke off all relations. For a very brief time, he entered his father's business. After his father's death, he took a *gymnasium* course, and then a university course, and a doctor's degree. He travelled in Italy, taught unsuccessfully for a year in the University of Berlin, and retired to Frankfort-am-Main where he lived, a bachelor in a boarding house, with his dog as his chief companion, until he died at the age of seventy-two. A sharp, vain recluse with a passion for controversy but also for the truth as he saw it, he lived to see his version of the truth world-famous before his death.

That version of the truth takes its cue and borrows its technique from Kant. "The world is my idea," Schopenhauer begins. The world of appearance is a structure of objects *for* a subject, but the *structure* of the world as idea is in the form of understanding of the subject. The world appears in that union of the forms of space and time which constitute causation, and the functioning constitutes what we call the world of matter. The order of the world is the order of understanding, to which Schopenhauer gives the inclusive name of the "principle of sufficient reason," whose forms are physical, logical, mathematical, and moral. The world of appearances appears *to* a subject. The principles of understanding are subjective; they are variants of the single principle of sufficient reason or of intelligibility. But the intellect to which and for which the world as idea appears is itself secondary. The intellect itself cannot probe to the reality beyond appearances for it itself is not primary. Beyond appearances Kant had put the world of realities. But reality for Schopenhauer lies not beyond the world of objects appearing for a subject, but in that primary aspect of the self, more primary than intellect, the will. Intellect arises as the instrument of the will. In the interest of the will the intellect erects that system of appearances, that systematic illusion, the *world as idea.* To know the real, one must transcend the principle of knowing. One must retire into that indubitable urgency in the interest of which the intellect and its train of illusions—and disillusions—arises. Descartes (and before him Augustine) had found the indubitable in thinking itself. Schopenhauer finds it in will, the primary irrational tension of desire, urgency, life, apparent in its immediacy in our hungers and lusts, and attributable, justly, to all nature as its inner being—illustrated by gravitation in organic nature, by growth in plants, impulse in animals, and will in man. At whatever level it appears, it is a phase or level of what Schopenhauer in general calls Will. The reality behind appearances is its inner assertion of will. That will is one throughout nature, a will to live. It is irrational, it is blind. It is an oscillation between the pain of frustration and the ennui of fulfillment. At a certain stage intellect appears, the servant of will. The latter invents a world of objects and relations, known through intellect under the principle of sufficient reason. The world which intellect knows can never satisfy the will in whose interest both intellect and its fiction, the world, have arisen. The world as idea is both illusion and disillusion.

There are two escapes possible, one radical and permanent, the other temporary. The temporary escape is from that willful knowledge of illusion, the world of ideas, to willess contemplation of eternal objects that transcend the principle of sufficient reason, that are beyond the illusions and precariousness of time and space. These are the Platonic essences revealed to creative genius and to the temporarily absorbed lover of essences; revealed in aesthetic objects created by, *i.e.* revealed by, genius. In beholding objects of art, and there alone, one beholds willessly essences that do not change and do not disappear, for the will is quieted, and there are no fictions to disillusion one. The escape to art is always temporary. For though the objects of art are timeless essences, the will is suspended only for the nonce. One returns to the tensions

of the will and of the world. The radical escape is that of
saintliness. Deny the will altogether and the world, in whose
interest and to whose discomfiture it has arisen, vanishes also.
The assertion of the will is the assertion of a world to satisfy
it. Deny the will; the world disappears. Schopenhauer recognizes the paradox: to deny the will may seem itself to be an
act of will. But denial means for him a relaxation, a lapse, a
surcease, into Nirvana. This radical relinquishment is possible only to a saint and through the vision opened by saintliness. The first step is through sympathy: the recognition in
other wills of the unanimity of will, its singleness in nature,
and its bonds of sympathy in suffering and in futility or
doom. Sympathy is the first abdication of assertiveness; it is
the first step toward the merging of individual wills with absolute *will*. The second step, open, Schopenhauer admits,
only to truly saintly spirits, is that of morally piercing
through the illusion of willfulness altogether, recognizing the
blindness and irrationality of the will itself wherever it appears, seeing, as the Buddhists do, through the veil of illusion,
and recognizing that save for the will there would be no
illusion, no hunger, no ennui, no suffering, no world. Nothingness would remain, and peace.

Much of Western philosophy has been devoted to a dialectical proof that this is the best of all possible worlds.
Philosophy has been the official certification of the established
disorder as essentially order and harmony, a proof of good
paramount in the midst of evil. Not the least of Schopenhauer's distinctiveness lies in his facing the fact of evil, and
finding the good life only in escaping life itself, the radical
source of evil. His is the only secular philosophy in the
Western world that has had a theory of redemption and salvation without recourse to the theological. But not without
recourse to mythology, for the Will to which he refers as the
source of all evil is a metaphysical creation of his own. In
terms of that creation, he has much to say of realistic and
romantic insight about good and evil, nature and art. And

what he called Will in absolute terms was an objectification of those aspects of desire, impulse, and action which the intellectualistic tradition in Western philosophy had hitherto largely ignored. In the hands of the biologists and pragmatists, the will, less metaphysical than in Schopenhauer, was to receive increasing attention. The origins of that attention are in Schopenhauer.

The World as Will and Idea

First Book
The World As Idea

First Aspect

The Idea Subordinated to the Principle of Sufficient Reason: The Object of Experience and Science

11 "THE world is my idea":—this is a truth which holds good for everything that lives and knows, though man alone can bring it into reflective and abstract consciousness. If he really does this, he has attained to philosophical wisdom. It then becomes clear and certain to him that what he knows is not a sun and an earth, but only an eye that sees a sun, a hand that feels an earth; that the world which surrounds him is there only as idea, *i.e.,* only in relation to something else, the consciousness, which is himself. If any truth can be asserted *a priori,* it is this: for it is the expression of the most general form of all possible and thinkable experience: a form which is more general than time, or space, or causality, for they all presuppose it; and each of these, which we have seen to be just so many modes of the principle of sufficient reason, is valid only for a particular class of ideas; whereas the antithesis of object and subject is the common form of all these classes, is that form under which alone any idea of whatever kind it may be, abstract or intuitive, pure or empirical, is possible and thinkable. No truth therefore is more certain, more independent of all others, and less in need of proof than this, that all that exists for knowledge, and therefore this whole world, is only object in relation to subject, perception of a perceiver, in a word, idea. This is obviously true of the past and the future, as well as of the present, of what is farthest off, as of what is near; for it is true of time and space themselves,

721

in which alone these distinctions arise. All that in any way belongs
or can belong to the world is inevitably thus conditioned through
the subject, and exists only for the subject. The world is idea. . . .

21 That which knows all things and is known by none is the subject. Thus it is the supporter of the world, that condition of all
phenomena, of all objects which is always presupposed throughout
experience; for all that exists, exists only for the subject. Every one
finds himself to be subject, yet only in so far as he knows, not in
so far as he is an object of knowledge. But his body is object, and
therefore from this point of view we call it idea. For the body is
an object among objects, and is conditioned by the laws of objects,
although it is an immediate object. Like all objects of perception,
it lies within the universal forms of knowledge, time and space,
which are the conditions of multiplicity. The subject, on the contrary, which is always the knower, never the known, does not come
under these forms, but is presupposed by them; it has therefore
neither multiplicity nor its opposite unity. We never know it, but
it is always the knower wherever there is knowledge.

So then the world as idea, the only aspect in which we consider
it at present, has two fundamental, necessary, and inseparable
halves. The one half is the object, the forms of which are space and
time, and through these multiplicity. The other half is the subject,
which is not in space and time, for it is present, entire and undivided, in every percipient being. So that any one percipient being,
with the object, constitutes the whole world as idea just as fully
as the existing millions could do; but if this one were to disappear,
then the whole world as idea would cease to be. These halves are
therefore inseparable even for thought, for each of the two has
meaning and existence only through and for the other, each appears with the other and vanishes with it. They limit each other
immediately; where the object begins the subject ends. The universality of this limitation is shown by the fact that the essential
and hence universal forms of all objects, space, time, and causality,
may, without knowledge of the object, be discovered and fully
known from a consideration of the subject, i.e., in Kantian language, they lie a priori in our consciousness. That he discovered
this is one of Kant's principal merits, and it is a great one. I however go beyond this, and maintain that the principle of sufficient

reason is the general expression for all these forms of the object of which we are *a priori* conscious; and that therefore all that we know purely *a priori* is merely the content of that principle and what follows from it; in it all our certain *a priori* knowledge is expressed. In my essay on the principle of sufficient reason I have shown in detail how every possible object comes under it; that is, stands in a necessary relation to other objects, on the one side as determined, on the other side as determining: this is of such wide application, that the whole existence of all objects, so far as they are objects, ideas and nothing more, may be entirely traced to this their necessary relation to each other, rests only in it, is in fact merely relative; but of this more presently. I have further shown, that the necessary relation which the principle of sufficient reason expresses generally, appears in other forms corresponding to the classes into which objects are divided, according to their possibility; and again that by these forms the proper division of the classes is tested. . . .

³¹ The chief distinction among our ideas is that between ideas of perception and abstract ideas. The latter form just one class of ideas, namely concepts, and these are the possession of man alone of all creatures upon earth. The capacity for these, which distinguishes him from all the lower animals, has always been called reason. We shall consider these abstract ideas by themselves later, but, in the first place, we shall speak exclusively of the *ideas of perception*. These comprehend the whole visible world, or the sum total of experience, with the conditions of its possibility. We have already observed that it is a highly important discovery of Kant's, that these very conditions, these forms of the visible world, *i.e.,* the absolutely universal element in its perception, the common property of all its phenomena, space and time, even when taken by themselves and apart from their content, can, not only be thought in the abstract, but also be directly perceived; and that this perception or intuition is not some kind of phantasm arising from constant recurrence in experience, but is so entirely independent of experience that we must rather regard the latter as dependent on it, inasmuch as the qualities of space and time, as they are known in *a priori* perception or intuition, are valid for all possible experience, as rules to which it must invariably conform. Accord-

ingly, in my essay on the principle of sufficient reason, I have treated space and time, because they are perceived as pure and empty of content, as a special and independent class of ideas. This quality of the universal forms of intuition, which was discovered by Kant, that they may be perceived in themselves and apart from experience, and that they may be known as exhibiting those laws on which is founded the infallible science of mathematics, is certainly very important. Not less worthy of remark, however, is this other quality of time and space, that the principle of sufficient reason, which conditions experience as the law of causation and of motive, and thought as the law of the basis of judgment, appears here in quite a special form, to which I have given the name of the ground of being. In time, this is the succession of its moments, and in space the position of its parts, which reciprocally determine each other *ad infinitum*.

Any one who has fully understood from the introductory essay the complete identity of the content of the principle of sufficient reason in all its different forms, must also be convinced of the important of the knowledge of the simplest of these forms, as affording him insight into his own inmost nature. This simplest form of the principle we have found to be time. In it each instant is, only in so far as it has effaced the preceding one, its generator, to be itself in turn as quickly effaced. The past and the future (considered apart from the consequences of their content) are empty as a dream, and the present is only the indivisible and unenduring boundary between them. And in all the other forms of the principle of sufficient reason, we shall find the same emptiness, and shall see that not time only but also space, and the whole content of both of them, *i.e.*, all that proceeds from causes and motives, has a merely relative existence, is only through and for another like to itself, *i.e.*, not more enduring.

4] Whoever has recognised the form of the principle of sufficient reason, which appears in pure time as such, and on which all counting and arithmetical calculation rests, has completely mastered the nature of time. Time is nothing more than that form of the principle of sufficient reason, and has no further significance. Succession is the form of the principle of sufficient reason in time, and succession is the whole nature of time. Further, whoever has recognised the principle of sufficient reason as it appears in the presentation of pure space, has exhausted the whole nature of space, which is absolutely nothing more than that possibility of the reciprocal determination of its parts by each other, which is called position. The detailed treatment of this, and the formulation in abstract conceptions of the results which flow from it, so that they may be more conveniently used, is the subject of the science of geometry. Thus also, whoever has recognised the law of causation, the aspect of the principle of sufficient reason which appears in what fills these forms (space and time) as objects of perception, that is to say, matter, has completely mastered the nature of matter as such, for matter is nothing more than causation, as any one will see at once if he reflects. Its true being is its action, nor can we possibly conceive it as having any other meaning. Only as action does it fill space and time; its action upon the immediate objects (which is itself matter) determines that perception in which alone it exists. The consequence of the action of any material object upon any other, is known only in so far as the latter acts upon the immediate object in a different way from that in which it acted before; it consists only of this. Cause and effect thus constitute the whole nature of matter; its true being is its action. The nature of all material things is therefore very appropriately called in German *Wirklichkeit,* a word which is far more expressive than *Realität.* Again, that which is acted upon is always matter, and thus the whole being and essence of matter consists in the orderly change, which one part of it brings about in another part. The existence of matter is therefore entirely relative, according to a relation which is valid only within its limits, as in the case of time and space.

But time and space, each for itself, can be mentally presented apart from matter, whereas matter cannot be so presented apart from time and space. The form which is inseparable from it presupposes space, and the action in which its very existence consists, always imports some change, in other words a determination in time. But space and time are not only, each for itself, presupposed by matter, but a union of the two constitutes its essence, for this, as we have seen, consists in action, *i.e.,* in causation. All the innumerable conceivable phenomena and conditions of things, might be co-existent in boundless space, without limiting each other, or might be successive in endless time without interfering with each other: thus a necessary relation of these phenomena to each other, and a law which should regulate them according to such a relation, is by no means needful, would not, indeed, be applicable: it therefore follows that in the case of all co-existence in space and change in time, so long as each of these forms preserves for itself its condition and its course without any connection with the other, there can be no causation, and since causation constitutes the essential nature of matter, there can be no matter. But the law of causation receives its meaning and necessity only from this, that the essence of change does not consist simply in the mere variation of things, but rather in the fact that at the *same part of space* there is now *one thing* and then *another,* and at *one* and the same point of time there is *here* one thing and *there* another: only this reciprocal limitation of space and time by each other gives meaning, and at the same time necessity, to a law, according to which change must take place. What is determined by the law of causality is therefore not merely a succession of things in time, but this succession with reference to a definite space, and not merely existence of things in a particular place, but in this place at a different point of time. Change, *i.e.,* variation which takes place according to the law of causality, implies always a determined part of space and a determined part of time together and in union. Thus causality unites space with time. But we found that the whole essence of matter consisted in action, *i.e.,* in causation, consequently space and time must also be united in matter, that is to say, matter must take to itself at once the distinguishing qualities both of space and time, however much these may be opposed to each other, and must unite in itself what is impossible for each of these independently, that is, the fleeting course of time, with the rigid unchangeable perduration of space: infinite divisibility it receives from both. It is for this reason that we find that co-existence, which could neither be in time alone, for time has no contiguity, nor in space alone, for space has no before, after, or now, is first established through matter. But the co-existence of many things constitutes, in fact, the essence of reality, for through it permanence first becomes possible; for permanence is only knowable in the change of something which is present along with what is permanent, while on the other hand it is only because something permanent is present along with what changes, that the latter gains the special character of change, *i.e.,* the mutation of quality and form in the permanence of substance, that is to say, in matter. If the world were in space alone, it would be rigid and immovable, without succession, without change, without action; but we know that with action, the idea of matter first appears. Again, if the world were in time alone, all would be fleeting, without persistence, without contiguity, hence without co-existence, and consequently without permanence; so that in this case also there would be no matter. Only through the union of space and time do we reach matter, and matter is the possibility of co-existence, and, through that, of permanence; through permanence again matter is the possibility of the persistence of substance in the change of its states. As matter consists in the union of space and time, it bears throughout the stamp of both. It manifests its origin in space, partly through the form which is inseparable from it, but especially through its persistence (substance), the *a priori* certainty of which is therefore wholly deducible from that of space (for variation belongs to time alone, but in it alone and for itself nothing is persistent). Matter shows that it springs from time by quality (accidents), without which it never exists, and which is plainly always causality, action upon other matter, and therefore change (a time concept). The law of this action, however, always depends upon space and time together, and only thus obtains meaning. The regulative function of causality is confined entirely to the determination of what must occupy *this time and this space.* The fact that we know *a priori* the unalterable characteristics of matter, depends upon this derivation of its essential nature from the forms of our knowledge of which we are conscious *a priori.*

But as the object in general is only for the subject, as its idea, so every special class of ideas is only for an equally special quality in the subject, which is called a faculty of perception. This subjective correlative of time and space, in themselves as empty forms, has been named by Kant pure sensibility; and we may retain this expression, as Kant was the first to treat of the subject, though it is not exact, for sensibility presupposes matter. The subjective correlative of matter or of causation, for these two are the same, is understanding, which is nothing more than this. To know causality is its one function, its only power; and it is a great one, embracing much, of manifold application, yet of unmistakable identity in all its manifestations. Conversely all causation, that is to say, all matter, or the whole of reality, is only for the understanding, through the understanding, and in the understanding. The first, simplest, and ever-present example of understanding is the perception of the actual world. This is throughout knowledge of the cause from the effect, and therefore all perception is intellectual. The understanding could never arrive at this perception, however, if some effect did not become known immediately, and thus serve as a starting-point. But this is the affection of the animal body. So far, then, the animal body is the *immediate object* of the subject; the perception of all other objects becomes possible through it. The changes which every animal body experiences, are immediately known, that is, felt; and as these effects are at once referred to their causes, the perception of the latter as *objects* arises. This relation is no conclusion in abstract conceptions; it does not arise from reflection, nor is it arbitrary, but immediate, necessary, and certain. It is the method of knowing of the pure understanding, without which there could be no perception; there would only remain a dull plant-like consciousness of the changes of the immediate object, which would succeed each other in an utterly unmeaning way, except in so far as they might have a meaning for the will either as pain or pleasure. But as with the rising of the sun the visible world appears, so at one stroke, the understanding, by means of its one simple function, changes the dull, meaningless sensation into perception. What the eye, the ear, or the hand feels, is not perception; it is merely its data. By the understanding passing from the effect to the cause, the world first appears as perception extended in space, varying in respect of form, persistent through all time in respect of matter; for the understanding unites space and time in the idea of matter, that is, causal action. As the world as idea exists only through the understanding, so also it exists only for the understanding. . . .

6] In this first book we consider everything merely as idea, as object for the subject. And our own body, which is the starting-point for each of us in our perception of the world, we consider, like all other real objects, from the side of its knowableness, and in this regard it is simply an idea. Now the consciousness of every

one is in general opposed to the explanation of objects as mere
ideas, and more especially to the explanation of our bodies as
such; for the thing in itself is known to each of us immediately in
so far as it appears as our own body; but in so far as it objectifies
itself in the other objects of perception, it is known only indirectly. But this abstraction, this one-sided treatment, this forcible
separation of what is essentially and necessarily united, is only
adopted to meet the demands of our argument; and therefore the
disinclination to it must, in the meantime, be suppressed and silenced by the expectation that the subsequent treatment will correct the one-sidedness of the present one, and complete our
knowledge of the nature of the world.

At present therefore the body is for us immediate object; that
is to say, that idea which forms the starting-point of the subject's knowledge; because the body, with its immediately known
changes, precedes the application of the law of causality, and thus
supplies it with its first data. The whole nature of matter consists, as we have seen, in its causal action. But cause and effect
exist only for the understanding, which is nothing but their subjective correlative. The understanding, however, could never come
into operation if there were not something else from which it
starts. This is simple sensation—the immediate consciousness of
the changes of the body, by virtue of which it is immediate object.
Thus the possibility of knowing the world of perception depends
upon two conditions; the first, *objectively expressed,* is the power
of material things to act upon each other, to produce changes
in each other, without which common quality of all bodies no
perception would be possible, even by means of the sensibility of
the animal body. And if we wish to express this condition *subjectively* we say: The understanding first makes perception possible; for the law of causality, the possibility of effect and cause,
springs only from the understanding, and is valid only for it, and
therefore the world of perception exists only through and for it.
The second condition is the sensibility of animal bodies, or the
quality of being immediate objects of the subject which certain
bodies possess. The mere modification which the organs of sense
sustain from without through their specific affections, may here
be called ideas, so far as these affections produce neither pain nor
pleasure, that is, have no immediate significance for the will, and

are yet perceived, exist therefore only for *knowledge*. Thus far, then, I say that the body is immediately *known*, is *immediate object*. But the conception of object is not to be taken here in its fullest sense, for through this immediate knowledge of the body, which precedes the operation of the understanding, and is mere sensation, our own body does not exist specifically as *object*, but first the material things which affect it: for all knowledge of an object proper, of an idea perceived in space, exists only through and for the understanding; therefore not before, but only subsequently to its operation. Therefore the body as object proper, that is, an idea perceived in space, is first known indirectly, like all other objects, through the application of the law of causality to the action of one of its parts upon another, as, for example, when the eye sees the body or the hand touches it. Consequently the form of our body does not become known to us through mere feeling, but only through knowledge, only in idea; that is to say, only in the brain does our own body first come to appear as extended, articulate, organic. A man born blind receives this idea only little by little from the data afforded by touch. A blind man without hands could never come to know his own form; or at the most could infer and construct it little by little from the effects of other bodies upon him. If, then, we call the body an immediate object, we are to be understood with these reservations.

In other respects, then, according to what has been said, all animal bodies are immediate objects; that is, starting-points for the subject which always knows and therefore is never known in its perception of the world. Thus the distinctive characteristic of animal life is knowledge, with movement following on motives, which are determined by knowledge, just as movement following on stimuli is the distinctive characteristic of plant-life. Unorganised matter, however, has no movement except such as is produced by causes properly so called, using the term in its narrowest sense. . . .

Besides the ideas we have as yet considered, which, according to their construction, could be referred to time, space, and matter, if we consider them with reference to the object, or to pure sensibility and understanding *(i.e., knowledge of causality)*, if we consider them with reference to the subject, another faculty of knowledge has appeared in man alone of all earthly creatures, an

entirely new consciousness, which, with very appropriate and significant exactness, is called *reflection*. For it is in fact derived
from the knowledge of perception, and is a reflected appearance
of it. But it has assumed a nature fundamentally different. The
forms of perception do not affect it, and even the principle of
sufficient reason which reigns over all objects has an entirely different aspect with regard to it. It is just this new, more highly
endowed, consciousness, this abstract reflex of all that belongs to
perception in that conception of the reason which has nothing to
do with perception, that gives to man that thoughtfulness which
distinguishes his consciousness so entirely from that of the lower
animals, and through which his whole behaviour upon earth is
so different from that of his irrational fellow-creatures. He far
surpasses them in power and also in suffering. They live in the
present alone, he lives also in the future and the past. They satisfy
the needs of the moment, he provides by the most ingenious
preparations for the future, yea for days that he shall never see.
They are entirely dependent on the impression of the moment,
on the effect of the perceptible motive; he is determined by
abstract conceptions independent of the present. Therefore he
follows predetermined plans, he acts from maxims, without reference to his surroundings or the accidental impression of the
moment. Thus, for example, he can make with composure deliberate preparations for his own death, he can dissemble past finding
out, and can carry his secret with him to the grave; lastly, he has
an actual choice between several motives; for only in the abstract
can such motives, present together in consciousness, afford the
knowledge with regard to themselves, that the one excludes the
other, and can thus measure themselves against each other with
reference to their power over the will. The motive that overcomes,
in that it decides the question at issue, is the deliberate determinant of the will, and is a sure indication of its character. The
brute, on the other hand, is determined by the present impression; only the fear of present compulsion can contrain its desires,
until at last this fear has become custom, and as such continues
to determine it; this is called training. The brute feels and perceives; man, in addition to this, *thinks* and *knows:* both *will*. The
brute expresses its feelings and dispositions by gestures and
sounds; man communicates his thought to others, or, if he wishes,

he conceals it, by means of speech. Speech is the first production, and also the necessary organ of his reason. Therefore in Greek and Italian, speech and reason are expressed by the same word; *ò logos, il discorso. Vernunft* is derived from *vernehmen,* which not a synonym for the verb to hear, but signifies the consciousness of the meaning of thoughts communicated in words. It is by the help of language alone that reason accomplishes its most important achievements,—the united action of several individuals, the planned co-operation of many thousands, civilisation, the state; also science, the storing up of experience, the uniting of common properties in one concept, the communication of truth, the spread of error, thoughts and poems, dogmas and superstitions. The brute first knows death when it dies, but man draws consciously nearer to it every hour that he lives; and this makes life at times a questionable good even to him who has not recognised this character of constant annihilation in the whole of life. Principally on this account man has philosophies and religions, though it is uncertain whether the qualities we admire most in his conduct, voluntary rectitude and nobility of feeling, were ever the fruit of either of them. As results which certainly belong only to them, and as productions of reason in this sphere, we may refer to the marvellous and monstrous opinions of philosophers of various schools, and the extraordinary and sometimes cruel customs of the priests of different religions.

It is the universal opinion of all times and of all nations that these manifold and far-reaching achievements spring from a common principle, from that peculiar intellectual power which belongs distinctively to man and which has been called reason. Besides this, no one finds any difficulty in recognising the manifestations of this faculty, and in saying what is rational and what is irrational, where reason appears as distinguished from the other faculties and qualities of man, or lastly, in pointing out what, on account of the want of reason, we must never expect even from the most sensible brute. The philosophers of all ages may be said to be on the whole at one about this general knowledge of reason, and they have also given prominence to several very important manifestations of it; such as, the control of the emotions and passions, the capacity for drawing conclusions and formulating general principles, even such as are true prior to all experience, and so forth.

The understanding has only one function—immediate knowledge of the relation of cause and effect. Yes the perception of the real world, and all common sense, sagacity, and inventiveness, however multifarious their applications may be, are quite clearly seen to be nothing more than manifestations of that one function. So also the reason has one function; and from it all the manifestations of reason we have mentioned, which distinguish the life of man from that of the brutes, may easily be explained. The application or the non-application of this function is all that is meant by what men have everywhere and always called rational and irrational.

91 Although concepts are fundamentally different from ideas of perception, they stand in a necessary relation to them, without which they would be nothing. This relation therefore constitutes the whole nature and existence of concepts. Reflection is the necessary copy or repetition of the originally presented world of perception, but it is a special kind of copy in an entirely different material. Thus concepts may quite properly be called ideas of ideas. The principle of sufficient reason has here also a special form. Now we have seen that the form under which the principle of sufficient reason appears in a class of ideas always constitutes and exhausts the whole nature of the class, so far as it consists of ideas, so that time is throughout succession, and nothing more; space is throughout position, and nothing more; matter is throughout causation, and nothing more. In the same way the whole nature of concepts, or the class of abstract ideas, consists simply in the relation which the principle of sufficient reason expresses in them; and as this is the relation to the ground of knowledge, the whole nature of the abstract idea is simply and solely its relation to another idea, which is its ground of knowledge. This, indeed, may, in the first instance, be a concept, an abstract idea, and this again may have only a similar abstract ground of knowledge; but the chain of grounds of knowledge does not extend *ad infinitum;* it must end at last in a concept which has its ground in knowledge of perception; for the whole world of reflection rests on the world of perception as its ground of knowledge. Hence the class

of abstract ideas is in this respect distinguished from other classes; in the latter the principle of sufficient reason always demands merely a relation to another idea of the *same* class, but in the case of abstract ideas, it at last demands a relation to an idea of *another* class.

Those concepts which, as has just been pointed out, are not immediately related to the world of perception, but only through the medium of one, or it may be several other concepts, have been called by preference *abstracta,* and those which have their ground immediately in the world of perception have been called *concreta.* But this last name is only loosely applicable to the concepts denoted by it, for they are always merely *abstracta,* and not ideas of perception. These names, which have originated in a very dim consciousness of the distinctions they imply, may yet, with this explanation, be retained. As examples of the first kind of concepts, *i.e., abstracta* in the fullest sense, we may take "relation," "virtue," "investigation," "beginning," and so on. As examples of the second kind, loosely called *concreta,* we may take such concepts as "man," "stone," "horse," &c. If it were not a somewhat too pictorial and therefore absurd simile, we might very appropriately call the latter the ground floor, and the former the upper stories of the building of reflection.

10] Reason is feminine in nature; it can only give after it has received. Of itself it has nothing but the empty forms of its operation. There is no absolutely pure rational knowledge except the four principles to which I have attributed metalogical truth; the principles of identity, contradiction, excluded middle, and sufficient reason of knowledge. For even the rest of logic is not absolutely pure rational knowledge. It presupposes the relations and the combinations of the spheres of concepts. But concepts in general only exist after experience of ideas of perception, and as their whole nature consists in their relation to these, it is clear that they presuppose them. No special content, however, is presupposed, but merely the existence of a content generally, and so logic as a whole may fairly pass for pure rational science. In all other sciences reason has received its content from ideas of perception; in mathematics from the relations of space and time, presented in intuition or perception prior to all experience; in pure natural science, that is, in what we know of the course of nature prior to any experience, the content of the science proceeds from the pure understanding, *i.e.,* from the *a priori* knowledge of the law of causality and its connection with those pure intuitions or perceptions of space and time. In all other sciences everything that is not derived from the sources we have just referred to belongs to experience. Speaking generally, *to know rationally (wissen)* means to have in the power of the mind, and capable of being reproduced at will, such judgments as have their sufficient ground of knowledge in something outside themselves, *i.e.,* are true. Thus only abstract cognition is *rational knowledge (wissen)*, which is therefore the result of reason, so that we cannot accurately say of the lower animals that they *rationally know (wissen)* anything, although they have apprehension of what is presented in perception, and memory of this, and consequently imagination, which is further proved by the circumstance that they dream. We attribute consciousness to them, and therefore although the word *(bewusstsein)* is derived from the verb to know rationally *(wissen)*, the conception of consciousness corresponds generally with that of idea of whatever kind it may be. Thus we attribute life to plants, but not consciousness. *Rational knowledge (wissen)* is therefore abstract consciousness, the permanent possession in concepts of the reason, of what has become known in another way.

12] *Rational knowledge (wissen)* is then all abstract knowledge,— that is, the knowledge which is peculiar to the reason as distinguished from the understanding. Now, as reason only reproduces, for knowledge, what has been received in another way, it does not actually extend our knowledge, but only gives it another form. It enables us to know in the abstract and generally, what first became known in sense-perception, in the concrete. But this is much more important than it appears at first sight when so expressed. For it depends entirely upon the fact that knowledge has become rational or abstract knowledge *(wissen)*, that it can be safely preserved, that it is communicable and susceptible of certain and wide-reaching application to practice. Knowledge in the form of sense-perception is valid only of the particular case, extends only to what is nearest, and ends with it, for sensibility and understanding can only comprehend one object at a time. Every enduring, arranged, and planned activity must therefore proceed from principles,—that is, from abstract knowledge, and it must be conducted in accordance with them. Thus, for example, the knowledge of the relation of cause and effect arrived at by the understanding, is in itself far completer, deeper and more exhaustive than anything that can be thought about it in the abstract; the understanding alone knows in perception directly and completely the nature of the effect of a lever, of a pulley, or a cog-wheel, the stability of an arch, and so forth. But on account of the peculiarity of the knowledge of perception just referred to, that it only extends to what is immediately present, the mere understanding can never enable us to construct machines and buildings. Here reason must come in; it must substitute abstract concepts for ideas of perception, and take them as the guide of action; and if they are right, the anticipated result will happen. In the same way we have perfect knowledge in pure perception of the nature and constitution of the parabola, hyperbola, and spiral; but if we are to make trustworthy application of this knowledge to the real, it must first become abstract knowledge, and by this it certainly loses its character of intuition or perception, but on the other hand it gains the certainty and preciseness of abstract knowledge. The differential calculus does not really extend our knowledge of the curve, it contains nothing that was not already in the mere pure perception of the curve; but it alters the kind of knowledge, it changes the intuitive into an abstract knowledge, which is so valuable for application.

This quality of concepts by which they resemble the stones of a mosaic, and on account of which perception always remains their asymptote, is the reason why nothing good is produced in art by their means. If the singer or the virtuoso attempts to guide his execution by reflection he remains silent. And this is equally true of the composer, the painter, and the poet. The concept always remains unfruitful in art; it can only direct the technical part of it, its sphere is science. We shall consider more fully in the third book, why all true art proceeds from sensuous knowledge, never from the concept. Indeed, with regard to behaviour also, and personal agreeableness in society, the concept has only a negative value in restraining the grosser manifestations of egotism and brutality; so that a polished manner is its commendable production. But all that is attractive, gracious, charming in behaviour, all affectionateness and friendliness, must not proceed from the concepts, for if it does, "we feel intention, and are put out of tune." All dissimulation is the work of reflection; but it cannot be maintained constantly and without interruption: "For no man can long time conceal his imperfections," says Seneca in his book *de clementia;* and so it is generally found out and loses its effect. Reason is needed in the full stress of life, where quick conclusions, bold action, rapid and sure comprehension are required, but it may easily spoil all if it gains the upper hand, and by perplexing hinders the intuitive, direct discovery, and grasp of the right by simple understanding, and thus induces irresolution.

Lastly, virtue and holiness do not proceed from reflection, but from the inner depths of the will, and its relation to knowledge. The exposition of this belongs to another part of our work; this, however, I may remark here, that the dogmas relating to ethics may be the same in the reason of whole nations, but the action of every individual different; and the converse also holds good; action, we say, is guided by *feelings,*—that is, simply not by concepts, but as a matter of fact by the ethical character. Dogmas occupy the idle reason; but action in the end pursues its own course independently of them, generally not according to abstract rules, but according to unspoken maxims, the expression of which is the whole man himself. Therefore, however different the religious dogmas of nations may be, yet in the case of all of them, a good action is accompanied by unspeakable satisfaction, and a bad action by endless remorse. No mockery can shake the former; no priest's absolution can deliver from the latter. Notwithstanding this, we must allow, that for the pursuit of a virtuous life, the application of reason is needful; only it is not its source, but has the subordinate function of preserving resolutions which have been made, of providing maxims to withstand the weakness of the moment, and give consistency to action. It plays the same part ultimately in art also, where it has just as little to do with the essential matter, but assists in carrying it out, for genius is not always at call, and yet the work must be completed in all its parts and rounded off to a whole. . . .

Second Book

The World As Will

First Aspect

The Objectification of the Will

17] What now impels us to inquiry is just that we are not satisfied with knowing that we have ideas, that they are such and such, and that they are connected according to certain laws, the general expression of which is the principle of sufficient reason. We wish to know the significance of these ideas; we ask whether this world is merely idea; in which case it would pass by us like an empty dream or a baseless vision, not worth our notice; or whether it is also something else, something more than idea, and if so, what. Thus much is certain, that this something we seek for must be completely and in its whole nature different from the idea; that the forms and laws of the idea must therefore be completely foreign to it; further, that we cannot arrive at it from the idea under the guidance of the laws which merely combine objects, ideas, among themselves, and which are the forms of the principle of sufficient reason.

Thus we see already that we can never arrive at the real nature of things from without. However much we investigate, we can never reach anything but images and names. We are like a man who goes round a castle seeking in vain for an entrance, and sometimes sketching the façades. And yet this is the method that has been followed by all philosophers before me.

18] In fact, the meaning for which we seek of that world which is present to us only as our idea, or the transition from the world as mere idea of the knowing subject to whatever it may be besides this, would never be found if the investigator himself were nothing more than the pure knowing subject (a winged cherub without a body). But he is himself rooted in that world; he finds himself in it as an *individual,* that is to say, his knowledge, which is the necessary supporter of the whole world as idea, is yet always

given through the medium of a body, whose affections are, as we
have shown, the starting-point for the understanding in the perception of that world. His body is, for the pure knowing subject, an
idea like every other idea, an object among objects. Its movements
and actions are so far known to him in precisely the same way as
the changes of all other perceived objects, and would be just as
strange and incomprehensible to him if their meaning were not
explained for him in an entirely different way. Otherwise he
would see his actions follow upon given motives with the constancy of a law of nature, just as the changes of other objects follow upon causes, stimuli, or motives. But he would not understand the influence of the motives any more than the connection
between every other effect which he sees and its cause. He would
then call the inner nature of these manifestations and actions of
his body which he did not understand a force, a quality, or a
character, as he pleased, but he would have no further insight
into it. But all this is not the case; indeed the answer to the riddle
is given to the subject of knowledge who appears as an individual, and the answer is *will*. This and this alone gives him the key
to his own existence, reveals to him the significance, shows him
the inner mechanism of his being, of his action, of his movements. The body is given in two entirely different ways to the
subject of knowledge, who becomes an individual only through
his identity with it. It is given as an idea in intelligent perception,
as an object among objects and subject to the laws of objects. And
it is also given in quite a different way as that which is immediately known to every one, and is signified by the word *will*. Every
true act of his will is also at once and without exception a movement of his body. The act of will and the movement of the body
are not two different things objectively known, which the bond
of causality unites; they do not stand in the relation of cause and
effect; they are one and the same, but they are given in entirely
different ways,—immediately, and again in perception for the
understanding. The action of the body is nothing but the act of
the will objectified, *i.e.*, passed into perception. It will appear
later that this is true of every movement of the body, not merely
those which follow upon motives, but also involuntary movements which follow upon mere stimuli, and, indeed, that the
whole body is nothing but objectified will, *i.e.*, will become idea.

All this will be proved and made quite clear in the course of this work. In one respect, therefore, I shall call the body the *objectivity of will;* as in the previous book, and in the essay on the principle of sufficient reason, in accordance with the one-sided point of view intentionally adopted there (that of the idea), I called it *the immediate object.* Thus in a certain sense we may also say that will is the knowledge *a priori* of the body, and the body is the knowledge *a posteriori* of the will. . . .

The double knowledge which each of us has of the nature and activity of his own body, and which is given in two completely different ways, has now been clearly brought out. We shall accordingly make further use of it as a key to the nature of every phenomenon in nature, and shall judge of all objects which are not our own bodies, and are consequently not given to our consciousness in a double way but only as ideas, according to the analogy of our own bodies, and shall therefore assume that as in one aspect they are idea, just like our bodies, and in this respect are analogous to them, so in another aspect, what remains of objects when we set aside their existence as idea of the subject, must in its inner nature be the same as that in us which we call *will.* For what other kind of existence or reality should we attribute to the rest of the material world? Whence should we take the elements out of which we construct such a world? Besides will and idea nothing is known to us or thinkable. If we wish to attribute the greatest known reality to the material world which exists immediately only in our idea, we give it the reality which our own body has for each of us; for that is the most real thing for every one. But if we now analyse the reality of this body and its actions, beyond the fact that it is idea, we find nothing in it except the will; with this its reality is exhausted. Therefore we can nowhere find another kind of reality which we can attribute to the material world. Thus if we hold that the material world is something more than merely our idea, we must say that besides being idea, that is, in itself and according to its inmost nature, it is that which we find immediately in ourselves as *will.* I say according to its inmost nature; but we must first come to know more accurately this real nature of the will, in order that we may be able to distinguish from it what does not belong to itself, but to its manifestation, which has many grades. Such, for example, is the circumstance of its being accompanied by knowledge, and the determination by motives which is conditioned by this knowledge. As we shall see farther on, this does not belong to the real nature of will, but merely to its distinct manifestation as an animal or a human being. If, therefore, I say,—the force which attracts a stone to the earth is according to its nature, in itself, and apart from all idea, will, I shall not be supposed to express in this proposition the insane opinion that the stone moves itself in accordance with a known motive, merely because this is the way in which will appears in man. We shall now proceed more clearly and in detail to prove, establish, and develop to its full extent what as yet has only been provisionally and generally explained.

20] As we have said, the will proclaims itself primarily in the voluntary movements of our own body, as the inmost nature of this body, as that which it is besides being object of perception, idea. For these voluntary movements are nothing else than the visible aspect of the individual acts of will, with which they are directly coincident and identical, and only distinguished through the form of knowledge into which they have passed, and in which alone they can be known, the form of idea.

But these acts of will have always a ground or reason outside themselves in motives. Yet these motives never determine more than what I will at *this* time, in *this* place, and under *these* circumstances, not *that* I will in general, or *what* I will in general, that is, the maxims which characterise my volition generally. Therefore the inner nature of my volition cannot be explained from these motives; but they merely determine its manifestation at a given point of time: they are merely the occasion of my will showing itself; but the will itself lies outside the province of the law of motivation, which determines nothing but its appearance at each point of time. It is only under the presupposition of my empirical character that the motive is a sufficient ground of explanation of my action. But if I abstract from my character, and then ask, why, in general, I will this and not that, no answer is possible, because it is only the manifestation of the will that is subject to the principle of sufficient reason, and not the will itself, which in this respect is to be called *groundless*.

If now every action of my body is the manifestation of an act of will in which my will itself in general, and as a whole, thus my character, expresses itself under given motives, manifestation of the will must be the inevitable condition and presupposition of every action. For the fact of its manifestation cannot depend upon something which does not exist directly and only through it, which consequently is for it merely accidental, and through which its manifestation itself would be merely accidental. Now that condition is just the whole body itself. Thus the body itself must be manifestation of the will, and it must be related to my will as a whole, that is, to my intelligible character, whose phenomenal appearance in time is my empirical character, as the particular action of the body is related to the particular act of the will. The whole body, then, must be simply my will become visible, must be my will itself, so far as this is object of perception, an idea of the first class. It has already been advanced in confirmation of this that every impression upon my body also affects my will at once and immediately, and in this respect is called pain or pleasure, or, in its lower degrees, agreeable or disagreeable sensation; and also, conversely, that every violent movement of the will, every emotion or passion, convulses the body and disturbs the course of its functions. Indeed we can also give an etiological account, though a very incomplete one, of the origin of my body, and a somewhat better account of its development and conservation, and this is the substance of physiology. But physiology merely explains its theme in precisely the same way as motives explain action. Thus the physiological explanation of the functions of the body detracts just as little from the philosophical truth that the whole existence of this body and the sum total of its functions are merely the objectification of that will which appears in its outward actions in accordance with a motive, as the establishment of the individual action through the motive and the necessary sequence of the action from the motive conflicts with the fact that action in general, and according to its nature, is only the manifestation of a will which itself has no ground. If, however, physiology tries to refer even these outward actions, the immediate voluntary movements, to causes in the organism,—for example, if it explains the movement of the muscles as resulting from the presence of fluids, even supposing it really could give a thorough explanation of this kind, yet this would never invalidate the immediately certain truth that every voluntary motion *(functiones animales)* is the manifestation of an act of will. Now, just as little can the physiological explanation of vegetative life *(functiones naturales vitales)*, however far it may advance, ever invalidate the truth that the whole animal life which thus develops itself is the manifestation of will. In general, then, as we have shown above, no etiological explanation can ever give us more than the necessarily determined position in time and space of a particular manifestation, its necessary appearance there, according to a fixed law; but the inner nature of everything that appears in this way remains wholly inexplicable, and is presupposed by every etiological explanation, and merely indicated by the names, force, or law of nature, or, if we are speaking of action, character or will. Thus, although every particular action, under the presupposition of the definite character, necessarily follows from the given motive, and although growth, the process of nourishment, and all the changes of the animal body take place according to necessarily acting causes (stimuli), yet the whole series of actions, and consequently every individual act, and also its condition, the whole body itself which accomplishes it, and therefore also the process through which and in which it exists, are nothing but the manifestation of the will, the becoming visible, *the objectification of the will.* Upon this rests the perfect suitableness of the human and animal body to the human and animal will in general, resembling, though far surpassing, the correspondence between an instrument made for a purpose and the will of the maker, and on this account appearing as design, *i.e.,* the teleological explanation of the body. The parts of the body must, therefore, completely correspond to the principal desires through which the will manifests itself; they must be the visible expression of these desires. Teeth, throat, and bowels are objectified hunger; the organs of generation are objectified sexual desire; the grasping hand, the hurrying feet, correspond to the more indirect desires of the will which they express. As the human form generally corresponds to the human will generally, so the individual bodily structure corresponds to the individually modified will, the character of the individual, and therefore it is throughout and in all parts characteristic and full of expression.

211 Whoever has now gained from all these expositions a knowledge *in abstracto,* and therefore clear and certain, of what every one knows directly *in concreto, i.e.,* as feeling, a knowledge that his will is the real inner nature of his phenomenal being, which manifests itself to him as idea, both in his actions and in their permanent substratum, his body, and that his will is that which is most immediate in his consciousness, though it has not as such completely passed into the form of idea in which object and subject stand over against each other, but makes itself known to him in a direct manner, in which he does not quite clearly distinguish subject and object, yet is not known as a whole to the individual himself, but only in its particular acts,—whoever, I say, has with me gained this conviction will find that of itself it affords him the key to the knowledge of the inmost being of the whole of nature; for he now transfers it to all those phenomena which are not given to him, like his own phenomenal existence, both in direct and indirect knowledge, but only in the latter, thus merely onesidedly as *idea* alone. He will recognise this will of which we are speaking not only in those phenomenal existences which exactly resemble his own, in men and animals as their inmost nature, but the course of reflection will lead him to recognise the force which germinates and vegetates in the plant, and indeed the force through which the crystal is formed, that by which the magnet turns to the north pole, the force whose shock he experiences from the contact of two different kinds of metals, the force which appears in the elective affinities of matter as repulsion and attraction, decomposition and combination, and, lastly, even gravitation, which acts so powerfully throughout matter, draws the stone to the earth and the earth to the sun,—all these, I say, he will recognise as different only in their phenomenal existence, but in their inner nature as identical, as that which is directly known to him so intimately and so much better than anything else, and which in its most distinct manifestation is called *will.* It is this application of reflection alone that prevents us from remaining any longer at the phenomenon, and leads us to the *thing-in-itself.* Phenomenal existence is idea and nothing more. All idea, of whatever kind it may be, all *object,* is *phenomenal* existence, but the *will* alone is a *thing-in-itself.* As such, it is throughout not idea, but *toto genere* different from it; it is that of which all idea, all object, is the phenomenal appearance, the visibility, the objectification. It is the inmost nature, the kernel, of every particular thing, and also of the whole. It appears in every blind force of nature and also in the preconsidered action of man; and the great difference between these two is merely in the degree of the manifestation, not in the nature of what manifests itself. . . .

24] Spinoza (Epist. 62) says that if a stone which has been projected through the air had consciousness, it would believe that it was moving of its own will. I add to this only that the stone would be right. The impulse given it is for the stone what the motive is for me, and what in the case of the stone appears as cohesion, gravitation, rigidity, is in its inner nature the same as that which I recognise in myself as will, and what the stone also, if knowledge were given to it, would recognize as will. In the passage referred to, Spinoza had in view the necessity with which the stone flies, and he rightly desires to transfer this necessity to that of the particular act of will of a person. I, on the other hand, consider the inner being, which alone imparts meaning and validity to all real necessity (*i.e.*, effect following upon a cause) as its presupposition. In the case of men this is called character; in the case of a stone it is called quality, but it is the same in both. When it is immediately known it is called will. In the stone it has the weakest, and in man the strongest degree of visibility, of objectivity.

26] The lowest grades of the objectification of will are to be found in those most universal forces of nature which partly appear in all matter without exception, as gravity and impenetrability, and partly have shared the given matter among them, so that certain of them reign in one species of matter and others in another species, constituting its specific difference, as rigidity, fluidity, elasticity, electricity, magnetism, chemical properties and qualities of every kind. They are in themselves immediate manifestations of will, just as much as human action; and as such they are groundless, like human character. Only their particular manifestations are subordinated to the principle of sufficient reason, like the particular actions of men. They themselves, on the other hand, can never be called either effect or cause, but are the prior and presupposed conditions of all causes and effects through which their real nature unfolds and reveals itself. It is therefore senseless to demand a cause of gravity or electricity, for they are original forces. Their expressions, indeed, take place in accordance with the law of cause and effect, so that every one of their particular manifestations has a cause, which is itself again just a similar particular manifestation which determines that this force must express itself here, must appear in space and time; but the force itself is by no means the effect of a cause, nor the cause of an effect. It is therefore a mistake to say "gravity is the cause of a stone falling"; for the cause in this case is rather the nearness of the earth, because it attracts the stone. Take the earth away and the stone will not fall, although gravity remains. The force itself lies quite outside the chain of causes and effects, which presupposes time, because it only has meaning in relation to it; but the force lies outside time. The individual change always has for its cause another change just as individual as itself, and not the force of which it is the expression. For that which always gives its efficiency to a cause, however many times it may appear, is a force of nature. As such, it is groundless, *i.e.*, it lies outside the chain of causes and outside the province of the principle of sufficient reason in general, and is philosophically known as the immediate objectivity of will, which is the "in-itself" of the whole of nature; but in etiology, which in this reference is physics, it is set down as an original force, *i.e.*, a *qualitas occulta*.

In the higher grades of the objectivity of will we see individuality occupy a prominent position, especially in the case of man, where it appears as the great difference of individual characters, *i.e.*, as complete personality, outwardly expressed in strongly marked individual physiognomy, which influences the whole bodily form. None of the brutes have this individuality in anything like so high a degree, though the higher species of them have a trace of it; but the character of the species completely predominates over it, and therefore they have little individual physiognomy. The farther down we go, the more completely is every trace of the individual character lost in the common character of the species, and the physiognomy of the species alone remains. We know the physiological character of the species, and from that we know exactly what is to be expected from the individual; while, on the contrary, in the human species every individual has to be studied and fathomed for himself, which, if we wish to forecast his action with some degree of certainty, is, on account of the possibility of concealment that first appears with reason, a matter of the greatest difficulty. It is probably connected with this difference of the human species from all others, that the folds and convolutions of the brain, which are entirely wanting in birds, and very weakly marked in rodents, are even in the case of the higher animals far more symmetrical on both sides, and more constantly the same in each individual, than in the case of human beings. It is further to be regarded as a phenomenon of this peculiar individual character which distinguishes men from all the lower animals, that in the case of the brutes the sexual instinct seeks its satisfaction without observable choice of objects, while in the case of man this choice is, in a purely instinctive manner and independent of all reflection, carried so far that it rises into a powerful passion. While then every man is to be regarded as a specially determined and characterised phenomenon of will, and indeed to a certain extent as a special Idea, in the case of the brutes this individual character as a whole is wanting, because only the species has a special significance. And the farther we go from man, the fainter becomes the trace of this individual character, so that plants have no individual qualities left, except such as may be fully explained from the favourable or unfavourable external influences of soil, climate, and other accidents. Finally, in the inorganic kingdom of nature all individuality disappears. The crystal alone is to be regarded as to a certain extent individual. It is a unity of the tendency in definite directions, fixed by crystallisation, which makes the trace of this tendency permanent. It is at the same time a cumulative repetition of its primitive form, bound into unity by an idea, just as the tree is an aggregate of the single germinating fibre which shows itself in every rib of the leaves, in every leaf, in every branch; which repeats itself, and to some extent makes each of these appear as a separate growth, nourishing itself from the greater as a parasite, so that the tree, resembling the crystal, is a systematic aggregate of small plants, although only the whole is the complete expression of an individual Idea, i.e., of this particular grade of the objectification of will. But the individuals of the same species of crystal can have no other difference than such as is produced by external accidents; indeed we can make at pleasure large or small crystals of every species. The individual, however, as such, that is, with traces of an individual character, does not exist further in unorganised nature. All its phenomena are expressions of general forces of nature, *i.e.*, of those grades of the objectification of will which do not objectify themselves (as is the case in organised nature), by means of the difference of the individualities which collectively express the whole of the Idea, but show themselves only in the species, and as a whole, without any variation in each particular example of it. Time, space, multiplicity, and existence conditioned by causes, do not belong to the will or to the Idea (the grade of the objectification of will), but only to their particular phenomena. Therefore such a force of nature as, for example, gravity or electricity, must show itself as such in precisely the same way in all its million phenomena, and only external circumstances can modify these. This unity of its being in all its phenomena, this unchangeable constancy of the appearance of these, whenever, under the guidance of causality, the necessary conditions are present, is called a *law of nature*. If such a law is once learned from experience, then the phenomenon of that force of nature, the character of which is expressed and laid down in it, may be accurately forecast and counted upon. But it is just this conformity to law of the phenomena of the lower grades of the objectification of will which gives them such a different aspect from the phenomena of the same will in the higher, *i.e.*, the more distinct, grades of its objectification, in animals, and in men and their actions, where the stronger or weaker influence of the individual character and the susceptibility to motives which often remain hidden from the spectator, because they lie in knowledge, has had the result that the identity of the inner nature of the two kinds of phenomena has hitherto been entirely overlooked.

If we start from the knowledge of the particular, and not from that of the Idea, there is something astonishing, and sometimes even terrible, in the absolute uniformity of the laws of nature. It might astonish us that nature never once forgets her laws; that if, for example, it has once been according to a law of nature that where certain materials are brought together under given conditions, a chemical combination will take place, or gas will be evolved, or they will go on fire; if these conditions are fulfilled, whether by our interposition or entirely by chance (and in this case the accuracy is the more astonishing because unexpected), to-day just as well as a thousand years ago, the determined phenomenon will take place at once and without delay. We are most vividly impressed with the marvellousness of this fact in the case of rare phenomena, which only occur under very complex circumstances, but which we are previously informed will take place if these conditions are fulfilled. For example, when we are told that if certain metals, when arranged alternately in fluid with which an acid has been mixed, are brought into contact, silver leaf brought between the extremities of this combination will suddenly be consumed in a green flame; or that under certain conditions the hard diamond turns into carbonic acid. It is the ghostly omnipresence of natural forces that astonishes us in such cases, and we remark here what in the case of phenomena which happen daily no longer strikes us, how the connection between cause and effect is really as mysterious as that which is imagined between a magic formula and a spirit that must appear when invoked by it. On the other hand, if we have attained to the philosophical knowledge that a force of nature is a definite grade of the objectification of will, that is to say, a definite grade of that which we recognise as our own inmost nature, and that this will, in itself, and distinguished from its phenomena and their forms, lies outside time and space, and that, therefore, the multiplicity, which is conditioned by time and space, does not belong to it, nor directly to the grade of its objectification, *i.e.*, the Idea, but only to the phenomena of the Idea; and if we remember that the law of causality has significance only in relation to time and space, inasmuch as it determines the position of the multitude of phenomena of the different Ideas in which the will reveals itself, governing the order in which they must appear; if, I say, in this knowledge the inner meaning of the great doctrine of Kant has been fully grasped, the doctrine that time, space, and causality do not belong to the thing-in-itself, but merely to the phenomenon, that they are only the forms of our knowledge, not qualities of things in themselves; then we shall understand that this astonishment at the conformity to law and accurate operation of a force of nature, this astonishment at the complete sameness of all its million phenomena and the infallibility of their occurrence, is really like that of a child or a savage who looks for the first time through a glass with many facets at a flower, and marvels at the complete similarity of the innumerable flowers which he sees, and counts the leaves of each of them separately.

Thus every universal, original force of nature is nothing but a low grade of the objectification of will, and we call every such grade an eternal *Idea* in Plato's sense. But a *law of nature* is the relation of the Idea to the form of its manifestation. This form is time, space, and causality, which are necessarily and inseparably connected and related to each other. Through time and space the Idea multiplies itself in innumerable phenomena, but the order according to which it enters these forms of multiplicity is definitely determined by the law of causality; this law is as it were the norm of the limit of these phenomena of different Ideas, in accordance with which time, space, and matter are assigned to them. This norm is therefore necessarily related to the identity of the aggregate of existing matter, which is the common substratum of all those different phenomena. If all these were not directed to that common matter in the possession of which they must be divided, there would be no need for such a law to decide their claims. They might all at once and together fill a boundless space throughout an endless time. Therefore, because all these phenomena of the eternal Ideas are directed to one and the same matter, must there be a rule for their appearance and disappearance; for if there were not, they would not make way for each other. Thus the law of causality is essentially bound up with that of the permanence of substance; they reciprocally derive significance from each other. Time and space, again, are related to them in the same way. For time is merely the possibility of conflicting states of the same matter, and space is merely the possibility of the permanence of the same matter under all sorts of conflicting states. Accordingly, in the preceding book we explained matter as the union of space and time, and this union shows itself as change of the accidents in the permanence of the substance, of which causality or becoming is the universal possibility. And accordingly, we said that matter is through and through causality. We explained the understanding as the subjective correlative of causality, and said matter (and thus the whole world as idea) exists only for the understanding; the understanding is its condition, its supporter as its necessary correlative. I repeat all this in passing, merely to call to mind what was demonstrated in the First

Book, for it is necessary for the complete understanding of these two books that their inner agreement should be observed, since what is inseparably united in the actual world as its two sides, will and idea, has, in order that we might understand each of them more clearly in isolation, been dissevered in these two books. . . .

In any case Malebranche is right: every natural cause is only an occasional cause. It only gives opportunity or occasion for the manifestation of the one indivisible will which is the "in-itself" of all things, and whose graduated objectification is the whole visible world. Only the appearance, the becoming visible, in this place, at this time, is brought about by the cause and is so far dependent on it, but not the whole of the phenomenon, nor its inner nature. This is the will itself, to which the principle of sufficient reason has not application, and which is therefore groundless. Nothing in the world has a sufficient cause of its existence generally, but only a cause of existence just here and just now. That a stone exhibits now gravity, now rigidity, now electricity, now chemical qualities, depends upon causes, upon impressions upon it from without, and is to be explained from these. But these qualities themselves, and thus the whole inner nature of the stone which consists in them, and therefore manifests itself in all the ways referred to; thus, in general, that the stone is such as it is, that it exists generally—all this, I say, has no ground, but is the visible appearance of the groundless will. Every cause is thus an occasional cause. We have found it to be so in nature, which is without knowledge, and it is also precisely the same when motives and not causes or stimuli determine the point at which the phenomena are to appear, that is to say, in the actions of animals and human beings. For in both cases it is one and the same will which appears; very different in the grades of its manifestations, multiplied in the phenomena of these grades, and, in respect of these, subordinated to the principle of sufficient reason, but in itself free from all this. Motives do not determine the character of man, but only the phenomena of his character, that is, his actions; the outward fashion of his life, not its inner meaning and content. These proceed from the character which is the immediate manifestation of the will, and is therefore groundless. That one man is bad and another good, does not depend upon motives or outward influences, such as teaching and preaching, and is in this sense quite inexplicable. But whether a bad man shows his badness in petty acts of injustice, cowardly tricks, and low knavery which he practises in the narrow sphere of his circumstances, or whether as a conqueror he oppresses nations, throws a world into lamentation, and sheds the blood of millions; this is the outward form of his manifestation, that which is unessential to it, and depends upon the circumstances in which fate has placed him, upon his surroundings, upon external influences, upon motives; but his decision upon these motives can never be explained from them; it proceeds from the will, of which this man is a manifestation. Of this we shall speak in the Fourth Book. The manner in which the character discloses its qualities is quite analogous to the way in which those of every material body in unconscious nature are disclosed. Water remains water with its intrinsic qualities, whether as a still lake it reflects its banks, or leaps in foam from the cliffs, or, artificially confined, spouts in a long jet into the air. All that depends upon external causes; the one form is as natural to it as the other, but it will always show the same form in the same circumstances; it is equally ready for any, but in every case true to its character, and at all times revealing this alone. So will every human character under all circumstances reveal itself, but the phenomena which proceed from it will always be in accordance with the circumstances. . . .

271 If several of the phenomena of will in the lower grades of its objectification—that is, in unorganised nature—come into conflict because each of them, under the guidance of causality, seeks to possess a given portion of matter, there arises from the conflict the phenomenon of a higher Idea which prevails over all the less developed phenomena previously there, yet in such a way that it allows the essence of these to continue to exist in a subordinate manner, in that it takes up into itself from them something which is analogous to them. This process is only intelligible from the identity of the will which manifests itself in all the Ideas, and which is always striving after higher objectification. We thus see, for example, in the hardening of the bones, an unmistakable analogy to crystallisation, as the force which originally had possession of the chalk, although ossification is never to be reduced to crystallisation. The analogy shows itself in a weaker degree in the flesh

becoming firm. The combination of humours in the animal body
and secretion are also analogous to chemical combination and
separation. Indeed, the laws of chemistry are still strongly operative in this case, but subordinated, very much modified, and mastered by a higher Idea; therefore mere chemical forces outside the
organism will never afford us such humours; but the more developed Idea resulting from this victory over several lower Ideas or
objectifications of will, gains an entirely new character by taking
up into itself from every Idea over which it has prevailed a
strengthened analogy. The will objectifies itself in a new, more
distinct way. It originally appears in *generatio œquivoca;* afterwards in assimilation to the given germ, organic moisture, plant,
animal, man. Thus from the strife of lower phenomena the higher
arise, swallowing them all up, but yet realising in the higher grade
the tendency of all the lower. Here, then, already the law applies
—"Unless the serpent eats a serpent, he does not become a dragon."

According to the view I have expressed, the traces of chemical
and physical modes of operation will indeed be found in the
organism, but it can never be explained from them; because it
is by no means a phenomenon even accidentally brought about
through the united actions of such forces, but a higher Idea which
has overcome these lower Ideas by *subduing assimilation;* for the
one will which objectifies itself in all Ideas always seeks the highest
possible objectification, and has therefore in this case given up the
lower grades of its manifestation after a conflict, in order to appear
in a higher grade, and one so much the more powerful. No victory
without conflict: since the higher Idea or objectification of will
can only appear through the conquest of the lower, it endures the
opposition of these lower Ideas, which, although brought into
subjection, still constantly strive to obtain an independent and
complete expression of their being. The magnet that has attracted
a piece of iron carries on a perpetual conflict with gravitation,
which, as the lower objectification of will, has a prior right to the
matter of the iron; and in this constant battle the magnet indeed
grows stronger, for the opposition excites it, as it were, to greater
effort. In the same way every manifestation of the will, including
that which expresses itself in the human organism, wages a constant war against the many physical and chemical forces which, as
lower Ideas, have a prior right to that matter. Thus the arm falls

which for a while, overcoming gravity, we have held stretched out;
thus the pleasing sensation of health, which proclaims the victory
of the Idea of the self-conscious organism over the physical and
chemical laws, which originally governed the humours of the body,
is so often interrupted, and is indeed always accompanied by
greater or less discomfort, which arises from the resistance of these
forces, and on account of which the vegetative part of our life is
constantly attended by slight pain. Thus also digestion weakens
all the animal functions, because it requires the whole vital force
to overcome the chemical forces of nature by assimilation. Hence
also in general the burden of physical life, the necessity of sleep,
and, finally, of death; for at last these subdued forces of nature,
assisted by circumstances, win back from the organism, wearied
even by the constant victory, the matter it took from them, and
attain to an unimpeded expression of their being. We may therefore say that every organism expresses the Idea of which it is the
image, only after we have subtracted the part of its force which
is expended in subduing the lower Ideas that strive with it for
matter. This seems to have been running in the mind of Jacob
Böhm when he says somewhere that all the bodies of men and
animals, and even all plants, are really half dead. According as
the subjection in the organism of these forces of nature, which
express the lower grades of the objectification of will, is more or
less successful, the more or the less completely does it attain to the
expression of its Idea; that is to say, the nearer it is to the *ideal*
or the further from it—the *ideal* of beauty in its species.

Thus everywhere in nature we see strife, conflict, and alternation of victory, and in it we shall come to recognise more distinctly that variance with itself which is essential to the will.
Every grade of the objectification of will fights for the matter, the
space, and the time of the others. The permanent matter must
constantly change its form; for under the guidance of causality,
mechanical, physical, chemical, and organic phenomena, eagerly
striving to appear, wrest the matter from each other, for each
desires to reveal its own Idea. This strife may be followed through
the whole of nature; indeed nature exists only through it. Yet
this strife itself is only the revelation of that variance with itself
which is essential to the will. This universal conflict becomes most
distinctly visible in the animal kingdom. For animals have the

whole of the vegetable kingdom for their food, and even within
the animal kingdom every beast is the prey and the food of another; that is, the matter in which its Idea expresses itself must
yield itself to the expression of another Idea, for each animal can
only maintain its existence by the constant destruction of some
other. Thus the will to live everywhere preys upon itself, and in
different forms is its own nourishment, till finally the human
race, because it subdues all the others, regards nature as a manu-
factory for its use. Yet even the human race, as we shall see in the
Fourth Book, reveals in itself with most terrible distinctness this
conflict, this variance with itself of the will, and we find *homo
homini lupus.* . . .

We should see the will express itself here in the lowest grade
as blind striving, an obscure, inarticulate impulse, far from susceptible of being directly known. It is the simplest and the weakest mode of its objectification. But it appears as this blind and
unconscious striving in the whole of unorganized nature, in all
those original forces of which it is the work of physics and chemistry to discover and to study the laws, and each of which manifests itself to us in millions of phenomena which are exactly
similar and regular, and show no trace of individual character,
but are mere multiplicity through space and time, *i.e.,* through
the *principum individuationis,* as a picture is multiplied through
the facets of a glass.

From grade to grade objectifying itself more distinctly, yet still
completely without consciousness as an obscure striving force, the
will acts in the vegetable kingdom also, in which the bond of its
phenomena consists no longer properly of causes, but of stimuli;
and, finally, also in the vegetative part of the animal phenomenon,
in the production and maturing of the animal and in sustaining
its inner economy, in which the manifestation of will is still always
necessarily determined by stimuli. The ever-ascending grades of
the objectification of will bring us at last to the point at which
the individual that expresses the Idea could no longer receive
food for its assimilation through mere movement following upon
stimuli. For such a stimulus must be waited for, but the food has
now come to be of a more special and definite kind, and with the
ever-increasing multiplicity of the individual phenomena, the
crowd and confusion has become so great that they interfere with

each other, and the chance of the individual that is moved merely by stimuli and must wait for its food would be too unfavourable. From the point, therefore, at which the animal has delivered itself from the egg or the womb in which it vegetated without consciousness, its food must be sought out and selected. For this purpose movement following upon motives, and therefore consciousness, becomes necessary, and consequently it appears as an agent, *mēchanē,* called in at this stage of the objectification of will for the conservation of the individual and the propagation of the species. It appears represented by the brain or a large ganglion, just as every other effort or determination of the will which objectifies itself is represented by an organ, that is to say, manifests itself for the idea as an organ. But with this means of assistance, this *mēchanē,* the *world as idea* comes into existence at a stroke, with all its forms, object and subject, time, space, multiplicity, and causality. The world now shows its second side. Till now *mere will,* it becomes also *idea,* object of the knowing subject. The will, which up to this point followed its tendency in the dark with unerring certainty, has at this grade kindled for itself a light as a means which became necessary for getting rid of the disadvantage which arose from the throng and the complicated nature of its manifestations, and which would have accrued precisely to the most perfect of them. The hitherto infallible certainty and regularity with which it worked in unorganized and merely vegetative nature, rested upon the fact that it alone was active in its original nature, as blind impulse, will, without assistance, and also without interruption, from a second and entirely different world, the world as idea, which is indeed only the image of its own inner being, but is yet of quite another nature, and now encroaches on the connected whole of its phenomena. Hence its infallible certainty comes to an end. Animals are already exposed to illusion, to deception. They have, however, merely ideas of perception, no conceptions, no reflections, and they are therefore bound to the present; they cannot have regard for the future. It seems as if this knowledge without reason was not in all cases sufficient for its end, and at times required, as it were, some assistance. . . .

Finally, when the will has attained to the highest grade of its objectification, that knowledge of the understanding given to brutes to which the senses supply the data out of which there arises mere perception confined to what is immediately present, does not suffice. That complicated, many-sided, imaginative being, man, with his many needs, and exposed as he is to innumerable dangers, must, in order to exist, be lighted by a double knowledge; a higher power, as it were, of perceptive knowledge must be given him, and also reason, as the faculty of framing abstract conceptions. With this there has appeared reflection, surveying the future and the past, and, as a consequence, deliberation, care, the power of premediated action independent of the present, and finally, the full and distinct consciousness of one's own deliberate volition as such. Now if with mere knowledge of perception there arose the possibility of illusion and deception, by which the previous infallibility of the blind striving of will was done away with, so that mechanical and other instincts, as expressions of unconscious will, had to lend their help in the midst of those that were conscious, with the entrance of reason that certainty and infallibility of the expressions of will (which at the other extreme in unorganized nature appeared as strict conformity to law) is almost entirely lost; instinct disappears altogether; deliberation, which is supposed to take the place of everything else, begets (as was shown in the First Book) irresolution and uncertainty; then error becomes possible, and in many cases obstructs the adequate objectification of the will in action. For although in the character the will has already taken its definite and unchangeable bent or direction, in accordance with which volition, when occasioned by the presence of a motive, invariably takes place, yet error can falsify its expressions, for it introduces illusive motives that take the place of the real ones which they resemble; as, for example, when superstition forces on a man imaginary motives which impel him to a course of action directly opposed to the way in which the will would otherwise express itself in the given circumstances. Agamemnon slays his daughter; a miser dispenses alms, out of pure egotism, in the hope that he will some day receive an hundredfold; and so on.

Thus knowledge generally, rational as well as merely sensuous, proceeds originally from the will itself, belongs to the inner being of the higher grades of its objectification as a means of supporting the individual and the species, just like any organ of the body. Originally destined for the service of the will for the accomplishment of its aims, it remains almost throughout entirely subjected to its service: it is so in all brutes and in almost all men. Yet we shall see in the Third Book how in certain individual men knowledge can deliver itself from this bondage, throw off its yoke, and, free from all the aims of will, exist purely for itself, simply as a clear mirror of the world, which is the source of art. Finally, in the Fourth Book, we shall see how, if this kind of knowledge reacts on the will, it can bring about self-surrender, *i.e.*, resignation, which is the final goal, and indeed the inmost nature of all virtue and holiness, and is deliverance from the world. . . .

Third Book

The World As Idea

Second Aspect

The Idea Independent of the Principle of Sufficient Reason: The Platonic Idea: The Object of Art

30] In the First Book the world was explained as mere *idea,* object for a subject. In the Second Book we considered it from its other side, and found that in this aspect it is *will,* which proved to be simply that which this world is besides being idea. In accordance with this knowledge we called the world as idea, both as a whole and in its parts, the *objectification of will,* which therefore means the will become object, *i.e.,* idea. Further, we remember that this objectification of will was found to have many definite grades, in which, with gradually increasing distinctness and completeness, the nature of will appears in the idea, that is to say, presents itself as object. In these grades we already recognised the Platonic Ideas, for the grades are just the determined species, or the original unchanging forms and qualities of all natural bodies, both organised and unorganised, and also the general forces which reveal themselves according to natural laws. These Ideas, then, as a whole express themselves in innumerable individuals and particulars, and are related to these as archetypes to their copies.

The multiplicity of such individuals is only conceivable through time and space, their appearing and passing away through causality, and in all these forms we recognise merely the different modes of the principle of sufficient reason, which is the ultimate principle of all that is finite, of all individual existence, and the universal form of the idea as it appears in the knowledge of the individual as such. The Platonic Idea, on the other hand, does not come under this principle, and has therefore neither multiplicity nor change. While the individuals in which it expresses itself are innumerable, and unceasingly come into being and pass away, it remains unchanged as one and the same, and the principle of sufficient reason has for it no meaning. As, however, this is the form under which all knowledge of the subject comes, so far as the subject knows as an *individual,* the Ideas lie quite outside the sphere of its knowledge. If, therefore, the Ideas are to become objects of knowledge, this can only happen by transcending the individuality of the knowing subject. The more exact and detailed explanation of this is what will now occupy our attention.

34] The transition which we have referred to as possible, but yet to be regarded as only exceptional, from the common knowledge of particular things to the knowledge of the Idea, takes place suddenly; for knowledge breaks free from the service of the will, by the subject ceasing to be merely individual, and thus becoming the pure will-less subject of knowledge, which no longer traces relations in accordance with the principle of sufficient reason, but rests in fixed contemplation of the object presented to it, out of its connection with all others, and rises into it.

If, raised by the power of the mind, a man relinquishes the common way of looking at things, gives up tracing, under the guidance of the forms of the principle of sufficient reason, their relations to each other, the final goal of which is always a relation to his own will; if he thus ceases to consider the where, the when, the why, and the whither of things, and looks simply and solely at the *what;* if, further, he does not allow abstract thought, the concepts of the reason, to take possession of his consciousness, but, instead of all this, gives the whole power of his mind to perception, sinks himself entirely in this, and lets his whole consciousness be filled with the quiet contemplation of the natural object actually present, whether a landscape, a tree, a mountain, a building, or whatever it may be; inasmuch as he *loses* himself in this object (to use a pregnant German idiom), *i.e.,* forgets even his individuality, his will, and only continues to exist as the pure subject, the clear mirror of the object, so that it is as if the object alone were there, without any one to perceive it, and he can no longer separate the perceiver from the perception, but both have become one, because the whole consciousness is filled and occupied with one single sensuous picture; if thus the object has to such an extent passed out of all relation to something outside it, and the subject out of all relation to the will, then that which is so known is no longer the particular thing as such; but it is the *Idea,* the eternal form, the immediate objectivity of the will at this grade; and, therefore, he who is sunk in this perception is no longer individual, for in such perception the individual has lost himself; but he is *pure,* will-less, painless, timeless *subject of knowledge.* This, which in itself is so remarkable (which I well know confirms the saying that originated with Thomas Paine, "It is only one step from the sublime to the ridiculous"), will by degrees become clearer and less surprising from what follows. It was this that was running in Spinoza's mind when he wrote: "The mind is eternal in so far as it conceives things under the form of eternity" (Eth. V. pr. 31, Schol.) In such contemplation the particular thing becomes at once the *Idea* of its species, and the perceiving individual becomes *pure subject of knowledge.* The individual, as such, knows only particular things; the pure subject of knowledge knows only Ideas. For the individual is the subject of knowledge in its relation to a definite particular manifestation of will, and in subjection to this. This particular manifestation of will is, as such, subordinated to the principle of sufficient reason in all its forms; therefore, all knowledge which relates itself to it also follows the principle of sufficient reason, and no other kind of knowledge is fitted to be of use to the will but this, which always consists merely of relations to the object. The knowing individual as such, and the particular things known by him, are always in some place, at some time, and are links in the chain of causes and effects. The pure subject of knowledge and his correlative, the Idea, have passed out of all these forms of the principle of sufficient reason: time, place, the individual that knows, and the individual that is known, have for them no meaning. When an individual knower has raised himself in the manner described to be pure subject of knowledge, and at the same time has raised the observed object to the Platonic Idea, the *world as idea* appears complete and pure, and the full objectification of the will takes place, for the Platonic Idea alone is its *adequate objectivity*. The Idea includes object and subject in like manner in itself, for they are its one form; but in it they are absolutely of equal importance; for as the object is here, as elsewhere, simply the idea of the subject, the subject, which passes entirely into the perceived object has thus become this object itself, for the whole consciousness is nothing but its perfectly distinct picture. Now this consciousness constitutes the whole *world as idea,* for one imagines the whole of the Platonic Ideas, or grades of the objectivity of will, in their series passing through it. The particular things of all time and space are nothing but Ideas multiplied through the principle of sufficient reason (the form of the knowledge of the individual as such), and thus obscured as regards their pure objectivity. When the Platonic Idea appears, in it subject and object are no longer to be distinguished, for the Platonic Idea, the adequate objectivity of will, the true world as idea, arises only when the subject and object reciprocally fill and penetrate each other completely; and in the same way the knowing and the known individuals, as things in themselves, are not to be distinguished. For if we look entirely away from the true *world as idea,* there remains nothing but *the world as will.* The will is the "in-itself" of the Platonic Idea, which fully objectifies it; it is also the "in-itself" of the particular thing and of the individual that knows it, which objectify it incompletely. As will, outside the idea and all its forms, it is one and the same in the object contemplated and in the individual, who soars aloft in this contemplation, and becomes conscious of himself as pure subject. These two are, therefore, in themselves not different, for in themselves they are will, which here knows itself; and multiplicity and difference exist only as the way in which this knowledge comes to the will, *i.e.,* only in the phenomenon, on account of its form, the principle of sufficient reason.

Now the known thing, without me as the subject of knowledge, is just as little an object, and not mere will, blind effort, as without the object, without the idea, I am a knowing subject and not mere blind will. This will is in itself, *i.e.,* outside the idea, one and the same with mine: only in the world as idea, whose form is always at least that of subject and object, we are separated as the known and the knowing individual. As soon as knowledge, the world as idea, is abolished, there remains nothing but mere will, blind effort. That it should receive objectivity, become idea, supposes at once both subject and object; but that this should be pure, complete, and adequate objectivity of the will, supposes the object as Platonic Idea, free from the forms of the principle of sufficient reason, and the subject as the pure subject of knowledge, free from individuality and subjection to the will. . . .

³⁶¹ History follows the thread of events; it is pragmatic so far as it deduces them in accordance with the law of motivation, a law that determines the self-manifesting will wherever it is enlightened by knowledge. At the lowest grades of its objectivity, where it still acts without knowledge, natural science, in the form of etiology, treats of the laws of the changes of its phenomena, and, in the form of morphology, of what is permanent in them. This almost endless task is lightened by the aid of concepts, which comprehend what is general in order that we may deduce what is particular from it. Lastly, mathematics treats of the mere forms, time and space, in which the Ideas, broken up into multiplicity, appear for the knowledge of the subject as individual. All these, of which the common name is science, proceed according to the principle of sufficient reason in its different forms, and their theme is always the phenomenon, its laws, connections, and the relations which result from them. But what kind of knowledge is concerned with that which is outside and independent of all relations, that which alone is really essential to the world, the true content of its phenomena, that which is subject to no change, and therefore is known with equal truth for all time, in a word, the *Ideas,* which are the direct and adequate objectivity of the thing-in-itself, the will? We answer, *Art,* the work of genius. It repeats or reproduces the eternal Ideas grasped through pure contemplation, the essential and abiding in all the phenomena of the world; and according to what the material is in which it reproduces, it is sculpture or painting, poetry or music. Its one source is the knowledge of Ideas; its one aim the communication of this knowledge. While science,

following the unresting and inconstant stream of the fourfold forms of reason and consequent, with each end attained sees further, and can never reach a final goal nor attain full satisfaction, any more than by running we can reach the place where the clouds touch the horizon; art, on the contrary, is everywhere at its goal. For it plucks the object of its contemplation out of the stream of the world's course, and has it isolated before it. And this particular thing, which in that stream was a small perishing part, becomes to art the representative of the whole, an equivalent of the endless multitude in space and time. It therefore pauses at this particular thing; the course of time stops; the relations vanish for it; only the essential, the Idea, is its object. We may, therefore, accurately define it as the *way of viewing things independent of the principle of sufficient reason,* in opposition to the way of viewing them which proceeds in accordance with that principle, and which is the method of experience and of science. This last method of considering things may be compared to a line infinitely extended in a horizontal direction, and the former to a vertical line which cuts it at any point. The method of viewing things which proceeds in accordance with the principle of sufficient reason is the rational method, and it alone is valid and of use in practical life and in science. The method which looks away from the content of this principle is the method of genius, which is only valid and of use in art. The first is the method of Aristotle; the second is, on the whole, that of Plato. The first is like the mighty storm, that rushes along without beginning and without aim, bending, agitating, and carrying away everything before it; the second is like the silent sunbeam, that pierces through the storm quite unaffected by it. The first is like the innumerable showering drops of the waterfall, which, constantly changing, never rest for an instant; the second is like the rainbow, quietly resting on this raging torrent. Only through the pure contemplation described above, which ends entirely in the object can Ideas be comprehended; and the nature of *genuis* consists in pre-eminent capacity for such contemplation. Now, as this requires that a man should entirely forget himself and the relations in which he stands, *genius* is simply the completest *objectivity, i.e.,* the objective tendency of the mind, as opposed to the subjective, which is directed to one's own self—in other words, to the will. Thus genius is the faculty of continuing in the state of pure perception, of losing oneself in perception, and of enlisting in this service the knowledge which originally existed only for the service of the will; that is to say, genius is the power of leaving one's own interests, wishes, and aims entirely out of sight, thus of entirely renouncing one's own personality for a time, so as to remain *pure knowing subject,* clear vision of the world; and this not merely at moments, but for a sufficient length of time, and with sufficient consciousness, to enable one to reproduce by deliberate art what has thus been apprehended, and "to fix in lasting thoughts the wavering images that float before the mind." It is as if, when genius appears in an individual, a far larger measure of the power of knowledge falls to his lot than is necessary for the service of an individual will; and this superfluity of knowledge, being free, now becomes subject purified from will, a clear mirror of the inner nature of the world. This explains the activity, amounting even to disquietude, of men of genius, for the present can seldom satisfy them, because it does not fill their consciousness. This gives them that restless aspiration, that unceasing desire for new things, and for the contemplation of lofty things, and also that longing that is hardly ever satisfied, for men of similar nature and of like stature, to whom they might communicate themselves; whilst the common mortal, entirely filled and satisfied by the common present, ends in it, and finding everywhere his like, enjoys that peculiar satisfaction in daily life that is denied to genius. . . .

381 In the æsthetical mode of contemplation we have found *two inseparable constituent parts*—the knowledge of the object, not as individual thing but as Platonic Idea, that is, as the enduring form of this whole species of things; and the self-consciousness of the knowing person, not as individual, but as *pure will-less subject of knowledge.* The condition under which both these constituent parts appear always united was found to be the abandonment of the method of knowing which is bound to the principle of sufficient reason, and which, on the other hand, is the only kind of knowledge that is of value for the service of the will and also for science. Morever, we shall see that the pleasure which is produced by the contemplation of the beautiful arises from these two constituent parts, sometimes more from the one, sometimes more from the other, according to what the object of the æsthetical contemplation may be.

All *willing* arises from want, therefore from deficiency, and therefore from suffering. The satisfaction of a wish ends it; yet for one wish that is satisfied there remain at least ten which are denied. Further, the desire lasts long, the demands are infinite; the satisfaction is short and scantily measured out. But even the final satisfaction is itself only apparent; every satisfied wish at once makes room for a new one; both are illusions; the one is known to be so, the other not yet. No attained object of desire can give lasting satisfaction, but merely a fleeting gratification; it is like the alms thrown to the beggar, that keeps him alive to-day that his misery may be prolonged till the morrow. Therefore, so long as our consciousness is filled by our will, so long as we are given up to the throng of desires with their constant hopes and fears, so long as we are the subject of willing, we can never have lasting happiness nor peace. It is essentially all the same whether we pursue or flee, fear injury or seek enjoyment; the care for the constant demands of the will, in whatever form it may be, continually occupies and sways the consciousness; but without peace no true well-being is possible. The subject of willing is thus constantly stretched on the revolving wheel of Ixion, pours water into the sieve of the Danaids, is the ever-longing Tantalus.

But when some external cause or inward disposition lifts us suddenly out of the endless stream of willing, delivers knowledge from the slavery of the will, the attention is no longer directed to the motives of willing, but comprehends things free from their relation to the will, and thus observes them without personal interest, without subjectivity, purely objectively, gives itself entirely up to them so far as they are ideas, but not in so far as they are motives. Then all at once the peace which we were always seeking, but which always fled from us on the former path of the desires, comes to us of its own accord, and it is well with us. It is the painless state which Epicurus prized as the highest good and as the state of the gods; for we are for the moment set free from the miserable striving of the will; we keep the Sabbath of the penal servitude of willing; the wheel of Ixion stands still. . . .

391 All these reflections are intended to bring out the subjective part of æsthetic pleasure; that is to say, that pleasure so far as it consists simply of delight in perceptive knowledge as such, in opposition to will. And as directly connected with this, there naturally follows the explanation of that disposition or frame of mind which has been called the sense of the *sublime*.

We have already remarked above that the transition to the state of pure perception takes place most easily when the objects bend themselves to it, that is, when by their manifold and yet definite and distinct form they easily become representatives of their Ideas, in which beauty, in the objective sense, consists. This quality belongs pre-eminently to natural beauty, which thus affords even to the most insensible at least a fleeting æsthetic satisfaction: indeed it is so remarkable how especially the vegetable world invites æsthetic observation, and, as it were, presses itself upon it, that one might say, that these advances are connected with the fact that these organisms, unlike the bodies of animals, are not themselves immediate objects of knowledge, and therefore require the assistance of a foreign intelligent individual in order to rise out of the world of blind will and enter the world of idea, and that thus they long, as it were, for this entrance, that they may attain at least indirectly what is denied them directly. But I leave this suggestion which I have hazarded, and which borders perhaps upon extravagance, entirely undecided, for only a very intimate and devoted consideration of nature can raise or justify it. As long as that which raises us from the knowledge of mere relations subject to the will, to æsthetic contemplation, and thereby exalts us to the position of the subject of knowledge free from will, is this fittingness of nature, this significance and distinctness of its forms, on account of which the Ideas individualised in them readily present themselves to us; so long is it merely *beauty* that affects us and the sense of the *beautiful* that is excited. But if these very objects whose significant forms invite us to pure contemplation, have a hostile relation to the human will in general, as it exhibits itself in its objectivity, the human body, if they are opposed to it, so that it is menaced by the irresistible predominance of their power, or sinks into insignificance before their immeasurable greatness; if, nevertheless, the beholder does not direct his attention to this eminently hostile relation to his will, but, although perceiving and recognising it, turns consciously away from it, forcibly detaches himself from his will and its relations, and, giving himself up entirely to knowledge, quietly contemplates those very objects that are so terrible to the will, comprehends only their Idea, which is foreign to all relation, so that he lingers gladly over its contemplation, and is thereby raised above himself, his person, his will, and all will:—in that case he is filled with the sense of the *sublime,* he is in the state of spiritual exaltation, and therefore the object producing such a state is called *sublime.* Thus what distinguishes the sense of the sublime from that of the beautiful is this: in the case of the beautiful, pure knowledge has gained the upper hand without a struggle, for the beauty of the object, *i.e.,* that property which facilitates the knowledge of its Idea, has removed from consciousness without resistance, and therefore imperceptibly, the will and the knowledge of relations which is subject to it, so that what is left is the pure subject of knowledge without even a remembrance of will. On the other hand, in the case of the sublime that state of pure knowledge is only attained by a conscious and forcible breaking away from the relations of the same object to the will, which are recognised as unfavourable, by a free and conscious transcending of the will and the knowledge related to it. . . .

When we say that a thing is *beautiful,* we thereby assert that it is an object of our æsthetic contemplation, and this has a double meaning; on the one hand, it means that the sight of the thing makes us *objective,* that is to say, that in contemplating it we are no longer conscious of ourselves as individuals, but as pure will-less subjects of knowledge; and, on the other hand, it means that we recognise in the object, not the particular thing, but an Idea; and this can only happen, so far as our contemplation of it is not subordinated to the principle of sufficient reason, does not follow the relation of the object to anything outside it (which is always ultimately connected with relations to our own will), but rests in the object itself. For the Idea and the pure subject of knowledge always appear at once in consciousness as necessary correlatives, and on their appearances all distinction of time vanishes, for they are both entirely foreign to the principle of sufficient reason in all its forms, and lie outside the relations which are imposed by it; they may be compared to the rainbow and the sun, which have

no part in the constant movement and succession of the falling
drops. Therefore, if, for example, I contemplate a tree æsthetically, *i.e.,* with artistic eyes, and thus recognise, not it, but its
Idea, it becomes at once of no consequence whether it is this tree
or its predecessor which flourished a thousand years ago, and
whether the observer is this individual or any other that lived
anywhere and at any time; the particular thing and the knowing
individual are abolished with the principle of sufficient reason,
and there remains nothing but the Idea and the pure subject of
knowing, which together constitute the adequate objectivity of
will at this grade. And the Idea dispenses not only with time, but
also with space, for the Idea proper is not this special form which
appears before me but its expression, its pure significance, its
inner being, which discloses itself to me and appeals to me, and
which may be quite the same though the spatial relations of its
form be very different.

Since, on the one hand, every given thing may be observed in
a purely objective manner and apart from all relations; and since,
on the other hand, the will manifests itself in everything at some
grade of its objectivity, so that everything is the expression of an
Idea; it follows that everything is also *beautiful.* That even the
most insignificant things admit of pure objective and will-less
contemplation, and thus prove that they are beautiful, is shown
by the Dutch pictures of still life. But one thing is more beautiful
than another, because it makes this pure objective contemplation
easier, it lends itself to it, and, so to speak, even compels it, and
then we call it very beautiful. This is the case sometimes because,
as an individual thing, it expresses in its purity the Idea of its
species by the very distinct, clearly defined, and significant relation of its parts, and also fully reveals that Idea through the
completeness of all the possible expressions of its species united
in it, so that it makes the transition from the individual thing to
the Idea, and therefore also the condition of pure contemplation,
very easy for the beholder. Sometimes this possession of special
beauty in an object lies in the fact that the Idea itself which
appeals to us in it is a high grade of the objectivity of will, and
therefore very significant and expressive. Therefore it is that man
is more beautiful than all other objects, and the revelation of his
nature is the highest aim of art. Human form and expression are

the most important objects of plastic art, and human action the most important object of poetry. Yet each thing has its own peculiar beauty, not only every organism which expresses itself in the unity of an individual being, but also everything unorganised and formless, and even every manufactured article. For all these reveal the Ideas through which the will objectifies itself at its lowest grades; they give, as it were, the deepest resounding bass notes of nature. Gravity, rigidity, fluidity, light, and so forth, are the Ideas which express themselves in rocks, in buildings, in waters. Landscape gardening or architecture can do no more than assist them to unfold their qualities distinctly, fully, and variously; they can only give them the opportunity of expressing themselves purely, so that they lend themselves to æsthetic contemplation and make it easier. Inferior buildings or ill-favoured localities, on the contrary, which nature has neglected or art has spoiled, perform this task in a very slight degree or not at all; yet even from them these universal, fundamental Ideas of nature cannot altogether disappear. To the careful observer they present themselves here also, and even bad buildings and the like are capable of being æsthetically considered; the Ideas of the most universal properties of their materials are still recognisable in them, only the artificial form which has been given them does not assist but hinders æsthetic contemplation. . . .

521 Now that we have considered all the fine arts in the general way that is suitable to our point of view, beginning with architecture, the peculiar end of which is to elucidate the objectification of will at the lowest grades of its visibility, in which it shows itself as the dumb unconscious tendency of the mass in accordance with laws, and yet already reveals a breach of the unity of will with itself in a conflict between gravity and rigidity—and ending with the consideration of tragedy, which presents to us at the highest grades of the objectification of will this very conflict with itself in terrible magnitude and distinctness; we find that there is still another fine art which has been excluded from our consideration, and had to be excluded, for in the systematic connection of our exposition there was no fitting place for it—I mean *music*. It stands alone, quite cut off from all the other arts. In it we do not recognise the copy or repetition of any Idea of existence in the

world. Yet it is such a great and exceedingly noble art, its effect
on the inmost nature of man is so powerful, and it is so entirely
and deeply understood by him in his inmost consciousness as a
perfectly universal language, the distinctness of which surpasses
even that of the perceptible world itself, that we certainly have
more to look for in it than an "an unconscious exercise in arithmetic in which the mind does not know that it is counting,"
which Leibnitz called it. Yet he was perfectly right, as he considered only its immediate external significance, its form. But if
it were nothing more, the satisfaction which it affords would be
like that which we feel when a sum in arithmetic comes out right,
and could not be that intense pleasure with which we see the
deepest recesses of our nature find utterance. From our standpoint,
therefore, at which the æsthetic effect is the criterion, we must
attribute to music a far more serious and deep significance, connected with the inmost nature of the world and our own self, and
in reference to which the arithmetical proportions, to which it
may be reduced, are related, not as the thing signified, but merely
as the sign. That in some sense music must be related to the world
as the representation to the thing represented, as the copy to the
original, we may conclude from the analogy of the other arts, all
of which possess this character, and affect us on the whole in the
same way as it does, only that the effect of music is stronger,
quicker, more necessary and infallible. Further, its representative
relation to the world must be very deep, absolutely true, and
strikingly accurate, because it is instantly understood by every
one, and has the appearance of a certain infallibility, because its
form may be reduced to perfectly definite rules expressed in
numbers, from which it cannot free itself without entirely ceasing
to be music. Yet the point of comparison between music and the
world, the respect in which it stands to the world in the relation
of a copy or repetition, is very obscure. Men have practised music
in all ages without being able to account for this; content to
understand it directly, they renounce all claim to an abstract conception of this direct understanding itself.

I gave my mind entirely up to the impression of music in all
its forms, and then returned to reflection and the system of thought
expressed in the present work, and thus I arrived at an explanation of the inner nature of music and of the nature of its imitative

relation to the world—which from analogy had necessarily to be presupposed—an explanation which is quite sufficient for myself, and satisfactory to my investigation, and which will doubtless be equally evident to any one who has followed me thus far and has agreed with my view of the world. Yet I recognise the fact that it is essentially impossible to prove this explanation, for it assumes and establishes a relation of music, as idea, to that which from its nature can never be idea, and music will have to be regarded as the copy of an original which can never itself be directly presented as idea. I can therefore do no more than state here, at the conclusion of this third book, which has been principally devoted to the consideration of the arts, the explanation of the marvellous art of music which satisfies myself, and I must leave the acceptance or denial of my view to the effect produced upon each of my readers both by music itself and by the whole system of thought communicated in this work. Moreover, I regard it as necessary, in order to be able to assent with full conviction to the exposition of the significance of music I am about to give, that one should often listen to music with constant reflection upon my theory concerning it, and for this again it is necessary to be very familiar with the whole of my system of thought.

The (Platonic) Ideas are the adequate objectification of will. To excite or suggest the knowledge of these by means of the representation of particular things (for works of art themselves are always representations of particular things) is the end of all the other arts, which can only be attained by a corresponding change in the knowing subject. Thus all these arts objectify the will indirectly only by means of the Ideas; and since our world is nothing but the manifestation of the Ideas in multiplicity, though their entrance into the *principium individuationis* (the form of the knowledge possible for the individual as such), music also, since it passes over the Ideas, is entirely independent of the phenomenal world, ignores it altogether, could to a certain extent exist if there was no world at all, which cannot be said of the other arts. Music is as *direct* an objectification and copy of the whole *will* as the world itself, nay, even as the Ideas, whose multiplied manifestation constitutes the world of individual things. Music is thus by no means like the other arts, the copy of the Ideas, but the *copy of the will itself*, whose objectivity the Ideas are. This is why the effect of music is so much more powerful and penetrating than that of the other arts, for they speak only of shadows, but it speaks of the thing itself. Since, however, it is the same will which objectifies itself both in the Ideas and in music, though in quite different ways, there must be, not indeed a direct likeness, but yet a parallel, an analogy, between music and the Ideas whose manifestation in multiplicity and incompleteness is the visible world. The establishing of this analogy will facilitate, as an illustration, the understanding of this exposition, which is so difficult on account of the obscurity of the subject.

I recognise in the deepest tones of harmony, in the bass, the lowest grades of the objectification of will, unorganised nature, the mass of the planet. It is well known that all the high notes which are easily sounded, and die away more quickly, are produced by the vibration in their vicinity of the deep bass note. When, also, the low notes sound, the high notes always sound faintly, and it is a law of harmony that only those high notes may accompany a bass note which actually already sound along with it of themselves (its *sons harmoniques*) on account of its vibration. This is analogous to the fact that the whole of the bodies and organisations of nature must be regarded as having come into existence through gradual development out of the mass of the planet; this is both their supporter and their source, and the same relation subsists between the high notes and the bass. There is a limit of depth, below which no sound is audible. This corresponds to the fact that no matter can be perceived without form and quality, *i.e.*, without the manifestation of a force which cannot be further explained, in which an Idea expresses itself, and, more generally, that no matter can be entirely without will. Thus, as a certain pitch is inseparable from the note as such, so a certain grade of the manifestation of will is inseparable from matter. Bass is thus, for us, in harmony what unorganised nature, the crudest mass, upon which all rests, and from which everything originates and develops, is in the world. Now, further, in the whole of the complemented parts which make up the harmony between the bass and the leading voice singing the melody, I recognise the whole gradation of the Ideas in which the will objectifies itself. Those nearer to the bass are the lower of these grades, the still unorganised, but yet manifold phenomenal things; the higher represent to me the world of plants and beasts. The definite intervals of the scale are parallel to the definite grades of the objectification of will, the definite species in nature. The departure from the arithmetical correctness of the intervals, through some temperament, or produced by the key selected, is analogous to the departure of the individual from the type of the species. Indeed, even the impure discords, which give no definite interval, may be compared to the monstrous abortions produced by beasts of two species, or by man and beast. But to all these bass and complemental parts which make up the *harmony* there is wanting that connected progress which belongs only to the high voice singing the melody, and it alone moves quickly and lightly in modulations and runs, while all these others have only a slower movement without a connection in each part for itself. The deep bass moves most slowly, the representative of the crudest mass. Its rising and falling occurs only by large intervals, in thirds, fourths, fifths, never by *one* tone, unless it is a bass inverted by double counterpoint. This slow movement is also physically essential to it; a quick run or shake in the low notes cannot even be imagined. The higher complemental parts, which are parallel to animal life, move more quickly, but yet without melodious connection and significant progress. The disconnected course of all the complemental parts, and their regulation by definite laws, is analogous to the fact that in the whole irrational world, from the crystal to the most perfect animal, no being has a connected consciousness of its own which would make its life into a significant whole, and none experiences a succession of mental developments, none perfects itself by culture, but everything exists always in the same way according to its kind, determined by fixed law. Lastly, in the *melody,* in the high, singing, principal voice leading the whole and progressing with unrestrained freedom, in the unbroken significant connection of *one* thought from beginning to end representing a whole, I recognise the highest grade of the objectification of will, the intellectual life and effort of man. As he alone, because endowed with reason, constantly looks before and after on the path of his actual life and its innumerable possibilities, and so achieves a course of life which is intellectual, and therefore connected as a whole; corresponding to this, I say, the *melody* has significant intentional connection from beginning to end. It records, therefore, the history of the intellectually-enlightened will. This will expresses itself in the actual world as the series of its deeds; but melody says more, it records the most secret history of this intellectually-enlightened will, pictures every excitement, every effort, every movement of it, all that which the reason collects under the wide and negative concept of feeling, and which it cannot apprehend further through its abstract concepts. Therefore it has always been said that music is the language of feeling and of passion, as words are the language of reason. . . .

Now the nature of man consists in this, that his will strives, is satisfied and strives anew, and so on for ever. Indeed, his happiness and well-being consist simply in the quick transition from wish to satisfaction, and from satisfaction to a new wish. For the absence of satisfaction is suffering, the empty longing for a new wish, languor, *ennui*. And corresponding to this the nature of melody is a constant digression and deviation from the keynote in a thousand ways, not only to the harmonious intervals to the third and dominant, but to every tone, to the dissonant sevenths and to the superfluous degrees; yet there always follows a constant return to the keynote. In all these deviations melody expresses the multifarious efforts of will, but always its satisfaction also by the final return to an harmonious interval, and still more, to the keynote. The composition of melody, the disclosure in it of all the deepest secrets of human willing and feeling, is the work of genius, whose action, which is more apparent here than anywhere else, lies far from all reflection and conscious intention, and may be called an inspiration. The conception is here, as everywhere in art, unfruitful. The composer reveals the inner nature of the world, and expresses the deepest wisdom in a language which his reason does not understand; as a person under the influence of mesmerism tells things of which he has no conception when he awakes. Therefore in the composer, more than in any other artist, the man is entirely separated and distinct from the artist. Even in the explanation of this wonderful art, the concept shows its poverty and limitation. I shall try, however, to complete our analogy. As quick transition from wish to satisfaction, and from satisfaction to a new wish, is happiness and well-being, so quick melodies without great deviations are cheerful; slow melodies, striking painful discords, and only winding back through many bars to the keynote are, as analogous to the delayed and hardly won satisfaction, sad. The delay of the new excitement of will, languor, could have no other expression than the sustained keynote, the effort of which would soon be unbearable; very monotonous and unmeaning melodies approach this effect. The short intelligible subjects of quick dance-music seem to speak only of easily attained common pleasure. On the other hand, the *Allegro maestoso,* in elaborate movements, long passages, and wide deviations, signifies a greater, nobler effort towards a more distant end, and its final attainment. The *Adagio* speaks of the pain of a great and noble effort which despises all trifling happiness. But how wonderful is the effect of the *minor* and *major!* How astounding that the change of half a tone, the entrance of a minor third instead of a major, at once and inevitably forces upon us an anxious painful feeling, from which again we are just as instantaneously delivered by the major. The *Adagio* lengthens in the minor the expression of the keenest pain, and becomes even a convulsive wail. Dance-music in the minor seems to indicate the failure of that trifling happiness which we ought rather to despise, seems to speak of the attainment of a lower end with toil and trouble. The inexhaustibleness of possible melodies corresponds to the inexhaustibleness of Nature in difference of individuals, physiognomies, and courses of life. The transition from one key to an entirely different one, since it altogether breaks the connection with what went before, is like death, for the individual ends in it; but the will which appeared in this individual lives after him as before him, appearing in other individuals, whose consciousness, however, has no connection with his.

But it must never be forgotten, in the investigation of all these analogies I have pointed out, that music has no direct, but merely an indirect relation to them, for it never expresses the phenomenon, but only the inner nature, the in-itself of all phenomena, the will itself. It does not therefore express this or that particular and definite joy, this or that sorrow, or pain, or horror, or delight, or merriment, or peace of mind; but joy, sorrow, pain, horror, delight, merriment, peace of mind *themselves,* to a certain extent in the abstract, their essential nature, without accessories, and therefore without their motives. Yet we completely understand them in this extracted quintessence. Hence it arises that our imagination is so easily excited by music, and now seeks to give form to that invisible yet actively moved spirit-world which speaks to us directly, and clothe it with flesh and blood, *i.e.,* to embody it in an analogous example. This is the origin of the song with words, and finally of the opera, the text of which should therefore never forsake that subordinate position in order to make itself the chief thing and the music a mere means of expressing it, which is a great misconception and a piece of utter perversity; for music always expresses only the quintessence of life and its events, never these themselves, and therefore their differencs do not always affect it. It is precisely this universality, which belongs exclusively to it, together with the greatest determinateness, that gives music the high worth which it has as the panacea for all our woes. Thus, if music is too closely united to the words, and tries to form itself according to the events, it is striving to speak a language which is not its own. No one has kept so free from this mistake as Rossini; therefore his music speaks *its own language* so distinctly and purely that it requires no words, and produces its full effect when rendered by instruments alone.

According to all this, we may regard the phenomenal world, or nature, and music as two different expressions of the same thing, which is therefore itself the only medium of their analogy, so that a knowledge of it is demanded in order to understand that analogy. Music, therefore, if regarded as an expression of the world, is in the highest degree a universal language, which is related indeed to the universality of concepts, much as they are related to the particular things. Its universality, however, is by no means that empty universality of abstraction, but quite of a different kind, and is united with thorough and distinct definiteness. In this respect it resembles geometrical figures and numbers, which are the universal forms of all possible objects of experience and applicable to them all *a priori*, and yet are not abstract but perceptible and thoroughly determined. All possible efforts, excitements, and manifestations of will, all that goes on in the heart of man and that reason includes in the wide, negative concept of feeling, may be expressed by the infinite number of possible melodies, but always in the universal, in the mere form, without the material, always according to the thing-in-itself, not the phenomenon, the inmost soul, as it were, of the phenomenon, without the body. This deep relation which music has to the true nature of all things also explains the fact that suitable music played to any scene, action, event, or surrounding seems to disclose to us its most secret meaning, and appears as the most accurate and distinct commentary upon it. This is so truly the case, that whoever gives himself up entirely to the impression of a symphony, seems to see all the possible events of life and the world take place in himself, yet if he reflects, he can find no likeness between the music and the things that passed before his mind. For, as we have said, music is distinguished from all the other arts by the fact that it is not a copy of the phenomenon, or, more accurately, the adequate objectivity of will, but is the direct copy of the will itself, and therefore exhibits itself as the metaphysical to everything physical in the world, and as the thing-in-itself to every phenomenon. We might, therefore, just as well call the world embodied music as embodied will; and this is the reason why music makes every picture, and indeed every scene of real life and of the world, at once appear with higher significance, certainly all the more in proportion as its melody is analogous to the inner spirit of the given phenomenon. It rests upon this that we are able to set a poem to music as a song, or a perceptible representation as a pantomime, or both as an opera. Such particular pictures of human life, set to the universal language of music, are never bound to it or correspond to it with stringent necessity; but they stand to it only in the relation of an example chosen at will to a general concept. In the determinateness of the real, they represent that which music expresses in the universality of mere form. For melodies are to a certain extent, like general concepts, an abstraction from the actual. This actual world, then, the world of particular things, affords the object of perception, the special and individual, the particular case, both to the universality of the concepts and to the universality of the melodies. But these two universalities are in a certain respect opposed to each other; for the concepts contain particulars only as the first forms abstracted from perception, as it were, the separated shell of things; thus they are, strictly speaking, *abstracta;* music, on the other hand, gives the inmost kernel which precedes all forms, or the heart of things. This relation may be very well expressed in the language of the schoolmen by saying the concepts are the *universalia post rem,* but music gives the *universalia ante rem,* and the real world the *universalia in re.* To the universal significance of a melody to which a poem has been set, it is quite possible to set other equally arbitrarily selected examples of the universal expressed in this poem corresponding to the significance of the melody in the same degree. This is why the same composition is suitable to many verses; and this is also what makes the *vaudeville* possible. But that in general a relation is possible between a composition and a perceptible representation rests, as we have said, upon the fact that both are simply different expressions of the same inner being of the world. When now, in the particular case, such a relation is actually given, that is to say, when the composer has been able to express in the universal language of music the emotions of will which constitute the heart of an event, then the melody of the song, the music of the opera, is expressive. But the analogy discovered by the composer between the two must have proceeded from the direct knowledge of the nature of the world unknown to his reason, and must not be an imitation produced with conscious intention by means of conceptions, otherwise the music does not express the inner nature of the will itself, but merely gives an inadequate imitation of its phenomenon. All specially imitative music does this; for example, "The Seasons," by Haydn; also many passages of his "Creation," in which phenomena of the external world are directly imitated; also all battle-pieces. Such music is entirely to be rejected.

The unutterable depth of all music by virtue of which it floats through our consciousness as the vision of a paradise firmly believed in yet ever distant from us, and by which also it is so fully understood and yet so inexplicable, rests on the fact that it restores to us all the emotions of our inmost nature, but entirely without reality and far removed from their pain. So also the seriousness which is essential to it, which excludes the absurd from its direct and peculiar province, is to be explained by the fact that its object is not the idea, with reference to which alone deception and absurdity are possible; but its object is directly the will, and this is essentially the most serious of all things, for it is that on which all depends. How rich in content and full of significance the language of music is, we see from the repetitions, as well as the *Da capo*, the like of which would be unbearable in works composed in a language of words, but in music are very appropriate and beneficial, for, in order to comprehend it fully, we must hear it twice. . . .

We found in the second book that the highest grade of the objectification of will, man, could not appear alone and isolated, but presupposed the grades below him, as these again presupposed the grades lower still. In the same way music, which directly objectifies the will, just as the world does, is complete only in full harmony. In order to achieve its full effect, the high leading voice of the melody requires the accompaniment of all the other voices, even to the lowest bass, which is to be regarded as the origin of all. The melody itself enters as an integral part into the harmony, as the harmony enters into it, and only thus, in the full harmonious whole, music expresses what it aims at expressing. Thus also the one will outside of time finds its full objectification only in the complete union of all the steps which reveal its nature in the innumerable ascending grades of distinctness. The following analogy is also very remarkable. We have seen in the preceding book that notwithstanding the self-adaptation of all the phenomena of will to each other as regards their species, which constitutes their teleological aspect, there yet remains an unceasing conflict between those phenomena as individuals, which is visible at every grade, and makes the world a constant battle-field of all those manifestations of one and the same will, whose inner contradiction with itself becomes visible through it. In music also there is something corresponding to this. A complete, pure, harmonious system of tones is not only physically but arithmetically impossible. The numbers themselves by which the tones are expressed have inextricable irrationality. There is no scale in which, when it is counted, every fifth will be related to the keynote as 2 to 3, every major third as 4 to 5, every minor third as 5 to 6, and so on. For if they are correctly related to the keynote, they can no longer be so to each other; because, for example, the fifth must be the minor third to the third, &c. For the notes of the scale may be compared to actors who must play now one part, now another. Therefore a perfectly accurate system of music cannot even be thought, far less worked out; and on this account all possible music deviates from perfect purity; it can only conceal the discords essential to it by dividing them among all the notes, *i.e.*, by temperament. . . .

I might still have something to say about the way in which

music is perceived, namely, in and through time alone, with absolute exclusion of space, and also apart from the influence of the knowledge of causality, thus without understanding; for the tones make the æsthetic impression as effect, and without obliging us to go back to their causes, as in the case of perception. I do not wish, however, to lengthen this discussion, as I have perhaps already gone too much into detail with regard to some things in this Third Book, or have dwelt too much on particulars. But my aim made it necessary, and it will be the less disapproved if the importance and high worth of art, which is seldom sufficiently recognised, be kept in mind. For if, according to our view, the whole visible world is just the objectification, the mirror, of the will, conducting it to knowledge of itself, and, indeed, as we shall soon see, to the possibility of its deliverance; and if, at the same time, the world as idea, if we regard it in isolation, and, freeing ourselves from all volition, allow it alone to take possession of our consciousness, is the most joy-giving and the only innocent side of life; we must regard art as the higher ascent, the more complete development of all this, for it achieves essentially just what is achieved by the visible world itself, only with greater concentration, more perfectly, with intention and intelligence, and therefore may be called, in the full significance of the word, the flower of life. If the whole world as idea is only the visibility of will, the work of art is to render this visibility more distinct. It is the *camera obscura* which shows the objects more purely, and enables us to survey them and comprehend them better. It is the play within the play, the stage upon the stage in "Hamlet."

The pleasure we receive from all beauty, the consolation which art affords, the enthusiasm of the artist, which enables him to forget the cares of life,—the latter an advantage of the man of genius over other men, which alone repays him for the suffering that increases in proportion to the clearness of consciousness, and for the desert loneliness among men of a different race,—all this rests on the fact that the in-itself of life, the will, existence itself, is, as we shall see farther on, a constant sorrow, partly miserable, partly terrible; while, on the contrary, as idea alone, purely contemplated, or copied by art, free from pain, it presents to us a drama full of significance. This purely knowable side of the world, and the copy of it in any art, is the element of the artist. He is chained to the contemplation of the play, the objectification of will; he remains beside it, does not get tired of contemplating it and representing it in copies; and meanwhile he bears himself the cost of the production of that play, *i.e.,* he himself is the will which objectifies itself, and remains in constant suffering. That pure, true, and deep knowledge of the inner nature of the world becomes now for him an end in itself: he stops there. Therefore it does not become to him a quieter of the will, as, we shall see in the next book, it does in the case of the saint who has attained to resignation; it does not deliver him for ever from life, but only at moments, and is therefore not for him a path out of life, but only an occasional consolation in it, till his power, increased by this contemplation and at last tired of the play, lays hold on the real. The St. Cecilia of Raphael may be regarded as a representation of this transition. To the real, then, we now turn in the following book.

Fourth Book

The World As Will

Second Aspect

The Assertation and Denial of the Will to Live, When Self-Consciousness Has Been Attained

541 The first three books will, it is hoped, have conveyed the distinct and certain knowledge that the world as idea is the complete mirror of the will, in which it knows itself in ascending grades of distinctness and completeness, the highest of which is man, whose nature, however, receives its complete expression only through the whole connected series of his actions. The self-conscious connection of these actions is made possible by reason, which enables a man constantly to survey the whole in the abstract.

The will, which, considered purely in itself, is without knowledge, and is merely a blind incessant impulse, as we see it appear in unorganised and vegetable nature and their laws, and also in the vegetative part of our own life, receives through the addition of the world as idea, which is developed in subjection to it, the knowledge of its own willing and of what it is that it wills. And this is nothing else than the world as idea, life, precisely as it exists. Therefore we called the phenomenal world the mirror of the will, its objectivity. And since what the will wills is always life, just because life is nothing but the representation of that willing for the idea, it is all one and a mere pleonism if, instead of simply saying "the will," we say, "the will to live."

Will is the thing-in-itself, the inner content, the essence of the world. Life, the visible world, the phenomenon, is only the mirror of the will. Therefore life accompanies the will as inseparably as the shadow accompanies the body; and if will exists, so will life, the world, exist. Life is, therefore, assured to the will to live; and so long as we are filled with the will to live we need have no fear for our existence, even in the presence of death. It is true we see the individual come into being and pass away; but the individual is only phenomenal, exists only for the knowledge which is bound to the principle of sufficient reason, to the *principium individuationis*. Certainly, for this kind of knowledge, the individual receives his life as a gift, rises out of nothing, then suffers the loss of this gift through death, and returns again to nothing. But we desire to consider life philosophically, *i.e.*, according to its Ideas, and in this sphere we shall find that neither the will, the thing-in-itself in all phenomena, nor the subject of knowing, that which perceives all phenomena, is affected at all by birth or by death. Birth and death belong merely to the phenomenon of will, thus to life; and it is essential to this to exhibit itself in individuals which come into being and pass away, as fleeting phenomena appearing in the form of time—phenomena of that which in itself knows no time, but must exhibit itself precisely in the way we have said, in order to objectify its peculiar nature. Birth and death belong in like manner to life, and hold the balance as reciprocal conditions of each other, or, if one likes the expression, as poles of the whole phenomenon of life. . . .

First of all, I wish the reader to recall the passage with which we closed the Second Book,—a passage occasioned by the question, which met us then, as to the end and aim of the will. Instead of the answer to this question, it appeared clearly before us how, in all the grades of its manifestation, from the lowest to the highest, the will dispenses altogether with a final goal and aim. It always strives, for striving is its sole nature, which no attained goal can put an end to. Therefore it is not susceptible of any final satisfaction, but can only be restrained by hindrances, while in itself it goes on for ever. We see this in the simplest of all natural phenomena, gravity, which does not cease to strive and press towards a mathematical centre to reach which would be the annihilation both of itself and matter, and would not cease even if the whole universe were already rolled into one ball. We see it in the other simple natural phenomena. A solid tends towards fluidity either by melting or dissolving, for only so will its chemical forces be free; rigidity is the imprisonment in which it is held by cold. The fluid tends towards the gaseous state, into which it passes at once as soon as all pressure is removed from it. No body is without relationship, *i.e.*, without tendency or without desire and longing, as Jakob Böhm would say. Electricity transmits its inner self-repulsion to infinity, though the mass of the earth absorbs the effect. Galvanism is certainly, so long as the pile is working, an aimless, unceasingly repeated act of repulsion and attraction. The existence of the plant is just such a restless, never satisfied striving, a ceaseless tendency through ever-ascending forms, till the end, the seed, becomes a new starting-point; and this repeated *ad infinitum*—nowhere an end, nowhere a final satisfaction, nowhere a resting-place. It will also be remembered, from the Second Book, that the multitude of natural forces and organised forms everywhere strive with each other for the matter in which they desire to appear, for each of them only possesses what it has wrested from the others; and thus a constant internecine war is waged, from which, for the most part, arises the resistance through which that striving, which constitutes the inner nature of everything, is at all points hindered; struggles in vain, yet, from its nature, cannot leave off; toils on laboriously till this phenomenon dies, when others eagerly seize its place and its matter.

We have long since recognised this striving, which constitutes the kernel and in-itself of everything, as identical with that which in us, where it manifests itself most distinctly in the light of the fullest consciousness, is called *will*. Its hindrance through an obstacle which places itself between it and its temporary aim we call *suffering,* and, on the other hand, its attainment of the end satisfaction, well-being, happiness. We may also transfer this terminology to the phenomena of the unconscious world, for though weaker in degree, they are identical in nature. Then we see them involved in constant suffering, and without any continuing happiness. For all efforts springs from defect—from discontent with one's estate—is thus suffering so long as it is not satisfied; but no satisfaction is lasting, rather it is always merely the starting-point of a new effort. The striving we see everywhere hindered in many ways, everywhere in conflict, and therefore always under the form of suffering. Thus, if there is no final end of striving, there is no measure and end of suffering.

But what we only discover in unconscious Nature by sharpened observation, and with an effort, presents itself distinctly to us in the intelligent world in the life of animals, whose constant suffering is easily proved. But without lingering over these intermediate grades, we shall turn to the life of man, in which all this appears with the greatest distinctness, illuminated by the clearest knowledge; for as the phenomenon of will becomes more complete, the suffering also becomes more and more apparent. In the plant there is as yet no sensibility, and therefore no pain. A certain very small degree of suffering is experienced by the lowest species of animal life—infusoria and radiata; even in insects the capacity to feel and suffer is still limited. It first appears in a high degree with the complete nervous system of vertebrate animals, and always in a higher degree the more intelligence develops. Thus, in proportion as knowledge attains to distinctness, as consciousness ascends, pain also increases, and therefore reaches its highest degree in man. And then, again, the more distinctly a man knows, the more intelligent he is, the more pain he has; the man who is gifted with genius suffers most of all. In this sense, that is, with reference to the degree of knowledge in general, not mere abstract rational knowledge, I understand and use here that saying of the Preacher: "Whoever augments our knowledge, increases our suffering as well." That philosophical painter or painting philosopher, Tischbein, has very beautifully expressed the accurate relation between the degree of consciousness and that of suffering by exhibiting it in a visible and clear form in a drawing. The upper half of his drawing represents women whose children have been stolen, and who in different groups and attitudes, express in many ways deep maternal pain, anguish, and despair. The lower half of the drawing represents sheep whose lambs have been taken away. They are arranged and grouped in precisely the same way; so that every human head, every human attitude of the upper half, has below a brute head and attitude corresponding to it. Thus we see distinctly how the pain which is possible in the dull brute consciousness is related to the violent grief, which only becomes possible through distinctness of knowledge and clearness of consciousness.

We desire to consider in this way, in *human existence,* the inner and essential destiny of will. Every one will easily recognise that same destiny expressed in various degrees in the life of the brutes, only more weakly, and may also convince himself to his own satisfaction, from the suffering animal world, *how essential to all life is suffering.*

571 At every grade that is enlightened by knowledge, the will appears as an individual. The human individual finds himself as finite in infinite space and time, and consequently as a vanishing quantity compared with them. He is projected into them, and, on account of their unlimited nature, he has always a merely relative, never absolute *when* and *where* of his existence; for his place and duration are finite parts of what in infinite and boundless. His real existence is only in the present, whose unchecked flight into the past is a constant transition into death, a constant dying. For his past life, apart from its possible consequences for the present, and the testimony regarding the will that is expressed in it, is now entirely done with, dead, and no longer anything; and, therefore, it must be, as a matter of reason, indifferent to him whether the content of that past was pain or pleasure. But the present is always passing through his hands into the past; the future is quite uncertain and always short. Thus his existence, even when we consider only its formal side, is a constant hurrying of the present into the dead past, a constant dying. But if we look at it from the physical side; it is clear that, as our walking is admittedly merely a constantly prevented falling, the life of our body is only a constantly prevented dying, an ever-postponed death: finally, in the same way, the activity of our mind is a

constantly deferred ennui. Every breath we draw wards off the death that is constantly intruding upon us. In this way we fight with it every moment, and again, at longer intervals, through every meal we eat, every sleep we take, every time we warm ourselves, &c. In the end, death must conquer, for we became subject to him through birth, and he only plays for a little while with his prey before he swallows it up. We pursue our life, however, with great interest and much solicitude as long as possible, as we blow out a soap-bubble as long and as large as possible, although we know perfectly well that it will burst.

We saw that the inner being of unconscious nature is a constant striving without end and without rest. And this appears to us much more distinctly when we consider the nature of brutes and man. Willing and striving is its whole being, which may be very well compared to an unquenchable thirst. But the basis of all willing is need, deficiency, and thus pain. Consequently, the nature of brutes and man is subject to pain originally and through its very being. If, on the other hand, it lacks objects of desire, because it is at once deprived of them by a too easy satisfaction, a terrible void and ennui comes over it, *i.e.*, its being and existence itself becomes an unbearable burden to it. Thus its life swings like a pendulum backwards and forwards between pain and ennui. This has also had to express itself very oddly in this way; after man had transferred all pain and torments to hell, there then remained nothing over for heaven but ennui.

But the constant striving which constitutes the inner nature of every manifestation of will obtains its primary and most general foundation at the higher grades of objectification, from the fact that here the will manifests itself as a living body, with the iron command to nourish it; and what gives strength to this command is just that this body is nothing but the objectified will to live itself. Man, as the most complete objectification of that will, is in like measure also the most necessitous of all beings: he is through and through concrete willing and needing; he is a concretion of a thousand necessities. With these he stands upon the earth, left to himself, uncertain about everything except his own need and misery. Consequently the care for the maintenance of that existence under exacting demands, which are renewed every day, occupies, as a rule, the whole of human life. To this is directly related the second claim, that of the propagation of the species. At the same time he is threatened from all sides by the most different kinds of dangers, from which it requires constant watchfulness to escape. With cautious steps and casting anxious glances round him he pursues his path, for a thousand accidents and a thousand enemies lie in wait for him. Thus he went while yet a savage, thus he goes in civilised life; there is no security for him.

The life of the great majority is only a constant struggle for this existence itself, with the certainty of losing it at last. But what enables them to endure this wearisome battle is not so much the love of life as the fear of death, which yet stands in the background as inevitable, and may come upon them at any moment. Life itself is a sea, full of rocks and whirlpools, which man avoids with the greatest care and solicitude, although he knows that even if he succeeds in getting through with all his efforts and skill, he yet by doing so comes nearer at every step to the greatest, the total, inevitable, and irremediable shipwreck, death; nay, even steers right upon it: this is the final goal of the laborious voyage, and worse for him than all the rocks from which he has escaped.

Now it is well worth observing that, on the one hand, the suffering and misery of life may easily increase to such an extent that death itself, in the flight from which the whole of life consists, becomes desirable, and we hasten towards it voluntarily; and again, on the other hand, that as soon as want and suffering permit rest to a man, ennui is at once so near that he necessarily requires diversion. The striving after existence is what occupies all living things and maintains them in motion. But when existence is assured, then they know not what to do with it; thus the second thing that sets them in motion is the effort to get free from the burden of existence, to make it cease to be felt, "to kill time," *i.e.*, to escape from ennui. Accordingly we see that almost all men who are secure from want and care, now that at last they have thrown off all other burdens, become a burden to themselves, and regard as a gain every hour they succeed in getting through, and thus every diminution the very life which, till then, they have employed all their powers to maintain as long as possible. Ennui is by no means an evil to be lightly esteemed; in the end it depicts on the countenance real despair. It makes beings who love each other so little as men do, seek each other eagerly, and thus becomes the source of social intercourse. Moreover, even from motives of policy, public precautions are everywhere taken against it, as against other universal calamities. For this evil may drive men to the greatest excesses, just as much as its opposite extreme, famine: the people require *panem et circenses*. The strict penitentiary system of Philadelphia makes use of ennui alone as a means of punishment, through solitary confinement and idleness, and it is found so terrible that it has even led prisoners to commit suicide. As want is the constant scourge of the people, so ennui is that of the fashionable world. In middle-class life ennui is represented by the Sunday, and want by the six week-days.

Thus between desiring and attaining all human life flows on throughout. The wish is, in its nature, pain; the attainment soon begets satiety: the end was only apparent; possession takes away the charm; the wish, the need, presents itself under a new form; when it does not, then follows desolateness, emptiness, ennui, against which the conflict is just as painful as against want. That wish and satisfaction should follow each other neither too quickly nor too slowly reduces the suffering, which both occasion to the smallest amount, and constitutes the happiest life. For that which we might otherwise call the most beautiful part of life, its purest joy, if it were only because it lifts us out of real existence and transforms us into disinterested spectators of it—that is, pure knowledge, which is foreign to all willing, the pleasure of the beautiful, the true delight in art—this is granted only to a very few, because it demands rare talents, and to these few, only as a passing dream. And then, even these few, on account of their higher intellectual power, are made susceptible of far greater suffering than duller minds can ever feel, and are also placed in lonely isolation by a nature which is obviously different from that of others; thus here also accounts are squared. But to the great majority of men purely intellectual pleasures are not accessible. They are almost quite incapable of the joys which lie in pure knowledge. They are entirely given up to willing. If, therefore, anything is to win their sympathy, to be *interesting* to them, it must (as is implied in the meaning of the word) in some way excite their *will*, even if it is only through a distant and merely problematical relation to it; the will must not be left altogether out of the question, for their existence lies far more in willing than in knowing,—action and reaction is their one element. We may find in trifles and everyday occurrences the naïve expressions of this quality. Thus, for example, at any place worth seeing they may visit, they write their names, in order thus to react, to affect the place since it does not affect them. Again, when they see a strange, rare animal, they cannot easily confine themselves to merely observing it; they must rouse it, tease it, play with it, merely to experience action and reaction; but this need for excitement of the will manifests itself very specially in the discovery and support of card-playing, which is quite peculiarly the expression of the miserable side of humanity.

But whatever nature and fortune may have done, whoever a man be and whatever he may possess, the pain which is essential to life cannot be thrown off. The ceaseless efforts to banish suffering accomplish no more than to make it change its form. It is essentially deficiency, want, care for the maintenance of life. If we succeed, which is very difficult, in removing pain in this form, it immediately assumes a thousand others, varying according to age and circumstances, such as lust, passionate love, jealousy, envy, hatred, anxiety, ambition, covetousness, sickness, &c, &c. If at last it can find entrance in no other form it comes in the sad, grey garments of tediousness and ennui, against which we then strive in various ways. If finally we succeed in driving this away, we shall hardly do so without letting pain enter in one of its earlier forms, and the dance begin again from the beginning; for all human life is tossed backwards and forwards between pain and ennui. Depressing as this view of life is, I will draw attention, by the way, to an aspect of it from which consolation may be drawn, and perhaps even a stoical indifference to one's own present ills may be attained. For our impatience at these arises for the most part from the fact that we regard them as brought about by a chain of causes which might easily be different. We do not generally grieve over ills which are directly necessary and quite universal; for example, the necessity of age and of death, and many daily inconveniences. It is rather the consideration of the accidental nature of the circumstances that brought some sorrow just to us, that gives it its sting. But if we have recognised that pain, as such, is inevitable and essential to life, and that nothing depends upon chance but its mere fashion, the form under which it presents itself, that thus our present sorrow fills a place that, without it, would at once be occupied by another which now is excluded by it, and that therefore fate can affect us little in what is essential; such a reflection, if it were to become a living conviction, might produce a considerable degree of stoical equanimity, and very much lessen the anxious care for our own well-being. But, in fact, such a powerful control of reason over directly felt suffering seldom or never occurs.

Besides, through this view of the inevitableness of pain, of the supplanting of one pain by another, and the introduction of a new pain through the passing away of that which preceded it, one might be led to the paradoxical but not absurd hypothesis, that in every individual the measure of the pain essential to him was determined once for all by his nature, a measure which could neither remain empty, nor be more than filled, however much the form of the suffering might change. Thus his suffering and well-being would by no means be determined from without, but only through that measure, that natural disposition, which indeed might experience certain additions and diminutions from the physical condition at different times, but yet, on the whole, would remain the same. This hypothesis is supported not only by the well-known experience that great suffering makes all lesser ills cease to be felt, and conversely that freedom from great suffering makes even the most trifling inconveniences torment us and put us out of humour; but experience also teaches that if a great misfortune, at the mere thought of which we shuddered, actually befalls us, as soon as we have overcome the first pain of it, our disposition remains for the most part unchanged; and, conversely, that after the attainment of some happiness we have long desired, we do not feel ourselves on the whole and permanently very much better off and more agreeably situated than before. Only the moment at which these changes occur affects us with unusual strength, as deep sorrow or exulting joy, but both soon pass away, for they are based upon illusion. For they do not spring from the immediately present pleasure or pain, but only from the opening up of a new future which is anticipated in them. Only by borrowing from the future could pain or pleasure be heightened so abnormally, and consequently not enduringly. It would follow, from the hypothesis advanced, that a large part of the feeling of suffering and of well-being would be subjective and determined *a priori,* as is the case with knowing; and we may add the following remarks as evidence in favour of it. Human cheerfulness or dejection are manifestly not determined by external circumstances such as wealth and position, for we see at least as many glad faces among the poor as among the rich. Further, the motives which induce suicide are so very different, that we can assign no motive that is so great as to bring it about, even with great probability, in every character, and few that would be so small that the like of them had never caused it, Now, although the degree of our serenity or sadness is not at all times the same, yet, in consequence of this view, we shall not attribute it to the change of outward circumstances, but to that of the inner condition, the physical state. For when an actual, though only temporary, increase of our serenity, even to the extent of joyfulness, takes place, it usually appears without any external occasion. It is true that we often see our pain arise only from some definite external relation, and are visibly oppressed and saddened by this only. Then we believe that if only this were taken away, the greatest contentment would necessarily ensue. But this is illusion. The measure of our pain and our happiness is on the whole, according to our hypothesis, subjectively determined for each point of time, and the motive for sadness is related to that, just as a blister which draws to a head all the bad humours otherwise disturbed is related to the body. The pain which is at that period of time essential to our nature, and therefore cannot be shaken off, would, without the definite external cause of our suffering, be divided at a hundred points, and appear in the form of a hundred little annoyances and cares about things which we now entirely overlook, because our capacity for pain is already filled by that chief evil which has concentrated in a point all the suffering otherwise dispersed. This corresponds also to the observation that if a great and pressing care is lifted from our breast by its fortunate issue, another immediately takes its place, the whole material of which was already there before, yet could not come into consciousness as care because there was no capacity left for it, and therefore this material of care remained indistinct and unobserved in a cloudy form on the farthest horizon of consciousness. But now that there is room, this prepared material at once comes forward and occupies the throne of the reigning care of the day. And if it is very much lighter in its matter than the material of the care which has vanished, it knows how to blow itself out so as apparently to equal it in size, and thus, as the chief care of the day, completely fills the throne.

Excessive joy and very often keen suffering always occur in the same person, for they condition each other reciprocally, and are also in common conditioned by great activity of the mind. Both are produced, as we have just seen, not by what is really present, but by the anticipation of the future. But since pain is essential to life, and its degree is also determined by the nature of the subject, sudden changes, because they are always external, cannot really alter its degree. Thus an error and delusion always lies at the foundation of immoderate joy or grief, and consequently both these excessive strainings of the mind can be avoided by knowledge. Every immoderate joy always rests on the delusion that one has found in life what can never be found there—lasting satisfaction of the harassing desires and cares, which are constantly breeding new ones. From every particular delusion of this kind one must inevitably be brought back later, and then when it vanishes must pay for it with pain as bitter as the joy its entrance caused was keen. So far, then, it is precisely like a height from which one can come down only by a fall. Therefore one ought to avoid them; and every sudden excessive grief is just a fall from some such height, the vanishing of such a delusion, and so conditioned by it. Consequently we might avoid them both if we had sufficient control over ourselves to survey things always with perfect clearness as a whole and in their connection, and steadfastly to guard against really lending them the colours which we wish they had. The principal effort of the Stoical ethics was to free the mind from all such delusion and its consequences, and to give it instead an equanimity that could not disturbed. It is this insight that inspires Horace in the well-known ode—

> "Remember to preserve an even mind
> When fortune frowns and in prosperity
> So keep your heart from all excess of joy."
>
> [*trans. G. F. Murison*]

For the most part, however, we close our minds against the knowledge, which may be compared to a bitter medicine, that suffering is essential to life, and therefore does not flow in upon us from without, but that every one carries about with him its perennial source in his own heart. We rather seek constantly for an external particular cause, as it were, a pretext for the pain which never leaves us, just as the free man makes himself an idol, in order to have a master. For we unweariedly strive from wish to wish; and although every satisfaction, however much it promised, when attained fails to satisfy us, but for the most part comes presently to be an error of which we are ashamed, yet we do not see that we draw water with the sieve of the Danaides, but ever hasten to new desires. Thus it either goes on for ever, or, what is more rare and presupposes a certain strength of character, till we reach a wish which is not satisfied and yet cannot be given up. In that case we have, as it were, found what we sought, something that we can always blame, instead of our own nature, as the source of our suffering. And thus, although we are now at variance with our fate, we are reconciled to our existence, for the knowledge is again put far from us that suffering is essential to this existence itself, and true satisfaction impossible. The result of this form of development is a somewhat melancholy disposition, the constant endurance of a single great pain, and the contempt for all lesser sorrows or joys that proceeds from it; consequently an already nobler phenomenon that that constant seizing upon ever-new forms of illusion, which is much more common.

581 All satisfaction, or what is commonly called happiness, is always really and essentially only *negative,* and never positive. It is not an original gratification coming to us of itself, but must always be the satisfaction of a wish. The wish, *i.e.,* some want, is the condition which precedes every pleasure. But with the satisfaction the wish and therefore the pleasure cease. Thus the satisfaction or the pleasing can never be more than the deliverance from a pain, from a want; for such is not only every actual, open sorrow, but every desire, the importunity of which disturbs our peace, and, indeed, the deadening ennui also that makes life a burden to us. It is, however, so hard to attain or achieve anything; difficulties and troubles without end are opposed to every purpose,

and at every step hindrances accumulate. But when finally everything is overcome and attained, nothing can ever be gained but
deliverance from some sorrow, or desire, so that we find ourselves
just in the same position as we occupied before this sorrow or
desire appeared. All that is even directly given us is merely the
want, *i.e.*, the pain. The satisfaction and the pleasure we can
only know indirectly through the remembrance of the preceding
suffering and want, which ceases with its appearance. Hence it
arises that we are not properly conscious of the blessings and
advantages we actually possess, nor do we prize them, but think of
them merely as a matter of course, for they gratify us only negatively by restraining suffering. Only when we have lost them do
we become sensible of their value; for the want, the privation,
the sorrow, is the positive, communicating itself directly to us.
Thus also we are pleased by the remembrance of past need, sickness, want, and such like, because this is the only means of enjoying the present blessings. . . .

651 In all the preceding investigations of human action, we have
been leading up to the final investigation, and have to a considerable extent lightened the task of raising to abstract and philosophical clearness, and exhibiting as a branch of our central thought
that special ethical significance of action which in life is with
perfect understanding denoted by the words *good* and *bad*. . . .

The *good* is, according to its concept, *tōn prōs ti;* thus every
good is essentially relative, for its being consists in its relation to a
desiring will. *Absolute good* is, therefore, a contradiction in terms;
highest good, *summum bonum,* really signifies the same thing—
a final satisfaction of the will, after which no new desire could
arise,—a last motive, the attainment of which would afford enduring satisfaction of the will. But, according to the investigations
which have already been conducted in this Fourth Book, such a
consummation is not even thinkable. The will can just as little
cease from willing altogether on account of some particular satisfaction, as time can end or begin; for it there is no such thing as
a permanent fulfilment which shall completely and for ever satisfy
its craving. It is the vessel of the Danaides; for it there is no highest good, no absolute good, but always a merely temporary good.
If, however, we wish to give an honorary position, as it were

emeritus, to an old expression, which from custom we do not like
to discard altogether, we may, metaphorically and figuratively, call
the complete self-effacement and denial of the will, the true absence of will, which alone for ever stills and silences its struggle,
alone gives that contentment which can never again be disturbed,
alone redeems the world, and which we shall now soon consider
at the close of our whole investigation—the absolute good, the
summum bonum—and regard it as the only radical cure of the
disease of which all other means are only palliations or anodynes.
In this sense the Greek *telos* and also *finis bonorum* correspond
to the thing still better. So much for the words *good* and *bad;*
now for the thing itself.

If a man is always disposed to do *wrong* whenever the opportunity presents itself, and there is no external power to restrain
him, we call him *bad.* According to our doctrine of wrong, this
means that such a man does not merely assert the will to live as
it appears in his own body, but in this assertion goes so far that
he denies the will which appears in other individuals. This is
shown by the fact that he desires their powers for the service of
his own will, and seeks to destroy their existence when they stand
in the way of its efforts. The ultimate source of this is a high
degree of egoism, the nature of which has been already explained.
Two things are here apparent. In the first place, that in such a
man an excessively vehement will to live expresses itself, extending
far beyond the assertion of his own body; and, in the second place,
that his knowledge, entirely given up to the principle of sufficient
reason and involved in the *principium individuationis,* cannot
get beyond the difference which this latter principle establishes
between his own person and every one else. Therefore he seeks
his own well-being alone, completely indifferent to that of all
others, whose existence is to him altogether foreign and divided
from his own by a wide gulf, and who are indeed regarded by
him as mere masks with no reality behind them. And these two
qualities are the constituent elements of the bad character. . . .

67] We have seen how justice proceeds from the penetration of
the *principium individuationis* in a less degree, and how from its
penetration in a higher degree there arises goodness of disposition
proper, which shows itself as pure, *i.e.,* disinterested love towards

others. When now the latter becomes perfect, it places other individuals and their fate completely on the level with itself and its own fate. Further than this it cannot go, for there exists no reason for preferring the individuality of another to its own. Yet the number of other individuals whose whole happiness or life is in danger may outweigh the regard for one's own particular well-being. In such a case, the character that has attained to the highest goodness and perfect nobility will entirely sacrifice its own well-being and even its life, for the well-being of many others. So died Codrus, and Leonidas, and Regulus, and Decius Mus, and Arnold von Winkelried; so dies every one who voluntarily and consciously faces certain death for his friends or his country. And they also stand on the same level who voluntarily submit to suffering and death for maintaining what conduces and rightly belongs to the welfare of all mankind; that is, for maintaining universal and important truths and destroying great errors. So died Socrates and Giordano Bruno, and so many a hero of the truth suffered death at the stake at the hands of the priests.

Now, however, I must remind the reader, with reference to the paradox stated above, that we found before that suffering is essential to life as a whole, and inseparable from it. And that we saw that every wish proceeds from a need, from a want, from suffering, and that therefore every satisfaction is only the removal of a pain, and brings no positive happiness; that the joys certainly lie to the wish, presenting themselves as a positive good, but in truth they have only a negative nature, and are only the end of an evil. Therefore what goodness, love, and nobleness do for others, is always merely an alleviation of their suffering, and consequently all that can influence them to good deeds and works of love, is simply the *knowledge of the suffering of others*, which is directly understood from their own suffering and placed on a level with it. But it follows from this that pure love is in its nature sympathy; whether the suffering it mitigates, to which every unsatisfied wish belongs, be great or small. Therefore we shall have no hesitation, in direct contradiction to Kant, who will only recognise all true goodness and all virtue to be such, if it has proceeded from abstract reflection, and indeed from the conception of duty and of the categorical imperative, and explains felt sympathy as weakness, and by no means virtue, we shall have no hesitation, I say, in direct contradiction to Kant, in saying: the mere concept is for genuine virtue just as unfruitful as it is for genuine art: all true and pure love is sympathy, and all love which is not sympathy is selfishness. Combinations of the two frequently occur. Indeed genuine friendship is always a mixture of selfishness and sympathy; the former lies in the pleasure experienced in the presence of the friend, whose individuality corresponds to our own, and this almost always constitutes the greatest part; sympathy shows itself in the sincere participation in his joy and grief, and the disinterested sacrifices made in respect of the latter. As a confirmation of our paradoxical proposition it may be observed that the tone and words of the language and caresses of pure love, entirely coincide with the tones of sympathy; and we may also remark in passing that in Italian sympathy and true love are denoted by the same word *pietà*.

68] I now take up the thread of our discussion of the ethical significance of action, in order to show how, from the same source from which all goodness, love, virtue, and nobility of character spring, there finally arises that which I call the denial of the will to live.

We saw before that hatred and wickedness are conditioned by egoism, and egoism rests on the entanglement of knowledge in the *principium individuationis*. Thus we found that the penetration of that *principium individuationis* is the source and the nature of justice, and when it is carried further, even to its fullest extent, it is the source and nature of love and nobility of character. For this penetration alone, by abolishing the distinction between our own individuality and that of others, renders possible and explains perfect goodness of disposition, extending to disinterested love and the most generous self-sacrifice for others.

If, however, this penetration of the *principium individuationis,* this direct knowledge of the identity of will in all its manifestations, is present in a high degree of distinctness, it will at once show an influence upon the will which extends still further. If that veil of Mâyâ, the *principium individuationis,* is lifted from the eyes of a man to such an extent that he no longer makes the egotistical distinction between his person and that of others, but takes as much interest in the sufferings of other individuals as in his own, and therefore is not only benevolent in the highest degree, but even ready to sacrifice his own individuality whenever such a sacrifice will save a number of other persons, then it clearly follows that such a man, who recognises in all beings his own inmost and true self, must also regard the infinite suffering of all suffering beings as his own, and take on himself the pain of the whole world. No suffering is any longer strange to him. All the miseries of others which he sees and is so seldom able to alleviate, all the miseries he knows directly, and even those which he only knows as possible, work upon his mind like his own. It is no longer the changing joy and sorrow of his own person that he has in view, as is the case with him who is still involved in egoism; but, since he sees through the *principium individuationis,* all lies equally near him. He knows the whole, comprehends its nature, and finds that it consists in a constant passing away, vain striving, inward conflict, and continual suffering. He sees wherever he looks suffering humanity, the suffering brute creation, and a world that passes away. But all this now lies as near him as his own person lies to the egoist. Why should he now, with such knowledge of the world, assert this very life through constant acts of will, and thereby bind himself ever more closely to it, press it ever more firmly to himself? Thus he who is still involved in the *principium individuationis,* in egoism, only knows particular things and their relation to his own person, and these constantly become new *motives* of his volition. But, on the other hand, that knowledge of the whole, of the nature of the thing-in-itself which has been described, becomes a *quieter* of all and every volition. The will now turns away from life; it now shudders at the pleasures in which it recognises the assertion of life. Man now attains to the state of voluntary renunciation, resignation, true indifference, and perfect will-lessness. If at times, in the hard experience of our own suffering, or in the vivid recognition of that of others, the knowledge of the vanity and bitterness of life draws nigh to us also who are still wrapt in the veil of Mâyâ, and we would like to destroy the sting of the desires, close the entrance against all suffering, and purify and sanctify ourselves by complete and final renunciation; yet the illusion of the phenomenon soon entangles us again, and its motives influence the will anew; we cannot tear ourselves free. The allurement of hope, the flattery of the present, the sweetness of pleasure, the well-being which falls to our lot, amid the lamentations of a suffering world governed by chance and error, draws us back to it and rivets our bonds anew. Therefore Jesus says: "It is easier for a camel to go through the eye of a needle, than for a rich man to enter into the kingdom of God."

If we compare life to a course or path through which we must unceasingly run—a path of red-hot coals, with a few cool places here and there; then he who is entangled in delusion is consoled by the cool places, on which he now stands, or which he sees near him, and sets out to run through the course. But he who sees through the *principium individuationis,* and recognises the real nature of the thing-in-itself, and thus the whole, is no longer susceptible of such consolation; he sees himself in all places at once, and withdraws. His will turns round, no longer asserts its own nature, which is reflected in the phenomenon, but denies it. The phenomenon by which this change is marked, is the transition from virtue to asceticism. That is to say, it no longer suffices for such a man to love others as himself, and to do as much for them as for himself; but there arises within him a horror of the nature of which his own phenomenal existence is an expression, the will to live, the kernel and inner nature of that world which is recognised as full of misery. He therefore disowns this nature which appears in him, and is already expressed through his body, and his action gives the lie to his phenomenal existence, and appears in open contradiction to it. Essentially nothing else but a manifestation of will, he ceases to will anything, guards against attaching his will to anything, and seeks to confirm in himself the greatest indifference to everything. His body, healthy and strong, expresses through the genitals, the sexual impulse; but he denies the will and gives the lie to the body; he desires no sensual gratification under any condition. Voluntary and complete chastity is the first step in asceticism or the denial of the will to live. It thereby denies the assertion of the will which extends beyond the individual life, and gives the assurance that with the life of this body, the will, whose manifestation it is, ceases. Nature, always true and naïve, declares that if this maxim became universal, the human race would die out; and I think I may assume, in accordance with what was said in the Second Book about the connection of all manifestations of will, that with its highest manifestation, the weaker reflection of it would also pass away, as the twilight vanishes along with the full light. With the entire abolition of knowledge, the rest of the world would of itself vanish into nothing; for without a subject there is no object. . . .

Asceticism then shows itself further in voluntary and intentional poverty, which not only arises *per accidens,* because the possessions are given away to mitigate the sufferings of others, but is here an end in itself, is meant to serve as a constant mortification of will, so that the satisfaction of the wishes, the sweet of life, shall not again arouse the will, against which self-knowledge has conceived a horror. He who has attained to this point, still always feels, as a living body, as concrete manifestation of will, the natural disposition for every kind of volition; but he intentionally suppresses it, for he compels himself to refrain from doing all that he would like to do, and to do all that he would like not to do, even if this has no further end than that of serving as a mortification of will. Since he himself denies the will which appears in his own person, he will not resist if another does the same, *i.e.,* inflicts wrongs upon him. Therefore every suffering coming to him from without, through chance or the wickedness of others, is welcome to him, every injury, ignominy, and insult; he receives them gladly as the opportunity of learning with certainty that he no longer asserts the will, but gladly sides with every enemy of the manifestation of will which is his own person. Therefore he bears such ignominy and suffering with inexhaustible patience and meekness, returns good for evil without ostentation, and allows the fire of anger to rise within him just as little as that of the desires. And he mortifies not only the will itself, but also its visible form, its objectivity, the body. He nourishes it sparingly, lest its excessive vigour and prosperity should animate and excite more strongly the will, of which it is merely the expression and the mirror. So he practices fasting, and even resorts to chastisement and self-inflicted torture, in order that, by constant privation and suffering, he may more and more break down and destroy the will, which he recognises and abhors as the source of his own suffering existence and that of the world. If at last death comes which puts an end to this manifestation of that will, whose existence here has long since perished through free-denial of itself, with the exception of the weak residue of it which appears as the life of this body; it is most welcome, and is gladly received as a longed-for deliverance. Here it is not, as in the case of others, merely the manifestation which ends with death; but the inner nature itself is abolished, which here existed only in the manifestation, and that in a very weak degree; this last slight bond is now broken. For him who thus ends, the world has ended also. . . .

According to what has been said, the denial of the will to live, which is just what is called absolute, entire resignation, or holiness, always proceeds from that quieter of the will which the knowledge of its inner conflict and essential vanity, expressing themselves in the suffering of all living things, becomes. The difference, which we have represented as two paths, consists in whether that knowledge is called up by suffering which is merely and purely *known,* and is freely appropriated by means of the penetration of the *principium individuationis,* or by suffering which is directly *felt* by a man himself. True salvation, deliverance from life and suffering, cannot even be imagined without complete denial of the will. Till then, every one is simply this will itself, whose manifestation is an ephemeral existence, a constantly vain and empty striving, and the world full of suffering we have represented, to which all irrevocably and in like manner belong. For we found above that life is always assured to the will to live, and its one real form is the present, from which they can never escape, since birth and death reign in the phenomenal world. The Indian mythus expresses this by saying "they are born again." The great ethical difference of character means this, that the bad man in infinitely far from the attainment of the knowledge from which the denial of the will proceeds, and therefore he is in truth *actually* exposed to all the miseries which appear in life as *possible;* for even the present fortunate condition of his personality is merely a phenomenon produced by the *principium individuationis,* and a delusion of Mâyâ, the happy dream of a beggar. The sufferings which in the vehemence and ardour of his will he inflicts upon others are the measure of the suffering, the experience of which in his own person cannot break his will, and plainly lead it to the denial of itself. All true and pure love, on the other hand, and even all free justice, proceed from the penetration of the *principium individuationis,* which, if it appears with its full power, results in perfect sanctification and salvation, the phenom-

enon of which is the state of resignation described above, the
unbroken peace which accompanies it, and the greatest delight
in death. . . .

711 I now end the general account of ethics, and with it the whole
development of that one thought which it has been my object to
impart; and I by no means desire to conceal here an objection
which concerns this last part of my exposition, but rather to point
out that it lies in the nature of the question, and that it is quite
impossible to remove it. It is this, that after our investigation has
brought us to the point at which we have before our eyes perfect
holiness, the denial and surrender of all volition, and thus the
deliverance from a world whose whole existence we have found
to be suffering, this appears to us as a passing away into empty
nothingness.

That which is generally received as positive, which we call the
real, and the negation of which the concept nothing in its most
general significance expresses, is just the world as idea, which I
have shown to be the objectivity and mirror of the will. Moreover,
we ourselves are just this will and this world, and to them belongs
the idea in general, as one aspect of them. The form of the idea
is space and time, therefore for this point of view of all that is
real must be in some place and at some time. Denial, abolition,
conversion of the will, is also the abolition and the vanishing of
the world, its mirror. If we no longer perceive it in this mirror
we ask in vain where it has gone, and then, because it has no
longer any where and when, complain that it has vanished into
nothing.

A reversed point of view, if it were possible for us, would
reverse the signs and show the real for us as nothing, and that
nothing as the real. But as long as we ourselves are the will to
live, this last—nothing as the real—can only be known and signified by us negatively, because the old saying of Empedocles, that
like can only be known by like, deprives us here of all knowledge,
as, conversely, upon it finally rests the possibility of all our actual
knowledge, i.e., the world as idea; for the world is the self-
knowledge of the will.

If, however, it should be absolutely insisted upon that in some
way or other a positive knowledge should be attained of that

which philosophy can only express negatively as the denial of the will, there would be nothing for it but to refer to that state which all those who have attained to complete denial of the will have experienced, and which has been variously denoted by the names ecstasy, rapture, illumination, union with God, and so forth; a state, however, which cannot properly be called knowledge, because it has not the form of subject and object, and is, moreover, only attainable in one's own experience and cannot be further communicated.

We, however, who consistently occupy the standpoint of philosophy, must be satisfied here with negative knowledge, content to have reached the utmost limit of the positive. We have recognised the inmost nature of the world as will, and all its phenomena as only the objectivity of will; and we have followed this objectivity from the unconscious working of obscure forces of Nature up to the completely conscious action of man. Therefore we shall by no means evade the consequence, that with the free denial, the surrender of the will, all those phenomena are also abolished; that constant strain and effort without end and without rest at all the grades of objectivity, in which and through which the world consists; the multifarious forms succeeding each other in gradation; the whole manifestation of the will; and, finally, also the universal forms of this manifestation, time and space, and also its last fundamental form, subject and object; all are abolished. No will: no idea, no world.

Before us there is certainly only nothingness. But that which resists this passing into nothing, our nature, is indeed just the will to live, which we ourselves are as it is our world. That we abhor annihilation so greatly, is simply another expression of the fact that we so strenuously will life, and are nothing but this will, and know nothing besides it. But if we turn our glance from our own needy and embarrassed condition to those who have overcome the world, in whom the will, having attained to perfect self-knowledge, found itself again in all, and then freely denied itself, and who then merely wait to see the last trace of it vanish with the body which it animates; then, instead of the restless striving and effort, instead of the constant transition from wish to fruition, and from joy to sorrow, instead of the never-satisfied and never-dying hope which constitutes the life of the man who wills, we shall see that peace which is above all reason, that perfect calm of the spirit, that deep rest, that inviolable confidence and serenity, the mere reflection of which, in the countenance, as Raphael and Correggio have represented it, is an entire and certain gospel; only knowledge remains, the will has vanished. We look with deep and painful longing upon this state, beside which the misery and wretchedness of our own is brought out clearly by the contrast. Yet this is the only consideration which can afford us lasting consolation, when, on the one hand, we have recognised incurable suffering and endless misery as essential to the manifestation of will, the world; and, on the other hand, see the world pass away with the abolition of will, and retain before us only empty nothingness. Thus, in this way, by contemplation of the life and conduct of saints, whom it is certainly rarely granted us to meet with in our own experience, but who are brought before our eyes by their written history, and, with the stamp of inner truth, by art, we must banish the dark impression of that nothingness which we discern behind all virtue and holiness as their final goal, and which we fear as children fear the dark; we must not even evade it like the Indians, through myths and meaningless words, such as reabsorption in Brahma or the Nirvâna of the Buddhists. Rather do we freely acknowledge that what remains after the entire abolition of will is for all those who are still full of will certainly nothing; but, conversely, to those in whom the will has turned and has denied itself, this our world, which is so real, with all its suns and milky-ways—is nothing.

Friedrich Wilhelm Nietzsche

Nietzsche

From its origins in the Romantic school the interpretation of the world as will developed in two directions; to the philosophy of renunciation in Schopenhauer and to an optimistic affirmation of the will in Nietzsche. Both of these philosophies, however, were attempts to answer a problem which had arisen out of a change of interest and emphasis in the field of speculation. The growth of interest in history and in historical studies of religion and philosophy had tended to the dissolution of absolute principles and the realization of the seeming relativism of values. Advances in the scientific field, particularly in biology and psychology, necessitated a consideration of man as a biological specimen, a member of the animal kingdom instead of a being apart. Traditional ethical systems were threatened on the one hand by the relativism of the historical treatment and on the other by the critique latent in the theory of evolution.

Some philosophers were content to retain the traditional values, rephrased in biological or psychological terms. To Nietzsche the need was apparent for a completely new system of values, consonant with the new view of man. The old ideals had lost their meaning; the God which had given to the old morality its dynamic quality was dead. The time had come for a "transvaluation of values" as Nietzsche called it.

The primary distinction in Nietzsche's interpretation of human existence was that between original life force and rationality. In his interpretation of Greek tragedy he called these two forces the Dionysian and the Apollonian; the former the passionate, heroic, superindividual affirmation of all life, the latter the search for harmony, simplicity and clarity. A happy combination of the two elements constituted the greatness of Greek tragedies in antiquity, of the music of Richard Wagner in Nietzsche's own day.

The Darwinian struggle for survival becomes in Nietzsche's hands an active, creative force. The human expression of this life force is the will for power. Upon this biological basis Nietzsche constructed his morality. This involved discarding the empty hull of traditional moral systems. The Christian ideal of humility and the democratic demand of equality were denials of the will to power, characteristic of a slave morality, outgrowths of the resentment of the common-herd *(Herdenmenschen)* towards the masters *(Herrenmenschen)*. The morality of the will for power was one for this natural nobility. "Good and bad" *(gut und schlecht)* to distinguish the excellent from the common replaced "good and evil" *(gut und böse),* the basic moral distinction.

The will for power was the motive force in the human evolutionary process. Its ultimate objective was the creation of the "superman," a creature as far beyond man as man is beyond the ape. This was the ideal for humanity with which Nietzsche replaced God.

There is always a temptation to interpret Nietzsche's philosophy as a compensation for his own weaknesses. There was a certain delicacy in his manner, resulting from a youth spent in the exclusive society of women, which earned him the nickname "the saint." Extreme ill-health which finally brought on a complete mental breakdown made it impossible for him to engage in strenuous physical activities or even to work at all for long periods.

Friedrich Nietzsche (1844-1900) first achieved notice in literary criticism with his *Birth of Tragedy* (1872). He held a professorship at the University of Basle but spent most of his life in search of health in the mountains of Switzerland and in Italy. He never completed a definitive exposition of his philosophic position; *The Will to Power,* which was to be such a work, was never completed. The poetic beauty of much of Nietzsche's writing and the striking expression of insights in many of his aphorisms attracted many followers. His ideas appear in aphoristic form or poetic dress in shorter works. Some may be gleaned from his discussions of his contemporaries or from essays on particular problems. His published works, in addition to the one already mentioned, were: *Thoughts out of Season* (1873-1876), *Human, all too Human* (1878-1880), *Dawn of Day* (1881), *The Joyous Science* (1882), *Thus Spake Zarathustra* (1883-1884), *Beyond Good and Evil* (1886), *The Genealogy of Morals* (1887), *The Case of Wagner* (1888), *The Twilight of the Idols* (1888). The present selection contains the first two essays of the *Genealogy of Morals*.

The Genealogy of Morals

First Essay

"Good and Evil," "Good and Bad"

1

THOSE English psychologists, who up to the present are the only philosophers who are to be thanked for any endeavour to get as far as a history of the origin of morality—these men, I say, offer us in their own personalities no paltry problem;—they even have, if I am to be quite frank about it, in their capacity of living riddles, an advantage over their books—*they themselves are interesting!* These English psychologists—what do they really mean? We always find them voluntarily or involuntarily at the same task of pushing to the front the *partie honteuse* of our inner world, and looking for the efficient, governing, and decisive principle in that precise quarter where the intellectual self-respect of the race would be the most reluctant to find it (for example, in the *vis inertiæ* of habit, or in forgetfulness, or in a blind and fortuitous mechanism and association of ideas, or in some factor that is purely passive, reflex, molecular, or fundamentally stupid)—what is the real motive power which always impels these psychologists in precisely *this* direction? Is it an instinct for human disparagement somewhat sinister, vulgar, and malignant, or perhaps incomprehensible even to itself? or perhaps a touch of pessimistic jealousy, the mistrust of disillusioned idealists who have become gloomy, poisoned, and bitter? or a petty subconscious enmity and rancour against Christianity (and Plato), that has conceivably never crossed the threshold of consciousness? or just a vicious taste for those elements of life which are bizarre, painfully paradoxical, mystical, and illogical? or, as a final alternative, a dash of each of these motives—a little vulgarity, a little gloominess, a little anti-Christianity, a little craving for the necessary piquancy?

But I am told that it is simply a case of old frigid and tedious frogs crawling and hopping around men and inside men, as if they were as thoroughly at home there, as they would be in a *swamp.*

I am opposed to this statement, nay, I do not believe it; and if, in the impossibility of knowledge, one is permitted to wish, so do I wish from my heart that just the converse metaphor should apply, and that these analysts with their psychological microscopes should be, at bottom, brave, proud, and magnanimous animals who know how to bridle both their hearts and their smarts, and have specifically trained themselves to sacrifice what is desirable to what is true, *any* truth in fact, even the simple, bitter, ugly, repulsive, unchristian, and immoral truths—for there are truths of that description.

2

All honour, then, to the noble spirits who would fain dominate these historians of morality. But it is certainly a pity that they lack the *historical sense* itself, that they themselves are quite deserted by all the beneficent spirits of history. The whole train of their thought runs, as was always the way of old-fashioned philosophers, on *thoroughly* unhistorical lines: there is no doubt on this point. The crass ineptitude of their genealogy of morals is immediately apparent when the question arises of ascertaining the origin of the idea and judgment of "good." "Man had originally," so speaks their decree, "praised and called 'good' altruistic acts from the standpoint of those on whom they were conferred, that is, those to whom they were *useful;* subsequently the origin of this praise was *forgotten,* and altruistic acts, simply because, as a sheer matter of habit, they were praised as good, came also to be felt as good—as though they contained in themselves some intrinsic goodness." The thing is obvious:—this initial derivation contains already all the typical and idiosyncratic traits of the English psychologists— we have "utility," "forgetting," "habit," and finally "error," the whole assemblage forming the basis of a system of values, on which the higher man has up to the present prided himself as though it were a kind of privilege of man in general. This pride *must* be brought low, this system of values *must* lose its values: is that attained?

Now the first argument that comes ready to my hand is that the real homestead of the concept "good" is sought and located in the wrong place: the judgment "good" did *not* originate among those to whom goodness was shown. Much rather has it been the good themselves, that is, the aristocratic, the powerful, the high-stationed, the high-minded, who have felt that they themselves were good, and that their actions were good, that is to say of the first order, in contradistinction to all the low, the low-minded, the vulgar, and the plebeian. It was out of this pathos of distance that they first arrogated the right to create values for their own profit, and to coin the names of such values: what had they to do with utility? The standpoint of utility is as alien and as inapplicable as it could possibly be, when we have to deal with so volcanic an effervescence of supreme values, creating and demarcating as they do a hierarchy within themselves: it is at this juncture that one arrives at an appreciation of the contrast to that tepid temperature, which is the presupposition on which every combination of worldly wisdom and every calculation of practical expediency is always based—and not for one occasional, not for one exceptional instance, but chronically. The pathos of nobility and distance, as I have said, the chronic and despotic *esprit de corps* and fundamental instinct of a higher dominant race coming into association with a meaner race, an "under race," this is the origin of the antithesis of good and bad.

(The masters' right of giving names goes so far that it is permissible to look upon language itself as the expression of the power of the masters: they say "this *is* that, and that," they seal finally every object and every event with a sound, and thereby at the same time take possession of it.) It is because of this origin that the word "good" is far from having any necessary connection with altruistic acts, in accordance with the superstitious belief of these moral philosophers. On the contrary, it is on the occasion of the *decay* of aristocratic values, that the antitheses between "egoistic" and "altruistic" presses more and more heavily on the human conscience—it is, to use my own language, the *herd instinct* which finds in this antithesis an expression in many ways. And even then it takes a considerable time for this instinct to become sufficiently dominant, for the valuation to be inextricably dependent on this antithesis (as is the case in contemporary Europe); for to-day the prejudice is predominant, which, acting even now with all the intensity of an obsession and brain disease, holds that "moral," "altruistic," and *"désintéressé"* are concepts of equal value.

3

In the second place, quite apart from the fact that this hypothesis as to the genesis of the value "good" cannot be historically upheld, it suffers from an inherent psychological contradiction. The utility of altruistic conduct has presumably been the origin of its being praised, and this origin has become *forgotten:*—But in what conceivable way is this forgetting *possible?* Has perchance the utility of such conduct ceased at some given moment? The contrary is the case. This utility has rather been experienced every day at all times, and is consequently a feature that obtains a new and regular emphasis with every fresh day; it follows that, so far from vanishing from the consciousness, so far indeed from being forgotten, it must necessarily become impressed on the consciousness with ever-increasing distinctness. How much more logical is that contrary theory (it is not the truer for that) which is represented, for instance, by Herbert Spencer, who places the concept "good" as essentially similar to the concept "useful," "purposive," so that in the judgments "good" and "bad" mankind is simply summarising and investing with a sanction its *unforgotten* and *unforgettable experiences* concerning the "useful-purposive" and the "mischievous-non-purposive." According to this theory, "good" is the attribute of that which has previously shown itself useful; and so is able to claim to be considered "valuable in the highest degree," "valuable in itself." This method of explanation is also, as I have said, wrong, but at any rate the explanation itself is coherent, and psychologically tenable.

4

The guide-post which first put me on the *right* track was this question—what is the true etymological significance of the various symbols for the idea "good" which have been coined in the various languages? I then found that they all led back to *the same evolution of the same idea*—that everywhere "aristocrat," "noble" (in the social sense), is the root idea, out of which have necessarily developed "good" in the sense of "with aristocratic soul," "noble," in the sense of "with a soul of high calibre," "with a privileged soul"—a development which invariably runs parallel with that other evolution by which "vulgar," "plebeian," "low," are made to change finally into "bad." The most eloquent proof of this last contention is the German word *"schlecht"* itself: this word is identical with *"schlicht"*—(compare *"schlechtweg"* and *"schlechterdings"*)—which, originally and as yet without any sinister innuendo, simply denoted the plebeian man in contrast to the aristocratic man. It is at the sufficiently late period of the Thirty Years' War that this sense becomes changed to the sense now current. From the standpoint of the Genealogy of Morals this discovery seems to be substantial: the lateness of it is to be attributed to the retarding influence exercised in the modern world by democratic prejudice in the sphere of all questions of origin. This extends, as will shortly be shown, even to the province of natural science and physiology, which *prima facie* is the most objective. The extent of the mischief which is caused by this prejudice (once it is free of all trammels except those of its own malice), particularly to Ethics and History, is shown by the notorious case of Buckle: it was in Buckle that that *plebeianism* of the modern spirit, which is of English origin, broke out once again from its malignant soil with all the violence of a slimy volcano, and with that salted, rampant, and vulgar eloquence with which up to the present time all volcanoes have spoken.

5

With regard to *our* problem, which can justly be called an *intimate* problem, and which elects to appeal to only a limited number of ears: it is of no small interest to ascertain that in those words and roots which denote "good" we catch glimpses of that arch-trait, on the strength of which the aristocrats feel themselves to be beings of a higher order than their fellows. Indeed, they call themselves in perhaps the most frequent instances simply after their superiority in power (*e.g.* "the powerful," "the lords," "the commanders"), or after the most obvious sign of their superiority, as for example "the rich," "the possessors" (that is the meaning of *arya;* and the Iranian and Slav languages correspond). But they also call themselves after some *characteristic idiosyncrasy;* and this

is the case which now concerns us. They name themselves, for
instance, "the truthful": this is first done by the Greek nobility
whose mouthpiece is found in Theognis, the Megarian poet. The
word *esthlós*, which is coined for the purpose, signifies etymo-
logically "one who *is*," who has reality, who is real, who is true;
and then with a subjective twist, the "true," as the "truthful":
at this stage in the evolution of the idea, it becomes the motto and
party cry of the nobility, and quite completes the transition to
the meaning "noble," so as to place outside the pale the lying,
vulgar man, as Theognis conceives and portrays him—till finally
the word after the decay of the nobility is left to delineate psychological *noblesse,* and becomes as it were ripe and mellow. In
the word *kakòs* as in *deilòs* (the plebeian in contrast to the
agathòs) the cowardice is emphasised. This affords perhaps an
inkling on what lines the etymological origin of the very ambiguous *agathòs* is to be investigated. In the Latin *malus* (which I
place side by side with *mélas*) the vulgar man can be distinguished as the dark-coloured, and above all as the black-haired
("hic niger est"), as the pre-Aryan inhabitants of the Italian soil,
whose complexion formed the clearest feature of distinction from
the dominant blondes, namely, the Aryan conquering race:—at
any rate Gaelic has afforded me the exact analogue—*Fin* (for
instance, in the name *Fin-Gal),* the distinctive word of the nobility, finally—good, noble, clean, but originally the blonde-haired
man in contrast to the dark black-haired aboriginals. The Celts,
if I may make a parenthetic statement, were throughout a blonde
race; and it is wrong to connect, as Virchow still connects, those
traces of an essentially dark-haired population which are to be
seen on the more elaborate ethnographical maps of Germany
with any Celtic ancestry or with any admixture of Celtic blood:
in this context it is rather the *pre-Aryan* population of Germany
which surges up to these districts. (The same is true substantially
of the whole of Europe: in point of fact, the subject race has
finally again obtained the upper hand, in complexion and the
shortness of the skull, and perhaps in the intellectual and social
qualities. Who can guarantee that modern democracy, still more
modern anarchy, and indeed that tendency to the "Commune,"
the most primitive form of society, which is now common to all
the Socialists in Europe, does not in its real essence signify a

monstrous reversion—and that the conquering and *master* race—the Aryan race, is not also becoming inferior physiologically?) I believe that I can explain the Latin *bonus* as the "warrior": my hypothesis is that I am right in deriving *bonus* from an older *duonus* (compare *bellum-duellum* = *duen-lum,* in which the word *duonus* appears to me to be contained). *Bonus* accordingly as the man of discord, of variance, "entzweiung" *(duo),* as the warrior: one sees what in ancient Rome "the good" meant for a man. Must not our actual German word *gut* mean *"the godlike, the man of godlike race"*? and be identical with the national name (originally the nobles' name) of the *Goths?*

The grounds for this supposition do not appertain to this work.

6

Above all, there is no exception (though there are opportunities for exceptions) to this rule, that the idea of political superiority always resolves itself into the idea of psychological superiority, in those cases where the highest caste is at the same time the *priestly* caste, and in accordance with its general characteristics confers on itself the privilege of a title which alludes specifically to its priestly function. It is in these cases, for instances, that "clean" and "unclean" confront each other for the first time as badges of class distinction; here again there develops a "good" and a "bad," in a sense which has ceased to be merely social. Moreover, care should be taken not to take these ideas of "clean" and "unclean" too seriously, too broadly, or too symbolically: all the ideas of ancient man have, on the contrary, got to be understood in their initial stages, in a sense which is, to an almost inconceivable extent, crude, coarse, physical, and narrow, and above all essentially *unsymbolical.* The "clean man" is originally only a man who washes himself, who abstains from certain foods which are conducive to skin diseases, who does not sleep with the unclean women of the lower classes, who has a horror of blood—not more, not much more! On the other hand, the very nature of a priestly aristocracy shows the reasons why just at such an early juncture there should ensue a really dangerous sharpening and intensification of opposed values: it is, in fact, through these opposed values that gulfs are cleft in the social plane, which a veritabe Achilles of free thought would shudder to cross. There is from the outset a certain *diseased taint* in such sacerdotal aristocracies, and in the habits which prevail in such societies—habits which, *averse* as they are to action, constitute a compound of introspection and explosive emotionalism, as a result of which there appears that ʼintrospective morbidity and neurasthenia, which adheres almost inevitably to all priests at all times: with regard, however, to the remedy which they themselves have invented for this disease—the philosopher has no option but to state, that it has proved itself in its effects a hundred times more dangerous than the disease, from which it should have been the deliverer. Humanity itself is still diseased from the effects of the naïvetés of this priestly cure. Take, for instance, certain kinds of diet (abstention from flesh), fasts, sexual continence, flight into the wilderness (a kind of Weir-Mitchell isolation, though of course without that system of excessive feeding and fattening which is the most efficient antidote to all the hysteria of the ascetic ideal); consider too the whole metaphysic of the priests, with its war on the senses, its enervation, its hair-splitting; consider its self-hypnotism on the fakir and Brahman principles (it uses Brahman as a glass disc and obsession), and that climax which we can understand only too well of an unusual satiety with its panacea of *nothingness* (or God:—the demand for a *unio mystica* with God is the demand of the Buddhist for nothingness, Nirvana—and nothing else!). In sacerdotal societies *every* element is on a more dangerous scale, not merely cures and remedies, but also pride, revenge, cunning, exaltation, love, ambition, virtue, morbidity:—further, it can fairly be stated that it is on the soil of this *essentially dangerous* form of human society, the sacerdotal form, that man really becomes for the first time an *interesting animal,* that it is in this form that the soul of man has in a higher sense attained *depths* and become *evil*—and those are the two fundamental forms of the superiority which up to the present man has exhibited over every other animal.

7

The reader will have already surmised with what ease the priestly mode of valuation can branch off from the knightly aristocratic mode, and then develop into the very antithesis of the latter: special impetus is given to this opposition, by every occasion when the castes of the priests and warriors confront each other with mutual jealousy and cannot agree over the prize. The knightly-aristocratic "values" are based on a careful cult of the physical, on a flowering, rich, and even effervescing healthiness, that goes considerably beyond what is necessary for maintaining life, on war, adventure, the chase, the dance, the tourney—on everything, in fact, which is contained in strong, free, and joyous action. The priestly-aristocratic mode of valuation is—we have seen—based on other hypotheses: it is bad enough for this class when it is a question of war! Yet the priests are, as is notorious, *the worst enemies*—why? Because they are the weakest. Their weakness causes their hate to expand into a monstrous and sinister shape, a shape which is most crafty and most poisonous. The really great haters in the history of the world have always been priests, who are also the cleverest haters—in comparison with the cleverness of priestly revenge, every other piece of cleverness is practically negligible. Human history would be too fatuous for anything were it not for the cleverness imported into it by the weak —take at once the most important instance. All the world's efforts against the "aristocrats," the "mighty," the "masters," the "holders of power," are negligible by comparison with what has been accomplished against those classes by *the Jews*—the Jews, that priestly nation which eventually realised that the one method of effecting satisfaction on its enemies and tyrants was by means of a radical transvaluation of values, which was at the same time an act of the *cleverest revenge*. Yet the method was only appropriate to a nation of priests, to a nation of the most jealously nursed priestly revengefulness. It was the Jews who, in opposition to the aristocratic equation (good = aristocratic = beautiful = happy = loved by the gods), dared with a terrifying logic to suggest the contrary equation, and indeed to maintain with the teeth of the most profound hatred (the hatred of weakness) this contrary equation, namely, "the wretched are alone the good; the poor, the weak, the lowly, are alone the good; the suffering, the needy, the sick, the loathsome, are the only ones who are pious, the only ones who are blessed, for them alone is salvation—but you, on the other hand, you aristocrats, you men of power, you are to all eternity the evil, the horrible, the covetous, the insatiate, the godless; eter-

nally also shall you be the unblessed, the cursed, the damned!"
We know who it was who reaped the heritage of this Jewish transvaluation. In the context of the monstrous and inordinately fate-
ful initiative which the Jews have exhibited in connection with
this most fundamental of all declarations of war, I remember the
passage which came to my pen on another occasion *(Beyond Good
and Evil,* Aph. 195)—that it was, in fact, with the Jews that the
revolt of the slaves begins in the sphere *of morals;* that revolt
which has behind it a history of two millennia, and which at the
present day has only moved out of our sight, because it—has
achieved victory.

8

But you understand this not? You have no eyes for a force which
has taken two thousand years to achieve victory?—There is nothing wonderful in this: all *lengthy* processes are hard to see and
to realise. But *this* is what took place: from the trunk of that tree
of revenge and hate, Jewish hate,—that most profound and sublime hate, which creates ideals and changes old values to new
creations, the like of which has never been on earth,—there grew
a phenomenon which was equally incomparable, *a new love,* the
most profound and sublime of all kinds of love;—and from what
other trunk could it have grown? But beware of supposing that
this love has soared on its upward growth, as in any way a real
negation of that thirst for revenge, as an antithesis to the Jewish
hate! No, the contrary is the truth! This love grew out of that
hate, as its crown, as its triumphant crown, circling wider and
wider amid the clarity and fulness of the sun, and pursuing in
the very kingdom of light and height its goal of hatred, its victory,
its spoil, its strategy, with the same intensity with which the roots
of that tree of hate sank into everything which was deep and evil
with increasing stability and increasing desire. This Jesus of
Nazareth, the incarnate gospel of love, this "Redeemer" bringing
salvation and victory to the poor, the sick, the sinful—was he not
really temptation in its most sinister and irresistible form, temptation to take the tortuous path to those very *Jewish* values and
those very Jewish ideals? Has not Israel really obtained the final
goal of its sublime revenge, by the tortuous paths of this "Redeemer," for all that he might pose as Israel's adversary and Israel's

destroyer? Is it not due to the black magic of a really *great* policy
of revenge, of a far-seeing, burrowing revenge, both acting and
calculating with slowness, that Israel himself must repudiate
before all the world the actual instrument of his own revenge
and nail it to the cross, so that all the world—that is, all the enemies of Israel—could nibble without suspicion at this very bait?
Could, moreover, any human mind with all its elaborate ingenuity
invent a bait that was more truly *dangerous?* Anything that was
even equivalent in the power of its seductive, intoxicating, defil-
ing, and corrupting influence to that symbol of the holy cross, to
that awful paradox of a "god on the cross," to that mystery of the
unthinkable, supreme, and utter horror of the self-crucifixion of
a god for the *salvation of man?* It is at least certain that *sub hoc
signo* Israel, with its revenge and transvaluation of all values, has
up to the present always triumphed again over all other ideals,
over all more aristocratic ideals.

9

"But why do you talk of nobler ideals? Let us submit to the
facts; that the people have triumphed—or the slaves, or the populace, or the herd, or whatever name you care to give them—if this
has happened through the Jews, so be it! In that case no nation
ever had a greater mission in the world's history. The 'masters'
have been done away with; the morality of the vulgar man has
triumphed. This triumph may also be called a blood-poisoning
(it has mutually fused the races)—I do not dispute it; but there is
no doubt but that this intoxication has succeeded. The 'redemption' of the human race (that is, from the masters) is progressing
swimmingly; everything is obviously becoming Judaised, or Chris-
tianised, or vulgarised (what is there in the words?). It seems
impossible to stop the course of this poisoning through the whole
body politic of mankind—but its *tempo* and pace may from the
present time be slower, more delicate, quieter, more discreet—
there is time enough. In view of this context has the Church nowadays any necessary purpose? Has it, in fact, a right to live? Or
could man get on without it? *Quæritur.* It seems that it fetters
and retards this tendency, instead of accelerating it. Well, even
that might be its utility. The Church certainly is a crude and

boorish institution, that is repugnant to an intelligence with any pretence at delicacy, to a really modern taste. Should it not at any rate learn to be somewhat more subtle? It alienates nowadays, more than it allures. Which of us would, forsooth, be a free-thinker if there were no Church? It is the Church which repels us, *not* its poison—apart from the Church we like the poison." This is the epilogue of a freethinker to my discourse, of an honourable animal (as he has given abundant proof), and a democrat to boot; he had up to that time listened to me, and could not endure my silence, but for me, indeed, with regard to this topic there is much on which to be silent.

10

The revolt of the slaves in morals begins in the very principle of *resentment* becoming creative and giving birth to values—a resentment experienced by creatures who, deprived as they are of the proper outlet of action, are forced to find their compensation in an imaginary revenge. While every aristocratic morality springs from a triumphant affirmation of its own demands, the slave morality says "no" from the very outset to what is "outside itself," "different from itself," and "not itself": and this "no" is its creative deed. This volte-face of the valuing standpoint—this *inevitable* gravitation to the objective instead of back to the subjective—is typical of "resentment": the slave-morality requires as the condition of its existence an external and objective world, to employ physiological terminology, it requires objective stimuli to be capable of action at all—its action is fundamentally a reaction. The contrary is the case when we come to the aristocrat's system of values: it acts and grows spontaneously, it merely seeks its antithesis in order to pronounce a more grateful and exultant "yes" to its own self;—its negative conception, "low," "vulgar," "bad," is merely a pale late-born foil in comparison with its positive and fundamental conception (saturated as it is with life and passion), of "we aristocrats, we good ones, we beautiful ones, we happy ones."

When the aristocratic morality goes astray and commits sacrilege on reality, this is limited to that particular sphere with which it is *not* sufficiently acquainted—a sphere, in fact, from the

real knowledge of which it disdainfully defends itself. It mis-
judges, in some cases, the sphere which it despises, the sphere of
the common vulgar man and the low people: on the other hand,
due weight should be given to the consideration that in any case
the mood of contempt, of disdain, of superciliousness, even on the
supposition that it *falsely* portrays the object of its contempt, will
always be far removed from that degree of falsity which will
always characterise the attacks—in effigy, of course—of the vindictive hatred and revengefulness of the weak in onslaughts on their
enemies. In point of fact, there is in contempt too strong an admixture of nonchalance, of casualness, of boredom, of impatience,
even of personal exultation, for it to be capable of distorting its
victim into a real caricature or a real monstrosity. Attention again
should be paid to the almost benevolent *nuances* which, for instance, the Greek nobility imports into all the words by which it
distinguishes the common people from itself; note how continuously a kind of pity, care, and consideration imparts its honeyed
flavour, until at last almost all the words which are applied to the
vulgar man survive finally as expressions for "unhappy," "worthy
of pity" (compare *deilós, deílaios, ponērós, mochtherós;* the latter
two names really denoting the vulgar man as labour-slave and
beast of burden)—and how, conversely, "bad," "low," "unhappy"
have never ceased to ring in the Greek ear with a tone in which
"unhappy" is the predominant note: this is a heritage of the old
noble aristocratic morality, which remains true to itself even in
contempt (let philologists remember the sense in which *oïzurós,
ánolthos tlēmōn, dustucheïn, xumphorá* used to be employed. The
"well-born" simply *felt* themselves the "happy"; they did not have
to manufacture their happiness artificially through looking at
their enemies, or in cases to talk and lie themselves into happiness
(as is the custom with all resentful men); and similarly, complete
men as they were, exuberant with strength, and consequently *necessarily* energetic, they were too wise to dissociate happiness from
action—activity becomes in their minds necessarily counted as happiness (that is the etymology of *eũ práttein*)—all in sharp contrast
to the "happiness" of the weak and the oppressed, with their fester-
ing venom and malignity, among whom happiness appears essentially as a narcotic, a deadening, a quietude, a peace, a "Sabbath,"
an enervation of the mind and relaxation of the limbs,—in short,

a purely *passive* phenomenon. While the aristocratic man lived in confidence and openness with himself *(gennaîos* "noble-born," emphasises the nuance "sincere," and perhaps also "naïf"), the resentful man, on the other hand, is neither sincere nor naïf, nor honest and candid with himself. His soul *squints;* his mind loves hidden crannies, tortuous paths and backdoors, everything secret appeals to him as *his* world, *his* safety, *his* balm; he is past master in silence, in not forgetting, in waiting, in provisional self-depreciation and self-abasement. A race of such *resentful* men will of necessity eventually prove more *prudent* than any aristocratic race, it will honour prudence on quite a distinct scale, as, in fact, a paramount condition of existence, while prudence among aristocratic men is apt to be tinged with a delicate flavour of luxury and refinement; so among them it plays nothing like so integral a part as that complete certainty of function of the governing *unconscious* instincts, or as indeed a certain lack of prudence, such as a vehement and valiant charge, whether against danger or the enemy, or as those ecstatic bursts of rage, love, reverence, gratitude, by which at all times noble souls have recognised each other. When the resentment of the aristocratic man manifests itself, it fulfills and exhausts itself in an immediate reaction, and consequently instills no *venom:* on the other hand, it never manifests itself at all in countless instances, when in the case of the feeble and weak it would be inevitable. An inability to take seriously for any length of time their enemies, their disasters, their *misdeeds—* that is the sign of the full strong natures who possess a superfluity of moulding plastic force, that heals completely and produces forgetfulness: a good example of this in the modern world is Mirabeau, who had no memory for any insults and meannesses which were practised on him, and who was only incapable of forgiving because he forgot. Such a man indeed shakes off with a shrug many a worm which would have buried itself in another; it is only in characters like these that we see the possibility (supposing, of course, that there is such a possibility in the world) of the real *"love* of one's enemies." What respect for his enemies is found, forsooth, in an aristocratic man—and such a reverence is already a bridge to love! He insists on having his enemy to himself as his distinction. He tolerates no other enemy but a man in whose character there is nothing to despise and *much* to honour! On the other hand, imagine the "enemy" as the resentful man conceives him—and it is here exactly that we see his work, his creativeness; he has conceived "the evil enemy," the "evil one," and indeed that is the root idea from which he now evolves as a contrasting and corresponding figure a "good one," himself—his very self!

11

The method of this man is quite contrary to that of the aristocratic man, who conceives the root idea "good" spontaneously and straight away, that is to say, out of himself, and from that material then creates for himself a concept of "bad"! This "bad" of aristocratic origin and that "evil" out of the cauldron of unsatisfied hatred—the former an imitation, an "extra," an additional nuance; the latter, on the other hand, the original, the beginning, the essential act in the conception of a slave morality—these two words "bad" and "evil," how great a difference do they mark, in spite of the fact that they have an identical contrary in the idea "good." But the idea "good" is *not* the same: much rather let the question be asked, "Who is really evil according to the meaning of the morality of resentment?" In all sternness let it be answered thus: —*just* the good man of the other morality, just the aristocrat, the powerful one, the one who rules, but who is distorted by the venomous eye of resentfulness, into a new colour, a new signification, a new appearance. This particular point we would be the last to deny: the man who learnt to know those "good" ones only as enemies, learnt at the same time not to know them only as *"evil enemies,"* and the same men who *inter pares* were kept so rigorously in bounds through convention, respect, custom, and gratitude, though much more through mutual vigilance and jealousy *inter pares,* these men who in their relations with each other find so many new ways of manifesting consideration, self-control, delicacy, loyalty, pride, and friendship, these men are in reference to what is outside their circle (where the foreign element, a *foreign* country, begins), not much better than beasts of prey, which have been let loose. They enjoy there freedom from all social control, they feel that in the wilderness they can give vent with impunity to that tension which is produced by enclosure and imprisonment in the peace of society, they *revert* to the innocence of the beast-of-prey conscience, like jubilant monsters, who perhaps come from a ghostly bout of murder, arson, rape, and torture, with bravado and a moral equanimity, as though merely some wild student's prank had been played, perfectly convinced that the poets have now an ample theme to sing and celebrate. It is impossible not to recognise at the core of all these aristocratic races the beast of prey; the magnificent *blonde brute,* avidly rampant for spoil and victory; this hidden core needed an outlet from time to time, the beast must get loose again, must return into the wilderness—the Roman, Arabic, German, and Japanese nobility, the Homeric heroes, the Scandinavian Vikings, are all alike in this need. It is the aristocratic races who have left the idea "Barbarian" on all the tracks in which they have marched; nay, a consciousness of this very barbarianism, and even a pride in it, manifests itself even in their highest civilisation (for example, when Pericles says to his Athenians in that celebrated funeral oration, "Our audacity has forced a way over every land and sea, rearing everywhere imperishable memorials of itself for *good* and for *evil"*). This audacity of aristocratic races, mad, absurd, and spasmodic as may be its expression; the incalculable and fantastic nature of their enterprises,— Pericles sets in special relief and glory the *rathumia* of the Athenians, their nonchalance and contempt for safety, body, life, and comfort, their awful joy and intense delight in all destruction, in all the ecstasies of victory and cruelty,—all these features become crystallised, for those who suffered thereby in the picture of the "barbarian," of the "evil enemy," perhaps of the "Goth" and of the "Vandal." The profound, icy mistrust which the German provokes, as soon as he arrives at power,—even at the present time,— is always still an aftermath of that inextinguishable horror with which for whole centuries Europe has regarded the wrath of the blonde Teuton beast (although between the old Germans and ourselves there exists scarcely a psychological, let alone a physical, relationship). I have once called attention to the embarrassment of Hesiod, when he conceived the series of social ages, and endeavoured to express them in gold, silver, and bronze. He could only dispose of the contradiction, with which he was confronted, by the Homeric world, an age magnificent indeed, but at the same time so awful and so violent, by making two ages out of one, which he henceforth placed one behind the other—first, the age of the heroes and demigods, as that world had remained in the memories of the aristocratic families, who found therein their own ancestors; secondly, the bronze age, as that corresponding age appeared to the descendants of the oppressed, spoiled, ill-treated, exiled, enslaved; namely, as an age of bronze, as I have said, hard, cold, terrible, without feelings and without conscience, crushing everything, and bespattering everything with blood. Granted the truth of the theory now believed to be true, that the very *essence of all civilisation* is to *train* out of man, the beast of prey, a tame and civilised animal, a domesticated animal, it follows indubitably that we must regard as the real *tools of civilisation* all those instincts of reaction and resentment, by the help of which the aristocratic races, together with their ideals, were finally degraded and over-powered; though that has not yet come to be synonymous with saying that the bearers of those tools also *represented* the civilisation. It is rather the contrary that is not only probable—nay, it is *palpable* to-day; these bearers of vindictive instincts that have to be bottled up, these descendants of all European and non-European slavery, especially of the pre-Aryan population—these people, I say, represent the *decline* of humanity! These "tools of civilisation" are a disgrace to humanity, and constitute in reality more of an argument against civilisation, more of a reason why civilisation should be suspected. One may be perfectly justified in being always afraid of the blonde beast that lies at the core of all aristocratic races, and in being on one's guard: but who would not a hundred times prefer to be afraid, when one at the same time admires, than to be immune from fear, at the cost of being perpetually obsessed with the loathsome spectacle of the distorted, the dwarfed, the stunted, the envenomed? And is that not our fate? What produces to-day our repulsion towards "man"?—for we *suffer* from "man," there is no doubt about it. It is not fear; it is rather that we have nothing more to fear from men; it is that the worm "man" is in the foreground and pullulates; it is that the "tame man," the wretched mediocre and unedifying creature, has learnt to consider himself a goal and a pinnacle, an inner meaning, an historic principle, a "higher man"; yes, it is that he has a certain right so to consider himself, in so far as he feels that in contrast to that excess of deformity, disease, exhaustion, and effeteness whose odour is beginning to pollute present-day Europe, he at any rate has achieved a relative success, he at any rate still says "yes" to life.

12

I cannot refrain at this juncture from uttering a sigh and one last hope. What is it precisely which I find intolerable? That which I alone cannot get rid of, which makes me choke and faint? Bad air! Bad air! That something misbegotten comes near me; that I must inhale the odour of the entrails of a misbegotten soul!—That excepted, what can one not endure in the way of need, privation, bad weather, sickness, toil, solitude? In point of fact, one manages to get over everything, born as one is to a burrowing and battling existence; one always returns once again to the light, one always lives again one's golden hour of victory—and then one stands as one was born, unbreakable, tense, ready for something more difficult, for something more distant, like a bow stretched but the tauter by every strain. But from time to time do ye grant me—assuming that "beyond good and evil" there are goddesses who can grant—one glimpse, grant me but one glimpse only, of something perfect, fully realised, happy, mighty, triumphant, or something that still gives cause for fear! A glimpse of a man that justifies the existence of man, a glimpse of an incarnate human happiness that realises and redeems, for the sake of which one may hold fast to *the belief in man!* For the position is this: in the dwarfing and levelling of the European man lurks *our* greatest peril, for it is this outlook which fatigues—we see to-day nothing which wishes to be greater, we surmise that the process is always still backwards, still backwards towards something more attenuated, more inoffensive, more cunning, more comfortable, more mediocre, more indifferent, more Chinese, more Christian—man, there is no doubt about it, grows always "better"—the destiny of Europe lies even in this—that in losing the fear of man, we have also lost the hope in man, yea, the will to be man. The sight of man now fatigues.—What is present-day Nihilism if it is not *that?* —We are tired of *man.*

13

But let us come back to it; the problem of *another* origin of the good—of the good, as the resentful man has thought it out—demands its solution. It is not surprising that the lambs should bear a grudge against the great birds of prey, but that is no reason for blaming the great birds of prey for taking the little lambs. And when the lambs say among themselves, "Those birds of prey are evil, and he who is as far removed from being a bird of prey, who is rather its opposite, a lamb,—is he not good?" then there is nothing to cavil at in the setting up of this ideal, though it may also be that the birds of prey will regard it a little sneeringly, and perchance say to themselves, "*We* bear no grudge against them, these good lambs, we even like them: nothing is tastier than a tender lamb." To require of strength that it should *not* express itself as strength, that it should not be a wish to overpower, a wish to overthrow, a wish to become master, a thirst for enemies and antagonisms and triumphs, is just as absurd as to require of weakness that it should express itself as strength. A quantum of force is just such a quantum of movement, will, action—rather it is nothing else than just those very phenomena of moving, willing, acting, and can only appear otherwise in the misleading errors of language (and the fundamental fallacies of reason which have become petrified therein), which understands, and understands wrongly, all working as conditioned by a worker, by a "subject." And just exactly as the people separate the lightning from its flash, and interpret the latter as a thing done, as the working of a subject which is called lightning, so also does the popular morality separate strength from the expression of strength, as though behind the strong man there existed some indifferent neutral *substratum,* which enjoyed a *caprice and option* as to whether or not it should express strength. But there is no such *substratum,* there is no "being" behind doing, working, becoming; "the doer" is a mere appanage to the action. The action is everything. In point of fact, the people duplicate the doing, when they make the lightning lighten, that is a "doing-doing"; they make the same phenomenon first a cause, and then, secondly, the effect of that cause. The scientists fail to improve matters when they say, "Force moves, force causes," and so on. Our whole science is still, in spite of all its coldness, of all its freedom from passion, a dupe of the tricks of language, and has never succeeded in getting rid of that superstitious changeling "the subject" (the atom, to give another instance, is such a changeling, just as the Kantian "Thing-in-itself"). What wonder, if the

suppressed and stealthily simmering passions of revenge and hatred exploit for their own advantage their belief, and indeed hold
no belief with a more steadfast enthusiasm than this—"that the
strong has the *option* of being weak, and the bird of prey of being
a lamb." Thereby do they win for themselves the right of attributing to the birds of prey the *responsibility* for being birds of prey:
when the oppressed, downtrodden, and overpowered say to themselves with the vindictive guile of weakness, "Let us be otherwise
than the evil, namely, good! and good is every one who does not
oppress, who hurts no one, who does not attack, who does not pay
back, who hands over revenge to God, who holds himself, as we
do, in hiding; who goes out of the way of evil, and demands, in
short, little from life; like ourselves the patient, the meek, the
just,"—yet all this, in its cold and unprejudiced interpretation,
means nothing more than "once for all, the weak are weak; it is
good to do *nothing for which we are not strong enough";* but this
dismal state of affairs, this prudence of the lowest order, which
even insects possess (which in a great danger are fain to sham death
so as to avoid doing "too much"), has, thanks to the counterfeiting
and self-deception of weakness, come to masquerade in the pomp
of an ascetic, mute, and expectant virtue, just as though the *very*
weakness of the weak—that is, forsooth, its *being,* its working, its
whole unique inevitable inseparable reality—were a voluntary result, something wished, chosen, a deed, an act of *merit.* This kind
of man finds the belief in a neutral, free-choosing "subject" *necessary* from an instinct of self-preservation, of self-assertion, in which
every lie is fain to sanctify itself. The subject (or, to use popular
language, the *soul*) has perhaps proved itself the best dogma in the
world simply because it rendered possible to the horde of mortal,
weak, and oppressed individuals of every kind, that most sublime
specimen of self-deception, the interpretation of weakness as freedom, of being this, or being that, as *merit.*

14

Will any one look a little into—right into—the mystery of how
ideals are *manufactured* in this world? Who has the courage to do
it? Come!

Here we have a vista opened into these grimy workshops. Wait just a moment, dear Mr. Inquisitive and Foolhardy; your eye must first grow accustomed to this false changing light—Yes! Enough! Now speak! What is happening below down yonder? Speak out! Tell what you see, man of the most dangerous curiosity—for now *I* am the listener.

"I see nothing, I hear the more. It is a cautious, spiteful, gentle whispering and muttering together in all the corners and crannies. It seems to me that they are lying; a sugary softness adheres to every sound. Weakness is turned to *merit,* there is no doubt about it—it is just as you say."

Further!

"And the impotence which requites not, is turned to 'goodness,' craven baseness to meekness, submission to those whom one hates, to obedience (namely, obedience to one of whom they say that he ordered this submission—they call him God). The inoffensive character of the weak, the very cowardice in which he is rich, his standing at the door, his forced necessity of waiting, gain here fine names, such as 'patience,' which is also called 'virtue'; not being able to avenge one's self, is called not wishing to avenge one's self, perhaps even forgiveness (for *they* know not what they do—we alone know what they do). They also talk of the 'love of their enemies' and sweat thereby."

Further!

"They are miserable, there is no doubt about it, all these whisperers and counterfeiters in the corners, although they try to get warm by crouching close to each other, but they tell me that their misery is a favour and distinction given to them by God, just as one beats the dogs one likes best; that perhaps this misery is also a preparation, a probation, a training; that perhaps it is still more something which will one day be compensated and paid back with a tremendous interest in gold, nay in happiness. This they call 'Blessedness.' "

Further!

"They are now giving me to understand, that not only are they better men than the mighy, the lords of the earth, whose spittle they have got to lick (*not* out of fear, not at all out of fear! But because God ordains that one should honour all authority)—not only are they better men, but that they also have a 'better time,' at any rate, will one day have a 'better time.' But enough!

Enough! I can endure it no longer. Bad air! Bad air! These work-shops *where ideals are manufactured*—verily they reek with the crassest lies."

Nay. Just one minute! You are saying nothing about the mas-terpieces of these virtuosos of black magic, who can produce whiteness, milk, and innocence out of any black you like: have you not noticed what a pitch of refinement is attained by their *chef d'œuvre*, their most audacious, subtle, ingenious, and lying artist-trick? Take care! These cellar-beasts, full of revenge and hate—what do they make, forsooth, out of their revenge and hate? Do you hear these words? Would you suspect, if you trusted only their words, that you are among men of resentment and nothing else?

"I understand, I prick my ears up again (ah! ah! ah! and I hold my nose). Now do I hear for the first time that which they have said so often: 'We good, *we are the righteous*'—what they demand they call not revenge but 'the triumph of *righteousness*'; what they hate is not their enemy, no, they hate 'unrighteousness,' 'god-lessness'; what they believe in and hope is not the hope of revenge, the intoxication of sweet revenge (—"sweeter than honey," did Homer call it?), but the victory of God, of the *righteous God* over the 'godless'; what is left for them to love in this world is not their brothers in hate, but their 'brothers in love,' as they say, all the good and righteous on the earth."

And how do they name that which serves them as a solace against all the troubles of life—their phantasmagoria of their antic-ipated future blessedness?

"How? Do I hear right? They call it 'the last judgment,' the advent of *their* kingdom, 'the kingdom of God'—but *in the mean-while* they live 'in faith,' 'in love,' 'in hope.' "

Enough! Enough!

15

In the faith in what? In the love for what? In the hope of what? These weaklings!—they also, forsooth, wish to be strong some time; there is no doubt about it, some time *their* kingdom also must come—"the kingdom of God" is their name for it, as has been mentioned:—they are so meek in everything! Yet in order to experience *that* kingdom it is necessary to live long, to live beyond death,—yes, *eternal* life is necessary so that one can make up for ever for that earthly life "in faith," "in love," "in hope." Make up for what? Make up by what? Dante, as it seems to me, made a crass mistake when with awe-inspiring ingenuity he placed that inscription over the gate of his hell, "Me too made eternal love": at any rate the following inscription would have a much better right to stand over the gate of the Christian Paradise and its "eternal blessedness"—"Me too made eternal hate"—granted of course that a truth may rightly stand over the gate to a lie! For what is the blessedness of that Paradise? Possibly we could quickly surmise it; but it is better that it should be explicitly attested by an authority who in such matters is not to be disparaged, Thomas of Aquinas, the great teacher and saint. "The saints in the kingdom of heaven," says he, as gently as a lamb, "will see the punishments of the damned, that their own beatitude may be more pleasing unto them." . . .

16

Let us come to a conclusion. The two *opposing values,* "good and bad," "good and evil," have fought a dreadful, thousand-year fight in the world, and though indubitably the second value has been for a long time in the preponderance, there are not wanting places where the fortune of the fight is still undecisive. It can almost be said that in the meanwhile the fight reaches a higher and higher level, and that in the meanwhile it has become more and more intense, and always more and more psychological; so that nowadays there is perhaps no more decisive mark of the *higher nature,* of the more psychological nature, than to be in that sense self-contradictory, and to be actually still a battleground for those two opposites. The symbol of this fight, written in a writing which has remained worthy of perusal throughout the course of history up to the present time, is called "Rome against Judæa, Judæa against Rome." Hitherto there has been no greater event *than* that fight, the putting of *that* question, *that* deadly antagonism. Rome found in the Jew the incarnation of the unnatural, as though it were its diametrically opposed monstrosity, and in Rome the Jew was held to be *convicted of hatred* of the whole human race: and rightly so, in so far as it is right to link the well-being and the future of the human race to the unconditional

mastery of the aristocratic values, of the Roman values. What, conversely, did the Jews feel against Rome? One can surmise it from
a thousand symptoms, but it is sufficient to carry one's mind back
to the Johannian Apocalypse, that most obscene of all the written
outbursts, which has revenge on its conscience. (One should also
appraise at its full value the profound logic of the Christian
instinct, when over this very book of hate it wrote the name of
the Disciple of Love, that self-same disciple to whom it attributed
that impassioned and ecstatic Gospel—therein lurks a portion of
truth, however much literary forging may have been necessary
for this purpose.) The Romans were the strong and aristocratic;
a nation stronger and more aristocratic has never existed in the
world, has never even been dreamed of; every relic of them, every
inscription enraptures, granted that one can divine *what* it is that
writes the inscription. The Jews, conversely, were that priestly
nation of resentment *par excellence,* possessed by a unique genius
for popular morals: just compare with the Jews the nations with
analogous gifts, such as the Chinese or the Germans, so as to
realise afterwards what is first rate, and what is fifth rate.

Which of them has been provisionally victorious, Rome or
Judæa? but there is not a shadow of doubt; just consider to whom
in Rome itself nowadays you bow down, as though before the
quintessence of all the highest values—and not only in Rome, but
almost over half the world, everywhere where man has been tamed
or is about to be tamed—to *three Jews,* as we know, and *one Jew-
ess* (to Jesus of Nazareth, to Peter the fisher, to Paul the tentmaker,
and to the mother of the aforesaid Jesus, named Mary). This is
very remarkable: Rome is undoubtedly defeated. At any rate there
took place in the Renaissance a brilliantly sinister revival of the
classical ideal, of the aristocratic valuation of all things: Rome
herself, like a man waking up from a trance, stirred beneath the
burden of the new Judaised Rome that had been built over her,
which presented the appearance of an œcumenical synagogue and
was called the "Church": but immediately Judæa triumphed
again, thanks to that fundamentally popular (German and English) movement of revenge, which is called the Reformation, and
taking also into account its inevitable corollary, the restoration of
the Church—the restoration also of the ancient graveyard peace
of classical Rome. Judæa proved yet once more victorious over

the classical ideal in the French Revolution, and in a sense which was even more crucial and even more profound: the last political aristocracy that existed in Europe, that of the *French* seventeenth and eighteenth centuries, broke into pieces beneath the instincts of a resentful populace—never had the world heard a greater jubilation, a more uproarious enthusiasm: indeed, there took place in the midst of it the most monstrous and unexpected phenomenon; the ancient ideal *itself* swept before the eyes and conscience of humanity with all its life and with unheard-of splendour, and in opposition to resentment's lying war-cry of *the prerogative of the most,* in opposition to the will to lowliness, abasement, and equalisation, the will to a retrogression and twilight of humanity, there rang out once again, stronger, simpler, more penetrating than ever, the terrible and enchanting counter-war-cry of *the prerogative of the few!* Like a final sign-post to other ways, there appeared Napoleon, the most unique and violent anachronism that ever existed, and in him the incarnate problem *of the aristocratic ideal in itself*—consider well what a problem it is:—Napoleon, that synthesis of Monster and Superman.

17

Was it therewith over? Was that greatest of all antitheses of ideals thereby relegated *ad acta* for all time? Or only postponed, postponed for a long time? May there not take place at some time or other a much more awful, much more carefully prepared flaring up of the old conflagration? Further! Should not one wish *that* consummation with all one's strength?—will it one's self? demand it one's self? He who at this juncture begins, like my readers, to reflect, to think further, will have difficulty in coming quickly to a conclusion,—ground enough for me to come myself to a conclusion, taking it for granted that for some time past what I mean has been sufficiently clear, what I exactly *mean* by that dangerous motto which is inscribed on the body of my last book: *Beyond Good and Evil*—at any rate that is not the same as "Beyond Good and Bad."

Second Essay

"Guilt," "Bad Conscience," and the Like

1

The breeding of an animal that *can promise*—is not this just that very paradox of a task which nature has set itself in regard to man? Is not this the very problem of man? The fact that this problem has been to a great extent solved, must appear all the more phenomenal to one who can estimate at its full value that force of *forgetfulness* which works in opposition to it. Forgetfulness is no mere *vis inertiæ*, as the superficial believe, rather is it a power of obstruction, active and, in the strictest sense of the word, positive—a power responsible for the fact that what we have lived, experienced, taken into ourselves, no more enters into consciousness during the process of digestion (it might be called psychic absorption) than all the whole manifold process by which our physical nutrition, the so-called "incorporation," is carried on. The temporary shutting of the doors and windows of consciousness, the relief from the clamant alarums and excursions, with which our subconscious world of servant organs works in mutual co-operation and antagonism; a little quietude, a little *tabula rasa* of the consciousness, so as to make room again for the new, and above all for the more noble functions and functionaries, room for government, foresight, predetermination (for our organism is on an oligarchic model)—this is the utility, as I have said, of the active forgetfulness, which is a very sentinel and nurse of psychic order, repose, etiquette; and this shows at once why it is that there can exist no happiness, no gladness, no hope, no pride, no real *present*, without forgetfulness. The man in whom this preventative apparatus is damaged and discarded, is to be compared to a dyspeptic, and it is something more than a comparison —he can "get rid of" nothing. But this very animal who finds it necessary to be forgetful, in whom, in fact, forgetfulness represents a force and a form of *robust* health, has reared for himself an opposition-power, a memory, with whose help forgetfulness is, in certain instances, kept in check—in the cases, namely, where promises have to be made;—so that it is by no means a mere passive inability to get rid of a once indented impression, not merely the indigestion occasioned by a once pledged word, which one cannot dispose of, but an *active* refusal to get rid of it, a continuing and a wish to continue what has once been willed, an actual *memory of the will;* so that between the original "I will," "I shall do," and the actual discharge of the will, its *act,* we can easily interpose a world of new strange phenomena, circumstances, veritable volitions, without the snapping of this long chain of the will. But what is the underlying hypothesis of all this? How thoroughly, in order to be able to regulate the future in this way, must man have first learnt to distinguish between necessitated and accidental phenomena, to think casually, to see the distant as present and to anticipate it, to fix with certainty what is the end, and what is the means to that end; above all, to reckon, to have power to calculate—how thoroughly must man have first become *calculable, disciplined, necessitated* even for himself and his own conception of himself, that, like a man entering a promise, he could guarantee himself *as a future.*

2

This is simply the long history of the origin of *responsibility.* That task of breeding an animal which can make promises, includes, as we have already grasped, as its condition and preliminary, the more immediate task of first *making* man to a certain extent, necessitated, uniform, like among his like, regular, and consequently calculable. The immense work of what I have called, "morality of custom" (cp. *Dawn of Day,* Aphs. 9, 14, and 16), the actual work of man on himself during the longest period of the human race, his whole prehistoric work, finds its meaning, its great justification (in spite of all its innate hardness, despotism, stupidity, and idiocy) in this fact: man, with the help of the morality of customs and of social strait-waistcoats, was *made* genuinely calculable. If, however, we place ourselves at the end of this colossal process, at the point where the tree finally matures its fruits, when society and its morality of custom finally bring to light that to which it was only the means, then do we find as the ripest fruit on its tree the *sovereign individual,* that resembles only himself, that has got loose from the morality of custom, the autonomous "supermoral" individual (for "autonomous" and "moral" are mutually exclusive terms),—in short, the man of the personal, long, and independent will, *competent to promise*,—and we find in him a proud consciousness (vibrating in every fibre), of *what* has been at last achieved and become vivified in him, a genuine consciousness of power and freedom, a feeling of human perfection in general. And this man who has grown to freedom, who is really *competent* to promise, this lord of the *free* will, this sovereign—how is it possible for him not to know how great is his superiority over everything incapable of binding itself by promises, or of being its own security, how great is the trust, the awe, the reverence that he awakes—he "deserves" all three—not to know that with this mastery over himself he is necessarily also given the mastery over circumstances, over nature, over all creatures with shorter wills, less reliable characters? The "free" man, the owner of a long unbreakable will, finds in this possession his *standard of value:* looking out from himself upon the others, he honours or he despises, and just as necessarily as he honours his peers, the strong and the reliable (those who can bind themselves by promises),—that is, every one who promises like a sovereign, with difficulty, rarely and slowly, who is sparing with his trusts but confers *honour* by the very fact of trusting, who gives his word as something that can be relied on, because he knows himself strong enough to keep it even in the teeth of disasters, even in the "teeth of fate,"—so with equal necessity will he have the heel of his foot ready for the lean and empty jackasses, who promise when they have no business to do so, and his rod of chastisement ready for the liar, who already breaks his word at the very minute when it is on his lips. The proud knowledge of the extraordinary privilege of *responsibility,* the consciousness of this rare freedom, of this power over himself and over fate, has sunk right down to his innermost depths, and has become an instinct, a dominating instinct—what name will he give to it, to this dominating instinct, if he needs to have a word for it? But there is no doubt about it— the sovereign man calls it his *conscience.*

3

His conscience?—One apprehends at once that the idea "conscience," which is here seen in its supreme manifestation, supreme in fact to almost the point of strangeness, should already have behind it a long history and evolution. The ability to guarantee one's self with all due pride, and also at the same time to *say yes* to one's self—that is, as has been said, a ripe fruit, but also a *late* fruit:—How long must needs this fruit hang sour and bitter on the tree! And for an even longer period there was not a glimpse of such a fruit to be had—no one had taken it on himself to promise it, although everything on the tree was quite ready for it, and everything was maturing for that very consummation. "How is a memory to be made for the man-animal? How is an impression to be so deeply fixed upon this ephemeral understanding, half dense, and half silly, upon this incarnate forgetfulness, that it will be permanently present?" As one may imagine, this primeval problem was not solved by exactly gentle answers and gentle means; perhaps there is nothing more awful and more sinister in the early history of man than his *system of mnemonics*. "Something is burnt in so as to remain in his memory: only that which never stops *hurting* remains in his memory." This is an axiom of the oldest (unfortunately also the longest) psychology in the world. It might even be said that wherever solemnity, seriousness, mystery, and gloomy colours are now found in the life of the men and of nations of the world, there is some *survival* of that horror which was once the universal concomitant of all promises, pledges, and obligations. The past, the past with all its length, depth, and hardness, wafts to us its breath, and bubbles up in us again, when we become "serious." When man thinks it necessary to make for himself a memory, he never accomplishes it without blood, tortures and sacrifice; the most dreadful sacrifices and forfeitures (among them the sacrifice of the first-born), the most loathsome mutilation (for instance, castration), the most cruel rituals of all the religious cults (for all religions are really at bottom systems of cruelty)—all these things originate from that instinct which found in pain its most potent mnemonic. In a certain sense the whole of asceticism is to be ascribed to this: certain ideas have got to be made inextinguishable, omnipresent, "fixed," with the object of hypnotising the whole nervous and intellectual system through these "fixed ideas"—and the ascetic methods and modes of life are the means of freeing those ideas from the competition of all other ideas so as to make them "unforgettable." The worse memory man had, the ghastlier the signs presented by his customs; the severity of the penal laws affords in particular a gauge of the extent of man's difficulty in conquering forgetfulness, and in keeping a few primal postulates of social intercourse ever present to the minds of those who were the slaves of every momentary emotion and every momentary desire. We Germans do certainly not regard ourselves as an especially cruel and hard-hearted nation, still less as an especially casual and happy-go-lucky one; but one has only to look at our old penal ordinances in order to realise what a lot of trouble it takes in the world to evolve a "nation of thinkers" (I mean: *the* European nation which exhibits at this very day the maximum of reliability, seriousness, bad taste, and positiveness, which has on the strength of these qualities a right to train every kind of European mandarin). These Germans employed terrible means to make for themselves a memory, to enable them to master their rooted plebeian instincts and the brutal crudity of those instincts: think of the old German punishments, for instance, stoning (as far back as the legend, the millstone falls on the head of the guilty man), breaking on the wheel (the most original invention and speciality of the German genius in the sphere of punishment), dart-throwing, tearing, or trampling by horses ("quartering"), boiling the criminal in oil or wine (still prevalent in the fourteenth and fifteenth centuries), the highly popular flaying ("slicing into strips"), cutting the flesh out of the breast; think also of the evil-doer being besmeared with honey, and then exposed to the flies in a blazing sun. It was by the help of such images and precedents that man eventually kept in his memory five or six "I will nots" with regard to which he had already given his *promise,* so as to be able to enjoy the advantages of society—and verily with the help of this kind of memory man eventually attained "reason"! Alas! reason, seriousness, mastery over the emotions, all these gloomy, dismal things which are called reflection, all these privileges and pageantries of humanity: how dear is the price that they have exacted! How much blood and cruelty is the foundation of all "good things"!

4

But how is it that that other melancholy object, the consciousness of sin, the whole "bad conscience," came into the world? And it is here that we turn back to our genealogists of morals. For the second time I say—or have I not said it yet?—that they are worth nothing. Just their own five-spans-long limited modern experience; no knowledge of the past, and no wish to know it; still less a historic instinct, a power of "second sight" (which is what is really required in this case)—and despite this to go in for the history of morals. It stands to reason that this must needs produce results which are removed from the truth by something more than a respectful distance.

Have these current genealogists of morals ever allowed themselves to have even the vaguest notion, for instance, that the cardinal moral idea of "ought" originates from the very material idea of "owe"? Or that punishment developed as a *retaliation* absolutely independently of any preliminary hypothesis of the freedom or determination of the will?—And this to such an extent, that a *high* degree of civilisation was always first necessary for the animal man to begin to make those much more primitive distinctions of "intentional," "negligent," "accidental," "responsible," and their contraries, and apply them in the assessing of punishment. That idea—"the wrong-doer deserves punishment *because* he might have acted otherwise," in spite of the fact that it is nowadays so cheap, obvious, natural, and inevitable, and that it has had to serve as an illustration of the way in which the sentiment of justice appeared on earth, is in point of fact an exceedingly late, and even refined form of human judgment and inference; the placing of this idea back at the beginning of the world is simply a clumsy violation of the principles of primitive psychology. Throughout the longest period of human history punishment was *never* based on the responsibility of the evil-doer for his action, and was consequently *not* based on the hypothesis that only the guilty should be punished;—on the contrary, punishment was inflicted in those days for the same reason that parents punish their children even nowadays, out of anger at an injury that they have suffered, an anger which vents itself mechanically on the author of the injury—but this anger is kept in bounds and modified through the idea that every injury has somewhere or other its *equivalent* price, and can really be paid off, even though it be by means of pain to the author. Whence is it that this ancient deep-rooted and now perhaps ineradicable idea has drawn its strength, this idea of an equivalency between injury and pain? I have already revealed its origin, in the contractual relationship between *creditor* and *ower*, that is as old as the existence of legal rights at all, and in its turn points back to the primary forms of purchase, sale, barter, and trade.

5

The realisation of these contractual relations excites, of course (as would be already expected from our previous observations), a great deal of suspicion and opposition towards the primitive society which made or sanctioned them. In this society promises will be made; in this society the object is to provide the promiser with a memory; in this society, so may we suspect, there will be full scope for hardness, cruelty, and pain: the "ower," in order to induce credit in his promise of repayment, in order to give a guarantee of the earnestness and sanctity of his promise, in order to drill into his own conscience the duty, the solemn duty, of repayment, will, by virtue of a contract with his creditor to meet the contingency of his not paying, pledge something that he still possesses, something that he still has in his power, for instance, his life or his wife, or his freedom or his body (or under certain religious conditions even his salvation, his soul's welfare, even his peace in the grave; so in Egypt, where the corpse of the ower found even in the grave no rest from the creditor—of course, from the Egyptian standpoint, this peace was a matter of particular importance). But especially has the creditor the power of inflicting on the body of the ower all kinds of pain and torture—the power, for instance, of cutting off from it an amount that appeared proportionate to the greatness of the debt; —this point of view resulted in the universal prevalence at an early date of precise schemes of valuation, frequently horrible in the minuteness and meticulosity of their application, *legally* sanctioned schemes of valuation for individual limbs and parts of the body. I consider it as already a progress, as a proof of a freer, less petty, and more *Roman* conception of law, when the Roman Code of the Twelve Tables decreed that it was immaterial how much or how little the creditors in such a contingency cut off, *"si plus minusve secuerunt, ne fraude esto."* Let us make the logic of the whole of this equalisation process clear; it is strange enough. The equivalence consists in this: instead of an advantage directly compensatory of his injury (that is, instead of an equalisation in money, lands, or some kind of chattel), the creditor is granted by way of repayment and compensation a certain *sensation of satisfaction*—the satisfaction of being able to vent, without any trouble, his power on one who is powerless, the delight *"de faire le mal pour le plaisir de la faire,"* the joy in sheer violence: and this joy will be relished in proportion to the lowness and humbleness of the creditor in the social scale, and is quite apt to have the effect of the most delicious dainty, and even seem the foretaste of a higher social position. Thanks to the punishment of the "ower," the creditor participates in the rights of the masters. At last he too, for once in a way, attains the edifying consciousness of being able to despise and ill-treat a creature—as an "inferior"—or at any rate of *seeing* him being despised and ill-treated, in case the actual power of punishment, the administration of punishment, has already become transferred to the "authorities." The compensation consequently consists in a claim on cruelty and a right to draw thereon.

6

It is then in *this* sphere of the law of contract that we find the cradle of the whole moral world of the ideas of "guilt," "conscience," "duty," the "sacredness of duty,"—their commencement, like the commencement of all great things in the world, is thoroughly and continuously saturated with blood. And should we not add that this world has never really lost a certain savour of blood and torture (not even in old Kant: the categorical imperative reeks of cruelty). It was in this sphere likewise that there first became formed that sinister and perhaps now indissoluble association of the ideas of "guilt" and "suffering." To put the question yet again, why can suffering be a compensation for "owing"?—Because the *infliction* of suffering produces the highest degree of happiness, because the injured party will get in exchange for his loss (including his vexation at his loss) an extraordinary counter-pleasure: the *infliction* of suffering—a real *feast*, something that, as I have said, was all the more appreciated the greater the paradox created by the rank and social status of the creditor. These observations are purely conjectural; for, apart from the painful nature of the task, it is hard to plumb such profound depths: the clumsy introduction of the idea of "revenge" as a connecting-link simply hides and obscures the view instead of rendering it clearer (revenge itself simply leads back again to the identical problem—"How can the inflection of suffering be a satisfaction?"). In my opinion it is repugnant to the delicacy, and still more to the hypocrisy of tame domestic animals (that is, modern men; that is, ourselves), to realise with all their energy the extent to which *cruelty* constituted the great joy and delight of ancient man, was an ingredient which seasoned nearly all his pleasures, and conversely the extent of the naïveté and innocence with which he manifested his need for cruelty, when he actually made as a matter of principle "disinterested malice" (or, to use Spinoza's expression, the *sympathia malevolens*) into a *normal* characteristic of man—as consequently something to which the conscience says a hearty *yes*. The more profound observer has perhaps already had sufficient opportunity for noticing this most ancient and radical joy and delight of mankind; in *Beyond Good and Evil*, Aph. 188 (and even earlier, in *The Dawn of Day*, Aph. 18, 77, 113), I have cautiously indicated the continually growing spiritualisation and "deification" of cruelty, which pervades the whole history of the higher civilisation (and in the larger sense even constitutes it). At any rate the time is not so long past when it was impossible to conceive of royal weddings and national festivals on a grand scale, without executions, tortures, or perhaps an *auto-da-fé*, or similarly to conceive of an aristocratic household, without a creature to serve as a butt for the cruel and malicious baiting of the inmates. (The reader will perhaps remember Don Quixote at the court of the Duchess: we read nowadays the whole of *Don Quixote* with a bitter taste in the mouth, almost with a sensation of torture, a fact which would appear very strange and very incomprehensible to the author and his contemporaries—they read it with the best conscience in the world as the gayest of books; they almost died with laughing at it.) The sight of suffering does one good, the infliction of suffering does one more good—this is a hard maxim, but none the less a fundamental maxim, old, powerful, and "human, all-too-human"; one, moreover, to which perhaps even the apes as well would subscribe: for it is said that in inventing bizarre cruelties they are giving abundant proof of their future humanity, to which, as it were, they are playing the prelude. Without cruelty, no feast: so teaches the oldest and longest history of man—and in punishment too is there so much of the *festive*.

7

Entertaining, as I do, these thoughts, I am, let me say in parenthesis, fundamentally opposed to helping our pessimists to new water for the discordant and groaning mills of their disgust with life; on the contrary, it should be shown specifically that, at the time when mankind was not yet ashamed of its cruelty, life in the world was brighter than it is nowadays when there are pessimists. The darkening of the heavens over man has always increased in proportion to the growth of man's shame *before man*. The tired pessimistic outlook, the mistrust of the riddle of life, the icy negation of disgusted ennui, all those are not the signs of the *most evil* age of the human race: much rather do they come first to the light of day, as the swamp-flowers, which they are, when the swamp to which they belong, comes into existence—I mean the diseased refinement and moralisation, thanks to which the "animal man" has at last learnt to be ashamed of all his instincts. On the road to angel-hood (not to use in this context a harder word) man has developed that dyspeptic stomach and coated tongue, which have made not only the joy and innocence of the animal repulsive to him, but also life itself:—so that sometimes he stands with stopped nostrils before his own self, and, like Pope Innocent the Third, makes a black list of his own horrors ("unclean generation, loathsome nutrition when in the maternal body, badness of the matter out of which man develops, awful stench, secretion of saliva, urine, and excrement"). Nowadays, when suffering is always trotted out as the first argument *against* existence, as its most sinister query, it is well to remember the times when men judged on converse principles because they could not dispense with the *infliction* of suffering, and saw therein a magic of the first order, a veritable bait of seduction to life.

Perhaps in those days (this is to solace the weaklings) pain did not hurt so much as it does nowadays: any physician who has treated negroes (granted that these are taken as representative of the prehistoric man) suffering from severe internal inflammations which would bring a European, even though he had the soundest constitution, almost to despair, would be in a position to come to this conclusion. Pain has *not* the same effect with negroes. (The curve of human sensibilities to pain seems indeed to sink in an extraordinary and almost sudden fashion, as soon as one has passed the upper ten thousand or ten millions of over-civilised humanity, and I personally have no doubt that, by comparison with one painful night passed by one single hysterical chit of a cultured woman, the suffering of all the animals taken together who have been put to the question of the knife, so as to give scientific answers, are simply negligible.) We may perhaps be allowed to admit the possibility of the craving for cruelty not necessarily having become really extinct: it only requires, in view of the fact that pain hurts more nowadays, a certain sublimation and subtilisation, it must especially be translated to the imaginative and psychic plane, and be adorned with such smug euphemisms, that even the most fastidious and hypocritical conscience could never grow suspicious of their real nature ("Tragic pity" is one of these euphemisms: another is *"les nostalgies de la croix"*). What really raises one's indignation against suffering is not suffering intrinsically, but the senselessness of suffering; such a *senselessness,* however, existed neither in Christianity, which interpreted suffering into a whole mysterious salvation-apparatus, nor in the beliefs of the naïve ancient man, who only knew how to find a meaning in suffering from the standpoint of the spectator, or the inflictor of the suffering. In order to get the secret, undiscovered, and unwitnessed suffering out of the world it was almost compulsory to invent gods and a hierarchy of intermediate beings, in short, something which wanders even among secret places, sees even in the dark, and makes a point of never missing an interesting and painful spectacle. It was with the help of such inventions that life got to learn the *tour de force,* which has become part of its stock-in-trade, the *tour de force* of self-justification, of the justification of

evil; nowadays this would perhaps require other auxiliary devices
(for instance, life as a riddle, life as a problem of knowledge).
"Every evil is justified in the sight of which a god finds edifica-
tion," so rang the logic of primitive sentiment—and, indeed, was
it only of primitive? The gods conceived as friends of spectacles of
cruelty—oh, how far does this primeval conception extend even
nowadays into our European civilisation! One would perhaps like
in this context to consult Luther and Calvin. It is at any rate
certain that even the Greeks knew no more piquant seasoning for
the happiness of their gods than the joys of cruelty. What, do you
think, was the mood with which Homer makes his gods look down
upon the fates of men? What final meaning have at bottom the
Trojan War and similar tragic horrors? It is impossible to entertain any doubt on the point: they were intended as festival games
for the gods, and, in so far as the poet is of a more godlike breed
than other men, as festival games also for the poets. It was in just
this spirit and no other, that at a later date the moral philosophers
of Greece conceived the eyes of God as still looking down on the
moral struggle, the heroism, and the self-torture of the virtuous;
the Heracles of duty was on a stage, and was conscious of the fact;
virtue without witnesses was something quite unthinkable for
this nation of actors. Must not that philosophic invention, so
audacious and so fatal, which was then absolutely new to Europe,
the invention of "free will," of the absolute spontaneity of man in
good and evil, simply have been made for the specific purpose of
justifying the idea, that the interest of the gods in humanity and
human virtue was *inexhaustible?*

There would never on the stage of this free-will world be a
dearth of really new, really novel and exciting situations, plots,
catastrophes. A world thought out on completely deterministic
lines would be easily guessed by the gods, and would consequently
soon bore them—sufficient reason for these *friends of the gods,*
the philosophers, not to ascribe to their gods such a deterministic
world. The whole of ancient humanity is full of delicate consideration for the spectator, being as it is a world of thorough pub-
licity and theatricality, which could not conceive of happiness
without spectacles and festivals.—And, as has already been said,
even in great *punishment* there is so much which is festive.

8

The feeling of "ought," of personal obligation (to take up again the train of our inquiry), has had, as we saw, its origin in the oldest and most original personal relationship that there is, the relationship between buyer and seller, creditor and owner: here it was that individual confronted individual, and that individual *matched himself against* individual. There has not yet been found a grade of civilisation so low, as not to manifest some trace of this relationship. Making prices, assessing values, thinking out equivalents, exchanging—all this preoccupied the primal thoughts of man to such extent that in a certain sense it constituted *thinking* itself: it was here that was trained the oldest form of sagacity, it was here in this sphere that we can perhaps trace the first commencement of man's pride, of his feeling of superiority over other animals. Perhaps our word "Mensch" (manas) still expresses just something of *this* self-pride: man denoted himself as the being who measures values, who values and measures, as the "assessing" animal *par excellence*. Sale and purchase, together with their psychological concomitants, are older than the origins of any form of social organisation and union: it is rather from the most rudimentary form of individual right that the budding consciousness of exchange, commerce, debt, right, obligation, compensation was first transferred to the rudest and most elementary of the social complexes (in their relation to similar complexes), the habit of comparing force with force, together with that of measuring, of calculating. His eye was now focussed to this perspective; and with that ponderous consistency characteristic of ancient thought, which, though set in motion with difficulty, yet proceeds inflexibly along the line on which it has started, man soon arrived at the great generalisation, "everything has its price, *all* can be paid for," the oldest and most naïve moral canon of *justice*, the beginning of all "kindness," of all "equity," of all "goodwill," of all "objectivity" in the world. Justice in this initial phase is the goodwill among people of about equal power to come to terms with each other, to come to an understanding again by means of a settlement, and with regard to the less powerful, to *compel* them to agree among themselves to a settlement.

9

Measured always by the standard of antiquity (this antiquity, moreover, is present or again possible at all periods), the community stands to its members in that important and radical relationship of creditor to his owners. Man lives in a community, man enjoys the advantages of a community (and what advantages! we occasionally underestimate them nowadays), man lives protected, spared, in peace and trust, secure from certain injuries and enmities, to which the man outside the community, the "peaceless" man, is exposed,—a German understands the original meaning of "Elend" (*êlend*),—secure because he has entered into pledges and obligations to the community in respect of these very injuries and enmities. What happens *when this is not the case?* The community, the defrauded creditor, will get itself paid, as well as it can, one can reckon on that. In this case the question of the direct damage done by the offender is quite subsidiary: quite apart from this the criminal is above all a breaker, a breaker of word and covenant *to the whole,* as regards all the advantages and amenities of the communal life in which up to that time he had participated. The criminal is an "ower" who not only fails to repay the advances and advantages that have been given to him, but even sets out to attack his creditor: consequently he is in the future not only, as is fair, deprived of all these advantages and amenities—he is in addition reminded of the *importance* of those advantages. The wrath of the injured creditor, of the community, puts him back in the wild and outlawed status from which he was previously protected: the community repudiates him—and now every kind of enmity can vent itself on him. Punishment is in this stage of civilisation simply the copy, the mimic, of the normal treatment of the hated, disdained, and conquered enemy, who is not only deprived of every right and protection but of every mercy; so we have the martial law and triumphant festival of the *væ victis!* in all its mercilessness and cruelty. This shows why war itself (counting the sacrificial cult of war) has produced all the forms under which punishment has manifested itself in history.

10

As it grows more powerful, the community tends to take the offences of the individual less seriously, because they are now regarded as being much less revolutionary and dangerous to the corporate existence: the evil-doer is no more outlawed and put outside the pale, the common wrath can no longer vent itself upon him with its old licence,—on the contrary, from this very time it is against this wrath, and particularly against the wrath of those directly injured, that the evil-doer is carefully shielded and protected by the community. As, in fact, the penal law develops, the following characteristics become more and more clearly marked: compromise with the wrath of those directly affected by the misdeed; a consequent endeavour to localise the matter and to prevent a further, or indeed a general spread of the disturbance; attempts to find equivalents and to settle the whole matter (*compositio*); above all, the will, which manifests itself with increasing definiteness, to treat every offence as in a certain degree capable of *being paid off,* and consequently, at any rate up to a certain point, to *isolate* the offender from his act. As the power and the self-consciousness of a community increases, so proportionately does the penal law become mitigated; conversely every weakening and jeopardising of the community revives the harshest forms of that law. The creditor has always grown more humane proportionately as he has grown more rich; finally the amount of injury he can endure without really suffering becomes the criterion of his wealth. It is possible to conceive of a society blessed with so great a *consciousness of its own power* as to indulge in the most aristocratic luxury of letting its wrong-doers go *scot-free.*—"What do my parasites matter to me?" might society say. "Let them live and flourish! I am strong enough for it."—The justice which began with the maxim, "Everything can be paid off, everything must be paid off," ends with connivance at the escape of those who cannot pay to escape—it ends, like every good thing on earth, by *destroying itself.*—The self-destruction of Justice! we know the pretty name it calls itself—*Grace!* it remains, as is obvious, the privilege of the strongest, better still, their super-law.

11

A deprecatory word here against the attempts, that have lately
been made, to find the origin of justice on quite another basis—
namely, on that of *resentment*. Let me whisper a word in the ear
of the psychologists, if they would fain study revenge itself at close
quarters: this plant blooms its prettiest at present among Anar-
chists and anti-Semites, a hidden flower, as it has ever been, like
the violet, though, forsooth, with another perfume. And as like
must necessarily emanate from like, it will not be a matter for
surprise that it is just in such circles that we see the birth of endeavours (it is their old birthplace—compare above), to sanctify
revenge under the name of *justice* (as though Justice were at bottom merely a development of the consciousness of injury), and
thus with the rehabilitation of revenge to reinstate generally and
collectively all the *reactive* emotions. I object to this last point
least of all. It even seems *meritorious* when regarded from the
standpoint of the whole problem of biology (from which standpoint the value of these emotions has up to the present been un-
derestimated). And that to which I alone call attention, is the
circumstance that it is the spirit of revenge itself, from which develops this new nuance of scientific equity (for the benefit of hate,
envy, mistrust, jealousy, suspicion, rancour, revenge). This scientific "equity" stops immediately and makes way for the accents of
deadly enmity and prejudice, so soon as another group of emotions comes on the scene, which in my opinion are of a much
higher biological value than these reactions, and consequently
have a paramount claim to the valuation and appreciation of
science: I mean the really *active* emotions, such as personal and
material ambition, and so forth. (E. Dühring, *Value of Life;
Course of Philosophy,* and *passim.*) So much against this tendency
in general: but as for the particular maxim of Dühring's, that the
home of Justice is to be found in the sphere of the reactive feelings, our love of truth compels us drastically to invert his own
proposition and to oppose to him this other maxim: the *last* sphere
conquered by the spirit of justice is the sphere of the feeling of
reaction! When it really comes about that the just man remains
just even as regards his injurer (and not merely cold, moderate, reserved, indifferent: being just is always a *positive* state); when,

in spite of the strong provocation of personal insult, contempt, and calumny, the lofty and clear objectivety of the just and judging eye (whose glance is as profound as it is gentle) is untroubled, why then we have a piece of perfection, a past master of the world—something, in fact, which it would not be wise to expect, and which should not at any rate be too easily *believed*. Speaking generally, there is no doubt but that even the justest individual only requires a little dose of hostility, malice, or innuendo to drive the blood into his brain and the fairness *from* it. The active man, the attacking, aggressive man is always a hundred degrees nearer to justice than the man who merely reacts; he certainly has no need to adopt the tactics, necessary in the case of the reacting man, of making false and biassed valuations of his object. It is, in point of fact, for this reason that the aggressive man has at all times enjoyed the stronger, bolder, more aristocratic, and also *freer* outlook, the *better* conscience. On the other hand, we already surmise who it really is that has on his conscience the invention of "bad conscience,"—the resentful man! Finally, let man look at himself in history. In what sphere up to the present has the whole administration of law, the actual need of law, found its earthly home? Perchance in the sphere of the reacting man? Not for a minute: rather in that of the active, strong, spontaneous, aggressive man? I deliberately defy the above-mentioned agitator (who himself makes this self-confession, "the creed of revenge has run through all my works and endeavours like the red thread of Justice"), and say, that judged historically law in the world represents the very war *against* the reactive feelings, the very war waged on those feelings by the powers of activity and aggression, which devote some of their strength to damning and keeping within bounds this effervescence of hysterical reactivity, and to forcing it to some compromise. Everywhere where justice is practised and justice is maintained, it is to be observed that the stronger power, when confronted with the weaker powers which are inferior to it (whether they be groups, or individuals), searches for weapons to put an end to the senseless fury of resentment, while it carries on its object, partly by taking the victim of resentment out of the clutches of revenge, partly by substituting for revenge a campaign of its own against the enemies of peace and order, partly by finding, suggesting, and occasionally enforcing settlements, partly by standardising certain equivalents for injuries, to which equivalents the element of resentment is henceforth finally referred. The most drastic measure, however, taken and effectuated by the supreme power, to combat the preponderance of the feelings of spite and vindictiveness—it takes this measure as soon as it is at all strong enough to do so—is the foundation of *law,* the imperative declaration of what in its eyes is to be regarded as just and lawful, and what unjust and unlawful: and while, after the foundation of law, the supreme power treats the aggressive and arbitrary acts of individuals, or of whole groups, as a violation of law, and a revolt against itself, it distracts the feelings of its subjects from the immediate injury inflicted by such a violation, and thus eventually attains the very opposite result to that always desired by revenge, which sees and recognises nothing but the standpoint of the injured party. From henceforth the eye becomes trained to a more and more *impersonal* valuation of the deed, even the eye of the injured party himself (though this is in the final stage of all, as has been previously remarked)—on this principle "right" and "wrong" first manifest themselves after the foundation of law (and *not,* as Dühring maintains, only after the act of violation). To talk of intrinsic right and intrinsic wrong is absolutely nonsensical; intrinsically, an injury, an oppression, an exploitation, an annihilation can be nothing wrong, inasmuch as life is *essentially* (that is, in its cardinal functions) something which functions by injuring, oppressing, exploiting, and annihilating, and is absolutely inconceivable without such a character. It is necessary to make an even more serious confession:—viewed from the most advanced biological standpoint, conditions of legality can be only *exceptional conditions,* in that they are partial restrictions of the real life-will, which makes for power, and in that they are subordinated to the life-will's general end as particular means, that is, as means to create *larger* units of strength. A legal organization, conceived of as sovereign and universal, not as a weapon in a fight of complexes of power, but as a weapon *against* fighting, generally something after the style of Dühring's communistic model of treating every will as equal with every other will, would be a principle *hostile to life,* a destroyer and dissolver of man, an outrage on the future of man, a symptom of fatigue, a secret cut to Nothingness.—

12

A word more on the origin and end of punishment—two problems which are or ought to be kept distinct, but which unfortunately are usually lumped into one. And what tactics have our
moral genealogists employed up to the present in these cases?
Their inveterate naïveté. They find out some "end" in the punishment, for instance, revenge and deterrence, and then in all their
innocence set this end at the beginning, as the *causa fiendi* of the
punishment, and—they have done the trick. But the patching up
of a history of the origin of law is the last use to which the "End
in Law" ought to be put. Perhaps there is no more pregnant principle for any kind of history than the following, which, difficult
though it is to master, *should* none the less be *mastered* in every
detail.—The origin of the existence of a thing and its final utility,
its practical application and incorporation in a system of ends, are
toto cælo opposed to each other—everything, anything, which
exists and which prevails anywhere, will always be put to new
purposes by a force superior to itself, will be commandeered afresh,
will be turned and transformed to new uses; all "happening" in
the organic world consists of *overpowering* and dominating, and
again all overpowering and domination is a new interpretation
and adjustment, which must necessarily obscure or absolutely extinguish the subsisting "meaning" and "end." The most perfect
comprehension of the utility of any physiological organ (or also of
a legal institution, social custom, political habit, form in art or in
religious worship) does not for a minute imply any simultaneous
comprehension of its origin: this may seem uncomfortable and
unpalatable to the older men,—for it has been the immemorial
belief that understanding the final cause or the utility of a thing,
a form, an institution, means also understanding the reason for its
origin: to give an example of this logic, the eye was made to see,
the hand was made to grasp. So even punishment was conceived
as invented with a view to punishing. But all ends and all utilities
are only *signs* that a Will to Power has mastered a less powerful
force, has impressed thereon out of its own self the meaning of a
function; and the whole history of a "Thing," an organ, a custom,
can on the same principle be regarded as a continuous "sign-
chain" of perpetually new interpretations and adjustments, whose

causes, so far from needing to have even a mutual connection,
sometimes follow and alternate with each other absolutely hap-
hazard. Similarly, the evolution of a "Thing," of a custom, is
anything but its *progressus* to an end, still less a logical and direct
progressus attained with the minimum expenditure of energy and
cost: it is rather the succession of processes of subjugation, more
or less profound, more or less mutually independent, which operate on the thing itself; it is, further, the resistance which in each
case invariably displayed this subjugation, the Protean wriggles
by way of defence and reaction, and, further, the results of successful counter-efforts. The form is fluid, but the meaning is even
more so—even inside every individual organism the case is the
same: with every genuine growth of the whole, the "function" of
the individual organs becomes shifted,—in certain cases a partial
perishing of these organs, a diminution of their numbers (for
instance, through annihilation of the connecting members), can
be a symptom of growing strength and perfection. What I mean is
this: even partial *loss of utility,* decay, and degeneration, loss of
function and purpose, in a word, death, appertain to the conditions of the genuine *progressus;* which always appears in the shape
of a will and way to *greater* power, and is always realised at the
expense of innumerable smaller powers. The magnitude of a
"progress" is gauged by the greatness of the sacrifice that it requires: humanity as a mass sacrificed to the prosperity of the one
stronger species of Man—that *would be* a progress. I emphasise all
the more this cardinal characteristic of the historic method, for the
reason that in its essence it runs counter to predominant instincts
and prevailing taste, which must prefer to put up with absolute
casualness, even with the mechanical senselessness of all phenomena, than with the theory of a power-will, in exhaustive play
throughout all phenomena. The democratic idiosyncrasy against
everything which rules and wishes to rule, the modern *misarchism*
(to coin a bad word for a bad thing), has gradually but so
thoroughly transformed itself into the guise of intellectualism, the
most abstract intellectualism, that even nowadays it penetrates and
has the right to penetrate step by step into the most exact and
apparently the most objective sciences: this tendency has, in fact,
in my view already dominated the whole of physiology and biology, and to their detriment, as is obvious, in so far as it has spirited

away a radical idea, the idea of true *activity*. The tyranny of this
idiosyncrasy, however, results in the theory of "adaptation" being
pushed forward into the van of the argument, exploited; adaptation—that means to say, a second-class activity, a mere capacity
for "reacting"; in fact, life itself has been defined (by Herbert
Spencer) as an increasingly effective internal adaptation to external
circumstances. This definition, however, fails to realise the real
essence of life, its will to power. It fails to appreciate the paramount superiority enjoyed by those plastic forces of spontaneity,
aggression, and encroachment with their new interpretations and
tendencies, to the operation of which adaptation is only a natural
corollary: consequently the sovereign office of the highest functionaries in the organism itself (among which the life-will appears as an active and formative principle) is repudiated. One
remembers Huxley's reproach to Spencer of his "administrative
Nihilism": but it is a case of something much *more* than "administration."

13

To return to our subject, namely *punishment,* we must make
consequently a double distinction: first, the relatively permanent
element, the custom, the act, the "drama," a certain rigid sequence
of methods of procedure; on the other hand, the fluid element, the
meaning, the end, the expectation which is attached to the operation of such procedure. At this point we immediately assume,
per analogiam (in accordance with the theory of the historic
method, which we have elaborated above), that the procedure itself is something older and earlier than its utilisation in punishment, that this utilisation was *introduced* and interpreted into the
procedure (which had existed for a long time, but whose employment had another meaning), in short, that the case is *different*
from that hitherto supposed by our *naïf* genealogists of morals and
of law, who thought that the procedure was *invented* for the purpose of punishment, in the same way that the hand had been
previously thought to have been invented for the purpose of
grasping. With regard to the other element in *punishment,* its
fluid element, its meaning, the idea of punishment in a very late
stage of civilisation (for instance, contemporary Europe) is not content with manifesting merely one meaning, but manifests a whole

synthesis "of meanings." The past general history of punishment, the history of its employment for the most diverse ends, crystallises eventually into a kind of unity, which is difficult to analyse into its parts, and which, it is necessary to emphasise, absolutely defies definition. (It is nowadays impossible to say definitely *the precise reason* for punishment: all ideas, in which a whole process is promiscuously comprehended, elude definition; it is only that which has no history, which can be defined.) At an earlier stage, on the contrary, that synthesis of meanings appears much less rigid and much more elastic; we can realise how in each individual case the elements of the synthesis change their value and their position, so that now one element and now another stands out and predominates over the others, nay, in certain cases one element (perhaps the end of deterrence) seems to eliminate all the rest. At any rate, so as to give some idea of the uncertain, supplementary, and accidental nature of the meaning of punishment and of the manner in which one identical procedure can be employed and adapted for the most diametrically opposed objects, I will at this point give a scheme that has suggested itself to me, a scheme itself based on comparatively small and accidental material.—Punishment, as rendering the criminal harmless and incapable of further injury.— Punishment, as compensation for the injury sustained by the injured party, in any form whatsoever (including the form of sentimental compensation).—Punishment, as an isolation of that which disturbs the equilibrium, so as to prevent the further spreading of the disturbance.—Punishment as a means of inspiring fear of those who determine and execute the punishment.—Punishment as a kind of compensation for advantages which the wrong-doer has up to that time enjoyed (for example, when he is utilised as a slave in the mines).—Punishment, as the elimination of an element of decay (sometimes of a whole branch, as according to the Chinese laws, consequently as a means to the purification of the race, or the preservation of a social type).—Punishment as a festival, as the violent oppression and humiliation of an enemy that has at last been subdued.—Punishment as a mnemonic, whether for him who suffers the punishment—the so-called "correction," or for the witnesses of its administration.—Punishment, as the payment of a fee stipulated for by the power which protects the evildoer from the excesses of revenge.—Punishment, as a compromise with the natural phenomenon of revenge, in so far as revenge is still maintained and claimed as a privilege by the stronger races.— Punishment as a declaration and measure of war against an enemy of peace, of law, of order, of authority, who is fought by society with the weapons which war provides, as a spirit dangerous to the community, as a breaker of the contract on which the community is based, as a rebel, a traitor, and a breaker of the peace.

14

This list is certainly not complete; it is obvious that punishment is overloaded with utilities of all kinds. This makes it all the more permissible to eliminate one *supposed* utility, which passes, at any rate in the popular mind, for its most essential utility, and which is just what even now provides the strongest support for that faith in punishment which is nowadays for many reasons tottering. Punishment is supposed to have the value of exciting in the guilty the consciousness of guilt; in punishment is sought the proper *instrumentum* of that psychic reaction which becomes known as a "bad conscience," "remorse." But this theory is even, from the point of view of the present, a violation of reality and psychology: and how much more so is the case when we have to deal with the longest period of man's history, his primitive history! Genuine remorse is certainly extremely rare among wrong-doers and the victims of punishment; prisons and houses of correction are not *the* soil on which this worm of remorse pullulates for choice—this is the unanimous opinion of all conscientious observers, who in many cases arrive at such a judgment with enough reluctance and against their own personal wishes. Speaking generally, punishment hardens and numbs, it produces concentration, it sharpens the consciousness of alienation, it strengthens the power of resistance. When it happens that it breaks the man's energy and brings about a piteous prostration and abjectness, such a result is certainly even less salutary than the average effect of punishment, which is characterised by a harsh and sinister doggedness. The thought of those *prehistoric* millennia brings us to the unhesitating conclusion, that it was simply through punishment that the evolution of the consciousness of guilt was most forcibly retarded—at any rate in the victims of the punishing power. In particular, let us not underestimate the extent to which, by the very sight of the judicial and executive procedure, the wrong-doer is himself prevented from feeling that his deed, the character of his act, is *intrinsically* reprehensible: for he sees clearly the same kind of acts practised in the service of justice, and then called good, and practised with a good conscience; acts such as espionage, trickery, bribery, trapping, the whole intriguing and insidious art of the policeman and the informer—the whole system, in fact manifested in the different kinds of punishment (a system not excused by passion, but based on principle), of robbing, oppressing, insulting, imprisoning, racking, murdering.—All this he sees treated by his judges, not as acts meriting censure and condemnation *in themselves*, but only in a particular context and application. It was *not* on this soil that grew the "bad conscience," that most sinister and interesting plant of our earthly vegetation—in point of fact, throughout a most lengthy period, no suggestion of having to do with a "guilty man" manifested itself in the consciousness of the man who judged and punished. One had merely to deal with an author of an injury, an irresponsible piece of fate. And the man himself, on whom the punishment subsequently fell like a piece of fate, was occasioned no more of an "inner pain" than would be occasioned by the sudden approach of some uncalculated event, some terrible natural catastrophe, a rushing, crushing avalanche against which there is no resistance.

15

This truth came insidiously enough to the consciousness of Spinoza (to the disgust of his commentators, who (like Kuno Fischer, for instance) give themselves no end of *trouble* to misunderstand him on this point), when one afternoon (as he sat raking up who knows what memory) he indulged in the question of what was really left for him personally of the celebrated *Morsus conscientiæ*—Spinoza, who had relegated "good and evil" to the sphere of human imagination, and indignantly defended the honour of his "free" God against those blasphemers who affirmed that God did everything *sub ratione boni* ("but this was tantamount to subordinating God to fate, and would really be the greatest of all absurdities"). For Spinoza the world had returned again to that innocence in which it lay before the discovery of the bad conscience: what, then, had happened to the *morsus conscientiæ?* "The antithesis of *gaudium,*" said he at last to himself,—"A sadness accompanied by the recollection of a past event which has turned out contrary to all expectation" *(Eth.* iii., Propos. XVIII. Schol. i, ii.). Evil-doers have throughout thousands of years felt when overtaken by punishment *exactly like Spinoza,* on the subject of their "offence": "here is something which went wrong contrary to my anticipation," *not* "I ought not to have done this."—They submitted themselves to punishment, just as one submits one's self to a disease, to a misfortune, or to death, with that stubborn and resigned fatalism which gives the Russians, for instance, even nowadays, the advantage over us Westerners, in the handling of life. If at that period there was a critique of action, the criterion was prudence: the real *effect* of punishment is unquestionably chiefly to be found in a sharpening of the sense of prudence, in a lengthening of the memory, in a will to adopt more of a policy of caution, suspicion, and secrecy; in the recognition that there are many things which are unquestionably beyond one's capacity; in a kind of improvement in self-criticism. The broad effects which can be obtained by punishment in man and beast, are the increase of fear, the sharpening of the sense of cunning, the mastery of the desires: so it is that punishment *tames* man, but does not make him "better"—it would be more correct even to go so far as to assert the contrary ("Injury makes a man cunning," says a popular proverb: so far as it makes him cunning, it makes him also bad. Fortunately, it often enough makes him stupid).

16

At this juncture I cannot avoid trying to give a tentative and provisional expression to my own hypothesis concerning the origin of the bad conscience: it is difficult to make it fully appreciated, and it requires continuous meditation, attention, and digestion. I regard the bad conscience as the serious illness which man was bound to contract under the stress of the most radical change which he has ever experienced—that change, when he found himself finally imprisoned within the pale of society and of peace.

Just like the plight of the water-animals, when they were compelled either to become land-animals or to perish, so was the plight of these half-animals, perfectly adapted as they were to the savage life of war, prowling, and adventure—suddenly all their instincts were rendered worthless and "switched off." Henceforward they had to walk on their feet "carry themselves," whereas heretofore they had been carried by the water: a terrible heaviness oppressed them. They found themselves clumsy in obeying the simplest directions, confronted with this new and unknown world they had no longer their old guides—the regulative instincts that had led them unconsciously to safety—they were reduced, were those unhappy creatures, to thinking, inferring, calculating, putting together causes and results, reduced to that poorest and most erratic organ of theirs, their "consciousness." I do not believe there was ever in the world such a feeling of misery, such a leaden discomfort—further, those old instincts had not immediately ceased their demands! Only it was difficult and rarely possible to gratify them: speaking broadly, they were compelled to satisfy themselves by new and, as it were, hole-and-corner methods. All instincts which do not find a vent without, *turn inwards*—this is what I mean by the growing "internalisation" of man: consequently we have the first growth in man, of what subsequently was called his soul. The whole inner world, originally as thin as if it had been stretched between two layers of skin, burst apart and expanded proportionately, and obtained depth, breath, and height, when man's external outlet became *obstructed*. These terrible bulwarks, with which the social organization protected itself against the old instincts of freedom (punishments belong pre-eminently to these bulwarks), brought it about that all those instincts of wild, free, prowling man became turned backwards *against man himself*. Enmity, cruelty, the delight in presecution, in surprises, change, destruction—the turning all these instincts against their own possessors: this is the origin of the "bad conscience." It was man, who, lacking external enemies and obstacles, and imprisoned as he was in the oppressive narrowness and monotony of custom, in his own impatience lacerated, persecuted, gnawed, frightened, and ill-treated himself; it was this animal in the hands of the tamer, which beat itself against the bars of its cage; it was this being who, pining and yearning for that desert home of which it had been deprived, was compelled to create out of its own self, an adventure, a torture-chamber, a hazardous and perilous desert— it was this fool, this homesick and desperate prisoner—who invented the "bad conscience." But thereby he introduced that most grave and sinister illness, from which mankind has not yet recovered, the suffering of man from the disease called man, as the result of a violent breaking from his animal past, the result, as it were, of a spasmodic plunge into a new environment and new conditions of existence, the result of a declaration of war against the old instincts, which up to that time had been the staple of his power, his joy, his formidableness. Let us immediately add that this fact of an animal ego turning against itself, taking part against itself, produced in the world so novel, profound, unheard-of, problematic, inconsistent, and *pregnant* a phenomenon, that the aspect of the world was radically altered thereby. In sooth, only divine spectators could have appreciated the drama that then began, and whose end baffles conjecture as yet—a drama too subtle, too wonderful, too paradoxical to warrant its undergoing a nonsensical and unheeded performance on some random grotesque planet! Henceforth man is to be counted as one of the most unexpected and sensational lucky shots in the game of the "big baby" of Heraclitus, whether he be called Zeus or Chance—he awakens on his behalf the interest, excitement, hope, almost the confidence, of his being the harbinger and forerunner of something, of man being no end, but only a stage, an interlude, a bridge, a great promise.

17

It is primarily involved in this hypothesis of the origin of the bad conscience, that that alteration was no gradual and no voluntary alteration, and that it did not manifest itself as an organic adaptation to new conditions, but as a break, a jump, a necessity, an inevitable fate, against which there was no resistance and never a spark of resentment. And secondarily, that the fitting of a hitherto unchecked and amorphous population into a fixed form, starting as it had done in an act of violence, could only be accomplished by acts of violence and nothing else—that the oldest "State" appeared consequently as a ghastly tryanny, a grinding ruthless piece of machinery, which went on working, till this raw material of a semi-animal populace was not only thoroughly kneaded and elastic, but also *moulded*. I used the word "State"; my meaning is self-evident, namely, a herd of blonde beasts of prey, a race of conquerors and masters, which with all its warlike organisation and all its organising power pounces with its terrible claws on a population, in numbers possibly tremendously superior, but as yet formless, as yet nomad. Such is the origin of the "State." That fantastic theory that makes it begin with a contract is, I think, disposed of. He who can command, he who is a master by "nature," he who comes on the scene forceful in deed and gesture—what has he to do with contracts? Such beings defy calculation, they come like fate, without cause, reason, notice, excuse, they are there as the lightning is there, too terrible, too sudden, too convincing, too "different," to be personally even hated. Their work is an instinctive creating and impressing of forms, they are the most unvoluntary, unconscious artists that there are:—their appearance produces instantaneously a scheme of sovereignty which is *live*, in which the functions are partitioned and apportioned, in which above all no part is received or finds a place, until pregnant with a "meaning" in regard to the whole. They are ignorant of the meaning of guilt, responsibility, consideration, are these born organisers; in them predominates that terrible artist-egoism, that gleams like brass, and that knows itself justified to all eternity, in its work, even as a mother in her child. It is not in *them* that there grew the bad conscience, that is elementary—but it would not have grown *without them*, repulsive as it was, it would be missing, had not a tremendous quantity of freedom been expelled from the world by the stress of their hammer-strokes, their artist violence, or been at any rate made invisible and, as it were, *latent*. This *instinct of freedom* forced them into being latent—it is already clear—this instinct of freedom forced back, trodden back, imprisoned within itself, and finally only able to find vent and relief in itself; this, only this, is the beginning of the "bad conscience."

18

Beware of thinking lightly of this phenomenon, by reason of its initial painful ugliness. At bottom it is the same active force which is at work on a more grandiose scale in those potent artists and organisers, and builds states, where here, internally, on a smaller and pettier scale and with a retrogressive tendency, makes itself a bad conscience in the "labyrinth of the breast," to use Goethe's phrase, and which builds negative ideals; it is, I repeat, that identical *instinct of freedom* (to use my own language, the will to power): only the material, on which this force with all its constructive and tyrannous nature is let loose, is here man himself, his whole old animal self—and *not* as in the case of that more grandiose and sensational phenomenon, the *other* man, *other* men. This secret self-tyranny, this cruelty of the artist, this delight in giving a form to one's self as a piece of difficult, refractory, and suffering material, in burning in a will, a critique, a contradiction, a contempt, a negation; this sinister and ghastly labour of love on the part of a soul, whose will is cloven in two within itself, which makes itself suffer from delight in the infliction of suffering; this wholly *active* bad conscience has finally (as one already anticipates)—true fountain-head as it is of idealism and imagination—produced an abundance of novel and amazing beauty and affirmation, and perhaps has really been the first to give birth to beauty at all. What would beauty be, forsooth, if its contradiction had not first been presented to consciousness, if the ugly had not first said to itself, "I am ugly"? At any rate, after this hint the problem of how far idealism and beauty can be traced in such opposite ideas as *"selfless-ness," self-denial, self-sacrifice,* becomes less problematical; and indubitably in future we shall certainly know the real and original character of the *delight* experienced by the self-less, the self-deny-ing, the self-sacrificing: this delight is a phase of cruelty.—So much provisionally for the origin of "altruism" as a *moral* value, and the marking out the ground from which this value has grown: it is only the bad conscience, only the will for self-abuse, that provides the necessary conditions for the existence of altruism as a *value.*

19

Undoubtedly the bad conscience is an illness, but an illness as pregnancy is an illness. If we search out the conditions under which this illness reaches its most terrible and sublime zenith, we shall see what really first brought about its entry into the world. But to do this we must take a long breath, and we must first of all go back once again to an earlier point of view. The relation at civil law of the ower to his creditor (which has already been discussed in detail), has been interpreted once again (and indeed in a manner which historically is exceedingly remarkable and suspicious) into a relationship, which is perhaps more incomprehensible to us moderns than to any other era; that is, into the relationship of the *existing* generation to its *ancestors*. Within the original tribal association—we are talking of primitive times—each living generation recognises a legal obligation towards the earlier generation, and particularly towards the earliest, which founded the family (and this is something much more than a mere sentimental obligation, the existence of which, during the longest period of man's history, is by no means indisputable). There prevails in them the conviction that it is only thanks to sacrifices and efforts of their ancestors, that the race *persists* at all—and that this has to be *paid back* to them by sacrifices and services. Thus is recognized the *owing* of a debt, which accumulates continually by reason of these ancestors never ceasing in their subsequent life as potent spirits to secure by their power new privileges and advantages to the race. Gratis, perchance? But there is no gratis for that raw and "mean-souled" age. What return can be made?—Sacrifice (at first, nourishment, in its crudest sense), festivals, temples, tributes of veneration, above all, obedience—since all customs are, *quâ* works of the ancestors, equally their precepts and commands —are the ancestors ever given enough? This suspicion remains and grows: from time to time it extorts a great wholesale ransom, something monstrous in the way of repayment of the creditor (the notorious sacrifice of the first-born, for example, blood, human blood in any case). The *fear* of ancestors and their power, the consciousness of owing debts to them, necessarily increases, according to this kind of logic, in the exact proportion that the race itself increases, that the race itself becomes more victorious, more independent, more honoured, more feared. This, and not the contrary, is the fact. Each step towards race decay, all disastrous events, all symptoms of degeneration, of approaching disintegration, always *diminish* the fear of the founders' spirit, and whittle away the idea of his sagacity, providence, and potent presence. Conceive this crude kind of logic carried to its climax: it follows that the ancestors of the *most powerful* races must, through the growing fear that they

exercise on the imaginations, grow themselves into monstrous dimensions, and become relegated to the gloom of a divine mystery
that transcends imagination—the ancestor becomes at last necessarily transfigured into a *god*. Perhaps this is the very origin of the
gods, that is, an origin from *fear!* And those who feel bound to
add, "but from piety also," will have difficulty in maintaining this
theory, with regard to the primeval and longest period of the human race. And, of course, this is even more the case as regards the
middle period, the formative period of the aristocratic races—the
aristocratic races which have given back with interest to their
founders, the ancestors (heroes, gods), all those qualities which
in the meanwhile have appeared in themselves, that is, the aristocratic qualities. We will later on glance again at the ennobling and
promotion of the gods (which, of course, is totally distinct from
their "sanctification"): let us now provisionally follow to its end
the course of the whole of this development of the consciousness
of "owing."

<h2 style="text-align:center">20</h2>

According to the teaching of history, the consciousness of owing
debts to the deity by no means came to an end with the decay of
the clan organisation of society; just as mankind has inherited the
ideas of "good" and "bad" from the race-nobility (together with
its fundamental tendency towards establishing social distinctions),
so with the heritage of the racial and tribal gods it has also inherited the incubus of debts as yet unpaid and the desire to discharge
them. The transition is effected by those large populations of slaves
and bondsmen, who, whether through compulsion or through submission and *"mimicry,"* have accommodated themselves to the religion of their masters; through this channel these inherited tendencies inundate the world. The feeling of owing a debt to the
deity has grown continuously for several centuries, always in the
same proportion in which the idea of God and the consciousness
of God have grown and become exalted among mankind. (The
whole history of ethnic fights, victories, reconciliations, amalgama-
tions, everything, in fact, which precedes the eventual classing of
all the social elements in each great race-synthesis, are mirrored
in the hotch-potch genealogy of their gods, in the legends of their
fights, victories, and reconciliations. Progress towards universal

empires invariably means progress towards universal deities; despotism, with its subjugation of the independent nobility, always paves the way for some system or other of monotheism.) The appearance of the Christian god, as the record god up to this time, has for that very reason brought equally into the world the record amount of guilt consciousness. Granted that we have gradually started on the *reverse* movement, there is no little probability in the deduction, based on the continuous decay in the belief in the Christian god, to the effect that there also already exists a considerable decay in the human consciousness of owing (ought); in fact, we cannot shut our eyes to the prospect of the complete and eventual triumph of atheism freeing mankind from all this feeling of obligation to their origin, their *causa prima*. Atheism and a kind of second innocence complement and supplement each other.

21

So much for my rough and preliminary sketch of the interrelation of the ideas "ought" (owe) and "duty" with the postulates of religion. I have intentionally shelved up to the present the actual moralisation of these ideas (their being pushed back into the conscience, or more precisely the interweaving of the *bad* conscience with the idea of God), and at the end of the last paragraph used language to the effect that this moralisation did not exist, and that consequently these ideas had necessarily come to an end, by reason of what had happened to their hypothesis, the credence in our "creditor," in God. The actual facts differ terribly from this theory. It is with the moralisation of the ideas "ought" and "duty," and with their being pushed back into the *bad* conscience, that comes the first actual attempt to *reverse* the direction of the development we have just described, or at any rate to arrest its evolution; it is just at this juncture that the very hope of an eventual redemption *has to* put itself once for all into the prison of pessimism, it is at this juncture that the eye *has to* recoil and rebound in despair from off an adamantine impossibility, it is at this juncture that the ideas "guilt" and "duty" have to turn backwards —turn backwards against *whom?* There is no doubt about it; primarily against the "ower," in whom the bad conscience now establishes itself, eats, extends, and grows like a polypus throughout its length and breadth, all with such virulence, that at last, with the impossibility of paying the debt, there becomes conceived the idea of the impossibility of paying the penalty, the thought of its inexpiability (the idea of "eternal punishment")—finally, too, it turns against the "creditor," whether found in the *causa prima* of man, the origin of the human race, its sire, who henceforth becomes burdened with a curse ("Adam," "original sin," "determination of the will"), or in Nature from whose womb man springs, and on whom the responsibility for the principle of evil is now cast ("Diabolisation of Nature"), or in existence generally, on this logic an absolute *white elephant,* with which mankind is landed (the Nihilistic flight from life, the demand for Nothingness, or for the opposite of existence, for some other existence, Buddhism and the like)—till suddenly we stand before that paradoxical and awful expedient, through which a tortured humanity has found a temporary alleviation, that stroke of genius called Christianity:—God personally immolating himself for the debt of man, God paying himself personally out of a pound of his own flesh, God as the one being who can deliver man from what man had become unable to deliver himself—the creditor playing scapegoat for his debtor, from *love* (can you believe it?), from love of his debtor! . . .

22

The reader will already have conjectured what took place on the stage and *behind the scenes* of this drama. That will for self-torture, that inverted cruelty of the animal man, who, turned subjective and scared into introspection (encaged as he was in "the State," as part of his taming process), invented the bad conscience so as to hurt himself, after the *natural* outlet for this will to hurt, became blocked—in other words, this man of the bad conscience exploited the religious hypothesis so as to carry his martydom to the ghastliest pitch of agonised intensity. Owing something to *God:* this thought becomes his instrument of torture. He apprehends in God the most extreme antitheses that he can find to his own characteristic and ineradicable animal instincts, he himself gives a new interpretation to these animal instincts as being against what he "owes" to God (as enmity, rebellion, and revolt against the "Lord," the "Father," the "Sire," the "Beginning of the world"), he places himself between the horns of the dilemma, "God" and "Devil." Every negation which he is inclined to utter to himself, to the nature, naturalness, and reality of his being, he whips into an ejaculation of "yes," uttering it as something existing, living, efficient, as being God, as the holiness of God, the judgment of God, as the hangmanship of God, as transcendence, as eternity, as unending torment, as hell, as infinity of punishment and guilt. This is a kind of madness of the will in the sphere of psychological cruelty which is absolutely unparalleled:—man's *will* to find himself guilty and blameworthy to the point of inexpiability, his *will* to think of himself as punished, without the punishment ever being able to balance the guilt, his *will* to infect and to poison the fundamental basis of the universe with the problem of punishment and guilt, in order to cut off once and for all any escape out of this labyrinth of "fixed ideas," his will for rearing an ideal—that of the "holy God"—face to face with which he can have tangible proof of his own unworthiness. Alas for this mad melancholy beast man! What phantasies invade it, what paroxysms of perversity, hysterical senselessness, and *mental bestiality* break out immediately, at the very slightest check on its being the beast of action! All this is excessively interesting, but at the same time tainted with a black, gloomy, enervating melancholy, so that a forcible veto must be invoked against looking too long into those abysses. Here is *disease,* undubitably, the most ghastly disease that has as yet played havoc among men: and he who can still hear (but man turns now deaf ears to such sounds), how in this night of torment and nonsense there has rung out the cry of *love,* the cry of the most passionate ecstasy, of redemption in *love,* he turns away gripped by an invincible horror—in man there is so much that is ghastly—too long has the world been a mad-house.

23

Let this suffice once for all concerning the origin of the "holy God." The fact that *in itself* the conception of gods is not bound to lead necessarily to this degradation of the imagination (a temporary representation of whose vagaries we felt bound to give), the fact that there exist *nobler* methods of utilising the invention of gods than in this self-crucifixion and self-degradation of man, in which the last two thousand years of Europe have been past masters—these facts can fortunately be still perceived from every glance that we cast at the Grecian gods, these mirrors of noble and grandiose men, in which the *animal* in man felt itself deified, and did *not* devour itself in subjective frenzy. These Greeks long utilised their gods as simple buffers against the "bad conscience"—so that they could continue to enjoy their freedom of soul: this, of course, is diametrically opposed to Christianity's theory of its god. They went *very far* on this principle, did these splendid and lion-hearted children; and there is no lesser authority than that of the Homeric Zeus for making them realise occasionally that they are taking life too casually. "Wonderful," says he on one occasion—it has to do with the case of Ægistheus, a *very* bad case indeed—

"Wonderful how they grumble, the mortals against the immortals
 Only from us, they presume, *comes evil,* but in their folly,
 Fashion they, spite of fate, the doom of their own disaster."

Yet the reader will note and observe that this Olympian spectator and judge is far from being angry with them and thinking evil of them on this score. "How *foolish* they are," so thinks he of the misdeeds of mortals—and "folly," "imprudence," "a little brain disturbance," and nothing more, are what the Greeks, even of the strongest, bravest period, have admitted to be the ground of much that is evil and fatal.—Folly, *not* sin, do you understand? . . . But even this brain disturbance was a problem—"Come, how is it even possible? How could it have really got in brains like ours, the brains of men of aristocratic ancestry, of men of fortune, of men of good natural endowments, of men of the best society, of men of nobility and virtue?" This was the question that for century on century the aristocratic Greek put to himself when confronted with every (to him incomprehensible) outrage and sacrilege with which one of his peers had polluted himself. "It must be that a *god* had infatuated him," he would say at last, nodding his head.— This solution is *typical* of the Greeks, . . . accordingly the gods in those times subserved the functions of justifying man to a certain

extent even in evil—in those days they took upon themselves not
the punishment, but, what is *more noble,* the guilt.

24

I conclude with three queries, as you will see. "Is an ideal actually set up here, or is one pulled down?" I am perhaps asked . . .
But have ye sufficiently asked yourselves how dear a payment has
the setting up of *every* ideal in the world exacted? To achieve that
consummation how much truth must always be traduced and misunderstood, how many lies must be sanctified, how much conscience has got to be disturbed, how many pounds of "God" have
got to be sacrificed every time? To enable a sanctuary to be set up
a sanctuary has got to be destroyed: that is a law—show me an instance where it has not been fulfilled! . . . We modern men, we
inherit the immemorial tradition of vivisecting the conscience,
and practising cruelty to our animal selves. That is the sphere of
our most protracted training, perhaps of our artistic prowess, at
any rate of our dilettantism and our perverted taste. Man has for
too long regarded his natural proclivities with an "evil eye," so
that eventually they have become in his system affiliated to a bad
conscience. A converse endeavour would be intrinsically feasible—
but who is strong enough to attempt it?—namely, to affiliate to the
"bad conscience" all those *unnatural* proclivities, all those transcendental aspirations, contrary to sense, instinct, nature, and ani-
malism—in short, all past and present ideals, which are all ideals
opposed to life, and traducing the world. To whom is one to turn
nowadays with *such* hopes and pretensions?—It is just the *good*
men that we should thus bring about our ears; and in addition, as
stands to reason, the indolent, the hedgers, the vain, the hysterical, the tired. . . . What is more offensive or more thoroughly
calculated to alienate, than giving any hint of the exalted severity
with which we treat ourselves? And again how conciliatory, how
full of love does all the world show itself towards us so soon as we
do as all the world does, and "let ourselves go" like all the world.
For such a consummation we need spirits of *different* calibre than
seems really feasible in this age; spirits rendered potent through
wars and victories, to whom conquest, adventure, danger, even
pain, have become a need; for such a consummation we need habi-

tuation to sharp, rare air, to winter wanderings, to literal and metaphorical ice and mountains; we even need a kind of sublime malice, a supreme and most self-conscious insolence of knowledge, which is the appanage of great health; we need (to summarize the awful truth) just this *great health!*

Is this even feasible to-day? . . . But some day, in a stronger age than this rotting and introspective present, must he in sooth come to us, even the *redeemer* of great love and scorn, the creative spirit, rebounding by the impetus of his own force back again away from every transcendental plane and dimension, he whose solitude is misunderstanded of the people, as though it were a flight *from* reality;—while actually it is only his diving, burrowing, and penetrating *into* reality, so that when he comes again to the light he can at once bring about by these means the *redemption* of this reality; its redemption from the curse which the old ideal has laid upon it. This man of the future, who in this wise will redeem us from the old ideal, as he will from that ideal's necessary corollary of great nausea, will to nothingness, and Nihilism; this tocsin of noon and of the great verdict, which renders the will again free, who gives back to the world its goal and to man his hope, this Antichrist and Antinihilist, this conqueror of God and of Nothingness—*he must one day come.*

25

But what am I talking of? Enough! Enough? At this juncture I have only one proper course, silence: otherwise I trespass on a domain open alone to one who is younger than I, one stronger, more *"future"* than I—open alone to *Zarathustra, Zarathustra the godless.*

William James

William James

JAMES was first of all a biological scientist and student of medicine; he approached philosophy, morals, religion and human experience in general from the clinical point of view. He was more interested in why men believe what they do believe than in the truth of what they should believe. He even extended this interest to the problem of truth itself. Why do men seek truth and how do they decide when they have found it? Out of this psychology of reason he then constructed a theory of experience and a theory of truth.

The background of his philosophy is Kantian. He began by accepting determinism as the basis of science and freedom as the basis of morals. But as a psychologist he found himself unable to keep scientific and moral considerations as distinct as they were in the Kantian tradition. Both the British empirical psychology (especially Bain) and the German experimental psychology (especially Wundt and Helmholtz) were mechanistic and had no use for a "soul." But they rested on a romantic metaphysics of "the will" and of moral striving to which reason seemed alien, if not opposed. To overcome this Kantian heritage, to understand both reason and will as phases of a single, living, organic process became his life work and his greatest contribution. He analyzed logical categories in terms of their biological functions.

It was this basic insight into the nature of the mind that led him to criticize both "gnosticism" and agnosticism, i.e., both the doctrine that regards the vision of truth as the end of thought and the doctrine that faith is a handicap to knowledge. Man is a creature of wants and desires, a will before he is a mind; hence the mind is biologically the servant of the will, not in the sense of being a slave to passion, but in the sense of being an instrument for gaining satisfactions. Truth must satisfy; not because it is man's nature to love truth, but because it is truth's nature to serve man. In his early writings, notably in the essays on *The Will to Believe, The Sentiment of Rationality,* and *Reflex Action and Theism,* James argued that, given two rival hypotheses or ideas, either of which might be true in the sense of explaining the facts, that one will be chosen as true which *in addition to* explaining the facts satisfies a "moral" or vital need or interest. In his later writings notably in his *Pragmatism,* he argued that verification itself can be explained in terms of satisfactions, and that, given two hypotheses or ideas which would explain any facts whatsoever, neither has any scientific or pragmatic value. In short, James began by believing that most philosophic creeds were accepted or rejected on sentimental or "moral" grounds: he ended by believing that most philosophic creeds are pragmatically meaningless.

An amusing and basic illustration of his way of treating metaphysical issues was his treatment of the Absolute. He argued first that the idealists believed in the Absolute not because they could prove the truth of their belief, but for "moral" reasons—the faith in the Absolute gave them a "moral holiday." Royce, against whom James' criticism was directed especially, repudiated any such "subjective" motives for his faith. Whereupon James replied as follows:

". . . Explaining why I do not believe in the absolute myself, yet finding that it may secure 'moral holidays' to those who need them, and is true in so far forth (if to gain moral holidays be a good), I offered this as a conciliatory olive-branch to my enemies. But they, as is only too common with such offerings, trampled the gift under foot and turned and rent the giver. I had counted too much on their good will—oh for the rarity of christian charity under the sun! Oh for the rarity of ordinary secular intelligence also! I had supposed it to be matter of common observation that, of two

competing views of the universe which in all other respects
are equal, but of which the first denies some vital human
need while the second satisfies it, the second will be favored
by sane men for the simple reason that it makes the world
seem more rational. To choose the first view under such circumstances would be an ascetic act, an act of philosophic self-
denial of which no normal human being would be guilty.
Using the pragmatic test of the meaning of concepts, I had
shown the concept of the absolute to *mean* nothing but the
holiday giver, the banisher of cosmic fear. One's objective
deliverance, when one says 'the absolute exists,' amounted,
on my showing, just to this, that 'some justification of a feeling of security in presence of the universe,' exists, and that
systematically to refuse to cultivate a feeling of security
would be to do violence to a tendency in one's emotional
life which might well be respected as prophetic.

"Apparently my absolutist critics fail to see the workings
of their own minds in any such picture, so all that I can do is
to apologize, and take my offering back. The absolute is true
in *no* way then, and least of all, by the verdict of the critics,
in the way which I assigned!"

The scientific ground on which James repudiated the Absolute was that the logical need for which the Absolute was
invented, namely, to bring unity into a world of atomic experiences, was an artificial need. Much of his greatest work,
The Principles of Psychology (1891), is devoted to proving
that conscious experience is connected from the start. Reason
is not required to synthesize "sensations" into "bundles" as
the followers of Hume and Kant had imagined, but to analyze
the "big, blooming, buzzing confusion" of immediate experience into discrete ideas. Distinctions arise out of a continuum
of feeling; or, to use the technical language of the dispute,
relations are more immediately sensed than terms are. James
used this psychological insight not only in criticizing the logic
of idealism, but also in exhibiting the psychology of mysticism. His *Varieties of Religious Experience* (1902) was one of
the most significant applications he made of his psychology
of belief.

James' writing on this theme of "the will to believe" had a peculiar forcefulness because of the personal struggles in his own life to which it was intimately related. In 1867, at the age of twenty-five, James had been compelled to abandon his biological researches at Harvard in order to seek in Europe a cure for his chronic insomnia, indigestion and melancholia. After almost two years of restless search for cure and comfort he returned to Harvard little improved. But on April 30, 1870, he wrote in a notebook these famous lines:

"I think that yesterday was a crisis in my life. I finished the first part of Renouvier's second 'Essais' and see no reason why his definition of Free Will—'the sustaining of a thought *because I choose to* when I might have other thoughts'—need be the definition of an illusion. At any rate, I will assume for the present—until next year—that it is no illusion. My first act of free will shall be to believe in free will. For the remainder of the year, I will abstain from the mere speculation and contemplative *Grüblei* in which my nature takes most delight, and voluntarily cultivate the feeling of moral freedom, by reading books favorable to it, as well as by acting. After the first of January, my callow skin being somewhat fledged, I may perhaps return to metaphysical study and skepticism without danger of my powers of action. For the present then remember: care little for speculation; much for the *form* of my action; recollect that only when habits of order are formed can we advance to really interesting fields of action—and consequently accumulate grain on grain of willful choice like a very miser; never forgetting how one link dropped undoes an indefinite number. *Principiis obsta*—Today has furnished the exceptionally passionate initiative which Bain posits as needful for the acquisition of habits. I will see to the sequel. Not in maxims, not in *Anschauungen*, but in accumulated *acts* of thought lies salvation. *Passer outre*. Hitherto, when I have felt like taking a free initiative, like daring to act originally, without carefully waiting for contemplation of the external world to determine all for me, suicide seemed the most manly form to put my daring into; now, I will go a step further with my will, not only act with it, but believe as will; believe in my individual reality and creative power. My belief, to be sure, *can't* be optimistic— but I will posit life (the real, the good) in the self-governing *resistance* of the ego to the world."

Thus the young William James cured his Kantian dilemma by an "act of will" long before he solved it dialectically. In fact, he struggled with the dialectic all his life, in spite of his pragmatism, and in his essays on "radical empiricism," written shortly before his death in 1910, he made a brave new start by denying the existence of consciousness and thus giving birth to the movements known as neo-realism and behaviorism, which have carried to its most radical conclusions James' biological conception of mind.

The Sentiment of Rationality

WHAT is the task which philosophers set themselves to perform; and why do they philosophize at all? Almost every one will immediately reply: They desire to attain a conception of the frame of things which shall on the whole be more rational than that somewhat chaotic view which every one by nature carries about with him under his hat. But suppose this rational conception attained, how is the philosopher to recognize it for what it is, and not let it slip through ignorance? The only answer can be that he will recognize its rationality as he recognizes everything else, by certain subjective marks with which it affects him. When he gets the marks, he may know that he has got the rationality.

What, then, are the marks? A strong feeling of ease, peace, rest, is one of them. The transition from a state of puzzle and perplexity to rational comprehension is full of lively relief and pleasure.

But this relief seems to be a negative rather than a positive character. Shall we then say that the feeling of rationality is constituted merely by the absence of any feeling of irrationality? I think there are very good grounds for upholding such a view. All feeling whatever, in the light of certain recent psychological speculations, seems to depend for its physical condition not on simple discharge of nerve-currents, but on their discharge under arrest, impediment, or resistance. Just as we feel no particular pleasure when we breathe freely, but a very intense feeling of distress when the respiratory motions are prevented,—so any unobstructed tendency to action discharges itself without the production of much cogitative accompaniment, and any perfectly fluent course of thought awakens but little feeling; but when the movement is inhibited, or when the thought meets with difficulties, we experience distress. It is only when the distress is upon us that we can be said to strive, to crave, or to aspire. When enjoying plenary freedom either in the way of motion or of thought, we are in a sort of anæsthetic

877

state in which we might say with Walt Whitman, if we cared to say anything about ourselves at such times, "I am sufficient as I am." This feeling of the sufficiency of the present moment, of its absoluteness,—this absence of all need to explain it, account for it, or justify it,—is what I call the Sentiment of Rationality. As soon, in short, as we are enabled from any cause whatever to think with perfect fluency, the thing we think of seems to us *pro tanto* rational.

Whatever modes of conceiving the cosmos facilitate this fluency, produce the sentiment of rationality. Conceived in such modes, being vouches for itself and needs no further philosophic formulation. But this fluency may be obtained in various ways; and first I will take up the theoretic way.

The facts of the world in their sensible diversity are always before us, but our theoretic need is that they should be conceived in a way that reduces their manifoldness to simplicity. Our pleasure at finding that a chaos of facts is the expression of a single underlying fact is like the relief of the musician at resolving a confused mass of sound into melodic or harmonic order. The simplified result is handled with far less mental effort than the original data; and a philosophic conception of nature is thus in no metaphorical sense a labor-saving contrivance. The passion for parsimony, for economy of means in thought, is the philosophic passion *par excellence;* and any character or aspect of the world's phenomena which gathers up their diversity into monotony will gratify that passion, and in the philosopher's mind stand for that essence of things compared with which all their other determinations may by him be overlooked.

More universality or extensiveness is, then, one mark which the philosopher's conceptions must possess. Unless they apply to an enormous number of cases they will not bring him relief, The knowledge of things by their causes, which is often given as a definition of rational knowledge, is useless to him unless the causes converge to a minimum number, while still producing the maximum number of effects. The more multiple then are the instances, the more flowingly does his mind rove from fact to fact. The phenomenal transitions are no real transitions; each item is the same old friend with a slightly altered dress.

Who does not feel the charm of thinking that the moon and the apple are, as far their relation to the earth goes, identical; of knowing respiration and combustion to be one; of understanding that the balloon rises by the same law whereby the stone sinks; of feeling that the warmth in one's palm when one rubs one's sleeve is identical with the motion which the friction checks; of recognizing the difference between beast and fish to be only a higher degree of that between human father and son; of believing our strength when we climb the mountain or fell the tree to be no other than the strength of the sun's rays which made the corn grow out of which we got our morning meal?

But alongside of this passion for simplification there exists a sister passion, which in some minds—though they perhaps form the minority—is its rival. This is the passion for distinguishing; it is the impulse to be *acquainted* with the parts rather than to comprehend the whole. Loyalty to clearness and integrity of perception, dislike of blurred outlines, of vague identifications, are its characteristics. It loves to recognize particulars in their full completeness, and the more of these it can carry the happier it is. It prefers any amount of incoherence, abruptness, and fragmentariness (so long as the literal details of the separate facts are saved) to an abstract way of conceiving things that, while it simplifies them, dissolves away at the same time their concrete fulness. Clearness and simplicity thus set up rival claims, and make a real dilemma for the thinker.

A man's philosophic attitude is determined by the balance in him of these two cravings. No system of philosophy can hope to be universally accepted among men which grossly violates either need, or entirely subordinates the one to the other. The fate of Spinoza, with his barren union of all things in one substance, on the one hand; that of Hume, with his equally barren "looseness and separateness" of everything, on the other,—neither philosopher owning any strict and systematic disciples to-day, each bring to posterity a warning as well as a stimulus,—show us that the only possible philosophy must be a compromise between an abstract monotony and a concrete heterogeneity. But the only way to mediate between diversity and unity is to class the diverse items as cases of a common essence which you discover in them. Classification of things into extensive "kinds" is thus the first step; and classification of their relations and conduct into extensive "laws" is the last step, in their philosophic unification. A completed theoretic philosophy can thus never be anything more than a completed classification of the world's ingredients; and its results must always be abstract, since the basis of every classification is the abstract essence embedded in the living fact,—the rest of the living fact being for the time ignored by the classifier. This means that none of our explanations are complete. They subsume things under heads wider or more familiar; but the last heads, whether of things or of their connections, are mere abstract genera, data which we just find in things and write down.

When, for example, we think that we have rationally explained the connection of the facts A and B by classing both under their common attribute x, it is obvious that we have really explained only so much of these items as *is* x. To explain the connection of choke-damp and suffocation by the lack of oxygen is to leave untouched all the other peculiarities both of choke-damp and of suffocation,—such as convulsions and agony on the one hand, density and explosibility on the other. In a word, so far as A and B contain $l, m, n,$ and $o, p, q,$ respectively, in addition to x, they are not explained by x. Each additional particularity makes its distinct appeal. A single explanation of a fact only explains it from a single point of view. The entire fact is not accounted for until each and all of its characters have been classed with their likes elsewhere. To apply this now to the case of the universe, we see that the explanation of the world by molecular movements explains it only so far as it actually *is* such movements. To invoke the "Unknowable" explains only so much as is unknowable. "Thought" only so much as is thought, "God" only so much as is God. *Which* thought? *Which* God?—are questions that have to be answered by bringing in again the residual data from which the general term was abstracted. All those data that cannot be analytically identified with the attribute invoked as universal principle, remain as independent kinds of natures, associated empirically with the said attribute but devoid of rational kinship with it.

Hence the unsatisfactoriness of all our speculations. On the one hand, so far as they retain any multiplicity in their terms, they fail to get us out of the empirical sand-heap world; on the other, so far as they eliminate multiplicity the practical man despises their empty barrenness. The most they can say is that the elements of the world are such and such, and that each is identical with itself wherever found; but the question Where is it found? the practical man is left to answer by his own wit. Which, of all the essences, shall here and now be held the essence of this concrete thing, the fundamental philosophy never attempts to decide. We are thus led to the conclusion that the simple classification of things is, on the one hand, the best possible theoretic philosophy, but is, on the other, a most miserable and inadequate substitute for the fulness of the truth. It is a monstrous abridgment of life, which, like all abridgments is got by the absolute loss and casting out of real matter. This is why so few human beings truly care for philosophy. The particular determinations which she ignores are the real matter exciting needs, quite as potent and authoritative as hers. What does the moral enthusiast care for philosophical ethics? Why does the *Æsthetik* of every German philosopher appear to the artist an abomination of desolation?

> Grau, theurer Freund, ist alle Theorie
> Und grün des Lebens goldner Baum.

The entire man, who feels all needs by turns, will take nothing as an equivalent for life but the fulness of living itself. Since the essences of things are as a matter of fact disseminated through the whole extent of time and space, it is in their spread-outness and alternation that he will enjoy them. When weary of the concrete clash and dust and pettiness, he will refresh himself by a bath in the eternal springs, or fortify himself by a look at the immutable natures. But he will only be a visitor, not a dweller in the region; he will never carry the philosophic yoke upon his shoulders, and when tired of the gray monotony of her problems and insipid spaciousness of her results, will always escape gleefully into the teeming and dramatic richness of the concrete world.

So our study turns back here to its beginning. Every way of classifying a thing is but a way of handling it for some particular purpose. Conceptions, "kinds," are teleological instruments, No abstract concept can be a valid substitute for a concrete reality except with reference to a particular interest in the conceiver. The interest of theoretic rationality, the relief of identification, is but one of a thousand human purposes. When others rear their heads, it must pack up its little bundle and retire till its turn recurs. The exaggerated dignity and value that philosophers have claimed for their solutions is thus greatly reduced. The only virtue their theoretic conception need have is simplicity, and a simple conception is an equivalent for the world only so far as the world is simple,— the world meanwhile, whatever simplicity it may harbor, being also a mightily complex affair. Enough simplicity remains, however, and enough urgency in our craving to reach it, to make the theoretic function one of the most invincible of human impulses. The quest of the fewest elements of things is an ideal that some will follow, as long as there are men to think at all.

But suppose the goal attained. Suppose that at last we have a system unified in the sense that has been explained. Our world can now be conceived simply, and our mind enjoys the relief. Our universal concept has made the concrete chaos rational. But now I ask, Can that which is the ground of rationality in all else be itself properly called rational? It would seem at first sight that it might. One is tempted at any rate to say that, since the craving for rationality is appeased by the identification of one thing with another, a datum which left nothing else outstanding might quench that craving definitively, or be rational *in se*. No otherness being left to annoy us, we should sit down at peace. In other words, as the theoretic tranquillity of the boor results from his spinning no further considerations about his chaotic universe, so any datum whatever (provided it were simple, clear, and ultimate) ought to banish puzzle from the universe of the philosopher and confere peace, inasmuch as there would then be for him absolutely no further considerations to spin.

This in fact is what some persons think. Professor Bain says,—

"A difficulty is solved, a mystery unriddled, when it can be shown to resemble something else; to be an example of a fact already known. Mystery is isolation, exception, or it may be apparent contradiction: the resolution of the mystery is found in assimilation, identity, fraternity. When all things are assimilated, so far as assimilation can go, so far as likeness holds, there is an end to explanation; there is an end to what the mind can do, or can intelligently desire. . . . The path of science as exhibited in modern ages is toward generality, wider and wider, until we reach the highest, the widest laws of every department of things; there explanation is finished, mystery ends, perfect vision is gained."

But, unfortunately, this first answer will not hold. Our mind is so wedded to the process of seeing an *other* beside every item of its experience, that when the notion of an absolute datum is presented to it, it goes through its usual procedure and remains pointing at the void beyond, as if in that lay further matter for contemplation. In short, it spins for itself the further positive consideration of a nonentity enveloping the being of its datum; and as that leads nowhere, back recoils the thought toward its datum again. But there is no natural bridge between nonentity and this particular datum, and the thought stands oscillating to and fro, wondering "Why was there anything but nonentity; why just this universal datum and not another?" and finds no end, in wandering mazes lost. Indeed, Bain's words are so untrue that in reflecting men it is just when the attempt to fuse the manifold into a single totality has been most successful, when the conception of the universe as a unique fact is nearest its perfection, that the craving for further explanation, the ontological wonder-sickness, arises in its extremest form. As Schopenhauer says, "The uneasiness which keeps the never-resting clock of metaphysics in motion, is the consciousness that the non-existence of this world is just as possible as its existence."

The notion of nonentity may thus be called the parent of the philosophic craving in its subtilest and profoundest sense. Absolute existence is absolute mystery, for its relations with the nothing remain unmediated to our understanding. One philosopher only has pretended to throw a logical bridge over this chasm. Hegel, by trying to show that nonentity and concrete being are linked together by a series of identities of a synthetic kind, binds everything conceivable into a unity, with no outlying notion to disturb the free rotary circulation of the mind within its bounds. Since such unchecked movement gives the feeling of rationality, he must be held, if he has succeeded, to have eternally and absolutely quenched all rational demands.

But for those who deem Hegel's heroic effort to have failed,

nought remains but to confess that when all things have been
unified to the supreme degree, the notion of a possible other than
the actual may still haunt our imagination and prey upon our
system. The bottom of being is left logically opaque to us, as
something which we simply come upon and find, and about which
(if we wish to act) we should pause and wonder as little as possible. The philosopher's logical tranquillity is thus in essence no
other than the boor's. They differ only as to the point at which
each refuses to let further considerations upset the absoluteness
of the data he assumes. The boor does so immediately, and is liable at any moment to the ravages of many kinds of doubt. The
philosopher does not do so till unity has been reached, and is
warranted against the inroads of those considerations, but only
practically, not essentially, secure from the blighting breath of the
ultimate Why? If he cannot exorcise this question, he must ignore
or blink it, and, assuming the data of his system as something
given, and the gift as ultimate, simply proceed to a life of contemplation or of action based on it. There is no doubt that this
acting on an opaque necessity is accompanied by a certain pleasure. See the reverence of Carlyle for brute fact: "There is an
infinite significance in fact." "Necessity," says Dühring, and he
means not rational but given necessity, "is the last and highest
point that we can reach. . . . It is not only the interest of ultimate
and definitive knowledge, but also that of the feelings, to find a
last repose and an ideal equilibrium in an uttermost datum which
can simply not be other than it is."

Such is the attitude of ordinary men in their theism, God's fiat
being in physics and morals such an uttermost datum. Such also
is the attitude of all hard-minded analysts and *Verstandesmen-
schen*. Lotze, Renouvier, and Hodgson promptly say that of experience as a whole no account can be given, but neither seek to
soften the abruptness of the confession nor to reconcile us with
our impotence.

But mediating attempts may be made by more mystical minds.
The peace of rationality may be sought through ecstasy when logic
fails. To religious persons of every shade of doctrine moments
come when the world, as it is, seems so divinely orderly, and the
acceptance of it by the heart so rapturously complete, that intel-

lectual questions vanish; nay, the intellect itself is hushed to sleep, —as Wordsworth says, "thought is not; in enjoyment it expires." Ontological emotion so fills the soul that ontological speculation can no longer overlap it and put her girdle of interrogation-marks round existence. Even the least religious of men must have felt with Walt Whitman, when loafing on the grass on some transparent summer morning, that "swiftly arose and spread round him the peace and knowledge that pass all the argument of the earth." At such moments of energetic living we feel as if there were something diseased and contemptible, yea vile, in theoretic grubbing and brooding. In the eye of healthy sense the philosopher is at best a learned fool.

Since the heart can thus wall out the ultimate irrationality which the head ascertains, the erection of its procedure into a systematized method would be a philosophic achievement of first-rate importance. But as used by mystics hitherto it has lacked universality, being available for few persons and at few times, and even in these being apt to be followed by fits of reaction and dryness; and if men should agree that the mystical method is a subterfuge without logical pertinency, a plaster but no cure, and that the idea of nonentity can never be exorcised, empiricism will be the ultimate philosophy. Existence then will be a brute fact to which as a whole the emotion of ontologic wonder shall rightfully cleave, but remain eternally unsatisfied. Then wonderfulness or mysteriousness will be an essential attribute of the nature of things, and the exhibition and emphasizing of it will continue to be an ingredient in the philosophic industry of the race. Every generation will produce its Job, its Hamlet, its Faust, or its Sartor Resartus.

With this we seem to have considered the possibilities of purely theoretic rationality. But we saw at the outset that rationality meant only unimpeded mental function. Impediments that arise in the theoretic sphere might perhaps be avoided if the stream of mental action should leave that sphere betimes and pass into the practical. Let us therefore inquire what constitutes the feeling of rationality in its *practical* aspect. If thought is not to stand forever pointing at the universe in wonder, if its movement is to be diverted from the issueless channel of purely theoretic contemplation, let us ask what conception of the universe will awaken active impulses capable of effecting this diversion. A definition of the world which will give back to the mind the free motion which has been blocked in the purely contemplative path may so far make the world seem rational again.

Well, of two conceptions equally fit to satisfy the logical demand, that one which awakens the active impulses, or satisfies other æsthetic demands better than the other, will be accounted the more rational conception, and will deservedly prevail.

There is nothing improbable in the supposition that an analysis of the world may yield a number of formulæ, all consistent with the facts. In physical science different formulæ may explain the phenomena equally well,—the one-fluid and the two-fluid theories of electricity, for example. Why may it not be so with the world? Why may there not be different points of view for surveying it, within each of which all data harmonize, and which the observer may therefore either choose between, or simply cumulate one upon another? A Beethoven string-quartet is truly, as some one has said, a scraping of horses' tails on cats' bowels, and may be exhaustively described in such terms; but the application of this description in no way precludes the simultaneous applicability of an entirely different description. Just so a thorough-going interpretation of the world in terms of mechanical sequence is compatible with its being interpreted teleologically, for the mechanism itself may be designed.

If, then, there were several systems excogitated, equally satisfying to our purely logical needs, they would still have to be passed in review, and approved or rejected by our æsthetic and practical nature. . . .

It is far too little recognized how entirely the intellect is built up of practical interests. The theory of evolution is beginning to do very good service by its reduction of all mentality to the type of reflex action. Cognition, in this view, is but a fleeting moment, a cross-section at a certain point, of what in its totality is a motor phenomenon. In the lower forms of life no one will pretend that cognition is anything more than a guide to appropriate action. The germinal question concerning things brought for the first time before consciousness is not the theoretic "What is that?" but the practical "Who goes there?" or rather, as Horwicz has admirably put it, "What is to be done?"—"Was fang' ich an?" In all our discussions about the intelligence of lower animals, the only test we use is that of their *acting* as if for a purpose. Cognition, in short, is incomplete until discharged in act; and although it is true that the later mental development, which attains its maximum through the hypertrophied cerebrum of man, gives birth to a vast amount of theoretic activity over and above that which is immediately ministerial to practice, yet the earlier claim is only postponed, not effaced, and the active nature asserts its rights to the end.

When the cosmos in its totality is the object offered to consciousness, the relation is in no whit altered. React on it we must in some congenial way. It was a deep instinct in Schopenhauer which led him to reinforce his pessimistic argumentation by a running volley of invective against the practical man and his requirements. No hope for pessimism unless he is slain!

Helmholtz's immortal works on the eye and ear are to a great extent little more than a commentary on the law that practical utility wholly determines which parts of our sensations we shall be aware of, and which parts we shall ignore. We notice or discriminate an ingredient of sense only so far as we depend upon it to modify our actions. We *comprehend* a thing when we synthetize it by identity with another thing. But the other great department of our understanding, *acquaintance* (the two departments being recognized in all languages by the antithesis of such words as *wissen* and *kennen; scire* and *noscere,* etc.), what is that also but a synthesis,—a synthesis of a passive perception with a certain tendency to reaction? We are acquainted with a thing as soon as we have learned how to behave towards it, or how to meet the behavior which we expect from it. . . .

Reflex Action and Theism

IN A general way, all educated people know what reflex action means. It means that the acts we perform are always the result of outward discharges from the nervous centres, and that these outward discharges are themselves the result of impressions from the external world, carried in along one or another of our sensory nerves. Applied at first to only a portion of our acts, this conception has ended by being generalized more and more, so that now most physiologists tell us that every action whatever, even the most deliberately weighed and calculated, does, so far as its organic conditions go, follow the reflex type. There is not one which cannot be remotely, if not immediately, traced to an origin in some incoming impression of sense. There is no impression of sense which, unless inhibited by some other stronger one, does not immediately or remotely express itself in action of some kind. There is no one of those complicated performances in the convolutions of the brain to which our trains of thought correspond, which is not a mere middle term interposed between an incoming sensation that arouses it and an outgoing discharge of some sort, inhibitory if not exciting, to which itself gives rise. The structural unit of the nervous system is in fact a triad, neither of whose elements has any independent existence. The sensory impression exists only for the sake of awaking the central process of reflection, and the central process of reflection exists only for the sake of calling forth the final act. All action is thus re-action upon the outer world; and the middle stage of consideration or contemplation or thinking is only a place of transit, the bottom of a loop, both whose ends have their point of application in the outer world. If it should ever have no roots in the outer world, if it should ever happen that it led to no active measures, it would fail of its essential function, and would have to be considered either pathological or abortive. The current of life which runs in at our eyes or ears is meant to run out at our

hands, feet, or lips. The only use of the thoughts it occasions while
inside is to determine its direction to whichever of these organs
shall, on the whole, under the circumstances actually present, act
in the way most propitious to our welfare.

The willing department of our nature, in short, dominates both
the conceiving department and the feeling department; or, in
plainer English, perception and thinking are only there for behavior's sake.

I am sure I am not wrong in stating this result as one of the
fundamental conclusions to which the entire drift of modern physiological investigation sweeps us. If asked what great contribution
physiology has made to psychology of late years, I am sure every
competent authority will reply that her influence has in no way
been so weighty as in the copious illustration, verification, and
consolidation of this broad, general point of view. . . .

I am not quite sure that its full scope is grasped even by those
who have most zealously promulgated it. I am not sure, for example, that all physiologists see that it commits them to regarding the
mind as an essentially teleological mechanism. I mean by this that
the conceiving or theorizing faculty—the mind's middle department—functions *exclusively for the sake of ends* that do not exist
at all in the world of impressions we receive by way of our senses,
but are set by our emotional and practical subjectivity altogether.*
It is a transformer of the world of our impressions into a totally
different world,—the world of our conception; and the transformation is effected in the interests of our volitional nature, and for no
other purpose whatsoever. Destroy the volitional nature, the definitive subjective purposes, preferences, fondnesses for certain effects,
forms, orders, and not the slightest motive would remain for the
brute order of our experience to be remodelled at all. But, as we
have the elaborate volitional constitution we do have, the remodelling must be effected; there is no escape. The world's contents are
given to each of us in an order so foreign to our subjective interests that we can hardly by an effort of the imagination picture to
ourselves what it is like. We have to break that order altogether,—
and by picking out from it the items which concern us, and connecting them with others far away, which we say "belong" with

* See some Remarks on Spencer's Definition of Mind, in the Journal of Speculative Philosophy for January, 1878.

them, we are able to make out definite threads of sequence and
tendency; to foresee particular liabilities and get ready for them;
and to enjoy simplicity and harmony in place of what was chaos.
Is not the sum of your actual experience taken at this moment and
impartially added together an utter chaos? The strains of my voice,
the lights and shades inside the room and out, the murmur of the
wind, the ticking of the clock, the various organic feelings you may
happen individually to possess, do these make a whole at all? Is it
not the only condition of your mental sanity in the midst of them
that most of them should become non-existent for you, and that a
few others—the sounds, I hope, which I am uttering—should evoke
from places in your memory that have nothing to do with this
scene associates fitted to combine with them in what we call a
rational train of thought,—rational, because it leads to a conclusion which we have some organ to appreciate? We have no organ
or faculty to appreciate the simply given order. The real world as
it is given objectively at this moment is the sum total of all its
beings and events now. But can we think of such a sum? Can we
realize for an instant what a cross-section of all existence at a definite point of time would be? While I talk and the flies buzz, a sea-
gull catches a fish at the mouth of the Amazon, a tree falls in the
Adirondack wilderness, a man sneezes in Germany, a horse dies in
Tartary, and twins are born in France. What does that mean? Does
the contemporaneity of these events with one another and with a
million others as disjointed, form a rational bond between them,
and united them into anything that means for us a world? Yet just
such a collateral contemporaneity, and nothing else, is the real
order of the world. It is an order with which we have nothing to
do but to get away from it as fast as possible. As I said, we break it:
we break it into histories, and we break it into arts, and we break
it into sciences; and then we begin to feel at home. We make ten
thousand separate serial orders of it, and on any one of these we
react as though the others did not exist. We discover among its
various parts relations that were never given to sense at all (mathematical relations, tangents, squares, and roots and logarithmic
functions), and out of an infinite number of these we call certain
ones essential and lawgiving, and ignore the rest. Essential these
relations are, but only *for our purpose,* the other relations being
just as real and present as they; and our purpose is to *conceive*

simply and to *foresee*. Are not simple conception and prevision subjective ends pure and simple? They are the ends of what we call science; and the miracle of miracles, a miracle not yet exhaustively cleared up by any philosophy, is that the given order lends itself to the remodelling. It shows itself plastic to many of our scientific, to many of our æsthetic, to many of our practical purposes and ends.

When the man of affairs, the artist, or the man of science fails, he is not rebutted. He tries again. He says the impressions of sense *must* give way, *must* be reduced to the desiderated form. They all postulate in the interests of their volitional nature a harmony between the latter and the nature of things. The theologian does no more. And the reflex doctrine of the mind's structure, though all theology should as yet have failed of its endeavor, could but confess that the endeavor itself at least obeyed in form the mind's most necessary law. . . .

Whether true or false, any view of the universe which shall completely satisfy the mind must obey conditions of the mind's own imposing, must at least let the mind be the umpire to decide whether it be fit to be called a rational universe or not. Not any nature of things which may seem to *be* will also seem to be *ipso facto* rational; and if it do not seem rational, it will afflict the mind with a ceaseless uneasiness, till it be formulated or interpreted in some other and more congenial way. The study of what the mind's criteria of rationality are, the definition of its exactions in this respect, form an intensely interesting subject into which I cannot enter now with any detail. But so much I think you will grant me without argument,—that all three departments of the mind alike have a vote in the matter, and that no conception will pass muster which violates any of their essential modes of activity, or which leaves them without a chance to work. By what title is it that every would-be universal formula, every system of philosophy which rears its head, receives the inevitable critical volley from one half of mankind, and falls to the rear, to become at the very best the creed of some partial sect? Either it has dropped out of its net some of our impressions of sense,—what we call the facts of nature,—or it has left the theoretic and defining department with a lot of inconsistencies and unmediated transitions on its hands; or else, finally, it has left some one or more of our fundamental active and emotional powers with no object outside of themselves to react-on or to live for. Any one of these defects is fatal to its complete success. Some one will be sure to discover the flaw, to scout the system, and to seek another in its stead. . . .

Just as within the limits of theism some kinds are surviving others by reason of their greater practical rationality, so theism itself, by reason of its practical rationality, is certain to survive all lower creeds. Materialism and agnosticism, even were they true, could never gain universal and popular acceptance; for they both, alike, give a solution of things which is irrational to the practical third of our nature, and in which we can never volitionally feel at home. Each comes out of the second or theoretic stage of mental functioning, with its definition of the essential nature of things, its formula of formulas prepared. The whole array of active forces of our nature stands waiting, impatient for the word which shall tell them how to discharge themselves most deeply and worthily upon life. "Well!" cry they, "what shall we do?" "Ignoramus, ignorabimus!" says agnosticism. "React upon atoms and their concussions!" says materialism. What a collapse! The mental train misses fire, the middle fails to ignite the end, the cycle breaks down half-way to its conclusion; and the active powers left alone, with no proper object on which to vent their energy, must either atrophy, sicken, and die, or else by their pent-up convulsions and excitement keep the whole machinery in a fever until some less incommensurable solution, some more practically rational formula, shall provide a normal issue for the currents of the soul.

Now, theism always stands ready with the most practically rational solution it is possible to conceive. Not an energy of our active nature to which it does not authoritatively appeal, not an emotion of which it does not normally and naturally release the springs. At a single stroke, it changes the dead blank *it* of the world into a living *thou,* with whom the whole man may have dealings. To you, at any rate, I need waste no words in trying to prove its supreme commensurateness with all the demands that department Number Three of the mind has the power to impose on department Number Two.

Our volitional nature must then, until the end of time, exert a constant pressure upon the other departments of the mind to induce them to function to theistic conclusions. No contrary for-

mulas can be more than provisionally held. Infra-theistic theories
must be always in unstable equilibrium; for department Number
Three ever lurks in ambush, ready to assert its rights; and on the
slightest show of justification it makes its fatal spring, and con-
verts them into the other form in which alone mental peace and
order can permanently reign.

The question is, then, *Can* departments One and Two, *can* the
facts of nature and the theoretic elaboration of them, always lead
to theistic conclusions?

The future history of philosophy is the only authority capable
of answering that question. I, at all events, must not enter into it
to-day, as that would be to abandon the purely natural-history
point of view I mean to keep.

This only is certain, that the theoretic faculty lives between two
fires which never give her rest, and make her incessantly revise her
formulations. If she sink into a premature, short-sighted, and idol-
atrous theism, in comes department Number One with its battery
of facts of sense, and dislodges her from her dogmatic repose. If
she lazily subside into equilibrium with the same facts of sense
viewed in their simple mechanical outwardness, up starts the practical reason with its demands, and makes *that* couch a bed of
thorns. From generation to generation thus it goes,—now a movement of reception from without, now one of expansion from
within; department Number Two always worked to death, yet
never excused from taking the most responsible part in the arrangements. To-day, a crop of new facts; to-morrow, a flowering
of new motives,—the theoretic faculty always having to effect the
transition, and life growing withal so complex and subtle and immense that her powers of conceiving are almost ruptured with the
strain. . . .

Here let me say one word about a remark we often hear coming
from the anti-theistic wing: It is base, it is vile, it is the lowest
depth of immorality, to allow department Number Three to interpose its demands, and have any vote in the question of what is
true and what is false; the mind must be a passive, reactionless
sheet of white paper, on which reality will simply come and register its own philosophic definition, as the pen registers the curve
on the sheet of a chronograph. "Of all the cants that are canted in

this canting age" this has always seemed to me the most wretched, especially when it comes from professed psychologists. As if the mind could, consistently with its definition, be a reactionless sheet at all! As if conception could possibly occur except for a teleological purpose, except to show us the way from a state of things our senses cognize to another state of things our will desires! As if "science" itself were anything else than such an end of desire, and a most peculiar one at that! And as if the "truths" of bare physics in particular, which these sticklers for intellectual purity contend to be the only uncontaminated form, were not as great an alteration and falsification of the simple "given" order of the world, into an order conceived solely for the mind's convenience and delight, as any theistic doctrine possibly can be!

Physics is but one chapter in the great jugglery which our conceiving faculty is forever playing with the order of being as it presents itself to our reception. It transforms the unutterable dead level and continuum of the "given" world into an utterly unlike world of sharp differences and hierarchic subordinations for no other reason that to satisfy certain subjective passions we possess.*

And, so far as we can see, the given world is there only for the sake of the operation. At any rate, to operate upon it is our only chance of approaching it; for never can we get a glimpse of it in the unimaginable insipidity of its virgin estate. To bid the man's subjective interests be passive till truth express itself from out the environment, is to bid the sculptor's chisel be passive till the statue express itself from out the stone. Operate we must! and the only choice left us is that between operating to poor or to rich results. The only possible duty there can be in the matter is the duty of getting the richest results that the material given will allow. The richness lies, of course, in the energy of all three departments of the mental cycle. Not a sensible "fact" of department One must be left in the cold, not a faculty of department Three be paralyzed; and department Two must form an indestructible bridge. It is natural that the habitual neglect of department One by theologians should arouse indignation; but it is most *un*natural that

---

* "As soon as it is recognized that our thought, as logic deals with it, reposes on our *will to think*, the primacy of the will, even in the theoretical sphere, must be conceded; and the last of presuppositions is not merely [Kant's] that 'I think' must accompany all my representations, but also that 'I will' must dominate all my thinking." (Sigwart: Logik, ii. 25.)

the indignation should take the form of a wholesale denunciation of department Three. It is the story of Kant's dove over again, denouncing the pressure of the air. Certain of our positivists keep chiming to us, that, amid the wreck of every other god and idol, one divinity still stands upright,—that his name is Scientific Truth, and that he has but one commandment, but that one supreme, saying, *Thou shalt not be a theist,* for that would be to satisfy thy subjective propensities, and the satisfaction of those is intellectual damnation. These most conscientious gentlemen think they have jumped off their own feet,—emancipated their mental operations from the control of their subjective propensities at large and *in toto*. But they are deluded. They have simply chosen from among the entire set of propensities at their command those that were certain to construct, out of the materials given, the leanest, lowest, aridest result,—namely, the bare molecular world,—and they have sacrificed all the rest.[1]

Man's chief difference from the brutes lies in the exuberant excess of his subjective propensities,—his pre-eminence over them simply and solely in the number and in the fantastic and unnecessary character of his wants, physical, moral, æsthetic, and intellectual. Had his whole life not been a quest for the superfluous, he would never have established himself as inexpugnably as he has done in the necessary. And from the consciousness of this he should draw the lesson that his wants are to be trusted; that even when their gratification seems farthest off, the uneasiness they occasion is still the best guide of his life, and will lead him to issues entirely beyond his present powers of reckoning. Prune down his extravagance, sober him, and you undo him. The appetite for immediate consistency at any cost, or what the logicians call the "law of parsimony,"—which is nothing but the passion for conceiving the universe in the most labor-saving way,—will, if made the exclusive law of the mind, end by blighting the development of the intellect itself quite as much as that of the feelings or the

[1] As our ancestors said, *Fiat justitia, pereat mundus,* so we, who do not believe in justice or any absolute good, must, according to these prophets, be willing to see the world perish, in order that *scientia fiat.* Was there ever a more exquisite idol of the den, or rather of the *shop?* In the clean sweep to be made of superstitions, let the idol of stern obligation to be scientific go with the rest, and people will have a fair chance to understand one another. But this blowing of hot and of cold makes nothing but confusion.

will. The scientific conception of the world as an army of mole-
cules gratifies this appetite after its fashion most exquisitely. But
if the religion of exclusive scientificism should ever succeed in suf-
focating all other appetites out of a nation's mind, and imbuing a
whole race with the persuasion that simplicity and consistency demand a *tabula rasa* to be made of every notion that does not form
part of the *soi-disant* scientific synthesis, that nation, that race, will
just as surely go to ruin, and fall a prey to their more richly constituted neighbors, as the beasts of the field, as a whole, have
fallen a prey to man. . . .

Surely, if the universe is reasonable (and we must believe that
it is so), it must be susceptible, potentially at least, of being reasoned *out* to the last drop without residuum. Is it not rather an
insult to the very word "rational" to say that the rational character of the universe and its creator means no more than that we
practically feel at home in their presence, and that our powers
are a match for their demands? Do they not in fact demand to be
understood by us still more than to be reacted on? Is not the
unparalleled development of department Two of the mind in man
his crowning glory and his very essence; and may not the *knowing
of the truth* be his absolute vocation? And if it is, ought he flatly
to acquiesce in a spiritual life of "reflex type," whose form is no
higher than that of the life that animates his spinal cord,—nay,
indeed, that animates the writhing segments of any mutilated
worm?

It is easy to see how such arguments and queries may result in
the erection of an ideal of our mental destiny, far different from
the simple and practical religious one we have described. We may
well begin to ask whether such things as practical reactions can
be the final upshot and purpose of all our cognitive energy. Mere
outward acts, changes in the position of parts of matter (for they
are nothing else), can they possibly be the culmination and consummation of our relations with the nature of things? Can they
possibly form a result to which our godlike powers of insight shall
be judged merely subservient? Such an idea, if we scan it closely,
soon begins to seem rather absurd. Whence this piece of matter
comes and whither that one goes, what difference ought that to
make to the nature of things, except so far as with the comings

and the goings our wonderful inward conscious harvest may be reaped?

And so, very naturally and gradually, one may be led from the theistic and practical point of view to what I shall call the *gnostical* one. We may think that department Three of the mind, with its doings of right and its doings of wrong, must be there only to serve department Two; and we may suspect that the sphere of our activity exists for no other purpose than to illumine our cognitive consciousness by the experience of its results. Are not all sense and all emotion at bottom but turbid and perplexed modes of what in its clarified shape is intelligent cognition? Is not all experience just the eating of the fruit of the tree of *knowledge* of good and evil, and nothing more?

These questions fan the fire of an unassuageable gnostic thirst, which is as far removed from theism in one direction as agnosticism was removed from it in the other; and which aspires to nothing less than an absolute unity of knowledge with its object, and refuses to be satisfied short of a fusion and solution and saturation of both impression and action with reason, and an absorption of all three departments of the mind into one. Time would fail us to-day (even had I the learning, which I have not) to speak of gnostic systems in detail. The aim of all of them is to shadow forth a sort of process by which spirit, emerging from its beginnings and exhausting the whole circle of finite experience in its sweep, shall at last return and possess itself as its own object at the climax of its career. This climax is the religious consciousness. At the giddy height of this conception, whose latest and best known form is the Hegelian philosophy, definite words fail to serve their purpose; and the ultimate goal,—where object and subject, worshipped and worshipper, facts and the knowledge of them, fall into one, and where no other is left outstanding beyond this one that alone is, and that we may call indifferently act or fact, reality or idea, God or creation,—this goal, I say, has to be adumbrated to our halting and gasping intelligence by coarse physical metaphors, "positings" and "self-returnings" and "removals" and "settings free," which hardly help to make the matter clear.

But from the midst of the curdling and the circling of it all we seem dimly to catch a glimpse of a state in which the reality to be known and the power of knowing shall have become so mutually adequate that each exhaustively is absorbed by the other and the twain become one flesh, and in which the light shall somehow have soaked up all the outer darkness into its own ubiquitous beams. Like all headlong ideals, this apotheosis of the bare conceiving faculty has its depth and wildness, its pang and its charm. To many it sings a truly siren strain; and so long as it is held only as a postulate, as a mere vanishing point to give perspective to our intellectual aim, it is hard to see any empirical title by which we may deny the legitimacy of gnosticism's claims. That we are not as yet near the goal it prefigures can never be a reason why we might not continue indefinitely to approach it; and to all sceptical arguments, drawn from our reason's actual finiteness, gnosticism can still oppose its indomitable faith in the infinite character of its potential destiny.

Now, here it is that the physiologist's generalization, as it seems to me, may fairly come in, and by ruling any such extravagant faith out of court help to legitimate our personal mistrust of its pretensions. I confess that I myself have always had a great mistrust of the pretensions of the gnostic faith. Not only do I utterly fail to understand what a cognitive faculty erected into the absolute of being, with itself as its object, can mean; but even if we grant it a being other than itself for object, I cannot reason myself out of the belief that however familiar and at home we might become with the character of that being, the bare being of it, the fact that it is there at all, must always be something blankly given and presupposed in order that conception may begin its work; must in short lie beyond speculation, and not be enveloped in its sphere.

Accordingly, it is with no small pleasure that as a student of physiology and psychology I find the only lesson I can learn from these sciences to be one that corroborates these convictions. From its first dawn to its highest actual attainment, we find that the cognitive faculty, where it appears to exist at all, appears but as one element in an organic mental whole, and as a minister to higher mental powers,—the powers of will. Such a thing as its emancipation and absolution from these organic relations receives no faintest color of plausibility from any fact we can discern. Arising as a part, in a mental and objective world which are both larger than itself, it must, whatever its powers of growth may be (and I am far from wishing to disparage them), remain a part to the end. This is the character of the cognitive element in all the mental life we know, and we have no reason to suppose that that character will ever change. On the contrary, it is more than probable that to the end of time our power of moral and volitional response to the nature of things will be the deepest organ of communication therewith we shall ever possess. In every being that is real there is something external to, and sacred from, the grasp of every other. God's being is sacred from ours. To co-operate with his creation by the best and rightest response seems all he wants of us. In such co-operation with his purposes, not in any chimerical speculative conquest of him, not in any theoretic drinking of him up, must lie the real meaning of our destiny. . . .

Pragmatism

Some Metaphysical Problems Pragmatically Considered

I AM now to make the pragmatic method more familiar by giving you some illustrations of its application to particular problems. I will begin with what is driest, and the first thing I shall take will be the problem of *Substance*. Every one uses the old distinction between substance and attribute, enshrined as it is in the very structure of human language, in the difference between grammatical subject and predicate. Here is a bit of blackboard crayon. Its modes, attributes, properties, accidents, or affections,—use which term you will,—are whiteness, friability, cylindrical shape, insolubility in water, etc., etc. But the bearer of these attributes is so much *chalk*, which thereupon is called the substance in which they inhere. So the attributes of this desk inhere in the substance "wood," those of my coat in the substance "wool," and so forth. Chalk, wood and wool, show again, in spite of their differences, common properties, and in so far forth they are themselves counted as modes of a still more primal substance, *matter*, the attributes of which are space-occupancy and impenetrability. Similarly our thoughts and feelings are affections or properties of our several *souls*, which are substances, but again not wholly in their own right, for they are modes of the still deeper substance "spirit."

Now it was very early seen that all *we know* of the chalk is the whiteness, friability, etc., all *we know* of the wood is the combustibility and fibrous structure. A group of attributes is what each substance here is known-as, they form its sole cash-value for our actual experience. The substance is in every case revealed through *them*; if we were cut off from *them* we should never suspect its existence; and if God should keep sending them to us in an unchanged order, miraculously annihilating at a certain moment the substance that supported them, we never could detect the moment, for our experiences themselves would be unaltered. Nominalists accordingly adopt the opinion that substance is a spurious idea due to our inveterate human trick of turning names into things. Phenomena come in groups—the chalk-group, the wood-group, etc.,— and each group gets its name. The name we then treat as in a way supporting the group of phenomena. The low thermometer to-day, for instance, is supposed to come from something called the "climate." Climate is really only the name for a certain group of days, but it is treated as if it lay *behind* the day, and in general we place the name, as if it were a being, behind the facts it is the name of. But the phenomenal properties of things, nominalists say, surely do not really inhere in names, and if not in names then they do not inhere in anything. They *ad*here, or *co*here, rather, *with each other,* and the notion of a substance inaccessible to us, which we think accounts for such cohesion by supporting it, as cement might support pieces of mosaic, must be abandoned. The fact of the bare cohesion itself is all that the notion of the substance signifies. Behind that fact is nothing.

Scholasticism has taken the notion of substance from common sense and made it very technical and articulate. Few things would seem to have fewer pragmatic consequences for us than substances, cut off as we are from every contact with them. Yet in one case scholasticism has proved the importance of the substance-idea by treating it pragmatically. I refer to certain disputes about the mystery of the Eucharist. Substance here would appear to have momentous pragmatic value. Since the accidents of the wafer don't change in the Lord's supper, and yet it has become the very body of Christ, it must be that the change is in the substance solely. The bread-substance must have been withdrawn, and the divine substance substituted miraculously without altering the immediate sensible properties. But tho these don't alter, a tremendous difference has been made, no less a one than this, that we who take the sacrament, now feed upon the very substance of divinity. The substance-notion breaks into life, then, with tremendous effect, if once you allow that substances can separate from their accidents, and exchange these latter.

This is the only pragmatic application of the substance-idea with which I am acquainted; and it is obvious that it will only be treated seriously by those who already believe in the "real presence" on independent grounds.

Material substance was criticised by Berkeley with such telling effect that his name has reverberated through all subsequent philosophy. Berkeley's treatment of the notion of matter is so well known as to need hardly more than a mention. So far from denying the external world which we know, Berkeley corroborated it. It was the scholastic notion of a material substance unapproachable by us, *behind* the external world, deeper and more real than it, and needed to support it, which Berkeley maintained to be the most effective of all reducers of the external world to unreality. Abolish that substance, he said, believe that God, whom you can understand and approach, sends you the sensible world directly, and you confirm the latter and back it up by his divine authority. Berkeley's criticism of "matter" was consequently absolutely pragmatistic. Matter is known as our sensations of colour, figure, hardness and the like. They are the cash-value of the term. The difference matter makes to us by truly being is that we then get such sensations; by not being, is that we lack them. These sensations then are its sole meaning. Berkeley doesn't deny matter, then; he simply tells us what it consists of. It is a true name for just so much in the way of sensations.

Locke, and later Hume, applied a similar pragmatic criticism to the notion of *spiritual substance*. I will only mention Locke's treatment of our "personal identity." He immediately reduces this notion to its pragmatic value in terms of experience. It means, he says, so much "consciousness," namely the fact that at one moment of life we remember other moments, and feel them all as parts of one and the same personal history. Rationalism had explained this practical continuity in our life by the unity of our soul-substance. But Locke says: suppose that God should take away the consciousness, should *we* be any the better for having still the soul-principle? Suppose he annexed the same consciousness to different souls, should *we*, as we realize *ourselves*, be any the worse for that fact? In Locke's day the soul was chiefly a thing to be rewarded or punished. See how Locke, discussing it from this point of view, keeps the question pragmatic:

"Suppose," he says, "one to think himself to be the same *soul* that once was Nestor or Thersites. Can he think their actions his own any more than the actions of any other man that ever existed? But let him once find himself *conscious* of any of the actions of Nestor, he then finds himself the same person with Nestor . . .

In this personal identity is founded all the right and justice of reward and punishment. It may be reasonable to think, no one shall be made to answer for what he knows nothing of, but shall receive his doom, his consciousness accusing or excusing. Supposing a man punished now for what he had done in another life, whereof he could be made to have no consciousness at all, what difference is there between that punishment and being created miserable?"

Our personal identity, then, consists, for Locke, solely in pragmatically definable particulars. Whether, apart from these verifiable facts, it also inheres in a spiritual principle, is a merely curious speculation. Locke, compromiser that he was, passively tolerated the belief in a substantial soul behind our consciousness. But his successor Hume, and most empirical psychologists after him, have denied the soul, save as the name for verifiable cohesions in our inner life. They redescend into the stream of experience with it, and cash it into so much small-change value in the way of "ideas" and their peculiar connexions with each other. As I said of Berkeley's matter, the soul is good or "true" for just *so much,* but no more.

The mention of material substance naturally suggests the doctrine of "materialism," but philosophical materialism is not necessarily knit up with belief in "matter," as a metaphysical principle. One may deny matter in that sense, as strongly as Berkeley did, one may be a phenomenalist like Huxley, and yet one may still be a materialist in the wider sense, of explaining higher phenomena by lower ones, and leaving the destinies of the world at the mercy of its blinder parts and forces. It is in this wider sense of the word that materialism is opposed to spiritualism or theism. The laws of physical nature are what run things, materialism says. The highest productions of human genius might be ciphered by one who had complete acquaintance with the facts, out of their physiological conditions, regardless whether nature be there only for our minds, as idealists contend, or not. Our minds in any case would have to record the kind of nature it is, and write it down as operating through blind laws of physics. This is the complexion of present day materialism, which may better be called naturalism. Over against it stands "theism," or what in a wide sense may be termed "spiritualism." Spiritualism says that mind not only witnesses and records things, but also runs and operates them: the world being thus guided, not by its lower, but by its higher element.

Treated as it often is, this question becomes little more than a conflict between æsthetic preferences. Matter is gross, coarse, crass, muddy; spirit is pure, elevated, noble; and since it is more consonant with the dignity of the universe to give the primacy in it to what appears superior, spirit must be affirmed as the ruling principle. To treat abstract principles as finalities, before which our intellects may come to rest in a state of admiring contemplation, is the great rationalist failing. Spiritualism, as often held, may be simply a state of admiration for one kind, and of dislike for another kind, of abstraction. I remember a worthy spiritualist professor who always referred to materialism as the "mud-philosophy," and deemed it thereby refuted.

To such spiritualism as this there is an easy answer, and Mr. Spencer makes it effectively. In some well-written pages at the end of the first volume of his Psychology he shows us that a "matter" so infinitely subtile, and performing motions as inconceivably quick and fine as those which modern science postulates in her explanations, has no trace of grossness left. He shows that the conception of spirit, as we mortals hitherto have framed it, is itself too gross to cover the exquisite tenuity of nature's facts. Both terms, he says, are but symbols, pointing to that one unknowable reality in which their oppositions cease.

To an abstract objection an abstract rejoinder suffices; and so far as one's opposition to materialism springs from one's disdain of matter as something "crass," Mr. Spencer cuts the ground from under one. Matter is indeed infinitely and incredibly refined. To any one who has ever looked on the face of a dead child or parent the mere fact that matter *could* have taken for a time that precious form, ought to make matter sacred ever after. It makes no difference what the *principle* of life may be, material or immaterial, matter at any rate cooperates, lends itself to all life's purposes. That beloved incarnation was among matter's possibilities.

But now, instead of resting in principles, after this stagnant intellectualist fashion, let us apply the pragmatic method to the question. What do we *mean* by matter? What practical difference can it make *now* that the world should be run by matter or by spirit? I think we find that the problem takes with this a rather different character.

And first of all I call your attention to a curious fact. It makes not a single jot of difference so far as the *past* of the world goes, whether we deem it to have been the work of matter or whether we think a divine spirit was its author.

Imagine, in fact, the entire contents of the world to be once for all irrevocably given. Imagine it to end this very moment, and to have no future; and then let a theist and a materialist apply their rival explanations to its history. The theist shows how a God made it; the materialist shows, and we will suppose with equal success, how it resulted from blind physical forces. Then let the pragmatist be asked to choose between their theories. How can he apply his test if a world is already completed? Concepts for him are things to come back into experience with, things to make us look for differences. But by hypothesis there is to be no more experience and no possible differences can now be looked for. Both theories have shown all their consequences and, by the hypothesis we are adopting, these are identical. The pragmatist must consequently say that the two theories, in spite of their different-sounding names, mean exactly the same thing, and that the dispute is purely verbal. [I am supposing, of course, that the theories *have* been equally successful in their explanations of what is.]

For just consider the case sincerely, and say what would be the *worth* of a God if he *were* there, with his work accomplished and his world run down. He would be worth no more than just that world was worth. To that amount of result, with its mixed merits and defects, his creative power could attain but go no farther. And since there is to be no future; since the whole value and meaning of the world has been already paid in and actualized in the feelings that went with it in the passing, and now go with it in the ending; since it draws no supplemental significance (such as our real world draws) from its function of preparing something yet to come; why then, by it we take God's measure, as it were. He is the Being who could once for all do *that;* and for that much we are thankful to him, but for nothing more. But now, on the contrary hypothesis, namely, that the bits of matter following their laws could make that world and do no less, should we not be just as thankful to them? Wherein should we suffer loss, then, if we dropped God as an hypothesis and made the matter alone responsible? Where would any special deadness, or crassness, come in? And how, experience being what is once for all, would God's presence in it make it any more living or richer?

Candidly, it is impossible to give any answer to this question. The actually experienced world is supposed to be the same in its details on either hypothesis, "the same, for our praise or blame," as Browning says. It stands there indefeasibly: a gift which can't be taken back. Calling matter the cause of it retracts no single one of the items that have made it up, nor does calling God the cause augment them. They are the God or the atoms, respectively, of just that and no other world. The God, if there, has been doing just what atoms could do—appearing in the character of atoms, so to speak—and earning such gratitude as is due to atoms, and no more. If his presence lends no different turn or issue to the performance, it surely can lend it no increase of dignity. Nor would indignity come to it were he absent, and did the atoms remain the only actors on the stage. When a play is once over, and the curtain down, you really make it no better by claiming an illustrious genius for its author, just as you make it no worse by calling him a common hack.

Thus if no future detail of experience or conduct is to be deduced from our hypothesis, the debate between materialism and theism becomes quite idle and insignificant. Matter and God in that event mean exactly the same thing—the power, namely, neither more nor less, that could make just this completed world— and the wise man is he who in such a case would turn his back on such a supererogatory discussion. Accordingly, most men instinctively, and positivists and scientists deliberately, do turn their backs on philosophical disputes from which nothing in the line of definite future consequences can be seen to follow. The verbal and empty character of philosophy is surely a reproach with which we are but too familiar. If pragmatism be true, it is a perfectly sound reproach unless the theories under fire can be shown to have alternative practical outcomes, however delicate and distant these may be. The common man and the scientist say they discover no such outcomes, and if the metaphysician can discern none either, the others certainly are in the right of it, as against him. His science is then but pompous trifling; and the endowment of a professorship for such a being would be silly.

Accordingly, in every genuine metaphysical debate some practical issue, however conjectural and remote, is involved. To realize this, revert with me to our question, and place yourselves this time in the world we live in, in the world that *has* a future, that is yet uncompleted whilst we speak. In this unfinished world the alternative of "materialism or theism?" is intensely practical; and it is worth while for us to spend some minutes of our hour in seeing that it is so.

How, indeed, does the program differ for us, according as we consider that the facts of experience up to date are purposeless configurations of blind atoms moving according to eternal laws, or that on the other hand they are due to the providence of God? As far as the past facts go, indeed, there is no difference. Those facts are in, are bagged, are captured; and the good that's in them is gained, be the atoms or be the God their cause. There are accordingly many materialists about us to-day who, ignoring altogether the future and practical aspects of the question, seek to eliminate the odium attaching to the word materialism, and even to eliminate the word itself, by showing that, if matter could give birth to all these gains, why then matter, functionally considered, is just as divine an entity as God, in fact coalesces with God, is what you mean by God. Cease, these persons advise us, to use either of these terms, with their outgrown opposition. Use a term free of the clerical connotations, on the one hand; of the suggestion of grossness, coarseness, ignobility, on the other. Talk of the primal mystery, of the unknowable energy, of the one and only power, instead of saying either God or matter. This is the course to which Mr. Spencer urges us; and if philosophy were purely retrospective, he would thereby proclaim himself an excellent pragmatist.

But philosophy is prospective also, and, after finding what the world has been and done, and yielded, still asks the further question "what does the world *promise?*" Give us a matter that promises *success,* that is bound by its laws to lead our world ever nearer to perfection, and any rational man will worship that matter as readily as Mr. Spencer worships his own so-called unknowable power. It not only has made for righteousness up to date, but it will make for righteousness forever; and that is all we need. Doing practically all that a God can do, it is equivalent to God, its function is a God's function, and in a world in which a God would be superfluous; from such a world a God could never lawfully be missed. "Cosmic emotion" would here be the right name for religion.

But *is* the matter by which Mr. Spencer's process of cosmic evolution is carried on any such principle of never-ending perfection as this? Indeed it is not, for the future end of every cosmically evolved thing or system of things is foretold by science to be death tragedy; and Mr. Spencer, in confining himself to the æsthetic and ignoring the practical side of the controversy, has really contributed nothing serious to its relief. But apply now our principle of practical results, and see what a vital significance the question of materialism or theism immediately acquires.

Theism and materialism, so indifferent when taken retrospectively, point, when we take them prospectively, to wholly different outlooks of experience. For, according to the theory of mechanical evolution, the laws of redistribution of matter and motion, though they are certainly to thank for all the good hours which our organisms have ever yielded us and for all the ideals which our minds now frame, are yet fatally certain to undo their work again, and to redissolve everything that they have once evolved. You all know the picture of the last state of the universe, which evolutionary science foresees. I can not state it better than is Mr. Balfour's words: "The energies of our system will decay, the glory of the sun will be dimmed, and the earth, tideless and inert, will no longer tolerate the race which has for a moment disturbed its solitude. Man will go down into the pit, and all his thoughts will perish. The uneasy consciousness which in this obscure corner has for a brief space broken the contented silence of the universe, will be at rest. Matter will know itself no longer. 'Imperishable monuments' and 'immortal deeds,' death itself, and love stronger than death, will be as if they had not been. Nor will anything that is, be better or worse for all that the labor, genius, devotion, and suffering of man have striven through countless ages to effect." [1]

That is the sting of it, that in the vast driftings of the cosmic weather, though many a jewelled shore appears, and many an

[1] *The Foundations of Belief,* p. 30.

enchanted cloud-bank floats away, long lingering ere it be dissolved—even as our world now lingers, for our joy—yet when these
transient products are gone, nothing, absolutely *nothing* remains,
to represent those particular qualities, those elements of precious-
ness which they may have enshrined. Dead and gone are they, gone
utterly from the very sphere and room of being. Without an echo;
without a memory; without an influence on aught that may come
after, to make it care for similar ideals. The utter final wreck
and tragedy is of the essence of scientific materialism as at present
understood. The lower and not the higher forces are the eternal
forces, or the last surviving forces within the only cycle of evolution which we can definitely see. Mr. Spencer believes this as
much as any one; so why should he argue with us as if we were
making silly æsthetic objections to the "grossness" of "matter and
motion," the principles of his philosophy, when what really dis-
mays us is the disconsolateness of its ulterior practical results?

No, the true objection to materialism is not positive but negative. It would be farcical at this day to make complaint of it for
what it *is,* for "grossness." Grossness is what grossness *does*--we
now know *that.* We make complaint of it, on the contrary, for
what it is *not*—not a permanent warrant for our more ideal
interests, not a fulfiller of our remotest hopes.

The notion of God, on the other hand, however inferior it
may be in clearness to those mathematical notions so current in
mechanical philosophy, has at least this practical superiority over
them, that it guarantees an ideal order that shall be permanently
preserved. A world with a God in it to say the last word, may
indeed burn up or freeze, but we then think of him as still mindful
of the old ideals and sure to bring them elsewhere to fruition; so
that, where he is, tragedy is only provisional and partial, and shipwreck and dissolution not the absolutely final things. This need
of an eternal moral order is one of the deepest needs of our breast.
And those poets, like Dante and Wordsworth, who live on the
conviction of such an order, owe to that fact the extraordinary
tonic and consoling power of their verse. Here then, in these different emotional and practical appeals, in these adjustments of our
concrete attitudes of hope and expectation, and all the delicate
consequences which their differences entail, lie the real meanings
of materialism and spiritualism—not in hair-splitting abstractions

about matter's inner essence, or about the metaphysical attributes of God. Materialism means simply the denial that the moral order is eternal, and the cutting off of ultimate hopes; spiritualism means the affirmation of an eternal moral order and the letting loose of hope. Surely here is an issue genuine enough, for any one who feels it; and, as long as men are men, it will yield matter for a serious philosophic debate.

But possibly some of you may still rally to their defence. Even whilst admitting that spiritualism and materialism make different prophecies of the world's future, you may yourselves pooh-pooh the difference as something so infinitely remote as to mean nothing for a sane mind. The essence of a sane mind, you may say, is to take shorter views, and to feel no concern about such chimæras as the latter end of the world. Well, I can only say that if you say this, you do injustice to human nature. Religious melancholy is not disposed of by a simple flourish of the word insanity. The absolute things, the last things, the overlapping things, are the truly philosophic concerns; all superior minds feel seriously about them, and the mind with the shortest views is simply the mind of the more shallow man.

The issues of fact at stake in the debate are of course vaguely enough conceived by us at present. But spiritualistic faith in all its forms deals with a world of *promise*, while materialism's sun sets in a sea of disappointment. Remember what I said of the Absolute: it grants us moral holidays. Any religious view does this. It not only incites our more strenuous moments, but it also takes our joyous, careless, trustful moments, and it justifies them. It paints the grounds of justification vaguely enough, to be sure. The exact features of the saving future facts that our belief in God insures, will have to be ciphered out by the interminable methods of science: we can *study* our God only by studying his Creation. But we can *enjoy* our God, if we have one, in advance of all that labor. I myself believe that the evidence for God lies primarily in inner personal experiences. When they have once given your God, his name means at least the benefit of the holiday. You remember what I said yesterday about the way in which truths clash and try to "down" each other. The truth of "God" has to run the gauntlet of all our other truths. It is on trial by them and they on trial by it. Our *final* opinion about God can be settled only after all the truths have straightened themselves out together. Let us hope that they shall find a *modus vivendi!*

Let me pass to a very cognate philosophic problem, the *question of design in nature.* God's existence has from time immemorial been held to be proved by certain natural facts. Many facts appear as if expressly designed in view of one another. Thus the woodpecker's bill, tongue, feet, tail, etc., fit him wondrously for a world of trees, with grubs hid in their bark to feed upon. The parts of our eye fit the laws of light to perfection, leading its rays to a sharp picture on our retina. Such mutual fitting of things diverse in origin argued design, it was held; and the designer was always treated as a man-loving deity.

The first step in these arguments was to prove that the design *existed.* Nature was ransacked for results obtained through separate things being co-adapted. Our eyes, for instance, originate in intra-uterine darkness, and the light originates in the sun, yet see how they fit each other. They are evidently made *for* each other. Vision is the end designed, light and eyes the separate means devised for its attainment.

It is strange, considering how unanimously our ancestors felt the force of this argument, to see how little it counts for since the triumph of the darwinian theory. Darwin opened our minds to the power of chance-happenings to bring forth "fit" results if only they have time to add themselves together. He showed the enormous waste of nature in producing results that get destroyed because of their unfitness. He also emphasized the number of adaptations which, if designed, would argue an evil rather than a good designer. *Here,* all depends upon the point of view. To the grub under the bark the exquisite fitness of the woodpecker's organism to extract him would certainly argue a diabolical designer.

Theologians have by this time stretched their minds so as to embrace the darwinian facts, and yet to interpret them as still showing divine purpose. It used to be a question of purpose against mechanism, of one *or* the other. It was as if one should say "My shoes are evidently designed to fit my feet, hence it is impossible that they should have been produced by machinery." We know that they are both: they are made by a machinery itself designed to fit the feet with shoes. Theology need only stretch similarly the designs of God. As the aim of a football-team is not merely to get the ball to a certain goal (if that were so, they would simply get up on some dark night and place it there), but to get it there by a fixed *machinery of conditions*—the game's rules and the opposing players; so the aim of God is not merely, let us say, to make men and to save them, but rather to get this done through the sole agency of nature's vast machinery. Without nature's stupendous laws and counter-forces, man's creation and perfection, we might suppose, would be too insipid achievements for God to have proposed them.

This saves the form of the design-argument at the expense of its old easy human content. The designer is no longer the old man-like deity. His designs have grown so vast as to be incomprehensible to us humans. The *what* of them so overwhelms us that to establish the mere *that* of a designer for them becomes of very little consequence in comparison. We can with difficulty comprehend the *character* of a cosmic mind whose purposes are fully revealed by the strange mixture of goods and evils that we find in this actual world's particulars. Or rather we cannot by any possibility comprehend it. The mere word "design" by itself has no consequences and explains nothing. It is the barrenest of principles. The old question of *whether* there is design is idle. The real question is what *is* the world, whether or not it have a designer— and that can be revealed only by the study of all nature's particulars.

Remember that *no matter what* nature may have produced or may be producing, the means must necessarily have been adequate, must have been *fitted to that production*. The argument from fitness to design would consequently always apply, whatever were the product's character. The recent Mont-Pelée eruption, for example, required all previous history to produce that exact combination of ruined houses, human and animal corpses, sunken ships, volcanic ashes, etc., in just that one hideous configuration of positions. France had to be a nation and colonize Martinique. Our country had to exist and send our ships there. *If* God aimed at just that result, the means by which the centuries bent their influences towards it, showed exquisite intelligence. And so of any state of things whatever, either in nature or in history, which we find actually realized. For the parts of things must always make *some* definite resultant, be it chaotic or harmonious. When we look at what has actually come, the conditions must always appear perfectly designed to ensure it. We can always say, therefore, in any conceivable world, of any conceivable character, that the whole cosmic machinery *may* have been designed to produce it.

Pragmatically, then, the abstract word "design" is a blank cartridge. It carries no consequences, it does no execution. *What* design? and *what* designer? are the only serious questions, and the study of facts is the only way of getting even approximate answers. Meanwhile, pending the slow answer from facts, any one who insists that there *is* a designer and who is sure he is a divine one, gets a certain pragmatic benefit from the term—the same, in fact, which we saw that the terms God, Spirit, or the Absolute, yield us. "Design," worthless tho it be as a mere rationalistic principle set above or behind things for our admiration, becomes, if our faith concretes it into something theistic, a term of *promise*. Returning with it into experience, we gain a more confiding outlook on the future. If not a blind force but a seeing force runs things, we may reasonably expect better issues. This vague confidence in the future is the sole pragmatic meaning at present discernible in the terms design and designer. But if cosmic confidence is right not wrong, better not worse, that is a most important meaning. That much at least of possible "truth" the terms will then have in them.

Let me take up another well-worn controversy, *the free-will problem*. Most persons who believe in what is called their free-will do so after the rationalistic fashion. It is a principle, a positive faculty or virtue added to man, by which his dignity is enigmatically augmented. He ought to believe it for this reason. Determinists, who deny it, who say that individual men originate nothing, but merely transmit to the future the whole push of the past cosmos of which they are so small an expression, diminish man. He is less admirable, stripped of this creative principle. I imagine that more than half of you share our instinctive belief in free-will, and that admiration of it as a principle of dignity has much to do with your fidelity.

But free-will has also been discussed pragmatically, and, strangely enough, the same pragmatic interpretation has been put upon it by both disputants. You know how large a part questions of *accountability* have played in ethical controversy. To hear some persons, one would suppose that all that ethics aims at is a code of merits and demerits. Thus does the old legal and theological leaven, the interest in crime and sin and punishment abide with us. "Who's to blame? whom can we punish? whom will God punish?"—these preoccupations hang like a bad dream over man's religious history.

So both free-will and determinism have been inveighed against and called absurd, because each, in the eyes of its enemies, has seemed to prevent the "imputability" of good or bad deeds to their authors. Queer antinomy this! Free-will means novelty, the grafting on to the past of something not involved therein. If our acts were predetermined, if we merely transmitted the push of the whole past, the free-willists say, how could we be praised or blamed for anything? We should be "agents" only, not "principals," and where then would be our precious imputability and responsibility?

But where would it be if we *had* free-will? rejoin the determinists. If a "free" act be a sheer novelty, that comes not *from* me, the previous me, but *ex nihilo,* and simply tacks itself on to me, how can *I,* the previous I, be responsible? How can I have any permanent *character* that will stand still long enough for praise or blame to be awarded? The chaplet of my days tumbles into a cast of disconnected beads as soon as the thread of inner necessity is drawn out by the preposterous indeterminist doctrine. Messrs. Fullerton and McTaggart have recently laid about them doughtily with this argument.

It may be good *ad hominem,* but otherwise it is pitiful. For I ask you, quite apart from other reasons, whether any man, woman or child, with a sense for realities, ought not to be ashamed to plead such principles as either dignity or imputability. Instinct and utility between them can safely be trusted to carry on the social business of punishment and praise. If a man does good acts we shall praise him, if he does bad acts we shall punish him,— anyhow, and quite apart from theories as to whether the acts result from what was previous in him or are novelties in a strict sense. To make our human ethics revolve about the question of "merit" is a piteous unreality—God alone can know our merits, if we have any. The real ground for supposing free-will is indeed pragmatic, but it has nothing to do with this contemptible right to punish which has made such a noise in past discussions of the subject.

Free-will pragmatically means *novelties in the world,* the right to expect that in its deepest elements as well as in its surface phenomena, the future may not identically repeat and imitate the past. That imitation *en masse* is there, who can deny? The general "uniformity of nature" is presupposed by every lesser law. But nature may be only approximately uniform; and persons in whom knowledge of the world's past has bred pessimism (or doubts as to the world's good character, which become certainties if that character be supposed eternally fixed) may naturally welcome free-will as a *melioristic* doctrine. It holds up improvement as at least possible; whereas determinism assures us that our whole notion of possibility is born of human ignorance, and that necessity and impossibility between them rule the destinies of the world.

Free-will is thus a general cosmological theory of *promise,* just like the Absolute, God, Spirit or Design. Taken abstractly, no one of these terms has any inner content, none of them gives us any picture, and no one of them would retain the least pragmatic value in a world whose character was obviously perfect from the start. Elation at mere existence, pure cosmic emotion and delight, would, it seems to me, quench all interest in those speculations, if the world were nothing but a lubberland of happiness already. Our interest in religious metaphysics arises in the fact that our empirical future feels to us unsafe, and needs some higher guarantee. If the past and present were purely good, who could wish that the future might possibly not resemble them? Who could desire free-will? Who would not say, with Huxley, "let me be wound up every day like a watch, to go right fatally, and I ask no better freedom." "Freedom" in a world already perfect could only mean freedom to *be worse,* and who could be so insane as to wish that? To be necessarily what it is, to be impossibly aught else, would put the last touch of perfection upon optimism's universe. Surely the only *possibility* that one can rationally claim is the possibility that things may be *better.* That possibility, I need hardly say, is one that, as the actual world goes, we have ample grounds for desiderating.

Free-will thus has no meaning unless it be a doctrine of *relief.* As such, it takes its place with other religious doctrines. Between

them, they build up the old wastes and repair the former desola-
tions. Our spirit, shut within this courtyard of sense-experience,
is always saying to the intellect upon the tower: "Watchman, tell
us of the night, if it aught of promise bear," and the intellect gives
it then these terms of promise.

Other than this practical significance, the words God, free-will,
design, etc., have none. Yet dark tho they be in themselves, or in-
tellectualistically taken, when we bear them into life's thicket with
us the darkness *there* grows light about us. If you stop, in dealing
with such words, with their definition, thinking that to be an intellectual finality, where are you? Stupidly staring at a pretentious
sham! "Deus est Ens, a se, extra et supra omne genus, necessarium,
unum, infinite perfectum, simplex, immutabile, immensum, aeter-
num, intelligens," etc.,—wherein is such a definition really instructive? It means less than nothing, in its pompous robe of adjectives.
Pragmatism alone can read a positive meaning into it, and for that
she turns her back upon the intellectualist point of view altogether. "God's in his heaven; all's right with the world!"—*That's*
the real heart of your theology, and for that you need no rationalist definitions.

Why shouldn't all of us, rationalists as well as pragmatists, confess this? Pragmatism, so far from keeping her eyes bent on the
immediate practical foreground, as she is accused of doing, dwells
just as much upon the world's remotest perspectives.

See then how all these ultimate questions turn, as it were, upon
their hinges; and from looking backwards upon principles, upon
an *erkenntnisstheoretische Ich,* a God, a *Kausalitätsprinzip,* a Design, a Free-will, taken in themselves, as something august and exalted above facts,—see, I say, how pragmatism shifts the emphasis
and looks forward into facts themselves. The really vital question
for us all is, What is this world going to be? What is life eventually
to make of itself? The centre of gravity of philosophy must therefore alter its place. The earth of things, long thrown into shadow
by the glories of the upper ether, must resume its rights. To shift
the emphasis in this way means that philosophic questions will fall
to be treated by minds of a less abstractionist type than heretofore,
minds more scientific and individualistic in their tone yet not irreligious either. It will be an alteration in "the seat of authority"
that reminds one almost of the protestant reformation. And as, to

papal minds, protestantism has often seemed a mere mess of anarchy and confusion, such, no doubt, will pragmatism often seem to ultra-rationalist minds in philosophy. It will seem so much sheer trash, philosophically. But life wags on, all the same, and compasses its ends, in protestant countries. I venture to think that philosophic protestantism will compass a not dissimilar prosperity.

Henri Bergson

Henri Bergson

BERGSON (born 1860, died 1941), when his *Creative Evolution* appeared in 1907, became a philosophical figure of world-wide popular reputation, and seemed at the time to no less a mind than that of William James to be a miraculous fresh voice in philosophy. He brought the gifts of an extraordinary lucid and elegant style, subtle psychological insight, and a refined analytic intelligence to bear upon the assumptions of the mechanistic physics and the mechanistic biology which, along with century-long commitment to the static and the logically formal, had come to dominate nineteenth-century philosophy. Bergson was not the first to have celebrated vitality, change, and growth. He was not the first to have revolted against intellectualism; the German romantic philosophers were his predecessors along this line. But he was the first to try to establish a metaphysics, a theory of knowledge, and, ultimately, a theory of morals and of religion which found their center in the facts of change, growth, creation, and duration. He was almost the first since Heraclitus to make the changing rather than the permanent the foundation of his philosophy.

Bergson did not ever produce a rounded and systematic philosophy. He did produce a philosophy with characteristic leading themes, which he applied to everything from biological evolution to changes in society, morals, and religion. Those themes grew out of his critique of mechanist science and of the methods of intelligence which were relevant to it. He hit upon the fact that nearly all modern philosophy is spatial in its concepts, and all analysis was relevant to a spatial

world. Even time was measured in spatial terms, by the movement of a pendulum in space. Thinking was obsessed by the
static and the geometrical. The real could never be known by
the spatial terms of the geometrizing intellect. For the real is,
he holds, movement, the stream of consciousness, the felt
duration of life. Matter is a pragmatic projection of the
geometrizing methods of the mind. Intuition must plumb
below the criss-cross of distinctions the intellect throws across
the flowing stream. It must identity itself with duration itself.
All necessity is a fiction of the spatializing intellect. At any
moment duration is indeterminate, change is real, creation
actual, the future a genuine adventure.

Bergson, in his *Creative Evolution,* turns his conception of
life, duration, change and creation and freedom upon the
process of evolution. The latter process is not the mechanical
elimination that Darwin called natural selection. It is not the
moving toward a fixed end or goal. It is a genuinely creative
process, inventing its ends, various and changing, as it goes
and grows. It is an impulsion, an *élan vital.* Evolution made
a great bifurcation, on the one hand, in the direction of practical tool-making, spatializing intellect, on the other hand, in
the direction of intuitive realization, instinct sensuously flowing in an identity with duration itself. Insofar as man geom-
etrizes he is more and more effective practically. He is less
and less in touch with the vital movement which is life and
reality as well as evolution. To have metaphysical insight, one
must turn one's back on space and stabilities and be one with
the vital duration, the living, changing indetermination
which is the real.

Like evolution itself, the evolution of society, morals, religion, and art reveal the compulsive and explosive *élan* of
change. Open societies break through the encrustations of
closed societies in the living intuitions of seers, poets, and
saints. Stability is the mark of death; growth the sign of life.
The saint, the poet, and the revolutionary prophet touch the
living depths of life and creation. Their insights become

formalized and institutionalized; a *rigor mortis* sets in until fresh insights emerge from new prophets with new intuitions, drawn from a fresh bathing in the living flux.

In an early work, *Matter and Memory*, Bergson enlarged upon that "intuition" which pierces below the artificial schemas of intellectual distinctions, the formulas of practical action. Intuition is a "realization" of duration, which is enriched with the cumulating flow of focussed memories. "Memory" enlarges the range of consciousness, of conscious alternatives, of choice, of freedom.

Bergson's philosophy is at once a celebration of the *élan vital,* the impulsive urgency of life, and of the intuition of freedom, change, and creative growth. It is also a critique of that "false secondary power by which we multiply distinctions." The emphasis on vitality as over against verbalism, on insight rather than on schemes, on change rather than inertness, were all symptoms of a revolt against materialism and dialectic. Bergson romanticized change into creative growth, and mystic indistinction into insight. But no philosopher, hereafter, can fail to take into account the fact of change and of life to which he pointed, or the limitations upon intellectualism which he pointed out.

The selection below from *Two Sources of Morality and Religion* (1932) illustrates in the field of morals and religion the contrast between mechanical necessity and living freedom which animates Bergson throughout his work. The distinction between intellect and life here becomes the distinction between obligation and spontaneity, between closed and open societies.

Two Sources of Morality and Religion

Chapter I

Moral Obligation

THE remembrance of forbidden fruit is the earliest thing in the memory of each of us, as it is in that of mankind. We should notice this, were not this recollection overlaid by others which we are more inclined to dwell upon. What a childhood we should have had if only we had been left to do as we pleased! We should have flitted from pleasure to pleasure. But all of a sudden an obstacle arose, neither visible nor tangible: a prohibition. Why did we obey? The question hardly occurred to us. We had formed the habit of deferring to our parents and teachers. All the same we knew very well that it was because they were our parents, because they were our teachers. Therefore, in our eyes, their authority came less from themselves than from their status in relation to us. They occupied a certain station; that was the source of the command which, had it issued from some other quarter, would not have possessed the same weight. In other words, parents and teachers seemed to act by proxy. We did not fully realize this, but behind our parents and our teachers we had an inkling of some enormous, or rather some shadowy, thing that exerted pressure on us through them. Later we would say it was society. And speculating upon it, we should compare it to an organism whose cells, united by imperceptible links, fall into their respective places in a highly developed hierarchy, and for the greatest good of the whole naturally submit to a discipline that may demand the sacrifice of the part. This, however, can only be a comparison, for an organism subject to inexorable laws is one thing, and a society composed of free wills another. But, once these wills are organized, they assume the guise of an organism; and in this more or less artificial organism habit plays the same rôle as necessity in the works of nature. From this first standpoint, social life appears to us a system of more or less deeply rooted habits, corresponding to the needs of the community. Some of them are habits of command, most of them are habits of obedience, whether we obey a person commanding by virtue of a mandate from society, or whether from society itself, vaguely perceived or felt, there emanates an impersonal imperative. Each of these habits of obedience exerts a pressure on our will. We can evade it, but then we are attracted towards it, drawn back to it, like a pendulum which has swung away from the vertical. A certain order of things has been upset, it *must be* restored. In a word, as with all habits, we feel a sense of obligation.

But in this case the obligation is immeasurably stronger. When a certain magnitude is so much greater than another that the latter is negligible in comparison, mathematicians say that it belongs to another order. So it is with social obligation. The pressure of it, compared to that of other habits, is such that the difference in degree amounts to a difference in kind. It should be noted that all habits of this nature lend one another mutual support. Although we may not speculate on their essence and on their origin, we feel that they are interrelated, being demanded of us by our immediate surroundings, or by the surroundings of those surroundings, and so on to the uttermost limit, which would be society. Each one corresponds, directly or indirectly, to a social necessity; and so they all hang together, they form a solid block. Many of them would be trivial obligations if they appeared singly. But they are an integral part of obligation in general, and this whole, which is what it is owing to the contributions of its parts, in its turn confers upon each one the undivided authority of the totality. Thus the sum-total comes to the aid of each of its parts, and the general sentence "do what duty bids" triumphs over the hesitations we might feel in the presence of a single duty. As a matter of fact, we do not explicitly think of a mass of partial duties added together and constituting a single total obligation. Perhaps there is really not an aggregation of parts. The strength which one obligation derives from all the others is rather to be compared to the breath of life drawn, complete and indivisible, by each of the cells from the depths of the organism of which it is an element. Society, present within each of its members, has claims which, whether great or small, each express the sum-total of its vitality. But let us again repeat that this is only a comparison. A human community is a collectivity of free beings. The obligations which it lays down, and which enable it to subsist, introduce into it a regularity which has merely some analogy to the inflexible order of the phenomena of life.

And yet everything conspires to make us believe that this regularity is comparable with that of nature. I do not allude merely to the unanimity of mankind in praising certain acts and blaming others. I mean that, even in those cases where moral precepts implied in judgments of values are not observed, we contrive that they should appear so. Just as we do not notice disease when walking along the street, so we do not gauge the degree of possible immorality behind the exterior which humanity presents to the world. It would take a good deal of time to become a misanthrope if we confined ourselves to the observation of others. It is when we detect our own weaknesses that we come to pity or despise mankind. The human nature from which we then turn away is the human nature we have discovered in the depths of our own being. The evil is so well screened, the secret so universally kept, that in this case each individual is the dupe of all: however severely we may profess to judge other men, at bottom we think them better than ourselves. On this happy illusion much of our social life is grounded.

It is natural that society should do everything to encourage this idea. The laws which it promulgates and which maintain the social order resemble, moreover, in certain aspects, the laws of nature. I admit that the difference is a radical one in the eyes of the philosopher. To him the law which enunciates facts is one thing, the law which commands, another. It is possible to evade the latter; here we have obligation, not necessity. The former is, on the contrary, unescapable, for if any fact diverged from it we should be wrong in having assumed it to be a law; there would exist another one, the true one, formulated in such a way as to express everything we observe and to which the recalcitrant fact would then conform like the rest. True enough; but to the majority of people the distinction is far from being so clear. A law, be it physical, social or moral—every law—is in their eyes a command. There is a certain order of nature which finds expression in laws:

the facts are presumed to "obey" these laws so as to conform with that order. The scientist himself can hardly help believing that the law "governs" facts and consequently is prior to them, like the Platonic Idea on which all things had to model themselves. The higher he rises in the scale of generalizations the more he tends, willy-nilly, to endow the law with this imperative character; it requires a very real struggle against our own prepossessions to imagine the principles of mechanics otherwise than as inscribed from all eternity on the transcendent tables that modern science has apparently fetched down from another Sinai. But if physical law tends to assume in our imagination the form of a command when it attains to a certain degree of generality, in its turn an imperative which applies to everybody appears to us somewhat like a law of nature. The two ideas, coming against each other in our minds, effect an exchange. The law borrows from the command its prerogative of compulsion; the command receives from the law its inevitability. Thus a breach of the social order assumes an anti-natural character; even when frequently repeated, it strikes us as an exception, being to society what a freak creation is to nature.

And suppose we discern behind the social imperative a religious command? No matter the relation between the two terms: whether religion be interpreted in one way or another, whether it be social in essence or by accident, one thing is certain, that it has always played a social rôle. This part, indeed, is a complex one: it varies with time and place; but in societies such as our own the first effect of religion is to sustain and reinforce the claims of society. It may go much further. It goes at least thus far. Society institutes punishments which may strike the innocent and spare the guilty; its rewards are few and far between; it takes broad views and is easily satisfied; what human scales could weigh, as they should be weighed, rewards and punishments? But, just as the Platonic Ideas reveal to us, in its perfection and fulness, that reality which we see only in crude imitations, so religion admits us to a city whose most prominent features are here and there roughly typified by our institutions, our laws and our customs. Here below, order is merely approximate, being more or less artificially obtained by man; above, it is perfect and self-creative. Religion therefore, in our eyes, succeeds in filling in the gap, already narrowed by our habitual way of looking at things, between a command of society and a law of nature.

We are thus being perpetually brought back to the same comparison, defective though it be in many ways, yet appropriate enough to the point with which we are dealing. The members of a civic community hold together like the cells of an organism. Habit, served by intelligence and imagination, introduces among them a discipline resembling, in the interdependence it establishes between separate individuals, the unity of an organism of anastomotic cells.

Everything, yet again, conspires to make social order an imitation of the order observed in nature. It is evident that each of us, thinking of himself alone, feels at liberty to follow his bent, his desire or his fancy, and not consider his fellowmen. But this inclination has no sooner taken shape than it comes up against a force composed of the accumulation of all social forces: unlike individual motives, each pulling its own way, this force would result in an order not without analogy to that of natural phenomena. The component cell of an organism, on becoming momentarily conscious, would barely have outlived the wish to emancipate itself when it would be recaptured by necessity. An individual forming part of a community may bend or even break a necessity of the same kind, which to some extent he has helped to create, but to which, still more, he has to yield; the sense of this necessity, together with the consciousness of being able to evade it, is none the less what he calls an obligation. From this point of view, and taken in its most usual meaning, obligation is to necessity what habit is to nature.

It does not come then exactly from without. Each of us belongs as much to society as to himself. While his consciousness, delving downwards, reveals to him, the deeper he goes, an ever more original personality, incommensurable with the others and indeed undefinable in words, on the surface of life we are in continuous contact with other men whom we resemble, and united to them by a discipline which creates between them and us a relation of interdependence. Has the self no other means of clinging to something solid than by taking up its position in that part of us which is socialised? That would be so if there were no other way of escape from a life of impulse, caprice and regret. But in our innermost selves, if we know how to look for it, we may perhaps discover another sort of equilibrium, still more desirable than the one on the surface. Certain aquatic plants as they rise to the surface are ceaselessly jostled by the current: their leaves, meeting above the water, interlace, thus imparting to them stability above. But still more stable are the roots, which, firmly planted in the earth, support them from below. However, we shall not dwell for the present on the effort to delve down to the depths of our being. If possible at all, it is exceptional: and it is on the surface, at the point where it inserts itself into the close-woven tissue of other exteriorised personalities, that our ego generally finds its point of attachment; its solidity lies in this solidarity. But, at the point where it is attached, it is itself socialized. Obligation, which we look upon as a bond between men, first binds us to ourselves.

It would therefore be a mistake to reproach a purely social morality with neglecting individual duties. Even if we were only in theory under a state of obligation towards other men, we should be so in fact towards ourselves, since social solidarity exists only in so far as a social ego is superadded, in each of us, to the individual self. To cultivate this social ego is the essence of our obligation to society. Were there not some part of society in us, it would have no hold on us; and we scarcely need seek it out, we are self-sufficient, if we find it present within us. Its presence is more or less marked in different men; but no one could cut himself off from it completely. Nor would he wish to do so, for he is perfectly aware that the greater part of his strength comes from this source, and that he owes to the ever-recurring demands of social life that unbroken tension of energy, that steadiness of aim in effort, which ensures the greatest return for his activity. But he could not do so, even if he wished to, because his memory and his imagination live on what society has implanted in them, because the soul of society is inherent in the language he speaks, and because even if there is no one present, even if he is merely thinking, he is still talking to himself. Vainly do we try to imagine an individual cut off from all social life. Even materially, Robinson Crusoe on his island remains in contact with other men, for the manufactured objects he saved from the wreck, and without which he could not get along, keep him within the bounds of civilization, and consequently within those of society. But a moral contact is still more

necessary to him, for he would be soon discouraged if he had
nothing else to cope with his incessant difficulties except an individual strength of which he knows the limitations. He draws
energy from the society to which he remains attached in spirit; he
may not perceive it, still it is there, watching him: if the individual ego maintains alive and present the social ego, he will
effect, even in isolation, what he would with the encouragement
and even the support of the whole of society. Those whom circumstances condemn for a time to solitude, and who cannot find
within themselves the resources of a deep inner life, know the
penalty of "giving way," that is to say of not establishing the individual ego at the level prescribed by the social ego. They will
therefore be careful to maintain the latter, so that it shall not re-
lax for one moment its strictness towards the former. If necessary,
they will seek for some material or artificial support for it. You
remember Kipling's Forest Officer, alone in his bungalow in the
heart of the Indian rukh? He dresses every evening for dinner, so
as to preserve his self-respect in his isolation.[1]

We shall not go so far as to say that this social ego is Adam
Smith's "impartial spectator," or that it must necessarily be identified with moral conscience, or that we feel pleased or displeased
with ourselves according as it is favourably or unfavourably affected. We shall discover deeper sources for our moral feelings.
Language here groups under one name very different things: what
is there in common between the remorse of a murderer and that
racking, haunting pain, also a remorse, which we may feel at having wounded someone's pride or been unjust to a child? To betray
the confidence of an innocent soul opening out to life is one of
the most heinous offences for a certain type of conscience, which
is apparently lacking in a sense of proportion, precisely because
it does not borrow from society its standards, its gauges, its system
of measurement. This type of conscience is not the one that is
most often at work. At any rate it is more or less sensitive in different people. Generally the verdict of conscience is the verdict
which would be given by the social self.

And also, generally speaking, moral distress is a throwing-out
of gear of the relations between the social and the individual self.
Analyse the feeling of remorse in the soul of a desperate criminal.

[1] Kipling, "In the Rukh," from *Many Inventions*.

You might mistake it at first for the dread of punishment, and indeed you find most minute precautions, perpetually supplemented and renewed, to conceal the crime and avoid being found out; at every moment comes the awful thought that some detail has been overlooked and that the authorities will get hold of the tell-tale clue. But look closer: what the fellow wants is not so much to evade punishment as to wipe out the past, to arrange things just as though the crime had never been committed at all. When nobody knows that a thing exists, it is almost as if it were non-existent. Thus it is the crime itself that the criminal wants to erase, by suppressing any knowledge of it that might come to the human ken. But his own knowledge persists, and note how it drives him more and more out of that society within which he hoped to remain by obliterating the traces of his crime. For the same esteem for the man he was is still shown to the man he is no longer; therefore society is not addressing him; it is speaking to someone else. He, knowing what he is, feels more isolated among his fellow-men than he would on a desert island; for in his solitude he would carry with him, enveloping him and supporting him, the image of society; but now he is cut off from the image as well as the thing. He could reinstate himself in society by confessing his crime: he would then be treated according to his deserts, but society would then be speaking to his real self. He would resume his collaboration with other men. He would be punished by them, but, having made himself one of them, he would be in a small degree the author of his own condemnation; and a part of himself, the best part, would thus escape the penalty. Such is the force which will drive a criminal to give himself up. Sometimes, without going so far, he will confess to a friend, or to any decent fellow. By thus putting himself right, if not in the eyes of all, at least he is near it, close to it; he no longer remains alienated from point, by a thread: even if he does not reinstate himself in it, at least he is near it, close to it; he no longer remains alienated from it; in any case he is no longer in complete rupture with it, nor with that element of it which is part of himself.

It takes this violent break to reveal clearly the nexus of the individual to society. In the ordinary way we conform to our obligations rather than think of them. If we had every time to evoke the idea, enunciate the formula, it would be much more tiring to do our duty. But habit is enough, and in most cases we have only to leave well alone in order to accord to society what it expects from us. Moreover, society has made matters very much easier for us by interpolating intermediaries between itself and us: we have a family; we follow a trade or a profession; we belong to our parish, to our district, to our county; and, in cases where the insertion of the group into society is complete, we may content ourselves, if need be, with fulfilling our obligations towards the group and so paying our debts to society. Society occupies the circumference; the individual is at the centre: from the centre to the circumference are arranged, like so many ever-widening concentric circles, the various groups to which the individual belongs. From the circumference to the centre, as the circles grow smaller, obligations are added to obligations, and the individual ends by finding himself confronted with all of them together. Thus obligation increases as it advances; but, if it is more complicated, it is less abstract, and the more easily accepted. When it has become fully concrete, it coincides with a tendency, so habitual that we find it natural, to play in society the part which our station assigns to us. So long as we yield to this tendency, we scarcely feel it. It assumes a peremptory aspect, like all deep-seated habits, only if we depart from it.

It is society that draws up for the individual the programme of his daily routine. It is impossible to live a family life, follow a profession, attend to the thousand and one cares of the day, do one's shopping, go for a stroll, or even stay at home, without obeying rules and submitting to obligations. Every instant we have to choose, and we naturally decide on what is in keeping with the rule. We are hardly conscious of this; there is no effort. A road has been marked out by society; it lies open before us, and we follow it; it would take more initiative to cut across country. Duty, in this sense, is almost always done automatically; and obedience to duty, if we restrict ourselves to the most usual case, might be defined as a form of non-exertion, passive acquiscence. How comes it, then, that on the contrary this obedience appears as a state of strain, and duty itself as something harsh and unbending? Obviously because there occur cases where obedience implies an overcoming of self. These cases are exceptions; but we notice them because they are accompanied by acute consciousness, as happens with all forms of hesitation—in fact consciousness is this hesitation itself; for an action which is started automatically passes almost unperceived. Thus, owing to the interdependence of our duties, and because the obligation as a whole is immanent in each of its parts, all duties are tinged with the hue taken on exceptionally by one or the other of them. From the practical point of view this presents no inconvenience, there are even certain advantages in looking at things in this way. For, however naturally we do our duty, we may meet with resistance within ourselves; it is wise to expect it, and not take for granted that it is easy to remain a good husband, a decent citizen, a conscientious worker, in a word an honest fellow. Besides, there is a considerable amount of truth in this opinion; for if it is relatively easy to keep within the social order, yet we have had to enrol in it, and this enrolment demands an effort. The natural disobedience of the child, the necessity of education, are proof of this. It is but just to credit the individual with the consent virtually given to the totality of his obligations, even if he no longer needs to take counsel with himself on each one of them. The rider need only allow himself to be borne along; he has had to get into the saddle. So it is with the individual in relation to society. In one sense it would be untrue, and in every sense it would be dangerous, to say that duty can be done automatically. Let us then set up as a practical maxim that obedience to duty means resistance to self.

But a maxim is one thing, an explanation another. When, in order to define obligation, its essence and its origin, we lay down that obedience is primarily a struggle with self, a state of tension or contraction, we make a psychological error which has vitiated many theories of ethics. Thus artificial difficulties have arisen, problems which set philosophers at variance and which will be found to vanish when we analyse the terms in which they are expressed. Obligation is in no sense a unique fact, incommensurate with others, looming above them like a mysterious apparition. If a considerable number of philosophers, especially those who follow Kant, have taken this view, it is because they have confused the sense of obligation, a tranquil state akin to inclination, with the violent effort we now and again exert on ourselves to break down a possible obstacle to obligation.

After an attack of rheumatism, we may feel some discomfort

and even pain in moving our muscles and joints. It is the general sensation of a resistance set up by all our organs together. Little by little it decreases and ends by being lost in the consciousness we have of our movements when we are well. Now, we are at liberty to fancy that it is still there, in an incipient, or rather a subsiding, condition, that it is only on the look-out for a chance to become more acute; we must indeed expect attacks of rheumatism if we are rheumatic. Yet what should we say of a philosopher who saw in our habitual sensations, when moving our arms and legs, a mere diminution of pain, and who then defined our motory faculty as an effort to resist rheumatic discomfort? To begin with, he would thus be giving up the attempt to account for motory habits, since each of these implies a particular combination of movements, and can be explained only by that combination. The general faculty of walking, running, moving the body, is but an aggregation of these elementary habits, each of them finding its own explanation in the special movements it involves. But having only considered the faculty as a whole, and having then defined it as a force opposed to a resistance, it is natural enough to set up rheumatism beside it as an independent entity. It would seem as though some such error had been made by many of those who have speculated on obligation. We have any number of particular obligations, each calling for a separate explanation. It is natural, or, more strictly speaking, it is a matter of habit to obey them all. Suppose that exceptionally we deviate from one of them, there would be resistance; if we resist this resistance, a state of tension or contraction is likely to result. It is this rigidity which we objectify when we attribute so stern an aspect to duty.

It is also what the philosophers have in mind, when they see fit to resolve obligation into elements. In order to resist resistance, to keep to the right paths, when desire, passion or interest tempt us aside, we must necessarily give ourselves reasons. Even if we have opposed the unlawful desire by another, the latter, conjured up by the will, could arise only at the call of an idea. In a word, an intelligent being generally exerts his influence on himself through the medium of intelligence. But from the fact that we get back to obligation by rational ways it does not follow that obligation was of a rational order. We shall dwell on this point later; we do not intend to discuss ethical theories for the present. Let us merely say that a tendency, natural or acquired, is one thing, another thing the necessarily rational method which a reasonable being will use to restore to it its force and to combat what is opposing it. In the latter case the tendency which has been obscured may reappear; and then everything doubtless happens as though we had succeeded by this method in reestablishing the tendency anew. In reality we have merely swept aside something that hampered or checked it. It comes to the same thing, I grant you, in practice: explain the fact in one way or another, the fact is there, we have achieved success. And in order to succeed it is perhaps better to imagine that things did happen in the former way. But to state that this is actually the case would be to vitiate the whole theory of obligation. Has not this been the case with most philosophers?

Let there be no misunderstanding. Even if we confine ourselves to a certain aspect of morality, as we have done up to now, we shall find many different attitudes towards duty. They line the intervening space between the extremes of two attitudes, or rather two habits: that of moving so naturally along the ways laid down by society as barely to notice them; or on the contrary hesitating and deliberating on which way to take, how far to go, the distances out and back we shall have to cover if we try several paths one after another. In the second case new problems arise with more or less frequency; and even in those instances where our duty is fully mapped out, we make all sorts of distinctions in fulfilling it. But, in the first place, the former attitude is that of the immense majority of men; it is probably general in backward communities. And, after all, however much we may reason in each particular case, formulate the maxim, enunciate the principle, deduce the consequences: if desire and passion join in the discussion, if temptation is strong, if we are on the point of falling, if suddenly we recover ourselves, what was it that pulled us up? A force asserts itself which we have called the "totality of obligation": the concentrated extract, the quintessence of innumerable specific habits of obedience to the countless particular requirements of social life. This force is no one particular thing and, if it could speak (whereas it prefers to act), it would say: "You must because you must." Hence the work done by intelligence in weighing reasons, comparing maxims, going back to first principles, was to introduce more logical consistency into a line of conduct subordinated by its very nature to the claims of society; but this social claim was the real root of obligation. Never, in our hours of temptation, should we sacrifice to the mere need for logical consistency our interest, our passion, our vanity. Because in a reasonable being reason does indeed intervene as a regulator to assure this consistency between obligatory rules or maxims, philososphy has been led to look upon it as a principle of obligation. We might as well believe that the fly-wheel drives the machinery.

Besides, the demands of a society dovetail into one another. Even the individual whose decent behaviour is the least based on reasoning and, if I may put it so, the most conventional, introduces a rational order into his conduct by the mere fact of obeying rules which are logically connected together. I freely admit that such logic has been late in taking possession of society. Logical co-ordination is essentially economy. From a whole it first roughly extracts certain principles and then excludes everything which is not in accordance with them. Nature, by contrast, is lavish. The closer a community is to nature, the greater the proportion of unaccountable and inconsistent rules it lays down. We find in primitive races many prohibitions and prescriptions explicable at most by vague associations of ideas, by superstition, by automatism. Nor are they without their use, since the obedience of everyone to laws, even absurd ones, assures greater cohesion to the community. But in that case the usefulness of the rule accrues, by a kind of reverse action, solely from the fact of our submission to it. Prescriptions or prohibitions which are intrinsically useful are those that are explicitly designed for the preservation or well-being of society. No doubt they have gradually detached themselves from the others and survived them. Social demands have therefore been co-ordinated with each other and subordinated to principles. But no matter. Logic permeates indeed present-day communities, and even the man who does not reason out his conduct will live reasonably if he conforms to these principles.

But the essence of obligation is a different thing from a requirement of reason. This is all we have tried to suggest so far. Our description would, we think, correspond more and more to reality as one came to deal with less developed communities and more rudimentary stages of consciousness. It remains a bare out-line so long as we confine ourselves to the normal conscience, such as is found to-day in the ordinary decent person. But precisely be-cause we are in this case dealing with a strange complex of feel-ings, of ideas and tendencies all interpenetrating each other, we shall avoid artificial analyses and arbitrary syntheses only if we have at hand an outline which gives the essential. Such is the out-line we have attempted to trace. Conceive obligation as weighing on the will like a habit, each obligation dragging behind it the accumulated mass of the others, and utilising thus for the pressure it is exerting the weight of the whole: here you have the totality of obligation for a simple, elementary, moral conscience. That is the essential: that is what obligation could, if necessary, be re-duced to, even in those cases where it attains its highest com-plexity.

This shows when and in what sense (how slightly Kantian!) obligation in its elementary state takes the form of a "categorical imperative." We should find it very difficult to discover examples of such an imperative in everyday life. A military order, which is a command that admits neither reason nor reply, does say in fact: "You must because you must." But, though you may give the soldier no reason, he will imagine one. If we want a pure case of the categorical imperative, we must construct one *a priori* or at least make an arbitrary abstraction of experience. So let us im-agine an ant who is stirred by a gleam of reflection and thereupon judges she has been wrong to work unremittingly for others. Her inclination to laziness would indeed endure but a few moments, just as long as the ray of intelligence. In the last of these moments, when instinct regaining the mastery would drag her back by sheer force to her task, intelligence at the point of relapsing into in-stinct would say, as its parting word: "You must because you must." This "must because you must" would only be the mo-mentary feeling of awareness of a tug which the ant experiences —the tug which the string, momentarily relaxed, exerts as it drags her back. The same command would ring in the ear of a sleep-walker on the point of waking, or even actually beginning to wake, from the dream he is enacting: if he lapsed back at once into a hypnotic state, a categorical imperative would express in words, on behalf of the reflexion which had just been on the point of emerging and had instantly disappeared, the inevitableness of the relapse. In a word, an absolutely categorical imperative is instinctive or somnambulistic, enacted as such in a normal state, represented as such if reflexion is roused long enough to take form, not long enough to seek for reasons. But, then, is it not evident that, in a reasonable being, an imperative will tend to become categorical in proportion as the activity brought into play, although intelligent, will tend to become instinctive? But an activity which, starting as intelligent, progresses towards an imitation of instinct is exactly what we call, in man, a habit. And the most powerful habit, the habit whose strength is made up of the accumulated force of all the elementary social habits, is necessarily the one which best imitates instinct. Is it then surprising that, in the short moment which separates obligation merely experienced as a living force from obligation fully realized and justified by all sorts of reasons, obligation should indeed take the form of the categorical imperative: "you must because you must"?

Let us consider two divergent lines of evolution with societies at the extremities of each. The type of society which will appear the more natural will obviously be the instinctive type; the link that unites the bees of a hive resembles far more the link which holds together the cells of an organism, coordinate and subordinate to one another. Let us suppose for an instant that nature has intended to produce at the extremity of the second line societies where a certain latitude was left to individual choice: she would have arranged that intelligence should achieve here results comparable, as regards their regularity, to those of instinct in the other; she would have had recourse to habit. Each of these habits, which may be called "moral," would be incidental. But the aggregate of them, I mean the habit of contracting these habits, being at the very basis of societies and a necessary condition of their existence, would have a force comparable to that of instinct in respect of both intensity and regularity. This is exactly what we have called the "totality of obligation." This, be it said, will apply only to human societies at the moment of emerging from the hands of nature. It will apply to primitive and to elementary societies. But, however much human society may progress, grow complicated and spiritualized, the original design, expressing the purpose of nature, will remain.

Now this is exactly what has happened. Without going deeply into a matter we have dealt with elsewhere, let us simply say that intelligence and instinct are forms of consciousness which must have interpenetrated each other in their rudimentary state and become dissociated as they grew. This development occurred on the two main lines of evolution of animal life, with the Arthropods and the Vertebrates. At the end of the former we have the instinct of insects, more especially the Hymenoptera; at the end of the second, human intelligence. Instinct and intelligence have each as their essential object the utilisation of implements: in the first case, organs supplied by nature and hence immutable; in the second, invented tools, and therefore varied and unforeseen. The implement is, moreover, designed for a certain type of work, and this work is all the more efficient the more it is specialized, the more it is divided up between diversely qualified workers who mutually supplement one another. Social life is thus immanent, like a vague ideal, in instinct as well as in intelligence: this ideal finds its most complete expression in the hive or the ant-hill on the one hand, in human societies on the other. Whether human or animal, a society is an organization; it implies a co-ordination and generally also a subordination of elements; it therefore exhibits, whether merely embodied in life or, in addition, specifically form-ulated, a collection of rules and laws. But in a hive or an ant-hill the individual is riveted to his task by his structure, and the or-ganization is relatively invariable, whereas the human community is variable in form, open to every kind of progress. The result is that in the former each rule is laid down by nature, and is neces-sary: whereas in the latter only one thing is natural, the necessity of a rule. Thus the more, in human society, we delve down to the root of the various obligations to reach obligation in general, the more obligation will tend to become necessity, the nearer it will draw, in its peremptory aspect, to instinct. And yet we should make a great mistake if we tried to ascribe any particular obliga-tion, whatever it might be, to instinct. What we must perpetually recall is that, no one obligation being instinctive, obligation as a whole *would have been* instinct if human societies were not, so to speak, ballasted with variability and intelligence. It is a virtual instinct, like that which lies behind the habit of speech. The morality of a human society may indeed be compared to its lan-

guage. If ants exchange signs, which seems probable, those signs
are provided by the very instinct that makes the ants communicate
with one another. On the contrary, our languages are the product
of custom. Nothing in the vocabulary, or even in the syntax, comes
from nature. But speech is natural, and unvarying signs, natural
in origin, which are presumably used in a community of insects,
exhibit what our language would have been, if nature in bestowing on us the faculty of speech had not added that function which,
since it makes and uses tools, is inventive and called intelligence.
We must perpetually recur to what obligation *would have been*
if human society had been instinctive instead of intelligent: this
will not explain any particular obligation, we shall even give of
obligation in general an idea which would be false, if we went no
further; and yet we must think of this instinctive society as the
counterpart of intelligent society, if we are not to start without
any clue in quest of the foundations of morality.

From this point of view obligation loses its specific character. It
ranks among the most general phenomena of life. When the elements which go to make up an organism submit to a rigid discipline, can we say that they feel themselves liable to obligation
and that they are obeying a social instinct? Obviously not; but
whereas such an organism is barely a community, the hive and
the ant-hill are actual organisms, the elements of which are united
by invisible ties, and the social instinct of an ant—I mean the force
by virtue of which the worker, for example, performs the task to
which she is predestined by her structure—cannot differ radically
from the cause, whatever it be, by virtue of which every tissue,
every cell of a living body, toils for the greatest good of the
whole. Indeed it is, strictly speaking, no more a matter of obligation in the one case than in the other, but rather of necessity. It
is just this necessity that we perceive, not actual but virtual, at the
foundations of moral obligation, as through a more or less transparent veil. A human being feels an obligation only if he is free,
and each obligation, considered separately, implies liberty. But it
is necessary that there should be obligations; and the deeper we
go, away from those particular obligations which are at the top,
towards obligation in general, or, as we have said, towards obligation as a whole, which is at the bottom, the more obligation appears as the very form assumed by necessity in the realm of life,

when it demands, for the accomplishment of certain ends, intelligence, choice, and therefore liberty.

Here again it may be alleged that this applies to very simple human societies, that is to say primitive or rudimentary societies. Certainly, but, as we shall have occasion to point out later, civilized man differs from primitive man above all by the enormous mass of knowledge and habits which he has absorbed, since the first awakening of his consciousness, from the social surroundings in which they were stored up. What is natural is in great measure overlaid by what is acquired; but it endures, almost unchangeable, throughout the centuries; habits and knowledge by no means impregnate the organism to the extent of being transmitted by heredity, as used to be supposed. It is true that we could consider what is natural as negligible in our analysis of obligation, if it had been crushed out by the acquired habits which have accumulated over it in the course of centuries of civilization. But it remains in excellent condition, very much alive, in the most civilized society. To it we must revert, not to account for this or that social obligation, but to explain what we have called obligation as a whole. Our civilized communities, however different they may be from the society to which we were primarily destined by nature, exhibit indeed, with respect to that society, a fundamental resemblance.

For they too are closed societies. They may be very extensive compared to the small agglomerations to which we were drawn by instinct and which the same instinct would probably tend to revive to-day if all the material and spiritual acquisitions of civilization were to disappear from the social environment in which we find them stored; their essential characteristic is none the less to include at any moment a certain number of individuals, and exclude others. We have said above, that underlying moral obligation there was a social demand. Of what society were we speaking? Was it of that open society represented by all mankind? We did not settle the matter, any more than one usually does when speaking of a man's duty to his fellows; one remains prudently vague; one refrains from making any assertion, but one would like to have it believed that "human society" is already an accomplished fact. And it is well that we should like to have it believed, for if incontestably we have duties towards man as man (although these duties have an entirely different origin, as we shall see a little later) we should risk undermining them, were we to make a radical distinction between them and our duties to our fellow-citizens. This is right enough so far as action is concerned. But a moral philosophy which does not emphasize this distinction misses the truth; its analyses will thereby be inevitably distorted. In fact, when we lay down that the duty of respecting the life and property of others is a fundamental demand of social life, what society do we mean? To find an answer we need only think what happens in time of war. Murder and pillage and perfidy, cheating and lying become not only lawful, they are actually praiseworthy. The warring nations can say, with Macbeth's witches: "Fair is foul, and foul is fair." Would this be possible, would the transformation take place so easily, generally and instantaneously, if it were really a certain attitude of man towards man that society had been enjoining on us up till then? Oh, I know what society says (it has, I repeat, its reasons for saying so); but to know what it thinks and what it wants, we must not listen too much to what it says, we must look at what it does. It says that the duties it defines are indeed, in principle, duties towards humanity, but that under exceptional circumstances, regrettably unavoidable, they are for the time being inapplicable. If society did not express itself thus, it would bar the road to progress for another morality, not derived from it, which it has every inducement to humour. On the other hand, it is consistent with our habits of mind to consider as abnormal anything relatively rare or exceptional, disease for instance. But disease is as normal as health, which, viewed from a certain standpoint, appears as a constant effort to prevent disease or to avoid it. In the same way, peace has always hitherto been a preparation for defence or even attack, at any rate for war. Our social duties aim at social cohesion; whether we will or no they compose for us an attitude which is that of discipline in the face of the enemy. This means that, however much society may endow man, whom it has trained to discipline, with all it has acquired during centuries of civilization, society still has need of that primitive instinct which it coats with so thick a varnish. In a word, the social instinct which we have detected at the basis of social obligation always has in view—instinct being relatively unchangeable—a closed society, however large. It is doubtless overlaid by another morality which for that very reason it supports and to which it lends something of its force, I mean of its imperative character. But it is not itself concerned with humanity. For between the nation, however big, and humanity there lies the whole distance from the finite to the indefinite, from the closed to the open. We are fond of saying that the apprenticeship to civic virtue is served in the family, and that in the same way, from holding our country dear, we learn to love mankind. Our sympathies are supposed to broaden out in a unbroken progression, to expand while remaining identical, and to end by embracing all humanity. This is *a priori* reasoning, the result of a purely intellectualist conception of the soul. We observe that the three groups to which we can attach ourselves comprise an increasing number of people, and we conclude that a progressive expansion of feeling keeps pace with the increasing size of the object we love. And what encourages the illusion is that, by a forunate coincidence, the first part of the argument chances to fit in with the facts; domestic virtues are indeed bound up with civic virtues, for the very simple reason that family and society, originally undifferentiated, have remained closely connected. But between the society in which we live and humanity in general there is, we repeat, the same contrast as between the closed and the open; the difference between the two objects is one of kind and not simply one of degree. How much greater it would be if, passing to the realm of feeling, we compared with each other the two sentiments, love of country and love of mankind! Who can help seeing that social cohesion is largely due to the necessity for a community to protect itself against others, and that it is primarily as against all other men that we love the men with whom we live? Such is the primitive instinct. It is still there, though fortunately hidden under the accretions of civilization; but even to-day we still love naturally and directly our parents and our fellow-countrymen, whereas love of mankind is indirect and acquired. We go straight to the former, to the latter we come only by roundabout ways; for it is only through God, in God, that religion bids man love mankind; and likewise it is through reason alone, that Reason in whose communion we are all partakers, that philosophers make us look at humanity in order to show us the pre-eminent dignity of the human being, the right of all to command respect. Neither in the one case nor the other do we come to humanity by degrees, through the stages of the family and the nation. We must, in a single bound, be carried far beyond it, and, without having made it our goal, reach it by outstripping it. Besides, whether we speak the language of religion or the language of philosophy, whether it be a question of love or respect, a different morality, another kind of obligation supervenes, above and beyond the social pressure. So far we have only dealt with the latter. The time has come to pass to the other.

We have been searching for pure obligation. To find it we have had to reduce morality to its simplest expression. The advantage of this has been to indicate in what obligation consisted; the disadvantage, to narrow down morality enormously. Not indeed because that part of it which we have left on one side is not obligatory: is there such a thing as a duty which is not compulsory? But it is conceivable that, starting from a primitive basis of obligation pure and simple, such as we have just defined, this obligation should radiate, expand, and even come to be absorbed into something that transfigures it. Let us now see what complete morality would be like. We shall use the same method and once more proceed, not downwards as up to now but upwards, to the extreme limit.

In all times there have arisen exceptional men, incarnating this morality. Before the saints of Christianity, mankind had known the sages of Greece, the prophets of Israel, the Arahants of Buddhism, and others besides. It is to them that men have always turned for that complete morality which we had best call absolute morality. And this very fact is at once characteristic and instructive; this very fact suggests to us the existence of a difference of kind and not merely one of degree between the morality with which we have been dealing up to now and that we are about to study, between the minimum and the maximum, between the two extremes. Whereas the former is all the more unalloyed and perfect precisely in proportion as it is the more readily reduced to impersonal formulae, the second, in order to be fully itself, must be incarnate in a privileged person who becomes an example. The generality of the one consists in the universal acceptance of a law, that of the other in a common imitation of a model.

Why is it, then, that saints have their imitators, and why do the great moral leaders draw the masses after them? They ask nothing, and yet they receive. They have no need to exhort; their mere existence suffices. For such is precisely the nature of this other morality. Whereas natural obligation is a pressure or a propulsive force, complete and perfect morality has the effect of an appeal.

Only those who have come into touch with a great moral personality have fully realized the nature of this appeal. But we all, at those momentous hours when our usual maxims of conduct strike us as inadequate, have wondered what such or such a one would have expected of us under the circumstances. It might have been a relation or a friend whom we thus evoked in thought. But it might quite as well have been a man we had never met, whose life-story had merely been told us, and to whose judgment we in imagination submitted our conduct, fearful of his censure, proud of his approval. It might even be a personality brought up from the depths of the soul into the light of consciousness, stirring into life within us, which we felt might completely pervade us later, and to which we wished to attach ourselves for the time being, as the disciple to his teacher. As a matter of fact this personality takes shape as soon as we adopt a model; the longing to resemble, which ideally generates the form, is an incipient resemblance; the word which we shall make our own is the word whose echo we have heard within ourselves. But the person matters little. Let us merely make the point that, whereas the first morality was the more potent the more distinctly it broke up into impersonal obligation, on the contrary the latter morality, at first dispersed among general precepts to which our intelligence gave its allegiance, but which did not go so far as to set our will in motion, becomes more and more cogent in proportion as the multiplicity and generality of its maxims merge more completely into a man's unity and individuality.

Whence does it derive its strength? What is the principle of action which here takes the place of the natural obligation, or rather which ends by absorbing it? To discover this, let us first see what is tacitly demanded of us. The duties dealt with so far are those imposed on us by social life; they are binding in respect of the city more than in respect of humanity. You might say that the second morality—if we *do* distinguish two—differs from the first in that it is human instead of being merely social. And you would not be entirely wrong. For we have seen that it is not by widening the bounds of the city that you reach humanity; between a social morality and a human morality the difference is not one of degree but of kind. The former is the one of which we are generally thinking when we feel a natural obligation. Superimposed upon these clearly defined duties we like to imagine others, the lines of which are perhaps a little blurred. Loyalty, sacrifice of self, the spirit of renunciation, charity, such are the words we use when we think of these things. But have we, generally speaking, in mind at such times anything more than words? Probably not, and we fully realize this. It is sufficient, we say, that the formula is there; it will take on its full meaning, the idea which is to fill it out will become operative, when the occasion arises. It is true that for many people the occasion will never arise or the action will be put off till later. With certain people the will does make a feeble start, but so feeble that the slight shock they feel can in fact be attributed to no more than the expansion of social duty broadened and weakened into human duty. But only let these formulae be invested with substance, and that substance become animate, lo and behold! a new life is proclaimed; we understand, we feel the advent of a new morality. Consequently, in speaking here of love of humanity we should doubtless be denoting this morality. And yet we should not be expressing the essence of it, for the love of humanity is not a self-sufficient force or one which has a direct efficacy. The teachers of the young know full well that you cannot prevail over egoism by recommending "altruism." It even happens that a generous nature, eager to sacrifice itself, experiences a sudden chill at the idea that it is working "for mankind." The object is too vast, the effect too diffuse. We may therefore conjecture that if a love of humanity constitutes this morality, it constitutes it in much the same way as the intention of reaching a certain point implies the necessity of crossing an intervening space. In one sense it is the same thing; in another sense it is something entirely different. If we think only of the interval and the various points, infinite in number, which we still have to pass one by one, we shall be discouraged from starting, like Zeno's arrow, and besides there would be no object, no inducement. But if we step across the intervening space, thinking only of the goal

or looking even beyond it, we shall easily accomplish a simple
act, and at the same time overcome the infinite multiplicity of
which this simplicity is the equivalent. What then, in this case, is
the goal, what the direction of the effort? What exactly, in a word,
is required of us?

Let us first define the moral attitude of the man we have been
considering up to now. He is part and parcel of society; he and it
are absorbed together in the same task of individual and social
preservation. Both are self-centred. True, it is doubtful whether
private interest invariably agrees with public interest: we know
against what insurmountable difficulties utilitarian ethics has always come up when it laid down the principle that the individual
could seek only his own good, while maintaining that this would
lead him to desire the good of others. An intelligent being, pursuing his personal advantage, will often do something quite different from what the general interest demands. Yet, if utilitarian
ethics persists in recurring in one form or another, this means that
it is not untenable, and if it is tenable the reason is precisely
because, beneath the intelligent activity, forced in fact to choose
between its own interests and those of others, there lies a substratum of instinctive activity, originally implanted there by nature,
where the individual and the social are well-nigh indistinguishable. The cell lives for itself and also for the organism, imparting
to it vitality and borrowing vitality from it; it will sacrifice itself
to the whole, if need be; and it would doubtless then say, if it were
conscious, that it made this sacrifice in its own interest. Such
would probably be the state of mind of an ant reflecting on her
conduct. She would feel that her activity hinges on something
intermediate between the good of the ant and the good of the ant-
hill. Now it is just with this fundamental instinct that we have
associated obligation as such; it implies at the beginning a state
of things in which the individual and society are not distinguishable. This is what enables us to say that the attitude to which it
corresponds is that of an individual and a community concentrated
on themselves. At once individual and social, the soul here moves
round in a circle. It is closed.

The other attitude is that of the open soul. What, in that case,
is allowed in? Suppose we say that it embraces all humanity: we
should not be going too far, we should hardly be going far enough,

since its love may extend to animals, to plants, to all nature. And yet no one of these things which would thus fill it would suffice to define the attitude taken by the soul, for it could, strictly speaking, do without all of them. Its form is not dependent on its content. We have just filled it; we could as easily empty it again. "Charity" would persist in him who possesses "charity," though there be no other living creature on earth.

Once again, it is not by a process of expansion of the self that we can pass from the first state to the second. A psychology which is too purely intellectualist, following the indications of speech, will doubtless define feelings by the things with which they are associated; love for one's family, love for one's country, love of mankind, it will see in these three inclinations one single feeling, growing ever larger, to embrace an increasing number of persons. The fact that these feelings are outwardly expressed by the same attitude or the same sort of motion, that all three *incline* us to something, enables us to group them under the concept "love," and to express them by one and the same word; we then distinguish them by naming three objects, each larger than the other, to which they are supposed to apply. This does in fact suffice to distinguish them. But does it describe them? Or analyse them? At a glance, consciousness perceives between the two first feelings and the third a difference of kind. The first imply a choice, therefore an exclusion; they may act as incentives to strife, they do not exclude hatred. The latter is all love. The former alight directly on an object which attracts them. The latter does not yield to the attraction of its object; it has not aimed at this object; it has shot beyond and reached humanity only by passing through humanity. Has it, strictly speaking, an object? We shall ask this question. But for the present we shall confine ourselves to noting that this psychic attitude, or rather psychic motion, is self-sufficient.

Nevertheless there arises in regard to it a problem which stands ready solved in the case of the other. For that other was ordained by nature; we have just seen how and why we feel bound to adopt it. But the second attitude is acquired; it calls for, has always called for, an effort. How comes it that the men who have set the example have found other men to follow them? And what is the power that is in this case the counterpart of social pressure? We have no choice. Beyond instinct and habit there is no direct action on the will except feeling. The impulse given by feeling can indeed closely resemble obligation. Analyse the passion of love, particularly in its early stages; is pleasure its aim? Could we not as well say it is pain? Perhaps a tragedy lies ahead, a whole life wrecked, wasted, ruined, we know it, we feel it, no matter, we must because we must. Indeed the worst perfidy of a nascent passion is that it counterfeits duty. But we need not go as far as passion. Into the most peaceful emotion there may enter a certain demand for action, which differs from obligation as described above in that it will meet with no resistance, in that it imposes only what has already been acquiesced in, but which none the less resembles obligation in that it does impose something. Nowhere do we see this more clearly than in those cases where the demand ceases to have any practical consequence, thus leaving us the leisure to reflect upon it and analyse what we feel. This is what occurs in musical emotion, for example. We feel, while we listen, as though we could not desire anything else but what the music is suggesting to us, and that that is just as we should naturally and necessarily act did we not refrain from action to listen. Let the music express joy or grief, pity or love, every moment we are what it expresses. Not only ourselves, but many others, nay, all the others, too. When music weeps, all humanity, all nature, weeps with it. In point of fact it does not introduce these feelings into us; it introduces us into them, as passers-by are forced into a street dance. Thus do pioneers in morality proceed. Life holds for them unsuspected tones of feeling like those of some new symphony, and they draw us after them into this music that we may express it in action.

It is through excess of intellectualism that feeling is made to hinge on an object and that all emotion is held to be the reaction of our sensory faculties to an intellectual representation. Taking again the example of music, we all know that it arouses in us well-defined emotions, joy, sorrow, pity, love, that these emotions may be intense and that to us they are complete, though not attached to anything in particular. Are you going to say that we are here in the realm of art and not among real things, that therefore we are playing at emotion, that our feeling is purely imaginative, and that, anyway, the musician could not produce this emotion in us, suggest it without causing it, if we had not already experienced it in real life, where it was caused by an object from which art had merely to detach it? That would be to forget that joy and sorrow, pity and love, are words expressing generalities, words which we must call upon to express what music makes us feel, whereas each new musical work brings with it new feelings, which are created by that music and within that music, are defined and delimited by the lines, unique of their kind, of the melody or symphony. They have therefore not been extracted from life by art; it is we who, in order to express them in words, are driven to compare the feeling created by the artist with the feeling most resembling it in life. But let us then take states of emotion caused in effect by certain things and, as it were, prefigured in them. Those ordained by nature are finite, that is to say limited in number. They are recognizable because they are destined to spur us on to acts answering to needs. The others, on the contrary, are real inventions, comparable to those of the musician, at the origin of which there has always been a man. Thus mountains may, since the beginning of time, have had the faculty of rousing in those who looked upon them certain feelings comparable with sensations, and indeed inseparable from mountains. But Rousseau created in connection with them a new and original emotion. This emotion has become current coin, Rousseau having put it into circulation. And even to-day it is Rousseau who makes us feel it, as much and more than the mountains. True, there are reasons why this emotion, sprung from the heart of Jean-Jacques, should fasten on to mountains rather than any other object; the elementary feelings, akin to sensations, which were directly aroused by mountains must have been able to harmonize with the new emotion. But Rousseau gathered them together, gave them their places, henceforth as mere harmonies in a sound for which he provided, by a true creation, the principal tone. It is the same with love of nature in general. Nature has ever aroused feelings which are almost sensations; people have always enjoyed the pleasant shade, the cool waters, etc., in fine all those things suggested in the word "amœnus" by which the Romans described the charm of the country. But a fresh emotion, surely the creation of some person or persons, has arisen and used these pre-existing notes as harmonics, and produced in this way something to be compared with the fresh tones of a new instrument, what we call in our respective countries the sentiment of nature. The fundamental tone thus introduced might have been different, as is the case in the East, in Japan especially: the *timbre* would then have been different. Feelings akin to sensation, closely bound up with the objects which give rise to them, are indeed just as likely to attract a previously created emotion as they are to connect with an entirely new one. This is what happened with love. From time immemorial woman must have inspired man with an inclination distinct from desire, but in immediate contact, as though welded to it, and pertaining both to feeling and to sensation. But romantic love has a definite date: it sprang up during the Middle Ages on the day when some person or persons conceived the idea of absorbing love into a kind of supernatural feeling, into religious emotion as created by Christianity and launched by the new religion into the world. When critics reproach mysticism with expressing itself in the same terms as passionate love, they forget that it was love which began by plagiarizing mysticism, borrowing from it its fervour, its raptures, its ecstasies: in using the language of a passion it had transfigured, mysticism has only resumed possession of its own. We may add that the nearer love is to adoration, the greater the disproportion between the emotion and the object, the deeper therefore the disappointment to which the lover is exposed—unless he decides that he will ever look at the object through the mist of the emotion and never touch it, that he will, in a word, treat it religiously. Note that the ancients had already spoken of the illusions of love, but these were errors akin to those of the senses, and they concerned the face of the beloved, her figure, her bearing, her character. Think of Lucretius' description: the illusion here applies only to the qualities of the loved one, and not, as with the modern illusion, to what we can expect of love. Between the old illusion and the illusion we have superadded to it there is the same difference as between the primitive feeling, emanating from the object itself, and the religious emotion summoned from without by which it has been pervaded and eventually submerged. The margin left for disappointment is now enormous, for it is the gap between the divine and the human.

That a new emotion is the source of the great creations of art, of science and of civilization in general there seems to be no doubt. Not only because emotion is a stimulus, because it incites the intelligence to undertake ventures and the will to persevere with them. We must go much further. There are emotions which beget thought; and invention, though it belongs to the category of the intellect, may partake of sensibility in its substance. For we must agree upon the meaning of the words "emotion," "feeling" and "sensibility." An emotion is an affective stirring of the soul, but a surface agitation is one thing, an upheaval of the depths another. The effect is in the first case diffused, in the second it remains undivided. In the one it is an oscillation of the parts without any displacement of the whole; in the other the whole is driven forward. Let us, however, get away from metaphors. We must distinguish between two kinds of emotion, two varieties of feeling, two manifestations of sensibility which have this one feature in common, that they are emotional states distinct from sensation, and cannot be reduced, like the latter, to the psychical transposition of a physical stimulus. In the first case the emotion is the consequence of an idea, or of a mental picture; the "feeling" is indeed the result of an intellectual state which owes nothing to it, which is self-sufficient, and which, if it does experience a certain reaction from the feeling, loses more than it gains. It is the stirring of sensibility by a representation, as it were, dropped into it. But the other kind of emotion is not produced by a representation which it follows and from which it remains distinct. Rather is it, in relation to the intellectual states which are to supervene, a cause and not an effect; it is pregnant with representations, not one of which is actually formed, but which it draws or might draw from its own substance by an organic development. The first is infra-intellectual; that is the one with which the psychologist is generally concerned, and it is this we have in mind when we contrast sensibility with intelligence, and when we make of emotions a vague reflection of the representation. But of the other we should be inclined to say that it is supra-intellectual, if the word did not immediately and exclusively evoke the idea of superiority of value: it is just as much a question of priority in time, and of the relation between that which generates and that which is generated. Indeed, the second kind of emotion can alone be productive of ideas.

This is just what the critic overlooks when he qualifies as "feminine," with a touch of contempt, a psychology which accords so extensive and so handsome a place to sensibility. First of all he should be blamed for abiding by the current commonplaces about women, when it is so easy to use one's eyes. I do not intend, for the mere sake of correcting an inappropriate word, to enter upon a comparative study of the two sexes. Suffice it to say that woman is as intelligent as man, but that she is less capable of emotion, and that if there is any faculty or power of the soul which seems to attain less development in woman than in man, it is not intelligence, but sensibility. I mean of course sensibility in the depths, not agitation at the surface. [1] But no matter. When the critic fancies that he would do injustice to man if he related to sensibility the highest faculties of the mind, he is still more to be blamed for not seeing precisely where the difference lies between that intelligence which understands, discusses, accepts or rejects— which in a word limits itself to criticism—and the intelligence which invents.

Creation signifies, above all, emotion, and that not in literature or art alone. We all know the concentration and effort implied in scientific discovery. Genius has been defined as "an infinite capacity for taking pains." True, we think of intelligence as something apart, and, too, as something equally apart a general faculty of attention which, when more or less developed, is supposed to produce a greater or less concentration of intelligence. But could this indeterminate attention, extraneous to intelligence, bring out of intelligence something which is not there? We cannot help feeling that psychology is once more the dupe of language when, having used the same word to denote all efforts of attention made in all possible cases, and having thus been deceived into assuming them to be all of the same quality, it perceives between them only differences of degree. The truth is that in each case attention takes on a distinctive colouring, as though individualized by the object to which it applies: this is why psychology has already a

[1] We need hardly say that there are many exceptions. Religious fervour, for example, can attain, in women, to undreamt-of depths. But nature has probably ordained, as a general rule, that woman should concentrate on her child and confine within somewhat narrow bounds the best of her sensibility. In this department she is indeed incomparable; here the emotion is supra-intellectual in that it becomes divination. How many things rise up in the vision of a mother as she gazes in wonder upon her little one? Illusion perhaps! This is not certain. Let us rather say that reality is big with possibilities, and that the mother sees in the child not only what he will become, but also what he would become, if he were not obliged, at every step in his life, to choose and therefore to exclude.

tendency to use the term "interest" as much as "attention," thus
implicity introducing sensibility, as being capable of more extensive variation according to particular cases. But then this diversity
is not sufficiently insisted upon; a general faculty of being interested is posited, which, while always the same faculty, once again
affords variety only through a greater or less application to its object. So do not let us speak of interest in general. Let us rather
say that the problem which has aroused interest is a representation
duplicated by an emotion, and that the emotion, being at one
and the same time curiosity, desire and the anticipated joy of
solving a stated problem, is, like the representation, unique. It is
the emotion which drives the intelligence forward in spite of obstacles. It is the emotion above all which vivifies, or rather vitalizes, the intellectual elements with which it is destined to unite,
constantly collecting everything that can be worked in with them
and finally compelling the enunciation of the problem to expand
into its solution. And what about literature and art? A work of
genius is in most cases the outcome of an emotion, unique of its
kind, which seemed to baffle expression, and yet which *had* to express itself. But is not this so of all work, however imperfect, into
which there enters some degree of creativeness? Anyone engaged
in writing has been in a position to feel the difference between
an intelligence left to itself and that which burns with the fire of
an original and unique emotion, born of the identification of the
author with his subject, that is to say of intuition. In the first
case the mind cold-hammers the materials, combining together
ideas long since cast into words and which society supplies in a
solid form. In the second, it would seem that the solid materials
supplied by intelligence first melt and mix, then solidify again
into fresh ideas now shaped by the creative mind itself. If these
ideas find words already existing which can express them, for each
of them this seems a piece of unexpected good luck; and, in truth,
it has often been necessary to assist fortune, and strain the meaning of a word, to mould it to the thought. In that event the effort
is painful and the result problematical. But it is in such a case
only that the mind feels itself, or believes itself, to be creative.
It no longer starts from a multiplicity of ready-made elements to
arrive at a composite unity made up of a new arrangement of the
old. It has been transported at a bound to something which seems

both one and unique, and which will contrive later to express itself, more or less satisfactorily, in concepts both multiple and common, previously provided by language.

To sum up, alongside of the emotion which is a result of the representation and which is added to it, there is the emotion which precedes the image, which virtually contains it, and is to a certain extent its cause. A play may be scarcely a work of literature and yet it may rack our nerves and cause an emotion of the first kind, intense, no doubt, but commonplace, culled from those we experience in the course of daily life, and in any case devoid of mental content. But the emotion excited within us by a great dramatic work is of quite a distinct character. Unique of its kind, it has sprung up in the soul of the poet and there alone, before stirring our own; from this emotion the work has sprung, to this emotion the author was continually harking back throughout the composition of the work. It was no more than a creative exigency, but it was a specific one, now satisfied once the work is finished, which would not have been satisfied by some other work unless that other had possessed an inward and profound resemblance with the former, such as that which exists between two equally satisfactory renderings, in terms of ideas or images, of one and the same melody.

Which amounts to saying that, in attributing to emotion a large share in the genesis of the moral disposition, we are not by any means enunciating a "moral philosophy of sentiment." For we are dealing with an emotion capable of crystallising into representations and even into an ethical doctrine. From this particular doctrine we could never have elicited the moral disposition any more than from any other; no amount of speculation will create an obligation or anything like it: the theory may be all very fine, I shall always be able to say that I will not accept it; and even if I do accept it, I shall claim to be free and do as I please. But if the atmosphere of the emotion is there, if I have breathed it in, if it has entered my being, I shall act in accordance with it, uplifted by it; not from constraint or necessity, but by virtue of an inclination which I should not want to resist. And instead of explaining my act by emotion itself, I might in this case just as well deduce it from the theory built up by the transposition of that emotion into ideas. We here get a glimpse of the possible reply to

a weighty question which we have just touched on incidentally
and with which we shall be confronted later. People are fond of
saying that if a religion brings us a new morality, it imposes that
morality by means of the metaphysics which it disposes us to accept, by its ideas on God, the universe, the relation of the one to
the other. To which the answer has been made that it is, on the
contrary, by the superiority of its morality that a religion wins over
souls and reveals to them a certain conception of things. But would
intelligence recognize the superiority of the proposed morality,
since it can appreciate differences of value only by comparing them
with a rule or an ideal, and this ideal and this rule are perforce
supplied by the morality which is already in occupation? On the
other hand, how could a new conception of the universal order
of things be anything but yet another philosophy to set alongside
of those we know? Even if our intelligence is won over, we shall
never see in it anything but an explanation, theoretically preferable to the others. Even if it seems to enjoin on us, as more in
harmony with itself, certain rules of conduct, there will be a wide
gap between this assent of the intellect and a conversion of the
will. But the truth is that the doctrine cannot, as a purely intellectual representation, ensure the adoption and, above all, the
practice of the corresponding morality, any more than the particular morality, considered by intelligence as a system of rules
of conduct, can render the doctrine intellectually preferable. Antecedent to the new morality, and also the new metaphysics, there
is the emotion, which develops as an impetus in the realm of the
will, and as an explicative representation in that of intelligence.
Take, for example, the emotion introduced by Christianity under
the name of charity: if it wins over souls, a certain behaviour
ensues and a certain doctrine is disseminated. But neither has its
metaphysics enforced the moral practice, nor the moral practice
induced a disposition to its metaphysics. Metaphysics and morality
express here the self-same thing, one in terms of intelligence, the
other in terms of will; and the two expressions of the thing are
accepted together, as soon as the thing is there to be expressed.

That a substantial half of our morality includes duties whose
obligatory character is to be explained fundamentally by the pressure of society on the individual will be readily granted, because
these duties are a matter of current practice, because they have

a clear precise formula, and it is therefore easy for us, by grasping them where they are entirely visible, and then going down to the roots, to discover the social requirements from which they sprang. But that the rest of morality expresses a certain emotional state, that actually we yield not to a pressure but to an attraction, many people will hesitate to acknowledge. The reason is that here we cannot, generally speaking, get back to the original emotion in the depths of our hearts. There exists formulae which are the residue of this emotion, and which have settled in what we may call the social conscience according as, within that emotion, a new conception of life took form—or rather a certain attitude towards life. Precisely because we find ourselves in the presence of the ashes of an extinct emotion, and because the driving power of that emotion came from the fire within it, the formulæ which have remained would generally be incapable of rousing our will, if older formulae, expressing the fundamental requirements of social life, did not by contagious influence communicate to them something of their own obligatory character. These two moralities, placed side by side, appear now to be only one, the first having lent to the second something of its imperative character and having, on the other hand, received from it in exchange a connotation less strictly social, more broadly human. But let us stir the ashes, we shall find some of them still warm, and at length the sparks will kindle into flame; the first may blaze up again; and, if it does, it will gradually spread. I mean that the maxims of the second morality do not work singly, like those of the first: as soon as one of them, ceasing to be abstract, becomes filled with significance and acquires the capacity to act, the others tend to do the same: at last they all fuse in the warm emotion which left them behind long ago, and in the men, now come to life again, who experienced it. Founders and reformers of religions, mystics and saints, obscure heroes of moral life whom we have met on our way and who are in our eyes the equals of the greatest, they are all there: inspired by their example, we follow them, as if we were joining an army of conquerors. They are indeed conquerors: they have broken down natural resistance and raised humanity to a new destiny. Thus, when we dispel appearances to get at reality, when we set aside the common form assumed, thanks to mutual exchanges, by the two moralities in conceptual thought and in speech, then, at the two extremes of the single morality we find pressure and aspiration: the former the more perfect as it becomes more impersonal, closer to those natural forces which we call habit or even instinct, the latter the more powerful according as it is more obviously aroused in us by definite persons, and the more it apparently triumphs over nature. True, if we went down to the roots of nature itself we should perhaps find that the same force which manifests itself directly, rotating on its own axis, in the human species once constituted, also acts later and indirectly, through the medium of privileged persons, in order to drive humanity forward.

But there is no need to resort to metaphysics to determine the relation between this pressure and this aspiration. Once again, there is some difficulty in comparing the two moralities because they are no longer to be found in a pure state. The first has handed on to the second something of its compulsive force; the second has diffused over the other something of its perfume. We find ourselves in the presence of a series of steps up or down, according as we range through the dictates of morality from one extreme or from the other; as to the two extreme limits, they have chiefly a theoretical interest; it is not often that they are actually attained. Let us, nevertheless, consider separately, in themselves, pressure and aspiration. Immanent in the former is the representation of a society which aims only at self-preservation; the circular movement in which it carries round with it individuals, as it revolves on the same spot, is a vague imitation, through the medium of habit, of the immobility of instinct. The feeling which would characterize the consciousness of these pure obligations, assuming they were all fulfilled, would be a state of individual and social well-being similar to that which accompanies the normal working of life. It would resemble pleasure rather than joy. The morality of aspiration, on the contrary, implicitly contains the feeling of progress. The emotion of which we were speaking is the enthusiasm of a forward movement, enthusiasm by means of which this morality has won over a few and has then, through them, spread over the world. "Progress" and "advance," moreover, are in this case indistinguishable from the enthusiasm itself. To become conscious of them it is not necessary that we should picture a goal that we are trying to reach or a perfection to which we are approximating. It is enough that the joy of enthusiasm involves something more than the pleasure of well-being: the pleasure not implying the joy, while the joy does imply and encompass the pleasure. We feel this to be so, and the certainty thus obtained, far from hinging on a metaphysical theory, is what will provide it with its firmest support.

But antecedent to this metaphysical theory, and far nearer to what we have directly experienced, are the simpler representations which in this case spring from the emotion in proportion as we dwell on it. We were speaking of the founders and reformers of religion, the mystics and the saints. Let us hearken to their language; it merely expresses in representations the emotions peculiar to a soul opening out, breaking with nature, which enclosed it both within itself and within the city.

They begin by saying that what they experience is a feeling of liberation. Well-being, pleasures, riches, all those things that mean so much to the common run of men, leave them indifferent. In breaking away from them they feel relief, and then exhilaration. Not that nature was wrong in attaching us by strong ties to the life she had ordained for us. But we must go further, and the amenities which are real comforts at home would become hindrances, burdensome, impedimenta, if we had to take them on our travels. That a soul thus equipped for action would be more drawn to sympathize with other souls, and even with the whole of nature, might surprise us, if the relative immobility of the soul, revolving in a circle in an enclosed society, was not due precisely to the fact that nature has split humanity into a variety of individuals by the very act which constituted the human species. Like all acts creative of a species, this was a halt on the road. By a resumption of the forward movement, the decision to halt is broken. True, to obtain a complete effect, the privileged soul would have to carry the rest of humanity with it. But if a few follow, and if the others imagine they would do likewise on occasion, this already means a great deal; henceforth, with the beginning of accomplishment, there will be the hope that the circle may be broken in the end. In any case, we cannot repeat too often that it is not by preaching the love of our neighbour that we can obtain it. It is not by expanding our narrower feelings that we can embrace humanity. However much our intelligence may convince itself that this is the line of advance, things behave differently. What is simple for our understanding is not necessarily so for our will. In cases where logic affirms that a certain road should be the shortest, experience intervenes, and finds that in that direction there is no road. The truth is that heroism may be the only way to love. Now, heroism cannot be preached, it has only to show itself, and its mere presence may stir others to action. For heroism itself is a return to movement, and enanates from an emotion—infectious like all emotions—akin to the creative act. Religion expresses this truth in its own way by saying that it is in God that we love all other men. And all great mystics declare that they have the impression of a current passing from their soul to God, and flowing back again from God to mankind.

Let no one speak of material obstacles to a soul thus freed! It will not answer that we can get round the obstacle, or that we can break it; it will declare that there is no obstacle. We cannot even say of this moral conviction that it moves mountains, for it sees no mountains to move. So long as you argue about the obstacle, it will stay where it is; and so long as you look at it, you will divide it into parts which will have to be overcome one by one; there may be no limit to their number; perhaps you will never exhaust them. But you can do away with the whole, at a stroke, if you deny its existence. That is what the philosopher did who proved movement by walking: his act was the negation pure and simple of the effort, perpetually to be renewed, and therefore fruitless, which Zeno judged indispensable to cover, one by one, the stages of the intervening space. By going deeply into this new aspect of morality, we should find an impression of coincidence, real or imaginary, with the generative effort of life. If seen from outside, the activity of life lends itself, in each of its works, to an analysis which might be carried on indefinitely; there is no end to a description of the structure of an eye such as ours. But what we call a series of means employed is, in reality, but a number of obstacles overcome; the action of nature is simple, and the infinite complexity of the mechanism which it seems to have built up piece by piece to achieve the power of vision is but the endless network of opposing forces which have cancelled one another out to secure an uninterrupted channel for the functioning of the faculty. So, if we took into account only what we saw, the simple act of an invisible hand plunged into iron filings would seem like an inexhaustible interplay of actions and reactions among the filings themselves in order that they might effect an equilibrium. If such is the contrast between the real working of life and the aspect it presents to the senses and the intelligence which analyse it, is it surprising that a soul which no more recognizes any material obstacle should feel itself, rightly or wrongly, at one with the principle of life?

Whatever heterogeneity we may at first find between the effect and the cause, and though the distance is great from a rule of conduct to a power of nature, it has always been from the contact with the generative principle of the human species that a man has felt he drew the strength to love mankind. By this I mean, of course, a love which absorbs and kindles the whole soul. But a more lukewarm love, faint and fleeting, can only be a radiation of the former, if not a still paler and colder image of it, left behind in the mind or deposited in speech. Thus, morality comprises two different parts, one of which follows from the original structure of human society, while the other finds its explanation in the principle which explains this structure. In the former, obligation stands for the pressure exerted by the elements of society on one another in order to maintain the shape of the whole; a pressure whose effect is prefigured in each of us by a system of habits which, so to speak, go to meet it: this mechanism, of which each separate part is a habit, but whose whole is comparable to an instinct, has been prepared by nature. In the second, there is still obligation, if you will, but that obligation is the force of an aspiration or an impetus, of the very impetus which culminated in the human species, in social life, in a system of habits which bears a resemblance more or less to instinct: the primitive impetus here comes into play directly, and no longer through the medium of the mechanisms it had set up, and at which it had provisionally halted. In short, to sum up what has gone before, we should say that nature, setting down the human species along the line of evolution, intended it to be sociable, in the same way as it did the communities of ants and bees; but since intelligence was there, the maintenance of social life had to be entrusted to an all but intelligent mechanism: intelligent in that each piece could be remodelled by human intelligence, yet instinctive in that man could not, without ceasing to be a man, reject all the pieces together and cease to accept a mechanism of preservation. Instinct gave place temporarily to a system of habits, each one of which became contingent, their convergence towards the preservation of society being alone necessary, and this necessity bringing back instinct with it. The necessity of the whole, felt behind the contingency of the parts, is what we call moral obligation in general—it being understood that the parts are contingent in the eyes of society only; to the individual, into whom society inculcates its habits, the part is as necessary as the whole. Now the mechanism designed by nature was simple, like the societies originally constituted by her. Did she foresee the immense development and the endless complexities of societies such as ours? Let us first agree as to the meaning of this question. We do not assert that nature has, strictly speaking, designed or foreseen anything whatever. But we have the right to proceed like a biologist, who speaks of nature's intentions every time he assigns a function to an organ: he merely expresses thus the adequateness of the organ to the function. In spite of humanity's having become civilized, in spite of the transformation of society, we maintain that the tendencies which are, as it were, organic in social life have remained what they were in the beginning. We can trace them back and study them. The result of this investigation is clear; it is for closed, simple societies that the moral structure, original and fundamental in man, is made. I grant that the organic tendencies do not stand out clearly to our consciousness. They constitute, nevertheless, the strongest element of obligation. However complex our morality has grown and though it has become coupled with tendencies which are not mere modifications of natural tendencies, and whose trend is not in the direction of nature, it is to these natural tendencies that we come in the end, when we want to obtain a precipitate of the pure obligation contained in this fluid mass. Such then is the first half of morality. The other had no place in nature's plan. We mean that nature foresaw a certain expansion of social life through intelligence, but it was to be a limited expansion. She could not have intended that this should go on so far as to endanger the original structure. Numerous indeed are the instances where man has thus outwitted nature, so knowing and wise, yet so simple-minded. Nature surely intended that men should beget men endlessly, according to the rule followed by all other living creatures; she took the most minute precautions to ensure the preservation of the species by the multiplication of individuals; hence she had not foreseen, when bestowing on us intelligence, that intelligence would at once find a way of divorcing the sexual act from its consequences, and that man might refrain from reaping without forgoing the pleasure of sowing. It is in quite another sense that man outwits nature when he extends social solidarity into the brotherhood of man; but he is deceiving her nevertheless, for those societies whose design was prefigured in the original structure of the human soul, and of which we can still perceive the plan in the innate and fundamental tendencies of modern man, required that the group be closely united, but that between group and group there should be virtual hostility; we were always to be prepared for attack or defence. Not, of course, that nature designed war for war's sake. Those leaders of humanity drawing men after them, who have broken down the gates of the city, seem indeed thereby to have placed themselves again in the current of the vital impetus. But this impetus inherent in life is, like life, finite. Its path is strewn with obstacles, and the species which have appeared, one after the other, are so many combinations of this force with opposing forces: the former urging us forward, the others making us turn in a circle. Man, fresh from the hands of nature, was a being both intelligent and social, his sociability being devised to find its scope in small communities, his intelligence being designed to further individual and group life. But intelligence, expanding through its own efforts, has developed unexpectedly. It has freed men from restrictions to which they were condemned by the limitations of their nature. This being so, it was not impossible that some of them, specially gifted, should reopen that which was closed and do, at least for themselves, what nature could not possibly have done for mankind. Their example has ended in leading others forward, in imagination at least. There is a genius of the will as there is a genius of the mind, and genius defies all anticipation. Through those geniuses of the will, the impetus of life, traversing matter, wrests from it, for the future of the species, promises such as were out of the question when the species was being constituted. Hence in passing from social solidarity to the brotherhood of man, we break with one particular nature, but not with all nature. It might be said, by slightly distorting the terms of Spinoza, that it is to get back to *natura naturans* that we break away from *natura naturata*.

Hence, between the first morality and the second, lies the whole distance between repose and movement. The first is supposed to be immutable. If it changes, it immediately forgets that it has changed, or it ackonwledges no change. The shape it assumes at any given time claims to be the final shape. But the second is a forward thrust, a demand for movement; it is the very essence of mobility. Thus would it prove, thus alone, indeed, would it be able at first to define, its superiority. Postulate the first, you cannot bring the second out of it, any more than you can from one or several positions of a moveable body derive motion. But, on the contrary, movement includes immobility, each position traversed by the moving object being conceived and even perceived as a virtual stop. But a detailed demonstration is unnecessary: the superiority is experienced before ever it is represented, and furthermore could not be demonstrated afterwards if it had not first been felt. There is a difference of vital tone. Those who regularly put into practice the morality of the city know this feeling of well-being, common to the individual and to society, which is the outward sign of the interplay of material resistances neutralizing each other. But the soul that is opening, and before whose eyes material objects vanish, is lost in sheer joy. Pleasure and well-being are something, joy is more. For it is not contained in these, whereas they are virtually contained in joy. They mean, indeed, a halt or a marking time, while joy is a step forward.

That is why the first morality is comparatively easy to formulate, but not the second. For our intelligence and our language deal in fact with things; they are less at home in representing transitions or progress. The morality of the Gospels is essentially that of the open soul: are we not justified in pointing out that it borders upon paradox, and even upon contradiction, in its more definite admonitions? If riches are an evil, should we not be injuring the poor in giving them what we possess? If he who has been smitten on the one cheek is to offer the other also, what becomes of justice, without which, after all, there can be no "charity"? But the paradox disappears, the contradiction vanishes, if we consider the intent of these maxims, which is to create a certain disposition of the soul. It is not for the sake of the poor, but for his own sake, that the rich man should give up his riches: blessed are the poor "in spirit"! The beauty lies, not in being deprived, not even in depriving oneself, but in not feeling the deprivation. The act by which the soul opens out broadens and raises to pure spirituality a morality enclosed and materialized in ready-made rules: the latter then becomes, in comparison with the other, something like a snapshot view of movement. Such is the inner meaning of the antitheses that occur one after the other in the Sermon on the Mount: "Ye have heard that it was said . . . I say unto you . . ." On the one hand the closed, on the other the open. Current morality is not abolished; but it appears like a virtual stop in the course of actual progression. The old method is not given up; but it is fitted into a more general method, as is the case when the dynamic reabsorbs the static, the latter then becoming a mere particular instance of the former. We should need then, strictly speaking, a means of expressing directly the movement and the tendency; but if we still want—and we cannot avoid it—to translate them into the language of the static and the motionless, we shall be confronted with formulae that border on contradiction. So we might compare what is impracticable in certain precepts of the Gospels to what was illogical in the first explanations of the differential calculus. Indeed, between the morality of the ancients and Christianity we should find much the same relation as that between the mathematics of antiquity and our own.

The geometry of the ancients may have provided particular solutions which were, so to say, an anticipated application of our general methods; but it never brought out these methods; the impetus was not there which would have made them spring from the static to the dynamic. But at any rate it carried as far as possible the imitation of the dynamic by the static. Now, we have just the same impression when we compare, for example, the doctrine of the Stoics with Christian morality. The Stoics proclaimed themselves citizens of the world, and added that all men were brothers, having come from the same God. The words were almost the same; but they did not find the same echo, because they were not spoken with the same accent. The Stoics provided some very fine examples. If they did not succeed in drawing humanity after them, it is because Stoicism is essentially a philosophy. The philosopher who is so enamoured of this noble doctrine as to become wrapped up in it doubtless vitalizes it by translating it into practice; just so did Pygmalion's love breathe life into the statue once it was carven. But it is a far cry from that to the enthusiasm which spreads from soul to soul, unceasingly, like a conflagration. Such an emotion may indeed develop into ideas which make up a doctrine, or even several different doctrines having no other resemblance between them than a kinship of the spirit; but it precedes the idea instead of following it. To find something of the kind in classical antiquity, we must go not to the Stoics, but rather to the man who inspired all the great philosophers of Greece without contributing any system, without having written anything, Socrates. Socrates indeed exalts the exercise of reason, and particularly the logical function of the mind, above everything else. The irony he parades is meant to dispose of opinions which have not undergone the test of reflection, to put them to shame, so to speak, by setting them in contradiction with themselves. Dialogue, as he understands it, has given birth to the Platonic dialectics and consequently to the philosophical method, essentially rational, which we still practice. The object of such a dialogue is to arrive at concepts that may be circumscribed by definitions; these concepts will become the Platonic Ideas; and the theory of Ideas, in its turn, will serve as a model for the systems, also essentially rational, of traditional metaphysics. Socrates goes further still; virtue itself he holds to be a science, he identifies the practice of good with our knowledge of it; he thus paves the way for the doctrine which will absorb all moral life in the rational function of thought. Reason has never been set so high. At least that is what strikes us at first. But let us look closer. Socrates teaches because the oracle of Delphi has spoken. He has received a mission. He is poor, and poor he must remain. He must mix with the common folk, he must become one of them, his speech must get back to their speech. He will write nothing, so that his thought shall be communicated, a living thing, to minds who shall convey it to other minds. He is indifferent to cold and hunger, though in no way an ascetic; he is merely delivered from material needs, and emancipated from his body. A "daemon" accompanies him, which makes its voice heard when a warning is necessary. He so thoroughly believes in this "daemonic voice" that he dies rather than not follow it; if he refuses to defend himself before the popular tribunal, if he goes to meet his condemnation, it is because the "daemon" has said nothing to dissuade him. In a word, his mission is of a religious and mystic order, in the present-day meaning of the words; his teaching, so perfectly rational, hinges on something that seems to transcend pure reason. But do we not detect this in his teaching itself? If the inspired, or at all events lyrical sayings, which occur throughout the dialogues of Plato, were not those of Socrates, but those of Plato himself, if the master's language had always been such as Xenophon attributes to him, could we understand the enthusiasm which fired his disciples, and which has come down the ages? Stoics, Epicureans, Cynics, all the Greek moralists spring from Socrates—not only, as has always been said, because they develop the teaching of the Master in its various directions, but also, and, above all, because they borrow from him the attitude which is so little in keeping with the Greek spirit and which he created, the attitude of the Sage. Whenever the philosopher, closeted with his wisdom, stands apart from the common rule of mankind—be it to teach them, to serve as a model, or simply to go about his work of perfecting his inner self—Socrates is there, Socrates alive, working through the incomparable prestige of his person. Let us go further. It has been said that he brought philosophy down from heaven to earth. But could we understand his life, and above all his death, if the conception of the soul which Plato attributes to him in the Phaedo had not been his? More generally speaking, do the myths we find in the dialogues of Plato, touching the soul, its origin, its entrance into the body, do anything more than set down in Platonic terms a creative emotion, the emotion present in the moral teaching of Socrates? The myths, and the Socratic conception of the soul to which they stand in the same relationship as the explanatory programme to a symphony, have been preserved along with the Platonic dialectics. They pursue their subterranean way through Greek metaphysics, and rise to the open air again with the Alexandrine philosophers, with Ammonius perhaps, in any case with Plotinus, who claims to be the successor of Socrates. They have provided the Socratic soul with a body of doctrine similar to that into which was to be breathed the spirit of the Gospels. The two metaphysics, in spite, perhaps because, of their resemblance, gave battle to each other, before the one absorbed the best that was in the other; for a while the world may

well have wondered whether it was to become Christian or Neo-
Platonic. It was Socrates against Jesus. To confine ourselves to
Socrates, the question is: what would this very practical genius
have done in another society and in other circumstances; if he had
not been struck, above all, by the danger of the moral empiricism
of his time, and the mental anarchy of Athenian democracy; if he
had not had to deal with the most crying need first, by establishing
the rights of reason; if he had not therefore thrust intuition and
inspiration into the background, and if the Greek he was had not
mastered in him the Oriental who sought to come into being?
We have made the distinction between the closed souls? There
was irony running through Socratic teaching, and outbursts of
lyricism were probably rare; but in the measure in which these
outbursts cleared the road for a new spirit, they have been decisive
for the future of humanity.

Between the closed soul and the open soul there is the soul in
process of opening. Between the immobility of a man seated and
the motion of the same man running there is the act of getting up,
the attitude he assumes when he rises. In a word, between the
static and the dynamic there is to be observed, in morality too, a
transition stage. This intermediate state would pass unnoticed if,
when at rest, we could develop the necessary impetus to spring
straight into action. But it attracts our attention when we stop
short—the usual sign of insufficient impetus. Let us put the same
thing in a different way. We have seen that the purely static morality might be called infra-intellectual, and the purely dynamic,
supra-intellectual. Nature intended the one, and the other is a contribution of man's genius. The former is characteristic of a whole
group of habits which are, in man, the counterpart of certain instincts in animals; it is something less than intelligence. The latter
is inspiration, intuition, emotion, susceptible of analysis into ideas
which furnish intellectual notations of it and branch out into infinite detail; thus, like a unity which encompasses and transcends
a plurality incapable of ever equalling it, it contains any amount
of intellectuality; it is more than intelligence. Between the two lies
intelligence itself. It is at this point that the human soul would
have settled down, had it sprung forward from the one without
reaching the other. It would have dominated the morality of the
closed soul; it would not have attained to, or rather it would not

have created, that of the open soul. Its attitude, the result of getting up, would have lifted it to the plane of intellectuality. Compared with the position it had just left—described negatively—such
a soul would be manifesting indifference or insensibility, it would
be in the "ataraxy" or the "apathy" of the Epicureans and the
Stoics. Considered in what it positively is, if its detachment from
the old sought to be an attachment to something new, its life
would be contemplation; it would conform to the Platonic and
the Aristotelian ideal. From whatever angle we look at it, its attitude would be upright, noble, truly worthy of admiration and reserved for the chosen few. Philosophies which start from very
different principles may find in it a common goal. The reason is
that there is only one road leading from action confined in a circle
to action developing in the freedom of space, from repetition to
creation, from the infra-intellectual to the supra-intellectual. Anyone halting between the two is inevitably in the zone of pure contemplation, and in any case, no longer holding to the one but
without having yet reached the other, naturally practises that half-
virtue, detachment.

We are speaking of pure intelligence, withdrawing into itself
and judging that the object of life is what the ancients called "science" or contemplation. We are speaking, in a word, of what
mainly characterizes the morality of the Greek philosophers. But
it would no longer be a matter of Greek or Oriental philosophy,
we should be dealing with the morality of everybody if we considered intelligence as a mere elaboration or co-ordinating agent
of the material, some of it infra-intellectual and some of it supra-
intellectual, with which we have been dealing in this chapter. In
order to define the very essence of duty, we have in fact distinguished the two forces that act upon us, impulsion on the one
hand, and attraction on the other. This had to be done, and it is
because philosophy had left it undone, confining itself to the intellectuality which to-day covers both, that it has scarcely succeeded,
so it would seem, in explaining how a moral motive can have a
hold upon the souls of men. But our description was thereby condemned, as we hinted, to remain a mere outline. That which is
aspiration tends to materialize by assuming the form of strict obligation. That which is strict obligation tends to expand and to
broaden out by absorbing aspiration. Pressure and aspiration agree

to meet for this purpose in that region of the mind where concepts are formed. The result is mental pictures, many of them of a compound nature, being a blend of that which is a cause of pressure and that which is an object of aspiration. But the result is also that we lose sight of pure pressure and pure aspiration actually at work on our wills; we see only the concept into which have been melted the two distinct objects to which pressure and aspiration were respectively attached. The force acting upon us is taken to be this concept: a fallacy which accounts for the failure of strictly intellectualist systems of morality, in other words, of the majority of the philosophical theories of duty. Not, of course, that an idea pure and simple is without influence on our will. But this influence would operate effectively only if it could remain in isolation. It has difficulty in resisting hostile influences, or, if it does triumph over them, it is because the pressure and the aspiration, which had each renounced its own right of action to be represented together in one idea, have reappeared in their individuality and their independence and have exerted their full strength.

We should have to open a very long parenthesis indeed if we had to give their due share to the two forces, the one social, the other supra-social, one of impulsion, the other of attraction, which impart to each moral motive its driving force. An honest man will say, for example, that he acts from self-respect, from a feeling of the dignity of man. Obviously he would not express himself thus, if he did not begin by splitting himself into two selves, the personality he would be if he simply let himself drift, and the one to which his will uplifts him; the ego that respects is not the same as the ego respected. What, then, is the latter? Wherein lies its dignity? Whence comes the respect it inspires? Let us leave aside the task of analysing this respect, in which we should find above all an impulse of self-effacement, the attitude of the apprentice towards the master, or rather, to use the language of Aristotle, of the accident in the presence of the essence. There would remain to be defined the higher ego to which the average personality defers. There is no doubt that it is in the first place the "social ego" within each of us, on which we have already touched. If we posit, simply for the sake of theoretical clearness, a "primitive" mentality, we shall see in it self-respect coinciding with the feeling of so firm a solidarity between the individual and the group that the group remains present in the isolated individual, keeps an eye on him, encourages or threatens him, demands, in a word, to be consulted and obeyed; behind society itself there are supernatural powers on which the group depends, and which make the community responsible for the acts of the individual; the pressure of the social ego is exerted with all these accumulated forces. The individual, moreover, does not obey merely from a habit of discipline or from fear of punishment; the group to which he belongs must, of course, exalt itself above the others, if only to rouse his courage in battle, and the consciousness of this superiority of strength secures for him greater strength, together with all the satisfactions that pride can give. If you want to make sure of this, take a state of mind already more fully "evolved." Think of all the pride, as well as all the moral energy which is represented by *civis Romanus sum:* self-respect, in the Roman citizen, must have been tantamount to what we call nationalism to-day. But we need not turn to history or prehistory to see self-respect coinciding with a group-pride. We need only observe what goes on under our very eyes in the small societies which form within the big one, when men are drawn together by a distinguishing badge which emphasizes a real or apparent superiority, separating them from the common herd. To the self-respect which every man, as a man, professes is then coupled an additional respect, that of the ego which is no more than man for an ego that stands out among men. All the members of the group behave as a group, and thus a common code of behaviour comes to be observed, a feeling of honour springs up which is identical with *esprit de corps*. These are the first components of self-respect. Looked at from this angle, a point of view which we to-day can isolate only by an effort of abstraction, it "binds" us by the prestige of the social pressure it brings with it. Now indeed the impulsion would obviously become attraction, if self-respect were the respect for a person admired and venerated, whose image we bore in our hearts and with whom we would aspire to become identified, as the copy to an original. In reality it is not so, for even if the word merely evokes the idea of an attitude towards one's self, nevertheless self-respect is, at the end of its evolution as at the beginning, a social feeling. But the great moral figures that have made their mark on history join hands across the centuries, above our human cities; they unite into a di-

vine city which they bid us enter. We may not hear their voices
distinctly, the call has none the less gone forth, and something
answers from the depth of our soul; from the real society in which
we live we betake ourselves in thought to this ideal society; to this
ideal society we bow down when we reverence the dignity of man
within us, when we declare that we act from self-respect. It is true
that the influence exerted on us by definite persons tends to become impersonal. And the impersonal character is still more
stressed when a philosopher explains to us that it is reason, present
in each of us, which constitutes the dignity of man. But here we
must take care to know what we mean. That reason is the distinguishing mark of man no one will deny. That it is a thing of
superior value, in the sense in which a fine work of art is indeed
valuable, will also be granted. But we must explain how it is that
its orders are absolute and why they are obeyed. Reason can only
put forward reasons, which we are apparently always at liberty to
counter with other reasons. Let us not then merely assert that
reason, present in each of us, compels our respect and commands
our obedience by virtue of its paramount value. We must add that
there are, behind reason, the men who have made mankind divine,
and who have thus stamped a divine character on reason, which is
the essential attribute of man. It is these men who draw us towards
an ideal society, while we yield to the pressure of the real one.

All moral ideas interpenetrate each other, but none is more
instructive than that of justice, in the first place, because it includes most of the others, and next, because it is expressed, in
spite of its extraordinary richness, in simpler formulae; lastly and
above all, because here the two forms of obligation are seen to
dovetail into each other. Justice has always evoked ideas of equality, of proportion, of compensation. *Pensare,* from which we derive
"compensation" and "recompense," means *to weigh.* Justice is
represented as holding the scales. Equity signifies equality. Rules
and regulation, right and righteousness, are words which suggest
a straight line. These references to arithmetic and geometry are
characteristic of justice throughout its history. The idea must
have already taken shape as far back as the days of exchange and
barter; however rudimentary a community may be, it barters,
and it cannot barter without first finding out if the objects exchanged are really equal in value, that is to say, both exchange-

able for a definite third object. Let this equality of value be set up as a rule, this rule be given a place among the customs of the group, the "totality of obligation," as we called it, adding its weight to the rule: here we have justice already, in a clearly defined shape, with its imperative character, and the ideas of equality and reciprocity involved.—But such justice will apply not only to the exchange of objects. It will extend gradually to intercourse between persons, though unable, for a long time to come, to shake off all idea of objects and exchanges. It will then consist mainly in the regulation of natural impulses by the introduction of the idea of a no less natural reciprocity, for example, the expectation of an injury equivalent to the injury done. In primitive societies, assaults on persons concern the community only exceptionally, when the act is likely to injure the community itself by bringing down upon it the wrath of the gods. The injured party or his family has only therefore to obey his instinct, react naturally, and avenge himself; and the reprisals might be out of all proportion to the offence, if this requital of evil for evil was not, to all appearances, vaguely subject to the general law of exchanges and barter. It is true that the quarrel might go on for ever, and "vendetta" might be kept up indefinitely by the two families, if one of them did not make up its mind to accept "damages" in cash; here the idea of compensation, already implied in the idea of exchange and barter, will clearly emerge. Now let the community itself undertake to exact punishment, to repress all acts of violence whatsoever, and it will be said that the community is dispensing justice, if the rule to which individuals and families referred for a settlement of their disputes were already being described by that term. Moreover, the community will assess the penalty according to the gravity of the offence, since otherwise there would be no object in stopping, once we have begun to do wrong; we should not run any greater risk by proceeding to extremities. An eye for an eye, a tooth for a tooth, the injury received must always be equivalent to the injury inflicted.—But is the price of an eye always an eye, the price of a tooth always a tooth? Quality must be borne in mind as well as quantity. The law of retaliation is applied only within a class; the same injury sustained, the same offence received, will call for greater compensation, or heavier punishment, if the victim belong to a higher class. In a word, equality may connote a ratio and become a proportion. Hence, though justice may embrace a greater and greater variety of things, it is always defined in the same way.—Nor will its formula alter when, in a more civilized state, it extends to the relations between the rulers and the ruled, and in a more general way to those between different social categories; into a state of things which only exists *de facto* it will introduce considerations of equality or proportion which will make of that state something mathematically defined, and, thereby, it would seem, apparently *de jure*. There is indeed no doubt that force lies at the origin of the division of ancient societies into classes subordinate to one another. But a subordination that is habitual ends by seeming natural, and by seeking for itself an explanation; if the inferior class has accepted its position for a considerable time, it may go on doing so when it has virtually become the stronger, because it will attribute to the governing class a superior value. And this superiority will be real, if the members of this class have taken advantage of the facilities they may have had for intellectual and moral improvement; but it may quite as well be a mere carefully-fostered appearance of superiority. However it may be, whether real or apparent, this superiority needs only to persist in order to seem a matter of birth; since hereditary privilege is there, there must be, people say to one another, some innate superiority. Nature, who intended ordered societies, has predisposed man to this illusion. Plato shared it in his Ideal Republic. If a class system is understood in this way, responsibilities and privileges are looked upon as a common stock, to be eventually distributed among the individuals according to their worth, consequently according to the services they render. Justice here still holds her scales, measuring and proportioning.—Now, from this justice, which, though it may not express itself in utilitarian terms, is none the less faithful to its mercantile origins, how shall we pass to the justice which implies neither exchange made nor service rendered, being the assertion pure and simple of the inviolability of right and of the incommensurability of the person with any values whatever? Before answering this question, let us pause to admire the magic property of speech, I mean the power which a word bestows on a newly created idea—when it extends to that idea after having been applied to a pre-existent object—of modifying that object and thus

retro-actively influencing the past. In whatever light we view the
transition from relative to absolute justice, whether it took place
by stages or all at once, there has been creation. Something has
supervened which might never have existed, which would not
have existed except for certain circumstances, certain men, perhaps one particular man. But instead of realizing that some new
thing has come and taken possession of the old and absorbed it
into a whole that was up to then unforeseeable, we prefer looking
upon the process as if the new thing had always been there, not
actually but virtually pre-existing, and as if the old had been a
part of it even then, a part of something yet uncreated; and on
this showing the conceptions of justice which followed one another
in ancient societies were no more than partial, incomplete visions
of an integral justice which is nothing more or less than justice
as we know it to-day. There is no need to analyse in detail this
particular example of a very general illusion, barely noticed by
philosophers, which has vitiated a goodly number of metaphysical
doctrines and which sets the theory of knowledge insoluble problems. Let us simply say that it is part of our habit of considering
all forward movement as a progressive shortening of the distance
between the starting-point (which indeed exists) and the goal,
which comes into being as a stopping-place only when the moving
object has chosen to stop there. It does not follow that, because
it can always be interpreted in this sense when it has attained
its end, the movement consisted in a progresssion towards this
end: an interval which has still but one extremity cannot diminish little by little, since it is not yet an interval: it *will have
diminished* little by little when the moving object has created, by
its actual or virtual stopping, a second extremity, and when we
consider it in retrospect or even simply trace the movement in its
progress while, in anticipation, reconstituting it in that way, backwards. But this is just what we do not realize for the most part;
we introduce into the things themselves, under the guise of the
pre-existence of the possible in the real, this retrospective anticipation. This illusion lies at the root of many a philosophical problem; Zeno's Dichotomy has provided the typical example. And it
is this same illusion which we find in ethics when the continually
expanding forms of relative justice are defined as growing ap-
proximations of absolute justice. The most we are entitled to say

is that once the latter is stated, the former might be regarded as so many halts along a road which, plotted out retrospectively by us, would lead to absolute justice. And even then we should have to add that there had been, not gradual progress, but at a certain epoch a sudden leap.—It would be interesting to determine the exact point at which this *saltus* took place. And it would be no less instructive to find out how it was that, once conceived (in a vague form), absolute justice long remained no more than a respected ideal, without there being any question of translating it into practice. Let us simply say, in so far as the first point is concerned, that the long-standing inequalities of class, doubtless imposed in the beginning by force, and accepted afterwards as inequalities of merit and services rendered, become more and more exposed to the criticism of the lower classes; the ruling elements *are,* moreover, deteriorating, because, being too sure of themselves, they are guilty of a slackening of that inner tension upon which they had called for a greater effort of intelligence and will, and which had consolidated their supremacy. They could indeed maintain their position if they held together; but because of their very tendency to assert their individuality, there will one day arise ambitious men from among them who mean to get the upper hand and who will seek support in the lower class, especially if the latter already has some share in affairs: on that day is shattered the belief in a native superiority of the upper class; the spell is broken. Thus do aristocracies tend to merge into democracy, simply because political inequality is an unstable thing, as, indeed, political equality, once it is established, will be, if it is only *de facto,* if therefore it admits of exceptions, if, for example, it tolerates slavery within the city.—But it is a far cry from such examples of equilibrium, arrived at mechanically and always transitory, like that of the scales held by the justice of yore, to a justice such as ours, the justice of the "rights of man," which no longer evokes ideas of relativity and proportion, but, on the contrary, of the incommensurable and the absolute. Of this justice we could form a complete idea only if we were to "draw it out to infinity," as the mathematicians say; it is formulated precisely and categorically, at any stated time, only by prohibitions; but on its positive side it proceeds by successive creations, each of them being a fuller realization than the last of personality and consequently of humanity. Such realization is possible only through the medium of laws; it implies the assent of society. It would, moreover, be futile to maintain that it takes place gradually and automatically, as a consequence of the state of mind of society at a given period of its history. It is a leap forward, which can take place only if society has decided to try the experiment; and the experiment will not be tried unless society has allowed itself to be won over, or at least stirred. Now the first start has always been given by someone. It is no use maintaining that this leap forward does not imply a creative effort behind it, and that we have not to do here with an invention comparable with that of the artist. That would be to forget that most great reforms appeared at first sight impracticable, as in fact they were. They could be carried out only in a society whose state of mind was already such as their realization was bound to bring about; and you had a circle from which there would have been no escape, if one or several privileged beings, having expanded the social ego within themselves, had not broken the circle and drawn the society after them. Now this is exactly what occurs in the miracle of artistic creation. A work of genius which is at first disconcerting may create, little by little, by the simple fact of its presence, a conception of art and an artistic atmosphere which bring it within our comprehension; it will then become in retrospect a work of genius; otherwise it would have remained what it was at the beginning, merely disconcerting. In a financial speculation, it is the success that causes the idea to have been a good one. Something much the same occurs in artistic creation, with this difference, that the success, if the work which at first repelled us eventually wins through, is due to a transformation of public taste brought about by the work itself, the latter being then force as well as matter; it has set up an impetus imparted to it by the artist, or rather one which is the very impetus of the artist, invisible and present within the work. The same can be said of moral invention, and more particularly of the creations which more and more enrich, one after the other, the idea of justice. They bear, above all, upon the substance of justice, but they modify its form as well.—To take the latter first, let us lay down that justice has always appeared as obligatory, but that for a long time it was an obligation like other obligations. It met, like the others, a social need; and it was the pressure of society on the individual which made justice obligatory. This being so, an injustice was neither more nor less shocking than any other breach of the rules. There was no justice for slaves, save perhaps a relative, almost an optional, justice. Public safety was not merely the supreme law, as indeed it has remained, it was furthermore proclaimed as such; whereas today we should not dare to lay down the principle that it justifies injustice, even if we accept any particular consequence of that principle. Let us dwell on this point, put to ourselves the famous question: "What should we do if we heard that for the common good, for the very existence of mankind, there was somewhere a man, an innocent man, condemned to suffer eternal torment?" Well, we should perhaps agree to it on the understanding that some magic philtre is going to make us forget it, that we shall never hear anything more about it; but if we were bound to know it, to think of it, to realize that this man's hideous torture was the price of our existence, that it was even the fundamental condition of existence in general, no! a thousand times no! Better to accept that nothing should exist at all! Better let our planet be blown to pieces. Now what has happened? How has justice emerged from social life, within which it had always dwelt with no particular privilege, and soared above it, categorical and transcendent? Let us recall the tone and accents of the Prophets of Israel. It is their voice we hear when a great injustice has been done and condoned. From the depths of the centuries they raise their protest. True, justice has singularly expanded since their time. The justice they preached applied above all to Israel, their indignation against injustice was the very wrath of Jehovah against His disobedient people, or against the enemies of this chosen people. If any of them, like Isaiah, may have thought of universal justice, it was because Israel, the chosen of God among the other peoples, bound to God by a covenant, was so high above the rest of mankind that sooner or later it was destined to be taken as a model. None the less, they imparted to justice the violently imperative character which it has kept, which it has since stamped on a substance grown infinitely more extensive.—But these extensions did not occur spontaneously either. On each one of them a competent historian could put a proper name. Each development was a creation, and indeed the door will ever stand open to fresh creations. The progress which was decisive for the substance of justice, as the era of the prophets had been for its form, consisted in the substitution of a universal republic, embracing all men, for that republic which went no further than the gates of the city, and, within the city, was limited to free men. It is from this that all the rest has followed, for, if the door has remained open to new creations, and probably will for all time stand open, yet it must have been opened. There seems to be no doubt that this second advance, the passage from the closed to the open, is due to Christianity, as the first was due to the Prophets of Judaism. Could it have been brought about by mere philosophy? There is nothing more instructive than to see how the philosophers have skirted round it, touched it, and yet missed it. Let us leave out Plato, who certainly includes the Idea of man among the transcendent Ideas: did it not follow that all men were of the same essence? From this to the idea that all men, *qua* men, were of equal worth and that the common essence conferred on them the same fundamental rights, was but one step. But the step was not taken. It would have meant condemning slavery, giving up the Greek idea that foreigners, being barbarians, could claim no rights. Was it, in fact, an essentially Greek idea? We find it, implied in others, wherever Christianity has not penetrated, in modern as well as in ancient times. In China, for example, there have arisen very noble doctrines, but they have not been concerned with laying down laws for humanity; though they do not expressly say so, they are in fact interested only in the Chinese community. Indeed, before Christianity, we find Stoicism and, among the Stoics, philosophers who proclaim that all men are brothers, and that the wise man is a citizen of the world. But these dicta were the expression of an ideal, an ideal merely conceived, and very likely conceived as impracticable. There is nothing to show that any of the great Stoics, not even the Stoic who was an emperor, considered the possibility of lowering the barrier between the free man and the slave, between the Roman citizen and the barbarian. Humanity had to wait till Christianity for the idea of universal brotherhood, with its implication of equality of rights and the sanctity of the person, to become operative. Some may say that it has been rather a slow process; indeed eighteen centuries elapsed before the rights of man were proclaimed by the Puritans of America, soon followed by the men of the French Revolution. It began, nevertheless, with the teachings of the Gospels, and was destined to go on indefinitely; it is one thing for an idea to be merely propounded by sages worthy of admiration, it is very different when the idea is broadcast to the ends of the earth in a message overflowing with love, invoking love in return. Indeed there was no question here of clear-cut wisdom, reducible, from beginning to end, into maxims. There was rather a pointing of the way, a suggestion of the means; at most an indication of the goal, which would only be temporary, demanding a constant renewal of effort. Such effort was bound to be, in certain individuals at least, an effort of creation. The method consisted in supposing possible what is actually impossible in a given society, in imagining what would be its effect on the soul of society, and then inducing some such psychic condition by propaganda and example: the effect, once obtained, would retrospectively complete its cause; new feelings, evanescent indeed, would call forth the new legislation seemingly indispensable to their appearance, and which would then serve to consolidate them. The modern idea of justice has progressed in this way by a series of individual creations which have succeeded through multifarious efforts animated by one and the same impulse.—Classical antiquity had known nothing of propaganda; its justice had the unruffled serenity of the gods upon Olympus. Spiritual expansion, missionary zeal, impetus, movement, all these are of Judaic-Christian origin. But because men went on using the same word, they too readily thought they were dealing with the same thing. We cannot too often repeat that successive creations, individual and contingent, will be generally grouped under the same heading, classified under the same idea and labelled by the same name, if each one has given rise to the one that follows it and if they appear, in retrospect, as continuations of one another. Let us go further. The name will not apply only to the terms already existing of the series thus obtained. Encroaching on the future, it will denote the whole series, and it will be placed at the end, nay, be drawn out to infinity; as the designation was created long ago, we shall imagine the idea which it represents as having been also created just as long ago, and indeed existing since the beginning of time, though still open to additions and of undetermined content; thus each advance is imagined to be so much gained over an entity conceived as pre-existing; reality is looked upon as eating its way into the ideal, incorporating into itself, bit by bit, the totality of eternal justice. —Now that is true not only of the idea of justice but also of the ideas which are cognate with it—equality and liberty, for example. We are fond of defining the progress of justice as a forward movement towards liberty and equality. The definition is unimpeachable, but what are we to derive from it? It applies to the past; it can seldom guide our choice for the future. Take liberty, for instance. It is commonly said that the individual is entitled to any liberty that does not infringe the liberty of others. But the granting of a new liberty, which might lead to an encroachment of all the different liberties on one another in present-day society, might produce the opposite effect in a society where feeling and custom had been modified by that very reform. So that it is often impossible to state *a priori* the exact degree of liberty which can be allotted to the individual without injury to the liberty of his fellow-men; change the quantity, and the quality is no longer the same. On the other hand, equality can hardly be obtained, save at the expense of liberty, so that we should first ask ourselves which of the two is preferable to the other. But the question admits of no general answer; for the sacrifice of this or that liberty, if it is fully agreed upon by the citizens as a whole, partakes still of liberty; and above all, the liberty which is left may be superior in quality if the reform, tending towards greater equality, has led to a society where men breathe more freely, where greater joy is found in action. Look at it how you will, you must always come back to the conception of moral creators who see in their mind's eye a new social atmosphere, an environment in which life would be more worth living, I mean a society such that, if men once tried it, they would refuse to go back to the old state of things. Thus only is moral progress to be defined; but it is only in retrospect that it can be defined, when some exceptional moral nature has created a new feeling, like a new kind of music, and passed it on to mankind, stamping it with his own vitality. Think in this way of "liberty," of "equality," of "the sanctity of the individual," and you will see that you have here no mere difference of degree, but a radical difference of nature between the two ideas of justice which we have distinguished, the one closed, the other open. For relatively stable justice, closed justice, which expresses the automatic equilibrium of a society fresh from the hands of nature, manifests itself in customs to which the totality of obligation is attached, and this totality of obligation ends by incorporating, as public opinion progressively accepts them, the decrees of the other justice, the justice which is open to successive creations. Thus the two substances, the one supplied by society, the other a product of man's genius, come to be cast in the same mould. Indeed, in practice, they may well be indistinguishable. But the philosopher must discriminate the one from the other; if not, he is sure to misunderstand the nature of social evolution as well as the origin of duty. Social evolution is not the evolution of a society which has developed according to a method destined to transform it later. Between the development and the transformation there is here neither analogy nor common measure. Because closed justice and open justice are incorporated in equally peremptory laws, expressing themselves in the same way, and outwardly similar, it does not follow that they must be explained in the same fashion. No example can bring out better than this the two-fold origin of morality and the two elements of obligation.

There can be no question that, in the present state of things, reason must appear the sole imperative; that it is to the interest of humanity to attribute an intrinsic force, an authority of their own to moral concepts; in a word that moral activity in a civilized society is essentially rational. How else could we tell what to do in each particular case? There are deep underlying forces here, one of impulsion, the other of attraction; we cannot refer directly to them each time we have to make a decision. To do so would, in most cases, simply amount to doing needlessly over again something which society, on the one hand, and the highest representatives of humanity on the other, have done for us. Their work has resulted in certain rules being laid down and an ideal being set up as a pattern: to live morally will mean to follow these rules, to conform to this ideal. In this way alone can we be sure of remaining in complete accord with ourselves: the rational alone is self-consistent. Only in this way can we compare various lines of conduct with one another; only in this way can we estimate their moral value. The thing is so obvious that we have barely hinted at it, we have nearly always taken it for granted. But the result was that our statement remained a mere diagram and might well

appear inadequate. Indeed, on the intellectual plane, all the precepts of morality interpenetrate one another in concepts of which
each one, like Leibnitz's monad, is more or less representative of
all the others. Above or below this plane, we find forces which,
taken singly, correspond only to a part of what has been projected
on the intellectual plane. Since this drawback to the method we
have adopted is undeniable, and indeed inevitable, since we perceive that we must use this method and since we feel that it cannot
fail to raise objections throughout its application, we think it
important, in conclusion, to dwell on it once more, define it yet
again, even if we are once more obliged to repeat at certain points,
and almost in the same terms, what we have already had occasion
to say.

A human society with its members linked together like the cells
of an organism, or, what amounts almost to the same thing, like
ants in an ant-hill, has never existed, but the groupings of primitive humanity were certainly nearer the ants than ours are to-day.
Nature, in making man a social animal, intended that this solidarity should be very close, while relaxing it sufficiently to enable
the individual to display, in the interests of society itself, the intelligence with which she had provided him. We went no further
than this contention in the first part of our argument. It would
be of slight importance for any moral philosophy that accepted
without question the belief in the heredity of acquired characteristics. Man might in that case be born to-day with very different
tendencies from those of his remotest ancestors. But we rely upon
experience, which teaches that the hereditary transmission of a
contracted habit, assuming that it ever happens, is an exceptional
and not a regular or frequent occurrence, sufficient in the long
run to bring about a far-reaching alteration in the nature of man.
However radical the difference may be between primitive man
and civilized man, it is due almost solely to what the child has
amassed since the first awakening of its consciousness; all the
acquisitions of humanity during centuries of civilization are there,
at his elbow, deposited in the knowledge imparted to him, in the
traditions, the institutions, the customs, the syntax and vocabulary
of the language he learns to speak, and even in the gestures of the
people about him. It is this thick humus which covers to-day the
bed-rock of original nature. It may indeed represent the slowly

accumulated effects of an infinite variety of causes; it has, nevertheless, had to follow the general configuration of the soil on
which it is deposited. In short, the obligation we find in the depths
of our consciousness and which, as the etymology of the word
implies, binds us to the other members of society, is a link of the
same nature as that which unites the ants in the ant-hill or the
cells of an organism; it would take this form in the eyes of an ant,
were she to become endowed with man's intelligence, or of an
organic cell, were it to become as independent in its movements
as an intelligent ant. I refer here of course to obligation taken in
this simple form, devoid of matter: it is the irreducible, the ever-
present element, even now, in our nature. It goes without saying
that the matter wrought into this form becomes more and more
intellectual and self-consistent as civilization progresses, and new
matter accrues incessantly, not inevitably at the direct bidding of
this form, but under the logical pressure of the intellectual matter
already introduced into it. And we have seen also how a certain
kind of matter which is intended to be run into a different mould,
whose introduction is not due, even indirectly, to the need for
social preservation, but to an aspiration of individual consciousness, adopts this form by settling down, like the rest of morality,
on the intellectual plane. But every time we come back to the
strictly imperative element in obligation, and even supposing we
found in it everything intelligence had put there to enrich it,
everything with which reason has hedged it round to justify it,
we find ourselves once again confronted by this fundamental
framework. So much for pure obligation.

Now, a mystic society, embracing all humanity and moving,
animated by a common will, towards the continually renewed
creation of a more complete humanity, is no more possible of
realization in the future than was the existence in the past of
human societies functioning automatically and similar to animal
societies. Pure aspiration is an ideal limit, just like obligation
unadorned. It is none the less true that it is the mystic souls who
draw and will continue to draw civilized societies in their wake.
The remembrance of what they have been, of what they have
done, is enshrined in the memory of humanity. Each one of us
can revive it, especially if he brings it in touch with the image,
which abides ever living within him, of a particular person who

shared in that mystic state and radiated around him some of its light. If we do not evoke this or that sublime figure, we know that we *can* do so; he thus exerts on us a virtual attraction. Even if we ignore individuals, there remains the general formula of morality accepted to-day by civilized humanity: this formula includes two things, a system of *orders* dictated by *impersonal* social requirements, and a series of *appeals* made to the conscience of each of us by *persons* who represent the best there is in humanity. The obligation relating to the orders is, in its original and fundamental elements, sub-rational. The potency of the appeal lies in the strength of the emotion it has aroused in times gone by, which it arouses still, or can arouse: this emotion, if only because it can indefinitely be resolved into ideas, is more than idea; it is supra-rational. The two forces, working in different regions of the soul, are projected on to the intermediary plane, which is that of intelligence. They will henceforth be represented by their projections. These intermingle and interpenetrate. The result is a transposition of orders and appeals into terms of pure reason. Justice thus finds itself continually broadened by pity; "charity" assumes more and more the shape of justice; the elements of morality become homogeneous, comparable, and almost commensurable with one another; moral problems are clearly enunciated and methodically solved. Humanity is asked to place itself at a certain level, higher than that of animal society, where obligation would be but the force of instinct, but not so high as an assembly of gods, where everything would partake of the creative impetus. Considering then the manifestations of moral life thus organized, we shall find them perfectly self-consistent, capable therefore of being referred to first principles. Moral life will be rational life.

Everybody will agree on this point. But because we have established the rational character of moral conduct, it does not follow that morality has its origin or even its foundation in pure reason. The important question is to find out why we are "obliged" in cases where following our inclination by no means suffices to ensure that our duty is done.

That in that case it is reason speaking, I am willing to admit; but, if it spoke only in its own name, if it did anything more than rationally express the action of certain forces which dwell behind it, how could it struggle against passion and self-interest? The philosopher who considers that reason is self-sufficient and claims to demonstrate this, succeeds in his demonstration only if he tacitly reintroduces these forces; in fact they have crept back themselves, unbeknown to him, surreptitiously. Just examine the demonstration. It takes two forms, according as it assumes reason to be void or grants it a content of matter, according as it sees in moral obligation the necessity, pure and simple, of remaining logically in agreement with itself, or an invitation logically to pursue a certain end. Let us take these two forms in turn. When Kant tells us that a deposit of money must be handed back because, if the recipient appropriated it, it would no longer be a deposit, he is obviously juggling with words. Either by "deposit" he means the material fact of placing a sum of money in the hands (say) of a friend, with an intimation that it will be called for later. But this material fact alone, with this intimation alone, would have no other effect than that of impelling the holder to give back the sum if he has no need of it, or simply to appropriate it if he is short of money; both proceedings are equally consistent, equally logical, so long as the word deposit evokes only a material image unaccompanied by moral conceptions. Or else moral considerations are involved, there is the idea that the deposit has been "entrusted" and that a trust "must not" be betrayed; the idea that the holder has pledged himself, that he has "given his word;" the idea that, even if he has said nothing, he is bound by a tacit "contract;" the idea that there exists a "right of property," etc. Then indeed it would be self-contradictory to accept a deposit and refuse to give it back; the deposit would no longer be a deposit; the philosopher might say that the breach of morality in this case pertains to the irrational. But it would be because the word "deposit" was taken in the sense that it has in a human group possessing fully developed moral ideas, conventions and obligations; the moral obligation would no longer pertain to the bare and empty necessity of not contradicting oneself, since the contradiction in this case would simply consist in rejecting, after having accepted it, a moral obligation which for this very reason was already there. But enough of these quibbles. It is quite natural that we should meet with a pretension to found morality on a respect for logic among philosophers and scholars, who are accustomed to bow to logic in speculative matters, and are thus in-

clined to believe that in all matters, and for the whole of humanity, logic must be accepted as the sovereign authority. But because
science must respect the logic of things and logic in general if it
wants to succeed in its researches, because such is the interest of
the scientist as a scientist, it is not to be concluded that we are
obliged always to conform to logic in our conduct, as though such
were the interest of man in general, or even the interest of the
scientist as man. Our admiration for the speculative function of
the mind may be great; but when philosophers maintain that it
should be sufficient to silence selfishness and passion, they prove
to us—and this is a matter for congratulation—that they have never
heard the voice of the one or the other very loud within themselves. So much for a morality claiming as its basis reason in the
guise of pure form, without matter.—Before considering the morality which adds matter to this form, we must note that people often
get no further than the first when they think they have reached
the second. That is the case with those philosophers who explain
moral obligation by the fact that the idea of the Good forces itself
upon us. If they take this idea from organized society, where
human actions are already classified according as they are more
or less appropriate for maintaining social cohesion and furthering
the progress of humanity, and, above all, where certain clearly
defined forces produce this cohesion and bring about this progress,
they can doubtless say that an activity is more moral, the more it
conforms to the Good; and they might also add that the Good is
conceived as claiming obedience. But this is because the Good
would be merely the heading under which men agree to classify
the actions which present one or the other feature and to which
they feel themselves prompted by the forces of impulsion and attraction which we have defined. The notion of a graduated scale
of these various lines of conduct, and therefore of their respective
values, and, on the other hand, the all but inevitable necessity
which forces them upon us, must then have existed before the idea
of Good, which appeared later simply to provide a label or name;
this idea, left to itself, would have lent no assistance to their
classification, and still less to their enforcement. But if, on the
contrary, it is maintained that the idea of the Good is at the source
of all obligation and all aspiration, and that it should also serve
to evaluate human actions, we must be told by what sign we shall

recognize that a given line of conduct is in conformity with it; we must therefore be furnished with a definition of the Good; and we fail to see how it can be defined without assuming a hierarchy of creatures, or at the very least, of actions, of varying elevation: but if the hierarchy exists by itself, there is no need to call upon the idea of the Good to establish it; besides, we do not see why this hierarchy ought to be maintained, why we should be bound to respect it; you can invoke in its favour only aesthetic reasons, allege that a certain line of conduct is "finer" than another, that it sets us more or less high up in the ranks of living beings: but what could you reply to the man who declared that he places his own interest before all other considerations? Looking more closely, one would see that this morality has never been self-sufficient. It has simply been added on, as an artistic makeweight, to obligations which existed before it, and rendered it possible. When Greek philosophers attributed a pre-eminent dignity to the pure idea of Good, and, more generally, to a life of contemplation, they were speaking for a chosen few, a small group formed within society, which would begin by taking social life for granted. It has been said that this morality was silent about duty and knew nothing of obligation as we understand it. True, it was silent about it; but that was precisely because it assumed obligation to be self-evident. The philosopher was supposed to have begun by doing his duty like anybody else, as demanded of him by the city. Only then did a morality supervene, destined to make his life more beautiful by treating it as a work of art. In a word, and to sum up the discussion, there can be no question of founding morality on the cult of reason.—It remains to be seen, as we have said, whether it could be founded on reason in so far as reason might supply our activity with a definite object, in conformity with reason, but supplementary to it, an object towards which reason would teach us to strive systematically. But it is easy to see that no objective—not even the twofold one we have indicated, not even the dual preoccupation of maintaining social cohesion and of furthering the progress of humanity—will impose itself peremptorily as a mere rational proposition. If certain really active forces, actually influencing our will, are already in possession, reason could and should intervene to co-ordinate their effects, but it could not contend with them, since one can always reason with reason, confront its arguments with others, or simply refuse all discussion and reply by a *"sic volo, sic jubeo."* In truth, a system of ethics which imagines it is founding obligation on purely rational considerations, unwittingly reintroduces, as we have pointed out already and as we shall point out again, forces of a different order. That is exactly why it succeeds so easily. Real obligation is already there, and whatever reason impresses upon it assumes naturally an obligatory character. Society, with all that holds it together and drives it forward, is already there, and that is why reason can adopt as a principle of morality one or the other of the ends towards which social man is striving; by building up a thoroughly consistent system of means destined to attain this end, reason will more or less rediscover morality, such as common sense conceives it, such as humanity in general practises, or claims to practise it. For each of these objectives, culled by reason from society, has been socialized and, by that very fact, impregnated with all the other aims to be found there. Thus, even if we set up personal interest as the moral principle, we shall find no great difficulty in building up a rational morality sufficiently resembling current morality, as is proved by the relative success of utilitarian ethics. Selfishness, indeed, for the man living among his fellow-men, comprises legitimate pride, the craving for praise, etc., with the result that purely personal interest has become impossible to define, so large is the element of public interest it contains, so hard is it to keep them separate. Think of the amount of deference for others included in what we call self-love, and even in jealousy and envy! Anyone wanting to practise absolute egoism would have to shut himself up within himself, and not care enough for his neighbour to be jealous or envious of him. There is a touch of sympathy in these forms of hate, and the very vices of a man living among his fellows are not without certain implications of virtue; all are saturated with vanity, and vanity means sociability. Still easier will it be, then, to draw all moral maxims, or nearly all, from feelings such as honour, or sympathy, or pity. Each of these tendencies, in a man living in society, is laden with all that social morality has deposited in it; and we should have to unload it first, at the risk of reducing it to very little indeed, if we wished to avoid begging the question in using it to explain morality. The ease with which theories of this kind are built up should make us suspicious: if the most varied aims can thus be transmuted by philosophers into moral aims, we may surmise, seeing that they have not yet found the philosopher's stone, that they had started by putting gold in the bottom of their crucible. Similarly it is obvious that none of these doctrines will account for obligation. For we may be obliged to adopt certain means in order to attain such and such ends; but if we choose to renounce the end, how can the means be forced upon us? And yet, by adopting any one of these ends as the principle of morality, philosophers have evolved from it whole systems of maxims, which, without going so far as to assume an imperative form, come near enough to it to afford satisfaction. The reason is quite simple. They have considered the pursuit of these ends, we repeat, in a society in which there are peremptory pressures, together with aspirations to match them and also to extend them. Pressure and attraction, specifying their objectives, would lead to any one of these systems of maxims, since each of them aims at the attainment of an end both individual and social. Each of these systems then already exists in the social atmosphere when the philosopher arrives on the scene; it comprises maxims which are near enough in substance to those which the philosopher will formulate, the former being obligatory. Rediscovered by philosophy, but no longer in the form of a command since they are now mere suggestions for the intelligent pursuit of an end, such as intelligence might easily repudiate, they are snapped up by the vaguer or perhaps merely virtual maxims which resemble them, but which are laden with obligation. They thus become obligatory, but the obligation has not come *down,* as might be imagined, from above, that is to say, from a principle from which the maxims have been rationally deduced; it has come *up* from below, I mean from that substratum of pressure, capable of being extended into aspiration, which is the basis of society. In a word, the moral theorists take society for granted and consequently also the two forces to which society owes its stability and its mobility. Taking advantage of the fact that all social ends interpenetrate one another, and that each of them, resting as it were on that stability and mobility, seems to be invested with these two forces, they have no difficulty in reconstituting the content of morals with one or other of the ends assumed as a principle, and then showing that such morality is obligatory. For, by taking society for granted, they have also taken for granted the matter of this morality and its form, all it contains and all the obligation with which it is clothed.

If we now delve down beneath that illusion which is common to all theoretical moral systems, this is what we should find. Obligation is a necessity with which one can argue, and which is therefore companioned by intelligence and liberty. This necessity is, in fact, similar to that which accompanies the production of a physiological or even a physical effect; in a humanity which nature had made devoid of intelligence, where the individual had no power to choose, the action destined to maintain the preservation and cohesion of the group would be accomplished inevitably; it would be accomplished under the influence of a definite force, the same that makes each ant toil for the ant-hill and each cell in the tissue work for the organism. But intelligence intervenes with its faculty of choice; this is a new force which maintains the other in a state of virtuality, or rather in a state of reality barely discernible in its action, yet perceptible in its pressure: just as the swinging to and fro of the pendulum in a clock, while it prevents the tension of the spring from manifesting itself by a sudden unwinding, is yet a consequence of this tension, being an effect which exerts an inhibitive or regulating action on its causes. What then will intelligence do? It is a faculty used naturally by the individual to meet the difficulties of life; it will not follow the direction of a force which, on the contrary, is working for the species, and which, if it considers the individual at all, does so in the interest of the species. It will make straight for selfish decisions. But this will be only its first impulse. It cannot avoid reckoning with the force of which it feels the invisible pressure. It will therefore persuade itself into thinking that an intelligent egoism must allow all other egoisms their share. And if the intelligence is that of a philosopher, it will build up a theory of ethics in which the interpenetration of personal and general interests will be demonstrated, and where obligation will be brought back to the necessity, realized and felt, of thinking of others, if we wish intelligently to do good to ourselves. But we can answer that it does not suit us to see our interests in this light, and it is therefore not obvious why we should still feel obliged. Yet we *are* obliged, and intelligence is well aware of it, since this is the very reason why it attempted the demonstration. But the truth is that its demonstration seems successful only because it clears the way for something it does not mention, and which is the essential: a necessity that pertains to experience and feeling, one which some argument has thrust into the background and which an opposing argument reinstates. What is therefore, strictly speaking, obligatory in obligation does not come from intelligence. The latter only supplies the element of hesitation in obligation. When it appears to be the basis of obligation, it is merely sustaining it in its resistance to a resistance, in the operation of inhibiting itself from inhibiting. And we shall see in the next chapter what helpers it enlists. For the present, let us revert to a comparison we have found useful. An ant, accomplishing her heavy task as if she never thought of herself, as if she lived only for the ant-hill, is very likely in a somanbulistic state; she is yielding to an irresistible necessity. Imagine her suddenly becoming intelligent. She would reason about what she had done, wonder why she had done it, would say it was very foolish not to take things easy and have a good time. "I have had enough of sacrifice, now is the time for a little self-indulgence." And behold the natural order completely upset. But nature is on the watch. She provided the ant with the social instinct; she has just added to it, perhaps in response to a transitory need of instinct, a gleam of intelligence. However slightly intelligence has thrown instinct out of gear, it must incontinently set things to rights and undo what it has done. An act of reasoning will therefore prove that it is all to the interest of the ant to work for the ant-hill, and in this way the obligation will apparently find a basis. But the truth is that such a basis would be very unsafe, and that obligation already existed in all its force; intelligence has merely hindered its own hindrance. Our ant-hill philosopher would be none the less disinclined to admit this; he would doubtless persist in attributing a positive and not a negative activity to intelligence. And that is just what most moral philosophers have done, either because they were intellectuals and afraid of not according enough importance to intelligence, or rather because obligation appeared to them as an indivisible entity, defying analysis; on the contrary, if we see in it something approximate to a compulsion which may be thwarted by a resistance, we realize that the resistance has come from intelligence, the resistance to the resistance likewise, and that the compulsion, which is the essential, has a different origin. In truth, no philosopher can avoid initially postulating this compulsion; but very often he postulates it implicitly, and not in words. We have postulated it and said so. We connect it, moreover, with a principle that it is impossible not to admit. For, to whatever school of philosophy you belong, you are bound to recognize that man is a living creature, that the evolution of life along its two main lines has been accomplished in the direction of social life, that association is the most general form of living activity, since life is organization, and that, this being so, we pass by imperceptible transitions from the relation between cells in an organism to the relation between individuals in society. We therefore confine ourselves to noting what is uncontroverted and incontrovertible. But, this being admitted, any theorising on obligation becomes unnecessary as well as futile: unnecessary because obligation is a necessity of life; ineffectual because the hypothesis presented can, at the utmost, afford justification in the eyes of intelligence, and very incomplete justification at that, for an obligation anterior to this intellectual reconstruction.

Now, life might have stopped at this point and done nothing more than create closed societies, whose members were bound together by strict obligations. Composed of intelligent beings, these societies would have presented variations not to be found in animal societies, which are governed by instinct; but the variations would not have gone so far as to encourage the dream of a root and branch transformation; society would not have become modified to the extent that a single society, embracing all mankind, could seem possible. In fact, this society does not yet, and perhaps never will, exist; in according to man the requisite moral conformation for living in groups, nature probably did all she could for the species. But, just as there have been men of genius to thrust back the bounds of intelligence, and, thus, far more has been granted to individuals, at certain intervals, than it was possible to grant all at once to the species, so exceptional souls have appeared who sensed their kinship with the soul of Everyman, who thus, instead of remaining within the limits of the group and going no further than the solidarity laid down by nature, were borne on a great surge of love towards humanity in general. The appearance of each one of them was like the creation of a new species, composed of one single individual, the vital impulse culminating at long intervals in one particular man, a result which could not have been obtained at one stroke by humanity as a whole. Each of these souls marked then a certain point attained by the evolution of life; and each of them was a manifestation, in an original form, of a love which seems to be the very essence of the creative effort. The creative emotion which exalted these exceptional souls, and which was an overflowing of vitality, has spread far and wide about them; enthusiasts themselves, they radiated enthusiasm which has never been completely quenched, and which can be readily fanned into flame again. To-day, when in imagination we call to life these great moral leaders, when we listen to their words and see them at work, we feel that they communicate to us something of their fervour, and draw us in their wake; this is no longer a more or less attenuated compulsion, it is a more or less irresistible attraction. But neither does this second force, any more than the first, call for an explanation. For you cannot reject these two data: a compulsion, or something like it, exerted by habits which correspond, in man, to what you call instinct in animals, and, besides this, a certain stirring up of the soul, which you call emotion; in the one case you have primal obligation, in the other, something which becomes an extension of it; but in both cases you are confronted by forces which are not strictly and exclusively moral, and whose origin, therefore, it is no special duty of the moralist to trace. Because they have nevertheless insisted on doing so, philosophers have misunderstood the compound nature of obligation in its present-day form: they have been led to attribute to this or that mental picture or operation the power of influencing the will: as if an idea could ever categorically demand its own realization! as if the idea were anything else, in this case, than an intellectual extract common to all, or, better still, the projection on to the intellectual plane of a whole set of tendencies and aspirations, some above, some beneath, pure intelligence! Reinstate the duality of origin, and the difficulties vanish. Nay, the duality itself merges into a unity, for "social pressure" and "impetus of love" are but two complementary manifestations of life, normally intent on preserving generally the social form which was characteristic of the human species from the beginning, but, exceptionally, capable of transfiguring it, thanks to individuals who each represent, as the appearance of a new species would have represented, an effort of creative evolution.

All teachers have not perhaps a full perception of this double origin of morality, but they perceive something of it as soon as they try to inculcate morality into their pupils instead of merely talking about it. We do not deny the utility, the necessity even, of a moral instruction which appeals to reason alone, defining duties and connecting them with a principle of which it follows out in detail the various applications. It is on the plane of intelligence, and on that plane alone, that discussion is possible, and there is no complete morality without reflexion, analysis and argument with others as well as with oneself. But if instruction directed to the intelligence be indispensable to give confidence and delicacy to the moral sense, if it makes us fully capable of carrying out our intention where our intention is good, yet the intention must exist in the first place, and intention marks a direction of the will as much as and more than of intelligence. How can we get a hold over the will? Two ways lie open to the teacher. The one is that of training, in the highest meaning of the word; the other the mystic way, the term being taken here, on the contrary, in its most restricted sense. By the first method is inculcated a morality made up of impersonal habits; by the second we obtain the imitation of a person, and even a spiritual union, a more or less complete identification. The primeval training, the training intended by nature, consisted in adopting the habits of the group; it was automatic; it took place spontaneously in those cases where the individual felt himself half merged in the collectivity. As society became differentiated through a division of labour, it delegated to the groups thus formed within itself the task of training the individual, of putting him in harmony with the group and thereby with society itself; but it was still nothing more than a system of habits formed for the sole benefit of society. That a morality of this type may suffice at a pinch, if it be complete, there is no doubt. Thus the man confined strictly within the limits of his calling or profession, wholly absorbed in his daily task, with his life organized so as to turn out the greatest possible quantity, the best possible quality of work, would generally fulfil *ipso facto* many other obligations. Discipline would have made him an honest man. This is the first method: it works in the sphere of the

impersonal. The other can supplement it, if need be; it may even
take its place. We do not hesitate to call it religious, and even
mystic; but we must agree upon the meaning of the words. People
are fond of saying that religion is the helpmeet of morality in that
it induces a fear of punishment and a hope of reward. This is
perhaps true, but they should add that, in this direction, religion
does little more than promise an extension and rectification of
human justice by divine justice: to the rewards and punishments
established by society, whose application is so far from perfect, it
adds others, infinitely higher, to be meted out to us in the City of
God, when we shall have left the city of men; still it is on the same
plane of the city of men that we thus remain; religion is brought
in, doubtless, but not in its specifically religious aspect; however
high the teaching may rise, it still looks upon moral education as
training, and upon morality as discipline; so that it still clings to
the first of our two methods, it has not yet sprung over to the second. On the other hand, it is of religious dogmas and the metaphysical theories they imply that we generally think as soon as the
word religion is mentioned: so that when religion is said to be the
foundation of morality, we picture to ourselves a group of conceptions relating to God and the world, the acceptance of which
is supposed to result in the doing of good. But it is quite clear
that these conceptions, taken as such, influence our will and our
conduct in the same way as theories may do, that is to say, ideas;
we are here on the intellectual plane, and, as I hinted above,
neither obligation nor the force which extends it can possibly
originate in bare ideas, bare ideas affecting our will only to the
extent which it pleases us to accept them or put them into practice.
Now if you distinguish this metaphysical system from all others by
saying that it compels our assent, you may again be right, but
then you are not thinking of its content alone, of ideas pure and
simple; you introduce something different, which underpins the
representation, which imparts to it some undeniable efficacy, and
which is the specifically religious element: but then it is this element, and not the metaphysics with which you have associated it,
which becomes the religious basis of morality. Here indeed we are
concerned with the second method, but then we are dealing with
mystic experience. I mean mystic experience taken in its immediacy, apart from all interpretation. True mystics simply open

their souls to the oncoming wave. Sure of themselves, because they feel within them something better than themselves, they prove to be great men of action, to the surprise of those for whom mysticism is nothing but visions, and raptures and ecstasies. That which they have allowed to flow into them is a stream flowing down and seeking through them to reach their fellow-men; the necessity to spread around them what they have received affects them like an onslaught of love. A love which each one of them stamps with his own personality. A love which is in each of them an entirely new emotion, capable of transposing human life into another tone. A love which thus causes each of them to be loved for himself, so that through him, and for him, other men will open their souls to the love of humanity. A love which can be just as well passed on through the medium of a person who has attached himself to them or to their evergreen memory and formed his life on that pattern. Let us go further. If a word of a great mystic, or some one of his imitators, finds an echo in one or another of us, may it not be that there is a mystic dormant within us, merely waiting for an occasion to awake? In the first case a person attaches himself to the impersonal and aims at finding room inside it. Here he responds to the call of a personality, perhaps that of a revealer of moral life or one of his imitators, or even in certain circumstances his own.

Whichever of these two methods be adopted, in both cases the foundations of human nature have been taken into account, whether considered statically in itself or dynamically in its origin. The mistake would be to think that moral pressure and moral aspiration find their final explanation in social life considered merely as a fact. We are fond of saying that society exists, and that hence it inevitably exerts a constraint on its members, and that this constraint is obligation. But in the first place, for society to exist at all the individual must bring into it a whole group of inborn tendencies; society therefore is not self-explanatory; so we must search below the social accretions, get down to Life, of which human societies, as indeed the human species altogether, are but manifestations. But this is not going far enough; we must delve deeper still if we want to understand, not only how society "constrains" individuals, but again how the individual can set up as a judge and wrest from it a moral transformation. If society is

self-sufficient, it is the supreme authority. But if it is only one of
the aspects of life, we can easily conceive that life, which has had
to set down the human species at a certain point of its evolution,
imparts a new impetus to exceptional individuals who have immersed themselves anew in it, so that they can help society further
along its way. True, we shall have had to push on as far as the
very principle of life. Everything is obscure if we confine ourselves to mere manifestations, whether they are all called indiscriminately social, or whether one examines, in social man, more
particularly the feature of intelligence. All becomes clear, on the
contrary, if we start by a quest beyond these manifestations for
Life itself. Let us then give to the word biology the very wide
meaning it should have, and will perhaps have one day, and let us
say in conclusion that all morality, be it pressure or aspiration, is
in essence biological.

Index

Index